ETHICAL ISSUES IN PROFESSIONAL LIFE

ETHICAL ISSUES IN PROFESSIONAL LIFE

Edited by
JOAN C. CALLAHAN

New York Oxford
OXFORD UNIVERSITY PRESS
1988

Oxford University Press

Oxford New York Toronto
Delhi Bombay Calcutta Madras Karachi
Petaling Jaya Singapore Hong Kong Tokyo
Nairobi Dar es Salaam Cape Town
Melbourne Auckland

and associated companies in
Beirut Berlin Ibadan Nicosia

Published by Oxford University Press, Inc.,
200 Madison Avenue, New York, New York 10016

Library of Congress Cataloging-in-Publication Data
Ethical issues in professional life.
Bibliography: p.
1. Professional ethics. I. Callahan, Joan C., 1946–
BJ1725.E73 1988 174 87-13275
ISBN 0-19-505362-1
ISBN 0-19-505026-6 (pbk.)

9 8 7 6 5 4 3 2 1

Printed in the United States of America
on acid-free paper

10. Reproduced by permission. © The Hastings Center.
11. Reproduced by permission. © The Hastings Center.
12. Reproduced by permission. © The Hastings Center.
13. Reprinted, with permission, from Joan C. Callahan, "Academic Paternalism," *The International Journal of Applied Philosophy,* Vol. 3, No. 1 (Spring 1986), pp. 21–31.
14. From *Professional Ethics* by Michael D. Bayles. © 1981 by Wadsworth, Inc. Reprinted by permission of the publisher.
15. Joseph Ellin, "Special Professional Morality and the Duty of Veracity," from *Business and Professional Ethics Journal,* 1982. Reprinted by permission of the author.
16. Copyright © 1927 by *Harper's Magazine.* All rights reserved. Reprinted from the June 8 issue by special permission.
17., 18. From *Lying: Moral Choice in Public and Private Life,* by Sissela Bok. Copyright © 1978 by Sissela Bok. Reprinted by permission of Pantheon Books, a Division of Random House, Inc.
19. From *Ethics, Free Enterprise, and Public Policy: Original Essays on Moral Issues in Business* by Richard T. De George and Joseph A. Pichler. Copyright © 1978 by Oxford University Press, Inc. Reprinted by permission.
20. Reprinted with permission of Macmillan Publishing Company from *Liberty, Justice, and Morals: Contemporary Value Conflict* by Burton M. Leiser. Copyright © 1979 by Burton M. Leiser.
21. Reprinted with permission from 464 F.2d 772. Copyright © 1973 by West Publishing Co.
22. Franz J. Ingelfinger, "Informed (but Uneducated) Consent," from *The New England Journal of Medicine,* Vol. 287, pages 465–466. Copyright © 1972 by *The New England Journal of Medicine.* Reprinted by permission of the publisher.
23. Samuel Gorovitz, "Informed Consent and Patient Autonomy," from *Doctors' Dilemmas: Moral Conflict and Medical Care.* Copyright © 1982 by Oxford University Press. Reprinted by permission of the publisher.
24. From *Kind and Unusual Punishment: The Prison Business* by Jessica Mitford. Copyright © 1973 by Jessica Mitford. Reprinted by permission of Alfred A. Knopf, Inc.
25. Carl Cohen, "Medical Experimentation on Prisoners," from *Perspectives in Biology.* Copyright © 1978 by The University of Chicago Press. Reprinted by permission of the author and publisher.
26. Copyright 1986 Newsweek Inc. All rights reserved. Reprinted by permission.
27. W. A. Parent, "Privacy, Morality, and the Law," *Philosophy & Public Affairs,* Vol. 12, No. 4 (Fall 1983). Copyright © 1983 by Princeton University Press. Reprinted with permission of Princeton University Press.
28. Tom L. Beauchamp, Ruth R. Faden, R. Jay Wallace, Jr., LeRoy Walters. *Ethical Issues in Social Science Research.* The Johns Hopkins University Press, Baltimore/London, 1982, pp. 263–272.
29. From *Secrets: On the Ethics of Concealment and Revelation* by Sissela Bok. Copyright © 1982 by Sissela Bok. Reprinted by permission of Pantheon Books, a Division of Random House, Inc.
30. Reprinted with permission from 131 Cal. Rptr. 14, Copyright © 1976 by West Publishing Co.
31. Reproduced by permission. © The Hastings Center.
32. Alan Donagan, "Confidentiality in the Adversary System," from David Luban, ed., *The Good Lawyer: Lawyers' Roles and Lawyers' Ethics* (Totowa, N.J.: Rowman and Allanheld, 1984).
33. Used by permission of the author. Copyright © 1977 by Peter A. French.
34. John Danley, "Corporate Moral Agency: The Case for Anthropological Bigotry," from *Action and Responsibility: Bowling Green Studies in Applied Philosophy,* Vol. II, 1980.
35. Used by permission of the author. Copyright Peter A. French 1981.
36. Dennis F. Thompson, "Ascribing Responsibility to Advisers in Government," from *Ethics.* Copyright © 1983 by The University of Chicago Press. Reprinted by permission of the author and publisher.
37. James L. Muyskens, *Moral Problems in Nursing* (Totowa, New Jersey: Rowman & Allanheld, 1982).
38. Reproduced by permission. © The Hastings Center.
39. James L. Muyskens, *Moral Problems in Nursing: A Philosophical Investigation* (Totowa, New Jersey: Rowman & Littlefield, 1982).
40. Gene G. James, "In Defense of Whistleblowing," from *Business Ethics: Readings and Cases in Corporate Morality,* edited by W. Michael Hoffman and Jennifer Mills Moore. Copyright © 1984. Reprinted by permission of the author. Professor James has revised and expanded his discussion in "Whistle Blowing: Its Moral Justification," in Hoffman and Mills, eds., 2nd ed., 1988.
41. Reproduced by permission. © The Hastings Center.
42. Sissela Bok, "Whistleblowing and Professional Responsibilities," from *Ethics Teaching in Higher Education,* edited by Sissela Bok and Daniel Callahan. Copyright © 1980 by Plenum Publishing Corporation. Reprinted by permission of the author and publisher.
43. Milton Friedman, "The Social Responsibility of Business," from *Capitalism and Freedom.* Copyright © 1962 by The University of Chicago Press. Reprinted by permission of the publisher.
44. All rights reserved to the trustees of Columbia University.
45. George Sher, "Justifying Reverse Discrimination in Employment," *Philosophy & Public Affairs,* Vol. 4, No. 2 (Winter 1975). Copyright © 1975 by Princeton University Press. Reprinted with permission of Princeton University Press.
46. Andrew Kaufman, *Problems in Professional Responsibility,* Second Edition. Bates and O'Steen v. State Bar of Arizona, pp. 536–552. Ohralik v. Ohio State Bar Assoc., pp. 555–564. Copyright © 1979 by Little, Brown and Company. Reprinted by permission of the publisher.
"Drafting Lawyers." Copyright © by the American Bar Association, 1979. All rights reserved. Reprinted with permission.
47. Professor Freedman has elaborated on these views and modified them somewhat in *Lawyers' Ethics in an Adversary System* (1975) (ABA Gavel Award Certificate of Merit, 1976) and in "Personal Responsibility in a Professional System," 27 *Catholic University Law Review,* 191 (1976).
48. Reprinted with permission from *Ethics in Science & Medicine,* Vol. 6. Laurence B. McCullough, "The Right to Health Care." Copyright 1979, Pergamon Press, Ltd.

49. Andreas Eschete, "Does a Lawyer's Character Matter?" from David Luban (ed.) *The Good Lawyer* (Totowa, New Jersey: Rowman & Allanheld, 1983).

50. Bernard Williams, "Politics and Moral Character," from *Public and Private Morality,* edited by Stuart Hampshire. Copyright © 1978 by Cambridge University Press. Reprinted by permission of the publisher.

51. William May, "Professional Virtue and Self-Regulation," from *Ethics Teaching in Higher Education,* edited by Sissela Bok and Daniel Callahan. Copyright © 1980 by Plenum Publishing Corporation. Reprinted by permission of the author and publisher.

52. Copyright © John Kultgen.

53. Reprinted by permission of the author.

54. Samuel Gorovitz, "Good Doctors." Copyright © 1982 by Oxford University Press. Reprinted by permission of the publisher.

App. 1. "Model Rules of Professional Conduct." Copyright © by the American Bar Association, August 1983. All rights reserved. Reprinted with permission.

App. 2. Reprinted as adopted by AMA House of Delegates, July 1980, with permission.

App. 3. The Code for Nurses was developed and published by the American Nurses' Association. Copyright © 1976.

App. 4. Copyright © 1953 The International Council of Nurses, Geneva, Switzerland.

App. 5. "Ethical Principles of Psychologists," Copyright © 1981 by the American Psychological Association. Reprinted by permission of the publisher.

App. 6. Reprinted with permission from *Applying Professional Standards and Ethics in the '80s.* Copyright © 1982 by the American Society for Public Administration, 1120 G Street NW, Suite 500, Washington, D.C. All rights reserved. Copies are available for $4.

App. 7. Copyright 1979, National Association of Social Workers, Inc.

App. 8. © Reprinted with permission of the National Society of Professional Engineers, 1987.

CASES

Chapter 1. Martin Benjamin and Joy Curtis, "The Nurse's Dilemma." From *Ethics in Nursing* by Martin Benjamin and Joy Curtis. Copyright © 1981 by Oxford University Press, Inc. Reprinted by permission.

Chapter 2. Martin Benjamin and Joy Curtis, "Professionalism and Nursing." From *Ethics in Nursing* by Martin Benjamin and Joy Curtis. Copyright © 1981 by Oxford University Press, Inc. Reprinted by permission.

Chapter 5. Robert Veatch, "The Potent Placebo." Adapted by permission of the publishers from *Case Studies in Medical Ethics* by Robert M. Veatch, Cambridge: Harvard University Press, Copyright © 1977 by Robert M. Veatch.

Chapter 7. Tom L. Beauchamp, Ruth R. Faden, R. Jay Wallace, Jr., and LeRoy Walters, "Tearoom Trade," from *Ethical Issues in Social Science Research,* edited by Tom L. Beauchamp, Ruth R. Faden, R. Jay Wallace, Jr., and LeRoy Walters. Copyright © 1982 by The Johns Hopkins University Press. Reprinted, with some variation, by permission of the publisher.

Chapter 8. Manuel Velasquez, "The Ford Pinto," from Manuel G. Velasquez, *Business Ethics: Concepts and Cases,* © 1982, pp. 94–96. Reprinted by permission of Prentice-Hall, Inc., Englewood Cliffs, New Jersey.

Chapter 9. Lee Jennings, "Leaking an Investigatory Report." Leslie Froehlich, "The Space Shuttle *Challenger.*" Reprinted by permission of Lee Jennings and Leslie Froehlich.

For my grandfather,

FRANCIS J. SMITH

To everyone who proposes to have a good career, moral philosophy is indispensible.

—CICERO, *De Officiis*, 44 B.C.

PREFACE

The recent rise of interest in professional ethics has spawned a variety of specialized ethics courses in colleges and universities (e.g., medical ethics, legal ethics, business ethics). Such courses are extremely important, but they fail to meet the needs of vast numbers of students who are preparing for a professional life. This is partly because most colleges and universities do not have the personnel available to offer a full complement of such courses on a regular basis. But it is also partly because many of the most popular specialized courses simply leave out the career interests of many students. Even though many of the general issues discussed in specialized ethics courses arise universally in professional life, this has not been emphasized in the promotion of these courses. Moreover, the practices and problems of various professions affect the interests of everyone. All of us, for example, are affected by business, journalism, political decisions, and the way the law is practiced. And, in one way or another, at one time or another, each of us is bound to become involved with, and be affected by, the health care system, its providers, and the way it distributes its services. Exploring the moral issues that arise within these professions can be valuable for us all.

Given these various kinds of considerations, a number of college and university philosophy departments have recently introduced nonspecialized courses in professional ethics. This book is designed to serve as a text for such courses.

One possible way of organizing such a course—and this book—is to devote a section to each of several different professions. Another way is to organize a course and book around philosophical issues that cut across the professions and that clarify the issues as they surface in one or more professions. In preparing my own course in professional ethics, it seemed to me that focusing on issues rather than professions was likely to most fully respond to the kinds of considerations which motivate a nonspecialized course in professional ethics.

I quickly found, however, that there was no anthology available which was organized in this way. For the last four years, I have had to rely on my students' patience, understanding of the reasons for the course structure, and robust goodwill to keep them marching to the library reserve shelves to read their text piecemeal. On further investigation, I discovered a number of colleagues who were in quite the same position as well as others who were interested in introducing a course in professional ethics organized in the way I have described but were unwilling to put their students through the same efforts. When it became clear to me that my thoughts concerning nonspecialized professional ethics courses were not entirely idiosyncratic, it also became evident that an important gap existed in the collection of currently available textbooks. This book is one attempt to help fill that gap.

Most of the readings and all of the cases* in this book focus on a particular profession, illustrating how the issue which is a chapter's subject arises in that profession. Focused as they are on particular professions, most of the readings and cases provide an opportunity to discuss the issues concretely, that is, as they surface in the fields of law, medicine, nursing, counseling, scientific research, politics, education, police work, journalism, social work, engineering, business management, pharmacology, public administration, veterinary medicine, and so forth.

However, the general organization of the book, the chapter introductions, and many of the study/discussion questions (as well as some of the questions included with the cases) ask readers to move beyond the particular focus of these materials and connect the issue to professions not discussed in a given set of readings and cases. Thus, even though a reading or case may be centered on, say, deception in medical practice or in politics or a breach of confidentiality in legal practice or in psychological counseling, the overall aim of the book is to help readers see that life in any profession is fraught with hard questions about the kinds of issues that form the skeletal structure of this collection.

The issues taken up, though separated by chapter divisions, are all of a piece in several important respects. For example, questions pertaining to the moral foundations of professional ethics are intimately connected to questions about the appropriate model of the professional/client relationship that are, in turn, intimately related to questions regarding client deception and informed consent, privacy and confidentiality, and the obligations of professionals to third parties and society at large. Thus, the chapter introductions not only acquaint readers with the selections and point out how the same ethical issues arise in professions not mentioned in the readings, but also help weave the various strands of the book together: for example, by pointing out how a question raised in one chapter flows naturally from questions in the previous chapter and leads naturally to questions in the following chapter; by pointing out how a position taken in a reading in some earlier chapter or some chapter to come relates to a position taken in a reading in the present chapter; or by pointing out how part of a reading in the present chapter adds to the discussion of a topic which is the focus of some earlier or later chapter. The primary goal of the chapter introductions, then, is to keep the book's interconnections always before the reader, making the book an integrated whole rather than simply a collection of readings and cases. At the same time, each chapter and reading can stand on its own. Thus, no chapter or reading is necessary to make another chapter or reading comprehensible, which leaves readers and instructors alike free to move about the book, reorganizing the material in any way that might prove helpful.

Needless to say, this book cannot possibly cover all the moral issues which arise in professional life. Nor does it pretend to even touch on every profession. And, certainly, no book of this kind can give to any profession the philosophical attention it merits. My hope, however, is that the book will go some way toward filling an important gap and that it will provide a reasonably good start for philosophical reflection on ethical issues that cut across the professions.

Lexington, Kentucky J.C.C.
June 1987

*Cases bearing no credit lines were prepared by the editor of this volume.

ACKNOWLEDGMENTS

Working with Oxford University Press editors Cynthia Read and Henry Krawitz has been a genuine pleasure; and editorial assistants Catherine Aman and Claire Holt have been models of good-natured efficiency in taking care of so many details as this book went to press. Although copy editors generally go without mention, Andrew Yockers deserves special thanks for his exceptionally diligent work on the manuscript, and for several substantive suggestions that have added to the book's content. I am grateful to each of these extremely capable people for all their help.

I am also grateful to Edward Henderson, chair of the philosophy department at Louisiana State University, for arranging a reduction in my teaching responsibilities during the spring of 1986 to provide time for work on the manuscript. During the same semester, my students in the professional ethics course made a number of helpful suggestions for the book. I hope it will meet their standards.

Reviewing the final page proofs would have been an ordeal without the cheerful assistance of Ronnie Sheehy and Nancy Oraftik. I hesitate to remind them how much I have added to my already unpayable debts to each of them.

This book would not have materialized without the early encouragement of Judy Andre, Ruth Heizer, Tziporah Kasachkoff, Hugh LaFollette, David Kline, John Peale, and Larry Stern. I am also grateful to David James, David Kline, Hugh LaFollette, Alan Perreiah, Gene Schlossberger, Larry Stern, and several anonymous reviewers for their helpful suggestions on the initial plan of the book and early chapters.

Special thanks must go to Tziporah Kasachkoff, whose infinite generosity and capacity for raising the right questions resulted in extensive comments and suggestions for maximizing the book's usefulness as a course text. I have run up an enormous debt to Tom Grassey for a great variety of suggestions, for his many detailed remarks on large portions of my own writing, and for his contributions to appendix 2. Finally, I am extremely grateful to Ruth Heizer for her comments on chapter 1 and for her continuing suggestions as the book developed.

Despite all this excellent help, I have not always acted on the counsel of able advisers. What faults remain here, then, are completely my own.

CONTENTS

PART I CONCEPTUAL AND FOUNDATIONAL ISSUES

ETHICAL ISSUES IN PROFESSIONAL LIFE

PART I

CONCEPTUAL AND FOUNDATIONAL ISSUES

1

BASICS AND BACKGROUND

A PLACE TO BEGIN: SOME CASES

Case 1: Divided Loyalties. Imagine that you are a physician and one of your patients is a four-year-old girl in severe renal failure. She is failing to thrive on dialysis and it has become evident that without a kidney transplant in the near future she will not survive. The chance of a successful transplant is roughly ninety percent if the kidney comes from a close relative whose tissue type is virtually identical to that of the recipient. A successful transplant is far less probable if the tissue match is less close, even if the kidney is from a near relative. And implanting a poorly matched kidney from a relative holds out no greater probability of success than the implantation of an equally poor match from a cadaver. The probability of getting a good tissue match from a cadaver is lower than getting one from within the family. You inform the child's family (her parents and two older siblings) of this; all agree to undergo tissue-typing to see if any of the family members are good candidates for donation. The tests reveal that the child's father is an excellent match. All the other family members are poor matches. You are about to contact the family with the good news when the father arrives and asks to speak with you about the test results. You tell him, but much to your surprise, he begins to cry and tells you that he is afraid to donate his kidney. He begs you to tell his family that none of them is an appropriate tissue match and asks you to begin the search for a cadaver kidney. The child's best chance for survival lies in receiving a kidney from her father. You feel quite certain that if you tell the man's wife, he will be shamed into donating. What should you do? On the basis of what considerations should you make your decision?[1]

Case 2: The Candid Client. Imagine now that you are a criminal lawyer defending a client who is on trial for murder. You are quite certain that she is innocent of the crime. The trial is going in her favor and the probability of acquittal is very high. You have established a good relationship with her and (bolstered by the prospect of acquittal) she tells you that although she did not commit this murder, she did commit another murder four years earlier. She goes on to tell you that another woman with a long criminal record was convicted of that murder and is serving a life sentence for it. You attempt to persuade her to confess to the crime, but she adamantly refuses. She has been in trouble with the law numerous times before and is an intelligent and exceptionally well-informed criminal. When you threaten to withdraw from the case, she reminds you that your withdrawal at this stage would prejudice her case and, therefore, is impermissible under the American Bar Association's *Model Rules of Professional Con-*

duct. Further, she reminds you that the *Model Rules* require strict confidentiality between attorney and client, permitting breach of confidentiality only under certain clearly circumscribed circumstances, none of which obtain in this case. What do you do? On the basis of what considerations should you make your decision?[2]

Case 3: University Rules and Student Welfare. Imagine now that you are an instructor at a large state university. You make a strong effort to get to know your students and are relatively successful in this. One day you are giving an in-class exam and, much to your distress, you see one of your students cheating. He is very bright and is one of the students who has come to your office several times to discuss the course material. You know from one conversation with him that his father recently died and that he has had some difficulty concentrating on his schoolwork since then. When you see him cheating, you realize that you could interrupt him during the exam, but you decide not to do so since this would humiliate him in front of his classmates. You could confront him after the exam, fail him for the test, and let the matter go at that. The university, however, has a firm policy on how cases of cheating are to be handled. The policy requires that all cases of cheating are to be reported by faculty to the administration. Faculty are expressly forbidden to use their own discretion in any case of cheating. The administration is highly intolerant of cheating and first offenses result in suspension for a semester. Second offenses result in explusion. What should you do? On the basis of what considerations should you make your decision?

Case 4: The Nurse's Dilemma. Imagine now that you are a nurse on a medical/surgical floor in a large private hospital. A woman is admitted on a Sunday for a series of medical tests. You are assigned as her primary nurse. The testing begins on Monday and you are off for the next few days. You return to work the following Saturday and resume your duties as the woman's primary nurse. When you arrive on the floor, you go over her chart and find that the tests have revealed she has chronic lymphocytic leukema and is being transfused in an attempt to put the disease into remission. As you approach her that morning, she greets you happily and asks if you know when she will be able to return to work. Given her diagnosis, you are a bit puzzled by her exuberance and you judiciously reply that you have not seen her physician since your return to work but that you will talk with the physician about her discharge from the hospital. On your way back to the nurses' station, one of the woman's two daughters approaches you and urges you to assure her mother that there is no reason for concern. The daughter tells you her mother has just been through a painful divorce and that she and her sister have decided her mother should not be burdened with the news that she has a terminal illness. You discuss the whole situation with your head nurse. She tells you to talk with the woman's physician, who is also the new director of the hospital's medical service. You avoid going to the woman's room until the physician arrives on the floor. When she arrives, you tell her about the woman's request for information regarding her discharge and about your conversation with the daughter. The physician informs you that the woman has been told simply that she has refractory anemia (which, in fact, is a result of the leukemia) and has not been told the true nature of her illness in order to spare her unnecessary anxiety. You protest that the woman does not seem mentally unsound in any way and, therefore, she has a right to know about her diagnosis and prognosis. But the physician interrupts you and says that further disclosure on your part would have to be considered inconsistent with the best medical care of this woman. You are deeply troubled and return to your head nurse, who is sympathetic but advises you to follow the physician's directions. She also says that if this sort of thing really bothers you, she will be careful to assign this physician's patients to someone else in the future. What should you do? On the basis of what considerations should you make your decision?[3]

Case 5: Veracity Versus a Variety of Values. Suppose now that you are the newest member of a civil engineering firm in a small southwestern Mexican-American city. The city has only four such firms and your company, which is the youngest and smallest, has been having difficulty getting contracts. The firm's engineers are excellent and its work is always very fine. Every member of the firm, from the president down, is deeply committed to technical excellence and determined to see the organization succeed. The difficulty in getting contracts has been the firm's inability to submit economically competitive project proposals. The situation has become so desperate that the company is struggling for survival and has been extending itself beyond its resources to avoid a lay off. The other firms are not hiring and, given the seniority policy of your company, you would be the first to go in a lay off. You have moved to this city because your spouse has a job teaching at the local community college, and the two of you have just decided to try to begin your family. The city is now considering putting in a new sewer system and has put out a request for proposals. Part of your job is to work on proposal preparation and to explain any questions about the proposal to the company's president, who, like you, is a registered engineer. The committee completes the proposal and you pass it to the president. The next day the president sends for you. He instructs you to alter the proposal so that it comes in at roughly three hundred thousand dollars less than the original figure. You tell him that this will not be possible—the committee has already arrived at the lowest figure it could honestly submit and changing the proposal would have to include gross falsifications of estimates. You have a fine record as a loyal employee and the president decides to take you into his confidence. He proceeds to tell you that he has spoken with the incumbent mayor, who is currently in the last stages of his campaign for reelection. The mayor is well liked in the large but poor Mexican-American community but has had trouble financing a campaign to register the Mexican-Americans and bring them out to vote. What is more, the sewer system will most benefit the Mexican-American community, which is clustered in the lowest part of the city where floods from the mountain rains and snowmelts are most damaging. Every summer at least one child is drowned in one of the runoff washes that make up the current system for handling flash waters. The mayor's opponent has been opposed to the sewer system because, she says, building and maintaining it would necessitate an increase in city taxes, which she has promised to avoid. She has made it clear that, if elected, she would not support the new sewer system. The timing is such that whoever wins what promises to be a close race will decide on the project. The president of your firm, whom you have previously found to be an honest, sensitive, and fair man, tells you that after much painful thought, he has privately arranged for a large contribution (which has been adequately laundered) to reach the mayor's campaign fund, thereby supplying more money for the mayor to get out the Mexican-American vote, that can carry him to reelection. He also tells you that in exchange for the contribution, the mayor, who has good friends on the city's board, has instructed him on how to write the proposal so that it will be accepted by the board with no challenge. Both the president and the mayor know that there will be cost overruns after the project is begun. But they also know that if your firm does the project, it will not cost the city all that much more than if one of the other firms does it and that there is no question whatever about its being done well. The mayor also strongly believes that increasing the choices among civil engineering firms is in the long-term best interest of the city and he wants to see your firm stay in business. If you refuse to alter the proposal, the president will do it himself and you will probably be "laid off." If your firm doesn't get the contract, there is every reason to believe not only that you will be laid off, but that this will also be the beginning of the end of the company, which (again) is a fine firm but has been unable to successfully compete with the older, larger organizations that have worked very hard to keep your company from getting established. What do you do? On the basis of what considerations should you make your decision?

MORAL ISSUES AND MORAL DILEMMAS

The cases presented are among the many kinds that raise hard ethical questions for professionals. They are cases which involve troubling moral issues. Moral issues are, roughly, those issues which raise *normative* questions about the rights and welfare of persons and other sentient beings, and about the character of the agent, in particular, about the kinds of persons we should strive to become. Normative questions are questions of value (e.g., "Was it morally permissible for Jane to have that abortion?") as opposed to questions of mere fact (e.g., "Did Jane decide to have the abortion?"). The distinction between matters of value and matters of fact is often called 'the normative/descriptive distinction.' Although, as we shall see shortly, matters of fact are extremely important in moral decision making, moral decisions as such involve making important value judgments in a way that merely factual decisions do not. For example, if you are the physician in our first case, you are confronted with a serious conflict of moral values. Should you decide to respect physician/client confidentiality and to prevent what might amount to coercion of the child's father? Or, should you decide in favor of honesty and to pursue the child's best interest at the expense of confidentiality and the father's strong moral right to privacy regarding his own feelings about donating his kidney as well as his right to maintain the integrity of his body? If you are the lawyer in our second case, doing nothing will preserve professional/client confidentiality, the welfare of your client, and a widely accepted standard of practice in the profession. It will also ensure that you will not be sued for malpractice. But if you choose to protect those values, it will be at the cost of the liberty and welfare of someone else who is being severely punished for a crime she did not commit. If you are the professor in our third case, you must decide between the welfare of your student and one of your institutional obligations as an employee of the university. If you are the nurse in our fourth case, you must choose between your client's right to information about her condition and the value of honesty on one side, and respect for the physician's judgment, the prevention of anguish, and, quite possibly, a threat to your job on the other side. If you are the engineer in our last case, your job is at stake as is the well-being of your spouse. In addition, loyalty to the company's president, the survival of the firm, the good of the city as a whole, and the prevention of harm in the Mexican-American community also press in favor of falsifying the proposal. But to decide in favor of those values is to opt against honesty, not only on your part, but in the system as well.

Moral issues, then, involve questions of value. And moral problems involve value dilemmas—dilemmas not only where deciding to preserve or protect or further one value or one set of values necessarily includes the sacrifice of some other value or set of values, but also where not to decide in favor of one value or set of values is equivalent to deciding in favor of the competing value or set of values. In none of our opening cases can the professional escape making a hard moral choice. In this book, we shall not be concerned with behaviors that are obviously morally indefensible (e.g., stealing from clients, gross negligence in practice). Rather, our concern will be with issues that require making hard moral choices, that is, with issues that involve serious conflicts among important values. Before we approach these issues themselves, however, it should be helpful to spend some time reflecting more generally on how to address moral questions.

MORAL PHILOSOPHY

Our five opening cases raise only some of the many significant moral problems that arise in professional life. When we attempt to get clearer on such problems and/or when we try to resolve them in an ethically satisfactory way, we are engaged in doing ethics or moral philosophy.

Ethics, as a formal field of philosophical inquiry, is the philosophical study of morality. As a field of philosophical inquiry, ethics or moral philosophy is generally understood to include three conceptually distinct but closely related enterprises or projects.

Metaethics is an analytical enterprise which involves trying to discern what moral terms (e.g., 'good,' 'right') are generally understood to mean, how justification proceeds in moral discourse, and what we are doing when we share moral judgments with others. For example: Are we really describing persons or actions in a unique way? Or are we merely expressing our own positive or negative attitudes? As such, metaethics does not involve actually making moral judgments. Rather, metaethics involves attempting to discern precisely what is going on when moral judgments are made and uttered and what conceptual features justification in moral discourse involves.

Theoretical normative ethics, on the other hand, does involve making moral judgments. Here, the moral judgments are at the most general levels, since the task in this branch of moral philosophy is to develop general moral theories. Theoretical normative ethics has three branches: *moral axiology,* which includes theories of good and evil; *virtue ethics,* which includes theories of what counts as moral excellence in character; and *the theory of moral obligation,* which includes theories regarding what kinds of actions and practices are morally permissible and impermissible and what is morally required of all moral agents.

Applied ethics is the third major branch of moral philosophy. The task in applied ethics, as opposed to theoretical normative ethics, is to resolve specific moral issues and morally problematic concrete cases which arise in different areas of life. Applied ethics borrows insights from metaethics and theoretical normative ethics (thus the name 'applied ethics'); but the concentration in applied ethics is on finding acceptable resolutions of moral problems of present and practical urgency.[4] As an area of inquiry, professional ethics is one area of applied ethics.

Although we can make conceptual distinctions which separate these divisions of moral philosophy, when one actually begins doing moral philosophy, questions from all these areas tend to arise in tandem. John Stuart Mill provides a good example of this. In his famous little book *Utilitarianism,* Mill's purpose is to explain and defend his utilitarian theory of moral obligation.[5] His theory (roughly speaking) holds that we should always choose that which will tend to produce the greatest good for the greatest number. On Mill's view, then, we are to maximize the good. But what *is* this good we are to maximize? Mill moves from the theory of moral obligation into axiology and tells us that the good to be pursued is happiness. That is, according to Mill, happiness alone is intrinsically good (good in itself) rather than good as a means to some further good. Happiness is, in turn, understood by Mill to include pleasure and the absence of pain.[6] Mill then proceeds to tell us what must go into a "proof" of a view like his, thereby departing from his theoretical normative endeavor and taking on a metaethical question. In several places, he also admonishes us to foster certain characteristics in our children, moving back to normative matters by touching on questions in virtue ethics. Mill ventures into applied ethics as well, taking up questions regarding quite specific practices (e.g., slavery), drawing out the implications of his utilitarian view for the evaluation of the moral rightness or wrongness of those practices.[7] Mill, then, provides a nice example of a theorist whose main project is in the theory of moral obligation but whose theory development illuminates the complex connections among questions that arise in the conceptually distinct branches and subbranches of moral philosophy.

Since the nineteenth century, much of moral philosophy has focused on questions in the theory of moral obligation. For the first half of the current century, however, metaethics was the focus in English-speaking philosophy. And so-called applied ethics has only come into its own as a major area of philosophical inquiry over the past quarter century. Even more recently, interest in axiology and virtue ethics has resurfaced.[8] Still, much work is being done in the theory of obligation. And in applied ethics there has been a concentration on questions pertaining to the moral rightness or wrongness of certain actions and policies or practices. For example, the abortion debate has centered around the question of the moral permissibility of killing human fetuses for reasons other than self-defense. And the euthanasia debate has centered around the question of the moral permissibility of assisting another person in dying.

Many of the questions in professional ethics are questions of moral right and wrong. The cases with which we began this chapter point this out, raising questions like these: When, if ever, is it morally permissible for a professional to breach client confidentiality? When, if ever, is a professional morally required to harm or permit harm to a client for the sake of the welfare or rights of another client—or of some other third party or of the public in general? When special institutional duties and the well-being of another person conflict, which should take priority? When, if ever, is it morally permissible for a professional to deceive a client for that client's own good? When, if ever, does one's own well-being override duties of veracity? These are just a few of the morally thorny questions that arise in trying to decide what is morally permissible, what is morally prohibited, and what is morally required in professional life. Our concentration in this book will be on questions of morally justified actions and morally justified practices in professional life. But it needs to be emphasized that questions of moral character in professional life are extremely important and should not be left out of an inquiry into professional ethics. We shall touch on such questions in the final chapter.

REFLECTIVE EQUILIBRIUM

We have already seen that moral dilemmas involve situations in which one cannot escape deciding, in which not to decide is to decide, and in which doing nothing has the moral status of doing something. And we have seen that genuine moral dilemmas always involve sacrificing something of significant moral value, since they involve conflicts of values we want to preserve or, minimally, values we think are worthy of respect—values like loyalty to a colleague, a client's right to privacy and confidentialy, a client's welfare, the public good, veracity, personal integrity, legitimate self-interest. But we need to begin to ask how such choices are made. What are we doing when we engage in moral deliberation?

Moral deliberation, in general, involves two major activities: (1) getting clear on our moral intuitions/considered moral judgments about what is right or wrong in certain cases and (2) trying to find principles which will explain why actions we think are clearly right or wrong *are* right or wrong so that we can use those principles to help us decide what should be done in other cases in which we have no strong moral convictions or in which our intuitions shift. So, in moral deliberation we try to get a kind of reflective equilibrium between our deepest moral convictions (e.g., that killing children for sport is wrong), other background beliefs or theories that we hold (e.g., about the nature of persons), and our moral principles as properly refined.[9]

It might help to illuminate the concept of reflective equilibrium by comparing it to medical diagnosis. The activity of diagnosis involves using certain data (e.g., symptoms) in clear-cut cases to generate a diagnosis. Then, that diagnosis is used to help decide appropriate treatment in similar but less clear-cut cases. That is, the diagnosis provides guidance for treatment when the diagnostician is not entirely sure what the problem is in cases that are other than textbook cases; it provides a "best guess" which points to a way to begin to deal with the client's difficulity. In ethics we also have certain data, namely, deep convictions in some cases that some action or practice is right or wrong. We then ask *why* that action or practice is right or wrong, generating a principle (or a set of principles) which can explain the rightness or wrongness, just as diagnosis is generated to explain symptoms in clear-cut cases. This process in ethics provides us with moral principles to help us decide what should be done in less clear-cut cases—again, those cases in which we either have no strong convictions about what is right or in which our intuitions about what is permissible or required shift. The principles that we generate out of clear-cut cases, then, provide a place to begin in more puzzling cases. As we engage in this process, we are often led to refine our principles, just as the diagnostician is often led by new cases to refine and make more precise his or her diagnoses.

More generally, think of how science proceeds. In science, we start with some observations (data); then, we generate hypotheses to explain the data and to predict what we should find in relevantly similar cases. Notice, however, that in science we sometimes reject observations. For example, high school students "falsify" well-established theories in their physics labs all the time. But we don't reject those theories on that account; rather, we assume that something has gone wrong in the experiment, yielding false data. On the other hand, in science we do sometimes reject a theory because it cannot explain irrefutable data. There is, however, no hard-and-fast general rule available in science for when we should reject data and when we should modify our theories.

Things are much the same in ethics. We begin with our "moral data" (i.e., our strongest convictions of what is right or wrong in clear-cut cases) and move from here to generate principles for behavior that we can use for decision making in cases where what should be done is less clear. But, as in science, we sometimes have to reject our initial intuitions about what is right or wrong since they violate moral principles we have come to believe are surely correct. Thus, we realize we must dismiss the initial judgment as being the product of mere prejudice or conditioning rather than a judgment that can be supported by morally acceptable principles.[10] On the other hand, sometimes we are *so* certain that a given action would be wrong (or right) that we see we must modify our moral principles to accommodate that judgment. But, as in science, there is in ethics no hard-and-fast rule for deciding when to ignore our initial intuitions and when to alter our moral principles. This, however, should give us no cause for alarm, since we know that science progresses and that diagnoses get more and more helpful. In just the same way, we should be able to hope to make progress in moral decision making.

But how is all this done? Before we can answer, we need to understand better what genuinely reflective morality is and to distinguish morality from some things with which it is sometimes confused.

SOME MAJOR DISTINCTIONS AND WHAT MORALITY IS NOT

Our interest is in a genuinely reflective morality. Social scientists often report on the mores or morality of a particular group or culture. But we need to distinguish between questions about mores or norms dominant in a culture or group and actually doing moral philosophy or actually developing a reflective morality. We need, then, to distinguish between conventional (or received) morality and reflective morality.

Conventional Versus Reflective Morality. To follow a conventional morality is simply to be directed by traditional or customary rules or practices without stopping to examine or criticize those rules or practices or customs. As the term suggests, reflective morality arises when an individual begins to reflect on what principles will govern his or her actions, particularly when those actions involve the rights and interests of other persons (or other sentient beings) or the integrity of the agent. An individual acts as an autonomous moral agent when he or she acts on the basis of principles which are not merely imposed from without (e.g., by peer pressure, by some authority) or which have been internalized as a matter of mere habit, but rather when those principles have been consciously evaluated and accepted by the individual as the correct principles to direct his or her behavior. The autonomous moral agent has a clear sense of why he or she acts as he or she does and deliberately accepts acting that way on the basis of a reasoned, reflective conviction that such action is morally right. Minimally, reflective morality involves the movement beyond conditioned or "knee-jerk" reactions and merely self-interested behaviors to principled action where acceptance of the principles governing one's behavior is the result of a careful reflection which takes into account the moral integrity of the agent and the rights and interests of others.

Sometimes, however, moral agents act on the basis of reasons which are to be distinguished from fully reflective moral reasons. That is, sometimes morality is confused with other things which can certainly be relevant to moral decision making but which need to be clearly distinguished from morality as such. Though we are all aware of these distinctions, it can be helpful to make them explicit, particularly since these distinctions can sometimes be overlooked in professional life. They are the distinctions between morality and law, morality and prudence, morality and economics, morality and religion, morality and obedience to authority in general, and morality and mere opinion, bias, or taste.

The Distinction Between Morality and Law. We are all aware that morality is not reducible to law. This is just to say that finding out what the law permits or requires is not necessarily to find out what is morally right. We know, for example, that the law permits many immoralities, including disloyalties to friends, breaking of promises that do not have the stature of legal contracts, and a great variety of deceptions. In short, the law permits many actions that will not bear moral scrutiny. What is more, we would not want these immoralities to be made illegal since making them illegal would simply open the door to too much interference with individual lives.

It is also the case that the law sometimes requires gross immoralities. In the United States, for example, the Fugitive Slave Law of 1850 required that citizens help in the return of runaway slaves to their masters. Such laws were given further support by the Supreme Court's infamous Dred Scott decision in 1857, which made clear not only that slaves or those whose ancestors were sold as slaves were not (and could not be) citizens, but also that slaves were property, no different from any other property.[11]

Finally, we all know that sometimes morality may permit or require breaking a just law. For example, speeding laws are not by their nature unjust laws. But if there is an emergency, for example, the need to get someone to the hospital for lifesaving care, we generally would not think a driver immoral for going at, say, seventy-five or eighty miles an hour on a dry, open highway with little traffic, even though the speed limit is sixty-five miles an hour.

So, we cannot necessarily settle moral questions by settling the legal questions. The law may permit immoral behavior, the law may require immoral behavior, or the law may be morally justified but circumstances may be such that transgressing the law is permissible or even morally required.

This is not to say that what the law requires is of no moral import. What the law permits or requires is often a morally relevant consideration if for no reason other than that breaking the law can have serious consequences for the liberty and well-being of the agent. But it is to say that we cannot simply assume that the law is the whole of the moral story. The law itself is always subject to moral scrutiny and moral criticism; and the question of whether one should obey the law is always, in principle, an open one.

The Distinction Between Morality and Prudence. In a certain clear way, we all understand that morality puts constraints on merely self-interested behavior. That is, morality takes us beyond mere self-interest by requiring that we take the rights and interests of others into account when we act. Sometimes doing what would maximize one's own interests is morally impermissible. For example, suppose that I could make myself invisible and successfully burgle all my neighbors with no real chance of being discovered. Suppose further that I am not a person who suffers any sort of guilt in the wake of burgling. Under such circumstances, it might well be in my own best interests to be a burglar. But burgling is simply not a morally acceptable activity, it involves gross violations of the rights of others.

One's own rights and interests are, of course, relevant considerations in making moral decisions. However, self-interested action becomes selfish (i.e., morally repugnant self-interested action) when it violates the rights or carelessly sacrifices the interests of others. Thus, the point is that morally acceptable action is not to be *identified with* action that maximizes the good of the agent. Morality, then, is not reducible to prudence.

The Distinction Between Morality and Economics. Professionals are often confronted with hard choices that involve making decisions about the distribution of scarce resources. These resources include not only money, but also time and personnel. The temptation can be to find the most economical solution for all cases. But finding the most economic solution to a problem may not be to find a morally permissible solution to that problem. Consider, as an example, the growing costs of health care. We know that we must do something about these costs, but certain ways of saving resources are simply unacceptable. We could, for example, save considerable amounts of money and other resources by routinely killing off people over seventy years of age. But we know this would not be morally permissible, and this tells us that there is a distinction between morality and economics.

Sometimes important moral considerations like fairness or the respect for individual rights to self-determination require that we take the more economically costly routes. Our criminal justice system, for example, is an expensive one. But because of the concern to ensure that innocent persons do not fall victim to the massive powers of the state, we support an expensive system, opting to pay the costs of ensuring the freedom of those who have a right to be at liberty.

Economic considerations, to be sure, are often of great moral import in making distributive decisions. We do live under conditions of moderate scarcity, thus a decision to expand limited resources in one way is necessarily a decision not to expend those resources in another way. In the area of health care provision, for example, we realize that expending public resources for, say, research on transplanting human organs limits what resources we have available for research on acquired immune deficiency syndrome (AIDS) or on developing a cure or more effective treatments for arthritis or cancer, and so on. There are serious moral questions about what counts as a fair distribution of public resources in this area as well as others. And professionals constantly face hard questions about how to allocate their time among their clients. But the point is that one does not necessarily discover the correct moral choice by finding the most economical alternative. Thus, morally acceptable decisions are not reducible to decisions to take the most economical alternative.

The Distinction Between Morality and Religion. On some level, we all know, too, that finding out what a religious leader or religious tradition says is not necessarily to find out what is morally right. Religious leaders can make moral mistakes; and religious leaders can do, and have done, morally reprehensible things. In 1970, for example, Jim Jones, leader of the People's Temple, commanded his followers to drink Kool-Aid laced with cyanide and to give the drink to their children as well. Those who would not follow the command were either injected with the poison or shot. The episode, known as 'the Guyana Massacre,' is a chilling example of how religious leadership can go wrong. The more traditional religions have been known to make serious moral mistakes as well. The Roman Catholic Inquisition, which involved the execution of religious heretics, provides a frightening example of moral error.

Religious reasons are perfectly good reasons for deciding how one will conduct one's own life when one's actions are self-regarding. But when the liberty and welfare of other persons are involved, interfering with liberty or harming another requires a moral justification that must be able to stand on its own philosophical feet, independent of appeals to religious authority. One does not have the right to violate the moral rights of others or to otherwise harm others for religious reasons those others do not share. If one is going to override another person's right to free action or his or her right not to be harmed, then (minimally) one's reasons must be reasons that do not rely simply on the appeal to some religious belief or religious authority. Thus, morality is not reducible to religion.

The Distinction Between Morality and Obedience to Authority in General. A moral agent always retains the right to question commands if there is *any* reason to believe that those commands involve an unjustifiable infringement of rights or will lead to harm to persons or other sentient beings. Again, genuine morality involves maintaining moral autonomy; it involves more than mere unreflective obedience to external authority.

It goes without saying, of course, that special roles (e.g., in the various professions) serve to define areas of proper authority and that in assuming a role in one of these divisions, one takes on a duty to respect the limits of that role. Still, reflective morality requires that even within relatively clearly defined roles, moral agents must always be free to work for changes in the parameters of their roles if such changes are needed to ensure respect for moral rights and avoidance of unjustifiable harm. Moral agents always retain not only the right, but the obligation to evaluate the moral appropriateness of any order they might be given as well as the right and duty to resist if, after *careful* reflection, they are convinced that they are being instructed to do something that will not bear moral scrutiny. As we have already seen, in moral matters not to decide is equivalent to deciding. To blindly obey orders is itself to make a decision in favor of what the orders require. And that is a decision for which one is morally accountable.

The Distinction Between Morality and Mere Opinion/Bias/Taste. It is sometimes claimed that morality is only a matter of opinion: that morality is radically subjective like mere taste, thus talking about ethics is a waste of time. But there are some important differences between judgments of mere taste and genuine moral judgments which should be useful to clarify.

Taste involves matters of choice which are, though value-laden, essentially morally neutral. This, indeed, is what we *mean* by a matter of mere taste—that it pertains simply to preference, to matters without moral import.

What is more, we have already seen that moral matters tend to involve the rights and interests of others and/or the moral integrity of the agent in an essential way. Because of this, decisions with a moral content simply must not be made in shabby ways. Moral decisions are by their very nature decisions which must be made with care, not with the shrug that appropriately accompanies choices involving mere taste.

Further, morality involves conviction in a way that mere preference does not. And conviction involves a principled willingness to sacrifice which moves far beyond the realm of mere taste.

Moreover, very few of us really do believe that morality is reducible to mere opinion or taste. That is, once we see what such a view really involves, few of us are genuinely willing to accept that radical subjectivism in morality ought to be embraced. Sometimes students taking their first course in ethics will express the view that morality is nothing more than mere opinion. But they are inclined to change their position when something like this is suggested: Suppose at the end of the semester, everyone, no matter what his or her performance in the course, is given a *D*. The subjectivist is not free to complain that this would be unfair, since he or she is committed to the view that there are no objective standards for moral evaluation of behavior. The students quickly see that they do not really believe that morality is reducible to the arbitrarties of taste or mere opinion. If the instructor is going to issue a *D* for a student, this requires justification. And the appropriate justification is a certain kind of academic performance in a course. All things are simply not permitted, and few of us really believe that they are.

This is not to suggest that settling moral questions is easy or that reasonable people will always agree on what is morally permitted or morally required. But it is to say that it is not the case that all judgments of moral import are equally well justified.

Finally, and most importantly, we cannot argue rationally about matters of mere taste or mere bias. Imagine trying to rationally persuade someone that she should prefer the taste of chocolate to vanilla ice cream or that he should experience more pleasure eating crawfish than eating lobster. Certainly, we can *condition* people to new preferences; but this is very different from persuading them by rational argument. We can, on the other hand, argue rationally about moral beliefs. It will be useful to spend a little time on seeing how this is done.

THE STRUCTURE OF MORAL REASONING[12]

I have suggested that one of the central differences between morality and mere taste or mere opinion is that we can argue rationally about moral beliefs. What this means is that moral reasoning is a form of reasoning, that is, there is a structure of reasoning proper to moral decision making that takes the form of a logical argument. Particular moral judgments (e.g., "Beth should lie to protect her client" or "Beth would be wrong to lie to protect her client") are derived as conclusions of moral arguments which include as their premises general moral principles and certain factual claims. These arguments have this general structure or form:

Premise 1: General Moral Principle (GMP)
Premise 2, 3, etc. Factual Claim(s) (FC)

Conclusion: Derivative/Particular Moral Judgment (DMJ)

Consider, for example, the following (somewhat simple) moral arguments:

(1) We should do what we can to protect the innocent by deterring murderers. (GMP) (1.1)
(2) Capital punishment deters murderers. (FC)

THEREFORE, we should practice capital punishment. (DMJ)

or

(1) That which is unnatural is immoral. (GMP) (1.2)
(2) Homosexual behavior is unnatural. (FC)

THEREFORE, homosexual behavior is immoral. (DMJ)

Given this structure and these examples, we can begin to see where a particular moral judgment can be rationally challenged, that is, where moral reasoning can go wrong.

MORAL DEBATE OR HOW TO EVALUATE DERIVATIVE MORAL JUDGMENTS

There are at least four ways of challenging a particular moral judgment. That is, there are at least four places where any given argument for a derivative moral judgment can run into philosophical trouble. These are (1) conceptual confusions in the general moral principle, (2) problems in the factual link, (3) unacceptable conclusions following from the general moral principle when it is combined with certain other factual claims, and (4) moral inconsistency on the part of the person advancing the particular moral judgment in question.

Conceptual Confusions/Unclarities in the General Moral Principle.[13] Consider our second example (1.2), the unnaturalness argument. What is the meaning of 'unnatural' in the argument? Perhaps the proponent of the argument means by 'unnatural,' 'violates the laws of nature.' But if this is what we are to understand 'unnaturalness' to mean in the principle, then the first premise of the argument can lead to no moral conclusion about actions, since the laws of nature are merely descriptive laws and are, by their very nature, laws which cannot be violated. That is, the laws of nature simply *describe* the way things behave. They are not, like civil laws or the "laws" of morality, prescriptions for how people should behave, that is, they are not the kinds of laws which can be violated. Since all this is the case, if this is what the proponent of the argument understands 'unnatural' to mean, he or she is conceptually confused about what the laws of nature are. What is more, this meaning of 'unnatural' renders the second premise false, since it is impossible for any behavior to violate the laws of nature. This meaning of 'unnatural,' then, cannot lead us to conclude that the behavior in question is morally impermissible.

Another possible meaning of 'unnatural' is 'artificial' or 'man-made.' But if this is what the proponent of the unnaturalness argument means by the term, the claim that homosexual behavior is unnatural is surely a strange one, since replacing 'unnatural' with 'artificial' in this context seems to defy coherence. What is more, all human behavior is in a certain clear sense man-made. This analysis of 'unnatural,' then, does not seem to help in the argument against the moral permissibility of homosexual behavior.

In other cases, the analysis of 'unnatural' as 'artificial' or 'man-made' is less confusing. We do, for example, talk about artifical insemination, understanding this (roughly) to mean insemination with a certain kind of assistance from technology as opposed to insemination by sexual intercourse. But even if translating 'unnatural' as 'artificial' makes sense in some arguments from unnaturalness, we do not think that artificiality by itself entails immorality. For example, we use man-made means of transportation all the time; it certainly is not (in the sense under discussion) ''natural'' for human beings to fly, but we do not think that flying is morally wrong. There is nothing wrong in any general way with deviating from the way we might do things without the assistance of technology. Indeed, we often think that bringing technology to ''interfere with nature'' is precisely what we should do (e.g., in giving antibiotics to cure infection). Artificial behavior *as such* is only considered unethical when we mean by 'artificial' that which is 'deceptive' or 'insincere.' If we understand 'unnatural' as 'artificial' or 'man-made,' then, the first premise of the argument seems clearly to be false.

Perhaps the person using the unnaturalness argument means by 'unnatural,' 'uncommon' or 'deviating from the norm.' If we turn to the use of the unnaturalness argument in the debate about the morality of homosexual behavior, the first thing to notice is that recent studies suggest that homosexual behavior is really quite common and that it is ''normal'' for there to be a standard percentage of people with homosexual preferences in any given population. That percentage, is lower than the percentage of people with heterosexual preferences. But this only raises the question of precisely what norms we are to use. Homosexual behavior is actually far more common than other behaviors we think are perfectly fine, for example, being an astronaut, teaching ethics, being governor of a state, or—as Jonathon Glover points out—singing in the opera.[14] We generally do not think that unusual behavior is wrong simply *because* it is unusual.

What is more, we do not think that something is morally acceptable simply because it is commonly done. At one time, slavery was a common practice in the United States just as persecuting Jews was common practice under the Nazis. But in neither case do we think the fact that the practice was common is sufficient to make it morally acceptable.

Perhaps 'unnatural' in these arguments means 'violates the will of God.' If this is what the proponent of the unnaturalness argument means by 'unnatural,' he or she is not involved in a conceptual confusion. Indeed, this may well be the most plausible interpretation of 'unnatural' in all of the arguments in which it commonly occurs. But the problem with this understanding of 'unnatural' is that it rests the claim of immorality on a religious belief, abandoning the search for a philosophical account of why the actions or practices condemned by the unnaturalness argument are to be considered immoral. That is, if this is the meaning of 'unnatural' in these arguments, the purported moral principle is, instead, a theological principle, and these arguments will not be convincing to those who do not share the proponent's religious convictions.

Perhaps 'unnatural' in these arguments actually *means* 'immoral.' If so, three problems immediately arise. The first problem is that the first premise is vacuous; it tells us nothing since it simply states ''That which is immoral is immoral.'' The second problem is that what looks like a genuine argument for a moral conclusion turns out to be no argument at all because the so-called argument assumes what it supposedly sets out to prove, namely, that the behavior or practice in question is immoral. Thus, the argument begs the question by assuming the truth of the conclusion in the second premise. To see this, we just substitute 'immoral' for 'unnatural', and we get the following ''argument,'' which duplicates the conclusion in the second premise:

(1) That which is immoral is immoral. (GMP) (1.3)
(2) Homosexual behavior is immoral. (FC)

THEREFORE, homosexual behavior is immoral. ((DMJ)

The third problem also becomes apparent as soon as we make the substitutions of 'immoral' for 'unnatural' in the argument. If 'unnatural' means 'immoral' in the argument, we see immediately that the purported factual link is not factual at all. That is, we see that the second premise contains a moral judgment that has been buried under the appearance of being a factual or descriptive claim. This leads directly to the second area in which a moral argument can go wrong.

Problems in the Factual Link. Two kinds of problems can arise in the factual links of moral arguments. We have just seen an example of the first kind, namely, the mistake of taking a normative judgment to be a descriptive one.

This mistake often occurs in the abortion debate when it is claimed that the fetus is a human being, or a human life. That people think this is a factual claim is evidenced by their asking scientists when life begins to gain support for their claim that a fetus is a human life. But people who seek this scientific support invariably mean by 'a human life,' 'a bearer of moral rights'; and they fail to realize that whether something is a rights-bearer or not is not a matter of scientific discovery. It is, rather, a matter of moral judgment. Precisely the same problem arises when advocates of the woman's-right-to-choose argument call human fetuses parasites, since to call a fetus a parasite (or mere tissue, a mere collection of molecules, etc.) is already to assert that the fetus has the moral status of a fungus or tumor and, thus, is *not* a bearer of moral rights.[15]

In the same regard, consider judgments that are sometimes made about withholding information from patients. Sometimes the claim will be made that giving a patient full information about his or her condition is medically contraindicated. The physician in one of our opening cases implicitly suggested this in her response to the leukemia patient's nurse.[16] But in many of these cases, the reality is that the health care provider has made the normative judgment that it would be better to avoid whatever harm or discomfort might come to a patient from telling the truth than it would be to respect the patient's right to have important information concerning his or her own medical condition.[17] To point out that there is a value judgment here is not to say that making such judgments is necessarily wrong. But it is to say that it is important to realize that judgments which sometimes look like mere factual judgments are really different in kind—they are value judgments. The factual link in a moral argument may be faulty, then, by failing to be factual at all.

The second problem that can arise in the factual link pertains to the truth of claims made. That is, an argument's factual link may indeed contain factual claims, but these may be false or seriously questionable.

Consider again the argument for capital punishment given earlier as an example (1.1). Studies show that it is not at all clear that capital punishment does deter potential murderers. In fact, there is even some evidence to suggest that it might incite some people to murder.[18] If a factual claim is false or clearly questionable, the proponent of the argument lacks sufficient justification for his or her conclusion. That is, the conclusion of the argument may indeed be true, but the problem is that the argument given for that conclusion fails to provide adequate evidence for the conclusion. Thus, the derivative moral judgment that X is morally right or morally wrong has not been justified and the proponent of the argument must search for another argument to defend his or her moral judgment.

Unacceptable Implications of the General Moral Principle. There are several ways in which general moral principles can have unacceptable implications. A common problem lies with principles that are too broad, that is, principles that require more than we think is acceptable. Suppose, for example, that someone's derivative moral judgment that we should practice capital punishment rests on the belief that we should do all we can to minimize harm in our society. This sounds like a noble principle, but, on scrutiny, it has unacceptable consequences. Doing *all* we can to minimize harm would involve the sacrifice of too many other important values, particularly individual liberty, since taking this principle seriously would involve enormous efforts to protect people from themselves and others. A broad principle like this, then, needs to be rejected in favor of a more narrowly circumscribed and carefully thought-out foundational principle.

A similar example often arises in debates about lifesaving medical treatment. That is, people sometimes say things like, "We must do everything we can to preserve life" or "Life is sacred," and use such assertions as fundamental principles to justify particular moral judgments about life-sustaining medical treatment. But we do not really believe that we must do *all* we can to preserve life in general or to sustain the lives of patients in particular. If we were to do *all* we can, we would have to spend the whole gross national product on life-sustaining enterprises. Similarly, we don't really believe that life is sacred, if being sacred means that life cannot be sacrificed. Most of us do not think that the life of a polio virus is of intrinsic value or even that we must preserve the life of every human egg and sperm. We need, then, to try to avoid vague, unclear, or overgeneral fundamental moral principles which have implications that we simply cannot accept.

Consistency Problems. Consistency problems are a little different from the previous kinds of problems since they are not problems in an argument itself, but are, rather, problems that arise for a proponent of some argument. That is, the proponent of a moral argument may involve himself or herself in inconsistencies in taking views on different moral questions. Using the abortion debate again, consider the person who holds that abortion is murder because it is the killing of an innocent person, but also wants to allow abortion in cases of rape and incest. If a human fetus *is* a person, then it has the full range of basic moral rights that attach to persons, including the right not to be killed for reasons less than self-defense. And this right obtains no matter *how* that person came into existence. We do not think that we can kill grown-up persons simply because they are the products of rape or incest. Principles *are* principles, and a large part of the task in constructing a reflective morality consists in developing an internally coherent and consistent moral framework so that one's principles are strong and precise enough to survive when the going gets rough. The person who wants to rule out elective abortion but who wants to retain the option of abortion for rape and incest cases can be perfectly consistent. But consistency requires arguing for these judgments about different cases on the basis of a complex principle or several different principles which coherently support these differences in treatment.

These, then, are some of the central ways in which moral arguments can go wrong. By carefully considering our own and others' justifications for particular moral judgments, we can distinguish well-defended from poorly defended judgments, and can, thereby, help to ensure that the moral judgments we make and/or accept will be responsible, that is, well-reasoned ones. Of course, a moral argument can go wrong in any of the ways mentioned here but still have a true conclusion. The point is just that insofar as any of our judgments affect the rights and interests of others, we are obligated to have *good* reasons for making those judgments. If the justification for a particular moral judgment is faulty in any of these ways, the proponent of that judgment needs to find another justification.

But all of this raises the question of what kinds of moral principles we might appeal to in moral decision making. It should be useful to spend a little time on this question since the readings which follow include arguments from importantly different kinds of moral reasons.

KINDS OF MORAL PRINCIPLES

In theoretical normative ethics, theories of moral obligation are generally classified according to two major categories, namely, teleological theories and deontological theories. The term 'teleological' comes from the Greek *telos,* meaning 'end' or 'goal.' Teleological theories are consequentialist theories. That is, they are theories which hold that the moral value (including disvalue) of an action or practice is a function of the consequences (real or probable) of that action or practice. A common example of a teleological or consequentialist theory is the classical utilitarian theory of John Stuart Mill, which we have already touched on, that is, the view that we should always choose that which will tend to produce the greatest good for the greatest number. Although Mill did not make the distinction, it is common today to think of utilitarianism as being of two major kinds. One kind, which focuses on individual actions, is called 'act utilitarianism,' 'extreme utilitarianism,' or 'unrestricted utilitarianism.' Its principle is (roughly): "Of alternative actions open to you, choose that one which will tend to produce the greatest good for the greatest number." This view is often attributed to Mill's utilitarian predecessor, Jeremy Bentham.[19] Mill, on the other hand, is commonly understood to have been defending what is now called 'rule utilitarianism' or 'restricted utilitarianism.' This view tells us that instead of focusing on choosing those acts which will tend to produce the greatest good for the greatest number, we should choose those rules or practices which, if adhered to or generally accepted, will tend to produce the greatest good for the greatest number.[20]

Another example of teleology in ethics is a theory called 'ethical egoism.' Ethical egoism is the view that the agent should choose that (act, rule) which will (tend to) produce the greatest good for the agent choosing. Like utilitarianism, this is a consequentialist view, since it holds that the moral value of an agent's choice lies in the (real, probable) outcomes of that choice. Unlike utilitarianism, however, this view restricts the good to be pursued or maximized to that of the agent.[21]

Opposed to teleological ethical theories are deontological theories. The term 'deontological' comes from the Greek *deon,* meaning 'duty' or 'that which is binding.' The deontologist denies what the teleologist asserts. That is, the deontologist denies that the moral value of actions or practices is exclusively a function of the (real or probable) consequences of those actions or practices. Some deontologists (e.g., Immanuel Kant) deny that consequences have any relevance whatever to the moral evaluation of actions or practices.[22] For example, Kant held that morality forbids us to lie, and there is simply no exception to this rule. Even the fact that the murder of some innocent person might be prevented by lying could not be sufficient to justify lying according to Kant.[23] For strict rule deontologists such as Kant, once a moral rule is established, it is exceptionless.

Other deontologists are more moderate in their views of the nature of moral rules. W. D. Ross, for example, held that we have a number of *prima facie* duties, or duties which can come into conflict with one another.[24] That is, Ross held that we have a variety of general duties which arise from our positions and relations in the world, including duties to avoid doing harm, to prevent harm, to repair harm done, to do good, to be loyal, to be truthful, to be grateful, to improve ourselves, to be just. In any given concrete situation, two or more of these duties might come into conflict and the task in being moral is, according to Ross, to discern which of our conflicting duties takes priority in that concrete situation.

Contemporary deontologists (and they are legion) tend to allow that consequences (particularly bad consequences which can be avoided) are morally important, even though they, too, deny that consequences are the only relevant consideration in moral decision making. Thus, even though a deontologist may have a teleological element in his or her moral theory, as long as the theory holds that consequences (the production of good ones or the avoidance of bad ones) are not the whole of the moral story, the theory is generally classified as a deontological one.[25]

KINDS OF MORAL REASONS IN PROFESSIONAL ETHICS

The teleological/deontological distinction in ethical theory can be useful for thinking about the kinds of moral reasons which may be brought forward in trying to resolve the moral problems that arise in applied ethics in general and in professional ethics in particular. Reasons which pertain to the production of good consequences (e.g., higher profits or employee benefits in business, the gaining of useful information in medical or social science research, a client's physical or mental health in medicine and counseling, the dissemination of knowledge in education, a client's acquittal or the gaining of a good settlement in law, etc.) or the avoidance of bad ones (e.g., the prevention of a variety of harms to individuals and the wider society in all the professions) are teleological in nature. When one appeals to a teleological reason to support a decision in favor of or against an action or practice, one is holding that the action or practice is morally justifiable or not morally justifiable (at least in part) because of something *extrinsic* to it, that is, something it will bring about in the world or will prevent coming about in the world.

On the other hand, when one adduces a deontological reason for or against an action or practice, one is holding that the action or practice is of a certain *kind* (e.g., it is fraudulent, it involves unfair treatment), which (at least tends to) make it wrong. To use deontological reasons in the moral evaluation of actions or practices is to appeal not to something *extrinsic* to the act or practice, but to some feature *intrinsic* to the act or practice.

As an example, take the much-debated question of truth telling in health care provision. One can defend truth telling on teleological grounds, deontological grounds, or both. Sissela Bok, for example, defends the practice of truth telling in health care provision on the ground that patients and their loved ones tend to be better off when patients are informed of their diagnoses and prognoses. She argues that patients are more likely to be able to participate in their own treatment when they understand their conditions, that they can make plans to best provide for their families, and so on.[26] Alternatively, one can argue that persons have a right to know what their conditions are and that withholding information from patients is wrong because it violates this right.[27] And, of course, one can combine both kinds of reasons for supporting a practice of truth telling in health care provision.

It is also the case, however, that one can argue against truth telling in health care provision on both teleological and deontological grounds. For example, Joseph Collins argues that telling patients with serious conditions the truth about their conditions tends to be harmful to them. But he also argues that most patients with serious conditions simply do not want to know the grim story, thereby implicitly claiming that withholding information from these patients is not a violation of their rights.[28]

If we stop to theorize about it, most of us would categorize ourselves as deontologists. But in practice, the temptation is often to function teleologically, that is, to attempt to produce good results without considering seriously enough what moral values might be sacrificed in the process. We are, in practice, sometimes not what we think we ought to be. We tend to be a goal-oriented people, and this is evidenced in many of our professions, which by their very nature tend to be goal-oriented practices.

Consider, for example, business and the pursuit of profits. The goal orientation of business tends to excuse the sacrifice of respect for persons by allowing harmful pollution, deception and manipulation in advertising, and any number of other morally repugnant actions and practices. And consider the practice of medicine. It was not until quite recently that physicians as a group began to realize that their pursuit of medically good results often leads to a morally unacceptable violation of people's rights to control what happens to their own bodies. Medicine's goal is a noble one to be sure. And there is nothing morally reprehensible about the pursuit of profit in a society like our own. But though conflicts can arise among goals and though conflicts can arise among nonconsequentialist considerations, many contemporary deontologists are most concerned with the conflicts between these two kinds of moral reasons for making choices, and they hold that the pursuit of even the most worthy goals (e.g., a client's health) must be constrained by deontological values (e.g., a client's right to give an adequately informed consent).

As you read the selections in this book, then, you will see that the moral dilemmas that arise in professional life involve (1) conflicts among worthy goals, (2) conflicts among important nonconsequentialist values, and (3) conflicts among principles that urge us to pursue desirable outcomes and principles that urge us to keep the pursuit of such outcomes within the bounds of rights, fairness, and other kinds of nonconsequentialist moral values. Much of the task in developing one's own reflective morality consists in getting clear on how one believes such conflicts should be resolved.

There is much more that could be said by way of background. But I hope this much will be enough to provide a good start for thinking about ethical issues in professional life and to provide some guidance on how one might begin to organize and approach those issues.

NOTES

1. This case is adapted from Robert M. Veatch, *Case Studies in Medical Ethics* (Cambridge, MA: Harvard University Press, 1977), case 72.

2. This case is adapted from Maynard E. Pirsig and Kenneth F. Kirwin, (eds.), *Professional Responsibility: Cases and Materials,* 3rd ed. (St. Paul, MN: West, 1976), pp. 331–34. See the American Bar Association, *Model Rules of Professional Conduct* (Washington, DC: American Bar Association, 1983); rpt. in *United States Law Week* 52:7 (1983): 1–27. See appendix I, sample code 1, of *Ethical Issues in Professional Life;* hereafter *EIPL.*

3. This case is adapted from Martin Benjamin and Joy Curtis, *Ethics in Nursing* (New York: Oxford University Press, 1981), p. 3.

4. 'Applied ethics' is, however, something of a misnomer since it suggests that the task is merely to apply ethical theory to specific problems; in other words, that engaging in applied ethics is doing some sort of philosophical technology in which high-level theory is simply brought over to practice. In fact, applied ethics raises a number of interesting theoretical and methodological questions that, in turn, are useful both in the development of more general normative theory and in answering questions of meaning and justification in metaethics. On the question of the nature of applied ethics see, e.g., Arthur L. Caplan, "Ethical Engineers Need Not Apply: The State of Applied Ethics Today," *Science, Technology, and Human Values* 6:33 (1980): 24–32.

5. John Stuart Mill, *Utilitarianism* (1863), in Mary Warnock (ed.), *Utilitarianism, On Liberty, and Essay on Bentham* (New York: New American Library, 1962).

6. Each of these concepts is extremely complex in Mill's theory; but, given our immediate purposes, we can ignore these complexities.

7. In addition to *Utilitarianism,* see, e.g., *On Liberty* (1859), in Warnock, *supra.*

8. See, e.g., Alasdair MacIntyre, *After Virtue* (South Bend, IN: University of Notre Dame Press, 1981; 2nd ed., 1984); and Michael Slote, *Goods and Virtues* (New York: Oxford University Press, 1983), as well as several other of the selected readings for chap. 11, *EIPL.*

9. On the method of reflective equilibrium in ethics, see, e.g., John Rawls, "The Independence of Moral Theory," *Proceedings of the American Philosophical Association* 48:1 (1974–75): 5–22; Norman Daniels, "Wide Reflective Equilibrium and Theory Acceptance in Ethics," *Journal of Philosophy* 76:5 (1979): 256–62; Kai Nielsen, "Our Considered Judgments," *Ratio* 19:1 (1977): 39–46; Nielsen, "Considered Judgments Again," *Human Studies* 5:2 (1982): 109–18; Jonathon Glover, *Causing Death and Saving Lives* (New York: Penguin, 1977), chap. 2. This method is not without its critics. See, e.g., Joseph Raz, "The Claims of Reflective Equilibrium," *Inquiry* 25:3 (1982): 312–14.

10. On the difference between genuine moral judgments and other judgments for which we do not have moral reasons, see Ronald Dworkin, "Lord Devlin and the Enforcement of Morals," *Yale Law Journal* 75 (1966): republished as "Liberty and Moralism," which comprises chap. 10 in his *Taking Rights Seriously* (Cambridge, MA: Harvard University Press, 1977), pp. 240–58. See also Joan C. Callahan, "On Harming the Dead," *Ethics* 97:2 (1987): 341–52.

11. See the majority opinion, authored by Chief Justice Roger B. Taney (6 March 1857). For a thorough account of the case, see Vincent C. Hopkins, *Dred Scott's Case* (New York: Fordham University Press, 1951; reissued New York: Atheneum, 1967).

12. The following discussions of the structure of moral reasoning and the evaluation of moral arguments are indebted to Stephen Stich, "The Recombinant DNA Debate: Some Philosophical Considerations," in Stephen P. Stich and David A. Jackson (eds.), *The Recombinant DNA Debate* (Englewood Cliffs, NJ: Prentice-Hall, 1979), pp. 183–202; as well as to Professor Stich's lectures on ethics at the University of Maryland. See also Glover, *supra,* chap. 2, for a discussion of how to evaluate derivative moral judgments.

13. The following discussion of the unnaturalness argument is indebted to Leiser's criticism of the argument in Burton M. Leiser, *Liberty, Justice and Morals: Contemporary Value Conflicts* (New York: Macmillan, 1973; 2nd ed., 1979), chap. 2. See also Samuel Gorovitz's discussion of the argument in *Doctors' Dilemmas: Moral Conflict and Medical Care* (New York: Macmillan, 1982; reissued New York: Oxford University Press, 1985), chap. 10.

14. Glover, *supra,* chap. 2.

15. For a fuller discussion of these points, see Joan C. Callahan, "The Fetus and Fundamental Rights," *Commonweal,* 11 April 1986, pp. 203–9.

16. Joseph Collins makes this sort of claim in "Should Doctors Tell the Truth?" *Harper's Magazine* 155 (Aug. 1927), pp. 320–26; rpt. chap. 5, sel. 16, *EIPL*.

17. For a discussion of the frequent confusion between genuine medical judgments and value judgments made in the medical context, see Benjamin and Curtis, *supra,* chap. 1.

18. See, e.g., Hugo Bedau, "Capital Punishment and Social Defense," in Tom Regan (ed.), *Matters of Life and Death,* 2nd ed. (New York: Random House, 1986), pp. 175–212.

19. See, e.g., Jeremy Bentham, *An Introduction to the Principles of Morals and Legislation* (1789), ed. J. H. Burns and H.L.A. Hart (London: University of London, Athlone Press, 1970). For a contemporary defense of this view see J.J.C. Smart's contribution in J.J.C. Smart and Bernard Williams, *Utilitarianism: For and Against* (New York: Cambridge University Press, 1973).

20. For a contemporary version of this view, see Richard B. Brandt, *A Theory of the Good and the Right* (New York: Oxford University Press, 1979).

21. Notice that ethical egoism reduces morality to prudence. Because of this, many deny that it qualifies as a genuine moral theory.

22. See, e.g., Immanuel Kant, *Foundations of the Metaphysics of Morals* (1785; 2nd ed., 1786), in Lewis White Beck, (ed. and trans.), *Critique of Practical Reason and Other Works in Moral Philosophy* (Chicago: University of Chicago Press, 1949). (This work is sometimes entitled *Groundwork of the Metaphysics of Morals.*)

23. See e.g., Kant's "On the Supposed Right to Lie from Benevolent Motives," in his *Critique of Practical Reason* (1788), in Beck, *supra,* pp. 346–50.

24. See W. D. Ross, *The Right and the Good* (Oxford: Clarendon, 1930).

25. Strictly speaking, deontological views are those, like Kant's and Ross', which frame moral obligation in terms of features internal to an act or practice. An action is, for example, of a kind which (depending on the strictness of the view) is wrong or tends to be wrong if it is deceitful, if it is unjust, and so forth, independent of considerations of consequences. However, it has become common to classify as deontologists theorists who are not pure teleologists but who have mixed views and will allow that consequences can be relevant considerations in moral decision making and moral evaluation. I follow this usage.

26. See Sissela Bok, *Lying: Moral Choice in Public and Private Life* (New York: Pantheon, 1978), chap. 15; rpt. chap. 5, sel. 17 *EIPL.*

27. This is the direction taken by Alexander Capron in "Informed Consent in Catastrophic Disease Research and Treatment," *University of Pennsylvania Law Review* 123 (1974): 340–438.

28. Collins, *supra;* chap. 5, sel. 16, *EIPL.* See also Donald VanDeVeer, "The Contractual Argument for Withholding Medical Information," *Philosophy and Public Affairs* 9:2 (1980): 198–205.

QUESTIONS FOR STUDY AND DISCUSSION

1. Explain the normative/descriptive distinction and offer several examples of each kind of claim to illustrate the distinction.

2. What is a moral dilemma? Take some profession or occupation which interests you and explain what you think the most common moral dilemmas might be in that profession or occupation.

3. Explain the major divisions in moral philosophy, giving examples of the kinds of questions asked in each division. Use the descriptive/normative distinction to explain the main distinction between metaethics and the other divisions of moral philosophy.

4. Explain the method of reflective equilibrium in moral reasoning, analogizing this method to scientific method. In what ways is moral reasoning unlike scientific reasoning?

5. Explain the distinction between customary and reflective morality and offer several examples of your own to illustrate the distinction.

6. Offer concrete examples that illustrate the distinctions between law and morality, prudence and morality, economics and morality, religion and morality, obedience to authority in general and morality, and taste and morality. Explain why all of these distinctions are instances of the more general descriptive/normative distinction.

7. Explain the general structure of moral reasoning and describe four of the ways in which a derivative/particular moral judgment can be rationally challenged on the basis of this structure.

8. Explain the distinction between teleological and deontological moral reasons. Select a case from the beginning of this chapter, list the moral considerations relevant to that case (e.g., preventing harm, lying, deceiving, respecting rights, etc.) and categorize these considerations as teleological or deontological in nature. Using the guide on how to prepare case responses in appendix II, offer your own resolution of the case you have selected.

SELECTED BIBLIOGRAPHY

Aristotle. *Nichomachean Ethics*. Trans. W. D. Ross. In *The Works of Aristotle Translated into English,* ed. W. D. Ross. Oxford: Oxford University Press, 1915.

Ayer, Alfred J. *Language, Truth and Logic*. London: Victor Gollancz, 1936.

Baier, Kurt. *The Moral Point of View*. New York: Random House, 1958.

Bentham, Jeremy. *An Introduction to the Principles of Morals and Legislation* (1789). Ed. J. H. Burns and H.L.A. Hart. London: University of London, Athlone Press, 1970.

Bradley, F. H. *Ethical Studies* (1876). Oxford: Oxford University Press, 1970.

Brandt, Richard B. *A Theory of the Good and the Right*. New York: Oxford University Press, 1979.

Butler, Joseph. *Fifteen Sermons on Human Nature Preached at the Rolls Chapel* (1726; 2nd ed., 1729). Excerpted in *Five Sermons,* ed. Stephen Darwell. Indianapolis, IN: Hackett, 1983.

Donagan, Alan. *The Theory of Morality*. Chicago: University of Chicago Press, 1977.

Fried, Charles. *An Anatomy of Values: Problems of Personal and Social Choice*. Cambridge, MA: Harvard University Press, 1970.

———. *Right and Wrong*. Cambridge, MA: Harvard University Press, 1978.

Geach, Peter. *The Virtues: The Stanton Lectures, 1973–74*. New York: Cambridge University Press, 1977.

Gert, Bernard. *The Moral Rules*. New York: Harper and Row, 1966.

Gewirth, Alan. *Reason and Morality*. Chicago: University of Chicago Press, 1978.

Hare, Richard M. *Freedom and Reason*. Oxford: Clarendon, 1963.

———. *The Language of Morals*. New York: Oxford University Press, 1952.

———. *Practical Inferences*. New York: Oxford University Press, 1971.

Hume, David. *An Enquiry Concerning the Principles of Morals* (1751). Ed. J. B. Schneewind. Indianapolis, IN: Hackett, 1983.

———. *A Treatise of Human Nature,* Bks. 2, 3 (1739–1740). Ed. L. A. Selby-Bigge. Oxford: Clarendon, 1960.

Kant, Immanuel. *Critique of Practical Reason* (1788). In *Critique of Practical Reason and Other Writings in Moral Philosophy,* ed. and trans. Lewis White Beck. Chicago: University of Chicago Press, 1949.

———. *Foundations of the Metaphysics of Morals* (1785; 2nd ed., 1786). In Beck, *supra.*

———. *Lectures on Ethics* (1775–1780). Trans. Louis Infield. London: Methuen, 1930; reissued New York: Harper and Row, 1963.

———. *Metaphysical Principles of Virtue* (1797). In *Ethical Philosophy,* ed. and trans. James W. Ellington. Indianapolis, IN: Hackett, 1983.

———. *Perpetual Peace* (1795). Ed. and trans. Lewis White Beck. Indianapolis, IN: Bobbs-Merrill, 1957.

MacIntyre, Alasdair. *After Virtue*. South Bend, IN: University of Notre Dame Press, 1981; 2nd ed., 1984.

Mill, John S. *On Liberty* (1859). In *Utilitarianism, On Liberty, and Essay on Bentham,* ed. Mary Warnock. New York: New American Library, 1962.

———. *Utilitarianism* (1863). In Warnock, *supra.*

Nagel, Thomas. "The Fragmentation of Value." In *Knowledge, Value, and Belief,* ed. H. Tristram Engelhardt and

Daniel Callahan. Hastings-on-Hudson, NY: Institute of Society, Ethics and the Life Sciences, 1977; rpt. as chap. 9 of Nagel's *Mortal Questions*. New York: Cambridge University Press, 1979.

———. *The Possibility of Altruism*. New York: Oxford University Press, 1970.

Rawls, John. *A Theory of Justice*. Cambridge, MA: Harvard University Press, 1971.

———. "Two Concepts of Rules." *Philosophical Review* 64:1 (1955): 3–32.

Ross, W. D. *The Right and the Good*. Oxford: Clarendon, 1930.

Sartre, Jean-Paul. *L'Existentialisme est un humanisme* (1946). Trans. P. Mairet as *Existentialism Is a Humanism*. New York: Philosophical Library, 1949.

Sidgwick, Henry. *The Methods of Ethics* (1874; substantive revisions through the 6th ed.) London: Macmillan, 1901.

———. *Outlines of the History of Ethics* (1886). Ed. Alban G. Widgery. New York: Macmillan, 1931; reissued Boston: Beacon, 1960.

Slote, Michael. *Goods and Virtues*. New York: Oxford University Press, 1983.

Stevenson, Charles. *Ethics and Language*. New Haven, CT: Yale University Press, 1944.

———. *Facts and Values*. New Haven, CT: Yale University Press, 1963.

2

PROFESSIONS AND PROFESSIONALIZATION

We are concerned in this book with ethical issues that arise in professional life. Before we can get on to addressing specific moral issues in professional life, however, we need to ask some conceptual and foundational questions. This chapter focuses on the concept of a profession and what it might mean for an occupation to be more or less professionalized. It is important to notice that these conceptual questions are not entirely separable from the moral questions to be addressed in the chapters to follow, since the very concept one has of one's role as a professional tends to shape one's professional ethics. And, as we shall see in chapter 11, the moral questions raised in the chapters to come will eventually lead us full circle to reexamine the place of professionalization in professional ethics. As a way of approaching the normative questions that concern us, then, we can begin by asking what, if anything, marks an occupation as a profession.

The concept of a profession is a slippery one that is not entirely fixed in our conceptual geography. The selections by Michael Bayles, Everett Hughes, and Bernard Barber in this chapter attempt to do some conceptual housekeeping. They suggest that we understand professions as occupations which have certain shared characteristics, and that whether or not an occupation is more or less professionalized depends on how thoroughly it manifests these characteristics. Perhaps the best way to understand this approach is to see it as suggesting that professions and marginal or emerging professions have certain family resemblances, that is, they have features which make them look somewhat alike if not identical in structure. Bayles, for example, says that we recognize genuine professions as involving extensive intellectual training and the provision of services which are important to the organized functioning of society. But he also points out that paradigm professions (e.g., medicine, law) include certain characteristics which other professions might lack (e.g., state licensing). Notice that Bayles insists that whatever our definition of 'profession' might be, it must be a purely descriptive definition, that is, it must not be normative or value-laden in any way. But it can be objected that since we generally reserve the term 'profession' for those occupations which are prestigious, the concept of a profession does seem to include a strong normative component. The selections from Hughes and Barber take this into account.

These two selections illuminate the sociological features of occupations which are more or less professionalized. Barber isolates the steps which are typically taken by an occupation's leaders when they decide to seek the autonomy, social status, and other rewards that accompany recognition of an occupation as a profession. Barber also points out that emerging or marginal professions are those which include important differences in educational background and service orientation among its members. Good examples of what Barber understands the emerging or marginal professions to include might be nursing, journalism, and public administration. Nursing, for example, has tended to close down its hospital training programs and attach its preparation programs to universities. And we have recently seen a sharp increase in schools of journalism and schools of public administration in universities. At the same time, unlike law, medicine, and the professoriate (where the preparation of practitioners is highly homogeneous), levels of education within nursing, journalism, and public administration vary enormously. As John Merrill points out, one can function as a journalist with no formal journalistic training at all. On the other hand, those who teach journalism and public administration may be highly trained and clearly recognizable as professionals. The situation is similar in nursing, where preparatory programs range in length from eighteen-month licensed practical nurse programs through the doctorate.

Close to Barber's point regarding differences in attitudes toward service in the emerging professions is Hughes' observation that genuine professionalism often involves a sense of having a ''calling'' or vocation and being part of a community. In the emerging or marginal professions, the sense of vocation and the sense of being an integral part of a community or fellowship tends to be far more heterogeneous than, say, in medicine or the religious professions. There are for example, many nurses and public managers for whom their work is ''just a job.'' Yet there are also many in nursing and public sector positions who have a genuine vocational commitment. It is just this disparity in education and vocational commitment to the service provided by the occupation which has led the leadership in nursing and public administration to take the steps Barber has isolated. In recent years the American Nurses' Association, for example, has been pressing for a legally-recognized distinction between professional and technical nurses and for higher entry levels into what the leadership wants to be recognized as professional nursing. And the new schools of public administration are urging those who work for state and federal governments to pursue certification as public managers.

It is precisely this press toward homogeneity in preparation and ideology which Merrill denounces in the professionalization of journalism. Considering characteristics like those discussed by Bayles, Hughes, and Barber, Merrill holds that journalism is not, and ought not to become, a profession. Thus, Merrill challenges the often-unarticulated but traditional view that professionalization of an occupation is always desirable.

The readings in this chapter presuppose certain moral underpinnings for various professions. In chapter 3, we shall focus on the moral foundations of professional ethics.

1. The Professions

Michael D. Bayles

. . . No generally accepted definition of the term *profession* exists, yet a working concept is needed for our study of professional ethics. Because the purpose of this study is to consider common ethical problems raised by and within professions, a good definition will delineate characteristics of occupations with similar ethical problems. (These characteristics may prove to be related to some of those problems in important ways.) One need not char-

From *Professional Ethics* (Belmont, CA: Wadsworth Publishing Co., 1981), pp. 7–11.

acterize professions by a set of necessary and sufficient features possessed by all professions and only by professions.[1] The variety of professions is simply too great for that approach. Rather, some features can be taken as necessary for an occupation to be a profession, and others as simply common to many professions and as raising similar ethical concerns.

Three necessary features have been singled out by almost all authors who have characterized professions. First, a rather extensive training is required to practice a profession. Lawyers now generally attend law school for three years, and in the past they underwent years of clerkship with an established lawyer. Many, if not most, professionals have advanced academic degrees, and one author has plausibly contended that at least a college baccalaureate is necessary to be a professional.[2]

Second, the training involves a significant intellectual component.[3] The training of bricklayers, barbers, and craftspeople primarily involves physical skills. Accountants, engineers, lawyers, and physicians are trained in intellectual tasks and skills. Although physical skill may be involved in, for example, surgery or dentistry, the intellectual aspect is still predominant. The intellectual component is characteristic of those professionals who primarily advise others about matters the average person does not know about or understand. Thus, providing advice rather than things is a characteristic feature of the professions.

Third, the trained ability provides an important service in society. Physicians, lawyers, teachers, accountants, engineers, and architects provide services important to the organized functioning of society—which chess experts do not. The rapid increase in the numbers of professions and professionals in the twentieth century is due to this feature. To function, technologically complex modern societies require a greater application of specialized knowledge than did the simpler societies of the past. The production and distribution of energy requires activity by many engineers. The operation of financial markets requires accountants, lawyers, and business and investment consultants. In short, professions provide important services that require extensive intellectual training.

Other features are common to most professions, although they are not necessary for professional status. Usually a process of certification or licensing exists. Lawyers are admitted to the bar and physicians receive a license to practice medicine. However, licensing is not sufficient to constitute an occupation a profession. One must be licensed to drive a car, but a driver's license does not make one a professional driver. Many professionals need not be officially licensed. College teachers are not licensed or certified, although they must usually possess an advanced university degree. Similarly, many accountants are not certified public accountants, and computer scientists are not licensed or certified.

Another feature common to professions is an organization of members.[4] All major professions have organizations that claim to represent them. These organizations are not always open to all members of a profession, and competing organizations sometimes exist. Some bar associations, at least in the past, did not admit all lawyers. The organizations work to advance the goals of the profession—health, justice, efficient and safe buildings, and so on—and to promote the economic well-being of their members. Indeed, one author has stated that "the ethical problem of the profession, then, is . . . to fulfill as completely as possible the primary service for which it stands while securing the legitimate economic interest of its members."[5] If this claim is even approximately correct, one must expect professional organizations to be deeply involved in securing the economic interests of their members. Nevertheless, such organizations do generally differ from trade unions, which are almost exclusively devoted to members' economic interests. One does not expect to find carpenters' or automobile workers' unions striking for well-designed and constructed buildings or automobiles, yet public school teachers do strike for smaller classes and other benefits for students, and physicians and nurses for improved conditions for patients.

A third common feature of the professional is autonomy in his or her work. . . . How far such autonomy would extend is an open question. The minimum lies perhaps in the tasks of the work itself.[6] For example, surgeons are free to use their own judgment about the details of operating procedure and lawyers to use their judgment about how to draft a contract, provided they remain within the bounds of acceptable professional practice. If professionals did not exercise their judgment in these aspects, people would have little reason to hire them. However, many professionals now work in large bureaucratic organizations in which their autonomy is limited by superiors who direct their activity and overrule their judgments. Nurses are often thought to have an equivocal status as professionals simply because their superiors can overrule their judgments about specific aspects of their work. In these cases, however, an element of autonomy remains since the professionals are expected to exercise a considerable degree of discretionary judgment within the work context. Thus, an element of autonomy is a common and partially defining feature of a profession, though it might not be a necessary feature and the extent of such autonomy is debatable.

One may bias an investigation of professional ethics by using normative features (those saying how matters *should* be) to define or characterize professions. One common bias is to characterize professionals as primarily devoted to providing service and only secondarily to making money.[7] Such claims may be legitimate contentions about what should govern professions and motivate professionals, but they do not define the professions. If lawyers are, in the words of one of the earliest American writers on legal ethics, George Sharswood, "a hord of pettifogging, barratrous, custom-seeking, money-making" persons, they nonetheless constitute a profession.[8] An extreme example of the use of normative features to define professions is the following "consideration" presented by Maynard Pirsig: "The responsibility for effectuating the rendition of these services to all that need them and in such a manner that the public interest will best be served is left to the profession itself."[9] In this one condition, Pirsig manages to assume three different normative principles. First, services should be provided to all who need them. Second, the services should be provided so as best to promote the public interest. Third, the profession itself should be the sole judge of the method for achieving the first two principles. Even if these normative principles are correct, they should not be erected into the defining features of a profession.

Distinctions among kinds of professions are usually related to the kinds of activities pursued by most but not all members of the professions. An important distinction in professional ethics is between *consulting* and *scholarly* professions.[10] The consulting professions, such as law, medicine, and architecture, have traditionally practiced on a fee-for-service basis with a personal, individual relationship between client and professional. A consulting professional (or a professional in a consulting role) acts primarily in behalf of an individual client. A scholarly professional, such as a college teacher or scientific researcher, usually has either many clients at the same time (students) or no personal client (jobs assigned by superiors in a corporation). A scholarly professional usually works for a salary rather than as an entrepreneur who depends on attracting individual clients. Of course, this distinction is blurred in many cases. For example, a junior lawyer in a large law firm is more like a scientific researcher, and nurses have individual clients even though they usually work for a large organization (hospital). Among the consulting professionals are physicians, lawyers, accountants, consulting engineers, architects, dentists, psychiatrists, and psychological counselors. Other persons with tasks similar to some of the consulting professions include nurses, pharmacists, stockbrokers, the clergy, insurance brokers, social workers, and realtors. Among the scholarly professions are non-consulting engineers, teachers, scientists, journalists, and technicians.

These differences between the roles of consulting and scholarly professionals are crucial in defining the kinds of ethical problems each confronts. The economic considerations of the consulting professional—fees, advertising, and so on—are not important problems for the professional employed by a large organization on a salary. Although consulting architects and accountants have many ethical problems in the professional–client relationship, research scientists or engineers in large organizations do not normally deal with clients. University teachers do have clients, but they typically confront them in a group and have fewer problems of confidentiality, and so forth. . . .

Three salient features of the role of the consulting professions in the United States during the last half of the twentieth century lie at the heart of the problem of their positions in a liberal society. First, they all provide an important service. Consulting engineers and architects design the structures and facilities essential to modern life—buildings, houses, power stations, transportation systems, and so on. Most of us depend on the medical and dental professions to protect our health and well-being, even our lives. The legal profession provides services essential for justice and equality before the law. Accountants, as auditors, testify to the financial integrity of institutions and keep track of the wealth in society. The services of professionals are important for individuals to realize the values they seek in their personal lives—health, wealth, justice, comfort, and safety.

Second, not only do the professions serve basic values, they also have a monopoly over the provision of services. In many professions, one must be legally certified to practice. Laws often make it a criminal offense to practice a profession without a license. Attempting to do without professionals or to be one's own professional can realistically have only minimal success. If one decides to be one's own physician, one cannot obtain access to the most useful medicines and technology; most drugs can only be obtained legally with a prescription from a licensed physician and from another professional, a pharmacist. Although one may legally represent oneself, the legal profession has waged continuous war against allowing people access to information that would enable them to handle their own legal problems, such as divorce and probate of wills.

The monopolistic aspect of professional practices

has frequently brought profession into conflict with each other and with other occupational groups over the provision of services. Architects and engineers have long debated their respective spheres of practice, as have lawyers and accountants. The legal profession has also been anxious to define the respective spheres of practice of realtors and insurance and title companies. The medical profession now confronts questions concerning the services provided by nurse practitioners and physician's assistants. A little noticed battle has concerned the practice of midwives, especially lay midwives, at home births. In many states, delivering a child is considered the practice of medicine and only licensed physicians may offer to do so.[11] In a recent California case, three lay midwives were prosecuted for the unlicensed practice of medicine, and the Supreme Court of California upheld the constitutionality of the law with respect to childbirth.[12] A woman's right of privacy, it held, does not extend to the choice of the manner and circumstances in which her baby is born.

The legal monopoly of professional services has an important implication for professional ethics. Professionals do not have a right to practice; it is a privilege conferred by the state. One must carefully distinguish between a right and a privilege in this context. A right is a sound claim that one be permitted (or assisted) to act in some manner without interference. A privilege is a permission to perform certain acts provided specified conditions are fulfilled. With a privilege, the burden is upon the person obtaining it to demonstrate that he or she has the necessary qualifications. For example, one must pass tests for the privilege of driving a car. In the case of a right, the burden is upon anyone who fails to respect it, for example, by prohibiting the publication of one's opinions. Individual professionals have only a privilege to practice; in addition, the profession as a whole is a privileged activity created by the state to further social values.

A third feature of the consulting professional's role is that although some professions have secured legally protected monopolies, none of them has been subject to much public control. Monopolies such as public utilities that provide essential services have usually been subject to strict public control as to the conditions and types of services provided. In contrast, the professions have claimed and been accorded a large degree of self-regulation. They have claimed that because of the intellectual training and judgment required for their practice, nonprofessionals are unable to properly evaluate their conduct. Thus, in addition to control over membership and the disciplining of members, the professions also control the conditions of practice (including until recently the setting of fees and the regulation of advertising). . . .

NOTES

1. Wilbert E. Moore, in *The Professions: Roles and Rules* (New York: Russell Sage Foundation, 1970), pp. 4–5, recognizes this point and offers a scale of professionalism. The definitional technique used here could be modified to a scale system by assigning points to the possession of those characteristics that are not necessary but are often found in professions. Both the scale system and that used here agree that an occupation may be a profession yet lack some features found in most professions.

2. Ibid., p. 11.

3. Professionals "profess to know better than others the nature of certain matters, and to know better than their clients what ails them or their affairs. This is the essence of the professional idea and the professional claim." Everett C. Hughes, "Professions," in *The Professions in America,* ed. Kenneth S. Lynn and the editors of *Daedalus* (Boston: Houghton Mifflin, 1965 [Beacon pbk., 1967], p. 2). [Rpt. chap. 2, sel. 2, *EIPL.* —ED.]

4. See Moore, op. cit., pp. 9–10, and Roscoe Pound, "What Is a Profession? The Rise of the Legal Profession in Antiquity," *Notre Dame Lawyer* 19 (1944): 204.

5. R. M. MacIver, "The Social Significance of Professional Ethics," in *Cases and Materials on Professional Responsibility,* 2nd ed., ed. Maynard E. Pirsig (St. Paul, MN: West, 1965), p. 48.

6. See Eliot Freidson, *Profession of Medicine: A Study of the Sociology of Applied Knowledge* (New York: Harper and Row, 1970), pp. xviii, 42, 70, 82.

7. John W. Wade, "Public Responsibilities of the Learned Professions," in Pirsig, op. cit., p. 38; MacIver, op. cit., p. 48. Moore's use of this feature as one item on a scale is less objectionable because the service orientation is not a necessary feature. See Moore, op. cit., pp. 13–15.

8. George Sharswood. *An Essay on Professional Ethics,* 6th ed. (Philadelphia: George T. Bird, 1844; rpt. 1930), pp. 147–48.

9. Pirsig, op. cit., p. 43.

10. Freidson, op. cit., pp. 70, 75, 188.

11. George J. Annas, "Childbirth and the Law: How to Work Within Old Laws, Avoid Malpractice, and Influence New Legislation in Maternity Care." In *21st Century Obstetrics Now!,* 2 vols., ed. David Stewart and Lee Stewart, (Chapel Hill, NC: NAPSAC, 1974), vol. 2, p. 588.

12. *Bowland* v. *Municipal Ct. for Santa Cruz City.* 18 Cal. 3d 479, 556 P.2d 1081, 134 Cal. Rptr. 630 (1976).

2. Professions

Everett C. Hughes

. . . A profession delivers esoteric services—advice or action or both—to individuals, organizations or government; to whole classes or groups of people or to the public at large. The action may be manual; the surgeon and the bishop lay on their hands, although in the one case manual skill is of the essence, while in the other it need not be great because the action is symbolic. . . . Even when manual, the action—it is assumed or claimed—is determined by esoteric knowledge systematically formulated and applied to problems of a client. The services include advice. The person for or upon whom the esoteric service is performed, or the one who is thought to have the right or duty to act for him, is advised that the professional's action is necessary. Indeed, the professional in some cases refuses to act unless the client—individual or corporate—agrees to follow the advice given.

The nature of the knowledge, substantive or theoretical, on which advice and action are based is not always clear; it is often a mixture of several kinds of practical and theoretical knowledge. But it is part of the professional complex, and of the professional claim, that the practice should rest upon some branch of knowledge to which the professionals are privy by virtue of long study and by initiation and apprenticeship under masters already members of the profession.

The *Oxford Shorter Dictionary* tells us that the earliest meaning of the adjective "professed" was this: "That has taken the vows of a religious order." By 1675, the word had been secularized thus: "That professes to be duly qualified; professional." "Profession" originally meant the act or fact of professing. It has come to mean: "The occupation which one professes to be skilled in and to follow. . . . A vocation in which professed knowledge of some branch of learning is used in its application to the affairs of others, or in the practice of an art based upon it. Applied specifically to the three learned professions of divinity, law and medicine; also the military profession." From this follows later the adjective "professional," with the meanings now familiar.

Professionals *profess*. They profess to know better than others the nature of certain matters, and to know better than their clients what ails them or their affairs. This is the essence of the professional idea and the professional claim. From it flow many consequences. The professionals claim the exclusive right to practice, as a vocation, the arts which they profess to know, and to give the kind of advice derived from their special lines of knowledge. This is the basis of the license, both in the narrow sense of legal permission and in the broader sense that the public allows those in a profession a certain leeway in their practice and perhaps in their very way of living and thinking. The professional is expected to think objectively and inquiringly about matters which may be, for laymen, subject to orthodoxy and sentiment which limit intellectual exploration. . . .

Since the professional does profess, he asks that he be trusted. The client is not a true judge of the value of the service he receives, furthermore, the problems and affairs of men are such that the best of professional advice and action will not always solve them. A central feature, then, of all professions, is the motto—not used in this form, so far as I know—*credat emptor*. Thus is the professional relation distinguished from that of those markets in which the rule is *caveat emptor,* although the latter is far from a universal rule even in exchange of goods. The client is to trust the professional; he must tell him all secrets which bear upon the affairs in hand. He must trust his judgment and skill. In return, the professional asks protection from any unfortunate consequences of his professional actions; he and his fellows make it very difficult for any one outside—even civil courts—to pass judgment upon one of their number. Only the professional can say when his colleague makes a mistake.

The mandate also flows from the claim to esoteric knowledge and high skill. Lawyers not only give advice to clients and plead their cases for them; they also develop a philosophy of law—of its nature and its functions, and of the proper way in which to administer justice. Physicians consider it their prerogative to define the nature of disease and of health, and to determine how medical services ought to be distributed and paid for. Social workers are not content to develop a technique of case work; they concern themselves with social legislation. Every profession considers itself the proper body to set the terms in which some aspect of society, life or nature is to be thought of, and to define the general lines, or even the details, of

From *Daedalus* 92 (Fall 1963): 655–68.

public policy concerning it. The mandate to do so is granted more fully to some professions than to others; in time of crisis it may be questioned even with regard to the most respected and powerful professions.

These characteristics and collective claims of a profession are dependent upon a close solidarity, upon its members constituting in some measure a group apart with an ethos of its own. This in turn implies deep and lifelong commitment. A man who leaves a profession, once he is fully trained, licensed and initiated, is something of a renegade in the eyes of his fellows; in the case of the priest, even in the eyes of laymen. It takes a rite of passage to get him in; another to read him out. If he takes French leave, he seems to belittle the profession and his former colleagues. To be sure, not all occupations called professions show these characteristics in full measure. But they constitute the highly valued professional syndrome as we know it. Professions come near the top of the prestige-ratings of occupations.

Many occupations, some new, some old, are endeavoring so to change their manner of work, their relations to clients and public, and the image which they have of themselves and others have of them, that they will merit and be granted professional standing. The new ones may arise from the development of some scientific or technological discovery which may be applied to the affairs of others. The people who "process" data for analysis by computers are a recent example. Some of the specialties within medicine are due largely to the invention of some diagnostic instrument, or to an extension of biological or chemical knowledge. After the virus came the virologist, who works alongside the bacteriologist and the person who knows about fungi—together they are the microbiologists, who work with microscopes, and lately with the electronic one. Other new professions or specialties (and specialties follow much the same course of development as professions themselves) may arise from some change in society itself. As impersonal insurance replaced the older, more personal ways of spreading the risk of death, injury, illness, unemployment and loss of property, actuarial knowledge was of necessity developed, and a new profession arose. The professional social worker is a product of social changes. In an epoch of great technological and organizational change, new techniques and new social demands work in some sort of interaction to produce new esoteric occupations.

Perhaps the way to understand what professions mean in our society is to note the ways in which occupations try to change themselves or their image, or both, in the course of a movement to become "professionalized" (a term here used to mean what happens to an occupation, but lately used to refer also to what happens to an individual in the course of training for his occupation). Courses and seminars entitled Professions, Occupations, or Sociology of Work—which I have been holding for more than twenty-five years—invariably attract many people from outside sociology. As often as not, they want to write a paper to prove that some occupation—their own—has become or is on the verge of becoming a true profession. The course gives them a set of criteria for their demonstration. Librarians, insurance salesmen, nurses, public relations people, YMCA secretaries, probation officers, personnel men, vocational guidance directors, city managers, hospital administrators, and even public health physicians have been among them.

These people are serious, often quite idealistic. The changes they want to bring about or to document are directed to the same *terminus ad quem,* but the starting points lie in different directions. The insurance salesmen try to free themselves of the business label; they are not selling, they are giving people expert and objective diagnosis of their risks and advising them as to the best manner of protecting themselves. They are distressed that the heads of families do not confide in them more fully. The librarians seek to make themselves experts on the effects of reading, on bibliography and reference, rather than merely custodians and distributors of books; in schools and colleges, librarians want status as members of the teaching staff. They insist that they are, or must become, jointly with social psychologists, investigators of communications. That is their science, or one of their sciences. People in business management work at developing a science of management which could presumably be applied to any organization, no matter what its purpose. The social workers earlier were at pains to prove that their work could not be done by amateurs, people who brought to their efforts naught but goodwill; it required, they said, training in casework, a technique based on accumulated knowledge and experience of human nature and its operation in various circumstances and crises. Their first goal was to establish the position of the professional and to separate it from the amateur friendly visitor or reformer. The nurse, whose occupation is old, seeks to upgrade her place in the medical system. Her work, she says, requires much more general education than formerly, and more special knowledge; as medicine advances, the physicians delegate more and more technical functions to the nurse, who delegates some of her simpler functions to practical nurses, aides and maids. The nurse wants a measure of independence, prestige and money in keeping with her enlarged functions, as she sees them. The YMCA secretary wants his occupation recognized not merely as that of offering young men from the country a pleasant road to Protestant righteousness in the city, but as a more universal one of dealing with groups of young people. All that is learned of adolescence, of behavior in small groups, of the nature and organization of community life is considered the intellectual base of his work. The vocational guidance people have trouble in bringing the teaching profession to recognize that theirs is a separate complex of skills, presumed to rest on psychology. The public health men have a double problem. They must convince other physicians that their work—which is generally not the diagnosing and treating of patients—is really medicine. They must also combat the belief of physicians that they should do for fees some of what the public health people do for a fixed salary.

In these examples appear the main themes of professionalization. Detachment is one of them; and that in the sense of having in a particular case no personal interest such as would influence one's action or advice, while being deeply interested in all cases of the kind. The deep interest in all cases is of the sort that leads one to pursue and systematize the pertinent knowledge. It leads to finding an intellectual base for the problems one handles, which, in turn, takes those problems out of their particular setting and makes them part of some more universal order. One aspect of a profession is a certain equilibrium between the universal and the particular. The priest who would fix his attention entirely on the universal aspects of religious behavior might find himself indifferent as to which religion he would attach himself to; and thus, a renegade and a heretic. Churches do not encourage such circulation of the elite. Great corporations, too, although they may seek men who know the science of management, want an executive's curiosity about and love of the universal aspects of human organization tempered with a certain loyalty and commitment to his employer. I suppose there may be a professional man so free-sweeping in his interests that he does not mind what client he serves and what aspects of the client's affairs he deals with. He would be a rarity—a rich outcast or a poor idealist.

The balance of the universal and the particular in a profession varies, but there is always some measure of both, with an appropriate equilibrium between detachment and interest. The balance between universal and particular is related to that between the theoretical and the practical. Branches of learning are not always very directly related to the ordinary business of life. If some occupations become professions by developing an intellectual interest, others do it by becoming more practical. A large number of chemists are now employed by industries. Psychologists are seeking and obtaining legislation giving them monopoly over the name and making it an offense for anyone to "practice" psychology without it. Some sociologists, especially those who do research by the "project" for "clients," would do likewise. Perhaps one should distinguish between professions in essence, such as medicine or engineering, which pursue knowledge to improve practice; and professions by accident, such as, say, archaeology, where the practices are merely the means to increasing knowledge. In both cases, the people engaged may make their living by their activities. There appears to be a trend in certain fields of knowledge for this distinction to disappear and for the learned societies to become professional guilds concerned with problems of practice, employment, licensing and distribution of their services. Many learned societies show strain between the intellectuals and the professionalizers.

This strain, incidentally, is found in some degree in all professions. A physician may be too devoted to research; a lawyer too concerned with comparative law; a social worker overcurious about the roots of human behavior. In fact, inside most professions there develops a tacit division of labor between the more theoretical and the more practical; once in a while conflict breaks out over issues related to it. The professional schools may be accused of being too "academic"; the academics accuse other practitioners of failure to be sufficiently intellectual.

Another set of themes in professionalizing movements has to do with a change of status of the occupation in relation to its own past, and to the other people—clients, public, other occupations—involved in its work drama. Changes sought are more independence, more recognition, a higher place, a cleaner distinction between those in the profession and those outside, and a larger measure of autonomy in choosing colleagues and successors. One necessary validation of such changes of status in our society is introduction of study for the profession in question into the universities. It may be as an undergraduate program, leading to a Bachelor's degree with a major in the theory and practice of the occupation. A large proportion of the university undergraduates in this country are in such professional courses. Other professions seek to have a Master's degree made the standard professional qualification; so it is in social work, hospital administration, business administration, laboratory technology, librarianship and many others. The Master's degree is also used as qualification for a professional or administrative elite in occupations for which the basic preparation is a Bachelor's degree. The Ph.D. or some substitute, such as the Doctor of Education, is also used as qualification for higher administrative and teaching positions in professional agencies and schools.

The older professions, law and medicine, have long been established in the universities; at present in this country, they can keep their aspirants in college for four years and in professional school for three or four years after that. Indeed, so sure are they of their place that they tend to encourage undergraduates to pursue what lines of study they will, so long as their achievements are high. One way in which an occupation—or a college—can document its high status is by being able to take its pick of the young people about to enter the labor market, and then to keep them in school a long time before admitting them to the charmed circle.

Some combination of scholastic aptitude, ambition and financial means is required to accomplish this educational aim. The ambition must have been fostered in some social setting, generally in the middle class family, although occasionally in a working class family with the aid of a sponsoring schoolteacher who sets sights high. . . .

Competition for status is accompanied by a trend toward prolonging the professional training at both ends: at the beginning by multiplying prerequisites for entry to professional school, at the finish by prolonging the course and the various apprentice or internship programs. This is held in check by the fact that many of the would-be professions cannot offer enough future income and prestige to get people early and keep them long in school. Parents of less income and education also press their children to seek security in known middle-level occupations. This pressure may also work against the movement to lift professional requirements.

Old and new alike, the professions cherish their recruits once they get them. Having picked their candidates with great care, medical schools, for instance, gnash their teeth and tear their hair over a sheep lost from the fold. They wonder what they have done wrong to make the lamb stray. They make it clear to the professional recruit that he owes it to himself, the profession and the school to stick with his choice. Has it not been discovered by all the tests that this is the one right outlet for his talents? Is it not his duty to use his talents for his country in the best possible way? Have not the profession and the professional school made a great investment in him? Has he the right not to give full return on it? The day has passed when the youngsters entering professional school are told to look well at their neighbors in the classroom, for few of them will be there next year. The theme is mutual commitment, reinforced by students' auxiliaries sponsored by the professional associations, and by the use of such terms as "student-physician," which stress that the student is already in the professional family. One owes allegiance for life to a family.

Thus we have a high degree of competition among the professions for talent, combined with a great feeling of possessiveness over the recruits as soon as they have crossed the threshold. The professional student is, to some extent, already an organization man.

But that is not the only respect in which the modern professional is an organization man. Professions are more and more practiced in organizations. The *Freie Berufe* in Germany were considered free not merely because they were worthy of free men, but because those who followed them had no employer. Even the *freier Gelehrte,* or independent scholar, once he had acquired the right to teach, received his income in fees from his clients, the students. The university merely gave him his validation and his forum, as the court gives lawyers a playing field and a referee for their contest. The true professional, according to the traditional ideology of professions, is never hired. He is retained, engaged, consulted, etc., by someone who has need of his services. He, the professional, has or should have almost complete control over what he does for the client.

Especially in medicine, the protest against working in organizations and for salary is very strong. Yet in this country, more than in England, where there is a national plan of medical practice, physicians work in organizations. . . . An increasing proportion of physicians are in specialties; the specialist characteristically must work with other physicians. Some specialties never get the first call from an ailing patient; they are reached only after one or more referrals. Some specialties are, like pathology and anaesthesiology, practiced only in hospitals or clinics. All physicians now work at least a year for salary as interns; many work for a salary for several years as residents. In some specialties—those far from the first call of ailing people—work for an organization, possibly for salary, is the rule. An increasing number of lawyers work in large firms where duties and cases are assigned, not completely chosen by the individual practitioner himself. The firm operates as a referral system and allows the individual lawyer enough cases of one kind to permit him to specialize. Many lawyers have but one client, a company; and when there is but one client, it becomes in fact an employer.

Law and medicine—the models which other professions try to approximate—in spite of nourishing free practice of the individual for a number of clients with a minimum of institutional apparatus, are in fact far along the road to practice in complicated organizations which intervene in many ways between them and their clients. Engineers, applied scientists and people in most of the newer professions nearly all work in organizations with others of their own profession, and with many people of related occupations. Indeed, it becomes hard to say who is the client in many cases; in the case of medicine, is it the insurance company or the patient? In the school, is it the child, the parent, the community at large or some class of people within it? In social work, is it the agency—which pays—or the so-called client, who is worked upon not always of his own free will? It is characteristic of modern professions that they do work in such institutional settings, often with capital goods which they do not own and with a great variety of people. Professional ideology prefers a two-party arrangement: the professional and his client. It prefers the client who can speak for himself and pay for himself. This is not the prevailing arrangement, nor is it likely to be.

Thus arise a great number of problems for professions. The problem of finding a clientele becomes that of finding a place in a system of organizations. The problem of colleague relationships becomes that of determining who, in a complex organization of many professions, are indeed one's colleagues, and in what degree. The problem of freedom becomes one of distinguishing between one's obligations to the person, if it be such a case, on which one performs some action or to whom one gives some advice, and to one's employer or organization. For example, does the college physician report the secrets of his student-patient to the dean and, if so, in what situations? There is also a problem of authority; what orders does one accept from an employer, especially one who is not a member of one's own profession and whose interests may not always be those of the professional and his clients?

The other side of this coin is that the employer, even in business, finds himself dealing with an increasing number of professional (staff) people, who will not be ordered about as freely as line people. . . .

As the professions become more organized, business organizations become more professionalized. The result is the development of new patterns of organization. If the professional man giving staff services to business or industry sets a certain pattern of freedom not common among the employees of business, he has also lost a certain kind of freedom which inhered in the private practice of professions for clients of whom enough were solvent to assure him a good income and a fitting style of life. . . .

3. Professions and Emerging Professions

Bernard Barber

. . . . .

TOWARD A DEFINITION OF THE PROFESSIONS

Theoretical and methodological consensus is not yet so great among sociologists that there is any absolute agreement on the definition of "the professions."[1] And of course among the public at large the debate over the boundary between "professional" and "nonprofessional" continues, a debate which is kept going by the fact that these terms carry an important assignment of differential occupational prestige. Still, considerable progress[2] toward a definition has been made, and [what follows] seeks to summarize that progress.

A sociological definition of the professions should limit itself, so far as possible, to the *differentia specifica* of professional behavior. For example, concepts like style of life, corporate solidarity and socialization structures and processes, which apply to all other groups as well as to professional ones, are not the *differentia specifica*.

There is no absolute difference between professional and other kinds of occupational behavior, but only relative differences with respect to certain attributes common to all occupational behavior. Some occupational behavior, seen in the light of these attributes . . . is fully professional; other behavior is partly professional; and some can be thought of as barely or not at all professional. On this view, for example, there may be some professional elements in some kinds of business behavior. Similarly, on the same view, the medical profession is more professional than the nursing profes-

From "Some Problems in the Sociology of the Professions," *Daedalus* 92 (Fall 1963): 669–88.

sion, and the medical doctor who does university research is more professional than the medical doctor who provides minor medical services in a steel plant. Professionalism is a matter of degree.

Professional behavior may be defined in terms of four essential attributes: a high degree of generalized and systematic knowledge; primary orientation to the community interest rather than to individual self-interest; a high degree of self-control of behavior through codes of ethics internalized in the process of work socialization and through voluntary associations organized and operated by the work specialists themselves; and a system of rewards (monetary and honorary) that is primarily a set of symbols of work achievement and thus ends in themselves, not means to some end of individual self-interest.[3] Some amplification of these four attributes will be useful.

All occupational behavior has some degree of knowledge as one of its attributes. As the phrase "the learned professions" vividly signifies, a high degree of generalized and systematic knowledge early became one of the commonly used defining characteristics of professional behavior. Generalized and systematic knowledge of professional degree exists in such diverse cultural realms as the physical and biological sciences, in religion or theology, in the law, literature, art, mathematics and philosophy. During the last one hundred years, the social sciences, including history, economics, psychology, anthropology and sociology, have developed generalized and systematic knowledge of a professional level.

Its relation to individual and community interest is another attribute of all occupational performance. Since generalized and systematic knowledge provides powerful control over nature and society, it is important to society that such knowledge be used primarily in the community interest. Where such knowledge exists, orientation primarily to community rather than individual interest is an essential attribute of professional behavior. Individual self-interest is, of course, not utterly neglected in professional behavior, but is subserved *indirectly*.

Social control depends in part, obviously, upon substantive understanding of the behavior to be controlled. In the case of behavior characterized by a high degree of knowledge, the requisite understanding is available in full measure only to those who have themselves been trained in and apply that knowledge. It follows that some kind of self-control, by means of internalized codes of ethics and voluntary in-groups, is necessary. In the realms of professional behavior, such codes and such associations for the setting and maintaining of standards proliferate. Further controls on professional behavior exist, of course, in the informal agencies of public opinion and in governmental-legal agencies. But these other forms of social control are less important than in nonprofessional areas.

Money income, general prestige and specific honors or symbols of achievement are among the different forms of social reward for occupational performance.[4] Since money income is a more appropriate reward for individual self-interest, and since prestige and honors are more appropriate for community interest, these latter types of reward are relatively more important in professional than in nonprofessional behavior. The actual reward system in the professions tends to consist, therefore, in a combination of prestige and titles, medals, prizes, offices in professional societies, and so forth, together with sufficient monetary income for the style of life appropriate to the honor bestowed. Although the professions are not so well paid, on the whole, as equal-ranking business roles in American society, all studies show that the public ranks the professions at the top of the occupational prestige hierarchy and that professionals themselves are more satisfied with their work-rewards than are other occupational groups.

These four essential attributes define a scale of professionalism, a way of measuring the extent to which it is present in different forms of occupational performance. The most professional behavior would be that which realizes all four attributes in the fullest possible manner. Justice of the United States Supreme Court, or professor of physics and Nobel Prize winner in a distinguished university, would be defined as very highly professional roles. A $100,000-a-year vice president in charge of legal affairs for a middle-size business corporation would be clearly less professional in these terms. And a $6000-a-year schoolteacher would be ranked as less professional still.

THE ROLE OF THE UNIVERSITY PROFESSIONAL SCHOOL

In the light of our definition, we can now more easily see several aspects of the essential role that the university professional school performs for the practicing profession it serves. Nearly all the well-established professions are located in some measure in the university; the more professional ones, according to our definition, having the more university-connected schools. Within a given profession, the "better" or more professional schools are more likely to be in a university, and the very best ones are typically in the very best universities. Where a well-established profession is not, for some special reasons, located in the university, it has usually sought to construct an institution that approximates one, as in the case of the war colleges for the training of top military personnel. This type of institution tries to staff itself, in part, with university caliber instructors and also to bring from various civilian universities, on at least a part-time basis, specialists in the different kinds of generalized and systematic knowledge it needs but cannot provide from among its own professionals. As we shall also see, the emerging or marginal professions, when they are trying to raise standards for themselves, seek to locate themselves in universities. If they already have a marginal connection there, they seek to improve their position in the university. Among the members of a profession, and probably also among the public at large, the university professional school staff tends to have as high occupational prestige as any in the professions, though typically not the highest income.

The university professional school has as one of its basic functions the transmission to its students of the generalized and systematic knowledge that is the basis of professional performance. Not only the substantive knowledge itself, but knowledge of how to keep up with continuing advances in professional knowledge is what the university school seeks to give its students. Where the body of professional knowledge is changing very rapidly, the university professional school may take a direct role in promoting the ''adult'' education of the members of its profession through postprofessional training courses, seminars and institutes.

Equally important is the university professional school's responsibility for the creation of new and better knowledge on which professional practice can be based. Its university position makes it possible for all members of its staff to be part-time scholars and researchers and for some to carry on these activities full time. The university professional school can borrow resources of knowledge from other university departments, either by coopting full-time teaching and research personnel or through more informal, part-time cooperation in the university community. The better the university professional school, the more likely it is to use resources from the other professional schools in the university and from all the other departments of basic knowledge insofar as they are relevant. In sum, the university professional schools are the leading, though not the sole, innovators and systematizers of ideas for their professions.

So far as normative standards of community orientation (or ''ethics'') are concerned, again the university professional school has certain essential functions. The university professional school sees to the ethical training of its students as well as to their other learning. Some of this ethical training is explicit, in the form of teaching professional codes; some of it is intermixed with what is ostensibly only the learning of substantive knowledge; and some of it is implicit in the behavior of the staff. University professional-school staff members often come to serve as ethical role models for their students and even as guides to conscience after the students have themselves become mature practicing professionals.

The staff of the university professional school are often the leaders in the continual codification and improvement of standards of ethics for practicing professionals. They criticize, sometimes within professional circles and sometimes in public, inadequacy and deviation among practicing professionals. This criticism is the more powerful when it is based on careful research of the kind that university professionals are able to carry out. But more than negative means, in the form of criticism, is available to them. University members are often responsible for the award to practicing professionals of a variety of medals, prizes and other honors for high standards of ethics as well as for intellectual achievement in the profession. In these several ways, the university professional school is a moral watchdog for its profession.

For both its knowledge and its ethical functions, the relative insulation of the university professional school has certain advantages. It is relatively freer of those commitments to other organizations and other interests that practicing professionals have, and therefore it is more nearly able to maintain the highest intellectual and moral standards. Also, it can use the general insulation of the university from certain pressures to fortify itself in the performance of its functions, sometimes even in the face of resistance or opposition from the practicing professionals themselves.

So much for the positive functions of the university professional schools. Unfortunately, the literature has not pointed out that these also have the defects of their virtues. The functions of the university professional school lead to a certain amount of ''structured strain'' between it and the practicing professionals. The university professional is ever pressing, with increasing knowledge and higher moral standards, on the practicing professional who has to meet other pressures, sometimes . . . from nonprofessional organizations in which he works, but also from other cultural and social interests. These other pressures may have a legitimacy and a force that the practicing professional feels is equal to the legitimate pressure from his university colleagues. Even when he manages successfully to accommodate the opposed pressures, he is likely to feel a certain resentment against the ''ivory-tower'' university professionals whose relatively insulated situation and perspective have dysfunctions as well as functions for the man outside.

THE EMERGING OR MARGINAL PROFESSION

Since new levels and types of generalized and systematic knowledge are constantly being developed in modern society, there is a constant push both on and from within certain nonprofessional and quasiprofessional occupational groups to become more professional and to claim public recognition as such. Hence arises the phenomenon of the emerging or marginal profession, a phenomenon comprising a number of recurrent patterns, and of especial interest because it highlights the essential characteristics of professional behavior.[5]

The emerging or marginal profession is an occupation which is not so clearly high or so clearly low in both of the first two attributes of professionalism—generalized knowledge and community orientation—that its status is clearly defined by itself and others. The emerging profession may be middle ranking on both of these dimensions or it may be higher on one dimension and lower on the other. Library work, social work, pharmacy and accountancy are all examples of the emerging or marginal profession.

It is typical of the structure of the occupational group that is emerging as a profession that its members are not homogeneous with respect to the amount of knowledge and community orientation they possess. In occupations like social work or library work, probably two thirds or more of the members are pretty clearly only marginally professional. But the elite of these occupations, such as the director of a university library or the dean of a major university school of social work, are clearly professional. It is the elite of an emerging profession that takes the lead in pushing for the advancement of professionalism in its occupational group and in claiming public recognition of its new status.[6] Toward these ends, they typically engage in behavior showing the following patterns.

The leaders of an emerging profession may acknowledge the present and obvious inadequacies of their group, but they compare these inadequacies to ones that existed in the past among professions now fully established. Thus the professionally aspiring leader of the American Management Association says, "It's something like medicine years ago, when the doctors came to the realization that working in a drugstore was not sufficient training for their profession. Now management is going through a similar transition."[7] The implication is that the emerging profession too can progress to full professional status.

In the attempt to express and strengthen the community orientation of their group, the leaders take pains to construct and publish a code of ethics. Unfortunately, because the knowledge on which their occupational performance is based is not highly developed, the codes they construct are full of value generalities, and therefore hard for the individual practitioner to apply in concrete cases. The emerging profession is also unable to construct the machinery of interpretation and enforcement of its codes that exists in the established professions.

The leaders establish or try to strengthen a professional association. In an established profession, such an association effectively carries on the several functions of self-control, socialization and education of the members, communications with the public, and the defense of professional interest against infringement by the public or other occupational groups.[8] The emerging profession's association seeks to increase its effectiveness in all these functions.

Within their own occupational ranks, the leaders establish measures and titles of more and less professional behavior, hoping, for example, to use such prestigious titles as "fellow" as an incentive for the less professional to become more so. They may also seek legal licensure from the state if it does not already exist. Because their prestige and even their right to work seems to be threatened by such moves, the less professional members of the emerging profession resist these innovations, sometimes violently. To forestall some of this resistance, the elite will provide a "grandfather clause" in all new informal and legal regulations about title and prestige.

The leaders will, of course, seek to establish or strengthen university professional schools. The flexibility of the American university system has permitted even marginal professions to get some kind of connection with some kind of university, thus holding open the door for any further possible development of professionalism. Because marginal professional schools are a threat to the standards of the university, it in turn tries to strengthen such schools out of its own resources. In some cases, thus, a beneficial spiral of progress for the emerging profession is helped along.

Desiring prestige and support from the general public, the leaders will engage in a program of public information about the "professional" services it provides and the "professional" standards of community orientation it maintains. Such campaigns are sometimes dismissed by outsiders as "mere" public relations, that is, an attempt to flimflam the public with half-truths and deceit. There may be such flimflammery in some public information campaigns by emerging professions, though often an aspiring profession is fooling itself as much as the public. Insofar as the public's ignorance is replaced with genuine facts about the emerging profession, facts which the public can test in the actual social reality, such public information campaigns will effectively raise the professional status of an occupational group. Similarly, with regard to professional titles, the public will respect only those titles the emerging profession gives itself which seem to symbolize actually realized standards of performance and morality.

And, finally, the leaders of an emerging profession will have to engage in some conflict with elements both inside and outside their occupational group. We have already seen that they may meet with some opposition from the less professional members within the group. But also, as they make claims to certain levels of technical performance and certain standards of community orientation, they may have to label those outsiders who fall short of these levels and standards as "charlatans," and they may themselves be branded as "encroachers" on other established occupational and professional specialties.[9] In such social situations, competition and conflict often have positive as well as negative functions.

NOTES

1. One sociologist has gone so far as to say that "labor itself is becoming professionalized." See Nelson Foote, "The Professionalization of Labor in Detroit," *American Journal of Sociology,* 58 (1953), 371–80.

2. Our discussion here follows very closely that in Bernard Barber, "Is American Business Becoming Professionalized? Analysis of a Social Ideology." In *Sociocultural Theory, Values, and Sociocultural Change: Essays in Honor of Pitirim A. Sorokin,* ed. E. A. Tiryakian (Glencoe, IL: Free Press of Glencoe, 1963), pp. 130–33. The essential contributions to the definition offered here can be found in: Talcott Parsons, *The Social System* (Glencoe, IL: Free Press, 1951); "Some Trends of Change in American Society: Their Bearing on Medical Education," in *Structure and Process in Modern Societies,* ed. Talcott Parsons (Glencoe, IL: Free Press, 1960); and especially his "The Professions and Social Structure," *Social Forces,* 17 (1939), 457–67. See also A. M. Carr-Saunders and P. A. Wilson, "Professions," *Encyclopedia of the Social Sciences* (New York: Macmillan, 1933); and R. K. Merton, "Some Thoughts on the Professions in American Society," Brown University Papers, No. 37, 1960.

3. Certain "derivative" attributes follow from these essential attributes. For a list of ten "derivatives," see W. J. Goode, "Encroachment, Charlatanism, and the Emerging Profession: Psychology, Sociology, and Medicine," *American Sociological Review,* 25 (1960), 902–14.

4. On occupational prestige, see Bernard Barber, *Social Stratification* (New York: Harcourt, Brace, 1957), pp. 100–11. On honors in science, see R. K. Merton, "Priorities in Scientific Discovery: A Chapter in the Sociology of Science," *American Sociological Review,* 22 (1957), 642–46.

5. The discussion in this section is much indebted to two papers by W. J. Goode: "Encroachment, Charlatanism, and the Emerging Profession"; and "The Librarian: From Occupation to Profession?" *Library Quarterly,* 31 (1961), 306–20.

6. Even in business, the ideology of professionalism flourishes chiefly among the managerial elite who are pacesetters in knowledge and practice. See Barber, "Is American Business Becoming Professionalized?" esp. p. 127.

7. *New York Times,* December 27, 1957.

8. See Robert K. Merton, "The Functions of the Professional Association," *American Journal of Nursing,* 58 (1958), 50–54.

9. For an account of the conflict among the emerging professions of psychology, sociology and psychiatry, see W. J. Goode, "Encroachment, Charlatanism, and the Emerging Profession."

4. The Professionalization of Journalism

John C. Merrill

. . . . .

THE ROAD TO PROFESSIONALISM

Journalists—at least many of them—like to think of themselves as "professionals" and journalism as a "profession." They have seen that respectability, general esteem, even awe tends to surround any institutionalized activity which goes by the name of a "profession." They have also noted that medicine and law, for instance, in being accepted generally as professions, have not only been endowed with a kind of prestigious or elite image but have been able to regulate the numbers and functioning of their members and to have some semblance of common expectations and order in their routine activities. The journalists have also seen that, usually, with increased professionalization comes increased financial remuneration. It is little wonder that journalists, often intellectuals or pseudo-intellectuals, find the lure of professionalism very

From *The Imperative of Freedom* (New York: Hastings House, 1974), pp. 133–42.

strong. Professionalism may give them an aura of respectability, of public acceptance, of dignity, and at least the collective psychological comfort which they fail to find as autonomous, individual tradesmen or craftsmen.

In spite of the fact that the idea of professionalism is growing in American journalism, individual journalists do not really know what journalistic professionalism entails, what being a "professional" really means. Even two journalists with similar backgrounds may act in ways which each would consider "unprofessional" by the other. The term "professional," of course, can be used—and is used—in different ways; but when journalists talk about their "profession," they are limiting the meaning to something that can be dealt with. One of America's foremost sociologists of recent years, William J. Goode, has insisted that professionals comprise a homogeneous community whose members share identity, values, definition of role and interests. He says that members of a profession "are bound by a sense of identity" and "share values in common."[1] (The observer looking at American journalism can see very easily that journalists really do not have a single identity, nor do they share the same values, nor do they have a definition in common of their role.)

Just what is a profession? Originally a "profession" meant simply the act or fact of professing; it has developed from that base to mean the "occupation which one professes to be skilled in and to follow. . . . A vocation in which professed knowledge of some branch of learning is used in its application to the affairs of others, or in the practice of an art based upon it"—*(Oxford Shorter Dictionary)*.

Professionals do profess—even now. They profess to know better than others the nature of certain matters, and to know better than their non-professionalized clients what they need to know and in what proportions they need to know it. Professionals claim the exclusive right to practice, as a vocation, the arts which they profess to know.

Other characteristics of a profession are given in the book *The Professions in America* . . .[2] Here are a few of them:

The professional is expected to think objectively and inquiringly about matters which may be, for the outsider, subject to "orthodoxy and sentiment which limit intellectual exploration."

The professional assumes that he can be trusted since he professes to have certain expertise which the layman does not have; therefore the professional journalist would say that a non-journalist is not a true judge of the value of the service he receives.

The professional asks protection from any unfortunate consequences of his professional actions; the professional journalist would, therefore, collaborate with fellow journalists to make it very difficult for any one outside to pass judgment on the performance of one of their number. In other words, only the professional can say when he or his colleagues make a mistake. (The extreme sensitivity to criticism which has marked portions of the press in recent years attests to the growing enchantment with this aspect of professionalism by some press elitists.)

A professional believes in close solidarity with other members and thinks that it is a good thing to present a "solid front" to those outside the profession.

The professional would be a person who is able to meet various minimum "entrance" standards for the profession. This might be a particular academic degree as a qualification for practice; it might also be a special license which would identify him as a professional member in good standing.

And, finally, according to Lynn in his introductory section of the book, the true professional is never hired. He is retained, engaged, consulted by someone who needs his services. The professional has, or should have, almost complete control over what he does for his client.

Bernard Barber, writing also in *The Professions in America,* says that professional behavior may be defined in terms of four essential attributes: (1) a high degree of generalized and systematic knowledge; (2) a primary orientation to the community interest rather than to individual self-interest; (3) a high degree of group-control of behavior through codes of ethics and through associations organized and operated by the work specialists themselves; and (4) a system of rewards (monetary and honorary) for those who conduct themselves most notably within these codes of ethics.[3]

Having presented these basic characteristics of a "profession," it is well to look at journalism and ask the question: Is it a profession? Obviously it is not, although it has some of a profession's characteristics. There is no direct relationship between the journalist and his client. There is, in journalism, no minimum entrance requirement; anybody can be a journalist who can get himself hired—experience or no experience, degree or no degree. No journalist is expected (or required) to abide by any professional ethos or Code of Ethics. No journalist is licensed, thereby giving the "profession" some kind of control over him. There are no professional standards commonly agreed upon, and followed, by journalists. Journalists do not share in common a "high degree of generalized and systematic knowledge.'' Journalists do not claim for themselves the exclusive right to practice the arts (all borrowed from other disciplines) of their trade. And finally, journalists in America do not ''comprise a homogeneous community.''

The same people who are hacking away at journalistic autonomy by extolling ''social responsibility'' of the press, access of the people to the media, the necessity for press councils and the like, are also the ones who are the advocates of journalistic professionalism. Even though they know that journalism is not *really* a profession, they seem to have their eyes on some great day in the future when journalistic professionalization will come about. Listen to William Rivers and Wilbur Schramm: ''The slow, even painful way to promote change in mass communication requires a long process in which change takes place in people before it affects the system. This is professionalization.''[4] While admitting that journalism is not really a profession, there is a kind of sadness about this fact which manifests itself in the expressions of many of the commentators on American journalism. There seems to be a hope that someday journalism will become a profession. Of course, most of the proponents of a profession of journalism would insist that professionalization should come about by journalists accepting an *individual* sense of responsibility.

Rivers and Schramm make the point of individual journalistic responsibility. But it is very difficult to imagine journalism becoming a *profession* without the individual having to sublimate his individual sense of responsibility to the profession with its elite leaders, its ethical codes, its licensing procedures and its minimum entrance requirements. As I see it, you cannot have both individual concepts of responsibility and a professional concept of responsibility. The latter would naturally tend to stamp out deviant and ''eccentric'' concepts and, ultimately, also the ''professionals'' who might embrace them.

Lewis H. Lapham, in a thoughtful article in *Harper's* (1973), writes of a kind of deep-rooted desire among press people to belong to a hierarchy (''hierarchical longing within the press''); he also observes in the press more and more talk about ''legitimate'' journalists, implying a willingness to accept some type of licensing or certification so that, presumably, a *bona fide* journalist can be identified. Lapham writes that the more the press becomes a profession, the more it will ''discourage the membership of rowdy amateurs'' and, as it is with other professions, ''encourage the promotion of people diligently second-rate.''[5] Lapham no doubt is right; professionalism will certainly restrict the ranks of journalism, eliminate the ''non-professionals'' from its practice, and make the press appear more respectable and responsible—at least from the perspective of the professional elitists.

Daniel P. Moynihan, in a significant article in *Commentary*[6] notes that journalism lacks ''an epistemology which is shared by all respected members of the profession''; he does not maintain that this epistemology be forced on journalism by some force such as a press council (he is antipress council), but he does feel that if journalism in this country is to be a profession there must be basic knowledge agreed upon by all the ''professionals.'' Presumably, this will only occur in a system where professionalism has progressed to the extent that all journalists will be products of a common education so that a standard body of knowledge and theory of ethics has been agreed upon. Of course, this millenium will likely never come, but education for journalism can, with sufficient professional motivation, go a long way in this direction.

Journalism, through increased emphasis on codes of conduct, press councils, peer pressure, entrance requirements checked by standard examinations and by more rigorous demand for professional journalism education, *can* become a true profession. There is no contention here that it is impossible; what is contended here is that it is undesirable, that what keeps our journalism vigorous and diversified (and to some, ''irresponsible'') is the very fact that it is not a profession. William Barrett, reflecting the existentialist view of professions, states this case very well in these words:

> The price one pays for having a profession is a *déformation professionelle,* as the French put it—a professional deformation. Doctors and engineers tend to see things from the viewpoint of their own specialty, and usually show a very marked blind spot to whatever falls outside this particular province. The more specialized a vision the sharper its focus; but also the more nearly total the blind spot toward all things that lie on the periphery of this focus.[7]

"PROFESSIONAL" JOURNALISM EDUCATION

Barrett has put his existentialist finger on the main weakness of professionalism: It narrows the focus and restricts the options and possibilities that lie beyond the confines of its values and concerns. This restriction of options and focus is especially dangerous in journalism, although it may well be helpful or even desirous—at least to a certain degree—in professions such as law or medicine. How a journalist is educated is, of course, at the very heart of any concept of professionalism. Although it is changing rather rapidly, training or education for journalism in the United States has been very much a piecemeal, spotty, uneven and diversified system. It has ranged from no formal schooling at all, through all levels and types of university and college work in the liberal arts and sciences, to the varied programs which have grown up in academic journalism departments, schools and colleges.

Editors and publishers, broadcast news directors, and advertising and public relations executives are every year hiring more and more of their new staffers from "professional" journalism education programs in our colleges and universities. It gets harder each year, happily attest the journalism educators, for the major in English or sociology or political science to get a job in the communications media. Usually this is said with great satisfaction as if this tendency in the direction of professionalization will assure the country of better journalism. Of course, there is absolutely no empirical evidence to confirm this, and there are still editors and other media executives who have their doubts about the journalism student's superiority over others. But their number is becoming smaller, it must be admitted, and presumably virtually all journalists hired by the year 2000 will be products of formalized journalism education.

Journalism-program accreditation is doing much to standardize the coursework in various universities across the country. Also the increase in the number and size of professional meetings, conventions, workshops for journalism educators, as well as the proliferation of literature dealing with journalism education, is having an impact on the development of a more coherent and unified program of education for journalism in the United States. Increasingly, journalism professors are reaching common objectives and understanding with their colleagues elsewhere, are moving more frequently from campus to campus, and are thereby spreading their educational philosophies and techniques nationwide—and even, in many cases, to other countries. All of this strengthens the growth of "professional" journalism education which, presumably, will in time weld the practicing journalists into a homogeneous professional society.

Emphasis more and more is on *professional* work in journalism. The *Columbia Journalism Review*, for instance, has stated that if journalism is to be taught in any college or university, it should be taught as a "professional" course of study: "It has little more place in a liberal arts faculty than would education for law, medicine or business administration."[8] It must be said, however, that there is still considerable disagreement among journalism educators about what they are supposed to do; some would only teach journalism in a "liberal arts faculty"; others would have journalism education only on the graduate level; others would abolish all graduate work in journalism; and there are others who see no real need for formal journalism education at all. And there are shadings and degrees of all of these positions, and undoubtedly quite a few others.

Within every journalism faculty are the so-called "green eyeshades" teachers who emphasize techniques such as news reporting, newspaper makeup, headline writing and copyreading. Also—and usually in another camp—are the "Chi-square" professors, the faculty members (usually with Ph.D.'s in communication theory and methodologies of research) who mainly teach graduate level courses and apply their "scientific" skills to a variety of rather esoteric media studies. And last—and probably least—come the "hybrids": those faculty members who probably have some journalistic experience and also an academic eclecticism and liberal arts orientation which places them somewhere in limbo between the "trades" teachers and the researching theoreticians (or "communicologists" as they are sometimes called). These "hybrids" teach a variety of courses, but often they tend to be general courses such as "Mass Media and Society," "Law of Journalism," "Book Reviewing," "Journalistic Ethics," "History of American Journalism," and "Comparative Press Systems."[9] Thus far, these three main faculty types in journalism education have retained a diversity and tension which has delayed the "professionalization" of very many students.

Pressures, however, are building up against this tension created by disagreements among the three groups. Within journalism education itself there is increasing talk about the need to eliminate these disagreements and have more "cooperation" among the three groups. Also, more and more retired (or disgruntled) editors and journalists of one kind or another are entering journalism education to begin a "second career." This is causing the balance of faculty to begin a shift from the teacher who is mainly an academic to the teacher who is mainly a "professional" journalist. There is no doubt that as this trend increases—with even journalism school and department administrators coming freshly from the "profession" with little or no academic background—great impetus will be given to the aspects of journalism education which lead to professionalization. This situation is, of course, considered good by some and bad by others, depending on their philosophy of education and their feelings about the value of journalism as a profession.

One often wonders just what a "professional" school of journalism is, or how it differs from one which is not considered "professional." Obviously the term is used very loosely by the schools themselves, since nobody really seems to be able to explain just when a school (a new one, for instance) ceases being non-professional and becomes professional. Perhaps it might be well just to call them all professional—or, if you wish, call them all non-professional. . . .

But the question persists: What is a professional journalism program?[10] Presumably it is one which will prepare a student to be a professional journalist, whatever that is. At least, it should prepare him somewhat to be a *practicing* journalist. The teachers of all journalism courses would contend that this is exactly what they are doing. There are many persons in American journalism who minimize the importance of the kind of journalism education a student gets and who believe that really all a journalist needs is native intelligence, curiosity, a desire to learn, imagination, basic literacy and energy. Higher education is not necessarily needed at all.

Louis Lyons, a veteran newspaperman who was curator of the Nieman Fellowships at Harvard for some twenty years, is one of those who would emphasize the capacity to learn—and not formal journalism education—for the practicing journalist. What Lyons would want to know is whether or not the journalist would grow on the job, because the editor or person doing the hiring can not really say what is needed for the journalist "since part of what we need is that he discover for us what is outside our reach and that he bring it within our ken."[11] Lyons concludes an *Atlantic* article with these words about a new journalist: "A capacity for discovery and interpretation is perhaps as close as we can come to what we need from him." Whether such a capacity can be taught in journalism school—or anywhere else in Academe—is a moot question. If, in truth, this is all that is expected of the journalist coming out of the university—this "capacity for discovery and interpretation"—then certainly journalism schools and departments are wasting tremendous time, effort, and money on a growing proliferation of *professional* courses.

I rather agree with Lyons, although there is no valid reason why journalism education cannot supplement a student's basic general education and make him better able to discover the world around him and to better interpret it to others. Certainly, all serious journalism teachers would claim this as an objective. It is quite likely, however, that journalism education generally, in its desire to be more "professional," is becoming more and more specialized, inward, parochial and conformist.

An increasing amount of journalism coursework is being required of the student, and fewer and fewer "electives" are left open for him; in some schools, the student cannot even "minor" in a non-journalism area or get a "double major" in journalism and something else—for example, history. As journalism education grows, as it becomes more "professional" and more complex, as departments become schools and schools become colleges, and as additional years of graduate work in journalism are tacked on, it is understandable that the student's horizons get narrower and narrower. Often the student learns more and more *about* journalism as he goes along, but increasingly has less and less to communicate. And what is worse, graduate students in journalism seem to write worse than undergraduates.

Journalism education does increase and encourage conformist journalism. This, of course, is to some degree unavoidable, and, as Charles Siepmann rightly points out, it is not the aim of education to cultivate eccentrics—although "that society is richest, most flexible, and most humane that best uses and most tolerates eccentricity." For, as Siepmann says, "conformity, beyond a point, breeds sterile minds and, therefore, a sterile society."[12] Perhaps to far too great a degree journalism education does tend to turn journalism students into robots who can walk "surefootedly" into the world of Establishment journalism. It does discourage "unprofessional" practices and techniques, creativity and individuality by instilling in all the students the "proper ways" of journalism.

Students who dare think for themselves, depart from the academic and journalistic conformist practices, are often punished by lower grades, poor letters of recommendation, and by a kind of silent but potent pressure from the institutionalized system which is engaged in producing standardized products. Admittedly, the above statement is a generalization; there are some students who are creative and who are not robotized by the journalism educational system. And, certainly, there are many professors who encourage individuality and creativity, but they are scattered rather thinly through journalism education, for the pressures of the system are also on them to conform.

Nevertheless, it is encouraging that some students, as well as some professors—brave souls, all—manage to fight the system, to develop and retain their authenticity and autonomy, and survive the educational treadmill in spite of its conforming and deadening aspects. But these are the exceptions, the ones who are proud of their own individual minds; these are the ones who have self-esteem and confidence that they can transcend the collectivizing influences of formal education and "professionalization" and inject into society their own sense of personality and authenticity. They are the committed ones; those who are certain that, with rational and skillful thought and action, they can succeed in institutionalized education and journalism without sacrificing themselves. These are the ones who form the "saving remnant" of libertarian journalism; it is they who will man the bulwarks in the fight against the forces of authoritarianism and conformity which are creeping in upon us from all sides.

NOTES

1. William J. Goode, "Encroachment, Charlatanism, and the Emerging Profession: Psychology, Sociology, and Medicine," *American Sociological Review* 25 (1960), pp. 902–14.

2. Kenneth S. Lynn, and the editors of *Daedalus* (eds.), *The Professions in America* (Boston: Houghton Mifflin Co., 1965). . . .

3. Ibid., pp. 17–18. [Excerpted in chap. 2, sel. 3, *EIPL*.—ED.]

4. William L. Rivers and Wilbur Schramm, *Responsibility in Mass Communication* (New York: Harper and Row, 1969), p. 240.

5. Lewis H. Lapham, "The Temptation of a Sacred Cow," *Harper's [Magazine]* (vol. 247, no. 1479, Aug. 1973), p. 52.

6. Daniel P. Moynihan, "The Presidency and the Press," *Commentary* (vol. 51, no. 3, Mar. 1971), p. 46.

7. William Barrett, *Irrational Man: A Study in Existential Philosophy* (Garden City, NY: Anchor Books, Doubleday, 1962), pp. 4–5. Although certainly not in sympathy with existentialism generally, Ayn Rand reflects Barrett's opinion about the dangers of professionalism. Here is part of what she says: "If there is any one way to confess one's own mediocrity, it is the willingness to place one's work in the absolute power of a group, particularly a group of one's *professional colleagues*. Of any form of tyranny, this is the worst: it is directed against a single human attribute: the mind—and against a single enemy: the innovator. The innovator, by definition, is the man who challenges the established practices of his profession. To grant a professional monopoly to any group, is to sacrifice human ability and abolish progress; to advocate such a monopoly, is to confess that one has nothing to sacrifice." (Ayn Rand, *The New Left: The Anti-Industrial Revolution* (New York: New American Library, 1971), 46–47.

8. John C. Merrill, "Answering the J-School Critics," *Seminar* (Sept. 1967), p. 22.

9. The present author discusses the three main types of journalism educators in the article, "The ABC's of a Journalism Faculty," *Journalism Educator* (Spring 1965). For a good look at varying roles of journalism education in the United States, as well as its history, see chap. 19—"Mass Communications Education"—in Edwin Emery, Phillip Ault and Warren Agee, *Introduction to Mass Communications* (New York: Dodd, Mead and Co., 4th ed., 1973). For a good, although somewhat dated look at journalism education in other countries, see a special edition of *Gazette: International Journal for Mass Communications Studies* (Amsterdam [, Neth.]: [vol.] 12, [no.] 1, 1966).

10. Increasing numbers of articles and portions of books are dealing with journalism education and are trying to define what is meant by "professional" education in journalism. A few of these from the early 1960s into the 1970s follow: B. R. Manago, "A Philosophy for a Liberal Journalism Education," *Add* 1 (Spring 1962); Richard L. Tobin, "Journalism's Mounting Storms," *Saturday Review* (Dec. 4, 1965); J. C. Merrill, "The Modern Journalist: Soul of an Artist and Mind of a Scientist," *Vidura* (New Delhi, May 1967); John H. Colburn, "Journalism Education—At a Crossroads?" *Quill* (Apr. 1969); Joseph P. Lyford, "New Directions in Journalism Education?" *Seminar* (Dec. 1969); M. L. Stein, "Journalism Education—A Matter of Coexistence," *Saturday Review* (Oct. 9, 1971); John L. Hulteng, "The J-Graduate—How Well Prepared?" *Quill* (Apr. 1972); Harvey Saalberg, "J-Schools Search for Ways to Alleviate Overcrowding," *Editor & Publisher* (Jan. 27, 1973); LaRue Gilleland, "Educators Show Concern for Making Classrooms Relevant, Exciting," *Journalism Educator* (Oct. 1972); "The Ph.D. Debate," *Journalism Educator* (July 1973).

11. Louis Lyons, "What a Journalist Needs," *Atlantic* (Dec. 1957), p. 154.

12. Charles A. Siepmann, *Radio, Television and Society* (New York: Oxford University Press, 1950), p. 225.

QUESTIONS FOR STUDY AND DISCUSSION

1. Bernard Barber treats emerging and marginal professions as a single category. But it may be the case that some occupations will never emerge as full professions. List at least five occupations you think resemble occupations widely acknowledged as professions, but that you think will always seem to be marginal professions at best. Explain as fully as you are able why you list these occupations as marginal professions.

2. Using this chapter's readings and your answers to the last question as resources, classify the following as members of full professions, emerging and/or marginal professions, or nonprofessional occupations and explain the reasons for your classifications:

accountants	civil engineers	master electricians
dentists	cosmetologists	plumbers
social workers	auto mechanics	paralegal personnel
veterinarians	x-ray technicians	physical therapists

3. It is a fact that some occupations are more prestigious than others. Rank the following roles in order of prestige and develop as full an explanation as you are able of these variations in prestige:

police officer	rabbi	prison warden
licensed practical nurse	social worker	attorney
family-practice physician	professional athlete	priest
electrical engineer	politician	neurologist
university professor	registered nurse	psychologist
corporation president	news anchorperson	funeral director

4. Explain what you think full professionalization of journalism would involve, and—given your explanation—say why you think that journalism should or should not professionalize as fully as possible. In your discussion, be sure to consider the points raised by John Merrill.

5. It was pointed out in the introduction to this chapter that in an attempt to gain full recognition as a profession, nursing has been taking the kinds of steps toward professionalization mentioned by Barber. Given your understanding of what it means for an occupation to professionalize, develop and defend a position on whether nursing should continue to strive for full professionalization.

6. Licensing of professionals serves to provide professionals with a state-enforced monopoly on the provision of professional services. Explain in what ways these state-protected monopolies may be both desirable and undesirable from the point of view of people in need of services from those classified by Michael Bayles as belonging to the consulting professions.

7. Even though we might be reluctant to categorize certain occupations as genuine professions, an individual in any occupation may coherently be categorized as "a real professional." Offer as complete an account as you are able of what you take the marks of a true professional to be.

CASE: PROFESSIONALISM AND NURSING

Diane MacIntyre has two years of experience as a staff nurse on a general medical floor that serves many diabetic and stroke patients. As a team leader, she both gives direct patient care and plans basic care for other nursing personnel to carry out. In the past, when she worked extra hours at home or in the hospital library writing procedures, the other nurses (especially another team leader, Arlene Estes, who is a single parent with three children) have said that Diane (who is single and has no children) was foolish to work without pay. During the last few months Diane's attendance at weekly meetings of a multidisciplinary team—composed of professionals from physical therapy, occupational therapy, and social services who are active in rehabilitation efforts on her floor—has strained her relationships with some nursing coworkers. According to Diane, "These other nurses think I'm crazy to come in on my own time. I go to practically every weekly meeting, which take place mainly on my days off. I get a lot of positive reinforcement from being with that group of people, and I think they have a little better impression of professionalism in nursing because of my participation."

Diane's decision to participate with the multidisciplinary team stems from her desire to get more out of

---

Case adapted from Martin Benjamin and Joy Curtis, *Ethics in Nursing* (New York: Oxford University Press, 1981), p. 122.

her job than just a paycheck. She wants to show that "nursing is an important profession and that nurses have more to contribute than passing meds and giving baths." Despite her justification for working extra hours, Diane, nevertheless, feels hurt by the other nurses' reactions, especially those of her friend, Arlene, whose skills and integrity she has always admired.

Diane and Arlene have lunch one day with Peggy Sayre, a nurse from a different unit, and the topic of Diane's extra hours comes up. Peggy asks them both to explain their views. Diane defends her coming in on her day off by pointing out that her involvement with the interdisciplinary team and working on hospital procedures will lead to better care for a larger number of clients. But Arlene argues that Diane's functioning as a "super nurse" puts those who have other responsibilities in a bad light. What is more, she argues, Diane's doing this sort of thing without pay simply increases the expectation that nurses (who are always in danger of being disadvantaged by the "compassion trap") will work overtime without pay. But such work, Arlene argues, is unfair to staff nurses, who are paid an hourly wage. Working overtime without pay, she argues, amounts to being paid less than one's contract provides and is unfair. Arlene finishes defending her position by arguing that nurses like Diane actually hold nurses down by contributing to exploitation rather than helping to raise nursing to the status of a profession because professionals like physicians and lawyers get paid (and paid well) for their professional work.

1. In taking the position she does, has Arlene in any way failed to understand the proper role of altruism in professionalism in general and in nursing in particular? Why or why not?

2. Is Arlene's position fully coherent with the provisions of the American Nurses' Association Code for Nurses? Why or why not? (See appendix I, sample code 3, *EIPL*.)

3. Arlene suggests that the fact staff nurses get paid an hourly wage is relevant to deciding whether what Diane is doing is a fair treatment of a nurse by the hospital administration. Is this correct? Explain the reasons for your answer. Is it unfair for nurses who must consistently work ten or fifteen minutes extra each day not to be paid for that time? Why or why not?

4. Is Arlene correct in believing that activities, such as Diane's coming in on her day off and taking work home, holds nurses down? Why or why not?

5. Since Diane's work with the team seems to depend on the willingness of a nurse to work extra time without pay, does Diane jeopardize the positive gains of her work by not pressing for a paid, regular, institutionalized position to ensure that the work is carried on if she should move to another position? Why or why not?

SELECTED BIBLIOGRAPHY

Abraham, Stanley. *The Public Accounting Profession: Problems and Prospects.* Lexington, MA: Heath, 1978.

Anderson, D., and W. Sharrock. "Biasing the News: Technical Issues in Media Studies." *Sociology* 13 (1979): 361–85.

Becher, Howard S., and James Carper. "The Elements of Identification with an Occupation." *American Sociological Review* 21 (1956): 341–47.

Bledstein, Burton J. *The Culture of Professionalism: The Middle Class and the Development of Higher Education in America.* New York: Norton, 1977.

Blizzard, Samuel W. "The Minister's Dilemma." *Christian Century* (25 April 1956): 508–10.

Boston Nurses Group. *The False Promise: Professionalism and Nursing.* Somerville, MA: New England Free Press, 1978.

Bucher, Rue, and Anselm Strauss. "Professions in Process." *American Journal of Sociology* 66 (1961): 325–34.

Chalk, Rosemary, Mark S. Frankel, and Sallie B. Chafer. *Professional Ethics Activities in the Scientific and Engineering Societies.* Washington, DC: American Association for the Advancement of Science, 1980.

Chaska, N. L., ed. *The Nursing Profession: Views Through the Mist*. New York: McGraw-Hill, 1978.

Clapp, Jane. *Professional Ethics and Insignia*. Metuchen, NJ: Scarecrow, 1974.

Cogan, Morris L. "Toward a Definition of Profession." *Harvard Educational Review* 23 (Winter 1953): 33–50.

Cullen, John B. *The Structure of Professionalism: A Quantitative Analysis*. New York: Petrocelli, 1978.

Cumont, Matthew P. "The Changing Face of Professionalism." *Social Policy* 1 (1970): 26–31.

Davis, Fred, ed. *The Nursing Profession: Five Sociological Essays*. New York: Wiley, 1966.

Dingwall, Robert, and Philip Lewis, eds. *The Sociology of the Professions*. New York: St. Martin's, 1983.

Feldstein, Donald. "Do We Need Professions in Our Society? Professionalization versus Consumerism." *Social Work* 16 (1971): 5–11.

Fichter, Joseph. *Religion as an Occupation*. South Bend, IN: University of Notre Dame Press, 1961.

Frankena, William K. "The Philosophy of Vocation." *Thought* 51 (December 1976): 393–408.

Friedson, Eliot. "The Formal Characteristics of a Profession." In *The Profession of Medicine*, pp. 71–84. New York: Dodd, Mead, 1973.

———. *Professional Dominance*. New York: Atherton, 1970.

———, ed. *The Professions and Their Prospects*. Beverly Hills, CA: Sage, 1973.

Goode, William J. "Community Within a Community: The Professions." *American Sociological Review* 22 (1960): 194–200.

———. "The Librarian: From Occupation to Profession." *Library Quarterly* 31 (1961): 306–18.

Hall, Robert T. "Émile Durkheim on Business and Professional Ethics." *Business and Professional Ethics Journal* 2:1 (1982): 51–60.

Hatt, Paul K. "Occupational and Social Stratification." *American Journal of Sociology* 55 (1950): 539–43.

Janowitz, Morris. *The Professional Soldier*. Glencoe, IL: Free Press of Glencoe, 1960.

Kamerman, Jack. "Thievery as a Profession: A Footnote on the History of a Curious Idea." In *Legality, Morality, and Ethics in Criminal Justice*, ed. Nicholas N. Kittrie and Jackwall Susman, pp. 294–306. New York: Praeger, 1979.

Larson, Magali S. *The Rise of Professionalism: A Sociological Analysis*. Berkeley: University of California Press, 1977.

Lewis, Roy, and Angus Maude. *Professional People*. London: Phoenix House, 1962.

Light, Donald J. "Introduction: The Structure of the Academic Professions." *Sociology of Education* 47 (1974): 2–28.

Lynn, Kenneth S., and the Editors of *Daedalus*, eds. *The Professions in America*. Boston: Houghton Mifflin, 1965; reissued Boston: Beacon, 1967.

McCulloch, Frank, ed. *Drawing the Line*. Washington, DC: American Society of Newspaper Editors, 1984.

Newton, Lisa H. "The Origin of Professionalism: Sociological Conclusions and Ethical Implications." *Business and Professional Ethics Journal* 1:4 (1982): 33–43.

———. "Professionalization: The Intractable Plurality of Values." In *Profits and Professions: Essays in Business and Professional Ethics*, ed. Wade L. Robison, Michael S. Pritchard, and Joseph S. Ellin, pp. 23–36. Clifton, NJ: Humana, 1983.

Niebuhr, H. Richard, and Daniel. D. Williams, eds. *The Ministry in Historical Perspective*. New York: Harper, 1956.

Nielsen, Richard P. "Pluralism in the Mass Media: Can Management Participation Help?" *Journal of Business Ethics* 3:4 (1984): 335–41.

Parsons, Talcott. "Professions." In *International Encyclopedia of the Social Sciences*, 2nd ed., ed. Daniel L. Sills, pp. 536–47. New York: Macmillan and The Free Press, 1968.

———. "The Professions and Social Structure." *Social Forces* 17 (1939): 457–67.

Pellegrino, Edmund D. "Toward a Reconstruction of Medical Morality." *Journal of Medicine and Philosophy* 4:1 (1979): 32–56.

Perrucci, Robert, and Joel Gustl. *Profession Without Community: Engineers in America*. New York: Random House, 1969.

Pirsig, Maynard E., and Kenneth F. Kirwin, eds. *Professional Responsibility: Cases and Materials*, 3rd ed., chap. 1. St. Paul, MN: West, 1976. *Supplement*, 1981.

Pound, Roscoe. "What Is a Profession?: The Rise of the Legal Profession in Antiquity." *Notre Dame Lawyer* 19 (1944): 203–28.

Schaefer, Thomas E. "Professionalism: Foundation for Business Ethics." *Journal of Business Ethics* 3:4 (1984): 269–77.

Schiller, Dan. *Objectivity and the News: The Public and the Rise of Commercial Journalism*. Philadelphia: University of Pennsylvania Press, 1981.

Schmuhl, Robert, ed. *The Responsibility of Journalism*. Notre Dame, IN: Notre Dame University Press, 1984.

Segal, Eleanor T. "Is Nursing a Profession?" *Nursing* 85 (June 1985): 41–43.

Seymour, F.J.C. "What is Professionalism?" *American Teachers' Association Magazine* 43:10 (1963): 20–23.

Sharswood, George. *An Essay on Professional Ethics*, 6th ed. Philadelphia: George T. Bird: 1944; rpt. 1930.

Starr, Paul. *The Social Transformation of American Medicine*. New York: Basic Books, 1982.

Strauss, George. "Professionalism and Occupational Associations." *Industrial Relations* 2:3 (1963): 8–9.

Taylor, M. Lee. "Professionalization: Its Functions and Dysfunctions in the Life Insurance Occupation." *Social Forces* 38 (1959): 110–14.

Vollmer, H., and D. Mills, eds. *Professionalization*. Englewood Cliffs, NJ: Prentice-Hall, 1966.

Weber, Max. "Politics as a Vocation" (1919). In *From Max Weber: Essays in Sociology*, ed. and trans. Hans H. Gerth and C. Wright Mills, pp. 77–128. New York: Oxford University Press, 1946.

———. "Science as a Vocation" (1919). In Gerth and Mills, pp. 129–56, *supra*.

Wilensky, Harold L. "The Professionalization of Everyone?" *American Journal of Sociology* 70 (1964): 137–58.

3

OCCUPATIONAL AND ORDINARY MORALITY

Since professions and occupations arise to provide for certain kinds of needs or interests, each will have a proper task. The profession of medicine, for example, exists because people have a need for medical care. And the profession of law exists because people have a need for legal services. This leads quite directly to the issue of professional roles and the kinds of rights and responsibilities which attach to those roles. In particular, the fact that various professions exist to serve certain needs or interests raises questions about whether professionals, because of their special occupational roles, have permission or even obligations to ignore the moral norms which are generally held to be binding on persons. In one sense, it seems quite clear that professionals are permitted to do things which are normally morally (and often legally) impermissible. As Samuel Govovitz has pointed out, physicians often puncture people with sharp instruments, render them unconscious, cut them open and remove and discard some of their internal parts—things which would be considered felonious assault under normal conditions.[1] But the fact that someone is a physician, standing in a professional relationship to a client importantly changes things, and the physician may do to a patient what even that person's parent or spouse may not do.

Special roles, then, seem clearly to create special moral rights and duties. But the question then arises as to the source and scope of these special rights and duties. And these questions involve asking whether and, if so, how the constraints of ordinary morality apply to professionals in their professional roles.

The question of role morality is a large and intriguing one which is not limited to the ethics of occupational roles. In the broadest sense, questions of role morality cut across roles as diverse as parent, spouse, small-town pharmacist, crossing guard, and so on. For the purposes of this book, we shall limit our inquiry into role morality to questions concerning occupational roles, including roles in business. Because the recognized professions tend to be marked by the kinds of characteristics discussed by most of our authors in chapter 2, many would deny that business roles are, properly speaking, professional roles. Business roles, however, are institutional roles, and traditional business practice has raised serious questions of occupational ethics. In particular, competitive business practices have raised the central question of role morality in an especially clear way. Although the conventional wisdom in business is that ''business is business,'' the literature on business ethics has increasingly raised the question of whether it is morally permissible for those in business roles to radically separate their occupational roles from their roles as ordinary moral agents—that is, agents bound by the strictures (e.g. against deception, harming innocent others, etc.) that normally bind persons. As we shall see in this chapter's readings, quite the same question arises in law and politics.

Though the readings in this chapter focus on law, business, and politics, it is important to realize that they raise the more general question of the apparent discontinuity between occupational and ordinary morality. That is, the general question raised by the readings is whether it is morally permissible for those in professional/occupational roles to elevate the values or goals central to their professions or occupations (e.g., health in health care provision, a client's interests in legal practice, the pursuit of profits in business, the will or interests of a constituency in politics, etc.) in a way such that the preservation of those values or pursuit of those goals always takes priority when a conflict arises between them and the demands of ordinary morality. Perhaps we can best understand the general question to be whether occupational roles free their occupants to ignore the ordinary moral rights of persons, for example, rights not to be harmed, rights not to be treated deceptively, and so on.

The selections by Monroe Freedman and Richard Wasserstrom raise some serious questions about the role morality of lawyers. Freedman defends several practices often used by lawyers (discrediting a truthful person, assisting a client in lying, acting in a way that encourages lying) which seem to violate the requirements of ordinary morality. Wasserstrom (whose article also contributes to the discussion of the features of a profession in chap. 2) points out that what he calls the 'role differentiation' of attorneys seems to allow them to inhabit a morally simplified universe. He further suggests that this tends to be true of professionals in general. We shall see additional defenses of this kind of moral simplification in later chapters, for example, in the selections from Joseph Ellin and Joseph Collins in chapter 5 and in the selection from Milton Friedman in chapter 10.

Albert Carr provides an example of what Wasserstrom understands as role differentiation in business practice. Carr analogizes business to a poker game, and he suggests that just as it would be wrongheaded to raise moral objections to bluffing in poker, it is wrongheaded to raise such objections to bluffing in business. It is important to notice that Carr's game model for business and the justification it provides for bluffing between those engaged in business might be extended to other areas of professional life. One could, for example, expand Carr's poker analogy to health care provision, arguing that part of the "game" in health care is to relinquish candor when the provider deems this to be in a patient's best interest. Similarly, one might use the game model to justify manipulation in, say, physical therapy, psychological counseling, and education or to justify deception and invasion of privacy in, say, journalism, social science research, politics, and so on. The game model of business can also easily be used to justify a host of morally questionable business practices in addition to bluffing one's business colleagues. For example, it can be, and has been, used to justify deceptive advertising practices and polluting the environment within the limits of law.

Norman Chase Gillespie's article rejects Carr's game model for business, thereby rejecting the claim that business creates a special context with a special morality of its own. More generally, Gillespie's argument implicitly suggests that roles do not create moralities distinct from ordinary morality. Rather, the ordinary sorts of considerations which affect our moral rights and duties can be used to justify changes in rights and duties that can arise in occupational contexts. Gillespie also argues that it is precisely when circumstances are such that the ordinary rules of morality do not apply (e.g., in contexts where everyone—or nearly everyone—acts dishonestly and the honest person is put at a disadvantage) that the circumstances themselves are morally unacceptable and therefore must be changed.

Thomas Nagel's essay represents a response to the question of role differentiation which differs from that of Gillespie but is more moderate than the views of Freedman and Carr. Nagel suggests that although role morality (what he calls 'public morality') is not derivable from ordinary morality (what he calls 'private morality'), both are derived from a common source. This source includes outcome-centered values—that is, values which emphasize *goals or consequences*—and action-centered values, which are independent of outcomes emphasizing the *kinds* of actions being performed. (In the language of chap. 1, this is the distinction between teleological and deontological values.) Nagel calls the moralities arising from these fundamentally different values 'the morality of outcomes' and 'the morality of actions.' Both public and private morality include recognition of these different types of values, but, says Nagel, there are significant discontinuities in emphasis. That is, public morality, which is tied to institutions, gives a greater emphasis to the morality of outcomes, whereas private morality gives a greater emphasis to the morality of actions. Despite this explanation and justification of certain discontinuities between public and private morality, Nagel argues that the action-centered, deontological concerns which dominate ordinary morality are not (as Freedman and Carr suggest) justifiably ignored in professional morality and that much of the sacrifice of these values by persons in special roles will not bear moral scrutiny.

However one decides to resolve the question of whether role morality is derivable from ordinary morality, roles clearly can make a significant moral difference in what we are morally permitted and required to do, and these selections begin our inquiry into that difference. In the chapters that follow, we shall take up more particular questions regarding the scope of the rights and responsibilities that follow from the assumption of special occupational roles.

NOTE

1. Samuel Gorovitz, *Doctors' Dilemmas: Moral Conflict and Medical Care* (New York: Macmillan, 1982); reissued New York: Oxford University Press, 1985), chap. 1.

5. Professional Responsibility of the Criminal Defense Lawyer: The Three Hardest Questions*†

Monroe H. Freedman

In almost any area of legal counseling and advocacy, the lawyer may be faced with the dilemma of either betraying the confidential communications of his client or participating to some extent in the purposeful deception of the court. This problem is nowhere more acute than in the practice of criminal

From *Michigan Law Review* 64 (1966): 1469–82.

*The substance of this paper was recently presented to a Criminal Trial Institute attended by forty-five members of the District of Columbia Bar. As a consequence, several judges (none of whom had either heard the lecture or read it) complained to the Committee on Admissions and Grievances of the District Court for the District of Columbia, urging the author's disbarment or suspension. Only after four months of proceedings, including a hearing, two meetings, and a de novo review by eleven federal district court judges, did the Committee announce its decision to "proceed no further in the matter."

†[For a further development of the discussion in this article, see Monroe H. Freedman, *Lawyers' Ethics in an Adversary System* (Indianapolis, IN: Bobbs-Merrill, 1975), chap. 3.—ED.]

law, particularly in the representation of the indigent accused. The purpose of this article is to analyze and attempt to resolve three of the most difficult issues in this general area:

1. Is it proper to cross-examine for the purpose of discrediting the reliability or credibility of an adverse witness whom you know to be telling the truth?
2. Is it proper to put a witness on the stand when you know he will commit perjury?
3. Is it proper to give your client legal advice when you have reason to believe that the knowledge you give him will tempt him to commit perjury?

These questions present serious difficulties with respect to a lawyer's ethical responsibilities. Moreover, if one admits the possibility of an affirmative answer, it is difficult even to discuss them without appearing to some to be unethical. It is not surprising, therefore, that reasonable, rational discussion of these issues has been uncommon and that the problems have for so long remained unresolved. In this regard it should be recognized that the Canons of Ethics, which were promulgated in 1908 "as a general guide,"[1] are both inadequate and self-contradictory.

I. THE ADVERSARY SYSTEM AND THE NECESSITY FOR CONFIDENTIALITY

At the outset, we should dispose of some common question-begging responses. The attorney is indeed an officer of the court, and he does participate in a search for truth. These two propositions, however, merely serve to state the problem in different words: As an officer of the court, participating in a search for truth, what is the attorney's special responsibility, and how does that responsibility affect his resolution of the questions posed above?

The attorney functions in an adversary system based upon the presupposition that the most effective means of determining truth is to present to a judge and jury a clash between proponents of conflicting views. It is essential to the effective functioning of this system that each adversary has, in the words of Canon 15, "entire devotion to the interest of the client, warm zeal in the maintenance and defense of his rights and the exertion of his utmost learning and ability." It is also essential to maintain the fullest uninhibited communication between the client and his attorney, so that the attorney can most effectively counsel his client and advocate the latter's cause. This policy is safeguarded by the requirement that the lawyer must, in the words of Canon 37, "preserve his client's confidences." Canon 15 does, of course, qualify these obligations by stating that "the office of attorney does not permit, much less does it demand of him for any client, violations of law or any manner of fraud or chicane." In addition, Canon 22 requires candor toward the court.

The problem presented by these salutary generalties of the Canons in the context of particular litigation is illustrated by the personal experience of Samuel Williston, which was related in his autobiography.[2] Because of his examination of a client's correspondence file, Williston learned of a fact extremely damaging to his client's case. When the judge announced his decision, it was apparent that a critical factor in the favorable judgment for Williston's client was the judge's ignorance of this fact. Williston remained silent and did not thereafter inform the judge of what he knew. He was convinced, and Charles Curtis[3] agrees with him, that it was his duty to remain silent.

In an opinion by the American Bar Association Committee on Professional Ethics and Grievances, an eminent panel headed by Henry Drinker held that a lawyer should remain silent when his client lies to the judge by saying that he has no prior record, despite the attorney's knowledge to the contrary.[4] The majority of the panel distinguished the situation in which the attorney has learned of the client's prior record from a source other than the client himself. William B. Jones, a distinguished trial lawyer and now a judge in the United States District Court for the District of Columbia, wrote a separate opinion in which he asserted that in neither event should the lawyer expose his client's lie. If these two cases do not constitute "fraud or chicane" or lack of candor within the meaning of the Canons (and I agree with the authorities cited that they do not), it is clear that the meaning of the canons is ambiguous.

The adversary system has further ramifications in a criminal case. The defendant is presumed to be innocent. The burden is on the prosecution to prove beyond a reasonable doubt that the defendant is guilty. The plea of not guilty does not necessarily mean "not guilty in fact," for the defendant may mean "not legally guilty." Even the accused who knows that he committed the crime is entitled to put the government to its proof. Indeed, the accused who knows that he is guilty has an absolute constitutional right to remain silent.[5] The moralist might quite reasonably understand this to mean that, under these circumstances, the defendant and his lawyer are privileged to "lie" to the court in pleading not guilty. In my judgment, the moralist is right. However, our adversary system and related notions of the proper administration of criminal justice sanction the lie.

Some derive solace from the sophistry of calling

the lie a "legal fiction," but this is hardly an adequate answer to the moralist. Moreover, this answer has no particular appeal for the practicing attorney, who knows that the plea of not guilty commits him to the most effective advocacy of which he is capable. Criminal defense lawyers do not win their cases by arguing reasonable doubt. Effective trial advocacy requires that the attorney's every word, action, and attitude be consistent with the conclusion that his client is innocent. As every trial lawyer knows, the jury is certain that the defense attorney knows whether his client is guilty. The jury is therefore alert to, and will be enormously affected by, any indication by the attorney that he believes the defendant to be guilty. Thus, the plea of not guilty commits the advocate to a trial, including a closing argument, in which he must argue that "not guilty" means "not guilty in fact."[6]

There is, of course, a simple way to evade the dilemma raised by the not guilty plea. Some attorneys rationalize the problem by insisting that a lawyer never knows for sure whether his client is guilty. The client who insists upon his guilt may in fact be protecting his wife, or may know that he pulled the trigger and that the victim was killed, but not that his gun was loaded with blanks and that the fatal shot was fired from across the street. For anyone who finds this reasoning satisfactory, there is, of course, no need to think further about the issue.

It is also argued that a defense attorney can remain selectively ignorant. He can insist in his first interview with his client that, if his client is guilty, he simply does not want to know. It is inconceivable, however, that an attorney could give adequate counsel under such circumstances. How is the client to know, for example, precisely which relevant circumstances his lawyer does not want to be told? The lawyer might ask whether his client has a prior record. The client, assuming that this is the kind of knowledge that might present ethical problems for his lawyer, might respond that he has no record. The lawyer would then put the defendant on the stand and, on cross-examination, be appalled to learn that his client has two prior convictions for offenses identical to that for which he is being tried.

Of course, an attorney can guard against this specific problem by telling his client that he must know about the client's past record. However, a lawyer can never anticipate all of the innumerable and potentially critical factors that his client, once cautioned, may decide not to reveal. In one instance, for example, the defendant assumed that his lawyer would prefer to be ignorant of the fact that the client had been having sexual relations with the chief defense witness. The client was innocent of the robbery with which he was charged, but was found guilty by the jury—probably because he was guilty of fornication, a far less serious offense for which he had not even been charged.

The problem is compounded by the practice of plea bargaining. It is considered improper for a defendant to plead guilty to a lesser offense unless he is in fact guilty. Nevertheless, it is common knowledge that plea bargaining frequently results in improper guilty pleas by innocent people. For example, a defendant falsely accused of robbery may plead guilty to simple assault, rather than risk a robbery conviction and a substantial prison term. If an attorney is to be scrupulous in bargaining pleas, however, he must know in advance that his client is guilty, since the guilty plea is improper if the defendant is innocent. Of course, if the attempt to bargain for a lesser offense should fail, the lawyer would know the truth and thereafter be unable to rationalize that he was uncertain of his client's guilt.

If one recognizes that professional responsibility requires that an advocate have full knowledge of every pertinent fact, it follows that he must seek the truth from his client, not shun it.[7] This means that he will have to dig and pry and cajole, and, even then, he will not be successful unless he can convince the client that full and confidential disclosure to his lawyer will never result in prejudice to the client by any word or action of the lawyer. This is, perhaps, particularly true in the case of the indigent defendant, who meets his lawyer for the first time in the cell block or the rotunda. He did not choose the lawyer, nor does he know him. The lawyer has been sent by the judge and is part of the system that is attempting to punish the defendant. It is no easy task to persuade this client that he can talk freely without fear of prejudice. However, the inclination to mislead one's lawyer is not restricted to the indigent or even to the criminal defendant. Randolph Paul has observed a similar phenomenon among a wealthier class in a far more congenial atmosphere:

> The tax adviser will sometimes have to dynamite the facts of his case out of the unwilling witnesses on his own side—witnesses who are nervous, witnesses who are confused about their own interest, witnesses who try to be too smart for their own good, and witnesses who subconsciously do not want to understand what has happened despite the fact that they must if they are to testify coherently.[8]

Paul goes on to explain that the truth can be obtained only by persuading the client that it would be a violation of a sacred obligation for the lawyer ever to reveal a client's confidence. Beyond any question, once a lawyer has persuaded his client of the obligation of confidentiality, he must respect that obligation scrupulously.

II. THE SPECIFIC QUESTIONS

The first of the difficult problems posed above will now be considered: Is it proper to cross-examine for the purpose of discrediting the reliability or the credibility of [an adverse] witness whom you know to be telling the truth? Assume the following situation. Your client has been falsely accused of a robbery committed at 16th and P Streets at 11:00 P.M. He tells you at first that at no time on the evening of the crime was he within six blocks of that location. However, you are able to persuade him that he must tell you the truth and that doing so will in no way prejudice him. He then reveals to you that he was at 15th and P Streets at 10:55 that evening, but that he was walking east, away from the scene of the crime, and that, by 11:00 P.M., he was six blocks away. At the trial, there are two prosecution witnesses. The first mistakenly, but with some degree of persuasion, identifies your client as the criminal. At that point, the prosecution's case depends on this single witness, who might or might not be believed. Since your client has a prior record, you do not want to put him on the stand, but you feel that there is at least a chance for acquittal. The second prosecution witness is an elderly woman who is somewhat nervous and who wears glasses. She testifies truthfully and accurately that she saw your client at 15th and P Streets at 10:55 P.M. She has corroborated the erroneous testimony of the first witness and made conviction virtually certain. However, if you destroy her reliability through cross-examination designed to show that she is easily confused and has poor eyesight, you may not only eliminate the corroboration, but also cast doubt in the jury's mind on the prosecution's entire case. On the other hand, if you should refuse to cross-examine her because she is telling the truth, your client may well feel betrayed, since you knew of the witness's veracity only because your client confided in you, under your assurance that his truthfulness would not prejudice him.

The client would be right. Viewed strictly, the attorney's failure to cross-examine would not be violative of the client's confidence because it would not constitute a disclosure. However, the same policy that supports the obligation of confidentiality precludes the attorney from prejudicing his client's interest in any other way because of knowledge gained in his professional capacity. When a lawyer fails to cross-examine only because his client, placing confidence in the lawyer, has been candid with him, the basis for such confidence and candor collapses. Our legal system cannot tolerate such a result.

> The purposes and necessities of the relation between a client and his attorney require, in many cases, on the part of the client, the fullest and freest disclosures to the attorney of the client's objects, motives and acts. . . . To permit the attorney to reveal to others what is so disclosed, would be not only a gross violation of a sacred trust upon his part, but it would utterly destroy and prevent the usefulness and benefits to be derived from professional assistance.[9]

The client's confidences must "upon all occasions be inviolable," to avoid the "greater mischiefs" that would probably result if a client could not feel free "to repose [confidence] in the attorney to whom he resorts for legal advice and assistance."[10] Destroy that confidence, and "a man would not venture to consult any skillful person, or would only dare to tell his counsellor half his case."[11]

Therefore, one must conclude that the attorney is obligated to attack, if he can, the reliability or credibility of an opposing witness whom he knows to be truthful. The contrary result would inevitably impair the "perfect freedom of consultation by client with attorney," which is "essential to the administration of justice."[12]

The second question is generally considered to be the hardest of all: Is it proper to put a witness on the stand when you know he will commit perjury? Assume, for example, that the witness in question is the accused himself, and that he has admitted to you, in response to your assurances of confidentiality, that he is guilty. However, he insists upon taking the stand to protest his innocence. There is a clear consensus among prosecutors and defense attorneys that the likelihood of conviction is increased enormously when the defendant does not take the stand. Consequently, the attorney who prevents his client from testifying only because the client has confided his guilt to him is violating that confidence by acting upon the information in a way that will seriously prejudice his client's interests.

Perhaps the most common method for avoiding the ethical problem just posed is for the lawyer to withdraw from the case, at least if there is sufficient time before trial for the client to retain another attorney.[13] The client will then go to the nearest law office, realizing that the obligation of confidentiality is not what it has been represented to be, and withhold incriminating information or the fact of his guilt from his new attorney. On ethical grounds, the practice of withdrawing from a case under such circumstances is indefensible, since the identical perjured testimony will ultimately be presented. More important, perhaps, is the practical consideration that the new attorney will be ignorant of the perjury and therefore will be in no position to attempt to discourage the client from presenting it. Only the original attorney, who knows the truth, has that opportunity, but he loses it in the very act of evading the ethical problem.

The problem is all the more difficult when the client is indigent. He cannot retain other counsel, and in many jurisdictions, including the District of Columbia, it is impossible for appointed counsel to withdraw from a case except for extraordinary reasons. Thus, appointed counsel, unless he lies to the judge, can successfully withdraw only by revealing to the judge that the attorney has received knowledge of his client's guilt. Such a revelation in itself would seem to be a sufficiently serious violation of the obligation of confidentiality to merit severe condemnation. In fact, however, the situation is far worse, since it is entirely possible that the same judge who permits the attorney to withdraw will subsequently hear the case and sentence the defendant. When he does so, of course, he will have had personal knowledge of the defendant's guilt before the trial began.[14] Moreover, this will be knowledge of which the newly appointed counsel for the defendant will probably be ignorant.

The difficulty is further aggravated when the client informs the lawyer for the first time during trial that he intends to take the stand and commit perjury. The perjury in question may not necessarily be a protestation of innocence by a guilty man. Referring to the earlier hypothetical of the defendant wrongly accused of a robbery at 16th and P, the only perjury may be his denial of the truthful, but highly damaging, testimony of the corroborating witness who placed him one block away from the intersection five minutes prior to the crime. Of course, if he tells the truth and thus verifies the corroborating witness, the jury will be far more inclined to accept the inaccurate testimony of the principal witness, who specifically identified him as the criminal.[15]

If a lawyer has discovered his client's intent to perjure himself, one possible solution to this problem is for the lawyer to approach the bench, explain his ethical difficulty to the judge, and ask to be relieved, thereby causing a mistrial. This request is certain to be denied, if only because it would empower the defendant to cause a series of mistrials in the same fashion. At this point, some feel that the lawyer has avoided the ethical problem and can put the defendant on the stand. However, one objection to this solution, apart from the violation of confidentiality, is that the lawyer's ethical problem has not been solved, but has only been transferred to the judge. Moreover, the client in such a case might well have grounds for appeal on the basis of deprivation of due process and denial of the right to counsel, since he will have been tried before, and sentenced by, a judge who has been informed of the client's guilt by his own attorney.

A solution even less satisfactory than informing the judge of the defendant's guilt would be to let the client take the stand without the attorney's participation and to omit reference to the client's testimony in closing argument. The latter solution, of course, would be as damaging as to fail entirely to argue the case to the jury, and failing to argue the case is "as improper as though the attorney had told the jury that his client had uttered a falsehood in making the statement."[16]

Therefore, the obligation of confidentiality, in the context of our adversary system, apparently allows the attorney no alternative to putting a perjurious witness on the stand without explicit or implicit disclosure of the attorney's knowledge to either the judge or the jury. Canon 37 does not proscribe this conclusion; the canon recognizes only two exceptions to the obligation of confidentiality. The first relates to the lawyer who is accused by his client and may disclose the truth to defend himself. The other exception relates to the "announced intention of a client to commit a crime." On the basis of the ethical and practical considerations discussed above, the Canon's exception to the obligation of confidentiality cannot logically be understood to include the crime of perjury committed during the specific case in which the lawyer is serving. Moreover, even when the intention is to commit a crime in the future, Canon 37 does not require disclosure, but only permits it. Furthermore, Canon 15, which does proscribe "violation of law" by the attorney for his client, does not apply to the lawyer who unwillingly puts a perjurious client on the stand after having made every effort to dissuade him from committing perjury. Such an act by the attorney cannot properly be found to be subornation—corrupt inducement—of perjury. Canon 29 requires counsel to inform the prosecuting authorities of perjury committed in a case in which he has been involved, but this can only refer to perjury by opposing witnesses. For an attorney to disclose his client's perjury "would involve a direct violation of Canon 37."[17] Despite Canon 29, therefore, the attorney should not reveal his client's perjury "to the court or to the authorities."[18]

Of course, before the client testifies perjuriously, the lawyer has a duty to attempt to dissuade him on grounds of both law and morality. In addition, the client should be impressed with the fact that his untruthful alibi is tactically dangerous. There is always a strong possibility that the prosecutor will expose the perjury on cross-examination. However, for the reasons already given, the final decision must necessarily be the client's. The lawyer's best course thereafter would be to avoid any further professional relationship with a client whom he knew to have perjured himself.

The third question is whether it is proper to give your client legal advice when you have reason to believe that the knowledge you give him will tempt him to commit perjury. This may indeed be the most difficult problem of all, because giving such advise creates the appearance that the attorney is encouraging and condoning perjury.

If the lawyer is not certain what the facts are when he gives the advice, the problem is substantially minimized, if not eliminated. It is not the lawyer's function to prejudge his client as a perjurer. He cannot presume that the client will make unlawful use of his advice. Apart from this, there is a natural predisposition in most people to recollect facts, entirely honestly, in a way most favorable to their own interest. As Randolph Paul has observed, some witnesses are nervous, some are confused about their own interests, some try to be too smart for their own good, and some subconsciously do not want to understand what has happened to them.[19] Before he begins to remember essential facts, the client is entitled to know what his own interests are.

The above argument does not apply merely to factual questions such as whether a particular event occurred at 10:15 or at 10:45.[20] One of the most critical problems in a criminal case, as in many others, is intention. A German writer, considering the question of intention as a test of legal consequences, suggests the following situation.[21] A young man and a young woman decide to get married. Each has a thousand dollars. They decide to begin a business with these funds, and the young lady gives her money to the young man for this purpose. Was the intention to form a joint venture or a partnership? Did they intend that the young man be an agent or a trustee? Was the transaction a gift or a loan? If the couple should subsequently visit a tax attorney and discover that it is in their interest that the transaction be viewed as a gift, it is submitted that they could, with complete honesty, so remember it. On the other hand, should their engagement be broken and the young woman consult an attorney for the purpose of recovering her money, she could with equal honesty remember that her intention was to make a loan.

Assume that your client, on trial for his life in a first-degree murder case, has killed another man with a penknife but insists that the killing was in self-defense. You ask him, "Do you customarily carry the penknife in your pocket, do you carry it frequently or infrequently, or did you take it with you only on this occasion?" It is entirely appropriate to inform him that his carrying the knife only on this occasion, or infrequently, supports an inference of premeditation, while if he carried the knife constantly, or frequently, the inference of premeditation would be negated. Thus, your client's life may depend upon his recollection as to whether he carried the knife frequently or infrequently. Despite the possibility that the client or a third party might infer that the lawyer was prompting the client to lie, the lawyer must apprise the defendant of the significance of his answer. There is no conceivable ethical requirement that the lawyer trap his client into a hasty and ill-considered answer before telling him the significance of the question.

A similar problem is created if the client has given the lawyer incriminating information before being fully aware of its significance. For example, assume that a man consults a tax lawyer and says, "I am fifty years old. Nobody in my immediate family has lived past fifty. Therefore, I would like to put my affairs in order. Specifically, I understand that I can avoid substantial estate taxes by setting up a trust. Can I do it?" The lawyer informs the client that he can successfully avoid the estate taxes only if he lives at least three years after establishing the trust or, should he die within three years, if the trust is found not to have been created in contemplation of death. The client then might ask who decides whether the trust is in contemplation of death. After learning that the determination is made by the court, the client might inquire about the factors on which such a decision would be based.

At this point, the lawyer can do one of two things. He can refuse to answer the question, or he can inform the client that the court will consider the wording of the trust instrument and will hear evidence about any conversations which he may have or any letters he may write expressing motives other than avoidance of estate taxes. It is likely that virtually every tax attorney in the country would answer the client's question, and that no one would consider the answer unethical. However, the lawyer might well appear to have prompted his client to deceive the Internal Revenue Service and the courts, and this appearance would remain regardless of the lawyer's explicit disclaimer to the client of any intent so to prompt him. Nevertheless, it should not be unethical for the lawyer to give the advice.

In a criminal case, a lawyer may be representing a client who protests his innocence, and whom the lawyer believes to be innocent. Assume, for example, that the charge is assault with intent to kill, that the prosecution has erroneous but credible eyewitness testimony against the defendant, and that the defendant's truthful alibi witness is impeachable on the basis of several felony convictions. The prosecutor, perhaps having doubts about the case, offers to permit the defendant to plead guilty to simple assault. If the defendant should go to trial and be convicted, he might well be sent to jail for fifteen years; on a plea of simple assault, the maximum penalty would be one year, and sentence might well be suspended.

The common practice of conveying the prosecutor's offer to the defendant should not be considered unethical, even if the defense lawyer is convinced of this client's innocence. Yet the lawyer is clearly in the position of prompting his client to lie, since the defendant cannot make the plea without saying to the judge that he is pleading guilty because he is guilty. Furthermore, if the client does decide to plead guilty, it would be improper for the lawyer to inform the court that his client is innocent, thereby compelling the defendant to stand trial and take the substantial risk of fifteen years' imprisonment.[22]

Essentially no different from the problem discussed above, but apparently more difficult, is the so-called *Anatomy of a Murder* situation.[23] The lawyer, who has received from his client an incriminating story of murder in the first degree, says, "If the facts are as you have stated them so far, you have no defense, and you will probably be electrocuted. On the other hand, if you acted in a blind rage, there is a possibility of saving your life. Think it over, and we will talk about it tomorrow." As in the tax case, and as in the case of the plea of guilty to a lesser offense, the lawyer has given his client a legal opinion that might induce the client to lie. This is information which the lawyer himself would have, without advice, were he in the client's position. It is submitted that the client is entitled to have this information about the law and to make his own decision as to whether to act upon it. To decide otherwise would not only penalize the less well-educated defendant, but would also prejudice the client because of his initial truthfulness in telling his story in confidence to the attorney.

III. CONCLUSION

The lawyer is an officer of the court, participating in a search for truth. Yet no lawyer would consider that he had acted unethically in pleading the statute of frauds or the statute of limitations as a bar to a just claim. Similarly, no lawyer would consider it unethical to prevent the introduction of evidence such as a murder weapon seized in violation of the fourth amendment or a truthful but involuntary confession, or to defend a guilty man on grounds of denial of a speedy trial.[24] Such actions are permissible because there are policy considerations that at times justify frustrating the search for truth and the prosecution of a just claim. Similarly, there are policies that justify an affirmative answer to the three questions that have been posed in this article. These policies include the maintenance of an adversary system, the presumption of innocence, the prosecution's burden to prove guilt beyond a reasonable doubt, the right to counsel, and the obligation of confidentiality between lawyer and client.

NOTES

1. American Bar Association, *Canons of Professional Ethics,* Preamble (1908).
2. Williston, *Life and Law,* 271 (1940).
3. Curtis, *It's Your Law,* 17–21 (1954). See also Curtis, "The Ethics of Advocacy," 4 *Stan. L. Rev.*, 3, 9–10 (1951); Drinker, "Some Remarks on Mr. Curtis' 'The Ethics of Advocacy,' " 4 *Stan. L. Rev.*, 349, 350–51 (1952).
4. Opinion 287, Committee on Professional Ethics and Grievances of the American Bar Association (1953).
5. *Escobedo* v. *Illinois,* 378 U.S. 478, 485, 491 (1964).
6. "The failure to argue the case before the jury, while ordinarily only a trial tactic not subject to review, manifestly enters the field of incompetency when the reason assigned is the attorney's conscience. It is as improper as though the attorney had told the jury that his client had uttered a falsehood in making the statement. The right to an attorney embraces effective representation throughout all stages of the trial, and where the representation is of such low caliber as to amount to no representation, the guarantee of due process has been violated." *Johns* v. *Smyth,* 176 F. Supp. 949, 953 (E.D. VA 1959); Schwartz, *Cases on Professional Responsibility and the Administration of Criminal Justice,* 79 (1962).
7. "[C]ounsel cannot properly perform their duties without knowing the truth," Opinion 23, Committee on Professional Ethics and Grievances of the American Bar Association (1930).
8. Paul, "The Responsibilities of the Tax Adviser," 63 *Harv. L. Rev.*, 377, 383 (1950).
9. 2 Mechem, *Agency* § 2297 (2d ed. 1914).
10. Opinion 150, Committee on Professional Ethics and Grievances of the American Bar Association (1936), quoting Thornton, *Attorneys at Law* § 94 (1914). See also Opinion 23, *supra* note 7.
11. *Greenough* v. *Gaskell,* 1 Myl. & K. 98, 103, 39 Eng. Rep. 618, 621 (Ch. 1833) (Lord Chancellor Brougham).
12. Opinion 91, Committee on Professional Ethics and Grievances of the American Bar Association (1933).
13. See Orkin, "Defense of One Known to Be Guilty," 1 *Crim. L.Q.*, 170, 174 (1958). Unless the lawyer has told the client at the outset that he will withdraw if he learns that the client is guilty, "it is plain enough as a matter of good morals and professional ethics" that the lawyer should not withdraw on this ground. Opinion 90, Committee on Professional Ethics and Grievances of the

American Bar Association (1932). As to the difficulties inherent in the lawyer's telling the client that he wants to remain ignorant of crucial facts, see note 7 *supra* and accompanying text.

14. The judge may infer that the situation is worse than it is in fact. In the case related in note 22 *infra*, the attorney's actual difficulty was that he did not want to permit a plea of guilty by a client who was maintaining his innocence. However, as is commonly done, he told the judge only that he had to withdraw because of "an ethical problem." The judge reasonably inferred that the defendant had admitted his guilt and wanted to offer a perjured alibi.

15. One lawyer, who considers it clearly unethical for the attorney to present the alibi in this hypothetical case, found no ethical difficulty himself in the following case. His client was prosecuted for robbery. The prosecution witness testified that the robbery had taken place at 10:15, and identified the defendant as the criminal. However, the defendant had a convincing alibi for 10:00 to 10:30. The attorney presented the alibi, and the client was acquitted. The alibi was truthful, but the attorney knew that the prosecution witness had been confused about the time, and that his client had in fact committed the crime at 10:45.

16. See note 6 *supra*.

17. Opinion 287, Committee on Professional Ethics and Grievances of the American Bar Association (1953).

18. Ibid.

19. See Paul, *supra* note 8.

20. Even this kind of "objective fact" is subject to honest error. See note 15 *supra*.

21. Wurzel, "Das Juristische Denken," 82 (1904), translated in Fuller, *Basic Contract Law*, 67 (1964).

22. In a recent case, the defendant was accused of unauthorized use of an automobile, for which the maximum penalty is five years. He told his court-appointed attorney that he had borrowed the car from a man known to him only as "Junior," that he had not known the car was stolen, and that he had an alibi for the time of the theft. The defendant had three prior convictions for larceny, and the alibi was weak. The prosecutor offered to accept a guilty plea to two misdemeanors (taking property without right and petty larceny) carrying a combined maximum sentence of eighteen months. The defendant was willing to plead guilty to the lesser offenses, but the attorney felt that, because of his client's alibi, he could not permit him to do so. The lawyer therefore informed the judge that he had an ethical problem and asked to be relieved. The attorney who was appointed in his place permitted the client to plead guilty to the two lesser offenses, and the defendant was sentenced to nine months. The alternative would have been five or six months in jail while the defendant waited for his jury trial, and a very substantial risk of conviction and a much heavier sentence. Neither the client nor justice would have been well served by compelling the defendant to go to trial against his will under these circumstances.

23. See Traver, *Anatomy of a Murder* (1958).

24. *Cf.* Kamisar, "Equal Justice in the Gatehouses and Mansions of American Criminal Procedure," in *Criminal Justice in Our Time* 77–78 (Howard ed. 1965):

Yes, the presence of counsel in the police station may result in the suppression of truth, just as the presence of counsel at the trial may, when a client is advised not to take the stand, or when an objection is made to the admissibility of trustworthy, but illegally seized, "real" evidence.

If the subject of police interrogation not only cannot be "coerced" into making a statement, but need not volunteer one, why shouldn't he be so advised? And why shouldn't court-appointed counsel, as well as retained counsel, so advise him?

6. Lawyers as Professionals: Some Moral Issues

Richard A. Wasserstrom

In this paper I examine two moral criticisms of lawyers which, if well founded, are fundamental. Neither is new but each appears to apply with particular force today. Both tend to be made by those not in the mainstream of the legal profession and to be rejected by those who are in it. Both in some sense concern the lawyer-client relationship.

The first criticism centers around the lawyer's stance toward the world at large. The accusation is that the lawyer-client relationship renders the lawyer at best systematically amoral and at worst more than occasionally immoral in his or her dealings with the rest of mankind.

The second criticism focuses upon the relationship between the lawyer and the client. Here the charge is that it is the lawyer-client relationship which is morally objectionable because it is a relationship in which the lawyer dominates and in which the lawyer typically, and perhaps inevitably, treats the client in both an impersonal and paternalistic fashion.

To a considerable degree these two criticisms of lawyers derive, I believe, from the fact that the lawyer is a professional. And to the extent to which this is the case, the more generic problems I will be exploring are those of professionalism generally.

From *Human Rights* 5:1 (1975): 1–24.

But in some respects, the lawyer's situation is different from that of other professionals. The lawyer is vulnerable to some moral criticism that does not as readily or as easily attach to any other professional. And this, too, is an issue that I shall be examining.[1]

Although I am undecided about the ultimate merits of either criticism, I am convinced that each is deserving of careful articulation and assessment, and that each contains insights that deserve more acknowledgment than they often receive. My ambition is, therefore, more to exhibit the relevant considerations and to stimulate additional reflection, than it is to provide any very definite conclusions.

As I have indicated, the first issue I propose to examine concerns the ways the professional-client relationship affects the professional's stance toward the world at large. The primary question that is presented is whether there is adequate justification for the kind of moral universe that comes to be inhabited by the lawyer as he or she goes through professional life. For at best the lawyer's world is a simplified moral world; often it is an amoral one; and more than occasionally, perhaps, an overtly immoral one.

To many persons, Watergate was simply a recent and dramatic illustration of this fact. When John Dean testified before the Select Senate Committee inquiring into the Watergate affair in the Spring of 1973, he was asked about one of the documents that he had provided to the Committee. The document was a piece of paper which contained a list of a number of the persons who had been involved in the cover-up. Next to a number of the names an asterisk appeared. What, Dean was asked, was the meaning of the asterisk: Did it signify membership in some further conspiracy? Did it mark off those who were decision makers from those who were not? There did not seem to be any obvious pattern: Ehrlichman was starred, but Haldeman was not; Mitchell was starred, but Magruder was not. Oh, Dean answered, the asterisk really didn't mean anything. One day when he had been looking at the list of participants, he had been struck by the fact that so many of them were lawyers. So, he marked the name of each lawyer with an asterisk to see just how many there were. He had wondered, he told the Committee, when he saw that so many were attorneys, whether that had had anything to do with it; whether there was some reason why lawyers might have been more inclined than other persons to have been so willing to do the things that were done in respect to Watergate and the cover-up. But he had not pursued the matter; he had merely mused about it one afternoon.

It is, I think, at least a plausible hypothesis that the predominance of lawyers was not accidental—that the fact that they were lawyers made it easier rather than harder for them both to look at things the way they did and to do the things that were done. The theory that I want to examine in support of this hypothesis connects this activity with a feature of the lawyer's professionalism.

As I have already noted, one central feature of the professions in general and of law in particular is that there is a special, complicated relationship between the professional and the client or patient. For each of the parties in this relationship, but especially for the professional, the behavior that is involved is, to a very significant degree, what I call role-differentiated behavior. And this is significant because it is the nature of role-differentiated behavior that it often makes it both appropriate and desirable for the person in a particular role to put to one side considerations of various sorts—and especially various moral considerations—that would otherwise be relevant if not decisive. Some illustrations will help to make clear what I mean both by role-differentiated behavior and by the way role-differentiated behavior often alters, if not eliminates, the significance of those moral considerations that would obtain, were it not for the presence of the role.

Being a parent is, in probably every human culture, to be involved in role-differentiated behavior. In our own culture, and once again in most, if not all, human cultures, as a parent one is entitled, if not obligated, to prefer the interests of one's own children over those of children generally. That is to say, it is regarded as appropriate for a parent to allocate excessive goods to his or her own children, even though other children may have substantially more pressing and genuine needs for these same items. If one were trying to decide what the right way was to distribute assets among a group of children all of whom were strangers to oneself, the relevant moral considerations would be very different from those that would be thought to obtain once one's own children were in the picture. In the role of a parent, the claims of other children vis-à-vis one's own are, if not rendered morally irrelevant, certainly rendered less morally significant. In short, the role-differentiated character of the situation alters the relevant moral point of view enormously.

A similar situation is presented by the case of the scientist. For a number of years there has been debate and controversy within the scientific community over the question of whether scientists should participate in the development and elaboration of atomic theory, especially as those theoretical advances could then be translated into development of atomic weapons that would become a part of the arsenal of existing nation-states. The dominant view, although it was not the unanimous one, in the scientific community was that the role of the scientist was to expand the limits of human knowledge. Atomic power was a force which had previously not been utilizable by human beings. The job of the scientist was, among other things, to develop ways and means by which that could now be done. And it was simply no part of one's role as a scientist to forego inquiry, or divert one's scientific explorations because of the fact that the fruits of the investigation could be or would be put to improper, immoral, or even catastrophic uses. The moral issues concerning whether and when to develop and use nuclear weapons were to be decided by others; by citizens and statesmen; they were not the concern of the scientist *qua* scientist.

In both of these cases it is, of course, conceivable that plausible and even thoroughly convincing arguments exist for the desirability of the role-differentiated behavior and its attendant neglect of what would otherwise be morally relevant considerations. Nonetheless, it is, I believe, also the case that the burden of proof, so to speak, is always upon the proponent of the desirability of this kind of role-differentiated behavior. For in the absence of special reasons why parents ought to prefer the interests of their children over those of children in general, the moral point of view surely requires that the claims and needs of all children receive equal consideration. But we take the rightness of parental preference so for granted, that we often neglect, I think, the fact that it is anything but self-evidently morally appropriate. My own view, for example, is that careful reflection shows that the *degree* of parental preference systematically encouraged in our own culture is far too extensive to be morally justified.

All of this is significant just because to be a professional is to be enmeshed in role-differentiated behavior of precisely this sort. One's role as a doctor, psychiatrist, or lawyer alters one's moral universe in a fashion analogous to that described above. Of special significance here is the fact that the professional *qua* professional has a client or patient whose interests must be represented, attended to, or looked after by the professional. And that means that the role of the professional (like that of the parent) is to prefer in a variety of ways the interests of the client or patient over those of individuals generally.

Consider, more specifically, the role-differentiated behavior of the lawyer. Conventional wisdom has it that where the attorney-client relationship exists, the point of view of the attorney is properly different—and appreciably so—from that which would be appropriate in the absence of the attorney-client relationship. For where the attorney-client relationship exists, it is often appropriate and many times even obligatory for the attorney to do things that, all other things being equal, an ordinary person need not, and should not do. What is characteristic of this role of a lawyer is the lawyer's required indifference to a wide variety of ends and consequences that in other contexts would be of undeniable moral significance. Once a lawyer represents a client, the lawyer has a duty to make his or her expertise fully available in the realization of the end sought by the client, irrespective, for the most part, of the moral worth to which the end will be put or the character of the client who seeks to utilize it. Provided that the end sought is not illegal, the lawyer is, in essence, an amoral technician whose peculiar skills and knowledge in respect to the law are available to those with whom the relationship of client is established. The question, as I have indicated, is whether this particular and pervasive feature of professionalism is itself justifiable. At a minimum, I do not think any of the typical, simple answers will suffice.

One such answer focuses upon and generalizes from the criminal defense lawyer. For what is probably the most familiar aspect of this role-differentiated character of the lawyer's activity is that of the defense of a client charged with a crime. The received view within the profession (and to a lesser degree within the society at large) is that having once agreed to represent the client, the lawyer is under an obligation to do his or her best to defend that person at trial, irrespective, for instance, even of the lawyer's belief in the client's innocence. There are limits, of course, to what constitutes a defense: A lawyer cannot bribe or intimidate witnesses to increase the likelihood of securing an acquittal. And there are legitimate questions, in close cases, about how those limits are to be delineated. But, however these matters get resolved, it is at least clear that it is thought both appropriate and obligatory for the attorney to put on as vigorous and persuasive a defense of a client believed to be guilty as would have been mounted by the lawyer thoroughly convinced of the client's innocence. I suspect that many persons find this an attractive and admirable feature of the life of a legal professional. I know that often I do. The justifications are varied and, as I shall argue below, probably convincing.

But part of the difficulty is that the irrelevance of the guilt or innocence of an accused client by no means exhausts the altered perspective of the lawyer's conscience, even in criminal cases. For in the course of defending an accused, an attorney may have, as a part of his or her duty of representation, the obligation to invoke procedures and practices which are themselves morally objectionable and of which the lawyer in other contexts might thoroughly disapprove. And these situations, I think, are somewhat less comfortable to confront. For example, in California, the case law permits a defendant in a rape case to secure in some circumstances an order from the court requiring the complaining witness, that is the rape victim, to submit to a psychiatric examination before trial.[2] For no other crime is such a pretrial remedy available. In no other case can the victim of a crime be required to undergo psychiatric examination at the request of the defendant on the ground that the results of the examination may help the defendant prove that the offense did not take place. I think such a rule is wrong and is reflective of the sexist bias of the law in respect to rape. I certainly do not think it right that rape victims should be singled out by the law for this kind of special pretrial treatment, and I am skeptical about the morality of any involuntary psychiatric examination of witnesses. Nonetheless, it appears to be part of the role-differentiated obligation of a lawyer for a defendant charged with rape to seek to take advantage of this particular rule of law—irrespective of the independent moral view he or she may have of the rightness or wrongness of such a rule.

Nor, it is important to point out, is this peculiar, strikingly amoral behavior limimted to the lawyer involved with the workings of the criminal law. Most clients come to lawyers to get the lawyers to help them do things that they could not easily do without the assistance provided by the lawyer's special competence. They wish, for instance, to dispose of their property in a certain way at death. They wish to contract for the purchase or sale of a house or a business. They wish to set up a corporation which will manufacture and market a new product. They wish to minimize their income taxes. And so on. In each case, they need the assistance of the professional, the lawyer, for he or she alone has the special skill which will make it possible for the client to achieve the desired result.

And in each case, the role-differentiated character of the lawyer's way of being tends to render irrelevant what would otherwise be morally relevant considerations. Suppose that a client desires to make a will disinheriting her children because they opposed the war in Vietnam. Should the lawyer refuse to draft the will because the lawyer thinks this a bad reason to disinherit one's children? Suppose a client can avoid the payment of taxes through a loophole only available to a few wealthy taxpayers. Should the lawyer refuse to tell the client of a loophole because the lawyer thinks it an unfair advantage for the rich? Suppose a client wants to start a corporation that will manufacture, distribute and promote a harmful but not illegal substance, for example, cigarettes. Should the lawyer refuse to prepare the articles of incorporation for the corporation? In each case, the accepted view within the profession is that these matters are just of no concern to the lawyer *qua* lawyer. The lawyer need not of course agree to represent the client (and that is equally true for the unpopular client accused of a heinous crime), but there is nothing wrong with representing a client whose aims and purposes are quite immoral. And having agreed to do so, the lawyer is required to provide the best possible assistance, without regard for his or her disapproval of the objective that is sought.

The lesson, on this view, is clear. The job of the lawyer, so the argument typically concludes, is not to approve or disapprove of the character of his or her client, the cause for which the client seeks the lawyer's assistance, or the avenues provided by the law to achieve that which the client wants to accomplish. The lawyer's task is, instead, to provide that competence which the client lacks and the lawyer, as professional, possesses. In this way, the lawyer as professional comes to inhabit a simplified universe which is strikingly amoral—which regards as morally irrelevant any number of factors which nonprofessional citizens might take to be important, if not decisive, in their everyday lives. And the difficulty I have with all of this is that the arguments for such a way of life seem to be not quite so convincing to me as they do to many lawyers. I am, that is, at best uncertain that it is a good thing for lawyers to be so professional—for them to embrace so completely this role-differentiated way of approaching matters.

More specifically, if it is correct that this is the perspective of lawyers in particular and professionals in general, is it right that this should be their perspective? Is it right that the lawyer should be able so easily to put to one side otherwise difficult problems with the answer: But these are not and cannot be my concern as a lawyer? What do we gain and what do we lose from having a social universe in which there are professionals such as lawyers, who, as such, inhabit a universe of the sort I have been trying to describe?

One difficulty in even thinking about all of this is that lawyers may not be very objective or detached in their attempts to work the problem through. For one feature of this simplified, intellectual world is that it is often a very comfortable one to inhabit.

To be sure, on occasion, a lawyer may find it uncomfortable to represent an extremely unpopular client. On occasion, too, a lawyer may feel ill at ease invoking a rule of law or practice which he or she thinks to be an unfair or undesirable one. Nonetheless, for most lawyers, most of the time, pursuing the interests of one's clients is an attractive and satisfying way to live in part just because the moral world of the lawyer is a simpler, less complicated, and less ambiguous world than the moral world of ordinary life. There is, I think, something quite seductive about being able to turn aside so many ostensibly difficult moral dilemmas and decisions with the reply: But that is not my concern; my job as a lawyer is not to judge the rights and wrong of the client or the cause; it is to defend as best I can my client's interests. For the ethical problems that can arise within this constricted point of view are, to say the least, typically neither momentous nor terribly vexing. Role-differentiated behavior is enticing and reassuring precisely because it does constrain and delimit an otherwise often intractable and confusing moral world.

It is good, so the argument goes, that the lawyer's behavior and concomitant point of view are role-differentiated because the lawyer *qua* lawyer participates in a complex institution which functions well only if the individuals adhere to their institutional roles.

For example, when there is a conflict between individuals, or between the state and an individual, there is a well-established institutional mechanism by which to get that dispute resolved. The mechanism is the trial in which each side is represented by a lawyer whose job it is both to present his or her client's case in the most attractive, forceful light and to seek to expose the weaknesses and defects in the case of the opponent.

When an individual is charged with having committed a crime, the trial is the mechanism by which we determine in our society whether or not the person is in fact guilty. Just imagine what would happen if lawyers were to refuse, for instance, to represent persons whom they thought to be guilty. In a case where the guilt of a person seemed clear, it might turn out that some individuals would be deprived completely of the opportunity to have the system determine whether or not they are in fact guilty. The private judgment of individual lawyers would in effect be substituted for the public, institutional judgment of the judge and jury. The amorality of lawyers helps to guarantee that every criminal defendant will have his or her day in court.

In addition, of course, appearances can be deceiving. Persons who appear before trial to be clearly guilty do sometimes turn out to be innocent. Even persons who confess their guilt to their attorney occasionally turn out to have lied or to have been mistaken. The adversary system, so this argument continues, is simply a better method than any other that has been established by which to determine the legally relevant facts in any given case. It is certainly a better method than the exercise of private judgment by any particular individual. And the adversary system only works if each party to the controversy has a lawyer, a person whose institutional role it is to argue, plead and present the merits of his or her case and the demerits of the opponent's. Thus if the adversary system is to work, it is necessary that there be lawyers who will play their appropriate, professional, institutional role of representative of the client's cause.

Nor is the amorality of the institutional role of the lawyer restricted to the defense of those accused of crimes. As was indicated earlier, when the lawyer functions in his most usual role, he or she functions as a counselor, as a professional whose task it is to help people realize those objectives and ends that the law permits them to obtain and which cannot be obtained without the attorney's special competence in the law. The attorney may think it wrong to disinherit one's children because of their views about the Vietnam war, but the attorney's complaint is really with the laws of inheritance and not with his or her client. The attorney may think the tax provision an unfair, unjustifiable loophole, but once more the complaint is really with the Internal Revenue Code and not with the client who seeks to take advantage of it. And these matters, too, lie beyond the ambit of the lawyer's moral point of view as institutional counselor and facilitator. If lawyers were to substitute their own private views of what ought to be legally permissible and impermissible for those of the legislature, this would constitute a surreptitious and undesirable shift from a democracy to an oligarchy of lawyers. For given the fact that lawyers are needed to effectuate the wishes of clients, the lawyer ought to make his or her skills available to those who seek them without regard for the particular objectives of the client.

Now, all of this certainly makes some sense. These arguments are neither specious nor without force. Nonetheless, it seems to me that one dilemma which emerges is that if this line of argument is sound, it also appears to follow that the behavior of the lawyers involved in Watergate was simply another less happy illustration of lawyers playing their accustomed institutional role. If we are to approve on institutional grounds of the lawyer's zealous defense of the apparently guilty client and the lawyer's effective assistance of the immoral cheat, does it not follow that we must also approve of the Watergate lawyer's zealous defense of the interests of Richard Nixon?

As I have indicated, I do not think there is any easy answer to this question. For I am not, let me hasten to make clear, talking about the easy cases—about the behavior of the lawyers that was manifestly illegal. For someone quite properly might reply that it was no more appropriate for the lawyer who worked in the White House to obstruct justice or otherwise violate the criminal law than it would be for a criminal defense lawyer to shoot the prosecution witness to prevent adverse testimony or bribe a defense witness in order to procure favorable testimony. What I am interested in is all of the Watergate behavior engaged in by the Watergate lawyers that was not illegal, but that was, nonetheless, behavior of which we quite properly disapprove. I mean lying to the public; dissembling; stonewalling; tape-recording conversations; playing dirty tricks. Were not these just effective lawyer-like activities pursued by lawyers who viewed Richard Nixon as they would a client and who sought, therefore, the advancement and protection of his interests—personal and political?

It might immediately be responded that the analogy is not apt. For the lawyers who were involved in Watergate were hardly participants in an adversary proceeding. They were certainly not participants in that institutional setting, litigation, in which the amorality of the lawyer *qua counselor* is clearly distinguishable from the behavior of the Watergate lawyers. Nixon as President was not a client; they, as officials in the executive branch, were functioning as governmental officials and not as lawyers at all.

While not wholly convinced by a response such as the above, I am prepared to accept it because the issue at hand seems to me to be a deeper one. Even if the involvement of so many lawyers in Watergate was adventitious (or, if not adventitious, explicable in terms of some more benign explanation), there still seems to me to be costs, if not problems, with the amorality of the lawyer that derives from his or her role-differentiated professionalism.

As I indicated earlier, I do believe that the amoral behavior of the *criminal* defense lawyer is justifiable. But I think that justification depends at least as much upon the special needs of an accused as upon any more general defense of a lawyer's role-differentiated behavior. As a matter of fact I think it likely that many persons such as myself have been misled by the special features of the criminal case. Because a deprivation of liberty is so serious, because the prosecutorial resources of the state are so vast, and because, perhaps, of a serious skepticism about the rightness of punishment even where wrongdoing has occurred, it is easy to accept the view that it makes sense to charge the defense counsel with the job of making the best possible case for the accused—without regard, so to speak, for the merits. This coupled with the fact that it is an adversarial proceeding succeeds, I think, in justifying the amorality of the criminal defense counsel. But this does not, however, justify a comparable perspective on the part of lawyers generally. Once we leave the peculiar situation of the criminal defense lawyer, I think it quite likely that the role-differentiated amorality of the lawyer is almost certainly excessive and at times inappropriate. That is to say, this special case to one side, I am inclined to think that we might all be better served if lawyers were to see themselves less as subject to role-differentiated behavior and more as subject to the demands of the moral point of view. In this sense it may be that we need a good deal less rather than more professionalism in our society generally and among lawyers in particular.

Moreover, even if I am wrong about all this, four things do seem to me to be true and important.

First, all of the arguments that support the role-differentiated amorality of the lawyer on institutional grounds can succeed only if the enormous degree of trust and confidence in the institutions themselves is itself justified. If the institutions work well and fairly, there may be good sense to deferring important moral concerns and criticisms to another time and place, to the level of institutional criticism and assessment. But the less certain we are entitled to be of either the rightness or the self-corrective nature of the larger institutions of which the professional is a part, the less apparent it is that we should encourage the professional to avoid direct engagement with the moral issues as they arise. And we are, today, I believe, certainly entitled to be quite skeptical both of the fairness and of the capacity for self-correction of our larger institutional mechanisms, including the legal system. To the degree to which the institutional rules and practices are unjust, unwise or undesirable, to that same degree is the case for the role-differentiated behavior of the lawyer weakened if not destroyed.

Second, it is clear that there are definite character traits that the professional such as the lawyer must take on if the system is to work. What is less clear is that they are admirable ones. Even if the role-differentiated amorality of the professional lawyer is justified by the virtues of the adversary system, this also means that the lawyer *qua* lawyer will be encouraged to be competitive rather than cooperative; aggressive rather than accommodating; ruthless rather than compassionate; and pragmatic rather than principled. This is, I think, part of the logic of the role-differentiated behavior of lawyers in particular, and to a lesser degree of professionals in general. It is surely neither accidental nor unimportant that these are the same character traits that are emphasized and valued by the capitalist ethic—and on precisely analogous grounds. Because the ideals of professionalism and capitalism are the dominant ones within our culture, it is harder than most of us suspect even to take seriously the suggestion that radically different styles of living, kinds of occupational outlooks, and types of social institutions might be possible, let alone preferable.

Third, there is a special feature of the role-differentiated behavior of the lawyer that distinguishes it from the comparable behavior of other professionals. What I have in mind can be brought out through the following question: Why is it that it seems far less plausible to talk critically about the amorality of the doctor, for instance, who treats all patients irrespective of their moral character than it does to talk critically about the comparable amorality of the lawyer? Why is it that it seems so obviously sensible, simple and right for the doctor's behavior to be narrowly and rigidly role-differentiated, that is, just to try to cure those who are ill? And why is it that at the very least it seems so complicated, uncertain, and troublesome to decide whether it is right for the lawyer's behavior to be similarly role-differentiated?

The answer, I think, is twofold. To begin with (and this I think is the less interesting point) it is, so to speak, intrinsically good to try to cure disease, but in no comparable way is it intrinsically good to try to win every lawsuit or help every client realize his or her objective. In addition (and this I take to be the truly interesting point), the lawyer's behavior is different in kind from the doctor's. The lawyer—and especially the lawyer as advocate—directly says and affirms things. The lawyer makes the case for the client. He or she tries to explain, persuade and convince others that the client's cause should prevail. The lawyer lives with and within a dilemma that is not shared by other professionals. If the lawyer actually believes everything that he or she asserts on behalf of the client, then it appears to be proper to regard the lawyer as in fact embracing and endorsing the points of view that he or she articulates. If the lawyer does not in fact believe what is argued by way of argument, if the lawyer is only playing a role, then it appears to be proper to tax the lawyer with hypocrisy and insincerity. To be sure, actors in a play take on roles and say things that the characters, not the actors, believe. But we know it is a play and that they are actors. The law courts are not, however, theaters, and the lawyers both talk about justice and they genuinely seek to persuade. The fact that the lawyer's words, thoughts, and convictions are, apparently, for sale and at the service of the client helps us, I think, to understand the peculiar hostility which is more than occasionally uniquely directed by lay persons toward lawyers. The verbal, role-differentiated behavior of the lawyer *qua* advocate puts the lawyer's integrity into question in a way that distinguishes the lawyer from the other professionals.[3]

Fourth, and related closely to the three points just discussed, even if on balance the role-differentiated character of the lawyer's way of thinking and acting is ultimately deemed to be justifiable within the system on systemic instrumental grounds, it still remains the case that we do pay a social price for that way of thought and action. For to become and to be a professional, such as a lawyer, is to incorporate within oneself ways of behaving and ways of thinking that shape the whole person. It is especially hard, if not impossible, because of the nature of the professions, for one's professional way of thinking not to dominate one's entire adult life. Thus, even if the lawyers who were involved in Watergate were not, strictly speaking, then and there functioning as lawyers, their behavior was, I believe, the likely if not inevitable consequence of their legal acculturation. Having been taught to embrace and practice the lawyer's institutional role, it was natural, if not unavoidable, that they would continue to play that role even when they were somewhat removed from the specific institutional milieu in which that way of thinking and acting is arguably fitting and appropriate. The nature of the professions—the lengthy educational preparation, the prestige and economic rewards, and the concomitant enhanced sense of self—makes the role of professional a difficult one to shed even in those obvious situations in which that role is neither required nor appropriate. In important respects, one's professional role becomes and is one's dominant role, so that for many persons at least they become their professional being. This is at a minimum a heavy price to pay for the professions as we know them in our culture, and especially so for lawyers. Whether it is an inevitable price is, I think, an open question, largely because the problem has not begun to be fully perceived as such by the professionals in general, the legal profession in particular, or by the educational institutions that train professionals.

II

The role-differentiated behavior of the professional also lies at the heart of the second of the two moral issues I want to discuss, namely, the character of the interpersonal relationship that exists between the lawyer and the client. As I indicated at the outset, the charge that I want to examine here is that the relationship between the lawyer and the client is typically, if not inevitably, a morally defective one in which the client is not treated with the respect and dignity that he or she deserves.

There is the suggestion of paradox here. The discussion so far has concentrated upon defects that flow from what might be regarded as the lawyer's excessive preoccupation with and concern for the client. How then can it also be the case that the lawyer *qua* professional can at the same time be taxed with promoting and maintaining a relationship of dominance and indifference vis-à-vis his or her client? The paradox is apparent, not real. Not only are the two accusations compatible; the problem of the interpersonal relationship between the lawyer and the client is itself another feature or manifestation of the underlying issue just examined—the role-differentiated life of the professional. For the lawyer can both be overly concerned with the interest of the client and at the same time fail to view the client as a whole person, entitled to be treated in certain ways.

One way to begin to explore the problem is to see that one pervasive, and I think necessary, feature of the relationship between any professional and the client or patient is that it is in some sense a relationship of inequality. This relationship of inequality is intrinsic to the existence of professionalism. For the professional is, in some respects at least, always in a position of dominance vis-à-vis the client, and the client in a position of dependence vis-à-vis the professional. To be sure, the client can often decide whether or not to enter into a relationship with a professional. And often, too, the client has the power to decide whether to terminate the relationship. But the significant thing I want to focus upon is that while the relationship exists, there are important respects in which the relationship cannot be a relationship between equals and must be one in which it is the professional who is in control. As I have said, I believe this is a necessary and not merely a familiar characteristic of the relationship between professionals and those they serve. Its existence is brought about by the following features.

To begin with, there is the fact that one characteristic of professions is that the professional is the possessor of expert knowledge of a sort not readily or easily attainable by members of the community at large. Hence, in the most straightforward of all senses the client, typically, is dependent upon the professional's skill or knowledge because the client does not possess the same knowledge.

Moreover, virtually every profession has its own technical language, a private terminology which can only be fully understood by the members of the profession. The presence of such a language plays the dual role of creating and affirming the membership of the professionals within the profession and of preventing the client from fully discussing or understanding his or her concerns in the language of the profession.

These circumstances, together with others, produce the added consequence that the client is in a poor position effectively to evaluate how well or badly the professional performs. In the professions, the professional does not look primarily to the client to evaluate the professional's work. The assessment of ongoing professional competence is something that is largely a matter of self-assessment conducted by the practising professional. Where external assessment does occur, it is carried out not by clients or patients but by other members of the profession, themselves. It is significant, and surely surprising to the outsider, to discover to what degree the professions are self-regulating. They control who shall be admitted to the professions and they determine (typically only if there has been a serious complaint) whether the members of the profession are performing in a minimally satisfactory way. This leads professionals to have a powerful motive to be far more concerned with the way they are viewed by their colleagues than with the way they are viewed by their clients. This means, too, that clients will necessarily lack the power to make effective evaluations and criticisms of the way the professional is responding to the client's needs.

In addition, because the matters for which professional assistance is sought usually involve things of great personal concern to the client, it is the received wisdom within the professions that the client lacks the perspective necessary to pursue in a satisfactory way his or her own best interests, and that the client requires a detached, disinterested representative to look after his or her interests. That is to say, even if the client had the same knowledge or competence that the professional had, the client would be thought to lack the objectivity required to utilize that competency effectively on his or her own behalf.

Finally, as I have indicated, to be a professional is to have been acculturated in a certain way. It is to have satisfactorily passed through a lengthy and allegedly difficult period of study and training. It is to have done something hard. Something that not everyone can do. Almost all professions encourage this way of viewing oneself; as having joined an elect group by virtue of hard work and mastery of the mysteries of the profession. In addition, the society at large treats members of a profession as members of an elite by paying them more than most people for the work they do with their heads rather than their hands, and by according them a substantial amount of social prestige and power by virtue of their membership in a profession. It is hard, I think, if not impossible, for a person to emerge from professional training and participate in a profession without the belief that he or she is a special kind of person, both different from and somewhat better than those nonprofessional members of the social order. It is equally hard for the other members of society not to hold an analogous view of the professionals. And these beliefs surely contribute, too, to the dominant role played by a professional in any professional-client relationship.

If the foregoing analysis is correct, then one question that is raised is whether it is a proper and serious criticism of the professions that the relationship between the professional and the client is an inherently unequal one in this sense.

One possible response would be to reject the view that all relationships of inequality (in this sense of inequality) are in fact undesirable. Such a response might claim, for example, that there is nothing at all wrong with inequality in relationships as long as the inequality is consensually imposed. Or, it may be argued, this kind of inequality is wholly unobjectionable because it is fitting, desired, or necessary in the circumstances. And, finally, it may be urged, whatever undesirability does attach to relationships by virtue of their lack of equality is outweighed by the benefits of role-differentiated relationships.

Another possible response would be to maintain that all human relationships of inequality (again in this sense of inequality) are for that reason alone objectionable on moral grounds—any time two or more persons are in a relationship in which power is not shared equally, the relationship is on that ground appropriately to be condemned. This criticism would solve the problem by abolishing the professions.

A third possible response, and the one that I want to consider in some detail, is a more sophisticated variant of the second response. It might begin by conceding, at least for purposes of argument, that some inequality may be inevitable in any professional-client relationship. It might concede, too, that a measure of this kind of inequality may even on occasion be desirable. But it sees the relationship between the professional and the client as typically flawed in a more fundamental way, as involving far more than the kind of relatively benign inequality delineated above. This criticism focuses upon the fact that the professional often, if not systematically, interacts with the client in both a manipulative and a paternalistic fashion. The point is not that the professional is merely dominant with the relationship. Rather, it is that from the professional's point of view the client is seen and responded to more like an object than a human being, and more like a child than an adult. The professional does not, in short, treat the client like a person; the professional does not accord the client the respect that he or she deserves. And these, it is claimed, are without question genuine moral defects in any meaningful human relationship. They are, moreover, defects that are capable of being eradicated once their cause is perceived and corrective action taken. The solution, so the argument goes, is to "deprofessionalize" the professions; not do away with the professions entirely, but weaken or eliminate those features of professionalism that produce these kinds of defective, interpersonal relationships.

To decide whether this would be a good idea we must understand better what the proposal is and how the revisions might proceed. Because thinking somewhat along these lines has occurred in professions other than the law, for example, psychiatry, a brief look at what has been proposed there may help us to understand better what might be claimed in respect to the law.

I have in mind, for example, the view in psychiatry that begins by challenging the dominant conception of the patient as someone who is sick and in particular need of the professional, the psychiatrist, who is well. Such a conception, it is claimed, is often inadequate and often mistaken. Indeed, many cases of mental illness are not that at all; they are merely cases of different, but rational behavior. The alleged mental illness of the patient is a kind of myth, encouraged, if not created, by the professionals to assure and enhance their ability to function as professionals. So, on this view one thing that must occur is that the accepted professional concepts of mental illness and health must be revised.[4]

In addition, the language of psychiatry and mental illness is, it is claimed, needlessly technical and often vacuous. It serves no very useful communicative purpose, but its existence does of course help to maintain the distinctive status and power of the psychiatric profession. What is called for here is a simpler, far less technical language that permits more direct communication between the patient and the therapist.

Finally, and most significantly, the program calls for a concomitant replacement of the highly role-differentiated relationship between the therapist and the patient by a substantially less differentiated relationship of wholeness of interaction and equality. There should not, for instance, be mental hospitals in which the patients are clearly identified and distinguished from the staff and the professionals. Instead, therapeutic communities should be established in which all of the individuals in the community come to see themselves both as able to help the other members of the community and as able to be helped by them. In such a community, the distinctions between the professionals and the patients will be relatively minor and uninteresting. In such a community the relationship among the individuals, be they patients or professionals, will be capable of being more personal, intimate and complete—more undifferentiated by the accident of prior training or status.

Now, if this is a plausible proposal to make, it is possible that it is because of reasons connected with therapy rather than with the professions generally. But I do not think this is so. The general analysis and point of view is potentially generic; and certainly capable, I think, of being taken seriously in respect to the law as well as in respect to psychiatry, medicine, and education. If the critique is extravagant even when applied to psychiatry, as I think it is, I am more impressed by the truths to be extracted from it than I am by the exaggerations to be rejected. For I do think that professionals generally and lawyers in particular do, typically, enter into relationships with clients that are morally objectionable in virtue of the paternalistic and impersonal fashion in which the client is viewed and treated.

Thus it is, for example, fairly easy to see how a number of the features already delineated conspire to depersonalize the client in the eyes of the lawyer *qua* professional. To begin with, the lawyer's conception of self as a person with special competencies in a certain area naturally leads him or her to see the client in a partial way. The lawyer *qua* professional is, of necessity, only centrally interested in that part of the client that lies within his or her special competency. And this leads any professional including the lawyer to respond to the client as an object—as a thing to be altered, corrected, or otherwise assisted by the professional rather than as a person. At best the client is viewed from the perspective of the professional not as a whole person but as a segment or aspect of a person—an interesting kidney problem, a routine marijuana possession case, or another adolescent with an identity crisis.[5]

Then, too, the fact already noted that the professions tend to have and to develop their own special languages has a lot to do with the depersonalization of the client. And this certainly holds for the lawyers. For the lawyer can and does talk to other lawyers but not to the client in the language of the profession. What is more, the lawyer goes out of his or her way to do so. It is satisfying. It is the exercise of power. Because the ability to communicate is one of the things that distinguishes persons from objects, the inability of the client to communicate with the lawyer in the lawyer's own tongue surely helps to make the client less than a person in the lawyer's eyes—and perhaps even in the eyes of the client.

The forces that operate to make the relationship a paternalistic one seem to be at least as powerful. If one is a member of a collection of individuals who have in common the fact that their intellects are highly trained, it is very easy to believe that one knows more than most people. If one is a member of a collection of individuals who are accorded high prestige by the society at large, it is equally easy to believe that one is better and knows better than most people. If there is, in fact, an area in which one does know things that the client doesn't know, it is extremely easy to believe that one knows generally what is best for the client. All this, too, surely holds for lawyers.

In addition there is the fact, also already noted, that the client often establishes a relationship with the lawyer because the client has a serious problem or concern which has rendered the client weak and vulnerable. This, too, surely increases the disposition to respond toward the client in a patronizing, paternalistic fashion. The client of necessity confers substantial power over his or her well-being upon the lawyer. Invested with all of this power both by the individual and the society, the lawyer *qua* professional responds to the client as though the client were an individual who needed to be looked after and controlled, and to have decisions made for him or her by the lawyer, with as little interference from the client as possible.

Now one can, I think, respond to the foregoing in a variety of ways. One could, to begin with, insist that the paternalistic and impersonal ways of behaving are the aberrant rather than the usual characteristics of the lawyer-client relationship. One could, therefore, argue that a minor adjustment in better legal education aimed at sensitizing prospective lawyers to the possibility of these abuses is all that is required to prevent them. Or, one could, to take the same tack described earlier, regard these features of the lawyer-client relationship as endemic but not as especially serious. One might have a view that, at least in moderation, relationships having these features are a very reasonable price to pay (if it is a price at all) for the very appreciable benefits of professionalism. The impersonality of a surgeon, for example, may make it easier rather than harder for him or for her to do a good job of operating successfully on a patient. The impersonality of a lawyer may make it easier rather than harder for him or for her to do a good job of representing a client. The paternalism of lawyers may be justified by the fact that they do in fact know better—at least within many areas of common concern to the parties involved—what is best for the client. And, it might even be claimed, clients want to be treated in this way.

But if these answers do not satisfy, if one believes that these are typical, if not systemic, features of the professional character of the lawyer-client relationship, and if one believes, as well, that these are morally objectionable features of that or any other relationship among persons, it does look as though one way to proceed is to "deprofessionalize" the law—to weaken, if not excise, those features of legal professionalism that tend to produce these kinds of interpersonal relationships.

The issue seems to me difficult just because I do think that there are important and distinctive competencies that are at the heart of the legal profession. If there were not, the solution would be simple. If there were no such competencies—if, that is, lawyers didn't really help people any more than (so it is sometimes claimed) therapists do—then no significant social goods would be furthered by the maintenance of the legal profession. But, as I have said, my own view is that there are special competencies and that they are valuable. This makes it harder to determine what to preserve and what to shed. The question, as I see it, is how to weaken the bad consequences of the role-differentiated lawyer-client relationship without destroying the good that lawyers do.

Without developing the claim at all adequately in terms of scope or detail, I want finally to suggest the direction this might take. Desirable change could be brought about in part by a sustained effort to simplify legal language and to make the legal processes less mysterious and more directly available to lay persons. The way the law works now, it is very hard for lay persons either to understand it or to evaluate or solve legal problems more on their own. But it is not at all clear that substantial revisions could not occur along these lines. Divorce, probate, and personal injury are only three fairly obvious areas where the lawyers' economic self-interest says a good deal more about resistance to change and simplification than does a consideration on the merits.

The more fundamental changes, though, would, I think, have to await an explicit effort to alter the ways in which lawyers are educated and acculturated to view themselves, their clients, and the relationships that ought to exist between them. It is, I believe, indicative of the state of legal education and of the profession that there has been to date extremely little self-conscious concern even with the possibility that these dimensions of the attorney-client relationship are worth examining—to say nothing of being capable of alteration. That awareness is, surely, the prerequisite to any serious assessment of the moral character of the attorney-client relationship as a relationship among adult human beings.

I do not know whether the typical lawyer-client relationship is as I have described it; nor do I know to what degree role-differentiation is the cause; nor do I even know very precisely what "deprofessionalization" would be like or whether it would on the whole be good or bad. I am convinced, however, that this, too, is a topic worth taking seriously and worth attending to more systematically than has been the case to date.

NOTES

1. Because of the significance for my analysis of the closely related concepts of a profession and a professional, it will be helpful to indicate at the outset what I take to be the central features of a profession.

But first there is an ambiguity that must be noted so that it can be dismissed. There is one sense of "professional" and hence of "profession" with which I am not concerned. That is the sense in which there are in our culture, professional athletes, professional actors, and professional beauticians. In this sense, a person who possesses sufficient skill to engage in an activity for money and who elects to do so is a professional rather than, say, an amateur or a volunteer. This is, as I have said, not the sense of "profession" in which I am interested.

I am interested, instead, in the characteristics of professions such as law, or medicine. There are, I think, at least six that are worth noting.

(1) The professions require a substantial period of formal education—at least as much if not more than that required by any other occupation.

(2) The professions require the comprehension of a substantial amount of theoretical knowledge and the utilization of a substantial amount of intellectual ability. Neither manual nor creative ability is typically demanded. This is one thing that distinguishes the professions both from highly skilled crafts—like glassblowing—and from the arts.

(3) The professions are both an economic monopoly and largely self-regulating. Not only is the practice of the profession restricted to those who are certified as possessing the requisite competencies, but the questions of what competencies are required and who possesses them are questions that are left to the members of the profession to decide for themselves.

(4) The professions are clearly among the occupations that possess the greatest social prestige in the society. They also typically provide a degree of material affluence substantially greater than that enjoyed by most working persons.

(5) The professions are almost always involved with matters which from time to time are among the greatest personal concerns that humans have: physical health, psychic well-being, liberty, and the like. As a result, persons who seek the services of a professional are often in a state of appreciable concern, if not vulnerability, when they do so.

(6) The professions almost always involve at their core a significant interpersonal relationship between the professional, on the one hand, and the person who is thought to require the professional's services: the patient or the client.

2. *Ballard* v. *Superior Court,* 64 Cal. 2d 159, 410 P.2d 838, 49 *Cal. Rptr.* 302 (1966).

3. I owe this insight, which I think is an important and seldom appreciated one, to my colleague, Leon Letwin.

4. On this and the points that follow, I am thinking in particular of the writings of Thomas Szasz, e.g., T. S. Szasz, *The Myth of Mental Illness* (1974), and of R. D. Laing, e.g., R. D. Laing and A. Esterson, *Sanity, Madness and the Family* (1964).

5. This and other features are delineated from a somewhat different perspective in an essay by Erving Goffman. *See* "The Medical Model and Mental Hospitalization: Some Notes on the Vicissitudes of the Tinkering cTrades" in E. Goffman, *Asylums* (1961), esp. pts. 5 and 6 of the essay.

7. Is Business Bluffing Ethical?

Albert Z. Carr

. . . . .

[T]he basis of private morality is a respect for truth . . . At the same time, . . . most bluffing in business might be regarded simply as game strategy—much like bluffing in poker, which does not reflect on the morality of the bluffer.

. . . Henry Taylor, the British statesman, pointed out that "falsehood ceases to be falsehood when it is understood on all sides . . . that the truth is not expected to be spoken"—an exact description of bluffing in poker, diplomacy, and business. [Compare] the criminal court, where the criminal is not expected to tell the truth when he pleads "not guilty." Everyone from the judge down takes it for granted that the job of the defendant's attorney is to get his client off, not to reveal the truth; and this is considered ethical practice.

[M]illions of [people in business] feel constrained every day to say *yes* to their bosses when they secretly believe *no* and . . . this is generally accepted as permissible strategy when the alternative might be the loss of a job. The essential point . . . is that the ethics of business are game ethics, different from the ethics of religion. . . .

PRESSURE TO DECEIVE

Most executives from time to time are almost compelled, in the interests of their companies or themselves, to practice some form of deception when negotiating with customers, dealers, labor unions, government officials, or even other departments of their companies. By conscious misstatements, concealment of pertinent facts, or exaggeration—in short, by bluffing—they seek to persuade others to agree with them. I think it is fair to say that if . . . individual executive[s] refuse to bluff from time to time—if [they] feel obligated to tell the truth, the whole truth, and nothing but the truth—[they are] ignoring opportunities permitted under the rules and [are] at a heavy disadvantage in [their] business dealings.

But . . . before . . . executive[s] can make profitable use of the strategy of the bluff, [they] need to make sure that in bluffing [they] will not lose self-respect or become emotionally disturbed. If [they are] to reconcile personal integrity and high standards of honesty with the practical requirements of business, [they] must feel that [their] bluffs are ethically justified. The justification rests on the fact that business, as practiced by individuals as well as by corporations, has the impersonal character of a game—a game that demands both special strategy and an understanding of its special ethics.

The game is played at all levels of corporate life, from the highest to the lowest. . . . [Consider] the recent experience of a Cornell honor graduate who applied for a job with a large company:

From *Harvard Business Review,* (Jan.–Feb. 1968): 143–53.

☐ This applicant was given a psychological test which included the statement, "Of the following magazines, check any that you have read either regularly or from time to time, and double-check those which interest you most. *Reader's Digest, Time, Fortune, Saturday Evening Post, New Republic, Life, Look, Ramparts, Newsweek, Business Week, U.S. News and World Report, Nation, Playboy, Esquire, Harper's, Sports Illustrated.*"

His tastes in reading were broad, and at one time or another he had read almost all of these magazines. . . . [B]ut he had a shrewd suspicion that if he confessed to an interest in *Ramparts* and *The New Republic,* he would be thought a liberal, a radical, or at least an intellectual, and his chances of getting the job, which he needed, would greatly diminish. He therefore checked five of the more conservative magazines. Apparently it was a sound decision, for he got the job.

He had made a game player's decision consistent with business ethics.

A similar case is that of a magazine space salesman who, owing to a merger, suddenly found himself out of a job:

☐ This man was 58, and, in spite of a good record, his chance of getting a job elsewhere in a business where youth is favored in hiring practice was not good. He was a vigorous, healthy man, and only a considerable amount of gray in his hair suggested his age. Before beginning his job search he touched up his hair with a black dye to confine the gray to his temples. He knew that the truth about his age might well come out in time, but he calculated that he could deal with that situation when it arose. He and is wife decided that he could easily pass for 45, and he so stated his age on his résumé.

This was a lie; yet within the accepted rules of the business game, no moral culpability attaches to it.

THE POKER ANALOGY

We can learn a good deal about the nature of business by comparing it with poker. While both have a large element of chance, in the long run the winner . . . plays with steady skill. In both games ultimate victory requires intimate knowledge of the rules, insight into the psychology of the other players, a bold front, a considerable amount of self-discipline, and the ability to respond swiftly and effectively to opportunities provided by change.

No one expects poker to be played on the ethical principles preached in churches. In poker it is right and proper to bluff a friend out of the rewards of being dealt a good hand. . . . In the words of an excellent poker player, former President Harry Truman, "If you can't stand the heat, stay out of the kitchen." If one shows mercy to a loser in poker, it is a personal gesture divorced from the rules of the game.

Poker has its special ethics, and here I am not referring to rules against cheating. . . .

In contrast to the cheat, the unethical poker player is one who, while abiding by the letter of the rules, finds ways to put the other players at an unfair disadvantage: perhaps [by unnerving] them with loud talk. . . . Ethical poker players frown on such tactics.

Poker's own brand of ethics is different from the ethical ideals of civilized human relationships. The game calls for distrust of the other. . . . It ignores the claim of friendship. Cunning deception and concealment of one's strength and intentions, not kindness and openheartedness, are vital in poker. No one thinks any the worse of poker on that account. And no one should think any the worse of the game of business because its standards of right and wrong differ from the prevailing traditions of morality in our society.

DISCARD THE GOLDEN RULE

. . . That most [people in business] are not indifferent to ethics in their private lives, everyone will agree. My point is that in their office lives they cease to be private citizens; they become game players who must be guided by a somewhat different set of ethical standards.

The point was forcefully made to me by a Midwestern executive who has given a good deal of thought to the question:

> So long as a businessman complies with the laws of the land and avoids telling malicious lies, he's ethical. If the law as written gives a man a wide-open chance to make a killing, he'd be a fool not to take advantage of it. If he doesn't, somebody else will. There's no obligation on him to stop and consider who is going to get hurt. If the law says he can do it, that's all the justification he needs. There's nothing unethical about that. It's just plain business sense.

This executive (call him Robbins) took the stand that even industrial espionage, which is frowned on by some [in] business . . . , ought not to be considered unethical. He recalled a recent meeting of the National Industrial Conference Board where an authority on marketing made a speech in which he deplored the employment of spies by business organizations. More and more companies, he pointed out, find it cheaper to penetrate the secrets of competitors with concealed cameras and microphones or by bribing employees than to set up costly research and design departments of their own. A whole branch of the electronics industry has grown up with this trend, he continued, providing equipment to make industrial espionage easier.

Disturbing? The marketing expert found it so. But when it came to a remedy, he could only appeal to "respect for the golden rule." Robbins thought this a confession of defeat, believing that the golden rule, for all its value as an ideal for society, is simply not feasible as a guide for business. . . . Robbins continued:

> Espionage of one kind or another has become so common in business that it's like taking a drink during Prohibition—it's not considered sinful. And we don't even have Prohibition where espionage is concerned; the law is very tolerant in this area. There's no more shame for a business that uses secret agents than there is for a nation. Bear in mind that there already is at least one large corporation—you can buy its stock over the counter—that makes millions by providing counterespionage service to industrial firms. Espionage in business is not an ethical problem; it's an established technique of business competition.

"We Don't Make the Laws"

Wherever we turn in business, we can perceive the sharp distinction between its ethical standards and those of the churches. Newspapers abound with sensational stories growing out of this distinction:

- ☐ We read one day that Senator Philip A. Hart of Michigan has attacked food processors for deceptive packaging of numerous products.[1]
- ☐ The next day there is a congressional to-do over Ralph Nader's book, *Unsafe at Any Speed,* which demonstrates that automobile companies for years have neglected the safety of car-owning families.[2]
- ☐ Then another senator, Lee Metcalf of Montana, and journalist Vic Reinemer show in their book, *Overcharge,* the methods by which utility companies elude regulating government bodies to extract unduly large payments from users of electricity.[3]

These are merely dramatic instances of a prevailing condition; there is hardly a major industry at which a similar attack could not be aimed. Critics of business regard such behavior as unethical, but the companies concerned know that they are merely playing the business game.

Among the most respected of our business institutions are the insurance companies. A group of insurance executives meeting recently in New England was startled when their guest speaker, social critic [and later New York Senator] Daniel Patrick Moynihan, roundly berated them for "unethical" practices. They had been guilty, Moynihan alleged, of using outdated actuarial tables to obtain unfairly high premiums. They habitually delayed the hearings of lawsuits against them in order to tire out the plaintiffs and win cheap settlements. In their employment policies they used ingenious devices to discriminate against certain minority groups.[4]

It was difficult for the audience to deny the validity of these charges. But these . . . were business game players. Their reaction to Moynihan's attack was much the same as that of the automobile manufacturers to Nader, of the utilities to Senator Metcalf, and of the food processors to Senator Hart. If the laws governing their business change, or if public opinion becomes clamorous, they will make the necessary adjustments. But morally they have in their view done nothing wrong. As long as they comply with the letter of the law, they are within their rights to operate their businesses as they see fit. . . .

I think it is fair to sum up the prevailing attitude . . . on ethics [in business] as follows:

☐ We live in what is probably the most competitive of the world's civilized societies. Our customs encourage a high degree of aggression in the individual's striving for success. Business is our main area of competition, and it has been ritualized into a game of strategy. The basic rules of the game have been set by the government, which attempts to detect and punish business frauds. But as long as a company does not transgress the rules of the game set by law, it has the legal right to shape its strategy without reference to anything but its profits. If it takes a long-term view of its profits, it will preserve amicable relations, so far as possible, with those with whom it deals. A wise [practitioner] will not seek advantage to the point [of generating] dangerous hostility among employees, competitors, customers, government, or the public at large. But decisions in this area are, in the final test, decisions of strategy, not of ethics. . . .

FOR OFFICE USE ONLY

An executive's family life can easily be dislocated if he fails to make a sharp distinction between the ethical systems of the home and the office . . .

An illuminating illustration of this comes from a Southern sales executive who related a conversation he had had with his wife at a time when a hotly contested political campaign was being waged in their state:

> "I made the mistake of telling her that I had had lunch with Colby, who gives me about half my business. Colby mentioned that his company had a stake in the election. Then he said, 'By the way, I'm treasurer of the citizens'

committee for Lang. I'm collecting contributions. Can I count on you for a hundred dollars?'

"Well, there I was. I was opposed to Lang, but I knew Colby. If he withdrew his business I could be in a bad spot. So I just smiled and wrote out a check then and there. He thanked me, and we started to talk about his next order. Maybe he thought I shared his political views. If so, I wasn't going to lose any sleep over it.

"I should have had sense enough not to tell Mary about it. She hit the ceiling. She said she was disappointed in me. She said I hadn't acted like a man, that I should have stood up to Colby.

"I said, 'Look, it was an either-or situation. I had to do it or risk losing the business.'

"She came back at me with, 'I don't believe it. You could have been honest with him. You could have said that you didn't feel you ought to contribute to a campaign for a man you weren't going to vote for. I'm sure he would have understood.'

"I said, 'Mary, you're a wonderful woman, but you're way off the track. Do you know what would have happened if I had said that? Colby would have smiled and said, "Oh, I didn't realize. Forget it." But in his eyes from that moment I would be an oddball, maybe a bit of a radical. He would have listened to me talk about his order and would have promised to give it consideration. After that I wouldn't hear from him for a week. Then I would telephone and learn from his secretary that he wasn't yet ready to place the order. And in about a month I would hear through the grapevine that he was giving his business to another company. A month after that I'd be out of a job.'

"She was silent for a while. Then she said, 'Tom, something is wrong with business when a man is forced to choose between his family's security and his moral obligation to himself. It's easy for me to say you should have stood up to him—but if you had, you might have felt you were betraying me and the kids. I'm sorry that you did it, Tom, but I can't blame you. Something is wrong with business!' "

This wife saw the problem in terms of moral obligation as conceived in private life; her husband saw it as a matter of game strategy. As a player in a weak position, he felt that he could not afford to indulge an ethical sentiment that might have cost him his seat at the table.

Playing to Win

Some . . . might challenge the Colbys of business—might accept serious setbacks to their business careers rather than risk a feeling of moral cowardice. They merit our respect—but as private individuals, not businessmen. When the skillful player of the business game is compelled to submit to unfair pressure, [this is not] moral weakness. . . .

[A]n occasional bluff may well be justified in terms of the game's ethics and warranted in terms of economic necessity. . . .

[To win, one] must play to win. This does not mean [being] ruthless, cruel, harsh, or treacherous. On the contrary, the better [one's] reputation for integrity, honesty, and decency, the better [one's] chances of victory will be in the long run. But from time to time [everyone in business], like every poker player, is offered a choice between certain loss or bluffing within the legal rules of the game. . . .

Whatever the form of the bluff, it is an integral part of the game, and the executive who does not master its techniques is not likely to accumulate much money or power.

NOTES

1. *New York Times,* November 21, 1966.
2. New York, Grossman Publishers, 1965.
3. New York, David McKay Company, 1967.
4. *New York Times,* January 17, 1967.

8. The Business of Ethics

Norman Chase Gillespie

It is the business of ethics to tell us what are our duties, or by what test we may know them.
—John Stuart Mill, *Utilitarianism*

The public image of business does not always inspire public confidence, since it is often assumed that talk of ethics in business is only talk, not something that makes a difference in practice. Business executives are pragmatic individuals, accustomed to dealing with their environment as they find it and not inclined to question how things ought to be. That frame of mind reinforces the public image of business as impervious to moral imperatives.

That image is often only confirmed in the press,

From *Profits and Professions: Essays in Business and Professional Ethics,* edited by Wade L. Robison, Michael S. Pritchard, and Joseph S. Ellin (Clifton, NJ: Humana Press, 1983), pp. 133–40 for instance, by such articles as those of Albert Carr,* which embrace the purest kind of moral conventionalism: That which is generally done in business sets the standard of ethical conduct, so that an executive acts ethically as long as he or she conforms to the general practice. Carr goes so far as to maintain that misrepresentation in business is as ethical as bluffing in poker, and that only needless concern and anxiety will result from applying the ordinary moral standards of society to the conduct of business.[1] On this score, I believe Carr is completely mistaken.

This paper will argue that ordinary moral standards do apply to business decisions and practices and will explain *how* they apply. This should result in a clearer picture of the relationship between business and ethics—what it is now and what it ought to be.

Carr, in setting forth the conventionalist position, argues:

(1) Business, like poker, is a form of competition.
(2) In this competition, the rules are different from what they are in ordinary social dealings.
(3) Anyone who abides by ordinary moral standards instead of the rules of business is placed at a decided disadvantage. Therefore,
(4) It is not unethical or immoral to abide by the current rules of business. (These rules are determined in part by what is generally done in business and in part by legal statutes governing business activities.)

In support of this position, three reasons might be offered:

(1) If a business practice is not illegal, it is thereby ethically acceptable.
(2) If a businessman does not take advantage of a legal opportunity, others will surely do so.
(3) If a practice is so widespread as to constitute the norm, everyone expects conformity.

The claim that it is ethically correct to do something because it is not illegal is, of course, one of the conventionalist's weakest arguments, since it should be obvious that legality does not establish morality—it may not be illegal for a teacher to favor some students over others for non-academic reasons, yet it is clearly unethical. When one speaks of ethics in business, it is to establish what business practices ought to be. The law, as written, does not settle that issue. The other two reasons, however, may appear to have some merit and require more detailed analysis.

* [See this chap., sel. 7.—ED.]

BUSINESS AS A GAME

Suppose that such things as industrial espionage, deception of customers, and shading the truth in published financial statements are common enough to be of broad concern, in effect comprising some de facto state of business affairs. What bearing would such a state have upon what is moral or ethical in conducting business? Would the existence of such "rules of the game" relieve owners, managers, and employees of otherwise appropriate ethical obligations? Or, would such behavior merely be a matter of business strategy and not a matter of ethics?

The obvious fallacy in the "business-as-a-game" idea is that, unlike poker, business is not a game. People's lives, their well-being, their plans, and their futures often depend upon business and the way it is conducted. Indeed, people usually exchange part of their lives (i.e., the portion spent earning money) for certain goods and services They have the right not to be misled or deceived about the true nature of those goods or services. Similarly, elected officials have a duty to legislate and act for the good of their country (or state). It can hardly be right for business executives to frustrate them in the performance of that duty by providing them with evasive answers or by concealing relevant facts.

THE PRICE OF DUTY

So, the poker analogy, while informative of the way things *are,* seems to have no bearing at all on the way they *ought* to be in business. Why, then, do so many people adopt the conventionalist position that "business is business and, when in business do as the others do"? Some take that position for essentially the same reason Yossarian offers to justify his conduct in the novel *Catch 22.* Yossarian has refused to fly any more combat missions and when asked, "But suppose everybody on our side felt that way?" he replies, "Then I'd be a damn fool to feel any other way. Wouldn't I?"[2] If everyone were refusing to fly, Yossarian says, he would be a fool to fly. In business, the position would be: If everyone is bluffing, an individual would be a fool not to do the same. On this point, Yossarian and the conventionalist are correct, but not because there are special rules (or special ethics) for airplane gunners and people in business. The reason, instead, is that our ordinary moral reasoning does, indeed, make allowance for just such cases. In other words, the idea that there is something ethically distinctive about a situation in which a person in business may find himself or herself is sound. But it is sound because ordinary moral reasoning allows for such circumstances, not because there are special ethical rules for people in business comparable to the rules of poker.

The sort of considerations I have in mind all involve the *cost* of doing what would normally be one's duty. There are at least three ways in which a normal or ordinary duty may cease to be so because the cost is too high. The first of these is widely recognized: Sometimes the *moral cost* of obeying a standard moral rule is too great, so one must make an exception to that rule. If the only way to save someone's life is by telling a lie, then one should normally lie. If treating an accident victim involves breaking a promise to meet someone on time, then one should normally be late. In a variety of circumstances obeying a moral rule might require breaking some other, more urgent, moral duty. In these circumstances, the more urgent duty dictates an exception to the lesser rule.

The second way in which an ordinary duty may cease to be a duty is when the *cost to the individual* of fulfilling that duty is too high. For example, when driving an automobile, one normally has the duty not to run into other cars, and one also has the general duty not to harm or injure other persons. But suppose one is driving down a steep mountain road and the brakes fail. One might have a choice among three options: cross into the oncoming lane of traffic, go off the cliff on one's right, or drive into the car in front. In such a case, a driver would not act wrongly by choosing the third option, even though there is a way in which the duty of not injuring others and not driving into other people's cars can be met, namely, by going off the cliff. In these circumstances, the cost to the individual of meeting the duty is simply too high, and virtually no one would blame the driver or condemn the action as morally wrong if he or she drove into the back of the car ahead rather than going off the cliff.

The third way in which a normal duty may turn out not to be a duty is the kind of situation described by Yossarian. If everyone else is not doing what ought to be done, then one would be a fool to act differently. This third consideration does not obviate all duties, for example, just because everyone else is committing murder does not make it right for you to do so, but it does apply to those cases in which the *morally desirable state of affairs can be produced only by everyone, or virtually everyone, doing his or her part*. With respect to such a duty, for example, jury duty, one person alone cannot accomplish anything; one can only be placed at a disadvantage vis-à-vis everyone else by doing what everyone ought to do but is not doing. This sort of situation can be described as a "state of nature situation,"[3] and by that I mean a situation in which certain moral rules are generally disobeyed either by everyone or by the members of a well-defined group.

In dealing with such situations, the fact that other people can be expected to act in certain ways is morally relevant in that it creates a special sort of moral dilemma. If one does what everyone ought to do but is not doing, then one will, in all likelihood, be at a disadvantage. The morally questionable behavior of others creates the circumstances in which one finds oneself and in those circumstances it may be necessary to fight fire with fire and resist deception with deception. But replying in kind only prolongs the state of nature situation, so one's primary goal should be to attempt to change the situation. No one ought to take unfair advantage of others, but no one is obligated to let others take unfair advantage of him or her.

It is absolutely essential to note, in connection with such situations, that people are not doing what they ought to be doing. The conventionalist recognizes that simple application of ordinary moral rules to such situations is inadequate. But it is a mistake to conclude (1) that ordinary rules do not apply *at all* to such cases, and (2) that business has its own distinctive set of rules that determines one's duties in such circumstances. Both points are incorrect because (1) the ordinary rules help define the situation as one in which people are not doing what they ought to be doing (we apply the ordinary moral rules to such cases and find that they are not being generally observed), and (2) the considerations that are relevant in determining one's duties in such circumstances do not constitute a special set of factors that are relevant only in business. The mitigating considerations apply generally and are an important part of ordinary moral reasoning.

When virtually everyone is not doing what ought to be done, it affects what we can morally expect of any one individual. That person does not have a duty to "buck the tide" if doing so will cause the individual substantial harm or not do any good. But, in conjunction with everyone else, the person *ought to be* acting differently. So the tension one may feel between what one does and what one ought to do is quite real and entirely appropriate.

In the conventionalist argument, these two considerations—the cost to the individual and what everyone else is doing—recur again and again: It is right to lie about one's age and one's magazine preferences when doing otherwise will prevent you from getting a job; right to engage in industrial espionage because everyone else is doing it; right to sell a popular mouthwash with a possibly deleterious form of alcohol in it because cigarettes are sold to the public; and right to sell master automobile keys through the mails (to potential criminals) because guns are sold.[4]

Of these four examples, the last two seem to me to be clearly wrong since neither the high cost to the individual of doing otherwise nor the existence of a general practice has been established. Industrial espionage, however, is a good illustration of a "state of nature situation," and if (1) one does it to others who are doing the same, and (2) it is necessary to "fight fire with fire" for the sake of survival, then it would not be morally wrong. For the job applicant, the conditions themselves are morally dubious, so here, too, it may be a case of fighting fire with fire for the sake of personal survival. But notice, in each of these examples, how distasteful the action in question is; most of us would prefer not to engage in such activities. The point is that conditions may be such that the cost of not engaging in them may be so great that an individual caught in such circumstances is blameless. At the same time, however, we do feel that *the circumstances* should be different.

The second consideration, distinct from the cost to the individual, is that one person doing what everyone ought to do (but is not doing) will accomplish nothing. This can be the case even where the individual cost is insignificant. To take a homely example, suppose there were a well-defined path across the local courthouse lawn as the result of shortcuts taken across it. It would not cost anyone very much to walk around instead of across the lawn, but if one knows his fellow citizens and knows that the path is there to stay, then walking around will accomplish nothing. So one may as well take the path unless, of course, one decides to set an example of how others ought to be acting. Since it costs so little, it might well be a good idea to set such an example. This would be one small way at least of trying to change the situation.

Although one's primary goal ought to be to change the situation, that statement like all claims about what one ought to do, is subject to the moral precept that individuals have a duty to do only what they can do. So, if it is impossible for one individual to change the situation, that person does not have a duty to change it. What is true is that the situation ought to be different, but to make it so may require the combined efforts of many people. All of them collectively have the duty to change it, so this is not a duty that falls solely or directly on the shoulders of any one person. For the individual executive, then, the question is primarily one of what he or she in conjunction with others can accomplish. Secondarily, it is a question of the likely personal cost to the executive of instituting or proposing needed changes.

A ROLE FOR THE INDIVIDUAL EXECUTIVE

At the very least, executives should not *thwart* the impetus for change on the ground that business sets its own ethical standards. Everyone has a legitimate interest in the way business is run, and Better Business Bureaus and legislative inquiries should be viewed as important instruments serving that interest. We know on the basis of ordinary moral rules that in certain business environments a new way of acting is a desirable goal. If no one else will join in the promotion of that goal, then the individual executive can, as the poet said, "only stand and wait." But according to that same poet, John Milton, "They also serve who only stand and wait."

The essential difference between the conventionalist position and ordinary moral reasoning comes out most clearly in the following example, provided by Carr in defense of his position. A businessman, Tom, is asked by an important customer in the middle of a sales talk to contribute to the election campaign of a candidate Tom does not support. He does so, and the talk continues with enthusiasm. Later, Tom mentions his action to his wife, Mary, and she is furious. They discuss the situation and the conversation concludes with her saying, "Tom, something is wrong with business when a man is forced to choose between his family's security and his moral obligation. . . . It's easy for me to say you should have stood up to him—but if you had, you might have felt you were betraying me and the kids. I'm sorry you did it, Tom, but I can't blame you. Something is wrong with business."

Carr comments that, "This wife saw the problem in terms of moral obligation as conceived in private life; her husband saw it as a matter of game strategy." Those who would refuse to make the contribution "merit our respect—but as private individuals, not businessmen."[5]

What Tom did was not morally wrong in those circumstances, but not for the reasons cited in Carr's paper. There is something wrong with *the situation* in which Tom found himself. It *ought not be the case* that one has to choose between one's family and being honest about one's political preferences. Carr fails to recognize this and either misses or ignores entirely the fact that Mary makes precisely this point: She does not blame her husband or say that he did the wrong thing in those circumstances; what she says, instead, is that *something is wrong with business* when a person has to act as her husband did. It is business and the way it is conducted that ought to be changed. The conventionalist position simply blocks out such an issue: It nowhere considers how business ought to be. It merely says that "the way it is" is all that need be taken into account in deciding what would be ethical.

An analogous situation exists in connection with the financing of political campaigns. No one blames candidates for taking contributions from lobbyists and other individuals since they need the money to run for office. But many people do think that the system ought to be changed. In other words, the current practices are not as honest or ethical as they ought to be. Now, how can the conventionalist handle such a claim? It seems obvious that he cannot, since he systematically rules out applying ordinary moral standards to business practices. But the correct position is that these standards do apply, and sometimes we find they are not being put into practice. In precisely those cases, the general practice ought to change.

THE NEED FOR CHANGE

There is a most important difference, then, between asking "What are the individual duties of a person doing business?" and "What are the ways in which business ought to be conducted?" Both are an essential part of the ethics of business but the conventionalist simply ignores the second question in attempting to answer the first. The answers to the second question can be found, for the most part, by consulting our ordinary moral standards of how people ought to act vis-à-vis one another. When we find that business is not as moral as we would like it to be, that *does* have some bearing upon the answer to the first question. But, as I have argued in this paper, ordinary moral reasoning is prepared to take those facts into account. It is not at all necessary to postulate a special ethical outlook or a distinctive set of ethical rules for business in order to explain the ethical relevance of such phenomena to the individual businessman.

Ordinary moral reasoning, then, is far richer than mere conventionalism and the factors it takes into account are relevant in many managerial and executive decisions. Ethics can be subtle, as well as realistic, and conventionalism is unrealistic when it obscures the moral imperative for change.

NOTES

1. Albert Carr advocates conventionalism in *Business as a Game* (New York, 1968); "Is Business Bluffing Ethical?" *Harvard Business Review* (January–February, 1968) pp. 143–53; and reiterates it in "Can an Executive Afford a Conscience?", *Harvard Business Review* (July–August, 1970), pp. 58–64. In defending himself against the criticism that he is condoning unethical behavior, Carr insists that an executive who acts according to prevailing business practices "is guilty of nothing more than conformity; he is merely playing the game according to the rules." "Showdown on Business Bluffing," *Harvard Business Review,* (May–June, 1968), p. 169.
2. Joseph Heller, *Catch 22,* (New York, Dell, 1961), chap. 9.
3. Marcus G. Singer uses this term in *Generalization in Ethics* (New York: Knopf, 1961), pp. 153, 156–57.
4. Examples from Carr's "Is Business Bluffing Ethical?" pp. 144, 146, 148.
5. Ibid., pp. 152–53.

9. Ruthlessness in Public Life*

Thomas Nagel

I

The great modern crimes are public crimes. To a degree the same can be said of the past, but the growth of political power has introduced a scale of massacre and despoliation that makes the efforts of private criminals, pirates, and bandits seem truly modest.

Public crimes are committed by individuals who play roles in political, military, and economic institutions. (Because religions are politically weak, crimes committed on their behalf are now rare.) Yet unless the offender has the originality of Hitler, Stalin, or Amin, the crimes don't seem to be fully attributable to the individual himself. Famous political monsters have moral personalities large enough to transcend the boundaries of their public roles; they take on the full weight of their deeds as personal moral property. But they are exceptional. Not only are ordinary soldiers, executioners, secret policemen, and bombardiers morally encapsulated in their roles, but so are most secretaries of defense

From *Public and Private Morality,* edited by Stuart Hampshire (New York: Cambridge University Press, 1978), pp. 75–91.

* I am grateful to Gerald Dworkin, Bernard Williams, and members of the Society for Ethical and Legal Philosophy for reactions to an earlier draft.

or state, and even many presidents and prime ministers. They act as officeholders or functionaries, and thereby as individuals they are insulated in a puzzling way from what they do: insulated both in their own view and in the view of most observers. Even if one is in no doubt about the merits of the acts in question, the agents seem to have a slippery moral surface produced by their roles or offices.

This is certainly true of several American statesmen responsible for the more murderous aspects of policy during the Vietnam War. Robert McNamara is president of the World Bank. McGeorge Bundy is present of the Ford Foundation. Elliot Richardson was secretary of defense under Nixon during the completely illegal bombing of Cambodia which went on *after* the Vietnam peace agreements were signed. He then became attorney general and was widely acclaimed for resigning that office rather than comply with Nixon's request that he fire Archibald Cox for demanding the White House tapes. His highly selective sense of honor has served him well: He has since been ambassador to Britain, secretary of commerce and ambassador at large, and we shall hear more of him. Kissinger is of course a highly esteemed figure, despite the Christmas bombing of 1972 and all that preceded it.

The judgments I am presupposing are controversial: not everyone agrees that American policy during the Vietnam War was criminal. But even those who do think so may find it hard to attach the crimes to the criminals, in virtue of the official role in which they were committed. Few old antiwar demonstrators would feel more than mildly uncomfortable about meeting one of these distinguished figures, unless it was just because we were unaccustomed to personal contact with anyone as powerful as the president of the World Bank.

There is, I think, a problem about the moral effects of public roles and offices. Certainly they have a profound effect on the behavior of the individuals who fill them, an effect partly restrictive but significantly liberating. Sometimes they confer great power, but even where they do not, as in the case of an infantryman or police interrogator, they can produce a feeling of moral insulation that has strong attractions. The combination of special requirements and release from some of the usual restrictions, the ability to say that one is only following orders or doing one's job or meeting one's responsibilities, the sense that one is the agent of vast impersonal forces or the servant of institutions larger than any individual—all these ideas form a heady and sometimes corrupting brew.

But this would not be so unless there were something to the special status of action in a role. If roles encourage illegitimate release from moral restraints it is because their moral effect has been distorted. It will help to understand the distortion if we consider another curiosity of current moral discourse about public life: the emphasis placed on those personal restrictions that complement the lack of official restraint—the other side of the coin of public responsibility and irresponsibility. Public figures are not supposed to use their power openly to enrich themselves and their families, or to obtain sexual favors. Such primitive indulgences are generally hidden or denied, and stress is laid on the personal probity and disinterest of public figures. This kind of personal detachment in the exercise of official functions is thought to guarantee their good moral standing, and it leaves them remarkably free in the public arena. No doubt private transgressions are widespread, but when they are inescapably exposed the penalty can be severe, for a delicate boundary of moral restraint that sets off the great body of public power and freedom has been breached. Spiro Agnew will never be head of the Ford Foundation.

The exchange seems fairly straightforward. The exercise of public power is to be liberated from certain constraints by the imposition of others, which are primarily personal. Because the office is supposedly shielded from the personal interests of the one who fills it, what he does in his official capacity seems also to be depersonalized. This nourishes the illusion that personal morality does not apply to it with any force, and that it cannot be strictly assigned to his moral account. The office he occupies gets between him and his depersonalized acts.

Among other things, such a picture disguises the fact that the exercise of power, in whatever role, is one of the most personal forms of individual self-expression, and a rich source of purely personal pleasure. The pleasure of power is not easily acknowledged, but it is one of the most primitive human feelings—probably one with infantile roots. Those who have had it for years sometimes realize its importance only when they have to retire. Despite their grave demeanor, impersonal diction, and limited physical expression, holders of public power are personally involved to an intense degree and probably enjoying it immensely. But whether or not it is consciously enjoyed, the exercise of power is a primary form of individual expression, not diminished but enhanced by the institutions and offices on which it depends.

When we try, therefore, to say what is morally special about public roles and public action, we must concentrate on how they alter the demands on the individual. The actions are his, whether they consist of planning to obliterate a city or only firing in response to an order. So if the moral situation is different from the case where he acts in no official capacity, it must be because the requirements are different.

II

It is hard to discuss this subject in general terms, since roles and offices differ so widely. Nevertheless, the question of the nature of the discontinuity between individual morality and public morality is in part a general one, because the answer must take one of two forms. Either public morality will be derivable from individual morality or it will not. The answer will vary greatly in detail from case to case, but if a significant element of public morality is not derivable from the moral requirements that apply to private individuals, it is probably a common feature of many different examples.

To give the question content, it is necessary to say more about derivability. The interesting question is whether the special features of public morality can be explained in terms of principles already present at the individual level, which yield apparent moral discontinuities when applied to the special circumstances of public life. If so, then public morality is in a substantive and not merely trivial sense derivable from private morality.[1] It emerges naturally from individual morality under the conditions that define the individual's public role.

This could still yield different moral requirements in two ways. Either the general principles could imply additional constraints on public action; or the principles could be such that certain requirements would cease to apply once one assumed a public role, because the conditions for their application would have disappeared. Or the change might involve some combination of the two. In view of the second kind of change, even if public morality is derivable from private, it is possible that the moral restraints on public action are weaker than those on individual action.

The alternative to derivability is that public morality is not grounded on individual morality, and that therefore people acting in certain official roles or capacities are required or permitted to do things that cannot be accounted for on that basis. This also might take two forms. They might come under restrictions in areas left free by individual morality: Public officials might be held to higher standards of concern for the general welfare, for example, than ordinary people. Or else those acting in official roles might be permitted or even required to do things which, considered from the point of view of individual morality, would be impermissible.

Both derivability and non-derivability are formally suited to explain either the addition or the removal of restrictions in public morality; both can therefore explain the appearance of discontinuity. The only way to decide between them is to see which form of explanation can be more plausibly filled out. I shall begin with a version of the derivability hypothesis, based on familiar concepts of individual morality. But while this can explain a good deal, it also leaves something out. I shall therefore go on to say what seems to me true in the non-derivability hypothesis, and this will involve giving an account of the alternative basis on which special conditions of public morality depend.

Even if public morality is not derivable from private, however, it does not mean that they are independent of one another. Both may derive from a common source that yields different results when applied to the generation of principles for action in the widely differing circumstances of private and public life. Neither private morality nor public morality is ultimate. Both result when the general constraints of morality are applied to certain types of action. Public morality would be derivable from private only if those constraints had to be applied first to the development of principles governing the conduct of persons acting individually, and could not be applied directly to public life. In that case one would have to reach the private principles from the general constraints of morality, and the public principles only from the private ones, as applied to public circumstances. But there is no a priori reason to think that ethics has this structure. If it does not, then public and private morality may share a common basis without one being derived from the other. I shall say more about this later. First I want to explore the more direct connections between them.

Part of my aim is to give a correct account of facts that are easily distorted by those defenders of political, diplomatic or military license who cloak themselves in the responsibilities of office. Whoever denies the application of moral restaints to certain public decisions is making a moral claim, and a very strong one. But there is something to the idea of a moral discontinuity between private and public, and to understand the distortions we must know what this is.

III

Some of the moral peculiarity of official roles can be explained by the theory of obligation. Whoever takes on a public or official role assumes the obligation to serve a special function and often the interests of a special group. Like more personal obligations, this limits the claim that other sorts of reasons can make on him. Recall E. M. Forster's remark: "I hate the idea of causes, and if I had to choose between betraying my country and betraying my friend, I hope I should have the courage to betray my country."[2] He was not talking about public office, but similar problems can arise there. In a rigidly defined role like that of a soldier or judge or prison guard, only a very restricted set of considerations is supposed to bear on what one decides to do, and nearly all general considerations are excluded. With less definition, other public offices limit their occupants to certain considerations and free them from others, such as the good of mankind. Public figures sometimes even say and believe that they are obliged to consider only the national or state interest in arriving at their decisions as if it would be a breach of responsibility for them to consider anything else.

This apparent restriction on choice is easy to accept partly because, looked at from the other direction, it lifts restraints that might otherwise be burdensome. But any view as absolute as this is mistaken: there are no such extreme obligations, or offices to which they attach. One cannot, by joining the army, undertake an obligation to obey any order whatever from one's commanding officer. It is not possible to acquire an obligation to kill indebted gamblers by signing a contract as a Mafia hit man. It is not even possible to undertake a commitment to serve the interests of one's children in complete disregard of the interests of everyone else. Obligations to the state also have limits, which derive from their moral context.

Every obligation or commitment reserves some portion of the general pool of motivated action for a special purpose. Life being what it is, each person's supply of time, power, and energy is limited. The kinds of obligations one may undertake, and their limits, depend on how it is reasonable to allocate this pool, and how much liberty individuals should have to allocate it in radically uneven ways. This is true for personal obligations. It applies to public ones as well.

In private life some exclusivity is necessary if we are to allow people to form special relations and attachments, and to make special arrangements with each other on which they can rely. For similar reasons larger groups should be able to cooperate for mutual benefit, or to form social units that may have a geographical definition. And it is natural that the organization of such cooperative units will include institutions, roles, and offices and that the individuals in them will undertake obligations to serve the interests of the group in special ways—by promoting its prosperity, defending it against enemies, etc. To a degree, large-scale social arrangements can be seen as extensions of more individual obligations and commitments.

It may be that the added power conferred by an institutional role should be used primarily for the benefit of that institution and its constituents. The interests of mankind in general have a lesser claim on it. But this does not mean that prohibitions against harming others, directly or indirectly, are correspondingly relaxed. Just because the power to kill thousands of people is yours only because you are the secretary of defense of a certain country, it does not follow that you should be under no restrictions on the use of that power which do not derive specifically from your obligations to serve that country. The same reasoning that challenges private obligations that imply too much of a free hand in carrying them out, will also disallow public commitments with inadequate restraints on their greater power. Insofar as public obligations work like private ones, there is no reason to think that individuals in public roles are released from traditional moral requirements on the treatment of others, or that in public life, the end justifies the means.

IV

Let me now say what such an account leaves out. The moral impersonality of public action may be exaggerated and abused, but there is something in it, which a general theory of obligation cannot explain. Such a theory fails to explain why the *content* of public obligations differs systematically from that of private ones. The impersonality suitable for public action has two aspects: It implies both a heightened concern for results and a stricter requirement of impartiality. It warrants methods usually excluded for private individuals, and sometimes it licenses ruthlessness. This can be explained only by a direct application of moral theory to those public institutions[3] that create the roles to which public obligations are tied. To account for the difference between public and private life we must return to a point mentioned earlier: that public morality may be underivable from private not because they come from different sources, but because each of them contains elements derived independently from a common source.[4]

Morality is complicated at every level. My basic claim is that its impersonal aspects are more prominent in the assessment of institutions than in the assessment of individual actions, and that as a result, the design of institutions may include roles whose occupants must determine what to do by principles different from those that govern private individuals. This will be morally justified, however, by ultimate considerations that underlie individual morality as well. I shall present the view only in outline, and mostly without defending the moral opinions it expresses. My main contention is that the degree to which ruthlessness is acceptable in public life—the ways in which public actors may have to get their hands dirty—depends on moral features of the institutions through which public action is carried out.

Two types of concern determine the content of morality: concern with what will happen and concern with what one is doing.[5] Insofar as principles of conduct are determined by the first concern, they will be outcome-centered or consequentialist, requiring that we promote the best overall results. Insofar as they are determined by the second, the influence of consequences will be limited by certain restrictions on the means to be used, and also by a loosening of the requirement that one always pursue the best results. The action-centered aspects of morality include bars against treating others in certain ways which violate their rights, as well as the space allotted to each person for a life of his own, without the perpetual need to contribute to the general good in everything he does. Such provisions are described as action-centered because, while they apply to everyone, what they require of each person depends on his particular standpoint rather than on the impersonal consequentialist standpoint that surveys the best overall state of affairs and prescribes for each person whatever he can do to contribute to it.

The interaction and conflict between these two aspects of morality are familiar in private life. They result in a certain balance that emphasizes restrictions against harming or interfering with others, rather than requirements to benefit them, except in cases of serious distress. For the most part it leaves us free to pursue our lives and form particular attachments to some people, so long as we do not harm others.

When we apply the same dual conception to public institutions and activities, the results are different. There are several reasons for this. Institutions are not persons and do not have private lives, nor do institutional roles usually absorb completely the lives of their occupants. Public institutions are designed to serve purposes larger than those of particular individuals or families. They tend to pursue the interests of masses of people (a limiting case would be that of a world government, but most actual institutions have a less than universal constituency). In addition, public acts are diffused over many actors and sub-institutions; there is a division of labor both in execution and in decision. All this results in a different balance between the morality of outcomes and the morality of actions. These two types of moral constraint are differently expressed in public life, and both of them take more impersonal forms.

Some of the same agent-centered restrictions on means will apply to public action as to private. But some of them will be weaker, permitting the public employment of coercive, manipulative, or obstructive methods that would not be allowable for individuals. There is some public analogue to the individual's right to lead his own life free of the constant demand to promote the best overall results, but it appears in the relations of states to one another rather than in their relations to their citizens: States can remain neutral in external disputes, and can legitimately favor their own populations—though not at any cost whatever to the rest of the world.

There is no comparable right of self-indulgence or favoritism for public officials or institutions vis-à-vis the individuals with whom they deal. Perhaps the most significant action-centered feature of public morality is a special requirement to treat people in the relevant population equally. Public policies and actions have to be much more impartial than private ones, since they usually employ a monopoly of certain kinds of power and since there is no reason in their case to leave room for the personal attachments and inclinations that shape individual lives.[6]

In respect to outcomes, public morality will differ from private in according them greater weight. This is a consequence of the weakening of certain action-centered constraints and permissions already described, which otherwise would have restrictive effects. The greater latitude about means in turn makes it legitimate to design institutions whose aim is to produce certain desirable results on a large scale, and to define roles in those institutions whose responsibility is mainly to further those results. Within the appropriate limits, public decisions will be justifiably more consequentialist than private ones. They will also have larger consequences to take into account.

To say that consequentialist reasons will be prominent is not to say what kinds of consequences matter. This is a well-worked field, and I shall avoid discussing the place of equality, liberty, autonomy and individual rights, as well as overall level of happiness, in a consequentialist view of the good. The point to remember is that consequentialist values need not be utilitarian; a consequentialist assessment of social institutions can be strongly egalitarian, in addition to valuing welfare, liberty, and individuality in themselves. Moreover, giving the members of a society the opportunity to lead their own lives free of consequentialist demands is one of the goods to be counted in a consequentialist social reckoning. But I won't try to present a complete system of public values here, for I am concerned with the more abstract claim that consequentialist considerations, together with impartiality, play a special role in the moral assessment and justification of public institutions.

The effect of these two deviations of public from private morality on the assessment of public action will be complex. The reason is that the constraints of public morality are not imposed as a whole in the same way on all public actions or on all public offices. Because public agency is itself complex and divided, there is a corresponding ethical division of labor, or ethical specialization. Different aspects of public morality are in the hands of different officials. This can create the illusion that public morality is more consequentialist or less restrictive than it is, because the general conditions may be wrongly identified with the boundaries of a particular role. But in fact those boundaries usually presuppose a larger institutional structure without which they would be illegitimate. (The most conspicuous example is the legitimacy conferred on legislative decisions by the limitation of constitutional protections enforced by the courts.)

By this rather complex route, the balance of outcome-oriented and action-oriented morality will justify the design of public institutions whose officials can do what would be unsuitable in private life. Some of the deviations will be conspicuously consequentialist; others will express the impersonality of public morality in other ways. Action-centered constraints will not be absent: there will still be restrictions on means. But those restrictions may be weaker in relation to the results than they are for individuals.

I have simply adapted a point made by Rawls in "Two Concepts of Rules,"[7] He argued that utilitarianism could justify practices that exclude utilitarian reasoning in some circumstances. I am arguing that a more complex morality than utilitarianism will likewise have different implications for human conduct when applied to its assessment directly and when applied indirectly via the assessment of institutions through which action occurs. The details of this morality cannot be explained here, but many of its features depend on an idea of moral universality different from that which underlies utilitarianism. Utilitarian assessment decides, basically, whether something is acceptable from a general point of view that combines those of *all* individuals. The method of combination is basically majoritarian. The alternative is to ask whether something is acceptable from a schematic point of view that represents in essentials the standpoint of each individual. The method of combination here is a form of unanimity, since acceptability from the schematic point of view represents acceptability to each person. Both of these moral conceptions can claim to count everyone equally, yet they are very different. My own opinion is that morality should be based on acceptability to each rather than on acceptability to all. The problem is to define the two points of view that express these opposed moral conceptions.[8]

It could also be said that the separate application of these basic constraints to social institutions and to individual conduct yields a moral division of labor between the individual and society, in which individual and social ideals are inseparably linked. The impersonal benevolence of public morality is intended to provide a background against which individualism in private morality is acceptable. It is a pressing and difficult question whether private individualism and public benevolence are socially compatible, or whether the tension between them makes this an unstable moral conception and an unstable social ideal.

V

Because they are specialized, not all public institutions are equally sensitive to overall consequences. An important exception is the judiciary, at least in a society where the courts are designed to protect individual rights against both public and private encroachment. Neither the institution itself nor the roles it defines—judge, juror, prosecutor—are dominated by a concern with overall results. They act on narrower grounds. To some extent this narrowing of grounds is itself justified by consequentialist reasoning about the overall effects of such an institution. However the courts also embody the state's action-centered moral constraints—impersonal but not consequentialist. Very importantly, they are supposed to enforce its impartiality in serious dealings with individual citizens. And by setting limits to the means that can be employed by other public institutions, they leave those institutions free to concentrate more fully on achieving results within those limits.

To illustrate the positive claim that these limits differ from those that operate in private life, let me consider two familiar examples of public action: taxation and conscription. Both are imposed by the legislature in our society, and it may be thought that they are therefore indirectly consented to by the population. I believe it is a desperate measure to impute consent to everyone who is drafted or pays income taxes on the ground that he votes or accepts certain public services. Consent is not needed to justify such legislative action, because the legislature is an institution whose authority to make such decisions on consequentialist grounds is morally justified in other ways. Its periodic answerability to the electorate is one feature of the institution (another being the constitutional protection of rights) that contributes to its legitiimacy—but not by implying each citizen's consent to its actions.[9] Particularly when those actions are coercive the defense of consent is not credible.

Some would describe taxation as a form of theft and conscription as a form of slavery—in fact some would prefer to describe taxation as slavery too, or at least as forced labor.[10] Much might be said against these descriptions, but that is beside the point. For within proper limits, such practices when engaged in by governments are acceptable whatever they are called. If someone with an income of $2,000 a year trains a gun on someone with an income of $100,000 a year and makes him hand over his wallet, that is robbery. If the federal government withholds a portion of the second person's salary (enforcing the laws against tax evasion with threats of imprisonment under armed guard) and gives some of it to the first person in the form of welfare payments, food stamps, or free health care, that is taxation. In the first case it is (in my opinion) an impermissible use of coercive means to achieve a worthwhile end. In the second case the means are legitimate, because they are impersonally imposed by an institution designed to promote certain results. Such general methods of distribution are preferable to theft as a form of private initiative and also to individual charity. This is true not only for reasons of fairness and efficiency, but also because both theft and charity are disturbances of the relations (or lack of them) between individuals and involve their individual wills in a way that an automatic, officially imposed system of taxation does not. The results achieved by taxation in an egalitarian welfare state would not be produced either by a right of individual expropriation or by a duty of charity. Taxation therefore provides a case in which public morality is derived not from private morality, but from impersonal consequentialist considerations applied directly to public institutions, and secondarily to action within those institutions. There is no way of analyzing a system of redistributive taxation into the sum of a large number of individual acts all of which satisfy the requirements of private morality.

In the case of conscription, the coercion is extreme, and so is what one is forced to do. You are told to try to kill people who are trying to kill you, the alternative being imprisonment. Quite apart from fighting, military service involves unusual restrictions of liberty. Even assuming agreement about when conscription is acceptable and what exemptions should be allowed, this is a kind of coercion that it would be unthinkable to impose privately. *A* can't force *B* to help him fight a gang of hoodlums who are robbing them both, if *B* would rather give his money. Again, the more impersonal viewpoint of public morality gives a different result.

But not everything is permitted. Restrictions on the treatment of individuals continue to operate from a public point of view, and they cannot be implemented entirely by the courts. One of the hardest lines to draw in public policy is the one that defines where the end stops justifying the means. If results were the only basis for public morality then it would be possible to justify anything, including torture and massacre, in the service of sufficiently large interests. Whether the limits are drawn by specific constitutional protections or not, the strongest constraints of individual morality will continue to limit what can be publicly justified even by extremely powerful consequentialist reasons.

VI

This completes my discussion of the continuities and discontinuities between public and private morality. I have argued that some of the special features of public morality can be explained in terms of a theory of obligation that also accounts for the steps individuals can take to restrict the grounds on which they will make certain choices. Public officials accept special obligations to serve interests that their offices are designed to advance—and to serve them in more or less well-defined ways. In doing so, they correlatively reduce their right to consider other factors, both their personal interests and more general ones not related to the institution or their role in it.

I have also argued, however, that the special character of public obligations—the weight they give both to results and to impartiality—reflects the relative impersonality of public action: its scale, its lack of individuality, its institutional structure. A theory of obligation explains only part of the change that occurs when an individual takes on a public role. It does not explain either the prominence of consequentialism or the shift in strength and character of action-centered reasons. I have tried to explain these differences as the result of a direct application of basic moral constraints to public institutions and therefore to the public functions that individuals may undertake.

Both of these sources of public morality generate limits to what a public official may do in the conduct of his office, even if he is serving institutional interests. It is easy to forget about those limits, for three reasons. First, restrictions against the use of public power for private gain can seem like a moral cushion that insulates whatever else is done officially from moral reproach. Second, the fact that the holder of public office takes on an obligation to a particular group may foster the idea that he is obliged not to consider anything except the interest of that group. Third, the impersonal morality of public institutions, and the moral specialization that inevitably arises given the complexity of public actions, lead naturally to the establishment of many roles whose terms of reference are primarily consequentialist. Lack of attention to the context that is necessary to make these roles legitimate can lead to a rejection of all limits on the means thought to be justified by ever greater ends. I have argued that these are all errors. It is important to remember that they are *moral* views: The opinion that in certain conditions a certain type of conduct is permissible has to be criticized and defended by moral argument.

Let me return finally to the individuals who occupy public roles. Even if public morality is not substantively derivable from private, it applies to individuals. If one of them takes on a public role, he accepts certain obligations, certain restrictions, and certain limitations on what he may do. As with any obligation, this step involves a risk that he will be required to act in ways incompatible with other obligations or principles that he accepts. Sometimes he will have to act anyway. But sometimes, if he can remember them, he will see that the limits imposed by public morality itself are being transgressed, and he is being asked to carry out a judicial murder or a war of unjust aggression. At this point there is no substitute for refusal and, if possible, resistance. Despite the impersonal character of public morality and its complex application to institutions in which responsibility is divided, it tells us not only how those institutions should be designed but also how people in them should act. Someone who has committed public wrongs in the exercise of his office can be just as guilty as a private criminal. Sometimes his responsibility is partly absorbed by the moral defects of the institution through which he acts; but the plausibility of that excuse is inversely proportional to the power and independence of the actor. Unfortunately this is not reflected in our treatment of former public servants who have often done far worse than take bribes.

NOTES

1. Public morality becomes trivially derivable from individual morality if individual morality is extended to include all true propositions of the form, 'if the individual is acting in public role X, he may (or must) do Y,' and so forth. This is compatible, however, with there being no connection between the grounds of the public and private requirements.

2. "What I Believe" in *Two Cheers for Democracy* (London, 1939).

3. What I say will be put in terms of the largest and most powerful institutions, the state and its agencies. But there is a wide range of public institutions including universities, political parties, charitable organizations, and revolutionary movements. Much of what I shall say about nation-states applies to these cases also in some degree. They too come under a kind of public morality.

4. This retracts something I said at pp. 139–40 of "Libertarianism Without Foundations," 85 *Yale Law Journal* (1975).

5. I discuss this distinction in "War and Massacre," *Philosophy and Public Affairs,* vol. 1, no. 2 (1972) 123–44.

6. Would a giant with immense power be obliged to act primarily on impersonal grounds if he were unique among millions of ordinary people whose lives he could affect? I doubt it. He would presumably have a personal life as well, which made some claims on him. The state is the closest thing we know to such a giant, and it is not similarly encumbered.

7. *Philosophical Review* 64 (1955) 3–32.

8. One attempt is made by Rawls in *A Theory of Justice* (Cambridge, MA, 1971), chap. 3.

9. This conception of legitimacy is found in Thomas M. Scanlon, "Nozick on Rights, Liberty, and Property," *Philosophy and Public Affairs,* vol. 6, no. 1 (1976) at pp. 17–20.

10. E.g., Robert Nozick, *Anarchy, State, and Utopia* (New York, 1974) pp. 169–74.

QUESTIONS FOR STUDY AND DISCUSSION

1. Monroe Freedman defends what Richard Wasserstrom calls 'role differentiation' of lawyers by arguing that the attorney is to maintain strict confidentiality in the lawyer/client relationship and that the attorney is always to be a zealous advocate of his or her client's cause, pursuing that cause as fully as possible within the limits of law. Much of Freedman's case for strong role differentiation in legal ethics rests on the purported virtues of the adversary system, which is central to the conduct of criminal and civil litigation in our society. Using Freedman and Wasserstrom as resources, explain as fully as you are able the presumed values of the adversary system and offer your own detailed evaluation of whether the adversary system does, in fact, protect the values it is assumed by many to protect. In your discussion, be sure to evaluate Wasserstrom's suggestion that the adversary system seems far less appropriate in the context of civil law than it does in the context of criminal law.

2. Albert Carr several times equates personal or ordinary morality with religious ethics. Evaluate this equation.

3. Carr argues that rightful conduct in business is limited to conduct within the law. Explain as fully as you are able Carr's reasons for holding this view. Also explain as fully as you are able what kinds of business practices this view endorses as perfectly ethical. Do you agree with Carr's position on business morality? Defend your answer; anticipate and respond to what you think is the strongest objection to your position.

4. Explain Norman Chase Gillespie's account of the considerations which change our moral duties. In considering what Gillespie (following Marcus Singer) calls a ''state of nature situation,'' Alan Goldman has argued that

> the consequence of allowing injustice on the ground that others are committing it with personal gain is that any injustice becomes excusable if it is widespread enough. And injustice is likely to be widespread once this excuse is granted. One cannot therefore claim a right to do wrong by complaining that others are benefitting from their wrong actions and that it is an unfair disadvantage when one cannot join in. If there is any force to this complaint, it is that the others should be made to stop, not that anyone who so chooses should be permitted to participate in the wrongdoing. The notion of an equal right to do wrong is simply contradictory. (Alan H. Goldman, *The Moral Foundations of Professional Ethics* [Totowa, NJ: Rowman and Littlefield, 1980], p. 272)

Does the fact that certain practices are common in business (e.g., deceptive packaging, pollution up to the limits permitted by law, etc.) provide a moral justification for those in business to behave in these ways? Does Goldman's position require people in business to be moral heroes by putting themselves at an unfair disadvantage? Does Gillespie's position require too little of those in business? Justify your answers.

5. Using the concept of role differentiation as it emerges in this chapter's introduction and readings, explain what role differentiation in journalism, psychological counseling, and education might involve. Given your answers, do you think that journalists, psychological therapists, and educators should be role differentiated? Explain the reasons for your answers.

6. Explain Thomas Nagel's account of how ''public'' and ''private'' morality are related, yet different; be sure to include in your explanation an account of Nagel's distinction between the morality of outcomes and the morality of actions. According to Nagel, are the obligations of public officials limited to the demands of their professional roles, that is, to the pursuit of the goals of the institutions in which they serve? Explain your answer carefully. Do you agree with Nagel on this point? Again, explain your answer carefully.

CASE: ZEALOUS ADVOCACY AND CROSS-EXAMINING THE TRUTHFUL WITNESS

You are the defense attorney for a twenty-one-year-old man accused of raping a young woman in a bar. The incident took place after the woman entered the bar to buy a pack of cigarettes. She was dressed in a miniskirt and tight sweater. She responded to the flirtations of several patrons (including your client) by sitting down at the bar and having several drinks. Your client began fondling her and she did not resist. Your client and the woman then began kissing and mutually intimate fondling. Your client then began to remove the woman's underpants; she resisted. As other patrons cheered him on, your client overpowered the woman, removed her underpants, and dragged here across the room where he lifted her onto a pool table and had intercourse with her despite her crying, verbal protests, and physical efforts to free herself. Your client has told you that these are the facts and that he ignored the woman's resistance because "she was asking for it."

The defense has been that because of the woman's passionate sexual interactions with your client, he did not believe that the woman was an unwilling sexual partner; he believed, you have argued, that her resistance was feigned. You have also argued that the evidence for this belief lies in the fact that when the woman fled from the bar, your client made no attempt to leave. When the woman returned twenty minutes later with the police, your client was still in the bar, joking and talking with other patrons. You are about to cross-examine the woman.

1. What moral relevance, if any, does the woman's behavior prior to your client's beginning to undress her have to the *moral* guilt of your client? Explain your answer carefully. Should the question of your client's moral blameworthiness for his actions enter into answering the question of how strenuously he should be defended? Why or why not?

2. Rape involves sexual penetration, forcibly and against the victim's will. Is your client guilty of rape? Explain your answer. In your considered judgment, should your client be convicted of rape? Why or why not?

3. Your conversations with your client have made it clear to you that your client knew the woman was unconsenting to intercourse but that he ignored this. Since "she was asking for it" or "she got what she deserved" does not constitute a defense to the charge of rape, the defense that you have mounted on your client's behalf asserts that he sincerely believed that the woman's resistance was a pretense. Is it morally justifiable for you to use this defense even though it contains a blatant lie? Explain your answer carefully and anticipate and respond to the most serious objection to your position.

4. You are about to cross-examine the woman. Would it be morally permissible for you to try to demoralize and confuse her as much as you can in an effort to either discredit her testimony or get her to say that her behavior indicated that she was not an unwilling partner to intercourse? Why or why not?

5. Assume that your client is legally guilty of rape. Is it morally permissible for you *not* to attempt to demoralize and confuse the woman in cross-examination if doing this might help your client's case? Defend your answer; anticipate and respond to the most serious objection that can be raised against your position.

SELECTED BIBLIOGRAPHY

Andre, Judith. "Role as a Complex Moral Concept." Unpublished typescript. Norfolk, VA: Old Dominion University.

Bowie, Norman. " 'Role' as a Moral Concept in Health Care." *Journal of Medicine and Philosophy* 7:1 (1982): 57–63.

Bradley, F. H. "My Station and Its Duties." In *Ethical Studies* (1876). Oxford: Oxford University Press, 1970.

Brandeis, Louis D. *Business—A Profession*. Boston: Small, Maynard, 1914.

Camenisch, Paul F. *Grounding Professional Ethics in a Pluralistic Society*. New York: Haven, 1983.

Carr, Albert Z. "Can an Executive Afford a Conscience?" *Harvard Business Review* (July-August 1970): 58–64.

Donagan, Alan. "Justifying Legal Practice in the Adversary System." In *The Good Lawyer: Lawyers' Roles and Lawyers' Ethics*, ed. David Luban, pp. 123–49. Totowa, NJ: Rowman and Allanheld, 1984.

Downie, R. S. "Responsibility and Social Roles." In *Individual and Collective Responsibility*, ed. Peter A. French, pp. 65–80. Cambridge, MA: Schenkman, 1972.

Emmet, Dorothy. *Rules, Roles, and Regulations*. New York: St. Martin's, 1966.

Freedman, Benjamin. "A Meta-Ethics for Professional Morality." *Ethics* 89:1 (1978): 1–19.

———. "What Really Makes Professional Morality Different: Response to Martin." *Ethics* 91:4 (1981): 626–30.

Freedman, Monroe H. *Lawyers' Ethics in an Adversary System*. Indianapolis, IN: Bobbs-Merrill, 1975.

———. "Personal Responsibility in a Professional System." *Catholic University Law Review* 27 (1975): 191–206.

Gewirth, Alan. "Professional Ethics: The Separatist Thesis." *Ethics* 96:2 (1986): 282–300.

Goldman, Alan H. *The Moral Foundations of Professional Ethics*. Totowa, NJ: Rowman and Littlefield, 1980.

Hannaford, Robert V. "The Theoretical Twist to Irresponsibility in Business." In *Profits and Professions: Essays in Business and Professional Ethics,* ed. Wade L. Robison, Michael S. Pritchard, and Joseph S. Ellin, pp. 101–12. Clifton, NJ: Humana Press, 1983.

Hefferman, William C. "The Moral Accountability of Advocates." *Notre Dame Law Review* 61 (1986): 36–87.

Held, Virginia. "The Division of Moral Labor and the Role of the Lawyer." In Luban, pp. 60–79, *supra*.

Howard W. Kenneth. "Must Public Hands Be Dirty?" *Journal of Value Inquiry* 11:1 (1977): 29–40.

Jones, W. T. "Public Roles, Private Roles, and Differential Assessments of Role Performance." *Ethics* 94:4 (1984): 602–620.

Kipnis, Kenneth. "Goldman on Professional Ethics." *Westminster Institute Review* 1:1 (1981): 8–10.

Koehn, Donald. "A Laissez-Faire Approach to Business Ethics." In Robison et al., pp. 113–32, *supra*.

Konrad, Armin R. "Business Managers and Moral Sanctuaries." *Journal of Business Ethics* 1:3 (1982): 195–200.

Kutak, Robert J. "The Adversary System and the Practice of Law." In Luban, pp. 172–87, *supra*.

Luban, David. "The Adversary System Excuse." In Luban, pp. 83–122, *supra*.

Martin, Mike W. "Professional and Ordinary Morality: A Reply to Freedman." *Ethics* 91:4 (1981): 631–33.

———. "Rights and the Meta-Ethics of Professional Morality." *Ethics* 91:4 (1981): 619–25.

Patterson, L. Ray. *Legal Ethics: The Law of Professional Responsibility*. New York: Matthew Bender, 1982.

Postema, Gerald. "Moral Responsibility in Professional Ethics." *New York University Law Review* 55 (1980): 63–89.

Simon, William H. "The Ideology of Advocacy: Procedural Justice and Professional Ethics." *Wisconsin Law Review* 1978 (1978): 30–144.

Taylor, Allen. "The Adversary System of Justice: An Ethical Jungle." *Journal of Critical Analysis* 3:1 (April 1971): 23–28.

Urmson, J. O. "Saints and Heroes." In *Essays in Moral Philosophy,* ed. A. I. Melden, pp. 198–216. Seattle: University of Washington Press, 1958.

Veatch, Robert M. "Medical Ethics: Professional or Universal?" *Harvard Theological Review* 65 (1972): 531–59.

———. "Professional Ethics: New Principles for Physicians?" *Hastings Center Report* 10:3 (1980): 16–18.

———. "Professional Medical Ethics: The Grounding of Its Principles." *Journal of Medicine and Philosophy* 4:1 (1979): 1–19.

Walzer, Michael. "Political Action: The Problem of Dirty Hands." *Philosophy and Public Affairs* 2:2 (1973): 160–80.

Wasserstrom, Richard A. "Roles and Morality." In Luban, pp. 25–37, *supra*.

Willard, L. Duane. "Is Action Within the Law Morally Sufficient in Business?" In Robison et al., pp. 89–99, *supra*.

4

PROFESSIONALS AND CLIENTS: MODELS AND METAPHORS

The selections in chapter 3 began our approach to the question of the rights and responsibilities of professionals when they are functioning in their occupational roles. The present chapter carries that inquiry forward by asking how we are to understand the special moral relationship which obtains between professionals and those whose interests they are engaged to serve. Though simply stated, this question is enormously complex: For the relationships which are of philosophical interest to us here range from relationships like that between a self-employed physician and his or her clients, through that between a hospital-employed nurse and the hospital—as well as the nurse's clients—to relationships between scientific advisors and their employers (including the federal government) and to relationships between engineers and the corporations which employ them as well as the public whose interests they are supposed to protect by ensuring safe designs.

Despite this great variety in employment relationships, there is a question implicitly raised by the readings in chapter 3 that pertains to all of them, namely, whether the engaged professional is to function solely as an agent in pursuit of his or her principal's interests, whether that principal is an individual person; or a local, state, or federal government; or some other corporate employer. In the context of legal practice, we have already seen Monroe Freedman defending what Michael Bayles in this chapter's reading calls the 'agency' model of the professional/principal relationship. Although Bayles limits his treatment of the professional/principal relationship to what he has called 'the consulting professions' (see sel. 1 in chap. 2), the agency model need not be limited in application to those professions. As a professional/principal model, it is also utilizable in thinking about professional responsibility in the employer/employee relationship even when the employers are as diverse in kind as those mentioned above. In chapter 10, for example, we shall see Milton Friedman arguing that the single moral responsibility of business managers is to maximize profits within the limits of law for the shareholders who have entrusted them with their funds.

The present chapter, however, addresses the question of the professional/principal relationship by focusing on the relationship between professionals and clients in several of the service professions, namely, medicine, nursing, and higher education. The candidates which emerge in this chapter as models to be captured in these relationships are contract, covenant, advocate, and fiduciary. It may well be the case that these models are not mutually exclusive. And it may also be the case that no single model will be appropriate to serve as the standard across all the service professions (or the professions Bayles categorizes as the consulting professions).

And it may also be the case that no single model fully captures all we want to capture in any one profession. Still, reflecting on the models and metaphors suggested in these readings can be useful in thinking through the rights and responsibilities of professionals toward their clients.

Central to our focus in this chapter is the question of power distribution in the professional/client relationship. As Richard Wasserstrom's article in chapter 3 pointed out, the lawyer/client relationship seems to have a decidedly paternalistic component. This component has not been limited to relationships between attorneys and principals. Indeed, some would argue that paternalism has traditionally been one of the clearest characteristics of the health care professions and education (even at its highest levels), among others. But paternalism, as Bayles points out, strips clients of important rights to self-direction. The following articles by Robert Veatch and William May reject a paternalistic model for medicine. Veatch supports a contract model, which incorporates respect for patient autonomy. But May contends that the contract model fails to capture important features of the physician/patient relationship, and he attempts to improve on the contract model by suggesting that the relationship between physicians and their patients should be more richly understood as covenant.

The article by Gerald Winslow addresses a metaphor which has recently been widely supported as providing the appropriate model for nursing, namely, the advocacy model. As Winslow points out, the advocacy model in nursing has its roots in law and is an interesting derivative of the agency model in legal practice. The advocacy model in nursing takes protection of the moral rights of patients to be central to nursing practice, suggesting that nurses are to assume the role of "moral watchdog" for patients in the health care system. Winslow traces the development of this metaphor in nursing and shows the obstacles nursing will need to overcome if nurses are to become effective patient advocates.

My own article addresses the question of whether the relationship between professors and students in higher education is to be understood, in any general way, as a paternalistic one. I suggest that it is not and that we would do best to understand the general structure of the ordinary relationship between professors and their students as contractual in nature. An objection to my position might be raised along the lines suggested by May in his discussion of medicine. But it is not clear to me that contract, properly understood in certain contexts, needs to be as cool and legalistic as May's criticism of the contract model suggests. What the contract model in this chapter's readings preserves are the relevant aspects of the fiduciary model proposed by Bayles as well as the social sanctions which, as Veatch points out, institutionalize and stand behind the professional/client relationship in case there is a violation of the contract. At the same time, the model assumes that professionals will, in general, faithfully and conscientiously fulfill their obligations. The contract model also avoids the identification of the professional person with his or her professional role, which seems to be involved in May's account of the covenant model.

Implicit in all the models of the professional/client relationship proposed in this chapter is a respect for professional autonomy, which is inadequately captured in the agency (or hired-gun) model of the professional/client relationship, as well as a respect for client autonomy, which is inadequately captured in the paternalistic model of the professional/client relationship. The articles by Veatch and Bayles as well as my own article begin a direct discussion of paternalism in the professions that will continue into the first part of chapter 5, where deceiving clients for their own good is the central issue.

10. Models for Ethical Medicine in a Revolutionary Age

Robert M. Veatch

Most of the ethical problems in the practice of medicine come up in cases where the medical condition or desired procedure itself presents no moral problem. Most day-to-day patient contacts are just not cases which are ethically exotic. For the woman who spends five hours in the clinic waiting room with two screaming children waiting to be seen for the flu, the flu is not a special moral problem; her wait is. When medical students practice drawing bloods from clinic patients in the cardiac care unit—when teaching material is treated as material—the moral problem is not really related to the patient's heart in the way it might be in a more exotic heart transplant. Many more blood samples are drawn, however, than hearts transplanted. It is only by moving beyond the specific issues to more basic underlying ethical themes that the real ethical problems in medicine can be dealt with. . . .

THE ENGINEERING MODEL

One of the impacts of the biological revolution is to make the physician scientific. All too often he behaves like an applied scientist. The rhetoric of the scientific tradition in the modern world is that the scientist must be "pure." He must be factual, divorcing himself from all considerations of value. It has taken atomic bombs and Nazi medical research to let us see the foolishness and danger of such a stance. In the first place the scientist, and certainly the applied scientist, just cannot logically be value free. Choices must be made daily—in research design, in significance levels of statistical tests, and in perception of the "significant" observations from an infinite perceptual field, and each of these choices requires a frame of values on which it is based. Even more so in an applied science like medicine choices based upon what is "significant," what is "valuable," must be made constantly. The physician who thinks he can just present all the facts and let the patient make the choices is fooling himself even if it is morally sound and responsible to do this at all the critical points where decisive choices are to be made. Furthermore, even if the physician logically could eliminate all ethical and other value considerations from his decision making and even if he could in practice conform to the impossible value-free ideal, it would be morally outrageous for him to do so. It would make him an engineer, a plumber making repairs, connecting tubes and flushing out clogged systems, with no questions asked. . . .

THE PRIESTLY MODEL

In proper moral revulsion to the model which makes the physician into a plumber for whom his own ethical judgments are completely excluded, some move to the opposite extreme, making the physician a new priest. Establishment sociologist of medicine Robert N. Wilson describes the physician-patient relationship as religious. "The doctor's office or the hospital room, for example," he says, "have somewhat the aura of a sanctuary"; ". . . the patient must view his doctor in a manner far removed from the prosaic and the mundane."

The priestly model leads to what I call the "As-a syndrome." The symptoms are verbal, but the disease is moral. The chief diagnostic sign is the phrase "speaking-as-a. . . ." In counseling a pregnant woman who has taken Thalidomide, a physician says, "The odds are against a normal baby and "speaking-as-a-physician that is a risk you shouldn't take." One must ask what it is about medical training that lets this be said "as-a-physician" rather than as a friend or as a moral man or as a priest. The problem is one of generalization of expertise: transferring of expertise in the technical aspects of a subject to expertise in moral advice.

The main ethical principle which summarizes this priestly tradition is "Benefit and do no harm to the patient." Now attacking the principle of doing no harm to the patient is a bit like attacking fatherhood. (Motherhood has not dominated the profession in the Western tradition.) But Fatherhood has long been an alternative symbol for the priestly model, "Father" has traditionally been a personalistic metaphor for God and for the priest. Likewise, the classical medical sociology literature (the same literature using the religious images) always uses the parent-child image as an analogy for the physician-patient relationship. It is this paternalism in the realm of values which is represented in the moral slogan "Benefit and do no harm to the patient." It takes the locus of decision making away from the patient and places it in the hands of the professional. In doing so it destroys or at least minimizes the other moral themes essential to a more balanced ethical system. While a

From *Hastings Center Report* 2:3 (1972): 5–7.

professional group may affirm this principle as adequate for a professional ethic, it is clear that society, more generally, has a much broader set of ethical norms. If the professional group is affirming one norm while society affirms another for the same circumstances, then the physician is placed in the uncomfortable position of having to decide whether his loyalty is to the norms of his professional group or to those of the broader society. What would this larger set of norms include?

Producing Good and Not Harm

Outside of the narrowest Kantian tradition, no one excludes the moral duty of producing good and avoiding harm entirely. Let this be said from the start. Some separate producing good and avoiding evil into two different principles placing greater moral weight on the latter, but this is also true within the tradition of professional medical ethics. The real difference is that in a set of ethical norms used more universally in the broader society producing good and avoiding harm is set in a much broader context and becomes just one of a much larger set of moral obligations.

Protecting Individual Freedom

Personal freedom is a funadmental value in society. It is essential to being truly human. Individual freedom for both physician and patient must be protected even if it looks like some harm is going to be done in the process. This is why legally competent patients are permitted by society to refuse blood transfusions or other types of medical care even when to the vast majority of us the price seems to be one of great harm. Authority about what constitutes harm and what constitutes good (as opposed to procedures required to obtain a particular predetermined good or harm) cannot be vested in any one particular group of individuals. To do so would be to make the error of generalizing expertise.

Preserving Individual Dignity

Equality of moral significance of all persons means that each is given fundamental dignity. Individual freedom of choice and control over one's own life and body contributes to that dignity. We might say that this more universal, societal ethic of freedom and dignity is one which moves beyond B. F. Skinner.

Many of the steps in the hospitalization, care, and maintenance of the patient, particularly seriously ill patients are currently an assault on that dignity. The emaciated, senile man connected to life by IV tubes, tracheotomy, and colostomy has difficulty retaining his sense of dignity. Small wonder that many prefer to return to their own homes to die. It is there on their own turf that they have a sense of power and dignity.

Truth Telling and Promise Keeping

As traditional as they sound, the ethical obligations of truth telling and promise keeping have retained their place in ethics because they are seen as essential to the quality of human relationships. It is disturbing to see these fundamental elements of human interaction compromised, minimized, and even eliminated supposedly in order to keep from harming the patient. This is a much broader problem than the issue of what to tell the terminal carcinoma patient or the patient for whom there has been an unanticipated discovery of an XYY chromosome pattern when doing an amniocentesis for mongolism. It arises when the young boy getting his measles shot is told "Now this won't hurt a bit" and when a medical student is introduced on the hospital floor as "Doctor." And these all may be defended as ways of keeping from harming the patient. It is clear that in each case, also, especially if one takes into account the long-range threat to trust and confidence, that in the long run these violations of truth telling and promise keeping may do more harm than good. Both the young boy getting the shot and the medical student are being taught what to expect from the medical profession in the future. But even if that were not the case, each is an assault on patient dignity and freedom and humanity. Such actions may be justifiable sometimes, but the case must be awfully strong.

Maintaining and Restoring Justice

Another way in which the ethical norms of the broader society move beyond concern for helping and not harming the patient is by insisting on a fair distribution of health services. What we have been calling the social revolution, as prefigurative as it may be, has heightened our concern for equality in the distribution of basic health services. If health care is a right, then it is a right for all. It is not enough to produce individual cases of good health or even the best aggregate health statistics. Even if the United States had the best health statistics in the world (which it does not have), if this were attained at the expense of inferior health care for certain groups within the society it would be ethically unacceptable.

At this point in history with our current record of discriminatory delivery of health services there is a special concern for restoring justice. Justice must also be compensatory. The health of those who have been discriminated against must be maintained and restored as a special priority.

THE COLLEGIAL MODEL

With the engineering model the physician becomes a plumber without any moral integrity. With the priestly model his moral authority so dominates the patient that the patient's freedom and dignity are extinguished. In the effort to develop a more proper balance which would permit the other fundamental values and obligations to be preserved, some have suggested that the physician and the patient should see themselves as colleagues pursuing the common goal of eliminating the illness and preserving the health of the patient. The physician is the patient's "pal." It is in the collegial model that the themes of trust and confidence play the most crucial role. When two individuals or groups are truly committed to common goals, then trust and confidence are justified and the collegial model is appropriate. It is a very pleasant, harmonious way to interact with one's fellow human beings. There is an equality of dignity and respect, an equality of value contributions, lacking in the earlier models.

But social realism makes us ask the embarrassing question: Is there, in fact, any real basis for the assumption of mutual loyalty and goals, of common interest which would permit the unregulated community of colleagues model to apply to the physician-patient relationship?

There is some proleptic sign of a community of real common interests in some elements of the radical health movement and free clinics, but for the most part we have to admit that ethnic, class, economic, and value differences make the assumption of common interest which is necessary for the collegial model to function . . . a mere pipedream. What is needed is a more provisional model which permits equality in the realm of moral significance between patient and physician without making the utopian assumption of collegiality.

THE CONTRACTUAL MODEL

The model of social relationship which fits these conditions is that of the contract or covenant. The notion of contract should not be loaded with legalistic implications, but taken in its more symbolic form as in the traditional religious or marriage "contract" or "covenant." Here two individuals or groups are interacting in a way where there are obligations and expected benefits for both parties. The obligations and benefits are limited in scope, though, even if they are expressed in somewhat vague terms. The basic norms of freedom, dignity, truth telling, promise keeping, and justice are essential to a contractual relationship. The premise is trust and confidence even though it is recognized that there is not a full mutuality of interests. Social sanctions institutionalize and stand behind the relationship, in case there is a violation of the contract, but for the most part the assumption is that there will be a faithful fulfillment of the obligations.

Only in the contractual model can there be a true sharing of ethical authority and responsibility. This avoids the moral abdication on the part of the physician in the engineering model and the moral abdication on the part of the patient in the priestly model. It also avoids the uncontrolled and false sense of equality in the collegial model. With the contractual relationship there is a sharing in which the physician recognizes that the patient must maintain freedom of control over his own life and destiny when significant choices are to be made. Should the physician not be able to live with his conscience under those terms the contract is not made or is broken. This means that there will have to be relatively greater open discussion of the moral premises hiding in medical decisions before and as they are made.

With the contractual model there is a sharing in which the patient has legitimate gounds for trusting that once the basic value framework for medical decision making is established on the basis of the patient's own values, the myriads of minute medical decisions which must be made day in and day out in the care of the patient will be made by the physician within that frame of reference.

In the contractual model, then, there is a real sharing of decision making in a way that there is realistic assurance that both patient and physician will retain their moral integrity. In this contractual context patient control of decision making in the individual level is assured without the necessity of insisting that the patient participate in every trivial decision. On the social level community control of health care is made possible in the same way. The lay community is given and should be given the status of contractor. The locus of decision making is thus in the lay community, but the day-to-day medical decisions can, with trust and confidence, rest with the medical community. If trust and confidence are broken the contract is broken.

Medical ethics in the midst of the biological and social revolutions is dealing with a great number of new and difficult ethical cases: in vitro fertilization, psychosurgery, happiness pills, brain death, and the military use of medical technology. But the real day-to-day ethical crises may not be nearly so exotic. Whether the issue is in an exotic context or one which is nothing more complicated medically than a routine physical exam, the ethos of ethical responsibility established by the appropriate selection of a model for the moral relationship between the professional and the lay communities will be decisive. This is the real framework for medical ethics in a revolutionary age.

11. Contract or Covenant?

William F. May

. . . While criticizing the ideal of philanthropy, I have emphasized the elements of exchange, agreement, and reciprocity that mark the professional relationship. This leaves us with the question as to whether the element of the gratuitous should be suppressed altogether in professional ethics. Does the physician merely respond to the social investment in his training, the fees paid for his services, and the terms of an agreement drawn up between himself and his patients, or does some element of the gratuitous remain?

To put this question another way: Is covenant simply another name for a contract in which two parties calculate their own best interests and agree upon some joint project in which both derive roughly equivalent benefits for goods contributed by each? If so, this essay would appear to move in the direction of those who would interpret the doctor-patient relationship as a legal agreement and who want, on the whole, to see medical ethics draw closer to medical law.

The notion of the physician as contractor has certain obvious attractions. First, it represents a deliberate break with more authoritarian models (such as priest or parent) for interpreting the role. At the heart of a contract is informed consent rather than blind trust; a contractual understanding of the therapeutic relationship encourages full respect for the dignity of the patient, who has not, because of illness, forfeited his sovereignity as a human being. The notion of a contract includes an exchange of information on the basis of which an agreement is reached and a subsequent exchange of goods (money for services); it also allows for a specification of rights, duties, conditions, and qualifications limiting the agreement. The net effect is to establish some symmetry and mutuality in the relationship between the doctor and patient.

Second, a contract provides for the legal enforcement of its terms—on both parties—and thus offers both parties some protection and recourse under the law for making the other accountable for the agreement.

Finally, a contract does not rely on the pose of philanthropy, the condescension of charity. It presupposes that people are primarily governed by self-interest. When two people enter into a contract, they do so because each sees it to his own advantage. This is true not only of private contracts but also of that primordial social contract in and through which the state came into being. So argued the theorists of the eighteenth century. The state was not established by some heroic act of sacrifice on the part of the gods or men. Rather men entered into the social contract because each found it to his individual advantage. It is better to surrender some liberty and property to the state than to suffer the evils that would beset men apart from its protection. Subsequent enthusiasts about the social instrument of contracts[1] have tended to measure human progress by the degree to which a society is based on contracts rather than status. In the ancient world, the Romans made the most striking advances in extending the areas in which contract rather than custom determined commerce between people. In the modern world, the bourgeoisie extended the instrumentality of contracts farthest into the sphere of economics; the free churches, into the arena of religion. Some educationists today have extended the device into the classroom (as students are encouraged to contract units of work for levels of grade); more recently some women's liberationists would extend it into marriage and still others would prefer to see it define the professional relationship. The movement, on the whole, has the intention of laicizing authority, legalizing relationships, activating self-interest, and encouraging collaboration.

In my judgment, some of these aims of the contractualists are desirable, but it would be unfortunate if professional ethics were reduced to a commercial contract. First, the notion of contract suppresses the element of gift in human relationships. Earlier I verged on denying the importance of this ingredient in professional relations, when I criticized the medical profession for its conceit of philanthropy, for its self-interpretation as the great giver. In fact, this earlier criticism was not an objection to the notion of gift but to the moral pretension of a professional whenever it pretends

---

From "Code and Covenant or Philanthropy and Contract," *Hastings Center Report* 5:6 (1975): 29–38.

to be the exclusiver giver. Factually, the professional is also the beneficiary of gifts received. It is unbecoming to adopt the pose of spontaneous generosity when the profession has received so much from the community and from patients, past and present.

But the contractualist approach to professional behavior falls into the opposite error of minimalism. It reduces everything to tit for tat. Do no more for your patients than what the contract calls for. Perform specified services for certain fees and no more. The commercial contract is a fitting instrument in the purchase of an appliance, a house, or certain services that can be specified fully in advance of delivery. The existence of a legally enforceable agreement in professional transactions may also be useful to protect the patient or client against the physician or lawyer whose services fall below a minimal standard. But it would be wrong to reduce professional obligation to the specifics of a contract alone.

Professional services in the so-called helping professions are directed to subjects whose needs are in the nature of the case rather unpredictable. The professional deals with the sickness, ills, crimes, needs, and tragedies of humankind. These needs cannot be exhaustively specified in advance for each patient or client. The professions therefore must be ready to cope with the contingent, the unexpected. Calls upon services may be required that exceed those anticipated in a contract or for which compensation may be available in a given case. These services moreover are more likely to be effective in achieving the desired therapeutic result if they are delivered in the context of a fiduciary relationship that the patient or client can really trust.

Contract and covenant, materially considered, seem like first cousins; they both include an exchange and an agreement between parties. But, in spirit, contract and covenant are quite different. Contracts are external; covenants are internal to the parties involved. Contracts are signed to be expediently discharged. Covenants have a gratuitous, growing edge to them that spring from ontological change and are directed to the upbuilding of relationships.

There is a donative element in the upbuilding of covenant—whether it is the covenant of marriage, friendship, or professional relationship. Tit for tat characterizes a commercial transaction, but it does not exhaustively define the vitality of that relationship in which one must serve and draw upon the deeper reserves of another.

This donative element is important not only in the doctor's care of the patient but in other aspects of health care. In a fascinating study of *The Gift Relationship*, the late economist, Richard M. Titmuss, compares the British system of obtaining blood by donations with the American partial reliance on the commercial purchase and sale of blood, without the exploitation of the indigent, which the American system has condoned and which our courts have encouraged when they refused to exempt non-profit blood banks from the antitrust laws. By court definition, blood exchange becomes a commercial transaction in the United States. Titmuss expanded his theme from human blood to social policy by offering a sober criticism of the increased commercialism of American medicine and society at large. Recent court decisions have tended to shift more and more of what had previously been considered as services into the category of commodity transactions with negative consequences he believes for the health of health delivery systems.[2] Hans Jonas has had to reckon with the importance of voluntary sacrifice to the social order in a somewhat comparable essay on "Human Experimentation."* Others have done so on the subject of organ transplants.

The kind of minimalism that a contractualist understanding of the professional relationship encourages produces a professional too grudging, too calculating, too lacking in spontaneity, too quickly exhausted to go the second mile with his patients along the road of their distress.

Contract medicine encourages not only minimalism, it also provokes a peculiar kind of maximalism, the name for which is "defensive medicine." Especially under the pressure of malpractice suits, doctors are tempted to order too many examinations and procedures for self-protection. Paradoxically, contractualism simultaneously tempts the doctor to do too little and too much for the patient—too little in that one extends oneself only to the limits of what is specified in the contract, yet, at the same time, too much in that one orders procedures useful in protecting oneself as the contractor even though not fully indicated by the condition of the patient. The link between these apparently contradictory strategies of too little and too much is the emphasis in contractual decisions on self-interest.

Three concluding objections to contractualism can be stated summarily. Parties to a contract are better able to protect their self-interest to the degree that they are informed about the goods bought and sold. Insofar as contract medicine encourages increased knowledge on the part of the patient, well and good. Nevertheless the physician's knowledge

*[See Hans Jonas, "Philosophical Reflections on Experimenting with Human Subjects," *Daedalus* 98 (Spring 1969): 219–47. —ED.]

so exceeds that of his patient that the patient's knowledgeability alone is not a satisfactory constraint on the physician's behavior. One must at least, in part, depend upon some internal fiduciary checks which the professional (and his guild) accept.

Another self-regulating mechanism in the traditional contractual relationship is the consumer's freedom to shop and choose among various vendors of services. Certainly this freedom of choice needs to be expanded for the patient by an increase in the number of physicians and paramedical personnel. However, the crisis circumstances under which medical services are often needed and delivered does not always provide the consumer with the kind of leisure or calm required for discretionary judgment. Thus normal marketplace controls cannot be relied upon fully to protect the consumer in dealings with the physician.

For a final,reason, medical ethics should not be reduced to the contractual relationship alone. Normally conceived, ethics establishes certain rights and duties that transcend the particulars of a given agreement. The justice of any specific contract may then be measured by these standards. If, however, such rights and duties adhere only to the contract, then a patient might legitimately be persuaded to waive his rights. The contract would solely determine what is required and permissible. An ethical principle should not be waivable (except to give way to a higher ethical principle). Professional ethics should not be so defined as to permit a physician to persuade a patient to waive rights that transcend the particulars of their agreement.

The Donative mode seems to provide for a more satisfactory analysis than the philanthropic or the contractual, but it shares their flaws. Analysis based on Donative elements suggests that the professional fulfills his contract, lives up to his specified technical code, and then, gratuitously, throws in something extra to sweeten the pot. All of these tools of analysis allow the analyst to evade the uncomfortable and demanding ontological implications of . . . profession as transformation. . . . A profession of a mystery, in theological terms changes one from damned to saved; in professional terms, from a man who studies medicine, to a man who at all times embodies healing. . . . A professional eats to heal, drives to heal, reads to heal, comforts to heal, rebukes to heal, and rests to heal. The transformation is radical, and total. The Hippocratic Oath, under this ontological aspect, can be summaried: *aut medicus aut nihil;* from this moment, I am a healer or I am (literally) nothing. He takes his identity from that which he professes, and that which he professes, to which he is covenanted, whose code he will embody, transcends him and transcends his colleagues.

Two characteristics of covenantal ethics have been developed in the course of contrasting it with the ideal of philanthropy and the legal instrument of contracts. As opposed to the ideal of philanthropy that pretends to wholly gratuitous altruism, covenantal ethics places the service of the professional within the full context of goods, gifts, and services received; thus covenantal ethics is responsive. As opposed to the instrument of contract that presupposes agreement reached on the basis of self-interest, covenantal ethics may require one to be available to the covenant partner above and beyond the measure of self-interest; thus covenantal ethics has an element of the gratuitous in it. . . .

Covenant ethics shies back from the idealist assumption that professional action is and ought to be wholly gratuitous and from the contractualist assumption that it be carefully governed by quotidian self-interest in every exchange.

A transcendent reference may also be important in laying out not only the proper context in which human service takes place but also the specific standards by which it is measured. Earlier we noted some dangers in reducing rights and duties to the terms of a particular contract. We observed the need for a transcendent norm by which contracts are measured (and limited). By the same token, rights and duties cannot be wholly derived from the particulars of a given covenant. What limits ought to be placed on the demands of an excessively dependent patient? At what point does the keeping of one covenant do an injustice to obligations entailed in others? These are questions that warn against a covenantal ethics that sentimentalizes any and all involvements, without reference to a transcendent by which they are both justified and measured.

FURTHER REFLECTIONS ON COVENANT

So far we have discussed those features of a covenant that affect the doctor's conduct toward his patient. The concept of convenant has further consequences for the patient's understanding of his role as patient, for the accountability of health institutions, for the placement of institutional priorities within other national commitments, and, finally, for such collateral problems as truth telling.

Every model for the doctor-patient relationship establishes not only a certain image of the doctor, but also a specific concept of the patient. The image of the doctor as priest or parent encourages dependency in the patient. The image of the doctor as skillful technician encourages the patient to think of himself as passive host to a disease. The doctor and his technical procedures are the only serious agent in the relationship. The image of the doctor as covenanter or contractor bids the patient to become a more active participant both in the prevention and the healing of disease. He must bring a will-to-live and a will-to-health to the partnership.

Differing views of disease are involved in these differing patterns of relationship to the doctor. Disease today is usually interpreted by the layman as an extraordinary state, discrete and episodic, disjunctive from the ordinary condition of health. Illness is a special time when the doctor is in charge and the layman renounces authority over his life. This view, while psychologically understandable, ignores the buildup, during apparent periods of health, of those pathological conditions that invite the dramatic breakdown when the doctor "takes over."

The cardiovascular accident is a case in point. Horacio Fabrega[3] has urged an interpretation of disease and health that respects more fully the processive rather than the episodic character of both disease and health. This interpretation, I assume, would encourage the doctor to monitor more continuously health and disease than ordinarily occurs today, to share with the patient more fully the information so obtained, and to engage the layperson in a more active collaboration with the doctor in health maintenance.

The concept of covenant has two further advantages for defining the professional relationship not enjoyed by models such as parent, friend, or technician. First, covenant is not so restrictively personal a term as parent or friend. It reminds the professional community that it is not good enough for the individual doctor to be a good friend or parent to the patient, it is important also that whole institutions—the hospital, the clinic, the professional group—keep covenant with those who seek their assistance and sanctuary. Thus the concept permits a certain broadening of accountability beyond personal agency.

At the same time, however, the notion of the covenant also permits one to set professional responsibility for this one human good (health) within social limits. The professional covenant concerning health should be situated within a larger set of covenant obligations that both the doctor and patient have to other institutions and priorities within the society at large. The traditional models for the doctor-patient relationship (parent, friend) tend to establish an exclusivity of relationship that obscures these larger responsibilities. At a time when health needs command $120 billion out of the national budget, one must think about the place that the obligation to the limited human good of health has among a whole range of social and personal goods for which men are compacted together as a society. . . .

NOTES

1. Sir Henry Sumner Maine, *Ancient Law* (London: Oxford University Press, 1931).

2. [Richard M. Titmuss, *The Gift Relationship* (New York: Pantheon, 1970)] Titmuss does not acknowledge that physicians in the United States have helped prepare for this commercialization of medicine by their substantial fees for services (as opposed to salaried professors in the teaching field or salaried health professionals in other countries).

3. Horacio Fabrega, Jr., "Concepts of Disease: Logical Features and Social Implications," *Perspectives in Biology and Medicine,* vol. 15, no. 4, Summer 1972.

12. From Loyalty to Advocacy: A New Metaphor for Nursing*

Gerald R. Winslow

Nurses are by far the largest group of health care professionals, numbering well over one million in the United States today. They are often the professionals with whom patients have the most sustained contact. And because of the profession's perceived tradition of holism and "care more than cure," nursing is often upheld as a hopeful paradigm for the future.

From *Hastings Center Report* 14:3 (1984): 32–40.

*An earlier version of this paper was presented to the 1983 National Endowment for the Humanities Summer Seminar, "Principles and Metaphors in Biomedical Ethics," under the direction of James F. Childress. I wish to thank Professor Childress for his thoughtful comments and encouragement. I also wish to thank the other participants in the seminar. J. Brian Benestad, Albert Howard Carter, Ruth Caspar, Daniel Friedman, David M. Holley, David N. James, Shannon Jordan, Janet Dickey McDowell, Phillip J. Miller, Debra C. Rosenthal, and W. D. White. Finally, for her thorough coments and criticisms, I am indebted to Betty Wehtje Winslow, a nurse.

But the paradigm is changing. For over a decade, professional nursing has been engaged in profound revision of its ethic. The evidence is abundant: revised codes of ethics, new legal precedents, a flood of books and articles on nursing ethics, and, what may be more significant than any other attestation, a shift in the central metaphors by which nursing structures its own self-perception.

The metaphors associated with nursing are numerous. Two examples that have received considerable attention recently are the nurse as traditional-mother substitute and the nurse as professional contractor.[1] As substitute mother, the nurse cares for sick children (patients) and follows the orders of the traditional father (the physician). As professional contractor, the nurse negotiates a plan for the care of clients (patients) and consults with other contractors (other health care professionals).

Such metaphors are not mere niceties of language. Rather, they interact with the more explicit features of nursing ethics, such as stated rules and principles, in ways that tend to be either mutually supportive or productive of change. The power of metaphors is due in part to their capacity to focus attention on some aspects of reality while concealing others.[2] For example, thinking of the nurse as a parent may highlight certain functions, such as nurture, protection, and domination, while hiding the patient's responsibility for decisions about his or her own care. The metaphor has the ability to create a set of expectations and make some forms of behavior seem more "natural" than others. Thus, if both nurse and patient begin to use the metaphor of nurse as contractor and its associated forms of expression, such as "negotiations," they may come to expect actions in keeping with a "businesslike" relationship.

This article examines the developing changes in nursing ethics by considering two basic metaphors and the norms and virtues consonant with them. The first is nursing as military effort in the battle against disease, a metaphor that permeates many of the early discussions of nursing ethics. It is associated with virtues such as loyalty and norms such as obedience to those of "higher rank" and the maintenance of confidence in authority figures. The second metaphor is nursing as advocacy of patient rights, an essentially legal metaphor that has pervaded much of the literature on nursing ethics within the past decade. The metaphor of advocacy is associated with virtues such as courage and norms such as the defense of the patient against infringements of his or her rights. I did not select these two metaphors for analysis randomly, but, in part, because they have played a prominent role in the formation of ethics within nursing's own literature. More than most others, these metaphors have been espoused by the leaders of nursing, and have had obvious effects on nursing education and practice. Metaphors such as the nurse as surrogate parent, nun, domestic servant, or "handmaiden of the physician" have often been discussed. But these discussions have been almost entirely intended to reject such metaphors and not to uphold them as representative of nursing ideals. Indeed, such metaphors have been used most often to serve as foils for images considered more adequate. On the other hand, the military metaphor, with its language of loyalty and obedience, and the legal metaphor, with its language of advocacy and rights, have served as basic models of ideal nursing practice as proposed in nursing literature.

THE MILITARY METAPHOR

It would be surprising if professional nursing had *not* early adopted the metaphor of military service. Modern nursing is generally acknowledged to have begun with the work of Florence Nightingale, superintendent of nurses in British military hospitals during the Crimean War in the 1850s.[3] Upon her return to England, she continued her work with the military and was instrumental in founding the British Army Medical School. Whatever else Nightingale was, she most certainly was a practitioner and proponent of strict military discipline. And though some have criticized Nightingale's work, the idealization of the "Lady with the Lamp" continues, with rare exceptions, in professional nursing to this day. As two nurses very recently declared: "We think of ourselves as Florence Nightingale—tough, canny, powerful, autonomous, and heroic."[4]

Not only was modern nursing born in a military setting, it also emerged at a time when medicine was appropriating the military metaphor: medicine as war.[5] It has now become difficult to imagine a more pervasive metaphor in contemporary medicine (unless, perhaps, it is medicine as economic enterprise).[6] Disease is the *enemy,* which threatens to *invade* the body and overwhelm its *defenses.* Medicine *combats* disease with *batteries* of tests and *arsenals* of drugs. And young staff physicians are still called house *officers.* But what about nurses?

Perhaps even more than medicine, nursing explicitly choose the military metaphor. It was used to engender a sense of purpose and to explain the training and discipline of the nurse. In the fledgling *American Journal of Nursing,* Charlotte Perry, an early leader, described the education required to produce the "nursing character." Upon entering training, wrote Perry, the student "soon learns the military aspect of life—that it is a life of toil and discipline. . . ." Such discipline, the author asserted, is part of the "ethics of nursing," and it should be evidenced in the "look, voice, speech, walk, and touch" of the trained nurse. The nurse's "whole being bristles with the effect of the military training she has undergone and the sacrifices she has been called upon to make. A professional manner is the result."[7]

The goal of the military discipline was to produce trained nurses with many of the qualities of good soldiers. The military imagery was neither subtle nor unusual, as a passage from an early book on nursing ethics illustrates:

> [An] excellent help to self devotion is the love a nurse has for the stern strife of her constant battle with sickness. . . . "The stern joy which warriors feel, in foemen worthy of their steel," should inspirit the valiant heart of the nurse as it does the heart of the brave soldier who bears long night watches, weary marches, dangerous battles, for the love of the conflict and the keen hope of victory. The soldier in a just war is upheld by this keen joy of battle. So will the nurse be spurred on to devotion by the love of conflict with disease.[8]

The moral force of the metaphor is obvious. Nurses should be prepared for the hardships of night duty, personal danger, weary walking, and so forth. And there can be little doubt that the military metaphor supported a number of nursing behaviors. A minor example is the uniform. Early discussions of nursing ethics almost always included sections on propriety regarding dress. The uniforms of different schools had characteristic differences, reminiscent of the differences signifying various military units. And as nurses progressed up the ranks, stripes were added to their caps and insignia pins to their uniforms. The uniform was always to be worn while "on duty" but never while "off duty." And ordinary clothing was even referred to as "civilian dress."[9]

Some traits are more important to good soldiers than the proper wearing of uniforms. More central, for example, is suitable respect for those of higher rank. Such respect is evidenced both in obedience and in various symbolic gestures of deference. Commenting on nursing ethics, Perry urged her fellow nurses to have proper respect for rank:

> Carrying out the military idea, there are ranks in authority. . . . "Please" and "Thank you" are phrases which may be exchanged between those of equal rank. The military command is couched in no uncertain terms. Clear, explicit directions are given, and are received with unquestioning obedience.

Later, Perry added that there are "necessary barriers" between those of different ranks and "familiarity" should not be allowed to dismantle these barriers.[10] The ideal of military obedience was applied often to the nurse's work with physicians. Physicians were the commanding officers. In a published lecture to nurses, one physician did not hesitate to use the military metaphor in explaining why there must be discipline in the hospital "just as in the regiment, [where] we have the captains, the lieutenants, and the sergeants. . . . Obedience to one's superiors is an essential duty of all." The author acknowledged that some of the rules are bound to "appear captious and unfair." Nevertheless, they must be obeyed. And such obedience should be not in a spirit of fear but rather in a spirit of "loyalty."[11]

Loyalty was one of the key virtues of the ideal nurse. In the words of the Nightingale pledge: "With loyalty will I endeavor to aid the physician in his work. . . ."[12] Nearly every early discussion of nursing ethics includes a major section on loyalty, and the link between loyalty and the military metaphor was strong. For example, the physician just quoted reminded nurses of their obligation: "As in the hospital loyalty to her superior officers is the duty of the nurse, so in private nursing she must be loyal to the medical man who is in attendance on her patient."[13] This sentiment is echoed in Charlotte Aikens's 1916 book on nursing ethics, a standard text for over twenty years:

> Loyalty to the physician is one of the duties demanded of every nurse, not solely because the physician is her superior officer, but chiefly because the confidence of the patient in his physician is one of the important elements in the management of his illness, and nothing should be said or done that would weaken his faith or create doubts as to the character or ability or methods of the physician. . . .[14]

What, then, did it mean for the "trained nurse" to be loyal? It meant, to be sure, faithful and self-sacrificial care of patients. But most of the discussions of loyalty were occupied more with another concern: the protection of confidence in the health care effort. Loyalty meant refusal to criticize the nurse's hospital or training school, fellow nurses, and most importantly, the physician under whom the nurse worked.

Ideally, all these loyalties should harmonize. And nurses were often reminded that being loyal to the physician by preserving the patient's confidence was the same as being loyal to the patient. As one doctor put it: "Loyalty to the physician means faithfulness to the patient, even if the treatment is not always in line with what [the nurse] has been taught in the training school. . . . Loyalty to the physician and faithfulness to the patient do not form a twofold proposition, but a single one."[15] The reasoning was supposed to be obvious: The patient's recovery could be aided powerfully by trust in the doctor and the prescribed regimen. Worry over the doctor's competence was likely to worsen the patient's condition not only because of the wasted energy but also because of the lost power of suggestion and the patient's failure to comply with the treatment. The author of a text on nursing ethics summed up the idea:

> Confidence and skepticism are both contagious, and we know very well how important it often is for a patient's cure that he should have the attitude of faith and confidence in his physician. . . . [It] is unkind indeed to destroy a confidence which is so beneficient and comforting.[16]

The moral power of this reasoning should not be overlooked. Nurses accepted as their solemn obligation assisting in the patient's recovery. And nurses were taught repeatedly that the "*faith* that people have in a physician is as much a healing element as is any medicinal treatment."[17] Thus, even if the physician blundered, the patient's confidence should usually be maintained at all costs. To quote an early nursing text:

> If a mistake has been made in treating a patient, the patient is not the person who should know it if it can be kept from him, because the anxiety and lack of confidence that he would naturally feel might be injurious to him and retard his recovery.[18]

But what if the nurse finally concluded that the confidence in the physician simply was not merited? It is one of the myths of a later generation that nurses of the past never questioned loyalty to the physician. In speeches, journals, and books, leading nurses complained that loyalty to the physician often was not deserved and even more often was not returned in kind.[19] And the difficult moral dilemmas faced by nurses were usually discussed in terms of conflicts of loyalties. For example, in an earlier editorial titled "Where Does Loyalty End?" the author claimed that many letters from nurses asked essentially the same questions: "Where does the nurse's loyalty to the doctor end? And is she required to be untruthful or to practice deceit in order to uphold the reputation of the physician at her own expense or that of the patient?"[20]

The published letters revealed the kinds of cases troubling nurses. One told how a physician inserted a catheter too far into the patient's bladder—a mistake that, according to the nurse, required surgery to correct. The nurse reported that she was blamed in order to protect the doctor's reputation. Another nurse told how a physician failed to remove a surgical sponge, causing the patient great suffering and neardeath. When the problem became apparent, the nurse was unable to keep the truth from the family. Later, the doctor chastised the nurse for failure to conceal the truth. The writer claimed that "nurses are taught that they must stand by the doctor whether he is right or wrong." But, she concluded, if this means lying to the patient in order "to defend the doctor then I don't care for the profession. . . ."[21]

Such letters (and many similar discussions in early nursing literature) indicate that conflicts of loyalties tended to focus on two main issues: truth telling and physicians' competency. Obviously, these two were often linked. Nurses felt obliged to protect doctors even if the care seemed deficient and the truth suffered. But in many cases the truth was concealed because physicians did not want their patients to know their diagnoses. In her text on ethics, Aikens complained: "From the beginning of her career [the nurse] is impressed with the idea that . . . it is an unpardonable sin to lie to a doctor about a patient but perfectly pardonable, and frequently very desirable, to lie to a patient about his own condition."[22] So, although lying was often roundly condemned, clearly it was often the "order" of the day. Dissonance was the inevitable result. Nurses were pleased, as Lena Dietz put it, to "enjoy a confidence such as is placed in no other women in the world. . . . The fact that they are nurses is accepted as an unquestionable guarantee of honesty."[23] But, at times, loyalty to the "superior officers" left the guarantee more than a little tattered.

In all likelihood loyal protection of the physician often was motivated, in no small measure, by the nurse's desire for self-protection. In the early years of nursing, the goal of most graduate nurses was to leave the hospital and become "private duty nurses."[24] The names of those available for this work were obtained from the local "registry" (kept variously by hospitals, nurses' associations, or medical associations) or simply by word of mouth. Technically, such nurses were hired directly by the patient. But in reality the attending physician was highly influential in the selection of the private nurse and, if need be, in the nurse's dismissal. Understandably, this arrangement led at times to conflicting interests and loyalties. One doctor grumbled: "Paid by the patient, or someone close to him, and not by the physician, [the nurse] sometimes seems to think that it is safest to 'stand in' with the patient, and actually obey him, rather than the physician."[25] The patient paid the wages of the nurse, but the doctor was supposed to be in charge. The financial implications of this arrangement were not lost on nurses. Aikens wrote: "Not infrequently, a nurse is torn between her desire to be loyal to the patient's interests, and not disloyal to the doctor, who has it in his power to turn calls in her direction, and influence other doctors to do the same, or the reverse."[26]

Troubled at times by conflicting loyalties and worried about employment, nurses advocated a number of strategies for coping with some doctors' apparent ineptitude. Of these strategies, four stand out.

First, the nurse could faithfully obey all orders and simply assume that the doctor knew best. Isabel Robb, in the first American book on nursing ethics, wrote: "Apart from the fact that [the nurse] may be quite wrong in her opinions, her sole duty is to obey orders, and so long as she does this, she is not to be held responsible for untoward results."[27] On this, the prevailing view, the nurse was supposed to be absolved from guilt so long as she followed orders. The doctrine of *respondeat superior* generally did offer nurses legal protection. But moral protection is not always so easily secured, hence the additional strategies.

Second, the nurse could gently question the doctor's orders. Sara Parsons suggested to her nursing colleagues that when the nurse "becomes sufficiently experienced to detect a mistake, she will, of course, call [the doctor's] attention to it by asking if her understanding of the order is correct."[28] This approach of nurses making what amounts to recommendations in the form of questions is apparently long-lived. Recent work indicates that it is still an expected part of the "doctor-nurse game."[29]

A third maneuver was consultation with some other authority figure.[30] In the hospital, the nursing supervisor was the most likely candidate. But the private duty nurse had no such recourse. This difficulty led one author to propose that the nurse call the family's "religious advisor" in a confidential attempt to engineer a change of physicians.[31]

Finally, the nurse could withdraw from the case, or refuse the physician's patients from the beginning. If the doctor was intolerably deficient, Robb counseled, the nurse could "always find some means of refusing to take charge of the nursing of his patients. . . ." Robb added, however, "Once having put herself under [the doctor], let her remain loyal and carry out his orders to the letter."[32] And in his lecture to nurses, a physician put the same point bluntly: "Better to be an honest deserter than a traitor in the camp."[33]

Better than deserter or traitor, however, was the nurse as loyal soldier. Then the world changed. Or at least the metaphors did.

THE LEGAL METAPHOR

It would be foolish to set a date to the changing of nursing's self-image. The process has been gradual, the way tortuous. As was noted earlier, nurses' criticism of the "one-sided loyalty" expected of them dates back nearly to the beginning of the profession. And by 1932, Annie Warburton Goodrich, an acknowledged leader, could speak of nursing's "militarism, that splendid drilling in subordination of self to the machine" as a feature that the profession was attempting to "modify, if not abolish."[34]

Even if the abolition has come slowly, some major events can be identified. For example, a significant blow to nursing's ethic of military loyalty occurred in an unlikely place in 1929. In Manila, a newly graduated nurse, Lorenza Somera, was found guilty of manslaughter, sentenced to a year in prison, and fined one thousand pesos because she followed a physician's order. The physician had mistakenly called for the preparation of cocaine injections (he meant procaine) for a tonsillectomy patient. Witnesses agreed that the physician ordered the cocaine, that Somera verified that order, and that the physician administered the injections. But the physician was acquitted and Somera found guilty because she failed to *question* the orders. The Supreme Court upheld the lower court's decision.[35]

Nurses around the world (and especially in the United States, because the Philippine Islands were under U.S. jurisdiction) were at first stunned and then incensed. A successful protest campaign was organized, and Somera was pardoned before serving a day of her sentence. But the whole affair left an enduring impression on nurses. The doctrine of *respondeat superior* turned out to be thin security. Never again could nurses be taught simply to follow doctors' orders. Even now, over fifty years later, nursing texts still refer to *Somera* as proof of nurses' independent accountability.[36]

But, despite *Somera* and later similar cases, the tradition of loyalty to the physician retained considerable power. This strength was illustrated by the first codes of nursing ethics. Nurses had been calling for a code of ethics before the turn of the century. But not until 1926 was the first "suggested code" for nurses proposed. By present standards this proposed code must be judged remarkably enlightened. It speaks of broad principles and, with regard to nurses' relationship to physicians, it says that "neither profession can secure complete results without the other." When the proposed code discusses loyalty, it says that "loyalty to the motive which inspires nursing should make the nurse fearless to bring to light any serious violation of the ideals herein expressed." Perhaps not surprisingly, the code failed to gain acceptance.[37] The next attempt came in 1940. This proposal was much more similar to what later became the accepted tenets.[38] Obligations to the physicians were central. For example, the code adopted by the American Nurses' Association (ANA) called for nurses to verify and carry out the physician's orders, sustain confidence in the physician, and report incompetency or unethical conduct "only to the proper authority."[39] A similar code, approved by the International Council of Nurses in 1953, spelled out the nurse's obligation to follow the physician's orders "loyally" and to maintain confidence in the physician.[40]

In the 1960s and 1970s the image of the loyal nurse began to be significantly revised. The forces for change in health care delivery during the past two decades are too numerous and complex to analyze here. In his social history of medicine, Paul Starr describes the "stunning loss of confidence" sustained by medicine during the 1970s. The formerly unquestioned mandate of the "sovereign profession" was challenged with increased frequency. Consumerism was strengthening. And the ever-higher costs of medical care along with the perceived arrogance of many in the medical profession irritated large numbers of consumers. Moreover, medicine was viewed increasingly as a large, impersonal institution, a privileged and protected castle constantly resisting needed modifications. For nursing, a profession populated almost entirely by women, the growth of feminism also proved a highly important development. These forces, and many others, achieved sharp focus in the patients' rights movement which, in Starr's words, "went beyond traditional demands for more medical care and challenged the distribution of power and expertise."[41] Few in the health care system seemed more eager for the challenge to succeed than nurses. It was hardly surprising, therefore, that leaders of the patients' rights movement turned to nurses in the search for "patient advocates." For example, George Annas, an attorney and author of *The Rights of Hospital Patients,* called for nurses to accept the new role of patient advocacy.[42] It is worthy of note that Annas prefaced his appeal to nurses by explicitly attacking the military metaphor. Nurses who accepted such traditional images would be poorly equipped to be patient advocates. At times, orders would have to be challenged. But, Annas argued, properly retrained nurses had the potential to play a "key role" in patient advocacy.[43]

In rejecting the metaphor of nurse as loyal soldier, Annas offered a replacement—the nurse as courageous advocate. The image was essentially legal. As a significant part of their retraining, for example, nurses needed "some clear understanding of the law" relating to patients' rights. *"The powers of the advocate would be precisely the legal powers of the patient."* Acceptance of the advocacy role entailed a readiness to enter disputes. Patients needed assurance that their advocate was "someone who could be trusted to fight for their rights." Included in Annas's list of rights are those that became the standards of the patient's rights movement: the right to adequate information about proposed medical procedures, the right to refuse or accept any or all such procedures, the right to full information about prognosis and diagnosis, the right to leave the hospital, and so forth. To these canons, Annas added the right of the patient to around-the-clock access to a patients' rights advocate. Clearly, the assumptions were that patients' rights were often being threatened and someone was needed continually to contend for patients. Annas hoped that nurses would be among those to take up the fight. He was not to be disappointed—not, that is, if the volume of nursing literature promoting the role of nurse as patient advocate is a measure of success.

From the mid-1970s to the present, literally scores of nursing books and articles have appeared advocating advocacy.[44] It is now not at all uncommon for nurses to argue, as one recently did, that "the nurse is the ideal patient advocate!"[45] And at least two thoughtful nurse-philosophers have argued that the concept of advocacy is the most appropriate philosophical foundation for the nursing profession.[46] After all, nurses usually have the most regular contact with the patient. And more than any other health care professionals, nurses tend to be concerned with the well-being of the *whole* patient. Moreover, nurses have a long tradition of educating patients, so it is entirely natural for nurses to accept responsibility for assuring that patients are properly informed. Finally, nurses and patients should make obvious and genuine allies since both groups have often suffered the indignities of powerlessness in the modern health care system. Who, then, could function better as a patient advocate than a nurse?

So the arguments go. And, the result has been more than a flurry of words. The metaphor has had a way of "working into life." For example, one school of nursing now requires all of its advanced students to devise and carry out an "Advocacy Project."[47] A student might discover, for instance, that elderly patients in a nursing home feel a need for legal advice. The student would develop a plan for securing such advice and then attempt to put the plan into action.

During the 1970s, the concept of advocacy was also incorporated into nursing's codes of ethics. In its 1973 revision, the International Council of Nurses' code dropped all mention of loyal obedience to the physician's orders.[48] Instead, the code said that the "nurse's primary responsibility is to those people who require nursing care," and the "nurse takes appropriate action to safeguard the individual when his care is endangered by a co-worker or any other person.'' Even more striking, in some respects, are the 1976 revisions of the ANA code. The revised code requires nurses to protect ''the client'' from the ''incompetent, unethical, or illegal practice of any person.''[49] In the interpretive statements on this point, the code makes explicit use of the language of advocacy: ''In the role of client advocate, the nurse must be alert to and take appropriate action regarding any instances of incompetent, unethical, or illegal practice(s) by any member of the health care team or the health care system itself, or any action on the part of others that is prejudicial to the client's best interests.'' The revised ANA code is revealing not only because of this addition but also because of its subtractions. Gone are the rules obliging nurses to maintain confidence in physicians or obey their orders. In fact, ''physician'' does not even appear in the revised code.

Nursing's adoption of the ethic of advocacy has brought to life a whole new genre of nursing literature: the nurse-as-advocate short story. In a recent example, a nurse detailed her attempts to become an ''advocate for the clients.'' While employed as director of nursing in a county health department, she became aware of the very poor record of maternity care at one hospital. The postpartum infection rate was nearly three times higher than the national average. And the Apgar scores of many newborns were lower than should have been expected statistically. But the hospital resented having the problems called to public attention and resisted any suggested changes. For her efforts, the nurse was ostracized by the health care community. Finally, she resigned before she could be fired. In her view, the theories about advocacy were fine, but ''the problem lies in putting these theories into action.''[50] Unfortunately, this account is typical of most published nurse-as-advocate stories.[51] They usually describe a nurse's attempt to defend a patient or group of patients against mistreatment. Most often, the endeavor fails because the system overpowers the nurse. The patient suffers or dies. The nurse gets fired or resigns in outrage. The system goes on. As literature, the stories tend to have the features of tragedy (though the flaw is in the character of the system rather than the advocate).

Of such stories, none has been more widely publicized as an example of patient advocacy than the case of Jolene Tuma.[52] In March 1976, Tuma, a clinical instructor of nursing, was asked by a cancer patient about alternatives to chemotherapy. The patient was apprehensive about the therapy. She did not want to question her physician further, however, because he had already indicated his conviction that chemotherapy was the only acceptable treatment. Tuma knew that discussing options with the patient would be risky. In fact, she told the patient that such a conversation would not be ''exactly ethical.'' Nevertheless, Tuma proceeded to discuss a number of alternatives about which the patient had questions, including nutritional therapy and Laetrile. The patient then decided to continue chemotherapy. But, in spite of the efforts, she died two weeks later. One of the patient's children informed the attending physician about Tuma's discussion with the patient. The physician protested to Tuma's employing college and to the Board of Nurse Examiners of Idaho. As a result, Tuma lost her job and her nursing license. The state's nursing board concluded that Tuma had interfered unethically with the physician-patient relationship. During the conflict, Tuma wrote to a nursing journal and described her predicament:

> Does the nurse have the right to assist the patient toward full and informed consent? Litigation against nurses already shows us we have the responsibility when we do not properly inform the patient. But do we have the authority to go along with this responsibility as the patient's advocate?[53]

Tuma's case might have ended like so many other nurse-as-advocate stories except for the fact that she appealed the state board's ruling. Three years later, the Supreme Court of Idaho ruled that the nursing board had been wrong in suspending Tuma's license.[54] It is difficult, however, to assess the extent of Tuma's victory. She did not regain her teaching position, she suffered through three years of legal appeals, and it was too late to change the outcome for the patient. Certainly, the physician and at least some of the patient's family were displeased by her actions. Still, Tuma believes that her actions were justified. She feels that her personal sacrifice has been repaid not only by the assurance that the patient's rights were defended but also by the public attention directed toward the rightful role of nurses as patient advocates.[55] And a recently published poll of 12,500 nurses reveals that Tuma has strong support from her colleagues. Over 80 percent of the respondents agreed that a nurse who acted as Tuma did would be doing the ''right thing.''[56]

The response of nurses to the Tuma case is a clear indication of the profession's changing self-perception. The new metaphor of nurse as advocate has risen to power. Indeed, if the profession's literature during the past decade is taken as primary evidence, then it can be said safely that no other symbol has so captured imagination or won acceptance within nursing as that of the advocate.

ASSESSING THE ADVOCACY METAPHOR

It is generally easier to criticize the metaphors of an earlier age than to evaluate those now regnant. But further criticism of the military metaphor is hardly in order. The nurse as loyal soldier is dead. Among nurses, mourners of the metaphor's passage are either nonexistent or well hidden. Meanwhile, the metaphor of nurse as patient advocate has nearly achieved the status of a slogan. Criticism of patient advocacy in nursing literature is virtually unknown.[57]

But those who hope that the rise of advocacy is a positive sign of a maturing profession (and I am among them) should give careful attention to the ambiguities and potential criticism of the advocacy role. I mention only five:

1. *The meaning of advocacy needs clarification.* Metaphors tend to be unruly. Part of their richness is their capacity to generate new and at times surprising perspectivies. Thus, referring to nurses as advocates opens apparently boundless possibilities for new understandings. And, as might be expected, a survey of the nursing literature on advocacy soon reveals that the metaphor is invoked in a variety of ways, some of which may be incompatible. At times, advocacy is construed so broadly that it seems to mean something like "doing the best for the patient." But most supporters of advocacy have in mind more specific actions such as helping the patient to obtain needed health care, assuring the quality of health care, defending the patient's rights (such as the right of informed consent), serving as a liaison between the patient and health care professionals, and counseling the patient in order to alleviate fear.

In one of the few thorough discussions, Sally Gadow proposes a model of "existential" advocacy. In her view, the ideal is "that individuals be *assisted* by nursing to *authentically* exercise their freedom of self-determination."[58] Gadow argues for a type of advocacy that avoids paternalistic manipulation of the patient on the one hand and reduction of the nurse to a mere technician who is unwilling to recommend alternatives on the other hand. Whether most nurses would agree entirely with Gadow's interpretation, most discussions of the nurse as advocate would benefit both from Gadow's example of careful analysis and from her thesis. In my view, the central, moral significance of the advocacy metaphor lies in its power to shape actions intended to protect and enhance the personal autonomy of patients. Further clarification of this significance is essential if the metaphor is to rise above the level of a simple slogan.

2. *The states' nurse practice acts need revision.* Since 1971, states have been revising practice acts to allow for newly expanded nursing roles.[59] But changes in the laws generally have not kept pace with nursing's adoption and understanding of advocacy. And, as *Tuma* illustrates, the legal limits are often unclear. What does it mean, for example, to interfere with the physician-patient relationship? Does unacceptable interference include suggesting a second medical opinion? What about recommending a change of physicians? As a result of such uncertainties, nurses who set out to be patient advocates may find themselves needing a lawyer. One nurse recently reported just such an experience. She was present when a surgical resident botched a tracheotomy and severed the patient's carotid artery. The patient bled to death. The nurse decided that for the sake of other patients she should report the resident. But the medical director cautioned the nurse not to pursue the matter unless she hired an attorney. As the nurse put it: "Dr. X kills the patient and I need a lawyer."[60] The threat of retaliation and the loss of professional and economic security are bound to have a chilling effect on nurses' willingness to function as patient advocates.

To be effective, the calls for nurses to become patient advocates must be accompanied by political action aimed at needed revision of the states' laws. But when it comes to politics, a more apt metaphor for nursing might be that of slumbering giant. Nursing's status as the largest health care profession generally has not translated into commensurate political strength. As the profession has adopted the ethic of advocacy, however, nurses have begun to pay more attention to the need for political action.[61] We should hope that the effect of such action will be to make patient advocacy a less dangerous activity.

3. *Patients (or their families) are often unprepared to accept the nurse as advocate.* In at least one important respect, nurses are unlike many other professionals whom the patient might engage for services. The patient is usually free to accept or reject the efforts of, say, a physician or an attorney. But in most instances the patient is not involved in the selection of his or her nurse. Thus, the nurse who functions as a patient advocate usually does so for one who has not chosen the nurse's services and who does not *expect* the nurse to serve as an advocate.

There is abundant evidence that society generally accepts a more traditional role for nurses. On this subject, nursing literature is peppered with analyses, laments, and calls for change.[62] But old metaphors die hard. And it is a frustrating fact that vestigial images of the nurse as loyal soldier, substitute parent, assistant physician, or even handmaiden will probably remain in the minds of the public long after most nurses have rejected them. For patient advocacy to be fully successful, further attention must be given to the mechanisms for appropriate public education.

4. *Advocacy is frequently associated with controversy.* It would be a rare advocacy story that did not include a measure of discord. The patient who needs an advocate is often being mistreated by someone's action or inaction. The nurse accepts the responsibility of contending for the rights of the patient, work that may involve conflict.

Some people may thrive on controversy. Many do not. Nursing educators who share the ethic of advocacy must ask how well the nursing curriculum prepares nurses to cope with the potential conflicts. They should also ask how an ethic that makes advocacy central avoids the risk of being *unduly* contentious.

5. *As advocate, the nurse is bound to be torn, at times, by conflicting interests and loyalties.* Metaphors can conceal as well as reveal facets of reality. The advocacy metaphor may hide the depths of potential conflicts by leaving the impression that only loyalty to the patient counts. But as Susan Thollaug, a nurse interested in patient advocacy, put it: "We can easily underestimate the difficulty of being a patient advocate, forgetting how divided our loyalties tend to be."[63] Patients come and go; the nurse's employing institution and professional colleagues tend to remain. To admit this is not merely to say that nurses may be tempted, along with other mortals, to place self-interest ahead of professional or moral obligations. The issue is more complicated morally. Most of us would acknowledge loyalty to associates as a virtue. An unwillingness to expose a colleague's shortcomings to public view and a desire to preserve confidence in one's institution are among the characteristic features of loyalty. Deeming such loyalty a vice would be a mistake likely to produce detrimental results for both the health care providers and their patients. The obvious difficulty is deciding when the role of advocacy must take precedence over the legitimate concerns of loyalty. Borderline cases, which bring us to the edges of our ability to reason morally, are inevitable. But no ethic of advocacy could be called adequate without a place for the virtue of loyalty.

These five concerns illustrate the impediments that must be overcome if nursing's new ethic of advocacy is to be most effective. But my discussion of these difficulties is in no way intended to suggest that nursing's adoption of advocacy is meaningless, undesirable, or impossible. I believe that nursing's change of images is a hopeful sign for a developing profession. Of course, no metaphor can convey fully the complexities of the profession's moral virtues and obligations. But the season for the nurse as advocate has arrived. Nursing is still a relatively new profession, and one that has often experienced the indignities of powerlessness. The language of advocacy provides a new way to express a growing sense of professional responsibility and power. Once an ethic of "good soldiers," with loyal obedience at its core, made sense to nurses. But nursing has been moving away from a heteronomous morality of constraint and toward a more autonomous morality of cooperation. An ethic of advocacy, with a concern for rights and the virtue of courage at its center, is an important development in this process of change.

NOTES

1. See, for example, Sheri Smith, "Three Models of the Nurse-Patient Relationship," in *Nursing: Images and Ideals,* Stuart F. Spicker and Sally Gadow, eds. (New York: Springer Publishing Company, 1980), pp. 176–88.

2. I am thinking of the work of George Lakoff and Mark Johnson, "Conceptual Metaphor in Everyday Language," *Journal of Philosophy* 78 (August 1980), 453–86. See also the same authors' book, *Metaphors We Live By* (Chicago: University of Chicago Press, 1980).

3. Richard H. Shryock, *The History of Nursing* (Philadelphia: W. B. Saunders Company, 1959), pp. 273–84. For an interesting and recent discussion of Nightingale's work see Irene Palmer, "From Whence We Came," in *The Nursing Profession: A Time to Speak Out,* Norma L. Chaska, ed. (New York: McGraw-Hill Book Company, 1983), pp. 1–28.

4. Claire Fagin and Donna Diers, "Nursing as Metaphor," *New England Journal of Medicine* 309 (July 14, 1983), 117.

5. Susan Sontag, *Illness as Metaphor* (New York: Farrar, Straus and Giroux, 1978). Sontag suggests that medicine adopted the military metaphor in the late nineteenth century about the time germ theory was accepted. My thoughts on medicine's use of the military metaphor have also been influenced by an unpublished paper by Virginia Warren, "Medicine as War," and by James F. Childress' *Who Should Decide? Paternalism in Health Care* (New York: Oxford University Press, 1982), p. 7.

6. Rashi Fein has recently complained that medicine is now being corrupted by "the language of the marketplace." "What Is Wrong with the Language of Medicine?" *New England Journal of Medicine* 306 (April 8, 1982), 863–64.

7. Charlotte M. Perry, "Nursing Ethics and Etiquette," *American Journal of Nursing* 6 (April 1906), 450–51.

8. Edward Francis Garsche, *Ethics and the Art of Conduct for Nurses* (Philadelphia: W. B. Saunders, 1929), p. 189.

9. Isabel Hampton Robb, *Nursing Ethics: For Hospital and Private Use* (Cleveland: E. C. Koeckert Publishing, 1900), p. 118.

10. Perry, "Nursing Ethics," p. 452.

11. T. Percy [and] C. Kirkpatrick, *Nursing Ethics* (Dublin: Dublin University Press, 1917). p. 24.

12. The Nightingale Pledge was first used by Farrand Training School, Harper Hospital, Detroit in 1893. For the text of the pledge, see Anne J. Davis and Mila A. Aroskar, *Ethical Dilemmas and Nursing Practice* (New York: Appleton-Century-Crofts, 1978), pp. 12–13.

13. [Percy and] Kirkpatrick, *Nursing Ethics,* p. 35.

14. Charlotte Albina Aikens, *Studies in Ethics for Nurses* (Philadelphia: W. B. Saunders Company, 1916), p. 44.

15. Thomas E. Satterthwaite, "Private Nurses and Nursing: With Recommendations for Their Betterment," *New York Medical Journal* 91 (January 15, 1910), 109.

16. Garesche, *Ethics and Conduct for Nurses,* p. 234.

17. Lena Dixon Dietz, *Professional Problems of Nurses,* 3rd, ed. rev. (Philadelphia: F. A. Davis Company, 1939), p. 165.

18. Sara E. Parsons, *Nursing Problems and Obligations* (Boston: Whitcomb and Barrows, 1916), p. 32. Parsons later allows for informing the patient about a mistake, after the patient has recovered sufficiently.

19. See for example Aikens, *Ethics for Nurses,* p. 297. See also S. H. Cabiniss, "Ethics," *American Journal of Nursing* 3 (August 1903), 875–79. Cabiniss wrote: "What of the ingratitude . . . of physicians who accept all courtesy and loyalty and give none in return?" p. 878.

20. "Where Does Loyalty End?" (editorial) *American Journal of Nursing* 10 (January 1910), 230–31.

21. "Where Does Loyalty to the Physician End?" (letters) *American Journal of Nursing* 10 (January 1910), 274, 276.

22. Aikens, *Ethics for Nurses,* p. 192.

23. Dietz, *Professional Problems,* p. 162.

24. Susan Reverby, "Re-forming the Hospital Nurse: The Management of American Nursing," in *The Sociology of Health and Illness: Critical Perspectives,* Peter Conrad and Rochelle Kern, eds. (New York: St. Martin's Press, 1981), pp. 220–33. See also Jo Ann Ashley, *Hospitals, Paternalism, and the Role of the Nurse* (New York: Teachers College Press, 1976).

25. Satterthwaite, "Private Nurses," p. 109.

26. Aikens, *Ethics for Nurses,* p. 297.

27. Robb, *Nursing Ethics,* p. 250.

28. Parsons, *Nursing Problems,* p. 58.

29. L. I. Stein, "The Doctor-Nurse Game," *Archives of General Psychiatry* 16 (1967), 699–703. See also Sandra Weiss and Naomi Remen, "Self-Limiting Patterns of Nursing Behavior Within a Tripartite Context Involving Consumers and Physicians," *Western Journal of Nursing Research* 5 (Winter 1983), 77–89.

30. Dietz, *Professional Problems,* p. 163.

31. Garesche, *Ethics and Conduct for Nurses,* p. 233.

32. Robb, *Nursing Ethics,* p. 251.

33. [Percy and] Kirkpatrick, *Nursing Ethics,* p. 24.

34. Annie Warburton Goodrich, *The Social Significance of Nursing* (New York: Macmillan, 1932), p. 167.

35. *Somera Case,* G. R. 31693 (Philippine Islands, 1929).

36. See, for example, Janine Fiesta, *The Law and Liability: A Guide for Nurses* (New York: John Wiley and Sons, 1983), p. 181.

37. For the entire text see "A Suggested Code," *American Journal of Nursing* 26 (August 1926), 599–601.

38. See "A Tentative Code," *American Journal of Nursing* 40 (September 1940), 977–80.

39. "A Code for Nurses," *American Journal of Nursing* 50 (April 1950), 196.

40. "International Code of Nursing Ethics," *American Journal of Nursing* 53 (September 1953), 1070. [See appendix 1, sample code 4, *EIPL.*—ED.]

41. Paul Starr, *The Social Transformation of American Medicine* (New York: Basic Books, 1982), pp. 379, 389.

42. George J. Annas, "The Patient Rights Advocate: Can Nurses Effectively Fill the Role?" *Supervisor Nurse* 5 (July 1974), 21–25. For another, similar work see George J. Annas and Joseph Healey, "The Patient Rights Advocate," *Journal of Nursing Administration* 4:3 (May–June 1974), 25–31.

43. Annas, "Patient Rights Advocate: Can Nurses Effectively Fill the Role?" p. 23.

44. Here is but a small sample: Jane E. Chapman and Harry Chapman, *Behavior and Health Care: A Humanistic Helping Process* (St. Louis: C. V. Mosby, 1975). This was one of the first works to set forth an "advocacy model" for health care delivery. Although it was not directed specifically to nurses, it had an obvious impact on subsequent nursing literature. M. Patricia Donahue, "The Nurse: A Patient Advocate?" *Nursing Forum* 17 (1978), 143–51. Corinne Sklar, "Patient's Advocate—A New Role for the Nurse?" *Canadian Nurse* 75 (June 1979), 39–41. Mary Elizabeth Payne, "The Nurse as Patient Advocate in the Rehab Setting," *ARN* (The Official Journal of the Association of Rehabilitation Nurses) 4 (September–October 1979), 9–11. Mary Kohnke, "The Nurse as Advocate," *American Journal of Nursing* 80 (November 1980), 2038–40. Ruth Purtilo and Christine Cassel, "Professionalism and Advocacy," in *Ethical Dimensions in the Health Professions* (Philadelphia: W. B. Saunders, 1981). Sally H. Durel, "Advocacy: A Function of the Community Mental Health Nurse," *Virginia Nurse* 49 (Spring 1981), 33–36. Marzena Laszewski, "Patient Advocacy in Primary Nursing," *Nursing Administration Quarterly* 5 (Summer 1981), 28–30. M. Josephine Flaherty, "This Nurse *Is* a Patient Advocate," *Nursing Management* 12 (September 1981), 12–13. George Castledine, "The Nurse as the Patient's Advocate: Pros and Cons," *Nursing Mirror* 153 (November 11, 1981), 38–40. H. Terri Brower, "Advocacy: What It Is," *Journal of Gerontological Nursing* 8 (March 1982), 141–43.

45. Payne, "The Nurse as Patient Advocate," p. 9.

46. Leah L. Curtin, "The Nurse as Advocate: A Philosophical Foundation for Nursing," *ANS (Advances in Nursing Science)* 1 (April 1979), 1–10. Sally Gadow, "Existential Advocacy: Philosophical Foundation of Nursing," in *Nursing: Images and Ideals,* pp. 79–101. Both authors wish to distinguish the concept of advocacy that they present as the philosophical basis for nursing from the concept of advocacy associated with the patient rights movement. But it is clear that most of their nursing colleagues who have written on the subject of advocacy have either failed to appreciate the distinction or rejected it.

47. M. Jo Namerow, "Integrating Advocacy into the

Gerontological Nursing Major,'' *Journal of Gerontological Nursing* 8 (March 1982), 149–51.

48. International Council of Nurses, ''Code for Nurses,'' reprinted in Davis and Aroskar, *Ethical Dilemmas,* pp. 13–14.

49. American Nurses' Association, *Code for Nurses with Interpretive Statements* (Kansas City, MO: American Nurses' Association, 1976), p. 8. [See appendix 1, sample code 3, *EIPL.*—ED.]

50. Christine Spahn Smith, ''Outrageous or Outraged: A Nurse Advocate Story,'' *Nursing Outlook* 28 (October 1980), 624–25.

51. See for example Flaherty, ''This Nurse *Is* a Patient Advocate.''

52. Of the many accounts of this case, the one I find most thorough and perceptive is in Purtilo and Cassel, *Ethical Dimensions,* pp. 126–137.

53. Jolene Tuma, Letter to the Editor, *Nursing Outlook* 25 (September 1977), 846.

54. *In re Tuma.* Supreme Court of the State of Idaho. 1977 Case 12587.

55. Purtilo and Cassel report this to be Tuma's position on the basis of personal communication. See *Ethical Dimensions,* p. 136.

56. Ronni Sandroff, ''Protecting the M.D. or the Patient: Nursing's Unequivocal Answer,'' *RN* 44 (February 1981), 28–33.

57. I know of only one significant essay that is critical of nurses' adoption of the advocacy role: Natalie Abrams, ''A Contrary View of the Nurse as Patient Advocate,'' *Nursing Forum* 17 (1978), 258–67. I have drawn on the thoughts in this essay in my discussion of the difficulties associated with the nurse as advocate.

58. Gadow, ''Existential Advocacy,'' p. 85. In addition to this essay and the one by Curtin (note 46), a very helpful discussion appears in James L. Muyskens, *Moral Problems in Nursing: A Philosophical Investigation* (Totowa, NJ: Rowman and Littlefield, 1982).

59. For a helpful article on the developments in the states' nurse practice acts see Bonnie Bullough, ''The Relationship of Nurse Practice Acts to the Professionalization of Nursing,'' in *The Nursing Profession: A Time to Speak,* pp. 609–633.

60. Patricia Murphy, ''Deciding to Blow the Whistle,'' *American Journal of Nursing* 81 (September 1981), 1691.

61. Sarah Archer and Patricia Goehner, *Speaking Out: The Views of Nurse Leaders* (New York: National League for Nursing, 1981).

62. See for example Linda Hughes, ''The Public Image of the Nurse,'' *ANS (Advances in Nursing Science)* 2 (April 1980), 55–72.

63. Susan Thollaug, ''The Nurse as Patient Advocate,'' *Imprint* 37 (December 1980), 37.

13. Academic Paternalism*

Joan C. Callahan

Though the campus unrest of the sixties is long over and a disquieting quietism sometimes seems to be the distinguishing mark of contemporary American university students as a group, it is sometimes objected by students in the university that a university, college, or department policy or practice, or that a policy, practice, decision, or behavior of an administrator or faculty member is paternalistic. The kinds of policies, practices, and behaviors which students complain about as being paternalistic fall into two major classes—academic and non-academic. In the academic class are university and college distribution requirements, departmental requirements for successful completion of a major or minor, and the particular educational practices and decisions of individual faculty members (e.g., requirements in courses). In the non-academic class are policies governing dormitory life (e.g., curfews and rules concerning visitors), policies governing faculty/student relationships, and hosts of decisions made by administrators governing all areas of student life, as well as the personal interactions of administrators and faculty with individual students.

I shall limit my remarks in this paper to the question of academic paternalism. I do not pretend, then, to offer an adequate account of paternalism in the university. Nor do I pretend to offer even an adequate account of the purported problem of academic paternalism in the university. Rather, I simply want to begin to understand whether the university and its departments and faculty in general function in a way that is to be understood as paternalistic at all. I shall, then, be primarily concerned with the appropriate model of the university/student and faculty/student relationship.

I begin with the assumption that university students are no longer children, and therefore, that treating them as children in any way requires a special justification. But even this presupposes an

From *International Journal of Applied Philosophy* 3:1 (1986): 21–31.

*An earlier version of this paper was prepared for presentation to the North American Society for Social Philosphy with support from the Louisiana State University Council on Research. I am grateful to Tziporah Kasachkoff, Hugh LaFollette, and the editors of this *Journal* for suggestions which have improved the paper.

understanding of paternalistic treatment that requires some clarification. Let me begin, then, with the paradigm case of paternalism in order to see what the problem-generating features of paternalism might be.[1]

THE PARADIGM CASE

'Paternalism' is an analogical concept derived from the special relationship between parents and children.[2] As John Kleinig points out, central to the paradigm case of paternalism is the picture of a relationship where one party acts on the presumption that he knows what is best for the other party.[3] There are at least three things to notice about the paradigm case: (1) that in acting paternalistically, a parent need not interfere with his or her child's liberty—parents are benevolent providers as well as benevolent enforcers; (2) that despite this, paternalism in the paradigm case often involves the imposition of the parent's will on the child, which does involve an interference with the child's liberty; and (3) that we think of paternalistic actions or policies in the paradigm case as involving protection or promotion of the child's well-being as their rationale—that is, the policy adopted or action undertaken is chosen (a) out of concern for the child's best interest and (b) on the basis of the parent's presumption that he or she *knows best* (what is in the child's best interest).

This last sub-feature of the paradigm case of paternalism, however, points to certain policies governing adults and behaviors toward adults that commonly lead to their classification as paternalistic policies and behaviors. These are policies and behaviors not grounded in some good of the targets of the policies or behaviors, but which assume an offensive and non-benevolent superiority on the part of those who set the policy or who behave in these ways. The management of a plant, for example, which, for the sake of greater efficiency, requires that workers get the permission of the supervisors to go to the restroom, treats its workers non-benevolently, yet is said to treat them paternalistically. That is, it acts in a way which is not intended to protect or promote the interests of the workers and is degrading of adults because it treats them like children who cannot be expected to act responsibly.[4]

Given these clues from the paradigm case and from other cases which we have come to classify as cases of paternalistic treatment, I take the problem of paternalism in higher education as arising in two major ways: (1) when policies, decisions, or behaviors involve an interference with the liberty of students for their own good; and (2) when policies, decisions, or behaviors toward students involve treating students in patronizing or other ways which fail to recognize their adult status.[5] Paternalism of the first kind is morally problematic because it involves the violation of the adult's right to make self-regarding choices. There is a general presumption against such interference in a free society; and when the interference is for the sake of benefitting an adult interferee, that presumption is very strong indeed. I shall focus most of my remarks on this form of paternalism; and I shall argue that much of what appears to be and is sometimes critized as being paternalism of this kind in the academic structure of the university and its departments and in the practices of its faculty need not be so, and should not, in any general way, be understood as falling under the paternalistic model.[6]

THE INSTRUCTOR/STUDENT RELATIONSHIP

Even though the paradigm case of the paternalistic relationship is appropriately described as involving a picture where one party acts on the presumption that he or she knows what is best for the other party, all policies adopted or actions undertaken on the basis of this presumption are not appropriately described as paternalistic actions or policies. In writing a brief, an attorney acts on the presumption that he knows what is best for his client; in bending the knees of her trainee in a certain way, the suburban golf pro acts on the presumption that she knows what is best for her pupil; in showing his apprentice how to use a lathe, the skilled cabinetmaker acts on the presumption that he knows what is best for his novice. Such actions fall under models other than that of the parent/child relationship. The attorney acts as a fiduciary in behalf of his principal; the golf instructor and cabinetmaker act as masters passing on skills. Parents, of course, can and do act in these ways; but central to the relationships in our examples is the fact that the trained professional uses his or her skills to provide a service *requested* by the client or trainee.[7] What is more, though the client or trainee must trust the professional's expertise, the client or trainee always retains the right to require a justification for professional decisions, a right (and the freedom) to ignore the professional's advice, and a right to withdraw from the relationship. At the same time, the professional retains the right to terminate the relationship if the client demands that he or she act in ways below acceptable professional standards; or, in the case of training, if the pupil simply refuses to cooperate in the learning process.

These features of professional/client and master/trainee-apprentice relationships serve to differentiate them from the relationship between parent and child. To be sure, within these relationships, the professional may impose his or her will on the client for the client's own good, or may treat the client in degrading (i.e., downgrading) ways; but the relationships themselves are not appropriately characterized as essentially paternalistic ones. They are, rather, relationships of contract, where a professional expertise is presumed, and where the client or trainee is justifiably assumed to have voluntarily entered into an arrangement for the purposes of benefiting from the professional's expertise, while retaining certain rights to accountability and rights of withdrawal.

The first suggestion I want to make, then, is that the relationship between university faculty and students more closely approximates the professional/client, specifically, the professional/trainee relationship, than the parent/child relationship. In part, this is to follow Kenneth Strike, who suggests that we understand the relationship between faculty and student as falling under the master/apprentice model.[8] We do need to distinguish in general, however, between graduate and undergraduate education and between undergraduate programs which complete professional training and those which do not. The master/apprentice model is most appropriate to the graduate student/faculty relationship. Although it may be true that the relationship between faculty and exceptionally gifted undergraduates or the relationship between faculty and undergraduates in certain undergraduate professional preparation programs often most closely approximates the master/apprentice relationship, the relationship between faculty and undergraduates is, in general, more like the suburban golf pro/trainee relationship than the cabinetmaker/apprentice relationship, insofar as the preparation being given is not assumed to be training for professional work in the faculty member's field, or is not late-stage training for work in that field. With this modification to Strike's analysis, my suggestion is that students should be understood as entering the university in much the same way that a client enters into a relationship with a trained and/or experienced professional, with the attending rights to professional accountability and rights to withdrawal of any professional/client relationship. In these relationships, the professional is presumed to have an expertise which, it is assumed by the client on contract, will be used to further the relevant interests of the client, but where pursuit of the client's relevant interests is also presumed to be constrained by some norms of professional practice.

THE UNIVERSITY/STUDENT RELATIONSHIP

But it must be acknowledged immediately that the university/student relationship is far more complex than relationships between clients and attorneys, and trainess and golf pros, and apprentices and master cabinetmakers. The university is not an individual; nor is the university expected to serve some single, relatively simple interest of its students. Rather, the university is an extremely complex institution which is expected to serve a variety of interests of its students, as well as interests of others, both within and outside the university community. Chief among the university's responsibilities toward its students and the wider community is the transmission of knowledge in particular fields which, in many cases, is part of preparation for a particular profession or occupation. Contemporary philosophers of education sometimes urge that we understand the main purpose of education to be to produce autonomous individuals. Kleinig, for example, argues that "the purpose of education, as a valuable enterprise, [is] to bring people with activated and developing capacities for autonomous agency" into being.[9] Other theorists urge that in addition to preparation for the professions, the university's main purposes include the formation of educated persons fit for citizenship in a free society, and the cultivation of individuals for their own purposes.[10] Let us assume for the sake of efficiency that such goals are proper to the university. But now it can be argued that goals like developing capacities for autonomous agency, preparation for citizenship, and cultivation of the person for his or her own purposes begin to make the university/student relationship more resemble the relationship between parent and child than the professional/client relationship. Thus, if we accept this variety of obligations towards its students, the university seems to share features of the professional/client relationship in general, and in particular the master/trainee relationship and the master/apprentice relationship, as well as the parent/child relationship. But even if it is the case that the university shares some responsibilities with parents, I want to suggest that the university/student relationship is more *unlike* the parent/child relationship than it is like these others. And this is essentially because (1) the student voluntarily enters into a relationship with another agent (in this case, a corporate agent), for the presumed purpose of forwarding certain interests or pursuing certain goods which the agent (or agency) has made clear it will pursue; (2) the student and the university are both free to terminate the contract for the variety of reasons already mentioned. Thus, these features of the student/university relationship seem to place it squarely in the class of contractual arrangements.

ACADEMIC PATERNALISM AND PATERNALISTIC RATIONALES

It might be suggested, however, that the student's so-called contract with the university is itself paternalistic, since, among other things, it is a contract which gives the university a right to forward certain (presumed) interests of the student. We could decide to describe the relationship this way; but to do so would obliterate any meaningful distinction between the contract model of relationships and the paternalistic model, since the description entails that any contract which involves serving some good of the client is to be classified as a paternalistic one. This muddies the conceptual waters in a way it seems preferable to avoid if we hope to retain any distinction between relationships between adults which, by their very nature, require a special justification and those which do not. Thus, for the purposes of conceptual clarity, it seems best to distinguish contracts for service from relationships which involve imposing benefits independent of considerations of the agreement of beneficiaries.

Despite this, it is important to emphasize that within a contractual relationship, a client may be treated paternalistically, either by having his wishes ignored for his own good, or by being otherwise treated (by agents or policies) as a child. Thus, even if we characterize faculty/student and university/student relationships as contractual, they may yet be quite unlike other professional/client contractual relationships where clients are assumed to have a veto power over actions (or policies) in service of the client's interest. When we think of academic requirements within the university, it is clear that students do not have such a veto power. Let me turn, then, to academic policies which are often thought to be paternalistically grounded; but which, I shall suggest, are not in reality grounded in paternalistic rationales (i.e., are not and should not be supposed by their proponents and enforcers to be justified primarily because they are assumed to be in the best interest of students) and are not policies which otherwise treat students as children, even though students are not free to decline completing these requirements as part of their coursework or degree programs.

DEPARTMENTAL REQUIREMENTS

Consider, for example, typical departmental requirements for the successful completion of a major—for example, a philosophy major. If we were to ask philosophy faculty in standard departments why we have such requirements, the initial response is likely to be something like, "These are things any philosophy major should know." I shall return to this "argument" for requirements in a moment, because I think it is a crucial part of the most plausible justification for major requirements; but first let us consider a concrete case.

Suppose that a major comes to the philosophy faculty and says that he would prefer not to meet the distribution requirements—he wants, let us suppose, to skip logic and the histories. We can imagine that at least some faculty might initially respond with the argument that having the required background is in his best interest. That this *is* in his best interest might be the case if he hopes to go on to graduate school in preparation for teaching philosophy at the university level. But suppose that the student has no such aspirations—suppose that he is already a successful entrepreneur or is preparing for a career in medicine—he simply likes French existentialism, or American pragmatism, or eastern philosophy and wants to do all his work in that area. Is it the least bit likely in such a case that the faculty would take its justification for insisting that he complete the requirements to rest on his interests? When pressed, the argument is surely that there are certain standards to be met for the completion of a major, and that, we might say, is that, whether meeting those standards is in this young man's best interest or not. In fact, "forcing" such a student through departmental requirements for a major in philosophy may not be in his interest at all. Of course, the faculty might try to persuade him of the value of a rounded background in the discipline, or advise him to take another major; but the fact that his interests would not be best served by completing the distribution requirements in philosophy will not suffice as a justification for waiving the requirements if he wants to complete his university tenure with a degree in philosophy.

This argument from standards implicitly appeals to the somewhat vague concepts of what I shall call 'academic ideals' and 'educational ideals.' I mean for these terms to cover a wide variety of paradigms which count for universities, departments (and other academic units), and instructors as standards of perfection or excellence to be approximated in university education. By an 'academic ideal' I mean (roughly) a notion of what any educated person should know. The core commitment here is to the transferral of a certain subject matter and the development of certain skills. Understood in this way, universities, departments, and instructors may each be said to have academic ideals. For example, a university committed to the ideal of providing a liberal education will require that all students distribute their coursework in ways which help to expose them to the questions, methods, factual content, and major theories in a wide variety of disciplines. Or a philosophy department concerned with providing its students with a broad substantive and methodolgical background may require that students show competence in (say) logic and complete courses which expose them to figures in the history of philosophy, various schools in contemporary philosophy, as well as various questions in metaphysics, epistemology, ethics, and so on. Some academic ideals may emphasize formal preparation in method over content, others may emphasize content over method. Thus, one philosophy program might require more training in, for example, logic, linguistic analysis, and/or phenomenology while another requires more in, e.g., the history of philosophy. Similar things might be said about various curricula in English, some of which might require more coursework in, for example, literary criticism, while others require more in literature proper. As regards instructors, they too can be expected to have academic ideals in the sense under discussion—general views regarding what any educated person should know, more specific views regarding what should be achieved in content and method in a given field, and quite particular views regarding what content and methods should be mastered in their own courses. In addition to all such views on content and methods, academic ideals may include certain standards of achievement, that is, criteria for judging incompetence, competence, and excellence in mastery of the content to be passed on and the skills to be developed.

I understand 'educational ideal' somewhat more broadly (and also roughly) to include academic ideals as well as the more general goals of university education as those goals are sought through academic requirements, and standards for *how* what is to be transmitted is to be transmitted, as well as standards for what kinds of personal characteristics an educator should manifest. Thus, a university's educational ideal may involve goals like those mentioned earlier (e.g., the preparation of qualified professionals, the development of persons with an activated and progressing capacity for autonomous agency, the preparation of persons capable of taking an intelligent part in a free society, etc.), a commitment to the academic ideal of liberal education, as well as to certain parameters governing characteristics educators should manifest. Departments and individual faculty may share the educational ideal of the university and may add to this as part of their educational ideal an academic ideal for education within a particular field of inquiry, and certain views on how content is to be passed on and skills developed. And an instructor's educational ideal may include special commitments—for example, to improving her students' abilities to argue orally, to conducting herself and her courses in ways which approximate certain standards which she takes to manifest excellence in teaching. Thus, an instructor might be committed to a lecture/discussion format, to providing class time for student debates or sustained discussion of concrete cases, etc., as well as to approximating certain standards governing how an educator should respond to various communications from students, including questions in class, responses to answers on examinations and student efforts in papers, and so on.

Although these remarks on academic and educational ideals still leave the boundaries of these concepts somewhat blurred and overlapping at points, they should be enough to make the point of my argument clear. And that point is just that universities, departments, and individual instructors may be said to have educational ideals which serve as the grounding of their academic requirements.

To return to our maverick philosophy major and departmental requirements—the example suggests that what might have the appearance of paternalism of the interfering kind is not paternalism of any kind at all. Requirements do limit student choices. But we begin to see that the most plausible fundamental justification of such requirements lies in a justifiable commitment to an academic ideal, which is believed to be captured in academic requirements, and which must be approximated if a department is to give its stamp of approval to someone's work in the form of a degree. This, of course, is not to suggest that *any* set of departmental distribution requirements will do. But it is to suggest that the real justification for departmental requirements does not lie in a paternalistic rationale, but in the attempt to approximate an academic ideal.

What is more, I do not mean to simply put forth an empirical prediction about how faculty would, when pressed, justify departmental requirements. My claim is stronger than that, and empirical predictions are meant to serve only as a bolstering consideration. Departments have an obligation to make public the meaning of having completed a course of study within them. And I mean to suggest that this obligation, coupled with an academic ideal believed to be captured in academic requirements, is *formally* sufficient to justify departmental requirements—that is, there is no need to make a direct appeal to the interests of students for a justification of such requirements. Again, any particular set of requirements must itself be justified, and what goes into that justification will involve the history and current status of a field of inquiry. The point is just that obligations of a university department other than the best interests of students (in general or in particular) play the crucial role in establishing the general right to impose certain program requirements on all its majors; and once we see this, it should be apparent that the charge of imposing departmental requirements on students for their own good is blunted.[11]

COLLEGE AND UNIVERSITY REQUIREMENTS

If we turn to typical college and university requirements, the same argument applies. The institution has duties not only to its students, but to the wider society as well. Part of the university's duty to the wider society consists in seeing that knowledge and skills are passed on from one generation to the next, and this involves making clear that certain standards in accord with an academic ideal will be met.[12] Thus, though a student may decide that he does not want to complete college or university requirements for a regular degree, the college or university may (and will) decide that he must complete them or forego the degree, and this without making any appeal whatever to the student's best interest. The university's commitments to certain academic requirements, as well as certain standards of excellence, is, then, prior to the contract with the student, and these commitments serve as the background conditions of that contract itself.

I have already suggested that the student enters the university freely. I do not want to underestimate parental pressures and the pressures of occupational preparation in modern life. But insofar as there are reasonable alternatives to entering the university in general, and any given university in particular, the assumption that the student enters the university voluntarily is justified (in the ordinary case).[13] When the student enters the university, she enters a system where, essentially, the agreement is that if she successfully fulfills the academic requirements, she will leave certified by the system as, minimally, having successfully completed a specified academic program.

Once in the system, there should be nothing to prevent the student's working for changes, including changes in the academic terms of the contract. For its part, the system (at all levels) needs to take well-considered requests for such changes seriously. This is merely a requirement of reasonableness, which binds any relationship between persons, and social systems generally. But if a system refuses to change the terms of a contract (e.g., by refusing to drop distribution requirements), it does not follow that it has acted outside of its just domain. It may refuse for good or bad reasons; but any complaint about refusal to change the academic terms must be based either on the claim that the initial terms were themselves unjust, or that the reasons for refusal to change the terms are themselves unreasonable.[14] It is not enough that one party to the academic contract (or even a majority of parties to the contract) want the terms changed—as an *academic* institution, the university is not and should not be a democratic community. If it were, the university could not fulfill its obligations to the wider society. If the original terms of the academic contract are fair and public, then the university does not act unjustly or paternalistically or otherwise immorally *simply* because it refuses to release students from established requirements.

IN-COURSE REQUIREMENTS

The same sorts of things can be said about the justification of teaching policies of individual faculty members. A faculty member need not act paternalistically in setting out requirements for a course. Though it may be true that Professor Writebedder assigns two papers instead of one in his lower level philosophy courses because he thinks this will be most helpful to the students both as regards writing and grades, his deepest justification for such a practice need not stop here. Indeed its stopping here would be more strange than one might at first think; for why should *this* instructor be requiring anything at all of *these* persons for their own good? Imagine that we question Professor Writebedder on his paper policy, asking if the policy is firm—that is, if no exceptions will be made for either those students who do not care about improving their writing and/or grades or for those who write excellent first papers. How might he answer? If he says the policy is firm, and we ask for a justification, what might he say? As regards students who do not care about improving their writing and/or grades, he might appeal to some educational ideal which he is convinced his position as a professional educator binds him to aspire to; and this, he might argue, includes requiring certain exercises of students, whether or not they care about the gains to be made from those exercises. As regards students who have done well in a first exercise, he might say quite the same thing—that a large part of his idea of what it means to be a good educator is to arrange a course so that *he* has done all he might to have his students leave the course taking all that might be taken from it.

But, again, the question arises as to why *this* instructor is involved with *these* students in pursuing *his* educational ideal. Were we to ask Professor Writebedder why he believes he is justified in imposing his academic ideals on these people, the most plausible reply is that *these* students, by coming into his course, are to be understood as having contracted him to do his best to educate them. They might, of course, attempt to persuade him to alter his ideal. But the point is that the most plausible deep justification of what might seem to be paternalistic course requirements and teaching methodologies is again tied to contract and professional standards which form part of the background assumptions of contract in the professional/client relationship.

The instructor who provides his students with the best education he finds it feasible to provide because it is to be understood as part of the background that this is what he has been hired to do does not, then, act in a way best captured by the paternalistic model. Rather, he acts as an employed professional; and if he is asked to lower his standards he acts within his moral right to refuse, just as a doctor who refuses to prescribe laetrile for the treatment of malignancy acts within her moral rights in so refusing. This is *not* to suggest that any such refusal will itself be justified, or that any educational ideal is as desirable as any other. Nor is it to deny more generally that well-meaning professionals can ever violate a client's rights by adhering to some wrongheaded professional ideal. But it is to hold that a faculty member who sets firm course policies has a general entitlement to do so—that the setting of such policies is within his or her proper sphere of authority, in just the same way that setting public policy is within the proper sphere of government authority—and that setting such policies is not plausibly understood as being in need of justification because it involves interference with the self-regarding choices of adults for their own good, or because it otherwise necessarily treats adults as children. A government may set a bad or unjust public policy; but when it does, the problem is not with public policy setting itself, but with the injustice or undesirability or harmfulness of a particular policy. And it is quite the same with universities and their faculties.

CONCLUSION

I have suggested that the most plausible moral underpinning for academic requirements in the university is not a paternalistic one insofar as paternalism is understood to involve the imposition of will on another for that other's own good or an offensive superiority which treats adults like children. Like the golf trainee or the cabinetmaker's apprentice, the student who comes to the university is expected to be relatively inexperienced in the fields she undertakes to study. And the university is expected to provide her with instructors who do indeed know better than she does what is good for her as regards her learning in those fields. This arrangement, I have argued, is not to be understood as a paternalistic one.

But this is a highly general point, which does no more than clear the way for addressing more concrete questions. Not the least among these is the question of deciding when the pursuit of an educational ideal might become an unjustifiable imposition of an educator's values on students. There is no such thing as value-free educating, just as there is no such thing as a value-free practice of medicine. And in both cases, the hard questions involve deciding precisely what values and where a practitioner's values appropriately enter into the professional/client relationship. Sometimes, it might seem that worries like this are not as troublesome in higher education as they might be in a practice like medicine, since students can more easily drop a course and pick up another than patients can drop a physician and pick up another; and, particularly, since what will be expected of the student is easily learned in advance of entering the university and (if faculty members are, as they should be, concerned with informed consent) since what will be required in a given course will be clearly explained to students before they commit themselves to that course. But taking this question as it arises in education as less worrisome than when it arises in other areas of professional practice is mistaken and morally dangerous. Indeed, it may well be the case that the imposition of values in the educator's pursuit of some educational ideal is far more worrisome than (say) the physician's refusal to prescribe laetrile. And this is because the educator's values might be more deeply hidden, and thus, the imposition of will may be less recognizable. This, then, is just one of the many issues that need to be dealt with in detail in a full discussion of academic paternalism.

I have not discussed non-academic policies and decisions governing student life, or the worrisome (benevolent and non-benevolent) attitudes toward students which sometimes motivate policies and individual behaviors on the parts of administrators and faculty in the university. But it should go without saying that policies and behaviors which treat students in degrading ways will not bear moral scrutiny. The university has a right to maintain order in its community, and faculty have a right to maintain order in their courses. But policies, practices, or behaviors which fail to accord students the respect due to generally competent adults in the wider society have no more place in the university than they have elsewhere. Student life is not and should not be life with father (or mother).

It is life in the free society, life among citizens; and the university must be a place where citizenship, with its attendant responsibilities and rights, is carefully practiced. Part of what this means in a free society is that matters pertaining to student life must be decided democratically within the bounds of the academic responsibilities of the university. In the past decade new democratic policies governing student life have emerged in many universities (e.g., those governing dormitory life). These are steps in the right direction. But student publications are still unduly influenced by administrators; and deans of students are still often too eager to be surrogate parents; and too many faculty still fail to realize that though many are young, university students are to be treated as adults and shown the same general respect for freedom of choice and freedom to dissent due any adults.

Adopting the contract model does not, then, do any more than establish the most general parameters for thinking about the relationship between the university and its personnel and students. The next, and most difficult, questions pertain to carefully specifying acceptable academic and non-academic terms of that contract.

NOTES

1. Although there are obvious reasons for preferring 'parentalism' (and its cognates) to 'paternalism' (and its cognates), I shall use the standard terminology, partly because linguistic behavior dies hard, and partly because the technical notion of 'paternalism' has come to include degrading treatment not associated with being a good parent. (See the next section in the text.)

2. See N. Fotion, "Paternalism," *Ethics* 89:2 (1979): 191–98, for an interesting comparison between the paradigm case of paternalism and so-called paternalistic public policies.

3. John Kleinig, *Paternalism* (Totowa, NJ: Rowman and Allenheld, 1984), p. 4.

4. The example comes from Joel Feinberg, *The Moral Limits of the Criminal Law, Volume 3: Harm to Self* (New York: Oxford University Press, 1986). The governance of student life, which involves so much in the way of concern about order in the university, constantly involves the challenge to avoid paternalism of this sort.

5. It is common in the contemporary philosophical literature to characterize paternalism as the interference with an individual for his own good. See, e.g., Gerald Dworkin, "Paternalism," in R. A. Wasserstrom (ed.), *Morality and the Law* (Belmont, CA: Wadsworth, 1971): 107–26; Jeffrie G. Murphy, "Incompetence and Paternalism." *Archiv für Rechts-und Socialphilosophie* 60:4 (1974): 465–85; Rosemary Carter, "Justifying Paternalism," *Canadian Journal of Philosophy* 7:1 (1977): 133–45; Dennis Thompson, "Paternalism in Medicine, Law, and Public Policy," in Daniel Callahan and Sissela Bok (eds.), *Ethics Teaching in Higher Education* (New York: Plenum Press, 1980): 245–75; John D. Hodson, "The Principle of Paternalism," *American Philosophical Quarterly* 14:1 (1977): 61–69; C. L. Ten, "Paternalism and Morality," *Ratio* 13 (1971): 55–66; David A. J. Richards, *The Moral Criticism of Law* (Encino, CA: Dickenson, 1977): chap. 5; and Bernard Gert and Charles Culver, "Paternalistic Behavior," *Philosophy and Public Affairs* 6:1 (1976): 45–57, among others. Although I believe there are significant problems with this as a general characterization of paternalistic behavior or policy (see my "Liberty, Beneficence, and Involuntary Confinement," *Journal of Medicine and Philosophy* 9:3 [1984]: 261–93), I shall accept it as a working characterization of the kind of paternalism I focus on in this paper.

6. In searching for the appropriate model of the university/student and faculty/student relationship, I want to find a description which is both empirically plausible (i.e., one which does not make false empirical assumptions about the parties involved) and morally attractive (i.e., one which takes rights and interests seriously). On this, see, e.g., Michael D. Bayles, *Professional Ethics* (Belmont, CA: Wadsworth, 1981): chap. 4. [Excerpted in chap. 4, sel. 14, *EIPL*.—ED.]

7. There are some cases, of course, where a professional/client relationship exists, but the client has not requested the professional's services—e.g., cases of involuntary psychiatric hospitalization and treatment. But in looking for a general model, one should not look to unusual cases, since these cases lack features of the normal case or have additional features. Again, see, e.g., Bayles, *supra*.

8. Kenneth Strike, *Liberty and Learning*, (New York: St. Martin's Press, 1982).

9. John Kleinig, *Philosophical Issues in Education* (New York: St. Martin's Press, 1982), p. 146.

10. See, e.g., Robert S. Morison, "Some Aspects of Policy-Making in the American University," *Daedalus* (Summer 1970): *Rights and Responsibilities: The University's Dilemma:* 609–44.

11. I do not mean to ignore the fact that departments sometimes put in requirements for self-serving reasons. The moral status of some reasons for adding requirements, however, is unclear. For example, a department might add to its requirements in order to justify hiring a specialist in some area, and a hefty part of the motivation might be to elevate the department's status in the eyes of the profession. Such an addition may or may not serve the genuine educational interests of that department's students. Though assessing academic ideals is beyond the scope of this paper, it should go without saying that any such additions which do not clearly serve an academic ideal conscientiously accepted by a department will not be justified.

12. Much of this assumes that we are discussing the typical university. But there is, of course, room in society for a variety of educational institutions with a variety of educational ideals. The traditional university functions according to the expert/trainee model—the experts are presumed to know their arts and presumed to have the capacity to make competent judgments about content and method in their areas of expertise; students are expected to be educated up to some level within those areas. But this need not be the only model of higher education. Some institutions elect to adopt a more Rogerian model,

where the exclusive aim of education is the development or revelation of natural capacities, and where it is held that the pressing of students through a preconceived process, designed by so-called experts is repressive and a genuine enemy of development. (See, e.g., A. S. Neill's *Summerhill* [New York: Hart Publishing Company, 1960] for an example of this view of the aims of education.) Traditional ways of educating can surely be (and certainly sometimes have been) repressive. But it is not necessary that education which guides and offers content be viciously restrictive, repressive, or otherwise growth inhibiting. See Strike, *supra,* for a thoughtful discussion of this point and the liberating function of traditional education.

13. I deal with the question of standards for presuming voluntariness in "Paternalism and Voluntariness," *Canadian Journal of Philosophy* 16:2 (1986): 199–220.

14. Unreasonable refusals to make a change might include refusals to alter methodologies or course offerings when such changes are needed to enhance understanding or keep a department current with widely accepted disciplinary standards.

14. The Professional–Client Relationship

Michael D. Bayles

. . . Many analyses have been offered of the professional–client relationship. Some analyses are empirical; they describe the relationship as it normally exists. That is not the purpose of this section. Rather, the purpose here is to develop an ethical model that should govern the professional–client relationship. However, ethical models and norms often assume certain facts. For example, an ethical model of the appropriate relationship between parent and child makes certain assumptions about a child's abilities. A model of full equality would not work for very young children simply because they lack the physical and mental abilities to engage in such a relationship. Thus, although an ethical model of the professional–client relationship is not simply to describe it, a model can be inappropriate because it makes false empirical assumptions about one or the other parties.

The impulse of philosophy is to generalize. The present aim is to develop general statements of obligation that can require different conduct depending on the situation. The obligations to keep promises and make reparations for past injustice remain constant although the required conduct varies with the situation. There is no a priori reason why general obligations of professionals to clients cannot be established even though their application to particular cases requires different conduct in different situations. This does not imply ethical relativism.

To develop an ethical model that has the broadest scope, the model should not be based on unusual situations, such as a defendant charged with a capital crime or an unconscious patient. Unusual situations are so simply because they lack features of the usual or have additional features. An analysis based on unusual situations is therefore likely to distort normal situations. Professional ethics should be based on the usual sort of contact average clients have with professionals. Individual citizens are most likely to see lawyers in connection with real estate transactions, divorces, making wills, and personal injury negligence cases. Lawyers also spend much time drafting commercial contracts and advising about business matters. The average client will probably have a physician's attendance during a fatal illness or injury, but most physician–patient contacts are for more mundane matters such as a bacterial infection or a broken bone. Only gross neglect by the patient or physician—for example, the failure of a patient to take any medicine at all or of a physician to ask whether the patient is allergic to penicillin before prescribing it—is apt to turn these matters into seriously life-threatening illnesses or injuries. Engineers are apt to be consulted by companies or governments that want a project designed. Similarly, certified public accounts are most often hired to audit the books of a corporation. Both accountants and architects also deal with individuals for such purposes as income tax preparation and designing houses.

The central issue in the professional–client relationship is the allocation of responsibility and authority in decision making—who makes what decisions. The ethical models are in effect models of different distributions of authority and responsibility in decision making. One may view the professional–client relationship as one in which the client has most authority and responsibility in decision making, the professional being his employee; one in which the professional and client are equals, either dealing at arm's length or at a more personal level; or as one in which the profes-

---

From *Professional Ethics* (Belmont, CA: Wadsworth Publishing Co., 1981), pp. 60–70.

sional, in different degrees, has the primary role. Each of these conceptions has been suggested by some authors as the appropriate ethical model of the relationship. Each has some commonsense support.

AGENCY

According to this view, the client has most of the authority and responsibility for decisions; the professional is an expert acting at the direction of the client.[1] The client hires a professional to protect or act for some interest; the professional provides services to achieve the client's goal—purchase of a house, removal of a gallbladder, design of a building. According to this conception, not only does the professional act for or in behalf of the client, but also acts under the direction of the client as in bureaucratic employer–employee relationships. This conception is especially plausible for lawyers. In filing a complaint or arguing for a client, a lawyer acts for and in behalf of the client. According to some people, a lawyer is merely a "mouthpiece" or "hired gun." It is not a plausible view of accountants performing public audits, for they are supposed to provide an independent review and statement of the clients' financial conditions.

In some contexts, professionals are prone to adopt the agency view of the professional–client relationship. Professionals are sometimes "identified" with their clients and charged with the client's alleged moral failings. Lawyers offer the defense that in representing clients, they do not thereby ascribe to or support clients' goals or aims.[2] They are merely employees hired to perform a specific task. If the projects are bad or immoral, the fault lies with the clients, or perhaps with the legal system for permitting them.

The agency model most clearly exemplifies what has been called the "ideology of advocacy." This ideology has two principles of conduct: (1) that the lawyer is neutral or detached from the client's purposes, and (2) that the lawyer is an aggressive partisan of the client working to advance the client's ends.[3] This ideology is readily applicable to physicians, architects, and engineers. A physician, for example, should not evaluate the moral worth of patients but only work to advance their health. The second element of the ideology does not apply to accountants performing audits, for they are to present independent statements of clients' financial conditions. It applies in other accounting activities though. For example, an accountant preparing a client's income tax statement should try to take every plausible deduction on behalf of the client.

Some aspects of this ideology appear inescapable in professional ethics. If professionals accepted only clients whose purposes they approved of and did not consider clients' interests any more than those of others, many persons with unusual purposes (such as wanting an architectural style of a building that is completely inconsistent with those nearby) might be unable to obtain professional services. And even if they did, the services might not be worth much, as no special consideration would be paid to their interests.[4] The chief problem with the ideology of advocacy, where it does become an ideology, is that sometimes devotion to a client's interests is thought to justify any lawful action advancing the client's ends, no matter how detrimental the effect on others.

The agency view of the professional–client relationship is unduly narrow. A number of considerations indicate limits to a professional's proper devotion to a client's interests, and consequently to a client's authority in decision making.

1. . . . Professionals have obligations to third persons that limit the extent to which they may act in behalf of client interests.
2. The agency view arises most often in the context of defending professionals, especially lawyers, from attribution of client sins. This focus is too narrow to sustain a general account of the professional–client relationship. It best pertains to an adversarial context in which two opposing parties confront one another. In counseling, a lawyer's advice "need not be confined to purely legal considerations. . . . It is often desirable for a lawyer to point out those factors which may lead to a decision that is morally just as well as legally permissible."[5]
3. Professionals emphasize their independence of judgment. Unlike a soldier who is not expected to think for himself but to do things the army's way, professionals should exercise their training and skills to make objective judgments. The agency view ignores this feature.
4. Except in cases of dire need—medical emergencies, persons charged with crimes—professionals may accept or reject specific clients. With a few restrictions, they may also stop the relationship. Consequently, the agency view is too strong. Professionals must also be ethically free and responsible persons. For their own freedom and the protection of others, they should not abdicate authority and responsibility in decision making.

The strongest possible claim of supremacy has been suggested, namely, that, like the common law doctrine of the merging of the identity of the husband and wife, the attorney and client are similarly merged in the identity of the client.[6] The proposal was made in the context of attempts by the Internal Revenue Service to obtain possibly incriminating documents from a client's attorney. By the Fifth Amendment to the U.S. Constitution, clients need not surrender possibly incriminating documents in their own possession, The IRS contends this Fifth Amendment privilege does not extend to lawyers, just as it does not extend to tax accountants. If the identities of client and attorney are merged, then the rights and privileges of a client would apply to the attorney.

Although this "legal fiction" could be useful in this narrow context, strong reasons are against adopting it. Fictions should be avoided in law and ethics if straightforward arguments lead to similar results. Once admitted, fictions can bewitch the understanding and lead to unjustifiable results in other areas. The analogy with the common law doctrine of the identity of husband and wife is quite weak. Except for dowry and a few other matters, the identities of husband and wife were completely merged for legal purposes. In contrast, the merger of attorney and client identities would be very limited. As the considerations against the agency view indicate, good grounds exist for separating the attorney and client in many contexts. Even with respect to incriminating materials, professionals should be permitted or even required to reveal confidences indicating a client's intention to commit a crime.[7]

CONTRACT

If a client ought not to be viewed as having most authority and responsibility, then perhaps the authority and responsibility should be shared equally. In law, a professional–client relationship is based on a contract, and the ethical concept of a just contract is of an agreement freely arrived at by bargaining between equals. If the relationship is a contractual one, then there are mutual obligations and rights, "a true sharing of ethical authority and responsibility."[8] As it recognizes the freedom of two equals to determine the conditions of their relationship, the contract model accords well with the liberal values of freedom and equality of opportunity.

However, no gain results from treating as equals people who are not relevantly equal in fact or from assuming a nonexistent freedom. The history of contracts of adhesion (the standard forms offered by monopolies or near monopolies such as airlines) indicates the injustice that can result from falsely assuming contracting parties have equal bargaining power. Many commentators have noted relevant inequalities between professionals and clients, especially in the medical context.[9] First, a professional's knowledge far exceeds that of a client. A professional has the special knowledge produced by long training, knowledge a client could not have without comparable training. Second, a client is concerned about some basic value—personal health, legal status, or financial status—whereas a professional is not as concerned about the subject matter of their relationship. The client usually has more at stake. Third, a professional often has a freedom to enter the relationship that a client lacks. A professional is often able to obtain other clients more easily than a client can obtain another professional. Especially if a potential client has an acute illness or has just been charged with a crime, he or she is not free to shop around for another professional. From this point of view, the bargaining situation is more like that between an individual and a public utility.

These considerations are not as important for the usual situation in architecture, accounting, and engineering. The clients of these professionals are often better informed about the subject matter of the transaction than are clients of lawyers and physicians. For example, businesses and corporations have accountants working for them who can give advice about auditors. Often firms hiring consulting engineers have had previous experience working with engineers in that field. Governments, even local ones, frequently have one or two engineers working for them who can advise and help. Moreover, they are freer than the professional to conclude an arrangement with another firm. Thus, in these situations the factual basis for the contract model is most nearly present. However, the consulting engineer or architect has some special knowledge and ability the client lacks, or else a professional would probably not be hired, so the contract model's empirical assumptions do not quite hold even in these cases.

FRIENDSHIP

Instead of viewing the relationship as one between two free and equal persons dealing at arm's length, some authors suggest that the relationship is more personal. One does not relate to a professional as one does to a grocer or public utility. The personal element is most closely captured by viewing the relationship as one of pals or friends. According to this view, professional and client have a close relationship of mutual trust and cooperation; they are involved in a mutual venture, a partnership.

Perhaps the most sophisticated version of this conception is that proposed by Charles Fried.[10] He is primarily concerned with the legal and medical professions. Fried seeks to justify professionals devoting special attention and care to clients and sometimes seeking ends and using means that they would not seek or use for themselves. Friends are permitted, even expected, to take each others' interests seriously and to give them more weight than they do those of other persons. Fried suggests that the attorney–client relationship is analogous to a one-way limited friendship in which the lawyer helps the client secure legal rights. The lawyer helps the client assert his autonomy or freedom within the bounds society permits. Others have suggested that the physician–patient relationship should similarly be viewed as a cooperative effort of friends or pals to deal with the patient's illness or injury.

The many dissimilarities between friendship and the professional–client relationship, however, destroy the analogy. First, as Fried recognizes, the professional–client relationship is chiefly in one direction; the professional has a concern for the client's interests but not vice versa. Second, friendship is usually between equals. Even in friendships between employer and employee, the employer's superiority in the office is changed to a position of equality in the bar for a drink. As the above discussion of the contract model indicates, professionals and clients are not equals. Third, the affective commitment of friendship is usually lacking.[11] Professionals accept clients for a fee, not out of concern for individuals. Thus, one commentator concludes that "Fried has described the classical notion, not of friendship, but of prostitution."[12] As the factual assumptions of this model are incorrect and the analogy supporting it is weak, its ethical implications are unfounded.

The friendship analogy is not needed to justify a professional paying special attention to a client's interests. The role of a professional is to provide services to clients, and the acceptance of a client is sufficient to justify the special attention. A barber who accepts a customer pays special attention to a customer's hair over that of others who need a haircut more. One need not postulate the barber as friend to justify this attention. It is presupposed by any system of services for a fee.

PATERNALISM

Once one abandons models that assume the professional and client are equal and accepts that the professional is to some extent in a superior position to the client, one faces the problem of the proper extent of professional authority and responsibility in decision making. Parents have knowledge and experience that children lack, and it is often ethically appropriate for them to exercise their judgment on behalf of their children. Similarly, as a professional has knowledge and experience a client lacks and is hired to further the client's interests, perhaps the relationship should be viewed as one of paternalism.

Paternalism is a difficult concept to analyze. A person's conduct is paternalistic to the extent his or her reasons are to do something to or in behalf of another person for that person's well-being. What is done can be any of a number of things, from removing an appendix to preventing the person from taking drugs. One can also have a paternalistic reason for acting in behalf of a person—for example, filing a counterclaim or asserting a legal defense. The key element of paternalism derives from the agent, *X*, acting regardless of the person's, *Y*'s, completely voluntary and informed consent. *X*'s reason is that he or she judges the action to be for *Y*'s well-being regardless of *Y*'s consent to it. *Y* may be incapable of consent, as when a physician treats an unconscious patient in an emergency, or *Y* may never have been asked, or may have refused to consent to the act.

Conduct can be paternalistic even when *Y* in fact consents.[13] For example, if *X* is prepared to do something to *Y* regardless of *Y*'s consent, then *X*'s reason is paternalistic even if *Y* does consent. Parents frequently manipulate a child into assenting to actions, although they were prepared to do them without the child's assent. The key element is that *X* would have done the action, if he could, even if *Y* had not consented. Such claims are difficult to establish, but this difficulty is a practical problem and does not affect the conceptual matter. In manufacturing consent, information can be withheld, false information provided, or more emphasis placed on some facts than others. Professionals sometimes manufacture consent when action cannot legally be taken without client consent, such as accepting a settlement or performing an operation.

The concept of doing something to or in behalf of someone includes failure to do something. Suppose *Y* requests *X* to do something for him, but *X* refuses because she thinks it would be detrimental to *Y*'s well-being; for example, a physician refuses to prescribe a tranquilizer for a patient. This also counts as doing something to or in behalf of a person without his consent; *Y* does not consent to the tranquilizers being withheld.

A voluminous literature exists concerning the justification of paternalism. The brief discussion here will outline only the major arguments. Paternalism requires justification because it involves doing something to or in behalf of another person regardless of that person's consent. It thus denies people the freedom to make choices affecting their lives. They lack the freedom of self-determination. . . . The loss of control over their own lives, especially to professionals, is one reason for people's concern about professional ethics. Thus, paternalism is of central importance in professional ethics.

Three arguments are often offered to justify paternalism.

1. The agent has superior knowledge as to what is in a person's best interest. Because the agent knows better than the person what is best, the agent is justified in acting to avoid significant harm to, or to procure a significant benefit for, the person. This argument is perhaps the central one in favor of paternalism by professionals. As noted before, a professional possesses a relevant knowledge the client lacks, so he or she is better able to perceive the advantages and disadvantages of alternative actions. Consequently, the professional rather than the client should have primary authority and responsibility for decisions.
2. The client is incapable of giving a fully free and informed consent. By "fully free" is meant without duress, psychological compulsion, or other emotional or psychological disturbance. By "informed" is meant with appreciation of the consequences of a course of conduct and its alternatives. If people cannot give such consent, then their decisions will not adequately reflect their reasonable desires and will not be expressions of their "true selves." This argument, which in some respects is a subcase of the previous one, is also popular in the professions, especially medicine. It is often claimed that people who are ill have a strong feeling of dependency, are worried by their illness, and are in a weakened state, and so lack their usual mental command. A somewhat similar argument can be made about lawyers' clients. If charged with a criminal offense, a person is fearful and disturbed. Even in civil suits, a client's emotions might be aroused, preventing an objective view of the situation.
3. A person will later come to agree that the decision was correct. Although the person does not now consent, he will later. For example, an unconscious accident victim with a broken limb will agree that a physician was correct to set the bone. Parents often require their children to do things, such as take music lessons, on the ground that later the children will be glad they did—"You'll thank me later!" An engineer might see a way to improve an agreed-upon rough design to better serve a client's needs, although it involves a significant alteration from the rough design. She might make the change in the belief that the client will agree when he sees the completed design.

To decide whether these justifications support viewing the professional–client relationship as paternalistic, it is useful to consider when reasonable people would allow others to make decisions for them. First, a person might not wish to bother making decisions because the differences involved are trivial. For example, an executive authorizes a secretary to order any needed office supplies, because the differences between brands of paper clips and so forth are not important. Second, the decisions might require knowledge or expertise a person does not possess. For example, an automobile mechanic knows whether a car's oil filter needs changing. One goes to a mechanic for knowledge and service. Third, a person might allow others to make judgments if he or she is or will be mentally incompetent. Some people voluntarily enter mental hospitals.

The first of these reasons does not directly relate to the arguments for paternalism, but the second and third do relate to the first two arguments for paternalism. Reasonable persons would allow others to make decisions for them when they lack the capacity to make reasonable judgments. However, most clients do not have sufficiently impaired judgment to reasonably allow others to make important decisions for them. This incapacity argument has little or no plausibility for the common clients of architects, engineers, and accountants. Business and corporate clients of lawyers are unlikely to have significantly impaired judgment, even if they are biased. Moreover, even with individuals, the view is not plausible for the common legal and medical cases. A person who wants to purchase a house or make a will, or who has the flu or an infection, is rarely so distraught as to be unable to make reasonable decisions. Consequently, the argument from incapacity does not support adopting a paternalistic conception of the professional–client relationship for most cases, although it supports using that conception in special cases.

The first argument for paternalism, that from superior knowledge, fits with reasonable persons allowing others to make decisions when they lack knowledge.

Moreover, clients go to professionals for their superior knowledge and skills; such knowledge and skill is a defining feature of a profession. However, many decisions require balancing legal or health concerns against other client interests. As many authors have noted, crucial professional decisions involve value choices.[14] They are not simple choices of technical means to ends, and even choices of means have a value component. Professionals have not had training in value choices. Even if they had, they might not know a client's value scheme sufficiently to determine what is best for him when everything is considered. An attorney might advise a client that he or she need not agree to such large alimony or child support payments, but the client might decide that for personal relations with the former spouse or the welfare of the children, the larger payments are best. Similarly, a physician can advise bed rest, but because of business interests a client can decide her overall interests are best promoted by continuing to work on certain matters. The client might especially need the income or be on the verge of completing a business deal that will earn a promotion. Physicians sometimes fail to realize that a patient's other concerns, even a vacation trip with the family, can precede health. They write and speak of the problem of patient noncompliance just as parents speak of noncompliance by children. Yet, one does not have everything when one has health. Similarly, a client might want an engineering or architectural design to use one type of construction rather than another because its subsidiary supplies such materials.

Although a professional and client are not equals, sufficient client competence exists to undermine the paternalistic model as appropriate for their usual relationship. Clients can exercise judgment over many aspects of professional services. If they lack information to make decisions, professionals can provide it. Sometimes professionals argue that clients can never have the information they have. This is true, but not directly to the point. Much of the information professionals have is irrelevant to decisions that significantly affect client values. The precise name of a disease and its manner of action are not relevant to deciding between two alternative drug therapies, but the fact that one drug reduces alertness is. Similarly, clients of engineers do not need to know the full weight a structure will bear, only that it is more than sufficient for all anticipated stress. To deny clients authority and responsibility by adopting the paternalistic model is to deny them the freedom to direct their own lives. Clients are not capable of determining the precise nature of their problem, or of knowing the alternative courses of action and predicting their consequences or carrying them out on their own. They need and want the technical expertise of a professional to do so. However, they are capable of making reasonable choices among options on the basis of their total values. They need professionals' information in order to make wise choices to accomplish their purposes.

Finally, when the professional–client relationship is conducted on the paternalistic model, client outcomes are not as good as when the client has a more active role. Douglas E. Rosenthal studied settlement awards in personal injury cases.[15] The actual awards received were compared to an expert panel's judgments of the worth of the claims. The less the client participated in the case by not expressing wants or seeking information from the lawyers, and so on, the more the awards fell short of the panel's estimates of the worth of claims. Not only does the paternalistic model sacrifice client freedom and autonomy, but as a result client values and interests are also often sacrificed.

FIDUCIARY

As a general characterization of what the professional–client relationship should be, one needs a concept in which the professional's superior knowledge is recognized, but the client retains a significant authority and responsibility in decision making. The law uses such a conception to characterize most professional–client relationships, namely, that of a fiduciary. In a fiduciary relationship, both parties are responsible and their judgments given consideration. Because one party is in a more advantageous position, he or she has special obligations to the other. The weaker party depends upon the stronger in ways in which the other does not and so must *trust* the stronger party.

In the fiduciary model, a client has more authority and responsibility in decision making than in the paternalistic model. A client's consent and judgment are required and he participates in the decision-making process, but the client depends on the professional for much of the information upon which he gives or withholds his consent. The term *consents* (the client consents) rather than *decides* (the client decides) indicates that it is the professional's role to propose courses of action. It is not the conception of two people contributing equally to the formulation of plans, whether or not dealing at arm's length. Rather, the professional supplies the ideas and information and the client agrees or not. For the process to work, the client must trust the professional to accurately analyze the problem, canvass the feasible alternatives, know as well as one can their likely consequences, fully convey this information to the client, perhaps make a recommendation, and work honestly and loyally for the client to effectuate the chosen alternatives. In short, the client must rely on the professional to use his or her knowledge and ability in the client's interests. Because the client cannot check most of the work of the professional or the information supplied, the professional has special obligations to the client to ensure that the trust and reliance are justified.

This is not to suggest that the professional simply presents an overall recommendation for a client's acceptance or rejection. Rather, a client's interests can be affected by various aspects of a professional's work, so the client should be consulted at various times. The extent of appropriate client participation and decision making can be determined by advertence to the reasons for allowing others to make decisions for one. Professionals do not have expertise in a client's values or in making value choices. Their superior knowledge and expertise do not qualify them to make value choices significantly affecting a client's life plans or style. However, they do have knowledge of technical matters. A patient will certainly let a physician determine the dosage of medicines. A client can reasonably allow an engineer to determine the general specifications of materials for a job. A lawyer may decide whether to stipulate facts, object to testimony, or agree to a postponement.[16] Clients allow professionals to make these judgments, because the effects on their values are small and they do not wish to be bothered. In short, client consent and involvement are not necessary when (1) the matter is chiefly a technical one or (2) the value effect is not significant.

The appropriate ethical conception of the professional–client relationship is one that allows clients as much freedom to determine how their life is affected as is reasonably warranted on the basis of their ability to make decisions. In most dealings of business and corporate clients with accountants, architects, engineers, and lawyers, the relationship is close to a contract between equals. As clients have less knowledge about the subject matter for which the professional is engaged, the special obligations of the professional in the fiduciary model become more significant. The professional must assume more responsibility for formulating plans, presenting their advantages and disadvantages, and making recommendations. Because of the increased reliance on the professional, he or she must take special care to be worthy of client trust. Thus, although the fiduciary model is appropriate throughout the range of competent clients and services, the less a client's knowledge and capacity to understand, the greater the professional's responsibilities to the client.

Finally, some clients are not competent to make decisions. In this case, the paternalistic model becomes appropriate. These cases of an incompetent client will almost always be restricted to members of the legal and health professions. Even then it does not follow that the professional should make the decisions. If a client is incompetent, a legal guardian should be appointed to make decisions. When this is done, the professional has a fiduciary relationship to the guardian. Consequently, the appropriate occasions for professionals to adopt a paternalistic role are restricted to those in which a client is incompetent and a guardian has not yet been appointed. . . .

NOTES

1. See Robert M. Veatch, "Models for Ethical Medicine in a Revolutionary Age." *Hastings Center Report* 2:3 (June 1972): 5–7, p. 5. Veatch calls this the engineering model of the physician, but this assumes it is appropriate for engineers. [See chap. 4, sel. 10, *EIPL*.—ED.]

2. See American Bar Association (ABA) Commission on Evaluation of Professional Standards, *Model Rules of Professional Conduct: Proposed Final Draft* (Chicago: American Bar Association, 30 May 1981), 1.2(b). [For the final draft, see appendix 1, sample code 1, *EIPL*.—ED.]

3. See William A. Simon, "The Ideology of Advocacy: Procedural Justice in Professional Ethics," 1978 *Wisconsin Law Review:* 29–144, p. 36.

4. Simon's [op. cit.] proposed alternative to the ideology of advocacy suffers these defects to some extent. He does not allow for professional roles. Thus, all professional obligations are at best specifications of ordinary norms. "The foundation principle of non-professional advocacy is that problems of advocacy be treated as a matter of *personal* ethics. . . . Personal ethics apply to people merely by virtue of the fact that they are human individuals. The obligations involved may depend on particular circumstances or personalities, but they do not follow from social role or station." Ibid., p. 131.

5. ABA, *Code of Professional Responsibility and Code of Judicial Conduct* (Chicago: ABA, 1979), EC [Ethical Consideration] 7–8; see also ABA Commission, *Proposed Model Rules,* op. cit., 2.1 and comment.

6. Roger M. Grace, "Invading the Privacy of the Attorney-Client Relationship." *Case and Comment* 81 (July-August 1976): 46–49, p. 47.

7. ABA, *Code of Professional Responsibility,* DR [Disciplinary Rule] 4-101(C)(3); ABA Commission, *Proposed Model Rules* 1.6(b).

8. Veatch, op. cit., p. 7.

9. See, for example, Roger D. Masters, "Is Contract an Adequate Basis for Medical Ethics?" *Hastings Center Report* 5:6 (December 1975): 24–28, p. 5; William F. May, "Code, Covenant, Contract, or Philanthropy?" *Hastings Center Report* 5:6 (December 1975): 29–38, p. 35 [see chap. 4, sel. 11, *EIPL*—ED.]; H. Tristram Englehardt, Jr. "Rights and Responsibilities of Patients and Physicians," in *Medical Treatment of the Dying: Moral Issues,* ed. Michael D. Bayles and Dallas M. High (Cambridge, MA: G. K. Hall and Schenkman, 1978), pp. 16–17; Richard Wasserstrom, "Lawyers as Professionals: Some Moral Issues," in *1977 Conference on Teaching Moral Responsibility: Pre-Conference Materials,* ed. Stuart C. Goldberg (Detroit: University of Detroit Law School, 1977), pp. 122–22 [rpt. chap. 4, sel. 6, *EIPL*—ED.].

10. Charles Fried, "The Lawyer as Friend: The Moral Foundations of the Lawyer-Client Relation," in Goldberg, op. cit., pp. 129–58; and Fried, *Right and Wrong* (Cambridge, MA: Harvard University Press, 1978) chap. 7; see also Veatch, op. cit., p. 7.

11. Edward A. Dauer and Arthur Allen Leff, "The Lawyer as Friend," in Goldberg, op. cit., p. 164.

12. Simon, op. cit., p. 108.

13. Cf. Joseph S. Ellin, "Comments on 'Paternalism in Health Care,' " in *Contemporary Issues in Biomedical Ethics*, ed. John W. Davis, Barry Hoffmaster, and Sarah Shorten (Clifton, NJ: Humana Press, 1978), pp. 245–46.

14. See, for example, Glenn C. Graber, "On Paternalism and Health Care," in Davis et al., eds., op. cit., p. 239; Allen E. Buchanan, "Medical Paternalism," *Philosophy and Public Affairs* 7:4 (1978): 370–90, p. 381; and Alan H. Goldman, *The Moral Foundations of Professional Ethics* (Totowa, NJ: Rowman and Littlefield, 1980), pp. 179–86.

15. Douglas E. Rosenthal, *Lawyer and Client: Who's in Charge?* (New York: Russell Sage Foundation, 1974), chap. 2.

16. See ABA, *Code of Professional Responsibility*, op. cit., EC7–7; but see ABA Commission, *Proposed Model Rules*, op. cit., 1.2(a), 1.4.

QUESTIONS FOR STUDY AND DISCUSSION

1. Using this chapter's readings as resources, compare and contrast the contract and covenant models of the physician/patient relationship. Does the covenant model substantially improve on the contract model of this relationship? Explain your answer as completely as possible.

2. Gerald Winslow supports adopting the advocacy metaphor in nursing, but he points out that nursing has a number of obstacles to overcome if nurses are to function effectively as patient advocates in the health care system. Explain as forcefully as you are able the case for nurses adopting the role of patient advocate. Explain as fully as possible the problems associated with this role for nurses (including problems relating to the power of nurses in the health care system) and what nursing as a profession would have to do to ensure the place of the nurses as effective patient advocates. Given these problems, do you believe that nurses can effectively assume the advocacy model? Explain. Do you believe that nursing should attempt to assume advocacy as its major model? Explain.

3. Joan Callahan offers a contract model of the professor/student relationship. Explain the central features of this model as described by Callahan and offer your own evaluation of accepting this model as an appropriate general model for the professor/student relationship.

4. What, in your considered judgment, is the most serious professional failing of college/university professors as regards their students? Explain precisely what model of the professional/client relationship your answer assumes. What do professors need to do to correct this problem? Can students contribute in any way to the correction? Explain.

5. Explain the central features of the five models of the professional/client relationship discussed by Michael Bayles and explain how he uses both empirical and moral considerations to evaluate these models; use examples to help your explanation.

6. Explain the concept of paternalism as articulated by Michael Bayles; be sure to emphasize in your explanation what he calls the 'key element' in paternalistic action and omission of action. Under what circumstances, according to Bayles, is it morally permissible for a professional to paternalistically substitute his or her judgment for a client's judgment? Offer your own evaluation of Bayles' view of justifiable paternalism in the professional/client relationship; be sure to say whether the paternalism Bayles will allow seems to be too little, too much, or about right.

CASE: POLICE AND PATERNALISM

James Michael was a twenty-six-year-old black male who worked in an oil refinery. One Friday night after work, James met several of his coworkers at a local bar to celebrate an across-the-board pay raise in their division. The party lasted five hours, during which James drank somewhere around a dozen mixed drinks, several of them doubles, thanks to a generous bartender. James left the bar shortly after 10:00 P.M. and proceeded to drive home. No one is certain how the accident took place; James either fell asleep, could not see properly, or lost control of his car and crashed into a telephone pole. The impact was on the passenger side of the vehicle. When the police arrived on the scene, they found James lying in a fetal position on the street next to his car. He had, apparently, managed to climb out of the car, but had not gotten very far. The police helped him to his feet. He had no visible injuries, but he was obviously intoxicated. The police asked him if he was all right, and he responded that he was—he just wanted to go home. He was arrested for driving while intoxicated and taken to the city jail. During the booking procedure, he was asked if he was under a doctor's care. He said that he was not. He was also asked if he needed medical care. He said that he did not. It was now nearly midnight, and James was placed in a cell with several other men, all of whom were sleeping. James promptly fell asleep himself. Several hours later, an officer came to see if James was sober enough to call a bail bondsman. But James was dead. An autopsy revealed that death was the result of massive internal injuries. James' family brought suit against the city's police department, charging the police with criminal negligence. The case went to trial. The jury found that the police had acted entirely appropriately and were guilty of no negligence or other wrongdoing. James' family left the court facing legal fees of seven thousand dollars.

1. Given the limited information that you have in this case, do you think that James was competent to make a judgment on his own need for medical care? Explain your answer carefully.

2. Ignoring questions of law (since one of the questions lurking in the background here is what the law *should* be), do you agree that the police acted entirely appropriately and were morally guilty of no negligence? If so, defend your answer, anticipating and responding to the most plausible objection to your view; also consider alternative actions available to the police, and say why these actions were appropriately avoided by the police.

3. If your view is that the police did not act fully appropriately and are (at least in some degree) morally blameworthy for James' death, explain what you believe should have been done and defend your answer; anticipate and respond to the most plausible moral objection to your view.

4. Offer your own comparison of the moral responsibility for James' death of the police and the bartender. In your discussion be sure to address these questions: Is the bartender any more or less blameworthy for the death than the police? In general, should bartenders be held morally and/or legally responsible for the behavior of clients who leave their establishments inebriated?

SELECTED BIBLIOGRAPHY

Abrams, Natalie. "A Contrary View of the Nurse as Patient Advocate." *Nursing Forum* 17 (1978): 258–67.

Ackerman, Terrence. "Medical Ethics and the Two Dogmas of Liberalism." *Theoretical Medicine* 5 (1984): 69–81.

Annas, George J., and Joseph M. Healey. "The Patient Rights Advocate: Redefining the Doctor-Patient Relationship in the Hospital Context." *Vanderbilt Law Review* 27 (1974): 243–69.

Aroskar, Mila, M. Josephine Flaherty, and James M. Smith. "The Nurse and Orders Not to Resuscitate." *Hastings Center Report* 7:4 (1977): 27–28.

Baca, M. Carlota, and Ronald H. Stein, eds. *Ethical Principles, Practices, and Problems in Higher Education.* Springfield, IL: Charles C. Thomas, 1983.

Bandman, Elsie L., and Bertram Bandman. *Nursing Ethics in the Lifespan.* Norwalk, CT: Appleton-Century-Crofts, 1985.

Barber, Bernard. "Compassion in Medicine: Toward New Definitions and New Institutions." *New England Journal of Medicine* 295 (1976): 939–40.

Benjamin, Martin, and Joy Curtis. *Ethics in Nursing,* chap. 3. New York: Oxford University Press, 1981; 2nd ed., 1986.

Brody, Howard. ''The Physician-Patient Contract: Legal and Ethical Aspects.'' *Journal of Legal Medicine* 4 (1976): 25–29.

Buchanan, Allan E. ''Medical Paternalism.'' *Philosophy and Public Affairs* 7:4 (1978): 371–90. Revised version in *Paternalism,* ed. Rolf Sartorius, pp. 61–81, *infra.*

Callahan, Joan C. ''Liberty, Beneficence, and Involuntary Confinement.'' *Journal of Medicine and Philosophy* 9:3 (1984): 261–93.

———. ''Paternalism and Voluntariness.'' *Canadian Journal of Philosophy* 16:2 (1986): 199–220.

Davidson, V. ''Psychiatry's Problems With No Name: Therapist-Patient Sex.'' *American Journal of Psychoanalysis* 37 (1977): 43–50.

Edwards, Rem B., ed. *Psychiatry and Ethics: Insanity, Rational Autonomy, and Mental Health Care,* chap. 3. Buffalo, NY: Prometheus, 1982.

Epstein, Richard A. ''Medical Malpractice: The Case for Contract.'' *American Bar Foundation Research Journal* 1 (1976): 87–149.

Feinberg, Joel. *The Moral Limits of the Criminal Law,* Volume 3: *Harm to Self.* New York: Oxford University Press, 1986.

Foster, H. M. ''The Conflict and Reconciliation of the Ethical Interests of Therapist and Patient.'' *Journal of Psychiatry and Law* 3 (1975): 39–48.

Freedman, Monroe H. *Lawyers' Ethics in an Adversary System,* chaps. 2–6. Indianapolis, IN: Bobbs-Merrill, 1975.

Fried, Charles. *Contract as Promise.* Cambridge, MA: Harvard University Press, 1981.

———. ''The Lawyer as Friend: The Moral Foundations of the Lawyer-Client Relation.'' *Yale Law Journal* 85 (1976): 1060–89.

———. *Right and Wrong,* chap. 7. Cambridge, MA: Harvard University Press, 1978.

Gadow, Sally, and Stuart Spicker, eds. *Nursing: Images and Ideals.* New York: Springer, 1980.

Gert, Bernard, and Charles Culver. ''The Justification of Paternalism.'' *Ethics* 89:2 (1979): 199–210.

———. ''Paternalistic Behavior.'' *Philosophy and Public Affairs* 6:1 (1976): 45–57.

Goldman, Alan H. *The Moral Foundations of Professional Ethics,* chaps. 3–4. Totowa, NJ: Rowman and Littlefield, 1980.

Greenhouse, Linda. ''In Corporate Law, Who's the Client?'' *New York Times,* 15 February 1981, sect. 4, p. 20.

Griffith, William B. ''Ethics and the Academic Professional: Some Open Problems and a New Approach.'' *Business and Professional Ethics Journal* 1:3 (1982): 75–95.

Husak, Douglas. ''Paternalism and Autonomy.'' *Philosophy and Public Affairs* 10:1 (1981): 27–46.

Jameton, Andrew L. ''The Nurse: When Roles and Rules Conflict.'' *Hastings Center Report* 7:4 (1977): 22–23.

Jasnow, A. ''The Psychotherapist—Artist and/or Scientist?'' *Psychotherapy: Theory, Research, and Practice* 15 (1978): 318–22.

Karasu, T. B. ''Psychotherapies: An Overview.'' *American Journal of Psychiatry* 134 (1977): 851–63.

Kasachkoff, Tziporah. ''Nursing Ethics and Hospital Work.'' In *Moral Rights in the Workplace,* ed. Gertrude Ezorsky, pp. 236–45. Albany: State University of New York Press, 1986.

Kleinig, John. *Paternalism.* Totowa, NJ: Rowman and Allanheld, 1984.

Lifton, Robert J. ''Advocacy and Corruption in the Healing Professions.'' *International Review of Psychoanalysis* 3 (1976): 385–98.

Mappes, E. Joy Kroeger. ''Ethical Dilemmas for Nurses: Physicians' Orders versus Patients' Rights.'' In *Biomedical Ethics,* 2nd ed., ed. Thomas A. Mappes and Jane S. Zembaty, pp. 127–34. New York: McGraw-Hill, 1986.

Marks, Joan, ed. *Advocacy in Health Care: The Power of a Silent Constituency.* Clifton, NJ: Humana, 1986.

Masters, Roger D. ''Is Contract an Adequate Basis for Medical Ethics?'' *Hastings Center Report* 5:6 (1975): 24–28.

May, William F. *The Physician's Covenant: Images of the Healer in Medical Ethics.* Philadelphia, PA: Westminster, 1983.

Mazor, Lester J. ''Power and Responsibility in the Attorney-Client Relation.'' *Stanford Law Review* 20 (1968): 1138–39.

McMahon, Thomas F. ''Models of the Relationship of the Firm to Society.'' *Business and Professional Ethics Journal* 5:3 (1986): 181–91.

Michalos, Alex C. "The Loyal Agent's Argument." In *Ethical Theory and Business,* 2nd ed., ed. Tom L. Beauchamp and Norman E. Bowie, pp. 247–54. Englewood Cliffs, NJ: Prentice-Hall, 1983.

Miller, Henry. "Value Dilemmas in Social Casework." *Social Casework* 13 (1968): 32–33.

Moore, R. A. "Ethics in the Practice of Psychiatry: Origins, Functions, Model, and Enforcement." *American Journal of Psychiatry* 135 (1978): 157–63.

Muyskens, James L. *Moral Problems in Nursing: A Philosophical Investigation,* chap. 4. Totowa, NJ: Rowman and Littlefield, 1982.

Pirsig, Maynard E., and Kenneth F. Kirwin, eds. *Professional Responsibility: Cases and Materials,* chap. 7. St. Paul, MN: West, 1976. *Supplement,* 1981.

Rich, William. "The Role of Lawyers: Beyond Advocacy." *Brigham Young University Law Review* 1980 (1980): 767–84.

Rosenthal, Douglas. *Lawyer and Client: Who's in Charge?* New York: Russell Sage Foundation, 1974.

Sartorius, Rolf. "Paternalistic Grounds for Involuntary Civil Commitment: A Utilitarian Perspective." In *Mental Illness: Law and Public Policy,* ed. Baruch A. Brody and H. Tristram Engelhardt, pp. 137–45. Dordrecht, Neth.: D. Reidel, 1980.

———, ed. *Paternalism.* Minneapolis, MN: University of Minnesota Press, 1983.

Schwartz, Murray. "The Zeal of the Civil Advocate." In *The Good Lawyer: Lawyers' Roles and Lawyers' Ethics,* ed. David Luban, pp. 150–71. Totowa, NJ: Rowman and Allanheld, 1984.

Sussman, Marvin B. "Professional Autonomy and the Revolt of the Client." *Social Problems* 71 (1969): 156–59.

Szasz, Thomas S., and H. Marc Hollender. "The Basic Models of the Doctor-Patient Relationship." *American Medical Association Archives of Internal Medicine* 97 (1956): 585–92.

VanDeVeer, Donald. "The Contractual Argument for Withholding Medical Information." *Philosophy and Public Affairs* 9:2 (1980): 198–205.

———. *Paternalistic Intervention: The Moral Bounds of Benevolence.* Princeton, NJ: Princeton University Press, 1986.

Veatch, Robert M. *A Theory of Medical Ethics,* chaps. 6–8. New York: Basic Books, 1981.

Walton, Douglas N. *Physician-Patient Decision-Making: A Study in Medical Ethics.* Westport, CT: Greenwood, 1985.

Wikler, Daniel. "Paternalism and the Mildly Retarded." *Philosophy and Public Affairs* 8:4 (1979): 377–92.

Zembaty, Jane S. "A Limited Defense of Paternalism in Medicine." In *Proceedings of the 13th Conference on Value Inquiry: The Life Sciences and Human Values,* pp. 145–58. State University of New York College at Geneseo, 1979. Rpt. in *Biomedical Ethics* 2nd ed., ed. Thomas A. Mappes and Jane S. Zembaty, pp. 60–66. New York: McGraw-Hill, 1986.

PART II

SOME RECURRING MORAL PROBLEMS

5

DECEPTION

The readings in chapter 4 began an examination of paternalistic treatment of clients that continues into the first part of this chapter and will be an implicit problem in chapters 6 and 7. In chapter 4, the papers by Joan Callahan and Michael Bayles outlined the concept of paternalistic treatment, and Bayles argued against accepting paternalism as a morally appropriate model for the professional/client relationship. Instead he suggested that the professional/client relationship should be understood as a fiduciary one in which the client must trust the professional, but also in which the client retains significant authority and responsibility for decisions within the relationship. The article by Joseph Ellin which opens the present chapter adds to the discussion in chapters 2 and 3 and also recommends a model for the professional/client relationship, thus adding to the discussion in chapter 4 as well. Like Bayles, Ellin understands his model of the professional/client relationship to be a fiduciary model. But Ellin's fiduciary model differs sharply from the one defended by Bayles in chapter 4. Indeed, Ellin's fiduciary model is significantly more like the paternalistic model Bayles rejects than it is like the fiduciary model Bayles offers.

One way of understanding the disagreement between Bayles and Ellin is to realize that Bayles' view of the professional/client relationship is fundamentally rights-based. In the language of chapter 3, Bayles rejects the view that professionals should be role differentiated. That is, according to Bayles, the ordinary moral rights of persons place moral constraints on how professionals may behave in their occupational roles. Part of what this involves is respecting the client's right to autonomy or self-direction, which generally requires that persons not be deprived by professionals of information they might need to make informed judgments about important matters in their lives. A rights-based moral framework leads Bayles to reject role differentiation in professional life and to hold, therefore, that deception in the professional/client relationship will seldom be justified.

Ellin, on the other hand, takes the professional/client relationship to be fundamentally duty-based. That is, Ellin argues that the professional is engaged by a client to pursue certain interests of that client (e.g., health in health care provision, interests in certain legal outcomes in law, interests in certain financial outcomes in various areas of business, etc.). Therefore, according to Ellin, in taking on a client, the professional undertakes an overriding duty to the client to pursue these special and clearly circumscribed interests. The professional, says Ellin, is not engaged to serve other special or general interests a client might have (e.g., the general interest in being told the truth); thus, the professional has a strong moral duty to place these interests below the interests he or she is engaged by the client to pursue. In the language of chapter 3, Ellin supports the view that professionals have a stringent moral duty to be role differentiated.

The particular focus of Ellin's article is on the question of deceiving clients for their own good, that is, on paternalistic deception of clients. Contrary to Bayles, the view taken by Ellin supports a considerable amount of such deception in the professions. In order to evaluate the competing views of Bayles and Ellin, one needs to evaluate the underlying moral frameworks and decide which seems more morally correct for determining rights and duties in the professional/clients relationship.

Focusing on medical practice, Joseph Collins also defends deception of clients for their own good. Collins' case for such deception in medical practice is two-pronged. On the one hand, he argues in a straightforwardly paternalistic way by suggesting that failing to deceive patients can be harmful to their health. This is a teleological argument (see chap. 1), since it rests on the goal of preventing harm. On the other hand, Collins implicitly appeals to the patient's right to self-direction by suggesting that patients who are seriously ill generally do not want to know the truth and should not have it imposed on them. This is a deontological argument (see chap. 1), since it appeals not to the purported consequences of truth telling, but to the implicit claim that one must respect people's rights. Notice that Ellin's duty-based justification for paternalistic deception by professionals is also deontological, since it does not simply appeal to the purported harmful consequences of being truthful but rather appeals to the implied agreement of professionals to pursue the relevant interests of their clients. That is, it is because the professional has assumed a responsibility to pursue his or her client's interest that he or she has a duty to prevent certain kinds of harm to the client.

Selection 17 by Sissela Bok offers responses to several aspects of the views found in Ellin and Collins. Is there a significant moral difference between lying and deception? Ellin holds that there is a significant moral difference between outright lying and other forms of deception. Bok, on the other hand, allows that there is a *conceptual* difference between lying and other forms of deception, but implicit in her view is the position that there is no genuine *moral* distinction between lying and intentionally deceiving without outright lies. Notice that Collins agrees with Bok that there is no significant moral distinction between lying and other forms of intentional deception.

Bok also challenges the factual assumptions made by Ellin and Collins that deception about serious illness is frequently in a patient's best interest. And she challenges Collins' claim that seriously ill people generally do not want to know the truth about their conditions.

Selection 18 by Bok focuses on political lies and deceptive practices in politics, told and undertaken for the public good. Bok examines the arguments given in favor of public deception in politics, and—congruent with what she says about lies to the sick and dying—she holds that the good assumed to be produced by deception in politics is overrated. And she suggests that the cumulative effects of even "innocent" political deceptions, seriously undermine public trust in government leadership. Bok concludes that only those deceptive practices which can be openly debated and consented to in advance are justifiable in a democracy. Her conclusion expresses a view like the one espoused by Terry Pinkard in his discussion of deception and invasions of privacy in social science research (see chap. 7).

The second part of chapter 5 raises the issue of nonpaternalistic deception, that is, deception designed to promote the interests of persons other than those deceived. The selections by Phillip Nelson and Burton Leiser focus on the question of misleading advertising. In chapter 3, Albert Carr argued that business is analogous to a poker game, thus bluffing to win is no more morally suspect in business than is bluffing in poker. In Nelson's article, we find a somewhat different argument to justify bluffing (puffery) in advertising, namely, the argument that even the most exaggerated advertising benefits consumers. Nelson's argument rests on the virtues traditionally ascribed to the free market system, and the view that the invisible hand of the free market will ultimately maximize societal good. (We shall see Milton Friedman appealing to this same claim in chap. 10.) Nelson buttresses his claim by arguing that the more stringently government attempts to keep advertising from being misleading, the more consumers are likely to be deceived by advertising. In essence, Nelson defends *caveat emptor* (let the buyer beware) as the best rule, not only for avoiding deception of consumers, but also for preventing an unjustifiable paternalism in limiting consumer choices.

The selection from Leiser directly challenges several of the assumptions made by Nelson. Leiser argues that not only is misleading advertising exploitative and unjust, it is also directly harmful to consumers who may be physically injured by harmful products or encouraged to waste their hard-earned money on ineffective ones. Contrary to Nelson, Leiser encourages more government involvement in the regulation of advertising.

Although the readings in this chapter focus on medicine, politics, and business, deception is an issue that arises with moral urgency across the professions. Deception is quite common, for example, in social science research, where it is generally held to be justified on teleological grounds, that is, on the basis of the benefits to society that result from such research. But there are several objections to be raised against deceptive social science research. Not the least among them is that such research violates the rights of persons by making them experimental subjects without obtaining an appropriately informed consent. Another is that deceptive social science research is often more harmful to subjects than researchers are generally willing to admit. A somewhat different problem is that social scientists in academia consistently train their students in deceptive research methods without giving careful consideration to the moral costs of deception. This raises a serious moral question for college and university educators. It should also be noted that the teaching of deceptive (and manipulative) techniques is not confined to social science curricula. Journalism students, for example, are often equally well trained in such techniques. And it should also be pointed out that professors' offering their students extra credit for participating as subjects in research projects raises some moral issues for academic social scientists that typically go ignored in colleges and universities.

The question of deception in professional life quite directly raises the question of informed consent (to medical care, to the goods and services we purchase as consumers, to human experimentation, etc.). In chapter 6 we shall focus on this question.

PATERNALISTIC DECEPTION

15. Special Professional Morality and the Duty of Veracity

Joseph S. Ellin

TWO THEORIES OF SPECIAL PROFESSIONAL MORALITY

Are there special rules and principles which govern professionals in their professional conduct? This question has been called (by Alan Goldman) "the most fundamental question for professional ethics."[1] But what exactly is being asked? Are we supposed to imagine the possibility of a fundamental conflict between ordinary morality and the special standards of the professions?[2] It certainly seems as if the standards of professional morality do not necessarily correspond with those of ordinary morality: lawyers, for example, are required to defend vigorously the interests of unsavory characters who by ordinary moral standards are entitled to no assistance from anyone. But the question is not whether professionals subscribe to such special standards, but whether such standards would amount to a departure, within certain limited circumstances, from ordinary moral rules. But departures from ordinary moral rules, it seems, can only be justified by reference to other, more basic, principles of morality. We must have good moral reasons for allowing such exceptions to our general principles. Where there are apparent conflicts between ordinary and special morality, these conflicts can generally be adjudicated by moral reasoning based on large moral considerations.

This view, which we may call "the priority of ordinary reflective morality," gives to ordinary morality a double function. First, ordinary reflective morality imposes the rules and standards which govern all of us in our ordinary, that is non-special, life encounters. Second, ordinary reflective morality plays an adjudicating role, resolving apparent conflicts between obligations in ordinary contexts and those in special contexts, such as those of professional life.

To hold the priority view is not, of course, to hold that in cases of apparent conflict, one's ordinary obligations always override, as if professionals could have no obligations inconsistent with those imposed on everybody by ordinary morality. There might be good moral reasons why we would want to impose special obligations on professionals in their professional life. Nor is it necessarily to hold that there can not be fundamental or irreconcilable moral conflicts which arise in the course of one's professional activities. The crux of the "priority" view is that whether there are such special obligations, and such irreconcilable conflicts, is to be determined by ordinary moral considerations. At bottom, no conflict can occur between an ordinary moral norm and a norm drawn from some special context; such conflicts that do occur are conflicts between the norms of ordinary morality itself. Suppose, for example, a professional finds a conflict between an obligation to tell the truth and an obligation to protect a client from a foolish blunder. The professional might conclude that he or she is forced simply to decide between inconsistent norms. On the priority view, such a conflict might be possible, but when it occurs, it does not arise because ordinary morality supports one norm and professional morality the other, but rather because ordinary morality supports both norms and provides no deeper principle of reconciliation.

The priority view holds that, since ordinary reflective morality is the only source of moral obligation, there is no such thing as a morality that is "internal" to special contexts such as professional life. The morality of the professions, rather, is imposed on them from above, by our usual values and common principles. Professional morality is, thus, [comprised of] a set of rules which is, in a sense, purely external to the professions. [These rules] do not grow out of any conception of professional life. The obligations of professionals must be assessed and determined strictly in accordance with our usual moral standards.

The priority view, then, gives us our first theory of special professional morality. According to it, there may well be special rules which govern professionals, and which impose duties inconsistent with the duties imposed on everybody in ordinary life. But the sole justification for imposing such special duties is that, judged by the norms of ordinary morality, "better moral consequences" (as Goldman puts it) will result.[3] Since every apparent conflict between ordinary and special morality can, by reflection, be resolved into a conflict within ordinary morality itself, the professional

From *Business and Professional Ethics Journal* 1:2 (1982): 75–90.

faces no greater moral difficulties than anybody else.[4]

However, this reduction of special professional to ordinary morality may seem to professionals themselves to distort their moral conflicts. Lawyers, for example, who defend the interests of clients whose interests are morally indefensible might think they are doing their duty *as lawyers,* and that in so doing they act in the face of ordinary morality, not with the ultimate sanction of ordinary morality. Doctors might believe that as doctors they have a special allegiance to the norm of health, a norm which they must respect even to the extent of sacrificing other moral interests a patient might have. It is such conflicts which make professionals even more morally uncomfortable than the rest of us. Since their obligations are derived from a certain conception of their profession, there may well be cases in which a conflict between two norms would be resolvable, were it simply a matter of resolving conflicting norms within ordinary morality; yet this does not settle the conflict between the professional and the ordinary norm.[5]

This gives us our second theory of special professional morality, according to which there are moral obligations which derive not from ordinary morality but from the nature of the professions. We may call this the parallel view, because according to it, professional morality is parallel with, not subordinate to, ordinary morality. The profession itself is a source of special moral obligations; hence fundamental conflicts with ordinary morality are possible, dilemmas of professional morality are not dissolvable into dilemmas of ordinary morality, and professionals are faced, at least potentially, with moral perplexities which are different than those faced by ordinary people.

. . . I propose to defend the "parallel" view. To do so, what is needed is some conception of professional ethics which makes fundamental conflicts possible. Of course it is not enough to point out that professions exist for certain ends, for example, medicine for health, as if this disposed of the question whether professionals are thereby obligated to pursue those ends even in violation of usual moral standards. What I suggest instead is that special professional morality internal to the professions may be derived through certain conceptions of what a profession is. Different conceptions are possible, and each different conception suggests different moral principles. More specifically, we can produce certain models of professional activities and relationships and examine these models to discover what obligations they suggest. For example, to conceive of a doctor on the model of a parent suggests certain obligations which would not be suggested were we to conceive of a doctor as a friend or counselor (a parent has paternalistic duties; a counselor gives advice). The obligations so suggested would be internal to the profession alone since they would depend on the nature of the model. Since these obligations would not be imposed on the professions by reflective ordinary morality, there might well be fundamental conflicts which ordinary morality could not resolve.

I intend to go further, however, and argue that there actually are such fundamental conflicts, at least if we accept a certain conception of a profession. My argument shall be relatively narrow in scope. I shall consider only one professional relationship, that of professional and client. I shall consider only one model of that relationship, the fiduciary. I shall use a modelling scheme according to which five models of the professional-client relationship are presented. Each of these models suggest somewhat different conceptions of the duty of veracity. I concentrate on one of the models, the fiduciary model, in order to contrast its conception of the duty of veracity with that of ordinary morality. These conceptions are not only significantly different, they are inconsistent. Hence, I will argue that if the relationship of professional to client is thought of as a fiduciary relationship, there is a fundamental conflict between ordinary and professional obligations.

THE ORDINARY DUTY OF VERACITY

In order to substantiate this claim, it is necessary to examine exactly what ordinary reflective morality tells us about veracity. Of course not every principle need be discussed, and I will consider only the distinction between lying and deception, and their relative moral wrongness. My main point is that ordinary morality provides reasons not only for condemning lying and deception, but also for considering deception a lesser wrong then lying. When we turn to the fiduciary relationship between professional and client, however, we find the "moral gap" between lying and deception much greater than in ordinary morality: Professional morality considers lying a more serious wrong than does ordinary morality, yet does not consider deception morally wrong at all. Hence, there might be situations in which, from the point of view of ordinary morality, it would be justifiable to lie, but not from the point of view of professional morality; there are also situations in which ordinary morality would, but professional morality would not, prohibit deception.

The distinction between lying and deception is fairly obvious, although the definition of lying is a question of some philosophical complexity.[6] We may consider a lie to be a statement which the speaker believes to be false.[7] What I call a deception, on the other hand, consists either in true statements which are nonetheless misleading, or in actions which convey a false impression, or in the deliberate withholding of information where the person not informed is misled into drawing a false conclusion. Deception can be inadvertent, but where it is deliberate, the agent must want someone to draw a false conclusion. Now most of us see a clear moral difference between lying and deception: Where we think it necessary to plant false beliefs, most of us would prefer to do so without actually lying, if we can.[8] Nonetheless this interesting moral distinction is commonly overlooked by philosophers, who seem to think that the duty of veracity is simply the duty not to deceive.[9] When, however, philosophers do acknowledge the distinction, they are apt to think that it is morally invalid; or else they accept its moral force but fail to explain it in any very satisfactory way. For example, Benjamin and Curtis, in their book *Ethics in Nursing,*[10] citing a case in which a nurse conveys a false impression about a patient's medication without actually lying to the patient, assert that the nurse would be "compounding deception with self-deception if she were to believe that there is a significant ethical difference." The authors leave the impression that in their view there can never be a "significant ethical difference" between deceiving and lying, although the example shows no more than that in the given case, in which the patient is assumed to have a clear right to the information, the wrong to the patient is so great as to make insignificant any difference in the way in which the deception is accomplished. But this does not show that in cases where deception is justified, there is no significant difference between deceiving by lying and deceiving by evasion or by withholding information; nor does it show that there are no cases in which it might be justified to deceive by evasive or misleading statements but *not* justified to deceive by telling a lie.

What would be an argument *against* the distinction between lying and deception? There might be many. It might be pointed out that lying and deception are equally harmful to the person deceived, since they deprive him of information rightfully his. It might be argued that whether one plants false beliefs by means of lying, or by means of evasive or misleading statements (or actions), is a question of means, whereas morality judges by intentions and consequences, and lying and deception are done with the same intention and (if successful) have the same consequence, namely, that someone is wrongfully made to have a false belief. Or it could be said that to deceive someone is to show that you do not respect that person, for you claim for yourself the right to give him false beliefs and thus to manipulate him: Hence deception is a form of contempt for others. Thus deception, no less than lying, harms a person's interest in having true beliefs, in having the information necessary to make intelligent decisions, in not being manipulated, and in being regarded with respect. What these arguments show, however, is that there are very good reasons why we should object to deception, and that some of them are the same reasons we have for objecting to lying. What they do not show is that there are no additional reasons for objecting to lying, which are not reasons for objecting to deception.

Let us consider some philosophers who acknowledge the distinction between lying and deception. Peter Geach, for instance, who counsels "total abstinence from lying,"[11] tells the amusing story of one St. Athanasius, who "was rowing on a river when the persecutors came rowing in the opposite direction: 'Where is the traitor Athanasius?' 'Not far away,' the Saint gaily replied." Here we have the concurrence of a contemporary moral philosopher with the opinion of a Christian Saint that when deception is justified, the gain in producing it without actually lying is great enough to be a cause for gaiety. No less a moralist than Kant, who even in the *Lectures on Ethics*[12] seems to take a position absolutely prohibiting lying (or what Kant calls lying), gives the following example: 'It is possible to deceive without making any statement whatever. I can make believe, make a demonstration from which others will draw the conclusion I want, though they have no right to expect that my action will express my real mind. In that case, I have not lied to them. . . . I may, for instance, wish people to think that I am off on a journey, and so I pack my luggage. . . ."[13] This is a case in which deception, at least in Kant's view, is not even morally problematic, although lying (suppose I told my neighbors, "I will soon be off on a journey") would be excluded.

The philosophers Chisholm and Feehan offer an explanation for the distinction. They write:

> *Why* is it thought wrong to lie? And why is lying thought to be *worse,* other things being equal, than other types of intended deception?
>
> The answer would seem to be this. It is assumed that, if a person L *asserts* a proposition p to another person D, then D has the *right to expect* that L himself believes p. And it is assumed that L knows, or at least that he ought to know that, if he asserts p to D, while believing himself that p is not true, then he violates this right of D's. But analogous assumptions are not made with respect to all other types of intended deception. When the man of Kant's example packs his luggage, he does not thereby give his friends the right to assume that he is about to

make a journey. Lying, unlike the other types of intended deception, is essentially a breach of faith.[14]

What this explanation fails to tell us is both why D *has* such a right against L when L asserts a proposition, and why D does *not* have an equivalent right when L does something without asserting a proposition. (Why do I not have a right to assume that if you pack your bags, then you are going on a journey?) Clearly Chisholm and Feehan, like Kant himself, are far too tolerant of "other forms of intended deception." Kant's neighbors would complain that they had been deceived, and there would be some merit in their complaint; though we might indeed concede that there is some merit in their friends' defense that he had not given them "the right to assume" that his action of packing his bags would in this case have its natural and expected consequence.

These authors fail to explain what is wrong with deception, and why deception, though wrong, is not as wrong as lying. They leave the impression that if deception is wrong, it must be wrong for some other reason altogether than the reason (breach of faith, according to Chisholm and Feehan) that makes lying wrong. But we must not defend the distinction in such a way that deception turns out either to be not wrong at all, or wrong for entirely different reasons than the wrong of lying. Ordinary morality holds that lying is worse than deception, not that it has another moral character altogether. Fortunately, we have already seen excellent reasons why deception should be considered morally wrong, and analogous to lying. I will now give three arguments to show why lying is a greater wrong. The first two distinguish between lying and deception by degree only: Lying is a greater violation of a principle which deception also violates. The third argument, drawn from Kant, does, however, introduce a new idea: that lying violates the social contract in a way that deception does not.

The first argument is that the liar takes advantage of weakness more than does the deceiver. Consider a typical case of deception in the professions: The surgeon, who smilingly enters the patient's room and reports that the operation went very well, but fails to mention that the findings were devastating. The deception occurs (the false belief is formed) only if the patient assumes that when the surgeon said the operation went well, he meant well from the patient's point of view rather than from the surgeon's (i.e., there were no complications or unexpected difficulties). This may be a natural inference, but it is an inference: If deception harms the victim's interest in the truth, this harm can occur only if the victim draws an inference grounded on what he has been told (or has observed, in Kant's example). We can defend ourselves against this harm by adopting the following maxim of prudence governing belief: "Believe everything you are told but draw no inferences unless supported by independent evidence." If we followed such a rule no one would ever be harmed by deception. Such a rule would impose far fewer burdens on life than a rule which protected against lying, to wit, "Believe nothing you hear unless it is supported by independent evidence." Most of us find the cost of following either rule excessive, hence we are vulnerable to the deceiver as well as to the liar. But the costs are not equal. Each rule may be regarded as a defense, where the cost of the defense against lying is greater than the cost of the defense against deception. Since weakness may be measured by the costs of defense (the more it costs to protect yourself against something, the weaker you are with respect to that thing), and since we are therefore weaker with respect to lying than we are with respect to deception, we can say that the liar takes advantage of our weakness to a greater degree than the deceiver, and is consequently morally worse, even though the harm produced by each is the same.

The second argument follows easily from the first. The liar is more responsible for the harm caused than is the mere deceiver. The reason for this is that in mere deception, the person deceived participates in his own deception, hence is in part responsible for causing it. This is usually obvious: In the case of the surgeon, the patient could have unmasked the deception simply by asking the surgeon a direct question about the findings. The patient is at fault for failing to ask. Even where there is a lie, of course, the victim must bear some responsibility for being deceived, since he has imprudently trusted the liar and failed to verify the statement made to him. But usually it is unreasonable for the victim to seek such verification: In the absence of reason to think otherwise, it is unreasonable not to accept for truth direct statements made to you. But the victim of deception does not simply believe what is said: He draws an inference which is based on, but not verified by, the evidence offered, and then fails to ask the speaker to confirm the inference. The victim of the lie fails to verify a direct statement, but the victim of deception fails to verify a conclusion of his own *and* fails to seek confirmation from the speaker, and hence is more responsible for the ensuing harm (his coming to hold a false belief).

We now come to the third difference between lying and deception. Suppose we adopted a social contract point of view and postulated that the duty of veracity depends on an original undertaking not to deceive. A lie would then be a violation of this implicit agreement. Such a view was held by Ross, who, however, confined the duty of veracity to the duty to use language truthfully: "Yet the peculiar stringency of the duty of veracity seems to spring from an implicit understanding that language shall be used to convey the real opinions of the speakers . . ."[15] We could even make the strong claim that unless there were such an implicit understanding, speech itself would be frustrated (and society as we know it impossible), since words establish their meaning only by being applied in standard situations, that is, by being spoken when they truly apply. Now the social contract point itself does not establish a difference with deception, since the undertaking is not to deceive, not merely not to lie. To establish a difference we would have to make one or both of two further points. The first is that the promise to speak the truth is more important than the promise not to deceive, since speech is necessary to *any* human society, whereas non-deception is necessary only for a tolerable or decent society. Truth we might say is an enabling condition for society, whereas non-deception is but an enhancing condition. This point, though powerful, rests on the assumptions above connecting meaningful speech with truth telling and with human society, assumptions clearly beyond our present scope.

The second point depends on our interpretation of the social contract, that is, how we affirm and reaffirm the promise to be truthful. Suppose we held that in addition to the underlying "implicit understanding," there is also a more explicit promise made every time we speak, so that to speak at all is virtually to warrant that our words are true. A lie would then amount to a violation of the very promise made by the speech act in which the lie is stated. If we further supposed that it would be implausible to make a parallel claim about deception, then a clear moral difference would emerge: A lie violates a warrant given by the very act of speech, whereas deception violates at most only the underlying "implicit understanding." Such a view would explain our feeling that a liar is less trustworthy than a mere deceiver, since the liar violates his promise in the very act of making it, whereas the deceiver violates only the remote understanding of the original agreement.

VERACITY AND THE PROFESSIONAL-CLIENT RELATIONSHIP

I now consider that I have both elucidated and defended what ordinary reflective morality has to say about veracity. According to it, lying and deception are both wrong for a number of basically similar reasons; but there are also good reasons for considering lying morally worse than deception. I now propose to argue that the situation is different with respect to professional morality. But first we must resolve a difficulty: What is professional morality? From what does it come, given that we are prevented by our previous rejection of the "priority" approach from simply deriving its precepts from ordinary morality. We have already indicated that some "conception" of the profession is needed, a conception according to which it might be possible to hold, for example, that the overriding obligation of the doctor is to the patient's health, or of the lawyer to the client's strictly legal rights. I propose to solve this problem by presenting models of a profession, or more precisely, models of the professional-client relationship. Modelling is a frequently used device, which enables us to understand basic relationships within the subject matter being modelled, by representing these relationships as something else, presumably more easily understood.

A number of interesting modelling proposals have been put forward in professional ethics, notably with respect to the doctor-patient relationship. I shall just note one, that of Szasz and Hollender.[16] They distinguish three models, which they call activity-passivity, guidance-cooperation, and mutual participation. Although they do not state explicitly what principle governs the derivation of the models, the idea seems to be the location of the control of the relationship: In the first two models the doctor controls, in the third, doctor and patient "mutually participate." (They do not consider the possibility that the patient might control the relationship.) The difference between the first and second models seems to be the kind of control exercised: The "cooperative" patient "is expected to . . . 'obey' his doctor . . . he is neither to question nor to argue or disagree with the orders he receives."[17]

Szasz and Hollender's principle, to distinguish models according to the location of the control of the relationship, is provocative, and I follow it in my own proposals. If we consider the ability to control the relationship, then we have the following possibilities. Either the position of the parties is one of equal power and control, or it is not. If the position is one of equality, then we have two possibilities: Either the relationship is competitive or it is cooperative. If competitive, then we have an adversary model characterized by arm's-length bargaining and contractual agreements; that is what both Veatch and May, in their analysis of doctor-patient relationships, call contract, but with explicit recognition that contract involves mutual wariness based on the need to compromise conflicting interests.[18] A cooperative relationship, on the other hand, also based on equality, is characterized by partnership, mutual trust and other-reliance; this is equivalent to the models of mutual participation which Szasz and Hollender advocate.[19]

If the position is not one of equality, then again we have two possibilities: either the professional is superior to the client, or the client to the professional. In the latter case, we have an agency model: The professional merely carries out the wishes of the client. The client determines the ends to be attained, and the professional acts to achieve these ends, being an instrument of the client's will. But if the professional is superior, then we have two further possibilities: Either the professional uses the client for his or her ends, which we call exploitation (this arises, for example, where the patient is an "interesting case" potentially suitable for write-up in the journals; or where the legal client has a novel problem which the lawyer may use to achieve a landmark legal victory); or the professional works for the client's ends, in which case we have a fiduciary model. Hence our principle gives us five models: adversary, cooperative, agency, exploitation, and fiduciary.

It is not my intention to discuss these models in detail, since I am primarily interested in the fiduciary.[20] The important distinction is that between the fiduciary model and the agency model. In each case the professional works entirely for the client, so it may seem that there is no difference. But there are two senses of "for the client." In the agency model, the agent works at the direction of the principal, that is, he does only those things the principal himself would do, if he had the ability, knowledge or inclination. When the agent acts, it is as if the principal were acting. In the fiduciary model, however, the fiduciary acts in the interests of the beneficiary. Here the fiduciary does not necessarily act as if he were the beneficiary nor does he do only those things which the beneficiary would do, were he in a position to act for himself. Hence the fiduciary has an independent responsibility for his acts on behalf of the beneficiary. He is not a mere instrument of the will of another, confined only to judgments about means and methods but never allowed to determine ends and principles. In a fiduciary relationship, the professional services the true interests of the client, not the client's immediate wishes or desires.[21]

When we reflect on the duties a fiduciary relationship might entail, we are struck with a paradox. On the one hand, a fiduciary relationship rests on trust. On the other hand, a fiduciary relationship encourages deception. I propose to resolve this paradox by widening the moral gap between deception and lying.

That professional-client relationships rest on trust is an oft-noted platitude; but it is in fact not true of any of our models but the fiduciary. It is only in this model that the professional uses his or her superior position to serve the client's interests, possibly contrary to the client's wishes or desires and possibly beyond the client's ability to understand the procedures the professional recommends.[22] If the professional merely carries out the client's wishes (agency) there is no need of trust, since the client can determine for himself whether the professional acts as desired. A contract model involves arm's-length bargaining between equals, which enables adversaries to reach agreements fair to each; trust is unnecessary. Partnerships indeed generate trust, but do not rest on it: If each partner is an equal, respectful of the other's knowledge and abilities, trust will naturally develop, but the partnership can carry on without it. Exploitation perhaps requires that the victim-client be trusting, but not that the professional-exploiter be trust*worthy*. Only in the fiduciary relationship must the professional act to protect the beneficiary's interests as he alone understands them. In the absence of trust, the client is unlikely to submit to the professional's authority, and will prefer an agency or contract model, in which the client may make use of the professional's services without the necessity of submitting to the professional's control. If the professional is not trustworthy, the relationship cannot be said to be fiduciary at all. It is not my intention to debate the merits of the models, but only to draw conclusions about one professional duty, that of veracity, within the fiduciary model.

VERACITY IN THE FIDUCIARY RELATIONSHIP

But why should the fiduciary relationship condone deception? The reason is that the relationship is governed by certain strictly defined ends. People enter into relations with professionals for specific and limited purposes: to improve their health, to protect their legal rights, to enhance their financial condition. If the relationship is fiduciary, the professional pledges to use his or her superior position to protect only those interests for the protection of which the relationship exists. One consults a doctor to protect one's health, not one's finances: It is not within the professional competence of a doctor to make judgments about financial matters. (This is not to say the doctor should not provide information about costs, but that he is not obligated to make judgments about them. The doctor tells me what, in this opinion, is the medically desirable treatment; my financial advisor tells me whether he thinks I can afford it.)

If we take this strict view of the fiduciary context, then we find a significant difference between ordinary morality and the special (professional) morality which governs the fiduciary relationship. Ordinary morality is designed to protect people's total package of interests which, as interests, are considered equally worthy of protection; but professional morality protects only those interests for which the professional relationship exists. Professional morality is thus spared the necessity of assigning weights to various interests in order to balance them in cases of conflict. Deception is thus not a violation of professional morality, since professionals are not mandated to protect the client's interest in having true beliefs, in not being manipulated or in being treated with respect. Nor can there be said to be any underlying contract beyond the pledge by the professional to use his or her superior position to further the goals of the relationship: health, legal rights, and so on. A patient's interest in the truth, for example, is exactly as relevant to the doctor's professional concern as the patient's interest in friends or enjoyable leisure: That is, all these interests are relevant to the physician's responsibility only as they might affect the patient's health. It is a medical judgment whether a person's health might be affected by the possession of certain information, and therefore, within the doctor's responsibility; but it is not a medical judgment, and so not within his responsibility whether a person's other interests ought to be respected at the price of some risk to the person's health. Insofar as information might affect a patient's health, what to tell the patient, whether to tell the patient, and how to tell the patient become purely medical questions, to be answered on medical grounds. Since the interests which deception harms are not otherwise relevant to the fiduciary medical context, there is no reason within that context to prohibit deception. To say this is at bottom only to say that a physician, acting as such, should make medical judgments, not financial judgments, not legal judgments, and not moral judgments either. . . .

It is important to be clear about what I am advocating. My point is that professional morality as it emerges from a certain conception of the professional-client relationship does not prohibit deception; but this is not to say that the professional may deceive for whatever reason he or she chooses. Ordinary morality governs all human relationships, and ordinary morality does not normally condone deception. Professional morality, however, as I understand it, allows deception where necessary to protect the client's relevant interests, but these interests only. It is at the point where, in the professional's best judgment, possession of certain information might harm the client's relevant interests, that professional and ordinary morality may conflict.

Let us consider two examples. Suppose a patient who has been in a serious accident has undergone surgery to restore mobility in an injured leg. After some days, the surgeon concludes that the operation has failed, and that chances of recovered mobility are slight. It is unlikely the patient will ever walk again. This news may be expected to depress the patient badly. Should the patient be informed? Assuming that the depression will not affect the patient's physical condition in a negative way, then ordinary morality must govern. It is not the doctor's professional duty to protect patients from depressing news, even if health-related. (It may, however, be his, that is anyone's, *moral* duty in these circumstances.)

Suppose another patient has undergone major heart surgery, from which he is recovering. While the patient is in the hospital, the patient's business suffers serious reverses. The patient's doctors fear this news will sufficiently upset the patient so as to impede or perhaps preclude complete recovery. Should they advise the family not to inform the patient? Although the information in question is not itself medical, the judgment about its effects is a medical judgment, and their duty is to so advise. Now suppose (implausibly, in my opinion)) ordinary morality might hold that the patient's right to know and to make all decisions concerning his own life, including his business affairs, outweighs the patient's interest in health, as Goldman seems to think.[23] If so, there is a conflict between ordinary and professional morality and professional morality must rule.

But given that professional morality has a significantly greater tolerance for deception than has ordinary morality, how can we resolve the paradox that the professional relationship depends on trust? My answer is to require a significantly greater preclusion of lying. Indeed, it is probably best if professional morality excluded lying altogether. We have already seen some reasons why lying should be considered a greater violation of trust than deception. First, deception cannot occur without some blame, even complicity, on the part of the person deceived. In the case of deception, we might say, trust has not been pushed to the limit, since the direct question which would prevent the deception has not been asked. To this we may add (second), that lying vitiates, but deception does not, what may be called the maxim of trust, "You may believe what you are told." Where this maxim is respected, then it, together with the prudent maxim, "Draw no inferences unless supported by independent evidence," will protect anyone from any kind of deliberate deception. Third, as we have seen, lying violates a promise made in the very act of speech, and so is a greater breach of trust than deception, which violates only the original understanding. And fourth, we may consider that the fiduciary relationship depends on a pledge, by the professional, to protect the interests of the client. But if the professional is capable of lying, how can the client expect that this pledge will be respected? If the professional will lie to the client in order to protect the client's interests, perhaps he will also lie to the client about whether he will protect his interests.

Finally, since lying is a great violation of trust, there is a strong reason for requiring a greater prohibition of lying in a relationship governed by trust, than in ordinary morality. The reason is that trust is not as important in the ordinary relationships of life for which ordinary morality is designed, first, because to a large extent ordinary relationships depend on the recognition by the parties that everyone's self-interest is served best in the long run if everyone obeys the rules of morality (this is the contract element underlying ordinary morality); and second because in ordinary life we do not consign our interests to the care of another. What distinguishes the fiduciary situation from ordinary life is that the client-beneficiary, being unable to control the relationship, must trust the fiduciary-professional to act in his, the beneficiary's, best interest, even where this contradicts the beneficiary's own judgment. This significant difference between ordinary life and the fiduciary relationship is sufficient to explain why the fiduciary relationship must impose a more stringent prohibition against lying than does ordinary morality.

There will, therefore, be situations in which a professional should tell the truth when ordinary morality would condone lying. A woman has been seriously injured in an automobile accident in which one of her children was killed, the others badly crippled.[24] She regains consciousness in the hospital and immediately inquires after her children. The nurses on duty are afraid that evasion will only arouse her suspicions and cause mounting anxiety. Ordinary morality might surely condone a lie in this situation. But if the woman insists on a straight answer, the nurses will be placed in a dilemma arising from their fiduciary responsibility not to lie. Only in an extreme case—for example, where they are certain beyond reasonable doubt that severe medical consequences would follow full disclosure—can a lie be justified. In a less clear case—where, for example, they are unable to judge how detrimental to the patient's subsequent recovery full disclosure would be—they are obligated to answer questions truthfully, even if ordinary morality might counsel lying. To do otherwise would jeopardize the fiduciary relationship which underlies the provision of future care of the patient.

NOTES

1. Alan Goldman, *The Moral Foundations of Professional Ethics* ([Totowa, NJ: Rowman and Littlefield] 1980), p. 1.

2. By ordinary morality, it is well to point out, we do not mean man-in-the-street morality, but rather the morality which governs us simply in virtue of the fact that we are moral agents. Ordinary morality is reflective or critical morality, that is, the views ordinary people should or would hold, were they properly reflective. Special morality, on the other hand, governs only those who have special status or engage in special relationships.

3. [Goldman, op. cit.], p. 22. It is our reflective moral consciousness which determines what consequences are "morally better."

4. Goldman's book [op. cit.] is the best sustained treatment incorporating this theory of professional morality. But the priority view seems to be widespread (if implicit) in the literature of professional ethics. Discussions of "medical paternalism" generally assume it; see inter alia [Allen E.] Buchanan, "Medical Paternalism," *Philosophy and Public Affairs,* vol. 7, no. 4 (1978), pp. 370–90; and the first two essays in [Michael S.] Pritchard and [Wade L.] Robison (eds.), *Medical Responsibility: Paternalism, Informed Consent, and Euthanasia* [Clifton, NJ: Humana Press] (1979), "The Justification of Paternalism" by [Bernard] Gert and [Charles] Culver and "Paternalism and Health Care" by [James F.] Childress.

5. A very fine discussion of this dual allegiance, and of the moral conflicts it generates, is offered by Gerald Postema, "Moral Responsibility in Professional Ethics," in *New York University Law Review,* vol. 55 (Apr. 1980), pp. 63–89. This essay appears as a chapter in Robison, Pritchard and Ellin (eds.), *Profits and Professions* [*: Essays in Business and Professional Ethics* (1983)].

6. For important contemporary discussions of the concept of lying, see Frederick Siegler, "Lying," *American Philosophical Quarterly,* vol. 3, no. 2 (Apr. 1966) [pp. 128–36]; and Roderick Chisholm and Thomas D. Feehan, "The Intent to Deceive" [(see note 14 below)]. Many passages from classical philosophers (Augustine, Aquinas, Kant, etc.) are conveniently reprinted in Bok, *Lying* (see note 9 [below]).

7. Two important conceptual questions which cannot be discussed here are whether the statement made by the liar must *be* false, or whether it is enough for the liar to believe it is false; and whether the liar must tell the lie with the intent to deceive the hearer. For discussion, see essays in note 6 above.

8. A recent article in the *New York Times* (Jan. 26, 1982) presents a nice illustration: "[President Franklin Delano] Roosevelt was not a liar," said Warren Moscow, who covered him for the Hearst papers and then for the *New York Times,* "He was a dissimulator. He had this habit of nodding and saying, 'Yes, yes, yes,' as if he was agreeing with you, and all he was doing was saying he heard you." Reporter Moscow expects the reader to

object to lying but to find "dissimulation" merely amusing.

9. One philosopher who does not see any distinction between lying and deception is Sissela Bok, *Lying* [*: Moral Choice in Public and Private Life* (New York: Pantheon)] (1978), especially chaps. 2 and 3, whose discussion moves back and forth between lying and deception as if there were no difference between them. [See chap. 5, sel. 17, *EIPL*.—ED.] Interestingly, Bok, who holds that a lie might be permissible in certain situations, also holds that "in any situation where a lie is a possible choice, one must first seek truthful alternatives. If lies and truthful statements appear to achieve the same result . . . the lies should be ruled out" (p. 33). What she fails to consider is that there is often a third alternative between lying and telling the truth, and that is deception. Our morality holds that where a lie is a possible choice, one must first seek deceptive alternatives which do not involve lying. More strongly, morality holds that even where a lie is not a possible choice, deception is not *thereby* excluded. The duty of veracity cannot be understood without reflection on this point.

10. [Martin] Benjamin and [Joy] Curtis, *Ethics in Nursing* [New York: Oxford University Press] (1981), p. 65.

11. [Peter] Geach, *The Virtues* [*: The Stanton Lectures, 1973–74,* New York: Cambridge University Press] (1977), p. 114.

12. [Immanuel Kant, *Lectures on Ethics,* Louis] Infield translation [Harper and Row] (1963), pp. 147–54. Reprinted in [Samuel] Gorovitz et al., eds., *Moral Problems in Medicine* [Englewood Cliffs, NJ: Prentice-Hall] (1976), pp. 94–97. Doubts on the attribution to Kant of the views expressed in the *Lectures* are discussed by Bok [op. cit.], pp. 315–16.

13. [Kant, op. cit.], p. 95.

14. [Roderick Chisholm and Thomas D. Feehan], "The Intent to Deceive," *Journal of Philosophy,* vol. 74, no. 3 (Mar. 1977), pp. 143–59; [quote] at p. 153.

15. Sir David [W. D.] Ross, *The Right and the Good* [Oxford: Clarendon] (1930), appendix i. Reprinted in [Wilfrid] Sellars and [John] Hospers, *Readings in Ethical Theory* [Englewood Cliffs, NJ: Prentice-Hall] (1952), p. 196.

16. Thomas S. Szasz and Marc H. Hollender, "The Basic Models of the Doctor-Patient Relationship," *American Medical Association Archives of Internal Medicine* 97 (1956), pp. 585–92. Reprinted in Gorovitz et al. [op. cit.], pp. 64–69.

17. Ibid., p. 66.

18. See Robert M. Veatch, "Models for Ethical Medicine in a Revolutionary Age," *Hastings Center Report* vol. 2, no. 3 (June 1972), pp. 5–7 [rpt. chap. 4, sel. 10, *EIPL*—ED.]; and William F. May, "Code and Covenant or Philanthropy and Contract," in *A Poynter Reader,* ed. David H. Smith (Bloomington, IN: Poynter Center, 1979). This is an extended version of an essay that appeared in *Hastings Center Report,* vol. 5, no. 2 (Dec. 1975), pp. 19–38. [Excerpted in chap. 4, sel. 11, *EIPL*.—ED.]

19. The partnership idea also, of course, underlies so-called holistic medicine. See among many sources [Sally] Guttmacher, "Whole in Body, Mind, and Spirit: Holistic Health and the Limits of Medicine," *Hastings Center Report,* vol. 9, no. 2 (Apr. 1979), pp. 15–21; and [Norman] Cousins, *Anatomy of an Illness as Perceived by the Patient* [*: Reflections on Healing and Regeneration,* New York: Norton] (1979), esp. chaps. 1, 5, 6.

20. Perhaps it is worth noting that the fiduciary relationship is popular in the law as well as in medicine and seems to be the underlying view of the lawyer-client relationship found (inter alia) in [Monroe H.] Freedman's *Lawyers' Ethics in an Adversary System* [Indianapolis, IN: Bobbs-Merrill] (1975) [see chap. 3, sel. 5; and chap. 10, sel. 47, *EIPL*—ED.]; in [Charles] Fried's "The Lawyer as Friend: The Moral Foundations of the Lawyer-Client Relation," 85 *Yale Law Journal* (1976) [pp. 1060–89); and in [Richard A.] Wasserstrom's "Lawyers as Professionals: Some Moral Issues," *Human Rights* vol. 5, no. 1 (1975), pp. 1–24. [Rpt. chap. 3, sel. 6, *EIPL*.—ED.]

21. The distinction between serving true needs or interests and merely appealing to taste and pleasure goes back at least as far as Plato; see *Gorgias* [ll.] 462ff., where Socrates distinguishes between cookery and "make-up," which simply gratify, and gymnastic and medicine, which improve. A recent use of the fiduciary-agency distinction may be found in Judith Swazey, "Health Professionals and the Public: Toward a New Social Contract?" (publication of the Society for Health and Human Values, 1979), esp. pp. 7, 24, 25. She basically accepts the view that "physicians have a special fiduciary relationship with their patients, which ought to be controlled by the physician because of his professional expertise, autonomy, and benevolent intent to use his skills in the best interest of the patient." Though she welcomes "legal and ethical affirmation of patients' rights" and advocates replacing "blind trust' by "a trust" that in some ways is more reasoned and realistic," she cautions against "a too radical shift from a paternalistic, authoritarian physician model to . . . a 'consumer model' in which the physician, or nurse, becomes a mere technician executing the patient's decisions." The "consumer model" is our agency model.

22. William May has also recognized the peculiar significance of trust in a fiduciary relationship. He points out that professionals deal with human needs that "cannot be exhaustively specified in advance for each patient or client. . . . Calls upon services may be required that exceed those anticipated in a contract. . . . [Professional] services . . . are more likely to be effective . . . if they are delivered in the context of a fiduciary relationship that the patient or client can really trust" (op. cit., [see note 18 above].)

23. Goldman's view is that the right to know is based on the right to make important life choices and decisions, and this right can never be violated for reasons of health. See note 1, above, chap. 4, passim, esp. p. 187 ("Personal autonomy over important decisions in one's life . . . is indeed so important that normally no amount of other goods . . . or avoidance of personal evils can take precedence"), and [see] pp. 214–16. I have chosen the example of business reverses since these may be expected to involve possible important decisions by the patient.

24. I take this example from Gert and Culver, op. cit., note 4 above, p. 7. However, I reach a different conclusion from theirs, which is that the patient may be deceived

since her desire to know is not "rational," given that the truth might "greatly increase her chance of dying." (By not rational, they mean that no one would adopt the principle, "Tell me the truth even if it might kill me.") I venture no judgment on the rationality of the patient's request.

16. Should Doctors Tell the Truth?

Joseph Collins

This is not a homily on lying. It is a presentation of one of the most difficult questions that confronts the physician. Should doctors tell patients the truth? Were I on the witness stand and obliged to answer the question with "yes" or "no," I should answer in the negative and appeal to the judge for permission to qualify my answer. The substance of this article is what that qualification would be.

Though few were willing to make the test, it is widely held that if the truth were more generally told, it would make for world welfare and human betterment. We shall probably never know. To tell the whole truth is often to perpetrate a cruelty of which many are incapable. This is particularly true of physicians. Those of them who are not compassionate by nature are made so by experience. They come to realize that they owe their fellowmen justice, and graciousness, and benignity, and it becomes one of the real satisfactions of life to discharge that obligation. To do so successfully they must frequently withhold the truth from their patients, which is tantamount to telling them a lie. Moreover, the physician soon learns that the art of medicine consists largely in skillfully mixing falsehood and truth in order to provide the patient with an amalgam which will make the metal of life wear and keep men from being poor shrunken things, full of melancholy and indisposition, unpleasing to themselves and to those who love them. I propose therefore to deal with the question from a pragmatic, not a moral standpoint.

"Now you may tell me the truth," is one of the things patients have frequently said to me. Four types of individuals have said it: those who honestly and courageously want to know so that they may make as ready as possible to face the wages of sin while there is still time; those who do not want to know, and who if they were told would be injured by it; those who are wholly incapable of receiving the truth. Finally, those whose health is neither seriously disordered nor threatened. It may seem an exaggeration to say that in forty years of contact with the sick, the patients I have met who are in the first category could be counted on the fingers of one hand. The vast majority who demand the truth really belong in the fourth category, but there are sufficient in the second—with whom my concern chiefly is—to justify considering their case.

One of the astonishing things about patients is that the more serious the disease, the more silent they are about its portents and manifestations. The man who is constantly seeking reassurance that the vague abdominal pains indicative of hyperacidity are not symptoms of cancer often buries family and friends, some of whom have welcomed death as an escape from his burdensome iterations. On the other hand, there is the man whose first warning of serious disease is lumbago who cannot be persuaded to consult a physician until the disease, of which the lumbago is only a symptom, has so far progressed that it is beyond surgery. The seriousness of disease may be said to stand in direct relation to the reticence of its possessor. The more silent the patient, the more serious the disorder.

The patient with a notebook, or the one who is eager to tell his story in great detail, is rarely very ill. They are forever asking, "Am I going to get well?" and though they crave assistance, they are often unable to accept it. On the other hand, patients with organic disease are very chary about asking point-blank either the nature or the outcome of their ailment. They sense its gravity, and the last thing in the world they wish to know is the truth about it; and to learn it would be the worst thing that could happen to them.

This was borne in upon me early in my professional life. I was summoned one night to assuage the pain of a man who informed me that he had been for some time under treatment for rheumatism—that cloak for so many diagnostic errors. His "rheumatism" was due to a disease of the spinal cord called locomotor ataxia. When he was told that he should submit himself to treatment wholly different from that which he had been receiving, the import of which any intelligent layman would have divined, he asked neither the nature nor the probable outcome of the disease. He did as he was

From *Harper's Magazine* 155 (August 1927), pp. 320–26.

counselled. He is now approaching seventy and, though not active in business, it still engrosses him.

Had he been told that he had a disease which was then universally believed to be progressive, apprehension would have depressed him so heavily that he would not have been able to offer the resistance to its encroachment which has stood him in such good stead. He was told the truth only in part. That is, he was told his "rheumatism" was "different"; that it was dependent upon an organism quite unlike the one that causes ordinary rheumatism; that we have preparations of mercury and arsenic which kill the parasite responsible for this disease, and that if he would submit himself to their use, his life would not be materially shortened, or his efficiency seriously impaired.

Many experiences show that patients do not want the truth about their maladies, and that it is prejudicial to their well-being to know it, but none that I know is more apposite than that of a lawyer, noted for his urbanity and resourcefulness in court. When he entered my consulting room, he greeted me with a bonhomie that bespoke intimacy, but I had met him only twice—once on the golf links many years before and once in court where I was appearing as expert witness, prejudicial to his case.

He apologized for engaging my attention with such a triviality, but he had had pain in one shoulder and arm for the past few months, and though he was perfectly well—and had been assured of it by physicians in Paris, London, and Brooklyn—this pain was annoying and he had made up his mind to get rid of it. That I should not get a wrong slant on his condition, he submitted a number of laboratory reports furnished him by an osteopath to show that secretions and excretions susceptible of chemical examinations were quite normal. His determination seemed to be to prevent me from taking a view of his health which might lead me to counsel his retirement. He was quite sure that anything like a thorough examination was unnecessary, but he submitted to it. It revealed intense and extensive disease of the kidneys. The pain in the network of nerves of the left upper arm was a manifestation of the resulting autointoxication.

I felt it incumbent upon me to tell him that his condition was such that he should make a radical change in his mode of life. I told him if he would stop work, spend the winter in Honolulu, go on a diet suitable to a child of three years, and give up exercise, he could look forward confidently to a recovery that would permit . . . a life of usefulness and activity in his profession. He assured me he could not believe that one who felt no worse than he did should have to make such a radical change in his mode of life. He impressed upon me that I should realize he was the kind of person who had to know the truth. His affairs were so diversified and his commitments so important that he *must* know. Completely taken in, I explained to him the relationship between the pain from which he sought relief and the disease, the degeneration that was going on in the excretory mechanisms of his body, how these were struggling to repair themselves, the procedure of recovery and how it could be facilitated. The light of life began to flicker from the fear that my words engendered, and within two months it sputtered and died out. He was the last person in the world to whom the truth should have been told. Had I lied to him, and then intrigued with his family and friends, he might be alive today.

The longer I practice medicine the more I am convinced that every physician should cultivate lying as a fine art. But there are many varieties of lying. Some are most prejudicial to the physician's usefulness. Such are: pretending to recognize the disease and understand its nature when one is really ignorant; asserting that one has effected the cure which nature has accomplished, or claiming that one can effect cure of a disease which is universally held to be beyond the power of nature or medical skill; pronouncing disease incurable which one cannot rightfully declare to be beyond cessation or relief.

There are other lies, however, which contribute enormously to the success of the physician's mission of mercy and salvation. There are a great number of instances in support of this but none more convincing than that of a man of fifty who, after twenty-five years of devotion to painting, decided that penury and old age were incompatible for him. Some of his friends had forsaken art for advertising. He followed their lead and in five years he was already to gather the first ripe fruit of his labor. When he attempted to do so he was so immobilized by pain and rigidity that he had to forego work. One of those many persons who assume responsibility lightly assured him that if he would put himself in the hands of a certain osteopath he would soon be quite fit. The assurance was without foundation. He then consulted a physician who without examining him proceeded to treat him for what is considered a minor ailment.

Within two months his appearance gave such concern to his family that he was persuaded to go to a hospital, where the disease was quickly detected, and he was at once submitted to surgery. When he had recovered from the operation, learning that I was in the country of his adoption, he asked to see me. He had not been able, he said, to get satisfactory information from the surgeon or the physician; all that he could gather from them was that he would have to have supplementary X-ray or radium treatment. What he desired was to get back to his business which was on the verge of success, and he wanted assurance that he could soon do so.

He got it. And more than that, he got elaborate explanation of what surgical intervention had accomplished, but not a word of what it had failed to accomplish. A year of activity was vouchsafed him, and during that time he put his business in such shape that its eventual sale provided a modest competency for his family. It was not until the last few weeks that he knew the nature of his malady. Months of apprehension had been spared him by the deception, and he had been the better able to do his work, for he was buoyed by the hope that his health was not beyond recovery. Had he been told the truth, black despair would have been thrown over the world in which he moved, and he would have carried on with corresponding ineffectiveness.

The more extensive our field of observation and the more intimate our contact with human activity, the more we realize the finiteness of the human mind. Every follower of Hippocrates will agree that ''judgment is difficult and experience fallacious.'' A disease may have only a fatal ending, but one does not know; one may know that certain diseases, such as general paresis, invariably cause death, but one does not know that tomorrow it may no longer be true. The victim may be reprieved by accidental or studied discovery or by the intervention of something that still must be called divine grace. . . .

17. Lying and Lies to the Sick and Dying

Sissela Bok

TRUTH AND TRUTHFULNESS

. . . ''Truth''—no concept intimidates and yet draws thinkers so powerfully. From the beginnings of human speculation about the world, the questions of what truth is and whether we can attain it have loomed large. Every philosopher has had to grapple with them. Every religion seeks to answer them. . . .

In all such speculation, there is great risk of a conceptual muddle, of not seeing the crucial differences between two domains: the *moral* domain of intended truthfulness and deception, and the much vaster domain of truth and falsity in general. The moral question of whether you are lying or not is not *settled* by establishing the truth or falsity of what you say. In order to settle this question, we must know whether you *intend your statement to mislead*. . . .

Any number of appearances and words can mislead us; but only a fraction of them are *intended* to do so. A mirage may deceive us, through no one's fault. Our eyes deceive us all the time. We are beset by self-delusion and bias of every kind. Yet we often know when we mean to be honest or dishonest. Whatever the essence of truth and falsity, and whatever the sources of error in our lives, *one* such source is surely the human agent, receiving and giving out information, intentionally deflecting, withholding, even distorting it at times. . . .

We must single out, therefore, from the countless ways in which we blunder misinformed through life, that which is done with the *intention to mislead;* and from the countless partial stabs at truth, those which are intended to be truthful. Only if this distinction is clear will it be possible to ask the moral question with rigor. And it is to this question alone—the intentional manipulation of information—that the court addresses itself in its request for ''the truth, the whole truth, and nothing but the truth.''

. . . . .

DEFINING INTENTIONAL DECEPTION AND LYING

When we undertake to deceive others intentionally, we communicate messages meant to mislead them, meant to make them believe what we ourselves do not believe. We can do so through gesture, through disguise, by means of action or inaction, even through silence. Which of these innumerable deceptive messages are also lies? I shall define as a lie any intentionally deceptive message which is

From *Lying: Moral Choice in Public and Private Life* (New York: Pantheon, 1978), selections from chapters 1, 2, 6, 14, and 15.

stated. Such statements are most often made verbally or in writing, but can of course also be conveyed via smoke signals, Morse code, sign language, and the like. Deception, then, is the larger category, and lying forms part of it. . . .

LYING AND CHOICE

Deceit and violence—these are the two forms of deliberate assault on human beings. Both can coerce people into acting against their will. Most harm that can befall victims through violence can come to them also through deceit. But deceit controls more subtly, for it works on belief as well as action. Even Othello, whom few would have dared to try to subdue by force, could be brought to destroy himself and Desdemona through falsehood. The knowledge of this coercive element in deception, and of our vulnerability to it, underlies our sense of the *centrality* of truthfulness. . . .

All our choices depend on our estimates of what is the case; these estimates must in turn often rely on information from others. Lies distort this information and therefore our situation as we perceive it, as well as our choices.

. . . . .

THE PERSPECTIVE OF THE DECEIVED

Those who learn that they have been lied to in an important matter—say, the identity of their parents, the affection of their spouse, or the integrity of their government—are resentful, disappointed, and suspicious. They feel wronged; they are wary of new overtures. And they look back on their past beliefs and actions in the new light of the discovered lies. They see that they were manipulated, that the deceit made them unable to make choices for themselves according to the most adequate information available, unable to act as they would have wanted to act had they known all along.

It is true, of course, that personal, informed choice is not the only kind available to them. They may *decide* to abandon choosing for themselves and let others decide for them—as guardians, financial advisors, or political representatives. They may even decide to abandon choice based upon information of a conventional nature altogether and trust instead to the stars or to throws of the dice or to soothsayers.

But such alternatives ought to be personally chosen and not surreptitiously imposed by lies or other forms of manipulation. Most of us would resist loss of control over which choices we want to delegate to others and which ones we want to make ourselves, aided by the best information we can obtain. We resist because experience has taught us the consequences when others choose to deceive us, even "for our own good." Of course, we know that many lies are trivial. But since we, when lied to, have no way to judge which lies are the trivial ones, and since we have no confidence that liars will restrict themselves to just such trivial lies, the perspective of the deceived leads us to be wary of *all* deception. . . .

Deception, then, can be coercive. When it succeeds, it can give power to the deceiver—power that all who suffer the consequences of lies would not wish to abdicate. . . .

THE PRINCIPLE OF VERACITY

. . . I believe that we must at the very least accept as an initial premise Aristotle's view that lying is "mean and culpable" and that truthful statements are preferable to lies in the absence of special considerations. This premise gives an initial negative weight to lies. It holds that they are not neutral from the point of view of our choices; that lying requires explanation, whereas truth ordinarily does not. It provides a counterbalance to the crude evaluation by liars of their own motives and of the consequences of their lies. And it places the burden of proof squarely on those who assume the liar's perspective.

This presumption against lying can also be stated so as to stress the positive worth of truthfulness or veracity. I would like . . . to refer to the "principle of veracity" as an expression of this initial imbalance in our weighing of truthfulness and lying. . . .

TYPES OF EXCUSES

What is it, then, that can conflict with the requirement for truthfulness so as to make lies permissible at times? Say you are caught in a compromising lie. What excuses might you offer? What kinds of excuses?

An excuse seeks to extenuate, sometimes to remove the blame entirely from something which would otherwise be a fault. It can seek to extenuate in three ways. First, it can suggest that what is seen as a fault is not really one. Secondly, it can suggest that, though there has been a fault, the agent is not really blameworthy, because he is not responsible. And finally, it can suggest that, though there has been a fault, and though the agent is responsible, he is not really to blame because he has good reasons to do as he did.

(a) Excuses of the first type may claim that the supposed lie is not really a lie, but a joke, perhaps, or an evasion, an exaggeration, a flight of fancy. Or else such an excuse may argue that since it is impossible to give objective distinctions between truth and falsehood, the supposed lie cannot be proved to be one.

(b) The second type of excuse holds that, though there may have been deception, the agent is not really or not completely responsible. The liar may claim he never meant to mislead, or was incompetent, perhaps drunk, or talking in his sleep, or coerced into deceiving. Or else he may take refuge in arguing that no one can ever be held responsible for lies, that free choice in that respect is a myth.

Both these types of excuses obviously cover a vast territory and are in constant use by liars. But it is the third type which will be the focus of [our] attention . . .—the type of excuse which is most fundamental for the process of evaluating deliberate lies. In this third type of excuse, the liar admits the lie, accepts responsibility for it, but offers reasons to show that he should be partially or even wholly cleared of blame. All three kinds of excuses are often present in the same effort to extenuate any one lie. . . .

(c) The third type of excuse, then, offers moral reasons for a lie, reasons to show that a lie ought, under the circumstances, to be allowed.

. . . . .

PATERNALISM

. . . To act paternalistically is to guide and even coerce people in order to protect them and serve their best interests, as a father might his children. . . .

The need for some paternalistic restraints is obvious. We survive only if protected from harm as children. Even as adults, we tolerate a number of regulations designed to reduce dangers such as those of infection or accidents. But it is equally obvious that the intention of guarding from harm has led, both through mistake and through abuse, to great suffering. The "protection" can suffocate; it can also exploit. Throughout history, men, women, and children have been compelled to accept degrading work, alien religious practices, institutionalization, and even wars alleged to "free" them, all in the name of what someone has declared to be their own best interest. And deception may well have outranked force as a means of subjection: duping people to conform, to embrace ideologies and cults—never more zealously perpetrated than by those who believe that the welfare of those deceived is at issue.

Apart from guidance and persuasion, the paternalist can manipulate in two ways: through force and through deception.

. . . . .

One reason for the appeal of paternalistic lies is that they, unlike so much deception, are felt to be without bias and told in a disinterested wish to be helpful to fellow human beings in need. On closer examination, however, this objectivity and disinterest are often found to be spurious. The benevolent motives claimed by liars are then seen to be mixed with many others much less altruistic—the fear of confrontation which would accompany a more outspoken acknowledgment of the liar's feelings and intentions; the desire to avoid setting in motion great pressures to change, as where addiction or infidelity are no longer concealed; the urge to maintain the power that comes with duping others (never greater than when those lied to are defenseless or in need of care). These are motives of self-protection and of manipulation, of wanting to retain control over a situation and to remain a free agent. So long as the liar does not see them clearly, his judgment that his lies are altruistic and thus excused is itself biased and unreliable.

The perspective of the deceived, then, challenges the "helpfulness" of many paternalistic lies. It questions, moreover, even the benefits that are thought to accrue to the liar. The effects of deception on the liars themselves—the need to shore up lies, keep them in good repair, the anxieties relating to possible discovery, the entanglements and threats to integrity—are greatest in a close relationship where it is rare that one lie will suffice. It can be very hard to maintain the deceit when one is in close contact with those one lies to. The price of "living a lie" often turns out not even to have been worth the gains for the liars themselves.

JUSTIFICATION?

The two simplest approaches to paternalistic lying, then, have to be ruled out. It is not all right to lie to people just because they are children, or unable to judge what one says, or indeed because they belong to any category of persons at all. And the simple conviction voiced by Luther and so many others that the "helpful lie" is excused by its own altruism is much too uncritical. It allows far too many lies to go unquestioned. Both of these views fail to take into consideration the harm that comes from lying, not only to the deceived but to the liars and to the bonds they share.

. . . . .

DECEPTION AS THERAPY

A forty-six-year-old man, coming to a clinic for a routine physical check-up needed for insurance purposes, is diagnosed as having a form of cancer likely to cause him to die within six months. No known cure exists for it. Chemotherapy may prolong life by a few extra months, but will have side effects the physician does not think warranted in this case. In addition, he believes that such therapy should be reserved for patients with a chance for recovery or remission. The patient has no symptoms giving him any reason to believe that he is not perfectly healthy. He expects to take a short vacation in a week.

For the physician, there are now several choices involving truthfulness. Ought he to tell the patient what he has learned, or conceal it? If asked, should he deny it? If he decides to reveal the diagnosis, should he delay doing so until after the patient returns from his vacation? Finally, even if he does reveal the serious nature of the diagnosis, should he mention the possibility of chemotherapy and his reasons for not recommending it in this case? Or should he encourage every last effort to postpone death?

In this particular case, the physician chose to inform the patient of his diagnosis right away. He did not, however, mention the possibility of chemotherapy. A medical student working under him disagreed; several nurses also thought that the patient should have been informed of this possibility. They tried, unsuccessfully, to persuade the physician that this was the patient's right. When persuasion had failed, the student elected to disobey the doctor by informing the patient of the alternative of chemotherapy. After consultation with family members, the patient chose to ask for the treatment.

Doctors confront such choices often and urgently. What they reveal, hold back, or distort will matter profoundly to their patients. Doctors stress with corresponding vehemence their reasons for the distortion or concealment: not to confuse a sick person needlessly, or cause what may well be unnecessary pain or discomfort, as in the case of the cancer patient; not to leave a patient without hope, as in those many cases where the dying are not told the truth about their condition; or to improve the chances of cure, as where unwarranted optimism is expressed about some form of therapy. Doctors use information as part of the therapeutic regimen; it is given out in amounts, in admixtures, and according to timing believed best for patients. Accuracy, by comparison, matters far less.

Lying to patients has, therefore, seemed an especially excusable act. Some would argue that doctors, and *only* doctors, should be granted the right to manipulate the truth in ways so undesirable for politicians, lawyers, and others.[1] Doctors are trained to help patients; their relationship to patients carries special obligations, and they know much more than laymen about what helps and hinders recovery and survival.

Even the most conscientious doctors, then, who hold themselves at a distance from the quacks and the purveyors of false remedies, hesitate to forswear all lying. Lying is usually wrong, they argue, but less so than allowing the truth to harm patients. B. C. Meyer echoes this very common view:

> [O]urs is a profession which traditionally has been guided by a precept that transcends the virtue of uttering truth for truth's sake, and that is, "so far as possible, do no harm."[2]

Truth, for Meyer, may be important, but not when it endangers the health and well-being of patients. This has seemed self-evident to many physicians in the past—so much so that we find very few mentions of veracity in the codes and oaths and writings by physicians through the centuries. This absence is all the more striking as other principles of ethics have been consistently and movingly expressed in the same documents.

The two fundamental principles of doing good and not doing harm—of beneficence and nonmaleficence—are the most immediately relevant to medical practitioners, and the more frequently stressed. To preserve life and good health, to ward off illness, pain, and death—these are the perennial tasks of medicine and nursing. These principles have found powerful expression at all times in the history of medicine. In the Hippocratic oath physicians promise to:

> use treatment to help the sick . . . but never with a view to injury and wrong-doing.[3]

And a Hindu oath of initiation says:

> Day and night, however thou mayest be engaged, thou shalt endeavor for the relief of patients with all thy heart and soul. Thou shalt not desert or injure the patient even for the sake of thy living.[4]

But there is no similar stress on veracity. It is absent from virtually all oaths, codes, and prayers. The Hippocratic Oath makes no mention of truthfulness to patients about their condition, prognosis, or treatment. Other early codes and prayers are equally silent on the subject. To be sure, they often refer to the confidentiality with which doctors should treat all that patients tell them; but there is no corresponding reference to honesty toward the patient. One of the few who appealed to such a principle was Amatus Lusitanus, a Jewish physician widely known for his skill, who, persecuted, died of the plague in 1568. He published an oath which reads in part:

> If I lie, may I incur the eternal wrath of God and of His angel Raphael, and may nothing in the medical art succeed for me according to my desires.[5]

Later codes continue to avoid the subject. Not even the Declaration of Geneva, adopted in 1948 by the World Medical Association, makes any reference to it. And the Principles of Medical Ethics of the American Medical Association[6] still leave the matter of informing patients up to the physician.

Given such freedom, a physician can decide to tell as much or as little as he wants the patient to know, so long as he breaks no law. In the case of the man mentioned at the beginning . . . some physicians might feel justified in lying for the good of the patient, others might be truthful. Some may conceal alternatives to the treatment they recommend; others not. In each case, they could appeal to the AMA Principles of Ethics. A great many would choose to be able to lie. They would claim that not only can a lie avoid harm for the patient, but that it is also hard to know whether they have been right in the first place in making their pessimistic diagnosis; a ''truthful'' statement could therefore turn out to hurt patients unnecessarily. The concern for curing and for supporting those who cannot be cured then runs counter to the desire to be completely open. This concern is especially strong where the prognosis is bleak; even more so when patients are so affected by their illness or their medication that they are more dependent than usual, perhaps more easily depressed or irrational.

Physicians know only too well how uncertain a diagnosis or prognosis can be. They know how hard it is to give meaningful and correct answers regarding health and illness. They also know that disclosing their own uncertainty or fears can reduce those benefits that depend upon faith in recovery. They fear, too, that revealing grave risks, no matter how unlikely it is that these will come about, may exercise the pull of the ''self-fulfilling prophecy.'' They dislike being the bearers of uncertain or bad news as much as anyone else. And last, but not least, sitting down to discuss an illness truthfully and sensitively may take much-needed time away from other patients.

These reasons help explain why nurses and physicians and relatives of the sick and dying prefer not to be bound by rules that might limit their ability to suppress, delay, or distort information. This is not to say that they necessarily plan to lie much of the time. They merely want to have the freedom to do so when they believe it wise. And the reluctance to see lying prohibited explains, in turn, the failure of the codes and oaths to come to grips with the problems of truth telling and lying.

But sharp conflicts are now arising. Doctors no longer work alone with patients. They have to consult with others much more than before; if they choose to lie, the choice may not be met with approval by all who take part in the care of the patient. A nurse expresses the difficulty which results as follows:

> From personal experience I would say that the patients who aren't told about their terminal illness have so many verbal and mental questions unanswered that many will begin to realize that their illness is more serious than they're being told. . . .
>
> Nurses care for these patients twenty-four hours a day compared to a doctor's daily brief visit, and it is the nurse many times that the patient will relate to, once his underlying fears become overwhelming. . . . This is difficult for us nurses because being in constant contact with patients we can see the events leading up to this. The patient continually asks you, ''Why isn't my pain decreasing?'' or ''Why isn't the radiation treatment easing the pain?'' . . . We cannot legally give these patients an honest answer as a nurse (and I'm sure I wouldn't want to) yet the problem is still not resolved and the circle grows larger and larger with the patient alone in the middle.[7]

The doctor's choice to lie increasingly involves co-workers in acting a part they find neither humane nor wise. The fact that these problems have not been carefully thought through within the medical profession, nor seriously addressed in medical education, merely serves to intensify the conflicts.[8] Different doctors then respond very differently to patients in exactly similar predicaments. The friction is increased by the fact that relatives often disagree even where those giving medical care to a patient are in accord on how to approach the patient. Here again, because physicians have not worked out to common satisfaction the question of whether relatives have the right to make such requests, the problems are allowed to be haphazardly resolved by each physician as he sees fit.

THE PATIENT'S PERSPECTIVE

The turmoil in the medical profession regarding truth telling is further augmented by the pressures that patients themselves now bring to bear and by empirical data coming to light. Challenges are growing to three major arguments for lying to patients: that truthfulness is impossible; that patients do not want bad news; and that truthful information harms them. . . .

The second argument for deceiving patients refers specifically to giving them news of a frightening or depressing kind. It holds that patients do not, in fact, generally want such information, that they prefer not to have to face up to serious illness and death. On the basis of such a belief, most doctors in a number of surveys stated that they do not, as a rule, inform patients that they have an illness such as cancer.

When studies are made of what patients desire to know, on the other hand, a large majority say that they *would* like to be told of such a diagnosis.[9] All these studies need updating and should be done with large numbers of patients and non-patients. But they do show that there is generally a dramatic divergence between physicians and patients on the factual question of whether patients want to know what ails them in cases of serious illness such as cancer. In most of the studies, over 80 percent of the persons asked indicated that they would want to be told.

Sometimes this discrepancy is set aside by doctors who want to retain the view that patients do not want unhappy news. In reality, they claim, the fact that patients say they want it has to be discounted. The more someone asks to know, the more he suffers from fear which will lead to the denial of the information even if it is given. Informing patients is, therefore, useless; they resist and deny having been told what they cannot assimilate. According to this view, empirical studies of what patients say they want are worthless since they do not probe deeply enough to uncover this universal resistance to the contemplation of one's own death.

This view is only partially correct. For some patients, denial is indeed well established in medical experience. A number of patients (estimated at between 15 percent and 25 percent) will give evidence of denial of having been told about their illness, even when they repeatedly ask and are repeatedly informed. And nearly everyone experiences a period of denial at some point in the course of approaching death.[10] Elisabeth Kübler-Ross sees denial as resulting often from premature and abrupt information by a stranger who goes through the process quickly to "get it over with." She holds that denial functions as a buffer after unexpected shocking news, permitting individuals to collect themselves and to mobilize other defenses. She described prolonged denial in one patient as follows:

> She was convinced that the X-rays were "mixed up"; she asked for reassurance that her pathology report could not possibly be back so soon and that another patient's report must have been marked with her name. When none of this could be confirmed, she quickly asked to leave the hospital, looking for another physician in the vain hope "to get a better explanation for my troubles." This patient went "shopping around" for many doctors, some of whom gave her reassuring answers, others of whom confirmed the previous suspicion. Whether confirmed or not, she reacted in the same manner; she asked for examination and reexamination.[11]

But to say that denial is universal flies in the face of all evidence. And to take any claim to the contrary as "symptomatic" of deeper denial leaves no room for reasoned discourse. There is no way that such universal denial can be proved true or false. To believe in it is a metaphysical belief about man's condition, not a statement about what patients do and do not want. It is true that we can never completely understand the possibility of our own death, any more than being alive in the first place. But people certainly differ in the degree to which they can approach such knowledge, take it into account in their plans, and make their peace with it.

Montaigne claimed that in order to learn both to live and to die, men have to think about death and be prepared to accept it.[12] To stick one's head in the sand, or to be prevented by lies from trying to discern what is to come, hampers freedom—freedom to consider one's life as a whole, with a beginning, a duration, an end. Some may request to be deceived rather than to see their lives as thus finite; others reject the information which would require them to do so; but most say that they want to know. Their concern for knowing about their condition goes far beyond mere curiosity or the wish to make isolated personal choices in the short time left to them; their stance toward the entire life they have lived, and their ability to give it meaning and completion, are at stake.[13] In lying or withholding the facts which permit such discernment, doctors may reflect their own fears (which, according to one study,[14] are much stronger than those of laymen) of facing questions about the meaning of one's life and the inevitability of death.

Beyond the fundamental deprivation that can result from deception, we are also becoming increasingly aware of all that can befall patients in the course of their illness when information is denied or distorted. Lies place them in a position where they no longer participate in choices concerning their own health, including the choice of whether to be a "patient" in the first place. A terminally ill person who is not informed that his illness is incurable and that he is near death cannot make decisions about the end of his life: about whether or not to enter a hospital, or to have surgery; where and with whom to spend his last days; how to put his affairs in order—these most personal choices cannot be made if he is kept in the dark, or given contradictory hints and clues.

It has always been especially easy to keep knowledge from terminally ill patients. They are most vulnerable, least able to take action to learn what they need to know, or to protect their autonomy. The very fact of being so ill greatly increases the likelihood of control by others. And the fear of being helpless in the face of such control is growing. At the same time, the period of dependency and slow deterioration of health and strength that people undergo has lengthened. There has been a dramatic shift toward institutionalization of the aged and those near death. (Over 80 percent of Americans now die in a hospital or other institution.)

Patients who are severely ill often suffer a further distancing and loss of control over their most basic functions. Electrical wiring, machines, intravenous administration of liquids, all create new dependency and at the same time new distance between the patient and all who come near. Curable patients are often willing to undergo such procedures; but when no cure is possible, these procedures merely intensify the sense of distance and uncertainty and can even become a substitute for comforting human acts. Yet those who suffer in this way often fear to seem troublesome by complaining. Lying to them, perhaps for the most charitable of purposes, can then cause them to slip unwittingly into subjection to new procedures, perhaps new surgery, where death is held at bay through transfusions, respirators, even resuscitation far beyond what most would wish.

Seeing relatives in such predicaments has caused a great upsurge of worrying about death and dying. At the root of this fear is not a growing terror of the *moment* of death, or even the instants before it. Nor is there greater fear of *being* dead. In contrast to the centuries of lives lived in dread of the punishments to be inflicted after death, many would now accept the view expressed by Epicurus, who died in 270 B.C.:

> Death, therefore, the most awful of evils, is nothing to us, seeing that, when we are, death is not come, and, when death is come, we are not.[15]

The growing fear, if it is not of the moment of dying nor of being dead, is of all that which now precedes dying for so many: the possibility of prolonged pain, the increasing weakness, the uncertainty, the loss of powers and chance of senility, the sense of being a burden. This fear is further nourished by the loss of trust in health professionals. In part, the loss of trust results from the abuses which have been exposed—the Medicaid scandals, the old-age home profiteering, the commercial exploitation of those who seek remedies for their ailments;[16] in part also because of the deceptive practices patients suspect, having seen how friends and relatives were kept in the dark; in part, finally, because of the sheer numbers of persons, often strangers, participating in the care of any one patient. Trust which might have gone to a doctor long known to the patient goes less easily to a team of strangers, no matter how expert or well-meaning.

It is with the working out of all that *informed consent*[17] implies and the information it presupposes that truth telling is coming to be discussed in a serious way for the first time in the health professions. Informed consent is a farce if the information provided is distorted or withheld. And even complete information regarding surgical procedures or medication is obviously useless unless the patient also knows what the condition is that these are supposed to correct.

Bills of rights for patients, similarly stressing the right to be informed, are now gaining acceptance.[18] This right is not new, but the effort to implement it is. Nevertheless, even where patients are handed the most elegantly phrased Bill of Rights, their right to a truthful diagnosis and prognosis is by no means always respected.

The reason why even doctors who recognize a patient's right to have information might still not provide it brings us to the third argument against telling all patients the truth. It holds that the information given might hurt the patient and that the concern for the right to such information is therefore a threat to proper health care. A patient, these doctors argue, may wish to commit suicide after being given discouraging news, or suffer a cardiac arrest, or simply cease to struggle, and thus not grasp the small remaining chance for recovery. And even where the outlook for a patient is very good, the disclosure of a minute risk can shock some patients or cause them to reject needed protection such as a vaccination or antibiotics.

The factual basis for this argument has been challenged from two points of view. The damages associated with the disclosure of sad news or risks are rarer than physicians believe; and the *benefits* which result from being informed are more substantial, even measurably so. Pain is tolerated more easily, recovery from surgery is quicker, and cooperation with therapy is greatly improved. The attitude that "what you don't know won't hurt you" is proving unrealistic; it is what patients do not know but vaguely suspect that causes them corrosive worry.

It is certain that no answers to this question of harm from information are the same for all patients. If we look, first, at the fear expressed by physicians that informing patients of even remote or unlikely risks connected with a drug prescription or operation might shock some and make others refuse the treatment that would have been best for them, it appears to be unfounded for the great majority of patients. Studies show that very few patients respond to being told of such risks by withdrawing their consent to the procedure and that those who do withdraw are the very ones who might well have been upset enough to sue the physician had they not been asked to consent beforehand.[19] It is possible that on even rarer occasions especially susceptible persons might manifest physical deterioration from shock; some physicians have even asked whether patients who die after giving informed consent to an operation, but before it actually takes place, somehow expire because of the information given to them.[20] While such questions are unanswerable in any one case, they certainly argue in favor of caution, a real concern for the person to whom one is recounting the risks he or she will face, and sensitivity to all signs of stress.

The situation is quite different when persons who are already ill, perhaps already quite weak and discouraged, are told of a very serious prognosis. Physicians fear that such knowledge may cause the patients to commit suicide, or to be frightened or depressed to the point that their illness takes a downward turn. The fear that great numbers of patients will commit suicide appears to be unfounded.[21] And if some do, is that a response so unreasonable, so much against the patient's best interest that physicians ought to make it a reason for concealment or lies? Many societies have allowed suicide in the past; our own has decriminalized it; and some are coming to make distinctions among the many suicides which ought to be prevented if at all possible, and those which ought to be respected.[22]

Another possible response to very bleak news is the triggering of physiological mechanisms which allow death to come more quickly—a form of giving up or of preparing for the inevitable, depending on one's outlook. Lewis Thomas, studying responses in humans and animals, holds it not unlikely that:

> There is a pivotal movement at some stage in the body's reaction to injury or disease, maybe in aging as well, when the organism concedes that it is finished and the time for dying is at hand, and at this moment the events that lead to death are launched, as a coordinated mechanism. Functions are then shut off, in sequence, irreversibly, and, while this is going on, a neural mechanism, held ready for this occasion, is switched on.[23]

Such a response may be appropriate, in which case it makes the moments of dying as peaceful as those who have died and been resuscitated so often testify. But it may also be brought on inappropriately, when the organism could have lived on, perhaps even induced malevolently, by external acts intended to kill. Thomas speculates that some of the deaths resulting from "hexing" are due to such responses. Lévi-Strauss describes deaths from exorcism and the casting of spells in ways which suggest that the same process may then be brought on by the community.[24]

It is not inconceivable that unhappy news abruptly conveyed, or a great shock given to someone unable to tolerate it, could also bring on such a "dying response," quite unintended by the speaker. There is every reason to be cautious and to try to know ahead of time how susceptible a patient might be to the accidental triggering—however rare—of such a response. One has to assume, however, that most of those who have survived long enough to be in a situation where their informed consent is asked have a very robust resistance to such accidental triggering of processes leading to death.

When, on the other hand, one considers those who are already near death, the "dying response" may be much less inappropriate, much less accidental, much less unreasonable. In most societies, long before the advent of modern medicine, human beings have made themselves ready for death once they felt its approach. Philippe Ariès describes how many in the Middle Ages prepared themselves for death when they "felt the end approach." They awaited death lying down, surrounded by friends and relatives. They recollected all they had lived through and done, pardoning all who stood near their deathbed, calling on God to bless them, and finally praying. "After the final prayer all that remained was to wait for death, and there was no reason for death to tarry."[25]

Modern medicine, in its valiant efforts to defeat disease and to save lives, may be dislocating the conscious as well as the purely organic responses allowing death to come when it is inevitable, thus denying those who are dying the benefits of the traditional approach to death. In lying to them, and in pressing medical efforts to cure them long past the point of possible recovery, physicians may thus rob individuals of an autonomy few would choose to give up.

Sometimes, then, the "dying response" is a natural organic reaction at the time when the body has no further defense. Sometimes it is inappropriately brought on by news too shocking or given in too abrupt a manner. We need to learn a great deal more about this last category, no matter how small. But there is no evidence that patients in general will be debilitated by truthful information about their condition.

Apart from possible harm from information, we are coming to learn much more about the benefits it can bring patients. People follow instructions more carefully if they know what their disease is and why they are asked to take medication; any benefits from those procedures are therefore much more likely to come about.[26] Similarly, people recover faster from surgery and tolerate pain with less medication if they understand what ails them and what can be done for them.[27]

NOTES

1. Plato, *The Republic,* 389b.
2. B. C. Meyer, "Truth and the Physician," *Bulletin of the New York Academy of Medicine* 45 (1969): 59–71.
3. W.H.S. Jones, trans., *Hippocrates,* Loeb Classical Library (Cambridge, MA: Harvard University Press, 1923), p. 164.
4. Reprinted in M. B. Etziony, *The Physician's Creed: An Anthology of Medical Prayers, Oaths and Codes of Ethics* (Springfield, IL: Charles C. Thomas, 1973), pp. 15–18.
5. See Harry Friedenwald, "The Ethics of the Practice of Medicine from the Jewish Point of View," *Johns Hopkins Hospital Bulletin,* no. 318 (Aug. 1917), pp. 256–61.
6. "Ten Principles of Medical Ethics," *Journal of the American Medical Association* 164 (1957): 1119–20.
7. Mary Barrett, Letter [to the Editor], *Boston Globe,* 16 November 1976, p. 1.
8. Though a minority of physicians have struggled to bring them to our attention. See Thomas Percival, *Medical Ethics,* 3d ed. (Oxford: John Henry Parker, 1849), pp. 132–41; Worthington Hooker, *Physician and Patient* (New York: Baker and Scribner, 1849), pp. 357–82; Richard C. Cabot, "Teamwork of Doctor and Patient Through the Annihilation of Lying," in *Social Service and the Art of Healing* (New York: Moffat, Yard and Co., 1909), pp. 116–70; Charles C. Lund, "The Doctor, the Patient, and the Truth," *Annals of Internal Medicine* 24 (1946): 955; Edmund Davies, "The Patient's Right to Know the Truth," *Proceedings of the Royal Society of Medicine* 66 (1973): 533–36.
9. For the views of physicians, see Donald Oken, "What to Tell Cancer Patients," *Journal of the American Medical Association* 175 (1961): 1120–28; and tabulations in Robert [M.] Veatch, *Death, Dying, and the Biological Revolution* (New Haven and London: Yale University Press, 1976), pp. 229–38. For the view of patients, see Veatch, ibid.; Jean Aitken-Swan and E. C. Easson, "Reactions of Cancer Patients on Being Told Their Diagnosis," *British Medical Journal* (1959), pp. 779–83; Jim McIntosh, "Patients' Awareness and Desire for Information About Diagnosed but Undisclosed Malignant Disease," *Lancet* 7 (1976): 300–303; William D. Kelly and Stanley R. Friesen, "Do Cancer Patients Want to Be Told?," *Surgery* 27 (1950): 822–26.
10. See Avery Weisman, *On Dying and Denying* (New York: Behavioral Publications, 1972); Elisabeth Kübler-Ross, *On Death and Dying* (New York: Macmillan, 1969); Ernest Becker, *The Denial of Death* (New York: Free Press, 1973); Philippe Ariès, *Western Attitudes Toward Death,* trans. Patricia M. Ranum (Baltimore and London: Johns Hopkins University Press, 1974); and Sigmund Freud, "Negation," *Collected Papers,* ed. James Strachey (London: Hogarth, 1950), 5: 181–85.
11. Kübler-Ross, *On Death and Dying,* p. 34.
12. Michel de Montaigne, *Essays,* bk. I, chap. 20.
13. It is in literature that these questions are most directly raised. Two recent works where they are taken up with striking beauty and simplicity are May Sarton, *As We Are Now* (New York: Norton, 1973); and Freya Stark, *A Peak in Darien* (London: John Murray, 1976).
14. Herman Feifel et al., "Physicians Consider Death," *Proceedings of the American Psychoanalytical Association,* 1967, pp. 201–2.
15. See Diogenes Laertius, *Lives of Eminent Philosophers,* p. 651. Epicurus willed his garden to his friends and descendants, and wrote on the eve of dying: "On this blissful day, which is also the last of my life, I write to you. My continual sufferings from strangury and dysentery are so great that nothing could augment them; but over against them all I set gladness of mind at the remembrance of our past conversation." (Letter to Idomeneus, Ibid, p. 549).
16. See Ivan Illich, *Medical Nemesis* (New York: Pantheon, 1976), for a critique of the iatrogenic tendencies of contemporary medical care in industrialized societies.
17. The law requires that inroads made upon a person's body take place only with the informed voluntary consent of that person. The term "informed consent" came into common use only after 1960, when it was used by the Kansas Supreme Court in *Nathanson* v. *Kline,* 186 Kan. 393,350, p.2d, 1093 (1960). The patient is now entitled to full disclosure of risks, benefits, and alternative treatments to any proposed procedure, both in therapy and in medical experimentation, except in emergencies or when the patient is incompetent, in which case proxy consent is required.
18. See, for example, "Statement on a Patient's Bill of Rights," reprinted in Stanley Joel Reiser, Arthur J. Dyck, and William J. Curran, [eds.] *Ethics in Medicine* (Cambridge, MA, and London: MIT Press, 1977), p. 148.
19. See Ralph Alfidi, "Informed Consent: A Study of Patient Reaction," *Journal of the American Medical Association* 216 (1971): 1325–29.
20. See Steven R. Kaplan, Richard A. Greenwald, and Arvey I. Rogers, Letter to the Editor, *New England Journal of Medicine* 296 (1977): 1127.
21. Oken, "What to Tell Cancer Patients"; Veatch, *Death, Dying, and the Biological Revolution;* Weisman, *On Dying and Denying.*
22. Norman L. Cantor, "A Patient's Decision to Decline Life-Saving Treatment: Bodily Integrity Versus the Preservation of Life," *Rutgers Law Review* 26 (1973): 228–64; Danielle Gourevitch, "Suicide Among the Sick in Classical Antiquity," *Bulletin of the History of Medicine* 18 (1969): 501–18. . . .
23. Lewis Thomas, "A Meliorist View of Disease and Dying," *Journal of Medicine and Philosophy,* 1 (1976): 212–21.
24. Claude Lévi-Strauss, *Structural Anthropology* (New York: Basic Books 1963), p. 167. See also Eric Cassell, "Permission to Die," in John Behnke and Sissela Bok, eds., *The Dilemmas of Euthanasia* (Garden City, NY: Doubleday, Anchor Books, 1975), pp. 121–31.

25. Ariès, *Western Attitudes Toward Death,* p. 11.

26. Barbara S. Hulka, J. C. Cassel, et al. "Communication, Compliance, and Concordance between Physicians and Patients with Prescribed Medications," *American Journal of Public Health* (Sept. 1976), pp. 847–53. The study shows that of the nearly half of all patients who do not follow the prescriptions of the doctors (thus foregoing the intended effect of these prescriptions), many will follow them if adequately informed about the nature of their illness and what the proposed medication will do.

27. See Lawrence D. Egbert, George E. Batitt, et al., "Reduction of Postoperative Pain by Encouragement and Instruction of Patients," *New England Journal of Medicine* 270 (1964), pp. 825–27. See also Howard Waitzskin and John D. Stoeckle, "The Communication of Information About Illness," *Advances in Psychosomatic Medicine* 8 (1972), pp. 185–215.

18. Lies for the Public Good

Sissela Bok

Hugo: And do you think the living will agree to your schemes?
Hoederer: We'll get them to swallow them little by little.
Hugo: By lying to them?
Hoederer: By lying to them sometimes.—Jean-Paul Sartre, *Dirty Hands*

THE NOBLE LIE

. . . Three circumstances have seemed to liars to provide the strongest excuse for their behavior—a crisis where overwhelming harm can be averted only through deceit; complete harmlessness and triviality to the point where it seems absurd to quibble about whether a lie has been told; and the duty to particular individuals to protect their secrets. Lies in times of crisis can expand into vast practices where the harm to be averted is less obvious and the crisis less and less immediate; . . . white lies can shade into equally vast practices no longer so harmless, with immense cumulative costs; and . . . lies to protect individuals and to cover up their secrets can be told for increasingly dubious purposes to the detriment of all.

When these three expanding streams flow together and mingle with yet another—a desire to advance the public good—they form the most dangerous body of deceit of all. These lies may not be justified by an immediate crisis nor by complete triviality nor by duty to any one person; rather, liars tend to consider them as right and unavoidable because of the altruism that motivates them. . . .

The most characteristic defense for these lies is . . . based on the benefits they may confer and the long-range harm they can avoid. The intention may be broadly paternalistic, as when citizens are deceived "for their own good," or only a few may be lied to for the benefit of the community at large. Error and self-deception mingle with these altruistic purposes and blur them. . . . But I shall try to single out, among these lies, the elements that are consciously and purposely intended to benefit society.

A long tradition in political philosophy endorses some lies for the sake of the public. Plato . . . first used the expression "noble lie" for the fanciful story that might be told to people in order to persuade them to accept class distinctions and thereby safeguard social harmony. According to this story, God Himself mingled gold, silver, iron, and brass in fashioning rulers, auxiliaries, farmers, and craftsmen, intending these groups for separate tasks in a harmonious hierarchy.

The Greek adjective which Plato used to characterize this falsehood expresses a most important fact about lies by those in power: this adjective is *"gennaion,"* which means "noble" in the sense of both "high minded" and "well bred."[1] The same assumption of nobility, good breeding, and superiority to those deceived is also present in Disraeli's statement that a gentleman is one who knows when to tell the truth and when not to. In other words, lying is excusable when undertaken for "noble" ends by those trained to discern these purposes.

Rulers, both temporal and spiritual, have seen their deceits in the benign light of such social purposes. They have propagated and maintained myths played on the gullibility of the ignorant, and sought stability in shared beliefs. They have seen themselves as high minded and well bred—whether by birth or by training—and as superior to those they deceive. Some have gone so far as to claim that those who govern have a *right* to lie.[2] The

From *Lying: Moral Choice in Public and Private Life* (New York: Pantheon, 1978), pp. 174–91.

powerful tell lies believing that they have greater than ordinary understanding of what is at stake; very often, they regard their dupes as having inadequate judgment, or as likely to respond in the wrong way to truthful information.

At times, those who govern also regard particular circumstances as too uncomfortable, too painful, for most people to be able to cope with rationally. They may believe, for instance, that their country must prepare for long-term challenges of great importance, such as a war, an epidemic, or a belt-tightening in the face of future shortages. Yet they may fear that citizens will be able to respond only to short-range dangers. Deception at such times may seem to the government leaders as the only means of attaining the necessary results.

The perspective of the liar is paramount in all such decisions to tell "noble" lies. If the liar considers the responses of the deceived at all, he assumes that they will, once the deceit comes to light and its benefits are understood, be uncomplaining if not positively grateful. The lies are often seen as necessary merely at one *stage* in the education of the public. Thus Erasmus, in commenting on Plato's views, wrote:

> He sets forth deceitful fictions for the rabble, so that the people might not set fire to the magistracy, and similar falsifications by which the crass multitude is deceived in its own interests, in the same way that parents deceive children and doctors the sick.
>
> . . . Thus for the crass multitude there is need of temporary promises, figures, allegories, parables . . . so that little by little they might advance to loftier things.[3]

Some experienced public officials are impatient with any effort to question the ethics of such deceptive practices (except actions obviously taken for private ends). They argue that vital objectives in the national interest require a measure of deception to succeed in the face of powerful obstacles. Negotiations must be carried on that are best left hidden from public view; bargains must be struck that simply cannot be comprehended by a politically unsophisticated electorate. A certain amount of illusion is needed in order for public servants to be effective. Every government, therefore, has to deceive people to some extent in order to lead them.

These officials view the public's concern for ethics as understandable but hardly realistic. Such "moralistic" concerns, put forth without any understanding of practical exigencies, may lead to the setting of impossible standards; these could seriously hamper work without actually changing the underlying practices. . . .

If we assume the perspective of the deceived—those who experience the consequences of government deception—such arguments are not persuasive. We cannot take for granted either the altruism or the good judgment of those who lie to us, no matter how much they intend to benefit us. We have learned that much deceit for private gain masquerades as being in the public interest. We know how deception, even for the most unselfish motive, corrupts and spreads. And we have lived through the consequences of lies told for what were believed to be noble purposes.

Equally unpersuasive is the argument that there always has been government deception, and always will be, and that efforts to draw lines and set standards are therefore useless annoyances. It is certainly true that deception can never be completely absent from most human practices. But there are great differences among societies in the kinds of deceit that exist and the extent to which they are practiced, differences also among individuals in the same government and among successive governments within the same society. This strongly suggests that it is worthwhile trying to discover why such differences exist and to seek ways of raising the standards of truthfulness.

The argument that those who raise moral concerns are ignorant of political realities, finally, ought to lead, not to a dismissal of such inquiries, but to a more articulate description of what these realities are, so that a more careful and informed debate could begin. We have every reason to regard government as more profoundly injured by a dismissal of criticism and a failure to consider standards than by efforts to discuss them openly. If duplicity is to be allowed in exceptional cases, the criteria for these exceptions should themselves be openly debated and publicly chosen. Otherwise government leaders will have free rein to manipulate and distort the facts and thus escape accountability to the public.

The effort to question political deception cannot be ruled out so summarily. The disparagement of inquiries into such practices has to be seen as the defense of unwarranted power—power bypassing the consent of the governed. . . . I shall take up just a few cases to illustrate both the clear breaches of trust that no group of citizens could desire, and circumstances where it is more difficult to render a judgment.

EXAMPLES OF POLITICAL DECEPTION

In September 1964, a State Department official, reflecting a growing administration consensus, wrote a memorandum advocating a momentous deceit of the American public.[4] He outlined possible courses of action to cope with the deteriorating military situation in South Vietnam. These included a stepping up of American participation in the "pacification'' in South Vietnam and a ''crescendo'' of military action against North Vietnam, involving heavy bombing by the United States. But an election campaign was going on; the president's Republican opponent, Senator Goldwater, was suspected by the electorate of favoring escalation of the war in Vietnam and of brandishing nuclear threats to the Communist world. In keeping with President Johnson's efforts to portray Senator Goldwater as an irresponsible war hawk, the memorandum ended with a paragraph entitled ''Special considerations during the next two months,'' holding that:

> During the next two months, because of the lack of ''rebuttal time'' before election to justify particular actions which may be distorted to the U.S. public, we must act with special care—signaling to . . . [the South Vietnamese] that we are behaving energetically despite the restraints of our political season, and to the U.S. public that we are behaving with good purpose and restraint.

As the campaign wore on, President Johnson increasingly professed to be the candidate of peace. He gave no indication of the growing pressure for escalation from high administrative officials who would remain in office should he win; no hint of the hard choice he knew he would face if elected.[5] Rather he repeated over and over again . . . :

> The first responsibility, the only real issue in this campaign, the only thing you ought to be concerned about at all, is: Who can best keep the peace?[6]

The stratagem succeeded; the election was won; the war escalated. Under the name of Operation Rolling Thunder, the United States launched massive bombing raids over North Vietnam early in 1965. In suppressing genuine debate about these plans during the election campaign and masquerading as the party of peace, government members privy to the maneuver believed that they knew what was best for the country and that history would vindicate them. They meant to benefit the nation and the world by keeping the danger of a Communist victory at bay. If a sense of *crisis* was needed for added justification, the domino theory strained for it: One regime after another was seen as toppling should the first domino be pushed over.

But why the deceit, if the purposes were so altruistic? Why not espouse these purposes openly before the election? The reason must have been that the government could not count on popular support for the scheme. In the first place, the sense of crisis and threat from North Vietnam would have been far from universally shared. To be forthright about the likelihood of escalation might lose many votes; it certainly could not fit with the campaign to portray President Johnson as the candidate most likely to keep the peace. Second, the government feared that its explanations might be ''distorted'' in the election campaign, so that the voters would not have the correct information before them. Third, time was lacking for the government to make an effort at educating the people about all that was at issue. Finally, the plans were not definitive; changes were possible, and the Vietnamese situation itself very unstable. For all these reasons, it seemed best to campaign for negotiation and restraint and let the Republican opponent be the target for the fear of United States belligerence.

President Johnson thus denied the electorate any chance to give or to refuse consent to the escalation of the war in Vietnam. Believing they had voted for the candidate of peace, American citizens were, within months, deeply embroiled in one of the cruelest wars in their history. Deception of this kind strikes at the very essence of democratic government. It allows those in power to override or nullify the right vested in the people to cast an informed vote in critical elections. Deceiving the people for the sake of the people is a self-contradictory notion in a democracy, unless it can be shown that there has been genuine consent to deceit. The actions of President Johnson were therefore inconsistent with the most basic principle of our political system.

What if all government officials felt similarly free to deceive provided they believed the deception genuinely necessary to achieve some important public end? The trouble is that those who make such calculations are always susceptible to bias. They overestimate the likelihood that the benefit will occur and that the harm will be averted; they underestimate the chances that the deceit will be discovered and ignore the effects of such a discovery on trust; they underrate the comprehension of the deceived citizens, as well as their ability and their right to make a reasoned choice. And, most important, such a benevolent self-righteousness disguises the many motives for political lying which could *not* serve as moral excuses: the need to cover up past mistakes; the vindictiveness; the desire to stay in power. These self-serving ends provide the impetus for countless lies that are rationalized as ''necessary'' for the public good.

As political leaders become accustomed to making such excuses, they grow insensitive to fairness and to veracity. Some come to believe that any lie can be told so long as they can convince themselves that people will be better off in the long run. From there, it is a short step to the conclusion that, even if people will not be better off from a particular lie, they will benefit by all maneuvers to keep the right people in office. Once public servants lose their bearings in this way, all the shabby deceits of Watergate—the fake telegrams, the erased tapes, the elaborate cover-ups, the bribing of witnesses to make them lie, the televised pleas for trust—become possible.

While Watergate may be unusual in its scope, most observers would agree that deception is part and parcel of many everyday decisions in government. Statistics may be presented in such a way as to diminish the gravity of embarrassing problems. Civil servants may lie to members of Congress in order to protect programs they judge important, or to guard secrets they have been ordered not to divulge. If asked, members of Congress who make deals with one another to vote for measures they would otherwise oppose deny having made such deals. False rumors may be leaked by subordinates who believe that unwise executive action is about to be taken. Or the leak may be correct, but falsely attributed in order to protect the source.

Consider the following situation and imagine all the variations on this theme being played in campaigns all over the United States, at the local, state, or federal level: A big-city mayor is running for reelection. He has read a report recommending that he remove rent controls after his reelection. He intends to do so, but believes he will lose the election if his intention is known. When asked, at a news conference two days before his election, about the existence of such a report, he denies knowledge of it and reaffirms his strong support of rent control.

In the mayor's view, his reelection is very much in the public interest, and the lie concerns questions which he believes the voters are unable to evaluate properly, especially on such short notice. In all similar situations, the sizable bias resulting from the self-serving element (the desire to be elected, to stay in office, to exercise power) is often clearer to onlookers than to the liars themselves. This bias inflates the alleged justifications for the lie—the worthiness, superiority, altruism of the liar, the rightness of his cause, and the inability of those deceived to respond "appropriately" to hearing the truth.

These common lies are now so widely suspected that voters are at a loss to know when they can and cannot believe what a candidate says in campaigning. The damage to trust has been immense. I have already referred to the poll which found 69 percent of Americans agreeing, both in 1975 and 1976, that the country's leaders had consistently lied to the American people over the past ten years. Over 40 percent of the respondents also agreed that

> most politicians are so similar that it doesn't really make much difference who gets elected.[7]

Many refuse to vote under such circumstances. Others look to appearance or to personality factors for clues as to which candidate might be more honest than the others. Voters and candidates alike are the losers when a political system has reached such a low level of trust. Once elected, officials find that their warnings and their calls to common sacrifice meet with disbelief and apathy, even when cooperation is most urgently needed. Lawsuits and investigations multiply. And the fact that candidates, should they win, are not expected to have meant what they said while campaigning, nor held accountable for discrepancies, only reinforces the incentives for them to bend the truth the next time, thus adding further to the distrust of the voters.

Political lies, so often assumed to be trivial by those who tell them, rarely are. They cannot be trivial when they affect so many people and when they are so peculiarly likely to be imitated, used to retaliate, and spread from a few to many. When political representatives or entire governments arrogate to themselves the right to lie, they take power from the public that would not have been given up voluntarily.

DECEPTION AND CONSENT

Can there be exceptions to the well-founded distrust of deception in public life? Are there times when the public itself might truly not care about possible lies, or might even prefer to be deceived? Are some white lies so trivial or so transparent that they can be ignored? And can we envisage public discussion of more seriously misleading government statements such that reasonable persons could consent to them in advance?

White lies, first of all, are as common to political and diplomatic affairs as they are to the private lives of most people. Feigning enjoyment of an embassy gathering or a political rally, toasting the longevity of a dubious regime or an unimpressive candidate for office—these are forms of politeness that mislead few. It is difficult to regard them as threats to either individuals or communities. As with all white lies, however, the problem is that they spread so easily, and that lines are very hard to draw. Is it still a white lie for a secretary of state to announce that he is going to one country when in reality he travels to another? Or for a president to issue a "cover story" to the effect that a cold is forcing him to return to the White House, when in reality an international crisis made him cancel the rest of his campaign trip? Is it a white lie to issue a letter of praise for a public servant one has just fired? Given the vulnerability of public trust, it is never more important than in public life to keep the deceptive element of white lies to an absolute minimum, and to hold down the danger of their turning into more widespread deceitful practices.

A great deal of deception believed not only innocent but highly justified by public figures concerns their private lives. Information about their marriages, their children, their opinions about others—information about their personal plans and about their motives for personal decisions—all are theirs to keep private if they wish to do so. Refusing to give information under these circumstances is justifiable—but the right to withhold information is not the right to lie about it. Lying under such circumstances bodes ill for conduct in other matters.

Certain additional forms of deception may be debated and authorized in advance by elected representatives of the public. The use of unmarked police cars to discourage speeding by drivers is an example of such a practice. Various forms of unannounced, sometimes covert, auditing of business and government operations are others. Whenever these practices are publicly regulated, they can be limited so that abuses are avoided. But they must be *openly* debated and agreed to in advance, with every precaution against abuses of privacy and the rights of individuals, and against the spread of such covert activities. It is not enough that a public official assumes that consent would be given to such practices.

Another type of deceit has no such consent in advance: the temporizing or the lie when truthful information at a particular *time* might do great damage. Say that a government is making careful plans for announcing the devaluation of its currency. If the news leaks out to some before it can be announced to all, unfair profits for speculators might result. Or take the decision to make sharp increases in taxes on imported goods in order to rescue a tottering economy. To announce the decision beforehand would lead to hoarding and to exactly the results that the taxes are meant to combat. Thus, government officials will typically seek to avoid any premature announcement and will refuse to comment if asked whether devaluation or higher taxes are imminent. At times, however, official spokesmen will go further and falsely deny that the actions in question will in fact take place.

Such lies may well be uttered in good faith in an effort to avoid harmful speculation and hoarding. Nevertheless, if false statements are made to the public only to be exposed as soon as the devaluation or the new tax is announced, great damage to trust will result. It is like telling a patient that an operation will be painless—the swifter the disproof, the more likely the loss of trust. In addition, these lies are subject to all the dangers of spread and mistake and deterioration of standards that accompany all deception.

For these reasons, it is far better to refuse comment than to lie in such situations. The objection may be made, however, that a refusal to comment will be interpreted by the press as tantamount to an admission that devaluation or higher taxes are very near. Such an objection has force only if a government has not already established credibility by letting it be known earlier that it would never comment on such matters, and by strictly adhering to this policy at all times. Since lies in these cases are so egregious, it is worth taking care to establish such credibility in advance, so that a refusal to comment is not taken as an invitation to monetary speculation.

Another form of deception takes place when the government regards the public as frightened, or hostile, and highly volatile. In order not to create a panic, information about early signs of an epidemic may be suppressed or distorted. And the lie to a mob seeking its victim is like lying to the murderer asking where the person he is pursuing has gone. It can be acknowledged and defended as soon as the threat is over. In such cases, one may at times be justified in withholding information; perhaps, on rare occasions, even in lying. But such cases are so rare that they hardly exist for practical purposes.

The fact that rare circumstances exist where the justification for government lying seems powerful creates a difficulty—these same excuses will often be made to serve a great many more purposes. For some governments or public officials, the information they wish to conceal is almost never of the requisite certainty, the time never the right one, and the public never sufficiently dispassionate. For these reasons, it is hard to see how a practice of lying to the public about devaluation or changes in taxation or epidemics could be consented to in advance, and therefore justified.

Are there any exceptionally dangerous circumstances where the state of crisis is such as to justify lies to the public for its own protection? We have already discussed lying to enemies in an acute crisis. Sometimes the domestic public is then also deceived, at least temporarily, as in the case of the U-2 incident. Wherever there is a threat—from a future enemy, as before World War II, or from a shortage of energy—the temptation to draw upon the excuses for deceiving citizens is very strong. The government may sincerely doubt that the electorate is capable of making the immediate sacrifices needed to confront the growing danger. (Or one branch of the government may lack confidence in another, for similar reasons, as when the administration mistrusts Congress.) The public may seem too emotional, the time not yet ripe for disclosure. Are there crises so exceptional that deceptive strategies are justifiable?

Compare, for instance, what was said and left unsaid by two United States presidents confronted by a popular unwillingness to enter a war: President Lyndon Johnson, in escalating the war in Vietnam, and President Franklin D. Roosevelt, in moving the country closer to participating in World War II, while making statements such as the following in his 1940 campaign to be reelected:

> I have said this before, but I shall say it again and again and again: Your boys are not going to be sent into any foreign wars.[8]

. . . President Johnson's covert escalation and his failure to consult the electorate concerning the undeclared war in Vietnam was clearly unjustifiable. Consent was bypassed; there was no immediate danger to the nation which could even begin to excuse deceiving the public in a national election on grounds of an acute crisis.

The crisis looming before World War II, on the other hand, was doubtless much greater. Certainly this case is a difficult one, and one on which reasonable persons might not be able to agree. The threat was unprecedented; the need for preparations and for support of allies great; yet the difficulties of alerting the American public seemed insuperable. Would this crisis, then, justify proceeding through deceit?

To consent even to such deception would, I believe, be to take a frightening step. Do we want to live in a society where public officials can resort to deceit and manipulation whenever they decide that an exceptional crisis has arisen? Would we not, on balance, prefer to run the risk of failing to rise to a crisis honestly explained to us, from which the government might have saved us through manipulation? And what protection from abuse do we foresee should we surrender this choice?

In considering answers to these questions, we must take into account more than the short-run effects of government manipulation. President Roosevelt's manner of bringing the American people to accept first the possibility, then the likelihood, of war was used as an example by those who wanted to justify President Johnson's acts of dissimulation. And these acts in turn were pointed to by those who resorted to so many forms of duplicity in the Nixon administration. Secrecy and deceit grew at least in part because of existing precedents.[9]

The consequences of spreading deception, alienation, and lack of trust could not have been documented for us more concretely than they have in the past decades. We have had a very vivid illustration of how lies undermine our political system. While deception under the circumstances confronting President Roosevelt may in hindsight be more excusable than much that followed, we could no more consent to it in advance than to all that came later.

Wherever lies to the public have become routine, then, very special safeguards should be required. The test of public justification of deceptive practices is more needed than ever. It will be a hard test to satisfy, the more so the more trust is invested in those who lie and the more power they wield. Those in government and other positions of trust should be held to the highest standards. Their lies are not ennobled by their positions; quite the contrary. Some lies—notably minor white lies and emergency lies rapidly acknowledged—may be more *excusable* than others, but only those deceptive practices which can be openly debated and consented to in advance are *justifiable* in a democracy.[10]

NOTES

1. The *gennaion pseudos* has generated much controversy. Some have translated it as ''pious fraud'' and debated whether such fraud can be perpetrated. Thus Hastings Rashdall, in *The Theory of Good and Evil,* 2d ed. (New York and London: Oxford University Press, 1924), bk. 1, p. 195, argued that such frauds would be justifiable ''if (when *all* their consequences are considered) they were socially beneficial.'' Other translations are: ''royal lie'' (Jowett), and ''bold flight of the imagination'' (Cornford). The latter represents an effort to see Plato as advocating not lies by the government but stories, and possible errors; an interpretation that is difficult to uphold in view of the other contexts in *The Republic* where lying is discussed, such as 389b: ''The rulers of the city may, if anybody, fitly lie on account of enemies or citizens for the benefit of the state.'' For Plato to have endorsed lying by the state is very significant, as truth for him was opposed, not just to falsehood, but to unreality.

2. Arthur Sylvester, ''The Government Has the Right to Lie,'' *Saturday Evening Post,* 18 November 1967, p. 10.

3. Erasmus, *Responsio ad Albertum Pium, Opera Omnia,* vol. 9 (Leiden, 1706; reprinted Hildesheim, 1962).

4. Senator Gravel Edition, *The Pentagon Papers* (Boston: Beacon Press, 1971), 3:556–59.

5. As early as March 1964, Lyndon Johnson knew that such a hard choice might have to be made. See telephone transcript cited by Doris Kearns in *Lyndon Johnson and the American Dream* (New York: Harper and Row, 1976), p. 197.

6. Theodore H. White, *The Making of the President 1964* (New York: Atheneum, 1965), p. 373.

7. *Cambridge Survey Research,* 1975, 1976.

8. *The Public Papers and Addresses of Franklin D. Roosevelt,* 1940, vol. 8, p. 517 (October 30, 1940).

9. See Arthur M. Schlesinger, Jr., *The Imperial Presidency* (Boston: Houghton Mifflin, 1973), p. 356: "The power to withhold and the power to leak led on inexorably to the power to lie . . . uncontrolled secrecy made it easy for lying to become routine." See also David Wise, *The Politics of Lying* (New York: Random House, 1973).

10. For discussions of lying and moral choice in politics, see Plato, *The Republic;* Machiavelli, *The Prince;* Grotius, *On the Law of War and Peace;* Werner Krauss, ed., *Est-il utile de tromper le peuple?*—a fascinating compilation of answers by Condorcet and others in a contest sponsored by Frederick II in 1780 (Berlin: Akademie-Verlag, 1966); Max Weber, "Politics as a Vocation," in *[From Max Weber:] Essays in Sociology,* [ed. and] trans. H. H. Gerth and C. Wright Mills (New York: Oxford University Press, 1946), pp. 77–128; and Michael Walzer, "Political Action: The Problem of Dirty Hands," *Philosophy and Public Affairs* 2 (Winter 1973): 160–80.

NONPATERNALISTIC DECEPTION: DECEPTIVE ADVERTISING

19. Advertising and Ethics

Phillip Nelson

. . . . .

DECEPTIVE ADVERTISING, REGULATION, AND FREE SPEECH

A lot of people think that there is far too much deceptive advertising and that active government intervention, policing every advertisement, is necessary to improve advertising.

But the amount of deceptiveness in advertising can be easily exaggerated if one simply looks at the incentives of the advertiser to deceive without considering the incentives of consumers not to be deceived. The circumstances under which advertisers have the greatest incentives to deceive if consumers believed them are precisely the circumstances under which consumers would be least inclined to believe advertising. Deception requires not only a misleading or untrue statement but somebody ready to be misled by that statement.

One possible source of deceptive advertising is consumer confusion. Though the decision rules that consumers need follow to avoid being deceived by advertising are relatively simple, some consumers will possibly be confused. They will possibly be gullible when they should not be, and inappropriately skeptical at other times.

But let us suppose that one tries to remove these deceptions by active government intervention to prohibit advertising that deceived anybody. Short of eliminating all advertising, such a government role would be self-defeating. Whatever the standards for fraudulence in advertising, it is unlikely that all consumers will know those standards. If the relatively simple decision rules necessary to avoid deception without government intervention are too confusing to some consumers, how much more confusing is the law on fraud? I know of no simple (or complicated) decision rule that would tell a consumer which advertising claims are legally required to be valid and which are not, or which advertisements are legally misleading and which are not.

The more the law protects against fraud, the more people think the law protects against fraud. Misinterpretation of the law's domain will exist, no matter how extensive that domain. Indeed, I believe, there is probably more deceptive advertising when laws on fraud exist than when they do not. Consumer market power generates information from advertising precisely because that information is in the self-interest of producers to provide. Hence, there is little incentive for deceptive advertising under the aegis of consumer market power. In contrast, state police power, involving the expenditure of resources, will never be enforced vigorously enough to eliminate all incentives for fraudulent advertising even in terms of the legal definition of fraud that prevails at the moment.

I am not saying that these laws against deceptive advertising are pointless. I am only asserting that most people have missed their point. The virtue of these laws is not that they reduce deceptive advertising. Rather, it is that they can make more infor-

From *Ethics, Free Enterprise, and Public Policy,* edited by Richard T. De George and Joseph A. Pichler (New York: Oxford University Press, 1978), pp. 187–98.

mation available to consumers than they would otherwise receive. Take, for example, the law prohibiting the mislabeling of the fabric content of clothing. If that law is sufficiently enforced, consumers will believe that a clothing label is usually correct. This will provide an incentive for some manufacturer to mislabel—unless the law is enforced so vigorously that nobody gains from breaking it (a non-optimal level of law enforcement). In the absence of the law, no one could trust any clothing label that it was not in the self-interest of the producer to specify correctly. Hence, these clothing labels, though incorrect, would not deceive many people. This law is not reducing deception in advertising, but it is enabling consumers to determine in many instances the fabric content of their clothing from the label. Laws can achieve the objective of more direct information at the price of both enforcement costs and costs to the consumer of being deceived where otherwise he would be appropriately distrustful.

Laws against fraudulent advertising are trying to accomplish something very important. People who feel that advertising is often wasteful have some real basis for that feeling. In the same sense that the engineer rates some kinds of engines as inefficient, the economist can declare that advertising is inefficient, that there is a significant potential for the improvement of advertising's performance. Whether that potential can be realized economically or not is, of course, another question. An inefficient motor may be the best motor we have. The indirect information which dominated the advertising of experience goods is inefficient compared to direct information. (By indirect information, I mean the information contained in the *fact* that the brand advertises. This is in contrast to direct information, which is the specific information contained in the advertising message.) First, direct information tells the consumer more, as evidenced by his preference for direct information. Second, more advertising is required to transmit indirect information than direct information. Any increase in the proportion of direct information in the advertising of experience goods would be an increase in advertising's efficiency. Laws that increase the range of believable statements in advertising can help advertising do a better job—unless, of course, they create even worse problems.

There are, indeed, some serious drawbacks to the way in which the Federal Trade Commission has been enforcing the law against fradulent advertising. Hyperbole plays a useful role in advertising. Exaggeration makes advertising more memorable. The more memorable the advertising, the more efficient it will be from both a private and social point of view, simply because memorability makes advertising perform its information function better. The FTC seems bent on eliminating these exaggerations. Take, for example, the famous case of the sandpaper shave. The FTC ruled that Rapid Shave must cancel this advertisement on the grounds that the conditions of the experiment were not quite kosher. An exceedingly memorable advertisement was eliminated. I believe virtually no new source of direct information was created by this decision.

Take another case on which the FTC would be on stronger ground: advertisements comparing Shell's performances with and without TCP, a gasoline additive. Obviously, it is an irrelevant comparison because Shell without TCP is not an option facing consumers. What harm is done by eliminating this advertisement? Its very existence suggests that it is a memorable advertisement. What good is done by this act? Nothing, by itself. The FTC would have to police carefully all advertisements using any purported tests or surveys to determine both the relevance and the appropriateness of the study design. Even then, it would take consumers quite a while to begin to believe the data quoted by advertisers, because it has been in their interest to distrust these data for so long. This herculean effort by the FTC would, in the process, have the unfortunate by-product of eliminating lots of memorable advertising.

AN ALTERNATIVE PROPOSAL

Can we do better? Laws designed to prevent deceptive advertising are not necessarily the best laws to help open up new bases of believable statements in advertising. The more strictly laws on fraud are interpreted, the less the opportunity for hyperbole, with its very real information payoff to society.

I think it is possible to design laws that at the same time: (1) create new bases for direct information, (2) allow hyperbole as much sway as the market desires, and (3) reduce enforcement costs as compared with the present legal structure. Remember, that is the heart of the problem. Advertisers provide indirect information for experience goods because, in the absence of laws, they are limited in the kinds of direct information they can authenticate. Let us attack that problem in the most direct way possible.

Let us create a dual set of standards for advertising authenticity. Suppose the advertiser were to utter some magic words such as, "We guarantee the validity and relevance of the information contained in this commercial." Then he would be strictly accountable in the courts for that information. Not only must that information be true, but it must not be misleading. Without such magic words, the advertiser is not accountable. Such a legal structure accomplishes the same objective as government authentication of advertising messages. The only differences are that the authentication process occurs after the advertisement rather than before, and the courts are the functioning government agency rather than the FTC.

This system seems to me to be vastly preferable to the present vigorous policing policies of the FTC against purportedly misleading advertising. It permits the authentication of direct information without destroying the effectiveness of indirect information. Certainly, the criterion that the FTC uses in policing advertising—does it mislead any consumers?—seems a self-defeating criterion to employ. The very act of policing makes other advertisements misleading to some consumers who would not have been previously misled.

It seems to me that, worthy though it may be, the goal of converting the advertising of experience qualities from indirect information cannot be completely achieved. Therefore, one has to remember that indirect information still has a role to play. One must be on guard against destroying the effectiveness of this indirect information while pursuing the goal of improving the information content of advertising.

In that sense, I am in favor of virtue rather than vice. But vice is not utterly vicious in its consequences. Consumers are, on the whole, better off as a result of being exposed to the essentially empty messages of experience goods advertising. That advertisements contain all sorts of non-credible statements does not prevent these advertisements from serving a social purpose, though that purpose could be better served if more credible statements were part of advertising.

Many of those who attack advertising are really attacking the market system in general. ''Advertisers,'' they say, ''are constantly pushing products which consumers either do not need or are possibly harmful to them. For shame!'' But these are always products that the consumer wants. Otherwise, the advertising could not succeed. In consequence, this is not an attack on advertising so much as an attack on consumer free choice.

It seems to me that consumer choice is the best way we have to determine what is valuable to consumers. Admittedly, consumers will make many mistakes in their choices. The information shortage that confronts consumers in their choice of brands is matched by the information shortage they face in choosing products. But consumers have a strong incentive to try to make the best decision, since their own well-being is at stake.

On the whole, government agencies will have even more severe information problems about which products are valuable to consumers than will consumers themselves. Consumers will, in general, know more about their own idiosyncracies than will any regulatory agency. The only class of cases in which the government could know more is that in which individual differences among consumers are largely irrelevant—not a very large class of cases.

While it is conceivable that in certain situations regulatory agencies will know more than will consumers, it is inconceivable that regulatory agencies will have as strong incentives to make the right choice as will consumers. Government officials are, on the whole, interested in their own well-being. Their own well-being is not closely related to consumer well-being because the voting market is a seriously defective market. People in general will have less incentive to acquire information as voters than they do as consumers, because the individual returns to them of voter information are less than the returns to them as individuals of consumer information. In consequence, government incentives to make decisions maximizing the well-being of voters are generally less than the incentives of consumers to achieve the same objective. In consequence, government decisions are likely to be worse than those of consumers.

The record of government regulation of consumer decisions is not one to encourage the case for government interference with consumer choice. Peltzman, for example, finds that the regulation of drugs by the Federal Drug Administration has made consumers far worse than they would have been otherwise.[1]

As far as advertising is concerned, the attack on consumer choice is particularly pointless. There is nothing in the process of advertising that makes advertisers systematically advertise the products that are bad for consumers rather than the products that are good for consumers. However, there is a process that seems to generate that result.

Advertising volume will be concentrated in the advertising of products that most consumers want rather than the products that satisfy minority taste. Best-sellers will be advertised more than poetry. Most critics of consumer choice would like consumers to have the tastes developed by a combined Ph.D. in English, art history, and music. Even supposing that Mozart provides more enjoyment than Elvis Presley, if one has developed the taste for Mozart, it is not clear whether such investment pays. It is assuredly clear that providing Mozart for people who prefer Presley will not work, since the Presleyites simply will not listen. The critics mistakenly attack advertising as catering to the products that are popular rather than unpopular.

They are mistaken not so much in their facts as in the inference they draw from this feature of advertising.

Furthermore, advertising is in many ways more useful to minor segments of the market than to majority groups. The continuation of activities for minor segments of the market is more dependent on advertising than is the continuation of majority activities. The smaller the group, the more difficult is the information problem of matching audience and activity. Anything which reduces that information problem—as does advertising—will tend, therefore, to be of particular benefit to minority groups.

While a critic (if pressed) might admit all of the above, he could still assert that an ethical advertiser should refuse to advertise a product which is not useful to consumers. This would be a largely pointless protest upon the part of advertisers unless many advertisers operated in this fashion since, otherwise, the consequence would be that somebody else, of roughly the same competence, would do the job at roughly the same price. If enough advertisers behaved this way, the price of ''unethical'' advertising would go up to some extent; but given actual behavior, the ethical advertiser would be making little social contribution.

It is even questionable whether advertising dominated by this much love of humanity is desirable or not. It is a maxim that, in a full-information world, the more people love one another, the better . . . . But with less than full information, this proposition no longer necessarily holds. One of the great advantages of selfish behavior in a market system is that it requires limited information to do a good job. The advertiser simply has to know how to advertise and at what price his services are demanded. But, now, let us convert the advertiser to a philanthropist, to a man who insists that he will advertise only those products which are best for consumers. To do his job right, he must now determine what are the consequences to consumers of all the alternative products that they face. The investments in necessary information required would be enormous, and a great deal of social waste would result. I would also be afraid of the results. The decisions people make about what others ought to consume differ in systematic ways from the decisions they make about what they themselves want. The fun in life tends to be eliminated in decisions for others. Sermons would be advertised heavily. Candy not at all. There are advantages to the maxim: Advertisers, stick to your copy.

NOTE

1. Sam Peltzman, ''An Evaluation of Consumer Protection Legislation: The 1962 Drug Amendments,'' *Journal of Political Economy,* vol. 81, no. 5 (September, 1973), pp. 1049–51.

20. Truth in the Marketplace

Burton M. Leiser

. . . . .

FALSE CLAIMS OF EFFECTIVENESS

An ad in a magazine directed at the teenage market carries a picture of a young girl whose tears are streaming down her cheeks. ''Cry Baby!'' the ad proclaims.

> That's right, cry if you like. Or giggle. You can even pout. Some things you can do just because you're a woman. And, also because you're a woman, you lose iron every month. The question is, are you putting that iron back? You may be among the 2 out of 3 American women who don't get enough iron from the food they eat to meet their recommended iron intake. . . . But One-A-Day Brand Multiple Vitamins Plus Iron does. . . . One-A-Day Plus Iron. One of the things you should know about, because you're a woman.

Two claims, at least, are made or implied by this advertisement. The first is that most American women do not get enough iron in their diets to make up for the ''deficiency'' that results from menstruation. The second is that One-A-Day tablets will fill the gap. As for the first claim, the American Medical Association pointed out long ago that ''the average diet of Americans is rich in iron.'' This statement was made during the AMA's campaign against Ironized Yeast, which also claimed to offer beneficial results from the Vitamin B that was included in its compound. The AMA showed that Vitamin B was found in sufficient quantities

From *Liberty, Justice, and Morals: Contemporary Value Conflicts,* 2nd ed. (New York: MacMillan, 1979), pp. 279–97.

in the average American diet to require no special supplement.[1] Now, if there is no significant lack of iron in the average person's diet (and this includes the average woman), there is no deficiency for One-A-Day tablets to fill. To be sure, some Americans do suffer from a lack of certain vitamins and minerals because they do not have an adequate diet. But the answer to this is not for them to take One-A-Day pills, but to eat more nutritious food.

Prior to 1922, Listerine had been advertised as "the best antiseptic for both internal and external use." It was recommended for treating gonorrhea and for "filling the cavity, during ovariotomy." During the years that followed, it was also touted as a safe antiseptic that would ward off cold germs and sore throat, and guard its users against pneumonia. Mothers were urged to rinse their hands in Listerine before touching their babies, and, after prayers, to "send those youngsters of yours into the bathroom for a goodnight gargle with Listerine." During the Depression the promoters of Listerine warned those who had jobs to hold on to them. To do that it was necessary to "fight colds as never before. Use Listerine."[2] Gerald B.Lambert, a member of the family that manufactured the product, told how Listerine came to be advertised as a mouthwash. He was deeply in debt, and, needing some cash to bail himself out, he decided to move into the family business. In discussing the advertising of the mixture, his brother asked whether it might be good for bad breath. Lambert was shocked at the suggestion that "bad breath" be used in advertising a respectable product. In the discussion that followed, the word *halitosis,* which had been found in a clipping from the British medical journal *Lancet,* was used. The word was unfamiliar to everyone at the meeting, but immediately struck Lambert as a suitable term to use in a new advertising campaign. The campaign caught on, Lambert paid off his debt, and in eight years made $25 million for his company.[3]

Now, how effective is Listerine for the ailments it claimed to cure? The AMA pointed out that the manufacturers of these antiseptics exaggerated the germ-killing powers of their products, that they did not tell of the hazardous germs that were not affected by Listerine, and that they failed to mention that the ability of a compound to kill germs in a test tube or on a glass plate in the laboratory is no indication of its capability of killing them in the mouth, the teeth, the gums, or the throat, let alone in other parts of the body.[4]

A recent case that is merely an echo of similar cases that go back many years is that in which the Federal Trade Commission ordered the ITT Continental Baking Company to stop promoting Profile bread as being less fattening than ordinary bread because it had fewer calories per slice. The advertisers neglected to mention that Profile bread had fewer calories per slice because it was sliced thinner, and that the difference between Profile and other bread slices was 58 as opposed to 63 calories, a rather insignificant amount. In addition, it had been claimed that people could lose weight by eating two slices of Profile before every meal. This was so, the FTC held, only if the consumer ate a lighter meal; and Profile bread had no special virtue, in this respect, over any other brand of bread.[5]

A similar misrepresentation was discovered in ads sponsored by the General Foods Corporation, claiming that two Toast'ems Pop-Ups contained at least as many nutrients as a breakfast of two eggs, two slices of bacon, and two slices of toast. In a commercial showing a child mulling over such a breakfast, a voice told parents whose children were unhappy at breakfast that "two hot Toast'ems provide 100 per cent of the minimum daily requirements of vitamins and iron. . . . As long as you know that—let them think it's just a big cookie." General Foods signed a consent order prohibiting it from making false nutritional claims for Toast' ems or any other consumer food product.[6] . . .

When a false claim of effectiveness is made, it is claimed that a product (treatment, remedy, or whatever) does *X*, when in fact that product does not do *X*. This is true of all false claims of effectiveness. But if a product does not do *X*, it does not follow that it does nothing else. Some products may do nothing; they may give the consumer no benefit, but at the same time do him no harm, other than the financial loss that he has suffered by buying the product. But some products may have *harmful* effects that are ignored in the promotional literature or advertisements that prompt people to buy them. Listerine may be harmless, though it will not prevent colds. Hoxsey's pastes* and many other preparations were (and are) harmful. Clearly, though the promoters of both Listerine and Hoxsey's treatments are guilty of false and misleading advertising, there is a further element of guilt in Hoxsey's kind of operation.

Still, the abuses go on, by some of the most respected firms in the food and drug line. In one recent year, the Food and Drug Administration seized shipments of Peritrate SA, a drug prescribed for the massive chest pain of the heart condition known as angina pectoris (Warner-Chilcott Laboratories); Serax, a tranquillizer (Wyeth Laboratories); Lincocin, an antibiotic (Upjohn); Lasix, a diuretic (Hoechst Pharmaceuticals); and Indoklon,

*[A paste, promoted as a cure for cancer, which was both ineffective and potentially deadly.—ED.]

an alternative to electroshock in some cases of depression (Ohio Chemical and Surgical Equipment Company)—all for false and deceptive promotion directed to the medical profession. Ayerst Laboratories was required by the FDA to send a "corrective letter" to some 280,000 doctors, retracting a claim that Atromid-S had a "beneficial effect" on heart disease, and the FDA ruled that Searle, Mead-Johnson, and Syntex had sent literature to physicians that misleadingly minimized the hazards of their birth control pills (Ovulen-21, Oracon, Norquen, and Norinyl-1).[7]

Unfortunately, moral suasion is not enough. Many persons, whatever their line of work, are not sufficiently resistant to the temptation to profit at the expense of others, and they are not touched by the moral arguments that might be brought to bear against their practices. One of the state's principal functions is the protection of its citizens against harm that might be done to them by others, even when they are unwitting collaborators in doing harm to themselves. It is the government's duty to require all hazardous substances to be labeled as such, so that everyone can see for himself what dangers he might expose himself to by ingesting them. It is no infringement on the citizen's freedom for the government to require of manufacturers of poisons that they clearly label their products with a warning that everyone may recognize. And the government is not interfering unreasonably with drug manufacturers when it demands that they print only scientifically verifiable facts in the literature that they distribute to the physicians who may be prescribing those products for their patients' use. Nor is it an unconscionable denial of freedom for the government to prevent persons who claim to cure diseases from practicing upon others unless they can offer some proof that the "cures" they offer are efficacious. For the government's right to protect its citizens against physical assault has never been questioned, and the purveyors of false and misleading information about harmful substances are as surely guilty of assault (if not in the legal sense, then at least in the moral sense) as they would have been had they poured their poisons into their victims' morning coffee. To argue that because the consumer has a choice and does not have to buy the product or use it, he is responsible for whatever happens to him, is like arguing that the poison victim had the choice of not drinking his coffee, and that by lifting the cup to his lips, he absolved the poisoner of all responsibility. The law has long maintained that a person who harms another is responsible for the harm that he does, even if he did so at the victim's request and with his active assistance. When a man is seeking relief from pain or illness and in that search relies upon the statements and claims made by drug salesmen, he is certainly entitled to no less protection than is offered to one who is determined to commit suicide.

THE PROMOTION OF DANGEROUS PRODUCTS

Any person who urges another to purchase and use a product or service assumes a responsibility toward him. The advertiser is not merely an innocent middleman who conveys a message from one person to another. He helps to create the message, using all the specialized skills of his art to persuade the potential consumer to act favorably upon his appeal. He shares in the rewards of successful advertising campaigns. He therefore assumes a responsibility for the product he induces the customer to purchase. In particular, if the product is dangerous or harmful, the advertiser who has persuaded the consumer to use it shares responsibility with the manufacturer for any harm that may result. This responsibility ought to be enforced by law, both with penal sanctions when the harm is particularly great and with appropriate remedies in tort. It is in any case a moral responsibility, for were it not for the advertiser's intervention, the consumer might never have suffered the damage done to him by the product he purchased.

By the same token, the advertiser has a right to feel . . . that he has contributed to the well-being of those who have been well served by the products and services he has helped to market. For every potential moral wrong that a person might commit, there must be an equivalent moral good that he might perform.

Those advertising agencies who have worked with the American Cancer Society to produce messages that have helped to persuade people to give up smoking or to refrain from becoming smokers have performed an important public service. Any utilitarian assessment of their performance would almost surely conclude that they had contributed to human happiness and significantly reduced the amount of pain and suffering in the world. Other advertising campaigns have assisted humanitarian organizations to raise funds for their operations and to further their causes. The government has employed advertising to discourage harmful behavior and to encourage beneficial activities. For example, during World War II, numerous ads reminded workers of the dangers inherent in talking about matters that might have helped the enemy and discouraged absenteeism at a time when the nation needed a steady supply of war matériel to carry its war effort to a successful conclusion. Similarly, advertising campaigns mounted by heavily over-populated nations have had some effect in encouraging their citizens to employ contraceptive devices so as to bring population growth down to a manageable level. The agencies that have helped to mount such campaigns can justly take pride in their work, for it is reasonable to believe that they have contributed to the sum of human happiness through their efforts.

On the other hand, some products that are heavily advertised are known—or ought to be known by those who market them—to be dangerous and capable of inflicting grave injuries upon those who use them. For example, Ultra Sheen Permanent Creme Relaxer is an emulsion used by consumers and professional beauticians to straighten curly hair. Ads represented it as "gentle" and "easy" to use. A woman in a television commercial for the product said that it "goes on cool while it really relaxes my hair. And the Conditioner and Hair Dress protects against moisture, so my hair doesn't go back." But the FTC found that Ultra Sheen's active ingredient was sodium hydroxide—lye—which straightens hair "by breaking down the cells of the hair shaft. . . . In some instances, [it] makes it brittle and causes partial or total hair loss." Moreover, the FTC found that it was neither cool nor gentle, but is "a primary skin irritant. It is caustic to skin and breaks down the cells which form the epidermis. Ultra Sheen relaxer in some instances causes skin and scalp irritation and burns, which may produce scars and permanent follicle damage. It also causes eye irritation and may impair vision." Because direct contact with eyes, scalp, or skin could cause irritation or injury, the FTC found that the product was not easy to use, contrary to the claims expressed in the ads. The FTC accordingly ordered the respondents to warn their customers of the product's dangers, to inform them of the presence of lye in it, to stop misrepresenting it, and to give clear instructions as to procedures to be followed in the event of injury to the customer.[8]

The law has for a long time recognized the duty a manufacturer owes to the purchaser of his product, particularly when the product is inherently dangerous. This duty has gradually been extended to others involved in the distribution and marketing of inherently dangerous products, so that persons and firms who retail automobiles, firearms, explosives, and poisons (for example) can be held liable in tort for damage caused by products that result from defects or negligence in the way they are labeled or handled.[9] At the very least, one would expect a warning to appear on the label of any product whose use might result in serious physical injury. The advertising and mass marketing of products that are prone to cause grave injury is a questionable practice.

This is not to say that dangerous products, including poisons, should not be sold. In the fifth chapter of *On Liberty,* John Stuart Mill argued that people ought to be permitted to purchase poisons, but that merchants who sold such substances were under a moral obligation (which should be a legal obligation as well) to label such substances clearly so that those who purchase them will know what they are buying. Mill's label rule should be extended to advertisements, because the decision to purchase a product is often made soon after an advertisement is seen. The product's hazards should be prominently displayed in advertisements so that the potential consumer may know what he or she is buying before the purchase is made. . . .

MISLEADING STATEMENTS OR CONTEXTS

Campbell Soup Company sponsored a television commercial that showed a thick creamy mixture that the announcer suggested was Campbell's vegetable soup. Federal investigators discovered that the bowl shown in the commercial had been filled with marbles to make it appear thicker than it really was and to make it seem to contain more vegetables than it did. Max Factor promoted a wave-setting lotion, Natural Wave, by showing how a drinking straw soaked in the lotion curled up. The FTC pointed out, however, that it did not logically follow that human hair would react as drinking straws did. The implication left in the viewer's mind, therefore, was false, because, in fact, straight hair did not curl after being soaked in Natural Wave. Such visual trickery is quite common in television commercials, in newspaper and magazine advertisements, in direct mail advertisements, and on package labels.

Misleading statements are also very common. Some agencies have advertised for talented men and women, and especially for children, who would be given an "excellent chance" of being put to work doing television commercials "at no fee." The agencies seldom placed anyone, and, though they charged no fees, they sent their clients to photographers who charged them substantial fees for taking their publicity pictures, or referred them to a firm that took "screen tests," also for lots of money. The photographers were always closely allied with the agencies, and the latter always shared a very healthy proportion of the fees charged.[10]

In none of these cases could one say that false statements were made. Strictly speaking, the advertisers were not guilty of lying to the public, if *lying* is defined as the deliberate utterance of an untrue statement. For, taken literally, none of the statements made in these advertisements is untrue. But the messages of the ads are misleading. Because of the pictorial matter in them, the reader or viewer makes inferences that are false, and the advertiser juxtaposes those pictures with the narrative in such a way that false inferences *will* be made. It is through those false inferences that he expects to earn enough money to pay for the ad and to have something left over for himself.

The land promoter who sends a glossy pamphlet advertising his ''retirement city'' in Arizona may not make a single false statement in the entire pamphlet. But by filling it with beautiful color photographs of swimming pools, golf links, and lush vegetation, none of which exists within 100 miles of the land he is selling, he leads his prospects to believe that certain features exist within that area which do *not* exist. Thus, without uttering or printing a single false statement, he is able to lead his prospects to believe what he knows is not true.

CONCEALMENT OF THE TRUTH

Merchants and producers have many ways of concealing truth from the customers—not by lying to them, but simply by not telling them facts that are relevant to the question of whether they ought to purchase a particular product or whether they are receiving full value for their money. An example that occurred a few years ago involved ham. Major packers, including Swift, Armour, and others, were selling ham that was advertised as being particularly juicy. The consumer was not told, however, that the hams were specially salted and that hypodermic syringes were used to inject large quantities of water into them. The ''juice'' was nothing but water that evaporated during cooking, leaving a ham some 40 percent smaller than the one that had been put into the oven. The housewife purchasing such a ham had no advance warning that she was purchasing water for the price of ham, unless she knew that the words *artificial ham* that were printed in small letters on the seal of the package meant that that was the case. Even that small warning was added only because of pressure brought to bear against the packers by the FTC. And there was no publicity to arouse the consumer to the special meaning of the term *artificial ham*.[11] . . .

A burglar or a thief may be heavily fined or sent to jail for many months for stealing a relatively small amount of money or valuables from a single person. But a salesman who cheats hundreds of people out of equal sums of money that total, in the aggregate, hundreds of thousands of dollars, is immune to prosecution, and may, in fact, be one of the community's most respected citizens. If Armour and Swift and other large corporations can bilk their customers out of enormous sums of money and do it with impunity, why, one might ask, should the petty thief be subjected to such severe penalties?

THE DUTY TO TELL THE WHOLE TRUTH

The advertising agency is hired by a firm to sell that firm's products. By signing a contract, it undertakes an obligation to do its utmost to fulfill that goal. Acceptance of that charge does not, however, relieve employees of the agency of their duties as citizens or as human beings. Their immediate goal as advertising men may be to obtain accounts and to keep them by increasing the customer's sales, but that goal should never be achieved at the expense of harm to unsuspecting persons. The duty not to direct advertising to children is related to this moral obligation, as is the duty to label hazardous substances with clear and unmistakable warnings. Such moral obligations may not be enforced by the law. Persons who are concerned with doing what is right need not set the limits of their conduct at the bounds delineated by the law, for the law does not always conform with standards of moral right. To be more specific, if the law permits an advertiser to refrain from mentioning a particular hazard that his product poses to his customer, it does not follow that he has a moral right to withold that information from them. If the law provides no sanctions against deceptive advertising, an ethical advertiser will nevertheless not engaged in willful deception of those who place their trust in him.

In a broad view of advertising, the small leaflets that are enclosed in the boxes in which drugs are packed may be regarded as advertisements of a sort. They contain technical information for the doctor's reference and are designed to prevent improper use of the drug. But they are also designed to influence physicians to use drugs for certain medical conditions, and may therefore be regarded as at least partially intended to serve as marketing devices.

A recent study revealed that certain drugs are advertised and packaged in Latin America in ways that the FDA would condemn (or has condemned) as unacceptable in the United States. Winstrol, a synthetic derivative of testosterone, is considered too toxic in the United States for all but the narrowest use. The AMA warns that such drugs "should not be used to stimulate growth in children who are small but otherwise normal and healthy." But in Latin America, Winstrol is widely promoted as an appetite stimulant for underweight children. A spokesman from the Winthrop Drug Company complained that the advertising was quoted out of context and that the company complied with the laws and medical practices of each country in which it did business.

Another Winthrop product, Commel (dipyrone), is a painkiller that may cause fatal blood diseases and may not be sold in the United States as a routine treatment for pain, arthritis, or fever. According to the AMA, the "only justifiable use [of dipyrone] is as a last resort to reduce fever when safer measures have failed." But a packet of the drug purchased in Brazil recommends that the drug be used for "migraine headaches, neuralgia, muscular or articular rheumatism, hepatic and renal colic, pain and fever which usually accompany grippe, angina, otitis, and sinusitis, toothache, and pain after dental extractions." The company's comments about the matter were as evasive as they were about Winstrol.

E. R. Squibb & Sons' Raudixin, which is occasionally used in this country to treat high blood pressure, was found to induce such deep depressions that hospitalization was often necessary, and suicide sometimes followed. But in Brazil, the package insert says it is the "ideal medicine for the treatment of emotional disturbances such as states of tension and anxiety, and in states characterized by nervousness, irritability, excitability and insomnia. . . . Raudixin is the drug of choice in daily practice." A company spokesman acknowledged that the insert had been written 20 years ago, conceded that the insert had not been rewritten in 20 years, but insisted that it complied with Brazilian drug regulations.

The aim of drug companies' ads, and even of their package inserts, is not so much to inform physicians of the uses and potential hazards of their products as to persuade them to prescribe them. When forced to do so by government regulations, they will write truthful and informative inserts, but when government regulations are lax, they will subject the public to needless hazards and rationalize their conduct by claiming that they are doing nothing unlawful. This not only is morally unacceptable but should be legally proscribed. Those who believe in minimal government interference in private affairs would prefer to see government regulations of all industries, including the drug industry, reduced as much as possible. But so long as an industry behaves irresponsibly and endangers the lives and health of the persons it is supposed to serve, the public has no alternative but to rely upon government for protection.

THE FORM OF THE ADVERTISEMENT

. . . Some firms advertise a product as if it were on sale at a reduced price when, in fact, the product never sold at the so-called regular price. A paint manufacturer, for example, advertised: "Buy 1 gallon for $6.98 and get a second gallon free." But it *never* sold its paint at $6.98 per gallon.

Encyclopedia salesmen sometimes misrepresent themselves as agents for school boards or as public opinion pollsters. They offer "free" sets of encyclopedias, allegedly as a public relations "service," but ask for a small monthly charge for a ten-year research service that will presumably guarantee the worried customer's children their places in medical school or law school.

Record clubs and book clubs falsely advertise "free" books which are not free at all but are consideration for a binding contract to purchase a number of books at a supposedly reduced price which, after postage and handling charges are added, is often higher than the retail price of the same books. The "club" members are customers and the "clubs" are profit-making businesses.

Insurance companies and other firms use photographs or drawings of impressive buildings in their ads and on their stationery to suggest that they are large, long-established firms, even though they may occupy no more than a single office. One firm recently hung its own sign on a large, modern municipal government building and filmed its commercials in front of the disguised structure, leaving the impression that its own offices were housed there.

Small-size type may be used to obscure limitations on insurance coverage, and bold type may emphasize irrelevant facts, such as coverage that is common to all policies of a given class.

Misleading words and phrases—particularly those having special technical meanings that are unfamiliar to the uninitiated—are used to create false impressions in the minds of laymen. Ordinary language may be used in such a way as to suggest to the uninitiated that certain conditions apply when they do not apply at all. For example, an ad saying, "This policy will pay your hospital and surgical bills" suggests (though it does not literally say) that *all* of the hospital and surgical bills of the insured will be paid; and "This policy will replace your income" suggests that *all* of the insured's income will be replaced if he becomes disabled—when, in fact, only a small portion of his bills or his income will be paid or replaced.

Some companies don't hesitate to make inconsistent claims for competing products that they manufacture or distribute. The Sterling Drug Company, for example, distributes Bayer aspirin in the United States and also manufactures Vanquish. In 1970, the company was simultaneously running ads that made the following claims:

> For Bayer: "Aspirin is already the strongest pain reliever you can buy." Combining Bayer with other drugs or buffering it would not improve it. "No one has ever found a way to improve Bayer Aspirin, because Bayer Aspirin is 100% Aspirin. None is faster or more effective than Bayer Aspirin. Even WE can't improve it though we keep trying."
>
> For Vanquish: It has "a unique way" of relieving headache "with extra strength and gentle buffers . . . . It's the only leading pain reliever you can buy that does."

Thus, Sterling Drug is both unable and able to produce a pain reliever that is more effective than Bayer. Buffering doesn't and does add to the strength or gentleness of aspirin.[12]

Another device is the half-truth which becomes an outright lie because it creates a completely false impression. Excedrin, for example, ran an ad reporting that a "major hospital study" showed that "it took more than twice as many aspirin tablets to give the same pain relief as two Excedrin." But the ad failed to point out that the Excedrin tablets contained twice as much aspirin as plain aspirin tablets and that another study had demonstrated that Excedrin had caused more intestinal upset than two brands of aspirin when given in equal doses.[13]

Although most of these examples have been derived from studies of the drug industry, that industry has no monopoly on deceptive advertising practices. Similar examples can be cited from industries as diverse as automobiles, lumber, oil, household cleaning products, and real estate. Unscrupulous and deceptive practices in many industries have caused severe financial losses to unsuspecting individuals. Even when the individual's loss is relatively small, collectively the damage may amount to hundreds of millions of dollars. With these financial losses there are inevitably other costs that are more difficult to assess, not the least of which is the emotional damage, the anger, and the resentment that must follow when the loss represents a major portion of an individual's earnings or savings. Some of this undoubtedly spills over into resentment against a system that permits what the victims perceive to be grave injustices against themselves and the classes or groups to which they belong. Advertising alone cannot be held responsible for any social dislocations that might result from such resentments, but the advertising industry cannot wholly escape responsibility for its contributions to the sense of injustice that prevails in so many quarters today. . . .

A FINAL WORD ON ADVERTISING

Advertising has an important and constructive role to play in the life of the nation. It is not true that all advertising men are unscrupulous or that all businessmen are concerned only with selling, no matter what the cost to their customers. Nor is it true that advertisements are necessarily misleading or fraudulent. . . .

. . . But even when the message is not distorted, those who use the mass media to disseminate it should do so with some sense of social and public responsibility. It is far worse, though, when the message is distorted. And even David Ogilvy, for all his insistence on honesty in advertising, admits that he is "continuously guilty of *suppressio veri* [the suppression of the truth]. Surely it is asking too much to expect the advertiser to describe the shortcomings of his product? One must be forgiven for putting one's best foot foward."[14] So the consumer is *not* to be told all the relevant information; he is *not* to be given all the facts that would be of assistance in making a reasonable decision about a given purchase. In particular, he will *not* be told about the weaknesses of a product, about its shock hazards, for example, if it is an electrical appliance; about the danger it poses to the consumer's health if it is a cleaning fluid; about the danger it poses to his life if it is an automobile tire that is not built to sustain the heavy loads of today's automobile at turnpike speeds; or, if one carries the doctrine to its final conclusion, about the possibly harmful side effects of a new drug that is advertised to the medical profession. Telling the truth combined with "*suppressio veri*" is *not* telling the truth. It is *not* asking too much of the advertiser to reveal such facts when they are known to him, and he should *not* be forgiven for "putting his best foot forward" at his customer's expense. . . . All aspirin is the same, for example, whether it is stamped *Bayer* and sells for $1.95 per hundred or whether it is an unadvertised brand of U.S.P. aspirin that sells for 35 cents per hundred. But the advertiser will try to convince you that what is true of Bayer aspirin is not true of the other product. This is unfair to the consumer, whether he is rich or poor; but it is particularly unfair to the poor consumer, who could use in other ways the money he spends paying for Bayer's advertising.

Advertising has an important role to fill in our society. It is not likely to disappear. But it is not always carried on in the most ethical manner. Its supporters tend to exaggerate the benefits that have flowed from it, and they are not at all shy about boasting about its effectiveness in their trade meetings and in their efforts to win new business. But they often shrug off any suggestion that their efforts may have harmful effects upon some segments of society by denying that they are all *that* effective. They cannot have it both ways. If advertising is as effective as its practitioners claim it to be, then it possesses enormous potential for harm as well as for good. Because many, though not all, advertisers are concerned primarily about selling their products and only secondarily, if at all, about telling the truth, it is reasonable to suggest that some government regulation be exercised over this industry; and in particular, that advertisers—both producers and agencies—be held liable for harm or damage that results to consumers from misleading or false claims in advertisements, and that they be required to make good any financial loss that consumers may suffer as a result of reliance upon any misleading advertisement, whether the advertisement was "fraudulent" in the criminal sense or not. If laws were passed, both on the federal level and at the state or provincial level, making agencies and producers responsible for restitution of damages suffered by customers who relied upon their "messages," there would be a great incentive for those concerned to confine their claims to those that could be substantiated and to resort to fewer misleading gimmicks. Though such legislation would not eliminate all abuses, it would go a long way toward assuring the public that the advertising messages to which it was exposed respected the truth.

NOTES

1. See James G. Burrow, *AMA: Voice of American Medicine* (Baltimore: Johns Hopkins [University] Press, 1963), p. 268; and Arthur J. Cramp, *Nostrums and Quackery and Pseudo-medicine* (Chicago: University of Chicago Press, 1936), vol. 3, pp. 29–31.

2. James H. Young, *The Medical Messiahs* (Princeton, NJ: Princeton University Press, 1967), pp. 147f.

3. See David Ogilvy, *Confessions of an Advertising Man* (New York: Atheneum, 1963), p. 86. Also Gerald B. Lambert, "How I Sold Listerine," in *The Amazing Advertising Business,* ed. the Editors of *Fortune* (New York: Simon and Schuster, 1957), chap. 5.

4. Young, op. cit., p. 155.

5. *Consumer Reports,* vol. 36 (September 1971), pp. 525f.

6. Ibid., p. 561.

7. Mortin Mintz, "Drugs: Deceptive Advertising," in David Sanford (ed.), *Hot War on the Consumer* (New York: Pitman, 1969), pp. 91ff.

8. *FTC in the Matter of Johnson Products Company, Inc., and Bozell & Jacobs, Inc.,* Docket no. C–2788 (February 10, 1976).

9. Cf. John G. Fleming, *The Law of Torts,* 4th ed. (Sydney, Austl.: Law Book Company, 1971), pp. 452ff.

10. *Consumer Reports,* [op. cit.] p. 560.

11. Cf. *Consumer Reports,* March and August, 1961; follow-up reports, April and August, 1962.

12. Select Committee Hearings, Pt. 1, *Analgesics* (Washington [,DC]: U.S. Government Printing Office, 1971), p. 230.

13. Ibid.

14. Ogilvy, [op. cit.], pp. 158f.

QUESTIONS FOR STUDY AND DISCUSSION

1. Carefully compare and contrast the fiduciary models of the professional/client relationship offered by Michael Bayles in chapter 4 and Joseph Ellin in this chapter. Offer your own defense of one of these models for the professional/client relationship, saying why you think it is the more acceptable model for that relationship.

2. Explain the conceptual distinction between lying and deception. One author has said, "evasive deception is at least a concession to the importance of autonomy, whereas the willingness to lie reveals a complete disregard for the rationality and autonomy of the other" (James L. Muyskens, *Moral Problems in Nursing: A Philosophical Investigation* [Totowa, NJ: Rowman and Littlefield], 1982, pp. 141–42.) Offer your own explanation and evaluation of this claim.

3. Explain the difference between Joseph Collins and Sissela Bok on the harmfulness of being truthful with patients. Which of these views do you believe is more correct? Defend your answer as fully as you are able, using concrete examples to help with your justification.

4. Offer your own account of what kinds of characteristics make advertising deceptive. Given your account, is all deceptive advertising morally impermissible? If so, explain why. If not, explain what kinds of deceptive advertising you think are morally permissible and what kinds, if any, are morally impermissible; justify any moral distinctions you make.

5. Compare and contrast Phillip Nelson and Burton Leiser on the question of rigorous government supervision of advertising; be sure to say why each author holds the position he does. Offer your own defense of one of these views over the other. Should advertisers, as Leiser suggests, be legally liable for harmful effects of the products they advertise? Explain.

6. In some rather well-known obedience studies, social science researcher Stanley Milgram deceived subjects into believing they were inflicting several electrical shocks on other people. (See Stanley Milgram, *Obedience to Authority: An Experimental View* [New York: Harper and Row, 1973]). The subjects were directed to keep adminstering higher and higher voltages despite the (feigned) cries of pain of those receiving the ''shocks''; much to the surprise of the researchers themselves, people went far beyond what anyone involved in the study had predicted. Milgram's studies have been defended on the ground that they provided powerful information on how susceptible ordinary people are to the demands of those in authority. But one author has objected that these studies did not tell us anything that we did not already know (e.g., from experiences like the Holocaust), namely, that ordinary human beings can become willing to do unthinkable things to other human beings when directed to do so by others in authority (Ruth Macklin, ''The Problem of Adequate Disclosure in Social Science Research,'' in Tom L. Beauchamp et al., eds., *Ethical Issues in Social Science Research* [Baltimore, MD: Johns Hopkins University Press, 1982], pp. 193–214; p. 202). Describe briefly some social science research experiment involving deception which has been performed by students at your own school as part of a course of study. (If you have not been involved in such an experiment either as a subject or researcher, you will need to ask around.) Offer your own moral evaluation of the experiment you describe; pay particular attention to the questions of whether the information gained was new information and precisely what the students conducting the experiment learned from it and whether what they learned could have been learned without using deception. Was the deception morally justified? Defend your answer.

7. Professors in social science courses often offer students extra credit for serving as subjects in research projects. Evaluate the morality of this practice. In your discussion, consider whether this practice raises any serious worries about exploitation and coercion.

8. It is sometimes the case that physicians training medical students on hospital floors introduce the students as ''young Doctor so-and-so.'' And some medical schools have issued medical students white coats and name tags reading ''Doctor ______'' to be worn when they are on the hospital floors. In defense of such practices, it has been argued that identifying students as ''young doctors'' (etc.) will help to relieve the anxiety of medical students when they start working on the floors and, even more importantly, that patients will only cooperate with students in ways helpful to their education if they are unaware that the students are students. As least one physician has suggested that as long as students are reporting their findings to the physicians responsible for a patient's care, ''there would be no question of of 'exploitive role playing' or 'fraud.' If students are addressed as 'Doctor' it would be because they would be assuming one of the essential functions of a physician.'' (Lewis Glickman, ''Student Doctors,'' letter, *New England Journal of Medicine* 284 [1971]: 1216.) Offer your own evaluation of the moral permissibility of these practices; be sure to include an evaluation of the kinds of reasons offered to justify them.

CASE: THE POTENT PLACEBO

Dorothy Abraham had been bedridden for the last twelve of her seventy-two years. Cancer of the colon had been treated through three operations and chemotherapy. During the active therapeutic intervention,

---

Case, with minor variation, from Robert M. Veatch, *Case Studies in Medical Ethics* (Cambridge, MA: Harvard University Press, 1977), case 46.

a period of about three years, Mrs. Abraham was in severe pain, for which she received meperidine, a narcotic analgesic. She also had a great deal of difficulty sleeping, for which her physician, Dr. Martha Little, gave her secobarbital one-half grain, a fast-acting barbiturate. Eventually Mrs. Abraham was able to decrease the dose of the analgesic and had not taken any for several years. As tolerance for the secobarbital developed, however, Dr. Little had increased the dose to one and one-half grains. Although . . . nothing organic could be found to account for the insomnia, the patient still was unable to sleep without the barbiturate. Mrs. Abraham continued taking the one and one-half grain secobarbital for about two more years, when Dr. Little became convinced she had a barbiturate addict on her hands. She did not object to sick patients getting the medication they needed, even if it meant addiction, but she saw no reason to support Mrs. Abraham's addiction, even if it had begun in the most innocent manner.

Through the local drugstore, which delivered all of Mrs. Abraham's medical supplies, Dr. Little arranged to prescribe a specifically formulated secobarbital with an increasing amount of lactose, the pharmacologically inert milk sugar, and a correspondingly decreasing amount of the barbiturate. The pharmacist began replacing ten percent of the active drug with lactose. After a month, the formula was changed to twenty-percent lactose. Special arrangement was made with the manufacturer of the drug to obtain the distinctive red, bullet-shaped capsules, so that they looked exactly like the full-strength barbiturate.

Over a period of about a year, the lactose proportion was gradually increased. For the last several years, once a month, Mrs. Abraham has had delivered to her apartment a prescription for thirty one-and-one-half-grain capsules of placebo. The pharmacist currently charged eight dollars a month, the same price he would have charged for the real barbiturate despite the fact that his labor cost for handfilling the capsules with lactose was much higher than would be the cost of the active drug. He had known Mrs. Abraham for many years and was aware that she and her husband lived on a modest Social Security check, so he felt he should give her the specially low price.

Dr. Little continued to see Mrs. Abraham and to write the monthly prescriptions for the pharmacist's files. She had reduced her charge for the prescription to two dollars a month out of a similar respect for the Abrahams' modest means. To give the prescriptions without charge, she feared, would run the risk of losing the therapeutic effect of the placebo.

A new pharmacist had just been hired to work evenings in the local drugstore to relieve the overworked owner. He had been asked to fill the placebo prescription for the thirty capsules. He was disturbed. The owner explained to him the long history of the case—the now-cured cancer, the barbiturate addiction, the gradual withdrawal several years ago. He ended with a plea that it would be cruel to Mrs. Abraham ever to suggest that she was not getting the real drug. The new pharmacist was still perplexed. He recognized how disturbing it would be to be told of the placebo. Mrs. Abraham would not only run the risk of insomnia and even real addiction, but also might lose confidence in her physician of many years. But he was also concerned about the expense to her—one hundred twenty dollars a year—for nothing more than milk sugar. More than that, he was deeply disturbed that he was becoming part of a conspiracy to deceive a patient, to trick her into thinking she was getting real pharmacological help. He conceded that Mrs. Abraham might be better off spending her last years happily thinking she was getting the potent drug, yet he found the whole enterprise demeaning, an insult to this patient and to patients in general. Was filling such orders, he wondered, consistent with his duties as a pharmacist?

1. What duties of a pharmacist do you think might be relevant to resolving this case?

2. Offer and defend your own views on the actions of Dr. Little, the first pharmacist, and the corporation which filled the request for the empty capsules when Dr. Little decided to deal with Mrs. Abraham's addiction by ordering a placebo.

3. Given that the conspiracy is in place and that the placebo seems clearly to be effective, should Dr. Little attempt to wean Mrs. Abraham from the placebo? Defend your answer.

4. Should the new pharmacist refuse to fill the prescription? Why or why not?

5. Suppose that the new pharmacist decides not only that filling the prescription would be inconsistent with his duties as a pharmacist, but also that continuing to give Mrs. Abraham the placebo cannot be morally justified. Suppose he contacts Dr. Little and urges her to wean Mrs. Abraham from the placebo. Suppose Dr. Little refuses. Given these suppositions, would it be morally permissible for the pharmacist to tell Mrs. Abraham that she has been receiving a placebo? Defend your answer carefully; be sure to say what place the pharmacist's duties as an individual and the pharmacist's duties as a professional have in your reasoning.

CASE: HIRING THE EX-CONVICT

In March 19—, our bank had an opening for a messenger/driver whose responsibility was to distribute interoffice mail and office supplies to various branch locations. One of the applicants interviewed on March —, was a black male who appeared to be in his early thirties. . . . The interviewer was impressed with the applicant's verbal ability, his friendliness, and his desire to obtain employment. Since his record was rather spotty, the interviewer pressed for more information and learned that he had had difficulties holding any job because employers fired him after it came to light that he had a prison record.

Banks fall under the Federal Deposit Insurance Act (12th U.S.C. 1829), and are prohibited from employing convicted criminals whose offenses involved dishonesty under Section 19. For the moment, then, the applicant was not eligible for employment. In further conversation, the interviewer learned that the applicant's last offense had occurred eight years previously and that he was convicted and started to serve time four months after the offense. The offense involved the theft of a vehicle, driving to endanger, and assault and battery of a police officer. He was released from prison after eighteen months and since that time had had no further difficulties with the law. (This was later substantiated by various sources, including his probation officer.) There was, then, ample evidence that this man had been rehabilitated, and the interviewer felt that the exclusion he was feeling from society was rooted in injustice. Had he not already paid the price society demanded for his crime? Consequently, the interviewer decided to press the issue on behalf of the applicant and her bank and learned, much to her delighted surprise, that the Federal Deposit Insurance Corporation (FDIC) had issued a memorandum to all banks in 1968 which gave general guidelines on how to petition for an exemption under Section 19. The FDIC verbally invited the bank to submit data which could result in an exemption for the applicant.

The applicant and the interviewer made the joint decision to pursue the exemption. In addition to the items listed as required for the application, a resolution of the bank's Board of Directors was required. The process was begun that March with a preliminary letter to the FDIC. Further information was forwarded to them at various intervals until all requirements, with the exception of the consent of the bonding company, had been assembled. In July, after nearly three months of negotiations, the bonding company wrote a letter declining to insure the applicant. Without a fidelity bond assurance for the person, the FDIC would not issue an exemption. At the end of July, the bank notified the applicant that the bonding company had refused to extend coverage on him and that it would not be in a position to hire him. The interviewer was deeply distressed.

We now know that there is a Catch 22 in the willingness of the FDIC to grant exemptions from their requirements. They will not consider an exemption without a fidelity bond coverage; yet the bonding company refuses to issue such a fidelity bond to persons they know have been convicted of crimes.

This case was prepared by a student who has asked not to be identified. I am grateful for her permission to use it. —ED.

1. Should private organizations be free to refuse to hire persons *simply* because they have a criminal record? Defend your answer; anticipate and respond to the strongest objection to your position.

2. Should bonding companies be free to refuse to issue fidelity bonds *simply* because an applicant has a criminal record? Defend your answer; anticipate and respond to the strongest objection to your position.

3. In future instances would this applicant be morally justified in lying about his criminal record? Defend your answer as fully as you are able.

4. In future instances would the interviewer in this case be morally justified in ignoring the law and Section 19 if she felt it would be just to hire an ex-offender? Justify your answer. Would the job a person was being hired for make any difference in your answer? Explain your answer as fully as you are able.

5. Suppose in some future instance the interviewer suspects that an applicant has an old criminal record but is lying about it. Suppose that she feels this is a strong applicant. Would she be morally justified in not pursuing the matter with the applicant? Why or why not?

SELECTED BIBLIOGRAPHY

Arendt, Hannah. "Lying in Politics." In *Crises of the Republic,* pp. 1–47. New York: Harcourt Brace Jovanovich, 1972.

Bok, Sissela. "Deceptive Social Science Research." In *Lying: Moral Choice in Public and Private Life,* chap. 13. New York: Pantheon, 1978.

———. "The Ethics of Giving Placebos." *Scientific American* 231 (November 1974): 17–23.

Bulmer, Martin. "The Research Ethics of Pseudo-Patient Studies: A New Look at the Merits of Covert Ethnographic Methods." *Sociological Review* 30 (1982): 627–46.

Carson, Thomas L., and Richard E. Wokutch. "The Moral Status of Bluffing and Deception in Business." In *Profits and Professions: Essays in Business and Professional Ethics,* ed. Wade L. Robison, Michael S. Pritchard, and Joseph S. Ellin, pp. 141–55. Clifton, NJ: Humana Press, 1983.

Carson, Thomas L., Richard E. Wokutch, and James E. Cox. "An Ethical Analysis of Deception in Advertising." *Journal of Business Ethics* 4:2 (1985): 93–104.

"Case—Police Informer in a Hospital Bed." *Hastings Center Report* 11:5 (1981): 17.

Chisholm, Roderick, and Thomas D. Feehen. "The Intent to Deceive." *Journal of Philosophy* 74:3 (1977): 143–59.

Durham, Taylor R. "Information, Persuasion, and Control in Moral Appraisal of Advertising." *Journal of Business Ethics* 3:3 (August 1984): 173–80.

Elms, Alan C. "Keeping Deception Honest: Justifying Conditions for Social Scientific Research Strategems." In *Ethical Issues in Social Science Research,* ed. Tom L. Beauchamp, Ruth R. Faden, R. Jay Wallace, Jr., and LeRoy Walters, pp. 232–45. Baltimore: Johns Hopkins University Press, 1982.

Emamalizadeh, Hossein. "The Informative and Persuasive Functions of Advertising: A Comment." *Journal of Business Ethics* 4:2 (1985): 151–53.

Fried, Charles. "On Lying." In *Right and Wrong,* pp. 54–78. Cambridge, MA: Harvard University Press, 1978.

Goldman, Alan H. "Ethical Issues in Advertising." In *Just Business: New Introductory Essays in Business Ethics,* ed. Tom Regan, pp. 235–70. Philadelphia: Temple University Press, 1983; reissued New York: Random House, 1984.

Henry, Jules. "Advertising as a Philosophical System." In *Culture Against Man,* pp. 45–99. New York: Random House, 1963.

Isenberg, Arnold. "Deontology and the Ethics of Lying." *Philosophy and Phenomenological Research* 24:4 (1964): 465–80.

Kant, Immanuel. "Duties Towards Others: Truthfulness." In *Lectures on Ethics* [1775–80], ed. Louis Infield, pp. 224–35. London: Methuen, 1930; reissued New York: Harper and Row, 1963.

———. "On the Supposed Right to Lie from Benevolent Motives." In *Critique of Practical Reason and Other Writings in Moral Philosophy,* ed. and trans. Lewis White Beck, pp. 346–50. Chicago: University of Chicago Press, 1949.

Kelly, William D., and Stanley R. Friesen. "Do Cancer Patients Want to Be Told?" *Surgery* 27 (1950): 822–26.

Milgram, Stanley. *Obedience to Authority: An Experimental View.* New York: Harper and Row, 1973.

Oken, Donald. "What to Tell Cancer Patients." *Journal of the American Medical Association* 175 (1961): 1120–28.

Santilli, Paul C. "The Informative and Persuasive Functions of Advertising: A Moral Appraisal." *Journal of Business Ethics* 2:1 (1983): 27–34.

Siegler, Frederick. "Lying." *American Philosophical Quarterly* 3:2 (1966): 128–36.

Wokutch, Richard E., Thomas L. Carson, and Kent F. Mursmann. "Bluffing in Labor Negotiations." *Journal of Business Ethics* 1:1 (1982): 13–22.

See also the selected bibliography for chap. 4: Buchanan, Callahan, Feinberg, Gert and Culver, Goldman (chap. 4), Husak, Kleinig, Sartorius, VanDeVeer, and Zembaty.

6

INFORMED CONSENT

Obtaining informed consent has only recently emerged as a significant and explicit moral concern in the professions. In the context of medical treatment, for example, there has not been a long or strong tradition of worry about obtaining informed consent from patients. The roots of the current emphasis on informed consent in health care provision date back to the Nuremburg trials and their shocking revelations of the horrifying experiments conducted by physicians on concentration camp prisoners. One significant outcome of the trials was the Nuremburg Code, which set out criteria for the moral acceptability of biomedical experiments on human subjects and underscored the moral necessity of gaining informed consent from research subjects.[1] The concern about informed consent in human biomedical experimentation later extended to include medical treatment. Today, the issue of informed consent is more and more widely discussed across the professions.

As the term suggests, informed consent involves two major components, namely, an informational component and a volitional component. For example (and roughly speaking), an individual gives a genuinely informed consent to some medical intervention when she both understands the risks and possible benefits of the treatment, and she voluntarily accepts the intervention. Informed consent (e.g., to medical intervention, to some action by one's attorney, as a subject in a biomedical or social science experiment, to dangerous pollutants in one's environment, to the risks one assumes on riding in a train or airplane or in using a product, etc.) can be vitiated in a number of ways, for example, if an agent is deprived of adequate information, or is incompetent to appreciate the information given, or is somehow coerced or manipulated into "consenting," and so forth. Problems with informed consent can arise, then, in the informational and/or in the volitional component.

The readings in this chapter concentrate on the question of informed consent in the biomedical context, examining the issue as it arises in ordinary medical treatment and in biomedical experimentation on human subjects, particularly prisoners, who have traditionally provided a substantial pool of subjects for such experiments. Despite the concentration of readings on the biomedical context, however, it cannot be emphasized strongly enough that there are equally important questions of informed consent in other contexts. For example, the issue of informed consent arises in education, in legal practice, and in various areas of business: What role must informed consent of students play in university education? Must it play any role at all in lower levels of education? What role must informed consent play in legal representation, or in the purchasing of products, or in the utilization of various corporate services? Such questions are intimately linked to the question of professional role differentiation (see chap. 3), to the question of the proper model of the professional/client relationship (see chap. 4), and to the problem of deception in business and the professions (see chap. 5).

The concern to secure informed consent to the assumption of risk, to impingements on privacy, to a variety of actions affecting one can be (and has been) justified on both teleological (consequentialist) grounds and deontological (nonconsequentialist) grounds. For instance, Sissela Bok's argument in "Lying and Lies to the Sick and Dying" (chap. 5) provides an example of a teleological argument for informing patients of their diagnoses and prognoses. Bok's central point is that individuals are generally in the best position to judge their own interests, and they are likely to be best able to provide for their welfare when they have information regarding matters affecting their welfare.[2]

The deontological argument for securing informed consent rests on a fundamental respect for persons as rational agents. For example, Alexander Capron has argued that the informed consent requirement in the biomedical context promotes individual autonomy, protects an individual's moral status as a human being, and avoids fraud and duress—all considerations grounded in a fundamental respect for persons as beings capable of, and entitled to, self-direction in matters affecting themselves.[3] Contemporary deontological arguments for requiring informed consent have much of their philosophical grounding in the Kantian position that persons are not to be used as means to good ends, whether those ends involve the good of others or their own good.[4] Respect for individual welfare and respect for individual autonomy, then, give rise to the concern about informed consent across the professions.

As we have already seen, informed consent involves an informational component and a volitional component. The selections in this chapter address each of these aspects of the issue. The selection from *Canterbury* v. *Spence* focuses on the informational component of informed consent in ordinary medical practice. The plaintiff, John Canterbury, had not been informed by his physician, William Spence, that a surgery to which he had consented held out a risk of paralysis. Judge Spotswood Robinson's argument in the decision includes a commitment to the view that adults of sound mind have a right to determine what will be done to their bodies. He argues that the exercise of this right is directly dependent on the informed exercise of choice, which requires that one be given the information necessary for a knowledgeable evaluation of the available options and their attendant risks. The general question raised by Judge Robinson is this: What information must an individual have in order to make an appropriately knowledgeable exercise of choice? The Court explores four possibilities, and it is important to notice that these possibilities might be suggested as informational criteria for informed consent in contexts other than medical treatment. After rejecting three of the candidates, Judge Robinson rules in favor of the reasonable person standard as the standard for fulfilling the informational requirement in obtaining an acceptably informed consent to medical intervention. In chapter 7, we shall see Terry Pinkard offer an interesting twist on the "reasonable person standard." In attempting to establish criteria for morally justifiable deception and invasions of privacy in social science research, Pinkard will suggest that social scientists should ask themselves what sorts of deceptions and privacy invasions reasonable persons would consent to, thereby attempting to preserve the element of respect for persons in research that precludes getting informed consent from subjects.

The selection from Franz Ingelfinger addresses problems in getting informed consent to biomedical research, and Ingelfinger points out that these problems arise in both the informational and volitional components. Ingelfinger argues that not even physicians can give a fully informed consent to being research subjects. And he suggests that patients who are asked by their physicians to participate in research do not give an uncoerced consent. This second claim is a particularly interesting one, since it raises the question of subtle coercion in the physician/patient relationship as well as concerns about exploitation of a vulnerable population—the ill.

The two major objections to the informed consent requirement in medical practice are that getting a genuinely informed consent is impossible and that it can be harmful to try to get a genuinely informed consent. This second claim has been made in chapter 5 by Joseph Collins, and it is addressed in selection 17 by Sissela Bok. In the present chapter, Samuel Gorovitz considers both traditional objections to the informed consent requirement. Addressing the kind of skepticism about the informational component found in Ingelfinger, Gorovitz argues that an *adequately* informed consent need not be a *fully* informed consent. Gorovitz also offers some help in thinking about claims that informing a patient is "medically contraindicated." His suggestion is that the best *medical* choice for an individual may not be the best choice for that individual, all things considered. Notice that these observations need not be limited to the medical context. It would be argued, for example, by Michael Bayles (see chap. 4) that clients across the professions must have a right to approve or veto the activities of professionals pursuing their interests. In the legal context, it might be argued (against a theorist like Joseph Ellin in chap. 5) that a client has a right to keep her lawyer from using a tactic which, though legal, is morally objectionable to her. Similarly, it might be argued that investors are entitled to direct their brokers not to buy stocks in corporations which promise to provide an excellent return, but which engage in practices the client feels are morally reprehensible. Professionals may, of course, terminate a relationship with a client when they believe they are being asked by clients to act in ways that are below professional standards (see Joan Callahan, chap. 4). But it does not follow from this that pursuit of the best medical outcome, the best legal outcome, the best financial outcome, and so forth, is the only relevant consideration in decision making in the professional/client relationship.

Although Gorovitz touches on the volitional component in informed consent, the last two readings in this chapter take this component as their focus. Jessica Mitford argues that because of their situation and the rewards attaching to participation in biomedical research, prisoners cannot give an acceptably voluntary consent to participation in such research. Mitford's position seems to be that research on prisoners is morally permissible if and only if (1) the studies conducted are scientifically sound, scientifically worthy, and morally responsible; (2) researchers are competent and can be trusted to adequately inform their subjects of the risks of the research; and (3) there are no rewards for participation in research projects. Although it seems that the first two requirements could be met by rigorous screening of projects and research personnel, it also seems that Mitford's third requirement for the moral permissibility of research on prisoners cannot ever be met. And that is because it seems that there will always be rewards to prisoners for participation in human experimentation: Given that prison life is intrinsically boring, the very break in routine afforded by research participation is enough to serve as a substantial reward to those who volunteer. On Mitford's account, then, the very living situation of prisoners necessarily precludes their giving an adequately voluntary consent to being research subjects.

Rejecting views like Mitford's, Carl Cohen argues that prisoners can give an adequately voluntary consent to research participation. Cohen's central point is that neither the attractiveness of a certain choice nor the desperateness of someone's situation is relevant to deciding whether the voluntariness of an individual's choice is vitiated. According to Cohen, a choice is genuinely coerced only when an individual is compelled or constrained to act as another wishes him to act as a result of measures taken by the coercer. On this understanding of coercion, prisoners are no more coerced into participating in research than the ordinary person who needs a job is coerced into taking a job which has been offered to her. The major disagreement between Mitford and Cohen, then, lies in their standards for accepting a choice as voluntary. Mitford's standards for voluntariness are extremely high, whereas Cohen's are extremely low. Mitford seems committed to holding that the very attractiveness of a choice detracts from the voluntariness in someone's making that choice. Cohen, on the other hand, seems unable to allow that there is any serious worry about diminished voluntariness of choice for prisoners participating in biomedical research. And both views have interesting implications for how we are to assess voluntariness of choice in a host of other contexts.

As we have seen, the concern about getting informed consent rests on the deeper moral requirements of respect for the well-being and self-direction of persons. Those same moral mandates underpin the requirements of respect for privacy and confidentiality in the professions. We shall focus on these issues in chapter 7.

NOTES

1. See the *Trials of War Criminals Before the Nuremburg Military Tribunals* (Washington, D.C.: U.S. Government Printing Office, 1948).

2. This argument also underpins John Stuart Mill's position that governments should not interfere with competent adult citizens for their own good. See Mill's *On Liberty* (1859), in *Utilitarianism, On Liberty, and Essay on Bentham,* ed. Mary Warnock (New York: New American Library, 1962).

3. See Alexander M. Capron, ''Informed Consent in Catastrophic Disease Research and Treatment,'' *University of Pennsylvania Law Review* 123 (1974): 340–438.

4. See, e.g., Immanuel Kant, *Foundations of the Metaphysics of Morals* (1785; 2nd ed., 1786), in *Critique of Practical Reason and Other Writings in Moral Philosophy,* ed. and trans. Lewis White Beck (Chicago: University of Chicago Press, 1949). In the Second Section, Kant offers the second formulation of his categorical imperative, which holds (roughly) that one must never treat a person—not even oneself—as a mere object. According to one interpretation, this excludes lying to or manipulating people for their own good, since doing so fails to treat persons as subjects.

THE INFORMATIONAL COMPONENT

21. Opinion in *Canterbury* v. *Spence**

Judge Spotswood W. Robinson, III

The record we review tells a depressing tale. A youth troubled only by back pain submitted to an operation without being informed of a risk of paralysis incidental thereto. A day after the operation he fell from his hospital bed after having been left without assistance while voiding. A few hours after

From U.S. Court of Appeals, District of Columbia Circuit, 19 May 1972. 464 *Federal Reporter*, 2nd Series, pp. 772–96, West Publishing Company.

*[Some notes have been deleted without indication.—ED.]

the fall, the lower half of his body was paralyzed, and he had to operated on again. Despite extensive medical care, he has never been what he was before. Instead of the back pain, even years later, he hobbled about on crutches, a victim of paralysis of the bowels and urinary incontinence. In a very real sense this lawsuit is an understandable search for reasons. . . .

Suits charging failure by a physician adequately to disclose the risks and alternatives of proposed treatment are not innovations in American law. They date back a good half-century, and in the last decade they have multiplied rapidly. There is, nonetheless, disagreement among the courts and the commentators on many major questions, and there is no precedent of our own directly in point. For the tools enabling resolution of the issues on this appeal, we are forced to begin at first principles.

The root premise is the concept, fundamental in American jurisprudence, that "[e]very human being of adult years and sound mind has a right to determine what shall be done with his own body. . . ."[1] True consent to what happens to one's self is the informed exercise of a choice, and that entails an opportunity to evaluate knowledgeably the options available and the risks attendant upon each.[2] The average patient has little or no understanding of the medical arts, and ordinarily has only his physician to whom he can look for enlightenment with which to reach an intelligent decision.[3] From these almost axiomatic considerations springs the need, and in turn the requirement, of a reasonable divulgence by physician to patient to make such a decision possible.[4]

A physician is under a duty to treat his patient skillfully[5] but proficiency in diagnosis and therapy is not the full measure of his responsibility. The cases demonstrate that the physician is under an obligation to communicate specific information to the patient when the exigencies of reasonable care call for it.[6] Due care may require a physician perceiving symptoms of bodily abnormality to alert the patient to the condition.[7] It may call upon the physician confronting an ailment which does not respond to his ministrations to inform the patient thereof.[8] It may command the physician to instruct the patient as to any limitations to be presently observed for his own welfare,[9] and as to any precautionary therapy he should seek in the future.[10] It may oblige the physician to advise the patient of the need for or desirability of any alternative treatment promising greater benefit than that being pursued.[11] Just as plainly, due care normally demands that the physician warn the patient of any risks to his well-being which contemplated therapy may involve.[12]

The context in which the duty of risk-disclosure arises is invariably the occasion for decision as to whether a particular treatment procedure is to be undertaken. To the physician, whose training enables a self-satisfying evaluation, the answer may seem clear, but it is the prerogative of the patient, not the physician, to determine for himself the direction in which his interests seem to lie.[13] To enable the patient to chart his course understandably, some familiarity with the therapeutic alternatives and their hazards becomes essential.[14]

A reasonable revelation in these respects is not only a necessity but, as we see it, is as much a matter of the physician's duty. It is a duty to warn of the dangers lurking in the proposed treatment, and that is surely a facet of due care. It is, too, a duty to impart information which the patient has every right to expect.[15] The patient's reliance upon the physician is a trust of the kind which traditionally has exacted obligations beyond those associated with arms–length transactions. His dependence upon the physician for information affecting his well-being, in terms of contemplated treatment, is well-nigh abject. As earlier noted, long before the instant litigation arose, courts had recognized that the physician had the responsibility of satisfying the vital informational needs of the patient.[16] More recently, we ourselves have found "in the fiducial qualities of [the physician-patient] relationship the physician's duty to reveal to the patient that which in his best interests it is important that he should know."[17] We now find, as a part of the physician's overall obligation to the patient, a similar duty of reasonable disclosure of the choices with respect to proposed therapy and the dangers inherently and potentially involved.

This disclosure requirement, on analysis, reflects much more of a change in doctrinal emphasis than a substantive addition to malpractice law. It is well established that the physician must seek and secure his patient's consent before commencing an operation or other course of treatment.[18] It is also clear that the consent, to be efficacious, must be free from imposition upon the patient. It is the settled rule that therapy not authorized by the patient may amount to a tort—a common law battery—by the physician.[19] And it is evident that it is normally impossible to obtain a consent worthy of the name unless the physician first elucidates the options and the perils for the patient's edification. Thus the physician has long borne a duty, on pain of liability for unauthorized treatment, to make adequate disclosure to the patient.[20] The evolution of the obligation to communicate for the patient's benefit as well as the physician's protection has hardly involved an extraordinary restructuring of the law.

There are, in our view, formidable obstacles to acceptance of the notion that the physician's obligation to disclose is either germinated or limited by medical practice. To begin with, the reality of any discernible custom reflecting a professional consensus on communication of option and risk information to patients is open to serious doubt.[21] We sense the danger that what in fact is no custom at all may be taken as an affirmative custom to maintain silence, and that physician-witnesses to the so-called custom may state merely their personal opinions as to what they or others would do under given conditions.[22] We cannot gloss over the inconsistency between reliance on a general practice respecting divulgence and, on the other hand, realization that the myriad of variables among patients[23] makes each case so different that its omission can rationally be justified only by the effect of its individual circumstances. Nor can we ignore the fact that to bind the disclosure obligation to medical usage is to arrogate the decision on revelation to the physician alone. Respect for the patient's right of self-determination on particular therapy demands a standard set by law for physicians rather than one which physicians may or may not impose upon themselves. . . .

Once the circumstances give rise to a duty on the physician's part to inform his patient, the next inquiry is the scope of the disclosure the physician is legally obliged to make. The courts have frequently confronted this problem but no uniform standard defining the adequacy of the divulgence emerges from the decisions. Some have said "full" disclosure,[24] a norm we are unwilling to adopt literally. It seems obviously prohibitive and unrealistic to expect physicians to discuss with their patients every risk of proposed treatment—no matter how small or remote—and generally unnecessary from the patient's viewpoint as well. . . .

The larger number of courts, as might be expected, have applied tests framed with reference to prevailing fashion within the medical profession.[25] Some have measured the disclosure by "good medical practice,"[26] others by what a reasonable practitioner would have bared under the circumstances,[27] and still others by what medical custom in the community would demand.[28] We have explored this rather considerable body of law but are unprepared to follow it. The duty to disclose, we have reasoned, arises from phenomena apart from medical custom and practice. The latter, we think, should no more establish the scope of the duty than its existence. Any definition of scope in terms purely of a professional standard is at odds with the patient's prerogative to decide on projected therapy himself. That prerogative, we have said, is at the very foundation of the duty to disclose, and both the patient's right to know and the physician's correlative obligation to tell him are diluted to the extent that its compass is dictated by the medical profession.[29]

In our view, the patient's right of self-decision shapes the boundaries of the duty to reveal. That right can be effectively exercised only if the patient possesses enough information to enable an intelligent choice. The scope of the physician's communications to the patient, then, must be measured by the patient's need, and that need is the information material to the decision. Thus the test for determining whether a particular peril must be divulged is its materiality to the patient's decision: all risks potentially affecting the decision must be unmasked.[30] And to safeguard the patient's interest in achieving his own determination on treatment, the law must itself set the standard for adequate disclosure.[31]

Optimally for the patient, exposure of a risk would be mandatory whenever the patient would deem it significant to his decision, either singly or in combination with other risks. Such a requirement, however, would summon the physician to second-guess the patient, whose ideas on materiality could hardly be known to the physician. That would make an undue demand upon medical practitioners, whose conduct, like that of others, is to be measured in terms of reasonableness. Consonantly with orthodox negligence doctrine, the physician's liability for nondisclosure is to be determined on the basis of foresight, not hindsight; no less than any other aspect of negligence, the issue on nondisclosure must be approached from the viewpoint of the reasonableness of the physician's divulgence in terms of what he knows or should know to be the patient's informational needs. If, but only if, the fact-finder can say that the physician's communication was unreasonably inadequate is an imposition of liability legally or morally justified.[32]

Of necessity, the content of the disclosure rests in the first instance with the physician. Ordinarily it is only he who is in position to identify particular dangers; always he must make a judgment, in terms of materiality, as to whether and to what extent revelation to the patient is called for. He cannot know with complete exactitude what the patient would consider important to his decision, but on the basis of his medical training and experience he can sense how the average, reasonable patient expectably would react.[33] Indeed, with knowledge of, or ability to learn, his patient's background and current condition, he is in a position superior to that of most others—attorneys, for example—who are called upon to make judgments on pain of liability in damages for unreasonable miscalculation.[34]

From these considerations we derive the breadth of the disclosure of risks legally to be required. The scope of the standard is not subjective as to either the physician or the patient; it remains objective with due regard for the patient's informational needs and with suitable leeway for the physician's situation. In broad outline, we agree that "[a] risk is thus material when a reasonable person, in what the physician knows or should know to be the patient's position, would be likely to attach significance to the risk or cluster of risks in deciding whether or not to forego the proposed therapy."[35]

The topics importantly demanding a communication of information are the inherent and potential hazards of the proposed treatment, the alternatives to that treatment, if any, and the results likely if the patient remains untreated. The factors contributing significance to the dangerousness of a medical technique are, of course, the incidence of injury and the degree of the harm threatened.[36] A very small chance of death or serious disablement may well be significant; a potential disability which dramatically outweighs the potential benefit of the therapy or the detriments of the existing malady . . . summons discussion with the patient.

There is no bright line separating the significant from the insignificant; the answer in any case must abide a rule of reason. Some dangers—infection, for example—are inherent in any operation; there is no obligation to communicate those of which persons of average sophistication are aware. Even more clearly, the physician bears no responsibility for discussion of hazards the patient has already discovered, or those having no apparent materiality to patients' decision on therapy. The disclosure doctrine, like others marking lines between permissible and impermissible behavior in medical practice, is in essence a requirement of conduct prudent under the circumstances. Whenever nondisclosure of particular risk information is open to debate by reasonable-minded men, the issue is for the finder of the facts.

Two exceptions to the general rule of disclosure have been noted by the courts. Each is in the nature of a physician's privilege not to disclose, and the reasoning underlying them is appealing. Each, indeed, is but a recognition that, as important as is the patient's right to know, it is greatly outweighed by the magnitudinous circumstances giving rise to the privilege. The first comes into play when the patient is unconscious or otherwise incapable of consenting, and harm from a failure to treat is imminent and outweighs any harm threatened by the proposed treatment. When a genuine emergency of that sort arises, it is settled that the impracticality of conferring with the patient dispenses with need for it. Even in situations of that character the physician should, as current law requires, attempt to secure a relative's consent if possible. But if time is too short to accommodate discussion, obviously the physician should proceed with the treatment.

The second exception obtains when risk-disclosure poses such a threat of detriment to the patient as to become unfeasible or contraindicated from a medical point of view. It is recognized that patients occasionally become so ill or emotionally distraught on disclosure as to foreclose a rational decision, or complicate or hinder the treatment, or perhaps even pose psychological damage to the patient.[37] Where that is so, the cases have generally held that the physician is armed with a privilege to keep information from the patient,[38] and we think it clear that portents of that type may justify the physician in action he deems medically warranted. The critical inquiry is whether the physician responded to a sound medical judgment that communication of the risk information would present a threat to the patient's well-being.

The physician's privilege to withhold information for therapeutic reasons must be carefully circumscribed, however, for otherwise it might devour the disclosure rule itself. The privilege does not accept the paternalisitc notion that the physician may remain silent simply because divulgence might prompt the patient to forego therapy the physician feels the patient really needs.[39] That attitude presumes instability or perversity for even the normal patient, and runs counter to the foundation principle that the patient should and ordinarily can make the choice for himself. Nor does the privilege contemplate operation save where the patient's reaction to risk information, as reasonably foreseen by the physician, is menacing.[40] And even in a situation of that kind, disclosure to a close relative with a view to securing consent to the proposed treatment may be the only alternative open to the physician. . . .

NOTES

1. *Schloendorff* v. *Society of New York Hospital,* 211 N.Y. 125, 105 N.E. 92, 93 (1914). See also *Natanson* v. *Kline,* 186 Kan. 393, 350 P.2d 1093, 1104 (1960), clarified, 187 Kan. 186, 354 P.2d 670 (1960). . . .

2. See *Dunham* v. *Wright,* 423 F.2d 940, 943–946 (3d Cir. 1970) (applying Pennsylvania law); *Campbell* v. *Oliva,* 424 F.2d 1244, 1250–1251 (6th Cir. 1970) (applying Tennessee law); *Bowers* v. *Talmage,* 159 So.2d 888 (Fla.App.1963); *Woods* v. *Brumlop,* 71 N.M. 221, 377 P.2d 520, 524–525 (1962); *Mason* v. *Ellsworth,* 3 Wash.App. 298, 474 P.2d 909, 915, 918–919 (1970).

3. Patients ordinarily are persons unlearned in the medical sciences. Some few, of course, are schooled in branches of the medical profession or in related fields. But even within the latter group variations in degree of medical knowledge specifically referable to particular therapy may be broad, as for example, between a specialist and a general practitioner, or between a physician and a nurse. It may well be, then, that it is only in the unusual case that a court could safely assume that the patient's insights were on a parity with those of the treating physician.

4. The doctrine that a consent effective as authority to form therapy can arise only from the patient's understanding of alternatives to and risks of the therapy is commonly denominated "informed consent." See, *e.g.*, Waltz and Scheuneman, Informed Consent to Therapy, 64 Nw.U.L. Rev. 628, 629 (1970). The same appellation is frequently assigned to the doctrine requiring physicians, as a matter of duty to patients, to communicate information as to such alternatives and risks. See, *e.g.*, Comment, Informed Consent in Medical Malpractice, 55 Calif.L.Rev. 1396 (1967). While we recognize the general utility of shorthand phrases in literary expositions, we caution that uncritical use of the "informed consent" label can be misleading. See, *e.g.*, Plante, An Analysis of "Informed Consent," 36 Ford.L.Rev. 639, 671–72 (1968).

In duty-to-disclose cases, the focus of attention is more properly upon the nature and content of the physician's divulgence than the patient's understanding or consent. Adequate disclosure and informed consent are, of course, two sides of the same coin—the former a *sine qua non* of the latter. But the vital inquiry on duty to disclose relates to the physician's performance of an obligation, while one of the difficulties with analysis in terms of "informed consent" is its tendency to imply that what is decisive is the degree of the patient's comprehension. . . . [T]he physician discharges the duty when he makes a reasonable effort to convey sufficient information although the patient, without fault of the physician, may not fully grasp it. . . . Even though the factfinder may have occasion to draw an inference on the state of the patient's enlightenment, the factfinding process on performance of the duty ultimately reaches back to what the physician actually said or failed to say. And while the factual conclusion on adequacy of the revelation will vary as between patients—as, for example, between a lay patient and a physician–patient—the fluctuations are attributable to the kind of divulgence which may be reasonable under the circumstances.

5. *Brown* v. Keaveny, 117 U.S.App.D.C. 117, 118, 326 F.2d 660, 661 (1963); *Quick* v. *Thurston,* 110 U.S.App.D.C. 169, 171, 290 F.2d 350, 362, 88 A.L.R.2d 299 (en banc 1961); *Rodgers* v. *Lawson,* 83 U.S.App.D.C. 281, 282, 170 F.2d 157, 158 (1948).

6. See discussion in McCoid, The Care Required of Medical Practitioners, 12 Vand.L.Rev. 549, 586–97 (1959).

7. See *Union Carbide and Carbon Corp.* v. *Stapleton,* 237 F.2d 229, 232 (6th Cir. 1956); *Maertins* v. *Kaiser Foundation Hosp.,* 162 Cal.App.2d 661, 328 P.2d 494, 497 (1958); *Doty* v. *Lutheran Hosp. Ass'n,* 110 Neb. 467, 194 N.W. 444, 445, 447 (1923); *Tvedt* v. *Haugen,* 70 N.D. 338, 294 N.W. 183, 187 (1940). See also *Dietze* v. *King,* 184 F.Supp. 944, 948, 949 (E.D.Va.1960); *Dowling* v. *Mutual Life Ins. Co.,* 168 So.2d 107, 116 (La.App.1964), writ refused, 247 La. 248, 170 So.2d 508 (1965).

8. See *Rahn* v. *United States,* 222 F.Supp. 775, 780–781 (S.D.Ga.1963) (applying Georgia law); *Baldor* v. *Rogers,* 81 So.2d 658, 662, 55 A.L.R.2d 453 (Fla.1955); *Manion* v. *Tweedy,* 257 Minn. 59, 100 N.W.2d 124, 128, 129 (1959); *Tvedt.* v. *Haugen, supra* note 7, 294 N.W. at 187; *Ison* v. *McFall,* 55 Tenn.App. 326, 400 S.W.2d 243, 258 (1964); *Kelly* v. *Carroll,* 36 Wash.2d 482, 219 P.2d 79, 88, 19 A.L.R.2d 1174, cert. denied, 340 U.S. 892, 71 S.Ct. 208, 95 L.Ed. 646 (1950).

9. *Newman* v. *Anderson,* 195 Wis. 200, 217 N.W. 306 (1928). See also *Whitfield* v. *Daniel Constr. Co.,* 226 S.C. 37, 83 S.E.2d 460, 463 (1954).

10. *Beck* v. *German Klinik,* 78 Iowa 696, 43 N.W. 617, 618 (1889); *Pike* v. *Honsinger,* 155 N.Y. 201, 49 N.E. 760, 762 (1898); *Doan* v. *Griffith,* 402 S.W.2d 855, 856 (Ky.1966).

11. The typical situation is where a general practitioner discovers that the patient's malady calls for specialized treatment, whereupon the duty generally arises to advise the patient to consult a specialist. . . . See also *Baldor* v. *Rogers, supra* note 8, 81 So.2d at 662; *Garafola* v. *Maimonides Hosp.,* 22 A.D.2d 85, 253 N.Y.S.2d 856, 858, 28 A.L.R.3d 1357 (1964); aff'd, 19 N.Y.2d 765, 279 N.Y.S.2d 523, 226 N.E.2d 311, 28 A.L.R.3d 1362 (1967); McCoid, The Care Required of Medical Practitioners, 12 Vand.L.Rev. 549, 597–98 (1959).

12. See, *e.g.*, *Wall* v. *Brim,* 138 F.2d 478, 480–481 (5th Cir. 1943), consent issue tried on remand and verdict for plaintiff aff'd., 145 F.2d 492 (5th Cir. 1944), cert. denied, 324 U.S. 857, 65 S.Ct. 858, 89 L.Ed. 1415 (1945); *Belcher* v. *Carter,* 13 Ohio App.2d 113, 234 N.E.2d 311, 312 (1967); *Hunter* v. *Burroughs,* 123 Va. 113, 96 S.E. 360 at 366; Plante, An Analysis of "Informed Consent," 36 Ford.L.Rev. 639, 653 (1968).

13. See text *supra* at notes 1–2.

14. See cases cited *supra* notes 3–4.

15. Some doubt has been expressed as to ability of physicians to suitably communicate their evaluations of risks and the advantages of optional treatment, and as to the lay patient's ability to understand what the physician tells him. Karchmer, Informed Consent: A Plaintiff's Medical Malpractice "Wonder Drug," 31 Mo.L.Rev. 29, 41 (1966). We do not share these apprehensions. The discussion need not be a disquisition, and surely the physician is not compelled to give his patient a short medical education; the disclosure rule summons the physician only to a reasonable explanation. . . . That means generally informing the patient in non-technical terms as to what is at stake: the therapy alternatives open to him, the goals expectably to be achieved, and the risks that may ensue from particular treatment and no treatment. See *Stinnett* v. *Price,* 446 S.W.2d 893, 894, 895 (Tex.Civ.App.1969). So informing the patient hardly taxes the physician, and it must be the exceptional patient who cannot comprehend such an explanation at least in a rough way.

16. See, *e.g.*, *Sheets* v. *Burman,* 322 F.2d 277, 279–280 (5th Cir. 1963); *Hudson* v. *Moore,* 239 Ala. 130, 194 So. 147, 149 (1940); *Guy* v. Schuldt, 236 Ind. 101,

138 N.E.2d 891, 895 (1956); *Perrin* v. *Rodriguez,* 153 So. 555, 556–557 (La.App. 1934); *Schmucking* v. *Mayo,* 183 Minn. 37, 235 N.W. 633 (1931); *Thompson* v. *Barnard,* 142 S.W.2d 238, 241 (Tex.Civ.App.1940), aff'd, 138 Tex. 227, 158 S.W.2d 486 (1942).

17. *Emmett* v. *Eastern Dispensary and Cas. Hosp.,* 130 U.S.App.D.C. 50, 54, 396 F.2d 931, 935 (1967). See also, Swan, The California Law of Malpractice of Physicians, Surgeons, and Dentists, 33 Calif.L.Rev. 248, 251 (1945).

18. Where the patient is incapable of consenting, the physician may have to obtain consent from someone else. See, *e.g., Bonner* v. *Moran,* 75 U.S.App.D.C. 156, 157–158, 126 F.2d 121, 122–123, 139 A.L.R. 1366 (1941).

19. See, *e.g., Bonner* v. *Moran, supra* note 18, 75 U.S.App.D.C. at 157, 126 F.2d at 122. . . .

20. We discard the thought that the patient should ask for information before the physician is required to disclose. Caveat emptor is not the norm for the consumer of medical services. Duty to disclose is more than a call to speak merely on the patient's request, or merely to answer the patient's questions; it is a duty to volunteer, if necessary, the information the patient needs for intelligent decision. The patient may be ignorant, confused, overawed by the physician or frightened by the hospital, or even ashamed to inquire. See generally Note, Restructuring Informed Consent: Legal Therapy for the Doctor-Patient Relationship, 79 Yale L. J. 1533, 1545–51 (1970). Perhaps relatively few patients could in any event identify the relevant questions in the absence of prior explanation by the physician. Physicians and hospitals have patients of widely divergent socio-economic backgrounds, and a rule which presumes a degree of sophistication which many members of society lack is likely to breed gross inequities. See Note, Informed Consent as a Theory of Medical Liability, 1970 Wis.L.Rev. 879, 891–97.

21. See, *e.g.,* Comment, Informed Consent in Medical Malpractice, 55 Calif.L.Rev. 1396, 1404–05 (1967); Comment, Valid Consent to Medical Treatment: Need the Patient Know?, 4 Duquesne L.Rev. 450, 458–59 (1966); Note, 75 Harv.L.Rev. 1445, 1447 (1962).

22. Comment, Informed Consent in Medical Malpractice, 55 Calif.L.Rev. 1396, 1404 (1967); Note, 75 Harv.L.Rev. 1445, 1447 (1962).

23. For example, the variables which may or may not give rise to the physician's privilege to withhold risk information for thereapeutic reasons. . . .

24. *E.g., Salgo* v. *Leland Stanford Jr. Univ. Bd. of Trustees,* 154 Cal.App.2d 560, 317 P.2d 170, 181 (1957); *Woods* v. *Brumlop, supra* note 2, 377 P.2d at 524–525.

25. *E.g., Shetter* v. *Rochelle,* 2 Ariz.App. 358, 409 P.2d 74, 86 (1965), modified, 2 Ariz. App. 607, 411 P.2d 45 (1966); *Ditlow* v. *Kaplan,* 181 So.2d 226, 228 (Fla.App.1965); *Williams* v. *Menehan,* 191 Kan. 6, 379 P.2d 292, 294 (1963); *Kaplan* v. *Haines,* 96 N.J.Super. 242, 232 A.2d 840, 845 (1967) aff'd, 51 N.J. 404, 241 A.2d 235 (1968); *Govin* v. *Hunter,* 374 P.2d 421, 424 (Wyo.1962). . . .

26. *Shetter* v. *Rochelle, supra* note 25, 409 P.2d at 86.

27. *E.g., Ditlow* v. *Kaplan, supra* note 25, 181 So.2d at 228; *Kaplan* v. *Haines, supra* note 25, 232 A.2d at 845.

28. *E.g., Williams.* v. *Menehan, supra* note 25, 379 P.2d at 294; *Govin* v. *Hunter, supra* note 25, 374 P2d at 424.

29. For similar reasons, we reject the suggestion that disclosure should be discretionary with the physician. See Note, 109 U.Pa.L.Rev. 768, 772–73 (1961).

30. See Waltz & Scheuneman, Informed Consent to Therapy, 64 Nw.U.L.Rev. 628, 639–41 (1970).

31. See Comment, Informed Consent in Medical Malpractice, 55 Calif.L.Rev. 1396, 1407–10 (1967).

32. See Waltz & Scheuneman, Informed Consent to Theraphy, 64 Nw.U.L.Rev. 628, 639–40 (1970).

33. *Id.*

34. *Id.*

35. *Id.* at 640. . . .

36. See Comment, Informed Consent in Medical Malpractice, 55 Calif.L.Rev. 1396, 1407 n. 68 (1967).

37. See, *e.g., Salgo* v. *Leland Stanford Jr. Univ. Bd. of Trustees, supra* note 24, 317 P.2d at 181 (1957); Waltz & Scheuneman, Informed Consent to Therapy, 64 Nw.U.L.Rev. 628, 641–43 (1970).

38. *E.g., Roberts* v. *Wood,* 206 F.Supp. 579, 583 (S.D.Ala.1962); *Nishi* v. *Hartwell,* 52 Haw. 188, 473 P.2d 116, 119 (1970); *Woods* v. *Brumlop, supra* note 2, 377 P.2d at 525; *Ball* v. *Mallinkrodt Chem. Works,* 53 Tenn.App. 218, 381 S.W.2d 563, 567–568 (1964).

39. *E.g., Scott* v. *Wilson,* 396 S.W.2d 532 at 534–535; Comment, Informed Consent in Medical Malpractice, 55 Calif.L.Rev. 1396, 1409–10 (1967); Note, 75 Harv.L.Rev. 1445, 1448 (1962).

40. Note, 75 Harv.L.Rev. 1445, 1448 (1962).

22. Informed (but Uneducated) Consent

Franz J. Ingelfinger

The trouble with informed consent is that it is not educated consent. Let us assume that the experimental subject, whether a patient, a volunteer, or otherwise enlisted, is exposed to a completely honest array of factual detail. He is told of the medical uncertainty that exists and that must be resolved by research endeavors, of the time and discomfort

From *New England Journal of Medicine* 287 (1972): 465–66.

involved, and of the tiny percentage risk of some serious consequences of the test procedure. He is also reassured of his rights and given a formal, quasi-legal statement to read. No exculpatory language is used. With his written signature, the subject then caps the transaction, and whether he sees himself as a heroic martyr for the sake of mankind, or as a reluctant guinea pig dragooned for the benefit of science, or whether, perhaps, he is merely bewildered, he obviously has given his "informed consent." Because established routines have been scrupulously observed, the doctor, the lawyer, and the ethicist are content.

But the chances are remote that the subject really understands what he has consented to—in the sense that the responsible medical investigator understands the goals, nature, and hazards of his study. How can the layman comprehend the importance of his perhaps not receiving, as determined by the luck of the draw, the highly touted new treatment that his roommate will get? How can he appreciate the sensation of living for days with a multi-lumen intestinal tube passing through his mouth and pharynx? How can he interpret the information that an intravascular catheter and radiopaque dye injection have an 0.01 per cent probability of leading to a dangerous thrombosis or cardiac arrhythmia? It is moreover quite unlikely that any patient-subject can see himself accurately within the broad context of the situation, to weigh the inconveniences and hazards that he will have to undergo against the improvements that the research project may bring to the management of his disease in general and to his own case in particular. . . .

Nor can the information given to the experimental subject be in any sense totally complete. It would be impractical and probably unethical for the investigator to present the nearly endless list of all possible contingencies; in fact, he may not himself be aware of every untoward thing that might happen. Extensive detail, moreover, usually enhances the subject's confusion. Epstein and Lasagna showed that comprehension of medical information given to untutored subjects is inversely correlated with the elaborateness of the material presented.[1] The inconsiderate investigator, indeed, conceivably could exploit his authority and knowledge and extract "informed consent" by overwhelming the candidate-subject with information.

Ideally, the subject should give his consent freely, under no duress whatsoever. The facts are that some element of coercion is instrumental in any investigator-subject transaction. Volunteers for experiments will usually be influenced by hopes of obtaining better grades, earlier parole, more substantial egos, or just mundane cash. These pressures, however, are but fractional shadows of those enclosing the patient-subject. Incapacitated and hospitalized because of illness, frightened by strange and impersonal routines, and fearful for his health and perhaps life, he is far from exercising a free power of choice when the person to whom he anchors all his hopes asks, "Say, you wouldn't mind, would you, if you joined some of the other patients on this floor and helped us to carry out some very important research we are doing?" When "informed consent" is obtained, it is not the student, the destitute bum, or the prisoner to whom, by virtue of his condition, the thumb screws of coercion are most relentlessly applied; it is the most used and useful of all experimental subjects, the patient with disease.

When a man or woman agrees to act as an experimental subject, therefore, his or her consent is marked by neither adequate understanding nor total freedom of choice. The conditions of the agreement are a far cry from those visualized as ideal. Jonas would have the subject identify with the investigative endeavor so that he and the researcher would be seeking a common cause: "Ultimately, the appeal for volunteers should seek . . . free and generous endorsement, the appropriation of the research purpose into the person's [i.e., the subject's] own scheme of ends."[2] For Ramsey, "informed consent" should represent a "covenantal bond between consenting man and consenting man [that] makes them . . . joint adventurers in medical care and progress."[3] Clearly, to achieve motivations and attitudes of this lofty type, an educated and understanding, rather than merely informed, consent is necessary.

Although it is unlikely that the goals of Jonas and of Ramsey will ever be achieved and that human research subjects will spontaneously volunteer rather than be "conscripted,"[4] efforts to promote educated consent are in order. . . . Little has been done to give the public a basic understanding of medical research and its requirements not only for the people's money but also for their participation. The public, to be sure, is being subjected to a bombardment of sensation-mongering news stories and books that feature "breakthroughs," or that reveal real or alleged exploitations—horror stories of Nazi-type experimentation on abused human minds and bodies. Muckraking is essential to expose malpractices, but unless accompanied by efforts to promote a broader appreciation of medical research and its methods, it merely compounds the difficulties for both the investigator and the subject when "informed consent" is solicited.

The procedure currently approved in the United States for enlisting human experimental subjects has one great virtue: Patient-subjects are put on notice that their management is in part at least an experiment. The deceptions of the past are no longer tolerated. Beyond this accomplishment, however, the process of obtaining "informed consent," with all its regulations and conditions, is no more than elaborate ritual, a device that, when the subject is uneducated and uncomprehending, confers no more than the semblance of propriety on human experimentation. The subject's only real protection, the public as well as the medical profession must recognize, depends on the conscience and compassion of the investigator and his peers.

NOTES

1. L. C. Epstein and Louis L. Lasagna, "Obtaining Informed Consent: Form or Substance?" *American Medical Association Archives of Internal Medicine* 123 (1969): 682–88.
2. Hans Jonas, "Philosophical Reflections on Experimenting with Human Subjects," *Daedalus* 98 (Spring 1969): 219–47.
3. Paul Ramsey, "The Ethics of a Cottage Industry in an Age of Community and Research Medicine," *New England Journal of Medicine* 284 (1971): 700–706.
4. Ibid.

23. Informed Consent and Patient Autonomy

Samuel Gorovitz

. . . Consider this actual case. A woman was hospitalized a few years ago for a biopsy to determine the character of a small lump in her breast. She knew that vigorous controversy existed within the medical profession about the various ways of dealing with malignancy—ranging from radiation and chemotherapy without surgery to radical mastectomy—and she knew that some physicians, but not all, favored performing a mastectomy immediately upon a diagnosis of malignancy, while the patient was still under the anesthesia that was employed in order to do the biopsy. She hoped for a negative finding, feared a positive finding, and resolved that if malignancy were found, she would look carefully into the therapeutic options, in consultation with several physicians, before deciding which treatment to elect. Since she knew that treatment standards in such cases varied to some extent from city to city, she saw the matter as involving a certain amount of fashion, and she determined that in a matter of such importance to her, the decision would be made on the most rational grounds that she could establish, rather than on the basis of the city she happened to be in. Not everyone approved of her resolve, but no one doubted her right to take such a stand.

The woman had recently suffered a marital separation. At best, such an experience is emotionally disorienting; at worst, it can be shattering. She knew that the truth about any marriage is elusive and that the truth about a failed marriage is often most distorted to those whose marriage it is. Struggling to gain a clear perspective on her circumstances, she had gone to a psychiatrist. But he saw her as having a sound and balanced sense of herself and her circumstances, with no need for psychiatric treatment. Nonetheless, when she later was admitted to the hospital for the biopsy, she replied to an inquiry on an admissions form that she had seen a psychiatrist recently. Unbeknownst to her, she was then classified as a patient with a psychiatric history. In consequence, although she was unaware of it at the time, she was given a double-strength dose of soporific medication at bedtime the night before the biopsy. Patients with psychiatric histories have difficulty sleeping, in the judgment of that hospital, and its convention of practice was to give them, automatically, a more powerful sleeping pill than is given to other patients. An hour after the medication the woman was nearly asleep. A surgical resident appeared with a consent form for her to sign. She had trouble reading it but had the presence of mind and fortitude to send the resident away, telling him to leave the form and return in the morning, when she would be clearheaded. And in the morning, when she examined the consent form, she saw that her signing it would have authorized the hospital and medical staff to perform any procedure that in their judgment would be in her best interest. She rejected the form, negotiated a revision that gave more limited consent, and then underwent the biopsy procedure.

The ethical issue raised by this case is that of informed consent. A large and growing literature on the subject gives testimony to its importance and to the disputes surrounding it. I do not propose to resolve those disputes here; I do propose to

From *Doctors' Dilemmas: Moral Conflict and Medical Care* (New York: Macmillan, 1982; reissued New York: Oxford University Press, 1985), pp. 35–54.

explore them as a way of gaining further understanding of medical transactions. The questions I will consider directly are these: What is informed consent, why is it required, can the requirement be met, and is it an aid or impediment to good medical care? Each of these questions gives rise to controversy.

Much medical treatment is in some way assaultive. . . . Some treatment that one would stop short of calling assaultive is nonetheless limiting of the patient's freedom of action. Such interventions on the part of the physicians in the lives of their patients require justification; it is important to seek clarity both about why justification is necessary and how it is possible. . . .

If this were a treatise on the foundations of political philosophy, it would be appropriate here to defend, rather than merely to affirm, the principle that individual persons are each, separately, of moral significance, worthy of respect, the bearers of basic rights and freedoms, and hence the final arbiters—subject to very limited constraints—of their own fates. Such a defense is not easy, however, for the principle represents so basic a commitment about the nature of persons that it would be difficult to find a more fundamental principle in terms of which to defend it, without relying on claims which themselves stand in even greater need of defense. In this respect, a commitment to human dignity is like a commitment to rationality; one who does not share it stands almost beyond the realm of discourse. . . .

Because we respect individuals, we subscribe to what has been called the Principle of Autonomy, the view that individuals are entitled to be and do as they see fit, so long as they do not violate the comparable rights of others. No person is to be merely the instrument of another person's plans; no person is to be treated in a manner that is blind to the plans, desires, and values that are the fabric of his or her life and identity. Roughly speaking, we believe that it is obligatory to leave people alone, unless we have powerful reasons for not doing so. . . .

The doctrine of informed consent is simple and clear on the surface. Physicians do the sorts of things to their patients that people in general cannot justifiably do to one another. If the patient understands what the physician proposes to do and, thus, informed, consents to its being done, then the medical intervention is not imposed on the patient in violation of the patient's autonomy; rather, that medical intervention is properly viewed as a service provided to the patient at the patient's request. Not only does this procedure of gaining informed consent respect the patient's autonomy, but it also protects the physician against the charge of imposing treatment on a patient who did not want that treatment—it protects the physician, in other words, against the charge of assault. On the face of it, the requirement should be applauded on all sides. But it is not.

In order to see why, we need to gain a clearer idea of what informed consent actually is. Obviously, it has two parts; informing and consenting. The physician does the former; the patient, the latter. At either point things can go wrong.

A common error to which professors are prone is instructive to consider here: the assumption that teaching is accomplished if the information to be taught is presented in a clear and accurate way. Ofttimes we tend to be so taken with the accuracy, insight, and eloquence of our lectures that it takes reading student examinations to remind us how far short we have fallen of achieving the goal, which is, after all, not to perform an entertainment that gives the impression to us or to the students of being uplifting or edifying, but to bring about specific changes in minds of the students. (If we do not succeed in changing the interiors of the students' heads, then our universities are simply overpriced day-care facilities for late adolescents, no matter how much illusion of edification there may be.) But teaching something to a student means bringing it about that the student understands it, and that may require more than simply saying it, no matter how well. Informed consent can go wrong in the informing because informing, like any other sort of teaching, is often harder to accomplish than one expects.

An attending surgeon sought permission to repair the heart of a newborn baby. In explaining to the mother that there was a leakage from one side of the heart to the other, he drew this diagram:

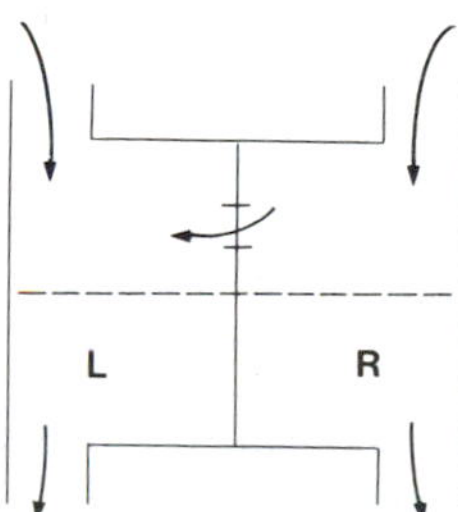

"The heart," he said, "has two chambers, the left and the right. In your baby's case, the two sides are connected by a little hole that lets blood get through from one side to the other. That's no good, and if we don't fix it, your baby won't do well at all and may not live. But that's the kind of problem we can fix. We just go in there and sew up that little hole, so the blood stays on the side it should be on. Then your baby will probably have a completely normal life."

Later the surgical resident went to see the mother to confirm her understanding of what was being done and why. He asked her if she understood; she said she did. "I want to make sure," he said, "so I'd like you to tell me in your own words what the problem is." "The problem," she replied, "is that my baby's got a square heart."

In this case the attending physician's efforts to explain had been conscientious, and some might argue that an adequate level of understanding had been achieved. It is enough, they could hold, that the woman understood there was some problem with the heart which the physician saw as serious but operable and that on such an understanding, she gave consent. But whether or not an adequate level of consent was achieved in this case, the resident was surprised by the distortion of information that was reflected in the mother's account of the problem, and he learned from the encounter how differently a patient and a physician can interpret the same language and visual images. Human physiology is largely a mystery to most people even at the level of gross anatomy. The woman in this case reacted more strongly to the drawing—which conflicted with her conception of what heart-shaped objects look like—than she did to the physician's words because of her misconception of human anatomy and her unexpectedly literal interpretation of the drawing. If the original physician had asked the mother to explain the problem in her own words, as the resident later did, he might have learned at the outset how limited a level of understanding he had achieved.

It is not just unusual interpretations or unexpected ignorance that can impede understanding. Heightened anxiety associated with illness, the effects of medication, the regression that is commonly exhibited by patients, the mechanisms of denial, and many other factors can also interfere, and commonly do. Recent empirical studies have shown that the cognitive capacities of patients are often diminished by the circumstances of their illness and hospitalization. Other studies have shown that patients often retain little of the information that is provided to them—a fact that practicing physicians have long known. (In one study, recordings were made of preoperative conversations between physicians and patients to establish a record of the informing process. Postoperative inquiries revealed substantial distortion and failures of memory when patients were asked to recall the conversations. One patient affirmed that he had been told nothing about his illness or the surgery that he faced, yet the recordings prove he had been provided with detailed information and an opportunity to raise questions and had reflected in his own conversation a good understanding of his medical circumstances.[1]) Finally, some medical procedures are so complicated or controversial that a layman can hardly be expected to have the necessary background information to understand what is really at issue in a decision about treatment.

Critics of the woman in the biopsy case held that it was foolish of her to think that she could make a better decision than her physicians about an issue so complicated that even the medical community was having difficulty deciding what the best course of treatment should be in cases like hers. Some physicians, summing up these barriers to patient understanding, have concluded that informed consent is impossible to achieve because patients are never actually well informed, and cannot be. "Are we to interrupt their illnesses," they ask, "in order to send them through medical school so that they can understand as we do what their problems and options are?"

The attempt to achieve patient understanding, moreover, incurs various costs. It is demanding of time; it requires the physician to draw on skills and sensitivities that have not typically been well developed in medical training; and, some critics have argued, it is dangerous to the health of the patients. The danger purportedly is of two kinds. Patients, because of their necessarily limited understanding, may make decisions that are detrimental to their own health. Also, there is a danger that patients will be directly harmed by the fears and anxieties induced by a more accurate understanding of the risks and discomforts they actually face. Informing patients in accordance with the doctrine requires that they come to understand the nature of their illness, the available choices of treatment, the risks and expected benefits of each choice, and the reasons for and against each of the options. But the list of risks is inexhaustible; not only can patients suffer ill effects from drugs, anesthesia, and surgical mishaps, they can be dropped off the cart coming back from the recovery room, and they can strangle themselves on their intravenous lines. Such outcomes are wildly improbable, but not impossible, and thus must be mentioned if *all* the risks must be mentioned. Any patient with the slightest inclination to timidity, and whose illness is not itself life threatening, will shrink in horror from such a panoply of risks and may then flee from treatment that would provide benefit with no undue risk.

These criticisms of the doctrine of informed consent have some force but are partly confused. It is true that patients cannot achieve a perfect understanding of their medical circumstances and of the options for action that are available to their physicians. For that matter, neither can the physician achieve a perfect understanding. . . . Still, in general, the patient will understand the medical aspects of the situation less well than the physician will. It is also true that some patients, given a reasonable understanding of their circumstances, will forget both the information and the fact that they once possessed it, and some patients will suffer heightened anxiety that may impede their treatment when they are informed about their circumstances. But what follows from these facts? Surely it does not follow that physicians may just do as they think best despite the wishes of the patients. That does not follow even in cases where the physician's judgment is clearly superior to that of the patient. First, the fact that the patient's knowledge will always be imperfect, and will often be inferior to the physician's, does not alter the fact that the patient has dominion over his or her own body, such that (except in an emergency or other circumstances of radically diminished capacity) treatment imposed without permission is abuse. Secondly, the fact that knowledge is *imperfect* does not imply that it is *inadequate* for the purpose at hand. Thirdly, the fact that a patient may, will, or does make the wrong decision about treatment does not entail that the patient lacks the right to make that decision. Fourthly, the fact that patients may misremember or entirely forget the information on which their decision, for better or ill, was made does not entail that the decision, when made, was uniformed or ill informed. Consider each point in turn.

Those who emphasize the impossibility of imparting *complete* understanding to the patient leave physicians themselves on the uninformed side of the line. Those who emphasize that patients cannot be as informed as their physicians have a more reasonable position. Both groups seem to think the point that patient understanding is limited has a significance that it simply does not have, however. The right not to be assaulted is not conditional on the extent to which one understands the motivation of the assault; the right to make choices about the fate of one's body does not presuppose a good understanding of the consequences of the choices one makes. . . .

Some patients, because of their own cognitive and psychological characteristics and the nature of their illness, can become well informed about their medical circumstances. (Norman Cousin's *Anatomy of an Illness*[2] documents the way he took over, in cooperation with his physicians, the management of a grave illness.) Other patients, in other circumstances, do not have and cannot be brought to have any reasonable understanding of their circumstances. So the extent to which the patient can be informed varies from not at all to comparably with the physician. Somewhere along that spectrum, patients have enough understanding of the medical aspects of their circumstances to exercise reasonable choice. Below that level, the case for paternalism builds; above it, the case for autonomy dominates. The situation is complicated by the fact that any patient's position on the spectrum of understanding is likely to depend on the quality of the physician's efforts to induce understanding in the patient. The better the physician is as an educator of the patient, the stronger the case is for respecting the autonomy of the patient. It becomes necessary, therefore, to make some assessment in the course of treatment—subject to revision at any point—of the extent to which the patient is, or can be made, capable of achieving a level of understanding that is adequate to support an autonomous choice.

. . . Medical decisions are often too important to be made on medical grounds alone. Consider again the woman who limited her consent to the biopsy procedure. Had the diagnosis been a finding of malignancy, many further technical questions about the nature of her disease and the possible modes of treatment would have arisen at once. The best source of knowledge about these matters is surely the medical profession and those in related areas. But nonmedical factors could also have an important bearing. If, for example, the woman were by profession and continuing aspiration a world-renowned nude model for painters and photographers, the prospect of a mastectomy might be even more distasteful than it ordinarily is. And that difference, at a given level of medical risk, might make the difference in what treatment the patient selects. Comparable considerations would apply to a man whose work as a model for bathing suit advertisements would be ended by the scarring that a coronary bypass operation would produce; he might on that account favor medical management of his angina, even if it seemed slightly less likely to be effective.

If it is assumed that the only rational option is the one with the best medical prognosis, then it follows trivially that a decision with a lower prospect of success is irrational. But there is no good reason to accept that assumption; there is no reason to believe that the prospect for medical success is the only relevant basis, or ought always to be the dominant basis, for exercising choice in medical situations. An individual has the right, in general, to determine what levels of risk to run in pursuit of the objectives that give his or her life its purpose and character; we recognize this in the case of dangerous occupations (the test pilot or high-wire artist, for example), dangerous recreations (hang gliding or American football), and dangerous lifestyles (dietary imprudence or smoking). Why, then, should we suppose that just because one is in the role of patient, one's freedom to choose medically inferior options suddenly is dissipated?

The woman in our example might have assessed the comparative risks and decided to trade a small increment in prospects for medical success in exchange for avoiding a treatment destructive of her career. Whether or not such a choice makes sense for the patient is, in any case, not a medical question; it is a question that arises out of her medical circumstances and depends importantly on the medical facts, but it is a question the answer to which will depend in the final analysis on her values and priorities and to the place among them that she accords to matters of physical well-being, compared with vanity, accomplishment, competing demands on time and economic resources, and the like. The wrong decision from a purely medical point of view may thus not be the wrong decision from the broader perspective of the patient's life; the medical experts therefore have an important place in the decisions that must be made about treatment, but they have no basis for presuming to be able always to reach decisions about what, all things considered—medical and nonmedical alike—is best for the patient.

Lastly, it should be clear that the notion of the right decision is itself liable to be somewhat misleading, as if there were a single choice that is correct, with the challenge facing both physician and patient being that of identifying that one right choice, and the penalty for missing it being some sort of clear failure. A choice can be wrong if it aims at achieving certain objectives which it then fails to achieve; such is the case in the choice of an antibiotic to which the offending bacteria are resistant, and such is the case if a treatment selected to maximize survival leads instead to hastening death. But if a choice of treatment (or a refusal to be treated) leads to a life that is shorter, while at the same time allows for achieving more of the goals in one's plan of accomplishment, it is hard to see how that choice can properly be called wrong, even though there is a clear sense in which medical personnel, who can be expected to grant pride of place to medical considerations, might reasonably see it as the wrong choice. Further, if the choice is wrong not only medically but from the point of view of the patient's overall perspective as well, it still does not follow that it is necessarily wrong for the patient to have been allowed to make the choice, although it would be appropriate for medical personnel to try to help the patient understand how the choice fails to accord with the patient's overall values.

Just as a respect for freedom requires us to allow people to make choices in other dimensions of life—choices that can be described only as folly from any point of view—so, too, is the patient's right of choice undiminished by the possibility of failure in choosing. The right to choose is not limited to the right to choose rightly. Lack of understanding can, in any area of choice that affects us, lead to our making choices we will later regret; the wise among us will seek where we can find it the best available evidence on which to base the choices we make. But being uninformed does not in general reduce our rights of choice in matters that concern us solely; the right to choose is not generally limited to the right to choose knowledgeably either.

That this fact is often obscured in medical situations may be due to the assumption—usually justified—that a single goal is shared by the patient and the medical staff, that being to maximize the health of the patient. On that assumption, a choice that serves the goals of the medical staff is necessarily the choice that serves the best interests of the patient, and it seems only efficient to have the choice made on the basis of the most sophisticated understanding of the issues involved—that is, to have the choice made by the physician, who, in consultation with peers, is medically best informed. Even this, however, is an erroneous judgment; that a physician and patient share a common objective does not nullify the patient's rights of autonomous decision, even when the physician is clearly better informed than the patient about how to achieve the objective they share.

Those who have shown that patients often remember badly—and sometimes not at all—what they have been told about their medical conditions and treatment options have not shown that informed consent is impossible. They have simply reported research confirming a phenomenon about patient memory. Still, it is tempting to conclude, as some in medical practice surely do, that since patients in the end don't know the difference anyway, the responsible physician will—indeed, must—decide and do what is best for the patient. But making an informed decision does not assure remembering the basis of the decision at a later time—especially when subsequent events are of a highly stressful sort. Ask a friend or yourself, for that matter, why you chose the career you did, or the spouse you have, let alone the car you drive or the neighborhood you live in, and you will be reminded of the difficulty of being able, after the fact, to give a clear account of the reasons that led to decisions that constitute a major influence on the course of our lives. Often, in the making of such decisions, we were never clear about the reasons. But often, even where there was clarity, that clarity quickly fades with the passage of time. A patient who does not remember being informed about the nature of an illness or the decisions that had to be made about its treatment may nonetheless have been well informed at the time the decision was made. Such lapses of memory may create a problem from the point of view of the psychological well-being of the patient, however, and, correspondingly, place the physician in greater jeopardy.

A patient who does not remember being informed may be discontent at the thought of not having been informed, and the physician may be concerned about the consequences of that discontent for the patient's recovery, the physician's reputation, or even, in an extreme case, the physician's legal responsibility. So it may be necessary to become more careful about documenting that patients have been informed; relying on their recollections is obviously not enough. But there is no reason to assume that informing them better would change the situation, for there is no reason to assume that the cause of faulty memories of the informing transactions is that the informing was inadequately done. Compare here what anyone remembers about a subject on the way in to a final examination with what that same individual remembers about the subject even a few weeks later. Knowledge is a transient phenomenon for most people about most things. . . .

The physician who has a conscientious concern with informing the patient is . . . faced with at least these questions: (1) How much understanding can the patient achieve? (2) What is the patient's background information on which to build that understanding? (3) What will it cost in time and effort to achieve that understanding? (4) What are the psychological barriers to understanding? (5) Does the patient want the information? (6) What is the likelihood that the information will harm the patient either directly or by impeding the processes of recovery? (7) How much of what the patient could be made to understand is necessary for a reasonable level of informedness in the actual circumstances? (8) What portion of the information, if any, must the patient be made to understand independently of the patient's desire for information? (9) How much of the physician's skepticism about the relevant information should be revealed to the patient? And finally, (10) When and how should the information be provided?

These questions are easy to answer in some cases but can be extremely hard in other cases. Rarely are they addressed explicitly; rather, the physician typically tends to respond to a case instinctively, relying on the clinical judgment that is an amalgam of what has been learned from previous successes and failures in practice and consultation with others when a case seems particularly problematic.

Our focus has been on the informing side of the requirement of informed consent; now consider the concept of consenting. On the way into the operating room a surgeon once asked the surgical resident, "Did you get the consent?" "Yes, here it is," replied the resident, handing the surgeon a consent form signed by the patient. But consent is not the sort of thing that one can carry in one's pocket to an operating room and hand to a surgeon. Just as numbers can be large or small, odd or even, but never heavy or blue, consent can be reluctant, coerced, freely given, or denied, but never carried around in a pocket. Consent is not a physical object; it is an act of the will—and therefore not a piece of paper that is, at best, evidence that the act took place. And evidence can be misleading. The reason it is important not to confuse the signed consent form with the consent itself is precisely that if one takes the signed form to be what is required, one can adopt a far less stringent standard regarding consent than if one remains aware that the consent requirement may not have been met even in cases where the document gives evidence that it has been.

If I have reason to want you to undergo a treatment that you do not want, I can produce a signed consent form by causing you to sign it under duress. I may hold a gun to your head and threaten you with loss of life if you do not sign. Or I may be your employer, who threatens you with a loss of your job in the hazardous chemicals laboratory if you do not agree to undergo a tubal ligation to eliminate any risk of a malformed child resulting from your exposure to chemicals or to radiation in the lab. In the case of the gun, no one could claim that an act of voluntary consent had occurred; rather, it would be clear to all, once the facts were known, that the signature on the consent form was obtained under duress, that the evidence was therefore fraudulent, and that the requirement of informed consent had not been met. In the case of coercion by the employer, the situation is less clear since the pressures brought to bear on the woman are far less direct, and the choices less sharply drawn. Faced with the choice of signing a consent form or being shot to death, most people in most circumstances would see themselves as having no choice—and therefore not acting freely. But the employee can refuse to accept the employer's terms.

These are, he would argue, conditions that must be met only if she wishes to retain employment that she is free to give up. One's life circumstances may be such that the loss of a job would be devastating, however, and hence a case that undue coercion has been brought to bear can be made in such situations.

Again, the consent form provides definitive evidence only of a physical act—the signing. In the normal course of events one assumes that the physical act of signing a consent form will occur only as a consequence of a cognitive act of agreement having taken place. And as a matter of statistical likelihood, the assumption may be well warranted. But it is not always true. The physician whose responsibility it is to gain consent thus has a responsibility to distinguish between a form bearing a signature and an act of consent. That requires understanding the *process* by which the form came to be signed and considering that process in awareness of all the ways such a process can go wrong.

Some have argued that consent is never freely given in the context of medical treatment because illness, medication, fear of death, and pain add up to a coercion as powerful as the gun. But even if this observation accurately describes some situations, it does not seem to cover many others, where the distortions of consciousness that can accompany illness may be wholly lacking. A subtler and more serious argument rests on the implicitly coercive power of the physician's role: Patients will do what their physicians want them to do, if for no other reason than because of fear—fear of a bad medical outcome and fear of the consequences of defying the wishes, however subtly they are expressed, of the physician. But this is a hard argument to make plausible to physicians, who have to deal with the problems of compliance that arise when patients openly reject, or simply ignore, clear and direct indications of what their physicians take to be medically advisable or even necessary. Yet the argument has some force, for physicians do communicate by subtle cues as well as by overt expression, and they can sometimes influence their patients more than they realize. A change in tone of voice or facial expression, while describing treatment options, can betray a preference that tacitly pressures the patient into consenting as the physician would wish. In the relationship between physician and patient, the differential of power is so massive that the patient may be unable to resist seeing the physician as providing only one real option. The physician, so the argument goes, must be meticulous in an effort to provide information in a neutral way that does not pressure the patient to choose one way or another because of the physician's preferences.

This argument, were it good, would entail that a patient's physician, who is most likely the best informed of anyone involved in the case, should be effectively barred from rendering advice of a medical sort—precisely the one sort of advice to which the physician can lay claim as an expert. We need not embrace such a bizarre outcome to be mindful of the problem of undue physician influence. There is nothing inappropriate about medical advice's being the dominant factor in decisions about medical treatment so long as the process of decision retains a place for the incorporation of other values that may be in conflict with a single-minded pursuit of medical objectives. If a physician is aware of the distinction between medical factors and those nonmedical factors that can play a role in the making of a medical decision, and if the physician is sensitive to the ways in which consent can be coerced, there should be no objection to the physician's expressing a preference explicitly about what would be medically best for the patient to do. The patient may not resist the force of that preference, but what is most important is that the circumstances allow for the possibility of such resistance.

The physician who has a conscientious concern with the patient's consent is thus faced with this additional question: (11) Is the consent voluntary, or is it the result of coercion or undue influence?

These eleven questions pose a challenge to the most conscientious physician. At the same time, they underscore the extent to which therapeutic transactions depend on an effective relationship between physician and patient. The more the patient understands, and the more the patient is willing and able to assume a share of the responsibility of entering into a collegial relationship with the physician in the management of medical care, the greater the likelihood that they will be able to join forces effectively in pursuit of shared objectives. . . .

NOTES

1. G. Robinson and A. Merav, "Informed Consent: Recall by Patients Tested Postoperatively," *Annals of Thoracic Surgery* 22 (1976), pp. 209–12.

2. Norman Cousins, *Anatomy of an Illness as Perceived by the Patient: Reflections on Healing and Regeneration* (New York: Norton, 1979).

THE VOLITIONAL COMPONENT

24. Cheaper Than Chimpanzees

Jessica Mitford

In 1947, 15 German doctors, distinguished medical men at the very top of their profession, were convicted by the Nuremberg war crimes tribunal of criminal responsibility for cruel and frequently murderous "medical experiments" performed on concentration camp inmates.

In their defense the accused doctors cited comparable experiments carried out on prisoners by American physicians: in 1906, a group of Philippine convicts were given "an abundance of cigarettes and also cigars if they desired them" for submitting to infection with plague and induction of beriberi. One died; others suffered paralysis, mental disturbances, and heart damage. In 1915, pellagra was induced in twelve Mississippi convicts, all of whom became seriously ill. They were rewarded by the promise of early parole. In 1944, several hundred Illinois and New Jersey prisoners were infected with malaria so that new cures could be tried out on them. They were paid in dollars. Some became extremely ill with malaria, others suffered horribly from the toxic effects of the experimental "cures."

Of the doctors tried in Nuremberg, seven were sentenced to death by hanging, others to long prison terms. Whatever deterrent effect these stiff sentences might have had elsewhere in the world, they surely have had none in the United States. The Nuremberg tribunal established standards for medical experimentation on humans which, if observed, would end the practice of using prisoners as subjects. Yet in the twenty-six years since the Nuremberg judgment there has been a huge expansion of medical "research programs" in many prisons in the U.S., sanctioned by federal health agencies and state prison administrations who do not choose to recognize these standards as applying to the captives in their custody.

Efforts by international medical societies to prohibit the use of prisoners as subjects have been effectively frustrated by American medical experimenters. The World Medical Association in 1961 proposed that prisoners, "being captive groups, should not be used as the subject of experiments." The recommendation was never formally adopted, largely because of the opposition of American doctors.

"Pertinax," writing in the *British Medical Journal* for January 1963, says: "I am disturbed that the World Medical Association is now hedging on its clause about using criminals as experimental material. The American influence has been at work on its suspension." He adds wistfully, "One of the nicest American scientists I know was heard to say, 'Criminals in our penitentiaries are fine experimental material—and much cheaper than chimpanzees.' I hope the chimpanzees don't come to hear of this."[1]

Behind the nice American scientists lurk a handful of pharmaceutical concerns with huge financial stakes in experimental testing on human subjects. FDA regulations require that all new drugs be tested on humans before being marketed. The testing, after the drug has cleared animal tests, is done in three stages: in Phase I, the new compound is tried out for effectiveness and possible toxic properties on a small group of normal, healthy individuals. If these survive without serious side effects and the drug appears promising, it is passed into Phase II, in which several hundred normal subjects are given the compound and the dosage is gradually increased until the experimenter decides the limit of safety has been reached. Once this is established, the drug is ready for Phase III, in which it is given as medication to patients to test its efficacy as a remedy for illness.

Dr. Robert Batterman, internist and specialist in pharmacology, told me, "Phase I is very big in prisons. FDA prefers Phase I to be on an in-patient basis—the only place available for large-scale toxicity studies is prison. But the vast majority of new drugs—more than 90 percent—never get into medical practice. They prove too toxic and fall by the wayside in Phase II."

There are formidable barriers to inquiries about medical experimentation on human subjects in prison. Yet horror stories crop up in the press with sufficient regularity to give some indication of the scope and nature of the experiments.

In 1963, *Time* magazine reported that the federal government was using prisoner "volunteers" for large-scale research, dispensing rewards ranging from a package of cigarettes to $25 cash plus

From *Kind and Unusual Punishment: The Prison Business* (New York: Alfred A. Knopf, 1971), pp. 151–361.

reduction of sentence; that prisoners in Ohio and Illinois were injected with live cancer cells and blood from leukemia patients to determine whether these diseases could be transmitted; that doctors in Oklahoma were grossing an estimated $300,000 a year from deals with pharmaceutical companies to test out new drugs on prisoners; that the same doctors were paying prisoners $5 a quart for blood which they retailed at $15.[2]

In July 1969, Walter Rugaber of the *New York Times* charged that "the federal government has watched without interference while many people sickened and some died in an extended series of drug tests and blood plasma operations . . . the immediate damage has been done in the penitentiary systems of three states. Hundreds of inmates in voluntary programs have been stricken with serious disease. An undetermined number of the victims have died."[3] . . .

There is something for everybody in the prison research studies. The drug companies, operating through private physicians with access to the prisons, can buy human subjects for a fraction—less than one tenth, according to many medical authorities—of what they would have to pay medical students or other "free-world" volunteers. They can conduct experiments on prisoners that would not be sanctioned for student subjects at any price because of the degree of risk and pain involved. Guidelines for human experimentation established by HEW and other agencies are easily disregarded behind prison walls.

Since the studies are carried out in the privacy of prison, if a "volunteer" becomes seriously ill, or dies, as a result of the procedures to which he is subjected, it is unlikely this will ever come to anybody's attention. As Rugaber discovered, . . . prison medical records that might prove embarrassing to the authorities have a habit of conveniently disappearing. There is minimal risk that subjects disabled by the experiments will bring lawsuits against the drug companies, for the prisoner is usually required as a condition of his participation to sign a waiver releasing everyone in sight from damage claims that may result. Such waivers are fraudulent, worthless, and illegal. They have been held legally invalid as contrary to public policy, and are prohibited by FDA regulations having the force of law, but the prisoner is hardly likely to be aware of such fine points. The psychological effect of signing the waiver, coupled with the general helplessness of prisoners, makes lawsuits a rarity.

For the prisoner, the pittance he gets from the drug company—generally around $1 a day for the more onerous experiments—represents riches when viewed in terms of prison pay scales: $30 a month compared with the $2 to $10 a month he might make if fortunate enough to have been granted a "pay slot" in an ordinary prison job.

Dr. Robert Batterman told me, "The prisoner-subject gets virtually nil." He cited an estimate given him for experimenting on prisoners in Vacaville, California: $15 a month for three months to be *lowered* to $12.50 a month should the experiment run for six months. "We would normally do it the other way around with 'free-world' volunteers. We'd give them more money if the experiment ran longer, because of the added risk involved." Dr. Batterman makes considerable use of student-subjects from a nearby Baptist divinity school. For a comparatively undemanding experiment—one requiring a weekly draw of blood—he would pay a student upward of $100 a month, he said.

The prisoner's view of the largesse dispensed by the drug companies is reflected in a series of interviews conducted in 1969 at Vacaville Prison, California, by Martin Miller, a graduate student at the University of California Department of Criminology.[4] Some of the prisoners' comments: "Yeah, I was on research, but I couldn't keep my chow down. Like I lost about 35 pounds my first year in the joint, so I started getting scared. I hated to give it up because it was a good pay test." "Hey, man, I'm making $30 a month on the DMSO thing [chronic topical application of dimethyl sulfoxide]. I know a couple of guys had to go to the hospital who were on it—and the burns were so bad they had to take *everyone* off it for a while. But who gives a shit about that, man? Thirty is a full canteen draw and I wish the thing would go on for years—I'd be lost without it." "I was on DMSO last year. It paid real good and it was better than that plague thing (bubonic plague vaccine immunization study) that fucked with guys last year. There was a lot of bad reactions to DMSO, but I guess that's why it paid so good." Of DMSO, Morton Mintz, staff writer for the *Washington Post,* had written three years earlier: "Human testing has now been severely curbed by FDA because of reports of serious adverse effects."[5]

The participating physician cashes in on the programs in various ways. He may make a direct deal with the drug company for financial backing, out of which he pays the expenses of research and pockets the rest as his fee. An individual research grant might run from $5,000 to upward of $50,000, enabling a doctor with good prison contacts to handily double or triple his regular income. Or if he is, as many are, a faculty member in a medical school, he can route the grant through the university to the acclaim of his colleagues and the tenure committee. His prestige and hence his worth in terms of salary will be greatly enhanced when the results of his research appear in a professional journal. . . . According to Dr. Irwin Feinberg of the University of California Medical Center, "Medical schools in the last two decades have increased their research activities dramatically, and the 'publish or perish' rule of other university departments is now applied relentlessly to the emerging full-time medical faculties."

Some of the vicissitudes the medical researcher may expect to find in his quest for prisoner-subjects are described by Dr. Robert E. Hodges in the *Journal of the American Medical Association.*[6] in the late forties, Dr. Hodges and his colleagues reached a "verbal working arrangement" with Iowa prison officials enabling them to canvass the prison population for volunteers who would submit to prolonged hospitalization in the University Hospitals as research subjects. "We knew this procedure was not specifically permitted by law," writes Dr. Hodges. "But neither was it specifically prohibited." Eventually the experiments came to the attention of Iowa's attorney general: "In his judgment, it was not legal for us to accept prison volunteers for medical research." There followed two fallow years in which the experiments were perforce halted, but Dr. Hodges, undaunted, put this time to good use: "We sought and obtained enactment of a specific law permitting the use of prisoners for medical research at University Hospitals." The path thus cleared, a total of 224 convicts were in the course of time delivered over to Dr. Hodges and his colleagues at the University Hospitals.

Speculating on the "incentives and motives" that induce prisoners to volunteer for research studies "which are usually somewhat unpleasant and in a few instances involve distinct risks," Dr. Hodges surmises that "for some, it probably represents a new experience which takes them away from the monotony and oppressiveness of prison routine." . . .

For some prisoners, "monetary gain may be the incentive, though inmates are paid only $1 daily." Iowa prisoners are not supposed to receive reduction of sentence in return for volunteering, but Dr. Hodges routinely sent a thank-you letter to the warden for each subject: "It is possible that this letter in the prisoner's file may favorably influence the parole board." As for the incentives and motives of researchers, Dr. Hodges reports that more than 80 scientific publications resulted from the Iowa studies on prisoners.

Dr. Hodges becomes almost lyrical in his discussion of the moral and ethical aspects of such experimentation. The prisoner-volunteers, he says, are "our companions in medical science and adventure"; the subject "in whatever degree derelict or forlorn, has sacred rights which the physician must always put ahead of his burning curiosity." Dr. Hodges, without elaborating on what these sacred rights might be, concludes: "A system of voluntary participation firmly based on legal and ethical standards has provided a rich opportunity for clinical investigators who wish to study metabolic, physiologic, pharmacologic, and medical problems. This has been a rewarding experience both for the physicians and for the subjects." . . .

One such rich opportunity is described by Dr. Hodges in one of these scientific publications: "Clinical Manifestations of Ascorbic Acid Deficiency in Man," in the *American Journal of Clinical Nutrition* of April 1971. The object: "to define the metabolism of this vitamin in the face of severe dietary deficiency." For the study, which consisted of experimentally induced scurvy, five companions in medical science and adventure were recruited from the Iowa State Penitentiary "and their informed consent was obtained." Among the rewarding experiences they encountered: for periods ranging from 84 to 97 days they were fed a liquid formula free of ascorbic acid by stomach tube: "because of the unpalatability of this formula, the men took it thrice daily via polyethylene gastric tube." They were exposed in a cold-climate "control room" to a temperature of 50 degrees for four hours each day. The volume of blood drawn "for laboratory purposes" was large enough to "cause mild anemia in all the men." In a throwaway line, Dr. Hodges observes that "the mineral supplement [recommended by the National Research Council] was inadvertently omitted from the diets during the first 34 days of the depletion period."

The experiment was a great success. It was, in fact, the second of its kind, Dr. Hodges having tried it once before with far less favorable results: "Despite a somewhat shorter period of deprivation in the second scurvy study, the subjects in the second study developed a more severe degree of scurvy . . . although none of the subjects in the first scurvy study developed arthralgia, this was a complaint in four out of five men who participated in the second scurvy study. Joint swelling and pain made themselves evident in Scurvy II, but had not been observed in the subjects participating in Scurvy I."

The gradual onset of scurvy in the five prisoners is traced by Dr. Hodges with the enthusiasm of a young mother recording Baby's first steps. "The first signs of scurvy to appear in both studies were petechial hemorrhage [hemorrhages in the skin]. Coiled hairs were observed in two of the men and first appeared on the forty-second and seventy-fourth days, respectively. The first definite abnormalities of the gums appeared between the forty-third and eighty-fourth days of depletion and progressed after the plasma ascorbic acid levels fell. . . . The onset of joint pains began between the sixty-seven and ninty-sixth days. . . . Beginning on the eighty-eighth day of deprivation there was a rapid increase in weight followed by swelling of the legs in the third man, who had the most severe degree of scurvy.''

By the time it was all over, Dr. Hodges was able to chalk up these significant accomplishments: all five subjects suffered joint pains, swelling of the legs, dental cavities, recurrent loss of new dental fillings, excessive loss of hair, hemorrhages in the skin and whites of the eyes, excess fluid in the joint spaces, shortness of breath, scaly skin, mental depression, and abnormalities in emotional responses. The youngest, a twenty-six-year-old, ''became almost unable to walk as a result of the rapid onset of arthropathy [painful joints] superimposed on bilateral femoral neuropathy [disease in both large nerves to the thighs and legs plus hemorrhage into nerve sheaths]. The onset of scurvy signaled a period of potentially rapid deterioration.'' Dr. Hodges's anticlimactic conclusion: ''Once again our observations are in accord with those of the British Medical Research Council.''

To doctors in the business of curing people rather than making them ill, the ''ascorbic acid deficiency'' study appears a senseless piece of savage cruelty visited on the five volunteers. ''This study was totally pointless,'' Dr. Ephraim Kahn of the California Department of Public Health said of Dr. Hodges's publication. ''The cause and cure of scurvy has been well known in the medical profession for generations. Some of the side effects he lists may well be irreversible—the young man who had the most severe case of scurvy may never have recovered. There's a clue here to the degree of competence of these so-called researchers—they 'inadvertently' omitted a mineral supplement from the diets. This no doubt weakened the men and exacerbated the other side effects. It might cause them to go into shock and to suffer severe cardiac abnormalities.'' Among the effects of the experiment recorded in the publication that could be permanent, Dr. Kahn cited heart damage, loss of hair, damage to teeth, hemorrhage into femoral nerve sheaths—the latter is ''terribly painful and could lead to permanent nerve damage.''

As seen by top brass in the American medical profession, the overriding ''ethical problem'' posed by use of prisoners for research is not, as one might have supposed, the trail of death and disease left in the wake of the experiments. Rather it is the danger that prisoner-subjects may be unduly rewarded for the pains of research by inappropriately large sums of cash and/or promise of early release. The reasoning is that the prisoner, not wishing to forego these benefits, may be tempted to conceal symptoms and side effects, thus calling into question the validity of the entire effort. The idea that a $1-a-day stipend to a healthy adult can be so overwhelmingly attractive as to invalidate the results of medical research is conceivable only in the irrational world of prison. Yet this is precisely the fear expressed by some spokesmen for the medical profession.

In the late forties, Governor Dwight H. Greene of Illinois appointed a prestigious committee of physicians, including Dr. Morris Fishbein (then editor of the *Journal of the American Medical Association*) to advise the Department of Public Safety on ''ethics governing the service of prisoners as subjects in medical experiments.''[7] A policy statement on this was needed because of widespread criticism of the wartime malaria experiments at Statesville Penitentiary in which, according to published accounts, subjects suffered severe abdominal pains, nausea, vomiting, transient changes in their electrocardiograms, fever, and a variety of other symptoms.

The committee's report disposes of the Statesville experiments in one line—it pronounced them ''ideal because of their conformity with . . . ethical rules''—and turns its attention to the problem of ''excessive rewards'' in the form of reduction of sentence held out to the prisoner-subjects.

There is, the committee found, ''reformative value in serving as a subject in a medical experiment,'' and in some cases ''a reduction of sentence in prison for serving as a subject may be considered favorable to the reformative purposes of imprisonment.'' But how should this be determined? Apparently the trick is to ferret out the prisoner's *real* reason for volunteering—is he motivated by a lofty desire to serve science and society, or does he just want to get out of prison?—and then reward him or not, accordingly. As the committee explains in this brainteaser: ''If the sole motive of the prisoner is to contribute to human welfare, any reduction in sentence would be a reward. If the sole motive of the prisoner is to obtain a reduction in sentence, an excessive reduction of sentence which would exercise undue influence in obtaining the consent of prisoners to serve as subjects would be inconsistent with the principle of voluntary participation.''

. . . . .

I asked Dr. Robert Hodges, now a professor of internal medicine in the University of California Medical School at Davis, how much he had paid the scurvy test volunteers. ''I think it was $1 or maybe $2 a day,'' he replied. ''Over the years, when I was in Iowa, as the cost of cigarettes and razor blades went up, we increased prisoners' pay somewhat. It's unethical to pay an amount of money that is too attractive. Oh, we had the money, we could have paid much more, of course—but we weren't just being cheap, we were considering the ethics of the situation. The prisoners got a bit extra for really unpleasant things—if we had to put a tube down their throats for several hours, or take a biopsy of the skin the size of a pencil eraser, we'd give them a few dollars more."

Doctors with whom I have discussed the matter are unanimously agreed that FDA regulations requiring drugs to be tested on humans before being marketed are sound and necessary. They point to the notorious greed and often criminal irresponsibility of the pharmaceutical industry, as evidenced by the thalidomide disaster and the sloppy fashion in which the birth control pill was released for mass consumption with harmful consequences for many women. But human experimentation, they say, must be conducted within a framework of stringent rules for the protection of the human subject.

Hence, one by-product of the enormous proliferation in recent decades of medical research on humans by government agencies and the drug industry is a parallel proliferation of "guiding principles" and "codes of ethics" developed by the medical profession to govern the conduct of the experiments, curb the overzealous researcher, and safeguard the human subjects. An American Medical Association resolution of 1946 on human research was in turn followed by FDA regulations of 1962 and the Helsinki Declaration of 1966.

These are largely repetitive. All affirm that human experiments must be based on prior laboratory work and research on animals, emphasize the grave responsibility of investigator to subject, exhort him to avoid experiments that are of no scientific value or that subject humans to unnecessary pain and risk.

The principle of informed consent is basic to all the codes. As stated in the Nuremberg judgment (and adopted almost verbatim by FDA), "the voluntary consent of the human subject is absolutely essential. This means the person involved should have legal capacity to give consent; should be so situated as to be able to exercise free power of choice . . . and should have sufficient knowledge and comprehension of the elements of the subject matter involved as to enable him to make an understanding, enlightened decision." Are prisoners, stripped of their civil rights when they enter the gates, subjected for years or decades to the iron compression chamber of the penitentiary, free agents capable of exercising freedom of choice? Are they furnished by the experimenters with "knowledge and comprehension" to enable them to make "understanding and enlightened" decisions? To ask these questions is to answer them.

NOTES

1. M. H. Pappworth: *Human Guinea Pigs* (Boston: Beacon Press; 1968), p. 64.
2. Ibid., pp. 65–6.
3. *New York Times*, July 29, 1969.
4. Martin Miller: unpubl. paper.
5. *Washington Post*, July 24, 1966.
6. Robert E. Hodges and William B. Bean: "The Use of Prisoners for Medical Research," *Journal of the American Medical Association*, vol. 202, no. 6 (November 6, 1967).
7. "Ethics Governing the Service of Prisoners as Subjects of Medical Experiments," Report of a Committee Appointed by Governor Dwight H. Greene of Illinois, *Journal of the American Medical Association*, vol. 136 no. 7 (February 14, 1948), pp. 447–58.

25. Medical Experimentation on Prisoners

Carl Cohen

PROLOG

Ought we to permit medical experimentation on prisoners? The issue is both practically important and morally complex. Some argue as follows: No human subject may be used in a medical experiment without his informed and freely given consent. But prisoners, by virtue of their total custody, cannot give free and uncoerced consent. Hence prisoners—no matter how valuable experimentation with their cooperation may prove—must be excluded from all populations of subjects in medical experimentation.

This argument, when expanded and reinforced, is very persuasive, as I shall show. I aim also to show that its key premise is simply mistaken, and the argument unsound.

. . . My question is this: *Should* we adopt the rule, now proposed by some, excluding all or

From *Perspectives in Biology and Medicine* 21:3 (1978): 357–72.

almost all experimentation involving prison volunteers?[1]

Some clarifications first. The principle that informed consent must be got from every human subject in a medical experiment is well established. It was eloquently formulated in the Nuremberg Code, and by the World Medical Association in their *Declaration of Helsinki*. It grounds a set of detailed regulations governing the operation of all institutions for medical research in this country funded in whole or in part by any Federal agency. . . . But "informed consent" involves more than information. Better thought of as "full consent," what is demanded in fact entails three elements; *information, competency,* and *voluntariness*. Where the consent received is defective in any one of these respects, we will rightly think the subject to have been improperly used.

Problematic defects of *information* arise when experiments are proposed in which the subjects cannot be told the truth, or the whole truth, about the investigation of which they are part—because their knowing what the investigator is after will have the effect of his not getting it. Deception is not uncommon in behavioral research, but I bypass the problem here. Problematic defects of *competency* arise when experiments call for subjects who are not (in fact or in law) competent to give their consent—infant children, the mentally disabled, the comatose, and so on. Some experiments with persons in these categories is essential, obviously, if care for them is to be improved; hence principles must be devised for determining who may give third-party consent ("proxy consent") for the incompetent, and under what restrictions it may be given. These issues of competency are sorely vexed, but here I bypass them also. Problematic defects of *voluntariness* arise when potential subjects, although fully informed and competent, are coerced into giving their consent by threat or excessive inducement, or other inappropriate manipulation. This is the more likely where the potential subjects are more vulnerable, more precariously placed. Among these precariously placed potential subjects, the case of prisoners is critical because, on the one hand, their incarceration renders them specially vulnerable, while on the other hand that same incarceration renders them peculiarly well suited for some very valuable long-term experiments. Some resolution of this matter is essential.

CAN A PRISONER GIVE VOLUNTARY CONSENT?

Voluntariness, the third element of full consent, is most difficult to specify. We insist that a subject's consent be freely given and uncoerced. What does that entail? Clear cases of "volunteers" who did not give their consent freely are not hard to recall or imagine. The archetype—which reality often approximates—is the army platoon, lined up before the First Sergeant who asks sternly for volunteers, and orders those who do not volunteer to take two steps forward. At the other extreme, cases of honest volunteering, genuinely autonomous, are legion. But very many cases fall between the extremes, and that of the prison volunteer is one of these.

It may well seem that, by virtue of the complete custody of their persons, prisoners lack the capacity to act with the kind of uncoerced voluntariness required. If they do lack it, they ought not be subjects. So I want now to put, more carefully than I have found it put anywhere, what precisely it is about the prisoner's condition that might render him or her unfit to be a consenting subject in a medical experiment.

The argument goes like this. The prison environment, both in fact and in principle, is such that consent without coercion is not possible there. This is not because of any defect in prisoners; it flows from the deeply intrusive, literally totalitarian character of prisons. One may take this as a condemnation of prisons, or simply as an unpleasant but unavoidable fact about them. Attitudes about prisons are not in contention here. Prisons being what they are, their inmates are in a state of constant coercion, from which there is no escape within the walls. No matter what the prisoner says, or we say to him, coercion is the essence of his condition. In that condition no consent to put oneself at risk should be accepted as full consent. Hence medical experimentation on prisoners should be forbidden, flatly.

That is the general thrust. Now, more concretely and specifically, see how this coercive spirit permeates the prison environment.

First. The body of the prisoner is simply not under his own control. Orders committing persons to prison are very blunt about this, generally containing the phrase: "the body of the defendant shall be delivered" to the custodial institution appropriately identified. No system of criminal punishment that relies upon prisons, however humane its intent, can evade this fact. . . .

Second. Not only is the prisoner's person unfree, but the control of that person, and the secure incarceration of his body, are his keepers' chief and overriding concerns. Prisons are closed, tightly guarded places. Anyone who has not visited a medium- or maximum-security prison can hardly imagine the impact of omnipresent locks, bars and armed guards. Supervision of hour-by-hour conduct is close; inspection is constant; privacy is nil; coercion is the flavor of every moment.

Third. Most prisoners are very poor and have tightly limited opportunity to earn the most puny wages. Some states pay no wages for prison labor; most states pay less than one dollar per day; only six states pay more than that. And even where wages are paid, not all prisoners have the chance to earn them. From this poverty any decent payment for service is partial rescue.

Fourth. Boredom, killing monotony, is that feature which, next to control, most pervades prison life. The state tells every prisoner when to sleep, when to rise, when to eat and what, when to work and when to play, what to do and how to do it—all with maddening sameness. From this barrenness, any change is relief.

Fifth, and finally. The dominant concern in every prisoner's life is release and the eventual date of it. In this country prison sentences of indeterminate length are very common. That single most important date is therefore subject to the judgment, even to the whim, of administrators whom the prisoner can rarely reach or even address. His behavior in prison—in ways he cannot be sure of—must affect, perhaps determine his date of release. Even for those with determinate sentences, that date remains indeterminate if there is, as usually, a parole board to be pleased. The felt need to please officials—doing what (at least in their own minds) prisoners think might please those who might be in a position to effect a somewhat earlier release—is an unavoidable pressure upon the behavior of prisoners.

It is in this environment that voluntariness of consent to subjection to medical experimentation must be assessed. However freely it appears that he consents, the prisoner is coerced so fully by his circumstances that even asking him must be unfair. His service as subject must be seen by him as a precious opportunity to escape, if only for short or infrequent periods, from the drabness and routine of prison life. He will see new faces, talk to interesting people who are neither inmates nor guards, leave his normal, grim surroundings on occasion for a setting that is lit by freedom and interest. And he is further coerced by the monetary rewards—dollars at a crack, even scores of dollars in a long experiment—promising opportunity for riches not possible otherwise. The risks run are overshadowed by the partial escape from state-imposed penury. Fifty dollars a month, say, for prison subjects in a malaria test—why, that is coercion turned green! And above all, what an opportunity to prove one's good will, one's eagerness to pay his debt to society, one's sincere intention to make up for past evils and be good! Surely they who have power in this sphere will note this evidence of good character. Surely it will not work against the prisoner when parole or release is being considered—and it may, it just *may* do some good. How can the rational prisoner not be coerced by such a concatenation of pressures? He cannot. It is not right (this argument concludes) even to ask the prisoner whether he wishes to put himself at risk when doing so is encouraged by his circumstances so strongly and so perniciously. No matter the circumspection and honest care of the investigator. If, as we have seen, full and uncoerced consent simply cannot be given by prisoners, the request for volunteers, must not, in fairness, be made to them.

The argument has two addenda:

(a) Everything above applies to prison experiments even when delicately and justly supervised. But the de facto circumstances in real prisons are such as to make delicacy rare, and justice less than universal. There is enormous potential for abuse in prisons; there *is* a great deal of abuse in prisons. Knowing that, we cannot in good conscience undertake medical experiments that may, in fact, be tainted by that abuse in various ways, but above all in the selection of subjects.

(b) Those who support medical experimentation in prisons quickly point to the great benefits they have yielded for mankind—experiments on polio virus strains, for example, which led directly to the selection of strains now used worldwide in the preparation of polio virus vaccine administered by mouth. Then there is the work on malaria, and dengue fever, and so on. All that is very fine—but if such experiments rely upon the wrongful use of human subjects, they simply shouldn't be done. The critical issues here concern what is right, what is just—not the balancing of benefits. Until the justice of such experimenting on prisoners has been shown, the calculation of benefits simply cannot be reached.

A CLOSER LOOK AT COERCION

There is the case, and it is a strong one. But it is not strong enough. The argument is rightly cautionary. Its several considerations show, I submit, that medical experiments using prisoners as subjects must go forward, if at all, under rules more constraining, and supervision more strict, than such experimentation in more ordinary contexts. It has not been shown, I contend, that a prisoner cannot give full consent in the sense that being a voluntary subject requires full consent.

I begin by granting much of the factual description of the prison environment presented above—although that account was deliberately put in rather purple language. But it is so; prison life is controlled, barren, poor, monotonous. Coercion is the spirit of the prison. Regretably, however, those who accept the argument above, or some variant of it, are led by their detestation of prisons to equivocate upon the word "coercion." When careful with it we find, reasonably enough, that there are respects in which the prisoner is coerced and respects in which he is not—and, indeed, that the same is true of everyone. We need to identify carefully that sense of coercion employed when we say that coercion vitiates an apparently free consent. Then we must decide whether, when given an opportunity to volunteer as subject, the prisoner is coerced in that sense. We will find upon reflection, I think, that another sense of coercion—looser and more suggestive, characterizing the flavor of prison activity—has been drawn upon. To make the argument work a transition is made, perhaps inadvertently, from that broad sense of coercion to a tighter, narrower sense that bears directly upon freedom in making choices.

By "coercion" our common meaning is compulsion by physical or moral pressures. *A* coerces *B* when *B* is compelled or constrained to act as *A* wishes him to, as a result of measures taken by *A* to effect just that result. The bandit coerces me, with his revolver, into handing over my wallet. The threat of criminal prosecution if I do not file an income tax return is a coercive instrument designed to constrain my behavior. We are tempted—and too many yield—to leap from this to calling coercive whatever restrains or limits or influences behavior. I may be coerced into giving to the United Fund, say by the threat of discharge or defamation; but I am not coerced into charitable giving by my strong desire to be admired as a public benefactor. Again, if my wealth were unlimited I should sail the seas in splendor; my means being what they are, I cast an admiring glance at every ocean racing yacht, and go on splashing about in my little sailing dinghy. It is an elastic use of English to say I am coerced into doing so. There are, too, desires of the utmost intensity which influence my conduct and with which I must come to terms. But these desires are not imposed (unless one holds a satanic view of the human condition) in order to bend my volition; they are the normal matrix of my life. It is facile or confused to suppose that I am coerced by my own wants. Even my most passionate wants, my sexual desires, cannot be said to coerce me into seduction.

We sometimes think powerful inducements, as well as threats, to be coercive. Sometimes they may be, but only when the subject in question is caused, by an extraordinary and deliberate temptation, to do what should not ever be done. If a poor person is tempted by a huge sum to accept a risk we think it not proper to urge upon anyone, the offer is . . . coercive. But if the reward be for conduct that is itself reasonable, the fact that one's condition renders that reward exceptionally attractive does not show that coercion has been applied. Professional football players are not coerced by huge salaries into risking their necks, nor are workers coerced into work by their need for earnings.

A definitive account of coercion I do not seek to provide here. No doubt any account, however refined, will leave some rough edges. But moderately thoughtful reflection will show, I believe, that the coercion that full consent precludes is the coercion flowing from the deliberate effort on the part of one who offers the choice (or his agent) to pressure the offeree into a particular decision. The pressure must be such that the offerer could have refrained from exerting it, but deliberately did not refrain.

If I seek admission to a research hospital specializing, say, in eye disease, desperate about my failing sight, and I am admitted upon the condition that I put myself at serious risk in an experiment having nothing to do with my condition, I have indeed been coerced improperly. Even in matters involving minor risks, if I am subjected to a moral barrage regarding the social value of medical research and for the importance of the experiment at hand to all mankind, when asked for my consent to serve as subject, I am coerced, if mildly, by the deliberate pressures of the investigator. We do not permit such distortions of potential subjects' volitions, rightly. But if I suffer from a serious disease for which cure is unknown, it is quite reasonable that I should find serving as subject, in an experiment aimed at enlarging knowledge about that disease, attractive in a way that one who does not suffer from that disease does not find attractive. My diseased condition does not coerce me. Or if one insists upon the lingo in which such sickness inevitably renders me "coerced"—then certainly that so-called coercion could not begin to establish that my freely expressed consent was really involuntary.

Our lives are led, and our decisions made, within a network of needs and wants, some natural, some arising from the acts of others, some aggravated by the acts of the state. We are all bored, or threatened, or tantalized in differing degrees by a perilous world, some hostile people, and not a very sensitive government. Sometimes, within that framework, we are coerced by the design of persons or institutions into choosing *X* rather than *Y*.

Such design, introduced in order to manipulate our choosing, is the coercion here chiefly of concern to us. The Nuremberg Code, in defining voluntary consent, puts the matter well. It insists that the person involved must in his situation be able to exercise free power of choice "without the intervention of any element of force, fraud, deceit, duress, overreaching, or other ulterior form of constraint or coercion. . . ."

Let's now apply the view of coercion to the case of the prisoner giving informed consent to serve as medical subject. The opportunity is given him, let us suppose, to respond by letter to a notice on a bulletin board, after which, if he proves a suitable subject, he is given full information about procedures, risks, pay and the rest by a research investigator. Is he coerced into giving consent by the fact of his imprisonment? On reflection I think we will see that he is not.

The question is not, "Are prisoners coerced?"—for we agree that, in general, theirs is a condition in which many more choices are foreclosed, and decisions compelled, than in conditions of ordinary life. But the pervasive presence of restraints in the prison leaves open the question of whether, with respect to a particular option put before him, he is coerced. He has a chance, say, to participate as subject in a set of drug tests, requiring intermittent hospital visits, small to moderate risks, occasional days of complete bed rest, and paying twenty dollars per month for the six months of the tests. Most experiments using human subjects involve less time, less money, and less risk. Some involve more. Take this one as a realistic illustration.

It is true that [the prisoner's] participation may promise occasional release from boredom. Boredom, however, is not a condition over which the investigator has any control, or in which he has any interest. It is simply the condition that the potential prisoner-subjects (as well as a good many non-prisoner-subjects) were in when the choice of participating or not was encountered by them. They are no more coerced into consenting by their boredom than I am coerced into seducing by my lust. The conditions in which we find ourselves powerfully affect our responses to choices put before us. If the standard of non-coercion be that potential subjects be free of all conditions that may significantly influence their willingness to consent, we will have no subjects and no experiments.

"But," the critic may reply, "although we are, indeed, all in conditions that constrain us in some respects, there remain enormous differences of degree. The prisoner's conditions are unusually severe, and that severity is what we underscore. When, for example, he supposes that giving his consent may help him, somehow, achieve an earlier release, he is in the special condition of desperately wanting release and blindly hoping that someone up there will be more moved to help him because he did consent. That is what is unusual about his condition."

This reply will not work; it does not serve to distinguish the prisoner's case from the case of others whom we do not regard as improperly coerced. It isn't only prisoners who have desperate desires that they hope may come nearer to fulfillment because of participation in experiments. Indeed, while the prisoner's hopes along that line may be tenuous and largely the result of his own wishful thinking, many non-prisoners are faced with the opportunity to participate in experiments involving considerable risk, which offer more serious hope of fulfilling desperate wants. Consider the person with psoriasis covering much of his body given the opportunity to participate in an experiment using a new and very powerful ultraviolet light that may increase the likelihood of his developing cancer and may injure his eyes. No pressure whatever is brought to bear on him by the researcher. But very great pressures he or she must feel from the intense longing to be rid of that disfiguring affliction. Is that potential subject coerced by virtue of the desperation of desire? Not in any sense that precludes his consent, surely; and if we thought he and others like him were truly coerced, we should have to forbid the experiment. Again, it is not rare for persons suffering from what appear to be terminal cancers to be offered the opportunity to participate in a controlled experiment with a new, highly toxic, chemical therapy that offers only slight hope of remission. All else has failed. Will the patient give consent to be [an] experimental subject? Very probably; he reaches for every chance to live. Is he coerced into being [a] guinea pig by the intensity of his desire? Not if the facts are presented to him truly and fairly. Indeed, we are likely to think that, though the new chemotherapy may have dreadful side effects, he is entitled, after being fully informed of the facts, to make up his own mind, and if given his circumstances he thinks it worth the risks, to consent to the desperate try.

If the researcher in this latter case had portrayed the patient's condition more grimly than the facts warranted, in order to get him to consent, we would think the patient to have been coerced, not by the intensity of his desire to live, but by that deceptive account. If the researcher had refrained deliberately from telling the patient of some alternative therapy offering equal hopes, in order to woo his participation, the patient would have been coerced, not by his needs or their grip on him, but by the manipulation of the investigator. Analogously, it is not the degree of boredom, or the passion of the desire for release, or the level of any condition that the prisoner is in that can coerce him. It is only deliberate conduct, conduct designed to deceive, to pressure, to constrain, that would coerce in the sense required. Therefore the boredom, the desire for early release, the being under constant guard—these cannot in themselves constitute coercion of a potential subject.

The critic may take another tack. "I see now (he may say) that it is not the intensity of desire that marks off the prisoner's case, or renders him coerced. Yet the precariousness of his condition is the key to the immortality I've been driving at. It is the deliberate choosing of prison populations to do experiments we would not do with others, taking advantage of their desperation, that is coercive. This, I now see, is the root of my complaint. By using prisoners the researcher gets away with an exploitation of subjects that would be impossible elsewhere—and that calculated exploitation must not be allowed."

Here the critic gives a caution that deserves to be taken seriously; but its scope must not be overblown. If we do on prisoners experiments we would not do on others, believing that for ordinary persons the risks clearly outweigh the potential benefits, the calculated choice of a precariously placed population enabling us to get away with that would, indeed, be wrongful. What troubles so about it, however, is that experiments would then be done which ought not be done at all. In the same way, where great risk far outweighs potential benefit we would not tolerate hugh sums used to inveigle the participation of indigent welfare recipients. To do with some, because we can get away with it, what we ought to do with no one is surely unconscionable. Some experiments in prisons, in the past, have been like that.

But this argument does not have the general force its advocates may suppose. When, for example, subject populations are enlisted both in and out of prisons on the same terms—as is often done—this objection has no place. When the judgment of experimental justifiability is made independently of the special circumstances of possible subject pools, an improper reliance upon those special circumstances cannot be complained of.

Moreover, the special circumstances of subjects may rightly enter when the experiment is of a kind that requires just that kind of subject for scientific reasons. Persons suffering from a given disease are reasonably chosen for experiments dealing with that disease, obviously, and any inclination they have to serve as subjects arising from that circumstance is neither avoidable nor pernicious. Again, some experiments have special requirements for long-term regularity and control, calling for subjects in unusually restricted circumstances. Seeking out those who fit the requirements of the investigation—an investigation whose worthiness is independently established—is equally reasonable, and no less so if those subjects be prisoners. It is a fact that for some scientific purposes prisoners are irreplaceable as subjects. Prisoners constitute extraordinarily stable populations, under constant and detailed observation. Diet, activity, whereabouts, and other factors possibly critical to the experiment are thoroughly known and dependable. And all of this is the case not as an imposed demand of the investigator, but as a consequence of the incarceration with which he had nothing to do. For experiments requiring repeated trials, over long periods, rigorously free of perturbing variables, there are no populations like these. One can imagine the sequestering of a non-prison subject pool for months or years, but there is no practical likelihood of it. Very few other persons, identifiable and accessible, are so situated that the time they must devote as subjects to lengthy experiments does not impose heavy burdens in removing them from what would be their alternate activities. The short of it is that for reasons having nothing to do with manipulative intent, but everything to do with scientific reliability, prison populations serve medicine as no other populations can. The critic rightly insists that prisoners should not be preyed upon, that we must not do in prisons what should not be done. This is a long way from showing that no experiments ought be conducted in prisons, or that prisoners ought not be allowed to volunteer as subjects.

What shall we say of payment to prisoners? That, after all, clearly is a factor under the researcher's full control. Moderate remuneration, of course, is widely given to subjects, in and out of prison. Insofar as those sums are deliberately offered to allure and tempt, they are, in every case, manipulative. And of course their manipulative force is the greater as the potential subject is the poorer. This argues against payment to subjects in any context, and I think that is an alternative worthy of serious consideration. On the other hand, the prospect of a small money reward (which does serve as a major motivating force in prisons)[2] neither threatens nor pressures nor tempts to do what should not be done. The very moderate sums involved—twenty or forty dollars or so—are also viewed by many not so much as lures as compensation for inconvenience. Some who would be pleased to volunteer cannot otherwise afford the time. In that spirit the sums involved do not coerce anyone. We ought no more permit large sums to tempt prisoners into undue hazards than we ought permit that among non-prisoners. Neither should we withhold from prisoners the minor compensations that serving as subject normally provides. One principle we surely wish to maintain is that prisoners not be in any way special targets for exploitation, and their not being special targets entails their being treated, in the matter of payment, just as non-prisoners are treated. They should be paid no more, no less.

How "more" or "less" ought to be calculated is a nice question. Is it equality of the absolute sum that is required? Or is it the same relative proportion of regular income that is called for? This is arguable. In my judgment it is the same dollar sum that should be used, both to be fair and to avoid the appearance of unfairness. The sums are in any event small; and adjusting them relatively entails the supposition of an "average regular income" of non-prisoner-subjects that must be wholly arbitrary.

It should be seen that even these small sums will be more alluring to prisoners than to most non-prisoners. If the payment be set at a regular standard, however, its allure is not the result of any deliberate effort by the researcher to twist the volition of the prisoner. Such twisting would be coercive. Given reasonable restrictions, that twisting can be avoided in the case of prisoners as it is in the case of non-prisoners.

I conclude that the argument against permitting prisoners to choose in this sphere, by virtue of their necessarily coerced condition, is simply mistaken. It confuses a wide sense of constraint (rightly characterizing the prison environment) with a different, narrow sense of constraint in the decision at hand—of which the prisoner can, with care, be entirely free. In the sense that one's condition coerces him, we are all coerced, and many of us as severely or more severely than prisoners. In the sense that choices before us, given our condition, may be made by us without ulterior manipulation in view of the merits of the case, the prisoners can, if fairly treated, be as free to choose as the rest of us.

Now it should be emphasized that prisoners and non-prisoners alike must be very carefully protected in making this choice—protected against "force, fraud, deceit, duress, over-reaching, or other ulterior form of constraint." Such protection against unfairness is a delicate and constantly ongoing business whose detail I cannot enter here. In the case of potential subjects in prisons, the fact of total custody, the evident potential for the abuses of power, place upon the protecting body stringent demands for caution. Membership of that body, its procedures and powers, reviews and appeals—all are matters requiring utmost circumspection. But seeing to it that the right rules are well enforced is essentially an administrative matter, though a hard one. Mine has been a moral concern, about the rightness of the rule that would forbid all experimentation on prisoners. The common argument supporting that rule, I conclude, is grounded on mistake, on a misunderstanding of what is required for genuinely free consent.

PROTECTION OR PATERNALISM?

The argument for that exclusionary rule is bad; the rule itself is worse. Reasons of two different kinds suggest that prisoners should be permitted to volunteer as subjects in medical experiments. Reasons of the first kind arise from the moral importance of protecting, for the prisoners, their right to give or withhold consent. Reasons of the second kind arise from the positive moral worth of the medical experimentation in which prisoners participate of their own volition. I deal briefly with the two categories in turn.

First. Without urging participation in experimentation upon anyone we may insist that prisoners are morally entitled to permission to volunteer. Not to permit them to do so is to deny bluntly the autonomy of the prisoner in this sphere. Persons in full custody need to be protected, not patronized. They need to be guarded from abuse, but not treated as less than the full human beings they are. Prisons are commonly condemned, with much truth, as inhuman environments, demeaning, debasing, decivilizing. Perhaps we ought not have them at all. But since we do have them, and are likely to retain them for a good while into the future, we ought to seek to create within them a spirit in which—so far as is consistent with security and punishment—the humanity of the inmate is respected. One way to register this respect is to give to prisoners, within some feasible contexts, opportunities to make serious decisions about their own lives, just as non-prisoners must. To say of prison inmates that they cannot reach genuine decisions, that they are so cramped in mind that they are not even to be allowed to make effective choices in their personal lives, is to deny them a chunk of that capacity for self-direction that must be as precious to them as to anyone else. Such denial, it seems to me, is not justifiable. It is a usurpation of their self-direction of body and person that prison itself was never intended to effect. I am frankly dismayed by the presumption of well-meaning reformers in this sphere. They will preserve the gentle heifer of freedom in the prisons by shooting it in the head.

The voice of prisoners themselves on this question is not dispositive, but it is worth hearing. Of prisoners who have been subjects, 98% of those interviewed in a University of Michigan study were either very willing or somewhat willing to participate again in a similar project, 87% were very willing.[3] This suggests strongly that they would oppose the denial of the opportunity to do so. I know of no large scale study of prison populations generally on the moral issue itself. But I submit that, were the question we discuss to be put before prisoners for vote: "Should prisoners be permitted to decide for themselves whether they choose to consent to be subjects in medical experiments?" it may be safely predicted that the endorsement of that right by prisoners would be overwhelming.[4] Of course they want the opportunity for relief and earnings, in exchange for discomfort or risk, when they think (based on an honest account of the facts) that they are getting a good deal. Their willingness to make the deal, the critic says, is only a product of their coerced condition. We've looked at that response and, I trust, put it behind us. Beyond any bargain or deal, many prisoners do very genuinely want to be of service to medicine and to fellow human beings. The altruism is genuine for a good number; there is substantial evidence for the seriousness and generality of that motivation.[5] Surely it is presumptuous of the reformer to decide for prisoners that this self-described motivation is not genuine, or is too small a factor in their real set of motivations, to allow them to decide for themselves. That, I submit, is heteronomy on stilts.

WHAT COUNTS AS MORAL?

The rule excluding prisoners from experimentation is bad for reasons of a second kind, having to do with the experiments themselves. The advantages accruing to society as a whole (prisoners included, of course) from the medical experiments taking place in prisons are very, very great. I shan't even begin to catalog the benefits that have resulted, and continue to flow, from such programs. "But," says the critic, "such benefits may not be taken as considerations bearing on the proposed exclusionary rule, since they are matters of utilitarian calculation, while the rule is a non-utilitarian protection of justice for prisoners." Allowing that the benefits are real, the critic insists that for judgment on this question the calculation of them cannot even be reached.

Again he errs. For utilitarian moralists his argument is utterly without sense, obviously. For those of us who are not thoroughgoing utilitarians this argument fails because it treats the process of experimentation and the effort to acquire knowledge that can alleviate suffering and disease as being purely non-moral, instruments for the attainment of sheer utilities having nothing to do with justice or duty. Not so. There are strong moral reasons to engage in medical experimentation, to serve the vital interests of persons numerous but unidentified. Reasons supporting such activities may include crass considerations like the reduction of absenteeism in factories, and so on, but also surely include considerations of human pain and longevity that cannot be thought crass. To the extent that there lies upon any of us the obligation to advance inquiry of a beneficent character, a proposed rule that would hinder the fulfillment of that obligation is morally objectionable. . . . If we allow that some (and perhaps all) of us have such obligations, the impact of the rule in question here upon the fulfillment of these obligations may certainly be reached in appraising that rule.

Is there a general principle of beneficence that does oblige us to be actively good? If there is, does that principle provide, perhaps, a *prima facie* obligation to advance (or not to obstruct) research aimed at knowledge to be used in healing the sick? I am not sure. It may be so. In any event we will want to insure that our rules do not unduly hinder any of us (including prisoners) who honestly believe that they have that beneficent obligation, or those of us whose special placement yields special duties.

The circumstances of the research investigator are special in this respect. The physician and the physician-researcher do take on, consciously and deliberately, the obligation to do what is reasonably within their power to ease pain, to heal, and to acquire the knowledge needed to promote these ends. The likely long-term consequences of the pursuit of such knowledge must therefore be weighed in the fully moral appraisal of any proposed principle that would restrict such pursuit.

What may mislead the critic here is the fact that while our duties to the subject in an experiment are reasonably precise—we must tell this person these things in this way—our duties to the unidentified beneficiaries of future experimentation are very imprecise. Toward them we have, as Kant would say, "imperfect" duties, because although obliged to serve them, the form of our service is not specifiable in advance. But imperfect duties are as real as those of more perfect form. That understood, we can have little remaining doubt that the results of medical experimentation for which prisoners volunteer is morally relevant in deciding whether they should be permitted to volunteer.

Finally, there are benefits of other kinds, arguably non-moral, that may also be worthy of consideration because they bear directly upon imprisonment, and the well-being of the prisoners concerned. Serving as genuinely voluntary subjects in medical experiments can and often does support the rehabilitative aims of the correctional institution. Studies have shown that such participation adds measureably to the prisoner's sense of self-esteem.[6] This becomes one of the few contexts in which he finds himself able to act purposefully in a larger world of serious affairs. In this role he can be full citizen, participant, taking some risks, gaining some advantages, being of service—in general grappling with serious matters in a way that supposes him to be the rational captain of his own fate. Rehabilitation in our prisons has not generally succeeded, as we know well. This device is no panacea, to be sure. But it does as much, perhaps more, to rehabilitate those it fully involves as any other activity in the prison. To eliminate it, out of regard for the prisoners, is to cut off our noses with theirs.

In sum. The reasons against permitting prisoners to give their consent are not sound. The moral reasons for permitting them to do so are forceful. The consideration of long-term benefits to all, and especially to the prisoners, that flow from the permission merely transforms an argument that is compelling into one that is more so.

EPILOG

Two concluding notes. Wherever I refer to the advantages or permissibility of medical experiments with voluntary prison subjects, I suppose that the caution in selecting subjects, in informing them, and in safeguarding their honest volition has been maximal. Horror stories abound; they are instructive in many contexts, but not in this one. Our question concerns the principles that ought to govern experimentation when fairly and honorably conducted.

And lastly. Early on I observed that prisoners are archetypical of persons precariously placed. But there are other categories of persons who, by virtue of their jobs, or custodial status, or the like, are particularly vulnerable to manipulation. The cautions that are rightly introduced in proposing to prisoners that they volunteer as subjects must of course be mirrored, in appropriate form and degree, for others in analogous circumstances: servicemen on military duty; patients in public hospital wards; employees in drug firms and laboratories; even students in school or university classes—all are in need of special protection for reasons like (but of course not identical with) the reasons we are specially concerned [about] with prisoners. By the same token, it is a mistake to assume that persons in such categories are incapable of giving their uncoerced consent, and that they therefore must not be permitted to do so. Of the larger class of the "precariously placed" the category [of] prisoners is the most extreme. Having dealt with it, I take myself—putting aside special situations—to have dealt, *a fortiori,* with all of the less extreme cases in the same family.

NOTES

1. The report and recommendations of the National Commission for the Protection of Human Subjects of Biomedical and Behavioral Research [*Research Involving Prisoners,* Washington, DC, Sept. 1976] is an important example. The commission recommends that "research involving prisoners should not be conducted or supported" unless a lengthy set of detailed conditions in the prison are fully realized. Voluntariness of consent is held to presuppose *grievance procedures* with elected prisoner representatives and prison advocates, and *living conditions* which, in turn, are specified to include such items as: single occupancy cells for all who desire them; arrangements for frequent, private visits; high standards for education, vocational training, health care, and recreation facilities, and so on. Since virtually no prisons are able to meet or approach the standards imposed, the recommendation (if adopted) would have the effect of forbidding almost all experimentation in prisons.

It would appear that the commission seeks to use permission to experiment in prisons as a social lever for what it views as needed prison reforms. Leaving aside the question of the necessity of the reforms demanded, it is unfortunate that the serious question of whether the consent of prisoners can be truly voluntary is there dealt with as an instrument to influence policy in other spheres rather than on its own merits.

2. See *Research in Prisons,* Survey Research Center, Institute for Social Research, the University of Michigan, Ann Arbor, 1976, pp. 47 ff.

3. Ibid., p. 57.

4. In April 1973, "96 of the 175 inmates of the Lancaster County, Pa., prison wrote to the local newspaper protesting the state's decision to stop all medical experiments on state prisoners" reads a report in the *Wall Street Journal* of 2 April 1974. Anecdotal evidence only, but not surprising.

5. *Research in Prisons,* op. cit. While this study shows that money is the reason most commonly given by prisoner subjects for volunteering, the second most common reason, cited by 27% of the many subjects interviewed, was "To help others, help society" (p. 47). Anecdotal but very persuasive support for this conclusion may be found also in the account of Dr. John C. McDonald, "Why Prisoners Volunteer to Be Experimental Subjects," JAMA, Nov. 6, 1967 (vol. 202, no. 6).

6. See: *Pharmacological Testing in a Correctional Institution,* S. H. Wells, P. Kennedy, et al., Charles C. Thomas, Publisher, Springfield, Ill., 1974. See also: *Proceedings,* Conference on Drug Research in Prisons, National Council on Crime and Delinquency, 1973.

QUESTIONS FOR STUDY AND DISCUSSION

1. In *Canterbury* v. *Spence,* the Court considers four possible standards for fulfilling the informational requirement in obtaining informed consent to medical intervention. Explain both what these suggested standards are and the Court's reasons for rejecting three of the proposed standards. What, in your considered judgment, is the most serious problem with the standard the Court finally accepts? Can a better standard be found? Explain your answer carefully.

2. In *Canterbury* v. *Spence,* Judge Robinson allows that there are two exceptions to the informed consent requirement in medical practice, and he explicitly rejects as an exception to the informed consent rule another reason. Explain the two exceptions to the informed consent requirement the Court accepts, and explain what the Court rules out as a legitimate exception to informed consent rule. What, in your considered judgment, is the most serious problem with these exceptions to the informed consent requirement accepted by the Court. How might the problem you raise be resolved?

3. Both Franz Ingelfinger and Samuel Gorovitz suggest problems in meeting the volitional requirement for informed consent. Write a short essay, focusing on law, medicine, counseling, physical therapy, university education, or some other field of interest to you which illuminates the problem of possible subtle coercion by professionals in the area you choose to discuss. Is there any way that such coercion can be avoided? If so, how? If not, why not?

4. Must one be completely informed to make an adequately knowledgeable choice in a matter pertaining to one's own welfare (e.g., regarding a medical intervention, regarding litigation when one is a plaintiff or defendant, regarding purchasing a product like an automobile, etc.)? Samuel Gorovitz suggests that we seem to have much higher standards for assuming that informed consent has been given in the medical context than in other areas of self-regarding decision making. Is there any justification for this discrepancy? Explain your answer carefully.

5. Compare and contrast Samuel Gorovitz's discussion of informed consent with Joseph Ellin's discussion of the values a professional is hired to promote (chap. 5). Carefully defend one of these views as morally superior to the other.

6. Using the readings in chapter 4 as a resource, offer your own account of what model of the professional/client relationship Gorovitz's discussion of informed consent presupposes.

7. Compare and contrast the views of Jessica Mitford and Carl Cohen on the question of voluntariness of consent; pay particular attention to each author's concept of coercion. Offer your own account of the merits and weaknesses of each author's position.

8. Suppose you are a legislator asked to vote on a bill which, if passed, will prohibit all biomedical experimentation on prisoners. Should you vote for or against the bill? Defend your answer; anticipate and respond to the most serious objection that might be raised against your view.

9. Explain the two major standard objections to the informed consent requirement in medical practice. Using the readings in this chapter and in chapter 5 as resources, construct a reply to each of these objections. Is the reply you have constructed strong enough to overcome the objections? Why or why not?

10. Is it ever morally permissible to conduct research on children too young to give an informed consent to research participation? If not, why not? If so, under what conditions? Whatever your answer, construct the strongest objection you can think of to your view and offer a reply to that objection.

CASE: BACK FROM THE DEAD

Dr. Cee, a veterinarian with a well-established practice in a small city, saw Ms. Kay's dog, Sandy, in March 1987. Dr. Cee diagnosed Sandy as having a rare blood disease. He knew of only one experimental treatment for the disease, but it was extremely expensive, lengthy, uncomfortable for the animal, and had been ninety-five percent ineffective in laboratory testing. Ms. Kay decided against trying the treatment and asked that Sandy be euthanized because she did not want him to suffer any longer. She was extremely attached to the dog and left him at Dr. Cee's with great sadness.

That afternoon, Dr. Cee began the experimental treatment on Sandy. He felt that most researchers on the disease had made a crucial mistake and that he might be able to treat Sandy effectively. But because he had never tried the experimental treatment and because of Ms. Kay's concern about Sandy's discomfort, he did not inform her. A month later, Sandy was free of all symptoms of the disease. Dr. Cee called Ms. Kay, and asked if he might stop in to see her. She assured him she would be happy to have him drop by. He arrived with Sandy, who was fit and simply delighted to be home again. Dr. Cee explained to Ms. Kay why he had decided to treat Sandy and that he had not told her because he did not want to raise her hopes. He did not ask Ms. Kay for any payment despite the fact that the hours and materials for the treatment totaled costs in excess of a thousand dollars.

1. Who is the veterinarian's client—the pet or the pet owner? Explain your answer as fully as you are able.

2. Is it ever morally acceptable for a veterinarian to do research on a pet without the pet owner's permission? If not, why not? If so, under what conditions?

3. Did Dr. Cee act in a morally acceptable way in this case? Defend your answer; anticipate and respond to the most serious objection to your view.

4. Suppose a man has died and his will stipulates that on his death his companion cat of thirteen years is to be euthanized. Suppose the family brings the cat to a veterinarian and requests euthanasia. Suppose the veterinarian can find a home for the cat, but the family insists that the man's will must be respected. Would it be morally acceptable for the veterinarian to take the animal, leading the family to believe she will euthanize him, but then place the cat in another home? Defend your answer; anticipate and respond to the most serious objection to your view.

CASE: PSYCHOSURGERY FOR A SEXUAL OFFENDER

John Doe has been detained for more than seventeen years in a psychiatric facility for the criminally insane. He is serving an indefinite commitment under his state's Criminal Sexual Psychopathic Law, having murdered and subsequently raped a student nurse while he was a patient in another psychiatric facility.

Doe is subject to episodes of what seem to be uncontrollable aggression, which issue in sexual violence. No drug or "talk" therapies have been effective with him, and he will not be released until the authorities are confident that he is safe to be at large.

Several physicians have just received funding from the state legislature to do a study on the treatment of uncontrollable aggression. The purpose of the study is to compare the effects of psychosurgery with the effects of medication in the treatment of sexual psychopaths in the state's psychiatric facilities. The long-term goal of the study is to discover how to relieve these inmates from their overpowering aggressive tendencies so that they can return to the community.

As it turns out, Doe is the only appropriate candidate in the state's facilities for the psychosurgery. His

---

Case adapted from *Kaimowitz* v. *Michigan Department of Mental Health,* Civil Action 73–19434–AW (Wayne County, MI Cir. Ct. 1973).

participation has been approved by a scientific review committee and a human rights review committee. Doe has signed an informed consent form which outlines the two-part procedure to be followed:

> Since conventional treatment efforts over a period of several years have not enabled me to control my outbursts of rage and anti-social behavior, I submit an application to be a subject in a research project which may offer me a form of elective therapy. The therapy is based upon the idea that episodes of anti-social rage and sexuality might be triggered by a disturbance in certain portions of my brain. I understand that in order to be certain that a significant brain disturbance exists, which might relate to my anti-social behavior, an initial operation will have to be performed. This procedure consists of placing fine wires into my brain, which will record the electrical activity from those structures which play a part in anger and sexuality. These electrical waves can be studied to determine the presence of abnormality.
>
> In addition, electrical stimulation with weak currents passed through these wires will be done in order to find out if one or several points in the brain can trigger my episodes of violence or unlawful sexuality. In other words, this stimulation may cause me to want to commit an aggressive or sexual act, but every effort will be made to have a sufficient number of people present to control me. If the brain disturbance is limited to a small area, I understand that the investigators will destroy this part of my brain with an electrical current. If the abnormality comes from a larger part of my brain, I agree that it should be surgically removed, if the doctors determine that it can be done so, without risk of side effects. Should the electrical activity from the parts of my brain into which the wires have been placed reveal that there is no significant abnormality, the wires will simply be withdrawn.
>
> I realize that any operation on the brain carries a number of risks which may be slight, but could be potentially serious. These risks include infection, bleeding, temporary or permanent weakness or paralysis of one or more of my legs or arms, difficulties with speech and thinking, as well as the ability to feel, touch, [and experience] pain and temperature. Under extraordinary circumstances, it is also possible that I might not survive the operation.
>
> Fully aware of the risks detailed in the paragraphs above, I authorize the physicians of Lafayette Clinic and Providence Hospital to perform the procedures as outlined above.

The decision to go ahead with the experiment on Doe is discovered by a local attorney. The attorney argues for an injunction forbidding the experiment on Doe on the ground that Doe's situation is intrinsically coercive, thus he cannot give an adequately voluntary consent to the procedure. The Court is moved by this argument and grants the injunction. Doe is denied permission to participate in the experiment.

1. Carefully examine the content of the informed consent form completed by Doe. How might the form be improved? As it stands, is the content of the form sufficient to convince you that Doe has the information he needs to make a knowledgeable judgment on the psychosurgery? Explain your answer. If you say the form is inadequate, can it be made adequate to ensure that Doe has the information he needs to make a knowledgeable decision? If not, why not? If so, explain how.

2. The attorney's argument against Doe's participation in the psychosurgery experiment rests on the features of Doe's circumstances rather than on Doe's actual mental state. Can it be assumed that a prisoner's situation is sufficient to render his or her choice to participate in a potentially beneficial experiment inadequately voluntary? Explain you answer with care.

3. Using your answer to the previous question as a resource, discuss the moral permissibility of paying the poor to participate in risky biomedical experimentation; pay particular attention to the question of whether an individual's financial need renders his or her decision to participate in such experiments less than adequately voluntary.

4. Consider the case of a patient in the late stages of a terminal disease. Suppose the patient is offered an opportunity to participate in a drug trial which holds out some remote hope that she will benefit from the drug. Given the assumption that without the experimental drug she will surely die, can her agreeing to participate in the drug trial be considered an acceptably voluntary choice? Explain clearly how cases like this might be said to be importantly parallel to cases like John Doe's. Explain any relevant differences you see in the terminal patient and the Doe cases.

SELECTED BIBLIOGRAPHY

Abernathy, Virginia, and Keith Lundin. ''Competency and the Right to Refuse Medical Treatment.'' In *Frontiers of Medical Ethics: Applications in a Medical Setting,* ed. Virginia Abernathy, pp. 79–98. Cambridge, MA: Ballinger, 1980.

Alfidi, Ralph J. ''Informed Consent: A Study of Patient Reaction.'' *Journal of the American Medical Association* 216 (1971): 1325–29.

Bartholome, William G., and Willard Gaylin. ''Correspondence: In Defense of a Child's Right to Assent.'' *Hastings Center Report* 12:5 (1982): 44–45.

Bayer, Ronald. ''Notifying Workers at Risk.'' *American Journal of Public Health* 76 (1986): 1352–56.

Beecher, Henry K. ''Consent in Clinical Experimentation: Myth and Reality.'' *Journal of the American Medical Association* 195 (1966): 34–35.

———. ''Experimentation in Man.'' *Journal of the American Medical Association* 169 (1959): 461–78.

———. ''Some Fallacies and Errors in the Application of the Principle of Consent in Human Experimentation.'' *Clinical Pharmacology and Therapeutics* 3 (1962): 141–45.

Callahan, Joan C. ''Paternalism and Voluntariness.'' *Canadian Journal of Philosophy* 16:2 (1986): 199–220.

Capron, Alexander M. ''Informed Consent in Catastrophic Disease Research and Treatment.'' *University of Pennsylvania Law Review* 123 (1974): 340–438.

Cobbs v. *Grant*. 502 P2d 1 (1972).

Donagan, Alan. ''Informed Consent in Therapy and Experimentation.'' *Journal of Medicine and Philosophy* 2:4 (1977): 307–29.

Faden, Ruth, and Tom L. Beauchamp. *A History of Informed Consent*. New York: Oxford University Press, 1986.

Fletcher, John. ''Human Experimentation: Ethics in the Consent Situation.'' *Law and Contemporary Problems* 32 (1967): 620–49.

Freedman, Benjamin. ''Competence, Marginal and Otherwise: Concepts and Ethics.'' *International Journal of Law and Psychiatry* 4 (1981): 53–72.

———. ''A Moral Theory of Informed Consent.'' *Hastings Center Report* 5:4 (1975): 32–39.

Freund, Paul A., ed. *Experimentation with Human Subjects*. New York: Braziller, 1970.

Gaylin, Willard. ''The Competence of Children: No Longer All or None.'' *Hastings Center Report* 12:2 1982: 33–38.

Katz, Jay. *Experimentation with Human Beings*. New York: Russell Sage Foundation, 1972.

LaForet, Eugene G. ''The Fiction of Informed Consent.'' *Journal of the American Medical Association* 235 (1976): 1579–85.

Lasagna, Louis L. ''Special Subjects in Human Experimentation.'' *Daedalus* (Spring 1969): 449–62.

Meisel, Alan. ''Informed Consent—the Rebuttal.'' *Journal of the American Medical Association* 234 (1975): 615.

———, Loren H. Roth, and Charles W. Lidz. ''Toward a Model of the Legal Doctrine of Informed Consent.'' *American Journal of Psychiatry* 134 (1977): 285–89.

Mills, Don H. ''Informed Consent—The Rejoinder.'' *Journal of the American Medical Association* 234 (1975): 616.

———. ''Whither Informed Consent?'' *Journal of the American Medical Association* 229 (1974): 305–10.

Montange, Charles. ''Informed Consent and the Dying Patient.'' *Yale Law Journal* 83 (1974): 1632–64.

Murphy, Jeffrie G. ''Consent, Coercion, and Hard Choices.'' *Virginia Law Review* 67 (1981): 79–95.

———. ''Total Institutions and the Possibility of Consent to Organic Therapies.'' In *Retribution, Justice, and Therapy: Essays in the Philosophy of Law,* pp. 183–201. Boston: D. Riedel, 1979.

Note. ''Restructuring Informed Consent: Legal Therapy for the Doctor-Patient Relationship.'' *Yale Law Journal* 79 (1972): 1535–37.

Olin, G. B., and H. S. Olin. "Informed Consent in Voluntary Mental Hospital Admissions." *American Journal of Psychiatry* 132 (1975): 938–41.

Plante, Marcus L. "An Analysis of 'Informed Consent.' " *Fordham Law Review* 36 (1968): 639–72.

Roth, Loren, Alan Meisel, and Charles Lidz. "Tests of Competency to Consent to Treatment." *American Journal of Psychiatry* 134 (1977): 279–84.

Spiegel, Mark. "Lawyering and Client Decision Making: Informed Consent and the Legal Profession." *University of Pennsylvania Law Review* 128 (1979): 41–140.

7

PRIVACY AND CONFIDENTIALITY

Like the issue of informed consent, systematic discussions of privacy and explicit concern about violations of privacy in business and the professions are a relatively recent phenomena. Even the U.S. Supreme Court's first formal recognition of a constitutional right to privacy appeared as recently as 1965.[1] The readings in the first part of this chapter concentrate on pointing out some contemporary practices that raise serious concerns about losses of privacy, on clarifying the concept of privacy, on understanding the value of various forms of privacy, and on determining when impingements on privacy are morally justified.

There is considerable disagreement on the precise analysis of the concept of privacy. W. A. Parent suggests that we should understand privacy as "the condition of not having undocumented personal knowledge about one possessed by others." As he clarifies and defends his definition, Parent outlines various other conceptions of privacy. Although he rejects them, the conceptions he mentions all offer some insight into our ordinary notion of privacy and why we recognize privacy as an important value. Terry Pinkard discusses invasions of privacy in social science research. Both Parent and Pinkard point out that respect for privacy is grounded in respect for persons.

Among other concerns, Parent's essay raises important questions about contemporary methods of collecting, storing, retrieving, and sharing information about individuals. For example, more and more hospitals are putting patient charts on computers. This immediately makes patient information available to persons not connected to patient care, for example, people running the hospital's computer system. In 1977, a U. S. government commission charged with studying the protection of privacy in contemporary society isolated five systematic features of personal data keeping in America today:

> [1] While an organization makes and keeps records about individuals to facilitate relationships with them, it also makes and keeps records about individuals for other purposes, such as documenting the record-keeping organization's own actions and making it possible for other organizations—government agencies, for example—to monitor the actions of individuals; [2] There is an accelerating trend, most obvious in the credit and financial areas, toward the accumulation in records of more and more personal details about an individual; [3] More and more records about an individual are collected, maintained, and disclosed by organizations with which the individual has no direct relationship but whose records help to shape his life; [4] Most record-keeping organizations consult the records of other organizations to verify the information they obtain from an individual and thus pay as much or more attention to what other organizations

> report about him than they pay to what he reports about himself; and [5] Neither law nor technology now gives an individual the tools he needs to protect his legitimate interests in the records organizations keep on him.[2]

As the selection from *Newsweek* points out, we have also recently seen a sharp rise in various forms of testing of individuals by employers as a way of ensuring safety, competence, and other virtues in the workplace. These tests range from mandatory drug screening through the use of polygraphs to screening for exposure to the AIDS virus. The five systematic and worrisome features of contemporary data keeping on persons and the proliferation of tests raise serious concerns about losses of privacy in contemporary society as well as serious questions about the scope of an employer's right to get the performance he or she pays for.

In his discussion of the justification of invasions of privacy (as well as the justification of deception) in social science research, Terry Pinkard appeals to some concepts which merit advance explication. First, Pinkard utilizes a rights-based moral framework to approach the question of invasion of privacy (see the introduction to chap. 5). Such a framework assumes that moral rights are always the most compelling of moral considerations. That is, the rights-based theorist holds that consequentialist (or in the language of chap. 1, teleological) considerations are always subordinate to considerations of moral rights. Thus, according to Pinkard (and theorists like him) the fact that good results can be produced by violating moral rights cannot be used as a justification for overriding moral rights. This is what Pinkard means when (rejecting Justice Rehnquist's argument for invading privacy and following Ronald Dworkin) he says that rights ''trump'' utilitarian considerations. Thus, invasions of privacy cannot be justified, according to Pinkard, on the ground that those invasions will produce even a substantial amount of individual or societal good.

On the other hand, Pinkard does allow that moral rights can sometimes be overridden. But as a rights-based theorist, his view is that this will only be the case when more morally compelling rights are at stake. Thus, Pinkard can allow that the strong right of innocent people not to be harmed can override the comparably less compelling right of others not to suffer minor invasions of privacy.

But how are such rights conflicts to be decided? In the final section of his paper, Pinkard appeals to the notions of tacit and hypothetical consent. Roughly speaking, tacit consent is that consent which we assume an individual gives on, for example, entering into certain customary arrangements. Pinkard uses the example of a poker game, where it can be assumed that individuals entering the game consent to the ''bluffing'' which is part of the game and thus are not treated wrongly when subjected to ''bluffs'' in the game (cf. the selection by Albert Carr in chap. 3). A related concept is that of hypothetical consent, which does not assume that an individual actually gives consent to otherwise wrongful treatment. Rather, the question for the method of hypothetical consent is whether a rational agent *would* consent to a certain impingement of his or her moral rights if he or she had all the relevant information. Although Pinkard does not completely distinguish these two concepts, they are importantly different. For even though we sometimes may not justifiably assume that an agent gives a real, though unexpressed, consent to certain impingements on his or her rights, it may be the case that we can be justified in assuming that a rational agent *would* consent to those impingements on his or her rights under certain conditions. And this, it might be argued, provides a justification for those impingements when getting actual consent is not possible. Pinkard ends his paper by arguing that because social science research is not like a poker game where the rules are (however implicitly) understood by all involved, people studied in most deceptive social science research are unjustifiably deceived, and their privacy is unjustifiably invaded. But it needs to be pointed out that this is an argument from lack of *tacit* consent, and it needs to be noticed that using the method of *hypothetical* consent need not yield so thorough a proscription on deceptive social science research or research which otherwise impinges on privacy.

Despite the conflation of tacit and hypothetical consent in Pinkard's paper, in appealing to these notions, Pinkard adds importantly to the discussion of informed consent in chapter 6. The method of hypothetical consent captures the concern for individual autonomy which underpins the informed consent requirement and the presumption against invading privacy, and it might be one way of approaching the placebo case at the end of chapter 5. Further, the method of hypothetical consent might be used more generally to think about paternalistic interventions in the professions as well as about justifiable breaches of confidentiality in the professional/client relationship, which is the topic of the second part of this chapter.[3]

Like the value of privacy, confidentiality in the professional/client relationship is important because respect for confidentiality is protective of individual self-direction, individual welfare, and, many argue, social good more generally. But the fact that confidentiality is important does not entail that it may never be overridden. The readings in the last section of this chapter focus on the question of when breaches of professional/client confidentiality might be justified.

Sissela Bok outlines several of the arguments for protecting confidentiality generally and in the professional/client relationship more particularly. But Bok argues that the duty of confidentiality is not absolute and must be moderated by the competence of the individual requesting confidentiality and the strong rights of innocent others not to be harmed. One interesting question implicitly raised by Bok's piece concerns the morally required extent of confidentiality between members of the clergy and those who consult them in confidence. Should a minister, priest, religious sister, or other pastoral counselor violate a counselee's request for confidence if maintaining confidence will be harmful to the counselee or others? Should a pastoral counselor go to the parents of a fourteen-year-old girl who reveals that she is pregnant and is thinking about an abortion? May the state require any breaches of confidence by the clergy? Should respect for clergy/counselee confidentiality be as/more/less rigorous than respect for confidentiality between patients and health care providers, between teachers and students, between attorneys and clients, between journalists and their sources?

The selections from Justices Tobriner and Clark address the issue of confidentiality in mental health care. Writing for the majority of the California Supreme Court in *Tarasoff* v. *Regents of the University of California,* Justice Tobriner contends that protection of others from violent assault outweighs a client's right to professional/client privilege. According to the Court, psychiatric counselors have a duty to warn individuals that they are in danger of assault by a violent patient. Writing for the dissenting minority, Justice Clark objects to a legal recognition of the duty to warn on the basis of public policy considerations and (implicitly) on the ground that individual rights will be violated by recognizing the duty in law. Clark argues that the position accepted by the majority will lead to an increase in violence because it will impair psychiatric treatment in several ways. Clark also argues that imposing a duty to warn will lead to increased involuntary confinement, since once the burden of protection of others is placed on psychiatric counselors, we can expect that they will protect themselves from liability by confining people who just might be dangerous to others. Implicit in this argument is a concern for a person's right not to be a "false positive"—that is, a person predicted to be assaultive who, in fact, will not be.[4]

The selection from Willard Gaylin raises the question of the professional's duties to the state and the use of professionals in apprehending criminals. If we are willing to require that physicians report gunshot wounds so that we may apprehend criminals, should we also be willing to have the FBI print posters of criminals with known physical ailments (or known histories of seeking psychiatric counseling) in professional journals? Just where do one's duties as a professional end and one's duties as a citizen begin? Or, alternatively, just where do one's duties as a citizen end and one's duties as a professional begin?

The selection from Alan Donagan challenges the strict confidentiality rule found in the American Bar Association's code of ethics for attorneys. Donagan attacks some of the standard teleological and deontological arguments for strict confidentiality in legal practice, and he argues that the attorney's *moral* duty to disclose certain information about a client is no different than the ordinary person's duty to disclose information about another person. In arguing as he does, Donagan's position is reminiscent of the discussion of occupational and personal morality in chapter 3 as well as the discussion of models of the professional/client relationship in chapter 4, since his view involves a rejection of what has earlier been called 'role differentiation' in the professions (see, esp., the introduction to chap. 3 and the selection from Richard Wassustrom in chap. 3). Donagan's article is also reminiscent of the selection from Bok in the present chapter insofar as he argues that lawyers should not promise strict confidentiality because there are some matters of information that they cannot escape a moral obligation to disclose.

Each of the readings in the second section of this chapter asks when confidentiality in the professional/client relationship may be overridden for the good or protection of others. This question paves the way for the next section, which will raise some additional questions about responsibility and the duties of professions and professionals to the wider society.

NOTES

1. *Griswold* v. *Connecticut* 381 U.S. 479 (1965).

2. Privacy Protection Study Commission, *Personal Privacy in an Information Society* (Washington, DC: U.S. Government Printing Office, 1977); excerpted in Deborah G. Johnson and John W. Snapper (eds.), *Ethical Issues in the Use of Computers* (Belmont, CA: Wadsworth, 1985), pp. 215–39. Excerpt here from Johnson and Snapper, p. 220.

3. The method of hypothetical consent is not without its critics. See, e.g., Ronald Dworkin's "The Original Position," in Norman Daniels (ed.), *Reading Rawls* (New York Basic Books, 1976), pp. 16–53. Dworkin's discussion is in terms of hypothetical contract, and he rightly points out that "a hypothetical contract is not simply a pale form of an actual contract; it is not contract at all" (p.18). But it does not follow that when we are trying to decide what to do in some morally dilemmic situation that the method of hypothetical consent is useless. Traditionally, asking what someone would want done to himself or herself or for someone else (e.g., a loved one) is a way of taking autonomy seriously, and, in certain contexts, often considered the morally crucial question to ask.

4. On the problems associated with predicting violence by psychiatric patients, see, e.g., John Monahan, *The Clinical Prediction of Violent Behavior* (Bethesda, MD: National Institute of Mental Health, 1980); and H. J. Steadman, "The Right Not to Be a False Positive: Problems in the Application of Dangerousness Standard," *Psychiatric Quarterly* 52:2 (1980), pp. 84–99. Steadman points out that the most accurate predictions of who in a group will engage in dangerous actions are those that say that none in the group will be dangerous.

PRIVACY

26. Can You Pass the Job Test?

When Arlo Guthrie sang his Vietnam-era ballad "Alice's Restaurant," his tormentor was that era's answer to Big Brother—the military draft board. Today John Sexton might cast someone else in the role of snooping archvillain: his former employer. Last year [1985] Sexton, then a $30,000-a-year dispatcher at Federal Express Corp. in Atlanta, was one of a group of employees ordered to submit urine samples for a drug test. Sexton tested positive; he says he had smoked marijuana at a party two weeks earlier, but he didn't appear impaired at the time of the test. Next he was ordered to take a lie-detector test or face suspension—but when he denied using drugs on the job or knowing anyone who did, the polygrapher running the test concluded he was holding something back. Fired last May, the 29-year-old college graduate hasn't been able to land another job since. Federal Express declines to comment on the episode but suggests that Sexton's firing was appropriate. Sexton, meanwhile, is preparing to sue Federal for wrongful discharge—and the American Civil Liberties Union (ACLU) of Georgia says he has a strong case.

Sexton's situation isn't unusual: in corporations across the United States, a frenzy of inspecting, detecting, selecting and rejecting is under way. Plans to test baseball players for illegal drug use have created a stir, but nearly a third of the corporations in the Fortune 500 also screen employees for abuse of even casual intake of such substances as marijuana and cocaine. Countless other firms monitor workers' honesty with lie detectors or written exams or probe their psyches with an array of personality tests. Some corporations have begun monitoring employees for diseases such as AIDS. And in quest of the perfect employee, many firms may one day be able to screen out workers with hundreds of genetic traits that could predispose them to serious and costly illnesses.

The boom in testing is fueling the growth of what was once a cottage industry: an array of labs, consulting firms, security specialists and other testing companies that together take in hundreds of millions of dollars in revenue each year. At the same time, it pits employees against management in a debate over whose interests tip the scales of justice. Which set of rights is paramount: those of companies seeking a productive and safe work force—or those of employees trying to protect their privacy? Does testing really identify drug abusers, in-house thieves and other undesirables, or are the innocent and employable also caught in the net? Is testing of employees the key to U.S. industrial competitiveness, or is it worsening labor-management relations at a time when more cooperation is needed? Does testing protect the commonweal, or does it run against the grain of American society—smacking of the oppressive utopias of Aldous Huxley's *Brave New World* or George Orwell's *1984?*

. . . Lawsuits and union grievances challenging the use of drug testing are on the rise; California has barred testing for the AIDS virus or antibody as a condition of employment, and Congress may soon approve legislation to outlaw the use of lie detectors by most private employers. But whether these developments will dampen the current enthusiasm for testing is unclear. Many companies, alarmed by growing drug use and fearful of everything from wrongful-discharge suits to liability for faulty products, are embracing the use of testing as a vital defense. And advances in technology have made testing almost irresistible, yielding procedures that are "good enough and cheap enough that they are now an [inexpensive] management tool," says Bill Maher, a San Francisco supervisor who helped draft a city ordinance that bars most blanket drug testing.

Testing employees and job applicants is hardly new; in fact, the 1950s may have marked an earlier zenith of testing, as companies gathered reams of information on their prospective workers through psychological profiles, employment histories, criminal records and personal data. The shifting values and mores of the 1960s and 1970s changed all that, says Columbia University professor of public law Alan Westin. Federal equal-employment-opportunity guidelines put the onus on employers to ensure that testing was a scientifically valid selection tool and that it didn't discriminate against specific racial or social groups. As privacy laws were passed to protect the public from intrusive or discriminatory data collection by government and institutions such as credit agencies, pri-

---

From *Newsweek* (5 May 1986): 46–53; story prepared by Susan Dentzer, Bob Cohn, George Raine, Ginny Carroll, and Vicki Quade.

vate employers also began weeding out their personnel files and testing less.

Now that companies are turning to testing again, the privacy issue is back with a vengeance. Through the Fourth Amendment, only government workers have constitutional protection against unreasonable searches and seizures by their employer—a by-product of the Founding Fathers' fear that unchecked government posed the greatest threat to citizens' rights. Nonetheless, many legal scholars believe that there also exists in society "a certain essential right of individuals to be left alone, and not to be subjected to . . . invasive activities without justification," as Geoffrey Stone, a professor of constitutional law at the University of Chicago, puts it. "Can you imagine the Founding Fathers saying that the major source of authority in [your] life"—your employer—"can make you drop your pants and urinate as a condition of getting or keeping a job?" asks Gene Guerrero, director of the Georgia ACLU. "It's ludicrous." But while employers argue that it's necessary, that's in a sense what many are compelling employees to do.

HONESTY TESTS: ARE THEY VALID?

The late Sen. Sam Ervin called them "20th-century witchcraft," but that hasn't stopped many employers from administering lie detectors, or polygraph tests. Almost 2 million are given to employees and job applicants each year—and they can be "a very effective tool in stopping employee crime," says Mark A. de Bernardo, a labor lawyer at the U.S. Chamber of Commerce. Brokerage firms such as E. F. Hutton and banks like Citicorp routinely give polygraphs—Hutton to all employees and Citicorp to most workers who physically handle money. Days Inns of America, a national motel chain based in Atlanta, testified in Congress last year that use of lie detectors helped cut its losses from employee crime to $115,000 in 1984, down from $1 million in 1975.

But polygraphs are undoubtedly more of a deterrent to crime than an effective means of determining an employee's guilt or innocence. The federal Office of Technology Assessment determined in 1983 that the scientific validity of lie-detector results couldn't be established. The American Psychological Association charges that polygraphs turn up "an unacceptable number of false positives"—that is, the subjects had not been lying. Because of these and other factors, few American courts will admit polygraph data as evidence.

Following the pattern of similar legislation in about 20 states, the House of Representatives last March passed the Polygraph Protection Act, which would prohibit private employers from giving lie-detector tests to most current or prospective employees. (Many utility workers, pharmaceutical workers handling controlled substances, day-care workers and employees of private security companies could still be polygraphed). Last week hearings were held on a similar measure introduced in the Senate by Republican Orrin Hatch of Utah, a conservative, and liberal Democrat Ted Kennedy. Opposed by the likes of attorney F. Lee Bailey—as well as polygraphers and many employers, who would prefer tighter regulation of the polygraph industry—the measure seems likely to pass.

To avoid the cost (about $40 to $50 per test) and ambiguity of polygraph tests, many companies have turned instead to written honesty tests. John E. Reid & Associates of Chicago, a pioneer in the field, markets its $9 tests to about 2,000 clients nationwide; Stanton Corp., based in Charlotte, N. C., sells about a million tests each year to hotel chains, clothing retailers, convenience stores and other companies whose workers regularly handle money or merchandise for sale. Jim Walls, vice president of Stanton, contends that such screening is a necessity in an age when people move or change jobs frequently. "There's no way that [companies] can ever get to know the people they're hiring before they're hired," he says.

Many honesty-test questions are almost disarmingly ingenuous. Dr. Homer B. C. Reed, a neuropsychologist at Tufts University's New England Medical Center and a consultant to Stanton, singles out one sample question: "The amount I stole from my employer was (a) 0 (b) $5 (c) $25 (d) $100 (e) $500." accompanied by a space for an explanation. Reed says many job applicants actually circle one of the last four answers. "You would think you can't identify scoundrels by asking them if they're scoundrels, but you can," he says.

Prompted by concerns that employers would use written tests to pry too much into employees' backgrounds, as some lie-detector tests have done, a new Massachusetts state law prohibits employers from giving honesty tests that amount to "paper and pencil" polygraphs. Many experts are troubled for different reasons, calling some tests a useless tool that could actually screen out capable, honest employees. Columbia Professor Westin derides the absolutism of some tests in requiring "a Fearless Fosdick, Dick Tracy response to every situation"; he thinks they may be used to screen out "people more likely to join a union or challenge something on a job as being morally or ethically improper." Michael Merbaum, a psychologist with St. Louis-based Psychological Associates Inc., a management-consulting and training firm, concurs. He believes that the "correct" answers to many tests are too often based on strict definitions of honesty that may not be shared by test takers; for example, an employee who admits he once took office supplies may not believe he did anything wrong. A far better approach, says Merbaum, is interviewing prospective employees carefully to determine their level of emotional maturity—and to discover whether they have "the capability to appraise situations . . . judiciously so they will make the proper decisions."

DRUG TESTS: LEGAL CHALLENGES

When guards conducted an early-morning drug sweep of the Albuquerque Publishing Co. last January, company officials said it was for good reason: an estimated 20 percent of the firm's employees have "an abuse problem," says company president Thompson Lang—and of all the job applicants who've taken drug tests in recent months, "no one has passed." Few companies face problems quite so dramatic, but drug use does take a serious toll: the U.S. Chamber of Commerce estimates that drug and alcohol abuse among workers costs employers $60 billion a year—the total tab for lost productivity, accidents, higher medical claims, increased absenteeism and theft of company property (the means by which many workers finance their drug habits). Relatively few companies seem to be tackling alcohol abuse with as much conviction, but concern about drugs is plainly growing, and it has spread well beyond the private workplace. Last week Boston's police commissioner called for mandatory drug testing of all officers, and in a recommendation hotly disputed by some panel members, President Reagan's Commission on Organized Crime recently called for testing of all federal workers in an attempt to control the spread of drugs.

To root out drug abusers among applicants or employees, meanwhile, companies such as Michigan-based Consumers Power Co., Westinghouse Electric Corp., the DuPont Co. and Albuquerque Publishing have turned to relatively inexpensive urine tests, such as the EMIT (Enzyme Multiplied Immunoassay Test) manufactured by Syva Co., a subsidiary of Syntex Corp. of Palo Alto, Calif. But whether use of these tests does much to control drug abuse is a matter of fierce debate. A major flaw of the most widely used tests is that they don't measure an employee's degree of impairment or level of job performance at the time of the test but show only traces of drugs in the urine. Cocaine may show up as much as three days after consumption; marijuana may be present from five days to three weeks afterward. A drug test, then, may nab even drug users who don't use them at the workplace. "What someone does outside the job isn't a concern for the employer unless it affects what they do on the job," argues Erwin Chemerensky, professor of constitutional law at the University of Southern California (USC).

An even bigger problem is that the tests aren't always accurate. Results can vary widely with the skills of the individuals carrying out the tests or the laboratories analyzing the results. Over-the-counter drugs such as Advil and Nuprin have shown up as illegal drugs on some tests, notes Kerry Shannon, marketing director of Bio-Analytical Technologies, a Chicago lab that conducts urinalysis tests. The most widely used tests claim a 95 to 99 percent accuracy rate; in companies where blanket testing is carried out, this means that, on average, 1 to 5 out of every 100 tests will produce inaccurate results. A recent Northwestern University study suggests an even worse record: it found that 25 percent of all EMIT tests that came up positive were really "false positives." And James Woodford, a forensic chemist in Atlanta and a consultant to the U.S. Public Health Service, contends that urinalysis tests may be racially biased. The reason: test results may be skewed by blacks' higher concentrations of the pigment melanin, which has an ion identical to THC, the active ingredient in Marijuana—and which may also soak up body substances similar to THC.

Manufacturers of urine tests acknowledge some of their deficiencies. Michelle Klaich, a spokeswoman for Syntex, stresses that a positive reading on one test shouldn't by itself be a ground for firing; she says Syntex recommends follow-up tests and other measures to verify the results. To improve accuracy, meanwhile, some companies are at work on the next generation of testing devices. National Patent Analytical Systems, Inc., of Roslyn Heights, N.Y., is awaiting results of clinical tests of its Veritas 100 Analyzer, which uses computer hardware and software to analyze the electrical stimuli given off by the brain in the presence of certain drugs. Company president Joseph Boccuzi says the device measures only the presence of drugs at the time of the test and cuts the false-positive rate to less than 5 percent.

But Ira Glasser, executive director of the ACLU, worries that the growing testing industry will become its own reason for being, propounding the use of testing to justify its existence. He recommends "an unused method for detecting [drug abuse]—it's called 'two eyes'." Most employees who are drug abusers reveal telltale signs of their problem, such as erratic behavior or inability to concentrate. A watchful supervisor, says Glasser, should be able to spot drug use and help an employee into a drug-rehabilitation program—an approach that ultimately may be most helpful in eliminating drug abuse.

Despite a growing number of lawsuits, courts so far have generally upheld the legality of drug testing. But some state and local legislatures are moving to restrict and regulate it. California Assemblyman Johan Klehs has proposed a bill that would require a company's testing policy to be in writing; test results would be kept confidential, and all labs that analyze tests of employees and job applicants would be licensed. The Civil Liberties Union of Massachusetts is drafting a bill that would allow testing of only those employees whose performance had a bearing on public safety—nuclear-plant operators, school-bus drivers and the like—and who show some signs of impairment. Similarly, in San Francisco, a new ordinance prohibits drug testing by private employers unless there is a high degree of what's known as individualized suspicion—that the employees to be tested are not only impaired but also pose a "clear and present danger" to themselves or others. Only through such measures will companies be barred from "rummaging through another person's biology," says San Francisco supervisor Maher, unless testing is absolutely necessary.

PERSONALITY TESTS: PROBING THE PSYCHE

Wanted: people with "kinetic energy," "emotional maturity" and the ability to "deal with large numbers of people in a fairly chaotic situation." No, not to be cohost of "Wheel of Fortune"; American Multi Cinema, the third largest theater chain in America, wants to hire candidates with these qualities to manage its movie houses. To identify the right employees, AMC is one of an increasing number of companies that administer personality or psychological tests to job applicants. Meanwhile, dozens of others such as General Motors, American Cyanamid, J. C. Penney and Westinghouse now rely on personality-assessment programs to evaluate and promote many current employees.

The tests that companies administer run the gamut. Some are standard psychological tests such as the 46-year-old MMPI (Minnesota Multiphasic Personality Inventory). Long used by psychiatrists and psychologists to test individuals for an array of personality traits, the MMPI consists of up to 566 statements and requires the answers "true," "false" or "cannot say" to questions such as "I avoid getting together with people" or "I have a great deal of self-confidence." Simpler tests include AMC's timed personality-profile exam, known as the PEP test, which among other things examines an applicant's level of mechanical interest and aptitude; people who score well "will be more likely to cope if the butter machine or the projection equipment develops problems," says an AMC district manager, Mario Marques.

Praendix Inc. of Wellesley Hills, Mass., produces a personality-assessment test that consists of a list of phrases and adjectives—including "life of the party," "sympathetic" and "aggressive"—and two questions: "Which of these adjectives describes how you think you are expected to act by others?" and "Which of these adjectives describes who you really are?" Arnold Daniels, founder of Praendix, explains that people who select "patient" as an apt description of themselves might be good "detail" workers, such as researchers, and comfortable reporting to a higher authority. But those who select "impatient"—and think others expect them to be less so—might be good managers, focused on the big picture and eager to see tasks completed.

Many companies swear by the tests. Bobbi Ciarfella, an administrator of Yankee Cos., Inc., an oil-and-gas firm based in Massachusetts, says the Praendix test has helped the firm cut its high turnover rate and hire employees who thrive in a fast-paced environment. "You can't afford to make a mistake when you're hiring somebody in the $45,000 range," she says. Others insist the objectivity of many tests benefits applicants by being even fairer than the typically subjective job interview.

Yet some employees may not fare so well. "For a large number of people, [tests] can predict" roughly who will perform a given job well, says Alexandra Wigdor of the National Research Council, which is currently conducting a study to devise an advanced testing system for the U.S. military. But for any one person, especially one who doesn't test well, "they can be hopeless," she concedes. Moreover, the human personality is so complex that not even the MMPI—considered by many psychiatrists to be the most objective of psychological tests—can give anything like a full and accurate reflection of the individual, says New York psychologist Juliet Lesser. Finally, there's the danger that employers will substitute test results for background checks or even old-fashioned intuition. "Anyone relying too much on tests is abdicating his responsibility as a manager," says New York industrial psychologist Brian Schwartz.

GENETIC TESTS: SCREENING FOR DISEASES

At Enserch Corp., a diversified energy company based in Dallas, officials were horrified: last summer the *maître d' hôtel* of the executive dining room was discovered to have AIDS. When the company summarily ordered mandatory AIDS tests for its other food-service workers, another was discovered to have the AIDS antibody. Both employees were suspended with full pay and medical benefits and escorted from the premises.

The consternation that followed among gay-rights groups and civil libertarians pointed up the controversy around a growing area of testing: monitoring employees' health. Examining blood or tissue samples for signs of disease or certain genetic traits could protect employees and the public from health risks—while sparing employers higher medical-insurance costs and reduced productivity. But as tests get increasingly sophisticated, they could also provide a powerful tool for discrimination against homosexuals, women, those predisposed to diseases or other groups of employees.

Testing for AIDS is especially problematic. Most of the tests offered have high rates of both false positives and "false negatives" (incorrect negative results)—traumatic with AIDS. Nor is it clear just what AIDS testing accomplishes, given most experts' belief that the disease isn't spread through the casual contact typical of the workplace but through sexual relations or contact with AIDS-contaminated blood. Yet so far, only California has acted to prohibit AIDS testing as a condition of employment.

Looming on the horizon is genetic testing. Each year 390,000 workers contract occupational illnesses including lung, bladder and other cancers; about 100,000 die. The belief that some workers possessed genetic "hypersusceptibility" to some of these conditions that could be triggered by exposure to toxins in the workplace led companies like Du Pont and Dow Chemical to conduct tests on workers beginning in the 1970s. But "after a number of years we were not seeing what we thought we might find," says Dr. John Venable, medical director of Dow. Negative publicity about tests—particularly Du Pont's testing of workers for sickle-cell trait, which leads to a condition that affects many blacks—further dampened corporate enthusiasm for testing. By the time a 1983 report by the Office of Technology Assessment determined that existing genetic tests couldn't predict what might happen on the job, most companies had quit the field.

Recently, however, biologists have discovered genetic "markers" for a number of genetic diseases such as cystic fibrosis and are now searching for others for more commonplace conditions such as Alzheimer's disease and breast cancer. "We're still many years away" from the time when genetic tests for such conditions could come into widespread use, asserts Alexander Morgan Capron, professor of law and medicine at USC. But since so many people may be prone to these diseases, there is the distant prospect that companies could one day undertake genetic screening—declining to hire employees who seem likely to become sick on the job, use up expensive medical benefits or die young.

As the technology of testing advances, say the experts, so must the public's attention to the range of economic, ethical and legal issues it raises. Columbia's Westin is confident that such awareness will increase; as a consequence, he predicts, within 10 years a "latticework of legislation" will be in place to balance employers' aims with employees' rights. Society has much to gain from careful and sophisticated testing—a potentially more productive corps of workers whose skills more closely match the requirements of their jobs. But the preeminent challenge for on-the-job testing will be whether it can avoid unwarranted encroachment on the rights and freedoms Americans hold dear.

27. Privacy, Morality, and the Law

W. A. Parent

I. THE DEFINITION OF PRIVACY

Defining privacy requires a familiarity with its ordinary usage, of course, but this is not enough since our common ways of talking and using language are riddled with inconsistencies, ambiguities, and paradoxes. What we need is a definition which is by and large consistent with ordinary language, so that capable speakers of English will not be genuinely surprised that the term "privacy" should be defined in this way, but which also enables us to talk consistently, clearly, and precisely about the family of concepts to which privacy belongs. Moreover the definition must not usurp or encroach upon the basic meanings and functions of the other concepts within this family. Drawing useful and legitimate distinctions between

From *Philosophy and Public Affairs* 12:4 (1983): 269–88.

different values is the best antidote to exploitation and evisceration of the concept of privacy.

Let me first state and then elaborate on my definition. Privacy is the condition of not having undocumented personal knowledge about one possessed by others. A person's privacy is diminished exactly to the degree that others possess this kind of knowledge about him. I want to stress that what I am defining is the condition of privacy, not the right to privacy. I will talk about the latter shortly. My definition is new, and I believe it to be superior to all of the other conceptions that have been proffered when measured against the desiderata of conceptual analysis above.

A full explication of the personal knowledge definition requires that we clarify the concept of personal information. My suggestion is that it be understood to consist of *facts* about a person[1] which most individuals in a given society at a given time do not want widely known about themselves. They may not be concerned that a few close friends, relatives, or professional associates know these facts, but they would be very much concerned if the information passed beyond this limited circle. In contemporary America facts about a person's sexual preferences, drinking or drug habits, income, the state of his or her marriage and health belong to the class of personal information. Ten years from now some of these facts may be a part of everyday conversation; if so their disclosure would not diminish individual privacy.

This account of personal information, which makes it a function of existing cultural norms and social practices, needs to be broadened a bit to accommodate a particular and unusual class of cases of the following sort. Most of us don't care if our height, say, is widely known. But there are a few persons who are extremely sensitive about their height (or weight or voice pitch).[2] They might take extreme measures to ensure that other people not find it out. For such individuals height is a very personal matter. Were someone to find it out by ingenious snooping we should not hesitate to talk about an invasion of privacy.

Let us, then, say that personal information consists of facts which most persons in a given society choose not to reveal about themselves (except to close friends, family, . . .) or of facts about which a particular individual is acutely sensitive and which he therefore does not choose to reveal about himself, even though most people don't care if these same facts are widely known about themselves.

Here we can question the status of information belonging to the public record, that is, information to be found in newspapers, court proceedings, and other official documents open to public inspection. (We might discover, e.g., that Jones and Smith were arrested many years ago for engaging in homosexual activities.) Should such information be excluded from the category of personal information? The answer is that it should not. There is, after all, nothing extraordinary about public documents containing some very personal information. I will hereafter refer to personal facts belonging to the public record as documented.

My definition of privacy excludes knowledge of documented personal information. I do this for a simple reason. Suppose that *A* is browsing through some old newspapers and happens to see *B*'s name in a story about child prodigies who unaccountably failed to succeed as adults. *B* had become an obsessive gambler and an alcoholic. Should we accuse *A* of invading *B*'s privacy? No. An affirmative answer blurs the distinction between the public and the private. What belongs to the public domain cannot without glaring paradox be called private; consequently it should not be incorporated within our concept of privacy.

But, someone might object. *A* might decide to turn the information about *B*'s gambling and drinking problems over to a reporter who then publishes it in a popular news magazine. Isn't *B*'s privacy diminished by this occurrence?[3] No. I would certainly say that his reputation might well suffer from it. And I would also say that the publication is a form of gratuitous exploitation. But to challenge it as an invasion of privacy is not at all reasonable since the information revealed was publicly available and could have been found out by anyone, without resort to snooping or prying. In this crucial respect, the story about *B* no more diminished his privacy than would have disclosures about his property interests, say, or about any other facts concerning him that belonged to the public domain.

I hasten to add that a person does lose a measure of privacy at the time when personal information about him first becomes a part of the public record, since the information was until that time undocumented. It is also important not to confuse documented facts as I define them here with facts about individuals which are kept on file for special purposes but which are not available for public consumption, for example, health records. Publication of the latter does imperil privacy; for this reason special precautions are usually taken to ensure that the information does not become public property.

I believe the personal knowledge definition isolates the conceptual one of privacy, its distinctive and unique meaning. It does not appropriate ideas which properly belong to other concepts. Unfortunately the three most popular definitions do just this, confusing privacy with quite different values.

1. *Privacy consists of being let alone.* Warren and Brandeis were the first to advocate this broad definition.[4] Brandeis movingly appealed to it again in his celebrated dissent to the U.S. Supreme Court's majority ruling in *Olmstead* v. *United States.*[5] Objecting to the Court's view that telephone wiretapping does not constitute a search and seizure, Brandeis delivered an impassioned defense of every citizen's right to be let alone, which he called our most cherished entitlement. Several other former U.S. Supreme Court Justices have endorsed this conception of privacy, among them Douglas, Fortas, and Stewart.[6] And a number of distinguished law professors have done likewise.[7]

What proponents of the Brandeis definition fail to see is that there are innumerable ways of failing to let a person alone which have nothing to do with his privacy. Suppose, for instance, that *A* clubs *B* on the head or repeatedly insults him. We should describe and evaluate such actions by appeal to concepts like force, violence, and harassment. Nothing in the way of analytical clarity and justificatory power is lost if the concept of privacy is limited, as I have suggested that it be, to cases involving the acquisition of undocumented personal knowledge. Inflationary conceptions of privacy invite muddled reasoning.

2. *Privacy consists of a form of autonomy or control over significant personal matters.* "If the right to privacy means anything, it is the right of the individual, married or single, to be free from unwarranted government invasion into matters so fundamentally affecting a person as the decision whether to bear or beget a child."[8] With these words, from the Supreme Court case of *Eisenstadt* v. *Baird,* Mr. Justice Brennan expresses a second influential theory of privacy.

Indeed, definitions of privacy in terms of control dominate the literature. Perhaps the most favored among them equates privacy with the control over personal information about oneself. Fried, Wasserstrom, Gross, and Beardsley all adopt it or a close variation of it.[9] Other lawyers and philosophers, including Van Den Haag, Altman, and Parker,[10] identify privacy with control over access to oneself, or in Parker's words, "control over when and by whom the various parts of us can be sensed by others."

All of these definitions should be jettisoned. To see why, consider the example of a person who voluntarily divulges all sorts of intimate, personal, and undocumented information about herself to a friend. She is doubtless exercising control, in a paradigm sense of the term, over personal information about herself as well as over (cognitive) access to herself. But we would not and should not say that in doing so she is preserving or protecting her privacy. On the contrary, she is voluntarily relinquishing much of her privacy. People can and do choose to give up privacy for many reasons. An adequate conception of privacy must allow for this fact. Control definitions do not.[11]

I believe the voluntary disclosure counterexample is symptomatic of a deep confusion underlying the thesis that privacy is a form of control. It is a conceptual confusion, the mistaking of privacy for a part of liberty. The defining idea of liberty is the absence of external restraints or coercion. A person who is behind bars or locked in a room or physically pinned to the ground is unfree[12] to do many things. Similarly a person who is prohibited by law from making certain choices should be described as having been denied the liberty or freedom to make them. The loss of liberty in these cases takes the form of a deprivation of autonomy. Hence we can meaningfully say that the right to liberty embraces in part the right of persons to make fundamentally important choices about their lives and therewith to exercise significant control over different aspects of their behavior. It is clearly distinguishable from the right to privacy, which condemns the unwarranted acquisition of undocumented personal knowledge.[13]

3. *Privacy is the limitation on access to the self.* This definition, defended by Garrett and Gavison[14] among others, has the virtue of separating privacy from liberty. But it still is unsatisfactory. If we understand "access" to mean something like "physical proximity," then the difficulty becomes that there are other viable concepts which much more precisely describe what is at stake by limiting such access. Among these concepts I would include personal property, solitude, and peace. If, on the other hand, "access" is interpreted as referring to the acquisition of personal knowledge, we're still faced with a seemingly intractable counterexample. *A* taps *B*'s phone and overhears many of her conversations, including some of a very intimate nature. Official restraints have been imposed on *A*'s snooping, though. He must obtain permission from a judge before listening in on *B*. This case shows that limitation of cognitive access does not imply privacy.

A response sympathetic with the Garrett-Gavison conception to the above criticism might suggest that they really meant to identify privacy with certain kinds of limitations on access to the self.

But why then didn't they say this, and why didn't they tell us what relevant limitations they had in mind?

Let us suppose that privacy is thought to consist of certain normal limitations on cognitive access to the self. Should we accept this conception? I think not, since it confuses privacy with the existential conditions that are necessary for its realization. To achieve happiness I must have some good luck, but this doesn't mean that happiness is good luck. Similarly, if I am to enjoy privacy there have to be limitations on cognitive access to me, but these limitations are not themselves privacy. Rather privacy is what they safeguard.

II. THE VALUE OF PRIVACY

Is privacy a basic human value? There are many unpersuasive arguments that it is. Consider one of the most well-known, that given by Fried: "to respect, love, trust, feel affection for others, and to regard ourselves as the objects of love, trust, and affection is at the heart of our notion of ourselves as persons among persons, and privacy is the necessary atmosphere for these attitudes and actions, as oxygen is for combustion."[15] Privacy is essential for intimate relationships because, in Fried's view, their defining mark is the sharing of information about oneself that is not shared with others, and without privacy this would be impossible.

The difficulty with Fried's argument is that it relies on a skewed conception of intimacy. Intimacy involves much more than the exclusive sharing of information. It also involves the sharing of one's total self—one's experiences, aspirations, weaknesses, and values. This kind of emotional commitment, and concomitant giving, is entirely overlooked by Fried. He furnishes no argument for the claim that it cannot survive the loss of privacy.

Several so-called functional arguments on behalf of privacy also fail. Thus it is sometimes said that privacy is needed for relaxation, emotional release, self-reflection, and self-analysis,[16] but this account confuses privacy with solitude, that is, the condition of being physically alone. Granted *A* might not be able to relax or think about her life unless she is left by herself, we are still not being told why *privacy* is important. Of course *A* might have to believe that her privacy is being respected if she is to relax and reflect successfully, but this still doesn't show that privacy itself (as opposed to the belief that we have it) is necessary to do these things.

Nor should we buy the thesis that privacy is necessary for individuality and freedom.[17] It is easy to imagine a person who has little or no privacy but who nonetheless possesses the determination and strength of will to think and act individually. Even those lacking in such determination might still be able to think and act for themselves so long as they believe (rightly or wrongly) that their privacy is intact. Similarly, persons without privacy might still enjoy considerable freedom. This will be true in cases where *A* is not aware of and has no reason for thinking that someone else is watching her every move and so is not deterred from pursuing various activities. It will also be true in cases where *A* simply doesn't care whether anyone else is watching her.

Lest you now begin to wonder whether privacy has any value at all, let me quickly point to several very good reasons why people in societies like ours desire privacy as I have defined it. First of all, if others manage to obtain sensitive personal knowledge about us they will by that very fact acquire power over us. Their power could then be used to our disadvantage. The possibilities for exploitation become very real. The definite connection between harm and the invasion of privacy explains why we place a value on not having undocumented personal information about ourselves widely known.

Second, as long as we live in a society where individuals are generally intolerant of life styles, habits, and ways of thinking that differ significantly from their own, and where human foibles tend to become the object of scorn and ridicule, our desire for privacy will continue unabated. No one wants to be laughed at and made to feel ashamed of himself. And we all have things about us which, if known, might very well trigger these kinds of unfeeling and wholly unwarranted responses.

Third, we desire privacy out of a sincere conviction that there are certain facts about us which other people, particularly strangers and casual acquaintances, are not entitled to know. This conviction is constitutive of "the liberal ethic," a conviction centering on the basic thesis that individuals are not to be treated as mere property of the state but instead are to be respected as autonomous, independent beings with unique aims to fulfill. These aims, in turn, will perforce lead people down life's separate paths. Those of us educated under this liberal ideology feel that our lives are our own business (hence the importance of personal liberty) and that personal facts about our lives are for the most part ours alone to know. The suggestion that all personal facts should be made available for public inspection is contrary to this view. Thus, our desire for privacy is to a large extent a matter of principle.[18]

For most people, this desire is perfectly innocent. We are not seeking to hurt or disadvantage anyone by exercising it. Unquestionably some people at times demand privacy for fraudulent purposes, for example, to hide discreditable facts about themselves from future employers who are entitled to this information. Posner emphasizes this motive for privacy.[19] But not everyone values privacy for this reason, and, even for those who do, misrepresentation is most often not the only or the overriding motive.

So there are several good reasons why we hold privacy to be an important value, one worth arguing for, and defending from unwarranted invasion. Now I want to suggest that anyone who deliberately and without justification frustrates or contravenes our desire for privacy violates the distinctively liberal, moral principle of respect for persons. Let us say that *A* frustrates *B*'s desire for privacy if he invades *B*'s privacy and *B* knows it. *A* acts in contravention of *B*'s desire for privacy if he invades *B*'s privacy without *B*'s knowing it. Assuming that *A* has no justification for doing either, we can and should accuse him of acting in disregard of *B*'s own desires and interests. *A*'s action displays contempt for *B* in the sense that it is undertaken with no effort to identify with her life purposes or to appreciate what the fulfillment of these purposes might mean to her. Specifically by gratuitously or indiscriminately invading *B*'s privacy (I will explain these terms shortly) *A* manifests disrespect for *B* in the sense that he ignores or counts as having no significance *B*'s desire, spawned and nutured by the liberal values of her society, not to have personal facts about herself known by ingenious or persistent snooping.[20]

III. THE MORAL RIGHT TO PRIVACY

The above argument establishes that privacy is indeed a moral value for persons who also prize freedom and individuality. That we should seek to protect it against unwarranted invasion should come, then, as no surprise. Advocating a moral right to privacy comprises an integral part of this effort. It expresses our conviction that privacy should only be infringed under exigent circumstances and for the most compelling reasons, for example, law enforcement and health care provision.

The moral right to privacy does not embody the rule "privacy may never be invaded." It is important to emphasize that there are such things as justifiable invasions of privacy. Our concern is not to condemn invasions but to declare our right not to become the victims of wrongful invasions (see Section IV). Discussion of a right to privacy presupposes that privacy is a good, vulnerable to loss by human contrivance. It does not presuppose that such loss is always bad.

Davis and Thomson[21] have recently tried to deflate the right to privacy. The latter's essay is the better known so I will now discuss it. Thomson wants us to believe that there is no one independently identifiable right to privacy. Instead there are a number of diverse rights under "privacy" each of which is a right of some other kind. Moreover, the right to privacy is derivative in the sense that we can explain why we possess each of the rights subsumable under privacy without ever mentioning the right of privacy itself. And we can also explain the wrongness of every violation of the right to privacy without once mentioning it. So according to Thomson we really don't need to talk about a distinct right to privacy at all. She supports her argument with the following analyses.

1. *A* owns a pornographic picture which he keeps locked up in a safe. *B* trains his special X-ray device on the safe and sees the picture. Thomson concedes that *B* has violated *A*'s right to privacy, but she thinks a more fundamental explanation of why *B* acted wrongly is in terms of *A*'s right that others not do certain things with what he owns. These include looking at them and selling them. These are property rights and it is by infringing one of them that *B* wrongs *A*.
2. *B* finds out by entirely legitimate means that *A* owns the pornographic picture. He proceeds to publish this fact in a newspaper. If anyone thinks that *B* has invaded *A*'s right to privacy, a very simple explanation is available: *A* has the right not to be caused mental distress, and it is this right that *B*'s action violates.
3. *A* doesn't want her face looked at and so keeps it covered. *B* uses his X-ray device to look at *A*'s face through the covering. In doing so *B* violates *A*'s right that her face not be looked at (how simple!). This is one of the rights over our person that we possess.
4. *A* is a great opera singer who no longer wants to be listened to. She only sings quietly behind closed doors and soundproof walls. *B* trains an amplifier on *A*'s home and listens to her sing. In so doing *B* transgresses *A*'s right not to be listened to, which according to Thomson is another one of those basic rights over the person we possess. Here, as in each of the preceding cases, we have no need to invoke the right to privacy.

Thomson's attempt to diminish the status of the right to privacy fails to persuade. It requires that we recognize a plethora of rights whose status is certainly more problematic than that of the right whose significance she wants to impugn. Do we really think of ourselves as possessing the rights not to be looked at and listened to? Must we talk about a right not to have our property looked at? Thomson's claim that we waive these rights all the time—a claim she has to make to avoid the absurd implication that our rights are violated thousands of times every day—flies in the face of common sense and common experience. Just ask whether you thought of yourself as having waived the right not to be listened to before speaking with people today. The idea seems preposterous. I certainly didn't conceive of myself as waiving a right not to be looked at before entering the classroom this morning. And I venture to add that it would bemuse my students to hear me speak of my right not to be looked at.

Thomson's simplifying strategy is unmistakably convoluted. It is possible to deal in a much less ad hoc and tortuous manner with her examples once we have settled on an adequate definition of privacy.

1. If *B*'s looking at *A*'s picture is unjustified, and if *A* is entitled to possess the pornographic picture, then by my account of the moral right to privacy *B* does violate this right in *A*. We could also say that *A* has a concrete moral right that her picture not be looked at which can be deduced from the more fundamental right of privacy when applied to the particular circumstances of this case.
2. If *B* has no justification for publishing the fact that *A* possesses a pornographic picture, then he has violated *A*'s right to privacy. And it is by virtue of violating this right that *B* causes *A* mental distress.
3. If *A* has no evil intention in covering her face and if *B* has no substantial reason for peeking at it, then *B*'s intrusion violates *A*'s right to privacy. We could express this point by saying that *A*'s right to privacy when applied to the particular circumstances of this case yields her concrete right not to be looked at. (Remember that a person's physical appearance can constitute personal information.)
4. If *B*'s snooping is without justification it should be condemned as a violation of *A*'s right to privacy.

The basic failing of Thomson's essay is that she makes no attempt to define privacy. We have good reason to ask how she hopes to convince anyone that the right to privacy is derivative and quite dispensable without first telling us what the right means. My position is that once the meaning of privacy is clarified and its value articulated no one will have cause to question the legitimacy of our talk about a fundamental right of privacy.

IV. CRITERIA OF WRONGFUL INVASION

Which invasions of privacy are justifiable and which are not? A complete conception of the right to privacy must address this question, providing general criteria of wrongful invasion, which will then have to be applied to specific cases. Whether the right to privacy has been violated in a specific case can often only be answered through a process of making difficult and controversial value judgments. No conception of the right to privacy, no matter how detailed and sophisticated will allow us to eliminate or bypass this process.

The following questions are central to assessing alleged violations of the right to privacy:

1. For what purpose(s) is the undocumented personal knowledge sought?
2. Is this purpose a legitimate and important one?
3. Is the knowledge sought through invasion of privacy relevant to its justifying purpose?
4. Is invasion of privacy the only or the least offensive means of obtaining the knowledge?
5. What restrictions or procedural restraints have been placed on the privacy-invading techniques?
6. What protection is to be afforded the personal knowledge once it has been acquired?

The first four questions all have to do with the rationale for invading privacy. We can say that the right to privacy is violated by *gratuitous* invasions and that these occur when: there is no purpose at all to them; when the purpose is less than compelling; when the personal facts sought have nothing to do with the justifying purposes; when the personal information could have been obtained by less intrusive measures. Among the legitimate purposes for acquiring undocumented personal information are efficient law enforcement, confirmation of eligibility criteria set forth in various government welfare programs, and the compilation of statistical data concerning important behavioral trends.

Question 5 pertains to the actual invasion of privacy itself. We can say that the right to privacy is violated by *indiscriminate* invasions and that these occur when insufficient procedural safeguards have been imposed on the techniques employed so that either: all sorts of personal information, some germane to the investigation but some totally irrelevant thereto, is obtained; or persons with no business knowing the personal facts acquired are allowed to gain cognitive access to them. One can argue against a proposed invasion of privacy on the grounds that it is too likely to be indiscriminate in either of these two senses.

Question 6 pertains to postinvasion safeguards.

We can say that the right to privacy is violated when the undocumented personal information acquired is not adequately protected against unwarranted cognitive intrusion or unauthorized uses. It is also violated, of course, by actual instances of such intrusions and uses.

Let us look at a concrete example. Suppose a large city is faced with the growing problem of welfare fraud. It decides that to combat this problem an elaborate system of surveillance must be initiated. Personal information regarding welfare recipients' income, family status, sexual habits, and spending habits is to be obtained. Search warrants are obtained permitting unlimited surveillance and specifying the kind of information being sought. Once obtained the information is to be stored on magnetic tapes and kept in the welfare department.

Any person who takes the right to privacy seriously will raise the following questions and make the following observations about this city's (*C*'s) action:

i. *C* presents no arguments or evidence in support of its belief that the problem of welfare fraud can be solved by resorting to large-scale surveillance. We should demand that *C* do so.
ii. *C* presents no arguments or evidence showing that surveillance is the only way to acquire the relevant personal information. Did it first try to obtain knowledge of welfare recipients' life style by asking them about it or sending them questionnaires? Were there other, less [intrusive] measures available for acquiring this knowledge?
iii. Search warrants permitting unlimited surveillance are insufficiently discriminating. So are warrants which do not particularly describe the places to be observed and the facts to be gathered. *C* should have insisted that the warrants place restrictions on the time periods of surveillance as well as on its scope.
iv. Why is it necessary to acquire information about welfare recipients' sexual habits? How is this knowledge relevant to the object of eradicating fraud?
v. What kind of security does *C* intend to provide for the magnetic tapes containing the acquired information? Who will enjoy access to these tapes? Will they eventually be erased or destroyed? *C* has the duty to guard against the potential abuse of the stored facts.

I hope this brief analysis is helpful in isolating some of the crucial issues and difficult questions that must be confronted when applying the right of privacy to particular cases. Often there will be strong disagreement over whether proposed programs of physical, psychological, and data surveillance are gratuitous or indiscriminate. This is to be expected. The results of these disputes will determine the contours of the privacy right.

V. THE LEGAL RIGHT TO PRIVACY

One final inquiry remains regarding how the moral right to privacy has fared in the law. To what extent is it receiving legal protection, and should it be receiving more? The account that follows is largely descriptive. My purpose is to show how contemporary privacy jurisprudence could have benefited from the use of disciplined philosophical analysis.

We must begin with the well-known U.S. Supreme Court case of *Griswold* v. *Connecticut,*[22] for this decision more than any other is responsible for the jurisprudential notoriety that now attends the right to privacy. In *Griswold* the Court struck down a law that made it a criminal offense for married couples to use contraceptives. Writing the majority opinion, Justice Douglas argued that even though the Constitution does not explicitly mention a right to privacy, one can still justifiably infer its existence from examining the penumbras or emanations of various specific constitutional provisions. The contraceptive law under challenge, according to Douglas, violated this right.

Unfortunately Douglas never explained why it did. Of course there is an obvious reason why the law's enforcement would invade privacy, but the Court made only passing reference to this problem. What precisely did Douglas mean by the expression "right of privacy"? *Eisenstadt* v. *Baird* provided an answer. In that case, decided seven years after *Griswold,* a majority of the Court equated the right to privacy with the right to make fundamentally important choices free from unwarranted government intrusion.[23] They went on to find a Massachusetts law forbidding the use of contraceptives among unmarried persons in violation of this right.

Since *Eisenstadt* the Supreme Court has invoked the right to privacy, conceived of as a species of the right to choose, in voiding several state laws which prohibited women from choosing an abortion except when necessary to save their lives.[24] And several state supreme courts have embraced this conception of the right to privacy and have applied it to cases involving euthanasia,[25] the use of marijuana,[26] and the prescription of laetrile as a cancer cure.[27]

All of these cases conflate the right to privacy with the right to liberty. I won't repeat my critique of the *Eisenstadt* definition set out in Section I. Suffice it to say that laws preempting the choice of citizens are coercive in an obvious sense of the term. Consequently they involve a denial of liberty and must therefore be evaluated against the Fourteenth Amendment's guarantee that citizens shall not be deprived of liberty without due process of law.[28] For years the U.S. Supreme Court decided cases like *Griswold* by Fourteenth Amendment interpretation. Thus legislation interfering with prospective employees' choice of work,[29] with students' choice whether to study foreign languages in private or public elementary schools,[30] and with parents' choice whether to send their children to public or private schools[31] was properly seen as implicating liberty interests and was assessed accordingly. That some of these decisions (I am thinking particularly of *Lochner)* met with severe criticism from later scholars and were even repudiated by later courts does not justify judicial indulgence in conceptual legerdemain. Confusing liberty with privacy only serves to impugn the intellectual integrity of the judiciary.

Another class of spurious privacy cases needs to be exposed. Consider the question whether a "music as you ride" program on buses and streetcars violates passengers' right to privacy; or whether solicitors and peddlers who go on private property and disturb homeowners infringe the latters' right to privacy; or whether sound trucks that emit loud and raucous noises in residential neighborhoods violate homeowners' right to privacy. The U.S. Supreme Court has had to consider such questions, and it has treated them as raising bona fide privacy interests.[32] This was a mistake. Unwanted or excessive solicitation or noise imperil homeowners' peace and their right to property, understood in the broad but widely accepted sense of the right to enjoy what one owns. Being exposed to music on buses might rattle the nerves and thereby threaten our peace. It certainly preempts the choice whether to listen or not while riding. But that is all. The concept of privacy has no useful role to play in any of these cases. Indeed, its introduction only obscures the gravamen of petitioners' complaints.

Invasion of privacy must consist of truthful disclosures about a person. Occasionally aggrieved parties will forget or ignore this. The case of *Paul* v. *Davis* will illustrate. The police distributed a five-page flyer to some eight hundred store owners in the Louisville, Kentucky, area which contained the names and photographs of persons identified as "known shoplifters." Davis's picture and name appeared there. He had been arrested for shoplifting but the charges against him were dropped shortly after the flyer's distribution. Davis brought an invasion of privacy suit against the police. He ought not to have done so, for the flyer did not reveal any personal facts about him. His only legitimate course would have been to bring a cause of action for defamation. Justice Rehnquist said precisely this in his majority opinion.[33]

The unfortunate view that cases like this can be argued in terms of privacy finds support in William Prosser's extraordinarily influential 1960 essay.[34] Prosser maintained that the law of privacy comprises four distinct torts, the third of which he identified with placing the plaintiff in a false light in the public eye. This false light categorization displays an egregious misunderstanding of privacy.

Are Prosser's remaining three torts similarly confused? The first form of privacy invasion he distinguishes is intrusion upon the plaintiff's seclusion or solitude, or into his private affairs. My personal knowledge definition shows that privacy is invaded by certain kinds of intrusions, namely those of a cognitive nature that result in the acquisition of undocumented personal facts. Other kinds of intrusion, for example, those involving causal access (see definition 3 discussed in Section I) and environmental disturbances, are more exactly and perspicuously described by concepts like trespass, nuisance, and peace.

Prosser's second privacy tort, the public disclosure of embarrassing private facts, is legitimate provided the facts are undocumented. The fourth tort, appropriation for the defendant's advantage of the plaintiff's name or likeness, should not be subsumed under privacy for the simple reason that such appropriation does not result in the obtaining of undocumented personal knowledge about the plaintiff. It does, however, preempt the choice whether or not to have one's name or likeness used (usually for advertising purposes) and could therefore be challenged on liberty grounds. It could also be challenged on property grounds, particularly in circumstances where the plaintiff is seeking financial remuneration for the use of his name or likeness.

Some First Amendment cases involving the disclosure of personal information implicate genuine privacy interests, others do not. Two well-known cases which ought not to have been decided in terms of privacy are *Cox Broadcasting Co.* v. *Cohn* and *Briscoe* v. *Reader's Digest.* In *Cohn* a newspaper published the name of a rape victim.[35] In *Briscoe,* the identity of a former truck hijacker was disclosed.[36] Because these facts belonged to the public record their disclosure cannot plausibly be condemned on privacy grounds.

However, the press sometimes does gratuitously invade privacy. One former case comes immediately to mind. William Sidis was a child prodigy (at the age of eleven he lectured to Harvard professors on the Fourth Dimension) who in his later years sought solitude and privacy. The *New Yorker* decided to do a story on him. The article focused on Sidis's life as a recluse. Sidis sued for invasion of privacy and lost.[37] In my judgment he should have won. Granted there is the First Amendment guarantee of a free press, but this has never been interpreted to mean that the press can publish anything it wants. There are limitations (e.g., pornography, libel), and invasions of privacy which serve no useful purpose should be included among them. The public had no need to know about Sidis's later life.

Other First Amendment-privacy cases are more difficult to decide. Much depends on the particular facts of the situation and the plaintiff's status. Public officials are not entitled to the same degree of protection as are private citizens. Warren and Brandeis took note of this many years ago when they wrote "[T]o publish of a modest and retiring individual that he suffers from an impediment of his speech or that he cannot spell correctly is an unwarranted, if not unexampled, infringement upon his privacy, while to state and comment on the same characteristic found in a would-be congressman would not be regarded as beyond the pale of propriety."[38]

Thus far our conclusion must be that privacy is not receiving significant legal protection. It is only when we look at Fourth Amendment cases that privacy enthusiasts can begin to take heart. In having to formulate criteria for unreasonable searches and seizures the Supreme Court has been slowly evolving a conception of the right to privacy.[39] In many of these cases the Court has provided substantial protection to privacy interests.[40]

Moreover, the Court may be sympathetic to privacy grievances not related to searches and seizures. Consider the recent and important case of *Whalen* v. *Roe*.[41] The State of New York required that the names and addresses of all persons obtaining schedule II drugs—opium, cocaine, amphetamines, and other drugs for which there is both a lawful and an unlawful use—be kept on record in a centralized computer file. This information was put on magnetic tapes which were then stored in a vault. After five years the tapes would be destroyed. A locked fence and alarm system provided security for the information-processing system. Public disclosure of the patient's identity was prohibited.

The Court unanimously agreed that this legislation did not infringe the patient's right to privacy. But in reaching this (reasonable, I believe) conclusion, the judges exhibited a genuine sensitivity to the privacy interests at stake. Thus Justice Stevens wrote:

> . . . The collecting of taxes, the distribution of welfare and society security benefits, the supervision of public health, the direction of our armed forces, and the enforcement of the criminal laws all require the orderly preservation of great quantities of information, much of which is personal in nature and potentially embarrassing or harmful if disclosed. The right to collect and use such data for public purposes is typically accompanied by a concomitant statutory or regulatory duty to avoid unwarranted disclosures.[42]

So the *Whalen* decision should not be a source of despair for privacy advocates. Privacy might yet come to occupy a significant place in American jurisprudence.

NOTES

1. The spreading of falsehoods or purely subjective opinions about a person does not constitute an invasion of his privacy. It is condemnable in the language of libel or slander.

2. I know a recently divorced man who doesn't want anyone to know the fact. He and his former wife still live together, so it is possible for him to conceal their marital status from most everyone.

3. I owe this example, as well as other useful comments and suggestions, to an editor of *Philosophy and Public Affairs*.

4. Samuel Warren and Louis Brandeis, "The Right to Privacy," *Harvard Law Review* 4 (1890): 205–7.

5. *Olmstead* v. *U.S.* 277 U.S. 438 (1928): 475–76.

6. See William Douglas, *The Rights of the People* (Westport, CT: Greenwood Press, 1958). See Fortas's decision in *Time* v. *Hill,* 385 U.S. 374 (1967): 412; and in *Gertz* v. *Robert Welch, Inc.,* 418 U.S. 323 (1974): 412–13. See Stewart's decision in *Katz* v. *U.S.,* 389 U.S. 347 (1967): 350; and in *Whalen* v. *Roe,* 429 U.S. 589 (1977): 608.

7. For example, Edward Bloustein, in "Group Privacy: The Right to Huddle," from his *Individual and Group Privacy* (New Brunswick, NJ: Transaction Books, 1978), pp. 123–86; Paul Freund "Privacy: One Concept or Many?" in *Nomos XIII: Privacy,* ed. J. Roland Pennock and John W. Chapman (New York: Atherton Press, 1971), pp. 182–98; Henry Paul Monagham, "Of 'Liberty' and 'Property,' " *Cornell Law Review* 62 (1977): 405–14; and Richard Posner, *The Economics of Justice* (Cambridge, MA: Harvard University Press, 1981), p. 123.

8. *Eisenstadt* v. *Baird,* 405 U.S. 438 (1972): 453.

9. Charles Fried, *An Anatomy of Values* (Cambridge, MA: Harvard University Press, 1970), chap. 9, p. 141; Richard A. Wasserstom, "Privacy: Some Assumptions and Arguments," in *Philosophical Law,* ed. Richard Bronaugh (Westport, CT: Greenwood Press. 1979), pp. 148–67; Hyman Gross, "Privacy and Autonomy," *Nomos XIII,* p. 170; Elizabeth Beardsley, "Private, Autonomy, and Selective Disclosure," *Nomos XIII,* p. 65.

10. Ernest Van Den Haag, "On Privacy," *Nomos XIII*, pp. 147ff.; Irwin Altman, "Privacy—A Conceptual Analysis," *Environment and Behavior* 8 (1976): 8; and "Privacy Regulation: Culturally Universal or Culturally Specific?" *Journal of Social Issues* 33 (1977): 67; Richard Parker, "A Definition of Privacy," *Rutgers Law Review* 27 (1974): 280.

11. Proponents of a control definition might respond by saying that they are really interested in identifying *the right to privacy* with the right to control personal information about or access to ourselves. But then they should have said so explicitly instead of formulating their contention in terms of privacy alone. And even if they had done so their position would still be confused, since the right to choose is an integral aspect of the right to liberty, not the right to privacy.

12. Here I use "unfree" to mean "lacking liberty." My concern is not with the metaphysical notion of free will.

13. I do not mean to ascribe to proponents of control definitions the view that every interference with liberty is by that very fact an infringement to privacy. I do mean to criticize them for failing to recognize that interferences with personal choice or control, taken by themselves and with no consideration given to undocumented personal knowledge that might be acquired from them, are not appropriately described or persuasively condemned in the language of privacy.

14. Roland Garrett, "The Nature of Privacy," *Philosophy Today* 18 (1974): 264; and Ruth Gavison, "Privacy and the Limits of the Law," *Yale Law Journal* 89 (1980): 428.

15. Charles Fried, "Privacy," *Yale Law Journal* 77 (1968): 477.

16. Westin, Bazelon, and Weinstein are among those who advance the relaxation argument. See, respectively: Alan Westin's *Privacy and Freedom* (New York: Atheneum Press, 1967). p. 34; David Bazelon, "Probing Privacy," *Georgia Law Review* 12 (1977): 588ff.; and Michael Weinstein, "The Uses of Privacy in the Good Life," *Nomos XIII*, p. 99. Westin (p. 36), Weinstein (p. 104), and Gavison (p. 449) are among those who defend the argument from query.

17. Westin (p. 33) and Bloustein, particularly in his essay, "Privacy as an Aspect of Human Dignity: An Answer to Dean Prosser," *New York University Law Review* 39 (1964): 970, are among those who defend the argument from individuality.

18. This argument from liberalism invites rebuttal from socialists and communists, of course, who want to maintain that the "ideal" of privacy does nothing but encourage unnecessary (and unnatural) conflict among human beings.

19. Richard Posner, "The Right to Privacy," *Georgia Law Review* 12 (1978): 491–522.

20. I don't mean to identify the liberal principle of respect for persons with Kant's conception of respect for humanity. Kant does not formulate his conception in terms of what persons desire. Instead he focuses on the property of rationality that all persons possess and that, in his view, confers intrinsic worth upon them.

21. Frederick Davis, "What Do We Mean by 'Right to Privacy'?" *San Diego Law Review* 4 (1959): 1–23; Judith Jarvis Thomson, "The Right to Privacy," *Philosophy and Public Affairs* 4 (1975): 295–315.

22. *Griswold* v. *Connecticut*, 381 U.S. 479 (1965).

23. *Eisenstadt* v. *Baird*, 405 U.S. 438 (1972): 453.

24. See, for example, *Roe* v. *Wade*, 410 U.S. 113 (1973).

25. *In the matter of Quinlan*, 355 A.2d 647 (1976). Here the New Jersey Supreme Court ruled that the right to privacy is broad enough to encompass a patient's decision to decline life-sustaining medical treatment under certain circumstances.

26. *Ravin* v. *State*, 537 P.2d 494 (1975). Here Alaska's Supreme Court ruled that a law forbidding the possession of marijuana by adults for their personal use in their homes violated the right of privacy.

27. *People* v. *Privitera*, 74 C.A. 3d (1977), and *People* v. *Privitera*, 23 Cal. 3d 687 (1979). The California Court of Appeal ruled that the right to privacy protects the choice of cancer patients to use laetrile as a treatment. The California Supreme Court disagreed. It accepted the privacy conceptualization of the issue but contended that the right is not broad enough to legitimate the choice of laetrile.

28. The Fourteenth Amendment provides in part that no state shall "deprive any person of life, liberty, or property, without due process of law." The Fifth Amendment protects liberty against arbitrary infringement by the federal government.

29. *Lochner* v. *New York*, 198 U.S. 45 (1905). In this controversial case the Court ruled that legislation forbidding employees for contracting to work more than sixty hours a week or ten hours a day in bakeries gratuitously infringed the right to liberty.

30. *Meyer* v. *Nebraska*, 262 U.S. 390 (1923). Here the Court invalidated a law that barred the teaching of foreign languages in private and public elementary schools on the grounds that it constituted an arbitrary infringement on the right to liberty.

31. *Pierce* v. *Society of Sisters*, 268 U.S. 510 (1925). In this case the Court invalidated a law that compelled children aged eight to sixteen to attend public schools on the ground that it unjustifiably abridged the right to liberty.

32. The cases are: *Public Utilities Commission* v. *Pollack*, 345 U.S. 451 (1952); *Breard* v. *Alexandria*, 341 U.S. 622 (1951); and *Kovacs* v. *Cooper* 336 U.S. 77 (1949).

33. *Paul* v. *Davis*, 424 U.S. 693 (1978).

34. William Prosser, "Privacy," *California Law Review* 48 (1960): 383–423.

35. *Cox Broadcasting Co.* v. *Cohn*, 420 U.S. 469 (1975). The U.S. Supreme Court correctly ruled that Cohn had no bona fide privacy complaint.

36. *Briscoe* v. *Reader's Digest*, 93 Cal. Rptr. 866 (1971). Briscoe won this case principally because so long a time had passed between his offense and the publication. The . . . Court should have realized, however, that personal information contained in official records which have not been destroyed is undeniably public.

37. *Sidis* v. *F-R Publishing Corp.*, 34 F. Supp. 19 (1938).

38. Warren and Brandeis, "The Right to Privacy," p. 205.

39. The Fourth Amendment reads: "The right of the people to secure in their persons, house, papers, effects, against unreasonable searches and seizures shall not be violated, and no warrants shall issue, but upon probable cause, supported by oath or affirmation, and particularly describing the place to be searched and the persons or things to be seized." One can plausibly argue that this amendment presupposes a right to privacy.

40. I have the following cases in mind: *Katz* v. *United States* 389 U.S. 347 (1967), where the Court ruled that the police may not attach electronic listening devices to the outside of a telephone booth in order to record the conversations on bets and wagers without first obtaining a search warrant; *Berger* v. *New York,* 388 U.S. 41 (1967), where the Court invalidated a permissive eavesdropping statute authorizing the indiscriminate use of electronic surveillance devices; *Stanley* v. *Georgia,* 394 U.S. 447 (1969), in which the Court ruled that allegedly pornographic movies seized without a search warrant from the defendant's home could not be used as evidence in his trial; *Lo-ji Sales, Inc.* v. *New York,* 442 U.S. 319 (1979) in which the Court declared that a search of an adult bookstore resulting in the seizure of several films and magazines violated petitioner's Fourth Amendment rights because the warrant issued failed to particularly describe the things to be seized; and *Steagold* v. *United States,* 101 S. Ct. 1642 (1981), where the Court ruled that the police may not search for the subject of an arrest warrant in the home of a third party without first obtaining a search warrant.

41. *Whalen* v. *Roe,* 429 U.S. 589 (1977).

42. Ibid., p. 605.

28. Invasions of Privacy in Social Science Research

Terry Pinkard

. . . . .

THE RIGHT TO PRIVACY

. . . Rights and goods belong together. A *right* to some good *x* shall be understood here as a valid claim to do or have *x,* where the claim satisfies the following two conditions: (1) the person who has the claim is permitted to do or have *x* (i.e., it would not be wrong for the person to do or have *x*); (2) the claim is the basis for another's obligation to the person, an obligation which can take two forms: *(a)* a positive obligation to provide the person with *x* or the means to do *x*; or *(b)* a negative obligation not to interfere with the person's doing or having *x.*[1] To have a right to do or have a good *x* thus presupposes a system of rules that imposes an obligation on someone to act or refrain from acting so that one is enabled to do or have something (if one wishes it); and a theory of rights requires a theory of obligation for its justification. This analysis accords with the widely accepted idea that the language of rights is translatable into the language of obligations—that is, that rights and obligations are logically correlative.

Moral rights are claims derivable from some set of moral principles or rules, and this distinguishes them from institutional and legal rights, which are claims derivable from some set of institutional and legal rules. Seen in this way, rights in general function to protect certain *goods.* A moral right to privacy is a claim derivable from one or more principles of morality to the effect that "being let alone" is a good with which it would be wrong to interfere. One of the basic such principles to which we might appeal in defending the validity of a claim to the protection of privacy is respect for persons. . . . This principle is notoriously difficult to ground in a general ethical theory, and may be, as Joel Feinberg has argued, " 'groundless'—a kind of ultimate attitude not itself justifiable in more ultimate terms."[2] Setting aside this grounding issue, perhaps the most important component of the concept of respect for persons is respect for their autonomy. To see people as autonomous is to see them as capable of forming conceptions of their own good and of how they should lead their lives; to *respect* this autonomy is to allow individuals, so far as possible, to act according to those conceptions. It is surely a truism that control over one's life entails control (to some degree) over what is known by others about oneself and control over some set of crucial (private) areas of one's life. From the general moral principle of respect for persons an *abstract* right to privacy thus follows. . . . We should . . . expect disputes about the commitments of this abstract right and its basis to surface wherever claims to *concrete* rights are at stake. There will be disputes as to its importance and goodness, as to *what* one is entitled by holding the right.

From *Ethical Issues in Social Science Research,* edited by Tom L. Beauchamp, Ruth R. Faden, R. Jay Wallace, Jr., and LeRoy Walters (Baltimore: Johns Hopkins University Press, 1982), pp. 257–73.

Consider, for example, the interactions that illustrate how the right to privacy may be *violated*. . . . One person may violate another's right to privacy by intruding and obtaining information about the other, revealing information that is embarrassing, eavesdropping on another's conversation, peeking in open windows, spreading certain kinds of gossip (even if true), entering closed doors without knocking, and so on. Some are trivial, some weighty, and not all are legally protected, but all contribute to the overall sense of privacy as "being let alone."

Although it is a substantial good, privacy is only one good among many. Moreover, not all aspects of privacy are equally important. Rational people can agree (and have agreed) to sacrifice some dimension of privacy for other goods. In this respect, privacy is somewhat like liberty: liberty is not unrestricted, and particular liberties are commonly surrendered in order to secure other goods. The claim that not all aspects of privacy are equally important amounts, then, to little more than the view now accepted almost everywhere that rights are not absolute; the right to privacy can legitimately be exercised and can create duties for others only when the right has an overriding status. While there is disagreement concerning the conditions sufficient to justify intruding upon privacy, . . . it is widely and properly recognized that some conditions are specifiable. I shall attempt such a specification for social science research in the concluding section. . . .

THE JUSTIFICATION OF INVASIONS OF PRIVACY

A moral right to privacy must be derived from some set of moral principles or rules that require persons to leave others alone. However, we have not addressed either the problem of valid restrictions on this right or the problem of its theoretical justification. This section explores these two problems in order, with particular emphasis on whether certain privacy-invading activities of social science investigators can be justified.

The analysis of the preceding sections might be thought sufficient to support the following strong criterion for limiting invasions of privacy in social science research (where, we shall assume, there is no consent to the invasion):

C_1: Social scientists unjustifiably invade their subjects' privacy whenever they manipulate subjects into doing something embarrassing or disclosing private embarrassing facts, and thereby place their subjects in a false public light or intrude into their private domains.

This criterion will strike many social scientists as indefensibly strong, for some methodologies *necessarily* involve deception or manipulation leading to embarrassment and intrusion into private domains. Without the use of such techniques the validity of their research would be imperiled. If Stanley Milgram had been forced to tell his subjects that his experiment was about obedience and that investigators actually were not shocking people, the experiment would have been lost.* Likewise, the element of deception is crucial in most participant-observer experiments that invade privacy—such as those in which people feigned heart attacks on Philadelphia subways to study "helping behavior." Social scientists who study cults and fringe groups by posing as believing members rely on deception that can involve revelations of private information. It would seem from the investigator's point of view, then, that criterion C_1 is too stringent and would, as the cliché goes, throw the baby out with the bathwater. Surely, one can hear the social scientist insisting, it cannot be *much* of a justification for prohibiting social science research involving human subjects if the only grounds are that it violates some loosely formulated idea of a right to . . . privacy, with no history of case law behind the formulation presented. But is the social scientist justified in this complaint about strong criterion C_1?

In order to address the question, let us first consider reformulating our "strong criterion," substituting the phrase "under certain conditions when" at the very beginning of the criterion for the word "whenever," so as to make the criterion weaker. Let us call this criterion C_2.

C_2: Social scientists unjustifiably invade their subjects' privacy under certain conditions when they manipulate subjects into doing something embarrassing or disclosing private embarrassing facts, and thereby place their subjects in a false public light or intrude into their private domains.

This formulation would make the proposed criterion far more acceptable to social scientists, though specification of the actual exceptive conditions would then of course make all the difference. This strategy will naturally seem to offer a more promising criterion than C_1, for no one would claim that *all* deceit or intrusion on privacy is wrong or that deceit or manipulation are *always* wrong when they lead to invasions of privacy. One may justifiably deceive one's opponents in poker, the enemy in wartime, even sometimes deceive and invade the

*[For a description of the Milgram studies, see chap. 5, study/discussion question 6.—ED.]

privacy of one's spouse—as when one plans a surprise party. Journalists are often regarded as justified in and admired for disclosing private embarrassing facts (under certain conditions, as in C_2). If deceit and invasion of privacy are not always wrong in these contexts, perhaps they are sometimes permissible in similar contexts of social science research, and for similar reasons. Still, the question remains: Can justifying conditions be added to C_2 that improve it over C_1—so as to permit enough social science research without permitting too much in the way of invasions of privacy?

One general answer has been given to these problems of justification by Justice William H. Rehnquist, who argues for a utilitarian approach to problems of privacy.[3] His argument does not uniquely apply to the social sciences, but it provides a perspective on the present issues that may be generalized to the social sciences. Rehnquist argues as follows: Government cannot escape certain conflicts between freedom and order. Both are respectable goods, and on some occasions we cannot have both. Efficient, intelligent law enforcement, which is necessary for the achievement of both goods, requires some sacrifice of privacy—for example, in dissemination of arrest records. So, Rehnquist argues, one must *balance* the goods of privacy and efficient law enforcement when rights to privacy conflict with rights to be protected. If damage to the individual in the dissemination of criminal and arrest records to relevant authorities is slight (with strictures on the use to which the information may be put so as to avoid abuse), while the gain in social utility is great, then even those whose privacy has been invaded ought not to object.

Rehnquist supports this position with the following example.[4] If a police officer parks in front of a tavern each evening from 5:30 to 7:30 and records the license numbers of cars coming and going into the tavern's parking lot during that time, many would consider the action a violation of the right to privacy, an unwarranted invasion. But suppose that on the previous two evenings a patron of the tavern had been killed shortly after leaving it, and evidence suggested that the culprit had been present at the bar when the patron left. Suddenly the picture changes; it is no longer so clear that privacy has been invaded, or at least not so clear that it has been wrongly or unjustifiably invaded.

Justice Rehnquist takes these conclusions to be justified on utilitarian grounds. I agree with him that they are justified, and I heartily endorse his example, but I do not think the proper justification is utilitarian, and I do not think the justification supports C_2 over C_1 either. Let me, then, offer a different justification, one that leads to a defense of C_1—a justification also suitable to handle privacy invasions in social research. This justification naturally starts from the conclusion reached in the previous section on the right to privacy. The analysis of rights as valid claims that are presumptive (or prima facie valid) does not mean that rights never have an overriding status. As Ronald Dworkin has pointed out in his *Taking Rights Seriously*, some rights are so basic that ordinary justifications for state interference—such as lessening inconvenience or promoting utility—are insufficient justifications for overriding rights.[5] In Dworkin's terms, the individual rights of citizens "trump" the reasons why we generally permit state control and planning over our lives. Indeed *everything* is trumped by a right *except another right with which it conflicts*. The citizen who bears a right does not hold a privilege and is not subject to the charity or professional etiquette of another. The right can justifiably be demanded as one's due precisely up to that point at which it comes into conflict with another right. There are numerous examples in social science research to illustrate this point. . . .

It is necessary for social justice and the institution of morality that what may be called "safe" areas of social life be carved out that are almost entirely free from intrusion. These are areas strictly protected by "rights," our most demanding moral rules. Within these areas, invasions of privacy, lying, and deception are virtually always wrong, especially where certain intimate relationships with important goods attached are at stake, because there is so seldom a warrant powerful enough to override a right. The "safe" areas are, however, only protected *areas;* they do not encompass the whole of everyday life and so cannot be protected against conflict with *other* areas that are also "safe." Rights, as we earlier remarked, can conflict with other rights. The alternative—that there are no "safe" areas protected by rights—is morally perilous, for it threatens to put morality on a shifting basis where clever legalistic reasoning with exception clauses can justify anything (e.g., on grounds of social utility).

The issues, then, turn out to be the following: no "safe" area has an ironclad safety about it, because someone's rights may always be of sufficient power to override someone else's rights in any given safe area. Social research leading to violations of rights (protected in a safe area) can *in theory* sometimes be morally justified, even when it involves deception and invasions of privacy. Thus "in theory" C_1 may seem wrong and indefensible, and C_2 therefore preferable. However, "in theory" is not good enough. I prefer C_1 over C_2 because I do not believe social science is actually justified in its practices of deception and invasion of privacy in safe areas where rights are violated. Accordingly, I shall now argue that social science research that invades a safe area is *always* morally unjustified.

APPLICATIONS TO SOCIAL SCIENCE RESEARCH

There are, no doubt, goods intrinsic to the pursuit of social science, knowledge being the obvious one. The *utility* of social science—its being a significant means to some other valued end such as the efficiency of police work sought by some criminologists—is less apparent. Certainly it is difficult to justify the involvement of human subjects where risk and no obvious benefit to the subjects is involved. . . . However, we can address both the invasion of privacy and the deception some social science research involves by placing them in the context of the obligation to respect persons and the right to privacy, as discussed above. First, we can quickly pass beyond the uncontroversial observation that with proper informed consent much research, including research that poses significant risks, would have nothing against it, even if it involved privacy invasions or deceptions. (Our strong criterion, it is to be remembered, exclude[s] activities having the prior consent of subjects.) If an investigator discloses to subjects in advance that there is a possibility of deception or invasion of privacy, then research becomes like a poker game—a structured situation where deception or invasion of privacy not only may occur but is expected. Adequate disclosures, provided to voluntary participants and informing them of the possibility of an invasion of privacy or deception, should satisfy the moral requirements of respect for persons.

Where obtaining such informed consent is impossible, as is often the case in social science research, the problem of justification is correspondingly stickier. Research into "helping behavior" by feigning heart attacks on subway trains is again a case in point. Here reasonable expectations are interfered with by deliberate intrusions. People in subways have their "private sphere" intruded upon much as they would by eavesdroppers or con artists. It is difficult to imagine an agreement among rational agents on this point that would permit such intrusions into their private sphere. Who could agree to conferring rights on people to manipulate others or oneself, where either oneself or the others are unwittingly manipulated, merely on grounds that knowledge of "helping behavior" would be accumulated?

This situation differs from the other situations where consent legitimated deceit and invasion of privacy. In the poker analogy, a socially structured situation is present in which deceit or intrusion into a private sphere is to be *expected* and in which the anticipated manipulation contributed to the value of the enterprise for the participant. Any rational agent would easily agree to such deception or limitation of privacy. Deceit to plan a surprise party for one's spouse is similar and easily endorsed by rational agents. But the subway case is significantly different. It is not a structured, understood and consensual situation like a game of poker. It is not even like an antagonistic international conflict such as war or a structured interpersonal relationship. In the latter contexts, there exist principles—however general—broadly delineating what is permitted and what is not. People studied in deceptive social science research are duped in a situation without familiar rules into revealing something about themselves that very likely they would rather not reveal. Their solitude—even though they are in public—is thus invaded. (The notion of "solitude in public" should not be troublesome. The earlier example of the police noting license plate numbers without any overriding justification is an example.) Such invasions are not covered by even tacit understandings, let alone by governing principles; and of course there is no prior expectation.

Participant-observer research where the researcher pretends to be a member or sympathizer of a group in order to elicit certain responses from the real participants provides another case in point, for here too no favorable analogy exists to the structured and consensual situations where deceit and invasion of privacy are legitimate. Typically, people studied feel both betrayed and invaded. . . . Structured social roles often carry with them an understanding of the amount of privacy *proper* to each. To have had someone pose as a friend only to extract private information from you is not only to have been deceived; it is to have had the bounds of what can legitimately be known about you overstepped. A gain in knowledge no more justifies this violation of one's rights than it could justify having a person pose as a lover to a member of a corporation so that the board of directors could discover his or her "real" attitude toward a task. One should add: no matter how much that knowledge furthered the aims of the corporation. Our judgments in these cases thus should be set in the context of a model of moral reasoning that focuses on principles that are *shared* between people and to which we can imagine people *contractually* agreeing. It is not the *consequences* (in the utilitarian sense) of adopting a principle that justifies it, but its being (at least hypothetically) *agreed upon*. This idea of hypothetical agreement rests on what we called earlier the principle of respect for persons, for the validity of the contract depends upon the consent of the contracting parties. Moral principles are justified when they are contracted to in order to balance conflicting interests and competing points of view.[6]

Of all people, social scientists do not need to be reminded of the complex ways in which societies are structured so that behavior which in one case is excusable may in another case be reprehensible. Lying to a close friend about a surprise party is among the excusable cases, but there one has already been granted access and privilege beyond those of the social *researcher* by virtue of a nondeceptive ongoing personal relationship. It is worth noting that no favorable analogy with governmental invasion of privacy exists here. The government has a right to collect certain types of potentially embarrassing information such as the information gathered in the census or that needed at IRS. Often there may be conflicts between rights of government and rights of individuals. But the social science researcher has no moral right to his or her investigations corresponding to the rights of government. At best, the researcher can argue that the research will have some great yield (in social utility, e.g.) and should be supported. But he or she cannot validly argue that the investigation should be supported even in face of its violating individual rights to privacy by intruding into our ''safe'' areas. In Ronald Dworkin's earlier mentioned phrase, rights trump utility, and certainly they trump the needs and interests of social science researchers. One can validly adjust or ''balance'' matters *only when rights compete*. However, there is no *right* to perform research which competes with the individual's right to privacy, and hence there is nothing to balance. Or, to state the thesis in a somewhat milder form: there may be *thin* constitutional grounds for claiming some form of First Amendment right to perform research . . ., but I know of no moral or legal grounds whatever that would support a right to perform research sufficient to override individual rights to privacy.

Of course [the] IRS, the Census Bureau, and other branches of government have a right to private information—and indeed a right to information that may place citizens in situations of legal and economic risk. The research done by such agencies is often social scientific; and thus it certainly appears that *at least in these contexts* social scientists (and society) have a right that can conflict with the ordinary citizen's right to privacy, one which trumps the individual's right to privacy. This thesis will not do, however, precisely because of the consent and contractual components of the analysis that has been presented above. The government obtains its rights through the consent (tacit or otherwise) of the governed, and in this respect promulgated government rules, regulations, and activities are unlike unanticipated or deceptive social scientific interventions—as represented by the example of studies into helping behavior.

Milgram's experiments occupy in the minds of some a deliciously grey area here, which might explain why so many people have conflicting intuitions about these experiments. They certainly did involve manipulation and deceit, and they do prompt people to reveal things about themselves that one would assume they would rather not have revealed. Yet they also took place in a laboratory setting voluntarily consented to by participants—a facility that was outside, so to speak, the normal course of life. In this respect, Milgram's investigations differ from those into helping behavior . . . Does this laboratory setting and the limited consent of subjects make a morally significant difference? I take it that some of the conflicting intuitions concerning Milgram's works are conflicts about whether or not the laboratory setting is enough like a poker game for the deception in it to be justified. To me, this seems implausible. Had a general warning been available to the participants beforehand that deception might be employed, intuitions about the rightness or wrongness of the experiments would no doubt have been considerably less divided. One would not expect this kind of change in intuition to occur if the laboratory were indeed the kind of ''structured situation'' in which deceit is to be suspected.[7]

To be sure, giving such a general warning would in some cases hamper or render impossible certain forms of research. But remember that putting restrictions on the admissibility of evidence hampers police work, and putting restrictions on the use of confidential information hampers banks. That restrictions hamper or prevent certain activities from reaching valuable goals efficiently should not be surprising; nor should it be surprising that morality as the regulation and guidance of life puts restrictions on even important constructive activities. We all complain and grouch with some good reason that *our* activities (whether they be law enforcement, social science, legislation, or what not) are restricted to the point of inefficiency or the diminishment of their final goal; and it should not be surprising that this complaint is pervasive. We should not, however, be blind to the cogency of ethical reasons for these restrictions when they exist. That clearly valuable work such as Milgram's might be hampered or rendered impossible by the desiderata introduced here may be unfortunate, but not on that account unjust.

In this final section, it has been shown that many

examples of social science research fall into the category of unjustified invasions of privacy, that they may not be justified by appealing to a similarity with situations from everyday life where deception or invasions of privacy are justified, and that if research occurs in a laboratory situation as opposed to an everyday one it is not *obviously* excused, though its justification cannot a priori be closed to further discussion. . . .

The argument of this paper is in the end a simple one: there is a right to privacy, even if vaguely defined and subject to challenge in *some ways*. Social scientists do not have a right to invade our privacy; they have no *right* to override our rights. And, on the view presented here, there can be no alternative utilitarian or knowledge-based justification for overriding the right to privacy. . . .

NOTES

1. This conception of the nature of rights is taken from Joel Feinberg, "The Nature and Value of Rights," [*Journal of Value Inquiry* 4 (1970),] as rpt. in David Lyons, ed., *Rights* (Belmont, CA: Wadsworth, 1979), pp. 78–91.
2. Joel Feinberg, *Social Philosophy* (Englewood Cliffs, NJ: Prentice-Hall, 1973), p. 93.
3. William H. Rehnquist, "Is an Expanded Right of Privacy Consistent with Fair and Effective Law Enforcement?" *Kansas Law Review* 23 (1974).
4. Ibid., pp. 9–11.
5. Ronald Dworkin, *Taking Rights Seriously* (Cambridge, MA: Harvard University Press, 1978).
6. We can place this approach to the justification of invasions of privacy in a more general theoretical framework: Society is a cooperative enterprise that requires public rules and principles of cooperation. Here, the *justice* of the terms of cooperation in the society is morally paramount. The terms of cooperation will be those established by legal, moral, and cultural rules and principles that structure the society and that individuals find binding on their behavior. How does one assess the justice of these "terms of cooperation"? One way might be to evaluate them in terms of their efficiency in promoting some overall goal such as utility (measured in terms of happiness or satisfaction of preferences). The way presupposed in this paper is to assess rules and principles in terms of their *fairness*. "Do the rules allow some persons to take undue advantage of others?" and "Is respect given to individual autonomy?" are typical questions that can be asked about the fairness of particular "terms of cooperation." The point of evaluating and justifying rights to privacy is to set them into the larger context of the terms of cooperation found in a particular society. The structure of justification which I am recommending, then, is the following: justice is a matter of fairness, specifically of the fairness of the terms of cooperation in a social order; what *counts* as fair, however, depends in large part on the conventions of that social order—on, as we have called them, "structured situations." The reason for the qualification "in large part" is that one must appeal to abstract principles of justice, such as those offered by John Rawls, which are *not* dependent on social convention, even though any understanding of how in a concrete case these principles are to be applied will involve some appeal to some set of conventions. Any justification of a right will thus appeal to both abstract principles of fairness and their mediation through a concrete social ordering. It follows from this argument that one must locate moral distinctions within the context of everyday social life.
7. One might, of course, still argue that a laboratory situation is in fact like many situations in life in which deceit is built into the rules of the game. But like what situations? Like selling used cars? Like real estate? These are not flattering analogies, and one would hardly expect social scientists to accept them.

CONFIDENTIALITY

29. The Limits of Confidentiality

Sissela Bok

THE PROFESSIONAL SECRET

. . . Doctors, lawyers, and priests have traditionally recognized the duty of professional secrecy regarding what individuals confide to them: personal matters such as alcoholism or depression, marital difficulties, corporate or political problems, and indeed most concerns that patients or clients want to share with someone, yet keep from all others.[1] Accountants, bankers, social workers, and growing numbers of professionals now invoke a similar duty to guard confidences. As codes of ethics take form in old and new professions, the

From *Secrets: The Ethics of Concealment and Revelation* (New York: Random House, 1983), pp. 116–35.

duty of confidentiality serves in part to reinforce their claim to professional status, and in part to strengthen their capacity to offer help to clients.

Confidential information may be more or less intimate, more or less discrediting, more or less accurate and complete. No matter how false or trivial the substance of what clients or patients convey, they may ask that it be kept confidential, or assume that it will be even in the absence of such a request, taking it for granted that professionals owe them secrecy. Professionals, in turn, must not only receive and respect such confidences; the very nature of the help they can give may depend on their searching for even the most deeply buried knowledge.

. . . But the duty of confidentiality is no longer what it was when lawyers or doctors simply kept to themselves the confidences of those who sought their help. How can it be, when office personnel and collaborators and team members must have access to the information as well, and when clients and patients with numerous interdependent needs consult different professionals who must in turn communicate with one another? And how can it be, given the vast increase in information collected, stored, and retrievable that has expanded the opportunities for access by outsiders? How can it be, finally, when employers, school officials, law enforcement agencies, insurance companies, tax inspectors, and credit bureaus all press to see some of this confidential information?

So much confidential information is now being gathered and recorded and requested by so many about so many that confidentiality, though as strenuously invoked as in the past, is turning out to be a weaker reed than ever. Employers, schools, government agencies, and mental health and social service organizations are among the many groups now delving into personal affairs as never before. Those with fewest defenses find their affairs most closely picked over. Schools, for instance, are looking into the home conditions of students with problems, sometimes even requesting psychiatric evaluations of entire families, regardless of objections from health professionals on grounds of confidentiality. And access to public welfare assistance, work training programs, and many forms of employment may depend on the degree to which someone is willing to answer highly personal questions.

At the same time, paradoxically, a growing number of discreditable, often unlawful secrets never even entered into computer banks or medical records have come to burden lawyers, financial advisers, journalists, and many others who take themselves to be professionally bound to silence. Faced with growing demands for both revelation and secrecy, those who have to make decisions about whether or not to uphold confidentiality face numerous difficult moral quandaries. Legislation can sometimes dictate their choice. But the law differs from state to state and from nation to nation, and does not necessarily prescribe what is right from a moral point of view. Even if it did, it could never entirely resolve many of the quandaries that arise, since they often present strong moral arguments on both sides. Consider, for example, the following case:

> A forty-seven-year-old engineer has polycystic kidney disease, in his case a genetic disorder, and must have his blood purified by hemodialysis with an artificial kidney machine. Victims of the disease [at the time of his diagnosis] usually die a few years after symptoms appear, often in their forties, though dialysis and transplants can stave off death for as much as ten years.
>
> The patient has two children: a son, eighteen, just starting college, and a daughter, sixteen. Though the parents know that the disease is genetic—that their children may carry it and might transmit it to their own offspring—the son and daughter are kept in the dark. The parents insist the children should not be told because it would frighten them unnecessarily, would inhibit their social life, and would make them feel hopeless about the future. They are firm in saying that the hospital staff should not tell the children; the knowledge, they believe, is privileged and must be kept secret. Yet the hospital staff worries about the children innocently involving their future spouses and victimizing their own children.[2]

It is not difficult to see the conflicting and, in themselves, quite legitimate claims on each side in this case: the parents' insistence on privacy and on the right to decide when to speak to their children about a matter of such importance to the family; and the staff members' concern for the welfare of the children. But the question of whether the parents are wrong to keep the information from the children must be separated from that of what the staff members should do about what they see as harmful secrecy. Should they reject their obligation of confidentiality in this case? . . .

These questions require us to look more closely at the nature of confidentiality and its powerful hold and to ask what it is that makes so many professionals regard it as the first and most binding of their duties.

Confidentiality refers to the boundaries surrounding shared secrets and to the process of guarding these boundaries. While confidentiality protects much that is not in fact secret, personal secrets lie at its core. The innermost, the vulnerable, often the shameful: these aspects of self-disclosure help explain why one name for professional confidentiality has been "the professional secret." Such secrecy is sometimes mistakenly confused with privacy; yet it can concern many matters in no way private, but that someone wishes to keep from the knowledge of third parties.

Confidentiality must also be distinguished from the testimonial privilege that protects information possessed by spouses or members of the clergy or lawyers against coerced revelations in court. While a great many professional groups invoke confidentiality, the law recognizes the privilege only in limited cases. In some cases, only lawyers can invoke it; in others, physicians and clergy can as well; more recently, psychiatrists and other professionals have been added to their number. Who ought and who ought not to be able to guarantee such a privilege is under ceaseless debate. Every newly established professional group seeks the privileges of existing ones. Established ones, on the other hand, work to exclude those whom they take to be encroaching on their territory.

The principle of confidentiality postulates a duty to protect confidences against third parties under certain circumstances. Professionals appeal to such a principle in keeping secrets from all outsiders and seek to protect even what they would otherwise feel bound to reveal. While few regard the principle as absolute, most see the burden of proof as resting squarely on anyone who claims a reason for overriding it. Why should confidentiality bind thus? And why should it constrain professionals to silence more than, say, close friends?

JUSTIFICATION AND RATIONALE

The justification for confidentiality rests on four premises, three supporting confidentiality in general and the fourth, professional secrecy in particular. They concern human autonomy regarding personal information, respect for relationships, respect for the bonds and promises that protect shared information, and the benefits of confidentiality to those in need of advice, sanctuary, and aid, and in turn to society.

The first and fundamental premise is that of individual autonomy over personal information. It asks that we respect individuals as capable of having secrets. Without some control over secrecy and openness about themselves, their thoughts and plans, their actions, and in part their property, people could neither maintain privacy nor guard against danger. But of course this control should be only partial. Matters such as contagious disease place individual autonomy in conflict with the rights of others. And a variety of matters cannot easily be concealed. No one can maintain control, for example, over others' seeing that they have a broken leg or a perennially vile temper.[3]

The second premise is closely linked to the first. It presupposes the legitimacy not only of having personal secrets but of sharing them, and assumes respect for relationships among human beings and for intimacy. It is rooted in loyalties that precede the formulation of moral justification and that preserve collective survival for one's tribe, one's kin, one's clan. Building on such a sense of loyalty, the premise holds that it is not only natural but often also right to respect the secrets of intimates and associates, and that human relationships could not survive without such respect.

This premise is fundamental to the marital privilege upheld in American law, according to which one spouse cannot be forced to testify against the other; and to the ancient Chinese legal tradition, so strongly attacked in the Maoist period, that forbade relatives to report on one another's misdeeds and penalized such revelations severely.[4] No more than the first premise, however, does this second one suffice to justify all confidentiality. It can conflict with other duties, so that individuals have to choose, say, between betraying country or friend, parents or children; and it can be undercut by the nature of the secret one is asked to keep.

The third premise holds that a pledge of silence creates an obligation beyond the respect due to persons and to existing relationships. Once we promise someone secrecy, we no longer start from scratch in weighing the moral factors of a situation. They matter differently, once the promise is given, so that full impartiality is no longer called for.

In promising one alienates, as Grotius said, either a thing or some portion of one's freedom of action: "To the former category belong promises to give; to the latter, promises to perform."[5] Promises of secrecy are unusual in both respects. What they promise to give is allegiance; what they promise to perform is some action that will guard the secret—to keep silent, at least, and perhaps to do more. Just what performance is promised, and at what cost it will be carried out, are questions that go to the heart of conflicts over confidentiality.[6] To invoke a promise, therefore, while it is surely to point to a prima facie ground of obligation, is not to close the debate over pledges of secrecy. Rather, one must go on to ask whether it was right to make the pledge in the first place, and right to accept it; whether the promise is a binding one, and even if it is, what circumstances might nevertheless justify overriding it.[7]

Individuals vary with respect to the seriousness with which they make a promise and the consequent weight of the reasons they see as sufficient to override it. Consider the CIA agents who take an oath of secrecy before gaining access to classified information; the White House butler who pledges never to publish confidential memoirs; the relatives who give their word to a dying author never to publish her diaries; the religious initiate who swears on all he holds sacred not to divulge the mysteries he is about to share; the engineer who signs a pledge not to give away company trade secrets as a condition of employment. Some of these individuals take the pledge casually, others in utter seriousness. If the latter still break their pledge, they may argue that they were coerced into making their promise, or that they did not understand how it bound them. Or else they may claim that something is important enough to override their promise—as when the relatives publish the author's diaries after her death for a sum of money they cannot resist, or in the belief that the reading public would be deprived without such documents.

For many, a promise involves their integrity and can create a bond that is closer than kinship, as the ceremonies by which people become blood brothers indicate. The strength of promising is conveyed in such early practices as those in which promisors might offer as a pledge their wife, their child, or a part of their body.[8] And promises of *secrecy* have been invested with special meaning, in part because of the respect for persons and for relationships called for by the first two premises.

Taken together, the three premises give strong prima facie reasons to support confidentiality. With certain limitations, I accept each one as binding on those who have accepted information in confidence. But of course there are reasons sufficient to override the force of all these premises, as when secrecy would allow violence to be done to innocent persons, or turn someone into an unwitting accomplice in crime. At such times, autonomy and relationship no longer provide sufficient legitimacy. And the promise of silence should never be given, or if given, can be breached.

It is here that the fourth premise enters in to add strength to the particular pledges of silence given by professionals.[9] This premise assigns weight beyond ordinary loyalty to professional confidentiality, because of its utility to persons and to society. As a result, professionals grant their clients secrecy even when they would otherwise have reason to speak out: thus lawyers feel justified in concealing past crimes of their clients, bankers the suspect provenance of investors' funds, and priests the sins they hear in confession.

According to this premise, individuals benefit from such confidentiality because it allows them to seek help they might otherwise fear to ask for; those most vulnerable or at risk might otherwise not go for help to doctors or lawyers or others trained to provide it. In this way, innocent persons might end up convicted of crimes for lack of competent legal defense, and disease could take a greater toll among those ashamed of the nature of their ailment. Society therefore gains in turn from allowing such professional refuge, the argument holds, in spite of the undoubted risks of not learning about certain dangers to the community; and everyone is better off when professionals can probe for the secrets that will make them more capable of providing the needed help.

The nature of the helpfulness thought to override the importance of revealing some confidences differs from one profession to another. The social worker can offer support, counsel, sometimes therapy; physicians provide means of relieving suffering and of curing disease; lawyers give assistance in self-protection against the state or other individuals. These efforts may conflict, as for army psychiatrists whenever their mission is both to receive the confidences of troubled military personnel and to serve as agents of the state, obligated to report on the condition of their patients. And the help held to justify confidentiality about informants by police and journalists is not directed to individuals in need of relief at all, but rather to society by encouraging disclosures of abuses and crime.

Such claims to individual and social utility touch on the *raison d' être* of the professions themselves; but they are also potentially treacherous. For if it were found that a professional group or subspecialty not only did not help but actually hurt individuals, and increased the social burden of, say, illness or crime, then there would be a strong case for not allowing it to promise professional confidentiality. To question its special reason for being able to promise confidentiality of unusual strength is therefore seen as an attack on its special purposes, and on the power it acquires in being able to give assurances beyond those which nonprofessionals can offer.

A purely strategic reason for stressing professional confidentiality is that, while needed by clients, it is so easily breached and under such strong pressures to begin with. In schools and in offices, at hospitals and in social gatherings, confidential information may be casually passed around. Other items are conveyed "off the record" or leaked in secret. The prohibition against breaching confidentiality must be especially strong in order to combat the pressures on insiders to do so, especially in view of the ease and frequency with which it is done.

Together with the first three premises for confidentiality, the defense of the fourth helps explain the ritualistic tone in which the duty of preserving secrets is repeatedly set forth in professional oaths and codes of ethics. Still more is needed, however, to explain the sacrosanct nature often ascribed to this duty. The ritualistic nature of confidentiality in certain religious traditions has surely had an effect on its role in law and medicine. A powerful esoteric rationale for secrecy linked the earliest practices of medicine and religion. Thus Henry Sigerist points out that in Mesopotamia medicine, like other sacred knowledge, was kept secret and not divulged to the profane; conversely, many religious texts ended with a warning that "he who does not keep the secret will not remain in health. His days will be shortened."[10]

However strong, these historical links between faith and professional practice give *no* added justification to professional confidentiality. The sacramental nature of religious confession is a matter of faith for believers. It may be respected even in secular law on grounds of religious freedom; but it adds no legitimacy to that of the four premises when it comes to what professionals conceal for clients.[11]

The four premises are not usually separated and evaluated in the context of individual cases or practices. Rather, they blend with the ritualistic nature attributed to confidentiality to support a rigid stance that I shall call the rationale of confidentiality. Not only does this rationale point to links with the most fundamental grounds of autonomy and relationship and trust and help; it also serves as a rationalization that helps deflect ethical inquiry. The very self-evidence that it claims can then expand beyond its legitimate applications. Confidentiality, like all secrecy, can then cover up for and in turn lead to a great deal of error, injury, pathology, and abuse.

When professionals advance confidentiality as a shield, their action is, to be sure, in part intentional and manipulative, but in part it also results from a failure to examine the roots of confidentiality and to spell out the limits of its application. It can lead them to sweeping claims such as that made by the World Medical Association in its 1949 International Code of Medical Ethics: "A doctor shall preserve absolute secrecy on all he knows about his patient because of the confidence entrusted in him."[12]

If such claims go too far, where and how should the lines be drawn? Granting the prima facie importance of the principle of confidentiality in the light of the premises which support it, when and for what reasons must it be set aside? I shall consider such limits with respect to the secrets of individual clients, of professionals themselves, and of institutional or corporate clients.

INDIVIDUAL CLIENTS AND THEIR SECRETS

Among the most difficult choices for physicians and others are those which arise with respect to confidences by children, mentally incompetent persons, and those who are temporarily not fully capable of guiding their affairs. While some such confidences—as about fear or hopes—can be kept secret without difficulty, others are more troubling. Consider the following case:

Janet M., a thirteen-year-old girl in the seventh grade of a small-town junior high school, comes to the office of a family physician. She has known him from childhood, and he has cared for all the members of her family. She tells him that she is pregnant, and that she has had a lab test performed at an out-of-town clinic. She wants to have an abortion. She is afraid that her family, already burdened by unemployment and illness, would be thrown into a crisis by the news. Her boyfriend, fifteen, would probably be opposed to the abortion. She asks the doctor for help in securing the abortion, and for assurance that he will not reveal her condition to anyone.

Cases such as Janet's are no longer rare. In small towns as in large cities, teen-age pregnancy is on the rise, teen-age abortion commonplace. Many families do provide the guidance and understanding so desperately needed at such times; but when girls request confidentiality, it is often out of fear of their families' reaction. Health professionals should clearly make every effort to help these girls communicate with their families. But sometimes there is no functioning family. Or else family members may have been so brutal or so unable to cope with crisis in the past that it is legitimate to be concerned about the risks in informing them. At times, it is even the case that a member of the girl's own family has abused her sexually.[13]

Health professionals are then caught in a conflict between their traditional obligation of confidentiality and the normal procedure of consulting with a child's parents before an irreversible step is taken. In this conflict, the premises supporting confidentiality are themselves in doubt. Just how autonomous should thirteen-year-olds be with respect to decisions about pregnancy? They are children still, but with an adult's choice to make. And what about even younger girls? In what relation does a physician stand to them, and to their parents, regarding such secrets?

Because the premises of autonomy and of relationship do not necessarily mandate secrecy at such times, deciding whether or not to pledge silence is much harder. Even the professional help that confidentiality allows is then in doubt. Pregnant young girls are in need of advice and assistance more than most others; confidentiality too routinely extended may lock them into an attitude of frightened concealment that can do permanent damage. Health professionals owe it to these patients, therefore, to encourage and help them to communicate with their families or others responsible for their support. But to *mandate,* as some seek to do, consultation with family members, no matter how brutal or psychologically abusive, would be to take a shortsighted view. Not only would it injure those pregnant girls forced into family confrontations; many others would end by not seeking professional help at all, at a time when they need it most.

Childhood and adolescent pregnancies are far from the only conditions that present professionals with conflicts over confidentiality. Veneral disease, drug and alcohol addiction among the young, as well as a great many problems of incompetent and disturbed individuals past childhood, render confidentiality similarly problematic.

Even where there is no question about maturity or competence, professionals worry about the secrecy asked of them when someone confides to them plans that seem self-injurious: to enter into a clearly disastrous business arrangement, or to give all his possessions to an exploitative "guru," or to abandon life-prolonging medical treatment. He may have no intention of hurting anyone else (though relatives and others may in fact be profoundly affected by his choice) and may be fully within his rights in acting as he does. But his judgment may itself be in doubt, depending on how self-destructive the plans are that he is confiding.

Here again, an absolute insistence on confidentiality would be unreasonable. No one would hesitate to reveal the secret of a temporarily deranged person about to do himself irreversible harm. Patients and clients do not have the requisite balance at such a time to justify silence—and thus complicity—regarding their self-destructive acts, the less so as the very revelation of such plans to a professional is often correctly interpreted as a call for help.

If, on the other hand, the act has been carefully thought through, breaches of confidentiality are much less justified, no matter how irrational the project might at first seem to outsiders. Say the person planning to give his money away wants to live the rest of his life as a contemplative, or that the patient planning to abandon medical treatment has decided to cease delaying death in view of his progressively debilitating and painful disease; it is harder to see the basis for a breach of professional confidentiality in such cases, since it is more difficult to prove that the person's act is necessarily self-destructive from his point of view. Professionals are constantly at risk of assuming too readily that the purposes they take to be overriding and to which they have dedicated their careers—financial prudence, for instance—are necessarily more rational for all others than conflicting aims. This professional bias has to be taken into account in any decision to override confidentiality on grounds of irrationality and self-harm.

Sometimes, however, a patient's insistence on confidentiality can bring quite unintended risks. Because people live longer, and often suffer from multiple chronic diseases, their records have to be accessible to many different health professionals. Their reluctance to have certain facts on their medical records may then be dangerous. One physician has pointed to some of the possible consequences of such concealment:

> The man who insists that no record be made of a psychiatric history, or the drugs that would suggest that there is one, and wants no record of his syphilis and penicillin injections and subsequent recovery, is the same man who must face squarely the risk of future syphilitic disease of the nervous system or even lethal penicillin reactions because future medical personnel never followed through in the right manner. They do not even know that the problem existed; they and the patient stumbled blindly into trouble.[14]

. . . . .

Do patients have the same claims to confidentiality about personal information when persons from whom it is kept run serious risks? Consider again the family mentioned earlier in which the father wishes to conceal from his children that he suffers from polycystic kidney disease. It is now two years later. The father, much closer to death, has told his two children about the genetic nature of his disease. He was prompted to do so, in part, by his daughter's plans to marry. She, however, fears disclosing to her future husband that the same disease may strike her and affect their children. Now it is her turn to insist on confidentiality, not only from her father but from all others who know the facts, including the health professionals involved.

The dilemma they face is in one sense very old, in another quite new. It resembles all the choices through the ages about whether or not to reveal to intimates and future spouses that someone suffers from incurable venereal disease, sexual problems, a recurring psychiatric condition, or a degenerative disease as yet in its early stages. But it has taken on a new frequency because there is now so much more information, especially of a genetic nature, than even a hundred years ago. The category of problematic and troubling predictions has expanded, raising new conflicts of secrecy for parents, prospective spouses, and many others, and of confidentiality for health professionals. Lacking the genetic information, this family would not have faced the same choice in an earlier period. With increased knowledge of risks, therefore, the collective burden of confidentiality has grown as well.

Does a professional owe confidentiality to clients who reveal plans or acts that endanger others directly? Such a question arises for the lawyer whose client lets slip that he plans a bank robbery, or that he has committed an assault for which an innocent man is standing trial; for the pediatrician who suspects that a mother drugs her children to keep them quiet; and for the psychiatrist whose patient discloses that he is obsessed by jealousy and thoughts of violence to his wife. . . .

The autonomy we grant individuals over personal secrets, first of all, cannot reasonably be thought to extend to plans of violence against innocent persons; at such times, on the contrary, someone who knows of plans that endanger others owes it to them to counteract those plans, and, if he is not sure he can forestall them, to warn the potential victims. Nor, in the second place, can patients who voice serious threats against innocent persons invoke confidentiality on the basis of their relationship with therapists or anyone else without asking them to be partially complicitous. The third premise, basing confidentiality in part on a promise, is likewise overridden, since in the absence of legitimacy for the first two, it ought to be clearly understood that no one, whether professionally trained or not, should give such a pledge. The benefits invoked in the fourth premise, finally, are not only not demonstrated in these cases; even if they were, they could not override the injustice done to those unwittingly placed at risk.*

Long before psychiatrists worried about these problems, Catholic theologians had studied them with a thoroughness often lacking in contemporary discussions. The distinctions they worked out over the centuries concerning different types of secrets and the obligations of professionals were detailed and well reasoned. Most theologians agreed that certain types of secrets were not binding on professional recipients, foremost among them grave threats against the public good or against innocent third persons.[15]

An example they often described is the following: What should a doctor do if he has a patient who suffers from an incurable and highly contagious veneral disease and who plans to marry without disclosing this fact to his fiancée? According to many theologians, the doctor's obligation of secrecy would then cease: the young man forfeits such consideration through his intent to act in a way that might gravely injure his fiancée. The doctor is therefore free to speak, but with certain limitations: he must reveal only so much of the secret as is necessary to avert the harm, and only to the person threatened, who has a right to this information, rather than to family members, neighbors, or the curious or gossip-hungry at large.

These commentators also discussed a subject that still divides the contemporary debate: Should the breach of secrecy to avert grave harm be obligatory, or merely permitted? Should the professional feel free to choose whether or not to warn the endangered person, or acknowledge a duty to do so? It is one thing to say that he no longer owes the client confidentiality; but does he also *owe* the endangered person the information? Do lawyers, for example, owe any information to persons who may be injured by their clients' unlawful tax schemes, plans for extortion, or threats of violence? And if they do recognize some such obligation, how does it weigh against that of confidentiality?

The duty of confidentiality clearly has some weight; as a result, the obligation to warn potential victims is not as great for professionals as it might be for others who happen to hear of the danger. Yet it is a strong one nevertheless, especially where serious harm is likely to occur. In such cases, the duty to warn ought to be overriding. Professionals should not then be free to promise confidentiality, nor should a client expect to be able to entrust them with such projects, any more than with stolen goods or lethal weapons.[16]

The same is true for confidences regarding past crimes. Here, too, confidentiality counts; but it must be weighed against other aims—of social justice and restitution. It is therefore hard to agree with those lawyers who argue as a matter of course that they owe clients silence about past, unsolved murders; it is equally hard to agree with Swiss bankers claiming that confidentiality suffices to legitimate the secret bank accounts that attract so many depositors enriched through crime, conspiracy, and political exploitation.

SECRECY AS A SHIELD

The greatest burden of secrecy imposed by confidentiality, however, is that of the secrets professionals keep to protect themselves rather than patients and clients. Confidentiality can be used, here as elsewhere, as a shield for activities that could ill afford to see the light of day. An example of how dangerous such shielding can be is afforded by the story of the death in 1976 of Anneliese Michel, a young German student, after ten months of exorcism.[17]

Anneliese Michel had been under periodic med-

*Such a conclusion carries with it line-drawing problems: how likely the danger should be before one assumes serious risk; how sure one should be about the identity of the potential victim; how much this individual already knows about the risk; the degree of precautions already in place, etc. But line-drawing problems would occur no matter what the conclusion unless one postulated either no duty to breach confidentiality under any conditions whatsoever, or, on the contrary, no obligation of confidentiality at all.

ical care since she was sixteen years old. She had been diagnosed as suffering both from recurrent epileptic seizures and from anorexia nervosa. When she was twenty-two, her parents persuaded her to withdraw from university studies. Ernst Alt, the local parish priest, suspected that she might be possessed by devils and that exorcism might cure her. He saw the seizures as evidence of such possession rather than of epilepsy, and decided to consult Germany's leading "satanologist," the eighty-three-year-old Adolf Rodewyk, S.J. Father Rodewyk concluded that the convulsions were trancelike states of possession in which, among other manifestations, a devil calling himself Judas made no secret of his identity.

Father Rodewyk recommended exorcism. The *Rituale Romanum* of 1614, still followed in cases of exorcism, prescribes that a bishop must agree to the procedure before it can be undertaken, and that the person thus treated must be beyond medical help. Father Rodewyk assured Bishop Joseph Stangl of Würzburg that Anneliese's case was one for exorcists, not for doctors; and the bishop authorized the rites, ordering "strictest secrecy and total discretion."

For ten months, the young woman took part in lengthy sessions with the parish priest and Father Wilhelm Renz, an expert called in for the exorcism. The two prayed with her and tried, by means of holy water, adjurations, and commands, to drive out the devils—by then thought to number at least six and calling themselves, in addition to Judas, by such names as Lucifer, Nero, and Hitler. Anneliese was convinced that she was thus possessed and that the powers of good and of evil were fighting over her soul. She wrote in her diary that the Savior had told her she was a great saint. Fearing that doctors might diagnose her voices and seizures as psychiatric symptoms and send her to a mental hospital, she avoided health professionals. As the months wore on, she grew weaker, eating and drinking next to nothing. During one particularly stormy session of exorcism, she rushed head first against the wall facing her bed, then lay back exhausted. The devils were finally declared to have left. The next morning, she was found dead in her bed.

In April 1978, her parents and the two priests who had conducted the exorcism were brought to trial. They were convicted of negligent homicide for having failed to seek medical help up to the very end. Physicians testified that, even as late as a few days before Anneliese died, her life could have been saved had she had medical attention. The four accused were sentenced to six months imprisonment.

The priests sincerely believed that they were doing their best to save Anneliese Michel. Insofar as they believed Father Rodewyk's attesting to the presence of devils, they could hardly think medical treatment appropriate. But they knew their belief that Anneliese was possessed by devils would be shared by few, and so they conspired with her parents to keep the sessions of exorcism secret to the very end. Two kinds of confidentiality come together here: that between priest and penitent, and that between caretaker and patient. But neither one should have been honored in this case, for while they protect much that is spoken by penitents and by patients, they were never intended to protect all that is done by priests or caretakers in response, least of all when it constitutes treatment of very sick persons by dangerous methods without medical assistance.

The case is an extreme one. Strict adherence to the stipulation in the *Rituale Romanum* of 1614 that someone must be beyond medical help would have required much more careful consultation with physicians before leaping to the conclusion that exorcism was called for. When publicity about the case arose, Catholics and non-Catholics alike were distressed at how the young woman had been treated. What is worth noting, however, is that her need for medical help went unnoticed because of the secrecy in which the exorcism was conducted. The case illustrates, therefore, what can happen in almost any system of advising and helping those in need whenever secrecy shrouds what is done to them. And it raises broader questions about confidentiality: Exactly whose secret should it protect? The patient's or client's alone? Or the professional's? Or all that transpires between them?

In principle, confidentiality should protect only the first. But in practice, it can expand, like all other practices of secrecy, to cover much more. It may even be stretched so far as to include what professionals hide *from* patients, clients, and the public at large.

The sick, the poor, the mentally ill, the aged, and the very young are in a paradoxical situation in this respect. While their right to confidentiality is often breached and their most intimate problems openly bandied about, the poor care they may receive is just as often covered up under the same name of confidentiality. That is the shield held forth to prevent outsiders from finding out about negligence, overcharging, unnecessary surgery, or institutionalization. And far more than individual mistakes and misdeeds are thus covered up, for confidentiality is also the shield that professionals invoke to protect incompetent colleagues and negligence and unexpected accidents in, for instance, hospitals, factories, or entire industries.

The word "confidentiality" has by now become

a means of covering up a multitude of questionable and often dangerous practices. When lawyers use it to justify keeping secret their client's plan to construct housing so shoddy as to be life-threatening, or when government officials invoke it in concealing the risks of nuclear weapons, confidentiality no longer serves the purpose for which it was intended; it has become, rather, a means for deflecting legitimate public attention.

Such invocations of confidentiality are facilitated by the ease with which many transpose the confidentiality owed to individuals to the collective level. Consider, for example, the prolonged collaboration between asbestos manufacturers and company physicians to conceal the risks from exposure to asbestos dust. These risks were kept secret from the public, from workers in plants manufacturing asbestos insulation, and even from those workers found in medical checkups to be in the early stages of asbestos-induced disease. When a reporter approached a physician associated with the concealment as consultant for a large manufacturer, the physician turned down his request for an interview on grounds of confidentiality owed as a matter of "the patient's rights," and explained, when the astonished reporter inquired who the "patient" was, that it was the *company*.[18]

Government agencies sometimes request confidentiality, not so much to deflect inquiry as to be able to conduct it in the manner most likely to resolve difficult problems. Thus the U.S. Center for Disease Control argued, in 1980, that it needed to be able to promise confidentiality to hospitals seeking its help for nosocomial, or hospital-induced, infections. Such infection is a major health risk, conservatively estimated as killing twenty thousand persons a year in the United States alone, and contributing to the deaths of over forty thousand others in a substantial manner. When a hospital experiences an outbreak of nosocomial infection, it can call on the expert advice of the Center for Disease Control in order to find the cause of the infection and to reverse its course; but to do so under conditions of publicity is to invite rumor, lawsuits, and patient anxiety, according to those who argued in favor of extending confidentiality to the hospitals.[19] The center saw a need to promise such confidentiality to a hospital in order to help it combat infection, much as a doctor might promise silence to an individual patient with a similar affliction.

The center's request for an exemption from the Freedom of Information Act on such grounds was turned down. No proof had been advanced that the dangers the hospitals feared were realistic. Patients did not appear to be staying away from hospitals that had experienced outbreaks of nosocomial infection; and no suit had been won on the basis of information provided by the center.

The step from patient confidentiality to hospital confidentiality is a large one, but it is often lightly taken in arguments that ignore the differences between the two. The first two premises underlying confidentiality, of autonomy regarding personal information and the respect for intimacy and human bonds, are obviously applicable, if at all, in a different manner when it comes to institutions. And the fourth premise, concerning the benefit to individuals from having somewhere to turn when vulnerable and in need of help, and the indirect benefit to society from allowing professionals to give counsel in strict confidence, must be scrutinized with care whenever the claim is made that it applies to government agencies, law firms, or corporations. We ask of them a much higher degree of accountability.

To be sure, these institutions should be able to invoke confidentiality for legitimate activities such as internal memoranda and personnel files; but it is a different matter altogether to claim confidentiality for plans that endanger others. Such protection attracts all who seek surreptitious assistance with bribery, tax evasion, and similar schemes. And because corporate or consulting law is so lucrative, the power to exercise confidentiality for such secrets then shields not merely the company and the client but the lawyer's own links to, and rewards from, highly questionable practices.

The premises supporting confidentiality are strong, but they cannot support practices of secrecy—whether by individual clients, institutions, or professionals themselves—that undermine and contradict the very respect for persons and for human bonds that confidentiality was meant to protect.

NOTES

1. See Robert E. Regan, *Professional Secrecy in the Light of Moral Principles* (Washington, DC: Augustinian Press, 1943); Alan H. Goldman, *The Moral Foundations of Professional Ethics* (Totowa, NJ: Rowman and Littlefield, 1980); LeRoy Walters, "Ethical Aspects of Medical Confidentiality," in Tom L. Beauchamp and LeRoy Walters, eds., *Contemporary Issues in Bioethics* (Encino, CA: Dickenson, 1978), pp. 169–75; Susanna J. Wilson, *Confidentiality in Social Work* (New York: Free Press, 1978); William Harold Tiemann, *The Right to Silence: Privileged Communication and the Pastor* (Richmond, VA: John Knox Press, 1964); William W. Meissner, "Threats to Confidentiality," *Psychiatric Annals* 2 (1979):54–71.

2. From the newsletter *Hard Choices*, Office for Radio and Television for Learning (Boston: 1980), p. 9.

3. For a discussion on whether this partial autonomy over personal information should be defended in terms of property, see Arthur R. Miller *The Assault on Privacy*

(Ann Arbor: University of Michigan Press, 1971), pp. 211–16.

4. For the marital privilege, see Sanford Levinson, *The State and Structures of Intimacy* (New York: Basic Books, forthcoming). For the Chinese tradition, see Derk Bodde and Clarence Morris, *Law in Imperial China* (Cambridge, MA: Harvard University Press, 1967), p. 40.

5. Hugo Grotius, *The Law of War and Peace,* trans. Francis Kelsey (Indianapolis, IN: Bobbs-Merrill, 1925), bk. 2, chap. 11, p. 331.

6. I discussed the question of lying to protect confidences in *Lying* [*: Moral Choice in Public and Private Life* (New York: Pantheon, 1978)], chap. 11.

7. For different views on the binding forces of promises, see William Godwin, *Enquiry Concerning Political Justice* (1793; 3rd ed. 1798), bk. 3, chap. 3; Richard Price, *A Review of the Principal Questions in Morals* (1758; 3rd ed. 1787), chap. 7 (both in D. H. Munro, ed., *A Guide to the British Moralists* [London: William Collins, 1972], pp. 187–97, 180–86). For more general treatments of promising, see Grotius, *Law of War and Peace,* bk. 2, chap. 11, pp. 328–42; John Searle, *Speech Acts* (Cambridge: Cambridge University Press, 1969); Charles Fried, *Contract as Promise* (Cambridge, MA: Harvard University Press, 1981).

8. Nietzsche, in *Ecce Homo,* trans. Kaufmann, p. 64, relates such pledges to the bond between debtor and creditor; he argues that the memory necessary for people to keep promises only developed through such painful, often cruel experiences.

9. For discussions of whether some or all of these premises should be accepted, and whether they are grounded on utilitarian or deontological considerations, see Goldman, *Moral Foundations of Professional Ethics,* Leo J. Cass and William J. Curran, ''Rights of Privacy in Medical Practice,'' partially reprinted in Samuel Gorovitz et al., *Moral Problems in Medicine* (Englewood Cliffs, NJ: Prentice-Hall, 1976), pp. 82–85; Benjamin Freedman, ''A Meta–Ethics for Professional Morality,'' *Ethics* 89:1 (1978):1–19; Benjamin Freedman, ''What Really Makes Professional Morality Different: Response to Martin,'' *Ethics* 91:4 (1981):626–30; Mike W. Martin, ''Rights and the Meta–Ethics of Professional Morality,'' *Ethics* 91:4 (1981):619–25.

10. Henry E. Sigerist, *A History of Medicine,* vol. 1, *Primitive and Archaic Medicine* (New York: Oxford University Press, 1951), p. 433.

11. Jeremy Bentham, otherwise opposed to testimonial privileges for professionals, argues in favor of ''excluding the evidence of a Catholic priest respecting the confessions intrusted to him,'' holding that freedom of religion outweighs the social costs of such practices. See *Works of Jeremy Bentham* [ed. John Bowring (Edinburgh: W. Tait, 1843)], 7:366–68.

12. [International] Code of [Medical] Ethics, 1949 World Medical Association, in *Encyclopedia of Bioethics* (New York: Free Press, 1978), pp. 1749–50.

13. I have discussed abortion in ''Ethical Problems of Abortion,'' *Hastings Center Studies* 2 (1974):33–52.

14. Lawrence Weed, *Your Health Care and How to Manage it* (Arlington, VT: Essex, 1978), p.79.

15. See Regan, *Professional Secrecy,* pp. 104–13.

16. For diverging views of the lawyer's responsibility of confidentiality, see American Bar Association, *Model Rules of Professional Conduct: Proposed Final Draft.* [Chicago: ABA, 30 May,] 1981, pp. 37–47; and the Roscoe Pound–American Trial Lawyers Foundation, *American Lawyer's Code of Conduct: Discussion Draft.* June 1980, pp. 101–10.

17. For accounts of the story of Anneliese Michel and of the trial after her death, I have relied on *Die Zeit,* July 30, 1976, and April 7, 1978; *Der Spiegel,* July 2, 1976, and April 3, 1978; and *Süddeutsche Zeitung,* which had stories almost daily during the period of the trial, March 30–April 24, 1978.

18. See Paul Brodeur, *Expendable Americans* (New York: Viking, 1973).

19. Ethics Advisory Board, Department of Health and Human Services, The Request of the Center for Disease Control for a Limited Exemption from the Freedom of Information Act. 1980.

30A. Majority Opinion in *Tarasoff* v. *Regents of the University of California**

Justice Mathew O. Tobriner

On October 27, 1969, Prosenjit Poddar killed Tatiana Tarasoff.[1] Plaintiffs, Tatiana's parents, allege that two months earlier Poddar confided his intention to kill Tatiana to Dr. Lawrence Moore, a psychologist employed by the Cowell Memorial Hospital at the University of California at Berkeley. They allege that on Moore's request, the campus police briefly detained Poddar, but released him when he appeared rational. They further claim that Dr. Harvey Powelson, Moore's superior, then directed that no further action be taken to detain Poddar. No one warned plaintiffs of Tatiana's peril. . . .

Plaintiffs' complaints predicate liability on two grounds: defendants' failure to warn plaintiffs of

From California Supreme Court, 1 July 1976. 131 *California Reporter,* pp. 14–33, West Publishing Company.

*[Some notes have been deleted without indication.—ED.]

the impending danger and their failure to bring about Poddar's confinement . . . Defendants, in turn, assert that they owed no duty of reasonable care to Tatiana and that they are immune from suit . . .

We shall explain that defendant therapists cannot escape liability merely because Tatiana herself was not their patient. When a therapist determines, or pursuant to the standards of his profession should determine, that his patient presents a serious danger of violence to another, he incurs an obligation to use reasonable care to protect the intended victim against such danger. The discharge of this duty may require the therapists to take one or more of various steps, depending upon the nature of the case. Thus it may call for him to warn the intended victim or others likely to apprise the victim of the danger, to notify the police, or to take whatever other steps are reasonably necessary under the circumstances.

In the case at bar, plaintiffs admit that defendant therapists notified the police, but argue on appeal that the therapists failed to exercise reasonable care to protect Tatiana in that they did not confine Poddar and did not warn Tatiana or others likely to apprise her of the danger. Defendant therapists, however, are public employees. Consequently, to the extent that plaintiffs seek to predicate liability upon the therapists' failure to bring about Poddar's confinement, the therapists can claim immunity . . . No specific statutory provision, however, shields them from liability based upon failure to warn Tatiana or others likely to apprise her of the danger . . .

Plaintiffs therefore can amend their complaints to allege that, regardless of the therapists' unsuccessful attempt to confine Poddar, since they knew that Poddar was at large and dangerous, their failure to warn Tatiana or others likely to apprise her of the danger constituted a breach of the therapists' duty to exercise reasonable care to protect Tatiana.

Plaintiffs, Tatiana's mother and father, filed separate but virtually identical second amended complaints. The issue before us on this appeal is whether those complaints now state, or can be amended to state, causes of action against defendants. We therefore begin by setting forth the pertinent allegations of the complaints.[2]

Plaintiffs' first cause of action, entitled "Failure to Detain a Dangerous Patient," alleges that on August 20, 1969, Poddar was a voluntary outpatient receiving therapy at Cowell Memorial Hospital. Poddar informed Moore, his therapist, that he was going to kill an unnamed girl, readily identifiable as Tatiana, when she returned home from spending the summer in Brazil. Moore, with the concurrence of Dr. Gold, who had initially examined Poddar, and Dr. Yandell, assistant to the director of the department of psychiatry, decided that Poddar should be committed for observation in a mental hospital. Moore orally notified Officers Atkinson and Teel of the campus police that he would request commitment. He then sent a letter to Police Chief William Beall requesting the assistance of the police department in securing Poddar's confinement.

Officers Atkinson, Brownrigg, and Halleran took Poddar into custody, but, satisfied that Poddar was rational, released him on his promise to stay away from Tatiana. Powelson, director of the department of psychiatry at Cowell Memorial Hospital, then asked the police to return Moore's letter, directed that all copies of the letter and notes that Moore had taken as therapist be destroyed, and "ordered no action to place Prosenjit Poddar in 72-hour treatment and evaluation facility."

Plaintiffs' second cause of action, entitled "Failure to Warn On a Dangerous Patient," incorporates the allegations of the first cause of action, but adds the assertion that defendants negligently permitted Poddar to be released from police custody without "notifying the parents of Tatiana Tarasoff that their daughter was in grave danger from Prosenjit Poddar." Poddar persuaded Tatiana's brother to share an apartment with him near Tatiana's residence; shortly after her return from Brazil, Poddar went to her residence and killed her.

Plaintiffs' third cause of action, entitled "Abandonment of a Dangerous Patient," seeks $10,000 punitive damages against defendant Powelson. Incorporating the crucial allegations of the first cause of action, plaintiffs charge that Powelson "did the things herein alleged with intent to abandon a dangerous patient, and said acts were done maliciously and oppressively."

Plaintiffs' fourth cause of action, for "Breach of Primary Duty to Patient and the Public," states essentially the same allegations as the first cause of action, but seeks to characterize defendants' conduct as a breach of duty to safeguard their patient and the public. Since such conclusory labels add nothing to the factual allegations of the complaint, the first and fourth causes of action are legally indistinguishable.

. . . [P]laintiffs' first and fourth cause of action, which seek to predicate liability upon the defendants' failure to bring about Poddar's confinement, are barred by governmental immunity. Plaintiffs' third cause of action succumbs to the decisions precluding exemplary damages in a wrongful death action. . . . We direct our attention, therefore, to the issue of whether plaintiffs' second cause of action can be amended to state a basis for recovery. . . .

The second cause of action can be amended to allege that Tatiana's death proximately resulted from defendants' negligent failure to warn Tatiana or others likely to apprise her of her danger. Plaintiffs contend that as amended, such allegations of negligence and proximate causation, with resulting damages, establish a cause of action. Defendants, however, contend that in the circumstances of the present case they owed no duty of care to Tatiana or her parents and that, in the absence of such duty, they were free to act in careless disregard of Tatiana's life and safety.

In analyzing this issue, we bear in mind that legal duties are not discoverable facts of nature, but merely conclusory expressions that, in cases of a particular type, liability should be imposed for damage done. As stated in *Dillon* v. *Legg* (1968) 68 Cal.2d 728, 734, 69 Cal.Rptr. 72, 76, 441 P.2d 912, 916: "The assertion that liability must . . . be denied because defendant bears no 'duty' to plaintiff 'begs the essential question—whether the plaintiff's interests are entitled to legal protection against the defendant's conduct . . . [Duty] is not sacrosanct in itself, but only an expression of the sum total of those considerations of policy which lead the law to say that the particular plaintiff is entitled to protection.' (Prosser, Law of Torts [3d ed. 1964] at pp. 332–333.)"

In the landmark case of *Rowland* v. *Christian* (1968) 69 Cal.2d 108, 70 Cal.Rptr. 97, 443 P.2d 561, Justice Peters recognized that liability should be imposed "for an injury occasioned to another by his want of ordinary care or skill" as expressed in section 1714 of the Civil Code. Thus, Justice Peters, quoting from *Heaven* v. *Pender* (1883) 11 Q.B.D. 503, 509 stated: " 'whenever one person is by circumstances placed in such a position with regard to another . . . that if he did not use ordinary care and skill in his own conduct . . . he would cause danger of injury to the person or property of the other, a duty arises to use ordinary care and skill to avoid such danger.' "

We depart from "this fundamental principle" only upon the "balancing of a number of considerations"; major ones "are the foreseeability of harm to the plaintiff, the degree of certainty that the plaintiff suffered injury, the closeness of the connection between the defendant's conduct and the injury suffered, the moral blame attached to the defendant's conduct, the policy of preventing future harm, the extent of the burden to the defendant and consequences to the community of imposing a duty to exercise care with resulting liability for breach, and the availability, cost and prevalence of insurance for the risk involved."[3]

The most important of these considerations in establishing duty is foreseeability. As a general principle, a "defendant owes a duty of care to all persons who are foreseeably endangered by his conduct, with respect to all risks which make the conduct unreasonably dangerous." (*Rodriguez* v. *Bethlehem Steel Corp.* (1974) 12 Cal.3d 382, 399, 115 Cal.Rptr. 765, 776, 525 P.2d 669, 680; *Dillon* v. *Legg, supra,* 68 Cal.2d 728, 739, 69 Cal.Rptr. 72, 441 P.2d 912; *Weirum* v. *R.K.O. General, Inc.* (1975) 15 Cal.3d 40, 123 Cal.Rptr. 468, 539 P.2d 36; see Civ.Code, § 1714.) As we shall explain, however, when the avoidance of foreseeable harm requires a defendant to control the conduct of another person, or to warn of such conduct, the common law has traditionally imposed liability only if the defendant bears some special relationship to the dangerous person or to the potential victim. Since the relationship between a therapist and his patient satisfies this requirement, we need not here decide whether foreseeability alone is sufficient to create a duty to exercise reasonabl[e] care to protect a potential victim of another's conduct.

Although, as we have stated above, under the common law, as a general rule, one person owed no duty to control the conduct of another[4] (*Richards* v. *Stanley* (1954) 43 Cal.2d 60, 65, 271, P.2d 23; *Wright* v. *Arcade School Dist.* (1964) 230 Cal.App.2d 272, 277, 40 Cal.Rptr. 812; Rest.2d Torts (1965) § 315), nor to warn those endangered by such conduct (Rest.2d Torts, *supra,* § 314, com. c.; Prosser, Law of Torts (4th ed. 1971) § 56, p. 341), the courts have carved out an exception to this rule in cases in which the defendant stands in some special relationship to either the person whose conduct needs to be controlled or in a relationship to the foreseeable victim of that conduct (see Rest.2d Torts, *supra,* §§ 315–320). Applying this exception to the present case, we note that a relationship of defendant therapists to either Tatiana or Poddar will suffice to establish a duty of care; as explained in section 315 of the Restatement Second of Torts, a duty of care may arise from either "(a) a special relation . . . between the actor and the third person which imposes a duty upon the actor to control the third person's conduct, or (b) a special relation . . . between the actor and the other which gives to the other a right of protection."

Although plaintiffs' pleadings assert no special relation between Tatiana and defendant therapists, they establish as between Poddar and defendant therapists the special relation that arises between a patient and his doctor or psychotherapist. Such a relationship may support affirmative duties for the benefit of third persons. Thus, for example, a hospital must exercise reasonable care to control the behavior of a patient which may endanger other persons.[5] A doctor must also warn a patient if the patient's condition or medication renders certain conduct, such as driving a car, dangerous to others.[6]

Although the California decisions that recognize this duty have involved cases in which the defendant stood in a special relationship *both* to the victim and to the person whose conduct created the danger, we do not think that the duty should logically be constricted to such situations. Decisions of other jurisdictions hold that the single relationship of a doctor to his patient is sufficient to support the duty to exercise reasonable care to protect others against dangers emanating from the patient's illness. The courts hold that a doctor is liable to persons infected by his patient if he negligently fails to diagnose a contagious disease (*Hoffman* v. *Blackmon* (Fla.App.1970) 241 So.2d 752), or, having diagnosed the illness, fails to warn members of the patient's family (*Wojcik* v. *Aluminum Co. of America* (1959) 18 Misc.2d 740, 183 N.Y.S.2d 351, 357–358; *Davis* v. *Rodman* (1921) 147 Ark. 385, 227 S.W. 612; *Skillings* v. *Allen* (1919) 143 Minn. 323, 173 N.W. 663; see also *Jones* v. *Stanko* (1928) 118 Ohio St. 147, 160 N.E. 456).

Since it involved a dangerous mental patient, the decision in *Merchants Nat. Bank and Trust Co. of Fargo* v. *United States* (D.N.D.1967) 272 F. Supp. 409 comes closer to the issue. The Veterans Administration arranged for the patient to work on a local farm, but did not inform the farmer of the man's background. The farmer consequently permitted the patient to come and go freely during nonworking hours; the patient borrowed a car, drove to his wife's residence and killed her. Notwithstanding the lack of any "special relationship" between the Veterans Administration and the wife, the court found the Veterans Administration liable for the wrongful death of the wife.

In their summary of the relevant rulings Fleming and Maximov conclude that the "case law should dispel any notion that to impose on the therapists a duty to take precautions for the safety of persons threatened by a patient, where due care so requires, is in any way opposed to contemporary ground rules on the duty relationship. On the contrary, there now seems to be sufficient authority to support the conclusion that by entering into a doctor–patient relationship the therapist becomes sufficiently involved to assume some responsibility for the safety, not only of the patient himself, but also of any third person whom the doctor knows to be threatened by the patient." (Fleming and Maximov, *The Patient or His Victim: The Therapist's Dilemma* (1974) 62 Cal.L.Rev. 1025, 1030.)

Defendants contend, however, that imposition of a duty to exercise reasonable care to protect third persons is unworkable because therapists cannot accurately predict whether or not a patient will resort to violence. In support of this argument amicus representing the American Psychiatric Association and other professional societies cites numerous articles which indicate that therapists, in the present state of the art, are unable reliably to predict violent acts; their forecasts, amicus claims, tend consistently to overpredict violence, and indeed are more often wrong than right.[7] Since predictions of violence are often erroneous, amicus concludes, the courts should not render rulings that predicate the liability of therapists upon the validity of such predictions.

The role of the psychiatrist, who is indeed a practitioner of medicine, and that of the psychologist who performs an allied function, are like that of the physician who must conform to the standards of the profession and who must often make diagnoses and predictions based upon such evaluations. Thus the judgment of the therapist in diagnosing emotional disorders and in predicting whether a patient presents a serious danger of violence is comparable to the judgment which doctors and professionals must regularly render under accepted rules of responsibility.

We recognize the difficulty that a therapist encounters in attempting to forecast whether a patient presents a serious danger of violence. Obviously we do not require that the therapist, in making that determination, render a perfect performance; the therapist need only exercise "that reasonable degree of skill, knowledge, and care ordinarily possessed and exercised by members of [that professional specialty] under similar circumstances." (*Bardessono* v. *Michels* (1970) 3 Cal.3d 780, 788, 91 Cal.Rptr. 760, 764, 478 P.2d 480, 484; *Quintal* v. *Laurel Grove Hospital* (1964) 62 Cal.2d 154, 159–160, 41 Cal.Rptr. 577, 397 P.2d 161; see 4 Witkin, Summary of Cal.Law (8th ed. 1974) Torts, § 514 and cases cited.) Within the broad range of reasonable practice and treatment in which professional opinion and judgment may differ, the therapist is free to exercise his or her own best judgment without liability; proof, aided by hindsight, that he or she judged wrongly is insufficient to establish negligence.

In the instant case, however, the pleadings do not raise any question as to failure of defendant therapists to predict that Poddar represented a serious danger of violence. On the contrary, the present complaints allege that defendant therapists did in fact predict that Poddar would kill, but were negligent in failing to warn.

Amicus contends, however, that even when a therapist does in fact predict that a patient poses a serious danger of violence to others, the therapist should be absolved of any responsibility for failing to act to protect the potential victim. In our view, however, once a therapist does in fact determine, or under applicable professional standards reasonably should have determined, that a patient poses a serious danger of violence to others, he bears a duty to exercise reasonable care to protect the foreseeable victim of that danger. While the discharge of this duty of due care will necessarily vary with the facts of each case, in each instance the adequacy of the therapist's conduct must be measured against the traditional negligence standard of the rendition of reasonable care under the circumstances. (Accord *Cobbs* v. *Grant* (1972) 8 Cal.3d 229, 243, 104 Cal.Rptr. 505, 502 P.2d 1.) As explained in Fleming and Maximov, *The Patient or His Victim: The Therapist's Dilemma* (1974) 62 Cal.L.Rev. 1025, 1067: ". . . the ultimate question of resolving the tension between the conflicting interests of patient and potential victim is one of social policy, not professional expertise. . . . In sum, the therapist owes a legal duty not only to his patient, but also to his patient's would–be victim and is subject in both respects to scrutiny by judge and jury."

Contrary to the assertion of amicus, this conclusion is not inconsistent with our recent decision in *People* v. *Burnick, supra,* 14 Cal.3d 306, 121 Cal.Rptr. 488, 535 P.2d 352. Taking note of the uncertain character of therapeutic prediction, we held in *Burnick* that a person cannot be committed as a mentally disordered sex offender unless found to be such by proof beyond a reasonable doubt. (14 Cal.3d at p. 328, 121 Cal.Rptr. 488, 535 P.2d 352.) The issue in the present context, however, is not whether the patient should be incarcerated, but whether the therapist should take any steps at all to protect the threatened victim; some of the alternatives open to the therapist, such as warning the victim, will not result in the drastic consequences of depriving the patient of his liberty. Weighing the uncertain and conjectural character of the alleged damage done the patient by such a warning against the peril to the victim's life, we conclude that professional inaccuracy in predicting violence cannot negate the therapist's duty to protect the threatened victim.

The risk that unnecessary warnings may be given is a reasonable price to pay for the lives of possible victims that may be saved. We would hesitate to hold that the therapist who is aware that his patient expects to attempt to assassinate the President of the United States would not be obligated to warn the authorities because the therapist cannot predict with accuracy that his patient will commit the crime.

Defendants further argue that free and open communication is essential to psychotherapy (see *In re Lifschutz* (1970) 2 Cal.3d 415, 431–434, 85 Cal.Rptr. 829, 467 P.2d 557); that "Unless a patient . . . is assured that . . . information [revealed by him] can and will be held in utmost confidence, he will be reluctant to make the full disclosure upon which diagnosis and treatment . . . depends." (Sen.Com. on Judiciary, comment on Evid. Code, § 1014.) The giving of a warning, defendants contend, constitutes a breach of trust which entails the revelation of confidential communications.

We recognize the public interest in supporting effective treatment of mental illness and in protecting the rights of patients to privacy . . ., and the consequent public importance of safeguarding the confidential character of psychotherapeutic communication. Against this interest, however, we must weigh the public interest in safety from violent assault. The Legislature has undertaken the difficult task of balancing the countervailing concerns. In Evidence Code section 1014, it established a broad rule of privilege to protect confidential communications between patient and psychotherapist. In Evidence Code section 1024, the Legislature created a specific and limited exception to the psychotherapist–patient privilege: "There is no privilege . . . if the psychotherapist has reasonable cause to believe that the patient is in such mental or emotional condition as to be dangerous to himself or to the person or property of another and that disclosure of the communication is necessary to prevent the threatened danger."

We realize that the open and confidential character of psychotherapeutic dialogue encourages patients to express threats of violence, few of which are ever executed. Certainly a therapist should not be encouraged routinely to reveal such threats; such disclosures could seriously disrupt the patient's relationship with his therapist and with the persons threatened. To the contrary, the therapist's obligations to his patient require that he not disclose a confidence unless such disclosure is necessary to avert danger to others, and even then that he do so discreetly, and in a fashion that would preserve the privacy of his patient to the fullest extent compatible with the prevention of the threatened danger. (See Fleming and Maximov, *The Patient or His Victim: The Therapist's Dilemma* (1974) 62 Cal.L.Rev. 1025, 1065–1066).[8]

The revelation of a communication under the above circumstances is not a breach of trust or a violation of professional ethics; as stated in the Principles of Medical Ethics of the American Medical Association (1957), section 9: "A physician may not reveal the confidence entrusted to him in the course of medical attendance . . . *unless he is required to do so by law or unless it becomes necessary in order to protect the welfare of the individual or of the community.''*[9] (Emphasis added.) We conclude that the public policy favoring protection of the confidential character of patient–psychotherapist communications must yield to the extent to which disclosure is essential to avert danger to others. The protective privilege ends where the public peril begins.

Our current crowded and computerized society compels the interdependence of its members. In this risk–infested society we can hardly tolerate the further exposure to danger that would result from a concealed knowledge of the therapist that his patient was lethal. If the exercise of reasonable care to protect the threatened victim requires the therapist to warn the endangered party or those who can reasonably be expected to notify him, we see no sufficient societal interest that would protect and justify concealment. The containment of such risks lie in the public interest. For the foregoing reasons, we find that plaintiffs' complaints can be amended to state a cause of action against defendants Moore, Powelson, Gold, and Yandell and against the Regents as their employer, for breach of a duty to exercise reasonable care to protect Tatiana. . . .

NOTES

1. The criminal prosecution stemming from this crime is reported in *People* v. *Poddar* (1974) 10 Cal.3d 750, 111 Cal.Rptr. 910, 518 P.2d 342.

2. Plaintiffs' complaints alleged merely that defendant therapists failed to warn plaintiffs—Tatiana's parents—of the danger to Tatiana. The complaints do not allege that defendant therapists failed to warn Tatiana herself, or failed to warn persons other than her parents who would be likely to apprise Tatiana of the danger. Such omissions can properly be cured by amendment. As we stated in *Minsky* v. *City of Los Angeles* (1974) 11 Cal.3d 113, 118–119, 113 Cal.Rptr. 102, 107, 520 P.2d 726, 731: "It is axiomatic that if there is a reasonable possibility that a defect in the complaint can be cured by amendment or that the pleading liberally construed can state a cause of action, a demurrer should not be sustained without leave to amend." . . .

3. See *Merrill* v. *Buck* (1962) 58 Cal.2d 552, 562, 25 Cal.Rptr. 456, 375 P.2d 304; *Biakanja* v. *Irving* (1958) 49 Cal.2d 647, 650, 320 P.2d 16; *Walnut Creek Aggregates Co.* v. *Testing Engineers Inc.* (1967) 248 Cal.App. 2d 690, 695, 56 Cal.Rptr. 700.

4. This rule derives from the common law's distinction between misfeasance and nonfeasance, and its reluctance to impose liability for the latter. (See Harper and Kime, *The Duty to Control the Conduct of Another* (1934) 43 Yale L.J. 886, 887.) Morally questionable, the rule owes its survival to "the difficulties of setting any standards of unselfish service to fellow men, and of making any workable rule to cover possible situations where fifty people might fail to rescue . . ." (Prosser, Torts (4th ed. 1971) § 56, p. 341.) Because of these practical difficulties, the courts have increased the number of instances in which affirmative duties are imposed not by direct rejection of the common law rule, but by expanding the list of special relationships which will justify departure from that rule. (See Prosser, *supra,* § 56, at pp. 348–350.)

5. When a "hospital has notice or knowledge of facts from which it might reasonably be concluded that a patient would be likely to harm himself *or others* unless preclusive measures were taken, then the hospital must use reasonable care in the circumstances to prevent such harm." (*Vistica* v. *Presbyterian Hospital* (1967) 67 Cal.2d 465, 469, 62 Cal.Rptr. 577, 580, 432, P.2d 193, 196.) (Emphasis added.) A mental hospital may be liable if it negligently permits the escape or release of a dangerous patient (*Semler* v. *Psychiatric Institute of Washington, D. C.* (4th Cir. 1976) 44 U.S.L.Week 2439; *Underwood* v. *United States* (5th Cir. 1966) 356 F.2d 92; *Fair* v. *United States* (5th Cir. 1956) 234 F. 2d 288). *Greenberg* v. *Barbour* (E.D.Pa. 1971) 322 F.Supp. 745, upheld a cause of action against a hospital staff doctor whose negligent failure to admit a mental patient resulted in that patient assaulting the plaintiff.

6. *Kaiser* v. *Suburban Transp. System* (1965) 65 Wash.2d 461, 398 P.2d 14; see *Freese* v. *Lemmon* (Iowa 1973) 201 N.W.2d 576 (concurring opn. of Uhlenhopp, J.).

7. See, e. g., *People* v. *Burnick* (1975) 14 Cal.3d 306, 325–328, 121 Cal.Rptr. 488, 535 P.2d 352; Monahan, *The Prevention of Violence,* in Community Mental Health in the Criminal Justice System (Monahan ed. 1975): Diamond, *The Psychiatric Prediction of Dangerousness* (1975) 123 U.Pa.L.Rev. 439; Ennis and Litwack, *Psychiatry and the Presumption of Expertise: Flipping Coins in the Courtroom* (1974) 62 Cal.L.Rev. 693.

8. Amicus suggests that a therapist who concludes that his patient is dangerous should not warn the potential victim, but institute proceedings for involuntary detention of the patient. The giving of a warning, however, would in many cases represent a far lesser inroad upon the patient's privacy than would involuntary commitment.

9. See also Summary Report of the Task Force on Confidentiality of the Council on Professions and Associations of the American Psychiatric Association (1975).

30B. Dissenting Opinion in *Tarasoff* v. *Regents of the University of California**

Justice William P. Clark

Until today's majority opinion, both legal and medical authorities have agreed that confidentiality is essential to effectively treat the mentally ill, and that imposing a duty on doctors to disclose patient threats to potential victims would greatly impair treatment. Further, recognizing that effective treatment and society's safety are necessarily intertwined, the Legislature has already decided effective and confidential treatment is preferred over imposition of a duty to warn.

The issue whether effective treatment for the mentally ill should be sacrificed to a system of warnings is, in my opinion, properly one for the Legislature, and we are bound by its judgment. Moreover, even in the absence of clear legislative direction, we must reach the same conclusion because imposing the majority's new duty is certain to result in a net increase in violence.

The majority rejects the balance achieved by the Legislature's Lanterman–Petris–Short Act. (Welf. & Inst. Code, § 5000 et seq., hereafter the act.)[1] In addition, the majority fails to recognize that, even absent the act, overwhelming policy considerations mandate against sacrificing fundamental patient interests without gaining a corresponding increase in public benefit. . . .

Having a grave impact on future treatment of the mentally ill in our state, the majority opinion clearly transcends the interests of the immediate parties and must discuss all applicable law. It abdicates judicial responsibility to refuse to recognize the clear legislative policy reflected in the act.

Effective 1 July 1969, the Legislature created a comprehensive statutory resolution of the rights and duties of both the mentally infirm and those charged with their care and treatment. The act's purposes include ending inappropriate commitment, providing prompt care, protecting public safety, and safeguarding personal rights. (§ 5001.) The act applies to both voluntary and involuntary commitment, and to both public and private institutions; it details legal procedure for commitment; it enumerates the legal and civil rights of persons committed; and it spells out the duties, liabilities, and rights of the psychotherapist. Thus the act clearly evinces the Legislature's weighing of the countervailing concerns presently before us—when a patient has threatened a third person during psychiatric treatment.

Reflecting legislative recognition that disclosing confidences impairs effective treatment of the mentally ill, and thus is contrary to the best interests of society, the act establishes the therapist's duty to *not* disclose. Section 5328 provides in part that "[a]ll information and records obtained in the course of providing services . . . to either voluntary or involuntary recipients of services *shall* be confidential." ([Emphasis] added.)

However, recognizing that some private and public interests must override the patient's, the Legislature established several limited exceptions to confidentiality. The limited nature of these exceptions and the legislative concern that disclosure might impair treatment, thereby harming both patient and society, are shown by section 5328.1. The section provides that a therapist may disclose "to a member of the family of a patient the information that the patient is presently a patient in the facility or that the patient is seriously physically ill . . . if the professional person in charge of the facility determines that the release of such information is in the best interest of the patient." Thus, disclosing even the fact of treatment is severely limited.

As originally enacted the act contained no provision allowing the therapist to warn anyone of a patient's threat. In 1970, however, the act was amended to permit disclosure in two limited circumstances. Section 5328 was amended, in subdivision (g), to allow disclosure "[*t*]*o governmental law enforcement agencies* as needed for the protection of federal and state elective constitutional officers and their families." ([Emphasis] added.) In addition, section 5328.3 was added to provide that when "necessary for the protection of the patient or *others* due to the patient's disappearance from, without prior notice to, a designated facility and his whereabouts is unknown, notice of such disappearance *may* be made to *relatives and governmental law enforcement agencies* designated by the physician in charge of the patient or the professional person in charge of the facility or his designee."([Emphasis] added.)

Obviously neither exception to the confidentiality requirement is applicable to the instant case. . . .

From California Supreme Court, 1 July 1976. 131 *California Reporter*, pp. 34–42, West Publishing Company.

*[Some notes have been deleted without indication.—ED.]

Under the act, there can be no liability for Poddar's premature release. It is likewise clear there exists no duty to warn. Under section 5328, the therapists were under a duty *to not disclose,* and no exception to that duty is applicable here. Establishing a duty to warn on the basis of general tort principles imposes a Draconian dilemma on therapists—either violate the act thereby incurring the attendant statutory penalties, or ignore the majority's duty to warn thereby incurring potential civil liability. I am unable to assent to such. . . .

Entirely apart from the statutory provisions, the same result must be reached upon considering both general tort principles and the public policies favoring effective treatment, reduction of violence, and justified commitment.

Generally, a person owes no duty to control the conduct of another. (*Richards* v. *Stanley* (1954) 43 Cal.2d 60, 65, 271 P.2d 23; *Wright* v. *Arcade School Dist.* (1964) 230 Cal.App.2d 272, 277, 40 Cal.Rptr. 812; Rest.2d Torts (1965) § 315.) Exceptions are recognized only in limited situations where (1) a special relationship exists between the defendant and injured party, or (2) a special relationship exists between defendant and the active wrongdoer, imposing a duty on defendant to control the wrongdoer's conduct. The majority does not contend the first exception is appropriate to this case.

Policy generally determines duty. (*Dillon* v. *Legg* (1968) 68 Cal.2d 728, 734, 69 Cal.Rptr. 72, 441 P.2d 912.) Principal policy considerations include foreseeability of harm, certainty of the plaintiff's injury, proximity of the defendant's conduct to the plaintiff's injury, moral blame attributable to defendant's conduct, prevention of future harm, burden on the defendant, and consequences to the community. (*Rowland* v. *Christian* (1968) 69 Cal.2d 108, 113, 70 Cal.Rptr. 97, 443 P.2d 561.)

Overwhelming policy considerations weigh against imposing a duty on psychotherapists to warn a potential victim against harm. While offering virtually no benefit to society, such a duty will frustrate psychiatric treatment, invade fundamental patient rights and increase violence.

The importance of psychiatric treatment and its need for confidentiality have been recognized by this court. (*In re Lifschutz* (1970) 2 Cal.3d 415, 421–422, 85 Cal.Rptr. 829, 467 P.2d 557.) "It is clearly recognized that the very practice of psychiatry vitally depends upon the reputation in the community that the psychiatrist will not tell." (Slovenko, *Psychiatry and a Second Look at the Medical Privilege* (1960) 6 Wayne L.Rev. 175, 188.)

Assurance of confidentiality is important for three reasons. . . .

First, without substantial assurance of confidentiality, those requiring treatment will be deterred from seeking assistance. (See Sen. Judiciary Com. comment accompanying § 1014 of Evid.Code; Slovenko, *supra,* 6 Wayne L.Rev. 175, 187–188; Goldstein and Katz, *Psychiatrist–Patient Privilege: The GAP Proposal and the Connecticut Statute* (1962) 36 Conn.Bar J. 175, 178). It remains an unfortunate fact in our society that people seeking psychiatric guidance tend to become stigmatized. Apprehension of such stigma—apparently increased by the propensity of people considering treatment to see themselves in the worst possible light—creates a well-recognized reluctance to seek aid. (Fisher, *The Psychotherapeutic Professions and the Law of Privileged Communications* (1964) 10 Wayne L.Rev. 609, 617; Slovenko, *supra,* 6 Wayne L.Rev. 175, 188; see also Rappeport, *Psychiatrist–Patient Privilege* (1963) 23 Md.L.J. 39, 46–47.) This reluctance is alleviated by the psychiatrist's assurance of confidentiality. . . .

Second, the guarantee of confidentiality is essential in eliciting the full disclosure necessary for effective treatment. (*In re Lifschutz, supra,* 2 Cal.3d 415, 431, 85 Cal.Rptr. 829, 467 P.2d 557; *Taylor* v. *United States* (1955), 95 U.S.App.D.C. 373, 222 F.2d 398, 401; Goldstein and Katz, *supra,* 36 Conn.Bar. J. 175, 178; Heller, *Some Comments to Lawyers on the Practice of Psychiatry* (1957) 30 Temp.L.Q. 401; Guttmacher and Weihofen, *Privileged Communications Between Psychiatrist and Patient* (1952) 28 Ind.L.J. 32, 34.)[2] The psychiatric patient approaches treatment with conscious and unconscious inhibitions against revealing his innermost thoughts. "Every person, however well-motivated, has to overcome resistances to therapeutic exploration. These resistances seek support from every possible source and the possibility of disclosure would easily be employed in the service of resistance." (Goldstein and Katz, *supra,* 36 Conn.Bar J. 175, 179; see also, 118 Am.J.Psych. 734, 735.) Until a patient can trust his psychiatrist not to violate their confidential relationship, "the unconscious psychological control mechanism of repression will prevent the recall of past experiences." (Butler, *Psychotherapy and Griswold: Is Confidentiality a Privilege or a Right?* (1971) 3 Conn.L.Rev. 599, 604.) . . .

Third, even if the patient fully discloses his thoughts, assurance that the confidential relationship will not be breached is necessary to maintain his trust in his psychiatrist—the very means by which treatment is effected. "[T]he essence of much psychotherapy is the contribution of trust in the external world and ultimately in the self, modelled upon the trusting relationship established during therapy." (Dawidoff, *The Malpractice of*

Psychiatrists, 1966 Duke L.J. 696, 704.) Patients will be helped only if they can form a trusting relationship with the psychiatrist. (*Id.* at p. 704, fn. 34; Burham, *Separation Anxiety* (1965) 13 Arch.Gen. Psychiatry 346, 356; Heller, *supra,* 30 Temp.L.Q. 401, 406.) All authorities appear to agree that if the trust relationship cannot be developed because of collusive communication between the psychiatrist and others, treatment will be frustrated. (See, e.g., Slovenko (1973) Psychiatry and Law, p. 61; Cross, *Privileged Communications Between Participants in Group Psychotherapy* (1970) Law and the Social Order, 191, 199; Hollender, *The Psychiatrist and the Release of Patient Information* (1960) 116 Am.J. Psychiatry 828, 829.)

Given the importance of confidentiality to the practice of psychiatry, it becomes clear the duty to warn imposed by the majority will cripple the use and effectiveness of psychiatry. Many people, potentially violent—yet susceptible to treatment—will be deterred from seeking it; those seeking it will be inhibited from making revelations necessary to effective treatment; and, forcing the psychiatrist to violate the patient's trust will destroy the interpersonal relationship by which treatment is effected.

By imposing a duty to warn, the majority contributes to the danger to society of violence by the mentally ill and greatly increases the risk of civil commitment—the total deprivation of liberty—of those who should not be confined. The impairment of treatment and risk of improper commitment resulting from the new duty to warn will not be limited to a few patients but will extend to a large number of the mentally ill. Although under existing psychiatric procedures only a relatively few receiving treatment will ever present a risk of violence, the number making threats is huge, and it is the latter group—not just the former—whose treatment will be impaired and whose risk of commitment will be increased.

Both the legal and psychiatric communities recognize that the process of determining potential violence in a patient is far from exact, being fraught with complexity and uncertainty.[3] . . . In fact precision has not ever been attained in predicting who of those having already committed violent acts will again become violent, a task recognized to be of much simpler proportions. (Kozol, Boucher and Garofalo, [*The Diagnosis and Treatment of Dangerousness* (1972)] 18 Crime & Delinquency 371, 384.)

This predictive uncertainty means that the number of disclosures will necessarily be large. As noted above, psychiatric patients are encouraged to discuss all thoughts of violence, and they often express such thoughts. However, unlike this court, the psychiatrist does not enjoy the benefit of overwhelming hindsight in seeing which few, if any, of his patients will ultimately become violent. Now, confronted by the majority's new duty, the psychiatrist must instantaneously calculate potential violence from each patient on each visit. The difficulties researchers have encountered in accurately predicting violence will be heightened for the practicing psychiatrist dealing for brief periods in his office with heretofore nonviolent patients. And, given the decision not to warn or commit must always be made at the psychiatrist's civil peril, one can expect most doubts will be resolved in favor of the psychiatrist protecting himself.

Neither alternative open to the psychiatrist seeking to protect himself is in the public interest. The warning itself is an impairment of the psychiatrist's ability to treat, depriving many patients of adequate treatment. It is to be expected that after disclosing their threats, a significant number of patients, who would not become violent if treated according to existing practices, will engage in violent conduct as a result of unsuccessful treatment. In short, the majority's duty to warn will not only impair treatment of many who would never become violent but worse, will result in a net increase in violence.[4]

The second alternative open to the psychiatrist is to commit his patient rather than to warn. Even in the absence of threat of civil liability, the doubts of psychiatrists as to the seriousness of patient threats have led psychiatrists to overcommit to mental institutions. This overcommitment has been authoritatively documented in both legal and psychiatric studies. (Ennis and Litwack, *Psychiatry and the Presumption of Expertise: Flipping Coins in the Courtroom, supra,* 62 Cal.L.Rev. 693, 711 et seq.; Fleming and Maximov, *The Patient or His Victim: The Therapist's Dilemma,* 62 Cal.L.Rev. 1025, 1044–1046; Am. Psychiatric Assn. Task Force Rep. 8 (July 1974) Clinical Aspects of the Violent Individual, pp. 23–24; see Livermore, Malmquist and Meehl, *On the Justifications for Civil Commitment,* 117 U.Pa.L.Rev. 75, 84.) This practice is so prevalent that it has been estimated that "as many as twenty harmless persons are incarcerated for every one who will commit a violent act." (Steadman and Cocozza, *Stimulus/Response: We Can't Predict Who is Dangerous* (Jan. 1975) 8 Psych. Today 32, 35.)

Given the incentive to commit created by the majority's duty, this already serious situation will be worsened, contrary to Chief Justice Wright's admonition "that liberty is no less precious because forfeited in a civil proceeding than when taken as a consequence of a criminal conviction." (*In re W.* (1971) 5 Cal.3d 296, 307, 96 Cal.Rptr. 1, 9, 486 P.2d 1201, 1209.)

NOTES

1. All statutory references, unless otherwise stated, are to the Welfare and Institutions Code.

2. One survey indicated that five of every seven people interviewed said they would be less likely to make full disclosure to a psychiatrist in the absence of assurance of confidentiality. (See, Comment, *Functional Overlap Between the Lawyer and Other Professionals: Its Implications for the Doctrine of Privileged Communications* (1962) 71 Yale L.J. 1226, 1255.)

3. A shocking illustration of psychotherapists' inability to predict dangerousness . . . is cited and discussed in Ennis, Prisoners of Psychiatry: Mental Patients, Psychiatrists, and the Law (1972): "In a well-known study, psychiatrists predicted that 989 persons were so dangerous that they could not be kept even in civil mental hospitals, but would have to be kept in maximum security hospitals run by the Department of Corrections. Then, because of a United States Supreme Court decision, those persons were transferred to civil hospitals. After a year, the Department of Mental Hygiene reported that one-fifth of them had been discharged to the community, and over half had agreed to remain as voluntary patients. During the year, only 7 of the 989 committed or threatened any act that was sufficiently dangerous to require retransfer to the maximum security hospital. Seven correct predictions out of almost a thousand is not a very impressive record. [¶] Other studies, and there are many, have reached the same conclusion: psychiatrists simply cannot predict dangerous behavior." (*Id.* at p. 227. Equally illustrative studies are collected in Rosenhan, *On Being Sane in Insane Places* [1973] 13 Santa Clara Law. 379, 384; Ennis and Litwack, *Psychiatry and the Presumption of Expertise: Flipping Coins in the Courtroom* [1974] 62 Cal.L.Rev. 693, 750–751.)

4. The majority concedes that psychotherapeutic dialogue often results in the patient expressing threats of violence that are rarely executed. (*Ante,* . . . p. 27 of 131 Cal.Rptr., p. 347 of 551 P.2d). The practical problem, of course, lies in ascertaining which threats from which patients will be carried out. As to this problem, the majority is silent. . . .

Thus, in effect, the majority informs the therapists that they must accurately predict dangerousness—a task recognized as extremely difficult—or face crushing civil liability. The majority's reliance on the traditional standard of care for professionals that "therapist need only exercise 'that reasonable degree of skill, knowledge, and care ordinarily possessed and exercised by members of [that professional specialty] under similar circumstances' " *(ante,* p. 25 of 131 Cal.Rptr., p. 345 of 551 P.2d) is seriously misplaced. This standard of care assumes that, to a large extent, the subject matter of the specialty is ascertainable. One clearly ascertainable element in the psychiatric field is that the therapist cannot accurately predict dangerousness, which, in turn, means that the standard is inappropriate for lack of a relevant criterion by which to judge the therapist's decision. The inappropriateness of the standard the majority would have us use is made patent when consideration is given to studies, by several eminent authorities, indicating that "[t]he chances of a second psychiatrist agreeing with the diagnosis of a first psychiatrist 'are barely better than 50–50; or stated differently, there is about as much chance that a different expert would come to some different conclusion as there is that the other would agree.' " (Ennis and Litwack, *Psychiatry and the Presumption of Expertise: Flipping Coins in the Courtroom, supra,* 62 Cal.L.Rev. 693, 701, quoting, Ziskin, Coping with Psychiatric and Psychological Testimony, 126.) The majority's attempt to apply a normative scheme to a profession which must be concerned with problems that balk at standardization is clearly erroneous.

In any event, an ascertainable standard would not serve to limit psychiatrist disclosure of threats with the resulting impairment of treatment. However compassionate, the psychiatrist hearing the threat remains faced with potential crushing civil liability for a mistaken evaluation of his patient and will be forced to resolve even the slightest doubt in favor of disclosure or commitment.

31. What's an FBI Poster Doing in a Nice Journal Like That?

Willard Gaylin

The pages of the *Archives of Dermatology,* with their full-color pictures of exotic skin diseases, are likely to strike the uninformed eye as bizarre and somewhat repellent. But even the best informed must have been startled by page 308 of the February 1972 issue. There, occupying almost the entire page, was an FBI wanted poster!

Appearing under the department heading, "News and Notes," the item looked identical to those appearing in police stations and post offices. But both of those are government agencies, and the *Archives* is an official publication of the American Medical Association. The graffiti that passes unnoticed in a subway station would outrage us if written on the wall of a church.

It seems ironic that the AMA, which has consistently opposed government intrusion into medical matters even where a legitimate public interest has been proved, should now have volunteered the services of organized medicine into a government function—and in an area so alien from the traditional medical mission as tracking down criminals.

From *Hastings Center Report* 2:2 (April 1972): 1–3.

Of course the thought occurs that it might not have been voluntary. The line between freedom and coercion is not so clearly drawn when the "petitioner" has the power of the Department of Justice. This thought, however, is only the first in the series of ethical and value questions inevitably raised by this eccentric utilization of a medical journal.

The notice, which also appeared in the *Archives of Internal Medicine,* described a 30-year-old woman indicted by a grand jury for "conspiring with another individual" in an act involving the interstate transportation of explosives. The alleged conspiracy violation occurred early in 1970. Along with the usual pictures in various poses, physical description, and biographical material, appeared the statement that she was known to be afflicted with an "acute and recurrent" skin condition. It further elaborates: "The recurrent aspect of this condition could necessitate treatment by a dermatologist." The reason for the FBI's wanting it in the *Archives of Dermatology* now becomes apparent. The reasons for the AMA's willingness to publish it are less immediately evident.

Before even the ethical questions, what is the legal responsibility of the physician reading this? Consultation with a professor of criminal law revealed that there were indeed open questions about liability and responsibility. If he had doubts—what of the average dermatologist?

The implications to the wanted person—who may or may not be a criminal—will also transcend ethical nicety. In this instance a fatal disease is not present—although it well might be in future cases, and it has been indicated that were the condition heart disease, diabetes, glaucoma, acute depression—the wanted notices would be referred to the appropriate journal. They would make it difficult, if not impossible, to get the necessary treatment.

The major question, however, seems to be whether medicine should be encouraged, or even allowed, to be an extension of the police functions of the society. There is no question that if this is seen as a legitimate function of medicine, it would represent a powerful and immense new ally for the police. In the files of physicians across the country are massive case records which would make an invaluable data bank (ready for computerization) of inestimable service in any police tracking function: the drugs one chronically uses, a tendency toward alcoholism, a hidden homosexual activity, proclivity for flirtations or other sexual idiosyncrasies, prescription glasses, specific allergies, dietary requirements, etc.

There is no question that all of this information would facilitate the police functions of the state. But is that the function of medicine? And in facilitating this other function *what would it do to the primary concern of medicine, which is relief of suffering, the treatment of illness, and the saving of life?* What happens to the tradition of confidentiality—so zealously protected over hundreds of years precisely because it has been seen as fundamental to the effective function of medicine? Such use of the profession by the police would represent the final destruction of the privacy, intimacy, and trust of a therapeutic relationship already seriously eroded.

It is conceivable that *in extremis* an institution must abandon its traditional role. The organized church has often supported the mass killing of war when it seemed essential for the survival of the state.

How are we to decide, however, *when* to violate our usual primary devotion and allegiance to the private person and his well-being, for the public purpose? How are we physicians to differentiate quantitatively among the various crimes and conditions of criminality in which we have no training? Are we prepared to assay indictment versus conviction, versus material witness, versus "wanted for questioning"? What are the relevant weights to be placed on conspiracy to blow up a heating system of the Pentagon versus armed robbery of a bank, versus possession of marijuana, versus massive embezzlement? How do we weigh these public dangers against the health or survival of a patient? Ought we be making these decisions—or should they be left to public decision making via the normal legislative process which, for example, now dictates that gunshot wounds demand violation of confidentiality, but by implication of exclusion allows a host of other material the protection of confidentiality?

Which raises the question of how such significant decisions should be made. How, for example, are the power and responsibility which influence the whole balance of medicine and government distributed by a major organization such as the American Medical Association?

The Association is formed of elected delegates. These delegates, in turn, as an organization, elect a board. There is an executive secretary who administers the organization. There is a Judicial Council with its own legal counsel that acts as an ethical watchdog. At what area of this complex apparatus was the decision discussed, debated, considered, and finally decided? A call to the editor of the *Archives of Dermatology* indicated that he had authority and responsibility only over the scientific articles and no responsibility for this particular poster. A call to the director, Division of Scientific Publications of the American Medical Association, confirmed that the editors of the specialty journal controlled only that localized aspect. The chairman of the Judicial Council said the matter had never been brought to the council, and, indeed, he was unaware of the publication of the posters when first consulted. He then suggested consulting the legal counsel of his committee who has had a long history of dealing with ethical issues and publication. *He* was unaware of the appearance of this FBI poster in the two publications until he was advised of the fact and, further, he could not recall its ever having been done before. He volunteered that when consulted in the past by various state journals, he had cautioned great prudence in publishing such material. Further calls to a variety of other sources in the American Medical Association (who must remain anonymous) indicate that it was "done somewhat experimentally" and spoke vaguely of "a great deal of pressure," having been exerted.

It was finally established that a request had been made in writing by the FBI to the chief of the Division of Scientific Publication of the AMA, and that he made the decision, seeing no need to consult the Judicial Council, the representatives of the board of the American Medical Association, or the executive secretary of the American Medical Association and his full-time professional staff. He indicated that in his mind it was an "editorial decision" of no great moment and implied that it was a part of an ongoing tradition that preceded his assumption of office three years ago. But Dr. John Talbott, who formerly held the post, said that, to his memory, never under his tenure was an FBI poster replicated in either the *Journal of the American Medical Association* or any of its specialty journals. (This seems indeed true, although investigation shows that three brief excerpts from "wanted" notices did appear in JAMA early in Dr. Talbott's editorship—1961 and 1962. None, apparently, has appeared in the past ten years.)

Equally interesting was the gradual shift of the attitude of the staff of the association when inquiries continued to indicate outside consternation. When they were first notified of the appearance of these pages, all seemed genuinely surprised, felt that the implications were of some moment, and suggested that, in a precedent-breaking move such as this, it seemed unlikely that one man, prudent though he be, would have initiated the action without extensive consultation.

But by the time this initial investigation was concluded, a new official profile was emerging, minimizing the innovation, suggesting it was a routine editorial-type decision, and denying even the presence of a problem. The man who made the decision stated that he would have no hesitation printing more such posters in the future, without advice or consultation, in whatever medical journals the AMA published, particularly when there was a specific medical potential for assisting the FBI, because "*no questions of medical ethics are involved.*"

The assumption that there are "no ethical issues involved" seems at this time to be the collective stance of the AMA. A formal statement read over the phone by the secretary of the AMA Judicial Council also starts with the statement that no issue of ethics is here involved. This may represent the most distressing aspect of this entire episode. Whether the publication of such material by an official medical journal is "ethical" or "unethical" may be debatable (and should be debated). That major ethical issues are raised, however, is indisputable. It involves such basic traditional questions as confidentiality and trust, private needs versus public rights, professional values versus personal ethics, the special role of the healer and saver of life, and the power of the state.

For an individual to want to avoid recognition of error is understandable. For a group to underestimate the implications of any ethical question is certainly no crime. If, however, an entire organization such as the AMA proves so insensitive to questions of ethics as to deny their existence here—it could be disastrous.

32. Confidentiality in the Adversary System

Alan Donagan

. . . . .

There can be no doubt that the adversary system imposes upon lawyers a strong duty of confidentiality with respect to their clients' affairs. According to Canon 4 of the American Bar Association's Code of Professional Responsibility (1970), "*A lawyer should preserve the confidences and secrets of a client.*"[1] And in the first of the "ethical considerations" in which this canon is explained, it adds:

> A client must feel free to discuss whatever he wishes with a lawyer and a lawyer must be equally free to obtain

From *The Good Lawyer: Lawyers' Roles and Lawyers' Ethics*, edited by David Luban (Totowa, NJ: Rowman and Allanheld, 1984), pp. 123–49.

information beyond that volunteered by his client. A lawyer should be fully informed of all the facts of the matter he is handling in order for his client to obtain the full advantage of our legal system. . . . The observance of the ethical obligation of a lawyer to hold inviolate the confidences and secrets of his client not only facilitates the full development of facts essential to proper representation of the client but also encourages laymen to seek early legal assistance.[2]

To anybody who accepts the adversary system because of the standard justification, this must seem loose in the extreme. The right of clients, by virtue of their human dignity, to get a hearing for their views both about their rightful due and about the facts of their case has been replaced by something quite different, the right of clients, *irrespective of anything they can possibly claim as their rightful due, and of what they confess in confidence to their lawyer the facts are,* "to obtain full advantage of our legal system." If the American Bar Association seriously asserts such a right as this, it has an obligation to make a public case for it. The standard justification of the adversary system is not such a case, nor is anything else I have encountered in the voluminous literature on the subject.

In answering general questions it is well to keep particular examples in mind; an example it is well to keep in mind in thinking about this general question has already given rise to a ruling by the New York Bar Association's Committee on Professional Ethics. It has become generally known as "the Lake Pleasant [bodies] case."[3] In presenting the pertinent facts of it, I substitute letters of the alphabet for the names of those who took part.

In the summer of 1973, *C* stood charged in ______ County with the crime of murder. The defendant was assigned two attorneys, *A* and *B*. A defense of insanity had been interposed by counsel for *C*. During the course of the discussions between *C* and his two counsel, three other murders were admitted by *C*. . . . On or about September 1973, *B* conducted his own investigation based upon what his client had told him and with the assistance of a friend the body of *D* was found. . . . *B* personally inspected the body and was satisfied, presumably, that this was the body of *D* that his client had told him that he murdered.

This discovery was not disclosed to the authorities, but became public during the trial of *C* in June of 1974, when to . . . establish the defense of insanity, these three other murders were brought before the jury by the defense. . . . Public indignation reached the fever pitch. . . . *A* was No Billed by the Grand Jury, but [an indictment] was returned as against *B*, accusing him of having violated § 4200 (1) of the Public Health Law, which, in essence, requires that a decent burial be accorded the dead, and § 4143 of the Public Health Law, which, in essence, requires anyone knowing of the death of a person without medical attendance, to report the same to the proper authorities. Defense counsel move[d] for dismissal of the Indictment on the grounds that a confidential, privileged communication existed between him and *C*.[4]

In a subsequent colloquy on the case, *B* divulged the following further information:

As we spoke to *C*, we knew of the particular murder he was charged with, but he was reluctant, very reluctant, to talk about the others in which *A* had indicated he was possibly involved. There were two known murders, because those bodies had been found. . . . [W]ith the suspicion we had of other murders, we knew that the only defense that we could have with this man was insanity. . . . I finally convinced *C* that the more murders we could reveal if necessary would show the jury that in fact he was insane. We gained his confidence, and after drawing a map we went up to the mountains . . . we finally found the body. . . . After taking some pictures, we went back to the car and *A* said, "What shall we do?" My answer was to go back and question *C* now on the second body. . . . There was never any question in our minds about keeping the secret. It was assumed from our training in law school.[5]

From tragedy to farce. The charges against *B* were dismissed in the county court, the judge virtually transcribing his judgment from an Amicus Curiae Memorandum of Law submitted by the National Association of Criminal Defense Lawyers.[6] The judge declared that

[t]here must always be a conflict between . . . obstruction of . . . justice and the preservation of the right against self-incrimination which permeates the mind of the attorney as the alter ego of his client. But that is not the situation before this court. We have the Fifth Amendment right, derived from the Constitution, on the one hand, as against the trivia of a pseudocriminal statute on the other, which has seldom been brought into play.[7]

Yet, if the court's finding was narrowly technical, the judge's parting compliments to *B* were not: "It is the decision of this Court that *B* conducted himself as an officer of the Court with all the zeal at his command to protect the constitutional rights of his client."[8] The Appellate Division's judgment, upholding the trial judge, was more circumspect:

In view of the fact that the claim of absolute privilege is not all-encompassing . . . we believe that an attorney must protect his client's interests, but also must observe basic human standards of decency.

We write to emphasize our serious concern regarding the consequences which emanate from a claim of an absolute attorney-client privilege. Because the only question . . . on this appeal was a legal one with respect to the sufficiency of the indictments, we limit our determination to that issue and do not reach the ethical questions underlying the case.[9]

The courts having washed their hands, the New York State Bar Association's Committee on Professional Ethics applauded their inaction as morally right:

> A lawyer should not reveal a client's confidences or secrets learned during the course of representation, even though they include the revelation by the client of his prior commission of serious undiscovered crimes.[10]

And finally, as its chairman, Robert J. Kutak, has proudly announced, in May 1981 the American Bar Association's Commission on the Evaluation of Professional Standards in the final draft of its proposed Model Rules went further than any representative body of lawyers until then in strengthening the principle of confidentiality "by expanding [it] to encompass all information relating to representation, and by narrowing the exceptions for disclosure."[11] If the proposed Model Rules become law by judicial legislation, honest lawyers will be forbidden on pain of such sanctions as disbarment to disclose any information whatever acquired from a client about completed crimes or frauds, except where their services were used in committing them, or any about crimes or frauds in progress or contemplation when their consequences are "insubstantial."

In this way, almost unnoticeably, the principle of confidentiality, already distorted to protect unjust lawyers in wronging their neighbors to serve unjust clients, will be transformed into an instrument for punishing just lawyers who refuse to commit such wrongs. If, as is probable, the public is helpless, protest is futile. Nevertheless, there is an intellectual duty to expose the shoddiness of the reasons offered not only for the final transformation but also for the original distortion.

Nobody denies that apart from special professional duties of confidentiality, information may be acquired by a member of the community of such a nature that it is his or her duty to communicate it either to some public authority or to other private individuals. Such information is of at least two kinds. The first is information for want of which public authorities are likely, by commission or omission, to act contrary to the common good: for example, information about crimes in progress or contemplation, or about matters the law requires to be publicly investigated, such as deaths or some personal injuries, or the whereabouts of illegal weapons, drugs, or property apparently lost or stolen. The second is information the withholding of which would wrong a private individual: for example, information about the whereabouts of the individual's lost or stolen property, and, more important still, about harm to members of his or her family or friends, whether suffered or in prospect. The duty to disclose such information is in some cases a legal one and in others not. In most jurisdictions, for example, it is not a legal duty to inform the public authorities that, while jogging in the park, you encountered a human body with its throat cut. Presumably it has not been made a legal duty because your duty as a human being and citizen—your moral duty—is evident, and the possibility that anybody with pretensions to moral decency would fail to discharge it has been thought negligible.

Nor is it seriously asserted that ordinary assurances of confidentiality could justify failure to communicate such information. Since it is wrong to promise to keep secret what you have no right to keep secret, it is wrong to give anyone expressly unlimited assurances of confidentiality and ordinary assurances are given with a tacit understanding as to their limits. Suppose that you ask one neighbor whether he knows where another is and he replies, "I'll tell you, if you promise to keep it secret." Were you to promise and were he then to tell you that the neighbor about whom you inquired was lying dead in her basement, would it be reasonable to consider that your promise of confidentiality obliged you to keep that information secret? There is a tacit understanding when such confidences are made that the information you are to be given is not such that it would be your duty to divulge it. And even if you had wrongly given an unlimited assurance, it would not bind you . . . promises to do wrong are invalid.

What reasons, then, can be given for maintaining that the professional relation of attorney to client justifies an attorney in keeping secrets confided by the client, even though no ordinary duty of confidentiality could justify it? Prima facie, the standard justification for the adversary system yields none. A client's dignity is violated if he or she is unable to be professionally represented in putting forward his or her view of the facts of any case to which he or she is a party and of its rights and wrongs. In representing a client, an attorney has a strict duty to keep secret any information the client may reveal about his or her doings, provided the client furnishes an innocent interpretation of them that can be accepted as possibly true. But there is no apparent reason why that should oblige an attorney to withhold information it would otherwise be one's moral duty to disclose. Nothing it might be one's duty as a citizen or as a human being to disclose would be about doings of a client that permit an innocent interpretation.

In the mountain of fervid special pleading on behalf of extending the lawyer's professional duty of confidentiality beyond what the standard justification of the adversary system plainly allows, I have found only two arguments of any weight. The first is set out in the Amicus Curiae brief of the

National Association of Criminal Defense Lawyers in the Lake Pleasant case:

> The Attorney is the alter ego of the client. . . . The client's Fifth Amendment rights cannot be violated by his attorney. . . . Because the discovery of the body of *D* would have presented *"a significant link in the chain of evidence tending to establish his guilt,"* *C* was constitutionally exempt from any statutory requirement to disclose the location of the body. And *B*, as *C*'s attorney, was not only equally exempt, but under a positive stricture precluding such disclosure. *C*, although constitutionally privileged . . . , was free to make such a revelation. . . . *B* was affirmatively required to withhold disclosure.[12]

In this argument, the right not to incriminate oneself is correctly taken to be a legal one. I do not question that a just and decent society must accord that legal right to all human beings, although I am acquainted with no theory of why it must that satisfies me.[13] But a legal right, even one that society is morally obliged to grant, is not necessarily a moral right. A murderer has no moral right whatever to escape incrimination by concealing the victim's body, although it would be wrong to compel him or her to reveal where it is. To the extreme wickedness of the original crime there has been added the wickedness of obstructing justice, of calculated cruelty to the victim's family and friends, and of desecrating a human body. That the legal right against self-incrimination should entitle the murderer to enlist professional associates in that obstruction, cruelty, and desecration is monstrous as moral theory. A morally decent attorney can be the client's alter ego only in actions that he or she believes the client may possibly have a moral right to do. That there are good moral reasons why a client should not be coerced into refraining from a wrong does not exculpate his attorney in also committing that wrong.

That the argument from an extended right against self-incrimination is confused and sophistical is shown by its acknowledged exceptions. Not even the Commission on the Evaluation of Professional Standards has had the effrontery to maintain that it is a lawyer's duty to withhold information about continuing crimes in which a client is implicated. Yet no such exception could be made if it were a true principle that a lawyer as the client's alter ego has a duty to withhold all incriminating information that the client has a legal right to withhold. Nor does it appear that the false principle can be amended in a morally coherent way to yield the exceptions the commission desires. Obviously a consequentialist solution will not do. More harm is sometimes caused by withholding information about past crimes than about continuing ones: for example, the parents of the murdered girl in the Lake Pleasant case may be presumed to have suffered more than would the multimillionaire victim of a continuing scheme for embezzling a few thousand dollars. And if a nonconsequentialist solution has been proposed, I do not know of it.

The second of the two serious arguments for extending lawyers' professional duty of confidentiality has been most clearly expressed by Monroe H. Freedman. It can be reduced to three steps:

1. The dignity of human individuals is not respected if lawyers, in defending their clients, cannot ascertain from them all they know about the facts of their cases.[14]
2. "The client can not be expected to reveal to the lawyer all information that is potentially relevant, including that which may well be incriminating, unless the client can be assured that the lawyer will maintain all such information in the strictest confidence."[15]
3. Therefore, the dignity of human individuals is not respected if they are denied the services of lawyers who will maintain even incriminating information in the strictest confidence.

The conclusion of this argument unquestionably follows from its premises. But are those premises, namely 1 and 2, true?

As they stand, neither is plausible, and I doubt whether Freedman himself would maintain either in its full generality. Consider 1: no intelligent client will disclose to his or her lawyer information revealing complicity in a continuing major crime, even though that information may ensure an acquittal on a lesser charge. However, it would be absurd to contend that the client's dignity is thereby violated. It is true that a client is disadvantaged if deterred from confiding to the lawyer all that he or she knows about the case; it is also true that some things that may deter the client would violate his or her dignity. But it does not follow that any client's dignity would be violated if he or she were deterred from confiding information to the lawyer by the normal moral limitations on the duty of confidentiality.

Yet would it not be in some cases? This question takes us to premise 2 and to a class of examples by which Freedman defends it. Clients who are in fact completely innocent may withhold information from their lawyers because, owing to misunderstandings of the law, they mistakenly believe it to establish that they are guilty of a crime. For example, a battered wife who has shot her brutal husband in self-defense may deny that she has shot him at all because, not knowing that killing in self-defense is lawful, she falsely believes herself guilty of murder. In such cases, Freedman contends,

> the lawyer must seek the truth from the client, not shun it. That means that [he] will have to dig and pry and cajole, and, even then, [he] will never be successful without convincing the client that full disclosure to the lawyer will never result in prejudice to the client by any word or action of the attorney.[16]

This seems reckless. It need not be denied that sometimes even the most adroit lawyer may be unable to persuade a timid and ignorant innocent to give information without promising strict confidentiality with respect to past crimes; but is there the slightest reason to suppose that this will be generally the case? It seems more probable that a lawyer of ordinary competence would be able to discern the nature of the fears that might prompt a client to lie or to conceal the truth, and that it would be enough to explain what the law in fact is. If that is so, premise 2 is not true as it stands and cannot bear the burden Freedman's argument places on it.

In sum, given the limited duty of professional confidentiality that can indisputably be derived from the standard justification of the adversary system, there is no reason to believe that, with reasonably competent lawyers, innocent clients will be deterred from confiding in them unless they are unreasonably timid and suspicious or unless they have reasons, independent of their beliefs about the legal system, for preferring to suffer a miscarriage of justice rather than to allow certain things they know to be used in their defense. In that case, no reason has been given why the respect owed to the dignity of clients who are in fact innocent requires that the duty of professional confidentiality be extended beyond any ordinary, morally bounded duty. *A fortiori,* no reason has been offered why it is required by the respect owed to the dignity of clients who are in fact guilty.

THE DUTY TO EXPOSE A CLIENT'S PERJURY

Those who maintain that it is a lawyer's professional duty to elicit from clients, by faithful promises of strict confidentiality, everything they know pertaining to their cases must also assert that the lawyer is restrained by those promises from exposing them should they then choose to offer perjured evidence. To others, this consequence is a *reductio ad absurdum.* The considerations that generate this conflict have been authoritatively expressed by Freedman as a "trilemma."[17] There are persuasive reasons for each of the following principles:

1. In criminal trials, counsel for the defense must ascertain all relevant facts known to the accused, because the lawyer cannot effectively defend the client if he or she is ignorant of anything that may affect the course of the trial.
2. Counsel must hold in strict confidence disclosures made by the client, because otherwise the client would not feel free to confide fully, and counsel would then be unable to ascertain all relevant facts.
3. The lawyer is an officer of the court, and his or her conduct before the court should be candid.

"As soon as one begins to think about these responsibilities," Freedman justly observes, "it becomes apparent that the conscientious attorney is faced with what we may call a trilemma—that is, the lawyer is required to know everything, to keep it in confidence, and to reveal it to the court."[18]

It is evident that such a conflict of obligations can be resolved only by weakening one or more of the principles that generate it, and which is to be weakened can be determined only by recourse to the foundations of the adversary system itself. Accordingly, Freedman reasons as follows. As an officer of the court, the task of counsel for the defense is to defend the client competently and zealously. Principle 1 lays down a fundamental condition for a competent defense, that the lawyer ascertain all relevant facts; principle 2 states a necessary condition for ascertaining them, that the lawyer reliably assure the client that all disclosures will be held in strict confidence. It follows that the lawyer's function as an officer of the court restricts an obligation of candor. Hence the principle that must be weakened is 3: the candor that counsel for the defense owes to the court must not be interpreted as requiring any breach of assurances to the client of confidentiality.

The defect of this reasoning has already been identified in analyzing Freedman's views about the duty of confidentiality. The assumption that lawyers cannot be expected to ascertain all the pertinent facts of a case unless they can assure their clients of unlimited confidentiality, although a dogma cherished by the National Association of Criminal Defense Lawyers, is unfounded with respect to clients who are in fact innocent. As for clients who are in fact guilty, while they have a legal right not to incriminate themselves, they have no moral right to enlist informed professional help in concealing their guilt. It is not a defect in the adversary system, properly understood, that it allows the guilty to plead innocence only under the disadvantage that their lawyers cannot be fully informed about the pertinent facts.

Once principles 1 and 2 have been independently weakened, there is no need to weaken 3. It is to the credit of the Canadian Bar Association that it has perceived this. Its Code of Professional Conduct requires a lawyer to warn clients that if, having disclosed incriminating information (for which, of course, they furnish innocent explanations), they proceed to deny it at trial, the lawyer cannot argue their untrue testimony to the jury and must explain to the court why he or she cannot.[19] In doing so, it has correctly deduced what the requirements of the adversary system, as founded on the fundamental principle of respect for human dignity, in fact are.

To this Freedman objects that "the inevitable result of the position taken by the Canadian Bar Association would be to caution the client not to be completely candid with the attorney. That, of course, returns us to resolving the trilemma by maintaining confidentiality and candor, but sacrificing complete knowledge."[20] Yes, but only in the case of guilty clients or of unreasonably timid ones, and that, I have argued, does not infringe the principle on which the adversary system rests. Freedman's remark that this solution "is denounced by the [ABA] Standards as 'unscrupulous,' 'most egregious,' and as 'professional impropriety,' "[21] savors of leg-pulling. The Canadian Bar Association lays it down that Canadian lawyers must warn clients that the information they vouchsafe cannot be kept confidential if it shows that evidence subsequently presented on their behalf is perjured. What the American Bar Association denounces is what moral theologians call "affected ignorance";[22] the description of it in the ABA Standards is: "the tactic . . . of advising the client at the outset not to admit anything to the lawyer which might handicap the lawyer's freedom in calling witnesses or in otherwise making a defense."[23] An intelligent scoundrelly client may well adopt the tactic on hearing a Canadian lawyer's warning, but the warning is not advice to adopt it. Freedman's observations about the perils of constructing a defense in ignorance of pertinent facts show that he or she would have cause to be apprehensive in doing so.

NOTES

1. The full text of the code is reprinted in Monroe H. Freedman, *Lawyers' Ethics in an Adversary System* (Indianapolis, IN: Bobbs-Merill, 1975), pp. 132–238. Canon 4 may be found at p. 178.

2. Ibid., p. 4. Quoting *American Bar Association Standards Relating to the Defense Function* (1971), pp. 145–46.

3. All information about this case is derived from Patrick A. Keenan, Stuart C. Goldberg, and G. Griffith Dick, eds., *Teaching Professional Responsibility: Materials and Proceedings from the National Conference* (Detroit: University of Detroit School of Law, 1979), pp. 237–325.

4. Keenan et al., *Teaching Professional Responsibility,* p. 277, quoting from Judge Ormand N. Gale in 83 Misc. 2d 186, 372 N.Y.S. 2d 798.

5. Ibid., pp. 316–18.

6. Ibid., pp. 279–81; cf. 265–75.

7. Ibid., p. 281.

8. Ibid.

9. Ibid., p. 285 (from a report in *New York Law Journal,* March 7, 1978).

10. Ibid., p. 282 (from N.Y. Appellate Division, Fourth Department, decisions filed December 17, 1975).

11. Robert J. Kutak, "The Adversary System and the Practice of Law," in David Luban, ed., *The Good Lawyer: Lawyers' Roles and Lawyers' Ethics* (Totowa, NJ: Rowman and Allanheld, 1984), pp. 172–187. That the discussion draft of the proposed Model Rules which the commission published in January 1980 was arguably in certain respects *weaker* than the present code had already been remarked by David Luban, "Professional Ethics: A New Code for Lawyers," *Hastings Center Report* 10:3 (1980), p. 14. [For the Model Rules, see appendix 1, sample code 1, *EIPL.*—ED.]

12. Keenan et al., *Teaching Professional Responsibility,* pp. 267–68.

13. David Luban, in "Corporate Counsel and Confidentiality," in *Ethics and the Legal Profession,* ed. by [Michael Davis and] Frederick A. Elliston (Buffalo, NY: Prometheus, 1986), perceives the difficulty of the problem and opens a promising line for investigation.

14. Freedman, *Lawyers' Ethics in an Adversary System,* p. 5.

15. Ibid.

16. Ibid., p. 30.

17. Ibid., pp. 27–42, esp. pp. 27–28. [See chap. 3, sel. 5, *EIPL.*—ED.]

18. Ibid., p. 28.

19. Ibid., p. 38; referring to *Canadian Bar Association, Code of Professional Conduct,* chap. 8, sect. 9, at 59–60, 62–64. Special Committee on Legal Ethics, Preliminary Report, June 1973.

20. Ibid.

21. Ibid.

22. Cf. St. Thomas Aquinas. *Summa Theologiae,* I–II, 6, 8.

23. *ABA Standards Relating to the Defense Function,* Commentary b to Sec. 3.2, at 205; quoted in Freedman, *Lawyers' Ethics in an Adversary System,* p. 36 note.

QUESTIONS FOR STUDY AND DISCUSSION

1. Using this chapter's readings as resources, offer your own articulation of the concept of privacy. What are the benefits to individuals and to the wider society of protecting privacy as you define it?

2. One often sees newspaper stories about the spouses of politicians entering treatment centers for chemical dependency. Do these stories violate the privacy of these people? If not, why not? If so, are these morally justifiable invasions of privacy? If not, why not? If so, why so?

3. Explain the distinction between tacit consent and hypothetical consent (see the introduction to this chapter) and offer examples of each to illustrate the distinction. What are the dangers of using the method of hypothetical consent to decide ethical questions (e.g., whether to sustain an unconscious person on life supports, when invasions of privacy are justified, etc.)? Do these dangers force the conclusion that the method of hypothetical consent should never be used? Explain.

4. Do employers have a moral right to use surprise urine tests on (all, some of) their employees to check for drug use? Defend your answer; anticipate and respond to the strongest objection that might be raised against your view.

5. Terry Pinkard points out that social science researchers sometimes get information about groups (e.g., religious groups) by infiltration. When, if ever, is it morally permissible for a researcher to infiltrate a group in order to gain information about that group? Justify your answer; anticipate and respond to the strongest potential objection to your view.

6. Using this chapter's readings as resources, explain as fully as you are able the value of confidentiality in general and in the professional/client relationship in particular.

7. Does the state have a right to demand breaches of confidentiality by members of the clergy? If not, why not? If so, under what conditions?

8. Explain in detail Justice Clark's objections to the majority view in *Tarasoff*. Are these objections strong enough to convince you that psychological counselors should not be held liable for assaults by their clients? Explain your answer in detail.

9. What are the reasons for a strong confidentiality rule in legal practice? In your considered judgment, does an attorney ever have a moral right or a moral duty to breach client confidentiality? If not, why not? If so, under what conditions?

10. Suppose a student tells a high school counselor that she is pregnant and asks for information on how to get an abortion. Suppose the student makes it clear that she does not want her parents to know. Would it be morally permissible for the counselor to tell the student's parents? Does the counselor have a moral obligation to tell the student's parents. Explain your answers in detail.

11. Do journalists have a strict moral duty to keep their sources confidential? Are there any conditions under which a journalist should reveal the name of a source even though that source has been promised confidentiality? If not, why not? If so, what are these conditions?

12. Some health care providers in hospital settings have argued that they should be informed if any patient with whom they might have to interact has tested positive for exposure to the AIDS virus. Others have argued that confidentiality on this matter should be maintained as strictly as is reasonably possible, and that providers should take the same precautions with all patients to protect themselves from exposure to the virus. Offer your own detailed defense of one of these positions.

CASE: TEAROOM TRADE

Laud Humphreys did a pioneering study of impersonal homosexual activity, carried out as dissertation research from 1965 to 1968. . . . Humphreys' topic was the sexual behavior and social position of men who frequent public rest rooms in search of quick and anonymous sexual encounters. . . . His results

---

Case, with some variation, as articulated by Tom L. Beauchamp, Ruth R. Faden, R. Jay Wallace, Jr., and LeRoy Walters (eds.), *Ethical Issues in Social Science Research* (Baltimore, MD: Johns Hopkins University Press, 1982), pp. 11–12.

suggested that, far from being the deviant and potentially dangerous social types commonly imagined, his subjects led conventional and routine public lives. Most turned out to be married (if not always happily) with children, and only fourteen percent were exclusively homosexual.

Since homosexual activity in public facilities tends not to take place in the presence of external observers, Humphreys found it necessary to conceal his identity as a social researcher. He did so by playing the part of a "watchqueen," an established role which requires that one look out for intruders while men are engaged in acts of fellatio. To study the social position and public behavior of his homosexual subjects outside the rest rooms, Humphreys . . . recorded the license numbers of his subjects' automobiles and on that basis obtained residential information about them from police registers and phone company records. A year later, after changing his hair style and attire, Humphreys interviewed his subjects in their homes as part of an ostensibly anonymous public health survey.

Humphreys . . . presented an extensive defense of his study which pointed to such beneficial consequences of the research as the destruction of dangerous stereotypes held about homosexual men. He regarded these consequences as powerful factors in any moral justification of the research. It is clear from this defense and from his book that Humphreys sympathized with the plight of his subject population. He considered them a disregarded and maligned group in American society, and he believed that widespread misperceptions played a significant role in perpetuating the social injustice affecting the group. To the extent that his findings challenged prevailing misunderstandings, Humphreys argued that they would help improve the social condition of homosexual men.

1. Was this study morally justified? Defend your answer, anticipating and responding to the strongest objection that might be raised to your position.

2. Suppose the study had been of members of the Klu Klux Klan and the researcher had infiltrated the group's ranks to learn about the identities and social positions of Klan members. Would your judgment about the moral permissibility of the study be the same? Why or why not?

3. Is the fact that the men studied were engaging in an illegal activity morally relevant to the question of whether the study was justified? Why or why not?

4. Would it be morally acceptable for a police agent to play the role Humphreys played for the purpose of prosecuting persons engaging in illegal homosexual activity? Why or why not?

5. As AIDS spreads more and more rapidly within the heterosexual community, would it be morally permissible for a public health researcher to play the role Humphreys played as part of a study gathering precise statistical information on bisexual behavior for the purpose of informing the public as fully as possible about one way in which the disease is passing into the wider community from one group at special risk for the disease? Defend your answer carefully; anticipate and respond to the strongest objection that might be raised against your position.

CASE: PROTECTING THE CHILD ABUSER

John Smith, M.D. is a psychiatrist with a private practice. He has been extremely successful in helping child-abusing parents. Many of his clients have sent him additional clients; at present, nearly seventy percent of his clients are people who have physically, mentally, or sexually abused their children.

Dr. Smith's provision of effective therapy is not the only reason for his exceptional concentration on child-abusing clients. He also systematically refuses to report child-abuse cases to the authorities, and he includes no mention of child abuse in his clients' files. Because of this, a number of his clients are serious abusers who have not previously sought counseling and who will not take their abused children to physicians because of their fear of being reported to authorities. Dr. Smith believes that by rigorously protecting confidentiality, he is able to help precisely those people who are most likely to profoundly injure their children.

1. Is Dr. Smith's confidentiality policy morally justifiable? Defend your answer carefully; anticipate and respond to the most serious objection that might be raised to your position. Would your answer be the same if Dr. Smith were a psychiatric social worker employed by a state agency? Explain.

2. Suppose Dr. Smith were treating unapprehended rapists, some of whom had murdered their victims. Would your judgment on his strict confidentiality policy remain the same? Why or why not?

3. Suppose Dr. Smith were treating airline pilots with active chemical dependency problems. Would his strict confidentiality policy be justifiable in these cases? Why or why not?

4. Suppose the government institutes a law requiring that individuals who test positive for exposure to the AIDS virus must be identified to the Public Health Department, which will then notify their known sexual partners. Suppose a physician believes that if confidentiality on this matter is maintained, more people will come forward for testing, with the result that those who test negative will be relieved, and those who test positive can be monitored closely and treated early if any symptoms of the disease should appear. Would this physician be morally justified in failing to report test results for these reasons? Defend your answer; anticipate and respond to the strongest objection that might be raised against your position.

SELECTED BIBLIOGRAPHY

''AIDS' Public Health and Civil Liberties.'' Special Supplement, *Hastings Center Report* 16:6 (1986): 1–36.

''The American Bar Association's Retreat on Whistleblowing.'' *Business Week* (31 August 1981): p. 56.

Appelbaum, Paul S. *''Tarasoff:* An Update on the Duty to Warn.'' *Hospital and Community Psychiatry* 32 (1981): 14–15.

Beck, James C., ed. *The Potentially Violent Patient and the ''Tarasoff'' Duty in Psychiatric Practice*. Washington, DC: American Psychiatric Press, 1985.

Bok, Sissela. ''Lies Protecting Peers and Clients.'' In *Lying: Moral Choice in Public and Private Life,* chap. 11. New York: Pantheon, 1978.

Bruce, Jo Anne Czecowski. *Privacy and Confidentiality of Health Care Information*. Chicago: American Hospital Publishing, 1984.

Brushwood, David B. ''Is There a Pharmacist-Patient Privilege?'' *Law, Medicine, and Health Care* 12:2 (1984): 63–67.

Burke, Maureen H. ''The Duty of Confidentiality and Disclosing Corporate Misconduct.'' *Business Lawyer* 36 (1981): 239–95.

Burnham, David. *The Rise of the Computer Society*. New York: Random House, 1983.

Carver, Charles B. ''The Inquisitional Process in Private Employment.'' *Cornell Law Review* 63 (1977): 1–64.

Chamberlain, Jeffrey F. ''Legal Ethics—Confidentiality and the Case of Garrow's Lawyers.'' *Buffalo Law Review* 25 (1975): 211–39.

Feldman, Douglas A., and Thomas M. Johnson, eds. *The Social Dimensions of AIDS: Method and Theroy*. New York: Praeger, 1986.

Flics, Martin. ''Employee Privacy Rights: A Proposal.'' *Fordham Law Review* 47 (1978): 155–202.

Freedman, Monroe H. ''Are the Model Rules Unconstitutional?'' *University of Miami Law Review* 35 (1981): 685–94.

Freid, Charles. *An Anatomy of Values: Problems of Personal and Social Choice,* chap. 9. Cambridge, MA: Harvard University Press, 1970.

Gaylin, Willard, and Daniel Callahan. ''The Psychiatrist as Double Agent.'' *Hastings Center Report* 4:4 (1974): 11–14.

Graffeo, Jane M. "Ethics, Law, and Loyalty: The Attorney's Duty to Turn Over Incriminating Physical Evidence." *Stanford Law Review* 32 (1980): 977–99.

Gurevitz, Howard. "*Tarasoff:* Protective Privilege versus Public Peril." *American Journal of Psychiatry* 292 (1977): 134–289.

"In the Service of the State: The Psychiatrist as Double Agent." Special Supplement, *Hastings Center Report* 8:7 (1978): 1–24.

Johnson, Deborah G., and John W. Snapper, eds. *Ethical Issues in the Use of Computers,* pt. 3. Belmont, CA: Wadsworth, 1985.

Kaufman, Andrew J., ed. *Problems in Professional Responsibility,* chaps. 3, 4. Boston: Little, Brown, 1976.

Landesman, Bruce M. "Confidentiality and the Lawyer-Client Relationship." *Utah Law Review* 1980 (1980): 765–86.

Laska, Eugene, and Rheta Bank, eds. *Safeguarding Psychiatric Privacy: Computer Systems and Their Uses.* New York: Wiley, 1976.

Lawry, Robert P. "Lying, Confidentiality, and the Adversary System of Justice." *Utah Law Review* 1977 (1977): 653–95.

Lowery v. *Cardwell.* 575 F2d 727 (1978).

Luban, David. *Corporate Counsel and Confidentiality.* College Park: Center for Philosophy and Public Policy, University of Maryland, 1981.

Meisel, Alan. "Confidentiality and Rape Counseling." *Hastings Center Report* 11:4 (1981): 5–7.

Minnesota v. *Andring.* 342 NW 2d 128 (1984).

Note. "Client Fraud and the Lawyer—An Ethical Analysis." *Minnesota Law Review* 62 (1977): 89–118.

Panner, Morris J., and Nicholas A. Cristakis. "The Limits of Science in On-the-Job Drug Screening." *Hastings Center Report* 16:6 (1986): 7–12.

Pennock, J. Roland, and John W. Chapman, eds. *Nomos XIII: Privacy.* New York: Atherton, 1971.

Pierce, Christine, and Donald VanDeVeer, eds. *AIDS: Ethics and Public Policy.* Belmont, CA: Wadsworth, 1987.

Rachels, James. "Why Privacy Is Important." *Philosophy and Public Affairs* 4:4 (1975): 323–33.

Roth, Loren H., and Alan Meisel. "Dangerousness, Confidentiality, and the Duty to Warn." *American Journal of Psychiatry* 134 (1977): 508–11.

Seitel, Max. "Privacy, Ethics, and Confidentiality." *Professional Psychiatry* 10 (1979): 249–58.

Shestack, Jerome J. "Psychiatry and the Dilemma of Dual Loyalties." In *Medical, Moral, and Legal Issues in Mental Health Care,* ed. Frank J. Ayd, chap. 2. Baltimore, MD: Williams and Wilkins, 1974.

Siegler, Mark. "Confidentiality—A Decrepit Concept." *New England Journal of Medicine* 307 (1982): 1516–21.

Smith, Robert Ellis. *Privacy: How to Protect What's Left of It.* Garden City, NY: Doubleday/Anchor Books, 1978.

Stone, Alan. "The *Tarasoff* Decision: Suing Psychotherapists to Safeguard Society." *Harvard Law Review* 90 (1976): 358–78.

Thompson, Dennis. "The Ethics of Social Experimentation: The Case of the DIME." *Public Policy* 29 (1981): 369–98.

Thomson, Judith Jarvis. "The Right to Privacy." *Philosophy and Public Affairs* 4:4 (1975): 295–315.

Thurman, Samuel D. "Limits to the Adversary System of Justice: Interests that Outweigh Confidentiality." *Journal of the Legal Profession* 5 (1980): 5–19.

Warshaw, Leon J. *AIDS and the Employer: Guidelines on the Management of AIDS in the Workplace.* New York: New York Business Group on Health, 1986.

Werhane, Patricia H. "Individual Rights in Business." In *Just Business: New Introductory Essays in Business Ethics,* ed. Tom Regan, pp. 100–128. Philadelphia: Temple University Press, 1983; reissued New York: Random House, 1984.

Westin, Alan. *Privacy and Freedom.* New York: Atheneum, 1967.

PART III

RESPONSIBILITY, DISSENT, JUSTICE, AND CHARACTER

8

INDIVIDUAL AND COLLECTIVE RESPONSIBILITY

Can a corporation act? Can a corporation, rather than individuals within it, be morally responsible for violating rights or causing harm? Thomas Nagel has said that the great modern crimes are public crimes—crimes committed by functionaries or officeholders, who are insulated in a puzzling way from what they do. Such people, says Nagel, seem to have a "slippery moral surface," created by their institutional roles (see the selection by Nagel in chap. 3).

The first two selections in this chapter address the question of corporatism, that is, whether the so-called actions of corporations can be completely translated into actions of indentifiable individuals. Peter French suggests that corporate acts are not translatable into individual acts or even collections of individual acts. Corporations are, on French's account, metaphysically separate persons, and should be granted full membership in the moral community, with the attendant rights, duties, and accountabilities of all persons in the moral community. If French's view (corporatism) is correct, it would help to account for the "slippery moral surfaces" of corporate officials (who are frequently not held personally accountable for the actions [or failings] of their corporations).

John Danley takes issue with corporatism. He argues on both logical and moral grounds against the organic metaphysics underlying the corporatist thesis and suggests that we should understand corporations (and, by implication, other institutions) on the mechanistic model. Corporations, says Danley, are more like machines than persons, and we should treat them as such. When a machine goes awry, we blame its creators and operators; and Danley argues that the same should be true of corporations and their creators and operators.

The positions of French and Danley on the question of corporatism create a kind of dilemma. If one accepts a full-blown corporatism, then the puzzles Danley points out do seem to follow; for example, given certain statements in their charters, it is logically impossible for a corporation to act illegally. And virtually any action of an individual done in his or her official capacity within a corporate structure is not ascribable to that individual as such. On the other hand, a thoroughgoing rejection of corporatism seems to entail that individuals are personally responsible for any good done by a corporation (e.g., the making of a charitable contribution) and for any harm done by a corporation (e.g., harm done by a defective product when all reasonable precautions were taken to ensure safety). But we do think there is a difference between a corporation's charity and an individual's charity. And we do not think that individuals should be liable for personal suit in all cases where harm results from corporate activity.

The second selection from Peter French directly addresses the issue of corporate responsibility for harm. French focuses on the 1974 DC-10 crash outside Paris, which killed 346 people. In discussing moral responsibility for the crash, French offers what he calls the 'Extended Principle of Accountability,' which holds that agents are morally accountable not only for intended or foreseen direct effects of their actions (or failures to act), but also for effects of the actions of others that were predictable, given their own actions. Thus, even though the Paris crash was caused by a defect that was passed over by low-level inspectors at McDonnell-Douglas, French argues that causal and moral responsibility for the crash does not end with those inspectors. Upper management, says French, should have known that its safety assurance procedures were inadequate to ensure rigor in the inspection process, and this makes the corporation as such responsible for the crash.

Although French wants to maintain his corporatist thesis through this second article, notice that the Extended Principle of Accountability might be used to isolate cases where individuals are to be held accountable for the so-called actions (or failures) of corporations, or, more generally, for the actions (or failures) of other persons. But notice, too, that the Extended Principle of Accountability when applied most generally to individuals is an extremely strong principle, since whenever I can predict that some action (or inaction) of mine will encourage others to act in harmful ways, it seems that I am (at least partially) accountable for that harm. Since it is predictable that some people will always abuse certain products (e.g., firearms, alcohol, automobiles), the principle may be too strong for universal application. But even if the principle is too strong to use for all cases, some principle like it might capture the insight that persons are at least sometimes at least partially accountable for the actions of others, even when they do not intend that others act in those ways.

Precisely when persons are so accountable is an interesting and important question in the moral life in general as well as in occupational life. In the most central way, it is one of Mary Shelley's questions in *Frankenstein:* When and to what extent are we responsible for the life history of what we create? For example, if a scientist participates in research isolating a particularly lethal virus and that virus is later used in a biological weapon, can the scientist fully escape accountability for that use of her research?

Dennis Thompson asks a closely related question: What responsibility do government advisers bear for the uses to which the information they provide is put? Like French and Danley, Thompson rejects the view that persons are accountable only for what they directly intend, and he argues that foreseeability is at least sometimes sufficient for ascribing moral responsibility to individuals. But Thompson also suggests that ascribing responsibility to more than one person need not diminish the responsibility of others: "There is no fixed pool of responsibility such that when one person's share goes up, another's must go down." And he argues that certain advisers (e.g., scientific advisers) cannot be shielded from moral responsibility for outcomes resulting from use of their advice or information they provide on the ground that their roles require them to act as mere technicians, avoiding recommendations about public policy. Thompson rejects the view, then, that advisers in government justifiably live in a morally simplified universe (see Richard Wasserstrom's article on attorneys in chap. 3), morally shielded from untoward outcomes resulting from what they do in their professional roles.

Several of Thompson's suggestions are captured in James Muyskens' essay on individual and collective responsibility in nursing, which ends the chapter. However, Muyskens argues that there is a "trade-off" in assigning responsibility to individuals and to groups or systems to which they belong. His focus is on nursing, and he suggests that insofar as nursing as a whole does not work to correct certain "forms of life" in health care provision that interfere with nurses' abilities to protect patient rights and interests, individual nurses who fail to protect those rights and interests are less blameworthy than they would be with a stronger profession supporting them. Muyskens' piece is reminiscent of Gerald Winslow's piece in chapter 4, since it points out some of the problems with the nurse's role as patient advocate, and the need for nursing to professionalize further (see chap. 2) if nurses are to effectively assume that role.

The readings in this chapter lead quite directly to the topic of chapter 9—the social responsibilities of professionals and the responsibility to dissent when professionals are unable to carry out those responsibilities.

33. Corporate Moral Agency*†

Peter A. French

In one of his *New York Times* columns of not too long ago Tom Wicker's ire was aroused by a Gulf Oil Corporation advertisement that "pointed the finger of blame" for the energy crisis at all elements of our society (and supposedly away from the oil company). Wicker attacked Gulf Oil as the major, if not the sole, perpetrator of that crisis and virtually every other social ill, with the possible exception of venereal disease. I do not know if Wicker was serious or sarcastic in making all of his charges; I have a sinking suspicion that he was in deadly earnest, but I have doubts as to whether Wicker understands or if many people understand what sense such ascriptions of moral responsibility make when their subjects are corporations. My interest is to argue for a theory that accepts corporations as members of the moral community, of equal standing with the traditionally acknowledged residents—biological human beings—and hence treats Wicker-type responsibility ascriptions as unexceptionable instances of a perfectly proper sort without having to paraphrase them. In short, I shall argue that corporations should be treated as full-fledged moral persons and hence that they can have whatever privileges, rights, and duties as are, in the normal course of affairs, accorded to moral persons.

There are at least two significantly different types of responsibility ascriptions that I want to distinguish in ordinary usage (not counting the laudatory recommendation, "He is a responsible lad"). The first type pins responsibility on someone or something, the who-dun-it or what-dun-it sense. Austin has pointed out that it is usually used when an event or action is thought by the speaker to be untoward. (Perhaps we are more interested in the failures rather than the successes that punctuate our lives.)

The second type of responsibility ascription, parasitic upon the first, involves the notion of accountability.[1] "Having a responsibility" is interwoven with the notion "Having a liability to answer," and having such a liability or obligation seems to imply (as Anscombe has noted[2]) the existence of some sort of authority relationship either between people, or between people and a deity, or in some weaker versions between people and social norms. The kernel of insight that I find intuitively compelling is that for someone to legitimately hold someone else responsible for some event, there must exist or have existed a responsibility relationship between them such that in regard to the event in question the latter was answerable to the former. In other words, a responsibility ascription of the second type is properly uttered by someone Z if he or she can hold X accountable for what he or she has done. Responsibility relationships are created in a multitude of ways, for example, through promises, contracts,

From *Business Ethics: Readings and Cases in Corporate Morality,* edited by W. Michael Hoffman and Jennifer Mills Moore (New York: McGraw-Hill, 1984), pp. 163–71.

*I am grateful to Professors Donald Davidson, J. L. Mackie, Howard Wettstein, and T. E. Uehling for their helpful comments on earlier versions of this paper. I wish also to acknowledge the support of the University of Minnesota Graduate School.

†[For an expanded discussion, see Peter A. French, "The Corporation as a Moral Person," *American Philosophical Quarterly* 16:3 (1979): 207–15.—ED.]

compacts, hirings, assignments, appointments, by agreeing to enter a Rawlsian original position, etc. The "right" to hold responsible is often delegated to third parties; but importantly, in the case of moral responsibility, no delegation occurs because no person is excluded from the relationship: Moral responsibility relationships hold reciprocally and without prior agreements among all moral persons. No special arrangement needs to be established between parties for anyone to hold someone morally responsible for his or her acts or, what amounts to the same thing, every person is a party to a responsibility relationship with all other persons as regards the doing or refraining from doing of certain acts: those that take descriptions that use moral notions.

Because our interest is in the criteria of moral personhood and not the content or morality, we need not pursue this idea further. What I have maintained is that moral responsibility, although it is neither contractual nor optional, is not a class apart but an extension of ordinary, garden-variety responsibility. What is needed in regard to the present subject, then, is an account of the requirements in *any* responsibility relationship.[3]

A responsibility ascription of the second type amounts to the assertion that the person held responsible is the cause of an event (usually an untoward one) and that the action in question was intended by the subject or that the event was the direct result of an intentional act of the subject. In addition to what it asserts, it implies that the subject is liable to account to the speaker (who the speaker is or what the speaker is, a member of the "moral community," a surrogate for that aggregate). The primary focus of responsibility ascriptions of the second type is on the subject's intentions rather than, though not to the exclusion of, occasions.[4]

For a corporation to be treated as a responsible agent it must be the case that some things that happen, some events, are describable in a way that makes certain sentences true, sentences that say that some of the things a corporation does were intended by the corporation itself. That is not accomplished if attributing intentions to a corporation is only a shorthand way of attributing intentions to the biological persons who comprise, for example, its board of directors. If that were to turn out to be the case, then on metaphysical if not logical grounds there would be no way to distinguish between corporations and mobs. I shall argue, however, that a corporation's CID Structure (the *C*orporate *I*nternal *D*ecision *S*tructure) is the requisite redescription device that licenses the predication of corporate intentionality.

It is obvious that a corporation's doing something involves or includes human beings' doing things and that the human beings who occupy various positions in a corporation usually can be described as having reasons for *their* behavior. In virtue of those descriptions they may be properly held responsible for their behavior, *ceteris paribus*. What needs to be shown is that there is sense in saying that corporations, and not just the people who work in them, have reasons for doing what they do. Typically, we will be told that it is the directors, or the managers, etc. that really have the corporate reasons and desires, etc. and that although corporate actions may not be reducible without remainder, corporate intentions are always reducible to human intentions.

Every corporation must have an internal decision structure. The CID Structure has two elements of interest to us here: (1) an organizational or responsibility flow chart that delineates stations and levels within the corporate power structure and (2) corporate decision recognition rule(s) (usually embedded in something called "corporate policy"). The CID Structure is the personnel organization for the exercise of the corporation's power with respect to its ventures, and as such its primary function is to draw experience from various levels of the corporation into a decision-making and ratification process. When operative and properly activated, the CID Structure accomplishes a subordination and synthesis of the intentions and acts of various biological persons into a corporate decision. When viewed in another way the CID Structure licenses the descriptive transformation of events seen under another aspect as the acts of biological persons (those who occupy various stations on the organizational chart) as corporate acts by exposing the corporate character of those events. A functioning CID Structure *incorporates* acts of biological persons. For illustrative purposes, suppose we imagine that an event E has at least two aspects, that is, can be described in two nonidentical ways. One of those aspects is "Executive X's doing *y*" and one is "Corporation C's doing *z*." The corporate act and the individual act may have different properties: indeed they have different causal ancestors though they are causally inseparable.[5]

Although I doubt he is aware of the metaphysical reading that can be given to this process, J. K. Galbraith rather neatly captures what I have in mind when he writes in his recent popular book on the history of economics:

> From [the] interpersonal exercise of power, the interaction . . . of the participants, comes the *personality* of the corporation.[6]

I take Galbraith here to be quite literally correct, but it is important to spell out how a CID Structure works this "miracle."

In philosophy in recent years we have grown accustomed to the use of games as models for understanding institutional behavior. We all have some understanding of how rules of games make certain descriptions of events possible that would not be so if those rules were nonexistent. The CID Structure of a corporation is a kind of constitutive rule (or rules) analogous to the game rules with which we are familiar. The organization chart of, for example, the Burlington Northern Corporation distinguishes "players" and clarifies their rank and the interwoven lines of responsibility within the corporation. The Burlington chart lists only titles, not unlike King, Queen, Rook, etc. in chess. What it tells us is that anyone holding the title "Executive Vice President for Finance and Administration" stands in a certain relationship to anyone holding the title "Director of Internal Audit" and to anyone holding the title "Treasurer," etc. Also it expresses, or maps, the interdependent and dependent relationships that are involved in determinations of corporate decisions and actions. In effect, it tells us what anyone who occupies any of the positions is vis-à-vis the decision structure of the whole. The organizational chart provides what might be called the grammar of corporate decision making. What I shall call internal recognition rules provide its logic.[7]

Recognition rules are of two sorts. Partially embedded in the organizational chart are the procedural recognitors: we see that decisions are to be reached collectively at certain levels and that they are to be ratified at higher levels (or at inner circles, if one prefers the Galbraithean model). A corporate decision is recognized internally not only by the procedure of its making, but by the policy it instantiates. Hence every corporation creates an image (not to be confused with its public image) or a general policy, what G. C. Buzby of the Chilton Company has called the "basic belief of the corporation,"[8] that must inform its decisions for them to be properly described as being those of that corporation. "The moment policy is sidestepped or violated, it is no longer the policy of that company."[9]

Peter Drucker has seen the importance of the basic policy recognitors in the CID Structure (though he treats matters rather differently from the way I am recommending). Drucker writes:

> Because the corporation is an institution it must have a basic policy. For it must subordinate individual ambitions and decisions to the *needs* of the corporation's welfare and survival. That means that it must have a set of principles and a rule of conduct which limit and direct individual actions and behavior.[10]

Suppose, for illustrative purposes, we activate a CID Structure in a corporation, Wicker's favorite, the Gulf Oil Corporation. Imagine then that three executives X, Y, and Z have the task of deciding whether or not Gulf Oil will join a world uranium cartel (I trust this may catch Mr. Wicker's attention and hopefully also that of Jerry McAfee, current Gulf Oil Corporation president). X, Y, and Z have before them an Everest of papers that have been prepared by lower echelon executives. Some of the reports will be purely factual in nature, some will be contingency plans, some will be in the form of position papers developed by various departments, some will outline financial considerations, some will be legal opinions, and so on. Insofar as these will all have been processed through Gulf's CID Structure system, the personal reasons, if any, individual executives may have had when writing their reports and recommendations in a specific way will have been diluted by the subordination of individual inputs to peer group input even before X, Y, and Z review the matter. X, Y, and Z take a vote. Their taking of a vote is authorized procedure in the Gulf CID Structure, which is to say that under these circumstances the vote of X, Y, and Z can be redescribed as the corporation's making a decision: that is, the event "X Y Z voting" may be redescribed to expose an aspect otherwise unrevealed, that is quite different from its other aspects, for example, from X's voting in the affirmative.

But the CID Structure, as already suggested, also provides the grounds in its nonprocedural recognitor for such an attribution of corporate intentionality. Simply, when the corporate act is consistent with the implementation of established corporate policy, then it is proper to describe it as having been done for corporate reasons, as having been caused by a corporate desire coupled with a corporate belief and so, in other words, as corporate intentional.

An event may, under one of its aspects, be described as the conjunctive act "X did *a* (or as X intentionally did *a*) and Y did *a* (or as Y intentionally did *a*) and Z did *a* (or as Z intentionally did *a*)" (where *a* = voted in the affirmative on the question of Gulf Oil joining the cartel). Given the Gulf CID Structure—formulated in this instance as the conjunction of rules: When the occupants of positions A, B, and C on the organizational chart unanimously vote to do something and if doing that something is consistent with an implementation of general corporate policy, other things being equal, then the corporation has decided to do it for corporate reasons—the event is redescribable as "the Gulf Oil Corporation did *j* for corporate reasons *f*" (where *j* is "decided to join the cartel" and *f* is any reason [desire + belief] consistent with basic policy of Gulf Oil, e.g., increasing profits) or simply as "Gulf Oil Corporation intentionally did *j*." This is a rather technical way of saying that in these circumstances the executives voting are, given its CID Structure, also the corporation deciding to do something, and that regardless of the personal reasons the executives have for voting as they do, and even if their reasons are inconsistent with established corporate policy or even if one of them has no reason at all for voting as he does, the corporation still has reasons for joining the cartel; that is, joining is consistent with the inviolate corporate general policies as encrusted in the precedent of previous corporate actions and its statements of purposes as recorded in its certificate of incorporation, annual reports, etc. The corporation's only method of achieving its desires or goals is the activation of the personnel who occupy its various positions. However, if X voted affirmatively purely for reasons of personal monetary gain (suppose he had been bribed to do so), that does not alter the fact that the corporate reason for joining the cartel was to minimize competition and hence pay higher dividends to its shareholders. Corporations have reasons because they have interests in doing those things that are likely to result in realization of their established corporate goals regardless of the transient self-interest of directors, managers, etc. If there is a difference between corporate goals and desires and those of human beings, it is probably that the corporate ones are relatively stable and not very wide ranging, but that is only because corporations can do relatively fewer things than human beings, being confined in action predominately to a limited socioeconomic sphere. It is, of course, in a corporation's interest that its component membership view the corporate purposes as instrumental in the achievement of their own goals. (Financial reward is the most common way this is achieved.)

It will be objected that a corporation's policies reflect only the current goals of its directors. But that is certainly not logically necessary nor is it in practice totally true for most large corporations. Usually, of course, the original incorporators will have organized to further their individual interests and/or to meet goals which they shared. But even in infancy the melding of disparate interests and purposes gives rise to a corporate long-range point of view that is distinct from the intents and purposes of the collection of incorporators viewed individually. Also corporate basic purposes and policies, as already mentioned, tend to be relatively stable when compared to those of individuals and not couched in the kind of language that would be appropriate to individual purposes. Furthermore, as histories of corporations will show, when policies are amended or altered it is usually only peripheral issues and matters of style that are involved. Radical policy alteration constitutes a new corporation. This point is captured in the incorporation laws of such states as Delaware. ("Any power which is not enumerated in the charter or which cannot be inferred from it is *ultra vires*[11] of the corporation.") Obviously underlying the objection is an uneasiness about the fact that corporate intent is dependent upon policy and purpose that is but an artifact of the sociopsychology of a group of biological persons. Corporate intent seems somehow to be a tarnished, illegitimate, offspring of human intent. But this objection is a form of the anthropocentric bias that pervades traditional moral theory. By concentrating on possible descriptions of events and by acknowledging only that the possibility of describing something as an agent depends upon whether or not it can be properly described as having done something for a reason, we avoid the temptation of trying to reduce all agents to human referents.

The CID Structure licenses redescriptions of events as corporate and attributions of corporate intentionality while it does not obscure the private acts of executives, directors, etc. Although X voted to support the joining of the cartel because he was bribed to do so, X did not join the cartel: Gulf Oil Corporation joined the cartel. Consequently, we may say that X did something for which he should be held morally responsible, yet whether or not Gulf Oil Corporation should be held morally responsible for joining the cartel is a question that turns on issues that may be unrelated to X's having accepted a bribe.

Of course Gulf Oil Corporation cannot join the cartel unless X or somebody who occupies position A on the organization chart votes in the affirmative. What that shows, however, is that corporations are collectivities. That should not, however, rule out the possibility of their having metaphysical status and being thereby full-fledged moral persons.

This much seems to me clear: We can describe many events in terms of certain physical movements of human beings and we also can sometimes describe those events as done for reasons by those human beings, but further we also can sometimes describe those events as corporate and still further as done for corporate reasons that are qualitatively different from whatever personal reasons, if any, component members may have for doing what they do.

Corporate agency resides in the possibility of

CID Structure licensed redescription of events as corporate intentional. That may still appear to be downright mysterious, although I do not think it is, for human agency, as I have suggested, resides in the possibility of description as well. On the basis of the foregoing analysis, however, I think that grounds have been provided for holding corporations *per se* to account for what they do, for treating them as metaphysical persons *qua* moral persons.

A. A. Berle has written:

> The medieval feudal power system set the "lords spiritual" over and against the "lords temporal." These were the men of learning and of the church who in theory were able to say to the greatest power in the world: "You have committed a sin; therefore either you are excommunicated or you must mend your ways." The lords temporal could reply: "I can kill you." But the lords spiritual could retort: "Yes that you can, but you cannot change the philosophical fact." In a sense this is the great lacuna in the economic power system today.[12]

I have tried to fill that gap by providing reasons for thinking that the moral world is not necessarily composed of homogeneous entities. It is sobering to keep in mind that the Gulf Oil Corporation certainly knows what "You are held responsible for payment in full of the amount recorded on your statement" means. I hope I have provided the beginnings of a basis for an understanding of what "The Gulf Oil Corporation should be held responsible for destroying the ecological balance of the bay" means.

NOTES

1. For which there are good lexical grounds. See *Oxford English Dictionary,* especially entry, Accountability.
2. G.E.M. Anscombe, "Modern Moral Philosophy," *Philosophy* 33, 1958, pp. 1–19.
3. For a more detailed discussion, see my *Foundations of Corporate Responsibility,* forthcoming. In that book I show that the notion of the juristic person does not provide a sufficient account. For example, the deceased in a probate case cannot be *held* responsible in the relevant way by anyone, even though the deceased is a juristic person, a subject of rights.
4. J. L. Austin, "Three Ways of Spilling Ink," in *Philosophical Papers* (Oxford: Clarendon Press, 1970), p. 273. "In considering responsibility, few things are considered more important than to establish whether a man *intended* to do A, or whether he did A intentionally." Moreover, to be the subject of a responsibility ascription of the second type, to be a party in responsibility relationships, hence to be a moral person, the subject must be, at minimum, what I shall call a Davidsonian agent. If corporations are moral persons, they will be noneliminatable Davidsonian agents. See, for example, Donald Davidson, "Agency," in *Agent, Action, and Reason,* ed. Binkley, Bronaugh, and Marros (Toronto: University of Toronto Press, 1971).
5. The causal inseparability of these acts I hope to show is a product of the CID Structure; X's doing *y* is not the cause of C's doing *z* nor is C's doing *z* the cause of X's doing *y,* although if X's doing *y* causes Event *E* then C's doing *z* causes *E* and vice versa.
6. John Kenneth Galbraith, *The Age of Uncertainty* (Boston: Houghton Mifflin, 1977), p. 261.
7. By "recognition rule(s)" I mean what Hart, in another context, calls "conclusive affirmative indication" that a decision on an act has been made or performed for corporate reasons. H.L.A. Hart, *The Concept of Law* (Oxford: Clarendon Press, 1961), chap. 6.
8. G. C. Buzby, "Policies—A Guide to What a Company Stands For," *Management Record* (March 1962), p. 5.
9. Ibid.
10. Peter Drucker, *Concept of the Corporation* (New York: John Day, 1946/1972), pp. 36–37.
11. Beyond the legal competence.
12. A. A. Berle, "Economic Power and the Free Society," in *The Corporate Take-Over,* ed. Andrew Hacker (Garden City, NY: Doubleday, 1964), p. 99.

34. Corporate Moral Agency: The Case for Anthropological Bigotry

John R. Danley

In "Corporate Moral Agency," Peter A. French argues for a position, increasingly popular, which would accept "corporations as members of the moral community, of equal standing with the traditionally acknowledged residents—biological human beings." This is but one implication of accepting the claim that one can legitimately ascribe moral responsibility to corporations. To put the matter somewhat differently, again in French's words, "corporations should be treated as full-

From *Action and Responsibility: Bowling Green Studies in Applied Philosophy,* vol. 2 (Bowling Green, OH: Bowling Green State University, 1980), pp. 172–79.

fledged moral persons and hence . . . have whatever privileges, rights, and duties as are, in the normal course of affairs, accorded to moral persons."

Unwilling to rest content with the usual assaults on prejudices against real persons based on race, creed, sex, religion, or national origin, French is among those[1] seeking to open yet another new front. The struggle is now being extended beyond real persons to eliminate discrimination against a particular class of *personae fictae,* fictitious persons, namely the corporation. Before too hastily endorsing this new "corporate" liberation movement let us pause for reflection. If after serious consideration we do vote to admit these peculiar entities into our rather exclusivist and elitist community of moral beings, we should insist on their having equal standing with the rest of us run-of-the-mill featherless bipeds. After all, what moral neighborhood worthy of the name would allow second-class citizens? After examining the case for admission, however, I find myself driven to the uncomfortable position of defending apartheid, biological apartheid that is, of defending anthropological bigotry. I contend that corporations should not be included in the moral community; they should not be granted full-fledged moral status. Within this emotionally charged atmosphere it is tempting to employ the standard *ad hominems* of bigotry ("Think of the value of your property"; or, "Before you know it your daughter will bring a corporation home to dinner"; "What about the children?"; and so forth), but I will attempt to ward off these temptations. My claim is that the corporatist programs of the kind represented by French would seriously disturb the logic of our moral discourse. Indeed, the corporatist position, while offering no substantial advantages, would entail the reduction of biological persons to the status of second-class citizens. Let us turn now to the dispute.

There is little doubt that we often speak of corporations as being responsible for this or that sin or charitable act, whether of microscopic or cosmic proportions. The question is what we mean when we speak in that way. Sometimes all we mean is that the corporation is the cause of such and such. In these instances we are isolating a cause for an event or state of affairs, an exercise not much more (or less) troublesome than saying "The icy pavement caused the accident." The debate revolves around a fuller sense of "responsibility," a sense which includes more than the idea of "causing to happen." In this richer sense, we ascribe responsibility only if the event or state of affairs caused was also intended by the agent.

When the concept of responsibility is unpacked in this fashion, the traditionalists appear to have victory already in hand. Whatever else we may say of them, collective entities are surely not the kinds of things capable of intending. Individuals within the corporation can intend, lust, have malice aforethought, and so forth, but the corporation cannot. Traditionalists, like myself, maintain that only persons, that is, entities with particular physical and mental properties, can be morally responsible. Corporations lack these. For the traditionalists, to speak of corporations being responsible is simply elliptical for speaking of certain individuals within the corporation being responsible. On this point, and perhaps this one alone, I do not believe Milton Friedman[2] to be in error.

Undaunted by this venerable line of reasoning, the corporatists proceed to press their case. Although it is French's view that I am treating, I am concerned not so much with the details of his argument as with the general outlines of the corporatist position. Using French's theory as representative, however, provides us with one of the most forceful, sophisticated theories developed. French has worked for years in the area of collective responsibility.[3] His strategy is to accept the traditionalists' analysis of "responsibility," and then to attempt to show that some sense can be made of ascribing "intentions" to a corporation.

The key to making some sense of corporate "intentions" is what French calls the Corporate Internal Decision Structure, the CID. The CID is that which allows one, "licenses" one, to redescribe the actions of certain individuals within a corporation as actions of the corporation. Although the notion is complicated, a CID contains two elements which are particularly relevant:

1. an organization or responsibility flow chart delineating stations and levels within the corporate power structure and
2. corporate decision recognition rules.

As French puts it, the organizational chart provides the grammar for corporate decision making; the recognition rules provide the logic. The purpose of the organizational chart is to locate which procedures will count as decisions for the corporation, and who may or must participate in those procedures. The recognition rules, we are informed, are of two sorts. The first sort are procedural recognitors, "partially embedded in the organizational chart." What these amount to, it seems, are directives more explicit than those contained in the chart, expanding upon it. The second sort of recognition rules are expressed primarily in corporate policy.

Employing the cumbersome apparatus of the CID, some acts may now be described in two non-identical ways, or so it is claimed.

> One of those . . . is "Executive X's doing *y*" and one is "Corporation C's doing *z*." The corporate act and the individual act may have different properties: indeed, they have different causal ancestors though they are causally inseparable.

The effect of this, of course, is that when certain individuals as specified by the organizational chart, engage in certain procedures as specified by the organizational chart and some recognition rules, and act in accordance with other recognition rules (corporate policy), then French claims we can redescribe the action as a corporate act, an intentional corporate act. It is critical to the corporatist position that the two descriptions are non-identical. Saying that "Corporation C did z" is not reducible to the statement that "Executives X, Y, and Z, voted to do y," even though y and z are the same. Since they are non-identical the traditionalist is supposedly prevented from ascribing responsibility only to these individuals. The acts of the individuals are necessary for a corporate act but not identical with it.

Like a child with a new toy, one is strongly inclined by the glitter of this technical hardware to dismantle it, to try to find out how it all works, to see whether it really fits together, to see how and whether it can handle hard cases. To be sure, there are some problems which one can detect immediately. Let me mention two. First of all, it is unclear what French means by an organizational chart. Since his examples are those of nice neat black lines and boxes on a page, like the ones found in business textbooks and corporate policy manuals, one is left with the impression that this is what he has in mind. If so, there are severe difficulties. Most everyone is aware of the extent to which corporate reality departs from the ethereal world of black lines and boxes. Will French maintain that any decisions made by the managers of corporations which do not conform to the organizational chart are not decisions of the corporation? Biting the bullet here may be the best course but it is probable that most decisions are not strictly corporate decisions then. Few corporations act at all, if this criterion is used. French needs a more positivistic interpretation[4] of the organizational chart, one which would insure that the flow chart realistically captured the actual procedures and personages holding the powers. The difficulty with this modification, however, is that the CID begins to lose its function as a normative criterion by which to determine which acts are corporate acts and which are not. The positivistic interpretation would mean that a corporate act is whatever some powerful person within the corporation manages to get others in the corporation to perform, or gets others outside to accept as a corporate act. That will not work at all. The CID appears nestled upon the familiar horns of a dilemma. At least more work is necessary here.

There is a second difficulty. A basic component of the CID must be the corporate charter. Recently the general incorporation charters have become little more than blank tablets for the corporation to engage in business for "any lawful purpose," although some aspects of the organizational chart and a few recognition rules are delineated. Even these permissive rules of recognition have pertinence for French. Suppose every aspect of the CID was followed except that the board of directors voted unanimously to engage the corporation in some unlawful activity. According to the charter, a part of the CID, this is not possible. One could not redescribe such an act as a corporate act. The result of this is that corporations can never act illegally. Unlike the Augustinian doctrine that for fallen man it is not possible not to sin, the French doctrine appears to be that for the corporation it is not possible to sin at all.

These are but two of many queries which might be addressed to French's proposal. However, it is not my concern to dwell on such technical points here, lest we be distracted from the larger issue. Suppose, for the sake of argument, that we accept some mode of redescribing individual acts such that one could identify these acts as constituting a corporate intentional act. Accept French's. Would that establish the corporatist case? I think not. French tips his hand, for instance, when he writes that what "needs to be shown is that there is sense in saying that corporations, and not just the people who work in them, have reasons for doing what they do." But, obviously, French needs to show much more. All that is established by a device which redescribes, is that there is *a sense* in saying that corporations have intentions. The significant question is whether that sense of "intend" is the one used by the traditionalists when explicating "responsibility," and when denying that corporations can have intentions. The traditionalists can easily, and quite plausibly, claim that the corporatist is equivocating on "intend." The sense in which a corporation intends is much different from that in which a biological person intends. The corporatist has further laid the foundation for this charge by finding it necessary to construct the apparatus so that the sense of "intend" involved can be made clear. The more clearly this sense of "intend" is articulated, the more clearly it diverges from what we usually mean by "intend." The arbitrariness of constructing a sense of "intend" should be evident when we consider the possibility of ascribing intentions to numerous other entities, such as plants, animals, or machines. One could go to extraordinary lengths to provide a sense for attributing intentionally to many of these. Yet, few would contend that it was very similar to what we mean in attributing "intention" to humans.

Consider a computer programmed to play chess which learns from previous mistakes. There is a sense in which the computer intends to respond P-K4 to my king pawn opening, but is this the same sense of "intend" as when I intended P-K4? Furthermore, even ascribing an intention to the computer by no means entails that we would be ready to ascribe responsibility to it. The point is that it remains for the corporatist to demonstrate the relationship between the sense of "intend" and the sense involved in ascriptions of responsibility to humans. Hence, a rather difficult task remains for the corporatist before the case is made.

Thus far I have established only that the corporatist has failed to establish the position. I must admit that I am not entirely enamored of the preceding line of argument. The dispute smacks of the theological controversies concerning whether "wisdom" or "goodness" when attributed to God have the same sense as when predicated of humans. Nonetheless, the corporatist has moved the debate in this direction by attempting to equate two markedly different senses. There are, fortunately, other factors to be considered in evaluating the corporatist position. These factors appear when one expands the focus of attention beyond the narrow conditions for ascribing "responsibility," and begins to examine the concept as it functions in the broader context of moral discourse.

Much hangs in the balance when ascribing "responsibility." Affixing responsibility is a prelude to expressing approbation or disapprobation—praise or blame. When the agent responsible is praised, that is the final move in the moral game. (Morality never pays very well.) But, when the responsibility is affixed and the agent in question is blameworthy, that is far from the end of the matter. In this case, affixing responsibility and expressing disfavor is itself a prelude to many further permissible or obligatory moves. Minimally, the blameworthy party is expected to express regret or remorse. More importantly, the agent may be required to pay compensation or be subject to punishment. Ascribing responsibility opens the door for these major moral moves. (There are other door openers as well, for example, the notion of cause in strict liability.) Any understanding of the concept of responsibility is incomplete without incorporating the role it plays in relation to these other moral moves. It is this which is lacking from the previous discussion of "intend." Such an analysis cannot be provided here. What can be done, however, is to sketch briefly how ascribing responsibility to corporations effectively blocks these moves, sundering many of the threads which tie "responsibility" so intimately with concepts like remorse, regret, compensation, or punishment. Let me elaborate.

An indication of the consequences of admitting the corporation into the moral community have been foreshadowed by admission into the legal corpus as a person. That legacy is an odious one, marred by an environment within which the corporation has enjoyed nearly all of the benefits associated with personhood while shouldering but few of the burdens or risks. Much the same would result from admission into the moral world. That legacy is not solely to be explained by jaundiced justices or bad judicial judgments, but is a natural consequence of attempting to pretend that the corporation is just another pretty face. While the law early began holding the corporation liable (read: responsible) for certain specified acts, and the scope of things for which it was liable has dramatically increased over the years, there has been a hesitancy to judge that corporations could be subject to most criminal statutes. One of the major stumbling blocks was just the one which is the subject of this paper. It was clear that many of the criminal statutes required criminal intent, or a criminal state of mind, and unable to locate the corporate mind, it was judged that the corporation was not subject to these. The relevance of proposals such as French's is that the justices would now have a method of determining when the corporation acts with intent, with malice aforethought, with premeditation or out of passion. What I am anxious to bring to light, however, is that these proposals offer no advantage over the traditionalist view and in fact create further problems. Consider now the moral moves involved in extracting compensation from, or punishing, a guilty person. How is one to make these moral moves against a corporate person? One cannot. An English jurist put the point well in an often quoted quip to the effect that corporations have no pants to kick, no soul to damn. We may concur with the sentiment of that jurist who concluded that "by God they ought to have both," but they have neither, although French has given them a surrogate soul, the CID.

The corporation cannot be kicked, whipped, imprisoned, or hanged by the neck until dead. Only individuals of the corporation can be punished. What of punishment through the pocketbook, or extracting compensation for a corporate act? Here too, the corporation is not punished, and does not pay the compensation. Usually one punishes the stockholders who in the present corporate climate have virtually no control over corporate actions. Or, if the corporation can pass on the cost of a fiscal punishment or compensation, it is in the end the consumer who pays for the punishment or compensation. If severe enough, hitting the pocketbook may result in the reduction of workforce, again resting the burden on those least deserving, more precisely, on those not responsible at all. Sooner or later, usually sooner, someone hits upon the solution of punishing those individuals of the corporation most directly responsible for the corporate act. There are also moral difficulties associated with this alternative. For example, many top executives are protected through insurance policies, part of the perks of the job. That would be satisfactory if the intent is simply to compensate, but it neutralizes any deterrent or retributive effect. But let us pass over these considerations and examine more closely these recommendations to "go inside" the corporation to punish an individual, whether stockholder, employee, agent, manager, or director of the corporation.

For the traditionalist there is little difficulty. The traditionalist recognizes the corporation as a legal fiction which for better or worse may have equal protection under the law of other persons, but the traditionalist may accept those legal trappings as at best a useful way of treating the corporation for legal purposes. After all, morally the corporation is not responsible; only individuals are. As long as those within the corporation pay for the deed, there is no theoretical difficulty.

What of the corporatist's position? The single advantage is that the adoption of the position would mean that some sense could be made of pointing an accusing finger or raising a fist in moral outrage at a fictitious person, a behavior which might otherwise appear not only futile but ridiculous. In the new corporatist scheme the behavior would no longer be ridiculous, only futile. The disadvantages, on the other hand, are apparent when one attempts to follow the responsibility assignment with the normally attendant moral moves as I have just shown. Either those moves are blocked entirely, since one may find no method by which to punish, or the moves are diverted away from the genuine culprit (the fictitious moral agent) and directed toward someone inside the corporation (non-fictitious moral agent). Either alternative is unacceptable. The former would entail that some citizens of the moral community, namely corporate persons, were not subject to the full obligations of membership. That reduces biological members to the status of second-class citizens, shouldering as they do all the burdens. The latter alternative, "going inside," is equally offensive. This alternative means that biological agents are sacrificed vicariously for the sins of the corporation. This solution not only reduces the biological agents to second-class citizens, but would make scapegoats or worse, sacrificial lambs, of them. Thus would the admission of the corporation into the moral community threaten to disturb the logic associated with the ascription of responsibility.

In addition to these problems, the corporatists face other theoretical obstacles. It is not clear that "going inside" a corporation is often, if ever, intelligible, given the analysis of a corporate act. To counter the traditionalist's claim that only individuals are responsible, French claims that the corporate act is not identical with the acts of individuals in the corporation. Given this, how is it possible now to reverse that claim and hold individuals responsible for something which they did not do? All they did at most was to vote for the corporation to do something, or to pay for something to be done on behalf of the corporation. The claim that individual acts and corporate acts are not identical opens the door to criminalless crime, a possibility admitted openly by French in another earlier paper. French there notes that a collective entity may be responsible yet no individual in that collectivity be responsible. Far from being an extreme case, that outcome may include all corporate acts. As mentioned above, such an alternative is unacceptable. But, again, can one make intelligible going inside to make one or more individuals responsible? In order to do so the corporatist must shift ground and concede that the individual acts and the corporate acts are identical, or perhaps that the individuals, by voting on a course of illegal or immoral action, coerced the hapless corporation to go along with the deed.

Although I have offered what I take to be a satisfactory defense of the traditionalist position, I would like to close by suggesting an alternative model for viewing the corporation. An alternative is needed because the corporatist's model has largely succeeded in warping many of our intuitions and is reinforced not only by legal idioms, but by managerial vocabulary. In many a corporatist's eye the corporation is an organism, and perhaps even much like a biological person. It has a brain, nerve receptors, muscle, it moves, reproduces, expands, develops, grows, in some periods the "fat is cut off," processes information, makes decisions, and so on. It adjusts to the environment. Such a metaphor may be useful but we have now begun to be victimized by the metaphorical model. Unfortunately, reformers have found it useful to accept that language and that model. It is useful to personify and then to vilify. The model, I fear, stands behind many attempts to endow the corporation with moral agency and personhood.

A more adequate model, especially for those who are reform-minded, I would maintain provides a different perspective from which to view contemporary trends. The corporation is more like a machine than an organism.[5] Like machines they are human inventions, designed by humans, modified by humans, operated by humans. Like many machines they are controlled by the few for the benefit of the few. They are no longer simple, easily understandable, organizations, but as complicated as the latest piece of electronic hardware. It takes years of training to learn how to operate and direct one. Like machines they are created, yet they create and shape humans.

If a complicated machine got out of hand and ravaged a community, there seems something perverse about expressing our moral outrage and indignation to the machine. More appropriately, our fervor should be addressed to the operators and to the designers of the machine. They, not the machines, are morally responsible. To ascribe responsibility to such machines, no matter how complicated, is tantamount to mistaking the created for the creator. This mystification is a contemporary form of animism. Such is the case for anthropological bigotry.

NOTES

1. Of those who apparently espouse this view to some degree are Norman Bowie and Tom L. Bauchamp in *Ethical Theory and Business* (Englewood Cliffs, NJ, Prentice-Hall, 1979), e.g., chap. 1 and comments on p. 128; and Christopher Stone in *Where the Law Ends* (New York: Harper, Colophon, 1975).

2. See *Capitalism and Freedom,* (Chicago, IL, University of Chicago Press, 1962), pp. 133–36.

3. One of French's earliest works is "Morally Blaming Whole Populations," which appears in *Philosophy, Morality, and International Affairs* (New York, Oxford University Press, 1974) ed. Virginia Held et al., pp. 266–85.

4. The positivistic interpretation is suggested by, among other things, French's references to Austin and H.L.A. Hart. The distinction between organizational chart and recognition rules also resembles the positivistic distinction between secondary and primary rules.

5. Although I do not follow Ladd's argument, one good example of taking this alternative model seriously is demonstrated in his "Morality and the Ideal of Rationality in Formal Organizations," in *Monist,* vol. 54 (October 1970), pp. 488–516.

35. What Is Hamlet to McDonnell-Douglas or McDonnell-Douglas to Hamlet: DC-10*

Peter A. French

1.

On the third of March 1974 on the outskirts of Paris, France, a Turkish Airlines plane carrying 346 passengers and crew fell from the sky killing all aboard. The plane was built by the McDonnell-Douglas Corporation, with major design subcontracts to the Convair Division of General Dynamics. It was Ship 29 of the DC-10 line. It became clear shortly after the event that the crash was no mere accident or an act of God or due to pilot or crew error. Ship 29 fell from the sky when its cargo-hold door blew open at approximately 10,000 feet, causing the floor of the passenger compartment to collapse, thereby breaking the electrical and hydraulic lines that run under that floor. Without electrical or hydraulic power the airplane is unflyable.

The Paris crash was not the first cargo door failure on an in-flight DC-10. Some two years earlier over Windsor, Ontario, an almost duplicate accident occurred, but not all hydraulic lines were severed. The pilot of that plane, owned by American Airlines, miraculously managed to land the airplane in Detroit, without fatalities. The history of DC-10 door failure and floor collapse, however, dates back to July 1970 when Ship 1 of the line, while under pressurization tests outside a hangar at the Douglas factory, blew its cargo door and the floor collapsed.

There can be little doubt that many engineers and managerial personnel at McDonnell-Douglas (and Convair) knew, well before the Paris crash, of the potential for a Class IV hazard[1] due to

From *Business and Professional Ethics Journal* 1:2 (1982); 1–13.

*The author acknowledges with appreciation support from the Exxon Education Foundation and the Center for the Study of Values, University of Delaware.

defective design of the DC-10 cargo door latching system and the floor structure. Not unexpectedly, McDonnell-Douglas tried to blame Turkish Airlines and its ground personnel for the Paris disaster. When that did not stick, it then suggested that some relatively low-ranking members within its own corporate structure had been contributorily negligent in the manufacture of Ship 29. There is, indeed, strong evidence that some employees of McDonnell-Douglas, through negligence, carelessness, or sloppiness, contributed to the design and manufacture of a defective airplane, but the authors of one of the books that provide the history of the corporate development of the DC-10 have also written:

> Some part of the blame [for the Paris disaster] must lie with the major subcontractor for the DC-10, the Convair division of General Dynamics. But the *central responsibility,* at least in terms of morality, must lie with McDonnell-Douglas and in particular with its Douglas Division.[2]

Evidence supporting that claim will be of primary concern here, but the moral responsibility of some individuals within the broader context of corporate responsibility will also be examined. I am not concerned with legal responsibility, which is a matter for the courts. The standard legal notions of strict liability, enterprise liability, and, the traditional ambit of corporate legal responsibility, vicarious liability would seem to provide adequate legal bases for recovery for wrongful death suits in this case, but the usual interpretation of such notions steadfastly sidesteps full-fledged corporate *moral* accountability and blameworthiness and hence does not locate a ground upon which a viable theory of corporate criminality and punishment may be built. That project has been the basic intent of my work on corporate moral responsibility. The Paris disaster happens to provide particularly clear examples to test my theory[3] regarding corporate and individual moral responsibility against our intuitions.

2.

In order to examine some of the morally significant aspects of this case, it will be necessary to introduce what I take to be rather commonly held views about the accountability of moral persons. A first condition of accountability (or moral responsibility) is what Bradley called ''self-sameness.'' Bradley wrote:

> If when we say, ''I did it,'' the I is not to be the one I, distinct from all other I's; or if the I now here is not the same I with the I whose act the deed was, then there can be no question whatever but that the ordinary notion of responsibility disappears.[4]

This condition is deeply grounded in our intuitions. It is, simply, the statement of the need for identity through time of moral subjects. If moral persons lack identity through time, in other words if there were *no* grounds for identifying one moral person now as the same person who existed at some previous time and did certain things, all sense of holding persons accountable for their deeds would be lost. The ''self-sameness'' condition, as I have argued elsewhere,[5] can be met by corporations as well as by natural persons.

In Book Three of the *Nicomachean Ethics,* Aristotle argues that only voluntary actions are properly praised or blamed. When behavior is involuntary, ''we are pardoned and sometimes even pitied.''[6] For Aristotle, behavior under constraint or compulsion or due to ignorance is involuntary. Let us concentrate on ignorance. Aristotle distinguishes two primary senses of ignorance. The first is ignorance of moral principle, which he tells us is not pardonable. He writes, ''Ignorance in moral choice does not make an act involuntary—it makes it wicked.''[7] Aristotle's second major sense of ignorance is ''ignorance of the particulars which constitute the circumstances and the issues involved in the action.''[8] Aristotle maintains that exculpability and pardon depend on what aspects of the circumstances are those of which the person is ignorant.

Consider Hamlet. Let us stipulate that he knows his moral principles, that he knows that intentionally killing an innocent human being is murder, is morally wrong. We also know that he is certainly ignorant of the fact that the person behind the arras in Gertrude's room is the rather harmless Polonius and not the murderous King Claudius. In fact, when he stabs that person, he believes he is stabbing the King. In keeping with Aristotle's point, it is clear that a person may be ignorant of many of the true descriptions of his action that are different from the one under which he intended the action. An action may be intended under one description but not intended under another. Hamlet intends to kill the person hiding behind the arras, and he intends to kill the king who he believes is hiding there, but he certainly does not intend to kill Polonius. Hamlet's ignorance of the identity of the person he intentionally stabs even may be offered in support of the claim that it is false that Hamlet *murdered* Polonius. (You can kill but you cannot unintentionally murder someone.) Of course, there is much more we should want to say about Hamlet's deed before we consider letting him off the moral hook. At the very least, however, it is clear that when accountability is at issue, it is crucial to know what a person intended as well as to know what actually happened. Insofar as ignorance limits what a person can actually intend, we see why true descriptions of a person's actions that are unknown or unforeseeable by him are not properly praised or blamed. Suppose Hamlet had stabbed into the arras thinking he was killing a rat and, lo and behold, the king, who had been hiding there, is dispatched on his way off this mortal coil. Would Hamlet deserve praise for so efficiently avenging his father? Not very likely!

These considerations may be captured in what I have elsewhere called the strict or Primary Principle of Accountability (PPA)[9]: a person can only be held accountable for that person's intentional acts.

PPA, however, is counterintuitive. It doesn't even satisfy in the Polonius stabbing case. A few minor modifications need to be made.

First, we do want to hold persons morally accountable, at least to some degree, for some of the unintended effects of their actions, those they should have or did know would occur. Suppose you know that you have inadequate skill for the performing of some task that when performed by the unskilled usually results in harm to someone else. The first time you perform the task, if you are unaware that harm will result and harm does result, we are likely to write off the harm as an accident or a misfortune and not hold you accountable. If you perform the task again, without sufficiently improving your skill, even if causing the harm is not your intention, it would generally be regarded as true that you were willing to have the harm occur. In such cases you can be held morally accountable for the harm. This explains why we are inclined to hold Hamlet morally accountable for Polonius' death. When he stabs through the arras with the intention of killing the person behind it (though he believes that it is the king), he is willing to kill Polonius if, as it happens, Polonius is the person in hiding. Polonius cries out from behind the arras, "Oh, I am slain!" The Queen asks Hamlet: "What hast thou done?" And Hamlet, somewhat befuddled, responds: "Nay, I know not. Is it the King?" When he learns it is Polonius, however, he says without apparent remorse: "Thou wretched, rash, intruding fool, farewell! I took thee for thy better." (His lack of regret at having killed Polonius shows again when he carts off the corpse.) It seems not unfair to describe Hamlet as having at least been willing to kill Polonius, though he certainly had no intention of doing so. Being willing to do something then does not entail intending to do it, but that means that moral accountability involves more than PPA allows. Not having intended the outcome, of course, might be treated as mitigatory in some cases. Holding Hamlet morally responsible for Polonius' death is not necessarily equivalent to accusing him of murder.

The second modification of PPA takes into account obliquely or collaterally intended second or non-original effects that involve other persons. Suppose we have two persons: John and Mary. Suppose John does *a* and Mary does *b* at some time later, but in direct response to John's doing *a*, and an outcome of Mary's doing *b* is harmful, and John was aware of that when he did *a*. Should John or Mary or both be held accountable for that harm? If Mary's doing *b* is a natural or (within some organizational structure) a required response to John's doing *a*, we usually hold only John primarily accountable for the harm (or John and the organization) by reason of what we may call oblique intention of a non-original effect. (We assume that John knows that to get Mary to do *b*, he has to do *a* or that he can get Mary to do *b* if he does *a*.) If Mary's doing *b*, although a response to John's doing *a*, is something she knows to be morally wrong and she can be truly described as willing for the harmful event to occur, even if not intending to cause harm, then Mary and not John may be held primarily accountable for the harm, *ceteris paribus*. But, if John's doing *a* is a clear temptation for Mary to do *b*, if John should know or does know it is such a temptation and John does *a*, (even if he does not intend that Mary do *b*) and harm occurs, then the moral responsibility for the harm would, to some extent or in some degree be distributed to both, but fall more heavily on John than Mary, *ceteris paribus*. Within certain organizational structures, however, Mary's doing *b* may be an established and automatic response to John's doing *a*, and that should be or is known by John. In such cases, when harm results, John is held more to account and Mary less so for the results of Mary's doing *b*. The historically more automatic Mary's response, the less she is held morally to account.

The principle of accountability that satisfies all of these considerations could be put in the following form: A person (pre-supposing Bradleyian self-sameness) may be held morally accountable for his intentional actions and for those actions that he was willing to perform under different descriptions of his intentional actions. Also, he may be held accountable for those non-original or second effects that involve the actions of other persons that he obliquely or collaterally intended or was willing to have occur as the result or under different descriptions of his actions. Let us call this the Extended Principle of Accountability (EPA). Armed with EPA, which may still need further modification but will suffice for present purposes, let us examine the DC-10 case. Remember that our first interest is with the ascription of moral responsibility to McDonnell-Douglas.

3.

What might justify such an ascription? It seems to me that we have at least three solid contenders: (1) McDonnell-Douglas would have to have decided to build Ship 29 intending that its design be defective such as would predictably result in a crash that kills hundreds of people; or (2) McDonnell-Douglas, not intending Ship 29 be defective or crash, would have to have taken steps in the development, design, and construction process of the airplane that it knew or should have known to be inadequate with regard to safety and highly likely to result in an in-flight Class IV hazard; or (3) it would have to have established policies and performed actions that it knew or should have known would prompt rather automatic responses by persons associated with the corporation that would increase the likelihood of the manufacture of a defective product, Ship 29.

Clearly McDonnell-Douglas did not design, manufacture, and sell DC-10s with the intention that they crash. It surely did not build Ship 29 and sell it to Turkish Airlines with the intention of killing 346 people. Our interest will have to focus on the other two possibilities, one that puts forth the claim that without intending to produce a defective airplane, McDonnell-Douglas was willing to do so and the other that claims that McDonnell-Douglas was willing to have a harmful outcome occur as the result of the predictable actions of other persons made in response to actions or policies of McDonnell-Douglas. In both claims appeal is made to EPA and not to the strict PPA. Surprisingly and sadly, the facts support both claims.

Before we examine those facts, it will help if we are clear about a few rudiments of DC-10 design.[10] We need concern ourselves only with cargo doors and passenger floors. The cargo doors on a DC-10 are large and cannot utilize the same plug design that secures the passenger entry doors. Instead, a latching system needs to be installed. There are two alternative types of systems that might be used. One is electrical, the other hydraulic. An electric latch actuator system is lighter, has fewer parts, and is easier to maintain than an hydraulic system. A hydraulic system, however, continuously exerts pressure on the latching device, holding it in place. An electrical system exerts pressure only when it is switched on. Electrically driven latches are prone to slip back if they are not made irreversible. When they achieve maximum force they must be fixed until the electric switch is again activated.

> An electric latch will behave very differently from a hydraulic one. A hydraulic latch, though positive, is *not* irreversible. If it fails to go over-center, it will in the nature of things "stall" at a point where the pressure inside the cylinder has reached equilibrium with the friction which is obstructing the travel of the latch. Thereafter, quite a small opposite pressure will move it in the reverse direction—and what this means in a pressure-hull door is that if the latches have not gone quite "over," they will slide open quite smoothly as soon as a little pressure develops inside the hull and starts pushing at the inside of the door. Thus, they will slide back and the door will open well before the pressure inside the aircraft hull is high enough to cause a dangerous decompression. The door will undoubtedly be ripped from its hinges by the force of the slip stream but, at low altitude, that poses no threat of structural damage to the plane and no danger to its passengers. The crew will immediately become aware of the problem, because the aircraft cannot be pressurized, and can simply return to the airport.
>
> However, if an irreversible electric latch fails to go over-center, the result will usually be quite different. Once current is switched off, the attitude of the latch is fixed, and if it has gone quite a long way over the spool, there will be considerable frictional forces between the two metal surfaces, holding the latch in place. Pressure building up inside the door cannot *slide* the latches open. It can only force the fixed part-closed latches off their spools. This, typically, will happen in a swift and violent movement, occurring only when pressure inside the airplane has built up to a level when sudden depressurization will be structurally dangerous.[11]

The underside of the passenger floor of a wide-bodied jet-liner is laced with the electrical and hydraulic lines that are absolutely necessary for the airplane to fly. The stability of that floor is crucial. In the event of a sudden decompressurization of the cargo area, enormous unoffset pressures from the passenger compartment are exerted on the floor. Without sufficient support, it will buckle and break and in so doing sever the electrical and hydraulic lines. The DC-10 was designed both with an electric cargo door latching system and with relatively few passenger floor supports, given the wide-bodied nature of the craft. Why? Certainly not because McDonnell-Douglas intended to build a dangerous airplane.

McDonnell-Douglas seems to have believed that by using technology that had proven successful during its long tradition of building passenger aircraft, it was manufacturing a safe product. DC-10 engineers, under express management orders, utilized the existing Douglas technology gained on the DC-3, DC-8 and DC-9 as the basic design for the wide-bodied DC-10.[12] That technology, though not clearly inappropriate to the jumbo craft, in the case of crucial systems, had been superceded by engineering advancements pioneered by Boeing and Lockheed on the 747 and the Tristar. The "state of the art" had developed, before McDonnell-Douglas had committed itself to its DC-10 design, beyond the design constraints with which McDonnell-Douglas had saddled its engineers, and the relevant technology was not proprietary.[13]

McDonnell-Douglas has an oft-stated[14] company policy of technological caution that, combined with its severe financial straits in the 1960s, was apparently interpreted by its engineers and manufacturing staff to dictate that corners be cut[15] and existing Douglas technology be used, even if that meant that some systems that were rejected as inferior by its competitors would be designed into the DC-10. It is of note that another engineering result of policy and financial constraint is less redundancy of key systems in the DC-10 than on 747s and Tristars. Both its competitors have four hydraulic systems each of which is capable of providing sufficient power for a landing. (Manual power is ineffective in moving control surfaces on a wide-bodied airplane). The DC-10 was engineered with only three redundant hydraulic systems, all running in parallel under the cabin floor. Its competitors can weather the loss of one more system than the DC-10. There is, of course, a point somewhere along the line where redundancy, even in essential systems, is waste. It probably is not reached, however, at three or four systems.[16] The DC-10 simply did not achieve the minimum state of the relevant engineering art. In the case of some products, that might be only quaint, but not, we should all allow, when the transportation of millions of people is involved.

The evidence supports the claim that McDonnell-Douglas designed an airplane that they *should have known* did not meet the engineering standards of the industry with respect to certain crucial systems. Manufacturing that airplane is arguably redescribable as being willing to produce a Class IV in-flight hazard, regardless of what McDonnell-Douglas might have intended. This sounds extremely harsh; unfortunately for McDonnell-Douglas matters are worse. Not only *should they have known* of the extreme hazard to life they were manufacturing, they *did* know. The evidence seems incontrovertible.[17] As it happens, in order to make the DC-10 case analogous to Hamlet's killing Polonius, we would have to imagine that Hamlet in fact knows that the chances are the person hiding behind the arras is not the king, yet he stabs away intending to kill the king, but willing to kill whoever is there, perhaps because he wants, at least, to terrify his mother.

In 1969 Convair was asked by McDonnell-Douglas to prepare a Failure Mode and Effects Analysis (an FMEA) for the DC-10's cargo door latching system. The FMEA is an assessment by the design engineers of the likelihood of failure of the system and its consequences for the airplane. FMEAs on the critical systems of a new airplane must be given to the FAA by the manufacturer when the airplane is certified. Convair's FMEA for the cargo door latching system shows that there were at least nine possible failure sequences that could result in life-endangering hazards. Four of those sequences would produce sudden depressurization in flight and the almost certainty of a crash of the airplane. One of those sequences in the FMEA reads as follows:

> Door will close and latch, but will not safety lock. Indicator light will indicate normal position. Door will open in flight—resulting in sudden depressurization and possibly structural failure of floor; also damage to empennage by expelled cargo and/or detached door. Class IV hazard in flight.[18]

Approximately five years later that is exactly what happened over the outskirts of Paris. (It may also be of note that McDonnell-Douglas never submitted that Convair-prepared FMEA to the FAA.[19]) If the FMEA was not enough evidence for McDonnell-Douglas to be said to *know* of the defects of its DC-10 design, one year later, in 1970, the cargo door blew and the floor collapsed in Ship 1, the prototype of the line, while it was undergoing standard pressurization tests.

If we apply EPA to the facts, it is clear that on the basis of this evidence alone McDonnell-Douglas can be held morally accountable for the Paris crash. Its knowledge of the defective Class IV hazard design of the cargo door latching system well before Ship 29 was built for Turkish Airlines provides us with adequate grounds to support the claim that McDonnell-Douglas was willing to manufacture and market an airplane that had a higher probability than the Boeing 747 or the Lockheed L-1011 of creating a Class IV hazard in flight. Again notice that I do not believe McDonnell-Douglas wanted or intended to manufacture a defective airplane. Its intentional actions regarding design decisions, however, clearly have a high probability, as shown in its own FMEAs, of certain consequences which, though unintended, ought, nonetheless, given the information available to McDonnell-Douglas, to have been expected by the manufacturer. Sadly, there is even evidence, in the form of company memos, that high-ranking engineering personnel expected Class IV hazards to occur on in-flight DC-10s.[20] It is as if Hamlet did not expect it was the king in hiding, hoped it was, and stabbed anyway.

In this analysis I have not tried to locate within the McDonnell-Douglas corporate structure any individual human beings who were significant contributors to the series of corporate decisions that resulted in the design and manufacture of the DC-10. Finding the Corporation morally accountable surely ought not to exculpate such persons. In cases such as this, however, the corporate "black box"[21] is not easily penetrated. The effects of what have been called the "Law of Diminishing Control" and "Cognitive Dissonance" as well as unintentional blocking of information, etc., in such large decentralized firms as McDonnell-Douglas, belie any simple reductionism to the beliefs, reasons, and intentions of human beings associated in the corporation. Australian corporate legal theorist W. B. Fisse has (with a nod to my work) recently written:

> The conventional assumption has been that corporate crime reduces to the willed acts of individual actors. However, this assumption fails to account for corporate behavior which cannot be explained exclusively in individualistic terms . . . corporate policy is not merely the sum of individual intentions but a collective choice influenced and constrained by organizational factors, including bargaining and teamwork. Nor are corporate acts simply the aggregation of individual acts: organization is a sine qua non. Accordingly, there is no oddity about regarding a corporation as a criminally responsible actor (or a moral person) where the act alleged has a sufficient organizational nexus.[22]

There is, however, another aspect of the unhappy history of Ship 29 in which both individual and corporate responsibility, in accord with EPA, may be assessed.

4.

After McDonnell-Douglas admitted possible difficulties with locking the cargo doors following the Windsor incident, an agreement with the FAA was reached that called for a modification of the doors. In July 1972, Ship 29 was in the "Rework for Delivery" area of the Long Beach Plant of McDonnell-Douglas. Included in the work to be done on Ship 29 were modifications to the cargo door. The plant records for July 1972 indicate that three inspectors stamped the work records for Ship 29 to indicate the modifications had been completed and that the plane was in compliance with FAA guidelines. None of the work on the cargo doors had actually been done. All three inspectors identified the stamps on the work record as theirs, but none of the three remembered having worked on Ship 29. There is no evidence that the stamps of all three, however, were stolen or borrowed during July 1972. It is company policy that:

> You are responsible for any work that your stamp appears on the record for accepting.[23]

One inspector, Edward Evans, conjectured that his stamp appears on the records of Ship 29 either because "it was high summer,"[24] that he had become confused between airplanes because of the summer heat and had stamped the wrong document, *or* that he had been interested in some other aspect of the reworking and had not carefully inspected the cargo door latching system. The other inspectors could not even offer conjectures as to how their stamps appeared on the records of Ship 29.

The president of the Douglas Division of McDonnell-Douglas, John Brizendine, who was responsible for "engineering, flight development, and production" of the DC-10, when questioned by attorneys, claimed no personal knowledge of misuse of inspection stamps. In fact, he insisted that he had nothing to do with insuring that design reworking actually was done. After the Paris crash he did reprimand the inspectors for misuse of stamps.

We could give two alternative accounts of what happened with regard to the inspections of Ship 29. The first is that three inspectors, whether singly or in concert, lied or conspired to lie about the inspections of Ship 29. But for what reasons? The second is that the McDonnell-Douglas system that is supposed to assure that individual responsibility is exercised by personnel at various stages of production to "insure quality in the tradition of the company" is fundamentally weak and easily compromised by employees who have fallen into a rather automatic pattern of behavior encouraged by that company policy and procedure. It is certainly impractical to insist that President Brizendine or any other high ranking corporate officer make all of the necessary inspections, etc., himself. However, it was not responsible for him to assume an uncompromised verification of inspection procedure.

The evidence[25] supports the view that over the years McDonnell-Douglas established an inspection procedure that invites or tempts inspectors to be lax and careless and some of those inspectors, either through inadvertence or because of conditioning to laxness, cursorily performed tasks that, given the basically poor design of the aircraft, called for the closest attention to detail to insure safety. McDonnell-Douglas policies and procedures constituted a temptation to carelessness, even though managerial superiors were unaware of such a temptation and that safety was at stake. Those corporate officers, we may say with some confidence, should have expected that their inspection procedures would be unintentionally compromised by inspectors.

The actions of the three inspectors are not excusable (if inadvertence is proved, that may be exculpatory), but it would be a grand offense to our moral intuitions, in the absence of any evidence of intentional sabotage, etc., to hold those inspectors primarily responsible for the crash of Ship 29. We are brought back to the principal actor in the design, manufacture, and sale of Ship 29, McDonnell-Douglas Corporation.

5.

When recently discussing this DC-10 case with certain economists and management professors, I was surprised to learn that they thought the whole matter should be resolved as a risk issue. On their account, McDonnell-Douglas, operating in the best of market traditions, simply had taken a not unreasonable, calculated risk in the manufacture of the DC-10. All machines are liable to failure or breakdown, and any manufacturer of a machine needs to take the probability of failure into account when marketing the product. For example, it buys product liability insurance. Also, any consumer of the machinery, I was told, can be presumed to know that machines are liable to breakdown. Turkish Airlines and its passengers can be presumed to have had such general knowledge of machinery. What then is the problem? If all that is meant by "taking a risk" in a business context is that the corporation, fully cognizant of certain product deficiencies, produces and markets the product in the hope (probably supported by statistically-based predictions of failure) that sales will offset any actual liabilities due to inadequate design, then evidence that such calculated risks were taken can only serve to strengthen the ascription of moral responsibility to the corporation on the occasion of harm. "It was a calculated risk" has no exculpatory or even mitigatory power. In fact, in cases of this sort, if anything, it is inculpating. There is, however, another side to the risk issue that is often confused with the matter of whether the corporation took a reasonable or calculated risk when it decided to manufacture and market its product. That is the matter of putting persons using the product "at risk" in cases where ordinarily they would be presumed to have taken or accepted the risk.

Clearly, risk, in this sense, is, in most cases, negotiable. A reasonable person will accept a certain amount of risk if the compensation is satisfactory. Everyone, we might say, has a risk budget. But risk cannot be negotiated in a unilateral contract nor can it be said to have been negotiated in the absence of knowledge by the parties of the relevant data. For risk to have been negotiated, the facts relevant to the potential for the causing of harm must be known by the parties, at least in general terms. Certainly every passenger who enters a commercial airliner should realize that there is a certain probability that the aircraft will develop a malfunction that could result in his death. In the case of most American commercial airplanes that probability is remarkably low. The benefits of fast travel, etc., far outweigh the risks in the minds of many travelers. The passenger pays for his ticket and boards the airplane. In effect, there is a certain, generally understood, risk to life involved in the use of a commercial airliner. Passengers can be presumed to understand that the risk is about the same for any craft on which they might fly.

None of this rather unexceptional business is, however, relevant to the DC-10 case. The DC-10 design was such as to drive it out of the risk probabilities of its sister craft. Risk budget calculations made in ignorance of the faulty design are not necessarily going to be the same as those that would have been made if the facts were known. The relevant design information was, of course, not widely known or easily accessible to consumers. In the case of Ship 29, Turkish Airlines clearly should have known of the previous cargo door locking failures, but it also had the assurances of McDonnell-Douglas that FAA-required modifications had been made.

Risk is simply not a unilateral matter. McDonnell-Douglas's decision to take a risk with the DC-10, of course, supports the view that is uncontested, that McDonnell-Douglas had no intention of building a defective airliner. The fact is McDonnell-Douglas was just wrong in its calculation of the risk it was taking with respect to product liability. It was creating a far greater risk for the passengers of its aircraft than they could have taken into account when deciding to fly the DC-10, and it should have known (indeed it did know) that it had miscalculated the risk. If the information about the defective design of the DC-10 had been public knowledge, it is unlikely McDonnell-Douglas would have been able to sell the airplane. (After the Chicago crash of 1978, attributed to engine mount failure, the entire DC-10 fleet was grounded for reworking and inspection. The resumption of DC-10 service, despite bargain rates and other allurements [compensations], was greeted with less than enthusiasm by the flying public. Even today many passengers report a preference to book flights on planes other than DC-10s. That is, of course, a good example of risk bargaining at work in the marketplace. No such circumstances surround the Paris crash.)

In short, the introduction of the notion of risk in the DC-10 case is totally irrelevant to the moral accountability concern. Even if all 346 people who boarded Ship 29 in Paris on March 3, 1974, knew they were entering a machine and that every machine has a statistical probability of breakdown for any moment of its operation, they cannot reasonably be said to have struck a bargain to accept the realistic risk probabilities of the *crash of Ship 29* for the compensation of the convenience of less in-travel time between Paris and London. McDonnell-Douglas' failure to engineer to the state of the art again enters the picture of our analysis because it accounts for the fact that the probabilities of harm generally understood to apply to American commercial aircraft were inapplicable to the calculation of the risk passengers were taking in the case of DC-10s. The facts are that McDonnell-Douglas knowingly exposed DC-10 passengers to a significantly higher probability of death than they would have been exposed to on other aircraft. The fact that McDonnell-Douglas performed acts that constituted creating such a risk and concealed pertinent evidence from the public and the regulatory agency only supports the moral indictment.

6.

In the absence of admission of corporations like McDonnell-Douglas to citizenry in the moral world, the moral responsibility for the Paris air disaster cannot reasonably be finally assessed. The aggregate of justifiable individual responsibilities for the production of Ship 29 simply does not ''add-up to'' that for its crash. Without a theory of the corporation as a moral person upon which to base the accountability ascriptions I have made in this analysis, the real villain of the piece will escape moral detection. A. A. Berle has written:

> The medieval feudal power system set the ''lords spiritual'' over and against the ''lords temporal.'' These were the men of learning and of the church who, in theory, were able to say to the greatest power in the world: ''You have committed a sin; therefore either you are excommunicated or you must mend your ways.'' The ''lords temporal'' could reply: ''I can kill you.'' But the ''lords spiritual'' could retort: ''Yes that you can, but you cannot change the philosophical fact.'' In a sense this is the great lacuna in the economic power system today.[26]

My theory of the corporation as a moral person[27] uncovers the grounds necessary to redescribe the actions of persons associated with a corporation as intentional acts of that corporation. If my account is cogent, we will have found the missing link that brings the corporate giants, today's ''lords temporal,'' into the scope of morality.

NOTES

1. A Class IV Hazard is a hazard involving danger to life.
2. Paul Eddy, Elaine Potter, and Bruce Page, *Destination Disaster* (New York: New York Times Book Co., 1976).
3. See my ''The Corporation as a Moral Person,'' *American Philosophical Quarterly* [16:3] July 1979 [pp. 297–317]. [See also chap. 8, sel. 33, *EIPL*.—ED.]
4. F. H. Bradley, *Ethical Studies* (Oxford: Oxford University Press, 1876; 1970 ed.), p. 5.
5. [Peter A. French,] ''Crowds and Corporations,'' *American Philosophical Quarterly* 19:3 (1982): 271–77.
6. Aristotle, *Nicomachean Ethics* (Ostwald translation) (Indianapolis, IN: Bobbs-Merrill Company, 1962), p. 52.
7. Ibid., p. 55.
8. Ibid., pp. 55–56.
9. [Peter A. French]. *The Scope of Morality* (Minneapolis: University of Minnesota Press, 1979), chap. I.
10. For a complete account see Eddy, Potter, and Page, op. cit.
11. Ibid., pp. 176–77.
12. Ibid., chap. 6. esp. pp. 96–99.
13. Ibid. Pp. 85–99 provide a clear and adequate account of the ''state of the art'' at the time of the development of the DC-10.
14. The authors of *Destination Disaster* [see n. 2] quote from McDonnell-Douglas company literature references to Pope's ''Be not the first by whom the new are tried/Nor yet the last to lay the old aside'' and Carnegie's ''Pioneering don't pay.'' Further accounts of corporate policy are cited in chap. 6.
15. Ibid., p. 97.
16. Ibid., p. 99.
17. Ibid., esp. chap. 10.
18. Ibid., p. 178.
19. Ibid., pp. 176–77.
20. Ibid., chap. 10.
21. See Christopher Stone, *Where the Law Ends* (New York: Harper and Row, 1975).
22. W. B. Fisse, ''The Retributive Punishment of Corporations'' (1980), unpublished.
23. Eddy, Potter, and Page, op. cit., p. 223.
24. Ibid., p. 224.
25. Ibid., pp. 223–35.
26. A. A. Berle, ''Economic Power and the Free Society,'' *The Corporate Take-Over*, ed. Andrew Hacker (Garden City, [NY:] Doubleday, 1964), p. 99.
27. See n. 3.

36. Ascribing Responsibility to Advisers in Government*

Dennis Thompson

In other times and other places, counselors often bore the responsibility for the consequences of their rulers' decisions—and with a vengeance. When for whatever reason the decisions of the Chinese emperors went awry, their ministers, it is said, could expect to have their hearts cut open, their feet cut off, or to be pickled in brine.[1] Today, advisers to government officials have less cause to worry. Rather than strict liability for the advice they give, advisers are commonly assumed to have no responsibility at all for the consequences of decisions made on the basis of their advice.[2] If anyone is to blame when decisions turn out badly, it is usually the official who made the decision, not the adviser who counseled him (unless of course the adviser deceives the officials or otherwise acts wrongly in ways the official could not be expected to take into account). I want to criticize the three most important theoretical claims that are put forward to absolve advisers of specifically moral responsibility: the first refers to causal criteria; the second, to the concept of intention; and the third, to role.[3] Each claim in effect takes one feature of the relationship between the adviser and the person he advises and turns it into the exclusive test for responsibility. None of these shortcuts will do, although each, substantially modified, may contribute something to a full account of the responsibility of advisers.[4]

I concentrate on only one kind of adviser since I suspect that any general theory of responsibility for advice will have to be constructed piecemeal from analyses of various particular kinds of advising. A good place to begin is the world of governmental advisers, whose influence in public life has expanded greatly in recent years.[5] Because these advisers work in institutional contexts, we are more likely to discover generalizations about their responsibility than if we were to consider (say) people who give occasional advice in everyday life. Because governmental advisers must sometimes decide whom their advice should serve (e.g., their immediate superior or the public), we also are more likely to notice problems in the definition of the role of adviser itself than if we were to consider (say) lawyers or doctors.

From *Ethics* 93:3 (1983): 546–60.

*I am grateful to Joel Feinberg, Albert Hirschman, Amy Gutmann, and Marion Smiley for advice on problems discussed in this article; since they could hardly have foreseen what I would do with their advice, they escape any blame for what I have written here.

I

The basic commonsense notion of responsibility derives from the idea of making something happen. Applied to relations between persons, the idea is that one person is responsible for what someone else does only if the first person causes the second to do it. On this view, as long as an adviser merely advises, we would not normally say that he causes the advisee to decide one way rather than another. Since the advisee remains free to accept or reject the advice, we would not blame the adviser for anything the advisee did. Just as in the law a voluntary intervention by another agent—a *novus actus interveniens*—breaks the chain of responsibility,[6] so in morality a subsequent voluntary decision by an official shifts the entire responsibility to him. Such a view may be appropriate for ascribing responsibility to agents who act independently in causal chains that produce physical effects. However, it fails completely to capture the complexities of the process of advising, which involves interaction among agents and influence that differs from the causing of physical events.

The key assumption of this version of the causal view—that causing an advisee to act is incompatible with his acting voluntarily—seems plausible only if one concentrates on instances in which an adviser makes an advisee do something and ignores the great variety of other ways an adviser may influence an advisee. An adviser often contributes significantly to the final decision an advisee makes. The way the adviser frames the alternatives, the weight he gives to various arguments, the language and the illustrations he uses (chosen perhaps to appeal especially to the advisee)—all these forms of influence may make the final decision different from what it would otherwise have been. On the causal view, such influences should count as causes of the outcome and therefore warrant ascribing some responsibility to the adviser. But at the same time, none of these forms of influence necessarily undermines the voluntariness of the advisee's decision. The nature of the process of advising itself, as a form of deliberation, requires that an advisee both make decisions voluntarily and respond to the influence of his advisers. Rather than causal influence being incompatible with voluntary decision, the presence of both is what characterizes a proper relationship between an adviser and an advisee.

An adviser's influence, moreover, need not always take the form of giving explicit reasons or arguments. When an official accepts advice more because of whom it comes from than because of what it says (as Roosevelt sometimes accepted Louis Howe's counsel; or Kennedy, his brother's and Ted Sorensen's),[7] we would want to impute some responsibility to the advisers and to do so without necessarily canceling or even reducing the responsibility of the official who made the decision. Stronger kinds of influence (such as advice accompanied by offers of support or threats of resignation), which even more clearly implicate the adviser in the consequences of an advisee's decision, would still allow us to call the decision voluntary.

More sophisticated proponents of the causal view, such as Hart and Honoré, recognize that "interpersonal transactions" (which include advising) constitute exceptions to their general principle that a subsequent voluntary intervention "negatives" causal connection and responsibility.[8] But Hart and Honoré still want to insist that (at least in legal theory) an adviser is not responsible for an advisee's actions based on the advice; they therefore must find some way to distinguish advice from other forms of influence that in their view do warrant the ascription of responsibility. In the law, a person who "merely advises" others is generally not liable for any harm the others commit; but a person who in some way "induces" others to act is generally liable.[9] To account for this distinction between inducing and advising (neither of which "negative" causal connection), Hart and Honoré suggest but do not develop two different criteria: one person is responsible for another's action insofar as the second person acted in the way the first person intended; or insofar as the first person advises the second person to follow a certain course of action rather than merely advising him about the course of action.[10] Both of these criteria have problems of their own that I discuss below, but the significant point to notice here is that by introducing the criteria Hart and Honoré have not only abandoned the principle that voluntary intervention breaks the causal chain but have moved well beyond the idea of one person's making another do something. All that remains of causal responsibility is the idea of one person's acting "in consequence" of another's influence, and to decide whether this is so in any particular instance. Hart and Honoré are forced to invoke what would normally be regarded as noncausal considerations (the intention of the adviser or the kind of advice he gives).

A similar problem confronts any attempt to determine responsibility exclusively according to the degrees of causal influence—for example, if we were to say that the adviser is more responsible to the degree that he has more influence over the person he advises. The problem is that an adviser who fails to discourage an official from pursuing a certain course of action may be just as culpable as one who encourages the official to follow it. To discriminate among the indefinite number of such omissions that "influence" a decision, we would have to invoke noncausal considerations, such as the expectations that attach to the role a particular adviser holds.[11] From among the many equally influential advisers who failed to try to prevent an official from implementing a harmful policy, we single out for blame those whose office should normally deal with the policy in question. The nature of an adviser's role may be even more significant than potential causal influence in determining how much responsibility we impute to him. A press secretary might have more potential influence over all the decisions a president makes than does the secretary of state, but if both failed to try to dissuade the president from undertaking a disastrous diplomatic initiative, we would usually blame the secretary of state more than the press secretary. We might not even blame the press secretary at all (although below I shall stress that the requirements of an adviser's role are not always sufficient grounds for absolving him from blame).

A causal criterion, then, does not get us very far in determining the responsibility of advisers. The most that we can coherently include in such a criterion would be the requirement that an adviser is responsible only if the person he advises would not have decided the way he did but for the advice (or the omission of the advice).[12] This requirement exonerates the adviser who, either by giving or refraining from giving advice, could have no influence on a decision maker (unless the adviser through negligence or some other act placed himself in position where he could have no such influence). The requirement would cancel or mitigate the responsibility of an adviser whose counsel was solicited after a decision maker had already made up his mind. Responding to the crisis in the Dominican Republic in 1965, Rusk and McNamara probably had already decided to order an American intervention when they asked the acting U.S. ambassador there if "he agreed with their view that a rebel victory would probably lead to a pro-communist government."[13] Given the ambassador's well-known anti-communist views and the form and timing of the request for the advice, we should not be inclined to impute much if any responsibility to the ambassador in this episode. No doubt the causal criterion will give rise to some difficult cases as we try to determine whether a decision would have been made but for some piece of advice (e.g., was a decision maker encouraged to act more vigorously because of the advice?), but I suspect that the critical questions of responsibility more often turn on other criteria. Even if an adviser is causally responsible (in the weak sense I have indicated) for harmful consequences of decisions based on his advice, he is far from being morally responsible. Advice (or its omission) may be misinterpreted. It may, for example, set off in the advisee's mind an entirely unexpected or unrelated chain of thought without which the advisee would not have made a particular decision but for which we could hardly blame the adviser.

II

Since the causal criterion by itself seems to spread responsibility too widely and indiscriminately, many theorists understandably look for a more restrictive criterion. Some notion of intention, drawn from a long and respectable philosophical tradition, has seemed the obvious candidate. Charles Fried presents a version of the criterion explicitly as a way of limiting moral responsibility: you are "personally" responsible only for what you intend. What you intend is to be understood as what you do, as distinguished from what you allow to happen.[14] Using this notion of intention certainly would shrink the scope of responsibility defined by the consequentialists against whom Fried explicitly develops his own theory. But where consequentialism (at least in unqualified form) places no limits on the harms that officials are responsible for preventing, theories like Fried's seem to insulate officials from responsibility for some harms for which we would intuitively want to blame them. On Fried's view, public officials who negligently or even corruptly divert money that should be spent for police protection are not morally responsible for any criminal assaults that occur as a result of the reduced protection, even when the officials could have anticipated that the assaults would occur.[15] By the same token, an adviser (like a lawyer) presumably is not culpable for harmful decisions made on the basis of his advice, so long as the adviser does not intend harm and so long as the adviser does not violate any duties of office in giving the advice (e.g., by lying to the advisee).[16]

Yet Fried evidently does not want to deny that sometimes we may morally criticize advisers for failing to anticipate the uses others make of their advice or that we may morally condemn officials for even remote consequences of their negligence or corruption. Thus it appears that, in some broader sense, Fried would hold officials responsible for consequences they do not intend.[17] But then we must wonder what is the force of holding someone personally responsible rather than merely morally responsible in this broader sense? Fried's answer seems to be that consequences for which we are personally responsible take precedence over other consequences in the sense that no remote consequences, side effects, or omissions can ever justify our intentionally doing wrong ("a person may not do wrong, even to prevent a greater wrong by others"). Fried therefore would have to hold that when an adviser's position requires that he give a certain kind of advice (such as merely technical analysis) to some other official, the adviser may be violating a trust (committing a wrong) if he refuses to provide that analysis or tries to offer some other kind of advice, even if he does so in order to prevent the official from committing a greater wrong.[18] Here a consequentialist response, which would compare the harm of violating the trust with the harm of fulfilling it, seems more plausible. We not only would want to justify a Defense Department analyst's refusal to provide his superiors with targeting plans for bombing medical facilities or civilian residences but also would hold him partly responsible for the bombing if he provided such plans.

Even if theories like Fried's could coherently find a place for moral criticism of unintended consequences, the priority these theories give to intention distorts the nature of responsibility in bureaucratic and other governmental institutions, where unintended consequences are so rife they might well be regarded as an occupational hazard. The standard counterexamples to such theories call into question the distinction between consequences that are means to one's end and those consequences that are merely side effects.[19] In these examples the agent achieves the end he intends, and the issue is whether he is responsible for certain foreseeable consequences: are they "means" or "side effects"? No doubt there are cases of this sort involving advisers: Consider an adviser who in helping pass a beneficial law knowingly ruins the reputation and destroys the career of the official whom he advises. But more common are instances where advisers do not achieve the ends they intend and indeed may intend just the opposite end. Such cases are instructive because at first glance they seem to support the use of the criterion of intention. Advisers to President Johnson who consistently opposed expansion of the Vietnam War and urged the withdrawal of American forces certainly did not intend their advice to have the effect of strengthening Johnson's resolve to continue the war. Yet dissenters such as George Ball became "domesticated," and their participation in the advisory process helped to legitimize the decisions they opposed.[20] They were welcomed as devil's advocates, their presence reassuring the president and others that the major objections to the administration's policy were being fully considered. To this extent, these dissenters, contrary to their own intentions, became part of the set of causes that sustained this policy.

It is of course difficult to know at what point one's objections serve mainly to further purposes one opposes, but at the point we could expect any reasonable person to recognize that his dissent has become counterproductive in this way, we would presumably consider a dissenting adviser at least a moral accessory.[21] Good intentions may make us think less badly of the adviser than of the advisee, but they cannot, at this point, absolve the adviser of responsibility for the consequences to which he contributes. Insofar as we are inclined to cancel or mitigate his responsibility, we would do so, not by citing an absence of intention, but by accepting either a plea that he could not have been expected to realize that he was promoting the result he opposed, or a plea that he could not have done anything to prevent that result. Notice, however, that even if we accept the latter plea (which in effect asserts that the official is not a cause even in the weak sense mentioned above), we might still want to criticize the official for continuing to serve as a member of a government pursuing immoral policies. Such criticism seems better framed in the language of complicity than of responsibility, however.[22] We would condemn him for his continued association with an immoral regime, without purporting to be able to show that this association actually helps perpetuate the regime or any of its policies. In any case, the official's intention does not appear to be the exclusive or even the chief factor in our assessment of his connection with the policies in question.

Another illustration of the insufficiency of the criterion of intention is the problem that sometimes confronts experts who serve on part-time advisory panels to various government agencies. It has been claimed that a series of advisory panels to the Food and Drug Administration provided advice that was intended, or at least should have been interpreted, as grounds for banning cyclamates, but FDA officials, allegedly for political reasons, presented the advice as being consistent with their decisions not to ban cyclamates completely.[23] Whatever the advisers intended, some of them—at least those who took part in the later phases of a process that went on for more than a decade—could have foreseen that the conclusions of the panels would be misinterpreted. Insofar as these advisers did not try to prevent their advice from being misused in this way, or did not dissociate themselves from its misuse, we should say that they too became partly responsible for the consequences of the failure to proscribe cyclamates.

Foreseeability, then, needs to be considered in ascribing responsibility, especially in the context of the organizations in which public officials and their advisers work. Many patterns of bureaucratic behavior, including practices that social scientists call pathological, are quite common in government and often could be anticipated by officials within these organizations, even if no one intends that the practices should exist, or that any harmful consequences they produce should occur.[24] Furthermore, some of these practices and consequences are also avoidable. Yet with a theory of responsibility that relies only on the criterion of intention, or that always gives intended consequences moral precedence over merely foreseen consequences, we are less likely to hold officials responsible for doing anything about these defective organizational practices and the harmful consequences that flow from them. Moreover, committing some lesser intentional wrong (breaking a promise to one's superior) may sometimes be necessary to prevent some greater wrong that would result from permitting the bureaucratic process to proceed as usual.

A criterion of foreseeability places some limitations on the scope of an adviser's responsibility: The less an adviser can reasonably be expected to anticipate the harmful consequences that result from his advice, the less responsible he is if he fails to prevent them.[25] But, to say that an adviser is more responsible because he could have foreseen the effects of his advice is not to imply that the person he advises is any less responsible for those effects. There is no fixed pool of responsibility such that when one person's share goes up, another's must go down (as with certain kinds of compensation in the law of torts). The advisee's responsibility must be appraised from the perspective of *his* location in the episode: In light of the advice he received and the options he faced, what could he have anticipated and controlled in the stream of consequences that flowed from his decision? The answer to such a question, though affected by the actions of his advisers, will not necessarily yield an ascription of responsibility that varies either directly or inversely with that of the advisers.

III

A third way to limit the responsibility of an adviser is to invoke the requirements of his official role.[26] An adviser may claim that by the formal or informal expectations of his office he is bound to give advice in certain specific ways (such as providing merely technical analysis), and so long as he does so properly, he cannot be held responsible for anything other officials do with his advice.

The classic source of a definition of the responsibility of advisers based on the requirements of their role is (or should be) chapter 25 of *Leviathan.*[27] There Hobbes clearly recognizes the special conditions that must obtain if a role is to shield an adviser from responsibility for the consequences of his advice. Hobbes distinguishes command, which purports to be directed to the benefit of the commander, from counsel, which purports to be directed only to the benefit of the person to whom it is given. No one may be "obliged" to do as he is counselled, because the hurt of not following it, is his own, and therefore no one should be blamed (accused or punished) for the counsel he gives. Up to this point, Hobbes's argument would appear to give much the same conclusions as would the doctrine of *novus actus interveniens.* But then Hobbes introduces a further distinction: counsel that is consistent with, and counsel that is contrary to, the duty of a counselor. The latter consists of counsel that is "vehemently pressed," in which the adviser urges action, appeals to "common passions and opinions" instead of "true reasoning," and hence may be supposed to be acting with regard to his own benefit rather than that of the person whom he advises.[28] A counselor who in this way acts contrary to the duty of his office may be accused and punished and presumably may also be blamed for consequences that follow from this advice.

This sharp distinction between two kinds of counsel is intelligible within the bounds of *Leviathan,* when shared standards of objective reasoning prevail in politics and where advisers speak to a single sovereign who authoritatively determines the public good. In modern democracies where these conditions do not exist, such a distinction, as a basis for insulating advisers, will be difficult to maintain, even with respect to scientific advisers, whose role most closely approximates that of Hobbes's dutiful counselors. The view nevertheless persists that some advisers can completely escape responsibility if they confine themselves to giving merely technical analysis (advice about means) and, conversely, that they risk blame if they overstep this role by recommending one public policy over another (advice about ends). In a report on the role of scientific advisers in the controversy in the late 1960s over the Anti-Ballistic Missile System (ABM), the Operations Research Society distinguished between analysts and advocates in a manner that recalls Hobbes's contrast between two kinds of counselors. The analyst restricts himself to the "quantifiable and logically structured aspects of the problem only," while the advocate need not admit the weaknesses of his positions and may put forward "unsupported allegations."[29] The report sharply criticized those scientific advisers who became advocates in the ABM debate. However, even on the highly technical questions in this debate, the kind of questions on which advisers on both sides chose to focus betrayed their partisanship and became a form of advocacy. Pro-ABM scientists concentrated on an analysis of the need for an ABM system, while the anti-ABM scientists stressed the evidence showing the inadequacy of an ABM system to meet this alleged need.[30] If on scientific questions such as this advisers are not able to purge their analyses of partisanship, we can hardly expect advisers on issues with even more economic and political content to sustain the role of Hobbesian analyst.[31]

It of course may be possible for an adviser only to analyze, not advocate. But even an adviser who presents a completely neutral analysis does not thereby escape moral responsibility for the consequences of his analysis. Under non-Hobbesian conditions, what the role of an adviser should be will often be contestable—morally so. A procedural controversy over the proper role of an adviser often simply reflects the substantive controversy in which the various advisers are engaged. The reaction to the ORS report, and its criticism of the scientists who advocated instead of analyzed, seemed to follow the divisions of the ABM controversy itself, pro-ABM scientists favoring the report and anti-ABM scientists disapproving of it.[32] When the nature of the role remains in such serious dispute, an adviser is responsible for the consequences of his choice of which role to play in the controversy.

To be sure, there must be a place in government for advisers who provide mainly technical analysis. The commissioner of the Food and Drug Administration, for example, should be able to insist that technical analysis of the safety and efficacy of drugs be given as impartially as possible and without any bias for or against regulation. The scientific personnel who provide such analysis should then not be held responsible for the consequences of some higher official's decision to ban, or not to ban, the drug. But to account for the limitation of responsibility of persons in technical or other similarly circumscribed roles, we do not have to attribute any intrinsic moral significance to the distinction between analysis and advocacy. The general utility of a division of labor in government, plus the obligation to fulfill one's freely assumed duties of office, are sufficient bases for excusing a technical adviser when his (properly provided) analysis leads to harmful consequences, or for accusing him when his (unauthorized) advocacy contributes to such consequences. Furthermore, these same kinds of considerations may also be reasons for overriding the requirements of role. An adviser may be blameworthy for failing to offer more than mere analysis—for example, when he realizes that unless he strongly opposes a particular policy some serious and irreversible harm will ensue, worse on balance than the harm of disturbing the normal practices of an advisory system. The advisers on the "Pesticides" Panel of the President's Science Advisory Committee in 1962 normally might have merely analyzed the scientific evidence of the effects of pesticides such as DDT, but instead they advocated steps to end their widespread use. Had they played their usual role, they would have been partially culpable for a significant delay in imposing the ban and hence for any irreversible harm to human health that occurred as a result of the delay.[33]

Beyond the realm of technical and scientific analysis, advisers are not likely to deny that advice almost inevitably involves advocacy and are not likely to rely on the distinction between analysis and advocacy to limit their responsibility. Instead, advocacy itself becomes a duty of counselors, and the more advocates, the better. We leave the territory of *Leviathan* and enter the world of *On Liberty*. It is often suggested that advice to public officials is a kind of microcosm of Mill's vision of a liberal society, where the free expression of many different perspectives is supposed to offer the best chance for arriving at policies that promote the public interest. An advisory system based on this model would populate government with advisers of diverse views and encourage each to advocate his particular and partial perspective. The official charged with making a decision would then be less likely in his deliberations to omit any important consideration and therefore more likely to discover the general interest (at whatever level of government the decision is made).[34] Given such a system, an adviser may well claim that he should not be held responsible for the decisions an official makes after listening to his advice, even if the official happens to follow his advice. The adviser himself may not subscribe to the position he is advocating but may be merely putting forward the partial point of view required by the role he plays in the advisory system.

If such a system exists and is understood to exist by advisers and the officials they counsel, any particular adviser's responsibility might be plausibly limited in this way. But no system of this kind is likely to be so well tuned that it will always produce an optimal balance of advice (let alone decisions in the public interest). Alexander George, who presents the most compelling design for such a system, specifies an elaborate set of structural conditions that would be necessary to make it function properly.[35] We may therefore wish to say that, when an adviser has good reason to believe that the advisory system in which he is participating is not yielding a reasonable balance of opinions or is otherwise distorting decisions and policies and his own expected role as advocate of a particular point of view is contributing to that distortion, he should abandon his normal role and seek to remedy the distortion in the process. If he fails to do so, he cannot, simply by appealing to the requirements of his role, disclaim responsibility for his part in the harmful decisions that the system produces.

It might be objected that to permit (or require) an adviser to transcend his role in this way is to create an advisory system that is self-defeating. One adviser decides that other advisers collectively are not providing balanced advice at a particular time, and he corrects his own advice to restore a proper balance. But in the meantime each of the other advisers, seeing the same original imbalance, acts to try to restore the balance. The result at best will be a return to the original imbalance and at worst, complete chaos. This objection, and the model of inherent disequilibrium on which it is based, must assume that the advisers act independently and simultaneously, and that none can inform the officials whom he is advising that his counsel takes into account certain faults in the advisory system. Since these assumptions do not usually hold in real systems, an adviser cannot readily appeal to the model to excuse his failure to compensate for defects in a system, even if his usual role would dictate that he ignore such defects.

A general problem with appeals to role, as ways to limit the responsibility of an adviser, is that they tend to confuse the responsibility of persons and the "responsibilities" of a role, permitting the latter to absorb the former. At the extreme, this predominance of role produces what has been called Pooh-Bahism, after the emperor's "Lord High Everything Else" in the *Mikado*.[36] When the emperor asks for advice about how much to spend on his wedding, Pooh-Bah in one short scene gives ten different answers, each from the perspective of one of the various official roles he holds. As private secretary, Pooh-Bah says, "Don't stint." But as chancellor of the exchequer he counsels frugality. Finally, even Pooh-Bah realizes that he must have a personal view that is not simply the sum of all the views given in the various roles he occupies. As it turns out, he thinks that the views of "all these distinguished people" can be "squared" if the emperor gives him "a very considerable bribe," which he will accept not in any particular role but simply as Pooh-Bah.

It is true that advisers seldom let their personal responsibility be so completely absorbed by their role. More often an adviser will simply claim that, as long as he stays in office, he is bound to provide counsel according to the requirements of his role, and if (as a person) he can no longer abide by these requirements, he should resign. Resignation thus becomes the last refuge of personal responsibility.[37] But this is surely too rigid a conception of the role of adviser. In most circumstances an adviser enjoys a great deal of discretion in how he fulfills the expectations of his role. This discretion involves not only shaping his advice according to different conceptions of his role (e.g., in deciding whether to analyze or advocate) but also varying his advice, within a particular conception of his role, according to general moral standards (e.g., in deciding what to include or exclude when he engages in advocacy). Moreover, an adviser trapped in a role that contributes to harmful policies often has many other options besides either resigning or carrying on as usual—including private and public criticism of the system of advising and the policies that it occasions. Given such discretion, an adviser's responsibility can hardly be said to be limited to the consequences of a choice of whether to resign or to continue in office acting strictly in accord with his normal role. How he exercises the discretion—perhaps even whether he creates whatever discretion is morally necessary—may often be an even more important factor in morally assessing his conduct and therefore in ascribing responsibility to him for the consequences of his advice.

IV

None of the shortcuts I have considered for ascribing responsibility to advisers seems adequate to account for the variety of relationships between advisers and the officials they advise, or the occasions on which advice is given. To hold that an adviser escapes responsibility if another person voluntarily intervenes after he presents his advice, or if the adviser does not intend the foreseeable consequences of his advice, or if he merely analyzes the pros and cons of a policy, or if he only plays his part in an advisory system that requires him to make recommendations that he himself does not necessarily favor—to accept any of these formulas or variations on them is to neglect important aspects of moral responsibility and produce counterintuitive results in some critical cases.

The analysis of each of these formulas, however, suggested some criteria that, taken together, could form a set of necessary and jointly sufficient conditions for ascribing responsibility to advisers. From the idea of causal responsibility comes the criterion that holds an adviser responsible only if his advisee would not have acted the way he did but for the advice (or its omission). That an adviser intended a certain result may be a further reason to criticize him, but such intent is not necessary to blame him for the result. An adviser is responsible for the consequences of decisions based on his advice insofar as he could reasonably be expected to foresee that they would follow from his advice. Finally, although the requirements of role can create a prima facie excuse, an adviser is responsible for any foreseeable harm his role-bound advice causes when that harm is greater than the harm that would result from breaching the requirements of his role.

These criteria remain quite schematic, but it should be clear that the scope of responsibility they define is likely to be more extensive than that found in everyday moral life. This expanded responsibility seems appropriate for public life not only because advisers to public officials can have great influence over the welfare of many people, but also because advisers voluntarily accept these positions of influence and therefore the greater risk of moral criticism that they invite. To expand the responsibility of advisers, however, is not to diminish the responsibility of the persons they advise. Often it is reasonable to assume that the official who makes a decision is more responsible than the adviser. It is reasonable to assume this because the official is usually "closer" to the consequences in the sense that we have stronger grounds for believing that he satisfies the criteria of responsibility. The consequences would not have occurred but for his decision, he could anticipate that his decision would produce them, and his role provided a clear opportunity or imposed a duty to prevent them. But however we apportion blame or praise among advisers and advisees, we are likely to find that the contours of responsibility of each are more complex than some general theories of moral responsibility and the pleas of some public officials would have us believe.

NOTES

1. Han Fei Tzū, *The Complete Works* (London: Probsthain, 1939), vol. 1, pp. 113–33 (cited by Herbert Goldhamer, *The Adviser* [New York: Elsevier/North-Holland Publishing Co., 1978], p. 118).

2. William R. Nelson, ed., *The Politics of Science* (New York: Oxford University Press, 1968), p. 119; and Lyman Bryson, "Notes on a Theory of Advice," in *Reader in Bureaucracy,* ed. Robert K. Merton et al. (New York: Free Press, 1952), p. 203.

3. The responsibility is moral in two senses: *what* an adviser is responsible for is assessed according to substantive principles of morality; and the extent to which *the adviser* is responsible is determined by criteria of moral agency. This paper concentrates on the second aspect of moral responsibility—what J. L. Austin calls excuses rather than justifications. ("A Plea for Excuses," *Proceedings of the Aristotelian Society* 57 [1956–57]: 1–

30, pp. 1–2). For another distinction between first- and second-order principles, see Alan Donagan, *The Theory of Morality* (Chicago: University of Chicago Press, 1977), pp. 52–57.

4. This account would have to be situated in a general framework for ascribing responsibility to public officials. Elsewhere, I have described such a framework in a way that accommodates, at least in a rough form, the chief features of the responsibility of advisers that I analyze in the present paper. See Dennis Thompson, "Moral Responsibility of Public Officials: The Problem of Many Hands," *American Political Science Review* 74 (1980): 905–16.

5. For an indication of the growth and variety of advising of governmental agencies in recent years, see Thomas E. Cronin and Norman C. Thomas, "Federal Advisory Processes: Advice and Discontent," *Science* 171 (February 26, 1971): 771–79.

6. H.L.A. Hart and A. M. Honoré, *Causation in the Law* (Oxford: Clarendon Press, 1959), pp. 69 ff., 94, 295.

7. Arthur M. Schlesinger, Jr., *The Coming of the New Deal* (Boston: Houghton Mifflin Co., 1959), pp. 514–15; and Graham Allison, *Essence of Decision* (Boston: Little, Brown and Co., 1971), pp. 203–4.

8. Hart and Honoré, pp. 48 ff., 171–72.

9. This is so even in many systems of criminal law; see ibid., pp. 338–39. Cf. Glanville Williams, *Criminal Law,* 2d ed. (London: Stevens and Sons, 1961), pp. 353–60, 381–83, 404–9; and George Fletcher, *Rethinking Criminal Law* (Boston: Little, Brown and Co., 1978), p. 755.

10. Hart and Honoré, pp. 51, 78, 338–40.

11. See Joel Feinberg, *Doing and Deserving: Essays in the Theory of Responsibility* (Princeton, NJ: Princeton University Press, 1970), esp. pp. 200–204; and John Casey, "Actions and Consequences," in *Morality and Moral Reasoning,* ed. John Casey (London: Methuen, 1971), pp. 185–86. For a criticism of this view, see Eric Mack, "Bad Samaritanism and the Causation of Harm," *Philosophy and Public Affairs* 9 (1980): 230–59, pp. 235–41.

12. The advice must thus in Feinberg's sense be a "causal factor": "A member of a set of jointly sufficient conditions whose presence was necessary to the sufficiency of the set" (p. 202n.). Although my interpretation of the causal criterion more closely follows Feinberg's analysis than that of Hart and Honoré, I am indebted to the latter authors' discussion of "causally relevant factors" and "conditions sine qua non" (pp. 103–22).

13. John Bartlow Martin, *Overtaken by Events* (Garden City, NY: Doubleday 1966), p. 659.

14. Charles Fried, *Right and Wrong* (Cambridge, MA: Harvard University Press, 1978), pp. 1–2, 20–28. For criticism of Fried's theory (specifically discussing responsibility for advice) see Brian Barry, "And Who Is My Neighbor?" *Yale Law Journal* 88 (1979): 629–58, pp. 647–49.

15. Fried, pp. 160, 22n.

16. Ibid., pp. 182–83.

17. Ibid., pp. 28, 41–42, 162–63.

18. Ibid., pp. 162, 67.

19. Fried himself presents two such examples, as well as an annotated bibliography on "intention" (pp. 23–24, 202–5).

20. James C. Thompson, "How Could Vietnam Happen? An Autopsy," *Atlantic Monthly* (April 1968), pp. 47–53; and George Reedy, *The Twilight of the Presidency* (New York: World Publishing Co., 1970), p. 11. Cf. Albert O. Hirschman, *Exit, Voice and Loyalty* (Cambridge, MA: Harvard University Press, 1970), pp. 115–19.

21. William Safire reminds us about "the Rejected Counsel": ". . . The White House staffer whose job it is to go into the Oval Office in times of crisis and say 'Mr. President—do the popular thing! Take the easy way!' The president can then say: 'Some of my advisers have suggested that I do what is politically popular. I have rejected such counsel' " ("Rejected Counsel's Return," *New York Times* [December 31, 1979], p. 15).

22. See Thomas A. Hill, Jr., "Symbolic Protest and Calculated Silence," *Philosophy and Public Affairs* 9 (1979): 83–102.

23. Joel Primak and Frank von Hippel, *Advice and Dissent: Scientists in the Political Arena* (New York: New American Library, 1976), pp. 87 ff., 34–35, 101.

24. For some examples, see Francis E. Rourke, *Bureaucracy, Politics and Public Policy,* 2d ed. (Boston: Little, Brown and Co., 1976), pp. 26–32, 154. Also see Michael Lipsky, "Toward a Theory of Street-Level Bureaucracy," in *Theoretical Perspectives on Urban Politics,* ed. Willis D. Hawley et al. (Englewood Cliffs, NJ: Prentice-Hall, Inc., 1976), pp. 196–213.

25. For an analysis of the general relation of foresight and intention, see Thomas Baldwin, "Foresight and Responsibility," *Philosophy* 54 (1979): 247–60. For an account of traditional morality that gives both intention and foreseeability important roles, see Donagan, esp. pp. 122–27.

26. Generally, on role responsibility, see Gerald A. Cohen, "Beliefs and Roles," *Proceedings of the Aristotelian Society* 67 (1966–67): 17–34; H.L.A. Hart, *Punishment and Responsibility* (New York: Oxford University Press, 1968), pp. 212–14; and R. S. Downie, *Roles and Values* (London: Methuen, 1971), pp. 121–45.

27. Thomas Hobbes, *Leviathan,* ed. M. Oakeshott (New York: Macmillan, 1962), pp. 191–97.

28. Ibid., pp. 192–93. Machiavelli also warns advisers not to "advocate any enterprise with too much zeal" and to give their advice "calmly and modestly." But he does so because he sees this as the only way counselors can cope with a common dilemma in their role: if they "do not advise what seems to them for the good of the republic or the prince . . . then they fail of their duty; and if they do advise it, then it is at the risk of their position and their lives" (Niccolo Machiavelli, *The Discourses,* bk. 3, chap. 35, in *The Prince and the Discourses,* trans. C. Detmold [New York: Random House, 1950], p. 514).

29. Operations Research Society of America, "Guidelines for the Practice of Operations Research," *Operations Research* 19 (1971): 1123–58, pp. 1134–35, 1144–48. Also see the "Reactions to the Guidelines. . . ," *Operations Research* 20 (1972): 205–44.

30. Paul Doty, "Can Investigations Improve Scientific Advice? The Case of the ABM," *Minerva* 10 (1972):

280–94, pp. 282–87. For another example, see Robert Gilpin, *American Scientists and Nuclear Weapons Policy* (Princeton, NJ: Princeton University Press, 1962), pp. 262–98.

31. See, e.g., Edward S. Flash, Jr., *Economic Advice and Presidential Leadership* (New York: Columbia University Press, 1965), pp. 276–325; T. E. Cronin and S. D. Greenberg, eds., *The Presidential Advisory System* (New York: Harper and Row, 1969); and Morton H. Halperin, *Bureaucratic Politics and Foreign Policy* (Washington, DC: Brookings Institution, 1974), pp. 158–72.

32. Doty, p. 281.

33. Primak and von Hippel, pp. 43–45.

34. Alexander George, "The Case for Multiple Advocacy in Making Foreign Policy," *American Political Science Review* 66 (1972): 751–85; Aaron Wildavsky, *The Politics of the Budgetary Process*, 2d, ed. (Boston: Little, Brown and Co., 1974), pp. 166–67; and Charles E. Lindblom, "Policy Analysis," *American Economic Review* 48 (1958): 298–312, p. 306.

35. George, pp. 784–85.

36. W. S. Gilbert, *The Savoy Operas* (London: Macmillan Publishing Co., 1926), pp. 325–26. This scene is cited and discussed by Cohen, pp. 19–20.

37. Edward Weisband and Thomas M. Franck, *Resignation in Protest* (New York: Penguin Books, 1976), esp. pp. 181–92.

37. The Nurse as a Member of a Profession

James L. Muyskens

Members of the nursing profession for a variety of reasons, including the nature of the profession but also economic exploitation and sexism,[1] have been "caught in the middle." On the one hand, for example, the nurse is hired to carry out the directives of the physician and to support the policy of the hospital administration. The system cannot function as presently constituted without such cooperation and support to carrying out the decisions and policies of those higher up in the hierarchy. Yet, on the other hand, the nurse is legally and morally accountable for her or his judgments exercised and actions taken. "Neither physician's prescriptions nor the employing agency's policies relieve the nurse of ethical or legal accountability for actions taken and judgments made."[2]

A common predicament of nurses is expressed in the April issue of *Nursing '78* by a nurse at a West Coast university hospital. She says:

> Our biggest problem right now is that our nursing leadership at the administrative level is completely impotent. They have no voting rights on any committee that has direct control over the hospital and/or nursing. Worse, the acting director and her associate have no idea of taking any power into their own hands, where it rightfully belongs. They ask permission to improve staffing ratios, by increasing or closing beds, and when they're turned down, say to us "Sorry girls! Work doubles."[3]

The overwork and understaffing not only make working conditions less than desirable for the nurse, they clearly endanger clients. When, for example, one registered nurse and an aide must try to care for 30 to 36 clients who have just undergone surgery, the situation is very dangerous and health care cannot be delivered in accordance with acceptable standards.

We can all sympathize with the nurse who wrote the following:

> I am supposed to be responsible for the control and safety of techniques used in the operating theatre. I have spent many hours teaching the technicians and the aides the routines necessary for maintaining aseptic conditions during surgery. They have learned to prepare materials and to maintain an adequate supply for all needs. They have learned to handle supplies with good technique.
>
> I find it is extremely difficult to have these appropriate routines carried out constantly by employees with little theoretical background or understanding. The surgeons are frequently breaking techniques and respond in a belligerent manner when breaks in technique are brought to their attention. I find a reminder of techniques often brings a determined response to ignore the reminder and proceed with surgery. For a male surgeon to be questioned by a female nurse is a serious breach of respect to them.
>
> One day a surgeon wore the same gown for two successive operations even though there were other gowns available. I quietly called this to his attention, but I had no authority which really allowed me to control his behavior for the good of the patient. In this situation even the hospital administrator was of no help to me.[4]

This nurse is responsible for the control and safety of techniques used in the operating rooms. The conditions over which she is responsible have fallen below acceptable standards. Although she has done her best, the assigned task has not been accomplished. The clients who have a right to expect, and have paid for, a safe and aseptic operating room have been let down.

Nursing is the largest group of health care professionals within the vast health care delivery

From *Moral Problems in Nursing: A Philosophical Investigation* (Totowa, NJ: Rowman and Littlefield, 1982), pp. 158–67.

system—a system that, despite some dramatic achievements, is increasingly under attack as dehumanizing, exploitative, and cost ineffective. Despite the seeming powerlessness of an individual nurse, taken collectively nursing, more than any other health care profession, is a necessary component in the delivery of health care. The present system could not have developed without nursing. If all nurses were to walk out tomorrow, the system would collapse. This cannot be said for any other group of health care professionals, including physicians. Hence, if the delivery of health care is substandard (as I believe it is), the nurse is not merely a victim of the system (along with the rest of us), but she or he is also an accomplice. As an accomplice she or he shares responsibility for the system's deficiencies. The nurse's plight is by no means unique. The paradoxical plight of the nurse who is both powerless and powerful, responsible yet not responsible, is a plight in which we almost all find ourselves in some aspects of our lives.

One way to try to make sense of these paradoxical situations—to be explored [here]—is to introduce the notion of collective responsibility. Two dramatic and widely discussed illustrations are the prosecution's case against certain middle-level Nazis after World War II and the defense's case for First Lieutenant William Calley, charged with murder at My Lai in Southeast Asia.

In the prosecution case, blame for the actions of certain individual members of the collective is ascribed to all members. Karl Jaspers expressed this view when he said: "Every German is made to share the blame for the crimes committed in the name of the Reich . . . inasmuch as we let such a regime arise among us."[5] In condemning every German, Jaspers is not merely blaming each German for his active or passive tolerance of the Nazis; he is saying that "the world of German ideas," "German thought," and "national tradition" are to blame. Collective responsibility is used as a net from which no member of the collective can escape.

In the defense case, the individual whose behavior has fallen below the acceptable standard is shielded from the full weight of blame, because the weight is shifted to the collective. It is the collective, the system, that must bear the brunt of the burden rather than the individual. In the Calley case it was claimed that Americans as a group failed to perform as they could have been expected to.

In a recent survey of nurses' attitudes,[6] this defense strategy was tacitly used. It was reported that, although nurses saw themselves as performing well given the work conditions, they "felt they ought somehow to deliver even when the system won't let them." The writers of the report indicate that this blame is misplaced ("not deserved"). Although performing below the acceptable standard, the nurses were not to be blamed because as individuals each was doing the best possible for him or her in the situation. The system itself was to be blamed.

If the blame appropriately ascribed in a situation is no greater than the sum of all the ascriptions of blame to the individuals, we do not have a case of collective responsibility except in a weak (distributive) sense. By collective responsibility in the strong (nondistributive) sense, as the term is to be used here, we mean that the responsibility of the group is not equivalent to that of the individuals; that is, the whole is not equal to the sum of its parts.

It is incontrovertible that we do ascribe responsibility to collectives in this strong sense. To use an example of D. E. Cooper's, if we say that the local tennis club is responsible for its closure, we do not necessarily or usually mean that the officers of the club or any particular members are responsible for its closure. The blame cannot be attributed to any particular individual or to the officers of the club, since no person failed to do what was expected of him. Yet something was missing. "It was just a bad club as a whole." From the claim that the local tennis club is responsible for its closure, no statements about particular individuals follow. "This is so," as Cooper says, "because the existence of a collective is compatible with a varying membership. No determinate set of individuals is necessary for the existence of a collective."[7]

As R. S. Downie has argued, "To provide an adequate description of the actions, purposes, and responsibilities of a certain range of collectives, such as governments, armies, colleges, incorporated business firms, etc., we must make use of concepts which logically cannot be analyzed in individualistic terms."[8]

The question to ask then is what set of conditions must obtain in order properly to ascribe nondistributive collective blame or responsibility. The conditions advanced by Cooper are sufficiently accurate and refined for [our] purposes. . . . These conditions are:

1. Members of a group perform undesirable acts.
2. Their performing these acts is partly explained by their acting in accordance with the "way of life" of the group (i.e., the rules, mores, customs, etc., of the group).
3. These characteristics of the group's "way of life" are below the standards we might reasonably expect the group to meet.

4. It is not necessarily the case that members of the group, in performing the acts, are falling below standards we can reasonably expect individuals to meet.[9]

A few comments about these conditions are in order. Clearly, we do not *hold* an individual or a group responsible—that is, following its etymology: having liability to answer to a *charge*—if undesirable acts have not been performed. When no undesirable acts occur, the question of blame or responsibility in the sense of liability does not arise. Hence the need for condition 1.

The second condition is not strictly necessary. It does seem, as Virginia Held has argued, that when special conditions obtain even a random collection of individuals can be held responsible[10] (a claim denied by condition 2). Nonetheless, for present purposes—consideration of collective responsibility of members of a profession—this stronger claim need not be defended. The most-plausible cases for ascribing collective responsibility are those cases in which the group has distinctive characteristics, has a sense of solidarity and cohesion (e.g., feels "vicarious pride and shame"[11]) and members identify themselves as members of the group (e.g., "Who are you?" "I am a nurse"), and some of these group feelings or characteristics are appealed to in explaining the acts in question. An illustration: If the citizens of Syldavia can be characterized as being rather hostile and distrustful of foreigners, and their customs, laws, and policies reflect this, then when some border guards—overzealously carrying out the Syldavian policy—kill some visiting dignitaries, we blame not only the border guards but the Syldavians. In contrast, if these border guards steal from the visiting dignitaries, in accounting for this behavior we would not be inclined to appeal to any larger group feelings or characteristics, and we definitely would not wish to ascribe collective blame.

We have seen in the variety of cases discussed above that it is when a collective fails to live up to what can reasonably be expected of it—that is, it falls below an acceptable standard—that it can incur collective blame. Hence the need for condition 3.

Condition 4 is necessary because the standards applied to groups may be different from those applied to individuals. For example, we may feel that the nurse (in the case cited above) who was charged with responsibility for the control and safety of techniques used in the operating rooms adequately met her obligations. She did not fall below standards we can reasonably expect an individual to meet. After all, as Joel Feinberg has argued, "No individual person can be blamed for not being a hero or a saint." Yet, as Feinberg goes on to say, "A whole people can be blamed for not producing a hero when the times require it, especially when the failure can be charged to some discernible element in the group's 'way of life' that militates against heroism."[12] Although Feinberg was not referring to this case or to the collective responsibility of the nursing profession (he was talking about a Jesse James train robbery case), his remarks are especially apt for this case and in many other situations within the nursing profession.

One can readily see that conditions outlined for properly ascribing nondistributive collective responsibility obtain in many situations within professions. Professions more than most other collectives are bound together by common aspirations, values, methodologies, and training. In too many cases, they also have similar socio-economic backgrounds and are of the same sex and ethnic group. As we have seen, the more cohesive the group, the less problematic the ascription of collective responsibility. The fact that professions such as nursing promulgate codes of ethics or standards of behavior, toward which they expect members to strive, provides a clear criterion for judging whether the actual practices of the profession fall below standards to which we can reasonably hold the group.

In addition to meeting these formal criteria for ascribing collective responsibility, there are several other reasons unique to the professions for ascribing collective responsibility in certain situations.

A. There are several ways by which one becomes responsible. One can be *saddled* with it by circumstances, one can have responsibility *assigned* to one, or one can deliberately *assume* responsibility.[13] Typically a profession is chosen. In choosing the profession, one *assumes* the responsibility concomitant with being a professional. One chooses to adopt the values, methodology, and "way of life" of the profession. Such choice is much less prominent with most other basic group affiliations. One does not choose family membership, region of birth, usually not citizenship, and often not military service. Once in the profession, of course, as one goes about his or her job he or she will also sometimes be saddled with responsibility by circumstances and be assigned responsibility. But these assignments are all within the context of choice: To assume professional responsibility provides the backdrop for all his or her professional activities. Hence, as a professional, more than most other group affiliations, one sees oneself as a member of the group and has—with eyes open—chosen the identification.

B. Nurses (as is, of course, also the case in several other professions) have been vested by the state with the power to regulate and control nursing practice. This collective power or right—given exclusively to the profession—has concomitant collective responsibility to see to it that acceptable standards are maintained. Since it is possible that each individual nurse, including officers of the American Nursing Association, is meeting acceptable standards in her or his own assignments and yet the group's "way of life" must be characterized as below an acceptable standard, appeal to collective responsibility is one of the tools the public has at its disposal to try to ensure adequate nursing and general health care. Obviously in these cases (when no individual has failed to meet her or his legal obligation), the public does not have recourse to law suits against individuals.

C. Supposedly as a means to protect the public, the licensing statutes of the states allow only those who have passed certain state requirements to practice nursing. One result of this is that the profession, which is by law also self-regulatory, becomes a protected monopoly. If a person is going to receive nursing care, this care must be provided by a member of the profession. If nursing care is to be upgraded, it must be from within with, at most, prodding from without. Quite clearly, one of the most-effective tools for such prodding is that of demonstrating collective responsibility, a responsibility that goes beyond the sum of each individual's responsibility.

From the discussion thus far, it is evident that the appeal to collective responsibility when some substandard behavior or undesirable act has occurred is a two-edged sword. It can be used to show that, despite undesirable performances or actions or conditions within a collective, a particular member of the collective is not individually responsible. But it can also be used to show that, despite the fact that the behavior of individuals does not fall below standards we can reasonably require individuals to meet (given that we cannot *demand* that an individual be a hero), the group's conduct is below the standards we can reasonably expect the group to meet. One of the reasons the weapon of collective responsibility looks suspect in the widely discussed World War II prosecution and Vietnam conflict defense cases is that only one edge of the sword is used, while the other edge is conveniently ignored.

If conditions for properly ascribing collective responsibility are satisfied, to the extent that the individual is exonerated, the group is indicted. To the degree the individual *qua* individual is indicted, the group is exonerated. Either way the individual group member bears responsibility. For any member of a collective but especially (for reasons cited above) for a professional, it is not enough to know that one has done all that could be expected of him or her as an individual. The arm of responsibility for a professional has a longer reach than that of the individual.

Specific situations within the nursing profession illustrate the two edges of the sword of collective responsibility. These situations should be seen within the context of the rapid evolution of the nursing profession. In recent years there has been considerable effort both within and outside the profession (e.g., the medical profession) to upgrade the requirements for licensure. These efforts have borne results. The scope of the professional nurse has expanded greatly, as exemplified by medical assistant programs and their use by medical doctors in certain areas. The history of the struggle first to adopt a code of ethics for American nurses and then to revise it reflects this evolution. Tentative codes were presented in the 1920s, 1930s, and 1940s. These efforts were met by opposition from those who feared the professionalization of nursing. A striking instance of this is the advice given by a physician to one of the earliest advocates of a code of ethics for American nurses: "Be good women but do not have a code of ethics."[14] Not until 1950 was a code of ethics adopted.

The code has been changed several times since then, the most recent being in 1976. Two of the most-interesting changes from our vantage point have been the following: Early versions of the code stated that the nurse had an obligation to carry out the physician's orders. [However,] the 1968 and 1976 versions of the code . . . stress the nurse's obligation to the client. The physician just mentioned who advised against having a code may have foreseen this development! Whereas earlier versions of the code pointed to an obligation to sustain confidence in associates, in the revised codes the nurse's obligation is to protect the client from incompetent, unethical, or illegal practice from any quarter.[15]

With this background, it is apparent why nursing is an especially interesting example of collective responsibility in the professions. The fundamental issue in the ongoing struggle to upgrade the profession—reflected in the code changes—has been that of accountability, the willingness to make decisions and to accept responsibility for these decisions. The crucial question in the attempt to upgrade the profession is that of the interface of individual and collective responsibility.

The author of an article in the *Quarterly Record of the Massachusetts General Hospital Nurses Alumnae Association* wrote about "blame-avoidance" behavior in nurses. As explained, blame-avoidance behavior is exhibited when the nurse says such things as "I did this because the supervisor told me to do it," or "The doctor ordered it," or "The hospital rules demanded it." The author maintains that accountability requires that the nurse can say, "I did this because in my best judgment it is what the patient needed."[16] Setting aside the many good qualities common to nurses, blame-avoidance behavior does seem to be one of the more-prevalent, endemic faults of the nursing profession. As we have seen, a concerted effort by many within the profession has made inroads on this "way of life" of the profession.

These efforts have been made without explicit appeal to the concept of collective responsibility. As a result, judgment in cases of blame-avoidance and other unacceptable or undesirable behavior has tended to be either too lenient or too harsh. That is, either (a) one judges that the individual nurse caught in the middle and in difficult circumstances has done all one can reasonably expect her or him to do. After all, we cannot expect or demand that she or he be a hero or a saint. Hence, the nurse is exonerated, but the unacceptable practice or condition continues unabated. Or (b) one focuses on professional responsibility and the fact that, if some individuals do not stand up against substandard practices—no matter what the odds of thereby improving the situation and no matter at what price to the individual—these practices likely will not be stopped. If the nurse does not take the action that would probably cost her her position, but that would ensure the best care possible for clients in her care, the nurse is judged to be a moral coward.

For example, in the case of the nurse charged with responsibility for maintaining a safe and aseptic operating room, without appeal to the concept of collective responsibility we are likely to say one of the following: (1) She has done all we can require of her (she has asked the surgeon to comply; she does not have the authority or status to demand compliance to proper procedures; the lack of compliance quite properly was followed by a report to the hospital administration.) Or (2) she has not done all we can require of her (she cannot allow dangerous violations of operating room aseptic standards to take place; in doing so, she is failing to carry out her assignment and is allowing the client's life to be placed in jeopardy; she should not be cowed by the surgeon's arrogance and sexism; even at the risk of losing her job, she cannot allow the operation to take place in these conditions).

The problem is that (1) is too lenient a judgment and (2) is too harsh. We cannot require the nurse qua individual to do more than she has done. But the nurse qua nurse shares blame with her colleagues in such cases, despite the much greater blame that must be placed on the surgeon who violates reasonable requirements. The lack of aggressive advocacy for the client's welfare and the willingness to be dominated by the (usually male) physician or surgeon (unfortunate if understandable "ways of life" of the nursing profession), which partially explain this nurse's behavior, are below the standard we can rightfully expect the group authorized to provide nursing services to meet. Appeal to collective responsibility yields a judgment neither too harsh nor too lenient.

This judgment conforms to the moral intuitions of the nurses surveyed who were mentioned earlier. Despite a feeling that as individuals they were doing all that could reasonably be required of them in their circumstances, they still felt dissatisfied with their performance. As nurses they felt blame for falling short of the mark set for the profession.

This dissatisfaction, when seen in the light of collective responsibility, can be turned to positive use. The nurse who has done all that is required of him or her as an individual need not suffer debilitating guilt. Guilt, in such cases, is misplaced; her or his individual actions do not warrant guilt. And, in contrast to nondistributive collective responsibility, there is no nondistributive collective guilt. "Guilt," as Feinberg has said, "consists in the intentional transgression of a prohibition. . . . There can be no such thing as vicarious guilt."[17] Nevertheless, although rightfully free of guilt, she or he cannot be complacent. She or he is a member of a group that stands judged (i.e., is liable) and must, with her or his colleagues, take appropriate steps to alleviate the undesirable conditions. It is not enough for a professional to do all that is required of her or him as an individual. Having freely accepted the privileges and benefits of the profession, one's responsibility in the areas of professional competence is greater than would be that of an equally skilled and knowledgeable individual who was not a member of the profession.

In order to meet this larger responsibility, as the American Nursing Association has recognized, "there should be an established mechanism for the reporting and handling of incompetent, unethical, or illegal practice within the employment setting so that such reporting can go through official channels and be done without fear of reprisal. The nurse should be knowledgeable about the mechanism and be prepared to utilize it if necessary."[18]

Paradoxically, if such machinery which collective responsibility requires were put in place, individual accountability would increase and the need to appeal to collective responsibility would decrease. If reporting incompetent, unethical, or illegal conduct could be done effectively through official channels and without fear of reprisal, such reporting—which under more-dangerous and less-effective circumstances is not required—would be morally required of the individual. Hence, it may be that a profession should strive to organize itself and regulate itself to such a degree that the conditions for proper ascription of collective responsibility do not arise. But this is not the situation within the nursing profession at the present. Therefore, the notion of collective responsibility is a timely weapon of considerable force for those who are working toward upgrading the nursing profession and the delivery of health care.

NOTES

1. See J. Ashley, *Hospitals, Paternalism, and the Role of the Nurse* (New York: Teachers College Press, 1976).
2. American Nurses' Association (ANA), *Code for Nurses with Interpretive Statements* (ANA: Kansas City, MO, 1976), p. 10.
3. M. A. Godfrey, "Job Satisfaction—Or Should That Be Dissatisfaction? How Nurses Feel About Nursing," Part 1: *Nursing '78* (April 1978): 89–102; Part 2: *Nursing '78* (May 1978): 105–20; quote from Part 1, pp. 101–2.
4. B. L. Tate, *The Nurse's Dilemma* (Geneva Switz.: International Council of Nurses, 1977); pp. 47–48.
5. D. E. Cooper, "Responsibility and the 'System,' " in *Individual and Collective Responsibility*, ed. P. A. French, pp. 81–100 (Cambridge, MA: Schenkman 1972), p. 86.
6. Godfrey, op. cit., Part 2, p. 110.
7. D. E. Cooper, "Collective Responsibility" *Philosophy* 43: 165 (July 1968): 258–68; pp. 260–62.
8. R. S. Downie, "Responsibility and Social Roles," in French, op. cit., pp. 65–80; p. 69.
9. Cooper, 1972, op. cit., pp. 90–91.
10. V. Held, "Can a Random Collection of Individuals Be Morally Responsible?" *Journal of Philosophy* 67:14 (July 1970): 471–81.
11. J. Feinberg, "Collective Responsibility," *Journal of Philosophy* 65:21 (November 1968): 674–88; p. 677.
12. Ibid., p. 687.
13. K. Baier, "Guilt and Responsibility," in French, op. cit., pp. 37–61; p. 52.
14. L. L. Dock, *A History of Nursing*, vol. 3 (New York: Putnam's Sons, 1912), p. 129.
15. K. M. Sward, "An Historical Perspective," in *Perspectives on the Code for Nurses*, ed. ANA (Kansas City, MO: ANA, 1978), pp. 1–9.
16. B. Durand, "A Nursing Practice Perspective," in ANA, *Perspectives on the Code for Nurses*, op. cit., pp. 18–22; p. 19.
17. Feinberg, op. cit., p. 676.
18. Sward, op. cit., p. 8.

QUESTIONS FOR STUDY AND DISCUSSION

1. Using the readings in this chapter as resources, develop and defend your own position on the question of whether the actions of corporations are always completely translatable into the actions of identifiable individuals.

2. Explain French's Extended Principle of Accountability in all its parts. Should we use this principle to decide when individuals are (at least partially) morally responsible for consequences of the actions of others? Explain your answer carefully; anticipate and respond to the strongest objection to your position.

3. In December 1984, a Union Carbide pesticide plant in Bhopal, India, leaked a deadly toxic gas (methyl isocyanate). Some two thousand people were killed; at least twenty thousand people were injured. There were a number of problems with safety measures which were supposed to be operative at the plant. After an in-house inquiry, Union Carbide's Chairman, Warren Anderson, distanced the Danbury, Connecticut, company headquarters from the disaster by blaming the Indian employees of Union Carbide who ran the Bhopal plant. "Safety," said Anderson, "is the responsibility of people who operate our plants. You can't run a $10 billion corporation all out of Danbury" (*Newsweek,* 1 April 1985). Offer your own evaluation of Anderson's suggestion that upper management at Union Carbide is exempt from any accountability for the disaster because maintaining safe plants is the responsibility of local managers.

3. Using this chapter's introduction and readings as resources, offer your own position on whether scientists are ever morally accountable for the uses to which their research is put by others. If you say they are not, explain why. If you say they are, explain why, and offer an account of the conditions under which you think they are accountable. Anticipate and respond to the strongest potential objection to your position.

5. James Muyskens uses the concept of collective responsibility to discuss some moral problems in nursing. Explain what Muyskens means by collective responsibility, comparing and contrasting it to individual responsibility. Why, according to Muyskens, is it sometimes difficult for nurses to discharge their moral duties? Is Muyskens correct in suggesting that there is such a thing as collective responsibility? Why or why not? What implications does Muyskens' view have for the profession of medicine? Explain.

CASE: THE FORD PINTO

With annual sales of over 6 million cars and trucks worldwide, Ford Motor Company has revenues of over $30 billion per year. In 1960, Ford's market position was eroded by competition from domestic and foreign subcompacts, especially Volkswagons. Lee Iacocca, then president of Ford, determined to regain Ford's share of the market by having a new subcompact, the Pinto, in production by 1970.

Although the normal preproduction testing and development of an automobile takes about forty-three months, Iacocca managed to bring the Pinto to the production stage in a little over two years. Internal memos showed that Ford crash-tested early models of the Pinto before production "at a top-secret site, more than forty times and . . . every test made at over 25 mph without special structural alteration of the car . . . resulted in a ruptured fuel tank."[1] Stray sparks could easily ignite any spilling gasoline and engulf the car in flames. Several years later, a spokesperson for Ford acknowledged that "early models of Pintos did not pass rear-impact tests at 20 mph."[2]

Nonetheless, the company went on with the production of the Pinto as designed since it met all applicable federal safety standards then in effect and was comparable in safety to other cars then being produced. Moreover, a later Ford Company study released by J. C. Echold, director of automotive safety for Ford, claimed that an improved design that would have rendered the Pinto and other similar cars less likely to burst into flames on collision would not be cost-effective for society. Entitled "Fatalities Associated with Crash Induced Fuel Leakage and Fires," the Ford study (which was intended to counter the prospect of stiffer government regulations on gasoline tank design) claimed that the costs of the design improvement ($11 per vehicle) far outweighed its social benefits:

> The total benefit is shown to be just under $50 million, while the associated cost is $137 million. Thus the cost is almost three times the benefits, even using a number of highly favorable benefit assumptions.

BENEFITS:	
Savings	— 180 burn deaths, 180 serious burn injuries, 2100 burned vehicles
Unit Cost	— $200,000 per death, $67,000 per injury, $700 per vehicle
Total Benefits	— 180 × ($2000,000) plus 180 × ($ 67,000) plus 2100 × ($ 700) = $49.15 million
COSTS:	
Sales	— 11 million cars, 1.5 million light trucks
Unit Cost	— $11 per car, $11 per truck
Total Costs	— 11,000,000 × ($11) plus 1,500,000 × ($11) = $137 million)[3]

Case description, with minor variations, taken from Manuel Velasquez, *Business Ethics*, Prentice-Hall, 1981, pp. 94–96.

Ford's estimate of the number of deaths, injuries, and vehicles that would be lost as a result of fires from fuel leakage were based on statistical studies. The $200,000 value attributed to loss of life was based on a study of the National Highway Traffic Safety Administration, which broke down the estimated social costs of death as follows.[4]

COMPONENT	1971 COSTS
Future Productivity Losses	
Direct	$132,000
Indirect	41,300
Medical Costs	
Hospital	700
Other	425
Property Damage	1,500
Insurance Administration	4,700
Legal and Court	3,000
Employer Losses	1,000
Victim's Pain and Suffering	10,000
Funeral	900
Assets (Lost Consumption)	5,000
Miscellaneous Accident Costs	200
TOTAL PER FATALITY:	$200,275

On 28 May, 1972, Mrs. Lily Gray was driving a six-month-old Pinto on Interstate 15 near San Bernardino, CA. With her was a thirteen-year-old boy, Richard Grimshaw. . . . Mrs. Gray was driving at about 55 mph when the Pinto stalled and was rear-ended by a 1963 Ford convertible. On impact, the Pinto's gas tank ruptured, and the car burst into flames. Mrs. Gray was burned to death, and Richard Grimshaw was severely burned over ninety percent of his body. Remarkably, Richard survived the accident; but he was severely disfigured and subsequently underwent seventy painful surgeries. As of early 1978, at least fifty-three people had died in accidents involving Pinto fires and many more have been severely burned.[5]

1. In your considered judgment, should managers at Ford be held morally responsible for Mrs. Gray's death and Richard Grimshaw's injuries? Should they be held legally liable for Mrs. Gray's death and Richard Grimshaw's injuries? Explain and defend your answers carefully; anticipate and respond to the strongest objections to your answer.

2. Was there anything morally wrong with the cost/benefit analysis Ford management used to decide whether to redesign the Pinto and light trucks? Explain and defend your answer; anticipate and respond the strongest objection to your position.

3. Would it have made any difference from a moral point of view if Ford management had informed its customers of the fire risks of these vehicles? Explain and defend your answer; anticipate and respond to the strongest objection to your answer.

4. Use the figures given in the memo to calculate the probability that a burn death would result from an accident involving one of these vehicles (i.e., divide the number of burn deaths by the total number of cars and trucks sold). In your considered judgment, is there a limit to the amount that Ford should have been willing to spend in order to reduce this figure to zero? If so, how much? Determine from your answer the price you place on life and compare that figure with the government's figure. If not, defend your position against the objection that society simply cannot afford to make automobiles that will ensure that no one will be killed in them.

NOTES

1. Mark Dowie, ''Pinto Madness,'' *Mother Jones* (September/October 1977): 20. See also Joanne Gamdin, ''Jury Slaps Massive 'Fine' on Ford in '72 Pinto Crash,'' *Business Insurance* (20 February 1978): 76.

2. ''Ford Rebuts Pinto Criticism,'' *National Underwriter* (9 September 1977).

3. From a memorandum attached to statement of J. C. Echold. See Ralph Drayton, ''One Manufacturer's Approach to Automobile Safety Standards,'' *CTLA News* 8:2 (February 1968): 11.

4. Dowie, ''Pinto Madness,'' p. 28.

5. ''Ford Fights Pinto Case: Jury Gives 128 Million,'' *Auto News* (13 February 1978): 3, 44.

SELECTED BIBLIOGRAPHY

Baldwin, Thomas. ''Foresight and Responsibility.'' *Philosophy* 54:209 (1979): 347–60.

Benjamin, Martin. ''Can Moral Responsibility Be Collective and Non-distributive?'' *Social Theory and Practice* 4 (1976): 93–106.

Boland, Richard J. ''Organizational Control, Organizational Power, and Professional Responsibility.'' *Business and Professional Ethics Journal* 2:1 (1982): 15–25.

Cooper, D. E. ''Collective Responsibility.'' *Philosophy* 43:165 (1968): 258–68.

———. ''Collective Responsibility Again.'' *Philosophy* 44:168 (1969): 153–55.

De George, Richard T. ''Ethical Responsibilities of Engineers in Large Corporations: The Pinto Case.'' *Business and Professional Ethics Journal* 1:1 (1981): 1–14.

Downie, R. S. ''Collective Responsibility.'' *Philosophy* 44:167 (1969): 67–69.

———. *Roles and Values*. London: Methuen, 1971.

Feinberg, Joel. ''Collective Responsibility.'' *Journal of Philosophy* 65:21 (1968): 674–88.

———. ''Sua Culpa.'' In *Doing and Deserving: Essays in the Theory of Responsibility*, pp. 187–221. Princeton: Princeton University Press, 1970.

Filios, Vassilios. ''Assessment of Attitudes Toward Corporate Accountability in Britain.'' *Journal of Business Ethics* 4:3 (1985): 155–73.

Flores, Albert, and Deborah Johnson. ''Collective Responsibility and Professional Roles.'' *Ethics* 93:3 (1983): 537–45.

French, Peter A. *Collective and Corporate Responsibility*. New York: Columbia University Press, 1984.

———. ''The Corporation as a Moral Person.'' *American Philosophical Quarterly* 16:3 (1979): 297–317.

———. ''Crowds and Corporations.'' *American Philosophical Quarterly* 19:3 (1982): 271–77.

———. ''The Principle of Responsive Adjustment in Corporate Moral Responsibility: The Crash on Mt. Erebus.'' *Journal of Business Ethics* 3:2 (1984): 101–11.

———. ''Types of Collectives and Blame.'' *The Personalist* 56 (1975): 160–69.

———, ed. *Individual and Collective Responsibility*. Cambridge, MA: Schenkman, 1972.

Haydon, Graham. ''On Being Responsible.'' *Philosophical Quarterly* 28:110 (1978): 46–57.

Held, Virginia. ''Can a Random Collection of Individuals Be Morally Responsible?'' *Journal of Philosophy* 67:14 (1970): 471–81.

Goodpaster, Kenneth. ''The Concept of Corporate Responsibility.'' In *Just Business: New Introductory Essays in Business Ethics*, ed. Tom Regan, pp. 292–322. Philadelphia: Temple University Press, 1983; reissued New York: Random House, 1984.

Kipnis, Kenneth. ''Engineers Who Kill: Professional Ethics and the Paramountcy of Public Safety.'' *Business and Professional Ethics Journal* 1:1 (1981): 77–91.

———. ''Professional Responsibility and the Responsibility of Professions.'' In *Profits and Professions: Essays in Business and Professional Ethics*, ed. Wade L. Robison, Michael S. Pritchard, and Joseph S. Ellin, pp. 9–22. Clifton, NJ: Humana Press, 1983.

Lachs, John. '' 'I Only Work Here'—Mediation and Irresponsibility.'' In *Ethics, Free Enterprise, and Public Policy*, ed. Richard T. De George and Joseph A. Pichler, pp. 201–13. New York: Oxford University Press, 1978.

Ladd, John. "Morality and the Ideal of Rationality in Formal Organizations." *Monist* 54 (1970): 488–516.

———. "Philosophical Remarks on Professional Responsibility in Organizations." In *Designing for Safety: Engineering Ethics in Organizational Contexts,* ed. Albert Flores, pp. 191–203. Troy, NY: Rensselaer Polytechnic Institute, 1982.

Manning Rita C. "Corporate Responsibility and Corporate Personhood." *Journal of Business Ethics* 3:1 (1984): 77–84.

Primak, Joel, and Frank von Hippel. *Advice and Dissent: Scientists in the Political Arena.* New York: New American Library, 1976.

Strobel, Lee Patrick. *Reckless Homicide? Ford's Pinto Trial.* South Bend, IN: AND Books, 1980.

Thompson, Paul B. "Collective Responsibility and Professional Roles." *Journal of Business Ethics* 5:2 (1986): 151–54.

9

SOCIAL RESPONSIBILITY AND PROFESSIONAL DISSENT

The previous chapter raised questions about the moral accountability and responsibility of individuals functioning within complex practices—like health care provision and business practice—and complex institutions—like corporations and governments. The readings in this chapter continue that discussion by focusing on professional dissent.

The first set of readings asks whether health care providers should participate in medical contingency planning in the event of nuclear confrontation. In 1981, the Department of Defense asked civilian hospitals to promise to make available a number of beds for use by military casualties from abroad. The list of potential casualties makes it clear that the Department of Defense plan is to provide for the care of Americans overseas in the event of nuclear confrontation. A number of physicians, many of whom belong to the group, Physicians for Social Responsibility (PSR), have argued that participation in such contingency planning is misleading because it suggests that the disease and injuries resulting from nuclear confrontation can be medically managed. They have also argued that participating in such planning will encourage nuclear confrontation. In response to this last claim, Jay Bisgard argues that PSR has erroneously concluded that there is an association between contingency plans and the threat of nuclear war. Instead, Bisgard suggests that *un*preparedness invites war. Bisgard also analogizes contingency planning for nuclear confrontation with contingency planning for natural disasters. He suggests, for example, that lack of preparedness for plane crashes will not prevent plane crashes, it will just put physicians in a position where they cannot discharge their duty to care for those in need of treatment. Refusal to participate in medical contingency planning, Bisgard argues, comes down to a refusal to provide care.

H. Jack Geiger argues for the position taken by PSR. He suggests that there are important differences between contingency medical planning for natural disasters, contingency medical planning for conventional war, and contingency medical planning for nuclear confrontation. Contingency planning for natural disasters, says Geiger, does not increase the likelihood of those disasters' occurring. But contingency medical planning for nuclear confrontation does increase the likelihood of such confrontation because it contributes to the confidence of the public and political leadership in the medical community's ability to manage the resultant casualties. And it is this difference in medical manageability, says Geiger, that makes for a moral difference between medical contingency planning for conventional war and such planning for nuclear war. Geiger's position is that physicians must make clear to the public and political leadership that an effective medical effort following a large scale nuclear confrontation is simply not possible. Implicit in his argument for resistance to the plan is the view that thinking that a nuclear confrontation will be ''limited'' and ''over there'' is unrealistic.

James Johnson focuses on the analogy to natural disasters offered by Bisgard, pointing out that wars sometimes surprise us—namely, when someone else is the aggressor. Thus, Johnson takes the analogical argument to be persuasive. The physician's duty to provide care holds whether a war is planned or unplanned, just or unjust, and a necessary condition of providing the best care that can be offered is planning for that care in advance.

Thomas Murray contends, against Bisgard, that the refusal to provide care is not at issue, and he offers another analogical argument to counter the analogy to natural disaster. Murray asks the reader to consider whether a physician should provide a plan for treating people who will be made ill by a sewer system that is in the planning stage and is known to be faulty. Even if medical management of the resulting disease is possible, Murray argues that the physician's duty is to refuse to offer the plan and to publicly resist the building of the system. Murray suggests that the physician's duty to protect the public health lies in this resistance. Notice that (unlike Geiger) Murray does not argue from medical unmanageability to a refusal to participate in contingency medical planning for nuclear war. Rather, Murray's argument is that physicians have a binding moral duty to come forward when any institution (including the military) threatens the public health. This set of readings, like the article by Dennis Thompson in chapter 8, raises the more general question of whether professionals should (or, indeed, must) use their professional positions to try to influence the political process.

James Muyskens raises the question of strikes by nurses; but his question can easily be generalized to other groups in the crucial service occupations, for example, physicians, ambulance personnel, firefighters, police. Even when motives for a strike are altruistic (e.g., to achieve the provision of more competent professional services), striking is morally dilemmic for these groups because an effective strike will require that needed services not be rendered. Muyskens argues that when such a genuine conflict of duty arises (i.e., the duty to provide care now versus the duty to improve the level of care), nurses should take the broader view and strike if this seems necessary for the provision of acceptable quality service by nursing. Notice that Muyskens also argues that questions of compensation are intimately linked to questions of quality of service. Low compensation, Muyskens suggests, is linked to low self-esteem, and low self-esteem contributes significantly to low-quality service.

One objection that might be raised to Muyskens' view is that in striking, professionals sacrifice the interests of persons in current need to the interests of persons in future need, thereby using some as a means to the good of others. Muyskens responds to this objection by contending that withdrawal of services necessary for the maintenance of life cannot be justified. But there are two problems with this. First, it does not address the sacrifice of interests less than life, but also extremely important—for example, maintaining a certain quality of life. Second, if we try to generalize Muyskens' position to other crucial service groups who specialize in emergency services (ambulance personnel, firefighters, police), it seems that strikes by these groups will never be justified. Perhaps one way of approaching the problem of strikes by emergency service providers would be to work toward a ''sympathy system,'' where other groups would strike for those unable to strike because they must provide continuing life-maintaining services. Such a system was effectively used in Britain when labor groups struck to raise compensation for nurses.

The last articles in this chapter address the question of whistleblowing. Each of these articles points out that the effects of whistleblowing on whistleblowers can be and have been severe. Myron Glazer's article is especially poignant in this regard. The articles by Gene James and Sissela Bok distinguish whistleblowing from other activities, like muckraking and civil disobedience. Both articles suggest sets of criteria that must be met for whistleblowing to be justified and/or morally obligatory. Notice that James addresses the Ford Pinto case (see Case for Discussion, chap. 8) and asks whether Ford engineers who knew of the Pinto's defect had an obligation to make that defect known when it became clear that Ford was not going to hold up production and marketing of the Pinto to correct the defect. Contrary to Richard De George, whose view he discusses, James concludes that Ford engineers did have an obligation to blow the whistle.

The present chapter raises questions about one kind of social responsibility of professionals—the obligation to dissent. The next chapter will address another set of questions about the social responsibility of professions and professionals, namely, questions related to social justice.

RESISTANCE AND STRIKES

38. Should Physicians Prepare for War?

Introduction

Joyce Bermel

In October 1981, sixty physicians at Contra Costa Hospital in San Francisco refused a request from the Defense Department to pledge at least fifty civilian beds for the care of military casualties who would be airlifted from overseas in the event of a large-scale war. The Defense Department argued, in a letter sent to Contra Costa and other civilian hospitals across the country . . . that the extra civilian beds were necessary because "a future large-scale conflict overseas could begin very rapidly and produce casualties at a higher rate than any other war in history." The plan has the support of the American Medical Association and the American Hospitals Association. In refusing to cooperate, the medical staff at Contra Costa responded that participation "would offer tacit approval for the planning of a nuclear war." The controversy raises ethical issues far beyond the question of whether to participate in this plan. What ought to be the moral role of the physician in preparations for a war that the Defense Department acknowledges will result in unprecedented injury, disease, and death? And should that role change depending on whether the conflict is conventional warfare, a limited nuclear conflict, or a total nuclear war?

The proliferation of nuclear weapons, the failure of arms limitation talks, deteriorating relationships between the United States and the Soviet Union, the growth in American and Soviet weapons arsenals—all these have raised anxiety levels about the possibilities of a nuclear war. The medical profession has responded strongly to what it perceives as this overwhelming threat to the public health. In December 1981, the American Medical Association passed a resolution calling on doctors to inform President Reagan and members of Congress about the medical consequences of nuclear war. The Harvard Medical School, among other medical schools, has introduced an elective course on the health effects of nuclear war. Physicians for Social Responsibility (PSR), an organization founded in 1961 to inform the public about the medical consequences of nuclear testing and nuclear war, holds seminars around the country for physicians. . . .

But eager as physicians are to inform politicians and the public about the catastrophic medical consequences of a nuclear war, many would stop short of refusing to participate in a plan to care for the wounded of a future conflict whose scope we cannot predict. . . .

From *Hastings Center Report* 12:2 (1982): 15–21.

The Obligation to Care for Casualties

Jay C. Bisgard, M.D.

The United States has combat-ready army and marine corps divisions and air forces that may be called upon at any time to defend the vital interests of this nation in one or more of the many potential trouble spots of the world. Given the sophisticated technology of modern conventional weapons and our ability to move forces quickly, we could very well see a high casualty rate applied to a sizable force at risk. From the Revolutionary War through the Vietnam conflict this country has always recognized a moral obligation to provide medical care for those we send into battle. Today the 15,000 beds in the military hospitals in the United States are no longer adequate to care for the numbers of servicemen and women who could easily become casualties in any large conventional conflict overseas. Recognizing our moral obligation to be able to care for these casualties should the need arise, we must then ask how to overcome a projected shortage of 50,000 acute care beds in the military health care system.

Obviously, we could build more military hospitals. This would be an extremely expensive proposition. In 1980, it cost about $180,000 per bed to build civilian hospitals in the United States. To this expense must be added the cost of equipping and manning military hospitals. A somewhat less costly alternative would be to ''mothball'' these hospitals against the wartime need. Since they would have to be manned quickly, we would have to staff them from the reserves. We could not draft people fast enough. But if this were done and we did not need these hospitals for ten to fifteen years, we would be providing less than optimal care. How would you like to be treated with ten-to-fifteen-year-old equipment that the nation could not afford to replace to keep up with advancing medical technology?

There is a third alternative—one that costs the taxpayer virtually nothing unless it is actually needed for casualty care and that also assures the best quality care. We have approximately one million acute care beds in the civilian private sector; 50,000 beds represents only five percent of this capability. Therefore, if civilian hospitals would agree to a totally voluntary partnership with the Department of Defense and the Veterans Administration to plan how we might most effectively cooperate, we could assure contingency care for military casualties, save the taxpayers an unnecessary burden, and make the most efficient use of the nation's health care manpower resources without increasing the size of the reserves or resorting to a draft. The logic of this approach readily won the enthusiastic support of key civil sector health care organizations, such as the American Medical Association and the American Hospital Association. It also won the blessing of the General Accounting Office, Congress, and other federal agencies, including the Department of Health and Human Services. Even more important, it was welcomed by civilian hospitals. Within a few months, over two hundred hospitals across the country had offered to provide more than 20,000 beds.

Then an organization called Physicians for Social Responsibility (or PSR) erroneously concluded that there was an association between this plan, called the Civilian-Military Contingency Hospital System (CMCHS), and nuclear war. PSR has, for many years, advocated nuclear arms limitation, and its members include many illustrious names in American medicine. I don't believe that any rational person, especially a physician, could oppose the concept of reducing the threat of nuclear war. That is not the issue. The ethical dilemma arose in October when PSR began to urge hospitals to refuse to participate in the CMCHS because participation would offer tacit approval to the concept of nuclear warfare.

Let us take a close look at the ethics of this situation. First, we must eliminate the ''red herring'' of nuclear war. The alleged association between CMCHS and planning for nuclear war was fabricated by PSR with absolutely no basis in fact. Even if there were some association, which there definitely is not, the medical ethical issue at hand is that of care for sick and injured young servicemen and women—not the morality of nuclear war.

I will not debate the morality of nuclear war. To me, the results of moral or immoral war are the same—sick and injured human beings. My sacred vow as a physician was to use my skills to save life and alleviate suffering. It would be a moral outrage for a physician to withhold care from any human being in need because of personal dislike of the victim's sex, color, religion, nationality, or mechanism of injury. If we don't hold that concept sacred, we could refuse care to the drunk driver or the person injured needlessly in an automobile accident because he didn't use his seat belt. Surely, no one would advocate closing emergency rooms to force people to be more responsible in their driving habits. This ethical principle is well founded in military medicine and is symbolized by the caduceus on the lapel of every army medical service officer. The caduceus is the wand of Hermes, the symbol of international neutrality. It is further symbolized by the presence of the Red Cross on the battlefield. Physicians are recognized under the Geneva Convention as neutral noncombatants. We care for anyone in need; ours, theirs, or the innocent civilian caught in a crossfire.

The single most important consideration, and what we must always remember, is our dedication to preserving human life. Regardless of our outside beliefs, we are always concerned primarily with humanity. The Oath of Geneva states that the physician: "Will not permit considerations of religion, nationality, race, party politics, or social standing to intervene between our duty and our patient." The daily prayer of Rabbi Moses ben Maimon, the twelfth-century physician better known as Maimonides, asks God to "preserve the strength of my body and soul so that they may be ever ready to help the rich and the poor, good and bad, enemy as well as friend. In the sufferer, let me only see the human being." These phrases and others like them from the Bible, the Torah, and other sacred and secular writings, are the only reminders that we need; they form the foundation for all medical ethics.

If the ethical question lies not in the actual delivery of care to patients, is it in the act of preparing to treat the casualties of war—any war? This is a more complex issue that has several facets.

One premise of the PSR is that preparation to receive casualties makes war more likely. History has shown that being ill prepared has never prevented a war from occurring: In fact, it has invited attack. When political leaders through the ages have weighed the prospect of going to war, do you think that the medical capabilities of the other side influenced their decisions? Would the United States have been able to stay neutral in World Wars I and II if we had not been prepared to deal with the resulting casualties? Did the medical readiness of Germany and Japan have any influence on our decisions to bomb Dresden, Hiroshima, and Nagasaki? Physicians have not made the decisions to make war. Those decisions have been made by politicians, who seldom have considered the consequences in suffering and loss of lives. In short, the issue is out of our hands, and the presence or absence of medical preparedness is not going to affect those decisions.

If we cannot prevent war by being medically unprepared, what then would be the result of unpreparedness? You know the answer—increased morbidity and mortality. We take for granted the need to prepare plans to deal with natural disasters and plane crashes, and we know it would be preposterous to suggest that destroying airport medical disaster plans would promote flying safety or prevent aircraft accidents. It would also be against medical ethics to take an action that could only result in increased human suffering. One of the cardinal principles of medical practice today has endured through twenty-two centuries. It was taught by Hippocrates: Above all, do no harm. Which then is the physician's ethical obligation: to prepare or not to prepare? The answer is obvious. Saving lives is the only constructive activity amid the mad destruction of war. The names of hospital ships are appropriate reminders: *The Comfort, The Solace, The Benevolence, The Sanctuary, The Haven.*

In thinking about the ethical issues, the following points are important to bear in mind:

1. The most important ethical consideration of any physician is a duty to the patient. Wartime activation of the CMCHS is consistent with this principle in that it will ensure the access to care for any casualty in need. To deny the availability of such care is unethical, irresponsible, and inconsistent with the precedents set through two hundred years of U.S. history.
2. The moral obligation to do no harm is also consistent with the planning aspect of the CMCHS. To oppose preparations to provide medical care to any in sudden need would clearly do harm if casualties were thereby deprived of necessary care. These preparations themselves lead to no harm, and preclude unnecessary expenditures of tax dollars to build, equip, and staff more military hospitals.

Why Survival Plans Are Meaningless

H. Jack Geiger, M.D.

For nearly a year now, the U.S. Department of Defense has been quietly—but actively—promoting a plan for a Civilian-Military Hospital Contingency System. The plan, in my view, poses the most profound ethical challenge to American physicians. As is often the case with such dilemmas, the most difficult step is the first one: recognizing that there is an ethical issue involved at all. In this instance, the Pentagon denies it, most physicians (and most of the public) don't even know that the plan exists, and only one medical organizational voice—that of Physicians for Social Responsibility—has been raised to question it.

The Pentagon's problem, as described in an official document entitled "In Combat, in the community, saving lives . . . together, CMCHS"[1] is as follows: "Because of technical advances in weaponry and the great mobility of armies today, a future large-scale war overseas will probably begin and end very rapidly and produce casualties at a higher rate than any other war in history." This war would produce casualties at a rate that "would very quickly exceed the capabilities of both the Veterans Administration and military systems,'' which total 120,000 beds. ''Within forty-eight hours,'' therefore, the Pentagon would organize a massive transoceanic casualty transport system to deliver these battlefield victims to beds and medical care in U.S. civilian hospitals.

How many? The document doesn't specify—but it asks each hospital administrator to prepare for the arrival of fifty acutely injured casualties with little or no advance notice. In the Boston metropolitan area, about forty hospitals were approached, with a request there for a total of about 2,000 beds. Thirty-four such areas have been identified across the United States, for a presumed total commitment of some 68,000 beds—or, adding in the military and VA capacities, total casualties in the first few *days* of the new war of some 188,000.[2] (In the fifteen *years* of the Vietnam war, in comparison, there were 57,000 deaths and 304,000 wounded, of whom 153,000 required hospitalization.[3])

Nowhere in the document does the word ''nuclear'' appear—but the scenario and the casualty rate immediately suggested a nuclear war. The Department of Defense has vacillated on the question. First it said no; in June 1981, Dr. John Moxley, then Assistant Secretary of Defense for Health Affairs, stated that ''it is possible, of course, that such a war could escalate to the use of chemical or tactical nuclear weapons within a combat theater.''[4] Subsequently, his successor has denied it. (Several physicians who called the CMCHS office at the Pentagon a few months ago and asked whether participating hospitals would need facilities for radioactive decontamination were specifically assured that they needn't worry—all that would be taken care of overseas before the casualties were sent back to the United States.) No one at DOD denies, of course, that U.S. forces are equipped at almost every level to fight with nuclear weapons, or that NATO doctrine calls for the use of tactical nuclear weapons if conventional weapons do not suffice to withstand a conventional attack.

And certainly, if the war the Pentagon envisions is nuclear, it is a so-called ''limited'' nuclear war; that is the only rationale consistent with the vision of an awesome conflict *there* (whether in Europe, the Middle East, or elsewhere) and intact, smoothly functioning civilian hospitals *here*.

My concerns were further heightened by the ''national profile'' of one hundred typical casualties the CMCHS office sent along to hospital administrators to assist them in their planning. About half of these are severe trauma and burn cases, which might occur in any kind of military conflict. The other half do not seem to be battle casualties by any definition, and it is difficult to understand why they would be admitted to any hospital either in peace- or war-time. The list includes four cases of neurosis, four cases of urinary system disease, three cases of disease of the oral cavity, three cases of infectious hepatitis, two cases of ulcer, and one case of normal pregnancy at seven months gestation.[5] It is not clear why such patients would require urgent intercontinental transportation to hastily emptied civilian beds in the United States—*unless they had suffered high-dose radiation exposure and were therefore high-risk patients in immediate need of tertiary care.*

What if the plan *were* designed as a medical response to the prospect of a ''limited'' nuclear war? The word itself is a distortion in this context, since it suggests something ''less than,'' when in fact even a modest nuclear exchange, totalling only fifteen or thirty megatons, would cause death, devastation, and destruction *greater* than anything in prior human experience. And the very concept of limited nuclear war may be a cruel and dangerous illusion, since no reliable analyst has proposed a credible scenario in which such a conflict could surely be halted, even if the will were there, before escalating into a major intercontinental nuclear exchange. No matter; it is the task of the military, presumably, to plan and prepare for such contingencies. And isn't it therefore the patriotic duty and the professional responsibility of physicians, committed as they are to the protection and preservation of human life, to take part?

I do not suggest—and no critic of CMCHS has ever suggested—that any physician, anywhere, refuse treatment to any wounded or injured person, soldier or civilian, under any circumstances. No one is saying ''hell no, we won't sew,'' despite some attempts to suggest that that is what criticism of CMCHS implies.[6] I contend, rather, that is it precisely the professional commitment to the protection and preservation of human life that would make it unethical for any physician to participate in either civilian or military ''disaster'' plans specifically designed to attempt to cope with the consequences of a nuclear war.

Such participation would be unethical, I believe, for two reasons—both related to the unique and unprecedented destructiveness of thermonuclear weapons, and to their capacity, quantitatively and qualitatively, to destroy the human social fabric (and the biologic and physical environments on which that fabric rests) so profoundly as to make survival meaningless, on a scale that conventional warfare can never approximate.

First, every major and detailed medical study of nuclear war makes it clear that an effective medical effort, in the face of death and injury of such unprecedented magnitude, is simply not possible.

The American Medical Association itself has recently formally stated that "there can be no adequate medical response to a nuclear war" (although, together with the American Hospital Association, the AMA has urged support of CMCHS). To participate in such a plan, even for a "limited" nuclear war, requires a suspension of professional judgment and an abandonment of reasonable reliance on medical and scientific data that cannot and should not be sanctioned even in the name of patriotism. If I were to sign up for a plan involving the massive distribution of laetrile to cancer patients I would be no more ethical if my reasons were patriotic, and no less responsible for abandoning my professional judgment if I did so at the request of my government.

Second—and this, I believe, is the heart of the matter—physician participation in nuclear war "disaster" planning may increase the risk that a nuclear war will occur. There is a critical distinction between nuclear war disaster plans and conventional medical disaster plans. Participation in the latter will not contribute to the likelihood of another Coconut Grove fire, an earthquake, a plane crash, a devastating flood, or even a massive civilian riot.

But the risk of nuclear war is different. We are unlikely to enter a nuclear exchange by considered public decision, congressional vote, or any other popularly approved definitive preparation; no one (I hope) "wants" it. We are far likelier to approach it step by step—each step in itself apparently innocuous—in a process that systematically escalates risk to the breaking point. An important contribution to that process, and to many of the steps along the way, is made by a series of false assurances: that nuclear war can be limited, that it is winnable, that it is survivable in any real meaning of that term beyond a biological body count; that shelters will afford adequate protection, that mass evacuations of populations are feasible—and that medical care will be available, and equal to the task.

If CMCHS is in fact a medical disaster plan for a limited nuclear war, the physician who participates is giving his or her colleagues, the public, and the government precisely such a false assurance. To do so is to help obliterate the distinction between conventional war (in which medical efforts can obviously be effective) and nuclear war; to do so is to ignore or misuse the role of physician as teacher. If I were to go to the nearest state with a death penalty, make my way to Death Row, and walk up and down the cell block saying, "Folks, I know things look desperate, but don't give up—I'm going to be right there in the execution chamber, using all my medical skill to revive you," no one would doubt that I was violating the most fundamental medical ethic.

Almost inevitably, the argument is made that CMCHS would be worth it if it saved even a single life. The moral calculation is the one that weighs the potential benefit (if any) against the increased risk to millions of others—and in addition judges the quality of the act in the light of the physician's commitment to the *prevention* of needless injury and death when palliation is insignificant and cure impossible.

As a casualty treatment plan for a conventional conflict, CMCHS is at best poorly conceived and unrealistic; it has been severely criticized, in various drafts, by the General Accounting Office, the VA, the U.S. Public Health Service, and the Federal Emergency Management Agency. As a plan for a nuclear conflict, CMCHS calls for the most searching inquiry and the broadest possible discussion—among physicians and public together—before decisions on participation are made by each of the proposed hospitals. We may then, at last, recognize what Albert Einstein wrote at the dawn of the nuclear age: "Everything has changed—except the way we think."

The Moral Bases of Contingency Planning

James T. Johnson

One of the most important features of the western moral tradition on war, ever since it began to coalesce during the Middle Ages, has been the requirement to respect noncombatant rights and care for injured noncombatants. The term "noncombatant" has various technical meanings; in the moral usage I follow here this term encompasses all persons who by reason of social function or infirmity are not actually engaged directly in the war effort. Modern techniques of counterpopulation warfare have eroded common consciousness of the moral obligations owed noncombatants, but even so these obligations remain.[7]

To act morally is above all to exercise an intentionality of control over events in terms of moral perceptions that are regarded as important. If modern warfare has undermined our awareness of the obligation to noncombatants, then the problem before us is twofold: to confront that obligation again and to seek to incorporate it into our actions, including our contingency planning. The CMCHS proposal represents one sort of planning clearly in accord with the fundamental moral obligations owed noncombatants. The fact that the particular noncombatants to be treated in the reserved hospital beds would be wounded military personnel has nothing to do with the matter. The wounded soldier in a hospital bed is no less a noncombatant than the chronically ill civilian down the hall or the clergyman walking the street: No one of them, by lack of capacity or social role, is in direct support of the war.

No one thinks it odd to anticipate natural disasters by contingency planning, training of personnel in specific procedures, and stockpiling of useful supplies. To think of the possibility of war in a similar way should be equally acceptable. Wars, like natural disasters, often have a distinctly accidental character. Who could have ever predicted that the worst war Europe had known up to that time would be precipitated by the assassination of an Austrian nobleman in an obscure Balkan city? That nuclear war might begin accidentally has been a problem confronted in much military and civilian planning since the *Dr. Strangelove* era. Indeed, it is characteristic of war that at least one side is almost always caught by surprise, so that the result is similar to the effect of a natural disaster. The whole matter of whether military preparedness encourages or retards the incidence of war is much debated, but that most certainly is not at issue in the CMCHS proposal. Here the issue is one of providing medical aid to the wounded, and the analogy with contingency civilian disaster planning seems very persuasive to me.

Does it matter whether the war is just or not? Emphatically, no. The justice or injustice of a particular war has nothing at all to do with the obligation to care for the victims of that war, whether they be military or civilians, whether they be our own nationals or not. This element in the moral obligation to persons involved in war follows from the recognition that justice and injustice are almost always inextricably mixed on both sides of a conflict. Though this argument had been made earlier, Francisco de Vitoria in the sixteenth century was the first person to spell it and its implications out fully. Grotius and others seconded him in following generations, and this has become a cardinal principle in international humanitarian law on war.

In the present connection, whatever particular critics of the CMCHS plan may think about the morality of war as such or about U.S. military preparedness in particular is not relevant to the question of contingency planning to care for wounded individuals. This is true whether we are thinking about the possibility of nuclear war or warfare using conventional weapons. In any conflict short of a general nuclear catastrophe, where there would be no hope at all of doing anything for most of the victims, the obligation to care for those who have been hurt would remain, and this implies being ready to provide such care. A limited war under contemporary conditions, even if nonnuclear, could easily cause an extremely high level of casualties over a short period of time, overwhelming purely military medical facilities. (The destructiveness of modern conventional weapons must not be forgotten in our preoccupation with nuclear weaponry.) What is different morally about limited war (nuclear or not) and general nuclear war, so far as treatment of the victims is concerned, is simply that in a limited war resources would remain to fulfill the obligation to care for victims.

Finally, consider the relation between the civilian and military spheres. Only comparatively recently in history has a standing military medical corps come into existence. The protection of medical personnel provided for in the original Red Cross Convention of 1864 or in the contemporaneous *Instructions for the Government of Armies of the United States in the Field*[8] arose in part from the life-preserving function these people served, but also in part from the fact that virtually all of them were not professional military; they were civilians drawn into military medical service because of the war. Most of these people, including one of my great-grandfathers, did not have military rank or even own uniforms, and many cared for wounded military personnel even while they attempted to carry on their civilian practice. The growth of the medical corps and the military hospital system has tended to parallel the separation of roles and functions elsewhere in modern societies, but this separation is inherently a fragile one. Nor is there any moral rationale for it, but only one rooted in convenience derived from social structure. Only when such separation is regarded (wrongly) as belonging to the necessary order of things is a proposal such as the CMCHS plan a threat to the civilian hospital sphere.

I am not qualified to comment on the particulars of the CMCHS proposal. But, provided that this plan represents intelligent policy, it is a responsible reaction to our moral obligation to care for persons harmed by the disaster of war, as well as an appropriate integration of civilian and military capabilities in the discharge of that obligation.

The Physician as Moral Leader

Thomas H. Murray

The refusal of sixty physicians at Contra Costa County Hospital in Martinez, California, to set aside a proportion of their civilian hospital beds in the event of war has conjured up a terrifying image:

doctors standing over the bleeding bodies of war victims, arms akimbo, jaws clenched, firmly shaking their heads "No!" An awful vision, but utterly beside the point.

It is one thing for a doctor to care for the casualties of war; quite another to participate in the planning for war. Imagine a community where an incompetent or corrupt political administration has contracted to build a profitable sewage system, knowing that it is insufficient and likely to lead to an increase in diseases of many kinds. Imagine further that you—a physician—have been asked to cooperate in designing a contingency plan to handle the epidemic that will almost certainly come. Should you comply? No, for two reasons. First, the existence of such a plan might make the project—the inadequate sewage system—more acceptable to the public, especially if you lend your public esteem as well as your expertise in health matters to the proposal. Second, you would be violating your principal loyalty, to the health and well-being of your patients and your community in general, to acquiesce in a policy you believe would be a danger to health. If the system is built over your objections, and the epidemic occurs, are you permitted to refuse care to the victims? No. Your commitment to health is overriding. In your social and political activities you may protest as loudly as you want, you may refuse all political help to those who threaten health. But when an individual needs your medical care, you are sworn to give it. The crucial difference is between caring for patients in need, which should always be done, and shaping the decisions that will alter the health of masses of people: that is, between *patients* and *public policies*.

The battlefield doctors in the movie and television series "MASH" have a fierce dedication to their patients that is matched only by their hatred for the politicians and generals who have created and sustained the war. I am not sure how Hawkeye Pierce would have responded to a request that he help plan a medical contingency system for casualties of the Korean War. But I am fairly certain what he would say to a similar request to plan for a tactical nuclear war that might generate as many casualties in one day as the Korean War did in three years.

That health is the principal end of medicine has been ably stated by Leon Kass.[9] But Kass limits his discussion to those individuals who are patients, demanding the physician's unswerving commitment to their good, which he believes includes health. What of those who are not the physician's patients, who, if physicians act effectively now, may be spared this manmade encounter with illness or death? Surely a physician's dedication to health is not limited to repair—after illness or calamity has struck. Just as the physician should instruct patients how to live a life as free from future illness as possible, so the physician should bear some responsibility toward others; if not affirmatively seeking them out and helping them, then at least using his or her powers—medical, political, or otherwise—to assure that their well-being is not risked frivolously.

There are several reasons why physicians should take a special interest in the planning for large-scale war. First, the medical profession is not merely a collection of individuals who happen to be doctors; it is an institution vested by society with special prerogatives and vital responsibilities in protecting the public health.

Second, because physicians are experts in detecting the causes of ill health and recommending the means for recovery, communities rely on them to bring to public attention neglected sources of disease and to suggest ways to improve the health of their members.

Finally, physicians are in an especially powerful position to focus public attention on policies that may endanger health. Physicians and clergy remain the most trusted professions in the United States. Whatever disparity exists in public reactions to appeals for godliness, the clamor for "health" remains a political trump card—almost as powerful as "defense" or "national security."

The Pentagon already had promises of 20,000 out of the planned 50,000 beds when the Martinez doctors registered their protest. What did they hope to accomplish? Even if they could have prevented the CMCHS plan from succeeding, did they believe that would lessen the probability of nuclear war? I doubt they were that naive. *Army* magazine understands their intentions: ". . . the only logical conclusion is that the Bay group has indeed embarked on a media hype job. . . ."[10] I would put it differently. The Martinez physicians seized on the plan as an issue on which doctors—acting as doctors—could alert the public to what they saw as the intolerable horrors of nuclear war. The impact is twofold: The public sees that many physicians are opposed to the nation's defense strategy; and the broader question—defense planning around tactical nuclear weapons—is dramatically brought to public attention.

Defense planning has become more and more the province of specialists; in abstract ways, they have learned to think dispassionately about kilotons and megadeaths. But being dispassionate about intensely passionate things, like mass death and suffering, is itself a kind of blindness. Defense planning is too important to be left to defense specialists. If the Martinez doctors succeed in intensifying the public debate over tactical nuclear weapons and international disarmament, they are discharging their special moral obligation born of public trust and their loyalty to health, and they will have done all of us a service.

In any society, values will collide, and institutions charged with those values will conflict. The mistake is to think that that is unfortunate. Just the opposite is true. In a well-functioning (dare I say "healthy"?) society, institutions will battle, and the values in conflict will be displayed to the public who in the end should make the decision about how to weigh and balance them. Any institution, left unchecked, will run wild, and the Defense Department is no exception. As its fortunes continue to rise, it is essential that its hegemony be challenged by some other respected institution. What better candidate do we have than medicine?

If special moral obligations flow from physicians' dedication to health, the public esteem in which they are held, and their institutional strength, then doctors do have a special duty to intervene whenever the health of individuals or the public is threatened by any powerful institution, not merely the military. The AMA has clearly accepted this principle where national health insurance is concerned; they claim to oppose NHI on grounds that it threatens the quality of health care. Is the possibility of a "future large-scale war" any less of a threat to public health? Whether the danger comes from incompetent bureaucracies, corrupt politicians, or ignorance from any source, when health is threatened doctors should act.

NOTES

1. Published by the Department of Defense, no date, no publication number. Available from the Department of Defense, The Pentagon, Room 3E-172, Washington, DC 20301.
2. Comptroller General, General Accounting Office, "DOD Needs Better Assessment of Military Hospitals' Capabilities to Care for Wartime Casualties," HRD-81-56, May 19, 1981, pp. 1–2.
3. Department of Defense, *In Connection with the Conflict in Vietnam,* fact sheet dated January 1976, as cited in Gloria Emerson, *Winners and Losers* (New York: Harcourt Brace Jovanovich, 1976), pp. 58–59.
4. Letter dated June 11, 1981, from John H. Moxley III, M.D., Assistant Secretary of Defense for Health Affairs, to Philip Shapiro, M.D., San Francisco, CA.
5. CMCHS, Appendix B.
6. "Medical Care and War," Editorial, *American Medical News,* December 18, 1981.
7. See further Paul Ramsey, *The Just War* (New York: Charles Scribner's Sons, 1968), pp. 59ff., as well as my own discussions in *Ideology, Reason, and the Limitation of War* (Princeton: Princeton University Press, 1975) and *Just War Tradition and the Restraint of War* (Princeton: Princeton University Press, 1981), *passim.*
8. The first of these represents the origination of the modern humanitarian international law on war; the second was the prototype of U.S. military manuals on the conduct of war. See further my discussion in *Just War Tradition,* pp. 306–22.
9. Leon R. Kass, "Regarding the End of Medicine and the Pursuit of Health," in A. L. Caplan, H. Tristram Engelhardt, Jr., and J. J. McCartney (eds.), *Concepts of Health and Disease* (Reading, MA: Addison Wesley, 1981).
10. "LJB," "Since When Have Doctors Become Dropouts?" *Army,* December 1981, p. 9.

39. The Nurse as an Employee

James L. Muyskens

Of all the moral issues facing the nurse as an employee, none is more difficult and divisive than deciding whether to go on strike. . . . Its difficulty as a moral dilemma arises from the fact that compelling moral reasons can be given in support of both sides of the question.

A nurse is quoted in a recent article in the *New York Times* (March 25, 1980) as saying that when nurses strike, "they talk about better patient care, but the bottom line is 'How much are you going to give me?' " Since bill collectors are as persistent with nurses as with professors, plumbers, and police officers, it is hardly surprising if, for most individual nurses on strike, wages are of greater and more compelling concern than demands for improved client care. Yet it would be a mistake to conclude from this that the expressions of concern about quality client care are no more than smoke screens. Nurses as professionals have and take seriously the collective responsibility of maintaining and improving the quality of nursing care. The question to be discussed is whether (and if so, when) the strike is a morally acceptable weapon for nurses to use in attempting to maintain and improve the conditions necessary for proper nursing practice and their self-respect.

From *Moral Problems in Nursing: A Philosophical Investigation* (Totowa, NJ: Rowman and Littlefield, 1982), pp. 168–78.

Too often, discussions of the moral duties of health professionals give the impression that the list of duties is exhausted when one has gone through those which pertain to the health professional as individual practitioner: the duty to respect a client's autonomy, the duty to obtain informed consent, the duty to maintain confidentiality, the duty to safeguard privacy. But health professionals do not work in a vacuum. Because of society's interest in their activity, their practice is regulated by the state. Specifically, . . . the nursing profession is given the legal status of a protected monopoly (no one may practice nursing unless licensed by the profession) and the authority to control its own practice. In exchange, society asks the profession to deliver high-quality nursing services. By accepting the role of nurse, one—along with one's colleagues—assumes responsibility (1) for maintaining and improving standards of nursing, (2) for maintaining conditions of employment conducive to high-quality nursing care, (3) for contributing to the development and implementation of community and national health needs, and (4) for making the most-efficient and [most]-effective use of nursing resources.

To exercise these duties, it is necessary for nurses to act in concert—for example, to work through professional associations or unions or to form independent groups within one's employment setting. If these collective efforts meet resistance or prove ineffectual, it may be difficult or impossible to fulfill these duties without taking further action, such as engaging in a strike or work slowdown. Yet such action may come into conflict with a variety of the nurses' other duties, including their collective duty to provide nursing care to all in need of it and their duties as practitioners to specific clients currently under their care. This potential for conflicts of duty is what makes the question of the nurses' right to strike a morally difficult and complex one.

The issue is compelling because many nurses find themselves in situations in which it is next to impossible to fulfill their collective responsibilities. Frequently . . . nurses lack power relative to administrators and other health professionals, such as doctors. Their proper place is often seen as being "at the physician's side"—a position of low esteem. Nurse supervisors often have neither the ability nor the desire forcefully to defend members of their staff in disputes with other health professionals or administrators. Far too often nurses are assigned too many clients or ordered to do tasks that lie outside the range of their training or expertise. These and many other factors militate against high-quality nursing care.

. . . [Among the most important] causes of nurses' relative powerlessness and low esteem . . . are the following:

1. The pervasive sexism of our culture. Sexist attitudes appear to have shaped society's expectations that nurses will perform the stereotypical female helping role. These same attitudes are reflected in (some) nurses' images of themselves as handmaidens of the physician or as surrogate mothers.
2. The class background of nurses. Whereas over the years most nurses have come from the lower half of the socio-economic spectrum, typically physicians have come from classes in the upper half.
3. Their relative lack of education. Many nurses lack a quality liberal arts education—a factor that sets them apart from most other professional groups. And their medical training is no match for that of doctors.
4. Their relatively low pay. This may be a consequence of the causes cited above, yet it in turn contributes to the low esteem accorded nurses. In our society esteem is, at least loosely, correlated with level of income. . . .

High-quality nursing care is unlikely to be widely available if nurses' positions of relative powerlessness and low esteem persist. Only if the conditions just cited are ameliorated is there a possibility of change—change that is essential if nurses are to fulfill the collective duties outlined above. Of course, to change these conditions is no easy task. Yet there is a growing awareness that things can and should be different. Through sheer dint of numbers (there are more nurses than any other health professionals) and because of the importance of nursing services, the *potential* for power to make these changes is undeniable.

In a variety of ways, these offending conditions and attitudes are being challenged. Two examples follow: New models of the nurse's role . . . have stressed independent, professional judgment and action primarily on behalf of the client, as opposed to being primarily an extension of the physician. These models emphasize the distinctive contribution of nursing (e.g., *caring* for the sick as opposed to physicians' contributions of diagnosing disease and attempting cures). Discussion and adoption of these models help somewhat to overcome the negative effects of the traditional, weak model. A second example . . . is the American Nursing Association's diligent (and controversial) efforts to upgrade nursing education. The association has been concerned that nurses' education be adequate to meet the challenges of high-quality nursing in today's world: care that requires skill in handling increasingly complex and sophisticated equipment, advanced training in nursing specialties and subspecialties, and the expertise to take on the lion's share of health education as our society places increasing emphasis on preventive care.

These are just two of any number of ways the nursing profession must work to satisfy its collective responsibility to provide quality nursing care. We turn now to the question of the appropriateness of a possible third way, collective action through strikes. Is the strike one of the paths nurses may follow in attempting to meet their collective responsibilities?

The strike is a technique usually used by labor organizations to exact economic concessions from management. It would be very unusual for a strike not to be premised in large part on demands for better pay and benefits. If such "self-serving" goals are incompatible with exercising professional responsibility, surely a strike by nurses could not be condoned. However, far from being incompatible with professional responsibility, the demand for better wages (we shall argue) is a requirement of professional responsibility.

An increase in compensation must go hand in hand with upgrading of the profession. Just as low pay is correlated with low esteem and low status, low status is linked to the lack of quality nursing care. Low status is a nearly insurmountable impediment to quality care. The economic issue is *not* detachable from the quality-of-care issue. The quest for higher wages as well as better working conditions is part and parcel of the struggle to fulfill the collective responsibilities of the profession.

It may be objected, however, that this line of reasoning blurs an important, traditional distinction between the professional and the laborer or worker. The worker does his or her job for pay, in part because the required tasks lack intrinsic worth. A professional's motives, it has often been argued, should be different. A professional is committed to his or her profession for its own sake and for the sake of those who are its recipients and beneficiaries. Therefore, the argument continues, a professional must refrain from using the strike weapon.

Is this argument persuasive? Its persuasiveness depends on our being able to detach the economic issues from the quality-of-care issues. We have argued, to the contrary, that they are not detachable. Let us consider this issue further. It would appear to be an empirical fact that we are unlikely to get quality people to enter a profession with poor working conditions, low esteem, and low pay. Even if we were to succeed in attracting highly qualified and highly motivated people, it is unlikely that their enthusiasm and morale could be sustained over the years. High drop-out rates, cynicism, and discouragement—all of which presently obtain in nursing—would have to be expected. If all professionals were motivated solely by love of their art and service to humanity, as proponents of the view under challenge wistfully imagine, a strike would indeed be incompatible with professional standing. But since professionals are humans of complex motivation, the image of the professional on which the argument rests is unrealistic.

Since other professional groups (e.g., teachers, interns, and residents) now engage in strike action and appear not to have lost their professional standing, attempts to show that striking is incompatible with professionalism are unlikely to be effective. If we are to find that striking is incompatible with the professional duties of a *nurse,* the conflict will arise from specific nursing duties rather than from general professional obligations.

Before we turn to those specific duties of the nurse, it will be helpful to look more closely at one's activities when striking. To strike is to take collective action, including the refusal to work, with the aim of extracting concessions from one's employer. The refusal to work imposes inconvenience and possibly hardship on those in need of one's services. In the case of strikes by employees such as nurses, the detrimental effect of the strike on the public (those in need of nursing care) is often more immediate and more grave than on the employer. The public's inconvenience is the means by which pressure is put on the employer to come to a settlement agreeable to the striking employees. Were the public in no way inconvenienced, the strike would likely be ineffectual.

Consider the conflict that appears to arise for the striking nurse, given that the means of achieving admittedly worthy goals is the inconvenience and perhaps even the hardship of clients. The modern nurse who functions in accordance with the client advocate model . . . is committed to working for the client, in that she or he has the special task of caring for the client as a person, of humanizing an otherwise impersonal and sometimes demeaning health care system. Of all health professionals, the nurse is uniquely situated so as to be the most-effective guardian of the client's interests and rights. Perhaps, then, it is this special role of the nurse that makes it wrong for nurses to strike. For a client advocate to be willing to sacrifice a particular client's interests, in order to achieve higher salaries for oneself and one's colleagues, or better care for future clients, at least appears to be contradictory and wrong.

One way out of this seeming impasse is to reject the special role of client advocate. But this is too heavy a price to pay. It would undermine the image and model of nursing that we have found is superior from the moral point of view and is one with which more and more responsible nurses are identifying themselves.

If—contrary to usual circumstances (as we have discussed)—a nurses' strike were *solely* for higher wages (if no quality-of-care issues were on the table and the situation happened to be such that the salary issue were unlikely to affect quality of care because the pay scale were already relatively high), we can see that a strike would be incompatible with the nurses' role as client advocate. Clients are being used as means for advancing nurses' interests. Clients' interests (which the nurse had pledged to advance) are being held hostage. What makes matters most difficult is that the especially stringent duty not to treat clients in this way is not counterbalanced by any other compelling moral duty. The moral duty of the nurse to her or his clients stands in conflict with self-interest—which, of course, does not provide one with a moral basis for failing to do one's moral duty.

On the other hand, if the strike were undertaken with an aim of advancing client care, the case would be quite different. We have the makings of a classic conflict-of-duty situation. The ongoing, collective duty to maintain and improve the quality of nursing care appears to be in conflict with specific duties to one's current clients and the collective duty to provide nursing care to the public. When all of these duties cannot be fulfilled, one has to decide which duty ought to take priority over the others.

For those nurses who find themselves in work contexts in which wages, standards, and practice are deficient, . . . concerted action to correct these conditions is obligatory. As is well known, the recent experience of many nursing groups within specific health care facilities is that the only effective way to effect the needed changes is strike action. If, as a matter of fact, a strike is the most-effective, or indeed the only effective, way in a particular situation to make the changes necessary for quality nursing care, the collective responsibilities of nurses require them to strike—*unless* there are other, more-stringent duties (to be considered below) which are binding on them and which would be violated were they to engage in a strike.

An initially appealing yet (as we shall see) unacceptable argument for giving priority to the duty to maintain and improve the quality of care (and, hence, to strike) is the following: the sacrifice of clients' interests resultant from a strike is for the improvement of future nursing care. That is, the sacrifice required of clients is for the good of clients. It would be shortsighted not to see that this is a reasonable price for clients to pay in order to have better care available in the future. Therefore, as in many other areas of our lives, it is reasonable to sacrifice the short-term interests for the long-term ones. Hence, clients cannot reasonably object to a strike under these conditions.

This argument would have some force if the *same* clients whose present interests and needs are sacrificed were the ones to benefit from the future gains. It is one thing to make X sacrifice now for X's (his or her own) later benefit. It is quite another to make X sacrifice now for Y's (another's) later benefit. But in most strikes, the sacrifice required now is for the benefit of others later. It is the yet-unknown client of the future, rather than the present client, whose welfare a strike can advance. The weakness of the argument is that it fails to consider the crucial question of justice (fair treatment of individuals to whom one already has obligations) and simply considers that of overall consequences.

In an article discussing the morality of strikes by interns and residents, David Bleich asks:

> May a person on the way to a class on first-aid instruction ignore the plight of a dying man, on the plea that he must perfect skills which may enable him to rescue a greater number of persons at some future time? . . . No person may plead that an activity designed to advance future societal benefits is justification for ignoring an immediate responsibility. . . . The "here and now" test is a general rule of thumb which may be applied to most situations requiring an ordering of priorities.[1]

No doubt we can all agree that the person failing to give aid on his way to first-aid instruction stands defenseless. Bleich suggests that this action violates a general principle to the effect that commitment to a course of action designed to increase future good is not a weighty enough reason to exempt one from immediate duties. Were we to apply this principle to the issue at hand in the manner Bleich proposes, we would conclude that a nurse going on strike even for the highest of motives, namely, to benefit future clients, is in the wrong, for she or he is violating immediate responsibilities to clients in need of nursing by inappropriately appealing to future benefits.

Such a conclusion need not be drawn even if we were to accept Bleich's argument. The sort of nurses' strike that would be analogous to his case of the man on his way to a first-aid class would be a case of nurses on strike to improve emergency nursing care and who refuse to respond to an emergency. In order to improve conditions so that more lives can be saved later, a life is lost here and now. Such a strike could not be morally justified—a fact that is generally recognized and honored by striking nurses, who see to it that nursing care in emergency rooms and intensive care units is not withdrawn. Bleich's example is useful in making it clear why withdrawal of services necessary for the maintenance of life cannot be justified.

The central moral question concerning nurses' strikes, however, is whether the withdrawal of nonemergency and nonlifesaving nursing services can be shown to be an acceptable means to the end of better nursing care for future clients. Bleich's general principle cited above (that one may not plead that one's attempt to advance future good exempts one from any immediate responsibility) prohibits withdrawal of these nursing services as well *if* doing so entails ignoring any immediate duties to clients.

Is Bleich's principle one we should accept? Whether or not we accept it will depend on how important we take considerations of consequences to be. We can imagine any number of cases in which greater overall good would be served if we were free to fail to meet an immediate conflicting responsibility. For example, suppose one were ready to proceed with a research project which, if successful, would probably provide us with the means to save numerous lives in the future. It has been determined that the only way the project can go forward is to select subjects from whom truly informed consent is not possible (for whatever reason). Most people would agree that, at least in general, one's immediate duty to his or her research subjects is to obtain genuine informed consent. Most would also agree that this is a very stringent requirement. . . . Yet if the risk to the research subjects were truly minimal and the potential for gain for those benefiting from the research were immense, we may feel that it is appropriate at least to consider whether an appeal to future societal benefits is sufficient to outweigh this immediate and serious responsibility. If we feel such a consideration is appropriate, our position entails a rejection of Bleich's principle. On the other hand, we may feel consideration of consequences is illegitimate here.

In deciding for or against Bleich's principle, the crux of the matter is how weighty we consider the duty to work for future societal benefits to be. The ethical principles [defended earlier[2]] allow for a middle position between that of the strict Kantian, who would see a consideration of consequences as illegitimate, and the utilitarian, who would see it as the only factor to be considered. We [take] the Kantian respect for persons principle and the principle of beneficence as basic. On this modified Kantian view, it is not wrong to consider consequences; however, in doing so one may not run roughshod over another's autonomy or fail to respect others as persons. The fundamental question that one must ask concerning this case is whether the proper balance has been struck between the duty to respect the research subjects as persons while carrying out one's duty of beneficence, which is the role of a research scientist.

We have established that nurses have a clear and compelling duty to see to it that future nursing care will be better than the substandard care available in certain facilities and locales. Contrary to Bleich, it is too stringent to declare a priori that all other immediate duties must take priority in conflict-of-duty situations. What must be determined is whether the duty to work toward better nursing care in the future should, in the particular situation at issue, take precedence over any other duty with which it conflicts.

In place of Bleich's principle, let us adopt the following procedural rule: All the various duties of nurses put forth in ethical codes, such as the *International Code of Nursing Ethics* and the ANA *Code for Nurses,** are binding on the nurse. The only time a nurse is excused from fulfilling any one of these duties is when doing so conflicts with fulfilling a more-stringent duty. As we have seen in the research example, how we determine which of several conflicting duties is the most stringent is a complicated issue that must be decided by an independent procedure. . . .

An obvious implication of following this procedural rule is that one must, in fact, be in a conflict-of-duty situation before one is relieved of any duties. If a strike could be conducted without violating any immediate responsibilities, such a course of action would be required. Certainly, in most situations ways can be found to minimize the failure to perform conflicting duties—for example, by directing nonemergency clients to other accessible facilities which provide nursing service and where nurses are not on strike, and by continuing to provide intensive care and emergency nursing services. A strike satisfying these conditions would not be morally objectionable. On the contrary, if a strike is the only means or clearly the most-effective way to change prevailing conditions that are incompatible with high-quality nursing care, then it is morally mandatory.

If other conditions obtain, it will be far more difficult to justify a strike. For example, if one were in a facility far from other facilities providing nursing care and a strike would leave many without the possibility of care, the duty to the public "here and now" might be the stronger duty. Or suppose a group of nurses has made a pledge to their employer not to strike or has signed a no-strike contract. Keeping that agreement is incompatible with strike action. Until 1968 the nursing profes-

*[See appendix 1, sample codes 3 and 4, *EIPL*.—ED.]

sion (through the ANA) took a no-strike stance. The duty of fidelity (keeping agreements), which conflicts with striking in these situations, may also be one that cannot be outweighed by the duty to provide quality care to future clients. Fortunately, the ANA no longer adheres to a no-strike position, and most nurses are not working under no-strike contracts.

The moderate position defended here—condoning strikes in certain carefully circumscribed situations, claiming they are morally mandatory in others, yet not justified in still others—is a position that would be taken were nurses and the public to draw up an original contract. Consider the following hypothetical situation, following John Rawls,[3] in which members of the public cannot know when or what nursing care they may need (they are under a veil of ignorance) and nurses also do not know in what situation they will find themselves. Nurses as nurses would want to be able to provide the best care under the best conditions. They would seek sufficient power to be able to overcome any impediments to quality nursing care and self-respect. The public would be concerned to have available to them the best care possible within the limits of allocated resources. Under no conditions would they be willing to barter away a constant availability of emergency or lifesaving care. (They never know when such care may make the difference between life and death.) If it were determined that in some situations—due to factors outside the control of either nurses or the public—the only way quality care could be obtained would be by use of the strike weapon, nurses would insist on the right to use it, and the public would concur as long as emergency and lifesaving care could not be withdrawn. The public would agree to suffer the necessary inconveniences and hardship of a strike in the event that it were the only way to achieve high-quality nursing services.

The way to determine in a particular situation whether nurses' obligations to their clients and the public are weightier than the collective and future-oriented duty to take strike action is to appeal to the original contract. Would the public as party to the agreement be willing to make this required sacrifice in order to benefit from this sought-for goal? If so, the duties to one's clients or to the public that conflict with strike activity can justly be set aside in favor of the strike action. If not, they cannot.

Even if a strike can be morally justified, everyone would agree that it is an awkward and tortuous means of settling disputes. A better way would result from a three-party initial compact, a compact which also included the nurses' employers. Such an agreement would commit both nurses and employers to binding arbitration. That is, if a dispute between nurses and their employer could not be resolved by collective bargaining, it would be turned over to a mutually acceptable arbitrator. (The mechanics of this could be worked out in a variety of ways.) Strikes could be avoided while achieving the end of improved care. Clearly, such an agreement would be advantageous to the public; they would not have to pay the price for the failure of other parties to reach an agreement. Nurses would also find this to be in their best interest. They could avoid being forced into the extremely awkward position of causing hardship or at least inconvenience to those whose interests they have sworn to advocate. Employers in the original position would also see that they stand to gain. They could not count on nurses' inability or disinclination to vigorously press their demands. Faced with the prospect of having to concede just as much or more to striking nurses than in binding arbitration, they would prefer binding arbitration. Everyone would avoid the loss of income and goodwill that inevitably results from a strike.

Of course, in the present real-life situation the employer's lot is quite different. He or she has little to gain by accepting binding arbitration. Perhaps through moral suasion employers will come to see that they ought to accept it. More likely, however, binding arbitration will be accepted only when it is in a particular employer's interest to do so. This will be the case if nurses are able to exact as many concessions from their employers by striking as would be possible through binding arbitration. Only strong, united action on the part of nurses will achieve such a breakthrough.

As client advocates, nurses should do all in their power to avoid strikes. But paradoxically, the best way to accomplish this is to be ready and able, in appropriate situations, to execute an effective strike.

NOTES

1. David Bleich and Robert M. Veatch, "Interns and Residents on Strike," *Hastings Center Report* 5:6 (1975): 7–9; quote from p. 9.

[2. James L. Muyskens, *Moral Problems in Nursing: A Philosophical Investigation* (Totowa, NJ: Rowman and Littlefield, 1982), chap. 1.]

3. John Rawls, *A Theory of Justice* (Cambridge, MA: Harvard University Press, 1971), pp. 136–42.

WHISTLEBLOWING

40. In Defense of Whistle Blowing

Gene G. James

Whistle blowing may be defined as the attempt by an employee or former employee of an organization to disclose what he or she believes to be wrongdoing in or by the organization. Like blowing a whistle to call attention to a thief, whistle blowing is an effort to make others aware of practices one considers illegal, unjust, or harmful. Whenever someone goes over the head of immediate supervisors to inform higher management of wrongdoing, the whistle blowing is *internal* to the organization. Whenever someone discloses wrongdoing to outside individuals or groups such as reporters, public interest groups, or regulatory agencies, the whistle blowing is *external*.

Most whistle blowing is done by people presently employed by the organization. However, people who have left the organization may also blow the whistle. The former may be referred to as *current* whistle blowers; the latter as *alumni* whistle blowers. If the whistle blower discloses his or her identity, the whistle blowing may be said to be *open;* if the person's identity is not disclosed, the whistle blowing is *anonymous*.

Whistle blowers differ from muckrakers because the latter do not have any ties to the organizations whose wrongdoing they seek to disclose. They differ from informers and stool pigeons because the latter usually have self-interested reasons for their disclosures, such as obtaining prosecutorial immunity. The term *whistle blower,* on the other hand, usually refers to people who disclose wrongdoing for moral reasons. However, unless whistle blowing is *defined* as disclosing wrongdoing for moral reasons, the distinction between whistle blowing and informing cannot be a sharp one. Thus, although most whistle blowers do it for moral reasons, one cannot take for granted that their motives are praiseworthy.

Whistle blowers almost always experience retaliation. If they work for private industry, they are likely to be fired. They also receive damaging letters of recommendation and may be blacklisted so they cannot find work in their profession. If they are not fired, or work for government agencies, they are still likely to be transferred, demoted, given less interesting work, and denied salary increases and promotions. Their professional competence is usually attacked. They are said to be unqualified to judge, misinformed, and so forth. Since their actions seem to threaten both the organization and their fellow employees, attacks on their personal lives are also frequent. They are called traitors, rat finks, and other names. They are also said to be disgruntled, known troublemakers, people who make an issue out of nothing, self-serving, and publicity seekers. Their life-styles, sex lives, and mental stability may be questioned. Physical assaults, abuse of their families, and even murder are not unknown as retaliation to whistle blowing.

WHISTLE BLOWING AND THE LAW[1]

The law does not at present offer whistle blowers very much protection. Agency law, the area of common law which governs relations between employees and employers, imposes a duty on employees to keep confidential any information learned through their employment which might be detrimental to their employers. However, this duty does not hold if the employee has knowledge that the employer either has committed or is about to commit a felony. In this case the employee has a positive obligation to report the offense. Failure to do so is known as misprision and makes one subject to criminal penalties.

The problem with agency law is that it is based on the assumption that unless there are statutes or agreements to the contrary, contracts between employees and employers can be terminated at will by either party. It therefore grants employers the right to discharge employees at any time for any reason or even for no reason at all. The result is that most employees who blow the whistle on their employers, even those who report felonies, are fired or suffer other retaliation. One employee of thirty years was even fired the day before his pension became effective for testifying under subpoena against his employer, without the courts doing anything to aid him.

This situation has begun to change somewhat in recent years. In *Pickering* v. *Board of Education* in 1968 the Supreme Court ruled that government employees have the right to speak out on policy issues affecting their agencies provided doing so does not seriously disrupt the agency. A number of similar decisions have followed and the right of government employees to speak out on policy issues now seems firmly established. But employees in private industry do not have the right to speak out on company policies without being fired. In one case involving both a union and a company doing a substantial portion of its business with the federal government, federal courts did award back pay to an employee fired for criticizing the union and the company, but did not reinstate him or award him punitive damages.

A few state courts have begun to modify the right of employers to dismiss employees at will. Courts in Oregon and Pennsylvania have awarded damages to employees fired for serving on juries. A New Hampshire court granted damages to a woman fired for refusing to date her foreman. A West Virginia court reinstated a bank employee who reported illegal interest rates. The Illinois Supreme Court upheld the right of an employee to sue when fired for reporting and testifying about criminal activities of a fellow employee. However, a majority of states still uphold the right of employers to fire employees at will unless there are statutes or agreements to the contrary. Only one state, Michigan, has passed a law prohibiting employers from retaliating against employees who report violations of local, state, or federal laws.

A number of federal statutes contain provisions intended to protect whistle blowers. The National Labor Relations Act, Fair Labor Standards Act, Title VII of the 1964 Civil Rights Act, Age Discrimination Act, and Occupational Safety and Health Act all have sections prohibiting employers from taking retaliatory actions against employees who report or testify about violations of the acts.

Although these laws seem to encourage and protect whistle blowers, to be effective they must be enforced. A 1976 study[2] of the Occupational Safety and Health Act showed that only about 20 percent of the 2300 complaints filed in fiscal years 1975 and 1976 were judged valid by OSHA investigators. About half of these were settled out of court. Of the sixty cases taken to court at the time of the study in November 1976, one had been won, eight were lost, and the others were still pending. A more recent study[3] showed that of the 3100 violations reported in 1979, only 270 were settled out of court and only 16 litigated.

Since the National Labor Relations Act guarantees the right of workers to organize and bargain collectively and most collective bargaining agreements contain a clause requiring employers to have just cause for discharging employees, these agreements would seem to offer some protection for whistle blowers. In fact, however, arbitrators have tended to agree with employers that whistle blowing is an act of disloyalty which disrupts business and injures the employer's reputation. Their attitude seems to be summed up in a 1972 case in which the arbitrator stated that one should not "bite the hand that feeds you and insist on staying for future banquets."[4] One reason for this, pointed out by David Ewing, is that unions are frequently as corrupt as the organizations on which the whistle is being blown. Such unions, he says, "are not likely to feed a hawk that comes to prey in their own barnyard."[5] The record of professional societies is not any better. They generally have failed to come to the defense of members who have attempted to live up to their professional codes of ethics by blowing the whistle on corrupt practices.

THE MORAL JUSTIFICATION OF WHISTLE BLOWING

Under what conditions, if any, is whistle blowing morally justified? Some people have argued that it is always justified because it is an exercise of free speech. But the right to free speech, like most other rights, is not absolute. Thus, even if whistle blowing is a form of free speech, that does not mean it is justified in every case. Others have argued that whistle blowing is never justified because employees have obligations of absolute loyalty and confidentiality to the organization for which they work. However, because the actions of organizations often harm or violate the rights of others, and one has an obligation to prevent harmful actions if one can, a universal prohibition against whistle blowing is not justifiable.

Assuming that we reject such extreme views, what conditions must be satisfied for whistle blowing to be morally justified? Richard De George believes that whistle blowing is morally permissible if it meets the following three conditions:

1. The company must be engaged in a practice or about to release a product which does *serious* harm to individuals or to society in general. The more serious the harm, the more serious the obligation.
2. The employee should report his concern or complaint to his immediate superior.
3. If no appropriate action is taken, the employee should take the matter up the managerial line. Before he or she is obliged to go public, the resources for remedy within the company should be exhausted.[6]

For whistle blowing to be morally obligatory, De George thinks two other conditions must be satisfied:

4. The employee should have documentation of the practice or defect. . . . Without adequate evidence his chances of being successful . . . are slim.
5. The employee must have good reason to believe that by going public he will be able to bring about the necessary changes.[7]

De George believes that because of the almost certain retaliation whistle blowers experience, whistle blowing is frequently morally permissible but not morally obligatory. He holds that this is true even when the person involved is a professional whose code of ethics requires him or her to put the public good ahead of personal good. He argues, for example:

> The myth that ethics has no place in engineering has . . . at least in some corners of the engineering profession . . . been put to rest. Another myth, however, is emerging to take its place—the myth of the engineer as moral hero. . . . The zeal . . . however, has gone too far, piling moral responsibility upon moral responsibility on the shoulders of the engineer. This emphasis . . . is misplaced. Though engineers are members of a profession that holds public safety paramount, we cannot reasonably expect engineers to be willing to sacrifice their jobs each day for principle and to have a whistle ever at their sides.[8]

He contends that engineers only have an obligation to do their jobs as best they can. This includes reporting observations about safety to management. But engineers do not have an "obligation to insist that their perceptions or their standards be accepted. They are not paid to do that, they are not expected to do that, and they have no moral or ethical obligation to do that."[9]

There are a number of problems with this analysis of whistle blowing.

The first condition is far too strong because it requires de facto wrongdoing instead of extremely probable evidence of wrongdoing before whistle blowing is morally justified. All that should be required of whistle blowers in this regard is that they be diligent in gathering evidence and act on the basis of the best evidence available to them. They should not be held to a more rigid standard than is usually applied to moral actions.

What constitutes serious and considerable harm? Must the harm be physical? Since De George was writing on business ethics, it is understandable that he only discussed whistle blowing involving corporations. But businesses, like governments, can be guilty of wrongs other than physically harming people. Should one, for example, never blow the whistle on such things as invasions of privacy?

If the harm is physical, how many people's health or safety must be endangered before the harm can be said to be considerable? And do professionals not have an obligation to inform the public of dangerous products and practices even if they will lose their jobs? Even though some Ford engineers had serious misgivings about the safety of Pinto gas tanks and several people were killed when tanks exploded after rear-end crashes, De George says that Ford engineers did not have an obligation to make their misgivings public. He maintains that although engineers are better qualified than other people to calculate cost versus safety, decisions about acceptable risk are not primarily engineering but managerial decisions. He believes that under ideal conditions the public itself would make this kind of decision. "A panel of informed people, not necessarily engineers, should decide . . . acceptable risk and minimum standards."[10] This information should then be relayed to car buyers who, he believes, are entitled to it.

One of the reasons it is difficult to decide when employees have an obligation to blow the whistle is that this is part of the larger problem of the extent to which people are responsible for actions by organizations of which they are members. The problem arises because it is extremely difficult to determine when a given individual in an organization is responsible for a particular decision or policy. Decisions are often the product of committees rather than single individuals. Since committee members usually serve temporary terms, none of the members who helped make a particular decision may be on the committee when it is implemented. Implementation is also likely to be the responsibility of others. Since committee membership is temporary, decisions are often made that contradict previous decisions. Even when decisions are made by individuals, these individuals seldom have control over the outcome of the decisions.

The result is that no one feels responsible for the consequences of organizational decisions. Top management does not because it only formulates policy; it does not implement it. Those in the middle and at the bottom of the chain of authority do not, because they simply carry out policy. If challenged to assume moral responsibility for their actions, they reply "I'm not responsible, I was simply carrying out orders" or "I was just doing my job." But, as De George points out, absence of a feeling of obligation does not mean absence of obligation.

Whenever one acts in such a way as to harm or violate the rights of others, one is justly held accountable for those actions. This is true regardless of one's occupation or role in society. Acting as a member of an institution or corporation does not relieve a person of moral obligations. To the contrary. Because most of the actions we undertake in such settings have more far-reaching consequences than those we undertake in our personal lives, our moral obligation is *increased*. The amount of responsibility one bears for organizational actions is dependent on the extent to which (a) one could foresee the consequences of the organizational action, and (b) one's own acts or failures to act are a cause of those consequences. It is important to include failures to act here because frequently it is easier to determine what will happen if we don't act than if we do and because we are morally responsible for not preventing evil as well as for causing it.

Although the foregoing discussion is brief and the ideas not fully worked out, if the criteria which are presented are applied to the engineers in the Pinto case, I think one must conclude that they had an obligation to blow the whistle. They knew the gas tanks were likely to explode, injuring or killing people, if Pintos were struck from behind by cars traveling thirty miles per hour. They knew that if they did not blow the whistle, Ford would market the cars. They were also members of a profession that, because of its special knowledge and skills, has a particular obligation to be concerned about public safety.

De George thinks that the Ford engineers would have had an obligation to blow the whistle only if they had also known that doing so would have been likely to prevent the deaths. But we have an obligation to warn others of danger even if we believe they will ignore our warnings. This is especially true if the danger will come about partly because we did not speak out. De George admits that the public has a right to know about dangerous products. If that is true, it would seem that those who have knowledge about such products have an obligation to inform the public. This is not usurping the public's right to decide acceptable risk; it is supplying it with the information necessary to exercise the right.

De George also believes we are not justified in asking engineers to blow the whistle if it would threaten their jobs. It is true that we would not be justified in demanding that they blow the whistle if that would place their or their families' lives in danger. But this is not true if only their jobs are at stake. Engineers are recognized as professionals and accorded respect and high salaries, not only because of their specialized knowledge and skills, but also because of the special responsibilities we entrust to them. All people have a prima facie obligation to blow the whistle on practices that are illegal, unjust, or harmful to others. But engineers who have special knowledge about, and are partially responsible for, dangerous practices or products have an especially strong obligation to blow the whistle if they are unsuccessful in getting the practices or products modified. Indeed, if they do not have an obligation to blow the whistle in such situations, no one ever has such an obligation.

A number of people have argued that for external whistle blowing to be justified the whistle blower must first make his or her concern known within the organization. "Surely," says Arthur S. Miller, "an employee owes his employer enough loyalty to try to work, first of all, within the organization to attempt to effect change."[11] De George even states that for whistle blowing to be morally justified one must first have informed one's immediate supervisor and exhausted all possible avenues of change within the organization. The problems with this kind of advice are: (1) It may be one's immediate supervisor who is responsible for the wrongdoing. (2) Organizations differ considerably in both their mechanisms for reporting and how they respond to wrongdoing. (3) Not all wrongdoing is of the same type. If the wrongdoing is one which threatens people's health or safety, exhausting all channels of protest within the organization could result in unjustified delay in correcting the problem. Exhausting internal channels of protest can also give people time to destroy evidence needed to substantiate one's allegations. Finally, it may expose the employee to possible retaliation that he or she would have some protection against if the wrongdoing were reported to an external agency.

It has also been argued that anonymous whistle blowing is never justified. It is said, for example, that anonymous whistle blowing violates the right of people to face their accusers. The fact that the whistle blower's identity is unknown also raises questions about his or her motives. But, as Frederick Elliston points out, anonymous whistle blowing can both protect whistle blowers from unjust retaliation and prevent those on whom the whistle is blown from engaging in an *ad hominem* attack to draw attention away from their wrongdoing. As he also points out, people should be protected from false accusations, but it is not necessary for the identity of whistle blowers to be known to accomplish this. "It is only necessary that accusations be properly investigated, proven true or false, and the results widely disseminated."[12] Discovering the whistle blower's motive is also irrelevant as far as immediate public policy is concerned. All that matters is whether wrongdoing has taken place and, if so, what should be done about it.

It has also been argued that anonymous whistle blowing should be avoided because it is ineffective. In fact, if anonymous whistle blowing is ineffective, it is more likely to be a function of lack of documentation and follow-up testimony than of its anonymity. Moreover, anonymity is a matter of degree. For whistle blowing to be anonymous, the whistle blower's identity does not have to be unknown to everyone, only to those on whom the whistle is blown and the general public. A few key investigators may know his or her identity. It should also not be forgotten that one of the most dramatic and important whistle-blowing incidents in recent years, Deep Throat's disclosure of Richard Nixon's betrayal of the American people, was an instance of anonymous whistle blowing.

FACTORS TO CONSIDER IN WHISTLE BLOWING

I have argued that because we have a duty to prevent harm and injustice to others, which holds even though we are members of organizations, we have a prima facie obligation to disclose organizational wrongdoing we are unable to prevent. The degree of the obligation depends on the extent to which we are capable of foreseeing the consequences of organizational actions and our own acts or failures to act are causes of those consequences. It also depends on the kind and extent of the wrongdoing. Even a part-time or temporary employee has an obligation to report serious or extensive wrongdoing. But, in general, professionals who occupy positions of trust and special responsibilities have a stronger obligation to blow the whistle than ordinary workers.

Although we have an obligation to document wrongdoings as thoroughly as possible, we can only act on the basis of probability, so it is possible for the whistle blower to be in error about the wrongdoing and the whistle blowing still be justified. Whether we have an obligation to express our concern within the organization before going outside depends on the nature of the wrongdoing, the kind of organization involved, and the likelihood of retaliation. Whether we have an obligation to blow the whistle openly rather than anonymously depends on the extent to which it helps us avoid unfair retaliation and is effective in exposing the wrongdoing. The same is true of alumni as opposed to current whistle blowing.

Since whistle blowing usually involves conflicting obligations and a wide range of variables and has far-reaching consequences for all people involved, decisions to blow the whistle are not easily made. Like all complicated moral actions, whistle blowing cannot be reduced to a how-to-do list. However, some of the factors whistle blowers should take into consideration, if they are to act prudently and morally, can be stated. The following is an attempt to do this.

- *Make sure the situation is one that warrants whistle blowing.*

  Make sure the situation involves illegal actions, harm to others, or violation of people's rights, and is not one in which you would be disclosing personal matters, trade secrets, customer lists, or similar material. If disclosure of the wrongdoing would involve the latter, make sure that the harm to be avoided is great enough to offset the harm from the latter.
- *Examine your motives.*

  Although it is not necessary for the whistle blower's motive to be praiseworthy for the action to be justified in terms of the public interest, examination of your motives will help in deciding whether the situation warrants whistle blowing.
- *Verify and document your information.*

  If at all possible, try to obtain evidence that would stand up in court or regulatory hearings. If the danger to others is so great that you believe you are justified in obtaining evidence by surreptitious methods such as eavesdropping or recording telephone calls, examine your motives thoroughly, weigh carefully the risks you are taking, and try to find alternative and independent sources for any evidence you uncover. In general, it is advisable to avoid surreptitious methods.
- *Determine the type of wrongdoing you are reporting and to whom it should be reported.*

  Determining the exact nature of the wrongdoing can help you decide both what kind of evidence to obtain and to whom it should be reported. For example, if the wrongdoing consists of illegal actions such as the submission of false test reports to government agencies, bribery of public officials, racial or sexual discrimination, or violation of safety, health, or pollution laws, then determining the nature of the laws being violated will also indicate which agencies have authority to enforce those laws. If, on the other hand, the wrongdoing consists of actions which are legal but contrary to the public interest, determining this will help you decide whether you have an obligation to publicize the actions and, if so, in what way. The best place to report this type of wrongdoing is usually a public interest group. Such an organization is more likely than the press to: (1) be concerned about and advise the whistle blower regarding retaliation, (2) maintain confidentiality, (3) investigate the whistle blower's allegations to try to substantiate them rather than sensationalize them by turning the issue into a "personality dispute." If releasing information to the press is the best way to remedy the situation, the public interest group can help with or do this.

- *State your allegations in an appropriate way.*

  Be as specific as possible without being unintelligible. If you are reporting violation of a law to a government agency and it is possible for you to do so, include information and technical data necessary for experts to verify the wrongdoing. If you are disclosing wrongdoing which does not require technical information to substantiate it, still be as specific as possible in stating the type of illegal or immoral action involved, who is being injured, and in what ways.

- *Stick to the facts.*

  Avoid name calling, slander, and being drawn into a mud-slinging contest. As Peter Raven-Hansen wisely points out: "One of the most important points . . . is to focus on the disclosure. . . . This rule applies even when the whistle blower believes that certain individuals are responsible. . . . The disclosure itself usually leaves a trail for others to follow to the miscreants."[13] Sticking to the facts also helps the whistle blower minimize retaliation.

- *Decide whether the whistle blowing should be internal or external.*

  Familiarize yourself with all available internal channels for reporting wrongdoing and obtain as many data as you can both on how people who have used these channels were treated by the organization and on what was done about the problems they reported. If you are considering blowing the whistle on an immediate supervisor, find out what has happened in the past in this kind of situation. If people who report wrongdoing have been treated fairly and problems corrected, use internal channels to report the wrongdoing. If not, decide to what external agencies you should report the wrongdoing.

- *Decide whether the whistle blowing should be open or anonymous.*

  If you intend to remain anonymous, decide whether partial or total anonymity is required. Also, make sure your documentation is as thorough as possible. Finally, since anonymity may be difficult to preserve, anticipate what you will do if your identity becomes known.

- *Decide whether current or alumni whistle blowing is required.*

  Sometimes it is advisable to resign your present position and obtain another before blowing the whistle. This protects you from being fired, receiving damaging letters of recommendation, or even being blacklisted from your profession. Alumni whistle blowing may also be advisable if you are anticipating writing a book about the wrongdoing. Since this can be profitable, anyone planning to take this step has a particularly strong obligation to examine his or her motives to make sure they are morally praiseworthy.

- *Find out how much protection is available for whistle blowers in your industry, state, or federal agency.*

  Follow any guidelines that have been established and make sure you meet all qualifications, deadlines, and so on for filing reports.

- *Anticipate and document retaliation.*

  Although it is not as certain as Newton's law of motion that for every action there is an equal reaction, whistle blowers whose identities are known can expect retaliation. Thus whether you decide to work within the organization or go outside, document every step with letters, records, tape recordings of meetings, and so forth. Unless you do this, you may find that regulatory agencies and the courts are of no help.

- *Consult a lawyer.*

  Lawyers are advisable at almost every stage of whistle blowing. They can help you determine if the wrongdoing violates the law, aid you in documenting information about it, inform you of any laws you might be breaking in documenting it, assist you in deciding to whom to report it, make sure reports are filed on time, and help you protect yourself against retaliation. However, since lawyers tend to view problems within a narrow legal framework and decisions to blow the whistle are moral decisions, in the final analysis you must rely on your conscience.

BEYOND WHISTLE BLOWING

What can be done to eliminate the wrongdoing which gives rise to whistle blowing? One solution would be to give whistle blowers greater legal protection. Another would be to try to change the nature of organizations so as to diminish the need for whistle blowing. These solutions of course are not mutually exclusive.

Many people are opposed to legislation protecting whistle blowers because they think it is unwarranted interference with the right to freedom of contract. However, if the right to freedom of contract is to be consistent with the public interest, it cannot serve as a shield for wrongdoing. It does this when threat of dismissal prevents people from blowing the whistle. The right of employers to dismiss at will has been restricted previously by labor laws which prevent employers from dismissing employees for union activities. It is ironic that we have restricted the right of employers to fire employees who are pursuing their economic self-interest, but allowed employers to fire employees acting in behalf of the public interest. The right of employers to dismiss employees in the interest of efficiency should be balanced against the right of the public to know about illegal, dangerous, and unjust practices of organizations. The most effective way to achieve the latter goal would be to pass a federal law protecting whistle blowers.

Laws protecting whistle blowers have also been opposed on the grounds that (1) employees would use them as an excuse to mask poor performance, (2) they would create an "informer ethos" within organizations, and (3) they would take away the autonomy of business, strangling it in red tape.

The first objection is illegitimate because only those employees who could show that an act of whistle blowing preceded their being dismissed or penalized and that their employment records were adequate up to the time of the whistle blowing could seek relief under the law.

The second objection is more formidable. A society that encourages snooping, suspicion, and mistrust is not most people's idea of the good society. Laws which encourage whistle blowing for self-interested reasons, such as the federal tax law, which pays informers part of any money that is collected, could help bring about such a society. However, laws protecting whistle blowers from being penalized or dismissed are quite different. They do not reward the whistle blower; they merely protect him or her from unjust retaliation. It is unlikely that federal or state laws of this sort would promote an informer society.

The third objection is also unfounded. Laws protecting whistle blowers would not require any positive duties on the part of organizations—only the negative duty of not retaliating against employees who speak out in the public interest. However, not every act of apparent whistle blowing should be protected. Only people who can show they had probable reasons for believing wrongdoing existed should be protected. Furthermore, the burden of proof should be on the individual. People who cannot show they had good cause to suspect wrongdoing may justly be penalized or dismissed. If the damage to the organization is serious, it should also be allowed to sue. Since these conditions would impose some risks on potential whistle blowers, they would reduce the possibility of frivolous action.

If, on the other hand, someone who has probable reasons for believing wrongdoing exists blows the whistle and is fired, the burden of proof should be on the organization to show that he or she was not fired for blowing the whistle. If the whistle blowing is found to be the reason for the dismissal, the whistle blower should be reinstated and awarded damages. If there is further retaliation after reinstatement, additional damages should be awarded.

What changes should be made in organizations to prevent the need for whistle blowing? Some of the suggestions which have been made are that organizations develop effective internal channels for reporting wrongdoing, reward people with salary increases and promotions for using these channels, and appoint senior executives, board members, ombudspersons, and so on whose primary obligations would be to investigate and eliminate organizational wrongdoing. These changes could be undertaken by organizations on their own or mandated by law. Other changes which might be mandated are requiring that certain kinds of records be kept, assessing larger fines for illegal actions, and making executives and other professionals personally liable for filing false reports, knowingly marketing dangerous products, failing to monitor how policies are being implemented, and so forth. Although these reforms could do much to reduce the need for whistle blowing, given human nature it is highly unlikely that this need can ever be totally eliminated. Therefore, it is important to have laws which protect whistle blowers and for us to state as clearly as we can both the practical problems and moral issues pertaining to whistle blowing.

NOTES

1. For discussion of the legal aspects of whistle blowing see Lawrence E. Blades, "Employment at Will vs. Individual Freedom: On Limiting the Abusive Exercise of Employer Power," *Columbia Law Review*, vol. 67 (1967); Philip Blumberg, "Corporate Responsibility and the Employee's Duty of Loyalty and Obedience: A Preliminary Inquiry," *Oklahoma Law Review*, vol. 24 (1971); Clyde W. Summers, "Individual Protection Against Unjust Dismissal: Time for a Statute," *Virginia Law Review*, vol. 62 (1976); Arthur S. Miller, "Whistle Blowing and the Law," in Ralph Nader, Peter J. Petkas, and Kate Blackwell [eds.], *Whistle Blowing*, New York: Grossman Publishers, 1972; Alan F. Westin [ed.], *Whistle Blowing*, New York: McGraw-Hill, 1981; Martin H. Marlin, "Current Status of Legal Protection for Whistleblowers," paper delivered at the Second Annual Conference on Ethics in Engineering, Illinois Institute of Technology, 1982. See also Gene G. James, "Whistle Blowing: Its Nature and Justification," *Philosophy in Context*, vol. 10, (1980) [pp. 99–117].

2. For a discussion of this study which was by Morton Corn see Frank von Hipple, "Professional Freedom and Responsibility: The Role of the Professional Society," *Newsletter on Science, Technology and Human Values*, vol. 22, January 1978.

3. See Westin, op. cit.

4. See Marlin, op. cit.
5. David W. Ewing, *Freedom Inside the Organization*, New York: E. P. Dutton, 1977, pp. 165–66.
6. Richard T. De George, *Business Ethics*, New York: Macmillan, 1982, p. 161. See also De George, "Ethical Responsibilities of Engineers in Large Organizations," *Business and Professional Ethics Journal*, vol. 1, no. 1, Fall 1981, pp. 1–14. He formulates the first criterion in a slightly different way in the last work, saying that the harm must be both serious and considerable before whistle blowing is justified.
7. Ibid.
8. De George, "Ethical Responsibilities of Engineers in Large Organizations," op. cit., p. 1.
9. Ibid., p. 5.
10. Ibid., p. 7.
11. Miller, op. cit., p. 30.
12. Frederick A. Elliston, "Anonymous Whistleblowing," *Business and Professional Ethics Journal*, vol. 1, no. 2, Winter 1982 [pp. 39–58].
13. Peter Raven-Hansen, "Dos and Don'ts for Whistleblowers: Planning for Trouble," *Technology Review*, May 1980 [pp. 34–44], p. 30. My discussion in the present section is heavily indebted to this article.

41. Ten Whistleblowers and How They Fared*

Myron Glazer

In 1959, Frank Serpico joined the New York City police force. For Serpico, the police had always represented the meshing of authority and service. His early days on the force propelled him into the conflict between the norms governing police behavior set by department regulations and the actual "code" generated by the police. Formal regulations precluded the taking of any items from neighborhood stores and sanctioned *[sic]* the acceptance of bribes. In the station house and out on patrol a different set of rules applied. "Shopping" for items of food at local stores was clearly acceptable and taking money to pardon a lawbreaker became standard fare. Serpico was caught in a dilemma that faces many rookie police. Which set of norms should he uphold?[1]

Like many other whistleblowers in industry, government, and the academic world, initially Serpico was caught between his desire to follow his moral beliefs, and the organizational pressures to conform. How do workers handle such a conflict? And what happens to their personal lives and their careers once they have blown the whistle? In an effort to understand the dynamics of the process, I have interviewed or exchanged letters with nine prominent whistleblowers and have corresponded with the wife of a tenth, who is deceased.[2] Their cases portray three distinct paths through which individuals move toward public disclosure:

Unbending resisters protest within the organization about unethical or illegal behavior that they have observed. They maintain a strict commitment to their principles, despite efforts to cajole or coerce them. Ultimately, as a consequence of neglect and retaliation within the organization, they take a public stand.

Implicated protestors speak out within their organizations, but acquiesce when they are ordered to conform. They find themselves drawn into illegal or unethical behavior, which they expose when they fear legal liability.

Reluctant collaborators become deeply involved in acts they privately condemn. They seek public remedy and personal expiation only when they leave the organization.

Once an employee has blown the whistle, the responses of his or her superiors can take two broad forms. There are "degradation ceremonies" to punish and alienate resisters and protesters; and "ceremonies of status elevation," which reinforce the whistleblower's feeling that what he or she is doing is right. Whether and when someone will blow the whistle will depend on the peculiar mixture of sustenance and punishment, as well as the person's courage and the circumstances of his or her life. My observations also reveal that the whistleblower's fate need not be grim.

From *Hastings Center Report* 13:6 (1983): 33–41.

*I am indebted to Julie Dobrow and Louise M. Rockey for their valuable research assistance, to Norma Lepine for her constant encouragement and typing, and to Michael Ford, Penina Migdal Glazer, Michael Lewis, Arthur Parsons, Gail Levi Perlman, Michael S. Perlman, Peter I. Rose and Miriam Slater for their thoughtful comments. Mark Kramer's line by line critique merits special recognition. The members of the Five-College Professional Ethics Seminar, particularly Joe Marcus, Janice Moulton, Barry O'Connell, George Robinson and Vere Chappell, provided an animated critique and Tom O'Connell and his staff in the Electronics Department assisted in the recording of the interviews as did Ruth Bryan who transcribed them.

An early version of this paper was presented as the keynote address at Speaker's Day ceremonies, Western New England College, 1 April 1981.

BLOWING THE WHISTLE

Like Serpico, Bob Leuci, the protagonist of *The Prince of the City,* was also caught in a net of conflicting loyalties. He has aptly described to me the "erosion process" by which young police officers became "bent":

> I remember the first time I was in a situation that scared me. We were in a police car and there was a fight in the street. I was working with this big, strong guy. I was nervous when I got out of the car and approached the fight. "Am I good enough to handle this kind of thing?" Two guys were going at each other with knives. I backed off a bit, but one guy came at me. My partner pushed me aside. "You move toward my partner again, and I'll kill you." And all of a sudden I got this feeling. He didn't say "You move toward me," but he said, "You move toward my partner." Whether he would have killed this guy or not, had the guy come at him, I don't know. But he would have killed him if the guy came at me. When hearing that, in that sort of context, you have this feeling of something very, very special about working with someone when your life may be in danger. So I was with a guy who was fifteen years my senior and a wonderful policeman. The first time he went in to get dinner, and came out with a sandwich I asked, "Did you pay for it?" He answered, "No, it's okay." It was in fact okay coming from him. It *was* okay. This man would not do anything wrong; he would not do anything criminal certainly, and what was so terrible about this? But what happens is that emotionally things are going on that you don't realize. There is an erosion process that is taking place, and it is changing you. That is something that I certainly didn't notice for many years. But it was happening to me—happening to a lot of people around me.[3]

Serpico felt similar pulls of loyalty born of comparable experiences. Yet he began to drift from the others on the force as he tired of the endless shoptalk. In a search for outside interests he took courses for a degree in sociology and moved to Greenwich Village where he spent time with aspiring women artists and dancers. Serpico's disenchantment peaked when, as a plainclothes officer, he accidentally received a $300 payoff, which he immediately took to one of the top men in the New York City Department of Investigation. The captain told Serpico that he could go before the grand jury, but that word would get out that he had been the chief witness and he might end "face down in the East River." Or, the captain continued, Serpico could forget the whole thing.

This is a crucial decision for the whistleblower. The organization counts on the threat of punishment to exercise control. But this can often backfire. Serpico's alienation toward the police force intensified. He felt powerless to require others to live up to their responsibilities. Doubting his own belief in the honesty of his comrades and leaders and knowing that serious rule-breaking was endemic at all levels of the department, he felt increasingly isolated from those whose trust was essential for his survival. He refused, however, to complete the cycle of self-alienation by turning his back on his own beliefs of proper police conduct. Serpico resisted the temptation to go along with the group, even though the pressure increased markedly when he transferred to the South Bronx with assurances by high-level police officials that it was free of corruption.

The combination of blatant police wrongdoing and the extreme poverty of the neighborhood aggravated his dilemma. In desperation, he bluffed to a superior that he had gone to "outside sources" about police payoffs. This threat generated an investigation and eight of his peers were eventually tried. But no higher-ups were indicted, despite promises from the district attorney. Ostracized by most police after testifying and feeling increasingly vulnerable, Serpico convinced his immediate superior to accompany him to the *New York Times.* This led to a series of front-page articles on police corruption and ultimately to the establishment of the Knapp Commission. Its lengthy, independent investigation verified all of Serpico's charges and led to important changes in the New York City Police Department. Serpico would leave his mark.[4]

Several months later, Serpico was shot and seriously wounded during a drug raid. Had he been set up by his comrades? He retired, received a pension, and left the country for a time. Serpico still maintains that a principled officer must resist. Serpico reappeared in 1981 and reported on a television news program that he was writing a book. Since Serpico's experiences, another police officer, detective Robert Ellis, has assisted investigators in the apprehension of corrupt fellow police. He reports the difficulty of his activities and the subsequent threats made upon his wife and daughter. "I don't want my friends in other commands to think that for eight years they were dealing with a spy," he said. "I want it simply to be said that I am an honest cop" (*New York Times,* July 3, 1977, p. 1).

The experience of other unbending resisters shows similar links between initial protest, retaliation against the whistleblower from one's superiors, and a continuing search for affirmation of professional ideals. In 1973 Joseph Rose, an experienced lawyer, joined the Associated Milk Producers Incorporated (AMPI) as an in-house attorney. Rose quickly became aware of illegal political payments to the Nixon reelection campaign, which were part of the Watergate investigation. In a phone interview in 1982, he told me:

My assignment in the corporation included fiduciary responsibilities. When I found out that so much money had gone under the table, I might have been able to take a moral posture of "All right—that's a past offense that I can indeed defend." But the criminal conspiracy was ongoing, and the law concerning criminal conspirators states that you don't have to participate in the original crime to be indicted as a co-conspirator later. All you need is to know about it and take steps to cover it up or otherwise further the conspiracy. Second, money was misused. The Watergate televised proceedings had started. An airline retrieved money that it had paid for similar purposes. When that broke, I went to the law books and became convinced of the duty to recover these assets. A whole chain of events led me more and more to believe that the current executives were in very deep themselves. I talked to a lawyer and former judge here in San Antonio named Joe Frazier Brown. He urged me to start keeping notes on everything I did. He also urged me to gather all of the documents that supported my position, to bypass the general manager, and to take the evidence to the board of directors. I was never allowed to do that. My attempt [to talk to the board] happened on a weekend during their convention in Minneapolis. Labor Day followed, and then Tuesday I went into work. I found a guard posted at my door; locks had been changed. The general manager demanded to see me. My services had become very, very unsatisfactory. When I was fired, I felt virtually a sense of relief. I was glad to be out of it, and I planned to keep my mouth shut. Then I had a call from one of the lawyers involved in an antitrust case against AMPI. He said, "They are really slandering you—making some very vicious attacks on you." I had indicated to AMPI executives that if the board would not listen to me, I would go right to the dairy farmers and they obviously felt my career and credibility had to be completely destroyed to protect their own tails. After I was terminated, I had a call both from the Watergate Special Prosecutor's Office and from the Congressional Committee's Subcommittee, wanting to know if they could fly down and talk to me. My answer was absolutely, unequivocally not. They both said they had subpoena power, and I said, "You have it. I suggest you use it if you want to talk to me." Of course, I was subpoenaed, first to Congress and then to Mr. Cox's grand jury.

Unlike Serpico who came forth on his own, Joseph Rose correctly feared he would be charged with breaking attorney-client privilege if he testified voluntarily. For Rose the path to public disclosure had been triggered by a series of events—his refusal to engage in illegal and unethical actions, corporate retaliation, and the government requirement that he testify against his former associates. Afterwards Rose was forced to confront the shame of being disreputable in the eyes of others, for as a result of his testimony he remained underemployed for eight years. Potential employers, who accepted AMPI's explanation that Rose had been disloyal, were unwilling to hire him. His father died believing that his son had irrevocably lost his ability to earn a living. A once-successful attorney and his family were forced to live on food stamps.

Rose's career opportunities began to improve appreciably only after the *Wall Street Journal* publicized his case. In the meantime, the AMPI was found guilty and heavily fined, and two of its officers were convicted and sentenced to prison terms. Its finance officers sought and received immunity from prosecution to testify against others.

Rose now looks at American society with cold cynicism.

> . . . I believe I can make a contribution to the young people in this country by continuing to respond with a strong warning that all of the public utterances of corporations and indeed our own government concerning "courage, integrity, loyalty, honesty, and duty" are nothing but the sheerest hogwash that disappear very rapidly when it comes to the practical application of these concepts by strict definition. The reason that there are very few Serpicos or Roses is that the message is too clearly out in this society that white-collar crime, or nonviolent crime, should be tolerated by the public at large, so long as the conduct brings a profit or a profitable result to the institution committing it. . . .

Public disclosure can also come about in an effort to clear one's personal reputation and establish the legitimacy of professionals to resist what they see as their superiors' unethical directives. Dr. Grace Pierce joined the Ortho Pharmaceutical Corporation, a division of Johnson & Johnson, in 1971 after eleven years in private medical practice, service in the Food and Drug Administration, and experience with another drug firm. In 1975 she was assigned to direct a research team attempting to develop Loperamide, a drug for the relief of acute and chronic diarrhea. The liquid Loperamide formulation originated with Janssen, a Johnson & Johnson company in Belgium, and had a very high saccharin content to hide the bitter taste. Dr. Pierce and all the Ortho team members agreed that there was a need to reformulate the drug to diminish the saccharine concentration, particularly with the ongoing controversy over its carcinogenic potential. While her colleagues ultimately acceded to management pressures to accept the high saccharin formulation, Dr. Pierce refused. As the only medical person on the team, she would not agree to begin clinical trials with what she considered a questionable formulation.

After her refusal, Dr. Pierce charged that her immediate superior questioned her judgment, loyalty, and competence. Later, he accused her of misusing company funds on a research trip and of taking an unauthorized vacation. Although she rejected and refuted the accusations, the critique was a clear signal of her diminished prospects.

When the situation came up and I couldn't get the other people to go along with me, I asked my superior whether we could get three objective consultants outside the company. If they say its okay, I'll do it. Or if you'll permit me to go to the FDA and put the situation to them openly and they say okay, I'll do it. I think I offered alternatives for a reasonable compromise. He refused. Use of saccharin remains a question yet. Nobody knows where this problem of carcinogens is heading. It probably won't be resolved soon, if ever. I was on the spot. I had to get with it or get out. I hated that. I was cornered. There was no compromise. Nobody from higher up came and said, "Why don't we do that or do this." They were just riding roughshod all over me. I always like to feel I'm a person, not a cog in a machine. . . . One of my colleagues said, "Grace, you're nuts. Why not write a lengthy memo for the files, make sure you're on record. They're responsible." If I do the research, I'm responsible. I feel responsibility as a physician first. My responsibility to the corporation is second. I think my colleagues' attitude is commonplace. People salve their conscience. They keep the benefits of the job. This memo gives them an escape hatch.

Pierce resigned. Unlike Joseph Rose, she was quickly approached by a colleague to affiliate in a group medical practice, which she joined on a part-time basis. Later the vice president of Personal Products, another subsidiary of Johnson & Johnson, invited her to join his research staff although she alerted him that she might sue Ortho. Within six months she had become director of research. While Dr. Pierce felt vindicated of charges against her integrity and competence, her work situation changed dramatically when she actually filed her suit for "damage to her professional reputation, dissipation of her career, loss of salary, as well as seniority and retirement benefits. . . ."[5]

Despite their excellent relationship, the vice president's attitude cooled. Not unexpectedly, he summoned her at the end of one work day.

I was fired. He said it was unconscionable that any one working for Personal Products would sue a sister company. I said I didn't think so. He had been aware of the legal thing with Ortho. He was dejected and hurt by the whole thing. The next morning he seemed very sad about seeing me go . . . I haven't seen him since.

Dr. Pierce carried her suit to the New Jersey Supreme Court, which broke constitutional ground by affirming a professional's right to challenge superiors where professional ethics are at stake. In Grace Pierce's case, however, five of the six judges for the New Jersey Supreme Court ruled that her judgment and Ortho's were simply at variance. Professional ethics were not the issue, according to the court, which sustained Ortho's actions.

POSTPONING THE WHISTLE

Some professionals delay taking a path of direct confrontation and, as a result, they become involved in unethical or illegal behavior. Implicated protesters include those who have spoken up within their organizations, have capitulated and gone along with the policies of their superiors, and have subsequently publicized inappropriate actions when they have become fearful of the consequences of their own involvement.

In the late 1960s, Kermit Vandivier, a technician, assisted in the production of an airplane brake whose faulty design could have endangered Air Force test pilots. He asserted that, despite his repeated pleas and those of several engineers including his supervisor, other engineers and managers in the Goodrich Corporation pushed a false report. When Air Force pilots tested the brakes with near fatal results, Vandivier approached a lawyer who advised him to go to the FBI.

Though Vandivier's account has been reprinted many times in the last decade,[6] he recently provided additional insight. Note how—as a relatively uneducated technician—he felt alienated and powerless. Note also his sense of anomie as people he trusted simply backed off, and his anxiety over his isolation.

At the time of the Goodrich fiasco I had six children of school age at home. My salary, if I remember correctly, was around \$125–\$135 per week. My only outside source of income was the pay I received from the *Troy Daily News* [TDN]—\$15 for the three columns per week I wrote. High principles notwithstanding, I couldn't—at that time—subject myself and my family to "retaliation." Please note I said "at that time," because I think there is one factor which I perhaps have not made entirely clear in the Goodrich story. I don't think anyone within the Goodrich organization really believed—until the moment it actually happened—that the report was going to be issued to the Air Force. Until such time as it was published and delivered to the Air Force, none of us who actually had a part in preparing the phony report was guilty of any criminal act. True, my attorney offered his opinion that we might be guilty of conspiracy to defraud, but qualified that opinion by adding there would have to be proof we knew at the outset a fraud would ultimately be committed. I can't describe the sense of incredulity I (and I'm sure others) experienced when I learned the report had really been issued, that Goodrich was actually going to try and pull this thing off. . . . Naturally, my editors at TDN knew what was going on right from the start. When the situation had developed sufficiently we considered whistleblowing in the TDN, but TDN attorneys were concerned that there was simply not enough proof of any wrongdoing at that time and felt that a libel suit could be certain. Meanwhile, I was gathering incriminating data, photographs, charts, movie film, notes of meetings and telephone conversations. I smuggled them out of the plant each day, copied them at night, and returned the originals the following day. Altogether, I amassed more than one thousand documents and other items (I still have them), which were invaluable evidence at the Senate hearing. When I finally was ready to blow the whistle I had all the evidence necessary to make a strong case. No one was indicted or charged in connection with the hearing, but the day following the hearing the Department of Defense quietly initiated sweeping changes in its inspection and procurement procedures. A DOD official later confirmed the changes were made as a direct result of the hearing. . . .

Vandivier's testimony underscores that the ties of loyalty can be broken and public criticism undertaken when the dangers of continued inaction appear more serious than the fears of retaliation. Under such circumstances, those who contemplate blowing the whistle have a potentially powerful and omnipresent ally in the weight of the law, which holds companies and individuals responsible for the production of faulty products.[7] Many implicated protesters might resist the orders of their superiors were there greater likelihood of apprehension, conviction, and severe punishment for white-collar crimes.[8]

In the early 1970s another serious breach of professional and managerial ethics unfolded. Frank Camps, a senior principal design engineer, was directly involved in the development of the Ford Pinto, which proved to have an unsafe windshield and a gas tank that might explode on impact. He questioned the design and testing procedure and later charged publicly that his superiors who knew of this danger were so anxious to produce a lightweight and cheap car to compete with the imports that they were determined to overlook serious design problems. Camp's level of anxiety grew as he contemplated the consequences of his own involvement.

We were still in the development stage. I had a certain degree of resentment; these people were not listening although we were having problems with the car. I can remember I went into my manager's office. He said, "Look, we're in the business of selling cars and every time we barrier crash a car and it causes problems, then we have one failure. If we get another car to crash, to see how the first failure happened, we may have two failures. This could compound itself until my bonus would be reduced." Now this was the kind of thinking—the corporate attitude—that my immediate superior had. He didn't say anything about crashing for occupant safety. He just didn't want his bonus to be cut down. I said to my wife, "This guy is a bad actor. This guy is going to get me in trouble if I don't start documenting and protecting myself." This was colossal arrogance, callous indifference toward the safety of people. It bothered me even if only one person should die or be disfigured because of something that I was responsible for.

Camps was a respected and longtime member of Ford's engineering staff and thus not totally without influence. Yet he felt powerless to affect company policy. To avoid complete absorption into a system of relationships and definitions that calibrated human life on a scale of company costs and to protect himself against legal liability, he sued the company.

Camps described the response of fellow engineers, a response that mitigated his sense of isolation.

Most of the working engineers were very supportive of me at that time. They are still supportive of me. I can recall, right after I filed the suit, other engineers said—"Go get 'em, we wish we could do it, there goes a man with brass balls." While I had tacit support, I was looking for an honest man to stand with me. I found that these guys were suddenly given promotions, nice increases in salary. Next thing I knew, I did not have the support any more.

Camps wasn't alone in his agony over the Pinto. From 1971 to 1978 fifty lawsuits were filed against Ford because of gas-tank explosions in rear-end accidents. In 1980 Ford was brought to trial on a criminal charge in the death of three Indiana girls. The case created national headlines and featured the testimony of a former high-ranking Ford engineer whose statements were similar to those made by Frank Camps within the company.[9] While Ford was found innocent in this trial, the Pinto has come to symbolize management's drive for profits over customer safety. Had Camps been treated as a voice to be heeded rather than a protester to be ignored and punished, Ford might have avoided fatalities and serious injuries, years of litigation, and the stigma of corporate irresponsibility.

WHISTLING LATE IN THE GAME

Many professionals who participate in illegal or unethical acts only blow the whistle once they have left the organization and have reestablished their careers in other companies or fields of work. They seek to make up for their past timidity and to ease their consciences.

The late Arthur Dale Console studied at Cornell Medical College and later practiced neurosurgery. In search of less strenuous work after a serious illness, he joined the E. R. Squibb and Sons pharmaceutical company in 1949 as associate director of research. He found Squibb an ethical company, still run by its founder and maintaining an orientation in which the physician in charge of research was defined as a "physician's physician." During the ensuing years, according to Dr. Console, much changed in the pharmaceutical industry. Larger companies bought out the smaller ones and the search for profit became more intense. The transformation affected all members of the company staff including the director of research, a position that Dr. Console had by then assumed. As he worked, he experienced an increasing tension between his sense of what was appropriate medical decision making and what was required by his more business-oriented superiors. He was particularly disturbed by those instances in which he had pressured physicians to certify drugs that they had not sufficiently tested. He resigned from his position in 1956 after six and a half years in the drug industry, and soon after began to train for a new career as a psychiatrist.

During the 1960s, Console's continuing sense of self-estrangement led him to take the initiative and testify several times before congressional committees. At one hearing he was asked why he had left Squibb. His answer captures the process of capitulating to the pressures of multinational corporations and the disillusionment that follows.

> I believe that the best answer can be found in my unfinished essay of *The Good Life of A Drug Company Doctor*. Toward the end I said: "These are only some of the things a drug company doctor must learn if he is to be happy in the industry. After all, *it is a business,* and there are many more things he must learn to rationalize. He must learn the many ways to deceive the FDA and, failing in this, how to seduce, manipulate or threaten the physician assigned to the New Drug Application into approving it even if it is incomplete. He must learn that anything that helps to sell a drug is valid even if it is supported by the crudest testimonial, while anything that decreases sales must be suppressed, distorted and rejected because it is not absolutely conclusive proof. He will find himself squeezed between businessmen who will sell anything and justify it on the basis that doctors ask for it and doctors who demand products they have been taught to want through the advertising and promotion schemes contrived by businessmen. If he can absorb all this, and more, and still maintain any sensibilities he will learn the true meaning of loneliness and alienation." During my tenure as medical director I learned the meaning of loneliness and alienation. I reached a point where I could no longer live with myself. I had compromised to the point where my back was against a wall and I had to choose between resigning myself to total capitulation, or resigning as medical director. I chose the later course.[10]

After he left the pharmaceutical industry, Dr. Console received a grant from Squibb to train for a career in psychiatry, which placed him outside the authority of all corporate structures. Console's widow, a respected psychiatrist in her own right, has provided additional insight into Dr. Console's background, his commitment to Squibb, and his ultimate decision to blow the whistle several years after entering private practice.

> He was one of two surviving brothers who both carried out their father's ambitions to complete medical school. Arthur did so with great distinction. . . . In spite of two bouts of tuberculosis during this period he went on and completed a neurosurgical residency—the first resident chosen in this separate specialty considered the most prestigious in surgery. Trouble really began when, in attempting to establish a practice, he fell ill a third time, necessitating complete bed rest at home. We had an infant son with club feet requiring frequent surgical intervention and casts, absolutely no income except mine from an also newly established practice and the resulting pressure on me from multiple conflicting responsibilities was overwhelming. It was apparent that he had to find a less physically demanding and an economically sound alternative. It was at this time he accepted the offer to join Squibb as an associate medical doctor. The decision to give up neurosurgery as a career was a bitter and lasting defeat. The coincidence of Dr. Console's tenure as medical director of Squibb with its changeover from an ethical drug house to a competitive business-oriented company could not have been foreseen, but his sense of having been condemned to second-class medicine then became more and more intolerable. Because of Dr. Console's increasing and outspoken alientation from the drug industry it was clear that an open break was pending. It was imperative for him to look elsewhere for the future. The choice of psychiatry was made after considerable discussion together. . . . When the opportunity arose to testify in the Kefauver hearings, Dr. Console had already distanced himself from almost all his former colleagues. . . . The real problem was one of conflict from some sense of loyalty to Squibb, which had been very generous to him, and the pressure of his need to speak out. I did not share this intensity and had some misgivings but felt that he had to follow his own conviction. His moments of "speaking out" appeared then to be an opportunity to vindicate himself in his own eyes before the world.

Dr. Console *chose* to reveal his own complicity in a large-scale effort to profit from unethical marketing procedures. Whistleblowing of this kind can result when people believe deeply that they should have acted earlier to resist illegitimate authority.[11] Although Dr. Console testified over a decade ago, recent scholarship reveals that many of the problems he highlighted continue to characterize the drug industry, particularly in its relationship with Third World countries.[12]

TABOOS AND DEGRADATION CEREMONIES

Those willing to breach the taboo against informing face potent challenges.[13] Their superiors have the power to harass them by questioning their competence and judgment, to terminate their employment, and to blacklist them from other positions. Attorney Joseph Rose learned that the extensive influence of the Associated Milk Producers could bring his career to a standstill.

After I left AMPI, they weren't content with the firing, they wanted to call my ex-employers and completely ruin me. There was an attorney up in New York and I answered one of his ads. It turned out that he was a friend of an executive of AMPI, and indeed his secretary was one of the executive's nieces. I accepted the job and he and I went out on one case. He said right in front of a client, "He doesn't know it yet, but at Christmas time, I am going to fire him." I thought he was kidding, and I didn't pay any attention to it, and then lo and behold, right at Christmas time, right on target before Christmas, he fired me. After he dismissed me, I had been under fire so long that I was about to have a damned nervous breakdown. I did a very peculiar thing. President Ford was in office, and I wrote Ford and said, "This is happening to me, because I wouldn't be a crook." The next thing I knew, John Sales of the Watergate prosecutor's office called me and he said, "How are you?" and the clear implication was "Are you keeping you sanity?" And I said, "John, I'm holding on, but it sure as hell isn't easy." And he said, "Well, we've got an interview for you with the Department of Labor in Dallas." I thought, all of a sudden, there is justice in the world, maybe somebody does care. So I drove to Dallas, and I interviewed with the guy who was the head of the Department of Labor there, and I'll be damned if he didn't know some of the AMPI people. He made the comment, "I didn't request to interview you, as far as I am concerned, I can throw your resume up to the ceiling and hope it sticks there."

AMPI's influence seemed also to extend into religious organizations. Rose, a devout man, was particularly hurt by this.

My wife and I were attending Castle Hills First Baptist Church in town. I was in very bad emotional shape. I mean *very* bad and one of the high guys at AMPI attended the same church. I went to talk to the leader of the church. I guess I just wanted somebody to talk to, to get this thing out of my system. The man literally turned his back on me and started talking to other people. I felt that I certainly was not abandoning Jesus Christ by abandoning the specific church building.

As Joseph Rose learned through bitter experience, those who break the taboo will experience degradation, which recasts the social identity of whistleblowers, labeling them as unreliable, of poor judgment, and of dangerous character.

Joseph Rose worked in private industry. What of the government employees? A prime example is Ernest A. Fitzerald, a staff analyst in the Pentagon. In 1969, he appeared before Proxmire's Senate subcommittee investigating the production of the C5A air transport. Fitzgerald "committed truth" by answering affirmatively that there had been a two-billion-dollar overrun in the plane's development.[14] He could have sidestepped the question or lied to the Senator. Had he done so, Fitzerald would have avoided being labeled as someone who no longer had a future at the Pentagon. Such a designation came from the highest levels of government, including the Secretary of the Air Force and the President of the United States, Richard M. Nixon.

A statement by Alexander Butterfield, White House aide (and the man who later revealed the existence of the secret Nixon tapes) best summed up the official view toward Fitzgerald.

Fitzerald is no doubt a top-notch cost expert, but he must be given very low marks in loyalty, and after all loyalty is the name of the game. Only a basic "nogoodnik" would take his official grievances so far from normal channels. We should let him bleed for a while at least.[15]

While such retaliation did not break Fitzgerald, it extracted a heavy price from him and his family. In a recent conversation he has spoken of the impact on his children as comparable to radiation—difficult to measure but potentially very damaging.

Butterfield's statement implicitly highlights some of the central characteristics of "successful degradation ceremonies" that Harold Garfinkel has identified: the whistleblower's actions are "out of the ordinary" and in contrast to those of a loyal employee or peer; the actions are not accidental and reflect on the entire person of the whistleblower; the denunciation reinforces the values of the group, which stress silence and loyalty.[16] The message is clear. Whether in industry or government or academia, the whistleblower who is determined to reject self-estrangement despite the attacks of superiors must be able to withstand the charge of being labeled incompetent and disloyal.

CEREMONIES OF STATUS ELEVATION

New York City detective Bob Leuci received crucial encouragement from government prosecutors Scoppetta and Shaw in his decision to do undercover work against racketeers and corrupt police. Note how Leuci's sense of self is directly tied to his identification with these two men.

I undertook this investigation because of the support that I received from Scoppetta and Shaw, incredible support. It was the same kind of support that I received from my partners when I was working out on the street. You have a sense that there is somebody who truly cares about you.

The experiences of James Boyd and Marjorie Carpenter offer a sharp example of the way in which efforts toward status elevation can alleviate the pressures toward self-estrangement. Boyd and Carpenter are credited with exposing and bringing down the powerful Senator Thomas Dodd of Connecticut in the late 1960s. Boyd, Dodd's assistant for twelve years, and Carpenter, Dodd's secretary, suspected that the senator was pocketing large amounts of campaign funds.[17] According to Boyd, Dodd sensed their suspicions, fired them both, and spread the word that they were disreputable employees who were dismissed when he discovered that they were engaged in a sordid love affair. Boyd suspected that the senator also intended to blacklist him from employment in Washington.

> I didn't come to the decision to really go at it, tooth and nail, until I saw him trying to keep me from getting a job. I didn't want to go back with him. I was trying to get away from him for some time, but he tried to use the power to keep me from getting a job, and then, in a roundabout way, boasting to me what he was doing, toying with me as if I were some kind of a creature, instead of a partner as we had started out.

Boyd had decided to expose Senator Dodd but could not act until he was approached by Drew Pearson and Jack Anderson.[18] The two journalists assessed his suspicion, and encouraged him to act against Dodd with their explicit promise that they would define the case as their highest priority, would never back off no matter how great the heat, and would continue to demand an investigation by the Senate and other legal authorities.

After this careful agreement, Boyd and Carpenter obtained keys to Dodd's office, and removed and copied thousands of documents that contained evidence of Dodd's financial dealings with major corporations and others who sought his intervention on their behalf. Boyd and Carpenter had taken bold and controversial action, which resulted in Dodd's eventual censure by the Senate.

HEALING THE WOUNDS

The available literature on whistleblowers often emphasizes the dead end that awaits those who break with peers and superiors. My evidence provides a more intricate mosaic. Virtually all the individuals discussed here have been able to rebuild their careers and belief in their competence and integrity. They found an escape hatch in private practice, consulting, and the media. Ironically perhaps the diversity of American economic and social institutions provides opportunities to those who have dared defy the authority of the established ones.

Although Frank Serpico never sought to develop a new career, he is a national figure who continues to be respected for his courageous stand. His name is synonymous with police integrity. Bob Leuci completed his twenty years in the New York City Police Department, is a popular speaker on college campuses, and is currently writing a novel about police work.

Joseph Rose is a successful attorney in San Antonio. Former colleagues who avoided him and believed the accusation that he had betrayed AMPI now treat him with respect. Some clients seek him out expressly because they know of his past difficulties and admire his toughness. When we spoke in the winter of 1983 his practice was flourishing.

Grace Pierce works exclusively in clinical medicine. She has expanded her work in the group clinic by opening an office in her home, believes she provides an important service to local patients, and has time to enjoy her garden.

"I really lucked out," she says. Her skills, the support of the medical community, and the receptiveness of her patients have provided an up-beat continuity to her work and personal life. She does, however, harbor many troubling questions about whistleblowing and its effectiveness in changing organizational policies. A few months ago she wrote:

> And now that the "whistleblowers" have been reestablished or resettled into other pursuits of living what has happened to the persons, institutions or corporations that created these dilemmas? Have there been corrective steps taken to avoid similar episodes of employee disenchantment? Have those offenders to the whistleblowers changed in any way—have there been any recriminations? Is there less deception or corruption or is it better concealed? Have the pathways of whistleblowers been kept open, or even broadened for other employees who may be confronted with similar ethical issues? Are the courts any more or less supportive? Were these struggles really worth it? Have our little pieces of this world actually improved because of these actions? Are there other ways and means available to resolve the whistleblower's conflicts—perhaps more effectively and perhaps less painfully with less personal sacrifice? Is there still a place for "idealists" in a world quite full of "realists"?

Unique opportunities arose for both Kermit Vandivier and Frank Camps after their break with former superiors. Vandivier has built a new career at the *Troy Daily News:*

> Looking back, I would say probably the best thing that ever happened to me was the Goodrich thing. That gave me the push I probably wouldn't have had otherwise. When you have six kids and you've got a job that looks fairly secure, and you like it—which I did—I liked the Goodrich job—and you feel like you're accomplishing something—you don't feel like quitting or starting a new career. I went into a different field. I would never have gotten a job at Goodyear or Bendix, the other two brake manufacturers. I don't think anyone in private industry would touch me. I am a troublemaker, you know. I went to work for the *Troy Daily News* the day following my abrupt departure from BFG. I have served as a general assignment reporter and have covered a variety of beats, including the police, city hall and political beats. . . . Two years ago the TDN became involved in cable television. I was named cable news director and given the responsibility of organizing and implementing the project.

Like Vandivier, Frank Camps found that others were interested in his skills and eager to hire him. Camps now serves as a consultant to attorneys involved in product liability litigations. He underscores how important those relationships have become in recreating his career and his sense of himself.

> When I filed my suit, six months before I left Ford, it gained wide publicity, not only in the Detroit papers but in many papers and in many television outlets in the cities where the Ford plants were located. It also got into the *Wall Street Journal*. I began getting calls from attorneys all over the country, and I couldn't quite comprehend what they were driving at until one of the attorneys said he would like me to help him on a case. He came up with an hourly figure and a retainer that was absolutely staggering, based on what I was making at Ford. He became my mentor. . . . All of those feelings I had—the anxiety, resentment, anger, helplesness, that's all gone, because of what I now accomplish. I am doing what I want to do, when I want to do it. I can speak my mind truthfully and openly in a court of law. There is nothing more gratifying than to know that you are now involved in due process. Incidentally, in all of the cases I have been involved in, I have not been on the losing side even one time.

Ernest Fitzgerald has spent more than a decade in litigation to secure his former position. He has defeated a bureaucracy committed to his expulsion and banishment. An out-of-court settlement with former President Richard Nixon, the return to previous duties, and the court-directed government payment of his legal fees have all provided clear evidence for his complete and public vindication. Fitzgerald has survived as the nation's best-known whistleblower.

Finally, James Boyd has taken a more circuitous route. He has published a book about his experiences in the Dodd case, has directed the Fund for Investigation Journalism, has written for the *New York Times Magazine,* and has completed several projects with Jack Anderson. He and Marjorie Carpenter Boyd live with their two children in a rural area far from Washington. She continues to believe that they acted appropriately and were guided by their need for a sense of inner satisfaction, which she finds characteristic of many whistleblowers. As Boyd reflects on the last fifteen years, he can count some of the costs and gains of his decision to take on a U.S. Senator.

> I have friends from that period of my life who are now retired. If I had done that, I would have been retired now for three years, and I would have been getting $35,000 a year. I realize that there is a tremendous material loss involved. Also you lose something—there's something in an institution, various supports—professional, friendship, life-support type things—that you lose when you are separated from that institution. What I have gained is a whole new outlook on life—a feeling of independence—of "being my own man"—working at my own hours—and all that sort of thing, which I find enormously attractive. . . .

In a recent note Rose aptly summarized his views.

> Gandhi said that noncooperation with evil is as much a duty as cooperation with good; Burke said the only thing necessary for the triumph of evil is for good men to do nothing. Both concepts are still viable . . . although expensive.

For each of these whistleblowers there was no going back. Yet there was a future.[19] That message is as vital as the severe price they paid.

NOTES

1. Peter Maas, *Serpico* (New York: Viking Press, 1973). For a participant observation account of police training see Richard Harris, *The Police Academy: An Inside View* (New York: John Wiley, 1973). Other studies of the policy support Serpico's experiences and observations. See Lawrence W. Sherman, *Police Corruption* (New York: [Douleday,] Anchor, 1974).

2. In those instances where the whistleblowers lived beyond driving distance, I exchanged letters with them and did a lengthy, taped, telephone interview during the summer of 1982. Unless otherwise noted all quoted material is from the interviews or letters. Since I was interested in the whistleblowers' perceptions of their experience, I did not interview other people involved in the cases. The material on Frank Serpico derives from published sources.

Three of the whistleblowers discussed in this article—Joseph Rose, Grace Pierce, and Frank Camps—also described their experiences in Alan Westin, ed. *Whistle Blowing: Loyalty and Dissent in the Corporation* (New York: McGraw-Hill, 1981).

For a study that reports on fifty-one cases of whistleblowers, see Lea P. Stuart, " 'Whistle Blowing' Implications for Organizational Communication," *Journal of Communication* 30:4 (Autumn 1980), 90–101. For an intensive case study read Robert M. Anderson, Robert Perrucci, Dan D. Schendel, and Leon E. Tractman, *Divided Loyalties: Whistle-Blowing at BART* (West Lafayette, IN: Purdue University Press, 1980).

3. Bob Leuci's experiences are recounted by Robert Daly, *Prince of the City* (Boston: Houghton Mifflin, 1978). This statement is taken from a class visit to Smith College, March 12, 1981. Since then, I have had numerous other discussions with Leuci.

4. David Burnham, "Graft Paid to Police Said to Run into Millions," *New York Times,* April 25, 1970. New York City, *The Knapp Commission Report on Police Corruption* (New York: George Braziller, 1973).

5. Alfred G. Feliu, "Discharge of Professional Employees: Protecting Against Dismissal for Acts Within a Professional Code of Ethics," *Columbia Human Rights Law Review,* 11 (1979–1980). See especially pp. 186–87.

6. Kermit Vandivier, "The Aircraft Brake Scandal," *Harper's,* April 1972, pp. 45–52.

7. For a discussion of the recent legislation to protect and encourage whistleblowing see Westin, *Whistle Blowing,* pp. 131–67.

8. For a pertinent instance, see Eberhard Faber, "How I Lost our Great Debate About Corporate Ethics," *Fortune,* November 1976, pp. 180–88.

9. Richard T. De George, "Ethical Responsibilities of Engineers in Large Organizations: The Pinto Case," *Business Professional Ethics Journal* I[:1] (Fall 1981), 1–14.

10. "A. Dale Console" in Ralph Nader, Peter J. Petkas, and Kate Blackwell, eds. *Whistle Blowing* (New York: Bantam, 1972), pp. 122–23. Also see, Hearings Before the Subcommittee on Monopoly of the Select Committee on Small Business. U.S. Senate, 91st Congress, 1st Session on Present Status of Competition in the Pharmaceutical Industry, Part II, March 13, 1959, p. 4484.

11. Other reluctant collaborators now have become international figures. See Philip Agee, *Inside the Company* (New York: Bantam Books, 1976). His decision to identify publicly CIA agents makes him the country's most controversial whistleblower. For a debate on his actions, see "On Naming C.I.A. Agents," *The Nation* (March 14, 1981), pp. 295–301.

12. See Ray H. Elling, "The Political Economy of International Health with a Focus on the Capitalist World-System," in Michael Lewis, ed. *Social Problems and Public Policy. vol. 2* (Stanford, CT: Jai Press, 1982).

13. For a recent and illuminating study of the role of the informer, see Victor Navasky, *Naming Names* (New York: Viking, 1980).

14. A. Ernest Fitzgerald, *The High Priests of Waste* (New York: W. W. Norton, 1972). For a pertinent study, see Mark Ryter, *A Whistle-blower's Guide to the Federal Bureaucracy* (Washington[, DC]: Institute for Policy Studies, 1977).

15. Media Transcripts Incorporated Program 20/20. December 18, 1980, p. 14.

16. Harold Garfinkel, "Conditions of Successful Degradation Ceremonies," *American Journal of Sociology* 61 (January 1956), 420–24: Victor W. Turner, *The Ritual Process* (Chicago: Aldine, 1969), pp. 168–203.

17. James Boyd, *Above the Law* (New York: New American Library, 1968).

18. Drew Pearson and Jack Anderson, *The Case Against Congress* (New York: Simon and Schuster, 1968). Part I: Portraits of a Senator. The Dodd case was one among other factors leading to the Senate's ultimate reconsideration of its principles of behavior and the revision of its own code of ethics. See the special section entitled "Revising the U.S. Senate Code of Ethics" *Hastings Center Report* [11:1] (February 1981), pp. 1–28.

19. These findings are confirmed by a recent government report. The U.S. Merit Systems Protection Board, *Whistle Blowing and the Federal Employee* (Washington, DC: U.S. Government Printing Office, October 1981), particularly p. 41.

42. Whistleblowing and Professional Responsibilities

Sissela Bok

RESPONSIBILITIES IN CONFLICT

"Whistleblowing" is a new word in the glossary of labels generated by our increased awareness of the ethical conflicts encountered at work. Whistleblowers sound an alarm from within the very organization in which they work, aiming to spotlight neglect or abuses that threaten the public interest.

The stakes in whistleblowing are high. Take the nurse who alleges that physicians enrich themselves in her hospital through unnecessary surgery; the engineers who disclose safety defects in the braking systems of a fleet of new rapid-transit vehicles; the Defense Department official who alerts Congress to military graft and overspending: All know that they pose a threat to those whom they denounce and that their own careers may be at risk.

Moral conflicts on several levels confront anyone who is wondering whether to speak out about abuses or risks or serious neglect. In the first place, he must try to decide whether, other things being equal, speaking out is in fact in the public interest. This choice is often made more complicated by factual uncertainties: Who is responsible for the abuse or the neglect? How great is the threat? And how likely is it that speaking out will precipitate changes for the better?

In the second place, a would-be whistleblower must weigh his responsibility to serve the public interest against the responsibility he owes to his colleagues and the institution in which he works. This conflict between responsibilities is reflected in conflicting messages within many professions: the professional ethic requires collegial loyalty, while the codes of ethics often stress responsibility to the public over and above duties to colleagues and clients.

Thus the U.S. Code of Ethics for government servants[1] asks them to "expose corruption wherever uncovered," and to "put loyalty to the highest moral principles and to country above loyalty to

From *Ethics Teaching in Higher Education,* edited by Daniel Callahan and Sissela Bok (New York: Plenum, 1980), pp. 277–95.

persons, party, or government." Similarly, the largest professional engineering association requires members to speak out against abuses threatening the safety, health, and welfare of the public.[2] And a number of business firms have codes making similar requirements.

A third conflict for would-be whistleblowers is personal in nature, and cuts across the first two: even in cases where they have concluded that the facts warrant speaking out, and that duty to do so overrides loyalties to colleagues and institutions, they often have reason to fear the results of carrying out such a duty. However strong this duty may seem in theory, they know that, in practice, retaliation is likely. As a result, their careers, and their ability to support themselves and their families, may be unjustly impaired.

Government service offers an insight into the variety of forms that retaliation can take. A handbook issued during the Nixon era recommends reassigning "undesirables" to places so remote that they would prefer to resign. Whistleblowers may also be downgraded, or given work without responsibility, or work for which they are not qualified; or else they may be given many more tasks than they can possibly perform.[3]

Another risk—devasting from the point of view of career plans—is that an outspoken civil servant may be ordered to undergo a psychiatric fitness-for-duty examination. Congressional hearings in 1978 uncovered a growing resort to such mandatory examinations, and found that they frequently result from conflicts between supervisors and employees.[4] A person declared unfit for service can then be "separated," as well as discredited from the point of view of any allegations he may be making. The chairman concluded that:

> There was general agreement . . . that involuntary psychiatric examinations were not helpful to the government, unfair to employees, and that the agencies placed psychiatrists in an impossible situation.

Outright firing, finally, is the most direct institutional response to whistleblowers. One civil servant, reflecting on her experiences and on that of others, stated:

> The reactions of those who have observed or exposed the truth about federal agencies have ranged from humiliation, frustration, and helpless rage to complete despair about our democratic process.[5]

Add to the conflicts confronting individual whistleblowers the claim to self-policing that many professions make, and professional responsibility is at issue in still another way. For an appeal to the public goes against everything that "self-policing" stands for.

The question for the different professions, then, is how to resolve, insofar as it is possible, the conflict between professional loyalty and professional responsibility toward the outside world. The same conflicts arise to some extent in all groups; but professional groups often have special cohesion, and claim special dignity and privileges. The strain between the ideals of public service and collegiality in the professions can therefore be especially strong; they add to the pressure on would-be whistleblowers.

The plight of whistleblowers has come to be documented by the press, and described in a number of books. Evidence of the hardships imposed on those who chose to act in the public interest has combined with a heightened awareness of professional malfeasance and corruption to produce a shift toward greater public support of whistleblowers. Public-service law firms and consumer groups have taken up their cause; institutional reforms and legislation have been proposed to combat illegitimate reprisals.[6] Some would encourage ever more employees to ferret out and publicize improprieties in the agencies and organizations where they work.

Given the indispensable services performed by so many whistleblowers—as during the Watergate period and after—strong public support is often merited. But the new climate of acceptance makes it easy to overlook the dangers of whistleblowing: of uses in error or in malice; of work and reputations unjustly lost for those falsely accused; of privacy invaded and trust undermined. There comes a level of internal prying and mutual suspicion at which no institution can function. And it is a fact that the disappointed, the incompetent, the malicious, and the paranoid all too often leap to accusations in public. Worst of all, ideological persecution throughout the world traditionally relies on insiders willing to inform on their colleagues or even on their family members, often through staged public denunciations or press campaigns.

No society can count itself immune from such dangers. But neither can it risk silencing those with a legitimate reason to blow the whistle. How, then, can we distinguish different instances of whistleblowing? A society that fails to protect the right to speak out even on the part of those whose warnings turn out to be spurious obviously opens the door to political respression. But, from the moral point of view, there are important differences in the aims, messages, and methods of dissenters from within.

THE NATURE OF WHISTLEBLOWING

The alarm of the whistleblower is intended to disrupt the status quo: to pierce the background noise, perhaps the false harmony or the imposed silence of "affairs as usual." For the act to be completed successfully, in the eyes of the person sounding the alarm, listeners must be aroused by the message, and capable of response. A signal must be sent, a voice raised, to an audience that gains new insight and takes action.

Three elements, each jarring, and triply jarring when conjoined, lend acts of whistleblowing special urgency and bitterness: dissent, breach of loyalty, and accusation.

Dissent

Like all dissent, whistleblowing makes public a disagreement with an authority of a majority view. But, whereas dissent can concern all forms of disagreement with, for instance, religious dogma, government policy, or court decisions, whistleblowing has the narrower aim of shedding light on negligence or abuse: of alerting to a risk, and assigning responsibility for this risk.

Would-be whistleblowers confront the conflict inherent in all dissent: between conforming and sticking their necks out. The more repressive the authority they challenge, the greater the personal risk they take in speaking out; at exceptional times, as in times of war, even ordinarily tolerant authorities may come to regard dissent as unacceptable, and even disloyal.[7]

Breach of Loyalty

The whistleblower hopes to stop the game; but since he is neither referee nor coach, and since he blows the whistle on his own team, his act is seen as a violation of loyalty. In holding his position, he has assumed certain obligations to his colleagues and clients: stepping out of channels to level accusations is regarded as a violation of these obligations. Loyalty to colleagues and to clients comes to be pitted against loyalty to the public interest, to those who may be injured unless the revelation is made.

Because the whistleblower is an insider in the very organization he criticizes, his act differs from muckraking and other forms of exposure by outsiders, as when reporters expose corruption within a government agency. Such acts are expected, sometimes even required of outsiders, and do not produce in them the same conflicts of loyalty. (Needless to say, the desire for "scoops" and for personal publicity presents moral conflicts all their own to critics from the outside.)

Pressure from within the institution adds to the internal conflict of loyalty. Fidelity to one's agency, to one's superiors, and to colleagues is stressed in countless ways. It may be supported by a loyalty oath, or a promise of confidentiality.

Not only is loyalty violated in whistleblowing; hierarchy as well is often opposed, since the whistleblower is not only a colleague, but a subordinate. Though aware of the risks inherent in such disobedience, he often hopes to keep his job.[8] At times, however, he plans his alarm to coincide with leaving the institution. If he is highly placed, or joined by others, resigning in protest may effectively direct public attention to the wrongdoing at issue.[9] Still another alternative, often chosen by those who wish to be safe from retaliation, is to leave the institution quietly, secure another post, and then blow the whistle. In this way, it is possible to speak with the authority and knowledge of an insider, without the vulnerability of that position.

Whistleblowing resembles civil disobedience in its openness; it differs from the anonymous warning as much as civil disobedience differs from covert breaches of the law.[10] Unlike civil disobedience, however, whistleblowing is usually not a breach of explicit rules and laws; rather, it is often protected by the right to free speech, but challenges unspoken bonds and loyalties. Its purpose, moreover, is narrower than that of civil disobedience; it aims for change through bringing to light new information of an accusatory nature, rather than through more general political disobedience.[11]

Accusation

It is the element of accusation, of calling "foul," that arouses the strongest reactions on the part of the hierarchy. The accusation may be of neglect, of willfully concealed dangers, or of outright abuse on the part of colleagues or superiors. It singles out specific persons or groups as responsible for threats to the public interest. If no one could be held responsible—as in the case of an impending avalanche—the warning would not constitute whistleblowing.

The accusation of the whistleblower, moreover, concerns a present or an imminent threat. Past errors or misdeeds occasion such an alarm only if they still affect current practices. And risks far in the future lack the immediacy needed to make the alarm a compelling one, as well as the close connection to particular individuals that would justify actual accusations. Thus, an alarm can be sounded about safety defects in a rapid-transit system that threaten or will shortly threaten passengers; but the revelation of safety defects in a system no longer in use, though of historical interest, would not constitute whistleblowing. Nor would the revelation of potential problems in a system not yet fully designed, and far from implemented.[12]

Not only immediacy, but also specificity, is needed for there to be an alarm capable of pinpointing responsibility. A concrete risk must be at issue, rather than a vague foreboding or a somber prediction. The act of whistleblowing differs in this respect from the lamentation or the dire prophecy.

An immediate and specific threat would usually be acted upon by those at risk. But the whistleblower assumes that his message will alert listeners to something that they do not know, or the significance of which they have not grasped. The reason that the danger is not known or understood is often that it has been kept secret by the organization, or by certain members within it who are at fault.

The desire for openness inheres in the temptation to reveal any secret: sometimes also the urge to self-aggrandizement and publicity, and the hope for revenge for past slights or injustices. There can be pleasure, too—righteous or malicious—in laying bare the secrets of co-workers, and in setting the record straight at last. Colleagues of the whistleblower often suspect his motives: they may regard him as a crank, as publicity-hungry, wrong about the facts, eager for scandal and discord, and driven to indiscretion by his personal biases and shortcomings.

EFFECTIVE WHISTLEBLOWING

Given the internal and external pressures exerted by the elements of dissent, disobedience, and accusation in whistleblowing, it is little wonder that such acts are the exception rather than the rule; little wonder that, once entered upon, most are destined to fail.

For whistleblowing to be effective, it must arouse its audience. Inarticulate whistleblowers are likely to fail from the outset. When they are greeted by apathy, their message dissipates. When they are greeted by disbelief, they elicit no response at all. And when the audience is unfree to receive or to act on the information—when censorship or fear of retribution stifles response—then the message rebounds to injure the whistleblower himself.

Whistleblowing requires *some* larger context, where secrecy, corruption, and coercion are less solidly entrenched, for the alarm to be possible—some forum where an appeal to justice can still be made. It also requires the possibility of concerted public response: the idea of whistleblowing in an anarchy is therefore merely quixotic.

Coercive regimes render whistleblowing an entirely different, often heroic practice, by their control over what is spoken, written, and heard. If not only are internal institutional protests blocked, but even national warnings thwarted, international appeals may be the only remaining possibility. Depending on the severity of repression, only the most striking injustices may then filter through with sufficient strength to alert ordinarily indifferent foreigners. Alarms, like rings in the water, weaken as they move away from their point of origin; if forced to go below the surface to emerge later, they may be further attenuated.

Such characteristics of whistleblowing, and strategic considerations for achieving an impact, are common to the noblest warnings, the most vicious personal attacks, and the delusions of the paranoid. How can one distinguish the many acts of sounding an alarm that are genuinely in the public interest from all the petty, biased, or lurid revelations that pervade our querulous and gossip-ridden society? Can we draw distinctions between different whistleblowers, different messages, different methods?

We clearly can, in a number of cases. Whistleblowing can be starkly inappropriate when in malice or error, or when it lays bare legitimately private matters having to do, for instance, with political belief or sexual life. It can, just as clearly, be the only way to shed light on an ongoing unjust practice, such as drugging political prisoners or subjecting them to electroshock treatment; it can be the last resort for alerting the public to an impending disaster.

Taking such clear-cut cases as benchmarks, and reflecting on what it is about them that weighs so heavily for or against speaking out, we can then work our way toward the admittedly more complex cases in between these extremes: cases in which whistleblowing is not so clearly the right or wrong choice, or where different points of view exist regarding its legitimacy: cases where there are moral reasons both for concealment and for disclosure, and where judgments conflict.

Consider the following three cases, chosen from the fields of government, business, and engineering:

> "This material might not be earth-shaking, but I thought you might be interested." With that modest opener, John Samuels (not his real name) proceeded to reveal the fruits of his private, unauthorized investigation into government corruption . . . to the Government Accountability Project (GAP) in Washington, DC.
>
> The corruption Samuels disclosed was pervasive. As a construction inspector for a federal agency, he had personal knowledge of shoddy and deficient construction practices by private contractors. He knew his superiors received free vacations and entertainment, had their homes remodeled, and found jobs for their relatives—all courtesy of a private contractor. These superiors later approved a multimillion no-bid contract with the same "generous" firm.
>
> Samuels also had evidence that other firms were hiring nonunion laborers at a low wage while receiving substantially higher payments from the government for labor costs. A former superior, unaware of an office dictaphone, had incautiously instructed Samuels on how to accept bribes for overlooking subpar performance. Whether all of this information would have sparked a congressional investigation, captured the attention of the public, or

initiated a cleansing of his agency will never be known. Samuels decided to remain silent.

As he prepared to volunteer this information to various members of Congress, he became tense and uneasy. His family was scared and the fears were valid. It might cost Samuels thousands of dollars to protect his job. Those who had freely provided Samuels with information would probably recant or withdraw their friendship. A number of people might object to his using a dictaphone to gather information. His agency would start covering up, and vent its collective wrath upon him. . . . As for reporters and writers, they would gather for a few days, then move on to the next story. He would be left without a job, with fewer friends, with massive battles looming, and without the financial means of fighting them.[13]

An attorney, working for a large company supplying medical products, becomes aware of practices of falsifying inventories by adding nonexistent sales and of attempts to influence federal regulatory personnel. She suspects, in addition, that machinery, sold by the company to hospitals for use in kidney dialysis, is unsafe. She brings these matters up with a junior executive, who assures her he'll look into the matters, and convey them to her chief executives if necessary. When she questions him a few weeks later, however, he answers her that all the problems have been taken care of, but without offering any evidence, and considerably irritated at her desire to learn exactly where the matter stands. She does not know how much further she can push her concern without jeopardizing her position in the firm.

Engineers of Company "A" prepared plans and specifications for machinery to be used in a manufacturing process, and Company "A" turned them over to Company "B" for production. The engineers of Company "B," in reviewing the plans and specifications, came to the conclusion that they included certain miscalculations and technical deficiencies of a nature that the final product might be unsuitable for the purposes of the ultimate users, and that the equipment, if built according to the original plans and specifications, might endanger the lives of persons in proximity to it. The engineers of Company "B" called the matter to the attention of appropriate officials of their employer who, in turn, advised Company "A." . . . Company "A" replied that its engineers felt that the design and specifications for the equipment were adequate and safe and that Company "B" should proceed to build the equipment as designed and specified. The officials of Company "B" instructed its engineers to proceed with the work.[14]

INDIVIDUAL MORAL CHOICE

What questions might those who consider sounding a public alarm ask themselves? How might they articulate the problem they see and weigh its injustice before deciding whether or not to reveal it? How can they best try to make sure that their choice is the right one?

In thinking about these questions, it helps to keep in mind the three elements mentioned earlier: dissent, breach of loyalty, and accusation. They impose certain requirements: of accuracy and judgment in dissent; of exploring alternative ways to cope with improprieties, thus minimizing the breach of loyalty; and of fairness in accusation. For each, careful articulation and testing of arguments are needed to limit error and bias.

Dissent by whistleblowers, first of all, is expressly claimed to be intended to benefit the public. It carries with it, as a result, an obligation to consider the nature of this benefit, and to consider also the possible harm that may come from speaking out: harm to persons or institutions and ultimately to the public interest itself. Whistleblowers must therefore begin by making every effort to consider the effects of speaking out versus those of remaining silent. They must assure themselves of the accuracy of their reports, checking and rechecking the facts before speaking out; specify the degree to which there is genuine impropriety; consider how imminent is the threat they see, how serious, and how closely linked to those accused of neglect or abuse.[15]

If the facts warrant whistleblowing, how can the second element—breach of loyalty—be minimized? The most important question here is whether the existing avenues for change within the organization have been explored. It is a waste of time for the public, as well as harmful to the institution, to sound the loudest alarm first. Whistleblowing has to remain a last alternative because of its destructive side effects: it must be chosen only when other alternatives have been considered and rejected. They may be rejected if they simply do not apply to the problem at hand, or when there is not time to go through routine channels, or when the institution is so corrupt or coercive that steps will be taken to silence the whistleblower should he try the regular channels first.

What weight should an oath or a promise of silence have in the conflict of loyalties? There is no doubt that one sworn to silence is under a stronger obligation because of the oath he has taken. He has bound himself, assumed specific obligations beyond those assumed in merely taking a new position. But even such promises can be overridden, when the public interest at issue is strong enough. They can be overridden if they were obtained under duress, or through deceit. They can be overridden, too, if they promise something that is in itself wrong or unlawful. The fact that one has promised silence is no excuse for complicity in covering up a crime or a violation of the public's trust.

The third element in whistleblowing—accusation—raises equally serious ethical concerns. They are concerns of fairness to the persons accused of impropriety. Is the message one to which the public is entitled in the first place? Or does it infringe on personal and private matters that one has no right to invade? Here, the very notion of what is in the public's best "interest" is at issue: "accusations" regarding an official's unusual sexual or religious experiences may well appeal to the public's interest, without therefore being information relevant to "the public interest."

Great conflicts arise here. We have witnessed excessive claims to executive privilege and to secrecy by government officials during the Watergate scandal, in order to cover up for abuses the public had every right to discover. Conversely, those hoping to profit from prying into private matters have become adept at invoking "the public's right to know." Some even regard such private matters as threats to the public: They voice their own religious and political prejudices in the language of accusation.

Such a danger is never stronger than when the accusation is delivered surreptitiously: The anonymous accusations made during the McCarthy period regarding political beliefs and associations often injured persons who did not ever know their accusers, or the exact nature of the accusations.

In fairness to those criticized, openly accepted responsibility for blowing the whistle should therefore be preferred to the secret denunciation or the leaked rumor: the more so, the more derogatory and accusatory the information. What is openly stated can more easily be checked, its source's motives challenged, and the underlying information examined. Those under attack may otherwise be hard put to defend themselves against nameless adversaries. Often they do not even know that they are threatened until it is too late to respond. The anonymous denunciation, moreover, common to so many regimes, places the burden of investigation on government agencies, that may thereby gain the power of a secret police.

From the point of view of the whistleblower, on the other hand, the choice is admittedly less easy. The anonymous message is safer for him in situations where retaliation is likely. But it is often less likely to be taken seriously. Newspaper offices, for example, receive innumerable anonymous messages without acting upon them. Unless the message is accompanied by indications of how the evidence can be checked, its anonymity, however safe for the source, speaks against it.

In order to assure transmission for the message—through the press for instance—yet be safe from reprisals, the whistleblower often resorts to a compromise: By making himself known to the journalist, he makes it possible to check the evidence; by asking that his identity not be given in the printed article, he protects himself from the consequences.

From the public's point of view, accusations that are openly made by identifiable individuals are more likely to be taken seriously. Since the open accusation is felt to be fairer to the accused, and since it makes the motives of the whistleblower open to inspection, the audience is more confident that his message may have a factual basis. As a result, if the whistleblower still chooses to resort to surreptitious messages, he has a strong obligation to let the accused know of the accusation leveled, and to produce independent evidence that can be checked.

During this process of weighing the legitimacy of speaking out, the method used, and the degree of fairness needed, whistleblowers must try to compensate for the strong possibility of bias on their part. They should be scrupulously aware of any motive that might skew their message; a desire for self-defense in a difficult bureaucratic situation, perhaps, or the urge to seek revenge, or inflated expectations regarding the effect that their message will have on the situation.[16]

Likewise, the possibility of personal gain from sounding the alarm ought to give pause. Once again, there is then greater risk of a biased message. Even if the whistleblower regards himself as incorruptible, his profiting from revelations of neglect or abuse will lead others to question his motives, and to put less credence in his charges. If the publicity gained through his act matters greatly to him, or if speaking out brings him greater benefits at work or a substantially increased income, such risks are present. If, for example, a government employee stands to make large profits from a book exposing the iniquities of his agency, there is danger that he will, perhaps even unconsciously, slant his report in order to cause more of a sensation. If he supports his revelation by referring to the Code of Ethics for Government Servants urging that loyalty to the highest moral principles and to country be put above loyalty to persons, party, and government, he cannot ignore another clause in the same code specifying that he "ought never to use any information coming to him confidentially in the performance of government duties as a means for making private profits."

Sometimes a warning is so cleary justifiable and substantiated that it carries weight no matter how tainted the motives of the messenger. But scandal can pay; and the whistleblower's motives ought ideally to be above suspicion, for his own sake as well as for that of the respect he desires for his warning. Personal gain from speaking out raises a presumption against it, a greater need to check the biases of the speaker.

A special problem arises in this regard whenever there is a high risk that the civil servant who speaks out will have to go through costly litigation. Might he not at least justifiably try to make money on his public revelations—say through books or public speaking—to offset his losses? In so doing, he will not, strictly speaking, have *profited* from his revelations: He merely avoids being financially crushed by their sequels. He will nevertheless still be suspected at the time of his revelation, and his message will therefore seem more questionable.

To weigh all these factors is not easy. The ideal case of whistleblowing—where the cause is a just one, where all the less dramatic alternatives have been exhausted, where responsibility is openly accepted, and the whistleblower is above reproach—is rare. The motives may be partly self-serving, the method questionable, and still we may judge that the act was in the public interest. In cases where the motives for sounding the alarm are highly suspect, for example, but where clear proof of wrongdoing and avoidable risk is adduced, the public may be grateful that the alarm was sounded, no matter how low its opinion of the whistleblower himself.

Reducing bias and error in moral choice often requires consultation, even open debate:[17] Such methods force articulation of the moral arguments at stake and challenge privately held assumptions. But acts of whistleblowing present special problems when it comes to open consultation. On the one hand, once the whistleblower sounds his alarm publicly, his arguments *will* be subjected to open scrutiny: He will have to articulate his reasons for speaking out and substantiate his charges. On the other hand, it will then be too late to retract the alarm, or to combat its harmful effects, should his choice to speak out have been ill-advised (in both senses of the word).

For this reason, the whistleblower owes it to all involved to make sure of two things: that he has sought as much and as objective advice regarding his choice as he can *before* going public and that he is aware of the arguments for and against the practice of whistleblowing in general so that he can see his own choice against as richly detailed and coherently structured a background as possible.

Satisfying these two requirements, once again, has special problems because of the very nature of whistleblowing: the more corrupt the circumstances, the more dangerous it may be to seek consultation before speaking out. And yet, since the whistleblower himself may have a biased view of the state of affairs, he may choose not to consult others when, in fact, it would have been not only safe, but advantageous to do so; he may see corruption and conspiracy where none exists. Given these difficulties, it would be especially important to seek more general means of considering the nature of whistleblowing and the arguments for and against different ways of combating abuse: to take them up in public debate and through teaching.

The public debate over whistleblowing is already under way. In the press, in articles and books, these problems have been described, and a number of remedies proposed. Institutional and legislative proposals are being made. Still lacking is work of a fact-finding, comparative, and analytical nature, on which practical decisions might be based, as well as the opportunity for individuals to give careful thought in advance to how they might respond, in their own working lives, to the conflicts where whistleblowing is one of the alternatives. . . .

INSTITUTIONAL QUESTIONS

What changes, outside and inside business organizations, government agencies, and other places of work, might serve to protect the right of dissenters, cut down on endless breaches of loyalty and on false accusations, while assuring public access to needed information?

The more far-reaching set of changes, and the hardest to implement, involves the cutting down on legitimate causes for alarm. Reducing practices of corruption and cover-up, as well as opportunities for errors to go undiscovered, would reduce also the need to call attention to them. The needed changes in review procedures, incentives, and obstacles go far beyond the scope of this paper; but so long as improprieties remain serious and frequent, whistleblowing will remain a last resort for calling attention to them.

The need to resort to whistleblowing can be reduced by providing mechanisms for taking criticism seriously before it reaches the press and the courtroom. These mechanisms must work to counteract the blockage of information within an organization, and the tendency to filter out negative information so that those who must make decisions ignore it.[18] The filtering process may be simple or intricate; well-intentioned or malevolent; more or less consciously manipulated. David Ewing gives examples of how it works:

> During 1976 and 1977, hundreds of newspapers gleefully reported the seamy and sexy ways used by Southwestern Bell to manipulate regulatory officials. The scandle came

to light after the suicide of T. O. Gravitt, an executive in San Antonio, and the firing of James Ashley, one of Gravitt's colleagues. It is difficult to think of any practice that Ma Bell frowns on more (as demonstrated by the prompt and decisive action by national headquarters once the lid came off the scandal). However, would-be whistleblowers were discouraged so firmly at the scene of the crimes that no early warnings seem to have found their way to New York. If they had, the company could have been spared a severe setback in public relations, to say nothing of the multimillion dollar damage suits it appears to have lost to Ashley and Gravitt's family.

A couple of years ago, when the Alaska pipeline was being built, some managers began ordering construction crews to take shortcuts in order to reduce costs and meet time deadlines for construction. According to reports confirmed by the *Wall Street Journal* and other sources, many batches of X-rays of weld joints were falsified so that flaws would not be detected. Some workers who objected were told to shut up. Nevertheless, news about the cover-up seeped out, and investigators were hired to look into the problem. Attempts were made to frustrate the investigation (one of the investigators died under mysterious circumstances), but the dreary mess finally came to the attention of responsible officials. It then became necessary for thousands of welds to be rechecked, and a great many corrected. This great extra cost in time and money, to say nothing of the bad publicity for the construction firms, can be charged to the lack of suitable mechanisms for whistle blowing.[19]

Ewing argues that industry has much to gain by not discouraging internal criticism. A number of managements do welcome the views of dissenters, and promise that no one will be unfairly dismissed or disciplined for having made their revelations.

Such an "open door" policy may suffice at times; but it is frequently inadequate, unless further buttressed. In the first place, the promises of protection given by top management cannot always be fulfilled. Though an employee may keep his job, there are countless ways of making his position difficult, to the point where he may be brought to resign of his own volition, or stay, while bitterly regretting that he had spoken out. Second, it would be naive to think that abuses in industry or in government are always unknown to top management and perpetrated against their will by subordinates. If the abuse—the secret bombardment of Cambodia, for instance, or the corporate bribing or conspiracy to restrict trade—is planned by those in charge, then the "open door" policy turns out to be a trap for the dissenter.

For these reasons, proposals have been made to protect dissenters in more formal ways. Independent review boards, ombudsmen, consumer or citizen representatives on boards of trustees, bills of rights for employees: These and other means have been suggested to protect dissenters while giving serious consideration to their messages.

These methods of protection spring up and sometimes die away with great rapidity. They are often instituted without careful comparison between different possibilities. Teaching and research could do much to study them, to compare their advantages and disadvantages and their differing suitability under different circumstances. The benefits from these methods, when they work, are strong. They allow for criticism with much less need for heroism; for a way to deflect the crank or the witch-hunter *before* their messages gain publicity; for a process of checking the accuracy of the information provided; for a chance to distinguish between urgent alarms and long-range worries; and for an arena for debating the moral questions of motive and of possible bias, of loyalty and responsibility to the public interest.

Many of these methods work well; others fail. They fail when they are but window dressing from the outset, meant to please or exhaust dissenters; or else they fail because, however independent at the outset, they turn into management tools. Such is the fate of many a patient-representative in hospitals; their growing loyalty to co-workers and to the institution once again leaves the dissenter little choice between submission and open revolt.

Still another reason for the failure of such intermediaries is their frequent lack of credibility. No matter how well-meaning, they will not be sought out if they cannot protect from retaliation those who turn to them for help. Even if they can give such protection, but cannot inspire confidence in those with grievances, their role will be largely a ceremonial one.

A comparative study of such intermediaries and means of protection would have to seek out the conditions of independence, flexibility, separateness from management, institutional good will, fairness, and objectivity needed for success. Moreover, in looking at the protection given to dissenters, the entire system must be kept in perspective so that changes in one area do not produce unexpected dislocations elsewhere. To what extent will increased due process make the entire institution more litigious? To what extent will protection in one place put increased pressure on another? Is it not possible, for example, that the increasing difficulties of firing incompetent federal employees have led to the growing resort to psychiatric fitness-for-duty examinations (mentioned above), and that these, in turn, have become a new weapon with which to combat critics?

A different method for reducing the tension and risk of whistleblowing is to state conditions expressly under which those who learn about an abuse *must* blow the whistle: times when to do so, far from being disloyal, is not only right, but obligatory. Laws or other regulations can require revelations and thus take the burden of choice off the individual critic.

Such requirements to report already exist in a number of places. The Toxic Substances Control Act, for instance, enacted in January 1977, requires companies producing chemicals to instruct their employees and officials to report chemicals that pose a substantial risk to health or to the environment. Once again, these requirements open up fields for study and for comparison. There is much to learn about how effective they are, how they may be combated within an industry, and how they compare with other ways of reducing neglect and abuse.

In order to be effective, requirements to report must be enforceable. It is, therefore, not appropriate for them to be as open-ended and exhortative as the U.S. Code of Ethics in urging government employees to "expose corruption wherever uncovered." Such requirements must be more specific than provisions in codes of ethics. They must be limited to clear-cut improprieties, and used as a last resort only. Once again, here the lines must be firmly drawn against requiring reporting on religious or political belief, or purely personal matters. In many societies, citizens are asked to report "deviations," fellow workers to spy on one another, and students to expose the subversive views of their teachers. No society can afford to ignore these precedents in its enthusiasm for eradicating corruption.

NOTES

1. Code of Ethics for Government Service, passed by the U.S. House of Representatives in the 85th Congress, and applying to all government employees and officeholders.

2. Code of Ethics of the Institute of Electrical and Electronics Engineers, Article IV.

3. For case histories and descriptions of what befalls whistleblowers, see Rosemary Chalk and Frank von Hippel, "Due Process for Dissenting Whistleblowers: Dealing with Technical Dissent in the Organization," *Technology Review* 81 (1979) pp. 48–55; Alan F. Westin and Stephan Salisbury, eds, *Individual Rights in the Corporation* (New York: Pantheon Books, 1980); Helen Dudar, "The Price of Blowing the Whistle," *New York Times Magazine* (30 October 1979, pp. 41–54); John Edsall, *Scientific Freedom and Responsibility* (Washington, DC: American Association for the Advancement of Science, 1975, p. 5); David W. Ewing, *Freedom Inside the Organization* (New York: E. P. Dutton, 1977); Ralph Nader, Peter Petkas, and Kate Blackwell, *Whistle Blowing* (New York: Grossman Publishers, 1972); and Charles Peters and Taylor Branch, *Blowing the Whistle* (New York: Praeger, 1972).

4. "Forced Retirement/Psychiatric Fitness for Duty Exams," Subcommittee on Compensation and Employee Benefits, Committee on Post Office and Civil Service, House of Representatives, 3 November 1978, pp. 2–4. See also the Subcommittee Hearings, 28 February 1978.

Psychiatric referral for whistleblowers has become institutionalized in government service, and is not uncommon in private employment. Even persons who make accusations without being "employed" in the organization they accuse have been classified as unstable, and thus as unreliable witnesses. See, for example, Jonas Robitscher, "Stigmatization and Stone-walling: The Ordeal of Martha Mitchell," *Journal of Psychohistory* 6 (Winter 1979), pp. 393–408.

5. Carol S. Kennedy, *Whistle-blowing: Contribution or Catastrophe?:* Address to the American Association for the Advancement of Science, 15 February 1978, p. 8.

6. For an account of strategies and proposals to support government whistleblowers, see *A Whistleblower's Guide to the Federal Bureaucracy*. Government Accountability Project, Institute for Policy Studies, 1977.

7. See, for example, Samuel Eliot Morison, Frederick Merk, and Frank Freidel, *Dissent in Three American Wars* (Cambridge, MA.: Harvard University Press, 1970).

8. In the scheme worked out by Albert Hirschman, in *Exit, Voice and Loyalty* (Cambridge, MA: Harvard University Press, 1970), whistleblowing then represents "voice" accompanied by a preference not to "exit," though forced "exit" is clearly a possibility, and "voice" after or during "exit" may be chosen for strategic reasons.

9. Edward Weisband and Thomas N. Franck, *Resignation in Protest* (New York: Grossman Publishers, 1975).

10. There are great variations in the degree of furtiveness or anonymity of any one message. Thus, a leak through a newspaper may be made by a person known to the reporter, but unknown to the readers—disguised, perhaps, as a "highly placed official," or even wrongly characterized in order to mislead those seeking to identify the source of the leak.

11. I rely on the definition of civil disobedience offered by John Rawls: A public, nonviolent, conscientious, yet political act, contrary to law, usually done with the aim of bringing about a change in the law or the policies of the government. See his *A Theory of Justice* (Cambridge, MA: Harvard University Press, 1971), p. 364. See also Hugo Bedau, "On Civil Disobedience," *Journal of Philosophy* 58 (1961), pp. 653–61. A *combination* of whistleblowing and civil disobedience occurs when, for instance, former CIA agents publish books to alert the public about what they regard as unlawful and dangerous practices in the intelligence community, and in so doing openly violate and thereby test the oath of secrecy that they have sworn, but that they now regard as having been unjustly required of them.

12. Future developments can, however, be a cause for whistleblowing if they are seen as resulting from steps

being taken, or to be taken soon, that render them inevitable.

13. From Louis Clark, "The Sound of Professional Suicide," *The Barrister* (Summer 1978), p. 10.

14. Case 5, in Robert J. Baum and Albert Flores, eds., *Ethical Problems of Engineering* (Troy, NY: Rensselaer Polytechnic Institute, 1978), p. 186.

15. In dissent concerning policy differences rather than specific improprieties, moreover, whistleblowing, with its accusatory element, is an inappropriate and dangerous form of warning. It threatens the public interest, in that it so easily derails into ideological persecution. Many other forms of dissent exist when there is reason to voice policy disagreement or ideological differences.

16. Needless to say, bias affects the silent as well as the outspoken. The motive for *holding back* important information about abuses and injustice ought to give similar cause for soul-searching. Civil servants who collaborate in the iniquities of so many regimes; businessmen who support them through bribes and silent complicity; and physicians the world over who examine the victims of torture, and return them to their tormentors: all have as much reason to examine *their* motives as those who may be speaking out without sufficient reason.

17. I discuss these questions of consultation and publicity with respect to moral choice in chap. 7 of *Lying: [Moral Choice in Public and Private Life]* (New York: Pantheon Books, 1978).

18. John C. Coffee, in "Beyond the Shut-eyed Sentry: Toward a Theoretical View of Corporate Misconduct and an Effective Legal Response," *Virginia Law Review,* 63 (1977) pp. 1099–1278, gives an informed and closely reasoned account of such "information blockages," such "filtering out," and of possible remedies.

19. David W. Ewing, "The Employee's Right to Speak Out: The Management Perspective," *Civil Liberties Review* 5 September–October (1978), pp. 10–15.

QUESTIONS FOR STUDY AND DISCUSSION

1. Many physicians have objected that the kind of resistance encouraged by Physicians for Social Responsibility against the Department of Defense plan is an attempt to use the physician's social position to influence the political process. Is it morally acceptable for professional groups to attempt to influence the political process, for example, by supporting certain candidates for office, by supporting or opposing a nuclear freeze, by supporting or opposing the Strategic Defense Initiative ("Star Wars"), or by supporting or opposing a liberal abortion policy? Defend your answer; anticipate and respond to the strongest objection that might be raised against your view.

2. Using this chapter's readings as resources, offer your own view on whether health care providers have a moral obligation to resist participating in contingency medical plans for nuclear confrontation. Defend your answer carefully; anticipate and respond to the most serious objection that might be raised against your view.

3. Explain James Muyskens' position on when it is morally permissible for nurses to strike. In your considered judgment, is it ever morally permissible for emergency service groups (e.g., ambulance personnel, firefighters, police) to strike? If not, why not? If so, under what conditions? Anticipate and respond to the most serious objection that might be raised against your view.

4. Is it morally objectionable for teachers to strike? If not, why not? If so, why?

5. Using the readings in this chapter as resources, offer your own account of when whistleblowing is morally justified. Is whistleblowing ever morally required? If not, why not? If so, under what conditions?

6. Might it be the case that of two professionals in parallel professional positions, one has an obligation to blow the whistle whereas the other does not? Consider, for example, two engineers (or nurses) in parallel positions, but one has three dependent children, whereas the other is single. Might it be the case that the single professional has an obligation to blow the whistle but that the professional with dependent children does not? Explain your answer; anticipate and respond to the strongest objection that might be brought against your view.

7. Consider the case of the Ford Pinto at the end of chapter 8. Did engineers at Ford (as Gene James suggests) have a moral responsibility to alert the public to the Pinto's defect? Defend your answer; anticipate and respond to the strongest potential objection to your view.

CASE: LEAKING AN INVESTIGATORY REPORT

Terry C. is a supervisor in the Office of Water Pollution at the Department of Environmental Quality. An investigatory team from Terry's enforcement section has just finished its report of a six-month study on the deep-wall injection of toxic chemical waste by several petrochemical processing plants. Preliminary chemical analysis indicates that there is sufficient evidence to believe that there is migration of these toxic materials toward the aquifier that is the sole source of drinking water for three rural communities. The report is complete, on Terry's desk, ready to be submitted to her supervisor, the assistant secretary for Air, Water, and Hazardous Waste.

Terry is very proud of the report, and has praised her staff for it. As she finishes going over it one final time, she recalls her last damaging report—on a major fish kill resulting from migrating toxic waste in the northern part of the state. When submitted up the chain of command, there was no response to the report for weeks. When Terry pressed for a response and suggested a course of action to remedy the condition, she was told that her report would not be passed on to the governor. She was further told that a private consultant had been hired by the department to examine the situation and that the consultant's preliminary findings were not in agreement with her report. The consultant found no wrongdoing on the part of the subject petrochemical plant (a plant that employs some two hundred workers in an economically depressed area). Terry recalls, also, that in this year's budget not only were three new positions she requested for the enforcement section denied, but two positions were also cut from her permanent staff.

Terry submits the report. Three months later she has still had no response. She finally calls the assistant secretary, and is told that her report has not been passed on to the governor, and, once again, that a private consultant has been hired and is just about finished her examination. Her prelimiary findings, Terry is told, do not agree with Terry's report. Terry's assistant (the leader of the investigatory team) walks in just as Terry is completing her conversation with the assistant secretary. She tells him what she has just learned. His response: "Maybe we should leak a copy to the press."

1. Should Terry leak the report? Does Terry have a moral obligation to leak the report? Defend your answers; anticipate and respond to the strongest objection that might be brought against your view(s).

2. Leaking is a form of anonymous whistleblowing. What are the problems with anonymous whistleblowing? In your considered judgment, is anonymous whistleblowing ever morally justified? If not, why not? If so, under what conditions? Defend your view; anticipate and respond to the most serious objection to your position.

3. Journalists are often happy to print or broadcast leaks by government personnel. Often, journalists will argue in favor of printing leaked stories on the ground that "the public has a right to know." Does the public have a right to know everything that is printed or broadcasted in the news? In answering this question, offer your best attempt to explain just what, if anything, the public's so-called right to know includes; say when, if ever, the press should decline to print or broadcast a story/report leaked by government personnel.

CASE: THE SPACE SHUTTLE *CHALLENGER*

On 28 January 1986, the Space Shuttle *Challenger* exploded approximately seventy-three seconds after liftoff. The seven-member crew included Christa McAuliffe, the first teacher in space. All were killed.

This case was initially prepared by Lee Jennings for discussion in the Public Management Certification Program at Louisiana State University's Government Services Institute. I am grateful for his permission to use it.

This case was prepared by Leslee Froehlich for the professional ethics course at Louisiana State University. I am grateful for her permission to use it.

The explosion was virtually certainly caused by a burn-through of the O-rings sealing two sections of *Challenger*'s right solid rocket booster (SRB). The SRB was designed and produced by Morton Thiokol, Inc.

The night before the disaster, engineers at Morton Thiokol were unanimously opposed to lauching.[1] The Thiokol engineers were concerned that the abnormally low temperatures would cause a failure of the O-ring seals on *Challenger*'s SRBs. The coldest previous launch had been at fifty-three degrees, and even at that temperature, hot gases had blown past and charred the primary seals in two of the SRB joints as well as one of the secondary seals. The O-ring seals had generated a long history of concern among Thiokol engineers. William L. Ray, an engineer who had worked on the initial design of the SRB had written memos as far back as 1971 complaining about inadequate design for the seal.[2] Another Thiokol engineer, Roger M. Boisjoly, had written a memorandum in the summer of 1985 warning that there "could be [a] catastrophe of the highest order" if the company did not improve the SRB's safety seals.[3] Another engineer said, "We all knew if the seals failed, the shuttle would blow up."[4] And another Thiokol engineer recalled watching the launch, thinking, "Oh God, we made it. We made it. . . . Then . . . the shuttle blew up. . . . And we all knew exactly what happened."[5] Despite the objections from the Thiokol engineers, NASA wanted to go ahead with the launch. Robert Lund, a vice president of Morton Thiokol, said of the attempt to persuade NASA not to launch: "We got ourselves in a thought process where we were trying to prove it *wouldn't* work and we couldn't do that."[6] The Thiokol engineers were overruled by their managers, and Thiokol signed off for launch. The temperature at liftoff was in the thirties. Upper managers at NASA subsequently denied that they had known about the Thiokol protest, and said that, had they known about it, they would have halted the launch.

1. Assume that upper management at NASA did not know of the Thiokol protest. Is this sufficient to exempt NASA's upper management for any moral responsibility for the *Challenger* crash? Explain your answer; anticipate and respond to the strongest objection that might be raised against your view.

2. What moral responsibility, if any, do managers at Morton Thiokol bear for the *Challenger* crash? Explain your answer carefully; anticipate and respond to the strongest objection that might be raised against your view.

3. In protesting the launch to their managers, who, in turn, brought the protest to the attention of upper management at Thiokol and middle management at NASA, did the Thiokol engineers fully discharge their moral duties? Did the engineers have a moral obligation to go directly to the director of NASA? Did the engineers have a moral obligation to try to contact the astronauts? Did the engineers have a moral obligation to go to the press? Explain your answers; anticipate and respond to the strongest objection(s) to your position(s).

NOTES

1. *New York Times,* 11 May 1986, p. 17.
2. *Times-Picayune/States Item,* 11 May 1986, p. A–10.
3. *New York Times,* 11 May 1986, p. 17.
4. *Newsweek,* 3 March 1986, p. 14.
5. *Newsweek,* 3 March 1986, p. 15.
6. *Newsweek,* 10 March 1986, p. 40.

SELECTED BIBLIOGRAPHY

Adams, R., and S. Cullen, eds. *The Final Epidemic: Physicians and Scientists on Nuclear War.* Chicago: Educational Foundation for Nuclear Science, 1981.

Anderson, Robert M., Robert Perrucci, Dan E. Schendel, and Leon E. Tractman. *Divided Loyalties: Whistle-Blowing at BART*. West Lafeyette, IN: Purdue University Press, 1980.

Bowman, James S., Frederick A. Elliston, and Paula Lockhart. *Professional Dissent: An Annotated Bibliography and Resource Guide*. New York: Garfield, 1984.

Burton, John F., Jr. "Public Sector Strikes: Legal, Ethical, and Practical Considerations." In *Ethics, Free Enterprise, and Public Policy,* ed. Richard T. De George and Joseph A. Pichler, pp. 127–54. New York: Oxford University Press, 1978.

Cassel, Christine, and Andrew L. Jameton. "Medical Responsibility and Thermonuclear War." *American Medical Association Annals of Internal Medicine* 97 (1982): 426–32.

Chalk, Rosemary. "The Miner's Canary." *Bulletin of the Atomic Scientists* 38 (Feb. 1982): 16–22.

Childress, James F. "Citizen and Physician: Harmonious or Conflicting Responsibilities?" *Journal of Medicine and Philosophy* 2:4 (1977): 401–9.

Curran, William J., and Ward Casscells. "The Ethics of Medical Participation in Capital Punishment by Intravenous Injection." *New England Journal of Medicine* 302 (1980): 226–30.

Daniels, Norman. "On the Picket Line: Are Doctors' Strikes Ethical?" *Hastings Center Report* 8:1 (1978): 24–29.

De George, Richard T. "Ethical Responsibilities of Engineers in Large Organizations: The Pinto Case." *Business and Professional Ethics Journal* 1:1 (1981): 1–14.

Elliston, Frederick A. "Anonymous Whistleblowing." *Business and Professional Ethics Journal* 1:2 (1982): 39–58.

———. "Civil Disobedience and Whistleblowing." *Journal of Business Ethics* 1:1 (1982): 23–28.

———, John Keenan, Paula Lockhart, and Jane van Schiack. *Whistleblowing: Managing Dissent in the Workplace*. New York: Praeger, 1985.

Ferren, John M. "The Corporate Lawyer's Obligation to the Public Interest." *Business Lawyer* 33 (1978): 1253–89.

Filios, Vassilios. "Corporate Social Responsibility and Public Accountability." *Journal of Business Ethics* 3:4 (1984): 305–14.

Hershman, M. "The Murky Divide—Professionalism and Professional Responsibility—Business Judgment and Legal Advice—What Is a Business Lawyer?" *Business Lawyer* 31 (1975): 457–63.

Hiatt, H. H. "Preventing the Last Epidemic." *Journal of the American Medical Association* 244 (1981): 2314–15.

———. "Preventing the Last Epidemic (2)." *Journal of the American Medical Association* 246 (1981): 2035–36.

James, Gene G. "Whistle-Blowing: Its Nature and Justification." *Philosophy in Context* 10 (1980): 99–117.

Jonsen, Albert R., and Andrew L. Jameton. "Social and Political Responsibility of Physicians." *Journal of Medicine and Philosophy* 2:4 (1977): 376–400.

Lipman, M. "When Should a Nurse Blow the Whistle?" *RN* 34 (October 1971): 54.

Lown, B. "Physicians and Nuclear War." *Journal of the American Medical Association* 246 (1981): 2331–33.

Mellinkoff, David. *The Conscience of a Lawyer*. St. Paul, MN: West, 1977.

Nader, Ralph, Peter J. Petkas, and Kate Blackwell, eds. *Whistle Blowing*. New York: Grossman, 1972.

Near, Janet P., and Marcia P. Micete. "Organizational Disobedience: The Case of Whistleblowing." *Journal of Business Ethics* 4:1 (1985): 1–16.

Nelkin, Dorothy. "Whistle Blowing and Social Responsibility in Science." In *Research Ethics: Progress in Clinical and Biological Research,* vol. 128, ed. Kåre Berg and Knut Erik Tranøy, pp. 351–57. New York: Alan R. Liss, 1983.

Peters, Charles, and Taylor Branch. *Blowing the Whistle: Dissent in the Public Interest*. New York: Praeger, 1972.

Presidential Commission on the Space Shuttle Challenger Accident. *Report to the President on the Space Shuttle Challenger Accident*. Washington, DC: U.S. Government Printing Office, 1986.

Raven-Hansen, P. "Dos and Don'ts for Whistleblowers: Planning for Trouble." *Technology Review* (May 1980): 34–44.

Stuart, Lea P. " 'Whistle Blowing': Implications for Organizational Communication." *Journal of Communication* 30:4 (1980): 90–101.

Swazey, Judith P., and Stephen R. Scher, eds. *Whistleblowing in Biomedical Research*. Washington, DC: U.S. Government Printing Office, 1981.

United States Merit Systems Protection Board. *Whistle Blowing and the Federal Employee*. Washington, DC: U.S. Government Printing Office, 1981.

Werhane, Patricia H. "Individual Rights in Business." In *Just Business: New Introductory Essays in Business Ethics*, ed. Tom Regan, pp. 100–128. Philadelphia: Temple University Press, 1983; reissued New York: Random House, 1984.

Westin, Alan, ed. *Whistle Blowing: Loyalty and Dissent in the Corporation*. New York: McGraw-Hill, 1981.

10

SOCIAL RESPONSIBILITY AND JUSTICE

The readings in the last chapter continued the discussion of the social responsibilities of professions and professionals begun in chapters 7 and 8. The readings in the present chapter take the discussion further by asking whether business and providers of crucial services have special responsibilities to contribute to the public good, to compensate for past social injustices, and to see that crucial professional services are provided to those who need them.

The selections from Milton Friedman and Melvin Anshen concentrate on corporate business, and address the question of whether corporations have any obligation to promote the public good. Friedman argues that the only social responsibility of corporate managers is to pursue profits for their shareholders within the "rules of the game," that is, "in open and free competition, without deception or fraud." Friedman's view takes the primary moral relationship in corporate business to be between corporate officials and stockholders, with the wider society entering in only to set legal constraints prohibiting deception and fraud (i.e., establishing the "rules of the game"). Underlying views like Friedman's is generally the deeper position that just as long as the moral prohibitions on fraud are respected, conducting business in society is a matter of the natural right to liberty. Natural rights are generally understood to be those entitlements that are held to obtain independent of any sort of voluntary agreement on the part of others. Conceptually, they are opposed to conventional or contractual rights, which are understood to arise out of voluntary agreement or action (e.g., the assumption of a role with special duties, giving rise to special rights). For example, those who hold that there are natural rights generally hold that such rights include rights not to be harmed or treated fraudulently and that the validity of these claims is not dependent on the agreement of others. By comparison, if I promise to feed your dog and water your plants while you are on vacation, you have a right to those actions from me; but you have that right only because I have agreed to perform those actions. Again, underlying views like Friedman's is generally the view that conducting business in society is a matter of the natural right to live one's life as one sees fit, provided (on Friedman's account) one does not act fraudulently.

Friedman also adopts the view of Adam Smith that individuals (and corporations) pursuing their own interests in open competition will, in fact, promote the public good. And he contends not only that business has no social responsibilities beyond the honest pursuit of shareholder profits; he takes the stronger position that it is morally wrong for corporate managers to attempt to serve the public good with corporate funds or to act in other ways in service of the public good that threaten to reduce shareholder profits. According to Friedman, not only are corporate managers unsuited to decide what is genuinely in the public interest, but promotion of the public good by corporations comes down to violating a contract with stockholders and simply spending someone else's money for one's own causes.

Melvin Anshen takes a different view of the primary moral relationship in corporate business. According to Anshen, this relationship is between those who conduct business and the wider society. Conducting business is not a matter of natural right, but a matter of permission or privilege, that is, contractual right, granted by society. The primary contract on this kind of view is a social contract, originally undertaken, according to Anshen, on the assumption made by Adam Smith and shared by Friedman that nonfraudulent pursuit of private interests will redound to the public good. According to Anshen, however, it is just this assumption that now seems to be mistaken; and the result is that business is being pressured not only to restrain its pursuit of profits, but also to correct social ills and to otherwise directly contribute to the public good. Somewhat implicit in Anshen's argument is the presupposition that if the empirical assumptions on which the permission was granted turn out to be false, the original contract is void. Thus, insofar as it is turning out that the pursuit of profits has not led to the social progress that was expected, the original contract between business and society is invalidated, a new contract must be developed, and Anshen advises business to take a role in developing the terms of that contract.

One of the social demands placed on business in recent years has been that business take affirmative steps to correct employment practices that have discriminated against women and minorities. The principle of compensatory justice holds that whenever there is a prior injustice resulting in harm, compensation is morally required. This is the principle most often used to argue for affirmative action programs and preferential treatment of women and minorities in hiring practices.

Women and blacks, for example, have clearly been systematically discriminated against in the past. Women were not guaranteed the right to vote until 1920 when the Nineteenth Amendment was ratified. And the practice of slavery in this country formally ended less than 150 years ago with the ratification of the Thirteenth Amendment in 1865. Despite that, as recently as the mid-1950s, blacks were required to ride at the back of buses and sit in the back of churches in Washington, DC. Such systematic injustice has harmed members of these groups in various ways, and society has now called on business to help work toward rectification by instituting hiring practices that will favor hiring members of these groups.

But there are at least two important questions about such practices that need to be addressed, namely, whether preferential hiring of women and minorities is an appropriate compensation for past injustices and whether such treatment amounts to an equally unjust reverse discrimination against white men, particularly young white men, who never set out to discriminate against women and minorities. The selection by George Sher addresses both these questions. Sher argues that what members of groups discriminated against have lost is the ability to compete equally with white men. If this is the harm that has been done by past discriminatory practices, Sher argues, then appropriate compensation will consist in removing the necessity of competing on equal terms with white men. What is more, according to Sher, this is not an unjust treatment of white men who have not themselves discriminated against women and minorities. Rather, Sher argues that white men have a competitive edge that is the result of past discrimination. Thus, to take away what amounts to an unfairly gained advantage is not, according to Sher, to treat white men unjustly.

The chapter's last three readings address the question of access to legal services and health care. The selections initially edited by Andrew Kaufman raise the issue of requiring private-practice attorneys to provide legal services to the poor, of attorney advertising, and of other forms of attorney solicitation of clients.

There is a long and strong tradition of a prohibition on advertising and personal solicitation of clients by professionals. This is one area in which business looks very unlike the paradigm professions. Monroe Freedman, however, argues that lawyers should not be prohibited from advertising or personally soliciting clients on the ground that such prohibitions interfere with getting legal services to those who need them and are entitled to them. Thus, according to Freedman, the limitations on competitive practices among lawyers is really contrary to the public good and violative of the rights of people who are entitled to the services they require. Indeed, Freedman argues that attorneys have a moral obligation to "stir up litigation" when people may be ignorant of their legal rights.

Another issue that merits mention here is the controversial practice of attorneys taking cases on the condition that if they win, they will receive some significant percentage of the award (e.g., forty percent is common). But if they lose, the plaintiff pays nothing or little for the legal services (e.g., perhaps some fees to outside consultants). One of the main arguments against attorneys' taking cases on a contingency basis is that the practice involves taking substantial portions of awards away from injured plaintiffs who are the ones who deserve the awards. But the standard reply to this objection is that without such arrangements, many people who have meritorious cases would not be able to bring suit because they would not be able to pay the standard legal fees. What is more, cases yielding high fees from high awards can then subsidize meritorious cases that will bring modest awards, and hence, modest remuneration to attorneys. Thus, the reply is that contingency fees increase access to legal services by those who are not in a position to purchase those services. But the response to this reply is that juries, in an effort to see that plaintiffs receive what they deserve, have made it common to give extremely high awards to cover the high-percentage contingency fees. A direct result of this has been a tremendous rise in insurance premiums, particularly for health care providers and health care facilities. As one of the cases at the end of this chapter makes clear, the "insurance crisis" has resulted in more and more physicians taking drastic steps, among them, leaving the profession and refusing to provide care for malpractice attorneys and their families.

The selection from Laurence McCullough, which concludes the chapter, suggests that there is a natural right to health care. McCullough suggests that this right involves an entitlement to care for illnesses that are fortuitous, that is, those that are not within our control. For such illnesses, says McCullough, we should recognize an equal right of all persons to health care.

But health care needs to be provided by practitioners. Robert Sade, whom McCullough quotes, argues that there is no right to health care. Rather, says Sade, health care provision is a service, like any other service, that may be purchased by those able and willing to pay for it. Sade's argument rests on the position that health care is provided by individuals who, through their own efforts, have developed certain skills. These individuals are, on this account, morally free to distribute their services as they see fit. But McCullough suggests that this ruggedly individualistic view is mistaken, that the knowledge and skills health care providers now have are, in large part, the result of enormous societal investments. Thus, providers have not come to their knowledge and skills on their own. Society has helped, and society may, therefore, make reciprocal demands for its members in need of care.

These last two readings bring us full circle, back to chapter 2, and the question raised there about professions and service orientation. Just what, if anything, do professionals owe society in the way of providing for the needs of the least well-off members of society? May society require that attorneys provide a certain amount of free representation or that physicians (and other health care providers) provide a certain amount of care at reduced costs (or no cost) to those who cannot afford standard costs? Do such requirements amount to unfairly exacting charity of professionals; or, alternatively, are such requirements a morally justified way of seeing that the moral rights of those in need of professional services are respected?

How one answers these questions will have much to say about whether one thinks that having a serious need is sufficient to create a strong moral entitlement. Moral and political philosophers are deeply divided on this issue. Some hold that people do have certain positive natural rights to goods from others who are in a position to provide those goods. But others hold that the only natural rights persons have are the negative rights not to be harmed or treated fraudulently and that positive rights to goods arise only out of the agreement of a benefactor to provide the good(s) in question.

The view which recognizes positive natural rights is shared by contemporary egalitarians and contemporary liberals.[1] Egalitarians and liberals generally differ according to how much relative weight they give to the fundamental moral values of respecting the equality of persons and respecting individual liberty. Egalitarians emphasize equality, and are willing to sacrifice more in the way of individual liberty to ensure equality of access to goods than are liberals, who are more concerned to establish a "trade-off" between liberty and equality that is careful to preserve high levels of individual liberty. The view which recognizes negative natural rights but rejects positive natural rights is held by contemporary libertarians.[2] Libertarians take the moral right to individual liberty (or noninterference) to be fundamental, and hold that individuals may not be interfered with to promote the good of others. Liberals, then, stand on the theoretical spectrum between egalitarians and libertarians.[3]

The libertarian position underpins Sade's view on the question of the right to health care. However, it should also be pointed out that one might hold that there is no natural positive right to health care (or legal services, or education, etc.), but that when a person enters into a crucial services profession, he or she tacitly agrees to help bring those services to those in society who need them, even if those in need cannot pay. It may be, then, (as McCullough's argument from reciprocity suggests) that the placement of professions in society and the help society renders in making skilled professional practice possible gives rise to a duty on the part of the crucial service professions to ensure that none in the society are excluded from access to those services.

All the questions that have been addressed in this and previous chapters have been questions about what is right or wrong in professional life. Before concluding this book, however, there is another kind of issue that needs to be raised, namely, the issue of virtue in professional life. In the final chapter, we shall take up this question, which has to do with whether a professional's character matters, with whether certain professions in our society seem to invite the cultivation of character traits that are morally undesirable, and with whether professionals should work to cultivate certain qualities of character. We shall also ask whether codes of professional ethics are helpful in deciding what should be done in morally hard cases, and whether they are helpful in developing and supporting professional virtue. The chapter and the book will end with some reflection on professional training and its relationship to ethical issues in professional life.

NOTES

1. For an example of a developed contemporary egalitarian theory, see Kai Nielsen, *Equality and Liberty: A Defense of Radical Egalitarianism* (Totowa, NJ: Rowman and Allanheld, 1985). For an example of a developed contemporary liberal theory, see John Rawls, *A Theory of Justice* (Cambridge, MA: Harvard University Press, 1971).
2. For an example of a developed libertarian theory, see Robert Nozick, *Anarchy, State, and Utopia* (New York: Basic Books, 1974).
3. For more on these comparisons, see Thomas Nagel, ''Libertarianism Without Foundations,'' *Yale Law Journal* 85 (1975): 136–49.

SOCIAL RESPONSIBILITY AND COMPENSATORY JUSTICE

43. The Social Responsibility of Business

Milton Friedman

The view has been gaining widespread acceptance that corporate officials and labor leaders have a ''social responsibility'' that goes beyond serving the interest of their stockholders or their members. This view shows a fundamental misconception of the character and nature of a free economy. In such an economy, there is one and only one social responsibility of business—to use its resources and engage in activities designed to increase its profits so long as it stays within the rules of the game, which is to say, engages in open and free competition, without deception or fraud. Similarly, the ''social responsibility'' of labor leaders is to serve the interests of the members of their unions. It is the responsibility of the rest of us to establish a framework of law such that an individual in pursuing his own interest is, to quote Adam Smith. . . ., ''led by an invisible hand to promote an end which was no part of his intention. . . . By pursuing his own interest, he frequently promotes that of the society more effectually than when he really intends to promote it. I have never known much good done by those who affected to trade for the public good.''[1]

Few trends could so thoroughly undermine the very foundations of our free society as the acceptance by corporate officials of a social responsibility other than to make as much money for their stockholders as possible. This is a fundamentally subversive doctrine. If businessmen do have a social responsibility other than making maximum profits for stockholders, how are they to know what it is? Can self-selected private individuals decide what the social interest is? Can they decide how great a burden they are justified in placing on themselves or their stockholders to serve that social interest? Is it tolerable that these public functions of taxation, expenditure, and control be exercised by the people who happen at the moment to be in charge of particular enterprises, chosen for those posts by strictly private groups? If businessmen are civil servants rather than the employees of their

From *Capitalism and Freedom* (Chicago: University of Chicago Press, 1962), pp. 133–36.

stockholders then in a democracy they will, sooner or later, be chosen by the public techniques of election and appointment.

And long before this occurs, their decision-making power will have been taken away from them. A dramatic illustration was the cancellation of a steel price increase by U.S. Steel in April 1962 through the medium of a public display of anger by President Kennedy and threats of reprisals on levels ranging from anti-trust suits to examination of the tax reports of steel executives. This was a striking episode because of the public display of the vast powers concentrated in Washington. We were all made aware of how much of the power needed for a police state was already available. It illustrates the present point as well. If the price of steel is a public decision, as the doctrine of social responsibility declares, then it cannot be permitted to be made privately.

The particular aspect of the doctrine which this example illustrates, and which has been most prominent recently, is an alleged social responsibility of business and labor to keep prices and wage rates down in order to avoid price inflation. Suppose that at a time when there was upward pressure on prices . . . every businessman and labor leader were to accept this responsibility and suppose all could succeed in keeping any price from rising, so we had voluntary price and wage control without open inflation. What would be the result? Clearly product shortages, labor shortages, gray markets, black markets. If prices are not allowed to ration goods and workers, there must be some other means to do so. Can the alternative rationing schemes be private? Perhaps for a time in a small and unimportant area. But if the goods involved are many and important, there will necessarily be pressure, and probably irresistible pressure, for governmental rationing of goods, a governmental wage policy, and governmental measures for allocating and distributing labor.

Price controls, whether legal or voluntary, if effectively enforced would eventually lead to the destruction of the free-enterprise system and its replacement by a centrally controlled system. And it would not even be effective in preventing inflation. History offers ample evidence that what determines the average level of prices and wages is the amount of money in the economy and not the greediness of businessmen or of workers. Governments ask for the self-restraint of business and labor because of their inability to manage their own affairs—which includes the control of money—and the natural human tendency to pass the buck.

One topic in the area of social responsibility that I feel duty bound to touch on, because it affects my own personal interests, has been the claim that business should contribute to the support of charitable activities and especially to universities. Such giving by corporations is an inappropriate use of corporate funds in a free-enterprise society.

The corporation is an instrument of the stockholders who own it. If the corporation makes a contribution, it prevents the individual stockholder from himself deciding how he should dispose of his funds. With the corporation tax and the deductibility of contributions, stockholders may of course want the corporation to make a gift on their behalf, since this would enable them to make a larger gift. The best solution would be the abolition of the corporate tax. But so long as there is a corporate tax, there is no justification for permitting deductions for contributions to charitable and educational institutions. Such contributions should be made by the individuals who are the ultimate owners of property in our society.

People who urge extension of the deductibility of this kind of corporate contribution in the name of free enterprise are fundamentally working against their own interest. A major complaint made frequently against modern business is that it involves the separation of ownership and control—that the corporation has become a social institution that is a law unto itself, with irresponsibile executives who do not serve the interests of their stockholders. This charge is not true. But the direction in which policy is now moving, of permitting corporations to make contributions for charitable purposes and allowing deductions for income tax, is a step in the direction of creating a true divorce between ownership and control and of undermining the basic nature and character of our society. It is a step away from an individualistic society and toward the corporate state.

NOTE

1. Adam Smith, *The Wealth of Nations* (1776) bk. IV, chap. ii, (Cannon ed., London, 1930) p. 421.

44. Changing the Social Contract: A Role for Business

Melvin Anshen

Among the problems confronting top corporate officers, none is more disturbing than the demand that they modify or abandon their traditional responsibility to devote their best talent and energy to the management of resources with the goal of maximizing the return on the owners' investment.

This demand takes many forms. It may appear as pressure:

- to withhold price increases to cover rising costs;
- to give special financial support to . . . properties and businesses [in minority neighborhoods];
- to provide special training and jobs for the hard-core unemployed;
- to invest in equipment designed to minimize environmental contamination by controlling, scrubbing or eliminating industrial process discharges into air or water;
- to contribute generously to the support of charitable, educational and artistic organizations and activities;
- to refuse to solicit or accept defense and defense-related contracts;
- to avoid or dispose of investments in countries where racial or political policies and practices offend elements of the citizenry;
- to provide for "public" or "consumer" representation on boards of directors;
- to make executives available to serve without compensation on public boards or other non-business assignments.

The common element in all these pressures is their departure from, even contradiction of, the economic considerations which have been regarded as appropriate criteria for determining the allocation and use of private resources. They challenge the thesis that decisions taken with a view to maximizing private profit also maximize public benefits. They deny the working of Adam Smith's "invisible hand."

This cluster of pressures is not limited to alleged deficiencies in the traditional elements of management decision making. It also raises fundamental questions about the intellectual ability of business managers—reflecting their education, experience and norms of behavior—to respond adaptively and creatively to new goals, new criteria for administering resources, new measures of performance.

. . . Society is approaching . . . a basic redefinition of the role and responsibility of private enterprise. . . .

One way of comprehending the whole development is to view it as an emerging demand for a new set of relationships among business, government, non-economic organizations and individuals. Some such set of relationships, of changing character and composition, has existed throughout recorded history. Without some implicit and broadly accepted design for living together, man's existence with his fellow men would be chaotic beyond endurance. . . .

The ultimate determinant of the structure and performance of any society is a set of reciprocal, institutionalized duties and obligations which are broadly accepted by its citizens. The acceptance may be described as an implicit social contract. Without such a contract, not less real or powerful for being implicit, a society would lack cohesiveness, order and continuity. Individuals would be confused about their own behavior and commitments as well as about their appropriate expectations with respect to the behavior and commitments of the private and public institutions which employ them, service them and govern them. . . .

The concept of the implied social contract is an old one in Western civilization. It found early expression in the writings of the Greek philosopher Epictetus. It was central to the intellectual system developed by Thomas Hobbes in the first half of the seventeenth century. Without such an implicit contract, he observed, man faces the terror of anarchy, for the natural condition of man is "solitary, short, brutish and nasty." Hobbes used his concept to rationalize the power of the state to compel obedience to the terms of the implied contract. A few decades later, John Locke converted this view of compulsion as the lever to the view of consent as the lever—the consent of the citizens to a relationship of reciprocal duties and obligations.

In the next century, Jean Jacques Rousseau expanded the idea into an intellectual system in which each member of society entered into an implicit contract with every other member, a contract that defined the norms of human behavior and the terms of exchanges and trade-offs among individuals and organizations, private and public. His view even provided for handling disagreements about ends and means. The implied social contract, he wrote,

From *Columbia Journal of World Business* 5:6 (1970): 6–14.

stipulated that the minority would accept the decisions of the majority, would express its opposition through legitimate channels of dissent, and would yield before proceeding to rebellion. To Rousseau, therefore, the act of rebellion signified not what it appeared to be on the surface—a rebellion against the ends and means favored by the majority—but rather a rejection of the very terms of the contract itself.

Most recently, the fundamental thrust of such a book as John Kenneth Galbraith's *The New Industrial State* challenges the terms of the implicit social contract that defines, among other things, the function and role of private enterprise in today's society, the popular view of the responsibilities and performance of private corporations and the network of reciprocal relationships among corporations, government, and citizens. Galbraith's description of the enterprise system is distorted and incomplete, but his perception of the fundamental contract and its pervasive influence is accurate.

The terms of the historic social contract for private business, now coming under critical attack, are brilliantly clear. They existed for more than a hundred years with only minor modifications. Indeed, they acquired a popular, almost mythic, concept which purported to define a set of institutional arrangements uniquely advantageous for the national well-being, superior to all alternatives. . . .

These contractual terms were an outgrowth of interlaced economic, social and technological considerations in which the economic issues were overwhelmingly dominant. Economic growth, summed in the grand measure of gross national product, was viewed as the source of all progress. The clear assumption was that social progress (including those benefits associated with ideas about the quality of life) was a by-product of economic progress and impossible to achieve without it. Technological advance both fueled economic progress and was fueled by it in a closed, self-generating system.

The engine of economic growth was identified as the drive for profits by unfettered, competitive, private enterprise. Natural and human resources were bought in an open market and were administered in the interest of profit maximization. Constraints were applied only at the margins and were designed either to assure the continuance of the system (as in anti-trust legislation and administration) or to protect those who could not protect themselves in the open market (as in legislation prohibiting child labor, assuring labor's right to organize or restraining deliberate injury to consumers). These and similar constraints were "the rules of the game," a suggestive term. The rules protected the game and assured its continuance as a constructive activity.

The implicit social contract stipulated that business could operate freely within the rules. Subject only to the constraints on conduct imposed by the rules, the responsibility of business was to search for and produce profits. In doing this competitively, business yielded benefits for society in the form of products and services wanted by consumers who earned the purchasing power to supply their wants by working at jobs created by business.

The social gains were viewed as so great that there was never any serious question about the costs of the system that were thrown out on society. For most of the period (until the cataclysm of the 1930s), there was no strong public demand that private firms absorb any share of the costs of unemployment or of retired workers. For an even longer period (until the last few years) there was no strong public demand that private firms carry any share of the costs of environmental contamination. . . . As long as business produced . . . growth, the only costs it had to carry were the internal costs of acquiring resources in the market and using them to produce and sell goods and services to the market. The external costs of the system were not even recognized as costs. They were not accounted for. When they were evidenced in the form of extreme personal hardship for individuals and groups, they were met by private charity, or they were not met at all.

Beyond the concept of social costs, the contract stipulated that private business had no responsibility for the general conditions of life or the specific conditions in local communities. The unresolved problems and strains of industrialized urban living were seen by none but a handful of radicals as in any way a proper concern of business firms or their managers.

Although there was a long history of efforts by individuals and groups to remove racial discrimination, for example, there was no strong public demand until recently that private business accept responsibility for eliminating discrimination within firms, much less for deliberately changing hiring policies in accordance with non-economic criteria, or for modifying lending policies to minority businesses and individuals in order to accept risks previously assessed as economically unrewarding.

The terms of the contract were so visibly defined by national norms of acceptable business behavior that they were rarely questioned by responsible managers. The relatively few and weak critics of some of the contract terms were identified by managers and even by themselves as radicals or revolutionaries interested not in reforming the system but in destroying it. This intellectual posture inhibited constructive criticism from within the system by impugning the patriotism, if not the rationality, of dissenters. One dangerous result has been to constrain flexible adaptation to dynamic economic and social changes which have been the inevitable by-products of advanced industrialization, urbanization and, broadly viewed, demonstration of the feasibility of universal affluence. . . .

The most dramatic element for business in the emerging new contract is a shift in the conceptual relation between economic progress and social progress. Until recently, the primacy of economic growth as the chief engine of civilization was generally not seriously questioned. Some of its unpleasant or wounding by-products were, to be sure, superficially deplored from time to time. But they were accepted by most people as fundamentally inevitable and were appraised as a reasonable price to pay for the benefits of a steadily rising gross national product. As a result, the by-products were rarely studied in depth, their economic and social costs were not measured—indeed, little was done even to develop accounting techniques for tooling such measurement.

Michael Harrington's book, *The Other America,* with its quantitative documentation of the existence of an unacknowledged poor nation within a rich nation, could strike with genuine shock on the mind and conscience of many professional and managerial leaders in public and private organizations. The facts of urban decay and the implications of trends projected into the future were not analyzed and reported in terms that would permit a realistic assessment of their present and future costs. Nor, certainly until the outbreak of mass riots in minority [neighborhoods], was there penetrating consideration of the relation of social disturbance to continued economic progress.

While much remains to be done in scientific research and analysis of the side effects of economic progress, the accumulating formal and informal documentation has begun to influence the set of general ideas that constitute[s] the terms of the contract for business. The clause in the contract that stipulated the primacy of economic growth, and thereby gave a charter to free enterprise within broad rules of competitive economic behavior, is now widely challenged. It is becoming clear that in the emerging new contract, social progress (the quality of life) will weigh equally in the balance with economic progress. . . .

Such equality foreshadows some drastic revisions in the rules of the game. As one example, it will no longer be acceptable for corporations to manage their affairs solely in terms of the traditional internal costs of doing business, while thrusting external costs on the public. Since the 1930s, of course, some external costs have been partially returned to business firms, as in the case of unemployment compensation. But most have not, and this situation is on the edge of revision. This means, as is even now beginning to occur, that the costs associated with environmental contamination will be transferred from the public sector to the business firms which generate the contamination. It also means that corporations whose economic activities are judged to create safety hazards (from automobiles to atomic power plants) will be compelled to internalize the costs of minimizing these hazards by conforming with stipulated levels of acceptable risk or of mandatory manufacturing and performance specifications.

To be rigorously correct, it should be noted that industry's new cost structure will be reflected in its prices. Purchasers of goods and services will be the ultimate underwriters of the increased expenses. But a moment's reflection on the supply-demand charts that sprinkle the pages of economics texts will demonstrate that a new schedule of supply prices will intersect demand curves at different points than formerly. This may lead to a changed set of customer purchase preferences among the total assortment of goods and services. What is implied is not a simple pass-through of newly internalized social costs. The ultimate results will alter relative market positions among whole industries and, within industries, among firms. Choices from available options in short-term technological adjustments to the new contamination and safety requirements and in long-term pricing strategies to reflect higher costs will, in the familiar competitive way, determine success or failure for a number of companies. Some interesting management decisions lie ahead.

The internalization of traditional social costs of private operations is the most obvious of the changes that will follow on striking a new balance between economic and social progress. More subtle, and eventually more radical, relocations of responsibility can be foreseen. The complex cluster of socioeconomic problems associated with urbanization, population shifts and the needs of disadvantaged minorities are already overwhelming the administrative capacities, probably also the resources, of city, county and state governments. Evidence is accumulating that the public expects private business to contribute brains and resources to the amelioration and resolution of these massive strains. History suggests that such expectations will be transformed into demands. . . .

If the thrust of this analysis is generally on target, the principal lesson for private management is clear. It must participate actively in the redesign of the social contract. There can be no greater danger than to permit the new rules to be formulated by either the small group of critics armed only with malevolence toward the existing system or the much larger group sincerely motivated by concern for ameliorating social ills but grossly handicapped by their ignorance of the techniques and dynamism of private enterprise. . . .

A good place to begin would be the uncharted jungle of cost estimates. We need concepts and techniques for measuring and accounting for the real costs of environmental contamination. We need to build a body of reliable information about what the costs are in all their complexity, where they originate, where they impact. We also need to evaluate present and potential technologies for suppressing or removing contaminants, along both engineering and economic parameters. . . .

A second area where business competence can make a contribution is the cluster of problems associated with poverty in the midst of plenty, unemployed or underemployed minorities, and urban decay. Less clearly defined than the contamination issue, this area possesses much greater potential for violent disruption that could mortally shred the fabric of our society. If this occurs (and there are too many recent examples of limited local disruptions to be comfortably skeptical about the possibilities ahead), many of the environmental conditions essential for the private enterprise system will disappear. There can be little doubt that what would follow would be an authoritarian, social-service, rigid society in which the conditions of production and distribution would be severely controlled. In such a setting, the dynamism, creativeness and flexibility of the economy would disappear, together with all the incentives for individual achievement in any arena other than, possibly, the political. . . .

The incentive for business management to enroll as a participant in the general exploration of ways and means for removing the cancerous growth in the vitals of society is classically selfish. Somehow, this cancer will be removed. The recognition is spreading rapidly that its continuance is intolerable. Some of the proposed or still-to-be-proposed lines of attack may be destructive of other elements in society, including the private enterprise system. Management is in a position to contribute rational analysis, technical competence and imaginative innovations. The interests served by continuing the enterprise system coincide here with other social interests.

These and comparable innovations [require of] private managers a willingness to think about new economic roles and social relationships that many will see as dangerous cracks in the wall of custom. It is not unreasonable, however, to suggest that we are considering nothing more adventurous than the explorations and commitments that managers have long been accustomed to underwrite in administering resources. The only significant difference is that the stakes are higher. In place of the marginal calculus of profit and loss, what may be involved is the preservation of the civilization that has created such an unparalleled record of wealth and growth.

45. Justifying Reverse Discrimination in Employment*

George Sher

A currently favored way of compensating for past discrimination is to afford preferential treatment to the members of those groups which have been discriminated against in the past. I propose to examine the rationale behind this practice when it is applied in the area of employment. I want to ask whether, and if so under what conditions, past acts of discrimination against members of a particular group justify the current hiring of a member of that group who is less than the best qualified applicant for a given job. Since I am mainly concerned about exploring the relations between past discrimination and present claims to employment, I shall make the assumption that each applicant is at least minimally competent to perform the job he seeks; this will eliminate the need to consider the claims of those who are to receive the services in question. Whether it is ever justifiable to discriminate in favor of an incompetent applicant, or a less than best qualified applicant for a job such as teaching, in which almost any increase in employee competence brings a real increase in services rendered, will be left to be decided elsewhere. Such questions, which turn on balancing the claim of the less than best qualified applicant against the competing claims of those who are to receive his services, are

From *Philosophy and Public Affairs* 4:2 (1975): 159–70.

*I am grateful to Michael Levin, Edward Erwin, and my wife Emily Gordon Sher for helpful discussion of this topic.

not as basic as the question of whether the less than best qualified applicant ever *has* a claim to employment.[1]

I

It is sometimes argued, when members of a particular group have been barred from employment of a certain kind, that since this group has in the past received *less* than its fair share of the employment in question, it now deserves to receive *more* by way of compensation.[2] This argument, if sound, has the virtue of showing clearly why preferential treatment should be extended even to those current group members who have not themselves been denied employment: if the point of reverse discrimination is to compensate a wronged *group,* it will presumably hardly matter if those who are preferentially hired were not among the original victims of discrimination. However, the argument's basic presupposition, that groups as opposed to their individual members are the sorts of entities that can be wronged and deserve redress, is itself problematic.[3] Thus the defense of reverse discrimination would only be convincing if it were backed by a further argument showing that groups can indeed be wronged and have deserts of the relevant sort. No one, as far as I know, has yet produced a powerful argument to this effect, and I am not hopeful about the possibilities. Therefore I shall not try to develop a defense of reverse discrimination along these lines.

Another possible way of connecting past acts of discrimination in hiring with the claims of current group members is to argue that even if these current group members have not (yet) been denied *employment,* their membership in the group makes it very likely that they have been discriminatorily deprived of *other* sorts of goods. It is a commonplace, after all, that people who are forced to do menial and low-paying jobs must often endure corresponding privations in housing, diet, and other areas. These privations are apt to be distributed among young and old alike, and so to afflict even those group members who are still too young to have had their qualifications for employment bypassed. It is, moreover, generally acknowledged by both common sense and law that a person who has been deprived of a certain amount of one sort of good may sometimes reasonably be compensated by an equivalent amount of a good of another sort. (It is this principle, surely, that underlies the legal practice of awarding sums of money to compensate for pain incurred in accidents, damaged reputations, etc.) Given these facts and this principle, it appears that the preferential hiring of current members of discriminated-against groups may be justified as compensation for the *other* sorts of discrimination these individuals are apt to have suffered.[4]

But, although this argument seems more promising than one presupposing group deserts, it surely cannot be accepted as it stands. For one thing, insofar as the point is simply to compensate individuals for the various sorts of privations they have suffered, there is no special reason to use reverse discrimination rather than some other mechanism to effect compensation. There are, moreover, certain other mechanisms of redress which seem prima facie preferable. It seems, for instance, that it would be most appropriate to compensate for past privations simply by making preferentially available to the discriminated-against individuals equivalent amounts of the very same sorts of goods of which they have been deprived; simple cash settlements would allow a far greater precision in the adjustment of compensation to privation than reverse discriminatory hiring ever could. Insofar as it does not provide any reason to adopt reverse discrimination rather than these prima facie preferable mechanisms of redress, the suggested defense of reverse discrimination is at least incomplete.

Moreover, and even more important, if reverse discrimination is viewed simply as a form of compensation for past privations, there are serious questions about its fairness. Certainly the privations to be compensated for are not the sole responsibility of those individuals whose superior qualifications will have to be bypassed in the reverse discriminatory process. These individuals, if responsible for those privations at all, will at least be no more responsible than others with relevantly similar histories. Yet reverse discrimination will compensate for the privations in question at the expense of these individuals alone. It will have no effect at all upon those other, equally responsible persons whose qualifications are inferior to begin with, who are already entrenched in their jobs, or whose vocations are noncompetitive in nature. Surely it is unfair to distribute the burden of compensation so unequally.[5]

These considerations show, I think, that reverse discriminatory hiring of members of groups that have been denied jobs in the past cannot be justified simply by the fact that each group member has been discriminated against in other areas. If this fact is to enter into the justification of reverse discrimination at all, it must be in some more complicated way.

II

Consider again the sorts of privations that are apt to be distributed among the members of those groups restricted in large part to menial and low-paying jobs. These individuals, we said, are apt to live in substandard homes, to subsist on improper and imbalanced diets, and to receive inadequate educations. Now, it is certainly true that adequate housing, food, and education are goods in and of themselves; a life without them is certainly less pleasant and less full than one with them. But, and crucially, they are also goods in a different sense entirely. It is an obvious and well-documented fact that (at least) the sorts of nourishment and education a person receives as a child will causally affect the sorts of skills and capacities he will have as an adult—including, of course, the very skills which are needed if he is to compete on equal terms for jobs and other goods. Since this is so, a child who is deprived of adequate food and education may lose not only the immediate enjoyments which a comfortable and stimulating environment bring but also the subsequent ability to compete equally for other things of intrinsic value. But to lose this ability to compete is, in essence, to lose one's access to the goods that are being competed for; and this, surely, is itself a privation to be compensated for if possible. It is, I think, the key to an adequate justification of reverse discrimination to see that practice, not as the redressing of *past* privations, but rather as a way of neutralizing the *present* competitive disadvantage *caused* by those past privations and thus as a way of restoring equal access to those goods which society distributes competitively.[6] When reverse discrimination is justified in this way, many of the difficulties besetting the simpler justification of it disappear.

For whenever someone has been irrevocably deprived of a certain good and there are several alternative ways of providing him with an equivalent amount of another good, it will *ceteris paribus* be preferable to choose whichever substitute comes closest to actually replacing the lost good. It is this principle that makes preferential access to decent housing, food, and education especially desirable as a way of compensating for the experiential impoverishment of a deprived childhood. If, however, we are concerned to compensate not for the experiential poverty, but for the effects of childhood deprivations, then this principle tells just as heavily for reverse discrimination as the proper form of compensation. If the lost good is just the *ability* to compete on equal terms for first-level goods like desirable jobs, then surely the most appropriate (and so preferable) way of substituting for what has been lost is just to remove the *necessity* of competing on equal terms for these goods—which, of course, is precisely what reverse discrimination does.

When reverse discrimination is viewed as compensation for lost ability to compete on equal terms, a reasonable case can also be made for its fairness. Our doubts about its fairness arose because it seemed to place the entire burden of redress upon those individuals whose superior qualifications are bypassed in the reverse discriminatory process. This seemed wrong because these individuals are, of course, not apt to be any more responsible for past discrimination than others with relevantly similar histories. But, as we are now in a position to see, this objection misses the point. The crucial fact about these individuals is not that they are more *responsible* for past discrimination than others with relevantly similar histories (in fact, the dirty work may well have been done before any of their generation attained the age of responsibility), but rather that unless reverse discrimination is practiced, they will *benefit* more than the others from its effects on their competitors. They will benefit more because unless they are restrained, they, but not the others, will use their competitive edge to claim jobs which their competitors would otherwise have gotten. Thus, it is only because they stand to *gain* the most from the relevant effects of the *original* discrimination that the bypassed individuals stand to *lose* the most from *reverse* discrimination.[7] This is surely a valid reply to the charge that reverse discrimination does not distribute the burden of compensation equally.

NOTES

1. In what follows I will have nothing to say about utilitarian justifications of reverse discrimination. There are two reasons for this. First, the winds of utilitarian argumentation blow in too many directions. It is certainly socially beneficial to avoid the desperate actions to which festering resentments may lead—but so too is it socially useful to confirm the validity of qualifications of the traditional sort, to assure those who have amassed such qualifications that "the rules of the game have not been changed in the middle," that accomplishment has not been downgraded in society's eyes. How could these conflicting utilities possibly be measured against one another?

Second and even more important, to rest a defense of reverse discrimination upon utilitarian considerations would be to ignore what is surely the guiding intuition of its proponents, that this treatment is *deserved* where discrimination has been practiced in the past. It is the intuition that reverse discrimination is a matter not (only) of social good but of right which I want to try to elucidate.

2. This argument, as well as the others I shall consider, presupposes that jobs are (among other things) *goods*, and so ought to be distributed as fairly as possible. This presupposition seems to be amply supported by the sheer economic necessity of earning a living, as well as by the fact that some jobs carry more prestige and are more interesting and pay better than others.

3. As Robert Simon has pointed out in "Preferential Hiring: A Reply to Judith Jarvis Thomson," *Philosophy and Public Affairs* 3:3 (1974): 312–20, it is also far from clear that the preferential hiring of its individual members could be a proper form of compensation for any wronged group that *did* exist.

4. A version of this argument is advanced by Judith Jarvis Thomson in "Preferential Hiring," *Philosophy and Public Affairs* 2:4 (1973): 364–84.

5. Cf. Simon, "Preferential Hiring," sec. 3.

6. A similar justification of reverse discrimination is suggested, but not ultimately endorsed, by Thomas Nagel in "Equal Treatment and Compensatory Discrimination" *Philosophy and Public Affairs* 2:4 (1973): 348–63. Nagel rejects this justification on the grounds that a system distributing goods solely on the basis of performance determined by native ability would itself be unjust, even if not *as* unjust as one distributing goods on a racial or sexual basis. I shall not comment on this, except to remark that our moral intuitions surely run the other way: the average person would certainly find the latter system of distribution *far* more unjust than the former, if, indeed, he found the former unjust at all. Because of this, the burden is on Nagel to show exactly why a purely meritocratic system of distribution would be unjust.

7. It is tempting, but I think largely irrelevant, to object here that many who are now entrenched in their jobs (tenured professors, for example) have already benefited from the effects of past discrimination at least as much as the currently best qualified applicant will if reverse discrimination is not practiced. While many such individuals have undoubtedly benefited from the effects of discrimination upon *their original* competitors, few if any are likely to have benefited from a reduction in the abilities of the *currently best qualified applicant's* competitor. As long as none of them have so benefited, the best qualified applicant in question will still stand to gain the most from that *particular* effect of past discrimination, and so reverse discrimination against him will remain fair. Of course, there will also be cases in which an entrenched person *has* previously benefited from the reduced abilities of the currently best qualified applicant's competitor. In these cases, the best qualified applicant will *not* be the single main beneficiary of his rival's handicap, and so reverse discrimination against him will *not* be entirely fair. I am inclined to think there may be a case for reverse discrimination even here, however; for if it is truly impossible to dislodge the entrenched previous beneficiary of his rival's handicap, reverse discrimination against the best qualified applicant may at least be the fairest (or least unfair) of the practical alternatives.

SOCIAL RESPONSIBILITY AND DISTRIBUTIVE JUSTICE

46. Access to Legal Services

Andrew Kaufman (Ed.)

Drafting Lawyers

The House of Delegates of the American Bar Association approved at its August 1975 meeting the following resolution proposed by its Special Committee on Public Interest practice:

Resolved, That it is a basic professional responsibility of each lawyer engaged in the practice of law to provide public interest legal services;

Further Resolved, That public interest legal service is legal service provided without fee or at a substantially reduced fee, which falls into one or more of the following areas:

1. Poverty Law: Legal services in civil and criminal matters of importance to a client who does not have the financial resources to compensate counsel.

2. Civil Rights Law: Legal representation involving a right of an individual which society has a special interest in protecting.

3. Public Rights Law: Legal representation involving an important right belonging to a significant segment of the public.

4. Charitable Organization Representation: Legal service to charitable, religious, civic, governmental and educational institutions in matters in furtherance of their organizational purpose, where the payment of customary legal fees would significantly deplete the organization's economic resources or would be otherwise inappropriate.

5. Administration of Justice: Activity, whether under bar association auspices, or otherwise, which is designed to increase the availability of legal services, or otherwise improve the administration of justice.

Further Resolved, That public interest legal services shall at all times be provided in a manner consistent with the Code of Professional Responsibility and the Code of Judicial Conduct;

Further Resolved, That so long as there is a need for public interest legal services, it is incumbent upon the organized bar to assist each lawyer in fulfilling his profes-

From *Problems in Professional Responsibility, 1979 Supplement* (Boston: Little, Brown, 1979), pp. 115–62.

sional responsibility to provide such services as well as to assist, foster and encourage governmental, charitable and other sources to provide public interest legal services.

Further Resolved, That the appropriate officials, committees or sections of the American Bar Association are instructed to proceed with the development of proposals to carry out the interest and purpose of the foregoing resolutions.

The report that accompanied the proposal discussed and justified its restrictive definition of "public interest legal service" by the most pressing needs of society. It also adverted to the possibility of meeting the need by financial contribution instead of service and of a law firm's meeting its obligation on a group rather than an individual basis. It did not seek to quantify the obligation but mentioned suggestions of five to ten percent of billable time. In a subsequent report, the committee noted the difficulty of deciding whether contributions should be related to time or income, but again referred to the fact that increasingly lawyers were being asked to contribute two to five weeks of their professional time per year. 1977 Report of the Special Committee on Public Interest Practice, p. 4.

The committee solicited the bar for comments. One reply, taking issue with its proposal, follows:

I believe very strongly that members of the legal profession ought to feel obligated to provide public-interest legal services on a volunteer basis. . . . On the other hand, I feel equally strongly that compelled service is not desirable. My reasons are both philosophical and practical.

I have a bias in favor of personal liberty and against the government (and especially a nongovernmental body exercising some governmental functions) telling people in substantial ways what to do with their lives. Sometimes, as with the draft in times of military necessity, recruitment becomes essential. Sometimes, as with the appointment of lawyers to serve as counsel to indigent criminal defendants, the intrusion is not so substantial. But an annual obligation to contribute five percent of one's professional time is a substantial compulsion. I think as a philosophical matter that the kind of situation that would justify that sort of compulsion must be of the sort that could fairly be called an emergency, and, as bad as problems are in the legal system, I do not think they create that kind of emergency. But, as I said, it all depends on how favorably inclined one is toward the idea of compulsion and how willing one is to set this kind of precedent.

On the practical side, I think that you must consider the dislocating effects of the proposal. Many lawyers contribute enormous amounts of time to the public interest, more broadly defined than your committee's conception—e.g., the lawyer who serves as an unpaid town selectman or an unpaid treasurer or board member of a charitable organization. Lawyering skills are certainly relevant to the job although the lawyer is not doing any "representing." My guess is that if lawyers are compelled to find tasks that will "qualify" they will tend to drop off many of those valuable public service tasks they would have preferred to do. The alternative is to spend even less time with their families than many of them do. Thus your proposal would be likely to cut down on a variety of important public tasks that lawyers currently perform.

A second practical problem relates to the competence of work done under compulsion. The problem already exists and has been much noted in criminal assignments. I think it will be even more massive when you involve the whole bar in it. Perhaps ideally it is erroneous even to consider the problem, but practically we must.

Involving the whole bar has further problems. The large percentage of the bar that is scraping to make ends meet will regard a five percent tax on their time as extraordinarily regressive as compared with the equivalent tax on a lawyer who is well off. Moreover, the "financial contribution instead of time" comes close to making a farce out of the notion of professional obligation involved in your proposal. The same holds true for the proposal for a "firm" contribution of total hours. If there is an individual professional obligation, then all should do it individually and with their own time. Compromises of this sort to make the proposal saleable are unworthy of the ideal your proposal is supposed to represent.

Having stated my agreement with your idea that lawyers should feel an obligation to do volunteer public work, I think I should do more than merely criticize your proposal. I think there is work to do. My sense is that there is a large reservoir of untapped willingness to do public service work in the profession. I see the major challenge as the devising of ways to tap that reservoir by creating mechanisms that would make it easier to plug lawyers in to needs. If bar associations had such mechanisms, so that lawyers could see what sort of tasks were available, I think many more of them could be encouraged into making commitments. That sort of mechanism would be a likely part of your proposal anyhow, and starting it at least with volunteers sounds preferable to me.

. . . . .

Lawyer Advertising: *Bates and O'Steen* v. *State Bar of Arizona,* 433 U.S. 350 (1977)*

Mr. Justice Blackmun delivered the opinion of the Court.

As part of its regulation of the Arizona Bar, the Supreme Court of that State has imposed and endorces a disciplinary rule that restricts advertising by attorneys. This case presents two issues: whether §§1 and 2 of the Sherman Act, 15 U.S.C. §§1 and 2, forbid such state regulation, and whether the operation of the rule violates the First Amendment, made applicable to the States through the Fourteenth.

---

*Extensive citations to the record and to other opinions in this case are omitted without indication.—ED. [Kaufman].

Appellants John R. Bates and Van O'Steen are attorneys licensed to practice law in the State of Arizona. As such, they are members of the appellee, the State Bar of Arizona.[1] After admission to the bar in 1972, appellants worked as attorneys with the Maricopa County Legal Aid Society.

In March 1974, appellants left the Society and opened a law office, which they call a "legal clinic," in Phoenix. Their aim was to provide legal services at modest fees to persons of moderate income who did not qualify for governmental legal aid. In order to achieve this end, they would accept only routine matters, such as uncontested divorces, uncontested adoptions, simple personal bankruptcies, and changes of name, for which costs could be kept down by extensive use of paralegals, automatic typewriting equipment, and standardized forms and office procedures. More complicated cases, such as contested divorces, would not be accepted. Because appellants set their prices so as to have a relatively low return on each case they handled, they depended on substantial volume.

After conducting their practice in this manner for two years, appellants concluded that their practice and clinical concept could not survive unless the availability of legal services at low cost was advertised and, in particular, fees were advertised. Consequently, in order to generate the necessary flow of business, that is, "to attract clients," appellants on February 22, 1976, placed an advertisement . . . in the *Arizona Republic,* a daily newspaper of general circulation in the Phoenix metropolitan area. . . . [T]he advertisement stated that appellants were offering "legal services at very reasonable fees," and listed their fees for certain services.

Appellants concede that the advertisement constituted a clear violation of Disciplinary Rule 2-101 (B), incorporated in Rule 29 (a) of the Supreme Court of Arizona, 17A Ariz. Rev. Stat. (Supp. 1976), p. 26. The disciplinary rule provides in part: "(B) A lawyer shall not publicize himself, or his partner, or associate, or any other lawyer affiliated with him or his firm, as a lawyer through newspaper or magazine advertisements, radio or television announcements, display advertisements in the city or telephone directories or other means of commercial publicity, nor shall he authorize or permit others to do so in his behalf."

Upon the filing of a complaint initiated by the president of the State Bar, a hearing was held before a three-member Special Local Administrative Committee, as prescribed by Arizona Supreme Court Rule 33. Although the committee took the position that it could not consider an attack on the validity of the rule, it allowed the parties to develop a record on which such a challenge could be based. The committee recommended that each of the appellants be suspended from the practice of law for not less than six months. Upon further review by the Board of Governors of the State Bar, pursuant to the Supreme Court's Rule 36, the Board recommended only a one-week suspension for each appellant, the weeks to run consecutively.

Appellants, as permitted by the Supreme Court's Rule 37, then sought review in the Supreme Court of Arizona, arguing, among other things, that the disciplinary rule violated §§1 and 2 of the Sherman Act because of its tendency to limit competition, and that the rule infringed their First Amendment rights. The court rejected both claims. *In re Bates,* 113 Ariz. 394, 555 P.2d 640 (1976). . . . Because the court, in agreement with the Board of Governors, felt that appellants' advertising "was done in good faith to test the constitutionality of DR 2-101 (B)," it reduced the sanction to censure only. 113 Ariz., at 400, 555 P.2d, at 646. . . .

. . . . .

III THE FIRST AMENDMENT

A

Last Term, in *Virginia Pharmacy Board* v. *Virginia Consumer Council,* 425 U.S. 748 (1976), the Court considered the validity under the First Amendment of a Virginia statute declaring that a pharmacist was guilty of "unprofessional conduct" if he advertised prescription drug prices. The pharmacist would then be subject to a monetary penalty or the suspension or revocation of his license. The statute thus effectively prevented the advertising of prescription drug price information. We recognized that the pharmacist who desired to advertise did not wish to report any particularly newsworthy fact or to comment on any cultural, philosophical, or political subject; his desired communication was characterized simply: " 'I will sell you the X prescription drug at the Y price.' " *Id.,* at 761. Nonetheless, we held that commercial speech of that kind was entitled to the protection of the First Amendment. . . .

We have set out [a] detailed summary of the *Pharmacy* opinion because the conclusion that Arizona's disciplinary rule is violative of the First Amendment might be said to flow *a fortiori* from it. Like the Virginia statutes, the disciplinary rule serves to inhibit the free flow of commercial information and to keep the public in ignorance. Because of the possibility, however, that the differences among professions might bring different constitutional considerations into play, we specifically reserved judgment as to other professions. . . .

B

The issue presently before us is a narrow one. First, we need not address the peculiar problems associated with advertising claims relating to the the *quality* of legal services. Such claims probably are not susceptible of precise measurement or verification and, under some circumstances, might well be deceptive or misleading to the public, or even false. Appellee does not suggest, nor do we perceive, that appellants' advertisement contained claims, extravagant or otherwise, as to the quality of services. Accordingly, we leave that issue for another day. Second, we also need not resolve the problems associated with in-person solicitation of clients—at the hospital room or the accident site, or in any other situation that breeds undue influence—by attorneys or their agents or "runners." Activity of that kind might well pose dangers of overreaching and misrepresentation not encountered in newspaper announcement advertising. Hence, this issue also is not before us. Third, we note that appellee's criticism of advertising by attorneys does not apply with much force to some of the basic factual content of advertising: information as to the attorney's name, address, and telephone number, office hours, and the like. The American Bar Association itself has a provision in its current Code of Professional Responsibility that would allow the disclosure of such information, and more, in the classified section of the telephone directory. DR 2-102(A)(6) (1976). We recognize, however, that an advertising diet limited to such spartan fare would provide scant nourishment.*

The heart of the dispute before us today [however] is whether lawyers also may constitutionally advertise the *prices* at which certain routine services will be performed. Numerous justifications are proffered for the restriction of such price advertising. We consider each in turn:

1. The Adverse Effect on Professionalism. Appellee places particular emphasis on the adverse effects that it feels price advertising will have on the legal profession. The key to professionalism, it is argued, is the sense of pride that involvement in the discipline generates. It is claimed that price advertising will bring about commercialization, which will undermine the attorney's sense of dignity and self-worth. The hustle of the marketplace will adversely affect the profession's service orientation, and irreparably damage the delicate balance between the lawyer's need to earn and his obligation selflessly to serve. Advertising is also said to erode the client's trust in his attorney: Once the client perceives that the lawyer is motivated by profit, his confidence that the attorney is acting out of a commitment to the client's welfare is jeopardized. And advertising is said to tarnish the dignified public image of the profession.

We recognize, of course, and commend the spirit of public service with which the profession of law is practiced and to which it is dedicated. The present Members of this Court, licensed attorneys all, could not feel otherwise. And we would have reason to pause if we felt that our decision today would undercut that spirit. But we find the postulated connection between advertising and the erosion of true professionalism to be severely strained. At its core, the argument presumes that attorneys must conceal from themselves and from their clients the real-life fact that lawyers earn their livelihood at the bar. We suspect that few attorneys engage in such self-deception. And rare is the client, moreover, even one of modest means, who enlists the aid of an attorney with the expectation that his services will be rendered free of charge. See B. Christensen, Lawyers for People of Moderate Means 152–53 (1970). In fact, the American Bar Association advises that an attorney should reach "a clear agreement with his client as to the basis of the fee charges to be made," and that this is to be done "[a]s soon as feasible after a lawyer has been employed." Code of Professional Responsibility, EC 2–19 (1976). If the commercial basis of the relationship is to be promptly disclosed on ethical grounds, once the client is in the office, it seems inconsistent to condemn the candid revelation of the same information before he arrives at that office.

Moreover, the assertion that advertising will diminish the attorney's reputation in the community is open to question. Bankers and engineers advertise, and yet these professions are not regarded as undignified. In fact, it has been suggested that the failure of lawyers to advertise creates public disillusionment with the profession. The absence of advertising may be seen to reflect the profession's failure to reach out and serve the community: Studies reveal that many persons do not obtain counsel even when they perceive a need because of the feared price of services or because of an inability to locate a competent attorney. Indeed, cynicism with regard to the profession may be created by the fact that it long has publicly es-

*[Disciplinary Rule 2–102(a)(6) permits the inclusion of certain biographical information (e.g., memberships in professional societies, scholastic distinctions, dates of degrees), as well as information regarding specialization of a law practice or individual attorney (provided such specializations are recognized in a jurisdiction), names of references, and fees for an initial consultation. The rule also permits providing a fee schedule and estimates of costs of services when they are requested.—ED.]

chewed advertising, while condoning the actions of the attorney who structures his social or civic associations so as to provide contacts with potential clients.

It appears that the ban on advertising originated as a rule of etiquette and not as a rule of ethics. Early lawyers in Great Britain viewed the law as a form of public service, rather than as a means of earning a living, and they looked down on "trade" as unseemly. See H. Drinker, Legal Ethics 5, 210–11 (1953). Eventually, the attitude toward advertising fostered by this view evolved into an aspect of the ethics of the profession. *Id.*, at 211. But habit and tradition are not in themselves an adequate answer to a constitutional challenge. In this day, we do not belittle the person who earns his living by the strength of his arm or the force of trade . . . [T]he historical foundation for the advertising restraint has crumbled.

2. The Inherently Misleading Nature of Attorney Advertising. It is argued that advertising of legal services inevitably will be misleading (a) because such services are so individualized with regard to content and quality as to prevent informed comparison on the basis of an advertisement, (b) because the consumer of legal services is unable to determine in advance just what services he needs, and (c) because advertising by attorneys will highlight irrelevant factors and fail to show the relevant factor of skill.

We are not persuaded that restrained professional advertising by lawyers inevitably will be misleading. Although many services performed by attorneys are indeed unique, it is doubtful that any attorney would or could advertise fixed prices for services of that type. The only services that lend themselves to advertising are the routine ones: the uncontested divorce, the simple adoption, the uncontested personal bankruptcy, the change of name, and the like—the very services advertised by appellants. Although the precise service demanded in each task may vary slightly, and although legal services are not fungible, these facts do not make advertising misleading so long as the attorney does the necessary work at the advertised price. The argument that legal services are so unique that fixed rates cannot meaningfully be established is refuted by the record in this case: The appellee State Bar itself sponsors a Legal Services Program in which the participating attorneys agree to perform services like those advertised by the appellants at standardized rates. Indeed, until the decision of this Court in *Goldfarb* v. *Virginia State Bar* [421 U.S. 773 (1975)], the Maricopa County Bar Association apparently had a schedule of suggested minimum fees for standard legal tasks. We thus find of little force the assertion that advertising is misleading because of an inherent lack of standardization in legal services.[2]

The second component of the argument—that advertising ignores the diagnostic role—fares little better.[3] It is unlikely that many people go to an attorney merely to ascertain if they have a clean bill of legal health. Rather, attorneys are likely to be employed to perform specific tasks. Although the client may not know the detail involved in performing the task, he no doubt is able to identify the service he desires at the level of generality to which advertising lends itself.

The third component is not without merit: Advertising does not provide a complete foundation on which to select an attorney. But it seems peculiar to deny the consumer, on the ground that the information is incomplete, at least some of the relevant information needed to reach an informed decision. The alternative—the prohibition of advertising—serves only to restrict the information that flows to consumers.[4] Moreover, the argument assumes that the public is not sophisticated enough to realize the limitations of advertising, and that the public is better kept in ignorance than trusted with correct but incomplete information. We suspect the argument rests on an underestimation of the public. In any event, we view as dubious any justification that is based on the benefits of public ignorance. See *Virginia Pharmacy Board* v. *Virginia Consumer Council,* 425 U.S., at 769–70. Although, of course, the bar retains the power to correct omissions that have the effect of presenting an inaccurate picture, the preferred remedy is more disclosure, rather than less. If the naiveté of the public will cause advertising by attorneys to be misleading, then it is the bar's role to assure that the populace is sufficiently informed as to enable it to place advertising in its proper perspective.

3. The Adverse Effect on the Administration of Justice. Advertising is said to have the undesirable effect of stirring up litigation.[5] The judicial machinery is designed to serve those who feel sufficiently aggrieved to bring forward their claims. Advertising, it is argued, serves to encourage the assertion of legal rights in the courts, thereby undesirably unsettling societal repose. There is even a suggestion of barratry. . . .

But advertising by attorneys is not an unmitigated source of harm to the administration of justice. It may offer great benefits. Although advertising might increase the use of the judicial machinery, we cannot accept the notion that it is always better for a person to suffer a wrong silently than to redress it by legal action. As the bar acknowledges, "the middle seventy percent of our population is not being reached or served adequately by the legal profession." ABA, Revised

Handbook on Prepaid Legal Services 2 (1972). Among the reasons for this underutilization is fear of the cost, and an inability to locate a suitable lawyer. Advertising can help to solve this acknowledged problem: Advertising is the traditional mechanism in a free-market economy for a supplier to inform a potential purchaser of the availability and terms of exchange. The disciplinary rule at issue likely has served to burden access to legal services, particularly for the not-quite-poor and the unknowledgeable. A rule allowing restrained advertising would be in accord with the bar's obligation to "facilitate the process of intelligent selection of lawyers, and to assist in making legal services fully available." ABA Code of Professional Responsibility EC 2–1 (1976).

4. The Undesirable Economic Effects of Advertising. It is claimed that advertising will increase the overhead costs of the profession, and that these costs then will be passed along to consumers in the form of increased fees. Moreover, it is claimed that the additional cost of practice will create a substantial entry barrier, deterring or preventing young attorneys from penetrating the market and entrenching the position of the bar's established members.

These two arguments seem dubious at best. Neither distinguishes lawyers from others, . . . and neither appears relevant to the First Amendment. The ban on advertising serves to increase the difficulty of discovering the lowest cost seller of acceptable ability. As a result, to this extent attorneys are isolated from competition, and the incentive to price competitively is reduced. Although it is true that the effect of advertising on the price of services has not been demonstrated, there is revealing evidence with regard to products; where consumers have the benefit of price advertising, retail prices often are dramatically lower than they would be without advertising. It is entirely possible that advertising will serve to reduce, not advance, the cost of legal services to the consumer.[6]

The entry-barrier argument is equally unpersuasive. In the absence of advertising, an attorney must rely on his contacts with the community to generate a flow of business. In view of the time necessary to develop such contacts, the ban in fact serves to perpetuate the market position of established attorneys. Consideration of entry-barrier problems would urge that advertising be allowed so as to aid the new competitor in penetrating the market.

5. The Adverse Affect of Advertising on the Quality of Service. It is argued that the attorney may advertise a given "package" of service at a set price, and will be inclined to provide, by indiscriminate use, the standard package regardless of whether it fits the client's needs.

Restraints on advertising, however, are an ineffective way of deterring shoddy work. An attorney who is inclined to cut quality will do so regardless of the rule on advertising. And the advertisement of a standardized fee does not necessarily mean that the services offered are undesirably standardized. Indeed, the assertion that an attorney who advertises a standard fee will cut quality is substantially undermined by the fixed-fee schedule of appellee's own prepaid Legal Services Program. Even if advertising leads to the creation of "legal clinics" like that of appellants—clinics that emphasize standardized procedures for routine problems—it is possible that such clinics will improve service by reducing the likelihood of error.

6. The Difficulties of Enforcement. Finally, it is argued that the wholesale restriction is justified by the problems of enforcement if any other course is taken. Because the public lacks sophistication in legal matters, it may be particularly susceptible to misleading or deceptive advertising by lawyers. After-the-fact action by the consumer lured by such advertising may not provide a realistic restraint because of the inability of the layman to assess whether the service he has received meets professional standards. Thus, the vigilance of a regulatory agency will be required. But because of the numerous purveyors of services, the overseeing of advertising will be burdensome.

It is at least somewhat incongruous for the opponents of advertising to extol the virtues and altruism of the legal profession at one point, and, at another, to assert that its members will seize the opportunity to mislead and distort. We suspect that with advertising, most lawyers will behave as they always have: They will abide by their solemn oaths to uphold the integrity and honor of their profession and of the legal system. For every attorney who overreaches through advertising, there will be thousands of others who will be candid and honest and straightforward. And, of course, it will be in the latter's interest, as in other cases of misconduct at the bar, to assist in weeding out those few who abuse their trust.

In sum, we are not persuaded that any of the proffered justifications rise to the level of an acceptable reason for the suppression of all advertising by attorneys. . . .

The constitutional issue in this case is only whether the State may prevent the publication in a newspaper of appellants' truthful advertisement concerning the availability and terms of routine legal services. We rule simply that the flow of such information may not be restrained, and we therefore hold the present application of the disciplinary rule against appellants to be violative of the First Amendment.

Chasing Ambulances: *Ohralik* v. *Ohio State Bar Association,* 436 U.S. 447 (1978)*

Mr. Justice Powell delivered the opinion of the Court. . . .

I

Appellant, a member of the Ohio Bar, lives in Montville, Ohio. Until recently he practiced law in Montville and Cleveland. On February 13, 1974, while picking up his mail at the Montville Post Office, appellant learned from the postmaster's brother about an automobile accident that had taken place on February 2 in which Carol McClintock, a young woman with whom appellant was casually acquainted, had been injured. Appellant made a telephone call to Ms. McClintock's parents, who informed him that their daughter was in the hospital. Appellant suggested that he might visit Carol in the hospital. Mrs. McClintock assented to the idea, but requested that appellant first stop by at her home.

During appellant's visit with the McClintocks, they explained that their daughter had been driving the family automobile on a local road when she was hit by an uninsured motorist. Both Carol and her passenger, Wanda Lou Holbert, were injured and hospitalized. In response to the McClintocks' expression of apprehension that they might be sued by Holbert, appellant explained that Ohio's guest statute would preclude such a suit. When appellant suggested to the McClintocks that they hire a lawyer, Mrs. McClintock retorted that such a decision would be up to Carol, who was 18 years old and would be the beneficiary of a successful claim.

Appellant proceeded to the hospital, where he found Carol lying in traction in her room. After a brief conversation about her condition,[7] appellant told Carol he would represent her and asked her to sign an agreement. Carol said she would have to discuss the matter with her parents. She did not sign the agreement, but asked appellant to have her parents come to see her.[8] Appellant also attempted to see Wanda Lou Holbert, but learned that she had just been released from the hospital. . . . He then departed for another visit with the McClintocks.

On his way appellant detoured to the scene of the accident, where he took a set of photographs. He also picked up a tape recorder, which he concealed under his raincoat before arriving at the McClintocks' residence. Once there, he reexamined their automobile insurance policy, discussed with them the law applicable to passengers, and explained the consequences of the fact that the driver who struck Carol's car was an uninsured motorist. Appellant discovered that the McClintocks' insurance policy would provide benefits of up to $12,500 each for Carol and Wanda Lou under an uninsured motorist clause. Mrs. McClintock acknowledged that both Carol and Wanda Lou could sue for their injuries, but recounted to appellant that "Wanda swore up and down she would not do it." The McClintocks also told appellant that Carol had phoned to say that appellant could "go ahead" with her representation. Two days later appellant returned to Carol's hospital room to have her sign a contract, which provided that he would receive one-third of her recovery.

In the meantime, appellant obtained Wanda Lou's name and address from the McClintocks after telling them he wanted to ask her some questions about the accident. He then visited Wanda Lou at her home, without having been invited. He again concealed his tape recorder and recorded most of the conversation with Wanda Lou.[9] After a brief, unproductive inquiry about the facts of the accident, appellant told Wanda Lou that he was representing Carol and that he had a "little tip" for Wanda Lou: The McClintocks' insurance policy contained an uninsured motorist clause which might provide her with a recovery of up to $12,500. The young woman, who was 18 years of age and not a high school graduate at the time, replied to appellant's query about whether she was going to file a claim by stating that she really did not understand what was going on. Appellant offered to represent her, also, for a contingent fee of one-third of any recovery, and Wanda Lou stated "O.K."[10]

Wanda's mother attempted to repudiate her daughter's oral assent the following day, when appellant called on the telephone to speak to Wanda. Mrs. Holbert informed appellant that she and her daughter did not want to sue anyone or to have appellant represent them, and that if they decided to sue they would consult their own lawyer. Appellant insisted that Wanda had entered into a binding agreement. A month later Wanda confirmed in writing that she wanted neither to sue nor to be represented by appellant. She requested that appellant notify the insurance company that he was not her lawyer, as the company would not release a check to her until he did so.[11] Carol also

*Extensive citations to the record and to other opinions in this case are omitted without indications.—ED. [Kaufman].

eventually discharged appellant. Although another lawyer represented her in concluding a settlement with the insurance company, she paid appellant one-third of her recovery[12] in settlement of his lawsuit against her for breach of contract.[13]

Both Carol McClintock and Wanda Lou Holbert filed complaints against appellant with the Grievance Committee of the Geauga County Bar Association. The County Bar Association filed a formal complaint with the Board of Commissioners on Grievance and Discipline of the Supreme Court of Ohio.[14] After a hearing, the Board found that appellant had violated Disciplinary Rules (DR) 2-103(A) and 2-104(A) of the Ohio Code of Professional Responsibility.* The Board rejected appellant's defense that his conduct was protected under the First and Fourteenth Amendments. The Supreme Court of Ohio adopted the findings of the Board,[15] reiterated that appellant's conduct was not constitutionally protected, and increased the sanction of a public reprimand recommended by the Board to indefinite suspension.

The decision in *Bates* was handed down after the conclusion of proceedings in the Ohio Supreme Court. We noted probable jurisdiction in this case to consider the scope of protection of a form of commercial speech, and an aspect of the State's authority to regulate and discipline members of the bar, not considered in *Bates*. 433 U.S. 350, 97 S. Ct. 2691, 53 L. Ed. 2d 810 (1977). We now affirm the judgment of the Supreme Court of Ohio.

II

The solicitation of business by a lawyer through direct, in-person communication with the prospective client has long been viewed as inconsistent with the profession's ideal of the attorney-client relationship and as posing a significant potential for harm to the prospective client. It has been proscribed by the organized Bar for many years. . . . The balance struck in *Bates* does not predetermine the outcome in this case. The entitlement of in-person solicitation of clients to the protection of the First Amendment differs from that of the kind of advertising approved in *Bates*, as does the strength of the State's countervailing interest in prohibition.

A

Appellant contends that his solicitation of the two young women as clients is indistinguishable, for purposes of constitutional analysis, from the advertisement in *Bates*. Like that advertisement, his meetings with the prospective clients apprised them of their legal rights and of the availability of a lawyer to pursue their claims. According to appellant, such conduct is "presumptively an exercise of his free speech rights" which cannot be curtailed in the absence of proof that it actually caused a specific harm that the State has a compelling interest in preventing. But in-person solicitation of professional employment by a lawyer does not stand on a par with truthful advertising about the availability and terms of routine legal services, let alone with forms of speech more traditionally within the concern of the First Amendment.

Expression concerning purely commercial transactions has come within the ambit of the Amendment's protection only recently. In rejecting the notion that such speech "is wholly outside the protection of the First Amendment," *Virginia Pharmacy*, 425 U.S. [748], at 761, we were careful not to hold "that it is wholly undifferentiable from other forms" of speech. *Id.*, at 771 n.24. We have not discarded the "commonsense" distinction between speech proposing a commercial transaction, which occurs in an area traditionally subject to government regulation, and other varieties of speech. *[Id.]* To require a parity of constitutional protection for commercial and noncommercial speech alike could invite dilution, simply by a leveling process, of the force of the Amendment's guarantee with respect to the latter kind of speech. Rather than subject the First Amendment to such a devitalization, we instead have afforded commercial speech a limited measure of protection, commensurate with its subordinate position in the scale of First Amendment values, while allowing modes of regulation that might be impermissible in the realm of noncommercial expression. . . .

In-person solicitation by a lawyer of remunerative employment is a business transaction in which speech is an essential but subordinate component. While this does not remove the speech from the protection of the First Amendment, as was held in *Bates* and *Virginia Pharmacy*, it lowers the level of appropriate judicial scrutiny.

As applied in this case, the disciplinary rules are said to have limited the communication of two kinds of information. First, appellant's solicitation imparted to Carol McClintock and Wanda Lou Holbert certain information about his availability and the terms of his proposed legal services. In this respect, in-person solicitation serves much the same function as the advertisement at issue in *Bates*. But there are significant differences as well. Unlike a public advertisement, which simply pro-

*[These rules proscribe giving unsolicited advice to a party that he or she should get an attorney and then accepting employment resulting from that advice or recommending for employment oneself, one's partner, or an associate.—ED.]

vides information and leaves the recipient free to act upon it or not, in-person solicitation may exert pressure and often demands an immediate response, without providing an opportunity for comparison or reflection.[16] The aim and effect of in-person solicitation may be to provide a one-sided presentation and to encourage speedy and perhaps uninformed decisionmaking; there is no opportunity for intervention or countereducation by agencies of the Bar, supervisory authorities, or persons close to the solicited individual. The admonition that "the fitting remedy for evil counsels is good ones" is of little value when the circumstances provide no opportunity for any remedy at all. In-person solicitation is as likely as not to discourage persons needing counsel from engaging in a critical comparison of the "availability, nature, and prices" of legal services, cf. *Bates,* . . . 433 U.S. at 364, 97 S. Ct. at 2699, it actually may disserve the individual and societal interest, identified in *Bates,* in facilitating "informed and reliable decisionmaking."*[Id.]*

It also is argued that in-person solicitation may provide the solicited individual with information about his or her legal rights and remedies. In this case, appellant gave Wanda Lou a "tip" about the prospect of recovery based on the uninsured motorist clause in the McClintocks' insurance policy, and he explained that clause and Ohio's guest statute to Carol McClintock's parents. But neither of the disciplinary rules here at issue prohibited appellant from communicating information to these young women about their legal rights and the prospects of obtaining a monetary recovery, or from recommending that they obtain counsel. DR 2-104(A) merely prohibited him from using the information as bait with which to obtain an agreement to represent them for a fee. The rule does not prohibit a lawyer from giving unsolicited legal advice; it proscribes the acceptance of employment resulting from such advice.

Appellant does not contend, and on the facts of this case could not contend, that his approaches to the two young women involved political expression or an exercise of associational freedom, "employ[ing] constitutionally privileged means of expression to secure constitutionally guaranteed civil rights." *NAACP* v. *Button,* 371 U.S. 415, 442 (1963). . . . A lawyer's procurement of remunerative employment is a subject only marginally affected with First Amendment concerns. It falls within the State's proper sphere of economic and professional regulation. . . . While entitled to some constitutional protection, appellant's conduct is subject to regulation in furtherance of important state interests.

B

The state interests implicated in this case are particularly strong. In addition to its general interest in protecting consumers and regulating commercial transactions, the State bears a special responsibility for maintaining standards among members of the licensed professions. . . . "The interest of the States in regulating lawyers is especially great since lawyers are essential to the primary governmental function of administering justice, and have historically been 'officers of the courts.' " *Goldfarb* v. *Virginia State Bar,* [421 U.S. 773 (1975)]. While lawyers act in part as "self-employed businessmen," they also act "as trusted agents of their clients, and as assistants to the court in search of a just solution to disputes." *Cohen* v. *Hurley,* 366 U.S. 117 (1961).

As is true with respect to advertising, . . . it appears that the ban on solicitation by lawyers originated as a rule of professional etiquette rather than as a strictly ethical rule. See H. Drinker, Legal Ethics 210–11, and n. 3 (1953). . . . But the fact that the original motivation behind the ban on solicitation today might be considered an insufficient justification for its perpetuation does not detract from the force of the other interests the ban continues to serve. . . . While the Court in *Bates* determined that truthful, restrained advertising of the prices of "routine" legal services would not have an adverse effect on the professionalism of lawyers, this was only because it found "the postulated connection between advertising and the erosion of *true professionalism* to be severely strained." 433 U.S., at 368. The *Bates* Court did not question a State's interest in maintaining high standards among licensed professionals. Indeed, to the extent that the ethical standards of lawyers are linked to the service and protection of clients, they do further the goals of "true professionalism."

The substantive evils of solicitation have been stated over the years in sweeping terms: stirring up litigation, assertion of fraudulent claims, debasing the legal profession, and potential harm to the solicited client in the form of overreaching, overcharging, underrepresentation, and misrepresentation. The American Bar Association, as *amicus curiae,* defends the rule against solicitation primarily on three broad grounds: It is said that the prohibitions embodied in Disciplinary Rules 2–103(A) and 2–104(A) serve to reduce the likelihood of overreaching and the exertion of undue influence on lay persons; to protect the privacy of individuals; and to avoid situations where the lawyer's exercise of judgment on behalf of the client will be clouded by his own pecuniary self-interest.

We need not discuss or evaluate each of these interests in detail as appellant has conceded that the State has a legitimate and indeed "compelling" interest in preventing those aspects of solicitation that involve fraud, undue influence, intimidation, overreaching, and other forms of "vexatious conduct." We agree that protection of the public from these aspects of solicitation is a legitimate and important state interest.

III

Appellant's concession that strong state interests justify regulation to prevent the evils he enumerates would end this case but for his insistence that none of those evils was found to be present in his acts of solicitation. He challenges what he characterizes as the "indiscriminate application" of the rules [to] him and thus attacks the validity of DR 2–103(A) and DR 2–104(A) not facially, but as applied to his acts of solicitation. And because no allegations or findings were made of the specific wrongs appellant concedes would justify disciplinary action, appellant terms his solicitation "pure," meaning "soliciting and obtaining agreements from Carol McClintock and Wanda Lou Holbert to represent each of them," without more. Appellant therefore argues that we must decide whether a State may discipline him for solicitation per se without offending the First and Fourteenth Amendments. . . .

[A]ppellant errs in assuming that the constitutional validity of the judgment below depends on proof that his conduct constituted actual overreaching or inflicted some specific injury on Wanda Holbert or Carol McClintock. His assumption flows from the premise that nothing less than actual proven harm to the solicited individual would be a sufficiently important state interest to justify disciplining the attorney who solicits employment in person for pecuniary gain.

Appellant's argument misconceives the nature of the State's interest. The rules prohibiting solicitation are prophylactic measures whose objective is the prevention of harm before it occurs. The rules were applied in this case to discipline a lawyer for soliciting employment for pecuniary gain under circumstances likely to result in the adverse consequences the State seeks to avert. In such a situation, which is inherently conducive to overreaching and other forms of misconduct, the State has a strong interest in adopting and enforcing rules of conduct designed to protect the public from harmful solicitation by lawyers whom it has licensed.

The State's perception of the potential for harm in circumstances such as those presented in this case is well-founded. The detrimental aspects of face-to-face selling even of ordinary consumer products have been recognized and addressed by the Federal Trade Commission, and it hardly need be said that the potential for overreaching is significantly greater when a lawyer, a professional trained in the art of persuasion, personally solicits an unsophisticated, injured, or distressed lay person. Such an individual may place his or her trust in a lawyer, regardless of the latter's qualifications or the individual's actual need for legal representation, simply in response to persuasion under circumstances conducive to uniformed acquiescence. Although it is argued that personal solicitation is valuable because it may apprise a victim of misfortune of his or her legal rights, the very plight of that person not only makes him or her more vulnerable to influence but also may make advice all the more intrusive. Thus, under these adverse conditions the overtures of an uninvited lawyer may distress the solicited individual simply because of their obtrusiveness and the invasion of the individual's privacy, even when no other harm materializes. Under such circumstances, it is not unreasonable for the State to presume that in-person solicitation by lawyers more often than not will be injurious to the person solicited.

The efficacy of the State's effort to prevent such harm to prospective clients would be substantially diminished if, having proved a solicitation in circumstances like those of this case, the State were required in addition to prove actual injury. Unlike the advertising in *Bates,* in-person solicitation is not visible or otherwise open to public scrutiny. Often there is no witness other than the lawyer and the lay person whom he has solicited, rendering it difficult or impossible to obtain reliable proof of what actually took place. This would be especially true if the lay person were so distressed at the time of the solicitation that he or she could not recall specific details at a later date. If appellant's view were sustained, in-person solicitation would be virtually immune to effective oversight and regulation by the State or by the legal profession, in contravention of the State's strong interest in regulating members of the Bar in an effective, objective, and self-enforcing manner. It therefore is not unreasonable, or violative of the Constitution, for a State to respond with what in effect is a prophylactic rule.

On the basis of the undisputed facts of record, we conclude that the disciplinary rules constitutionally could be applied to appellant. He approached two young accident victims at a time when they were especially incapable of making informed judgments or of assessing and protecting their own interests. He solicited Carol McClintock in a hospital room where she lay in traction and sought out Wanda Lou Holbert on the day she came home from the hospital, knowing from his prior inquiries that she had just been released. Appellant urged his services upon the young women and used the information he had obtained from the McClintocks, and the fact of his agreement with Carol, to induce Wanda to say "O.K." in response to his solicitation. He employed a concealed tape recorder, seemingly to insure that he would have evidence of Wanda's oral assent to the representation. He emphasized that his fee would come out of the recovery, thereby tempting the young women with what sounded like a cost-free and therefore irresistible offer. He refused to withdraw when Mrs. Holbert requested him to do so only a day after the initial meeting between appellant and Wanda Lou and continued to represent himself to the insurance company as Wanda Holbert's lawyer.

The court below did not hold that these or other facts were proof of actual harm to Wanda Holbert or Carol McClintock but rested on the conclusion that appellant had engaged in the general misconduct proscribed by the disciplinary rules. Under our view of the State's interest in averting harm by prohibiting solicitation in circumstances where it is likely to occur, the absence of explicit proof or findings of harm or injury is immaterial. The facts in this case present a striking example of the potential for overreaching that is inherent in a lawyer's in-person solicitation of professional employment. They also demonstrate the need for prophylactic regulation in furtherance of the State's interest in protecting the lay public. We hold that the application of Disciplinary Rules 2–103(A) and 2–104(A) to appellant does not offend the Constitution.

Accordingly, the judgment of the Supreme Court of Ohio is Affirmed.

NOTES*

1. Rule 27 (a) of the Supreme Court of Arizona, 17A Ariz. Rev. Stat. 84–85 (1973) reads in part:

[1] In order to advance the administration of justice according to law, . . . the Supreme Court of Arizona does hereby perpetuate, create and continue under the direction and control of this Court an organization known as the State Bar of Arizona, and all persons now or hereafter licensed in this state to engage in the practice of law shall be members of the State Bar of Arizona in accordance with the rules of this Court. . . .

[3] No person shall practice law in this state or hold himself out a one who may practice law in this state unless he is an active member of the state bar.

See Ariz. Const., Art. 3; Ariz. Rev. Stat. §§32–201, 32–237, 32–264 (1976). The Arizona Bar, thus, is an integrated one. See *Lathrop* v. *Donohue*, 367 U.S. 820 (1961).

2. The Chief Justice and Mr. Justice Powell argue in dissent that advertising will be misleading because the exact services that are included in an advertised package may not be clearly specified or understood by the prospective client. . . . The bar, however, retains the power to define the services that must be included in an advertised package, such as an uncontested divorce, thereby standardizing the "product." We recognize that an occasional client might fail to appreciate the complexity of his legal problem and will visit an attorney in the mistaken belief that his difficulty can be handled at the advertised price. The misunderstanding, however, usually will be exposed at the initial consultation, and an ethical attorney would impose, at the most, a minimal consultation charge or no charge at all for the discussion. If the client decides to have work performed, a fee could be negotiated in the normal manner. The client is thus in largely the same position as he would be if there were no advertising. In light of the benefits of advertising to those whose problem can be resolved at the advertised price, suppression is not warranted on account of the occasional client who misperceives his legal difficulties.

3. The same argument could be made about the advertising of abortion services. Although the layman may not know all the details of the medical procedure and may not always be able accurately to diagnose pregnancy, such advertising has certain First Amendment protection. *Bigelow* v. *Virginia*, 421 U.S. 809 (1975).

4. It might be argued that advertising is undesirable because it allows the potential client to substitute advertising for reputational information in selecting an appropriate attorney. . . . Since in a referral system relying on reputation an attorney's future business is partially dependent on current performance, such a system has the benefit both of providing a mechanism for disciplining misconduct and of creating an incentive for an attorney to do a better job for his present clients. Although the system may have worked when the typical lawyer practiced in a small, homogeneous community in which ascertaining reputational information was easy for a consumer, commentators have seriously questioned its current efficacy. . . . The trends of urbanization and specialization long since have moved the typical practice of law from its small-town setting. . . . Information as to the qualifications of lawyers is not available to many. . . . And, if available, it may be inaccurate or biased.

5. It is argued that advertising also will encourage fraudulent claims. We do not believe, however that there is an inevitable relationship between advertising and dishonesty. . . . Unethical lawyers and dishonest laymen are likely to meet even though restrictions on advertising exist. The appropriate response to fraud is a sanction addressed to that problem alone, not a sanction that unduly burdens a legitimate activity.

6. On the one hand, advertising does increase an attorney's overhead costs, and, in light of the underutilization of legal services by the public, . . . it may increase substantially the demand for services. Both these factors will tend to increase the price of legal services. On the other hand, the tendency of advertising to enhance

*[Note numbers have been regularized—ED.]

competition might be expected to produce pressures on attorneys to reduce fees. The net effect of these competing influences is hard to estimate. We deem it significant, however, that consumer organizations have filed briefs as *amici* urging that the restriction on advertising be lifted. And we note as well that, despite the fact that advertising on occasion might increase the price the consumer must pay, competition through advertising is ordinarily the desired norm.

Even if advertising causes fees to drop, it is by no means clear that a loss of income to lawyers will result. The increased volume of business generated by advertising might more than compensate for the reduced profit per case.

7. Carol also mentioned that one of the hospital administrators was urging a lawyer upon her. According to his own testimony, appellant replied: "Yes, this certainly is a case that would entice a lawyer. That would interest him a great deal."

8. Despite the fact that appellant maintains that he did not secure an agreement to represent Carol while he was at the hospital, he waited for an opportunity when no visitors were present and then took photographs of Carol in traction.

9. Appellant maintains that the tape is a complete reproduction of everything that was said at the Holbert home. Wanda Lou testified that the tape does not contain appellant's introductory remarks to her about his identity as a lawyer, his agreement to represent Carol McClintock, and his availability and willingness to represent Wanda Lou as well. Appellant disputed Wanda Lou's testimony but agreed that he did not activate the recorder until he had been admitted to the Holbert home and was seated in the living room with Wanda Lou.

10. Appellant told Wanda that she should indicate assent by stating "Okay," which she did. Appellant later testified: "I would say that most of my clients have essentially that much of a communication. . . . I think most of my clients, that's the way I practice law."

In explaining the contingency fee arrangement, appellant told Wanda Lou that his representation would not "cost [her] anything" because she would receive two-thirds of the recovery if appellant were successful in representing her but would not "have to pay [him] anything" otherwise.

11. The insurance company was willing to pay Wanda Lou for her injuries but would not release the check while appellant claimed, and Wanda Lou denied, that he represented her. Before appellant would "disavow further interest and claim" in Wanda Lou's recovery, he insisted by letter that Wanda Lou first pay him the sum of $2,466.66, which represented one-third of his "conservative" estimate of the worth of her claim.

12. Carol recovered the full $12,500 and paid appellant $4,166.66. She testified that she paid the second lawyer $900 as compensation for his services.

13. Appellant represented to the Board of Commissioners at the disciplinary hearing that he would abandon his claim against Wanda Lou Holbert because "the rules say that if a contract has its origin in a controversy, that an ethical question can arise." Yet in fact appellant filed suit against Wanda for $2,466.66 after the disciplinary hearing. *Albert Ohralik* v. *Wanda Lou Holbert,* Case No. 76–CV–F–66, filed February 2, 1976, Chardon Municipal Court, Geauga County, Ohio. Appellant dismissed that suit with prejudice on January 27, 1977, after the decision of the Supreme Court of Ohio had been filed.

14. The Board of Commissioners is an agent of the Supreme Court of Ohio. Counsel for appellee stated at oral argument that the Board has "no connection with the Ohio State Bar Association whatsoever."

15. The Board found that Carol and Wanda Lou "were, if anything, casual acquaintances" of appellant; that appellant initiated the contact with Carol and obtained her consent to handle her claim; that he advised Wanda Lou that he represented Carol, had a "tip" for Wanda, and was prepared to represent her, too. The Board also found that appellant would not abide by Mrs. Holbert's request to leave Wanda alone, that both young women attempted to discharge appellant, and that appellant sued Carol McClintock.

16. The immediacy of a particular communication and the imminence of harm are factors that have made certain communications less protected than others. Compare *Cohen* v. *California,* 403 U.S. 15 (1971), with *Chaplinsky* v. *New Hampshire,* 315 U.S. 568 (1942); see *Brandenburg* v. *Ohio,* 395 U.S. 444 (1969); *Schenck* v. *United States,* 249 U.S. 47 (1919).

47. Access to the Legal System: The Professional Obligation to Chase Ambulances

Monroe H. Freedman

Ernest Gene Gunn, a five-year-old boy, was seriously injured as a result of negligent driving attributed to John J. Washek. Shortly after the accident, the boy's mother was visited at home by an adjuster from Mr. Washek's insurance company. The adjuster told her that there was no need to retain an attorney, because the company would make a settlement as soon as the boy was out of his doctor's care; if Ms. Gunn were not satisfied at that time, she could retain an attorney and file suit.

From *Lawyers' Ethics in an Adversary System* (Indianapolis, IN: Bobbs-Merrill, 1974), pp. 113–25.

The boy's injuries were sufficiently severe to require a doctor's care for twenty-three months. At the end of that time Ms. Gunn made repeated efforts to reach the insurance company adjuster, but without success. She then retained a lawyer, who promptly filed suit for her. Ms. Gunn's boy never did have his day in court, however, because the attorneys for the insurance company successfully pleaded a two-year statute of limitations.[1]

The *Gunn* case illustrates two important issues of professional responsibility, which unfortunately, have never been adequately dealt with by the organized Bar. First, however, let us dispose of some preliminary issues of professional responsibility.

If counsel for the insurance company had no prior knowledge of the adjuster's actions, then it would not have been unprofessional to raise the defense of the statute of limitations. A client is entitled to have the benefit of the presentation of any lawful defense.[2] However, it would have been entirely proper—indeed, ethically required—for counsel at least to have urged the company to forego pleading the statutory bar because of the unjust circumstances of the case.[3] Moreover, an attorney would be justified in refusing to accept a retainer in such a case, because, contrary to popular belief, an attorney has no obligation to take a case (as distinguished from continuing in a case already under way) that would require the attorney to act in a way offensive to the attorney's personal judgment.[4] Indeed, if an attorney's personal objections are sufficiently strong about a particular matter, the attorney would be obligated to refrain from taking the case because of the potential conflict of interest.

Yet what if counsel was, in advance, aware of (or prompted) the adjuster's actions? For a lawyer to participate in a scheme to trick a lay person out of effective representation of counsel would constitute counselling or assisting the client in fraudulent conduct in violation of the Code of Professional Responsibility.[5] There is reason to believe, however, that it is not uncommon for some lawyers, acting alone or in connivance with insurance adjusters, to take advantage of claimants' ignorance and to mislead them into foregoing legal rights. Nevertheless, it is rare, if ever, that a lawyer has been disciplined for such perversion of professional knowledge and skills.

On the contrary, the thrust of Bar discipline has been directed toward restricting lay persons' knowledge of their rights and their access to legal redress. For example, not long after Ms. Gunn had lost her fight to overcome the effects of the insurance adjuster's deceitful actions, the Committee of Censors of the Philadelphia Bar Association undertook a $125,000 investigation—not of insurance adjusters, but of ''unethical'' solicitation of clients by plaintiffs' lawyers. The resulting report recognized the need on behalf of plaintiffs ''to counter the activity of [insurance] carriers' adjusters,'' but casually suggested that that problem could be dealt with ''by the exercise of restraint on the part of carriers.''[6] The Report also acknowledged the propriety and ''social value'' of automobile wrecking companies listening to police calls in order to be the first to arrive at accident scenes to carry off the damaged vehicles, but it found no justification at all in a similar effort directed toward protecting the legal rights of the injured people.[7]

The basis for disciplinary action that interferes with lawyers' efforts to advise people of their rights are, of course, the ABA Code strictures against advertising and solicitation.[8] Those provisions continue long-standing rules against maintenance, champerty, and barratry—commonly referred to as ambulance chasing or stirring up litigation.

A common justification for such rules is that advertising would lead to abuses such as false and misleading claims. Why lawyers would be more prone to engage in that kind of dishonesty, however, than are sellers of other services or of commodities has never been articulated. Nor has it been explained why it is feasible to regulate the size and content of professional cards, which is done now,* but impossible to regulate false and misleading advertising by lawyers. What is clear is that the principal purpose of the anti-solicitation rules is to limit competition among lawyers. Illustrative is a case permitting a bar association to advertise its lawyer referral service in a newspaper.[9] The court expressly justified its decision on the ground that the real evil in advertising is competition among lawyers, which is not present when the Bar advertises as a whole.[10]

It is not surprising, therefore, that a number of leading authorities have criticized the anti-solicitation rules as unrelated to professional ethics as distinguished from what Harvard Law Professor Andrew Kaufman calls ''the rules of a guild.''[11] That is, they are directed against competition rather than for the maintenance of moral standards in the public interest. Other authorities have also emphasized the effect of those rules in protecting established lawyers and large firms from undesired competition from young lawyers and small firms.[12]

Nevertheless, there are those who object that advertising for clients would ''degrade the profession'', and the ABA Code informs us that: ''His-

---

*In the Province of Quebec, which includes Montreal, lawyers are permitted to advertise in newspapers and in the Yellow Pages. Regulation of such advertising includes a limitation that: ''Such advertisements shall never exceed 16 square inches in size.'' Regulation of the Bar of Quebec, § 18, ¶ 72(2).

tory has demonstrated that public confidence in the legal system is best preserved by strict, self-imposed controls over, rather than by unlimited advertising.''[13] No historical reference is provided, however, to support that assertion. Similarly, the Philadelphia Report, referred to above, suggests that solicitation of clients in violation of the rules has led to intense public dissatisfaction with the Bar.[14] In fact, the opposite may be true—that is, that dissatisfaction with the Bar stems in major part from lawyers' aloofness and from their failure to reach out to those whom they purport to serve.

For example, in a survey conducted by two law professors at the University of Edinburgh for the Law Society of Scotland, people were asked whether they would resent or welcome an attorney who approached them to offer legal services in six situations (if you were in an accident; if you were considering buying a house; if you were going into a new business venture; etc.). The study revealed that less than two percent of the people in the survey would resent an attorney's contact, while about half would welcome the unrequested proffer of services by an attorney in all six cases.[15] Generally, about seventy percent fell in the ''welcome'' category. Moreover, the least well-educated people were those who, most of all, would welcome being solicited by attorneys. The study concludes: ''The extraordinarily high proportions of people who would welcome the solicitor's initiating contact in the different situations we have posed must seriously question many commonly held assumptions about the correct stance for members of the profession. Taken with the data noted which showed that few members of the public have adequate knowledge of the services solicitors could provide, and would like to know about these (*i.e.*, want more advertisement), there is a coherent and very emphatic call for a more active and positive legal profession.''[16]

A similar conclusion was reached by the Special Committee on Legal Ethics of the Canadian Bar Association. The Committee found that the increasing complexity and specialization in law make it more and more difficult for a potential client to have confidence in the selection of a lawyer. Accordingly, the committee recommended that the permitted forms of advertising by attorneys ''should be enlarged and extended'' to include ''publication of professional cards, in an institutional form in newspapers, shopping center guides, and other like publications.''[17]

Those who object to solicitation of clients are typically ignorant of the fact that the strictures against it are themselves only minor exceptions to the more fundamental rule of professional responsibility expressed in Canon Two of the Code of Professional Responsibility: ''A Lawyer Should Assist the Legal Profession in Fulfilling Its Duty to Make Legal Counsel Available.'' The Code thus recognizes an affirmative obligation of the profession to provide access to the legal system—and that access, presumably, is for the benefit of all people, not just a select few.

Oddly enough, however, the solicitation limitation appears in the Disciplinary Rules under that same Canon Two. Disciplinary Rule 2–104 reads, in part: ''A lawyer who has given unsolicited advice to a layman that he should obtain counsel or take legal action shall not accept employment resulting from that advice. . . .'' Disciplinary Rule 2–103 says: ''A lawyer shall not recommend employment as a private practitioner of himself, his partner, or associate to a non-lawyer who has not sought his advice.''

Those rules appear on first reading to be broad and absolute. But they are practically meaningless—at least for a particular class of lawyers and clients—because of certain exceptions to the anti-solicitation rules. For example, DR 2–104 provides further that: ''A lawyer [who has volunteered advice] may accept employment by a close friend, relative, [or a] former client. . . .'' That refinement means that those who are accustomed to retaining lawyers, say, for their tax or estates work, and those who have attorneys as relatives and friends, are the kind of people who can be solicited despite the rule. As to that socioeconomic class of people, there is no impropriety in solicitation. In addition, consistent with DR 2–104, lawyers have been known to take tax deductions for membership fees in country clubs, on the ground that such fees are an ordinary and necessary business expense—that is, a means for discreetly soliciting business. One prominent federal judge resigned from several exclusive clubs upon going on the Bench, explaining to friends that he no longer needed to attract clients.

Another device approved by the ABA for soliciting clients is the law list, such as in the impressive volumes of *Martindale-Hubbell*. This is purely and simply a self-laudatory advertisement, euphemistically called a ''card,'' and directed to potential clients. Yet not every attorney is permitted to advertise his or her professional autobiography, prestigious associations, and important clients in *Martindale-Hubbell*. One must await an invitation from the publisher to apply for an ''a'' rating, which can be achieved only upon submission of favorable references from sixteen judges and attorneys who have themselves already received an ''a'' rating. For all other members of the profession, *Martindale-Hubbell* is a closed book.

A similar service is *The Attorneys' Register*.

Their brochure boasts that the register holds a certificate of compliance from the American Bar Association, and explains that: "The primary purpose of *The Attorneys' Register* is to continue to be a valuable forwarding medium aimed at securing SUBSTANTIAL legal business for our listees. . . ." (The word SUBSTANTIAL is written in capital letters throughout the brochure.) Further, it offers the attorney "an opportunity to be recognized in association with other reputable members of the Bar," and the publishers promise that they will do "everything they properly can to encourage active forwardings to our listees." The brochure also provides a partial list of "important corporations which . . . have requested, and will receive, a copy of our current edition . . . for use when seeking qualified . . . counsel." The list contains about one hundred corporations, including Abbott Laboratories, American Sugar, Continental Can, DuPont, General Electric, and U.S. Plywood—corporations that will look for the attorney's name and qualifications in the paid advertisement in the register. In addition, the register is distributed free to "a careful selection of banks and trust companies, important industrial corporations, insurance companies, financing institutions, and the like, who are believed to be prolific forwarders of SUBSTANTIAL legal matters."

That is the way solicitation is carried on with impunity by lawyers seeking to represent those of wealth and privilege, such as John J. Washek's insurance company. The problem of impropriety arises, of course, only for those who seek to represent that other socioeconomic group typified by the mother of Ernest Gene Gunn or, say, by tenants as distinguished from landlords, or by consumers as distinguished from manufacturers. For such unsophisticates—that is for those who are most in need of that access to the legal system which is promised by Canon Two—the organized Bar, through its disciplinary rules and actions, discourages any realistic opportunity to take controversies "out of the streets and into the courtrooms."

Imagine, for example, the following situation. A woman arrives at a metropolitan courthouse holding a small boy by the hand. She speaks almost no English at all. She is intimidated by the imposing surroundings, and she is frightened and confused. All that she knows is that she is required to be some place in that building because her son has been arrested or her landlord is attempting to evict her family. People brush by her, concerned with their own problems. Then a man appears, smiles at her, and asks her in her own language whether he can help her. Through him, she meets and retains the man's employer, a lawyer who guides her to the proper place and who represents her interests. In my view, that lawyer should have been given a citation as Attorney of the Year. Instead, he was prosecuted as a criminal, convicted of the misdemeanor of soliciting business on behalf of an attorney, subjected to disciplinary proceedings, and censured by the court.*

If the profession has an obligation to "[Fulfill] Its Duty to Make Legal Counsel Available," strictures against advertising and soliciting are precisely the wrong way to go about it. Instead attorneys have a professional duty to stir up litigation when they are acting to advise people, who may be ignorant of their rights, to seek justice in the courts. As expressed by one authority:

> We must . . . discard . . . the assumption of Medieval Society that a law suit is an evil in itself. It is hard to see how either the legal profession or our court machinery can justify its existence, if we go on the assumption that it is always better to suffer a wrong than to redress it by litigation. . . . If we have so little confidence in the process of law as to think otherwise, we shall do well to consider a fundamental overhauling of our system.[18]

Fortunately, there is authority, as well as notions of humanity, equal protection, freedom of speech, and the right to petition, in support of the view that the legal system exists to be used by people, and that people who need legal advice are entitled to have it. Indeed, the new ABA Code at one point makes such advice a matter of professional duty: "The legal profession should assist laymen to recognize legal problems because such problems may not be self-revealing and often are not timely noticed."[19] Advice regarding legal rights is therefore held proper when it is "motivated by a desire to protect one who does not recognize that he may have legal problems or who is ignorant of his legal rights or obligations."[20] At the same time, however, the Code properly condemns the instigation of litigation that is intended "merely to harass or injure another."[21]

The Code does suggest that an attorney should not solicit a client solely for the purpose of obtaining a fee.[22] However, when the lawyer's motives are mixed—that is, when the attorney acts with both a proper motive (to provide needed advice) and an "improper" motive (to earn a fee)—it is

---

**In re Solomon Cohn,* N.Y.L.J., February 19, 1974, at 1:6–7, 3:3. The opinion of the court notes that the attorney had an unblemished record and that before he undertook to represent people in court, he had worked as a volunteer for, and then as a staff member of, the Legal Aid Society. The last paragraph of the opinion reads: "We cannot, of course, condone respondent's unprofessional conduct. However, after giving due consideration to all the circumstances here involved, including respondent's expressions of self-reproach and the humiliation he has already suffered, we believe leniency to be warranted in this instance. Accordingly, the respondent should be censured. . . ."

the proper motive that is determinative. For example, during the New Deal period, an organization was formed called the Liberty League, which was a group of lawyers opposed to such New Deal innovations as the National Labor Relations Act. The league published advertisements expressing its view that the Act was unconstitutional and offering to represent anyone who wanted to litigate against it. In Formal Opinion No. 148, the Committee on Professional Ethics of the American Bar Association held that the lawyers' activities were not only professionally proper but "wholesome and beneficial." Moreover, the Committee made it clear that the propriety of the advertisement would not be affected by a motive on the part of the lawyers to serve the interests of fee-paying clients:

> . . . We need not assume that these lawyers were actuated solely by altruistic motives. It would be extraordinary indeed if some of the lawyers in the list do not have some clients whose rights may be adversely affected by the legislation which the lawyers condemn, but their right to organize and declare their views cannot for that reason be denied, and no ethical principle is thereby violated.

It is clear, therefore, that even though an attorney may receive compensation, the solicitation of a client is not unethical if the client might otherwise have lost the opportunity to vindicate legal rights through ignorance of the law or of the availability of effective legal services.

As the foregoing discussion indicates, the Code of Professional Responsibility takes a schizophrenic position on solicitation and advertising. On one hand, it is good to advise people of their rights, even if a fee might result. On the other hand, there are some lawyers, for some clients, who had better not try to do it. One result of that inconsistency in the anti-solicitation rules has been that bar association disciplinary committees have been using it to harass public interest lawyers—even those working without fees from clients—who represent unpopular clients or causes.

In part because of that particular abuse of the rules, the Stern Community Law Firm in Washington, DC (of which I was then Director), decided to challenge the anti-solicitation rules as applied to non-fee cases. The test case related to child adoption. The District of Columbia then kept a larger proportion of its homeless children in public institutions than did any other American city. The District of Columbia institutions were notoriously overcrowded and understaffed. In the view of the Firm, the situation in the District of Columbia was in substantial part the result of arbitrary rules and bureaucratic policies and practices relating to adoption and foster care. For example, potential adoptive parents had been turned down or discouraged because they were single, because both parents were working, or because they were white and were seeking a black child.[23] Those parents did not meet the agencies' "textbook ideal" standards, but they were nevertheless able to provide healthy and loving homes that were far superior to the grossly inadequate institutions that were the sole actual alternative for the children.

The adoption agencies contended, on the other hand, that there were no such adoptive parents available, that no such arbitrary rules or practices existed, and that there was therefore no practical alternative to keeping the children in the institutions. It was therefore essential to the Firm's position that it demonstrate that potential adoptive parents were in fact available but were being arbitrarily rejected, despite the agencies' claims to the contrary. In order to produce such adoptive parents, the Firm published a Public Interest Legal Opinion in newspapers, magazines, and over radio and television to advise members of the community of the need for adoptive parents, the invalidity of the restrictive rules, and the availability of free legal services.

A second Public Service Legal Opinion published by the Firm related to our efforts to have the Food and Drug Administration declare certain toys to be hazardous to children and to provide that prior purchasers were entitled to return any such toys for a full refund. Despite having had such power through an act of Congress for nearly a year, and despite demands of consumer groups, the FDA had refused to act. Accordingly, Assistant Dean Harriet Rabb of Columbia Law School, then a staff attorney with the Firm, brought an action against the Secretary of HEW on behalf of the Consumers Union and the Children's Foundation to compel the FDA to take appropriate action. The agency at first opposed the litigation, but, while the case was on appeal, the FDA issued the requested ban on over three dozen named toys, declaring them to be capable of killing or maiming children. The FDA then failed, however, to act expeditiously to promulgate regulations providing for return of the toys for refund, so the Firm published a Public Service Legal Opinion setting forth the names and manufacturers of the toys found by the FDA to be hazardous, and expressing the legal opinion that purchasers were entitled immediately to return the toys for refund.

Predictably, some members of the bench and bar complained to the Committee on Legal Ethics and Grievances of the Bar Association of the District of Columbia. Although the Committee began with an attitude hostile to the idea of advertising, the members changed their views in the course of lengthy consideration of the merits of the issue. As a result, the Committee wrote the first Bar Association opinion in the country approving solicitation of clients by public interest lawyers serving without fees.[24] In its opinion, the Legal Ethics and Grievances Committee held that solicitation of clients by the Stern Firm was "consistent with the spirit and letter of the Code of Professional Responsibility" and "in keeping with the highest responsibilities of the legal profession". Fred Graham commented in *the New York Times:* "[F]or a profession that has forbidden lawyers to wear tie clasps bearing their state bar emblem or to send Christmas cards to prospective clients on the ground that such activities were unethical 'advertising,' the activities approved in the new ruling are unprecedented."

That appraisal, however, is somewhat exaggerated. In fact, the Supreme Court has held in a series of cases of major importance that rules of professional ethics must give way to constitutional rights. As the Stern Firm argued in its Memorandum to the Legal Ethics and Grievances Committee, the First Amendment protects solicitation as freedom of speech of the attorney and as an essential aspect of the client's right to petition for redress of grievances.[25] For example, the case of *NAACP v. Button* considered solicitation of clients in the context of efforts of the NAACP to recruit plaintiffs for school desegregation cases. The NAACP called a series of meetings, inviting not only its members and not only poor people, but all members of the community. At those meetings, the organization's paid staff attorneys took the platform to urge those present to authorize the lawyers to sue in their behalf.* The NAACP maintained the ensuing litigation by defraying all expenses, regardless of the financial means of a particular plaintiff.

Virginia contended that the NAACP's activities constituted improper solicitation under a state statute and fell within the traditional state power to regulate professional conduct. The Supreme Court held, however, that "the State's attempt to equate the activities of the NAACP and its lawyers with common-law barratry, maintenance and champerty, and to outlaw them accordingly, cannot obscure the serious encroachment . . . upon protected freedoms of expression." The Court concluded: "Thus it is no answer to the constitutional claims asserted by petitioner to say, as the Virginia Supreme Court of Appeals has said, that the purpose of these regulations was merely to insure high professional standards and not to curtail free expression. For a State may not, under the guise of prohibiting professional misconduct, ignore constitutional rights."[26]

Subsequently, in *Brotherhood of Railroad Trainmen v. Virginia ex rel. Virginia State Bar,* the Supreme Court considered the question of solicitation in a case in which a union's legal services plan resulted in channeling all or substantially all of the railroad workers' personal injury claims, on a private fee basis, to lawyers selected by the union and touted in its literature and at meetings. The Court again upheld the solicitation on constitutional grounds, despite the objection of the two dissenting Justices that by giving constitutional protection to the solicitation of personal injury claims, the Court "relegates the practice of law to the level of a commercial enterprise," "degrades the profession," and "contravenes both the accepted ethics of the profession and the statutory and judicial rules of acceptable conduct."[27]

In the *United Mine Workers* case the Supreme Court dealt with the argument that *Button* should be limited to litigation involving major political issues and not be extended to personal injury cases. The Court held that: "The litigation in question is, of course, not bound up with political matters of acute social moment, as in *Button,* but the First Amendment does not protect speech and assembly only to the extent it can be characterized as political. 'Great secular causes, with small ones are guarded. . . .' "[28] Finally, in the *United Transportation Union* case, the Court reversed a state injunction designed, in Justice Harlan's words, "to fend against 'ambulance chasing.' "[29] In that case a union paid investigators to keep track of accidents, to visit injured members, taking contingent fee contracts with them, and to urge the members to engage named private attorneys who were selected by the union and who had agreed to charge a fee set by prior agreement with the union. The investigators were also paid by the union for any time and expenses incurred in transporting potential clients to the designated lawyers' offices to enter retainer agreements.

In approving that arrangement, the Court reiterated that "collective activity undertaken to obtain meaningful access to the courts is a fundamental right within the protection of the First Amendment."[30] What is important to bear in mind, however, is that: (1) the attorneys in question were not in-house counsel for the union, but were private practitioners; (2) the attorneys earned substantial fees; (3) the cases were not "public interest" cases in the restricted sense, but were ordinary personal injury cases; and (4) the attorneys were retained as a result of the activities of "investigators," paid by the union, whose job it was to find out where

---

*The Court has recognized the critical importance of solicitation to public interest litigation in noting that proscription of solicitation in *Button* would have "seriously crippled" the efforts of the NAACP. *United Mine Workers* v. *Illinois State Bar Ass'n, infra* note 25, at 223, 19 L. Ed. 2d at 431.

accidents had occurred, to visit the victims as promptly as possible, to "tout" the particular lawyers and, if necessary, to take the victim to the lawyers' office to get a contingent fee contract signed.

The only question not decided by the Court was whether the investigators could properly have been paid directly by the lawyers. The dissenting Justices would have disapproved it, while the majority simply did not reach that issue, on the ground that it was not in the record before them. It is difficult, however, to see why a significant distinction should turn upon who pays the investigator. An unsophisticated person like Ms. Gunn needs information about the availability of legal services, regardless of whether she is a member of a union and regardless of who pays her informant. Furthermore, although the Court happened to be dealing in the union cases with group legal services, the people solicited in *Button* were not limited to members of NAACP.

We began with *Gunn* v. *Washek,* and it is an appropriate case with which to close. If lawyers are to take seriously the overriding rule expressed in Canon Two, the Bar must reverse the pattern illustrated by *Gunn*. First, we must vigorously discipline attorneys who abuse their training, skills, and status by misleading, overbearing, or overreaching unrepresented lay people. Second, we must encourage, rather than forbid, lawyers to seek out people like Ms. Gunn who have legal rights and who may, by ignorance, be deprived of access to the legal system.

In short, we should recognize that when Ernest Gene Gunn was injured by John J. Washek, the legal profession failed doubly in its duties when an insurance adjuster rather than a plaintiff's attorney was the first to call on Ms. Gunn.

NOTES

1. *Gunn* v. *Washek,* 405 Pa. 521, 176, A.2d 635 (1961); M. Freedman, Contracts 245 (1973).

2. DR [Disciplinary Rule] 7–101 (A) (1); EC [Ethical Consideration] 7–1, 7–4, 7–8.

3. EC 7–9, 7–8.

4. EC 2–26; DR 2–109, 2–110(C)(1)(e).

5. DR 7–102 (A) (7); *see also,* DR 7–102 (A) (1).

6. Jaffe, Report to the Committee of Censors of the Philadelphia Bar Association of the Investigation into Unethical Solicitation by Philadelphia Lawyers 41 (March 1, 1971). The Report also mentioned the possibility of remedial legislation, but no effort appears to have been made by the Bar Association toward that end.

7. *Id.* at 40.

8. DR 2–101–105.

9. *Jacksonville Bar Ass'n* v. *Wilson,* 102 So. 2d 292 (Fla. S. Ct. 1958). *See also,* EC 2–9.

10. *Id.* at 195.

11. Kaufman, *The Lawyers' New Code,* 22 Harv. L. Sch'l Bull. 19 (1970).

12. Shuchman, *Ethics and Legal Ethics: The Propriety of the Canons as a Group Moral Code,* 37 Geo. Wash. L. Rev. 244 (1968); Cohen, *Confronting Myth in the American Legal Profession: A Territorial Perspective,* 22 Ala. L. Rev. 513 (1970).

13. EC 2–9.

14. Jaffe, *supra* note 6, at 5.

15. Campbell and Wilson, Public Attitudes to the Legal Profession in Scotland 69 (Mimeograph, 1973).

16. *Id.* at 68.

17. Special Committee on Legal Ethics, Canadian Bar Association, Code of Professional Conduct, Recommendation V, at vii (Preliminary Report, June 1973). At the same time, the Committee expressed its opposition to "unregulated competitive advertising or professional touting or any other act or thing designed primarily to attract professional work". *Id.* at 88–89.

18. Radin, *Maintenance by Champerty,* 24 Calif. L. Rev. 48, 72 (1935).

19. EC 2–2.

20. EC 2–3.

21. *Id.*

22. *Id.*

23. Virtually all of the institutionalized children in the District were black.

24. *See,* 41 D.C.B.J. 102 (1974). The opinion (which was issued in 1971) indicated that the advertisements could not include the name of an individual attorney and that the word "Law" could not be used in the Firm's name ("Stern Community Law Firm"). The Firm publicly rejected those limitations, which I consider to be unconstitutional. *See,* Freedman, *Solicitation of Clients,* Juris Doctor, April 1971.

25. *NAACP* v. *Button,* 371 U.S. 415, 83 S. Ct. 328, 9 L. Ed. 2d 405 (1963); *Brotherhood of R.R. Trainmen* v. *Virginia ex rel. Virginia State Bar,* 377 U.S. 1, 84 S. Ct. 1113, 12 L. Ed. 2d 89 (1964); *United Mine Workers* v. *Illinois State Bar Ass'n* 389 U.S. 217, 88 S. Ct. 353, 19 L. Ed. 2d 426 (1967); *United Transp. Union* v. *State Bar,* 401 U.S. 576, 91 S. Ct. 1076, 28 L. Ed. 339 (1971).

26. *NAACP* v. *Button, supra* note 25, at 438–39, 9 L. Ed. 2d at 421.

27. *Brotherhood of R.R. Trainmen* v. *Virginia ex rel. Virginia State Bar, supra* note 25, at 9, 12 L. Ed. 2d at 95 (dissent by Justice Clark).

28. *United Mine Workers* v. *Illinois Bar Ass'n, supra* note 25, at 223, 19 L. Ed. 2d at 431.

29. *United Transp. Union* v. *State Bay, supra* note 25, at 597, 28 L. Ed. 2d at 353 (dissent by Justice Harlan).

30. *Id.* at 585, 28 L. Ed. 2d at 347.

48. The Right to Health Care

Laurence B. McCullough

"Health care is in a state of crisis," is a refrain become all too common in recent years. One of the many responses to this "crisis" has been a concern and even a demand for the right to health care. It is thought that everyone, regardless of their ability to pay or their geographical circumstances is entitled to adequate health care. The temptation of many is to extend this initial claim to a right to quality health care. That is, what is sought is not merely health maintenance but the kind of medical care and services ministered to the well-to-do. The rhetoric of such language is to expose what is taken to be an unjust or unfair state of affairs: people are being deprived of that which they are entitled to claim for themselves.

What is perceived to be unjust is the present structure of health care. It is such that possibilities for human life are frequently diminished or even eliminated. What I propose to do here is to reflect on talk about a right to health care as a way of exposing this injustice. I shall frame my reflections in terms of natural rights since this concept of rights is best suited to analyzing what is involved in this talk of a right to health care.

Historically, rights have been spoken of in three ways, determined by their origin: whether in God, in man, or in nature. Divine rights are known by revelation and are thought to be conferred upon men by the will of God. Quite clearly, then, for any divine right, God could have refrained from granting it. Consider, for example, the older notion of the divine right of kings. We can just as easily think in terms of a divine right of self-government. The one is just as plausible as the other. There is no necessity, therefore, that one should obtain and the other not. Divine rights are contingent and, because they could have failed to obtain, they cannot serve as those constraints on a moral or political order by which we determine the justice of that order.

Man-made rights—the conferred, societal, or civil rights—are those rights men agree to respect for one another. Like divine rights, they also could fail to obtain: Men could, quite simply, disagree on whether or not to create or respect this or that right. Men might, for example, decide to dispense with the legal right of due process under law or the right to vote. Man-made rights, therefore, cannot serve as a basis for providing a fundamental critique of a moral or political order as talk of a right to health is meant to do. Instead, man-made rights reflect and give expression to such orders.

Natural rights differ from both divine and man-made rights in that these rights could not fail to obtain. They obtain—that is, men possess them—no matter what the circumstances of a particular moral or political order. They can, therefore, serve as fundamental, moral constraints by which the justice of a political order is to be judged.

In my judgment, claims of a right to health care are best analyzed in terms of natural rights, because only such an analysis displays adequately the critique that such claims are meant to advance, namely that the present structure of medicine and health care appears to be unjust and that this structure must be changed in accordance with fundamental (in the sense of unavoidable) constraints placed upon *any* just social order. By contrast, talk of a right to health care, as either a divine or man-made right, is not adequate, as a logical matter, to the thrust of current discussion of the future of medicine and health care. There is, therefore, good reason to cast talk of a right to health care in terms of a natural right.

RIGHTS: SOME PRELIMINARY OBSERVATIONS

Claiming rights, of whatever sort, is a powerful moral and political move—thus, it is one frequently made. This is so despite the present-day discomfort with rights talk on the part of some philosophers.[1] When someone says that he has a right to something, he does so, in part, to arrest our attention. Rights talk signals that what is at issue is not taken by the claimant(s) to be some private matter that others can ignore but is, instead, something that has a claim on someone. The point of announcing something as a right is to express to others an interest in something one might not have, retain, or acquire in the absence of recognition of that right. So, for example, if I were to claim as a right a certain freedom of expression, this freedom is announced as something that I *ought* to enjoy, and not merely as something that I happen to enjoy or would like to enjoy. I am, so I claim in my right, entitled to freedom of expression and others are, therefore, bound to acknowledge that freedom.

Moreover, when a right is claimed, it is announced to someone, including society at large, governments, and other individuals. Rights and

From *Ethics in Science and Medicine* 6 (1979): 1–9.

rights talk have, then, a *public* character. First, rights are not private, else they would be empty. That is, if there can be no one morally bound to me by obligation regarding my right, then I would have no such right. Second, rights are not idiosyncratic. Instead, they are general, even universal: anyone similarly situated can and ought to enjoy the same rights. Finally, if one is to succeed in claiming something as a right, one must be prepared to adduce reasons in support of this claim, that is, to display the grounds of the right.

Any talk of a right to health care as a natural right, then, must be preceded by some consideration of the grounding of natural rights. This I propose to do in two parts. First, I shall consider the main themes of Locke's theory of natural rights. His account of natural rights is useful here in that it is especially revealing of the logic of natural rights and of claims made in terms of them. Second, I shall propose a revision of Locke's theory. This revised theory of natural rights will then serve as the basis for discussion of talk of the right to health care. This discussion will focus on (a) the different senses of the right to health care, and (b) the moral constraints that these different senses of the right place upon us.

LOCKE ON NATURAL RIGHTS

Locke argued that man possesses certain basic rights independently of—that is, logically and morally prior to—any political order. Indeed, natural rights constitute the fundamental moral order to which any political order must conform, if it is to be just. Locke used "natural rights" to designate the rights man possesses in this state, the state of nature.

In the state of nature, men are free and equal. In this state, freedom and equality obtain with respect to preservation. Preservation means freedom from harm in those conditions necessary to realize freedom and equality in the community and, subsequently, in the political order, namely, life, health, liberty, and possessions (one's body and one's property). Men, then, are entitled, under the law of nature, to those things required for their preservation "and such other things as Nature affords for their Subsistence."[2] Because these conditions have been met, men can realize their nature as free and equal creatures living the life of reason, that is, living in accord with the law of nature.

Although its metaphysical origin is in God's will, natural law can be known by man without the aid of revelation.[3] It can be known by reason alone. Hence, all rational creatures must assent to it. To refuse to assent to it is to abandon the very ground of rationality and, hence, of moral judgment. With this is lost, as well, the means to assess and defend on moral grounds any political order. In short, denial of the law of nature entails the abandonment of any rational, common basis for moral, civil, or political order.[4]

Reason, Locke maintains, discovers and does not invent or create the law of nature. "Positive laws of Commonwealths," on the other hand, *are* created by men.[5] The law of nature, therefore, enjoys logical and, hence, moral, priority over man's laws.

> . . . Yet it is certain there is such a law, and that too, as intelligible and plain to a rational Creature, and a Studier of the Law, as the positive Laws of Commonwealths, nay possibly plainer; As much as Reason is easier to be understood, than the Phansies and intricate Contrivances of Men, following contrary and hidden interest put into Words: For so truly are a great part of the Municipal Laws of Countries, which are only so far right, as they are founded on the Law of Nature, by which they are to be regulated and interpreted.[6]

Since the Law of Nature does not follow from the "phansies and contrivances of men" but from the requirements of reason, it is not "contrary and hidden," that is, contingent, but is, instead, clear and necessary.

Employing the law of nature, men can know with certainty that necessarily they are equal and free. These elements in man's nature are tempered by and realized in preservation. Whatever is entailed by preservation as its immediate necessary conditions is a natural right for Locke. These rights, in turn, *imply* (the relation is contingent) other rights. The natural right to liberty, for example, implies a right to self-government or the possibility of justifying the breaking of the compact of trust with governors in the political order. Hence, political self-determination is derivative of a natural right.

Locke maintained that man is a creature possessed of reason. What reason knows clearly—by the "light of nature"—is what is necessary. Among the things known in this way is the law of nature. And what we know when we reason according to the law of nature is something about the very nature, or essence, of man. In particular, we know that to *be* a man includes certain inalienable rights. Such rights can, therefore, never be justifiably ignored. Hence, they serve as fundamental constraints on any moral, social, or political order.

NATURAL RIGHTS: A REVISED THEORY

From the above, it should be clear that a natural right is an entitlement one possesses principally by virtue of being a certain kind of thing, namely, a human being: A natural right is grounded in our nature. Natural rights are best understood, therefore, as metaphysical, as well as moral claims. They are claims about what it is to be, what is included in being, a human being. Though metaphysical, natural rights are not wholly so. They do have serious pragmatic implications bearing on what one can will to do: they possess a profound moral dimension. That is, claims of natural rights are meant to determine the wills of others *always* to regard us in certain specified manners, for example, as entitled to possession of property that is the product of our own labors. To fail to satisfy such a right, that is, to fail to treat the claimant as the kind of being that he is clearly would be irrational. Hence the origin of the compelling character of natural rights: Failure to acknowledge them is a patent absurdity. Natural rights, therefore, always have a claim on us insofar as we are rational social beings. The difficult issue at this point is to determine the nature of this claim.

In discussing rights it is commonplace to distinguish absolute from *prima facie* rights. That is, rights may be construed such that their *exercise* is without limit or constraint: That exercise is never to be denied. This is the way Locke seems at times to have understood natural rights: Their exercise must be respected no matter what other rights or duties conflict with the duties created by natural rights. On the other hand, rights may be construed in more limited terms. It may be held that, where significant duties and/or rights conflict with the duty generated by a right, the claimant of that right has no absolute purchase on what he claims. So, for example, the right to own property—which Locke treated as a natural right—may be, and in practice is, restricted in scope, despite Locke's apparent views to the contrary. One has the right to possess property up to that point where other rights must give way, for example, another's right to property or even to life. In this way natural rights are but *prima facie* in their exercise. Natural rights, like all *prima facie* rights, are difficult to implement.

There is an important sense, however, in which natural rights are absolute.

> Those who have spoken of human rights as universal and inalienable have not intended to assert that the actual exercise of those rights on a given substantive human right may properly be denied or overridden if the force of other morally relevant considerations is stronger in a given situation. What we can *never* do is rule out a human right as a morally relevant consideration.[7]

Thus, natural rights, as was said at the beginning of this section, must always be *acknowledged:* They shall always enjoy a central place in moral reasoning and discourse. As a moral matter, one ought never to fail to consider obligations originating in natural rights when one seeks to determine the morally proper course of action. This is the nature of their claim upon us.

Natural rights, then, may not be absolute constraints on action. For example, I may not have an absolute duty to give my life to save another, say by hurling myself on the proverbial live handgrenade. Nor is it clear that I am morally constrained to refrain from killing another to save a life: I may be justified in killing someone who is trying to murder another. At the same time, though, I am *not* morally free to ignore altogether others' rights to life in trying to determine the proper course of action. There are two points to emphasize here; (a) that those obliged to another because of his natural rights are not bound absolutely to fulfill those duties, since more compelling obligations may bind them;[8] but (b) that natural rights must always be induced in moral discourse as fundamental constraints upon it.

Some considerations concerning the conditions under which rights obtain or fail to obtain are in order next. It has been maintained that only beings of a certain sort have rights. After all, a right is a claim to something. A claim to something, though, entails a choice of that something and someone's ability to realize that choice. Making choices, it seems, is the activity only of a being that can be aware of what it chooses as distinct from itself. Also, the realization of choices entails the capacity to form action in accordance with what is chosen, that is, to act in a reasoned matter. In short, only rational, self-conscious, and free beings have rights. As Professor Engelhardt has put it, only *persons* have rights. Non-persons, including some human beings, he says, have no rights.[9]

I take issue with his conclusion, for it is not adequate to the character of natural rights. Those entitlements that derive from our nature as human beings must always be recognized *since such conditions do not affect our nature*. Infants, children, the mentally retarded, the senile, and the comatose, for example, do not fail—simply as a result of being in such conditions—to possess those natural rights also belonging to a fully competent and rational adult. The senile or retarded, for example, are not non-human, though their capacity to realize that nature may be diminished. Therefore, natural rights can always be claimed, on behalf of others or for oneself. In particular, if some human being (distinguished as a genus from persons, one of the species of human, the other being non-persons) cannot claim his natural rights, one must acknowledge his entitlements nonetheless and claim them as rights for him, since he cannot fail to possess them and we cannot fail to claim them for him. A natural right, then, is a right that obtains for any being in virtue of its being of its kind; a human being with the *capacity* or potential for, if not always the actuality of, rational, self-conscious, free life is entitled to those special freedoms appropriate to that essence. Here, the language of essence enters into our consideration of natural rights. An examination of the different senses of essence reveals dimensions of natural rights which Locke overlooked, and which come to play a central role in understanding the right to health care.

Let me explain what I mean here in terms of a tradition that predates Locke. Following Aristotle, I maintain that essence includes the form of the thing (and sometimes matter). Form, for the present purposes, can be understood as that principle by which it is the kind of thing that it is. This is of course, the formal cause of the thing. Second, the form is the principle toward the realization of which the thing tends. It is the principle of what it is to *become* or *enjoy* the fullness of being that kind. This tending is the final cause. By the formal cause I exist as a man. By the final cause I strive to realize in my life history the fullness of human life.

Natural rights, if we follow Locke are to be understood as those rights included in man's nature by entailment: Natural rights are the necessary conditions for man's essence. But what Locke failed to appreciate is that natural rights take on one of two emphases or aspects, according to the two aspects of essence. The first concerns those conditions for humanity qua formal cause. The second concerns those conditions that permit not merely the existence of humanity but its fulfilment or full realization in each of us: the necessary conditions for humanity qua final cause.

This revision of Locke's theory and the revision of the sense in which natural rights are absolute are important for understanding the various senses of the right to health care.

THE RIGHT TO HEALTH CARE AS A NATURAL RIGHT

A right to health care, I said at the outset, is claimed in order to call attention to a state of affairs perceived to be unjust. The remedy for this injustice is to extend our awareness of the full scope of rights talk and to arrange the world accordingly. What is gained by the former is a recognition that all men have a certain entitlement to health care, independent of their socio-politico-economic status. What is gained by the latter is justice. At issue is the guarantee of comprehensive health services for everyone irrespective of income or geographical location. Failure of the socio-political order to recognize and to secure the exercise of this right would be judged unjust. The logic of this argument is the logic of natural rights.

Before explaining how that is, we must get clear as to what we mean by "health care" and "a right to health care." First, health care usually means *medical* care. But this is not an adequate rendering, since it is also meant to include requirements for good health like nutrition and clean water. (The latter seems already to be recognized as a fundamental right.) I shall not attempt to give a full definition here. Indeed, the concept of health care seems so open-textured as to defy final definition. In what follows, I shall use the term in a broad sense, not in the restricted sense of medical care (though I shall use its medical aspect as my paradigm).

Second, if "health care" is ambiguous, then the term "right to health care" cannot be unequivocal either. There are at least two ways of understanding it. The first sense of the term is that in which "right to health care" means equality of (access to) health care, irrespective of any considerations other than the fact that one is a human being subject to losses of health. Consideration of merit or capacity to pay, and so on, are to be put aside. This sense emphasizes that no one should be deprived of available health care and services. Each is equally entitled to health care resources already available.

The second sense is more penetrating. It suggests that health care of a variety not now available to all ought to be. The second sense of the right to health care can itself be taken in two ways. The first is what I want to call its negative aspect: What is claimed are those conditions of health necessary for survival as a human being. Hence, preventive medicine, cure of (curable) life-threatening ailments (like acute appendicitis), proper nutrition, etc. can be claimed as the right of all men, because in their absence we would not exist at all. The positive aspect of the right to health care is considerably more ambitious in scope than the negative sense. Under this rubric are claimed those facets of health care that *enhance* human life and do not simply or exclusively permit or maintain human life. It is not clear to me what exactly is to be included here. The revisionary emphasis of this aspect of talk of a right to health care is, in spite of the vagueness concerning the scope of the claim, a prominent feature in contemporary talk of a right to health care. The two major senses of a right to health care require separate analysis.

The first sense of the right to health care has been analyzed recently by Professor Outka. He begins by pointing out that we are all equal with respect to "being randomly susceptible to (health) crises."[10] That is, the loss of health and the occurrence of disease are by and large not a matter of will but are "acts of God." It makes no sense, then, to treat individuals or classes of individuals as unequal regarding their vulnerability. In particular, "health crises seem non-meritarian because they occur so often for reasons beyond our control or power to predict."[11]

Clearly, though, it is not true of all losses of health that they are non-meritarian. We do know, for example, that smoking is causally linked with the occurrence of various cancers. Outka, though, is aware of this obvious point. "People suffer in varying ratios the effects of their natural and undeserved vulnerabilities, the irresponsibility and brutality of others and their own desires and weakness."[12] Outka goes on, though, to discount this qualification of his position on pragmatic grounds.

> In some final reckoning, then, desert considerations seem not irrelevant to many health crises. The practical applicability of this admission, however, in the instance of health care delivery, appears limited. . . . Would it be feasible to allocate additional tax monies from taxes on alcohol and tobacco to the man with leukemia before [allocating them to] the overweight man suffering a heart attack on the ground of difference of desert? At the point of emergency care at least, it seems impracticable for the doctor to discriminate between these cases, to make meritarian judgments at the points of catastrophe. And the number of people who are in need of medical treatment for reasons utterly beyond their control remains a datum with tenacious relevance.[13]

Surely it is true that we persistently fall prey to the villainies of man and the "fate" of nature. But we also fall prey to our own folly and pernicious lack of self-regard. With respect to the villainies of man against man, it may well be impracticable, even unjust, to discriminate among losses of health. In such cases, the villainy of man may be taken as equivalent to the vicissitudes of nature, the so-called acts of God: We are all equally likely to fall prey to misfortune, whether at the hands of our fellows or of nature. But, unlike Outka, I do want to separate those losses of health whose causes *are* within "our control and power to predict" and consequently, to prevent, from those that are not. It is not at all clear to me that a person who has contracted lung cancer after fifteen or twenty years of smoking is like the five-year-old stricken with acute appendicitis. They are, indeed, not alike. Of the cancer-ridden man we can say, reasonably, that the outcome of his habit was predictable. In some measure, therefore, he was responsible for the results of a habit whose dangers have been well-known for some time. It would be unreasonable, even nonsensical, to say the same of the small child with appendicitis. His affliction is fortuitous.

Now, admittedly, the distinction between deserved and undeserved losses of health may be hard to draw exactly. But the absence of a sharp distinction does not entail the absence of the distinction altogether, as Outka would have it. Hence, those who can for good reasons be said to deserve their losses of health will be excluded from the set of those who have a right to health care *on the basis of the right to equality*. With regard to those cases, then, where losses of health are within our control, a natural right of equality does not apply. Otherwise one can speak in terms of a natural right to equal treatment for losses of health.

The sense of a right to health care just outlined is understood as depending on another right, that to equal treatment. By contrast, the right to health care in the second of our two senses is understood directly as a natural right and not as depending on one. That is, it is claimed that the right to health care is an ingredient in what it is to be a human being. The analysis here differs for each of the two aspects of this sense of the right to health care.

The first aspect is the negative one: a right to health care cast in terms of necessary conditions for one's very survival as human. At issue here is the denial of those conditions. It will help at this point to recall Locke's views on the natural right to health. For Locke, what is entailed by preservation can be claimed as a natural right and it is unjustifiable to take away what tends to the preservation of health. Hence, without at least minimal health care, preservation of health and life itself would be impossible. Any health care delivery system that fails to provide such care to all men would, therefore, be unjust and must be altered according to the conditions necessary for survival as human. It would appear, then, that the negative sense of the right to health care falls within the scope of natural rights. More exactly, the analysis turns on taking the natural right to health care as entailed by man's essence qua formal cause.

The requirements for taking the positive sense of the right to health care as a natural right are different. Recall that under this rubric are claimed those aspects of health care that enhance life and do not merely maintain or preserve it. Thus, the necessary conditions for the realization of the fullness of human life (essence qua final cause) may also be claimed in a right to health care: In the absence of these conditions, we would be deprived of that to which we are entitled to become, by virtue of being the kinds of things we are. Claims of a right to sophisticated medical treatment, for example, corrective surgery for physical defects, can be analyzed in this way.

The analysis so far has proceeded by displaying the nature of the different restraints that claims regarding a right to health care place upon us.

What this analysis shows is that these claims are not homogeneous and that care should, consequently, be taken in distinguishing which sense (or senses) is (are) appropriate in particular cases. One, should, therefore, not expect public policy formed in response to claims to a right to health care to be woven all of a single fabric. In whatever sense the right to health care is taken, however, it is, in its exercise, a *prima facie* and not an absolute right. This important point is apparent upon consideration of conflicts of the duties generated by the right to health care and other rights and/or duties of health practitioners.

In an interesting article, ''Medical Care as a Right: A Refutation,'' Dr Robert Sade takes up this issue. His argument is illustrative in the way it raises problems concerning conflicting exercise of rights. He fails, however, to understand the roots of his own position adequately and so skews his argument badly. Putting that argument back on the right track will help here, by bringing into focus what is at issue in the conflicts of the right to health care with other rights, in particular, conflicts with the rights of health care practitioners.

Dr Sade points to two kinds of conflicts which may defeat the right to health care. The first is a conflict with the natural right of any man to his property, what Locke called the right to Possessions. The second is a conflict with the natural right of freedom. On the first of these two points, as I shall show, Dr Sade's position fails. On the second, his argument can be taken to illuminate a point that should not be ignored by anyone advocating the right to health care (in any of its senses).

Dr Sade's first claim is that a physician's knowledge and skills are within the scope of the natural right to property. He argues as follows:

> In a free society, man exercises his right to sustain his own life by producing economic values in the form of goods and services that he is, or should be free to exchange with other men who are similarly free to trade with him or not. The economic values produced, however, are not given as gifts by nature, but exist only by virtue of the thought and effort of individual men. Goods and services are thus owned as a consequence of the right to sustain life by one's own physical and mental effort. . . . Medical care is neither a right nor a privilege: it is a service that is provided by doctors and others to people who wish to purchase it.[14]

In this claim, however, Dr Sade is incorrect. In answering his argument, I shall depend on Locke, as Dr Sade himself has done in an explicit way.[15]

According to Locke, possessions to which man is entitled as a natural right are the product of *his own individual* labor ''mixed with'' the material of nature.[16] Dr Sade captures this point in the phrase: ''the thought and individual effort of individual men.'' But the thought and effort of the individual practitioner is not produced by him *alone* and nature. On the contrary, it is reasonable to argue that the knowledge and skills of the contemporary practitioner are, without exception, made possible only by virtue of the enormous investment that society has made in the form of expenditures, facilities, and institutions of medical education, research, and care. Hence, it is the individual's labor, *only as mediated by society* and not as that individual's labor alone, that produces the ''property'' of medical knowledge and skills rendered in service to patients. If this analysis is correct, then it clearly follows that the practitioner has no *natural* right to his services as property. At most, he has a civil right to them.

The more significant sort of conflict that could be generated in the wake of a claim to health care would be with the freedom and not the property of the practitioner.

> American medicine is now at the point in the story where the state has proclaimed the nonexistent ''right'' to medical care as a fact of public policy, and has begun to pass laws to enforce it. The doctor finds himself less his own master and more and more controlled by forces outside his own judgment.[17]

This passage shows that Sade is aware of this kind of conflict in his consideration of what he terms the ''outrages'' of Senator Kennedy's proposed legislation.[18] Some of these are serious violations of the natural right to freedom and not to property. An interesting example of this is the bill's provision of forcing health care personnel to locate and practice in specified areas. This situation, if it came to pass, would result in a conflict of the right to health care with the right to freedom. In whatever way the right to health care is understood, it must eventually give way before the demands of freedom, because freedom itself is one of the natural rights, if any is.[19] This conflict is more difficult to resolve. The resolution should turn on which of the two rights in conflict are primary. As a natural right, health care is necessary to preservation of life. Without freedom, it seems, we would be no better off. Similarly, the denial of either or both diminishes the prospects for a full life. Here we encounter an invincible difficulty accompanying natural rights theory: balancing competing claims of natural rights in the simultaneous implementation of them.

The dual emphasis of natural rights has special application at this point. Clearly, a natural right in its aspect as a necessary condition for existing as a human being is logically prior to its aspect as an entitlement to an enhanced or fuller life. Hence, the moral status or authority of the former is greater than the latter. *Ceteris paribus,* the claims of natural rights to an enhanced human life must give way before the claims of natural rights to exist as a human being. Thus, for example, if one claims a natural right to health care in the negative aspect of the second sense and if making good this claim would, say, halve the average income of physicians, then it is morally justifiable, indeed imperative, to provide that health care, since at even half their average wage physicians could exist, quite comfortably, as human beings. . . .

NOTES

1. See, for example, Ruth Macklin. ''Moral Concerns and Appeals to Rights and Duties.'' *Hastings Center Report* 6:5, 31–38, 1976.
2. John Locke, *Two Treatises of Government,* with introduction and notes by Peter Laslett, Mentor Books, New York, second treatise, para. 25, 1965.
3. See ibid., Laslett's introduction, p. 104.
4. For a good discussion of this point, see Leo Strauss. *Natural Right and History,* University of Chicago Press, Chicago, p. 229, 1974.
5. John Locke, op. cit., second treatise, para. 12.
6. Ibid.
7. W. T. Blackstone. ''Equality and Human Rights.'' *Monist* 52, 627–28, 1968, his emphasis.
8. See Richard B. Brandt. *Ethical Theory,* Prentice-Hall, Inc., Englewood Cliffs, NJ, p. 444, 1959.
9. H. T. Engelhardt, Jr. ''The Ontology of Abortion.'' *Ethics* 84, 217–34, 1974.
10. Gene Outka. ''Social Justice and Equal Access to Health Care. *J. Religious Ethics* 2, 11, 1974.
11. Ibid.
12. Ibid., 17.
13. Ibid.
14. Robert M. Sade, ''Medical Care as a Right: A Refutation.'' *New England J. Med.* 285, 1289, 1971.
15. Ibid., 1288.
16. John Locke, op. cit., second treatise, para. 25ff. especially para. 27.
17. Robert M. Sade, op. cit., 1289.
18. Ibid., 1289–90.
19. H. L. A. Hart, ''Are There any Natural Rights?'' *Philosoph. Rev.* 64, 175–91, 1955.

QUESTIONS FOR STUDY AND DISCUSSION

1. Discuss the moral place of business and the professions in the wider society. In your discussion, explain the similarities in the views of Milton Friedman on the social responsibilities of business, the opponent of the ABA House of Delegates proposal on ''drafting'' lawyers to serve the poor, and Robert Sade on the question of access to health care (discussed in the introduction to this chapter and by Laurence McCullough), and contrast these views to those of Melvin Anshen on the social responsibilities of business, the ABA House of Delegates on attorney service to the poor, Monroe Freedman on the right of access to legal services, and Laurence McCullough on the right of access to health care.

2. Does business have a moral obligation to do any of the following: sacrifice profits to avoid price increases, provide special training programs and jobs for the hard-core unemployed, expend resources to minimize environmental pollution (beyond what is required by law), avoid or dispose of lucrative investments in nations that systematically violate human rights? Defend your answers carefully.

3. Explain George Sher's argument in favor of preferential treatment. It may be argued against Sher's position that especially competent members of groups that are given preferential treatment will suffer from the reinforcement of stereotyping, that is, it will be assumed of all members of these groups that they have the positions they have because they are black, female, and so on. Offer your own evaluation of this objection, and say whether and why you think the objection is or is not strong enough to overcome Sher's argument in favor of preferential treatment of members of groups that have been discriminated against.

4. It is sometimes argued that preferential treatment of women and minorities gives rise to a vicious logical circle. That is, if we must discriminate in favor of women and minorities now because we discriminated in favor of white men in the past, we shall have to discriminate in favor of white men in the future, and on and on the circle goes. Offer your own evaluation of this argument against preferential treatment of women and minorities.

5. Offer your own evaluation of the ABA House of Delegates' suggestion that private-practice attorneys be required to render service to indigent clients. It has been suggested that physicians should be required to spend several of their early years in practice in areas where there are currently physician shortages (e.g., rural and inner-city areas). How might someone argue for such a requirement? What are the most serious objections to such a requirement? In your considered judgment, could such a requirement be morally justified? Defend your answer.

6. Using the readings in this chapter as resources, explain as thoroughly as you are able the case for and the case against advertising by professionals. In your considered judgment, should professionals (e.g., physicians, lawyers, psychological counselors) advertise? If not, why not? If so, to what extent? If you place any limits on advertising, explain why.

7. Using the readings in this chapter as resources, develop your own view on whether people have a natural right to health care. If you say people do not have such a right, say why. If you say people do have such a right, what does this right include (e.g., a right to emergency life-saving treatment, a right to the best care currently available, etc.)? Anticipate and respond to the strongest objection to your view.

8. Using the introduction to this chapter as a resource, develop and defend your own position in support of or against allowing contingency fees for attorneys. As part of the defense of your position, invent a case (make it as realistic as possible) to help support your position. Anticipate and respond to the strongest potential objection to your view.

CASE: PREFERENTIAL HIRING

The mathematics department at a large state University advertised a position for an assistant professor with a specialization in set theory. Ninety-eight applications were received. The department search committee selected ten of the applications as outstanding and brought them to the full department to generate a short list of candidates for on-campus interviews. Of the ten applicants, three were selected to visit on campus for two days each, during which time each would teach an undergraduate class and read a professional paper. The three finalists consisted of two white men and a black woman. The candidates came to the university over a period of two weeks. One of the white men taught poorly and presented a mediocre paper. The other two candidates taught equally well and presented equally interesting professional papers. The field was narrowed to these two.

The department looked very closely at the professional credentials of each of the two finalists. The white man had gone to a highly prestigious graduate school, and had finished his work with a 4.0 grade-point average. The black woman had gone to a slightly less prestigious graduate school and had finished her work with a 3.97 grade-point average. The white man had published five articles in international journals. The black woman had published three articles in comparable journals. Both candidates had equally active and interesting research programs under way.

The chair of the search committee suggested that since the white man's credentials were slightly superior to those of the black woman, the former candidate deserved to get the job. But the department chair argued that the black woman was obviously extremely well qualified for the position and, since they had no blacks and few women in the department, they should hire her. He added that the slight edge the former candidate had might well be accounted for on the basis of traditional discrimination against blacks and women and that the latter really deserved the job. Another member of the department argued against the department chair that race and sex are improper criteria to use in deciding who should be hired. But a fourth member argued that given that both candidates were highly qualified, considerations like sex and race are entirely appropriate criteria to consider. He went on to point out that this woman would provide a good role model for blacks and women who might not otherwise consider scholarship in mathematics as a career. A fifth member of the department walked out of the meeting, furious. She felt that using sex and race as criteria against the white man was completely unfair to him.

1. Is it morally wrong for people in charge of hiring to use sex, race, or other "minority" statuses as criteria in a hiring decision? If so, explain why. If not, explain under what conditions you think these criteria may be used in hiring decisions.

2. Assume that the department hires the black woman. Has the white man been treated unfairly? Has the black woman been treated unfairly? Defend your answers; anticipate and respond to the most serious objection(s) to your position(s).

3. It is sometimes argued that there are strong teleological or utilitarian reasons for practicing preferential treatment of women and minorities—for example, that resources will be tapped that have gone untapped in the past, that tensions between the sexes, races, and ethnic groups will be diminished, and so on. But it is also sometimes argued that there are strong utilitarian reasons for avoiding preferential treatment of women and minorities—for example, that the less qualified will be hired (or admitted to professional schools, etc.), leading to inferior services, that preferential treatment increases the tensions between the sexes, races, and ethnic groups, and so on. Construct the strongest utilitarian arguments you can, both for and against preferential treatment of women and minorities. Which of these arguments, in your considered judgment, is the stronger one? Explain your answer.

CASE: CARE FOR THE UNINSURED

Manuel C. had grown up in a poor suburb of Los Angeles that was riddled with crime. After dropping out of high school, he had taken work as he could find it, sometimes in construction, sometimes as a migrant on California farms. In the summer of 1985, Manuel found clean-up work with a local construction company. He was paid "under the table" by the supervisor so the company could avoid paying standard benefits for him, like workmen's compensation. Manuel was happy to have the work; and as a healthy young man of twenty-two, he never thought about not having any medical insurance.

One day, Manuel was involved in an accident that broke a number of bones in his foot. The supervisor took him to the emergency room and paid to have his foot taken care of. Manuel was grateful for the help, but he would be unable to work for several months. A few nights later, Manuel went out with a group of unemployed friends from his neighborhood. They stopped in at an uptown club; after several hours, they were leaving when two of Manuel's friends got into an argument with a group of young men from a neighborhood near their own. On the street in front of the club, the argument grew more heated, and one of Manuel's friends drew a knife. A fight broke out, and when it was over, Manuel had been stabbed seven times. The police had been called, and when the young men heard the sirens, they fled, leaving Manuel on the sidewalk, conscious, but bleeding profusely. The local ambulance service was called. The ambulance driver called the nearest hospital. It was a private hospital, however, and they refused to accept Manuel because he did not have private insurance. The ambulance driver called the next nearest hospital, but was told the same thing. After trying a total of four local private hospitals, the ambulance driver headed for the nearest public hospital, which was downtown, twenty minutes away. Manuel was taken into emergency surgery, but the staff was unable to save him. The head surgeon was extremely upset. He said that had Manuel been taken by any of the local hospitals, he could have survived.

1. Do private, for-profit hospitals have a moral right to refuse to accept patients without private insurance? Should private, for-profit hospitals be required by law to accept emergency patients who have no insurance? Defend your answers; anticipate and respond to the most serious objections to your positions.

2. Should individuals who do not carry private insurance receive the same care as those whose insurance can pay for that care? Defend your answer; anticipate and respond to the most serious objection that might be brought against your view.

3. Should health care providers refuse to take positions with private hospitals that will not provide emergency care to the uninsured? Defend your answer; anticipate and respond to the strongest objection that might be brought against your position.

CASE: DOCTORS PUNISH LAWYERS

On June 6, 1986, papers across the United States ran a story headlined: ''Some Doctors Now Refusing to Treat Malpractice Lawyers and Their Families.'' Attorneys who make their living by suing doctors may discover it's easier to get through medical school than to find a physician to treat them.

Attorneys and medical experts are not calling it a trend yet, but they agree that many doctors are refusing to care for malpractice lawyers and the climate is right for others to follow suit.

The most concerted effort, described by some as a boycott, is in rural Brunswick, a paper mill town in south Georgia where the six obstetricians have refused to treat the wives, employees and families of several attorneys who have sued them or are aggressive in the field.

''It's obviously a sign of the times,'' explained Dr. Henry Flournoy, a Brunswick obstetrician. ''This is a desperate sort of thing. We don't like doing it. We just don't have a choice. Maybe if this gets around, other doctors will think about it.''

The decision demonstrates what can happen when the Hippocratic oath, an ethical pledge of patient care, runs headlong into a distrust of attorneys and fear of a lawsuit.

Although the Brunswick obstetricians consider their move an act of desperation, they predict other doctors may do the same to get attorneys and burgeoning malpractice premiums off their backs.

Malpractice premiums for Georgia obstetricians cost $35,000 annually and are expected to increase about fifty percent this year.

Trial attorneys acknowledge that doctors are in an insurance bind, but say they are reacting hysterically and out of spite.

''I would call it a deep-seated resentment on the part of physicians. . . . They just can't stand the concept of being held accountable to mere mortals,'' said Chris Searcy, president-elect of the Academy of Florida Trial Lawyers.

For many years in Florida, some doctors have turned down certain attorneys and their families as patients. At one point in the late 1970s, Searcy said a group of about 50 physicians in Palm Beach County drew up a list of despised attorneys and their families whom they would not treat. The list included Searcy.

Miami attorney J. B. Spence, a high-profile malpractice specialist, said his family has been refused medical treatment by several Dade County doctors even though he never has sued them.

Spence said when his son, John, injured his knee three years ago in a sporting accident, he was turned away from the first hospital emergency room. ''The doctor there said, 'I don't want to treat him, his name is Spence.' ''

Today some of the state's most active malpractice attorneys say they have had trouble finding doctors to treat them or their families.

The problem has spread and intensified.

Some state and national medical spokesmen believe the Brunswick doctors' action could be a signal to attorneys that the medical adage ''heal thyself'' might eventually apply to them.

Alex Beasley/KNT News Service, *Baton Rouge State Times*, 3 June 1986.

The prospect is alarming, said attorney Amanda Williams, one of the lawyers blacklisted in Brunswick. "If every doctor would take that position, then attorneys would have to think twice before they represent a client because they might not be able to find a doctor themselves. It could have a chilling effect on the public," she said.

Williams, who gave birth to her third child three months ago, had to drive nearly one hundred miles to Savannah for the delivery. Her pregnant law clerk also has been refused obstetrical care, and the wives of three other lawyers in Brunswick may face the same problem.

Although Williams never has sued Flournoy, the doctor said he refused to treat her as a defensive measure because he considers her one of the town's most aggressive malpractice attorneys.

Flournoy has been sued four times in his twelve years of practice, and two of the suits still are pending. He said he could not risk another lawsuit. He is afraid of being tagged a high risk and dropped from his insurance company. If he is unable to get insurance, he cannot practice at the town's only hospital because it will not grant privileges to doctors unless they carry $1 million of malpractice coverage.

So far the doctors' stand in the town of 17,000 has been directed mainly at attorneys who have sued them, but they are considering expanding the action to other personal injury lawyers, said Dr. Carl Dohn, Jr.

"We take it real personally when we get sued," he said, adding that the decision not to treat the attorneys was easy for him. "We didn't see any way at all to trust each other when we already were adversaries. If there is an attorney who is causing some problem for a doctor, he doesn't have to treat him. In the U.S. a private physician can refuse to take care of anyone he doesn't want to care for."

The Medical Association of Georgia is not taking a position on what the doctors have done, but spokeswoman Sherry Waronker said she could see others in the state following the example "because of the climate here."

That feeling is shared by the American College of Obstetricians and Gynecologists.

"I'm sure there are other doctors who may think this is the thing to do. They are very frustrated," said spokeswoman Laurie Hall. "But the problem can't be pinpointed to lawyers or insurance companies. It's broader than that."

If letters to Flournoy are any indication, doctors nationwide do indeed believe not treating malpractice attorneys is the way to go.

"I've got a stack of fan mail about eight-inches thick, about eighty percent of them from doctors from California to Maine," he said. "We are sort of regarded as the Don Quixote of the times."

1. Are physicians morally entitled to treat only those they choose to treat? Defend your answer carefully; anticipate and respond to the strongest potential objection to your view.

2. Are the physicians mentioned in this case morally justified in refusing to treat malpractice attorneys and their families? Defend your answer carefully; anticipate and respond to the strongest potential objection to your view.

3. Suppose a person in a small town has a reputation for bringing legal suits. Would the physicians in that town be justified in refusing to treat this person? Defend your answer carefully; anticipate and respond to the strongest potential objection to your view.

SELECTED BIBLIOGRAPHY

America, Richard F. "Affirmative Action, Redistributive Ethics." *Journal of Business Ethics* 5:1 (1986): 73–77.

Anderson, H. B. "Public Lawyers Group Gives Poor Defendants Big-Firm Advantage." *Wall Street Journal,* 21 September 1977, p. 1.

Arras, John D. "Health Care Vouchers for the Poor." *Hastings Center Report* 11:1 (1981): 29–39.

———, and Andrew L. Jameton. "Medical Individualism and the Right to Health Care." In *Intervention and Reflection: Basic Issues in Medical Ethics,* ed. Ralph Munson, pp. 462–71. Belmont, CA: Wadsworth, 1979.

Auerback, Jerold S. *Unequal Justice: Lawyers and Social Change in Modern America.* New York: Oxford University Press, 1976.

Barry, Brian. *The Liberal Theory of Justice.* Oxford: Clarendon, 1973.

Bayles, Michael D. "Compensatory Reverse Discrimination in Hiring." *Social Theory and Practice* 2 (1973): 301–12.

Beauchamp, Dan E. "Public Health and Individual Liberty." *Annual Review of Public Health* 1 (1980): 121–36.

———. "Public Health as Social Justice." *Inquiry* 13:1 (1976): 3–14.

Bell, Derrick A. "Black Students in White Law Schools: The Ordeal and the Opportunity." *University of Toledo Law Review* 1970 (1970): 539–58.

Blackstone, William T., and Robert D. Heslep, eds. *Social Justice and Preferential Treatment.* Athens: University of Georgia Press, 1977.

Boxill, Bernard. "The Morality of Preferential Hiring," *Philosophy and Public Affairs* 7:3 (1978): 246–68.

Buchanan, Allen E. "The Right to a Decent Minimum of Health Care." *Philosophy and Public Affairs* 13: (1984): 55–78.

Cheatham, Elliott E. *Cases on the Legal Profession,* 2nd ed., pp. 126–39. Brooklyn, NY: Foundation Press, 1955.

Childress, James F. "Who Shall Live When Not All Can Live?" *Soundings* 53 (1970): 339–55.

Cohen, Marshall, Thomas Nagel, and Thomas Scanlon, eds. *Equality and Preferential Treatment: A "Philosophy and Public Affairs" Reader.* Princeton, NJ: Princeton University Press, 1977.

Daniels, Norman. "Fair Equality of Opportunity and Decent Minimums: A Reply to Buchanan." *Philosophy and Public Affairs* 14:1 (1985): 106–10.

———. "Health Care Needs and Distributive Justice." *Philosophy and Public Affairs* 10:2 (1981): 146–79.

———. *Just Health Care.* Cambridge: Cambridge University Press, 1986.

———. "The Right to a Decent Minimum of Health Care." *Philosophy and Public Affairs* 13 (1984): 55–78.

———. "Rights to Health Care: Programmatic Worries." *Journal of Medicine and Philosophy* 4:2 (1979): 174–91.

Dolenc, Danielle A., and Charles J. Daugherty. "DRGs: The Counterrevolution in Financing Health Care." *Hastings Center Report* 15:3 (1985): 19–29.

Fisk, Milton. *Ethics and Society: A Marxist Interpretation of Values.* New York: New York University Press, 1980.

Frankel, Marvin E. *Partisan Justice.* New York: Hill and Wang, 1980.

Fullwinder, Robert K. *The Reverse Discrimination Controversy: A Moral and Legal Analysis.* Totowa, NJ: Rowman and Littlefield, 1980.

Goldman, Alan H. *Justice and Reverse Discrimination.* Princeton, NJ: Princeton University Press, 1979.

Gray, Bradford, ed. *For-Profit Enterprise in Health Care.* Washington, DC: National Academy Press, 1986.

Greenawalt, Kent. *Discrimination and Reverse Discrimination.* New York: Knopf, 1983.

Gross, Barry R., ed. *Reverse Discrimination.* Buffalo, NY: Prometheus, 1977.

Held, Virginia. "Reasonable Progress and Self-Respect." *Monist* 57:1 (1973): 12–27.

Katz, Michael. "Black Law Students in White Law Schools—Law in a Changing Society." *University of Toledo Law Review* (1970): 589–606.

Kaufman, Andrew J., ed. *Problems in Professional Responsibility,* chap. 8. Boston: Little, Brown, 1976. *Supplement,* 1979.

MacKinnon, F. B. *Contingent Fees for Legal Services.* Chicago: Aldine, 1964.

Marks, F. Raymond. *The Lawyer, the Public, and Professional Responsibility.* Chicago: American Bar Foundation, 1972.

Meyers, Diana T. *Inalienable Rights: A Defense.* New York: Columbia University Press, 1985.

Miles, Steven H., and Timothy J. Crimmins. "Orders to Limit Emergency Treatment for an Ambulance Service in a Large Metropolitan Area." *Journal of the American Medical Association* 245 (1985): 525–27.

Newton, Lisa. "Bakke and Davis: Justice, American Style." *National Forum* 58 (Winter 1978): 22–23.

Nielsen, Kai. *Equality and Liberty: A Defense of Radical Egalitarianism.* Totowa, NJ: Rowman and Allanheld, 1985.

Note. "Advertising, Solicitation, and the Professional's Duty to Make Legal Counsel Available." *Yale Law Journal* 81 (1972): 1181–1208.

Nozick, Robert. *Anarchy, State, and Utopia*. New York: Basic Books, 1974.

Purdy, Laura M. "In Defense of Hiring Apparently Less Qualified Women." *Journal of Social Philosophy* 15:2 (1984): 26–33.

Rescher, Nicholas. "The Allocation of Exotic Medical Lifesaving Therapy." *Ethics* 79:2 (1979): 173–80.

———. *Distributive Justice*. Indianapolis, IN: Bobbs-Merrill, 1966.

Rawls, John. *A Theory of Justice*. Cambridge, MA: Harvard University Press, 1971.

Sandel, Michael. *Liberalism and Its Critics*. New York: New York University Press, 1984.

Schwartz, Robert L. "Teaching Physicians and Lawyers to Understand Each Other." *Journal of Legal Medicine* 2 (1981): 131–49.

Sheldon, Mark. "Ethical Issues in the Cost-Containment of Modern Medicine." *Urban Health* 13:8 (1984): 25–48.

Shelp, Earl E. *Justice and Health Care*. Boston: D. Reidel, 1981.

Sher, George. "Reverse Discrimination, the Future, and the Past." *Ethics* 90:1 (1979): 81–87.

Siegler, Mark, and Harry Schwartz. "Treating the Jobless for Free: Do Doctors Have a Special Duty? A Debate on Professional Responsibility." *Hastings Center Report* 13:4 (1983): 12–14.

Smith, Reginald H. *Justice and the Poor*. New York: Scribner's, 1919.

Stewart, Potter. "Professional Ethics for the Business Lawyer: The Morals of the Marketplace." *Business Lawyer* 31 (1975): 463–68.

Taylor, Paul. "Reverse Discrimination and Compensatory Justice." *Analysis* 33:4 (1973): 177–82.

Wasserstrom, Richard A. "A Defense of Programs of Preferential Treatment." *National Forum* 58 (Winter 1978): 15–18.

Wexler, Stephen. "Practicing Law for Poor People." *Yale Law Journal* 79 (1970): 1049–67.

Winslow, Gerald R. *Triage and Justice: The Ethics of Rationing Life-saving Medical Resources*. Berkeley: University of California Press, 1982.

11

CHARACTER, REGULATION, AND TRAINING

The issue of professional virtue or moral character in professional life has not been discussed as frequently as have been questions of morally right and wrong actions and practices in the professions. The first three readings in this last chapter take up the issue of professional virtue.

The concept of virtue reaches back to the Greek concept of *arete,* meaning 'excellence' in characteristic or trait. The Greeks used the term *arete* to refer to excellence in objects as well as in persons. Consider, for example, a knife. A knife has a certain work (*ergon*) or job to do, namely, to cut. For a knife to do its work well, it must have a certain excellence (*arete*), namely, sharpness. A sharp knife, then, has the trait or characteristic or excellence that allows it to cut well. An excellence in a thing is thus a condition of the thing that "makes the work of that thing be done well."[1]

Notice that understanding virtue or excellence this way requires that one know the proper function of a thing. Although identifying a proper function for objects like knives is a rather easy business, when we get to living things, the issue can become much more complex. It is commonly held, however, that the work (*ergon*) of living beings is to live well. Thus, excellence in a living being will consist in those traits or conditions of a thing that allow it to live its life well or to flourish. But in order to know what it means for a living being to live its life well or to flourish as a being of that kind, we have to know something about the life of that kind of being. Thus, the characteristics that allow a plant to flourish will be importantly different from those that allow a nonhuman animal to flourish. And traits that make for properly *human* flourishing will be different again, and far more complex, because characteristically human lives are lives that involve a great variety of roles. Thus virtue or excellence in the human being will consist in characteristics that contribute to flourishing as human beings as such, as well as characteristics that allow the person to do well what is required for "good work" in his or her various roles.

In chapter 3, we raised the issue of role differentiation in professional life (i.e., of the professional's placing the values pursued by his or her profession above the requirements of ordinary morality) and one of the questions running through this book has pertained to this apparent gap between professional and ordinary morality: Is the professional justified in laying aside the strictures of ordinary morality because of his or her professional role? A similar question arises in the ethics of professional virtue. That is, it sometimes seems that certain professional roles may require that their occupiers have certain traits of character that we find morally undesirable or, as it were, vicious, when thought about from the point of view of ordinary morality or what we generally consider morally virtuous in the human being as such. The readings from Andreas Eshete and Bernard Williams raise this issue in their discussions of character in law and politics. Eshete suggests that our adversarial legal system fosters morally unsavory characteristics in attorneys. And he argues that the character traits fostered by our adversarial legal system also impair the lawyer's capacity to function in at least one important way, namely, as a political representative in seeking changes in the law.

Bernard Williams' article is in many ways reminiscent of Thomas Nagel's article on ruthlessness in public life (chap. 3). But whereas Nagel concentrates his discussion on the morality of actions and practices in public life, Williams concentrates his discussion on the question of the politician's character. Williams holds that for the politician to function well, he or she must sometimes get ''dirty hands,'' that is, do things that are, in Williams' language, ''morally disagreeable.'' To use the language of chapter 1, Williams has in mind violating or laying aside certain deontological values for the achievement of good political ends—the kinds of value that we think morally conscientious people would be disinclined to set aside. Although Williams concedes that it is sometimes necessary for politicians to do this, he argues that we should be reluctant to appoint to office leaders who are too easily willing to dirty their hands to bring about even the most desirable of political ends. A politician's character matters, according to Williams, because politicians too willing to dirty their hands in justifiable cases possess characteristics that may allow them to do morally reprehensible things in unjustifiable cases. Thus, for example, the politician who finds it too easy to mislead the public for the sake of national security is likely to find it too easy to appeal to national security to cover unnecessary deceptions or too easy to mislead the public for the sake of his or her own personal gain.

Both Eshete and Williams point to features of institutional systems that tend to select for persons with morally questionable character traits and/or that encourage the nurturing of character traits that may lead them to be morally inadequate in certain contexts or to act in morally unjustifiable ways. Although Eshete and Williams concentrate on legal and political systems, the question they ask about the fostering of traits can (and needs to be) asked of other occupations. What characteristics, for example, does health care provision select for and foster in its practitioners? What characteristics does counseling or education or business or journalism select for and foster in its practitioners? Are any of these characteristics in any way morally troubling?

Eshete and Williams raise the question of the influence of professional life on moral character. William May, on the other hand, suggests a short list of the characteristics professionals (particularly consulting professionals) should cultivate. May also addresses the question of the enforcement of professional standards, which, in its turn, raises the question of the value of professional codes.

The question of the nature and value of professional codes of ethics is addressed by John Kultgen and Norman Bowie. Kultgen frames his discussion in terms of what he takes to be a number of myths that are captured in what he calls ''the ideology of the professions'', and he suggests that professional codes all too often function to promote or protect the interests of a profession and its members rather than the interests of those served by the profession. He goes on, however, to make some interesting and useful suggestions for how professional codes might be reformed to rid them of purely self-serving provisions, and how they might add provisions more helpful to professionals in resolving hard moral questions.

Bowie suggests that effective codes of ethics in business can serve as an alternative to government regulation. He also suggests, however, that if a code of business ethics is to be more than "window dressing," its provisions must be enforceable and enforced. Bowie's remarks on this are reminiscent of Peter French's article on the crash of the DC-10 (chap. 8). McDonnell-Douglas had a quality control system, but it was not rigorously enforced: the result was that 346 people died in a single crash. Such failures in conscientiousness invite stiffer government regulation of business (and professions more generally). Codes that are enforced (either by officials within corporations or by professional associations) are preservative of self-regulation in business (and professions more generally).

The essays by Kultgen and Bowie point out various problems that can arise with codes of professional ethics. Another kind of problem is one that commonly arises in codes of government ethics, namely, the problem of being painfully narrow in focus by dealing virtually exclusively with questions of conflict of interest in financial matters. Such codes are poor codes because they have little or nothing to say by way of guidance in morally troubling cases that arise in professional life, cases that involve conflicts between other kinds of moral value.

Despite the ways in which codes can go wrong (and there are other ways as well), as both Kultgen and Bowie suggest, a good code can be useful in raising the quality of services provided. A good professional code will make clear to practitioners what considerations they must keep in mind while practicing within the profession. Consider the American Nurses' Association Code for Nurses (see appendix 1, sample code 3), which makes reference to many of the kinds of virtue mentioned by May, for example, respect for individual rights and welfare, diligence in remaining competent, devotion to public education and the protection of public health, honesty and intolerance of unethical activity. The code itself is unlikely to give an unambiguous answer to a nurse involved in some morally complex case, but it will, at least, make clear what values must be kept in mind when trying to make hard moral choices.

Similarly, the *Workbook and Study Guide for Public Administrators* (the developing ethical guidelines for those in public administration [see appendix 1, sample code 6]) has many of the marks of a good code. Among these marks are: (1) The notion of moral constraints on actions. The central idea here is that no matter how good the consequences a professional might produce from acting in certain ways, there are some actions that are simply morally impermissible. In general, these actions involve violating the rights of persons. (2) Clear recognition of the values of those to be served by the professional. (3) An emphasis on responsibility for one's decisions and actions. (4) An articulation of the virtues or characteristics appropriately expected of professionals, among them: diligence in work and maintaining competence; self-examination, including an awareness of personal biases; fairness in action; assertiveness; trustworthiness; awareness of potential conflicts of duty; action undertaken on the basis of principle; openness to opposing views and to criticism; sincerity/honesty/candor; accuracy/precision in work; commitment; integrity, that is, integrating one's professional activities with one's personal morality; the nurturing of certain attitudes, for example, respect for those served by the practitioner; loyalty; and moral courage.

Chapter 2 raised the question of whether certain occupations should "professionalize" by continuing to take the kinds of steps outlined by Bernard Barber. The article by Bowie in this last chapter points to some of the advantages of having strong professional codes and strong professional societies, two of the marks of professionalization discussed in several of the readings in chapter 2. Professional organizations often function in several ways that tend to elevate the quality of service. In addition to setting standards for professional practice, they draw practitioners together to share resources. Insofar as they enforce professional codes, they function as "watchdogs," working to ensure that accepted standards are met by all practitioners. And they generally encourage increased and continuing education for members of the occupation/profession. Lengthening educational requirements allows practitioners to acquire a deeper understanding of their roles and responsibilities and also provides time for acquiring more and better technical tools for executing those responsibilities. In addition, as leaders in professional associations move training to the university, those preparing for practice receive input from a number of sources that are importantly different in kind, bringing various perspectives to understanding the role of the professional in the wider society. It is also true that strong professional associations that stand behind careful and meaningful professional codes can serve not only to check unethical activity in a profession, but also to provide needed support for conscientious professionals who may be pressured to act unethically or to otherwise cooperate with or overlook unethical activity on the part of others. For example, public administrators are often under pressure to make decisions that will promote the interests of the elected officials under whom they serve but that are not in the public interest. Without a code to appeal to and without a strong professional association to support them, it can be very difficult for public administrators to maintain moral autonomy and resist such pressures, since resistance can involve serious threats to their jobs. The discussion of professional codes, then, leads us full circle—back to the discussion of professions and the value of professionalization with which we began.

Both the first and the last readings in this chapter address the question of preparation for the professions. Eschete points out that preparation for legal practice focuses on preparing students to be zealous advocates of client interests without questioning what legal interests are good to pursue. Attorneys need not take all cases offered to them, and Eshete's remarks suggest that legal education is faulty insofar as it leaves out questions regarding the moral desirability of taking on certain cases.

The concluding selection, by Samuel Gorovitz, asks what makes a good doctor and what should go into the formation of good doctors. As Gorovitz points out, his remarks, motivated by a more general concern about the education of professionals, are applicable beyond the area of preparation for the practice of medicine. Gorovitz suggests that the good doctor (and, by extension, the good professional more generally) is not merely a good technician, but also is a morally sensitive practitioner. He ends with a point that, generalized, is appropriately made as the final point in this book, namely, that professional life is fraught with moral hazards, and only a reflective individual can confront the moral challenges in professional life insightfully. Long ago, in introducing his inquiry into ethics, Aristotle said that we should not expect more precision of an inquiry than that inquiry permits, warning his reader that ethics is not a precise science.[2] In the moral realm, we frequently labor under conditions of uncertainty, and the best we can do often reduces to doing what we can to ensure that our moral judgments are made with great care and with sensitivity to the variety of morally relevant considerations surrounding an issue. As Gorovitz suggests, there will always be vexing moral problems in professional life, and the task in reflecting on those problems is often not so much to solve them once and for all, but to increase the quality of thought that is brought to bear on them. The purpose of this book has been to provide some help with making explicit some of the ethical issues that arise in professional life, and to go some way toward clarifying the considerations that need to be taken into account in dealing with those issues.

NOTES

1. Aristotle, *Nichomachean Ethics,* Bk. 1 chap. 7; Bk. 2, chap. 6, trans. W. D. Ross, in *The Works of Aristotle Translated into English,* ed. W. D. Ross (Oxford: Oxford University Press, 1915).
2. Ibid., Bk. 1, chaps. 3, 7.

CHARACTER

49. Does a Lawyer's Character Matter?*

Andreas Eshete

Lawyers sometimes find themselves in the unenviable position of offering what appears to be a farfetched rationale for their conduct. They say that in performing their professional tasks they are required to act in ways that are morally questionable—for example, vigilantly protecting clients they know to be in the wrong. Yet they claim that in so doing they attain morally important ends, and that there are no better ways in which they could secure these ends. The story sounds disingenuous for we are being told that, at times, good can be accomplished in this profession only by acting badly.

I first indicate how lawyers fall into morally compromising positions. In particular, certain aspects of what lawyers are asked to do, the training that prepares them for their work, the conception governing their professional activities, and the problems they meet in certain areas of legal practice draw them into dubious conduct. I then suggest that recognizing the forces that make lawyers susceptible to morally suspect attitudes and actions does not remove all our worries over the profession. I finally identify legal situations in which it is easier to see that lawyers cannot justifiably engage in squalid conduct. Here lawyers directly encounter issues that arise in other areas of public life, and whose resolution calls for various excellences of character. If lawyers were generally guided by a conception of their role suited to these settings, they might be able to avoid many of the dangers now attending their work.

I

To understand the lawyer's ways, it is useful to notice a few obvious features of the lawyer's work that do not figure in other professional work in which the important responsibilities also involve rendering direct service to individuals. For one thing, the interests that the lawyer serves are not always good.[1] (This is, I think, connected to Hume's thought, which I here leave unexamined, that particular acts of justice are not always good.)[2] In this respect, the lawyer's role is suspect from the start in a way in which, say, the doctor's is not. For generally, unless the doctor uses his skills to serve nonmedical purposes, the interests he protects are unquestionably good. This difference between the doctor's and lawyer's roles is often concealed by characterizing the interests that the lawyer safeguards as the client's legal rights. But the interests

From *The Good Lawyer: Lawyers' Roles and Lawyers' Ethics,* edited by David Luban, (Totowa, NJ: Rowman and Allanheld, 1984), pp. 270–85.

*For a better understanding of the issues discussed in the paper, I am indebted to the participants in the Working Group on Legal Ethics: I am especially grateful to David Luban for insightful criticisms. I owe thanks to Claudia Mills for helpful editorial suggestions. I would also like to thank Richard Warner for conversations on the problems touched on here.

that the lawyer protects may not be legal rights at all. Further, in an unjust legal system a person may not be morally entitled to his legal rights. Even in a just legal system, it is sometimes wrong to exercise one's legal rights. Another way in which the lawyer's position differs from the doctor's is that typically the way in which a lawyer promotes a client's interests has direct consequences on the interests of others. Not infrequently, a lawyer may be able to further the client's interests only by obstructing or defeating the interests of other persons. Unless a doctor works either in a society in which there are grave distributive injustices in medical services or in emergency situations such as wars, famines, and earthquakes, he can provide professional services to a patient without having to do anything that worsens the conditions of other patients. Thus the kind of interests that lawyers are asked to serve and the characteristic ways in which they offer service make them vulnerable to wrongdoing.

Formal education in the law does not prepare lawyers for the moral perils of the profession. Irrespective of its content, the ultimate aim of legal training is to enable the student to become an able advocate.[3] That legal education fosters the skills and attitudes of advocacy may not be evident from a consideration of many of the subjects covered in a law school curriculum. The analysis of statutes or high court decisions is not obviously geared to the extrinsic aim of cultivating the art of advocacy. In the examination of the structure and rationale of legal rules from an economic or historical perspective, the law is treated much like any other academic subject. Yet, even in its more academic dimensions, legal training does not serve the usual aims of scholarship. Students are not encouraged or expected to master the procedures and traditions that define law as an academic subject. Relatedly, law professors do not address their students as future law teachers or scholars. The main object of theoretical and practical instruction in the law is to prepare the student for the quite different role of advocate. Knowledge is important therefore insofar as it serves what adroit advocacy requires above all: the ability to make a convincing case for any side in a dispute. What this sort of learned cleverness does not require is either a developed capacity to judge what is right or a disposition to seek it. Indeed moral insight may get in the way of cleverness and hinder the capacity to determine and carry out the best means to given ends with worldly disregard for whether the ends are worthy or unworthy.

The moral liabilities of the lawyer's work and education are exacerbated by the adversarial conception of the role. Under this conception, the lawyer is required to present the client's case in the best possible light. This in turn requires indifference to the moral merits of the client's interests so that the lawyer's zeal is not tempered by his personal attitude toward the client's cause. The adversarial lawyer is required, moreover, to place the client's interests ahead of the interests of the adversary and of third parties, as well as of public values such as justice. He is required to assume the risk of infringing upon legitimate interests in serving the client's interests. In short, the adversarial lawyer must take sides in social disputes, without being disquieted by the possibility of landing on the morally worse side. The adversarial conception of the lawyer thus transforms the role's unfortunate hazards into its virtues.

Certain areas of legal practice—notably criminal defense—encourage the curious moral stance of the adversarial lawyer. Criminal conviction is a very serious matter. The public censure of one's conduct cannot be reasonably welcomed by anyone. The condemnation is made in an arena open to public view in which wider attention is drawn to a person's failings than in personal rebuke; as a result, the ill effects are more likely to resound throughout an individual's life. And since the person is condemned by the impersonal authorities of the state, who are presumably influenced by personal bias and partiality, condemnation carries a great deal of weight. Besides, the impersonal authorities issuing the verdict are largely ignorant of the details of the life of the condemned and are only marginally concerned with the effects of condemnation on the general course of the individual's life. In criminal conviction, therefore, an individual is censured in a manner that is designed to have wide consequences on his life by persons whose judgment is invested with authority but who know or care little about the effects of their judgment on the individual.

The penalties visited upon those convicted of crimes, even in societies that take pride in describing themselves as civilized, have few defenders. Prison inmates are subjected to treatment that is cruel and humiliating by most standards of decent conduct. So even if we are certain that, in particular cases, the public censure of convicted individuals is deserved, it is hard to see how we can go on to justify exposing them to the treatment accorded in most penal institutions. Nor does the humiliation of the criminally convicted terminate upon completion of the term of imprisonment. Those who have paid the penalties of the law often continue to be deprived of their liberties in such matters as choice of occupation and residence. Criminal conviction thus inflicts deep and long-standing evils on an individual. If the individual convicted of a crime happens to be innocent the evil suffered is, of course, incalculably greater. . . .

Against this background, it is possible to understand how the adversarial lawyer can be reasonably countenanced. In light of the perils of criminal conviction, lawyers need not worry much over the merits of their clients' interests. For, in protecting a criminal defendant, the lawyer can rest assured that he is promoting an individual's worthy aims to remain free and to avoid cruel and degrading treatment. . . . These are compelling reasons for giving special weight to the client's interests.

In sum, then, the general character of the lawyer's work, the nature of legal training, and the rather special problems of criminal defense together encourage and strengthen adversarial attitudes. Indeed, these attitudes continue to inform and guide a lawyer's activities in functions that are removed from the contentious setting of litigation: lawyers serving as advisers, for example, tend to seek arrangements that would avoid litigation against their side or that would place potential adversaries at a disadvantage should litigation transpire.[4]

II

Appreciating the various forces that make adversarial advocacy the pervasive conception of lawyering does not relieve our moral discomfort over the profession. The source of this discomfort can be brought to light by considering a simple and plausible hypothesis in moral psychology that John Rawls formulates.

> When an individual decides what to be, what occupation or profession to enter, say, he adopts a particular plan of life. In time his choice will lead him to acquire a definite pattern of wants and aspirations (or the lack thereof), some aspects of which are peculiar to him while others are typical of his occupation or way of life.[5]

In the proficient performance of the duties of the role, the lawyer cannot altogether avoid doing unsavory acts, acquiring unattractive traits, and developing dubious aspirations. Effective adversarial advocacy on behalf of a criminal defendant demands measures that are unacceptable from a moral point of view. For example, it may not be enough to show that the defendant has some worthy aims or that the prosecutor has not met the burden of proof: the lawyer may have to deliberately convey the impression that the client is completely innocent of wrongdoing; the lawyer may conclude that it is crucial to discredit an opposing witness whose testimony is known to be truthful, or to be less than forthright about information damaging to the client's case. Protracted engagement in these and similar practices must leave its trace on a person. And since the practices are undertaken as part of an accepted and socially rewarded professional calling, there is little to encourage the lawyer either to retain character traits contrary to these actions or to resist the cultivation of traits corresponding to them. A firm and settled disposition to truthfulness, fairness, goodwill, and the like would thwart the lawyer's capacity to do his tasks well. To excel as a lawyer, combative character traits such as cunning are most beneficial. In this way, the conduct required of an adversarial lawyer gradually produces undesirable features on his character.

The moral damage to character that lawyers in time tend to sustain in executing their important professional tasks can vary in degree and kind. Persons of good character who resort to the shady means of their trade while managing to maintain a lively picture of the justified, ultimate aims of their vocation will no doubt regret their infidelity to truth and justice as well as their unfairness to particular individuals. Remaining attached both to the ultimate aspirations of their office and to their good character, they cannot serenely undertake the everyday tasks that seem to go against their own personal and social ideals. Such persons would suffer the strain born of the knowledge that living fully and well the kind of life that they have chosen cannot yield a life that is of a piece: Their moral integrity is constantly imperiled. Others who have less self-mastery and a less firm attachment to ideals are more likely to lose sight of the more distant justifying aims of the profession. Instead, they shift their attachments to more immediate goods such as the wealth and status with which society rewards the successful exercise of their combative skills. Still different lawyers may acquire unworthy aspirations: They prize the acts of cunning, manipulation, and humiliation for their own sake. For them, the satisfactions of the profession consist in the enjoyment of the spectacle of others being subject to their power.

I do not, of course, mean to suggest that adversarial lawyers can be neatly classified into the three groups. What is outlined is a rough and crude classification of types of character that could be acquired upon entering the adversarial role. Accordingly, it is possible that a lawyer in his professional life would progress through the different types or oscillate between types at different stages of life. It is clear, for example, that the first type of character is unstable. Nagging feelings of regret and self-contempt may inhibit these lawyers' adversarial instincts. And since succumbing to these feelings might be entirely incapacitating, they may react by retreating from the ideals that endanger them. Such lawyers may decide to throw themselves into the adversarial role, switching their allegiance to its social rewards. Nor are inner collision and instability excluded by the other types of character. For instance, self-deception could arise in the second type of character as a result of what might be called the "halo effect."[6] The halo effect is produced when a person makes himself believe that worldly success in a profession or a way of life is a sure sign of success in other dimensions that are less accessible to public appreciation and appraisal.

An objection to this grim portrait of how a lawyer's conduct affects his character might be mounted by challenging the psychological hypothesis on which it rests. Conceding that effective adversarial lawyers have to engage in shabby conduct, one may nevertheless deny that their professional conduct shapes their personal attitudes and aspirations. It might be suggested that once lawyers step out of the legal sphere, they resume their ordinary personal character.[7] . . . In short, character is screened from professional conduct. Now, for such screening to be possible, lawyers must adopt a rather strange attitude toward their work: They must see what they do professionally as a form of acting. And there are, of course, aspects of the lawyer's work that lend themselves to a portrayal of the lawyer as actor. Effective adversarial representation can require self-identification with clients and their plight. To win the sympathies of those sitting in judgment, it may be essential for lawyers to enact what they have identified with in imagination. The element of performance is highlighted by the fact that stylized display of the lawyer's combative and persuasive skills—including those involving cunning and deception—is institutionally taught and openly practiced.

Notwithstanding the part that pretense plays in advocacy, the conception of the adversarial lawyer as actor and the division between personal character and professional conduct that it yields is unconvincing. It is true that theater can exert deep and lasting influence on our emotions and beliefs. In a particular performance, we sympathize and empathize with some of the characters while being repelled by others. If the characters are in conflict, we may even find ourselves taking sides. Still, a sharp gulf separates us from a stage performance: There is no decision we can make or action we can take that would alter the characters' fate. And it is in just this crucial respect that the lawyer's representation departs from the actor's. The lawyer's effort to make a client appear to be innocent or a witness to be a liar is intended to secure judgments that affect the lives of individuals. In the light of the practical consequences of such conduct, the lawyer's claim to be merely acting rings hollow: There is no way in which the official words and deeds can be fastened to the role. And if, barring elaborate self-deception, the lawyer cannot convince himself that the beliefs he asserts and the actions he takes belong to the role, it is hard to know what supports the screen separating self from conduct.

There is another quite different counter to the claim that the lawyer's conduct corrupts his character. In Book III of the *Nichomachean Ethics,* which has the virtue of courage as one of its subjects, Aristotle considers how courage figures in the man of complete virtue and then says: "It is quite possible that the best soldiers may not be men of this sort [i.e., completely virtuous] but those who are less brave and have no other good; for these are ready to face danger, and they sell their life for trifling gains."[8] It is important to be clear on just how the best soldiers fall short of complete excellence. Aristotle does not subscribe to the modern view that some acts of state necessitate viciousness; he does not ascribe vices to his good soldiers. Nor is he suggesting that the best soldiers lack virtue: they have not yielded to their baser desires and passions; they are not deflected from what they judge to be the right course by an infirm will; they do not choose the noble and just only upon subduing unruly desires and feelings. Unlike these types wanting in virtue, persons of moderate virtue do not have dispositions falling outside a mean. Rather, their fault consists in cherishing certain aims too highly. It is their judgment of ends that is unsound, and it is on account of this very defect that Aristotle concludes that they are better suited to certain tasks than men of superior practical judgment. So Aristotle's thought is that those of moderate virtue make the best soldiers because they zealously pursue ends for which those of higher moral vision cannot muster enthusiasm. And the thought appears to rest on an unexceptionable psychological insight: If his gaze were fixed on the sun above, it is unlikely that the man chained down in Plato's Cave could be lured by the sight of the flickering shadows before him.

After the model of Aristotle's good soldier, we can form a more attractive image of the lawyer. In doing disagreeable acts under the adversarial procedure, lawyers are not simply giving in to their baser desires and feelings. Nor are they being steered from right choices and acts because the procedure somehow saps the strength of their will. On the Aristotelian interpretation, the adversarial procedure forces lawyers to lower their sights. By adhering to the procedure, lawyers withdraw their vision from the higher aims of justice, such as whether the decision sought makes good law or whether it results in the wicked receiving the punishment they deserve. Instead, the lawyer's focus descends to the humbler good ends of a client's triumph and an opponent's defeat. These aims, which would not move someone commanding an exalted perspective, draw the zeal of the person with a modest professional calling. And lawyers need not apologize for the modesty of the objectives to which their attention is exclusively devoted. For one might say that the aims of justice as they pertain to disputants in law are in fact humble. Justice here does not aim to bring about some outcome that improves everyone's lot or to establish a more equal social arrangement. Here justice dictates, crudely, that individuals stay out of each other's way, and when their paths cross, it determines who should have the right of way. If the demands of justice in the settlement of legal conflict are of this order, by having his sights lowered the lawyer's energies are not only properly harnessed, they are also thereby rightly channeled.

Although the present image of the good lawyer is faithful to the Aristotelian model of the good soldier, it does not vindicate the lawyer: The trouble is that Aristotle's conception of the good soldier is, I think, seriously defective. In the first place, Aristotle's conclusion that men of less than complete virtue make the best soldiers is based on too narrow a construal of aims. Many actions—such as making a drawing, winning a battle, taking a trip—are comprised of a host of interrelated ends. So, in executing these complex actions, we are not always accurately described as striving after what seems to be our then immediate end: sketching the hand, taking this bridge, crossing that ridge. These immediate ends are pursued as constituents of the larger and more remote aims, though how they fit into the final end may be unclear to the agent or others before, during, or after the project. But if this is so, it will not do to say from some lofty perspective, how nice it is that these soldiers risk so much only to take a bridge or a hill, for it is not their intention to do merely that. Save the vicious and reckless, nobody would willingly face fire to capture Dien Bien Phu with utter disregard for the objectives of the conquest.

If aims are conceived more generously, say, to cover the objectives of a war, it is still not obvious that Aristotle can maintain that those of moderate virtue make the best soldiers by pointing to how inconsequential a war can be: This judgment would be unduly influenced by the importance of outcomes. People take great risks in combat not only when they believe that winning the contest is of paramount importance; they may also sacrifice themselves to help their comrades. Moreover, we can unexpectedly encounter formidable hardships in the pursuit of what we take to be humble ends, and in meeting them we may well have to display great courage. But, then, there is little reason to think that persons of less, rather than more, virtue make the best soldiers. More generally, there is no good deed that can always be better accomplished by a person of less virtue.

The difficulties attending the Aristotelian notion of military courage arise in the conception of the lawyer as combatant. The lawyer's aims cannot be confined to the immediate goal of seeing that the client prevails. Since the lawyer is in a particularly good position to know that this goal is often futile or wrong, he must see it as part of a wider system of aims. To envision the lawyer as always engaged in the single-minded pursuit of the client's triumph, we would have to endow lawyers with a psychology far more impoverished than that of most people. Even if the lawyer's aims are so implausibly diminished, to reach them may require being able to overcome formidable hazards and temptations: for instance, unsparing pursuit of the client's aims may bring grave harm to the lawyer. So in the proper pursuit even of modest aims, the lawyer may need the various excellences of character.

The problems in the conception of the lawyer as combatant are connected to the problems of seeing a legal system, or indeed a legal contest, as a game. Most games are carefully segregated from the moral world. In games, the aims of the activity as well as the proper and improper ways in which they are to be attained are defined by the rules of the game. Within these rules, the players can give free play to their talents, skills, and ingenuity without having to deliberate about the worth of their ends or the moral propriety of their means. Though there may be rational disagreement over how much of morality and which dimensions of it figure in the law, there is little doubt that the law, even in its mundane moments, is not, like a sport or an Aristotelian skirmish, an institution sealed off from moral life.[9] Accordingly, lawyers cannot use the permissible skills of their trade with ruthless efficiency for the sake of the client's triumph without working wrong.

At any rate, if lawyers were to succeed in the unlikely course of fashioning themselves after the Aristotelian soldier, they would rescue their characters from the corrupting influence of professional conduct only at a high price: they would have to be engulfed in their role.[10] The lawyer's personal character cannot then be tainted by his professional conduct because he is practically without a personal character. Whether or not it is worse to be without a personal character than to be saddled with a corrupt one, deprivation of character cannot be an enticing feature of a profession. . . .

III

It is possible to allow that the adversarial lawyer cannot avoid doing damage to his character and nonetheless to deny that this seriously matters. Anyone who is not in the grip of some unworldly perspective cannot fail to recognize that realizing some important social goals compels personal sacrifice. And since lawyers choose their occupation, we are not in the awkward position of having to ask some to sacrifice themselves for the good of others or for the common good. The lawyer's loss of good character is a case of self-sacrifice. . . . I shall suggest a few reasons why it would be bad for lawyers, in particular, to relinquish their good characters. There are significant legal situations in which the adversarial stance of the lawyer is inappropriate and where the combative traits and skills, fitting in that role, are obstacles to performing professional functions well. The lawyer's self-sacrifice of good character would not then be merely the loss of a personal good, but the loss of important public goods as well.

To see how a lawyer's character matters it is important to guard against a narrow interpretation of the purposes of legal action. The object of legal suits is not always to resolve factual disputes between private parties under clear and settled laws. In a wide range of cases—both criminal and civil—litigation is sometimes aimed at bringing about changes in the law. Decisions that result in legal change have far-reaching effects: Their direct consequences are not confined to the parties to the suit. A striking example of this kind of litigation is provided in suits seeking to rectify institutional wrongs such as racial discrimination in schools or official lawlessness and brutality in police departments.[11]

In litigation directed against institutional wrongs, the defendants—the principal of a school or an officer of a police force—may not be charged with or be guilty of intentional wrongdoing. The real target of the suit is the institution that produces structural injustice. And the defendants may have little or no responsibility for establishing or maintaining the institution that brings about the social wrongs. Accordingly, the remedy sought is some form of institutional reform that would bring the institution in line with the public values upheld in the legal system—a remedy that the defendants are not in a position to provide. Similarly, the individuals bringing the suit may not be the victims of the institutional wrong. If the plaintiffs happen to be victimized by the institution, vast numbers of victims may not be parties to the suit. Indeed, in some cases, such as racial discrimination, it would be very difficult to identify those unjustly treated by an institution of the state. Finally, neither the plaintiffs nor the victims may be the actual beneficiaries of the remedies sought in the way of institutional reform. The only possible or fair rectification could consist of forward-looking measures designed to protect persons in the future from the institutional injustice in question.

In legal disputes over institutional wrongs, lawyers cannot maintain their adversarial role. The first problem is captured in a question that Abram Chayes poses:

> [I]n the absence of a particular client, capable of concretely defining his interest, can we rely on the assumptions of the adversary system as a guide to the conduct and duty of the lawyers?[12]

The adversarial lawyer is supposed to take the client's interests as given and to further them zealously in legally permissible ways. But there seems to be no clear or sensible way in which the lawyer representing those seeking to rectify institutional wrongs can follow this procedure. The identities of the parties and the nature of their interests may be difficult to determine, and it is not obvious that the lawyer is in an especially favorable position to make such a determination. Even if the lawyer successfully disentangles these problems, he may find that different parties of those opposed to the institutional wrong suffer different kinds of harms to their interests at the hands of the institution. The lawyer then has to ascertain which of the conflicting interests of the victims should be represented, and this decision cannot be easy or noncontroversial. It would not be reasonable to represent the interests of the most numerous, the most vocal, or the most powerful. A decision among competing interests along these dimensions cannot, for example, be determinate or credible in respect to the interests of future persons. Confronted with these problems, the lawyer cannot sidestep a deliberation on the merits of the interests at stake in the specific institutional wrong he aims to correct, and deliberation cannot go very far without appeal to relevant interest-independent principles.

The lawyer would run into similar difficulties in attempting to strike a partisan posture. In litigation directed at institutional wrongs, there may be deep differences over the reforms desired. For instance, those aspiring to abolish racial discrimination in schools may disagree on whether equal access to schools or equal access to minimally decent education contributes to a more just arrangement.[13] And if it were established that the parents of minority children prefer a decent education to an integrated school, the lawyer would have to consider if the interests of future schoolchildren and future generations as a whole would be served well by racially divided educational institutions. Hence in deciding what institutional reform to advocate, the lawyer does not have ready-made interests to champion. And a responsible decision must look beyond the conflicting interests to the underlying public values of the legal system.

It would be misleading, of course, to think that the lawyer engaged in legal action against institutional wrongs is an officer of the court whose overriding professional goal is to advance the cause of legal justice. Like the judge, the lawyer is independent of the state. And this independence is here especially important since the legal action is taken against the institutions of the state. But unlike the judge, the lawyer is not exempted from the responsibility of representing certain interests. The difficulty is that the lawyer cannot properly discharge these representative duties by adhering to an adversarial role.

Perhaps a better way of understanding the conduct and responsibility of a lawyer acting against institutional injustices would be under the traditional conception of fair political representation. Fair political representation has at least three distinct justifying aims. First, since public decisions promote the interests of some and obstruct those of others, fair representation of all affected by a decision is required to ensure that the interests of those excluded are not disregarded. Second, public decisions are principled, and people seek decisions that best realize the principles to which they subscribe. Fair representation is required to make certain that views that would lead to decisions that better satisfy the shared principles do not go unheard. Third, public decisions must result in practical arrangements that those participating in them can endure. Fair representation is required to guarantee that personal or social circumstances that would make abiding by a decision a severe strain do not pass unnoticed.

An ideal of representation needs to satisfy all three aims. Attention to the first form in isolation creates the risk that the decision reached will favor the strongest interests over the most legitimate. The second aim alone could lead to decisions that are principled only relative to the interests of those who happen to be represented.[14] Without the third, there is the danger that the decisions reached cannot be followed with ease by those to whom they are addressed. For example, an impartial, principled policy of nationalization in land reform or busing in school desegregation may be impracticable. But the third form of representation by itself may lead to feasible and even harmonious social arrangements that are seriously wrong.

In litigation intended to secure institutional reform, the lawyer should attempt to realize all three aims embodied in the ideal of fair representation. He must see that no important interests that are affected by the decision of the court are excluded from consideration. In arriving at a judgment on the right remedy to plead, the lawyer must find out the considered opinions of those he represents and weigh them carefully. In addition, by seeking the advice and organized participation of interested parties, the lawyer should make sure that the proposed institutional reform would not impose needless psychological and sociological stress on the beneficiaries and others. Even if some of these duties of representation are shared by the attorney for the state, by lawyers representing special interests and, most importantly, by the judge, our lawyer would bear heavy responsibilities. And what it would take to carry them out with excellence may well be difficult to specify, at least in the form of a body of specific rules of conduct. But without going into the details, it is not hard to see that the adversarial lawyer is not well suited to live up to the ideal of fair political representation. A hard-hearted person, armed with entrenched combative traits and perhaps suffering from feelings of self-contempt, cannot be expected either to attend to the interests and ideals of others with sympathy or to follow the dictates of principle with care. If we need someone to represent us well in cases concerning public values, we had better look for a lawyer equipped with different character traits and talents.[15]

Lawyers guided by a conception of their role as political representatives would perform the valuable service of extending the institutional scope of democratic ideals in public life. The importance of the lawyer's office as political representative and the urgency of training lawyers with character traits and talents tailored to this office are more likely to be felt if two general beliefs about modern society are well founded.[16] First, in modern societies many of the basic goods of social life—health; education; transportation; defense from external attack; security against personal injury, unemployment, and the infirmities of old age—are increasingly provided by public institutions. Second, legislatures in modern societies do not afford strategic or fair protection against the invasion of public values by powerful public institutions.

NOTES

1. Richard Wasserstrom draws attention to this feature; he also makes the point, which I discuss later, that the criminal defense lawyer is a rather special case in "Lawyers as Professionals: Some Moral Issues," *Human Rights* 5:1 (1975): 1–24. [See chap. 3, sel. 6, *EIPL*.—ED.] See also David Luban, "The Adversary System Excuse," in

The Good Lawyer: Lawyers' Roles and Lawyers' Ethics, ed. David Luban (Totowa, NJ: Roman and Allanheld, 1984), pp. 83–122.

2. "[I]f we examine all the questions, that come before any tribunal of justice, we shall find, that, considering each case apart, it would as often be an instance of humanity to decide contrary to the laws of justice as conformable to them. Judges take from a poor man to give to a rich; they bestow on the dissolute the labour of the industrious; and put into the hands of the vicious the means of harming both themselves and others." David Hume, *A Treatise of Human Nature* [1739–40], ed. L. A. Selby-Bigge (Oxford: Clarendon Press, 1960), p. 579.

3. I have benefited from the interesting discussion of the limits of legal education in Anthony T. Kronman, "Foreword: Legal Scholarship and Moral Education," *Yale Law Journal* 90 (1981): 955–69; and Robert Condlin, "The Moral Failure of Clinical Legal Education," in Luban, *The Good Lawyer,* pp. 317–49.

4. Luban, "The Adversary System Excuse."

5. John Rawls, *A Theory of Justice* ([Cambridge, MA: Harvard University Press, 1971]) pp. 415–16. The claim that social positions shape the psychological makeup of individuals is a constant theme in the writings of Karl Marx. For an interesting discussion of the theme in Marx's early writings, see Gerald A. Cohen, "Bourgeois and Proletarians," *Journal of the History of Ideas* 29 (1968): 211–20. In his defense of liberty and his arguments for representative government, John Stuart Mill relies on psychological considerations similar to that expressed in Rawls's hypothesis. *On Liberty* [1859], ed. Currin V. Shields (Indianapolis, IN: Liberal Arts, 1956); *Considerations on Representative Government* [1861] (South Bend, IN: Gateway, 1926), p. 62. A clear example of an application of these considerations is found in his *The Subjection of Women* [1869], ed. Sue Mansfield (Arlington Heights, IL: Crofts, 1980), p. 62. A novel and interesting interpretation of Mill that stresses the importance of psychology for his moral views is offered in Richard Wollheim, "John Stuart Mill and Isaiah Berlin: The Ends of Life and the Preliminaries of Morality," *The Idea of Freedom: Essays in Honor of Isaiah Berlin,* ed. Alan Ryan (Oxford: Oxford University Press, 1979), pp. 253–69.

6. The "halo effect" figures importantly in Marx's analysis of alienation and fetishism. Robert Nozick discusses it briefly in *Anarchy, State, and Utopia* (New York: Basic Books, 1974), p. 243n.

7. See Gerald Postema's discussion of what he calls the "Montaigne strategy" in "Moral Responsibility in Professional Ethics," *New York University Law Review* 55 (1980): 63–89; and in Luban, *The Good Lawyer,* pp. 286–314.

8. *Ethica Nichomacea,* trans. W. D. Ross (Oxford: Clarendon Press, 1925), 1117 b 17–19.

9. Lord Devlin considers the analogy between adversarial advocacy and military combat in *The Judge* (Oxford: Oxford University Press, 1979), chap. 3.

10. Engulfment in roles is discussed in Gerald A. Cohen, "Beliefs and Roles," *Proceedings of the Aristotelian Society* 67 (1966–67): 17–34.

11. For excellent discussions of this form of litigation, see Abram Chayes, "The Role of the Judge in Public Law Litigation," *Harvard Law Review* 89 (1976): 1281–1316; and Owen M. Fiss, "The Supreme Court, 1978 Term—Foreward: The Forms of Justice," *Harvard Law Review* 93 (1979): 1–58. Ronald Dworkin remarks on the relevance of this form of adjudication to his theory of law in "Seven Critics," *Georgia Law Review* 11 (1977): 1257–58. H.L.A. Hart suggests that this kind of adjudication is peculiar to American courts in "American Jurisprudence Through English Eyes: The Nightmare and the Noble Dream," *Georgia Law Review* 11 (1977): 969–89.

12. Chayes, "The Role of the Judge," p. 1291.

13. See Derrick A. Bell, Jr., "Serving Two Masters: Integration Ideals and Client Interests in School Desegregation Litigation," *Yale Law Journal* 85 (1976): 470–516.

14. Brian Barry draws attention to principled decisions that are group-relative in a discussion of the right to equal representation in *The Liberal Theory of Justice* (Oxford: Clarendon Press, 1973), p. 136. A detailed examination of interest-relative agreements and their importance to liberal and Marxian political theory is provided in an unpublished essay by Joshua Cohen, "Marxism and Politics: Or, Trouble in Paradise."

15. This is a difficulty for the Leninist revolutionary as well. His austere and combative attitudes may be essential in the struggle to capture state power from the enemy, but quite different character traits are appropriate in relations with comrades in the revolutionary struggle and with citizens in the postrevolutionary state. This is an aspect of the notorious problem of succession in socialist states. I discuss the nature and importance of the various excellences of character in "Character, Virtue, and Freedom," *Philosophy* 57 (October 1982): 495–513.

16. The first belief is so deeply entrenched in sociological thinking—in theories as different as those of Max Weber and Karl Marx—that it is practically a dogma of modern sociology. The second is more controversial because of conceptual unclarity surrounding the notion of representation and important empirical differences among legislatures in different democratic societies. Owen M. Fiss defends both beliefs in "The Supreme Court, 1978 Term."

50. Politics and Moral Character

Bernard Williams

What sorts of persons do we want and need to be politicians? This question, and the broader question of what we morally want from politics, are importantly different from the question of what the correct answers are to moral problems which present themselves within political activity. We may want—we may *morally* want—politicians who on some occasions ignore these problems. Moreover, even in cases where what we want the politician to do is to consider, and give the right answer to, such a problem, it is not enough to say that we want him to be the sort of person who can do that. Since some of the correct answers involve actions which are nonetheless very disagreeable, further questions arise about the sorts of persons who will give—in particular, who may find it too easy to give—those right answers.

It is cases where the politician does something morally disagreeable, that I am concerned with: the problem that has been called that of *dirty hands*. The central question is: how are we to think about the involvement of politicians in such actions, and about the dispositions that such involvement requires? This is not in the first place a question about what is permissible and defensible in such connections; though something, obviously, will have to be said about what it means to claim that a politician has adequate reason to do something which is, as I put it, 'morally disagreeable'.

The discussion assumes that it makes some difference what politicians are like, what dispositions they have. I do not want to stress an individualist picture of political action too much, but I assume that there is something to be said in the moral dimension about the actions of individual politicians. Even someone who denied that might admit, I suppose, that it could make some difference, of the sort which concerns us morally, what politicians were like. Someone who denies all that will probably think that morality has nothing to do with politics at all, and for him the whole area of discussion lapses.

It is widely believed that the practice of politics selects at least for cynicism and perhaps for brutality in its practitioners. This belief, and our whole subject, notoriously elicit an uncertain tone from academics, who tend to be either over-embarrassed or under-embarrassed by moralizing in the face of power. Excited, in either direction, by the subject, they often take rather large-scale or epic examples, such as the conduct of international relations by hostile powers, or ruthless policies which may or may not be justified by history. I will touch marginally on those kinds of issue at the end, but my first concern is more with the simply squalid end of the subject, and with the politician not so much as national leader or maker of history, but as professional. I shall defer the more heady question of politicians being criminals in favor of the more banal notion that they are crooks.

There is of course one totally banal sense of the claim that they are crooks, namely that some break the law for their own advantage, take bribes, do shady things which are not actually illegal for personal gain. This dimension of effort is for the purpose of the present discussion beside the point. It does raise one or two interesting questions, for instance the absence from politics of any very robust notion of professional ethics. Some professions, such as [law and medicine], have elaborate codes of professional ethics: I take it that this is not because their vocation rises nobly above any thoughts of personal gain, but because their clients need to be protected, and be seen to be protected, in what are particularly sensitive areas of their interests. Some areas of business have similar provisions, but in general the concept of a professional business ethic is less developed than that of a professional medical or legal ethic. One might think that politics was concerned quite generally with sensitive areas of the clients' interests, yet even in places where it is recognized that these restrictions govern the activities of doctors and lawyers, the politician's professional conduct is perceived as more like that of the businessman. The explanation of this fact I take not to be very mysterious: roughly, there are several reasons why it is in the interest of most in these professions to belong to a respectable cartel, but in the case of politicians, the circumstances in which they are able to run a cartel are circumstances in which they have little motive to keep it respectable.

How are the morally dubious activities which belong to this, irrelevant, class, distinguished from those which concern our enquiry? Certainly not by the first sort being *secret*. For the first sort are often not secret, and in some cultures are barely meant to be so, it being an achievement calling for admiration that one has stolen extensively and conspicuously from the public funds. Even more

From *Public and Private Morality*, edited by Stuart Hampshire (New York: Cambridge University Press, 1978), pp. 55–73.

obviously, many dubious acts of the more strictly political kind are themselves secret. The point rather is that not all acts done by politicians are political acts, and we are concerned with those that are. Relative to some appropriate account of what the politician is supposed to be up to as a politician, stealing from public funds is likely to count as a diversion of effort. However, it is to be recognized that not all classifications which would be made on these principles by the most respectable northwest European or North American opinion would come out the same elsewhere: thus bribery can be an integral and functional part of a political system. What must count as a political activity anywhere, however, is *trying to stay in office*. There are, needless to say, unacceptable ways of staying in office, and there are among them ways of staying in office which defeat the purposes of the methods for acquiring office (rigging the ballot). But this is a matter of means—the *objective* of staying in office, though it cannot by every means or in every circumstance be decently attained, is itself highly relevant to the business of politics, whereas the objectives of enriching oneself or of securing sinecures for one's family are not.

We shall leave aside the dubious activities of politicians which are not primarily political activities. But since the question we shall be concerned with is primarily what dispositions we want in politicians, we should not at the same time forget the platitude that the psychological distance between the two sorts of activity may be very small indeed. Not every politically ruthless or devious ruler is disposed to enrich himself or improperly advance his friends: the ones who are not are usually morally and psychologically more interesting. But the two sorts of tendency go together often enough, and cries for 'clean government' are usually demands for the suppression of both.

There is another aspect of the subject that I shall mention only in passing: I shall consider the politician as the originator of action, or at least as a joint originator of action, rather than as one who participates in a party or government, or acquiesces, with respect to decisions which he does not help to make. Some of the issues we shall consider apply to those who originate at any level; other larger issues apply only to those who originate at some higher level, such as a president or prime minister or (in the British system) a cabinet minister. This emphasis leaves on one side the question of a politician's responsibility, and hence the view one should take of him, when he agrees with a measure but did not originate it. It also leaves aside the more interesting question of his responsibility when he does not agree with it but acquiesces in it or stays in a position where he is identified with it—what is, in a democratic system at least, the *resigning problem*.

One remark is perhaps worth making here in relation to that problem. Resigning, or again refraining from resigning, cannot be straightforwardly either instrumental or expressive acts. Instrumental considerations of course bear on the issue, as in the classical 'working from within' argument which has kept many queasy people tied to many appalling ventures for remarkably long periods. Yet such decisions cannot, in the nature of the case, be purely and in all cases instrumental, since the decision has a class of consequences which themselves depend on the agent's being perceived as not being entirely consequentialist about it. Among the consequences of the act are some that depend on what it is taken to mean, so that the purely consequentialist agent would be faced, if he fully considered the consequences, with the fact that what he is doing is by its nature something which cannot be adequately thought about purely in terms of its consequences. On the other hand, to view resignation as the mere equivalent of saying 'I agree' or 'I disagree' in a private and uncoerced conversation would be an elementary misunderstanding, entertained only by someone who neglected the difference between a commitment to ongoing political activity, and a one-off example of political expression. It is also, therefore, to neglect the point that for a politician such a decision is, in a substantial and relevant sense, part of his life.

When that point is seen, moreover, it is often seen in the wrong terms: it naturally invites being seen in the wrong terms. For a career politician, resignation is likely to affect the relation of his life to politics altogether. He must consider the decision to resign in the context of a commitment to a political life, and that can of course be read as his attending to his career. No doubt it is true of some in this situation that they are simply attending to their career, but it is important, both for the public and for the politician, to recognize that there is a structural reason why it should be difficult to tell whether that is true or not.

Among political acts are some for which there are good political reasons, as that important and worthy political projects would fail without these acts, but which are acts which honorable, scrupulous, etc. people might, prima facie at least, be disinclined to do. Besides those, there are more, and more insidious, cases in which the unpalatable act seems necessary not to achieve any such clear-cut and noble objective, but just to keep going, or to preempt opposition to a worthy project, or more generally to prevent a worthy project becoming impossible later. What the unpalatable acts may be depends on the political environment; at present we are concerned with a relatively ordered situation where political activity involves at least bargaining and the expression of conflicting interests and ideals. In such a situation a politician might find himself involved in, or invited to, such things as: lying, or at least concealment and the making of misleading statements; breaking promises; special pleading; temporary coalition with the distasteful; sacrifice of the interests of worthy persons to those of unworthy persons; and (at least if in a sufficiently important position) coercion up to blackmail. We are not at this point considering more drastic situations in which there is a question, for instance, of having opponents killed. (I mean by that, that *there is no question of it,* and it would be thought outrageous or insane to mention it as an option. The situation is not one of those in which such options are mentioned and then, all things considered, laid aside.)

The less drastic, but still morally distasteful, activities are in no way confined to politics. That they should seem necessary follows just from there being large interests involved, in a context of partly unstructured bargaining. It is the same, for instance, with a lot of business of the more active variety. But it attracts more obloquy in politics than elsewhere: the use of such means is thought more appropriate to the pursuit of professedly self-interested ends than where larger moral pretensions are entertained. But the fact that there are larger moral pretensions is itself not an accident. Besides the point that some objectives other than the self-interest of the professional participants are necessary—at the limit, are necessary for the activity even to be politics—there is the point that democracy has a tendency to impose higher expectations with regard even to the means, since under democracy control of politicians is precisely supposed to be a function of the expectations of the electorate.

I have mentioned acts, done in pursuit of worthy political ends, which 'honorable, scrupulous, etc. people might, prima facie at least, be disinclined to do'. But, it will be said, if it is for some worthy political objective and the greater good, does not that merely show that it is an act which these honorable people should *not* be disinclined to do? At most, the characteristic which the act possesses is that it is of a type which these people would be disinclined to do if it were not in this interest; and that, it may be said, is irrelevant. But this Utilitarian response either does not get to the question which concerns us, or else gives an inadequate answer to it. It does not get to the question if it merely insists that the otherwise discreditable act is the one, in these circumstances, to be done, and says nothing about the dispositions of the agent, and how his dispositions express themselves in a view of this act. It gives an inadequate answer if it says that the only disposition such an agent needs is the disposition to do what is Utilitarianly right. Even Utilitarians have found that answer inadequate: it is not self-evident, and many Utilitarians agree that it is not even true, that the best way to secure their objective of the greatest happiness all round is to have agents each of whom is pursuing, as such, the greatest happiness all round. Beyond that level of discussion, again, there is the deeper point that moral dispositions other than Utilitarian benevolence may themselves figure in people's conceptions of 'happiness'.

In any case, it is not enough to say that these are situations in which the right thing to do is an act which would *normally* be morally objectionable. That description best fits the case in which an act and its situation constitute an *exception.* We may recall the repertoire, familiar from Ross and other writers, of obligations properly overridden in emergencies. There, the decision is often easy—of course we break the routine promise to save the drowning child, and to doubt it, or to feel uneasy about having done it, would be utterly unreasonable. It is a clear overriding circumstance. While it is not as though the promise or other defeated obligation had never existed (one still has the obligation at least to explain), nevertheless it is quite clearly and unanswerably overridden, and complaints from the disadvantaged party would, once things had been explained, be unacceptable. Of course, not all cases of the straight overriding kind are clear cases of that kind. One can be in doubt what to do, and here there is room for unease. But the unease, within this structure, is directly related to the doubt or unclarity: the question will be 'did I really do the right thing?' If one has an uneasy sense that one may have done wrong to the victim, it is because one has an uneasy sense that one may have done the wrong thing.

Some situations in politics are no doubt of that structure. But the situations I have in mind (of course, as I have said, they are not confined to politics) are of a different structure. In these, the sense that a discreditable thing has been done is not the product of uncertainty, nor again of a recognition that one has made the wrong choice. A sense that something discreditable has been done will, moreover, be properly shared by the victims, and they will have a complaint that they have been wronged. The politician who just could not see that they had a complaint, and who, after he had explained the situation to them, genuinely thought that their complaint was based on a misunderstanding and that they were unreasonable to make it (as one might properly think in the first kind of case) is a politician whose dispositions are already such as to raise our questions in a very pressing form.

I do not have in mind here drastic cases of tragic choice, where one might say that whatever the agent did was wrong.[1] They, though not merely exceptions, are certainly exceptional. The cases we are considering are not just what our normal categories count as exceptions, nor are they of the exceptional kind that reaches beyond our normal categories. Nor, again, need the decision be at all uncertain. It will often be true of these cases that so long as the agent takes seriously the moral frames of reference or reasons which support each of the courses of action, it will not be unclear what he should do. But the clarity in such a case is not that of the vivid emergency exception; nor is it the clarity of the impossible, which can attend the tragic case. It is clear because it is everyday, part of the business: Not too often part of the business, one hopes, but part of the business all the same. If the politician is going to take the claims of politics seriously, including the moral claims of politics, and if he is going to act at anything except a modest and largely administrative level of responsibility, then he has to face at least the probability of situations of this kind. If he shares the highest responsibilities, it is virtually certain that he will encounter them. Below that level, he may perhaps not. He may operate in a very docile and citizenly environment. He may be lucky. He may even have, as a few seem to have, a virtue or a moral cunning which drives such situations away. But it is a predictable and probable hazard of public life that there will be these situations in which something morally disagreeable is clearly required. To refuse on moral grounds ever to do anything of that sort is more than likely to mean that one cannot seriously pursue even the moral ends of politics.

Yet, at the same time, the moral disagreeableness of these acts is not merely cancelled, and this comes out above all in the consideration that the victims can justly complain that they have been wronged. It is undeniable, for instance, that the agent has lied, or deliberately misled them, or bullied them, or let them down, or used them. It may be that when it is all explained, they understand, but it is foolish to say, even then, that they have no right to complain.

It may be said that the victims do not have a right to complain because their relation to the action is not the same in the political context as it would be outside it: perhaps it is not even the same action. There is some truth, sometimes, in this claim. It does apply to some victims themselves involved in politics: a certain level of roughness is to be expected by anyone who understands the nature of the activity, and it is merely a misunderstanding to go on about it in a way which might be appropriate to more sheltered activities. But this consideration—which might be called *Truman's kitchen-heat principle*—does not go all the way. There are victims outside politics, and there are victims inside it who get worst than they could reasonably expect; and in general there are political acts which no considerations about appropriate expectations or the going currency of the trade can in themselves adequately excuse.

I mentioned the 'moral claims' of politics. In some cases, the claims of the political reasons are proximate enough, and enough of the moral kind, to enable one to say that there is a moral justification for that particular political act, a justification which has outweighed the moral reasons against it. Even so, that can still leave the moral remainder, the uncancelled moral disagreeableness I have referred to. The possibility of such a remainder is not peculiar to political action, but there are features of politics which make it specially liable to produce it. It particularly arises in cases where the moral justification of the action is of a consequentialist or maximizing kind, while what has gone to the wall is a right: there is a larger moral cost attached to letting a right be overridden by consequences, than to letting one consequence be overridden by another, since it is part of the point of rights that they cannot just[2] be overridden by consequences. In politics the justifying consideration will characteristically be of the consequentialist kind. Moreover, an important aspect of consequentialist reasoning lies in maximizing *expectation,* the product of the size of the payoff and its probability. Since in the political sphere of action the payoffs are, or can readily be thought to be, very large, the probabilities can be quite small, and the victims may find that their rights have been violated for the sake of an outside chance.

Where the political reasons are of the less proximate kind, for instance defensive, or preemptive, or concerned with securing an opportunity, we may speak, not of the moral claims of politics, but merely of the claims of politics against morality. While an anxious politician may hope still to find some moral considerations bearing the situation, he may discover that they have retreated merely to the overall justification of the pursuit of his, or his party's, worthwhile objectives, or some similar overarching concern. The Olympian point of retreat is notoriously so distant and invulnerable that the rationale of seriously[3] carrying on the business of politics ceases to be disturbed by any moral qualms or any sense of non-political costs at all. Decent political existence lies somewhere between that—or its totally cynical successor, from which even the distant view of Olympus has disappeared—and an absurd failure to recognize that if politics is to exist as an activity at all, some moral considerations must be expected to get out of its way.

If that space is to have any hope of being occupied, we need to hold on to the idea, and to find some politicians who will hold on to the idea, that there are actions which remain morally disagreeable even when politically justified. The point of this is not at all that it is edifying to have politicians who, while as ruthless in action as others, are unhappy about it. Sackcloth is not suitable dress for politicians, least of all successful ones. The point—and this is basic to my argument—is that only those who are reluctant or disinclined to do the morally disagreeable when it is really necessary have much chance of not doing it when it is not necessary.

There are two different reasons for this. First, there is no disposition which just consists in getting it right every time, whether in politics or in anything else. Whether judgment is well exercised, whether immediate moral objections are given the right weight, or any, against large long-term issues, is, on any sensible view of those processes, something that involves patterns of sentiment and reaction. In a body of persons considering a practical question, it essentially involves their shared dispositions and their mutual expectations—what considerations can be heard, what kinds of hesitation or qualification or obstacle it is appropriate or effective to mention. (There is a remark attributed to Keynes, about an American official: 'a man who has his ear so close to the ground that he cannot hear what an upright man says'). That is the first, and main, reason, and one which any reasonable view of deliberation must accept: a habit of reluctance is an essential obstacle against the happy acceptance of the intolerable.

The second reason, which I have already included in my account, is something less widely acceptable: that reluctance in the necessary case, is not only a useful habit, but a correct reaction *to that case,* because that case does involve a genuine moral cost. The fact that reluctance is justified even in the necessary case—and in speaking of 'reluctance', I mean not just initial hesitation in reaching for the answer, but genuine disquiet when one arrives at it—is in fact something that helps to explain the nature, and the value, of the habit of reluctance which was appealed to in the first reason. It embodies a sensibility to moral costs. Utilitarianism, which hopes (in some of its indirect forms) to appeal to habits of reluctance, cannot in fact make any sense of them at this level, because it lacks any sense of *moral* cost, as opposed to costs of some other kind (such as utility) which have to be considered in arriving at the moral decision. Utilitarianism has its special reasons for not understanding the notion of a moral cost, which are connected with its maximizing conceptions; but much other moral philosophy shares that incapacity. Yet it is a notion deeply entrenched in many people's moral consciousness. Why so many moral philosophers learn to forget it is a harder question, and perhaps a deeper one, than why some politicians do.

If, then, there can be agents who in this way have good moral reason to do things which they have good reason to think are, and remain, morally distasteful, a way of understanding their situation might be to see it as one in which the agent has some special relationship to parties involved, which will give him an honorable motive for overruling his objections to such acts. This is the model which Charles Fried in a recent paper (''The Lawyer as Friend: The Moral Foundations of the Lawyer-Client Relation'': 85 *Yale Law Journal,* 1060–89 [1976]) has applied to the case (in some ways similar) of the lawyer who is required on behalf of his client to do things one would not feel morally well-disposed toward doing, such as harrassing witnesses or pressing a formal advantage of well-off persons against the vital interests of less well-off persons. Fried invokes in this connection the relationship of friendship, modeling the lawyer's relationship to his client on the kind of personal relationship which would be widely acknowledged to permit or even require departures from what would otherwise be the demands of impartiality. Fried honestly raises and confronts the problem, but it is hard to be convinced by the model that he has brought to bear on it. For one thing—a point which he mentions but, it seems to me, does not dispose of—one is not paid to be someone's friend; for another, the honorable man who is in question might not be expected to have friends who are like some of the lawyer's clients, or who expect him to do what some of the lawyer's clients expect him to do.

There are some analogies to a special relationship model in politics, inasmuch as politics involves loyalties or allegiances which require one to be something other than impartial. But while there are some allegiances of this kind, to country or party or electorate, and they play some role, they are not adequate, any more than a personal relationship to the client in the legal case, to cover the full range of these issues. Rather, the legal case very readily presses on us a different sort of question which is not only a useful question to ask but also, I think, *the* useful question to ask in these connections: namely, what sort of system does one want, and what sort of disposition do you want in the person acting? We then have to think about how the answers to these questions can be harmonized, in the light of the question: what dispositions does the system require or favor?

The example of the law raises some interesting questions in this connection, and I shall pursue it a little further. One has to ask how the desired product of legal activity, justice, is related to an adversarial system, and to what extent the sorts of behavior that concern Fried are encouraged or required by such a system. That is, in fact, only the start of the problem, for if the adversarial system succeeds in producing justice, one factor in that must be the presence of a judge—and judges are lawyers, and usually former advocates. The judicial disposition is not the same as the adversarial disposition, but as our system of recruitment for judges works, the one has somehow to issue from the other.

Let us, however, stick to the adversarial case. Concentrating on the morally disagreeable activities which may be involved in the enforcement of some legal rights (e.g., some legal rights of the strong against the weak), we might be tempted by the following argument:

(1) In any complex society (at least) the enforcement of some legal rights involves morally disagreeable acts.
(2) It is bad that legal rights which exist should not be enforceable.
(3) Enforcement of many rights of the kind mentioned in (1) requires lawyers.
(4) Any lawyer really effective in enforcing those rights must be fairly horrible.
ERGO (5) It is good that some lawyers are fairly horrible.

How might this argument be met, if at all? The conventional answer presumably lies in denying (1); but in our context of discussion, we will not accept as sufficient the conventional reason for denying it, namely that there is a sufficient moral justification for the system that requires those acts (which is in effect equivalent to (2)). Another line would be to deny (2). This is perhaps the approach of Wasserstrom,[4] who inclines to the view that if (1) carries much weight with regard to some rights, then it may just be better that those rights be not enforced. If this goes beyond the position of refusing to act when one knows that someone else will (not necessarily an objectionable position), it runs into difficulties about the operation of the law as a roughly predictable system. Fried denies (4), by putting the acts required in (1) into the framework of loyalty and friendship. Others might combat (4) by using notions of professionalism, insisting that since those acts are done in a professional role, in the name of a desirable system, it cannot follow that they express a horrible disposition—they are not, in that sense, personal acts at all.

The phenomenology of the states of mind invoked by that answer is very complex. The limitations of the answer are, however, fairly obvious and indeed notorious. One limitation, for instance, must lie in the consideration that it is a personal fact about somebody that that is his profession. However, whatever we think in general about those ideas of professionalism, there is at least one thing that can be allowed to the lawyer's situation which it is hard to allow to the politician's. Even if we accepted (5), the disagreeable conclusion of the argument, we could at least agree that the professional activities of lawyers are delimited enough to make the fact that some are fairly horrible of limited account to the public: the ways in which the argument, if sound, shows them to be horrible are ways which their clients, at any rate, have no reason to regret. But there is much less reason for such comfort in the politicians' case, and if a comparable argument can be mounted with them, then the public has reason to be alarmed. The professional sphere of activity is very much less delimited, and there are important asymmetries, for example in the matter of concealment. The line between the client and the other side is one which in an adversarial system governs a great deal of the lawyer's behavior, and certainly the sorts of reasons he has for concealing things from the opposition are not characteristically reasons for concealment from his client. But the reasons there are for concealing things in politics are always reasons for concealing them from the electorate.

Another reason for concern in the political case lies in the professional (and in itself perfectly proper) commitment to staying in power. I have already suggested that it involves an essential ambivalence: it is impossible to tell, at the limit, where it merges into simple ambition, and into that particular deformation of political life, under all systems, which consists in the inability to consider a question on its merits because one's attention is directed to the consequences of giving (to one's colleagues, in the first instance) a particular answer. Where that has widely taken over, the citizens have reason to fear their politicians' judgment.

The dispositions of politicians are differently related to their tasks and to their public than are those of a profession such as the legal profession for which partly analogous questions arise. Those differences all give greater reason for concern, and make more pressing the question: what features of the political system are likely to select for those dispositions in politicians which are at once morally welcome and compatible with their being effective politicians? What features of the system can help to bring it about that fairly decent people can dispose of a fair degree of power? How does one ensure a reasonable succession of colonists of the space between cynicism and political idiocy?

It is a vast, old, and in good part empirical question. If one adapts Plato's question, *how can the good rule?*, to Machiavelli's, *how to rule the world as it is?*, the simplest conflation—*how can the good rule the world as it is?*—is merely discouraging. It is also, however, excessively pious: the conception of the good that it inherits from Plato invites the question of how the good could do anything at all, which the Machiavellian conception of the world as it is raises the question of how anyone could do anything with it. (A popular sense of 'realism' gets its strength from the fact that the second of those questions has some answers, while the first has none.) But if one modifies from both ends, allowing both that the good need not be as pure as all that, so long as they retain some active sense of moral costs and moral limits; and that the society has some genuinely settled politics and some expectations of civic respectability: then there is some place for discussing what properties we should like the system, in these respects, to have. There are many: I will mention, only in barest outline, four dimensions of a political system which seem to bear closely on this issue.

(a) There is the question, already touched on, of the balance of publicity, and the relations of politician and public, particularly of course in a democracy. The assumption is widespread, particularly in the USA, that public government and a great deal of public scrutiny must encourage honest government, and apply controls to the cynicism of politicians. There is, however, no reason to suppose that the influence of such practices and institutions will be uniformly in one direction. The requirements of instant publicity in a context which is, as we are supposing, to some mild degree moralized, has an evident potential for hypocrisy, while, even apart from that, the instant identification of particular political acts, as they are represented at the degree of resolution achievable in the media, is a recipe for competition in preemptive press releases.

(b) A similar question is that of the relations of politicians to one another; and there is another approved belief, that it is in the interest of good government that politicians should basically be related to one another only functionally, that they should not share a set of understandings which too markedly differentiate them from people who are not politicians. Yet it is not clear how far this is true, either. For it is an important function of the relations of politicians to one another, what courses of action are even discussible, and that is a basic dimension of a moral culture. Very obviously, a ruthless clique is worse than a clique checked by less ruthless outsiders, but that is not the only option. Another is that of a less ruthless clique resisting more ruthless outsiders.

(c) A very well-known point is that of the relation of potential politicians to actual ones, the question of political recruitment. Notoriously, systems where succession is problematic or discontinuous have the property of selecting for the ruthless. No sensible critic will suggest that if that is so, it is at all easy to change, but it is nevertheless an important dimension of assessment of a political system.

(d) A slightly less obvious variant of the same sort of issue concerns the promotion-pattern within a political organization: in particular, the position of the bottleneck between very top jobs and rather less top jobs. Except in very favored circumstances, it is likely to be the case that getting to the top of a political system will require properties which, while they need not at all necessarily be spectacularly undesirable or even regrettable, may nevertheless perhaps lean in the direction of the kind of ambition and professionalism which does not always make for the best judgment, moral or practical. It is desirable that the system should not put too heavy stress on those properties too soon in the business; there can then be an honorable and successful role, below the final bottleneck, for persons without the elbow-power to get into or through the bottleneck. Government concentrated on a few personalities of course tends to weaken this possibility. Related is the question of the prestige of jobs below the top one. It was a notable fact, remarked by some commentators, that when the English politician R. A. (now Lord) Butler retired from politics, it was suggested that his career had been a failure because—and although—he had held almost every major office of state except the premiership itself.

These are, of course, only hints at certain dimensions of discussion. The aim is just to suggest that it is such ways that one should think about the disagreeable acts involved in (everyday) politics—that fruitful thought should be directed to the aspects of a political system which may make it less likely that the only persons attracted to a profession which undoubtedly involves some such acts will be persons who are insufficiently disposed to find them disagreeable.

Last, I should like to make just one point about the further dimension of the subject, in which one is concerned not just with the disagreeable or distasteful but with crimes, or what otherwise would be crimes. This is a different level from the last: here we are concerned not just with business but, so to speak, with the Mafia. My question, rather as before, is not directly whether actions of a certain kind—in this case such things as murders, torture, etc.—are ever justified, but rather, if they are justified, how we should think of those who politically bring them about. I shall call the actions in question, for short, *violence*. It might be worth distinguishing, among official acts of violence, what could be called *structured* and *unstructured* violence: the former related to such processes as executions under law, application of legal force by the police, etc., while the latter include acts (it may be, more abroad than at home) pursued in what is regarded as the national interest.

I shall set out a list of four propositions which some would regard as all true, and which, if they were all true, would make the hope of finding politicians of honorable character, except in minor roles and in favorable circumstances, very slim.

(i) There are violent acts which the state is justified in doing which no private citizen as such would be justified in doing.
(ii) Anything the state is justified in doing, some official such as, often, a politician is justified in ordering to be done.
(iii) You are not morally justified in ordering to be done anything which you would not be prepared to do yourself.
(iv) Official violence is enough like unofficial violence for the preparedness referred to in (iii) to amount to a criminal tendency.

I take it that no one except anarchists will deny (i), at least so far as structured violence is concerned (it is admitted that the distinction between structured and unstructured violence is imprecise). It may be said that structured violence constitutes acts which none but the state could even logically perform: thus nothing done by a private citizen as such could constitute a judicial execution. But I take it that while this is true, it does not cut very deep into the essential issues: thus there is another description of the act which is a judicial execution under which that act could logically, but ought not to be, performed by a private citizen. A more substantial issue is whether the only violence that is legitimate for the state is structured violence. This I doubt, too. Even if regular military operations are counted as structured violence, there may be other acts, bordering on the military or of an irregular character, which a state may be lucky if it is in a position to do without altogether.

An important issue connected with this is the extent to which a political leader's task, particularly in a democracy, is defined in terms of defending the interests of the state; and whether, if the interests of some other, rival, state will be advanced unless some act of violence is authorized, he can be justified in refusing to authorize that act. A similar problem arises in the case where he thinks that the interests of another state should, in justice, prevail. He certainly has a right to that opinion; to what extent has he the right to act on it while still performing that role?

The (imprecise) distinction between structured and unstructured violence also bears on (iv); (iv) is perhaps more plausible with unstructured than with structured violence. It is very widely agreed that the distinction between the official and the unofficial can make a moral difference to the estimation of acts of violence; there are similarly psychological differences in the dispositions underlying the two kinds of acts, even if it is unclear how deep those differences may, in many cases, go (an unclarity which itself makes some people unduly nervous about the legitimacy of official violence). If that is right, then (iv) will fail, and the disobliging conclusion will not follow from the argument, even granted the truth of (i) and the platitudinous truth of (ii). At least, it will be enough to prevent its following with full generality. But while we may certainly agree that (iv) is not exceptionlessly true, it is quite plausible to claim that there are acts, particularly perhaps of unstructured violence, for which (iv) really does hold true, but which nevertheless would be justified under (i). To suppose that there could be no such acts, to suppose in particular that if an act is such that (iv) applies to it, then it must follow that it could not be justified, would be, it seems to me, to take a highly unrealistic view either of politics, or of the possible psychology of agents who will do that act.

In this case, attention turns to (iii); (iii) seems to me false, and more interestingly so than (iv). If so, then there is perhaps a larger class of arguments which have some currency in moral discussion which will have to be abandoned or given extra help: as that one should be a vegetarian unless one would be prepared to work in an abattoir, or that one should not accept experimentation on animals unless one were prepared to conduct it (assuming that one had the skills) oneself. However it may be with those cases, at any rate our understanding of honesty and decency in politicians should be modified by reflection on (iii). The consideration that they should not order something unless they were prepared to do it themselves should be counterweighted with the consideration that if they were prepared to do it themselves, they might be far too willing to order it.

NOTES

1. I have said something about such cases in "Ethical Consistency," reprinted in *Problems of the Self* (Cambridge 1973), chap. 11.

2. I assume that rights can sometimes be overridden. To define 'rights' so that this should not ever be possible would have wider consequences—since one must say something about possible conflicts of rights among themselves—and is anyway undesirable: if all rights have to be *absolute* rights, then it is plausible to conclude that there are no rights at all.

3. I have known a politician, now dead, who used to say 'that is not a *serious* political argument' to mean, more or less, 'that is an argument about what to do in politics which mentions a non-political consideration'—in particular, a moral consideration. This posture was to some degree bluff.

4. "Lawyers as Professionals: Some Moral Issues," 5:1 *Human Rights* (1975), pp. 1–24. [See chap. 3, sel. 5, *EILP*.—ED.] I am grateful for discussion of these issues to Dick Wasserstrom, Andy Kaufman, and other participants in the Council for Philosophical Studies Institute on Law and Ethics, Williams College, MA, 1977.

51. Professional Virtue and Self-regulation

William F. May

. . . . .

PROFESSIONAL CHARACTER AND VIRTUE

Moralists make a mistake when they concentrate solely on the quandaries that practitioners face, or on the defects of the structures in which they operate. Inquiry into these matters already assumes specific dispositions of character, which themselves need to be clarified and criticized. The quandary-oriented professional tends to assume and prize the virtue of conscientiousness. The critic of structures often brings to the inquiry a specifically aroused moral indignation. Important to professional ethics is the moral disposition the professional brings to the structure in which he operates, and that shapes his or her approach to problems. The practitioner's perception of role, character, virtues and style can affect the problems he sees, the level at which he tackles them, the personal presence and bearing he brings to them, and the resources with which he survives moral crises to function another day. At the same time, his moral commitments, or lack of them, the general ethos in which he and his colleagues function, can frustrate the most well-intentioned structural reforms.

Unfortunately, contemporary moralists have been much less interested than their predecessors in the clarification and cultivation of those virtues upon which the health of personal and social life depends. Reflection is this area is likely to seem rather subjective, elusive, or spongy ("I wish my physician were more personal"), as compared with the critical study of decisions and structures. And yet, especially today, attention must be paid to the question of professional virtue. The growth of large-scale organizations has increased that need. Although bureaucracies offer increased opportunity for monitoring performance (and therefore would appear to lessen the need for internalized virtue), in another respect they make the society increasingly hostage to the virtue of professionals who work for them. Huge organizations wield enormous defensive power with which to cover the mistakes of their employees. Further, and more important, the opportunity for increased specialization which they provide means that few others—whether lay people or other professionals—know what any given expert is up to. He had better be virtuous. Few may be in a position to discredit him. The knowledge explosion is also an ignorance explosion; if knowledge is power, then ignorance is powerlessness. Although it is possible to devise structures that limit the opportunities for the abuse of specialized knowledge, ultimately one needs to cultivate virtue in those who wield that relatively inaccessible power. One test of character and virtue is what a person does when no one else is watching. A society that rests on expertise needs more people who can pass that test.

A short list of professional virtues should include at least the following.

Perseverence is a lowly virtue, but indispensable for the acquisition of technical competence in the course of lengthy professional training. A young physician once conceded that medical school required more stamina than brains. Most holders of Ph.Ds would have to confess the same about their

From "Professional Ethics: Setting, Terrain, and Teacher," in *Ethics Teaching in Higher Education*, edited by Daniel Callahan and Sissela Bok (New York: Plenum, 1980), pp. 205–41.

own graduate-school education, though it takes the virtue of modesty to concede that fact.

Public-spiritedness orients the professional to the common good. The term, "profession," and the more ancient though less often invoked words, "vocation" and "calling," have a public ring to them that the terms "job" and "career" do not. Professionals are often licensed by the state; the society invests in their education; they generate their own public standards of excellence; and they are expected to conform to these standards, and to accept responsibility for their enforcement in the guild. Apart from public-spiritedness, the professional degenerates into a careerist, and his education becomes a private stock of knowledge to be sold to the highest bidder.

Integrity marks the professional who is upright or integral (whole). Integrity gets tested at the outset in the forward scramble for admissions to professional schools, and in the competition for grades and position. Uprightness has to do with moral posture: The upright professional refuses to put his nose to the ground, sniffing out opportunities at the expense of clients and colleagues; he equally refuses to bow before the powerful client, the influential colleague, and outside pressures. Integrity also signifies a wholeness or completeness of character; it does not permit a split between the inner and the outer, between word and deed. As such, it makes possible the fiduciary bond between the professional and the client.

The professional virtue of *veracity* requires more than truthfulness or the avoidance of lying. Professionals are the knowledge experts in our society. They can, of course, hoard what they know, and dispense it guardedly in the form of technical services. But the success of professional work often requires the active and intelligent collaboration of the client in the pursuit of professional purpose. . . . The professional must be a teacher, to do his or her work well. Professional veracity, at this point, expands beyond the duty to tell the truth, and includes the enabling act of sharing it.

Although veracity has to do with sharing the truth, *fidelity* is a matter of being true to the client. It means keeping faith with the original promise to take the case, to keep confidences, and to work for the client's best interests, within the limits of the law and moral constraint. The philosopher J. L. Austin once distinguished between declarative and performative utterances. The first are statements that describe the world (it is raining), but the second are statements that change someone's world (I, John, take thee, Mary). A promise need not have the legal status of the marriage vow to qualify as a kind of performative utterance. Promises, to some degree, alter the world of the person to whom they are extended. The professional promise, "I will be your lawyer," alters importantly the client's world, even before the lawyer proceeds to do anything. That is why it is a serious matter when a professional agrees to take, or withdraws from, a case.

The professional transaction also depends upon a pair of virtues associated with giving and receiving—*benevolence* (or *love*), and *humility*. The virtue of benevolent service is the sine qua non of the professional relationship. The professional is giver; the client, receiver. The client depends upon the specialized service that the professional has to offer to meet his needs. The professional, of course, is paid for his work, and, like any seller, should be legally accountable for the delivery of goods promised. Compliance is essential; but the legal minimum should hardly be the norm. The professional transaction is giving and receiving, not just buying and selling. Contractualism based on self-interest alone suppresses the donative element in the professional relationship. It encourages a minimalism, a grudging tit for tat—just so much service for so much money, and no more. This minimalism is especially unsatisfactory in those professions that deliver help to persons with contingent, unpredictable, future needs, that can only be covered by the habits of service.

Humility is not a virtue that one usually associates with professionals. Quite the contrary; long training and specialized knowledge set them apart, and touch them with assumptions of superiority. In popular literature, the professional often takes liberties denied to others as a sign of skill and hard work. We are treated to the reckless, swinging style of the surgeons in "Mash," the final insouciance of the student lawyer in "The Paper Chase," or the authoritarian law professor who presides over language as an accomplished hostess, over her silver.

Clearly, the virtue of humility can have nothing to do with obsequiousness, or ritual expressions of self-doubt over competence. No one needs to see his lawyer nervous before the trial, or his surgeon shaky with doubt about his skill. Humility can only be understood as a necessary counterpart to the virtue of benevolence or love.

Idealistic members of the helping professions like to define themselves by their giving or serving alone—with others indebted to them. The young professional identifies himself with his competence; he pretends to be a relatively self-sufficient monad, unspecified by human need, while others appear before him in their distress, exposing to him their illness, their crimes, their secrets, or their ignorance, for which the professional as doctor, lawyer, priest, or teacher offers remedy.

A reciprocity, however, of giving and receiving is at work in the professional relationship that needs to be acknowledged. In the profession of teaching, to be sure, the student needs the services of the teacher to assist him in learning; but so also the professor needs his students. They provide him with regular occasion and forum to work out what he has to say, and to discover his subject afresh through the discipline of sharing it with others. The young rabbi or priest has more than once paused before the door of the sickroom, wondering what to say to a member of his congregation, only to discover the dying patient ministering to his own needs. Likewise, the doctor needs his patients; the lawyer, his clients. No one can watch the professional nervously approach retirement without realizing how much he needs his clients to be himself.

The discipline of receiving is important in still further ways. The successful client interview requires addressing, but also being addressed; giving, but also taking in; it means both speaking and hearing. . . . The professional's debts, moreover, extend beyond direct obligations to current clients; they also include public monies spent on education, the earlier contributions of clients upon whom he "practiced" while learning his craft, and the research traditions of his profession, upon which he daily draws. Humility, finally, is essential to professional self-renewal. No teacher stays alive if he or she does not remain a student. No preacher can preach the word if he no longer hears it. No physician can long dispense a range of professional services, if not serviced himself by the research arm of his profession.

This brief sketch of some of the virtues germane to professional life has, of course, its shadow side—the problems associated with professional incompetence and vice. . . .

THE ENFORCEMENT OF PROFESSIONAL STANDARDS: SELF-REGULATION AND DISCIPLINE

The subject of professional self-regulation and discipline appears in the professional codes; it preoccupies the layman when he thinks angrily about professional behavior. But, unfortunately, academic ethicists largely ignore the subject, and the guilds themselves only too often neglect it. A self-protective code of ethics, a politics too narrowly defensive of guild interests, and monopolistic practices contribute to this neglect.

No one can doubt, however, the importance of the problem of lax professional self-regulation. A former president of the American Medical Association has conceded that some five percent of physicians and surgeons are incompetent, or otherwise unsuitable for practice. Surely the figure is conservative, if one considers the source, and reflects on the probable percentages in one's own line of work. Since there are 300,000–400,000 practicing physicians in the United States, a minimum of 15,000–20,000 are incompetent. Yet, on the average in recent years, only 65–75 physicians annually have had their licenses revoked. (Some have argued that the extent of self-regulation in the professions should not be measured entirely on the basis of the number of instances of revocation and disbarment. Subtler devices are available to a profession in disciplining its members. The incompetent or unethical practitioner can be blocked out of referrals. The reckless physician may have hospital privileges revoked, without being drummed out of the profession. Although such lesser disciplinary action must be considered in any total assessment of the extent of professional self-regulation, it hardly solves the problem. The practitioner who is driven out of a given referral system often relocates in another circle sufficiently mediocre or indifferent to put him beyond the reach of professional criticism.) . . .

. . . Practitioners are as loath to regulate themselves as academics are reluctant to discuss regulation. First, within any guild a network of friendship and courtesy develops that tends to make loyalty to colleagues take precedence over obligations to clients, or to the wider public that the guild serves. Inevitably professional colleagues exchange favors, information, and services. By comparison, the ties to clients seem transient. A profession organizes itself around certain ends—to serve a specific set of clients—but a sense of community develops among colleagues that becomes an end in itself. In the language of the sociologists: Every *Gesellschaft* (organization) tends to become a *Gemeinschaft* (community). Americans exacerbate the problem in that they do not distinguish (and separate) as clearly as Europeans the public order of work from the private order of friendship. It is extremely painful to bring charges against a colleague who is also a friend.

The peculiar source of authority in at least two of the professions (the law and medicine) adds to the difficulties in achieving self-regulation. These professions draw their power from fear—the patient's concern about suffering and death, the client's fear of the loss of property, liberty, or life. (No academic is engaged in a war on ignorance quite comparable to the physician's battle against disease.) This negative source of authority provides great prestige and/or financial reward for the physician and lawyer in the modern world, but, at the same time, it renders their authority inherently unstable. Members of these professions are the object of great anger, and are subject to retaliation if through incompetence, greed, or thirst for power they help to impose on the patient/client what they were commissioned to resist. (The military profession also derives its authority from a negative, and suffers from the same instability of attitudes in the wider population it serves.) Since the stakes are so high, and since whole institutions (hospitals, clinics, and courts) can suffer from the publicized incompetence of a single practitioner, the temptation is strong to draw around the endangered colleague like a herd around a wounded elephant.

American professionals may also be reluctant to bring charges against their colleagues because of a morally wholesome, national aversion of officiousness. Unlike some of their European counterparts, Americans show little stomach for playing amateur policeman, prosecutor, and judge when they themselves are not directly or officially involved in an accident. Our libertarian and equalitarian instincts combine to produce a reluctance to interfere. In many respects, this is an admirable trait in the American character. Yet our distaste for officiousness cannot justify a laxness in enforcing professional standards. Professional status confers the duties of privilege, but not a limitless liberty; a respect for colleagues as equals, but not at the expense of clients in the inequality of their power.

In order to guarantee to the public that certain standards shall be maintained, the state limits the license to practice to those who have completed a course of professional education. Professionals as a group profit from this state-created monopoly. They fall short of their responsibilities for the maintenance of standards if they merely practice competently and ethically as individuals. The individual's license to practice depends upon the prior license to license which the state has, to all intents and purposes, bestowed upon the guild. If the license to practice carries with it the obligation to practice well, then the license to license carries with it the obligation to judge and monitor well. Not only the individual, but also the collectivity itself, is accountable for standards. . . .

PROFESSIONAL CODES

52. The Ideological Use of Professional Codes*

John Kultgen

Engineer's Creed

As a Professional Engineer, I dedicate my professional knowledge and skill to the advancement and betterment of human welfare. I pledge:

To give the utmost of performance;

To participate in none but honest enterprise;

To live and work according to the laws of man and the highest standards of professional conduct;

To place service before profit, the honor and standing of the profession before personal advantage, and the public welfare above all other considerations.

In humility and with need for Divine Guidance, I make this pledge.[1]

It would be instructive to determine how much influence pious professions such as the Engineer's Creed, Radio Broadcaster's Creed, Hippocratic Oath, Boy Scout Promise and Pledge of Allegiance to the Flag have on conduct. Very little, one would guess. They are better suited to fan the embers of group identification and self-congratulation than to demand hard decisions about how to behave in difficult situations. Some of the largest and most influential professional associations have, therefore, conceived a need for more detailed guidance for their members. The 1980 Principles of Medical Ethics of the American Medical Association (AMA) has 7 provisions, supplemented by some 59 interpretive Opinions of the Judicial Council. The 1980 Code of Professional Responsibility of the American Bar Association (ABA) contains 9 Canons, construed according to some 138 Ethical Considerations and implemented by a comparable number of parallel Disciplinary Rules. The Rules of Conduct of the American Institute of Certified Public Accountants (AICPA) has 15 major principles, each with numerous specifications. The American Psychological Association (APA) 1963

From *Business and Professional Ethics Journal* 1:3 (1982): 53–69.

*I wish to thank Norman Bowie, Peter Markie, and Jane Uebelhoer for criticisms of early drafts of this paper.

Ethical Standards for Psychologist contains 9† Principles with several provisions under each. Other associations with no codes or rudimentary ones are under pressure to follow suit as a mark of professionalism.

In this paper I argue that professional codes of ethics have served an ideological function comparable to that of the Engineer's Creed, though more subtle. I investigate the problem this poses for determining legitimate ethical norms of professionalism. I will use the 1974 Code of Ethics for Engineers of the Engineer's Council for Professional Development (ECPD)[2] as my prime example, and I will compare some of its provisions with those of other codes to justify my generalizations. But first I will discuss the nature of professional ideologies and the perspective from which I will view them.

I

The term "professional ideology" is frequently used, but rarely defined by sociologists. The general concept of ideology has been abstracted from the political context, where it designates world-views used to defend or attack entire social systems,[3] and generalized, as by Parsons, to any system of beliefs "oriented to the evaluative integration of [a] collectivity, by interpretation of the empirical nature of the collectivity and of the situation in which it is placed, the processes by which it has developed to its given state, the goals to which its members are collectively oriented, and their relation to the future course of events."[4]

Some sociologists conceive "ideology" as a descriptive category, whose definition does not stipulate that its content is false or that the will to believe behind its adoption is self-serving. However, authors most prone to utilize the term "professional ideology" are critics of professionalism such as Johnson, Larson, Collins and Noble.[5] They do have in mind false and self-serving beliefs. For them the term does not belong exclusively to social science or social ethics, but is a bridge-term leading from one to the other and back again.

I shall develop the professional ideology and criticize its distortions at greater length below. Before doing so I want to mention an alternative account which, while inadequate in some significant ways, also provides valuable insights. Magali Larson argues persuasively that the image of professionalism in the professional ideology both is false and has served well the "professional project" of many occupational groups in achieving monopolistic control over their markets and superior status in society.[6] She clearly does not think that professionalization serves, any longer, the interests of humanity or even of most professionals as measured by her social ideal. Hence, she calls for the "proletarianization of educated labor" as part of a large, unspecified program of social reform in the name of economic justice, an end of alienation, and conditions for individual human fulfillment.[7]

Larson identifies four basic inconsistencies between professional ideologies and true depictions of the professions. 1) Professional ideologies portray their groups as oriented to service rather than profit, with no affiliations with any particular social class. The reality is that professions pursue high socio-economic status and differentially serve the interests of the ruling elite. 2) The ideology justifies the exceptional rewards of professionals by imputing to them superior ability and merit, ignoring the fact that the privileges of education and autonomous practice are provided by society. 3) The ideology depicts professional work as somehow more elevated than non-professional, thus establishing a social distance between professionals and other workers. The work of most professionals in fact is more akin to that of certain non-professionals rather than that of the idealized professionals depicted in the ideology. 4) The ideology depicts professions as collegial communities voluntarily subscribing to a superior ethic which makes them trustworthy to manage a monopoly over services vital to the remainder of society. The reality is that self-regulation, other than that designed to make professionals faithful agents of whoever pays their keep, is an illusion.

Larson sees this ideology as a peculiar blend of (a) the bourgeois myth of atomic individuals voluntarily erecting a neutral and objective state, which maintains a free market for the benefit of all, and stratifying themselves according to differences in natural talent and effort; and (b) the anti-market-myth of the intrinsic value of work, gentlemanly disinterestedness, and noblesse oblige.[8]

Whatever its weaknesses, Larson's analysis does show that professionalism cannot be understood, much less evaluated, apart from a social ideal for the organization of work. I accept many of the elements of Larson's ideal, though her evaluation of professionalism is one-sided; but I entertain the hope that valid ideals can be culled from the professional ideology, that an exposure of the forces of distortion will enable us to wash the sand and pan the nuggets to be found there.

†[The 1981 revision contains 10 Principles. See appendix 1, sample code 5, *EIPL*.—ED.]

II

According to my conception, professional ideology consists of ideas about professions, professionals and professionalism to which an occupational group appeals to mobilize its members and appeals to those in positions of power, in order to gain or retain the control over the market for their services and the social standing which recognized professions enjoy. It is a matter of empirical investigation to determine which ideas in the ideology are true and false.

We cannot assume a priori that any given idea in a professional ideology is false. Still it is evident that the ideologies as a whole are mixtures of truth and falsity due to the social environment in which they have evolved. They have had to be grounded in reality to be persuasive; hence, they appeal to obvious facts and accepted norms. They have been promulgated to win superior position over competing occupations; hence, they have had to give lip service to ideals which the group does not pursue and attribute to it characteristics which it does not possess. Consequently, each element of a professional ideology must be examined critically on its own merits.

Professional ideologies are conveyed by all manner of formal and informal statements and nonverbal communications. The codes of ethics of professional associations are related to professional ideologies in two ways. First, the ideology provides the semantic background which shapes the way the code is interpreted. Of necessity, any brief set of rules or ideals is elliptical. One would be at a loss to understand what a code requires apart from some broad image of professionalism. Second the code is itself utilized for ideological ends. The existence of a code conveys the impression that a profession is concerned about ethics and the content of its code defines what the profession would like to be considered ethical practice.

The ideological purpose of professional codes is evident from the sorts of claims that are made about them in speeches and informal remarks of leaders, editorials and articles in house journals, and publications meant to supplement them.[9] In this paper, however, I will concentrate on evidence provided by the content and structure of the codes themselves as most relevant to my purposes.

Let us consider some details of the ECPD Code.* It is one of the better constructed documents, and my criticisms should not be read as a wholesale condemnation of it or its authors. I am quite aware of the limitations of any set of rules for moral guidance and the compromises required to secure acceptance by an entire profession or even its leadership.

The Code begins with a statement of principles as vague and general as the Engineer's Creed:

> Engineers uphold and advance the integrity, honor and dignity of the engineering profession by
>
> i. using their knowledge and skill for the enhancement of human welfare;
> ii. being honest and impartial, and serving with fidelity the public, their employers and clients;
> iii. striving to increase the competence and prestige of the engineering profession; and
> iv. supporting the professional and technical societies of their disciplines.

The Principles are specified somewhat in seven Fundamental Canons, which parallel other major codes in defining responsibilities roughly to (A) "the public" or humanity; (B) clients and employers; and (C) fellow professionals and "the profession":

	ECPD Canons	AMA Principles	ABA Canons	APA Principles	AICPA Rules
(A)	1,2,3	I,III,VII	2,8	1,3,4,5	—
(B)	2,3,4	IV,VI	4,5,6,7	6,7,8,18	1,2,3
(C)	5,6,7	IV,V	1,3,9	2,10–17,19	4,5

The reader will observe the attention devoted to (C). ECPD provides Guidelines for Use* with the Fundamental Canons, which are particularly extensive for C 5, 6 and 7.† Until ruled in recent Supreme Court decisions to be in violation of the Sherman Anti-Trust Act, many codes included sections such as the following (which have now been deleted from the ECPD Code).

> Engineers may advertise professional services only as a means of identification . . . and only in limited ways. (5.g)

> Engineers shall not enter competitions for designs for the purpose of obtaining commissions for specific projects, unless provision is made for reasonable compensation for all designs submitted. (5.l)

An apology was often given for such provisions to the effect that in service occupations in a compet-

*[Cf. the National Society of Professional Engineers' (NSPE) 1987 Code, appendix 1, sample code 8, *EIPL*.—ED.]

*[Cf. the NSPE Rules of Practice.—ED.]

†[Cf. the NSPE Professional Obligations.—ED.]

itive economy, practitioners have particularly delicate duties not to encroach on the turf of others, must maintain the appearance as well as the substance of disinterestedness (= "dignity") to nourish the trust of clients, and ought to offer competence not price. Duties which coincidently redound to the financial, prestigial and political advantage of the profession are intended for the benefit of those who it serves. The ingenuousness of these claims has naturally been met with scepticism by critics and the Supreme Court saw them as being clearly monopolistic. Ideologically, the association of "duties to the profession" with avowed duties to the public and clients bestows on them moral authority which they would not enjoy if they stood alone.

III

The charge that self-serving provisions of professional codes are ideological is plausible on the face. Less so is the charge that statements of obligation to the public and clients are. Let us look closely at ECPD's Canon 1:

> Engineers shall hold paramount the safety, health and welfare of the public in the performance of their professional duties.

In recognition of the vagueness of key words such as "public welfare," Canon 1 is supplemented with six Guidelines dealing with (a) engineers' recognition of the effect of their judgments on public welfare, and their obligation (b) not to approve unsafe specifications, (c) to notify proper authority if the public is endangered when their judgment is overruled or (d) when another person or firm violates the Guidelines, (e) to participate in civic affairs, and (f) to protect the environment.

These provisions are morally laudable and reasonably specific. Nevertheless, they suffer from a number of semantic, logical, and pragmatic limitations. In the first place, the Code itself has not been adopted by many specialized engineering societies, including the largest one, the Institute of Electrical and Electronic Engineers (IEEE). Other societies have adopted the Principles and Canons without the Guidelines, effectively demoting them to the role of the Engineer's Creed.

For those groups that have adopted it, the ECPD Code gives relatively little attention to matters of global importance: Canon 1 has only eleven specific provisions under its Guidelines. The six other Canons relate to the details of practice. Canon 4, which instructs engineers how to serve as "faithful agents" for employers and clients (and assures employers that engineers are not disposed to rock boats) has twenty-three provisions, and Canon 5, which limits acceptable forms of competition among engineers has twenty-four. This suggests that engineers are less receptive to detailed advice about how to promote the public welfare than about how to enhance the reputation of their profession, to avoid conflict with fellow engineers, or to serve their employers faithfully. Either they are confident that they can decide global questions for themselves or are convinced that the activities mandated by the remaining provisions of the Code take care of the matter. Being professional in specific tasks, they may think, automatically promotes the public good.

The tepidity of ECPD's social conscience is typical of professional codes. The 1979 National Association of Social Workers Code of Ethics is unusual in setting seven specific aims of social reform for its group, though these compose only one of sixteen coordinate sections. Other personal service occupations state no such aims at all. While the 1972 American Personnel and Guidance Association asserts that it "exalts services to the individual and society above personal gain," its silence is deafening about how to do so beyond duties to individual clients and employing organizations. The same is true of the 1963 American Psychological Association Code; and the American Psychiatric Association merely defers to the AMA Code. The American Institute of Certified Public Accountants view themselves as technicians with no responsibilities beyond service to honest employers. The 1962 Code of Ethics of the National Association of Realtors, in a statement that is worth quoting, baldly asserts that it promotes the public good maximally by going about its business:

> Under all is the land. Upon its wise utilization and widely allocated ownership depend the survival and growth of free institutions and of our civilization. The Realtor is the instrumentality through which the land resource of the nation attains the widest distribution. He is a creator of homes, a builder of cities, a developer of industries and productive farms.

More like ECPD, other codes take a stand on public issues that can be handled without disturbing the present social system or the organization of the profession. The American Bar Association devotes approximately five percent of its code to Canon 8. "A lawyer should assist in improving the legal system," and more attention to promoting accessibility of legal services within the present system. The American Medical Association addresses issues such as abortion and genetic engineering, but has nothing to say about the soaring costs of medical care or maldistribution of services. One must conclude that ECPD is representative in its general insouciance to what many critics see as the grave flaws in the social system in which its members flourish.

In respect to specific problems relating to public welfare, Guidelines 1.c and 1.d under Canon 1 of the ECPD Code attempt to come to grips with the need for whistleblowing, a practice fraught with risk for the engineer.

> Should the Engineers' professional judgment be overruled under circumstances where the safety, health, and welfare of the public are endangered, the Engineers shall inform their clients or employers of possible consequences and notify other proper authority of the situation, as may be appropriate. (Beginning of 1.c)*

Any guidance here is to the good and few other professional codes even address the problem. However, the guidelines are rather toothless. The engineer is enjoined to inform "proper authority." The casual reader may assume that this assigns a duty to "go public" or at least to warn an employer's customers or report him to the appropriate government agency when dangerous services or products are about to be released. The cautious engineer, however, may interpret "proper authority" to refer to superiors in the organization in which he or she works. Under this construction, the provision enjoins only whistleblowing on colleagues, lower-level superordinates, and competitors, not on top management. Whistleblowing becomes a relatively safe activity, but by the same token offers limited protection for the public.

The adventures of engineers in whistleblowing have not been inspired by the Code. There is little evidence that many have paid any attention to it. Nevertheless, the problem which G.1.c and G.1.d address is a real one. The whistleblowing engineers in the Bay Area Rapid Transit (BART) case, for example, thought that the engineering ethic required them to go over the heads of BART management to a member of the political Governing Board. Their superiors, who included engineers, and many of their colleagues in and outside the organization disagreed. Their professional association (the California Society of Professional Engineers, which subscribes to the Code of The National Society of Professional Engineers, whose provision on whistleblowing uses the same phraseology as ECPD) was too divided to offer effective support,[10] although IEEE filed an *amicus curiae* brief on behalf of the engineers. Where opinion is this divided, there are no standards for a profession, whatever the personal morality of its members. The best one can say about G.1.c and G.1.d is that they are a step toward clarification, with many steps left to go.

As a second example of a well-intentioned principle with ideological consequences, consider G.1.f, which reads in its entirety:

> Engineers should be committed to improving the environment to enhance the quality of life.

I shall not comment on the brevity of this provision, the vagueness of the phrases "improving the environment" to "enhance the quality of life," or the significance of the substitution of "should" for the "shall" that appears in other Guidelines. But what must we infer from the placement of the provision? No statements are provided in or about the Code to explain the order of its provisions. However, the Canons seem to be listed more or less in order of "moral gravity." The earlier ones state fundamental aims and values, and the later ones, instrumental obligations. Thus engineers are urged first to dedicate themselves to the public welfare, then to be competent and truthful in serving it, and to serve employers, to compete fairly, to protect the reputation of the profession, and to develop themselves and their professional associations as means to promote public welfare. Does the same order obtain for the Guidelines under each Canon? G.1.f is the last of six under Canon 1. This leads one to infer that concern for the environment is the last thing that need enter the engineer's mind in considering the public good, after he or she has conscientiously reviewed specifications, tattled to proper authority about wrongdoing, and participated in civic clubs. Environmental impact is apparently an afterthought. And this is the only place where the ECPD Code mentions the environment at all. There is no recognition of the massive cumulative effect of engineering decisions, each perhaps competent and justifiable in isolation, on the environment. There is no indication in the Code that engineers have a serious obligation to consider the environmental impact of everything they do.

The point that I wish to make by these two illustrations is that vagueness in provisions relating to service allows members of a profession to avoid difficult and dangerous responsibilities, while the profession can point to the provisions as proof of its dedication to the public good. It is significant that provisions become more specific, clear, numerous, and hence more effective, as they pertain to behavior that promotes the interests of the profession.

IV

Every communicative act is indeterminate apart from the assumptions which particular audiences bring to bear in interpreting it. Where language

---

*[Cf. NSPE code Rules of Practice, 1.a.—ED.]

remains vague under shared assumptions, the communicative instrument may fail altogether. More often, different audiences receive different meanings because their assumptions differ. It is a thesis of this paper that what I have called the professional ideology provides a semantic context for the way professions and a large part of their public construe professional codes, with differences between the insiders' and outsiders' perspectives generating a degree of systematic ambiguity. I shall now attempt to reconstruct the ideology as it has been developed by functionalist sociologists.[11]

The old and still popular image of professions is derived from paradigm occupations, the "high" professions or "learned arts," law, architecture, divinity, and especially medicine (the all-time success story of professionalization). This image is dressed out in the trappings of social science, whose concepts are enlisted by occupations to justify the support they need from the public. This support is not only material (finances for hospitals, courts, laboratories, universities, churches, etc.), but includes social practices and statutory laws to insure to the professional group a monopoly of competence in activities for which others will pay a very high price.

To justify this level of support, professions claim a number of characteristics. By the "substantive" characteristics, I will mean those that define professional activity and the professional qua professional. By "structural" characteristics, I will mean the way professional groups are organized internally and in relation to other groups in society. By "ideational" characteristics, I will mean the values and beliefs to which the professional is supposed to be committed—if you will, the ideology which ideology ascribes to the members of professions. Codes of ethics are official expressions of normative components in the self-images of professions, as well as the ideas to which the professional is alleged to be committed.

A. *Substantive Characteristics.* A profession involves complex and specialized activities that require a great amount of skill and arcane theoretical knowledge. Through these activities the professional renders important services to clients. In particular, the professional decides matters of vital importance for his client on grounds that are highly technical. This requires creativity, judgment, and wisdom. To acquire and maintain competence, the professional needs ability, lengthy preparation, continuing study and practice, and intense dedication. A profession thus is a vocation in the sense of a lifelong career to which individuals are "called"—by nature, as it were, since their native endowment equips and therefore obligates them to serve mankind in a special way through an arduous discipline.

B. *Structural Characteristics.* According to sociologists such as Talcott Parsons and Bernard Barber, a "true" profession has an autonomous, collegial, and meritocratic social structure. Because of the substantive character of the profession, professionals are the only ones qualified to judge professional work. Hence, the profession must rule itself with a minimum of interference and a maximum of support from society. Entry into the profession is determined by a course of professional training and testing in educational institutions manned and managed by professionals. The credentialed professional is allowed to practice and he is supplied clients by a system of licensure, referral, access to places, instruments, and resources for practice, etc. His work is monitored by peers. The primary agency that sets standards and punishes flagrant abuses is the professional society. Both schools and societies are manned by the most able members of the profession, as determined by their peers and especially by prior leaders. Hence, professions are autonomous collegial meritocracies.

C. *Ideational Characteristics.* The animating purpose of a profession is to contribute maximally and efficiently to human welfare. This aim determines all of its characteristics, substantive, structural, and indeed ideational. The same purpose (together with great interest in the work itself) is the motive of the true professional, not desire for compensation. Of course, professionals must be supported materially in money, perquisites, status, and power because their vocations are so demanding as to preclude any other livelihood. They *should* be supported exceedingly well for many reasons: because they need special resources for their work; because those who serve mankind should be rewarded; and because rewards are necessary to entice an adequate supply of practitioners into arduous disciplines. Nevertheless, the professionals' aim is to serve mankind and they are expected to affirm ("profess") this by accepting their professions' codes of ethics.

While the profession as a whole devises its code as well as its standards of technical competence, individual professionals need an unusual amount of freedom from interference and criticism (not only by lay people, but by colleagues as well) because of the personal judgment involved in professional decisions. Hence, society must rely on their individual consciences acquired during professional socialization and sustained by the professional subculture to guarantee that they will conform to technical standards and moral principles. The professional thus is a person of unusually high character. The professional code of ethics articulates what most professionals do by habit and personal conviction.

V

Is the ideology of the professions truth or mythology? A number of presuppositions on which the ideology depends are palpably false:[12]

A. *The Myth of Independence*. The professional is usually depicted as a self-employed, solitary agent, voluntarily selected by clients for personal, fiduciary, and confidential relationships.[13] The fact is, however, that the majority of practitioners, such as engineers, scientists, teachers, social workers, accountants, and management specialists, work in large corporate settings, public or private. This is the trend in the traditional professions, medicine, the law, and the ministry. In such settings, decisions are frequently made at the top of the hierarchy. The practitioner works on limited tasks, sometimes without knowing the uses to which the work will be put. Practitioners risk expulsion from both the organization and the profession if they object to immoral or imprudent acts of their superiors.

   Even self-employed practitioners may be encumbered with elaborate organizations—clinics, partnerships, consulting firms—with large overheads and payrolls. Economic constraints determine the kinds of tasks they can take on. The marketplace severely limits their freedom of choice.

   Thus, the latitude for individual judgment ascribed to the professional is exaggerated. Consequently, the rights and privileges claimed as appropriate to such responsibility are also exaggerated.

B. *The Myth of Altruism*. No evidence is adduced that lawyers are more dedicated to the public good than barbers, or doctors than plumbers. Perhaps the illusion is a residue from the day of the gentleman scientist, professor, divine, or physician, whose independent income or noble patron permitted devotion to an occupation without worry about material support. In present society professional identity is a means of upward mobility. (This is reflected in the eagerness with which engineers, lawyers, accountants, academicians, etc. abandon their professions for managerial posts.) Among those who practice, income is a primary goal and the avenue to the costume and setting in which status is confirmed, clients attracted, and respect nourished.

   The intrinsic interest of the work for the professional is no guarantee that it will be directed to the service of humanity. Indeed, fascination with technical feats may encourage subtle compromises of the rights of the public and individual clients. The theoretical basis for professional work does not guarantee the wisdom or morality of its aims.

   I am not condemning material rewards as intrinsically immoral, but I suggest that provisions in codes of ethics that aggrandize their adherents (such as those that promote the prestige of the profession and govern etiquette between professionals) be viewed with a jaundiced eye. Strictures against advertising, soliciting clients, competitive bidding, fee cutting, etc., are said to be necessary for the "dignity" of the profession, which in turn is said to nurture the trust of the client. A similar justification is given for high pay and prestige in corporate settings. But surely, as the Supreme Court has done in several decisions, we should demand strong empirical proof that these are the consequences of special privilege, since the facade of altruism can easily cover self-interest in cases of double motivation. Spokespersons for the professions show little interest in testing the social benefits claimed for their privileges in the face of obvious inequities in the distribution of such services as medical care, legal representation, and education in society.

C. *The Myth of Peer Review*. A professional is the best judge of technical aspects of work of a fellow professional. But to make an authoritative judgment, he or she must be informed of that work in detail. This is frequently not possible among private practitioners who work in isolation from one another or in corporate settings where the professional works under the cover of governmental or commercial secrecy. The chance of exposure for immoral, unwise, or unprofessional actions is further reduced by strictures in ethical codes against public criticism of colleagues. These formalize customary proprieties. Code and custom conspire to deny information not only to the public, but to the peer group itself.

   An institutional dilemma confronts society: (1) Professions might be empowered by law to enforce compliance with their codes of ethics, for example, by revoking the license to practice. But this enhances the power to exploit a monopoly of competence for competitive advantage over other occupational groups. (2) The power of regulation can be assigned to external groups. But these must be staffed *either* by professionals, in which case cross-over between regulators and regulated and their common socialization makes this another form of self-regulation, *or* by lay persons, who, while they may represent the public interest more faithfully, lack the background for informed judgments.

D. *The Myth of Wisdom*. According to the ideology, professionals can be trusted to monitor their work for the public good because they are wiser and more altruistic than individuals in other occupations. They are made this way by their education. This myth of noblesse oblige perhaps had a basis when professionals enjoyed a genteel upbringing and liberal education. Even this fragile basis has collapsed with the democratization and specialization of professional education. Intensive training in technical matters does not engender breadth of vision—just the opposite. Nor are those who rise to the top of the professional hierarchy particularly equipped by that experience to determine the proper role of their profession in society.

Thus the structural notions that professions are or should be characterized by autonomy, collegiality, and meritocracy are gravely flawed. The standards of competence in which professions justifiably take such pride control entry into the occupation, limit the supply of practitioners, and produce important material benefits for the profession. Until an occupation demonstrates that all of its practices are necessary for the public good and that the function of its code is morality rather than profit, we should view its claims for special privilege with scepticism.

VI

This discussion suggests that the codification of moral rules is not an unmixed blessing for society. Something like this frequently happens in the moral sphere: Ethical persons reflect on actions that are clearly right or clearly wrong and generalize principles for difficult cases. They formulate codes that carry moral authority. Society recognizes the value of actions promoted by the code and rewards them. The actions come to be performed by morally insouciant individuals for the sake of the rewards. Others find that they can gain the rewards by only appearing to conform to the code or, more deviously, by insinuating self-serving provisions into the code itself. This moral inversion occurs when vocational ideals are modified for ideological use and compromised as ideals. Society's commitment to morality is exploited to win competitive advantage for some occupations.

We must concede that the actual consequences of the professional ideology are hard to measure. It is obvious that fair shares of medical care, legal counsel, education, engineering, etc., do not go to economically, racially, ethically, sexually, or geographically disadvantaged groups in our own society, not to mention in the rest of the world. Professional services are not distributed in proportion either to need or contribution to society; the requirements of justice, under whatever concept of fairness, are not met. It is also clear that the professions are integral parts of the system that is responsible. They serve those who are able to command their services by virtue of power and financial resources. The ECPD Code is silent on this issue and few codes of professional ethics acknowledge the injustice of the system of distribution. They do little more than call for palliative measures. For example, Section 7 of the AMA Principles of Medical Ethics states that the physician's fee "should be commensurate with the services rendered and the patient's ability to pay" (while the codes concede to the lawyer and physician the right to choose clients). Such provisions may promote limited goods, but they encourage complacency about the status quo. Indeed sociologists cite professionalism as a major source of stability in society, that is, as a main obstacle to radical reform.

These facts are obvious. What is impossible to estimate is the contribution of professional ideology and codes of professional ethics to creating them.

VII

The moral of my criticisms is not that professional codes should be jettisoned, but that they should be reformed. I will conclude with some suggestions along this line.[14] There is no space for argument; development of the possibilities must await other occasions and further reflection.

My first suggestions have to do with purging the codes of false impressions and self-serving norms and adding provisions more relevant to actual moral dilemmas of professionals. For example:

(1) To come to terms with the realities of modern society, a sharper distinction needs to be drawn between the entrepreneural ethic appropriate to self-employed professionals and the bureaucratic ethic appropriate to professionals in corporate settings. The latter ethic is embryonic,

would be hard to develop, and will be less flattering to the professions' image than present codes.

(2) Professional obligations could be reformulated to fit together into a tighter hierarchical or means–end structure than present codes display. Genuine moral obligations to one's profession, colleagues, and employer are those which are necessary to provide legitimate services to clients or consumers. Services to the latter are limited by obligations not to harm the larger public unnecessarily and to rectify harms that flow from service to special clienteles. Provisions of an ideal code would mesh with the rules of the ideal social system, which would maximize and fairly distribute the benefits of social labor under contemporary conditions. It is incumbent on those propagating a code to justify its provisions in these terms.

(3) This goes double for rights and privileges. Only those demonstrably necessary for discharging the professional obligations should be mentioned in a code of ethics. On the other hand, more attention is due rights which must be guaranteed by corporate employers to allow professionals to follow their codes without undue sacrifice or heroic virtue.

(4) The paternalism in many codes (e.g., prominent in AMA's, condemned in ABA's, not mentioned in ECPD's) should be curtailed. Professionals are obligated to provide data to clients and the public on which the latter can make informed decisions. They should not make decisions *for* them except under carefully circumscribed conditions. It should be realized, that curtailment of paternalism would depose professionals from the throne of authority and dissipate their mystique—thus debilitating their efforts to determine their compensation unilaterally.

(5) It is understandable that the Code of Ethics of the American Football Coaches Association should stipulate that a "man" should see that "the boys who have played under him are finer and more decent men for having done so"; but there is little excuse for the codes of the major professions, which have a predominantly male membership but ought to include a significant percentage of women, to eschew feminine or gender-neutral terminology. Change here would be cosmetic if chauvinistic language were not recognized to be symptomatic of gate-keeping mechanisms, in professional socialization, education, credentialing, etc., which have systematically limited the admission of women and minorities. Language reform and affirmative action pledges are hollow if aggressive action is not taken to change practices and attitudes.

Such changes in the content and structure of codes will be decorative if the codes continue to be ignored in practice. They can make codes more relevant to work contexts and increase somewhat the likelihood that persons of good will would want to follow them. But structural changes in the institutions involving professionals are necessary to protect the ethical individual against unethical conduct of others and, once again, to permit him or her to do what is right without heroic virtue. For example,

1. The time is ripe for experimentation with new functions for professional associations and new kinds of association, new arrangements within corporate organizations, and new legislation, to guide and protect those who blow the whistle on unethical conduct. For example, ethics ombudsmen and a moral bill of rights for employees have been proposed for corporations. Stephen Unger among others has suggested that other professional associations take on mediational and support functions following the model of the American Association of University Professors.
2. There is a need for and perhaps a growing disposition to accept arrangements to involve lower level professionals in policy decisions of public and private organizations that affect the ethical character of their work, for example, its environmental impact, its cost in resources, and the distribution of its results to those in need. Contracts of employment might guarantee such conditions.
3. Leaders of professions should overcome the reflex reaction against external scrutiny and regulation. Agencies outside a profession are sometimes needed to protect the ethical practitioner from unfair competition. Not all wisdom about the proper role of professions in society reposes in those at the top of the professional heap; informed lay people and politicians have perspectives which they lack. Mechanisms should be developed to insure public contribution to the formulation and implementation of professional codes and the ethical bent of professional education.
4. Professions in America are products of the technological revolution and competitive capitalistic economy. Nevertheless, they can assume a role as agencies for the good of humanity. Their functions in this role should be clearly distinguished from their contribution to any specific socioeconomic system. The present system is the context in which codes have to be applied,

but there should be no implication that the professional is obligated to support this system if a better alternative is available.

5. Critical reflection on ethics should be recognized as an important component of professional education. Educators have concentrated on technical training and left moral training to outside agencies (the home, church, lower schools, etc.), to the models provided by established practitioners (including the educators themselves), and to the subculture which the individual enters upon admission to practice. At most, professional schools have provided a brief indoctrination in the profession's code and rites. Effective ethical training would confront students with concrete problems of the sorts they will encounter in professional life. They would be required to criticize or defend not only the various actions possible in those circumstances, but the principles proposed to determine action, including those in the professional code. This would require a grounding in general ethical theory.

My last proposals deal with qualities that should be developed in the individual professional.

1. Professionals should cultivate role distance which will enable them to question whether they ought always do what their peers and superiors expect. They should view ethical codes as hypotheses for critical debate, not final dogmas. Reflections such as those here about the functions of ethical codes, the distinction between an ideal professional and ideal human being, and the role of professions in society contribute to such a distancing. What is needed is a measure of moral leadership on a par with the intellectual leadership which professionals exercise in technical matters.
2. Professionals need ethical sensitivity to conflicting values and confusions of obligation which occur in concrete situations, in contrast to the clear-cut issues that often characterize technical problems. They need to be practiced in ethical reasoning, not just mindful of codes packaged by professional associations.
3. Professionals need a sense of limits—of their power to meet human needs as distinguished from their boundless fascination with their discipline; of just compensation for groups permitted a monopoly over expertise as distinguished from what they are able to extort by the sometimes desperate needs of others; of their rightful claim on resources that must be shared with other occupations as distinguished from their insatiable appetite.

The reader will recognize that these modest proposals are no more than piecemeal engineering designed to edge professional practice a bit toward an ideal organization of work on the order of that projected in Larson's critique and, as a means of doing so, reforming professional ethics to make it consonant with the ideal. I should like to end by restating the ideal, emphasizing the positive side of professionalism which Larson neglects. All members of an ideal society would voluntarily work at genuinely useful jobs, for a fair living, which utilized their special talents, for which they were optimally educated, adhering to professional standards of competence and care, with due consideration of the human consequences of their work under a "wisdom of the whole," and without invidious comparisons of the forms of work or status stratification. Under such conditions each would voluntarily do what would best serve the rest and each would will that every other be doing what the other was doing voluntarily. The moral dignity of professions lies in their potentiality to serve humanity in this way. But this is a dignity in which every useful occupation can share, once the obfuscations of ideology have been dissipated.

NOTES

1. Adopted by the National Society of Professional Engineers in 1954.

2. ECPD has been replaced by the Accreditation Board of Engineering and Technology (ABET) and some of its functions have been assumed by the newly formed umbrella organization, the American Association of Engineering Societies (AAES). The ECPD Code had been adopted in whole or part by about two-thirds of its participating associations, which included most of the major specialized engineering societies. AAES and these same societies are now attempting to revise the ECPD Code with the hope of developing a unified code for all engineers.

3. See John Plamenatz's concept of total ideology in *Ideology* (New York: Praeger Publishers, 1970). I have adopted my conception of professional ideology from his of partial ideologies.

4. Talcott Parsons, *The Social System* (Glencoe, IL: Free Press, 1951), p. 349.

5. Terence Johnson, *Professionalism and Power* (London: Macmillan, 1972); Magali Larson, *The Rise of Professionalism* (Berkeley, CA: University of California Press, 1977); Randall Collins, *The Credential Society* (New York: Academic Press, 1979); David Noble, *America by Design* (New York: Alfred Knopf, 1977).

6. Larson, pp. 8, 66, 105.

7. Larson, pp. 232–37, 243–44.

8. The bourgeois and anti-market ideologies are summarized in Larson on pp. 220–24. The incorporation of their various elements is discussed in many places throughout the book.

9. For example, "Your Engineering Kit," available from ECPD in 1979, included "The Young Engineer: A Professional Guide," "Personal Development Check List," "Professional Guide for Young Engineers," "Faith of the Engineer," "Canons of Ethics" (but not the "Guidelines"), "The Second Mile" and "The Unwritten Laws of Engineering," the last three being inspirational in character.

10. The details of this case are explored by Robert M. Anderson et al. in *Divided Loyalties: Whistle–Blowing at BART* (West Lafayette, IN: Purdue University Press, 1980). See especially the discussion of professional ethics in the organizational context in chap. 1 and the views of the whistleblowers in chap. 6.

11. The most frequently cited sources among seminal thinkers include Parsons, *The Social System* [see n. 4] and "Profession and Social Structure," [in] *Essays in Sociological Theory* (Glencoe, IL: Free Press, 1954); A. M. Carr-Saunders and P. A. Wilson, *The Professions* (Oxford: Clarendon Press, 1933); and Everett Hughes, *Men and Their Work* (Glencoe, IL: Free Press, 1958). Geoffrey Millerson provides a convenient summary of this literature in *The Qualifying Associations* (London: Routledge and Kegan Paul, 1964), chap. 1.

12. The works cited in n. 5 provide comprehensive arguments for these claims. They utilize an accumulating body of empirical studies confirming the separate points. The reader is referred to them for references to this literature.

13. This impression is reinforced by two recent works on professional ethics, Alan H. Goldman's *The Moral Foundations of Professional Ethics* (Totowa, NJ: Rowman and Littlefield, 1980); and Michael Bayles' *Professional Ethics* (Belmont, CA: Wadsworth Publishing, 1981). One would gather from these books that almost all ethical questions for professionals pertain to one-to-one relations with clients though most "professionals" work for employers in corporate settings.

14. I formulated these recommendations before the report, *AAAS Professional Ethics Project* (Washington, DC, 1980), by Rosemary Chalk, Mark Frankel, and Sallie Chafer came to my attention. Their recommendations (pp. 104–6) are complementary to mine, though written from a less sceptical point of view.

53. Business Codes of Ethics: Window Dressing or Legitimate Alternative to Government Regulation?

Norman E. Bowie

The problem is to find some mechanism for ensuring that *all* corporations adhere to the minimum conditions of business ethics. Most corporations believe that it is clearly in the enlightened self-interest of the free enterprise system to ensure adherence to ethical standards through self-regulation. Unethical conditions should not be allowed to develop to the point where government regulation takes over. Government regulation of corporate ethics is viewed on a scale from distrust to horror. There are several reasons why government regulation is opposed. These include:

1. A recognition that government regulation would diminish the power and the prestige of corporate officials.
2. A fear that government officials would interfere with incentives and efficiency and hence reduce profit.
3. A judgment that government officials do not understand business and hence that its regulations would be unrealistic and hence unworkable.
4. A judgment that government officials are in no position to comment on the ethics of others.
5. A judgment that the federal government is already too powerful in a pluralistic society so that it is inappropriate to increase the power of government in this way.
6. A judgment that government regulation violates the legitimate freedom and moral rights of corporations.

When compared to the spectre of government regulations, codes of ethics at least deserve a second look. Codes of good business practice do serve a useful function and are not new. After all, one of the purposes of the Better Business Bureau is to protect both the consumer and the legitimate business operator from the "fly-by-night operator." The lesson we learn from the Better Business Bureau is that business ethics is not simply in the interest of the consumer, it is in the vital interest of the business community as well. Business activity depends on a high level of trust and confidence. If a firm or industry loses the confidence of the public, it will have a difficult time in selling its products. . . . An important result follows from the argument that business codes are in the general interest of business. To be effective, codes of

From *Ethical Theory and Business*, edited by Tom L. Beauchamp and Norman E. Bowie (Englewood Cliffs, NJ: Prentice-Hall, 1979), pp. 234–39.

business ethics must be adopted industry-wide. Otherwise, it is not to the competitive advantage of the individual firm to follow them. For example, it would not make sense for Bethlehem Steel to initiate the installation of anti-pollution devices for their own plants. In the absence of similar initiatives on the part of other steel companies, Bethlehem's steel would become more expensive and hence Bethlehem would suffer at the hands of its competitors.

An industry-wide code based on rational self-interest would help rebut a frequent criticism of the codes of individual firms. Often the cynical reaction of the public to any individual code is that it is a mere exercise in public relations. . . . There is good reason for that public reaction. An individual code by a particular firm on matters of industry-wide significance runs the danger of being nothing but window dressing if the firm is not to be at a competitive disadvantage. However an industry-wide code designed to protect legitimate businesses from the unethical acts of their competitors is not mere public relations; it is designed to preserve the trust and confidence of the public which is necessary for the survival of the industry itself. For the purpose of protecting the consumer and hence ultimately for the protection of industry itself, industry-wide codes of ethics are in theory a viable alternative to government regulation.

If industry-wide codes of ethics make sense on grounds of self-interest, why don't we have more successful examples? Two factors explain the basic situation. The first has to do with the scope of the regulations, and the second has to do with enforcement.

First, it is hard to make regulations flexible enough to meet a wide variety of situations, especially new situations, and yet simple enough to guide people's behavior in ways that will hold them accountable. Many criticize professional codes of ethics because they are too broad and amorphous. For example, consider four of the first six standards of the Public Relations Society of America.

1. A member has a general duty of fair dealing towards his clients or employees, past and present, his fellow members and the general public.
2. A member shall conduct his professional life in accord with the public welfare.
3. A member has the affirmative duty of adhering to generally accepted standards of accuracy, truth, and good taste.
6. A member shall not engage in any practice which tends to corrupt the integrity of channels of public communication.

By using such terms as "fair dealing," "public welfare," "generally accepted standards," and "corrupt the integrity," the code of standards of the PRSA could be charged with being too general and vague.

Before giving up on codes on this account, a few comments about the nature of language are in order. Except in the use of proper names, language is always general and is always in need of interpretation. Consider a municipal law: "No vehicles are allowed in the park." What counts as a vehicle? A bicycle? A skateboard? A baby carriage? Moreover, whenever we have a definition, there are certain borderline cases. When is a person bald or middle-aged? I used to think thirty-five was middle-aged. Now I am not so sure. The point of these comments is to show that some of the criticisms of business codes are really not criticisms of the codes but of language itself.

One should note, however, that none of these remarks refutes the criticism that business codes of ethics are too general and amorphous. Indeed these codes must be supplemented by other forms of self-regulation. First, the codes must provide procedures for interpreting what the code means and what it requires. Just as the Constitution needs the Supreme Court, a code of business ethics needs something similar. A serious code of business ethics can have its vagueness and generality corrected in ways not dissimilar from the mechanisms used by the law to correct vagueness problems in statutes and precedents. Perhaps a professional association could serve as the necessary analogue. Business codes of ethics do not have unique problems here.

Now we come to the second basic factor underlying the lack of successful existing codes of ethics: the difficulty of adequate enforcement procedures. There is a validity to the saying that a law which is unenforceable is really not a law at all. Any code of ethics worth having is worth enforcing and enforcing effectively.

First, the codes must be taken seriously in the sense that failure to follow them will carry the same penalties that failure to meet other company objectives carries. The trouble with many corporate codes of ethics is that employees see the codes as peripheral to their main concerns. After all, what is important is the bottom line. Experience demonstrates that when the crunch comes, ethics take a back seat.

If they were philosophers, the employees could put their point in the form of a syllogism. (1) If management is serious about a policy, management will enforce it; (2) management doesn't enforce its codes of ethics; (3) therefore management isn't really serious about its codes of ethics.

If codes of ethics are to work they must be enforced, and the first step in getting them enforced is to get them taken seriously by the management. How is that to be done? Phillip T. Drotning of Standard Oil of Indiana puts it this way:

> Several generations of corporate history have demonstrated that any significant corporate activity must be locked into the mainstream of corporate operations or it doesn't get done. Social policies will remain placebos for the tortured executive conscience until they are implemented with the same iron-fisted management tools that are routinely employed in other areas of activity to measure performance, secure accountability, and distribute penalties and rewards.[1]

In a home where discipline is taken seriously, a certain atmosphere pervades. I submit that in a company where ethics is taken seriously, a certain atmosphere will also pervade. Since I do not work in a business corporation, I cannot identify all the signs which indicate that the right atmosphere exists, but I can mention some possibilities discussed in the literature. These include:

1. Recognition that ethical behavior transcends the requirements of the law. The attitude that if it's not illegal it's okay is wrong. It's wrong first because at most the law prescribes minimum standards of ethical behavior. The public desires higher standards and the desire of the public is legitimate although I will not argue for this point here. Moreover, the attitude "if it's not illegal, it's okay" is wrong because it is ultimately self-defeating. By depending upon the law, one is encouraging the government regulations most business persons strongly object to. The American Institute for Certified Public Accountants recognizes this point when it describes its code of professional ethics as a voluntary assumption of self-discipline above and beyond the requirements of law.
2. A high-level officer, presumably a vice-president, with suitable staff support, being empowered to interpret and enforce the code. This vice-president should have the same status as the vice-presidents for marketing, production, personnel, etc. The vice-president should also be responsible for measuring performance.
3. Utilization of the device of the corporate social audit as part of the measurement of performance. The corporate social audit has come to have a number of different meanings. What I have in mind, however, is a revision of the corporation's profit and loss statement and balance sheet. Following the ideas of David Linowes, on the credit side all voluntary expenditures not required by law aimed at improving the employees and the public would be entered. On the debit side would be known expenditures which a reasonably prudent socially aware management would make, but didn't make. Such debit entries represent lost opportunities which the company should not have lost.[2]

I recognize that many of these suggestions are highly controversial and I do not want the discussion to shift away from our main topic. This discussion does reiterate, however, an important point made before. Codes of ethics by themselves are not sufficient devices to provide the climate for a desirable record on business ethics. Codes of ethics must be buttressed by internal mechanisms within the corporation if they are to be effective. They must be adequately interpreted and effectively enforced.

Given these criticisms, we should remind ourselves why written codes, both legal and moral, are viewed as desirable despite their inadequacies. Laws or codes of conduct provide more stable permanent guides to right or wrong than do human personalities. As you recall, God recognized that the charismatic leadership of Moses needed to be replaced by the Ten Commandments. Codes of ethics or rules of law provide guidance especially in ethically ambiguous situations. When one is tempted to commit a wrong act, laws also provide the basis for appeal in interpersonal situations. Professor Henry P. Sims, Jr., Professor of Organizational Behavior at Penn State, has done some research with graduate students confronted with decision-making opportunities. His results show that a clear company policy forbidding kickbacks lowers the tendency of the graduate students to permit kickbacks. A business code of ethics can provide an independent ground of appeal when one is urged by a friend or associate to commit an unethical act. "I'm sorry, but company policy strictly forbids it," is a gracious way of ending a conversation about a "shady" deal.

Codes of ethics have another advantage. They not only guide the behavior of average citizens or employees, they control the power of the leaders and employers. For Plato, questions of political morality were to be decided by philosopher kings. Plato had adopted this approach after observing the bad decisions of the Athenian participatory democracy. Aristotle, however, saw the danger that Plato's elitism could easily lead to tyranny. The actions of human beings needed to be held in check by law. The English and American tradition is similar. One means for controlling the king or other governing officials is through a constitution. The Bill of Rights of our own Constitution protects the individual from the tyranny of the majority. A strict company code of ethics would help provide a needed defense for an employee ordered by a superior to do something immoral. "I'm sorry but company regulations forbid that" does have some bite to it.

Finally, during the time when conflicting standards of ethics are being pushed on the business community, a code of ethics would help clarify the ethical responsibilities of business. One of the most frustrating aspects of the current debate about business ethics is that no one knows what the rules are. Most business leaders recognize that the social responsibilities of business must expand and that businessmen and women will be held to higher ethical standards than in the past. However there are some obvious limits. A blanket ethical demand that business solve all social problems is arbitrary and unrealistic. Business codes of ethics acceptable both to the business community and to the general public would help bring some order out of the chaos.

Let me conclude by providing some suggestions for writing an effective code of ethics. I am taking these suggestions directly from an article by Neil H. Offen, senior vice-president and legal counsel of the Direct Selling Association.

1. Be clear on your objectives, and make sure of your constituent's support. It is important to get the commitment from the president of each company.
2. Set up a realistic timetable for developing and implementing your code.
3. Know the costs of running a code program, and be sure you have long-term as well as short-term funding.
4. Make sure to provide for changing the code to meet new situations and challenges. It should be a living document.
5. Gear your code to the problems faced by your industry or profession.
6. Be aware of the latest developments and trends in the area of self-regulation. Pay particular attention to FTC, Justice Department, and congressional activities.
7. Make sure legal counsel is consulted and the code is legally defensible.
8. Get expert advice on how to promote the code and how to go about educating the public.
9. Watch your rhetoric. Don't promise more than you can deliver.
10. Write it as simply as possible. Avoid jargon and gobbledygook.
11. Be totally committed to being responsive and objective.
12. Select an independent administrator of unquestionable competence and integrity.
13. Be patient, maintain your perspective, and don't lose your sense of humor.[3]

NOTES

1. Phillip T. Drotning, "Organizing the Company for Social Action," in S. Prakash Sethi, *The Unstable Ground: Corporate Social Policy in a Dynamic Society* (Los Angeles: Melville Publishing Co., 1974), p. 259.

[2. David F. Linowes, *The Corporate Conscience* (New York: Hawthorn, 1974).]

3. Neil H. Offen, "Commentary on Code of Ethics of Direct Selling Association," in *The Ethical Basis of Economic Freedom* (Chapel Hill, NC: American Viewpoint, Inc. 1976), pp. 274–75.

PROFESSIONAL PREPARATION

54. Good Doctors

Samuel Gorovitz

. . . The behavior of physicians can fail to meet the expectations that patients and the public might reasonably impose on them. But . . . the burdens faced by physicians are severe, the problems complex, and the expectations sometimes unreasonable. In this [essay] I will offer an account of what is involved in being a good doctor and some recommendations about how medical training could increase the likelihood that doctors will turn out that way. So the [essay] will focus on medical

From *Doctors' Dilemmas: Moral Conflict and Medical Care* (New York: Macmillan, 1982; reissued New York: Oxford University Press, 1985), pp. 191–224.

education. That seems, on the face of it, a rather specialized concern, and the general reader may wonder why it is included here.

There are several reasons. First, the physician is the central player in the transactions of medical care. To the extent that we all are concerned with the quality and character of medical care—as health care professionals, patients, or citizens—we are concerned with what physicians do and how well they are prepared to face their responsibilities. We each stand to be directly touched by the effects of medical training, in various ways, at various times. Also, medical education is largely supported at public expense. Even after the substantial reductions in public support for education that have been proposed in the early 1980s, the costs of educating physicians will continue to be largely borne by public resources. Since we all are affected by the results of medical education and since we largely pay for it in the first place, it is surely appropriate to pay some attention to what it is and how well it is working. The better we all understand what is involved in being and becoming a good doctor, the easier it will be for us to be supportive of the efforts physicians make to maintain a high standard of performance.

An independent reason for attending to the training of physicians, especially to their preparation for dealing with moral issues, is that we have good reason to be concerned about the professions generally, and the medical profession can be an instructive case study for those whose concerns lie elsewhere. Whether it is a mark of increased social complexity, greater public awareness, or other causes, all our professions are having to grapple with the ethical dimensions of their professional lives. Scientists, teachers, lawyers, jurists, politicians, and others have come under the same sort of moral scrutiny that has been brought to bear more visibly on the more visible profession of medicine. To the extent that we can gain an increased understanding of what is involved in being a good doctor and what is likely to make doctors good, we will also have gained a model for the illumination of professional standards and professional training more generally. It is with this broader agenda in mind that I invite you now to consider the question, in both its senses, What makes a good doctor?

The need for reform in medical education persists because clinical medicine is based on a rapidly changing body of scientific information, because of changing social expectations in regard to health services, and because of a changing understanding of how people learn and of what it is most important for them to learn. I do not presume to offer a comprehensive view of what medical education should be or to suggest that it can ever be structured in a definitively correct way. I merely offer some suggestions about how it can be improved in some respects.

The objective of medical education is primarily the training of good physicians. It is not possible to provide an uncontroversial definition of the species. But I will emphasize those characteristics that are central to the concerns of this discussion. . . . I then want to consider how the goal of producing such physicians can be more successfully achieved.

Primary among the characteristics that I associate with the good physician are these: The good physician

—has and maintains a high level of technical competence, including both the knowledge and the skills appropriate to his specialty;
—is unfailingly thorough and meticulous in his approach to his specialty;
—is aware of the dependence of clinical medicine on medical research and equally aware of the experimental nature of clinical medicine;
—sees patients as persons with life stories, not merely as bodies with ailments;
—sees beyond simplistic slogans about health, nature, and life to the complexity involved in selecting goals for treatment;
—has a breadth of understanding that enables transcending the parochialism of his own specialty;
—understands his own values and motivation well enough to recognize that they can be in conflict with the patient's interests;
—is sensitive to the diversity of cultural, interpersonal, and moral considerations that can influence a patient's view of what is best, in process or outcome, in the context of medical care, and has the judgment to respect that diversity without undermining the integrity of his own moral commitments;
—has a respect for persons that shapes his interactions with patients, staff, and colleagues alike;
—has the humility to respect patient autonomy, the dedication to promote it through patient education, and the courage to override it when doing so seems justified;
—has the honesty to be truthful both with himself and with his patients about his own fallibility and that of his art; and
—has the sensitivity to recognize moral conflict where it exists, the motivation to face it where it is recognized, the understanding to consider it with intelligent reflection where it is faced, and the judgment to decide wisely following such consideration.

It is a tall order. But many physicians meet it, and more approximate to it reasonably well. The question is whether it is possible to increase the extent to which physicians on the whole are of this character.

A good physician obviously must know a great many things. Medical schools are notorious for requiring the assimilation of an enormous mass of factual material and for requiring little in the way of reflection. This is not peculiar to medical schools, of course, but is characteristic of professional training generally. As Daniel Callahan and Sissela Bok write, in their 1980 report *The Teaching of Ethics in Higher Education:*

> It is striking how few professional schools offer students an opportunity to examine the nature of their profession—its historical roots, its function in society, its sociological characteristics, and its assumptions about the political and social order. Such questions will of course arise during a professional education, but few professional schools seem to think it valuable to confront them in any systematic fashion.[1]

This phenomenon led one of my college roommates, an outrageously bright man who went on to a leading medical school, to enroll simultaneously, after one semester of medicine, in a graduate program in another discipline; this he reported doing to temper the tedium of medical education with something conceptually interesting.

It should be clear that acquiring the characteristics listed above does not, in the main, depend on the accumulation of information. Rather, they are largely dispositions to behave in certain ways—aspects of character, not merely of mind. Recall that Plato held right actions to be a matter of understanding: To know the good is to seek the good. But for Aristotle, understanding alone would not suffice: Right action flows from the will, not from the understanding alone. It was perhaps the Watergate story that most effectively brought to the public consciousness the wisdom of Aristotle's view, for the Watergate rogues were largely intelligent and highly trained professionals. As Arjay Miller (former dean of the Stanford Business School and previously head of the Ford Motor Company) put it in a newspaper interview, "It is a problem of motivation and basic human values. There are a lot of people in jail today who have passed ethics courses."[2]

No wonder, then, that there is dispute about the possibility of increasing the extent to which physicians have these characteristics. In one view it is beyond the reach of education. One hopes the admissions process will select only people of sterling character, for with those of sterling character no moral education is needed, whereas for those who lack it, nothing can be done. A second view holds that character and moral judgment are, in fact, subject to educational influence, even though they may not be wholly a matter of cognitive understanding; it then becomes incumbent upon medical schools to provide the right kinds of educational influences. And here the sides divide again, on the matter of effective pedagogy.

Aristotle saw habituation as the only effective route to moral improvement: If you would become virtuous, act as a virtuous man does until the patterns of behavior that make him virtuous become habit with you. Then you, too, will have become a man of virtue.[3] This viewpoint is defended by many medical educators. Students learn not merely what they are taught explicitly but also what they gather from the behavior of teachers who serve as role models. A kind of imprinting goes on, apart from the transactions of textbook and classroom, that determines a student's approach to people and decisions. No other method of teaching morality or character should be employed,, the argument goes, because no other method works. One must instead rely on the selection processes for students and faculty, so that the students are inclined to develop the proper habits of behavior and their faculty mentors will present exemplary standards of behavior.

This view has strengths and weaknesses. Surely much learning and patterning of behavior do result from the implicit influence on us of the people we admire. The power of the faculty member as a role model is often underestimated by teachers, perhaps because it is more comfortable to concentrate on the presentation of one's discipline than to concentrate on the presentation of oneself. But it is a failure of responsibility to rely solely on this phenomenon, for various reasons. First, faculty members are selected primarily for disciplinary expertise and are not all exemplars of the good physician. Secondly, there is the obvious problem of selecting the paragons of virtue from among the panoply of behavioral types that are available as models. If one does not yet understand what virtue is, how is one to know which behavior to emulate? For Aristotle, it is a matter of parental responsibility and of legislation. The ideal state will constrain people, through its system of laws, to act in accordance with virtue until such actions become so much a matter of habit that they persist even in the absence of constraint. Only then is virtue achieved, in Aristotle's view.[4] But it is plainly impossible to write rules of specific behavior that will habituate students of medicine to the behavior of the good physician. Nor does it suffice to tell them to model themselves after those who exemplify whatever sense they have already developed of excellence in clinical behavior. Rather, there must be an interplay between the understanding that can be achieved through thinking about questions of morality and the internalization of standards that does come from a repeated pattern of behavior. Virtue is not a purely cognitive capacity, but neither is it wholly independent of the understanding.

I once presented to a class a case that was hypothetical but based on cases that are real. At issue was the treatment of the irreversibly comatose. The patient was a young child, hopelessly ill, devoid of sentience, capable of an indeterminate life with the support of medical treatment, but threatened with a curable infection that would end the life if left untreated. This is a standard sort of class exercise in grappling with problems of medical ethics. As expected, the class debate centered on questions of the right to life, whether considerations of the quality of a life could be legitimately taken into account, why life has value, what the physician's obligations are, whether considerations of what consequences would be "for the best" should settle the matter, whether the high costs of sustaining the life had any bearing on the case, and the like. Some members of the class were uncertain about what to do, but many of them thought it was quite clear what to do. They divided, of course, into two camps—those who thought it obvious that this child's life must be preserved and those who thought that this former child, now but a vegetating relic of humanity, should be dispatched as promptly as circumstances would allow. Each group viewed the other with uncomprehending horror. We discussed the case at length, reached what common understanding we could, made as much sense as possible of the remaining conflict, and moved on.

A year later the hypothetical case came to life. A physician presented an actual case in which the circumstances of the patient were essentially the same. The discussion and debate were replayed. But then the physician arranged for us all to go into the hospital to see the patient. We discussed the case in a conference room for a while, and then the child was brought in. She was barely three, a beautiful little blond girl, sleeping deeply without concern for the tubes that linked her to the surrounding outside world. She breathed unaided, and responded to nothing. She had been in such a state for months, her condition was one of slow but inexorable decline, and no physician held out any hope for recovery. Moments before, the debate had been spirited and positions had been emphatic. Now the class was subdued, awed almost into silence by the presence of a tragedy that shredded their arguments into irrelevance, shattered their confidence, and terrified them. With tears in their eyes they stared mutely into the face of the horrible, hopeless reality. Then, slowly, they began to challenge that reality. Couldn't this be tried, or that, they wondered. But there was no escape; the medical evidence was overwhelming. And as they gradually accepted the reality of the case they had so easily discussed when it did not confront them, there was very little certainty in the air. Those who had argued for a calculated, coldly consequentialist case for withdrawing support were struck by the obvious humanity, by the beauty, by the seeming peace of the sleeping child. One student volunteered that she would never again refer to any patient as a vegetable, that although she had argued for the withdrawal of treatment, she now had no idea what was right. But another, who had argued for continued treatment, was overcome with the hopelessness that he so reluctantly came to accept. He'd always had a respect for life, he explained, but this life was so impoverished, so limited, so searingly painful for all those around it that he was no longer certain what he would do either.

At the next class meeting the discussion revealed that a number of students, including several who had offered opinions previously, were uncertain about what should be done. And among those who were able to take a side, there were several who had switched from the position they had previously taken to the one they had previously opposed; this crossing over had occurred both ways. Yet no additional information of any substantial sort had been imparted to the class in the interim—none, that is, of the sort that can be apprehended by the intellect alone. Instead, the feelings of many students had been powerfully engaged in a way that influenced their beliefs about what ought to be done. They were then challenged to consider the extent to which this impact of feelings on their judgment was legitimate. For on one account, the best decision is most likely to emerge from a dispassionate analysis based on the relevant factors that can be abstracted from a situation without regard to the emotionalism that can distort the judgment of those immediately involved in a case. Yet the feelings of the involved parties are among the relevant facts, and it is irrational not to give due weight to the nonrational factors that swirl around a tragic situation. So we discussed how the students' feelings arose, what effect those feelings had on their judgments, and whether their judgments were likely to be better or worse when they were thus influenced by an emotional response to a situation they had previously been able to discuss in a more detached way. I believe that the students gained an enhanced appreciation of the interplay of emotions and judgment; in any event, I gained an enhanced sense of the shallowness of discussion that is wholly detached from the emotional impact, and the attendant stresses, of the situation in question.

The phenomenon of detachment is central in medical practice, and it may in part explain some of the interpersonal failings that physicians often exhibit under close scrutiny. For physicians must do terrible things to people, and it may be a psychological necessity to maintain a certain degree of detachment from the patient when such things are being done. The clearest case is that of surgery; surgeons are notoriously more remote and aloof than the practitioners of other specialties and often strike their patients as being brusque, mechanical, calculating, or cold. But think of what they have to do! A surgeon who identifies sensitively with the patient on the operating table may be less effective for it, to the ultimate disadvantage of the patient. The apparent detachment of the surgeon may be a mechanism which, by defending the surgeon against the natural sentiments that could arise from and impede the doing of surgery, makes it possible to do it well. A certain amount of detachment is also a necessary consequence of the professionalization of the physician—of the development of a sense of identification with a peer group from which standards and conventions of behavior are derived over the course of a career. It is impossible to march to the beat of one's profession's drum without at least partially distancing oneself from other constituencies.

Yet this comes at a price. For he who usefully adopts the mechanisms of detachment cannot be expected to exhibit sensitive identification with the patient on passing through the operating room door. As Aristotle noted, the patterns of behavior we adopt shape the character we assume, and we become what we do. The physician who suffers along with each patient, however, will not likely be any more successful than the one for whom the patient is merely an object presenting a challenge to technical expertise. There is thus a tension between detachment and sensitivity that calls upon the physician to strike a balance between letting emotions run rampant and suppressing them to a point that dehumanizes the physician beyond the point of successful interpersonal interactions.

To learn to strike such a balance, one must experience a range of emotional responses to the highly charged situations that clinicians face—the repugnance of delivering a monstrosity, the elation of a dramatic intervention, the revulsion of mutilating surgery, the frustration of dealing with an uncooperative patient, the discomfort of reporting a death to a spouse, the anger and humiliation of botching a case, the satisfaction of doing a difficult procedure well, and all the rest. It does not suffice simply to learn in the classroom that such responses occur and can influence the way one makes decisions. But neither does it suffice simply to experience such responses along the way to becoming an independent practitioner, for it takes an understanding of the essence of good medical practice to develop the ability to strike the elusive balance. So, unsurprisingly, there are both cognitive and affective dimensions to learning to be a good physician, and there is a constant interplay between them. This has consequences for the way medical education should be structured.

Thinking about moral conflicts in medicine will not by itself prepare physicians to deal with them; the case of the comatose girl illustrates this point. Neither will feeling the impact of such cases by itself enhance the capacity to confront them wisely. Rather, what is required is a prolonged interplay of thinking about problems, facing them (in reality or through as realistic a simulation as possible), and then thinking about them again with others who can bring critical scrutiny to bear on the quality of that thought. At first the result is likely to be the kind of confusion felt by the students who saw the comatose girl. But eventually a habit of response can emerge—a pattern of thinking and feeling about cases in a reflective and informed way that strikes many balances at once: between consequentialist and nonconsequentialist values, between the patient's desires and the physician's medical knowledge, between the demands of the physician's moral integrity and those of the patient's values, between detachment from the patient and identification with the patient, and between the affective and cognitive factors that influence how one decides what to do. This pattern is a large part of what in the end is called clinical judgment, but it doesn't just happen. It is cultivated with greater or less success, depending on the qualities both of the student and of the educational experience that is provided.

If we assume that what makes a good physician is not merely factual knowledge and technical skill but is, beyond that, a kind of character and quality of judgment that comes only from reflection on the interplay of cognitive and affective learning, it follows that certain lines of approach to the improvement of medical education will be more promising than others. Let me consider a few.

There is nothing like being a patient to open the eyes of a physician to the perils and indignities associated with receiving medical care. Testimony to this effect is eloquently presented in the medical literature, in which physicians report on their own experiences as patients. Much the same message appears in conversations with physicians who have recovered from major illnesses, many of whom see themselves as better physicians because of the experience of life on the receiving end. Rarely does the experience provide them with technical data or other factual knowledge about medical care that was not previously known to them. Rather, what they gain is a sense of what it feels like to be a patient—to undergo the fears, confusions, angers, and hopes that even they face when cast in the patient's role.

This awareness of what it is like to be ill and to be treated—of the phenomenology of illness—is hard to come by in any indirect way. Descriptive lectures in medical school are perhaps better than nothing, but probably just barely. To be told that illness is boring, indeed, to know that fact and to bear it in mind in managing the treatment of a patient, still falls far short of having endured the long, empty hours waiting for the physician's brief and perhaps all-too-facile visit to a patient's room, after which the long, empty hours begin again. To be told that postoperative patients can become discouraged and depressed, as they impatiently wait for their strength to return to a level that allows the resumption of work, still falls far short of living with the irrational anxiety of fearing that one's career is over, while a glib physician, oozing confidence, uncomprehendingly says that there is nothing to worry about because these things always take a bit of time. And so on.

The pedagogical point should be obvious: A prerequisite for receipt of the medical degree should be having fallen victim to and survived a serious illness and its treatment! I have no doubt that medical care would be the better for it. But the proposal is unrealistic to the point of seeming whimsical. Yet we can approximate the benefits that would result with milder measures. Medical training incorporates a small bit of patient experience already. Students learn to draw blood samples by drawing them from one another, and various other relatively innocuous procedures are learned this way. The students are sometimes provided with material that is descriptive of patients' experiences, they spend some time talking with patients or hearing them talk during rounds, and some students will inevitably have been patients at one time or another. Still, many students reach the end of their formal training without having so much as spent a day in a hospital bed.

Why not require that each student spend a forty-eight-hour period in a hospital ward, in a bed, playing a patient role as a participant-observer of the full hospital day in the life of an inpatient? This could be done late in the clinical years and scheduled on the basis of availability of beds. Since it is hard to predict when vacant beds will be available in a teaching hospital, or in what wards, the students would receive their hospitalization assignments on short notice. They would be unable to tell before the last moment where they would be placed, or when, and the assignment would in all likelihood be disruptive of their otherwise busily scheduled lives. So much the better; so much the move valid the experience. (The incremental cost to the hospital of filling otherwise empty beds would *not* be a serious barrier.)

Additional appreciation of the phenomenology of illness can be gained through the judicious use of films or videotapes, and medical schools have developed some fine materials of this sort. One of the best tells the story of, shows an interview with, and shows the treatment of a man who was badly burned, blinded, and crippled in a gas leak explosion. The man pleads to be allowed to die; he asks that treatment be terminated and he presents an articulate and reasoned defense of his position. He even seeks legal redress, but to no avail; the forces of medical intervention press on inexorably, and his treatment continues. The film provokes lively debate about the right to refuse treatment, the value of life, and related issues. But that is not the point here. Rather, it is the impact that such a film can have. It captures the attention of the viewer, who becomes drawn into it, wholly absorbed in it, and often deeply affected by it. It can prompt nausea, rage, and tears; viewers tend to to identify with the patient, to begin in a limited way to feel his frustration and despair, to share in his experience. The film has this capacity because in addition to being a documentary, it is good drama—despite its reality, it commands belief like a work of art.[5]

What gives the film its impact is its quality as art, rather than its literal veracity. This suggests a way to enhance the physician's understanding of the patient's perspective through simulated experience. For there is a rich heritage of literature that illuminates the phenomenology of illness as nothing else can short of illness itself. Yet it is rare indeed for a medical school to provide for any significant exposure to such material. One reform that would improve medical education is precisely the incorporation of the literary perspective on illness and treatment, despite its apparent remove from the day-to-day practicalities of clinical treatment or laboratory research.

Consider this passage on reactions to illness, from Hicks's *Patient Care Techniques*. (Note that this text is primarily for allied health workers; one searches in vain for any discussion of the patient's reaction to illness in such classical medical texts as *Price's Textbook of the Practice of Medicine*,[6] *Conybeare's Textbook of Medicine*,[7] or the massive fifteenth edition of the *Cecil Textbook of Medicine*.[8])

> It is generally accepted that illness poses a threat to which persons respond with behavior like that associated

with mourning. The process of mourning can be divided into four sequential phases: denial, anger, grief-depression, and acceptance. . . . It is often difficult to determine the difference between the normal range of behaviors in the phases of mourning and those behaviors which might indicate a pathological response that requires professional help. Careful attention should be given to a patient's behavior so that expert assistance can be sought to maintain mental health. . . .

Denial is described as a defensive behavior unconsciously used by a person to cope with thoughts and feelings that he is unable to face consciously. The denial phase is considered a necessary reaction to give the patient time to absorb the emotional shock of illness and to mobilize the constructive behavior needed to cope with the condition. This is especially true in critical illness or severe disability.

In working with patients during this phase it is important to give emotional support by showing concern for them and acceptance of them as persons. . . .

Anger or hostility is a sign that the patient can no longer completely deny his condition. This state is frequently one of the most difficult with which families and health care personnel must deal. The patient may direct his anger in many directions, such as toward those who are caring for him, toward the institution, and toward the family. He may become demanding and make frequent, and sometimes conflicting, requests.

When caring for angry patients, it is helpful to try to understand the reason for their anger. Illness interrupts a person's life—the plans for the future. The individual is afraid. . . .

Grief-depression is the normal manifestation of a recognized loss. It is part of an increased awareness by the patient of the reality of his condition. He may be quiet and withdrawn, or may give the appearance of sadness. He may cry or may talk about past experiences when he was able to function more ably.[9]

These observations are reasonable and important. But compare the impact of Solzhenitsyn's description of Pavel Nikolayevich's (Rusanov's) first day of hospitalization, in *The Cancer Ward:*

He needed support, but instead he was being pushed down into a pit. In a matter of hours he had as good as lost all his personal status, reputation and plans for the future—and had turned into one hundred and fifty-four pounds of hot, white flesh that did not know what tomorrow would bring. . . .

The lump of his tumor was pressing his head to one side, made it difficult for him to turn over, and was increasing in size every hour. Only here the doctors did not count the hours. All the time from lunch to supper no one had examined Rusanov and he had had no treatment. And it was with this very bait that Dr. Dontsova had lured him here—immediate treatment. Well, in that case she must be a thoroughly irresponsible and criminally negligent woman. Rusanov had trusted her, and had lost valuable time in this cramped, musty, dirty ward when he might have been telephoning and flying to Moscow.

Resentment at the delay and the realization of having made a mistake, on top of the misery of his tumor, so stabbed at Pavel Nikolayevich's heart that he could not bear anything from the noise of dishes scraped by spoons, to the iron bedsteads, the rough blankets, the walls, the lights, the people. He felt that he was in a trap, and that until the next morning any decisive step was impossible.

Deeply miserable, he lay there covering his eyes from the light and from the whole scene with the towel he had brought form home.[10]

Or consider his account of the psychological impact of hospital dress:

It was the shabby gray dressing gowns of rough cotton, so untidy-looking even when perfectly clean, as well as the fact that they were about to undergo surgery, that set these women apart, deprived them of their womanliness and their feminine charm. The dressing gowns had no cut whatever. They were all enormous, so that any woman, however fat, could easily wrap one around her. The drooping sleeves looked like wide, shapeless smokestacks. The men's pink and white striped jackets were much neater, but the women were never issued dresses, only those dressing gowns without buttons or buttonholes. Some of them shortened the dressing gowns, others lengthened them. They all had the same way of tightening the cotton belt to hide their nightdresses and of holding the flaps across their breasts. No woman suffering from disease and in such a drab dressing gown had a chance of gladdening anyone's eye, and they all knew it.[11]

A sympathetic understanding of the patient's perspective is necessary for the good doctor, but not sufficient. Some address to the moral dimensions of medical practice is needed as well. But what sort? There are basically four positions. The first is that there is no point to a formal consideration of ethical issues. This view can result from the belief that the diversity and confusion in ethical argumentation make complete moral skepticism the only reasonable position, so that there is nothing to discuss. . . . [But] this is overly pessimistic and . . . enough light can be shed by a systematic inquiry into matters of morality to make the undertaking worthwhile. Opposition also arises from the belief that the behavior of physicians depends on the moral outlook they have established prior to their medical training. This, too, I see as overly pessimistic; given an initial disposition on the part of the student to take matters of morality seriously, the quality of moral judgment can be enhanced by a systematic and guided exploration of the issues.

Three remaining positions hold that the consideration of ethics should take place early, late, and throughout the curriculum. As Callahan and Bok report:

A common problem in professional schools is whether it is better, comparatively, to introduce ethics at the beginning of a professional education, or to wait until the end. The main argument for introducing it at the beginning is to alert students to the ethical problems they will encounter in other courses, and to serve notice of the importance of ethical concerns. The argument for putting it at the end of a professional education is that, by then, students will better understand the nature of their profession and its problems, and thus be in a stronger position to appreciate the moral dilemmas—something not always possible when students, at the very beginning, have yet to really discover the nature of the professional problems themselves. . . .

A frequent comment, at both the undergraduate and especially the professional school level, is that ethics ought not to be taught in a specific course at all, but should be built into all other courses in the curriculum.[12]

Providing formal consideration of ethical issues at the start of professional training is the inoculation method. Give them a good dose at the outset, and they will be immune from moral crisis thereafter! The odd booster shot may be needed from time to time, but basic protection should be provided.

This method is unlikely to succeed. The initial dose is often small and dilute—a few guest lectures in the first-year program, a series of lunch-hour discussions, or something of the kind. More important, there is a mismatch between the methods and the goals. For there are two distinct stages of ethical sophistication [that are] often conflated. One is the heightening of moral sensitivity—making the physician aware of value assumptions, value conflicts, and perhaps different theoretical accounts of the nature and origin of values. This much may well be accomplished in a single course. But the other objective is the more crucial, and that is to go beyond a heightened awareness of ethical issues to an enhanced capacity to exercise ethical judgment. And this requires the internalization of a habit of mind that can come only through prolonged and reflective grappling with the issues. Even a large and potent single dose cannot accomplish that.

For the same reason, the single dose will fail when administered at the end of a professional program. Further, such late administration lets pass the opportunity to provide an enriched perspective for viewing the experiences to be encountered throughout a medical school career. So it may seem that the method of building ethical consideration into all the courses—what has come to be known as the pervasive method—is the method of choice. But it is even less satisfactory than the others.

What is everyone's responsibility too easily becomes no one's, and the time devoted to ethical issues in the context of other pursuits is likely to be insignificant. Worse, what consideration does occur is likely to be untutored, providing the form without the substance. One cannot expect the entire faculty of a medical school to be competent in the analysis of ethical issues—any more than one should expect them all to be competent in, say, anesthesiology. But whereas no one without qualifications in anesthesiology would consider trying to teach it, anyone can conduct a meandering discussion of some moral dilemma or other or can ruminate aloud about ethical conflicts faced and conquered. As likely as not, the result will be, at best, to increase the student's awareness of the reality of moral conflict and, at worst, to give the consideration of ethical issues a bad name.

I favor the intermittent method. Students should be sensitized to the reality and importance of ethical issues as early as possible in their medical training. And surely at the end, before they go on to residencies, there should be another systematic exploration of ethical issues, linked to the clinical experiences they will have confronted. Along the way there should be some thread of continuity—structuring and guiding the reflections that the students bring to bear on ethical matters. For the point is not to provide information, but to cultivate habits of mind and attitude. Only if the students' exposure to ethical reflection is a continuing presence in their consciousness will this result be achieved.

The details are where such proposals come to grief because of battles about who has to give up what to transform them from noble plans into operating programs. A medical school would have to go to some lengths to make such a program a reality, but some have already done it, thereby demonstrating their collective concern with the humanistic dimensions of medical practice.

Every discussion of curriculum reform comes rapidly to dispute about whether new programs should be required. Many medical schools offer courses in medical ethics and related areas as electives to interested students. However, they play little role in increasing the likelihood that the school will produce good physicians. For the students who elect them tend to be those who need them least. The chap who is most likely to become a cold medical technician will give such courses wide berth.

In a recent BBC series on the British public schools one headmaster put his position well. "Any lad worth 'is salt," he said, "will find the easy path. That's why they must be coerced into valuable experience." The point has broad applicability, for higher education generally has suffered a crisis of confidence and a failure of responsibility in the planning of educational programs. In the tumultuous period from 1964 through the mid-1970s, many long-overdue educational reforms were adopted at colleges and universities, but some excesses were embraced along the way. One of them was an overready acceptance of the notion that students know enough to determine not only what general course of studies they wish to pursue but what the fine structure of that pursuit should be. They do not. The faculty has no infallible insight into such matters, but it does have a broader base of judgment and a responsibility to exercise it. On the basis of that responsibility, medical schools should require a sustained consideration of the moral issues in clinical practice.

Increasingly, matters of medical practice become entangled with matters of public policy. Whenever there are issues to decide about such matters as expansion of hospital beds, the financing of medical care, or the establishment of environmental or industrial safety standards, physicians are called upon in the deliberation. Although their role may in principle be thought of as value-free, providing just the relevant technical facts, it is not possible in reality to separate the issues as sharply as that. The physician as a citizen is called upon to exercise judgment in hearings, at civic meetings, on committees, and at the ballot box, on matters that pertain to medicine and health. Yet there is typically nothing in the training of a physician to provide for an informed sense of social responsibility where such matters are concerned. This, too, needs redress in the curriculum.

I have argued against the position that the morality of medical students is wholly determined by the selections of the admissions committee. I believe that students who have the moral capacity and inclination to become good physicians are far more likely to do so if they are exposed to the kinds of influences I have been describing. Of course, some students will become good physicians, as many have before them, independently of the content of their training. And others will be interpersonal thugs no matter what they are exposed to in or after medical school. But that is no argument against reforms—no more than it is an argument against driving safely that doing so only modifies the likelihood of survival.

The extent to which students benefit from such programs along the way to becoming good doctors will depend to a great degree on who they are at the outset. So, although I reject the view that admissions decisions wholly determine the moral character of the class, I want to focus now on the importance of such decisions. There is probably no greater influence on the products of any educational institution than the raw material on which it exercises its influence—the students chosen for admission. Much of their ultimate character is already shaped, and they constitute one of the primary influences on one another. Present circumstances make medical school admissions highly competitive, and admissions decisions are often made on the basis of marginal considerations. There is a substantial literature concerning admissions policies, and medical sociologists strive to understand what sort of policies have what sorts of results. My views on the matter are not offered as the results of any study, but rather as suggestions for consideration.

Some years ago I was privy to admissions deliberations at a prestigious medical school. There were more than five thousand applications for just over one hundred seats. Most of the applications were from very good students, and perhaps the top ten percent—five hundred or so—were indistinguishably excellent. There were even two hundred applicants who already held the Ph.D. In a situation like that, an admissions committee can be very fussy. In the scramble to gain admission, the premedical student will do whatever there is a hint that admissions committees look on with favor. So if it were known that a particular school needed a new kettle-drum player for its anatomy lab band, drum sales would boom near college campuses across the land. And if an admissions committee rather favored fans of surrealistic art, campus bookstores would be stripped overnight of posters by Magritte. Because of this immense power, admissions policies must be fashioned and promulgated with great care.

Typically a candidate must have taken courses in mathematics, biology, and chemistry. But there is no requirement to have specialized in such subjects. Rather, the student may have taken a degree in linguistics, art history, philosophy, or anything else, so long as the premedical requirements are met. Yet most premedical students do major in biological or natural sciences largely because of the belief that doing so will enhance their prospects for admission. Further, they show no particular propensity to study such areas as abnormal psychology, moral philosophy, or sociology of the family, which have potential bearing on the practice of medicine. The quest for the perfect grade dominates all decisions, and the quest for breadth of learning takes a back seat.

A handful of medical schools could modify this pattern by explicitly favoring, among those with superb records in the premedical requirements, students who demonstrate an active concern with the humanistic dimensions of health care, manifested in the sustained pursuit of programs in the humanities or social sciences or in other ways. Such students do gain admission to medical school now, but increasing their number—a transformation that could be accomplished in short order—could substantially alter the intellectual climate within medical education and increase receptivity to the programs most likely to nurture the character traits that make good physicians good. No diminution of technical competence would result; selections would still be from among the technically superior. But parochialism might well diminish, and better clinical judgment could result. The experiment could be safely tried, given the strength of the admissions committees' position in the marketplace. Of course, the occasional brilliant psychopath would continue to slip through the net, but not likely any more often.

Medical schools do not have the sole responsibility for confronting issues in medical ethics. On the contrary, training in the early postgraduate years is of comparable importance, and it is gratifying to see new programs designed to help physicians learn to grapple with the moral problems they face in these early years of practice. Nor are these matters for the medical profession alone. I have argued that a good physician must develop moral sensitivity and good ethical judgment. But as I argued earlier, the moral problems in clinical practice, although they may center on what the physician does, are the proper concern of others as well. The exploration of these issues should not be limited to physicians because such issues are also the burden of the rest of us. Those who practice medicine should be good physicians, and that is too seldom the case. But good physicians should have the support of a broader community that understands the problems they face and accepts the responsibility of sharing them.

Medical science proceeds, answering old questions and replacing them with new, often harder questions, so that it becomes impossible to conceive of the enterprise's ever reaching an end. So, too, does medical ethics change and grow. Issues in medical ethics can be explored in medical training, but medical ethics cannot be taught as if it were a body of information any more than the skills of philosophical reflection can. For new problems arise to humble old conclusions, and only an appropriately reflective individual can confront them insightfully. So no amount of change in medical education or public education will solve the moral problems in medicine; at best it can merely increase the quality of thought that is brought to bear on them.

NOTES

1. Daniel Callahan and Sissela Bok, *The Teaching of Ethics in Higher Education* (Hastings-on-Hudson, NY: Hastings Center, 1980), p. 37.
2. Arjay Miller, quoted in Edward B. Fiske, "Ethics Courses Now Attracting More U.S. College Students," *New York Times* (February 20, 1978).
3. Aristotle, *Nichomachean Ethics,* Bk. II, many translations.
4. Ibid.
5. The videotape "Please Let Me Die" was developed by Dr. Robert White of the University of Texas Medical Branch at Galveston (1974).
6. Ronald B. Scott, ed. *Price's Textbook of the Practice of Medicine* (New York: Oxford University Press, 1978).
7. W. N. Mann, *Conybeare's Textbook of Medicine,* 16th ed. (New York: Churchill, 1975).
8. Paul B. Berson et al., *Cecil Textbook of Medicine,* 2 vols., 15th ed. (Philadelphia: Saunders, 1979).
9. Dorothy J. Hicks, *Patient Care Techniques* (Indianapolis, IN: Bobbs-Merrill, 1975), pp. 12–13.
10. Alexander Solzhenitsyn, *The Cancer Ward,* trans. Nicholas Bethell and David Berg (New York: Farrar, Straus and Giroux, 1969), pp. 11, 15.
11. Ibid., p. 42.
12. Callahan and Bok, *The Teaching of Ethics in Higher Education,* p. 74.

QUESTIONS FOR STUDY AND DISCUSSION

1. Using this book's chapter introductions, readings, and cases as resources, list any morally troubling characteristics you think are fostered in the practice of law and in politics. (They may not be the same characteristics in each profession.) Explain why you think these characteristics are morally troubling. Can lawyers and politicians function as effective professionals without exercising these characteristics? Explain your answers carefully.

2. Using this book's chapter introductions, readings, and cases as resources, list any morally troubling characteristics you think are fostered in practitioners of medicine and nursing. (They may not be the same characteristics in each profession.) Explain why you think these characteristics are morally troubling. Can physicians and nurses function as effective professionals without exercising these characteristics? Explain your answers carefully.

3. Using this book's chapter introductions, readings, and cases as resources, list any morally troubling characteristics you think are fostered in the practices of education and psychological counseling. (They may not be the same characteristics in each profession.) Explain why you think these characteristics are morally troubling. Can educators and counselors function as effective professionals without exercising these characteristics? Explain your answers carefully.

4. Using this book's chapter introductions, readings, and cases as resources, list any morally troubling characteristics you think are fostered in business practice and in journalism. (They may not be the same characteristics in each profession.) Explain why you think these characteristics are morally troubling. Can businesspersons and journalists function as effective professionals without exercising these characteristics? Explain your answers carefully.

5. Using this book's chapter introductions, readings, and cases as resources, list any morally troubling characteristics you think are fostered in police work and in the military. (They may not be the same characteristics in each profession.) Explain why you think these characteristics are morally troubling. Can police and career military personnel function as effective professionals without exercising these characteristics? Explain your answers carefully.

6. Using this chapter's introduction and readings as resources, choose some profession that interests you and generate as complete a list as you are able of the virtues you believe should be cultivated by practitioners in the profession. Be sure to explain why you select the characteristics you select. Anticipate and respond to any objections you think might be brought against your list.

7. Using this chapter's introduction and readings as resources, explain as clearly as you are able the problems that codes of professional ethics can have. In what ways, if any, can codes of professional ethics be beneficial?

8. Compare and contrast the two codes of nursing ethics included in appendix I, saying how the codes are similar and how the codes are different; pay particular attention to any differences in the portrait of the professional nurse in the codes. Which of these codes, in your considered judgment, is the preferable professional code for nurses? Explain your answer carefully.

9. What does John Kultgen mean by "the ideology of the professions"? Explain in detail how this concept figures into Kultgen's criticism of many existing codes of professional ethics.

10. Codes of professional ethics are usually drawn up by professional associations. It was noted by Bernard Barber in chapter 2 that the formation of professional societies and the development of professional codes are two common steps taken by occupations that seek social recognition as professions. Using the chapter introductions, readings, and cases in this book as resources, explain as fully as you are able the case for any two of the following occupations' strengthening their professional societies and the force of their professional codes: nursing, journalism, chemical engineering, civil engineering, public administration, social work, veterinary medicine.

11. Although Samuel Gorovitz focuses on medicine, one of his broader concerns is to suggest that training for every professional area should include substantial inquiry into the moral problems that arise in that profession. Offer your own evaluation of this suggestion.

CASE: VIRTUE IN THE CORPORATION

Quasar Stellar company is a subsidiary of Universal Nucleonics Company. Several years ago, Quasar submitted two falsified monthly financial reports to Universal. By the time Universal realized that it had been misinformed of Quasar's status, the parent company had projected fourth-quarter earnings that were

---

For a fuller description, see John J. Fendrock, "Crisis in Conscience at Quasar," *Harvard Business Review* (March–April 1968); reprinted in *Ethics for Executives Series: Reprints from the Harvard Business Review*, publication no. 21075 (Boston: Harvard Business Review, nd.), pp. 2–10. Page references in the case description refer to the reprint.

significantly higher than the earnings it was able to report at the end of the year. On investigation, Universal's executive vice president and the vice president for industrial relations found that Quasar's president and financial vice president (controller) had directed the falsification of the reports.

Quasar had been pursuing two large contracts, and the decision to falsify began when Quasar's president informally told headquarters that Quasar's chances of getting the contracts were less than fifty percent. The board suggested that the president was being pessimistic, and the president subsequently focused much of Quasar's marketing efforts on winning the two contracts, which led to a loss of other, smaller contracts.

When it became evident to Quasar's vice president of marketing that the company was unlikely to win the contracts, he reported this to Quasar's president. The president, however, elected to go forward with the attempt to recruit the contracts and did not inform Universal that the probability of getting them was diminishing. When asked by representatives of Universal why he did not report his reservations about Quasar's chances of getting the contracts directly to Universal's vice president of marketing, Quasar's vice president of marketing replied that he was not required by policy to do so. What is more, he said that he felt his loyalty was to his supervisor (Quasar's president) and that his obligation was to support whatever his supervisor decided to do with information he was given.

On being asked why he didn't alert Universal about the falsified reports, Quasar's vice president of manufacturing answered that he had expressed his views to Quasar's president and that in considering his responsibility to Quasar, Universal, himself, and his supervisor, he felt he could do no more: "The fact is, so long as we have a characteristic line and staff organizational structure, we can only follow the channels of communication that the CEO [chief executive officer] decides on. No self-respecting manager would consider surreptitiously reporting behind his superior's back" (p. 6).

A similar response was given by the vice president of engineering, who said, "No mechanism existed, or perhaps should ever exist, for circumventing top management. On a few occasions I might have had the opportunity to mention to the corporate vice president of engineering what was happening, but I certainly would not do that" (p. 9).

Finally, the chief accountant was asked why the accounting department did not report the fraud. His response: "As standard company policy on reports, we generate our financial statements from whatever information is given to us. Our statements, in turn, are sent to the controller's office, and he does what he sees fit with them. Should we receive instructions from his office to reorganize, let's say, or otherwise manipulate the reports, there is very little we can do but follow instructions. This is particularly true when matters of judgment are involved, [for example] if a project is reported as being behind schedule by the program manager and, after review by the controller's office it is decided that it is not all that far behind, naturally adjustments are made. . . . So far as I can see, this is nothing more than exercising management prerogative. I will summarize my position by saying that I do pretty much what I am told. Sometimes I may not like it, but my job is not to set policy or to question decisions. Rather, it is to follow instructions" (p. 10).

1. On being asked why they took no action when they realized that Quasar's president was ignoring their advice and when they learned that falsified reports had been sent to corporate headquarters, several of the vice presidents at Quasar cited loyalty to their supervisor. Offer your own evaluation of the importance of loyalty to supervisors and colleagues in professional life; say when (if ever) loyalty to a superior or colleague overrides other moral considerations and when (if ever) other moral considerations must take priority over the virtue of loyalty to those with whom one works. Given your account, did the Quasar employees who explained their silence on the ground of loyalty act in a morally defensible way? Defend your answer; anticipate and respond to the strongest objection to your view.

2. The accountant in this case draws a sharp distinction between the role of the corporate accountant and the role of the corporate manager. If we accept this sharp distinction as articulated by Quasar's accountant, what kinds of characteristics should people have in order to function well as corporate accountants? Are any of these characteristics morally troubling? Explain. Offer your own account of what virtues corporate and private accountants should cultivate in themselves.

3. Should we accept the distinction between the role of the corporate accountant and the role of corporate managers as the distinction is articulated by Quasar's chief accountant? If so, why so? If not why not? Anticipate and respond to the most serious objection that might be raised against your view.

CASE: THE LOYAL AGENT FALTERS

Eileen P. is a fifty-three-year-old factory pieceworker at ABC Widget Company. Her job involves several inspection and sorting tasks. While on the job one day, Eileen is hit in the eye by a bolt thrown from a piece of heavy equipment. Her compensation (two-thirds of her average pay while recuperating) is paid by XYZ Insurance Agency, a private insurance company, which carries Workmen's Compensation for a number of plants in that area of the state. After twelve weeks of recuperation, Eileen is told by the adjustor for XYZ Insurance that she is to return to work. Although she is still having considerable difficulty seeing, Eileen accepts the adjustor's judgment and returns to her job. The adjustor for XYZ informs the agency's legal division that Eileen has been instructed to return to work, and Frank D., one of the insurance agency's attorneys, is instructed by his supervisor to send Eileen a formal notice of termination of benefits. Frank sends the notification, as instructed; but in going over the record he feels that Eileen is probably entitled to considerably more compensation than she has received. Since returning to work, her productivity has slowed noticeably, significantly reducing her earnings, and Frank feels that she is probably entitled to compensation for the pay lost. The record also shows that Eileen is scarred from the injury, and scarring with an eye injury is often sufficient to provide a strong argument for full loss of the organ. Frank raises the matter with his supervisor, who tells him to forget it; if Eileen doesn't protest, there is nothing they can do. Frank finally decides to call Jim M., an attorney with considerable experience in insurance cases. He explains the case to Jim, who agrees that Eileen seems certainly entitled to compensation for the loss in pay and that she is probably able to win compensation for effective loss of the eye. Jim contacts Eileen and sets up an appointment to discuss her case. At their meeting, he explains that she is probably entitled to far more compensation than she has received. Eileen, a widow and sole support of two teen-age sons, has been alarmed by her reduction in productivity and consequent reduction in earnings. She is greatly interested in pursuing the matter. But she tells Jim that even if she were making the pay she made before the accident, she could not afford to hire a lawyer. Jim explains that his firm can take the case on a contingency basis, which will cost Eileen virtually nothing if they lose the case, and will bring his firm one-third of the award if they win. Eileen is greatly relieved and asks Jim to take the case. After roughly a year, Eileen is awarded approximately $100,000 and put on a continual pay supplement. Jim's firm receives one-third of the $100,000 award.

1. In contacting Jim, Frank violated his duty as a zealous advocate of the insurance company. In your considered judgment, was Frank's action morally wrong? Defend your answer in light of the strongest potential objection to your view.

2. Although there was never any agreement between Frank and Jim, it is customary in legal practice for attorneys who are successful in such cases to give referring attorney's one-third of the amount they receive in compensation for representing the client. If Jim's firm follows the convention in this case, however, it could be discovered that Frank referred the case to Jim, and both attorneys could be liable to disbarment for conspiracy against Frank's client. Would Jim's firm be wrong not to follow the convention in Eileen's case? Is Frank morally entitled to the conventional compensation? Explain.

3. If it were to be discovered that Frank brought Eileen's case to the attention of a plaintiff's attorney, should the attorneys be disbarred for conspiracy against Frank's client? Defend your answer in light of the strongest objection to your view.

4. Since Frank's action violated the Model Rules' requirements of zealous advocacy, explain how your answers to (1), (2), and (3) reflect your views on this part of the code for attorneys.

5. What, in your considered judgment, are the kinds of characteristics insurance company attorneys need to nurture in themselves to function comfortably and consistently as zealous advocates for their clients?

6. Read through the Model Rules (appendix 1). Offer your own account and evaluation of the character traits you think attorneys need to nurture in themselves if they are to follow the requirements of the Model Rules. (Keep in mind that attorneys function in a variety of roles: as representatives for the state, as criminal defense lawyers, as agents for business, as agents for individuals, etc.) In your discussion, be sure to say which of these traits (if any) you think are desirable and why they are desirable, which of these traits (if any) are undesirable and why they are undesirable, and/or which of these traits (if any) have both desirable and undesirable features; explain the reasons for your judgments.

SELECTED BIBLIOGRAPHY

Abel, Richard, "Why Does the American Bar Association Promulgate Ethical Rules?" *Texas Law Review* 59 (1981): 639–88.

Adams, R. M. "Motive Utilitarianism." *Journal of Philosophy* 73:14 (1976): 467–81.

American Medical Association Council on Ethical and Judicial Affairs. *Current Opinions of the Council on Ethical and Judicial Affairs of the American Medical Association*. Chicago: American Medical Association, 1986.

Aristotle. *Nichomachean Ethics*, esp. Bk. 7. Trans. W. D. Ross. In *The Works of Aristotle Translated into English*, ed. W. D. Ross. Oxford: Oxford University Press, 1915.

Baier, Kurt. "Duties to One's Employer." In *Just Business: New Introductory Essays in Business Ethics*, ed. Tom Regan, pp. 60–99. Philadelphia: Temple University Press, 1983; reissued New York: Random House, 1984.

———. "Moral Value and Moral Worth." *Monist* 54 (1970): 18–30.

Baron, Marcia. "On Admirable Immorality." *Ethics* 96:4 (1986): 557–66.

Bean, Lee Randolph. "Entrepreneurial Science and the University." *Hastings Center Report* 12:5 (1982): 5–9.

Blair, Roger D., and Stephen Rubin, eds. *Regulating the Professions*. Lexington, MA: Heath, 1980.

Bosk, Charles L. *Forgive and Remember: Managing Medical Failure*. Chicago: University of Chicago Press, 1979.

Brandt, Richard B. "Traits of Character: A Conceptual Analysis." *American Philosophical Quarterly* 7:1 (1970): 23–37.

Broad, William, and Nicholas Wade. *Betrayers of the Truth: Fraud and Deceit in the Halls of Science*. New York: Simon and Schuster, 1982.

Cheatham, Elliott. "What Law Schools Can Do to Raise the Standards of the Legal Profession." *American Law Society Review* 7 (1932): 716–35.

Comment. "The Lawyer's Moral Paradox." *Duke Law Journal* 1979 (1979): 1335–58.

Cowger, Nancy. "Do Lawyers Really Need a Detailed Code of Ethics?" *American Bar Association Journal* 64 (1978): 522.

Dworkin, Gerald. "Fraud and Science." In *Research Ethics: Progress in Clinical and Biological Research*, vol. 128, ed. Kåre Berg and Knut Erik Tranøy, pp. 65–74. New York: Alan R. Liss, 1983.

Feinberg Joel. "Supererogation and Rules." *Ethics* 71:4 (1961): 276–88

Flynn, John J. "Professional Ethics and the Lawyer's Duty to Self." *Washington University Law Quarterly* 1976 (1976): 429–44.

Foot, Philippa. "Virtues and Vices." In *Virtues and Vices*, chap. 1. Oxford: Basil Blackwell, 1978.

Geach, Peter. *The Virtues: The Stanton Lectures, 1973–74*. New York: Cambridge University Press, 1977.

Gorlin, Rena A., comp. *Codes of Professional Responsibility*. Washington, DC: Bureau of National Affairs, 1986.

Gorovitz, Samuel. "Preparing for Practice." *Hastings Center Report* 14:6 (1984): 38–41.

Gulick, Walter B. "Is It Ever Morally Permissible for Corporate Officers to Break the Law?" *Business and Professional Ethics Journal* 2:3 (1982): 25–49.

Hare, Richard M. "What Is Wrong with Slavery?" *Philosophy and Public Affairs* 8:2 (1979): 103–21.

Hellman, Lawrence K. "Considering the Future of Legal Education: Law Schools and Social Justice." *Journal of Legal Education* 29 (1978): 170–93.

Hughes, Everett C. "Institutional Office and the Person." *American Journal of Sociology* 43 (1937): 404–13.

Katz, Jay. "Why Doctors Don't Disclose Uncertainty." *Hastings Center Report* 14:1 (1984): 35–44.

Kelly, Michael. *Legal Ethics and Legal Education*. Hastings-on-Hudson, NY: Hastings Center, 1980.

Kipnis, Kenneth. "Professional Responsibility and the Responsibility of Professionals." in *Profits and Professions: Essays in Business and Professional Ethics*, ed. Wade L. Robison, Michael S. Pritchard, and Joseph S. Ellin, pp. 9–22. Clifton, NJ: Humana Press, 1983.

Kultgen, John. "Evaluating Codes of Professional Ethics." In Robison et al., pp. 225–64, *supra*.

Ladd, John. "Loyalty." In *Encyclopedia of Philosophy*, ed. Paul Edwards, pp. 97–98. New York: Macmillan, 1967.

Luban, David. "Professional Ethics—A New Code for Lawyers." *Hastings Center Report* 10:3 (1980): 11–15.

MacIntyre, Alasdair, *After Virtue*. South Bend, IN: Notre Dame University Press, 1981; 2nd ed., 1984.

———. "The Nature of the Virtues." *Hastings Center Report* 11:2 (1981): 27–34.

Martin, Mike W. "Why Should Engineering Ethics Be Taught?" *Engineering Education* 71:4 (1981): 275–78.

May, William F. *The Virtues in a Professional Setting*. Nashville, TN: Society for Values in Higher Education, 1985.

McDowell, John. "Virtue and Reason." *Monist* 62 (1979): 331–50.

McIntyre, Neil, and Karl Popper. "The Critical Attitude in Medicine: The Need for a New Ethics." *British Medical Journal* 287 (1983): 1919–23.

Nagel, Thomas. "Moral Luck." In *Mortal Questions*, chap. 3. Cambridge: Cambridge University Press, 1979.

Patterson, L. Ray. "The Function of a Code of Legal Ethics." *University of Miami Law Review* 35 (1981): 695–726.

Postema, Gerald. "Self-Image, Integrity, and Professional Responsibility." In *The Good Lawyer: Lawyers' Roles and Lawyers' Ethics*, ed. David Luban, pp. 286–314. Totowa, NJ: Rowman and Allanheld, 1984.

Schnapper, Eric. "The Myth of Legal Ethics: The Moral Platitudes Found in the Code of Professional Responsibility Have Little to Do With Legal Ethics as Actually Enforced." *American Bar Association Journal* 64 (1978): 202–5.

Shelp, Earl A., ed. *Virtue and Medicine: Explorations in the Character of Medicine*. Dordrecht, Neth.: D. Reidel, 1985.

Slote, Michael. "Admirable Immorality," In *Goods and Virtues*, chap. 4. New York: Oxford University Press, 1983.

Sommers, Christina Hoff. "Ethics Without Virtue: Moral Education in America." *American Scholar* (Summer 1984): 381–89.

———, ed. *Vice and Virtue in Everyday Life: Introductory Readings in Ethics*. New York: Harcourt Brace Jovanovich, 1985.

Stern, Philip M. *Lawyers on Trial*. New York: New York Times Books, 1980.

Wallace, James D. *Virtues and Vices*. Ithaca, NY: Cornell University Press, 1978.

Walzer, Michael. "Political Action and the Problem of Dirty Hands." *Philosophy and Public Affairs* 2:2 (1973): 160–80.

Williams, Bernard. *Moral Luck*. Cambridge: Cambridge University Press, 1981.

——. "Professional Morality and Its Dispositions." In Luban, pp. 259–69, *supra*.

Wolf, Patricia. "Fraud in Science." *Hastings Center Report* 11:5 (1981): 9–14.

APPENDIX I: SAMPLE CODES OF PROFESSIONAL ETHICS

1. AMERICAN BAR ASSOCIATION'S MODEL RULES OF PROFESSIONAL CONDUCT*

Preamble: A Lawyer's Responsibilities

A lawyer is a representative of clients, an officer of the legal system and a public citizen having special responsibility for the quality of justice.

As a representative of clients, a lawyer performs various functions. As advisor, a lawyer provides a client with an informed understanding of the client's legal rights and obligations and explains their practical implications. As advocate, a lawyer zealously asserts the client's position under the rules of the adversary system. As negotiator, a lawyer seeks a result advantageous to the client but consistent with requirements of honest dealing with others. As intermediary between clients, a lawyer seeks to reconcile their divergent interests as an advisor and, to a limited extent, as a spokesman for each client. A lawyer acts as evaluator by examining a client's legal affairs and reporting about them to the client or to others.

In all professional functions a lawyer should be competent, prompt and diligent. A lawyer should maintain communication with a client concerning the representation. A lawyer should keep in confidence information relating to representation of a client except so far as disclosure is required or permitted by the Rules of Professional Conduct or other law.

A lawyer's conduct should conform to the requirements of the law, both in professional service to clients and in the lawyer's business and personal affairs. A lawyer should use the law's procedures only for legitimate purposes and not to harass or intimidate others. A lawyer should demonstrate respect for the legal system and for those who serve it, including judges, other lawyers and public officials. While it is a lawyer's duty, when necessary, to challenge the rectitude of official action, it is also a lawyer's duty to uphold legal process.

As a public citizen, a lawyer should seek improvement of the law, the administration of justice and the quality of service rendered by the legal profession. As a member of a learned profession, a lawyer should cultivate knowledge of the law beyond its use for clients, employ that knowledge in reform of the law and work to strengthen legal education. A lawyer should be mindful of deficiencies in the administration of justice and of the fact that the poor, and sometimes persons who are not poor, cannot afford adequate legal assistance, and should therefore devote professional time and civic influence in their behalf. A lawyer should aid the legal profession in pursuing these objectives and should help the bar regulate itself in the public interest.

Many of the lawyer's professional responsibilities are prescribed in the Rules of Professional Conduct, as well as substantive and procedural law. However, a lawyer is also guided by personal conscience and the approbation of professional peers. A lawyer should strive to attain the highest level of skill, to improve the law and the legal profession and to exemplify the legal profession's ideals of public service.

A lawyer's responsibilities as a representative of clients, an officer of the legal system and a public citizen are usually harmonious. Thus, when an opposing party is well represented, a lawyer can be a zealous advocate on behalf of a client and at the same time assume that justice is being done. So also, a lawyer can be sure that preserving client confidences ordinarily serves the public interest

---

* [Annotations deleted.—ED.]

because people are more likely to seek legal advice, and thereby heed their legal obligations, when they know their communications will be private.

In the nature of law practice, however, conflicting responsibilities are encountered. Virtually all difficult ethical problems arise from conflict between a lawyer's responsibilities to clients, to the legal system and to the lawyer's own interest in remaining an upright person while earning a satisfactory living. The Rules of Professional Conduct prescribe terms for resolving such conflicts. Within the framework of these Rules many difficult issues of professional discretion can arise. Such issues must be resolved through the exercise of sensitive professional and moral judgment guided by the basic principles underlying the Rules.

The legal profession is largely self-governing. Although other professions also have been granted powers of self-government, the legal profession is unique in this respect because of the close relationship between the profession and the processes of government and law enforcement. This connection is manifested in the fact that ultimate authority over the legal profession is vested largely in the courts.

To the extent that lawyers meet the obligations of their professional calling, the occasion for government regulation is obviated. Self-regulation also helps maintain the legal profession's independence from government domination. An independent legal profession is an important force in preserving government under law, for abuse of legal authority is more readily challenged by a profession whose members are not dependent on government for the right to practice.

The legal profession's relative autonomy carries with it special responsibilities of self-government. The profession has a responsibility to assure that its regulations are conceived in the public interest and not in furtherance of parochial or self-interested concerns of the bar. Every lawyer is responsible for observance of the Rules of Professional Conduct. A lawyer should also aid in securing their observance by other lawyers. Neglect of these responsibilities compromises the independence of the profession and the public interest which it serves.

Lawyers play a vital role in the preservation of society. The fulfillment of this role requires an understanding by lawyers of their relationship to our legal system. The Rules of Professional Conduct, when properly applied, serve to define that relationship. . . .

Model Rules of Professional Conduct

Client-Lawyer Relationship

Rule 1.1 Competence

A lawyer shall provide competent representation to a client. Competent representation requires the legal knowledge, skill, thoroughness and preparation reasonably necessary for the representation.

Rule 1.2 Scope of Representation

(a) A lawyer shall abide by a client's decisions concerning the objectives of representation, subject to paragraphs (c), (d) and (e), and shall consult with the client as to the means by which they are to be pursued. A lawyer shall abide by a client's decision whether to accept an offer of settlement of a matter. In a criminal case, the lawyer shall abide by the client's decision, after consultation with the lawyer, as to a plea to be entered, whether to waive jury trial and whether the client will testify.

(b) A lawyer's representation of a client, including representation by appointment, does not constitute an endorsement of the client's political, economic, social or moral views or activities.

(c) A lawyer may limit the objectives of the representation if the client consents after consultation.

(d) A lawyer shall not counsel a client to engage, or assist a client, in conduct that the lawyer knows is criminal or fraudulent, but a lawyer may discuss the legal consequences of any proposed course of conduct with a client and may counsel or assist a client to make a good faith effort to determine the validity, scope, meaning or application of the law.

(e) When a lawyer knows that a client expects assistance not permitted by the Rules of Professional Conduct or other law, the lawyer shall consult with the client regarding the relevant limitations on the lawyer's conduct.

Rule 1.3 Diligence

A lawyer shall act with reasonable diligence and promptness in representing a client.

Rule 1.4 Communication

(a) A lawyer shall keep a client reasonably informed about the status of a matter and promptly comply with reasonable requests for information.

(b) A lawyer shall explain a matter to the extent reasonably necessary to permit the client to make informed decisions regarding the representation.

Rule 1.5 Fees

(a) A lawyer's fee shall be reasonable. The factors to be considered in determining the reasonableness of a fee include the following:

(1) the time and labor required, the novelty and difficulty of the questions involved, and the skill requisite to perform the legal service properly;
(2) the likelihood, if apparent to the client, that the acceptance of the particular employment will preclude other employment by the lawyer;
(3) the fee customarily charged in the locality for similar legal services;
(4) the amount involved and the results obtained;
(5) the time limitations imposed by the client or by the circumstances;
(6) the nature and length of the professional relationship with the client;
(7) the experience, reputation, and ability of the lawyer or lawyers performing the services; and
(8) whether the fee is fixed or contingent.

(b) When the lawyer has not regularly represented the client, the basis or rate of the fee shall be communicated to the client, preferably in writing, before or within a reasonable time after commencing the representation.

(c) A fee may be contingent on the outcome of the matter for which the service is rendered, except in a matter in which a contingent fee is prohibited by paragraph (d) or other law. A contingent fee agreement shall be in writing and shall state the method by which the fee is to be determined, including the percentage or percentages that shall accrue to the lawyer in the event of settlement, trial or appeal, litigation and other expenses to be deducted from the recovery, and whether such expenses are to be deducted before or after the contingent fee is calculated. Upon conclusion of a contingent fee matter, the lawyer shall provide the client with a written statement stating the outcome of the matter and, if there is a recovery, showing the remittance to the client and the method of its determination.

(d) A lawyer shall not enter into an arrangement for, charge, or collect:

(1) any fee in a domestic relations matter, the payment or amount of which is contingent upon the securing of a divorce or upon the amount of alimony or support, or property settlement in lieu thereof; or
(2) a contingent fee for representing a defendant in a criminal case.

(e) A division of fee between lawyers who are not in the same firm may be made only if:

(1) the division is in proportion to the services performed by each lawyer or, by written agreement with the client, each lawyer assumes joint responsibility for the representation;
(2) the client is advised of and does not object to the participation of all the lawyers involved; and
(3) the total fee is reasonable.

Rule 1.6 Confidentiality of Information

(a) A lawyer shall not reveal information relating to representation of a client unless the client consents after consultation, except for disclosures that are impliedly authorized in order to carry out the representation, and except as stated in paragraph (b).

(b) A lawyer may reveal such information to the extent the lawyer reasonably believes necessary:

(1) to prevent the client from committing a criminal act that the lawyer believes is likely to result in imminent death or substantial bodily harm; or
(2) to establish a claim or defense on behalf of the lawyer in a controversy between the lawyer and the client, to establish a defense to a criminal charge or civil claim against the lawyer based upon conduct in which the client was involved, or to respond to allegations in any proceeding concerning the lawyer's representation of the client.

Rule 1.7 Conflict of Interest: General Rule

(a) A lawyer shall not represent a client if the representation of that client will be directly adverse to another client, unless:

(1) the lawyer reasonably believes the representation will not adversely affect the relationship with the other client; and
(2) each client consents after consultation.

(b) A lawyer shall not represent a client if the representation of that client may be materially limited by the lawyer's responsibilities to another client or to a third person, or by the lawyer's own interests, unless:

(1) the lawyer reasonably believes the representation will not be adversely affected; and
(2) the client consents after consultation. When representation of multiple clients in a single matter is undertaken, the consultation shall include explanation of the implications of the common representation and the advantages and risks involved.

Rule 1.8 Conflict of Interest: Prohibited Transactions

(a) A lawyer shall not enter into a business transaction with a client or knowingly acquire an ownership, possessory, security or other pecuniary interest adverse to a client unless:

(1) the transaction and terms on which the lawyer acquires the interest are fair and reasonable to the client and are fully disclosed and transmitted in writing to the client in a manner which can be reasonably understood by the client;
(2) the client is given a reasonable opportunity to seek the advice of independent counsel in the transaction; and
(3) the client consents in writing thereto.

(b) A lawyer shall not use information relating to representation of a client to the disadvantage of the client unless the client consents after consultation.

(c) A lawyer shall not prepare an instrument giving the lawyer or a person related to the lawyer as parent, child, sibling, or spouse any substantial gift from a client, including a testamentary gift, except where the client is related to the donee.

(d) Prior to the conclusion of representation of a client, a lawyer shall not make or negotiate an agreement giving the lawyer literary or media rights to a portrayal or account based in substantial part on information relating to the representation.

(e) A lawyer shall not provide financial assistance to a client in connection with pending or contemplated litigation, except that:

(1) a lawyer may advance court costs and expenses of litigation, the repayment of which may be contingent on the outcome of the matter; and
(2) a lawyer representing an indigent client may pay court costs and expenses of litigation on behalf of the client.

(f) A lawyer shall not accept compensation for representing a client from one other than the client unless:

(1) the client consents after consultation;
(2) there is no interference with the lawyer's independence of professional judgment or with the client-lawyer relationship; and
(3) information relating to representation of a client is protected as required by Rule 1.6.

(g) A lawyer who represents two or more clients shall not participate in making an aggregate settlement of the claims of or against the clients, or in a criminal case an aggregated agreement as to guilty or nolo contendere pleas, unless each client consents after consultation, including disclosure of the existence and nature of all the claims or pleas involved and of the participation of each person in the settlement.

(h) A lawyer shall not make an agreement prospectively limiting the lawyer's liability to a client for malpractice unless permitted by law and the client is independently represented in making the agreement, or settle a claim for such liability with an unrepresented client or former client without first advising that person in writing that independent representation is appropriate in connection therewith.

(i) A lawyer related to another lawyer as parent, child, sibling, or spouse shall not represent a client in a representation directly adverse to a person who the lawyer knows is represented by the other lawyer except upon consent by the client after consultation regarding the relationship.

(j) A lawyer shall not acquire a proprietary interest in the cause of action or subject matter of litigation the lawyer is conducting for a client, except that the lawyer may:

(1) acquire a lien granted by law to secure the lawyer's fee or expenses; and
(2) contract with a client for a reasonable contingent fee in a civil case.

Rule 1.9 Conflict of Interest: Former Client

A lawyer who has formerly represented a client in a matter shall not thereafter:

(a) represent another person in the same or a substantially related matter in which that person's interests are materially adverse to the interests of the former client unless the former client consents after consultation; or

(b) use information relating to the representation to the disadvantage of the former client except as Rule 1.6 would permit with respect to a client or when the information has become generally known.

Rule 1.10 Imputed Disqualification: General Rule

(a) While lawyers are associated in a firm, none of them shall knowingly represent a client when any one of them practicing alone would be prohibited from doing so by Rules 1.7, 1.8(c), 1.9 or 2.2.

(b) When a lawyer becomes associated with a firm, the firm may not knowingly represent a person in the same or a substantially related matter in which that lawyer, or a firm with which the lawyer was associated, had previously represented a client whose interests are materially adverse to that person and about whom the lawyer had acquired information protected by Rules 1.6 and 1.9(b) that is material to the matter.

(c) When a lawyer has terminated an association with a firm, the firm is not prohibited from thereafter representing a person with interests materially adverse to those of a client represented by the formerly associated lawyer unless:

(1) the matter is the same or substantially related to that in which the formerly associated lawyer represented the client; and
(2) any lawyer remaining in the firm has information protected by Rules 1.6 and 1.9(b) that is material to the matter.

(d) A disqualification prescribed by this Rule may be waived by the affected client under the conditions stated in Rule 1.7.

Rule 1.11 Successive Government and Private Employment

(a) Except as law may otherwise expressly permit, a lawyer shall not represent a private client in connection with a matter in which the lawyer participated personally and substantially as a public officer or employee, unless the appropriate government agency consents after consultation. No lawyer in a firm with which that lawyer is associated may knowingly undertake or continue representation in such a matter unless:

(1) the disqualified lawyer is screened from any participation in the matter and is apportioned no part of the fee therefrom; and
(2) written notice is promptly given to the appropriate government agency to enable it to ascertain compliance with the provisions of this Rule.

(b) Except as law may otherwise expressly permit, a lawyer having information that the lawyer knows is confidential government information about a person acquired when the lawyer was a public officer or employee, may not represent a private client whose interests are adverse to that person in a matter in which the information could be used to the material disadvantage of that person. A firm with which that lawyer is associated may undertake or continue representation in the matter only if the disqualified lawyer is screened from any participation in the matter and is apportioned no part of the fee therefrom.

(c) Except as law may otherwise expressly permit, a lawyer serving as a public officer or employee shall not:

(1) participate in a matter in which the lawyer participated personally and substantially while in private practice or nongovernmental employment, unless under applicable law no one is, or by lawful delegation may be, authorized to act in the lawyer's stead in the matter; or
(2) negotiate for private employment with any person who is involved as a party or as attorney for a party in a matter in which the lawyer is participating personally and substantially.

(d) As used in this Rule, the term "matter" includes:

(1) any judicial or other proceeding, application, request for a ruling or other determination, contract, claim, controversy, investigation, charge, accusation, arrest or other particular matter involving a specific party or parties; and
(2) any other matter covered by the conflict of interest rules of the appropriate government agency.

(e) As used in this Rule, the term "confidential government information" means information which has been obtained under governmental authority and which, at the time this Rule is applied the government is prohibited by law from disclosing to the public or has a legal privilege not to disclose, and which is not otherwise available to the public.

Rule 1.12 Former Judge or Arbitrator

(a) Except as stated in paragraph (d), a lawyer shall not represent anyone in connection with a matter in which the lawyer participated personally and substantially as a judge or other adjudicative officer, arbitrator or law clerk to such a person, unless all parties to the proceeding consent after disclosure.

(b) A lawyer shall not negotiate for employment with any person who is involved as a party or as attorney for a party in a matter in which the lawyer is participating personally and substantially as a judge or other adjudicative officer, or arbitrator. A lawyer serving as a law clerk to a judge, other adjudicative officer or arbitrator may negotiate for employment with a party or attorney involved in a matter in which the clerk is participating personally and substantially, but only after the lawyer has notified the judge, other adjudicative officer or arbitrator.

(c) If a lawyer is disqualified by paragraph (a), no lawyer in a firm with which that lawyer is associated may knowingly undertake or continue representation in the matter unless:

(1) the disqualified lawyer is screened from any participation in the matter and is apportioned no part of the fee therefrom; and
(2) written notice is promptly given to the appropriate tribunal to enable it to ascertain compliance with the provisions of this Rule.

(d) An arbitrator selected as a partisan of a party in a multi-member arbitration panel is not prohibited from subsequently representing that party.

Rule 1.13 Organization as Client

(a) A lawyer employed or retained by an organization represents the organization acting through its duly authorized constituents.

(b) If a lawyer for an organization knows that an officer, employee or other person associated with the organization is engaged in action, intends to act or refuses to act in a matter related to the representation that is a violation of a legal obligation to the organization, or a violation of law which reasonably might be imputed to the organization, and is likely to result in substantial injury to the organization, the lawyer shall proceed as is reasonably necessary in the best interest of the organization. In determining how to proceed, the lawyer shall give due consideration to the seriousness of the violation and its consequences, the scope and nature of the lawyer's representation, the responsibility in the organization and the apparent motivation of the person involved, the policies of the organization concerning such matters and any other relevant considerations. Any measures taken shall be designed to minimize disruption of the organization and the risk of revealing information relating to the representation to persons outside the organization. Such measures may include among others:

(1) asking reconsideration of the matter;
(2) advising that a separate legal opinion on the matter be sought for presentation to appropriate authority in the organization; and
(3) referring the matter to higher authority in the organization, including, if warranted by the seriousness of the matter, referral to the highest authority that can act in behalf of the organization as determined by applicable law.

(c) If, despite the lawyer's efforts in accordance with paragraph (b), the highest authority that can act on behalf of the organization insists upon action, or a refusal to act, that is clearly a violation of law and is likely to result in substantial injury to the organization, the lawyer may resign in accordance with Rule 1.16.

(d) In dealing with an organization's directors, officers, employees, members, shareholders or other constituents, a lawyer shall explain the identity of the client when it is apparent that the organization's interests are adverse to those of the constituents with whom the lawyer is dealing.

(e) A lawyer representing an organization may also represent any of its directors, officers, employees, members, shareholders or other constituents, subject to the provisions of Rule 1.7. If the organization's consent to the dual representation is required by Rule 1.7, the consent shall be given by an appropriate official of the organization other than the individual who is to be represented, or by the shareholders.

Rule 1.14 Client Under a Disability

(a) When a client's ability to make adequately considered decisions in connection with the representation is impaired, whether because of minority, mental disability or for some other reason, the lawyer shall, as far as reasonably possible, maintain a normal client-lawyer relationship with the client.

(b) A lawyer may seek the appointment of a guardian or take other protective action with respect to a client, only when the lawyer reasonably believes that the client cannot adequately act in the client's own interest.

Rule 1.15 Safekeeping Property

(a) A lawyer shall hold property of clients or third persons that is in a lawyer's possession in connection with a representation separate from the lawyer's own property. Funds shall be kept in a separate account maintained in the state where the lawyer's office is situated, or elsewhere with the consent of the client or third person. Other property shall be identified as such and appropriately safeguarded. Complete records of such account funds and other property shall be kept by the lawyer and shall be preserved for a period of [five years] after termination of the representation.

(b) Upon receiving funds or other property in which a client or third person has an interest, a lawyer shall promptly notify the client or third person. Except as stated in this Rule or otherwise permitted by law or by agreement with the client, a lawyer shall promptly deliver to the client or third person any funds or other property that the client or third person is entitled to receive and, upon request by the client or third person, shall promptly render a full accounting regarding such property.

(c) When in the course of representation a lawyer is in possession of property in which both the lawyer and another person claim interests, the property shall be kept separate by the lawyer until there is an accounting and severance of their interests. If a dispute arises concerning their respective interests, the portion in dispute shall be kept separate by the lawyer until the dispute is resolved.

Rule 1.16 Representation

(a) Except as stated in paragraph (c), a lawyer shall not represent a client or, where representation has commenced, shall withdraw from the representation of a client if:

(1) the representation will result in violation of the Rules of Professional Conduct or other law;
(2) the lawyer's physical or mental condition materially impairs the lawyer's ability to represent the client; or
(3) the lawyer is discharged.

(b) Except as stated in paragraph (c), a lawyer may withdraw from representing a client if withdrawal can be accomplished without material adverse effect on the interests of the client, or if:

(1) the client persists in a course of action involving the lawyer's services that the lawyer reasonably believes is criminal or fraudulent;
(2) the client has used the lawyer's services to perpetrate a crime or fraud;
(3) a client insists upon pursuing an objective that the lawyer considers repugnant or imprudent;
(4) the client fails substantially to fulfill an obligation to the lawyer regarding the lawyer's services and has been given reasonable warning that the lawyer will withdraw unless the obligation is fulfilled;
(5) the representation will result in an unreasonable financial burden on the lawyer or has been rendered unreasonably difficult by the client; or
(6) other good cause for withdrawal exists.

(c) When ordered to do so by a tribunal, a lawyer shall continue representation notwithstanding good cause for terminating the representation.

(d) Upon termination of representation, a lawyer shall take steps to the extent reasonably practicable to protect a client's interests, such as giving reasonable notice to the client, allowing time for employment of other counsel, surrendering papers and property to which the client is entitled and refunding any advance payment of fee that has not been earned. The lawyer may retain papers relating to the client to the extent permitted by other law.

Counselor

Rule 2.1 Advisor

In representing a client, a lawyer shall exercise independent professional judgment and reader candid advice. In rendering advice, a lawyer may refer not only to law but to other considerations such as moral, economic, social and political factors, that may be relevant to the client's situation.

Rule 2.2 Intermediary

(a) A lawyer may act as intermediary between clients if:

(1) the lawyer consults with each client concerning the implications of the common representation, including the advantages and risks involved, and the effect on the attorney-client privileges, and obtains each client's consent to the common representation;
(2) the lawyer reasonably believes that the matter can be resolved on terms compatible with the clients' best interests, that each client will be able to make adequately informed decisions in the matter and that there is little risk of material prejudice to the interests of any of the clients if the contemplated resolution is unsuccessful; and
(3) the lawyer reasonably believes that the common representation can be undertaken impartially and without improper effect on other responsibilities the lawyer has to any of the clients.

(b) While acting as intermediary, the lawyer shall consult with each client concerning the decisions to be made and the considerations relevant in making them, so that each client can make adequately informed decisions.

(c) A lawyer shall withdraw as intermediary if any of the clients so requests, or if any of the conditions stated in paragraph (a) is no longer satisfied. Upon withdrawal, the lawyer shall not continue to represent any of the clients in the matter that was the subject of the intermediation.

Rule 2.3. Evaluation for Use by Third Persons

(a) A lawyer may undertake an evaluation of a matter affecting a client for the use of someone other than the client if:

(1) the lawyer reasonably believes that making the evaluation is compatible with other aspects of the lawyer's relationship with the client; and
(2) the client consents after consultation.

(b) Except as disclosure is required in connection with a report of an evaluation, information relating to the evaluation is otherwise protected by Rule 1.6.

Advocate

Rule 3.1. Meritorious Claims and Contentions

A lawyer shall not bring or defend a proceeding, or assert or controvert an issue therein, unless there is a basis for doing so that is not frivolous, which includes a good faith argument for an extension, modification or reversal of existing law. A lawyer for the defendent in a criminal proceeding, or the respondent in a proceeding that could result in incarceration, may nevertheless so defend the proceeding as to require that every element of the case be established.

Rule 3.2. Expediting Litigation

A lawyer shall make reasonable efforts to expedite litigation consistent with the interests of the client.

Rule 3.3. Candor Toward the Tribunal

(a) A lawyer shall not knowingly:

(1) make a false statement of material fact or law to a tribunal;
(2) fail to disclose a material fact to a tribunal when disclosure is necessary to avoid assisting a criminal or fraudulent act by the client;
(3) fail to disclose to the tribunal legal authority in the controlling jurisdiction known to the lawyer to be directly adverse to the position of the client and not disclosed by opposing counsel; or
(4) offer evidence that the lawyer knows to be false. If a lawyer has offered material evidence and comes to know of its falsity, the lawyer shall take reasonable remedial measures.

(b) The duties stated in paragraph (a) continue to the conclusion of the proceeding, and apply even if compliance requires disclosure of information otherwise protected by Rule 1.6.

(c) A lawyer may refuse to offer evidence that the lawyer reasonably believes is false.

(d) In an ex parte proceeding, a lawyer shall inform the tribunal of all material facts known to the lawyer which will enable the tribunal to make an informed decision, whether or not the facts are adverse.

Rule 3.4. Fairness to Opposing Party and Counsel

A lawyer shall not:

(a) unlawfully obstruct another party's access to evidence or unlawfully alter, destroy or conceal a document or other material having potential evidentiary value. A lawyer shall not counsel or assist another person to do any such act;

(b) falsify evidence, counsel or assist a witness to testify falsely, or offer an inducement to a witness that is prohibited by law;

(c) knowingly disobey an obligation under the rules of a tribunal except for an open refusal based on an assertion that no valid obligation exists;

(d) in pretrial procedure, make a frivolous discovery request or fail to make reasonably diligent effort to comply with a legally proper discovery request by an opposing party;

(e) in trial, allude to any matter that the lawyer does not reasonably believe is relevant or that will not be supported by admissible evidence, assert personal knowledge of facts in issue except when testifying as a witness, or state a personal opinion as to the justness of a cause, the credibility of a witness, the culpability of a civil litigant or the guilt or innocence of an accused; or

(f) request a person other than a client to refrain from voluntarily giving relevant information to another party unless:

(1) the person is a relative or an employee or other agent of a client; and
(2) the lawyer reasonably believes that the person's interests will not be adversely affected by refraining from giving such information.

Rule 3.5. Impartiality and Decorum of the Tribunal

A lawyer shall not:

(a) seek to influence a judge, juror, prospective juror or other official by means prohibited by law;

(b) communicate ex parte with such a person except as permitted by law; or

(c) engage in conduct intended to disrupt a tribunal.

Rule 3.6. Trial Publicity

(a) A lawyer shall not make an extrajudicial statement that a reasonable person would expect to be disseminated by means of public communication if the lawyer knows or reasonably should know that it will have a substantial likelihood of materially prejudicing an adjudicative proceeding.

(b) A statement referred to in paragraph (a) ordinarily is likely to have such an effect when it refers to a civil matter triable to a jury, a criminal matter, or any other proceeding that could result in incarceration, and the statement relates to:

(1) the character, credibility, reputation or criminal record of a party, suspect in a criminal investigation or witness, or the identity of a witness, or the expected testimony of a party or witness;
(2) in a criminal case or proceeding that could result in incarceration, the possibility of a plea of guilty to the offense or the existence or contents of any confession, admission, or statement given by a defendant or suspect or that person's refusal or failure to make a statement;
(3) the performance or results of any examination or test or the refusal or failure of a person to submit to an examination or test, or the identity or nature of physical evidence expected to be presented;
(4) any opinion as to the guilt or innocence of a defendant or suspect in a criminal case or proceeding that could result in incarceration;
(5) information the lawyer knows or reasonably

should know is likely to be inadmissible as evidence in a trial and would if disclosed create a substantial risk of prejudicing an impartial trial; or

(6) the fact that a defendant has been charged with a crime, unless there is included therein a statement explaining that the charge is merely an accusation and that the defendant is presumed innocent until and unless proven guilty.

(c) Notwithstanding paragraph (a) and (b)(1–5), a lawyer involved in the investigation or litigation of a matter may state without elaboration:

(1) the general nature of the claim or defense;
(2) the information contained in a public record;
(3) that an investigation of the matter is in progress, including the general scope of the investigation, the offense or claim or defense involved and, except when prohibited by law, the identity of the persons involved;
(4) the scheduling or result of any step in litigation;
(5) a request for assistance in obtaining evidence and information necessary thereto;
(6) a warning of danger concerning the behavior of a person involved, when there is reason to believe that there exists the likelihood of substantial harm to an individual or to the public interest; and
(7) in a criminal case:
(i) the identity, residence, occupation and family status of the accused;
(ii) if the accused has not been apprehended, information necessary to aid in apprehension of that person;
(iii) the fact, time and place of arrest; and
(iv) the identity of investigating and arresting officers or agencies and the length of the investigation.

Rule 3.7. Lawyer as Witness

(a) A lawyer shall not act as advocate at trial in which the lawyer is likely to be necessary witness except where:

(1) the testimony relates to an uncontested issue;
(2) the testimony relates to the nature and value of legal services rendered in the case; or
(3) disqualification of the lawyer would work substantial hardship on the client.

(b) A lawyer may act as advocate in a trial in which another lawyer in the lawyer's firm is likely to be called as a witness unless precluded from doing so by Rule 1.7 or Rule 1.9.

Rule 3.8. Special Responsibilities of a Prosecutor

The prosecutor in a criminal case shall:

(a) refrain from prosecuting a charge that the prosecutor knows is not supported by probable cause;

(b) make reasonable efforts to assure that the accused has been advised of the right to, and the procedure for obtaining, counsel and has been given reasonable opportunity to obtain counsel;

(c) not seek to obtain from an unrepresented accused a waiver of important pretrial rights, such as the right to a preliminary hearing;

(d) make timely disclosure to the defense of all evidence or information known to the prosecutor that tends to negate the guilt of the accused or mitigates the offense, and, in connection with sentencing, disclose to the defense and to the tribunal all unprivileged mitigating information known to the prosecutor, except when the prosecutor is relieved of this responsibility by a protective order of the tribunal; and

(e) exercise reasonable care to prevent investigators, law enforcement personnel, employees or other persons assisting or associated with the prosecutor in a criminal case from making an extrajudicial statement that the prosecutor would be prohibited from making under Rule 3.6.

Rule 3.9. Advocate in Nonadjudicative Proceedings

A lawyer representing a client before a legislative or administrative tribunal in a nonadjudicative proceeding shall disclose that the appearance is in a representative capacity and shall conform to the provisions of Rules 3.3(a) through (c), 3.4(a) through (c), and 3.5.

Transactions with Persons Other Than Clients

Rule 4.1. Truthfulness in Statements to Others

In the course of representing a client a lawyer shall not knowingly:

(a) make a false statement of material fact or law to a third person; or

(b) fail to disclose a material fact to a third person when disclosure is necessary to avoid assisting a criminal or fraudulent act by a client, unless disclosure is prohibited by Rule 1.6.

Rule 4.2 Communication with Person Represented by Counsel

In representing a client, a lawyer shall not communicate about the subject of the representation with a party the lawyer knows to be represented by another lawyer in the matter, unless the lawyer has the consent of the other lawyer or is authorized by law to do so.

Rule 4.3 Dealing with Unrepresented Person

In dealing on behalf of a client with a person who is not represented by counsel, a lawyer shall not state or imply that the lawyer is disinterested. When the lawyer knows or reasonably should know that the unrepresented person misunderstands the lawyer's role in the matter, the lawyer shall make reasonable efforts to correct the misunderstanding.

Rule 4.4 Respect for Rights of Third Persons

In representing a client, a lawyer shall not use means that have no substantial purpose other than to embarrass, delay, or burden a third person, or use methods of obtaining evidence that violate the legal rights of such a person.

Law Firms and Associations

Rule 5.1 Responsibilities of a Partner or Supervisory Lawyer

(a) A partner in a law firm shall make reasonable efforts to ensure that the firm has in effect measures giving reasonable assurance that all lawyers in the firm conform to the Rules of Professional Conduct.

(b) A lawyer having direct supervisory authority over another lawyer shall make reasonable efforts to ensure that the other lawyer conforms to the rules of professional conduct.

(c) A lawyer shall be responsible for another lawyer's violation of the rules of professional conduct if:

(1) the lawyer orders or, with knowledge of the specific conduct, ratifies the conduct involved; or
(2) the lawyer is a partner in the law firm in which the other lawyer practices, or has direct supervisory authority over the other lawyer, and knows of the conduct at a time when its consequences can be avoided or mitigated but fails to take reasonable remedial action.

Rule 5.2 Responsibilities of a Subordinate Lawyer

(a) A lawyer is bound by the Rules of Professional Conduct notwithstanding that the lawyer acted at the direction of another person.

(b) A subordinate lawyer does not violate the Rules of Professional Conduct if that lawyer acts in accordance with a supervisory lawyer's reasonable resolution of an arguable question of professional duty.

Rule 5.3 Responsibilities Regarding Nonlawyer Assistants

With respect to a nonlawyer employed or retained by or associated with a lawyer:

(a) A partner in a law firm shall make reasonable efforts to ensure that the firm has in effect measures giving reasonable assurance that the person's conduct is compatible with the professional obligations of the lawyer;

(b) A lawyer having direct supervisory authority over the nonlawyer shall make reasonable efforts to ensure that the person's conduct is compatible with the professional obligations of the lawyer; and

(c) A lawyer shall be responsible for conduct of such a person that would be a violation of the rules of professional conduct if engaged in by a lawyer if:

(1) the lawyer orders or, with the knowledge of the specific conduct, ratifies the conduct involved; or
(2) the lawyer is a partner in the law firm in which the person is employed, or has direct supervisory authority over the person, and knows of the conduct at a time when its consequences can be avoided or mitigated but fails to take reasonable remedial action.

Rule 5.4 Professional Independence of a Lawyer

(a) A lawyer or law firm shall not share legal fees with a nonlawyer, except that:

(1) an agreement by a lawyer with his firm, partner, or associate may provide for the payment of money, over a reasonable period of time after his death, to his estate or to one or more specified persons;
(2) a lawyer who undertakes to complete unfinished legal business of a deceased lawyer may pay to the estate of the deceased lawyer that proportion of the total compensation which fairly represents the services rendered by the deceased lawyer; and
(3) a lawyer or law firm may include nonlawyer employees in a compensation or retirement plan, even though the plan is based in whole or in part on a profit-sharing arrangement.

(b) A lawyer shall not form a partnership with a nonlawyer if any of the activities of the partnership consist of the practice of law.

(c) A lawyer shall not permit a person who recommends, employs, or pays him to render legal services for another to direct or regulate his professional judgment in rendering such legal services.

(d) A lawyer shall not practice with or in the form of a professional corporation or association authorized to practice law for a profit, if:

(1) a nonlawyer owns any interest therein, except that a fiduciary representative of the estate of a lawyer may hold the stock or interest of the lawyer for a reasonable time during administration;
(2) a nonlawyer is a corporate director or officer thereof; or

(3) a nonlawyer has the right to direct or control the professional judgment of a lawyer.

Rule 5.5 Unauthorized Practice of Law

A lawyer shall not:

(a) practice law in a jurisdiction where doing so violates the regulation of the legal profession in that jurisdiction; or

(b) assist a person who is not a member of the bar in the performance of activity that constitutes the unauthorized practice of law.

Rule 5.6 Restrictions on Right to Practice

A lawyer shall not participate in offering or making:

(a) a partnership or employment agreement that restricts the rights of a lawyer to practice after termination of the relationship, except an agreement concerning benefits upon retirement; or

(b) an agreement in which a restriction on the lawyer's right to practice is part of the settlement of a controversy between private parties.

Public Service

Rule 6.1 Pro Bono Publico Service

A lawyer should render public interest legal service. A lawyer may discharge this responsibility by providing professional services at no fee or a reduced fee to persons of limited means or to public service or charitable groups or organizations, by service in activities for improving the law, the legal system or the legal profession, and by financial support for organizations that provide legal services to persons of limited means.

Rule 6.2 Accepting Appointments

A lawyer shall not seek to avoid appointment by a tribunal to represent a person except for good cause, such as:

(a) representing the client is likely to result in violation of the rules of professional conduct or other law;

(b) representing the client is likely to result in an unreasonable financial burden on the lawyer; or

(c) the client or the cause is so repugnant to the lawyer as to be likely to impair the client-lawyer relationship or the lawyer's ability to represent the client.

Rule 6.3 Membership in Legal Services Organization

A lawyer may serve as a director, officer or member of a legal services organization, apart from the law firm in which the lawyer practices, notwithstanding that the organization serves persons having interests adverse to a client of the lawyer. The lawyer shall not knowingly participate in a decision or action of the organization:

(a) if participating in the decision would be incompatible with the lawyer's obligations to a client under Rule 1.7; or

(b) where the decision could have a material adverse effect on the representation of a client of the organization whose interests are adverse to a client of the lawyer.

Rule 6.4 Law Reform Activities Affecting Client Interests

A lawyer may serve as a director, officer or member of an organization involved in reform of the law or its administration notwithstanding that the reform may affect the interests of a client of the lawyer. When the lawyer knows that the interests of a client may be materially benefitted by a decision in which the lawyer participates, the lawyer shall disclose that fact but need not identify the client.

Information About Legal Services

Rule 7.1 Communications Concerning a Lawyer's Services

A lawyer shall not make a false or misleading communication about the lawyer or the lawyer's services. A communication is false or misleading if it:

(a) contains a material misrepresentation of fact or law, or omits a fact necessary to make the statement considered as a whole not materially misleading;

(b) is likely to create an unjustified expectation about results the lawyer can achieve, or states or implies that the lawyer can achieve results by means that violate the Rules of Professional Conduct or other law; or

(c) compares the lawyer's services with other lawyers' services, unless the comparison can be factually substantiated.

Rule 7.2 Advertising

(a) Subject to the requirements of Rule 7.1, a lawyer may advertise services through public media, such as a telephone directory, legal directory, newspaper or other periodical, outdoor sign, radio or television, or through written communication not involving solicitation as defined in Rule 7.3.

(b) A copy or recording of an advertisement or written communication shall be kept for two years after its last dissemination along with a record of when and where it was used.

(c) A lawyer shall not give anything of value to a person for recommending the lawyer's services, except that a lawyer may pay the reasonable cost of advertising or written communication permitted by this Rule and may pay the usual charges of a not-for-profit lawyer referral service or other legal service organization.

(d) Any communication made pursuant to this Rule shall include the name of at least one lawyer responsible for its content.

Rule 7.3 Direct Contact with Prospective Clients

A lawyer may not solicit professional employment from a prospective client with whom the lawyer has no family or prior professional relationship, by mail, in-person or otherwise, when a significant motive for the lawyer's doing so is the lawyer's pecuniary gain. The term ''solicit'' includes contact in person, by telephone or telegraph, by letter or other writing, or by other communication directed to a specific recipient, but does not include letters addressed or advertising circulars distributed generally to persons not known to need legal services of the kind provided by the lawyer in a particular matter, but who are so situated that they might in general find such services useful.

Rule 7.4 Communication of Fields of Practice

A lawyer may communicate the fact that the lawyer does or does not practice in particular fields of law. A lawyer shall not state or imply that the lawyer is a specialist except as follows:

(a) a lawyer admitted to engage in patent practice before the United States Patent and Trademark Office may use the designation ''patent attorney'' or a substantially similar designation;

(b) a lawyer engaged in admiralty practice may use the designation ''admiralty,'' ''proctor in admiralty'' or a substantially similar designation; and

(c) (Provisions on designation of specialization of the particular state).

Rule 7.5 Firm Names and Letterheads

(a) A lawyer shall not use a firm name, letterhead or other professional designation that violates Rule 7.1. A trade name may be used by a lawyer in private practice if it does not imply a connection with a government agency or with a public or charitable legal services organization and is not otherwise in violation of Rule 7.1.

(b) A law firm with offices in more than one jurisdiction may use the same name in each jurisdiction, but identification of the lawyers in an office of the firm shall indicate the jurisdictional limitations on those not licensed to practice in the jurisdiction where the office is located.

(c) The name of a lawyer holding a public office shall not be used in the name of a law firm, or in communications on its behalf, during any substantial period in which the lawyer is not actively and regularly practicing with the firm.

(d) Lawyers may state or imply that they practice in a partnership or other organization only when that is the fact.

Maintaining the Integrity of the Profession

Rule 8.1 Bar Admission and Disciplinary Matters

An applicant for admission to the bar, or a lawyer in connection with a bar admission application or in connection with a disciplinary matter, shall not:

(a) knowingly make a false statement of material fact; or

(b) fail to disclose a fact necessary to correct a misapprehension known by the person to have arisen in the matter, or knowingly fail to respond to a lawful demand for information from an admissions or disciplinary authority, except that this Rule does not require disclosure of information otherwise protected by Rule 1.6.

Rule 8.2 Judicial and Legal Officials

(a) A lawyer shall not make a statement that the lawyer knows to be false or with reckless disregard as to its truth or falsity concerning the qualifications or integrity of a judge, adjudicatory officer or public legal officer, or of a candidate for election or appointment to judicial or legal office.

(b) A lawyer who is a candidate for judicial office shall comply with the applicable provisions of the Code of Judicial Conduct.

Rule 8.3 Reporting Professional Misconduct

(a) A lawyer having knowledge that another lawyer has committed a violation of the Rules of Professional Conduct that raises a substantial question as to that lawyer's honesty, trustworthiness or fitness as a lawyer in other respects, shall inform the appropriate professional authority.

(b) A lawyer having knowledge that a judge has committed a violation of applicable rules of judicial conduct that raises a substantial question as to the judge's fitness for office shall inform the appropriate authority.

(c) This Rule does not require disclosure of information otherwise protected by Rule 1.6.

Rule 8.4 Misconduct

It is professional misconduct for a lawyer to:

(a) violate or attempt to violate the Rules of Professional Conduct, knowingly assist or induce another to do so, or do so through the acts of another;

(b) commit a criminal act that reflects adversely

on the lawyer's honesty, trustworthiness or fitness as a lawyer in other respects;

(c) engage in conduct involving dishonesty, fraud, deceit or misrepresentation;

(d) engage in conduct that is prejudicial to the administration of justice;

(e) state or imply an ability to influence improperly a government agency or official; or

(f) knowingly assist a judge or judicial officer in conduct that is a violation of applicable rules of judicial conduct or other law.

Rule 8.5 Jurisdiction

A lawyer admitted to practice in this jurisdiction is subject to the disciplinary authority of this jurisdiction although engaged in practice elsewhere.

2. AMERICAN MEDICAL ASSOCIATION'S PRINCIPLES OF MEDICAL ETHICS*

Preamble

The medical profession has long subscribed to a body of ethical statements developed primarily for the benefit of the patient. As a member of this profession, a physician must recognize responsibility not only to patients, but also to society, to other health professionals, and to self. The following Principles adopted by the American Medical Association are not laws, but standards of conduct which define the essentials of honorable behavior for the physician.

I. A physician shall be dedicated to providing competent medical service with compassion and respect for human dignity.

II. A physician shall deal honestly with patients and colleagues, and strive to expose those physicians deficient in character or competence, or who engage in fraud or deception.

III. A physician shall respect the law and also recognize a responsibility to seek changes in those requirements which are contrary to the best interests of the patient.

IV. A physician shall respect the rights of patients, of colleagues, and of other health professionals, and shall safeguard patient confidences within the constraints of the law.

V. A physician shall continue to study, apply and advance scientific knowledge, make relevant information available to patients, colleagues, and the public, obtain consultation, and use the talents of other health professionals when indicated.

VI. A physician shall, in the provision of appropriate patient care, except in emergencies, be free to choose whom to serve, with whom to associate, and the environment in which to provide medical services.

VII. A physician shall recognize a responsibility to participate in activities contributing to an improved community.

* [Annotations deleted.—ED.]

3. AMERICAN NURSES' ASSOCIATION CODE FOR NURSES†

Preamble

. . . . .

Recipients and providers of nursing services are viewed as individuals and groups who possess basic rights and responsibilities, and whose values and circumstances command respect at all times. Nursing encompasses the promotion and restoration of health, the prevention of illness, and the alleviation of suffering. The statements of the *Code* and their interpretation provide guidance for conduct and relationships in carrying out nursing responsibilities consistent with the ethical obligations of the profession and quality in nursing care.

Code for Nurses

1. The nurse provides services with respect for human dignity and the uniqueness of the client unrestricted by considerations of social or economic status, personal attributes, or the nature of health problems.
2. The nurse safeguards the client's right to privacy by judiciously protecting information of a confidential nature.

† [Annotations deleted.—ED.]

3. The nurse acts to safeguard the client and the public when health care and safety are affected by the incompetent, unethical, or illegal practice of any person.
4. The nurse assumes responsibility and accountability for individual nursing judgments and actions.
5. The nurse maintains competence in nursing.
6. The nurse exercises informed judgment and uses individual competence and qualifications as criteria in seeking consultation, accepting responsibilities, and delegating nursing activities to others.
7. The nurse participates in activities that contribute to the ongoing development of the profession's body of knowledge.
8. The nurse participates in the profession's efforts to implement and improve standards of nursing.
9. The nurse participates in the profession's efforts to establish and maintain conditions of employment conducive to high-quality nursing care.
10. The nurse participates in the profession's effort to protect the public from misinformation and misrepresentation and to maintain the integrity of nursing.
11. The nurse collaborates with members of the health professions and other citizens in promoting community and national efforts to meet the health needs of the public.

4. INTERNATIONAL COUNCIL OF NURSES' INTERNATIONAL CODE OF NURSING ETHICS*

Professional nurses minister to the sick, assume responsibility for creating a physical, social and spiritual environment which will be conducive to recovery, and stress the prevention of illness and promotion of health by teaching and example. They render health-service to the individual, the family, and the community and coordinate their services with members of other health professions.

Service to mankind is the primary function of nurses and the reason for the existence of the nursing profession. Need for nursing service is universal. Professional nursing service is therefore unrestricted by considerations of nationality, race, creed, colour, politics, or social status.

Inherent in the code is the fundamental concept that the nurse believes in the essential freedoms of mankind and in the preservation of human life.

The profession recognizes that an international code cannot cover in detail all the activities and relationships of nurses, some of which are conditioned by personal philosophies and beliefs.

(1) The fundamental responsibility of the nurse is threefold: to conserve life, to alleviate suffering, and to promote health.

(2) The nurse must maintain at all times the highest standards of nursing care and of professional conduct.

(3) The nurse must not only be well prepared to practice but must maintain her knowledge and skill at a consistently high level.

(4) The religious beliefs of a patient must be respected.

(5) Nurses hold in confidence all personal information entrusted to them.

(6) A nurse recognises not only the responsibilities but the limitations of her or his professional functions; recommends or gives medical treatment without medical orders only in emergencies and reports such action to a physician at the earliest possible moment.

(7) The nurse is under an obligation to carry out the physician's orders intelligently and loyally and to refuse to participate in unethical procedures.

(8) The nurse sustains confidence in the physician and other members of the health team: incompetence or unethical conduct of associates should be exposed but only to the proper authority.

(9) A nurse is entitled to just remuneration and accepts only such compensation as the contract, actual or implied, provides.

(10) Nurses do not permit their names to be used in connection with the advertisement of products or with any other form of self advertisement.

(11) The nurse cooperates with and maintains harmonious relationships with members of other

---

International Council of Nurses, 1953. Reprinted with permission from *The Physician's Creed,* compiled by M. B. Etziony (Springfield: Charles C. Thomas, 1973). Copyright © by the Israel Journal of Medical Science.

*[This code was revised in 1973. It is included to illustrate the recent changes in nursing's self-concept. For the revised International Code, see Anne J. Davis and Mila A. Aroskar, *Ethical Dilemmas and Nursing Practice* (New York: Appleton-Century-Crofts, 1978), pp. 13–14.—ED.]

professions and with her or his nursing colleagues.

(12) The nurse in private life adheres to standards of personal ethics which reflect credit upon [the] profession.

(13) In personal conduct nurses should not knowingly disregard the accepted patterns of behaviour of the community in which they live and work.

(14) A nurse should participate and share responsibility with other citizens and other health professions in promoting efforts to meet the health needs of the public—local, state, national and international.

5. AMERICAN PSYCHOLOGICAL ASSOCIATION'S ETHICAL PRINCIPLES OF PSYCHOLOGISTS*

Preamble

Psychologists respect the dignity and worth of the individual and strive for the preservation and protection of fundamental human rights. They are committed to increasing knowledge of human behavior and of people's understanding of themselves and others and to the utilization of such knowledge for the promotion of human welfare. While pursuing these objectives, they make every effort to protect the welfare of those who seek their services and of the research participants that may be the object of study. They use their skills only for purposes consistent with these values and do not knowingly permit their misuse by others. While demanding for themselves freedom of inquiry and communication, psychologists accept the responsibility this freedom requires: competence, objectivity in the application of skills, and concern for the best interests of clients, colleagues, students, research participants, and society. In the pursuit of these ideals, psychologists subscribe to principles in the following areas: 1. Responsibility, 2. Competence, 2. Moral and Legal Standards, 4. Public Statements, 5. Confidentiality, 6. Welfare of the Consumer, 7. Professional Relationships, 8. Assessment Techniques, 9. Research with Human Participants, and 10. Care and Use of Animals.

Acceptance of membership in the American Psychological Association commits the member to adherence to these principles.

Psychologists cooperate with duly constituted committees of the American Psychological Association, in particular, the Committee on Scientific and Professional Ethics and Conduct, by responding to inquiries promptly and completely. Members also respond promptly and completely to inquiries from duly constituted state association ethics committees and professional standards review committees.

Principle 1: Responsibility

In providing services, psychologists maintain the highest standards of their profession. They accept responsibility for the consequences of their acts and make every effort to ensure that their services are used appropriately.

Principle 2: Competence

The maintenance of high standards of competence is a responsibility shared by all psychologists in the interest of the public and the profession as a whole. Psychologists recognize the boundaries of their competence and the limitations of their techniques. They only provide services and only use techniques for which they are qualified by training and experience. In those areas in which recognized standards do not yet exist, psychologists take whatever precautions are necessary to protect the welfare of their clients. They maintain knowledge of current scientific and professional information related to the services they render.

Principle 3: Moral and legal standards

Psychologists' moral and ethical standards of behavior are a personal matter to the same degree as they are for any other citizen, except as these may compromise the fulfillment of their professional responsibilities or reduce the public trust in psychology and psychologists. Regarding their own behavior, psychologists are sensitive to prevailing community standards and to the possible impact that conformity to or deviation from these standards may have upon the quality of their performance as psychologists. Psychologists are also aware of the possible impact of their public behavior upon the ability of colleagues to perform their professional duties.

---

*[Annotations deleted.—ED.]

Principle 4: Public statements

Public statements, announcements of services, advertising, and promotional activities of psychologists serve the purpose of helping the public make informed judgments and choices. Psychologists represent accurately and objectively their professional qualifications, affiliations, and functions, as well as those of the institutions or organizations with which they or the statements may be associated. In public statements providing psychological information or professional opinions or providing information about the availability of psychological products, publications, and services, psychologists base their statements on scientifically acceptable psychological findings and techniques with full recognition of the limits and uncertainties of such evidence.

Principle 5: Confidentiality

Psychologists have a primary obligation to respect the confidentiality of information obtained from persons in the course of their work as psychologists. They reveal such information to others only with the consent of the person or the person's legal representative, except in those unusual circumstances in which not to do so would result in clear danger to the person or to others. Where appropriate, psychologists inform their clients of the legal limits of confidentiality.

Principle 6: Welfare of the consumer

Psychologists respect the integrity and protect the welfare of the people and groups with whom they work. When conflicts of interest arise between clients and psychologists' employing institutions, psychologists clarify the nature and direction of their loyalties and responsibilities and keep all parties informed of their commitments. Psychologists fully inform consumers as to the purpose and nature of an evaluative, treatment, educational, or training procedure, and they freely acknowledge that clients, students, or participants in research have freedom of choice with regard to participation.

Principle 7: Professional relationships

Psychologists act with due regard for the needs, special competencies, and obligations of their colleagues in psychology and other professions. They respect the prerogatives and obligations of the institutions or organizations with which these other colleagues are associated.

Principle 8: Assessment techniques

In the development, publication, and utlitzation of psychological assessment techniques, psychologists make every effort to promote the welfare and best interests of the client. They guard against the misuse of assessment results. They respect the client's right to know the results, the interpretations made, and the bases for their conclusions and recommendations. Psychologists make every effort to maintain the security of tests and other assessment techniques within limits of legal mandates. They strive to ensure the appropriate use of assessment techniques by others.

Principle 9: Research with human participants

The decision to undertake research rests upon a considered judgment by the individual psychologist about how best to contribute to psychological science and human welfare. Having made the decision to conduct research, the psychologist considers alternative directions in which research energies and resources might be invested. On the basis of this consideration, the psychologist carries out the investigation with respect and concern for the dignity and welfare of the people who participate and with cognizance of federal and state regulations and professional standards governing the conduct of research with human participants.

Principle 10: Care and use of animals

An investigator of animal behavior strives to advance understanding of basic behavioral principles and/or to contribute to the improvement of human health and welfare. In seeking these ends, the investigator ensures the welfare of animals and treats them humanely. Laws and regulations notwithstanding, an animal's immediate protection depends upon the scientist's own conscience.

6. AMERICAN SOCIETY FOR PUBLIC ADMINISTRATION'S WORKBOOK AND STUDY GUIDE FOR PUBLIC ADMINISTRATORS

Introduction

An Overview of Professional Standards and Ethics

Administrators in the public sector are confronted with two primary imperatives—satisfying their individual standards of professional performance, conduct, and ethics and adhering to those imposed upon them by their agencies, public policies, and a critical public. But the dual expectations that result vary frequently from situation to situation, place to place, and time to time, creating thorny conflicts.

Diversification of the roles of public administrators in modern society has added to the difficulty and complexity of meeting these dual expectations. Indeed, enactment of public policies and creation of numerous governmental entities to serve the public in what is assumed to be an even-handed, impersonal way may have lessened the public administrator's *perceived individual responsibility* for her or his actions. In this way, barriers to maintaining a strong commitment to *individual* and *professional* standards and ethics may have been unwittingly created.

Another challenge involves reconciling the requirements of law and the realities of situations encountered in the daily lives of administrators. Increasingly visible, for example, is the array of dilemmas associated with public sector transactions involving people, contracts, and grants. Such transactions call for exercise of discretion; they affect not only ethical codes of administrators but their standards of performance as well.

Considerable ambiguity has arisen over how public administrators should respond to the dual, and sometimes competing, demands of their professional roles and their individual codes of conduct. The challenge is complex, not susceptible to easy solution by applying pat "rules of thumb."

Throughout a career, every administrator ultimately confronts dilemmas in meeting standards and applying ethical guidelines; he or she must face them as an individual. Although it is possible to develop a long list of "thou shalts" and "thou shalt nots," ultimate responsibility for applying standards and ethics still falls upon the individual.

Given the nature of the individual decisions involved, we believe that one of the most effective ways to address such problems is through meaningful *self-evaluation*.

We suggest that this process may be approached from two perspectives: (a) consideration of the ethical dimensions of individual behavior, and (b) an examination of the ethical issues inherent in the administration of particular public policies. . . .

Responsibility and Accountability

. . . . .

Background—Responsibility

The administrator is responsible for performing tasks effectively: for taking care of, managing, and reliably discharging various functions. The administrator is expected to be trustworthy, willing, and able to carry out tasks with competence and conformity to professional standards. Obviously, public managers/administrators *must deal with* defining their ultimate responsibility to the public. . . .

Background—Accountability

Accountability is based on the idea that the public administrator is answerable first to the public and second to his or her organization for the results of work performed. It also involves generating and providing credible, accurate information that facilitates evaluations of performance by the public, the employing agency, client groups, and the profession. Accountability also calls for disclosures that illuminate how responsibilities were assigned, methods adopted to accomplish tasks, tasks executed, and outcomes realized. . . .

Commitment

Background

Commitment in public administration reflects the desire to administer the public's business in the most competent manner possible. It encompasses dedication to and enthusiasm for the work of government, one's organization, and the programs for which one carries responsibility. It calls for use of one's energy and talent to see that the job gets done, not halfheartedly, but rather through full effort and involvement of self in the area of responsibility. It nurtures innovation and imagination.

Edited by Herman Mertins, Jr., and Patrick J. Hennigan. Professional Standards and Ethics Committee, American Society for Public Administration, copyright © 1982, American Society for Public Administration.

The results of commitment do not occur in a vacuum; they are based on a sense of public morality, values, precedents, and personal conduct which are expected by the public and the public administration profession.

Commitment also implies a willingness to struggle with myriad dilemmas and frustrations. These result from the diverse collection of laws, codes, regulations, client pressures, technical requirements, organizational goals, professional standards of behavior, and political realities faced by the public administrator. . . .

Responsiveness

Background

Responsiveness reflects the degree to which public administrators are sensitive to dealing with new circumstances, changing conditions, or evolving demands and needs of the public. It touches on their reaction to societal norms, the goals of the agency or institution, the influences, actions, or appeals of various client groups, and the environment in which decision making and democratic processes take place. . . .

Knowledge and Skills

Background

The need for public services and leadership on a wide range of fronts is increasing, yet the resources available to many governments are diminishing. Increasing public concern about governmental spending, expanding activities of taxpayer groups, constitutional amendments to limit public spending—all underscore the seriousness of the problems. Pressure has never been greater on government at all levels to economize and perform well. Compared to the past 30 years, public administrators in the 1980s encounter unrelenting pressure to do more with less.

Some assistance in meeting this dilemma has been provided by progress in the social, behavioral, and natural sciences and supporting technologies. In many cases, promising opportunities have been created by the advancing ''state of the art'' of public administration. But these advances have frequently brought with them some hidden costs—new administrative problems.

Given these challenges, public administrators must keep abreast of expanding knowledge, retain the best of existing knowledge, acquire new capabilities, and sharpen skills. . . .

Professional Development and Achievement of Potential

Background

Maintaining professional growth and achieving full potential are vital for the public administrator. Uniform expectations in these areas, however, are difficult to define because public administration has characteristics of a ''supraprofession,'' embracing many professions and fields. Altogether, it encompasses a wide range of both general and technical knowledge, vocational skills, and academic preparation. These often result in the setting of unique qualifications for the individual professions that play roles in it.

A rapidly changing environment is also a fact of life in public service; it imposes pressure on individuals to adapt to new requirements, needs, and demands. Sometimes, it fosters displacement from chosen jobs or fields. At other times, it creates new roles and positions that call for uncommon combinations of skills and qualifications. Consequently, efforts to achieve self-development and achievement of potential must satisfy a broad spectrum of needs ranging from entry level positions to senior level roles that require new learning, rethinking, and continuous professional growth.

Given all this, several sources can be tapped to meet individual needs. These include:

1. Formal education of all types, including degree programs and in-service courses.
2. Institutional resources, such as public, university, and agency libraries, or agency-maintained education centers or self-learning laboratories.
3. Intergovernmental personnel exchanges, or exchanges between government and academia.
4. Job-related community involvement as, for example, when an individual employed in drug abuse program planning or evaluation performs volunteer work on his or her own time at a drop-in center for troubled teenagers.
5. Participation (as distinguished from dues paying membership) in professional societies.
6. Individual initiatives, such as authoring articles for professional journals and other publications, teaching in an agency or for an educational institution, reading to keep abreast of developments in one's field, or designing a career ladder and planning job changes to promote personal growth.

. . . . .

Citizenship and the Political Process

Background

The public administrator's relationship to government is different from that of most other persons. It grows out of the dual nature of the role played by the public administrator as an employee and a citizen. As an employee of the public, the administrator is responsible for the nonpartisan conduct of his or her duties. As a citizen in a democratic society, the administrator participates directly in the political process.

Administrators who allow *partisan* politics to subvert the performance of their duties as public employees can neglect the legal obligation to serve the citizenry impartially. Public adminstrators who insulate themselves from the political process, however, risk abdicating their responsibilities as citizens. . . .

Conflicts of Interest

Background

Although conflicts of interest characterize all professions, they are particularly accentuated in public administration, where the need to maintain the public trust is crucial. Public administrators frequently find themselves in situations in which public objectives and private goals, as well as the means to attain them, are in conflict. So, too, must public administrators deal with conflicts in their loyalties to supervisors and subordinates, immediate unit and agency, and individual programs and broad organizational missions.

These conflicts may be minimized if there is a close match between the personal codes of the public administrator and the mission and practices of her or his organization. But given the high degree of individuality evident among public administrators, the usual case is one of some conflict and lack of matching.

Public management responsibilities also extend well beyond simply determining matters that might be considered technically legal or illegal. Involved are such concerns as:

1. Reflecting on actions of yours that result in personal gains as opposed to organizational benefits.
2. Examining the impact of your personal belief system on organizational programs and practices.
3. Considering the numerous forms of offering or accepting favors.
4. Reflecting on your use of personal power and influence in the organization and the conflicts that may result.
5. Observing and possibly intervening in conflict of interest situations involving colleagues.
6. Considering the dilemmas created for you by responsibilities imposed by agency missions, citizenship, and codes of conduct.
7. Dealing with the potential conflicts between your organization's goals and tactics and pursuing the general welfare within the political subdivision involved.

. . . . .

Whistle Blowing

Background

Public administrators who disclose previously hidden organizational or employee activities which they consider potentially harmful to the public interest are labeled "whistle blowers." These activities may include violations of laws, rules, or regulations; mismanagement, gross waste of funds, or abuse of authority; actions that pose a substantial danger to public health or safety.

Whistle blowing is a contentious activity for a public administrator. On the positive side, it may be considered a responsible expression of accountability. On the negative side, it can appear to be the ultimate form of organizational disloyalty, representing little more than the spiteful behavior of a disgruntled employee.

The ASPA National Council has endorsed a policy statement on whistle blowing which states, in part, that ". . . organizations should protect from retaliation responsible and conscientious public employees who, after much forethought, disclose information about situations potentially harmful to the public interest. Agencies should focus on the message rather than the messenger." . . .

Public Disclosure and Confidentiality

Background

This area covers two elements of the administrator's role that sometimes move in opposite directions.

On the one hand, he or she must be cognizant of the public's right to know about the actions of government agencies, except when information sharing would be harmful to the security and welfare of the nation or its citizens. Thus, new emphasis has been placed on openness, full participation, and disclosure in the conduct of public business. These goals are buttressed by the Freedom of Information Act; the underlying theme suggests that we all would be better served if governance were exposed to open scrutiny.

"Sunshine laws" provide an example of the application of disclosure to various agencies and units of government. On the personal level, one finds increasing expectations for full financial disclosure by public officials who seek elective or high policy-making posts in government.

On the other hand, a countervailing force exists. Each person, whether a citizen-at-large or a public administrator, has rights of privacy to be safeguarded. Included are protections against illegal domestic surveillance, unauthorized sharing of credit information, unauthorized access to confidential personal files, and the like.

The coexistence of these two thrusts presents obvious dilemmas for the public administrator. . . .

Professional Ethics

Background

The ethical dimensions of a public administrator's professional activity are generating increasing concern. If the definition and application of professional ethics are to be effective, the thrust cannot be simply directed toward "catching" people engaged in unacceptable behavior. The basic goal is more fundamental—to spur development of professional integrity. This calls for assisting public administrators in being self-reflective about whether their expressed values coincide with the values that they actually apply in their daily conduct.

Definitions

Values may be viewed as beliefs that model our assessments of relative worth and importance. They influence our approaches to:

1. How one ought or ought not to behave.
2. The desirability or undesirability of achieving certain ends.

In these terms, values influence and shape both our goals and our patterns of activity. Our values often make conflicting demands upon our behavior because they relate to roles which are not always consistent and congruent.

Ethics involves applying principles so that we might order our values in particular situations. When two or more values make conflicting claims on our conduct, ethical reflection helps us decide the paramount value in that particular context. Principles, such as those dealing with justice, freedom, honesty, beauty, order, and loyalty are employed to sort out our values and establish priorities among them. These principles are derived from a variety of sources, including the family, schooling, religion, socio-cultural environments, and professional identities.

Key Principles

Professional ethics of public administrators address a number of critical elements such as:

1. *Equality*—One of the basic virtues of rational, bureaucratic organization is often represented to be identical treatment of clients. This means that a consistent quality of service is to be rendered to all, regardless of political affiliation and status. A common assumption is that the same treatment is tantamount to fair treatment. Following this line of reasoning, one achives fairness by rendering no special favors.
2. *Equity*—One of the limitations of *equality* of treatment as a sole criterion is that it does not always lead to justice and fairness. A pluralistic society, in which some people have been subjected to long-term discrimination, exhibits a great spectrum of problems and needs. In such a social environment, *equality* may demand *equal* treatment in some instances (to end discrimination in employment, housing, and so forth) and *unequal* treatment in others (for example, to provide compensatory education, special job training programs, subsidized housing).
3. *Loyalty*—A major problem in applying this principle is maintaining an awareness of one's *ultimate loyalties*. Loyalties to the Constitution, the structures of government, the law, and to superiors, subordinates and peers within an organization are related in a highly complex fashion. They are laced with different levels of intensity and are difficult to keep in perspective as specific demands for decisions are encountered.
4. *Responsibility*—when one functions within a hierarchical organization, it is easy to fall into the "I am just following orders" syndrome. Yet each public official must be prepared to accept responsibility for whatever is done and explain his or her reasons for "following orders." Sustaining this principle is difficult yet crucial. . . .

7. NATIONAL ASSOCIATION OF SOCIAL WORKERS' CODE OF ETHICS*

Preamble

This code is intended to serve as a guide to the everyday conduct of members of the social work profession and as a basis for the adjudication of issues in ethics when the conduct of social workers is alleged to deviate from the standards expressed or implied in this code. It represents standards of ethical behavior for social workers in professional relationships with those served, with colleagues, with employers, with other individuals and professions, and with the community and society as a whole. It also embodies standards of ethical behavior governing individual conduct to the extent that such conduct is associated with an individual's status and identity as a social worker.

This code is based on the fundamental values of the social work profession that include the worth, dignity, and uniqueness of all persons as well as their rights and opportunities. It is also based on the nature of social work, which fosters conditions that promote these values.

In subscribing to and abiding by this code, the social worker is expected to view ethical responsibility in as inclusive a context as each situation demands and within which ethical judgement is required. The social worker is expected to take into consideration all the principles in this code that have a bearing upon any situation in which ethical judgement is to be exercised and professional intervention or conduct is planned. The course of action that the social worker chooses is expected to be consistent with the spirit as well as the letter of this code.

In itself, this code does not represent a set of rules that will prescribe all the behaviors of social workers in all the complexities of professional life. Rather, it offers general principles to guide conduct, and the judicious appraisal of conduct, in situations that have ethical implications. It provides the basis for making judgements about ethical actions before and after they occur. Frequently, the particular situation determines the ethical principles that apply and the manner of their application. In such cases, not only the particular ethical principles are taken into immediate consideration, but also the entire code and its spirit. Specific applications of ethical principles must be judged within the context in which they are being considered. Ethical behavior in a given situation must satisfy not only the judgement of the individual social worker, but also the judgement of an unbiased jury of professional peers.

This code should not be used as an instrument to deprive any social worker of the opportunity or freedom to practice with complete professional integrity; nor should any disciplinary action be taken on the basis of this code without maximum provision for safeguarding the rights of the social worker affected.

The ethical behavior of social workers results not from edict, but from a personal commitment of the individual. This code is offered to affirm the will and zeal of all social workers to be ethical and to act ethically in all that they do as social workers.

The following codified ethical principles should guide social workers in the various roles and relationships and at the various levels of responsibility in which they function professionally. These principles also serve as a basis for the adjudication by the National Association of Social Workers of issues in ethics.

In subscribing to this code, social workers are required to cooperate in its implementation and abide by any disciplinary rulings based on it. They should also take adequate measures to discourage, prevent, expose, and correct the unethical conduct of colleagues. Finally, social workers should be equally ready to defend and assist colleagues unjustly charged with unethical conduct.

Summary of Major Principles

I. The Social Worker's Conduct and Comportment as a Social Worker

A. Propriety. The social worker should maintain high standards of personal conduct in the capacity or identity as social worker.

B. Competence and Professional Development. The social worker should strive to become and remain proficient in professional practice and the performance of professional functions.

C. Service. The social worker should regard as primary the service obligation of the social work profession.

D. Integrity. The social worker should act in accordance with the highest standards of professional integrity.

---

*[Annotations deleted.—ED.]

E. Scholarship and Research. The social worker engaged in study and research should be guided by the conventions of scholarly inquiry.

II. The Social Worker's Ethical Responsibility to Clients

F. Primacy of Clients' Interests. The social worker's primary responsibility is to clients.

G. Rights and Prerogatives of Clients. The social worker should make every effort to foster maximum self-determination on the part of clients.

H. Confidentiality and Privacy. The social worker should respect the privacy of clients and hold in confidence all information obtained in the course of professional service.

I. Fees. When setting fees, the social worker should ensure that they are fair, reasonable, considerate, and commensurate with the service performed and with due regard for the clients' ability to pay.

III. The Social Worker's Ethical Responsibility to Colleagues

J. Respect, Fairness, and Courtesy. The social worker should treat colleagues with respect, courtesy, fairness, and good faith.

K. Dealing with Colleagues' Clients. The social worker has the responsibility to relate to the clients of colleagues with full professional consideration.

IV. The Social Worker's Ethical Responsibility to Employers and Employing Organizations

L. Commitments to Employing Organizations. The social worker should adhere to commitments made to the employing organizations.

V. The Social Worker's Ethical Responsibility to the Social Work Profession

M. Maintaining the Integrity of the Profession. The social worker should uphold and advance the values, ethics, knowledge, and mission of the profession.

N. Community Service. The social worker should assist the profession in making social services available to the general public.

O. Development of Knowledge. The social worker should take responsibility for identifying, developing, and fully utilizing knowledge for professional practice.

VI. The Social Worker's Ethical Responsibility to Society

P. Promoting the General Welfare. The social worker should promote the general welfare of society.

8. NATIONAL SOCIETY OF PROFESSIONAL ENGINEERS' CODE OF ETHICS FOR ENGINEERS AND STATEMENT BY NSPSE EXECUTIVE COMMITTEE

Preamble

Engineering is an important and learned profession. The members of the profession recognize that their work has a direct and vital impact on the quality of life for all people. Accordingly, the services provided by engineers require honesty, impartiality, fairness and equity, and must be dedicated to the protection of the public health, safety and welfare. In the practice of their profession, engineers must perform under a standard of professional behavior which requires adherence to the highest principles of ethical conduct on behalf of the public, clients, employers and the profession.

I. Fundamental Canons

Engineers, in the fulfillment of their professional duties, shall:

1. Hold paramount the safety, health and welfare of the public in the performance of their professional duties.

2. Perform services only in areas of their competence.

3. Issue public statements only in an objective and truthful manner.

4. Act in professional matters for each employer or client as faithful agents or trustees.

5. Avoid improper solicitation of professional employment.

II. Rules of Practice

1. Engineers shall hold paramount the safety, health and welfare of the public in the performance of their professional duties.

a. Engineers shall at all times recognize that their primary obligation is to protect the safety, health, property and welfare of the public. If their professional judgment is overruled under circumstances where the safety, health, property

---

NSPE Publication No. 1102, as revised January 1987.

or welfare of the public are endangered, they shall notify their employer or client and such other authority as may be appropriate.

b. Engineers shall approve only those engineering documents which are safe for public health, property and welfare in conformity with accepted standards.

c. Engineers shall not reveal facts, data or information obtained in a professional capacity without the prior consent of the client or employer except as authorized or required by law or this Code.

d. Engineers shall not permit the use of their name or firm name nor associate in business ventures with any person or firm which they have reason to believe is engaging in fraudulent or dishonest business or professional practices.

e. Engineers having knowledge of any alleged violation of this Code shall cooperate with the proper authorities in furnishing such information or assistance as may be required.

2. Engineers shall perform services only in the areas of their competence:

a. Engineers shall undertake assignments only when qualified by education or experience in the specific technical fields involved.

b. Engineers shall not affix their signatures to any plans or documents dealing with subject matter in which they lack competence, nor to any plan or document not prepared under their direction and control.

c. Engineers may accept assignments and assume responsibility for coordination of an entire project and sign and seal the engineering documents for the entire project, provided that each technical segment is signed and sealed only by the qualified engineers who prepared the segment.

3. Engineers shall issue public statements only in an objective and truthful manner.

a. Engineers shall be objective and truthful in professional reports, statements or testimony. They shall include all relevant and pertinent information in such reports, statements or testimony.

b. Engineers may express publicly a professional opinion on technical subjects only when that opinion is founded upon adequate knowledge of the facts and competence in the subject matter.

c. Engineers shall issue no statements, criticisms or arguments on technical matters which are inspired or paid for by interested parties, unless they have prefaced their comments by explicitly identifying the interested parties on whose behalf they are speaking, and by revealing the existence of any interest the engineers may have in the matters.

4. Engineers shall act in professional matters for each employer or client as faithful agents or trustees.

a. Engineers shall disclose all known or potential conflicts of interest to their employers or clients by promptly informing them of any business association, interest, or other circumstances which could influence or appear to influence their judgment or the quality of their services.

b. Engineers shall not accept compensation, financial or otherwise, from more than one party for services on the same project, or for services pertaining to the same project, unless the circumstances are fully disclosed to, and agreed to, by all interested parties.

c. Engineers shall not solicit or accept financial or other valuable consideration, directly or indirectly, from contractors, their agents, or other parties in connection with work for employers or clients for which they are responsible.

d. Engineers in public service as members, advisors or employees of a governmental body or department shall not participate in decisions with respect to professional services solicited or provided by them or their organizations in private or public engineering practice.

e. Engineers shall not solicit or accept a professional contract from a governmental body on which a principal or officer of their organization serves as a member.

5. Engineers shall avoid deceptive acts in the solicitation of professional employment.

a. Engineers shall not falsify or permit misrepresentation of their, or their associates', academic or professional qualifications. They shall not misrepresent or exaggerate their degree of responsibility in or for the subject matter of prior assignments. Brochures or other presentations incident to the solicitation of employment shall not misrepresent pertinent facts concerning employers, employees, associates, joint venturers or past accomplishments with the intent and purpose of enhancing their qualifications and their work.

b. Engineers shall not offer, give, solicit or receive, either directly or indirectly, any political contribution in an amount intended to influence the award of a contract by public authority, or which may be reasonably construed by the public of having the effect or intent to influence the award of a contract. They shall not offer any gift, or other valuable consideration in order to secure work. They shall not pay a commission, percentage or brokerage fee in order to secure work except to a bona fide employee or bona fide established commercial or marketing agencies retained by them.

III. Professional Obligations

1. Engineers shall be guided in all their professional relations by the highest standards of integrity.

a. Engineers shall admit and accept their own errors when proven wrong and refrain from distorting or altering the facts in an attempt to justify their decisions.

b. Engineers shall advise their clients or employers when they believe a project will not be successful.

c. Engineers shall not accept outside employment to the detriment of their regular work or interest. Before accepting any outside employment they will notify their employers.

d. Engineers shall not attempt to attract an engineer from another employer by false or misleading pretenses.

e. Engineers shall not actively participate in strikes, picket lines, or other collective coercive action.

f. Engineers shall avoid any act tending to promote their own interest at the expense of the dignity and integrity of the profession.

2. Engineers shall at all times strive to serve the public interest.

a. Engineers shall seek opportunities to be of constructive service in civic affairs and work for the advancement of the safety, health and well-being of their community.

b. Engineers shall not complete, sign, or seal plans and/or specifications that are not of a design safe to the public health and welfare and in conformity with accepted engineering standards. If the client or employer insists on such unprofessional conduct, they shall notify the proper authorities and withdraw from further service on the project.

c. Engineers shall endeavor to extend public knowledge and appreciation of engineering and its achievements and to protect the engineering profession from misrepresentation and misunderstanding.

3. Engineers shall avoid all conduct or practice which is likely to discredit the profession or deceive the public.

a. Engineers shall avoid the use of statements containing a material misrepresentation of fact or omitting a material fact necessary to keep statements from being misleading or intended or likely to create an unjustified expectation; statements containing prediction of future success; statements containing an opinion as to the quality of the Engineers' services; or statements intended or likely to attract clients by the use of showmanship, puffery, or self-laudation, including the use of slogans, jingles, or sensational language or format.

b. Consistent with the foregoing, Engineers may advertise for recruitment of personnel.

c. Consistent with the foregoing, Engineers may prepare articles for the lay or technical press, but such articles shall not imply credit to the author for work performed by others.

4. Engineers shall not disclose confidential information concerning the business affairs or technical processes of any present or former client or employer without his consent.

a. Engineers in the employ of others shall not without the consent of all interested parties enter promotional efforts or negotiations for work or make arrangements for other employment as a principal or to practice in connection with a specific project for which the Engineer has gained particular and specialized knowledge.

b. Engineers shall not, without the consent of all interested parties, participate in or represent an adversary interest in connection with a specific project or proceeding in which the Engineer has gained particular specialized knowledge on behalf of a former client or employer.

5. Engineers shall not be influenced in their professional duties by conflicting interests.

a. Engineers shall not accept financial or other considerations, including free engineering designs, from material or equipment suppliers for specifying their product.

b. Engineers shall not accept commissions or allowances, directly or indirectly, from contractors or other parties dealing with clients or employers of the Engineer in connection with work for which the Engineer is responsible.

6. Engineers shall uphold the principle of appropriate and adequate compensation for those engaged in engineering work.

a. Engineers shall not accept remuneration from either an employee or employment agency for giving employment.

b. Engineers, when employing other engineers, shall offer a salary according to professional qualifications.

7. Engineers shall not attempt to obtain employment or advancement or professional engagements by untruthfully criticizing other engineers, or by other improper or questionable methods.

a. Engineers shall not request, propose, or accept a professional commission on a contingent basis under circumstances in which their professional judgment may be compromised.

b. Engineers in salaried positions shall accept part-time engineering work only to the extent consistent with policies of the employer and in accordance with ethical consideration.

c. Engineers shall not use equipment, supplies, laboratory, or office facilities of an employer to carry on outside private practice without consent.

8. Engineers shall not attempt to injure, maliciously or falsely, directly or indirectly, the professional reputation, prospects, practice or employment of other engineers, nor untruthfully criticize other engineers' work. Engineers who believe others are guilty of unethical or illegal practice shall present such information to the proper authority for action.

a. Engineers in private practice shall not review the work of another engineer for the same client, except with the knowledge of such engineer, or unless the connection of such engineer with the work has been terminated.
b. Engineers in governmental, industrial or educational employ are entitled to review and evaluate the work of other engineers when so required by their employment duties.
c. Engineers in sales or industrial employ are entitled to make engineering comparisons of represented products with products of other suppliers.

9. Engineers shall accept personal responsibility for all professional activities; provided, however, that Engineers may seek indemnification for professional services arising out of their practice for other than gross negligence, where the Engineer's interests cannot otherwise be protected.

a. Engineers shall conform with state registration laws in the practice of engineering.
b. Engineers shall not use association with a non-engineer, a corporation, or partnership, as a "cloak" for unethical acts, but must accept personal responsibility for all professional acts.

10. Engineers shall give credit for engineering work to those to whom credit is due, and will recognize the proprietary interests of others.

a. Engineers shall, whenever possible, name the person or persons who may be individually responsible for designs, inventions, writings, or other accomplishments.
b. Engineers using designs supplied by a client recognize that the designs remain the property of the client and may not be duplicated by the Engineer for others without express permission.
c. Engineers, before undertaking work for others in connection with which the Engineer may make improvements, plans, designs, inventions, or other records which may justify copyrights or patents, should enter into a positive agreement regarding ownership.
d. Engineers' designs, data, records, and notes referring exclusively to an employer's work are the employer's property.

11. Engineers shall cooperate in extending the effectiveness of the profession by interchanging information and experience with other engineers and students, and will endeavor to provide opportunity for the professional development and advancement of engineers under their supervision.

a. Engineers shall encourage engineering employees' efforts to improve their education.
b. Engineers shall encourage engineering employees to attend and present papers at professional and technical society meetings.
c. Engineers shall urge engineering employees to become registered at the earliest possible date.
d. Engineers shall assign a professional engineer duties of a nature to utilize full training and experience, insofar as possible, and delegate lesser functions to subprofessionals or to technicians.
e. Engineers shall provide a prospective engineering employee with complete information on working conditions and proposed status of employment, and after employment will keep employees informed of any changes.

"By order of the United States District Court for the District of Columbia, former Section 11(c) of the NSPE Code of Ethics prohibiting competitive bidding, and all policy statements, opinions, rulings or other guidelines interpreting its scope, have been rescinded as unlawfully interfering with the legal right of engineers, protected under the antitrust laws, to provide price information to prospective clients; accordingly, nothing contained in the NSPE Code of Ethics, policy statements, opinions, rulings or other guidelines prohibits the submission of price quotations or competitive bids for engineering services at any time or in any amount."

Statement by NSPE Executive Committee

In order to correct misunderstandings which have been indicated in some instances since the issuance of the Supreme Court decision and the entry of the Final Judgment, it is noted that in its decision of April 25, 1978, the Supreme Court of the United States declared: "The Sherman Act does not require competitive bidding."

It is further noted that as made clear in the Supreme Court decision:

(1) Engineers and firms may individually refuse to bid for engineering services.
(2) Clients are not required to seek bids for engineering services.
(3) Federal, state, and local laws governing procedures to procure engineering services are not affected, and remain in full force and effect.
(4) State societies and local chapters are free to

actively and aggressively seek legislation for professional selection and negotiation procedures by public agencies.

(5) State registration board rules of professional conduct, including rules prohibiting competitive bidding for engineering services, are not affected and remain in full force and effect. State registration boards with authority to adopt rules of professional conduct may adopt rules governing procedures to obtain engineering services.

(6) As noted by the Supreme Court, "nothing in the judgment prevents NSPE and its members from attempting to influence governmental action. . . ."

APPENDIX 2: PREPARING CASES AND POSITION PAPERS

GUIDELINES FOR PREPARING CASES*

As you are preparing cases, either for group discussion, in preparation for writing a paper, or simply for the sake of attempting to resolve a morally problematic case, it will be helpful to work through the following steps.

1. Getting Out the Relevant Facts:[1] Generate as complete a set of lists as possible of the *facts* (known, possible, probable) that might be used to support *various* positions on how the case should be resolved. Not every fact about a case is relevant to resolving the moral issue(s) the case raises. But for every morally dilemmic case, there will be facts that support resolving the case in opposing ways. Set out the options you see as ways to decide the case; under each option, list the facts about the case that you think are relevant to resolving the case in that way. This will help to clarify what assumptions you are making about what the facts actually are and what they might be/will be if some decision is taken; and it will help to ensure that you have thought carefully about the morally relevant implications of alternative resolutions before you make a decision on the case. Relevant facts might include: someone will be or is likely to be harmed (physically, financially, emotionally, in reputation, etc.) if a certain resolution is chosen; resources expended in one place could be expended elsewhere where there is need; some decision will interfere with the autonomy/liberty of an individual; some choice involves deception, manipulation, violation of trust, coercion, keeping a promise, breaking a promise, permitting exploitation, inequitable treatment, equitable treatment, and so on.

2. Clarifying the Conflicting Moral Values and Moral Principles: Generate as complete a set of lists as possible of the *moral values and moral principles* that might be used to support *various* positions on how the case should be resolved. Again, set out the options you see as possible ways to decide the case, and under each option, list out the moral values and moral principles supportive of selecting that option. Keep in mind that genuinely dilemmic cases are not cases where what is right or wrong is obvious. On the contrary, such cases are *dilemmic* precisely because they confront us as "this kind of good versus that kind of good; this kind of evil versus that kind of evil; this kind of right versus that kind of right; this kind of wrong versus that kind of wrong." It is just these kinds of conflict of important values and principles that make dilemmic cases hard to decide. Despite this, clearly setting out the conflicts can often make more evident the relative importance of competing values and principles in a given case—as one sets out the conflicts, it can become clear that one kind of right takes precedence over another or that one sort of wrong action seems less evil than any of the alternatives. At the very least, setting out the conflicts in an orderly way gives us a full and clear appreciation of what is at stake when we are forced to decide. Articulating these values and principles will also make explicit the moral relevance of the facts you list as important considerations in resolving the case in various ways. Relevant moral principles might include: prevent harm, do good, be loyal, be fair, be honest, do not inflict harm on others, maintain integrity, be candid, live up to the moral requirements of your office or role, it is morally permissible to pursue/protect one's own legitimate self-interest, respect the autonomy of

*Cowritten with Tom Grassey.

others, and so on. It will not be uncommon to have one moral principle supporting two opposing options.

3. Reflections on Your Lists: Before making your decision, look over your list of options. You may have identified an alternative that is very difficult or demanding or repugnant for some reason but that is among possible resolutions. The morally right thing to do (as we all know) is not always easy or pleasant. Sometimes acting morally requires great courage and involves considerable pain. And sometimes considering the arguments for and against various resolutions reveals that the alternative one was inclined to choose at the outset cannot be supported in the light of arguments for some other decision. Ask yourself if your lists of facts and values/principles have given each option a full hearing, and if, in your own thinking, you have given serious consideration to the weights of competing arguments. If the case is a complex one that admits of more than two options, ask yourself if you have identified all the options a decision-maker might reasonably take. One of the greatest deficiencies in decision making is the failure to identify promising possible solutions that allow a decision-maker to act without compromising his or her values or principles. And sometimes the person making the decision in a particular case is not the person who should be making it. If the case admits of more than two alternatives, then, be sure that you have taxed your imagination, and have not left out some option that was not initially an obvious or plausible one.

4. Make and Articulate Your Decision: After being sure that your lists and your reflection on them have taken into careful and sensitive consideration the available options and the facts and moral values and principles relevant to conflicting positions on how the case might be resolved, make a decision on how the case should be resolved and articulate your decision clearly.

5. Justify Your Decision: Make clear your reasons for your answer on how the case should be resolved, that is, set out your *positive* reasons for selecting this option.

6. Anticipate Criticism/Clarify the Costs: Go back to your lists a final time; look at the facts and values/principles supportive of options other than the one you have chosen, and ask what the most serious objection to your decision might be. Offer your response to this objection, clarifying why—despite this objection—you take your decision to be the morally preferable decision. Finish your analysis by clarifying what you take to be the "downside" aspects or consequences of your decision. That is, clarify what you think the greatest moral costs are of deciding the case the way you have decided it.

Proceeding in this way will help to crystallize the arguments for resolving the case in various ways. Thus, it should be helpful in ensuring that your response to a case has not oversimplified the issue(s) and has taken into careful account the morally relevant considerations which need to be taken into account in resolving a dilemmic case. Keep in mind that sometimes resolving a case will have to consist in finding the least morally problematic resolution, that is, the resolution that seems to involve the least sacrifice of moral value.

Note

1. See chapter 1 for an account of the distinction between descriptive (factual) and normative (value) claims. If you are writing the case, claims for this section are descriptive in form; claims for the section on values and principles are normative in form.

GUIDELINES FOR PREPARING POSITION PAPERS

The purpose of writing position papers in ethics is to do just what the term suggests, namely, to develop and defend one's own position on a morally problematic issue or case. Although well-argued position papers should reflect familiarity with the views of others on the issue or on similar cases, the main task is for the author to make his or her own serious, careful, and sustained attempt to resolve the case or issue in the most morally acceptable way. A position paper, then, should not simply be an account of the positions of others.

Much that has already been said about preparing cases has application to writing position papers, particularly if you are writing on a concrete case. The remarks that follow should be understood to supplement the remarks on preparing cases.

It is always helpful to work up a detailed prospectus of a paper before actually writing the paper.

Many students do less well than they might in their papers because they wait too long to begin writing. It is a good idea to start writing your paper some time before it is due, working up a draft, then putting it away before going back to it and writing the final version. Taking advantage of this one, simple procedure can help a paper enormously.

Students sometimes think that because they are writing a philosophy paper, the paper must be obscure if it is to be profound. But this is a mistake. Clarity is a literary and philosophical virtue. Write your essays, then, as if you were writing for an intelligent, interested, but uninformed reader. Explain all problems clearly, define all technical terminology (in notes if necessary to save space), check the paper for unclarities and ambiguities, possible incoherencies, and for statements that might be obscure to your reader. And be sure to offer a justification for all potentially controversial assumptions. Such checks will help to ensure that you do not assume too much or leave any crucial steps out of your arguments.

You should also carefully check your paper for grammatical and typographical errors, errors in punctuation, and proper footnote or endnote style. Good papers are generally careful in style and presentation as well as careful in content.

The first step in writing any paper is getting clear on precisely what question the paper is undertaken to answer, what problem the paper is intended to solve, or what point the paper is meant to establish. Structurally, papers should always begin with an introduction that clearly states the problem/question to be addressed or the point to be established, and which gives a clear indication of how you will approach the problem or answer the question or argue for the point in the essay. Every essay must have a solution to a problem to offer or a point to establish; it should not just be an unfocused discussion around some topic. Be sure, then, to make the purpose of your essay clear at the outset. The introduction should motivate the paper; it should give your reader a good reason for reading the paper.

As you defend positions in your papers, it is really crucial that you keep in mind potential objections to your views. That is, you should include in your discussion consideration of the strongest arguments you can think of that can be brought against your views, and say why those objections do not defeat your positions. Thus, it will often be appropriate to say something like, "It might be objected that . . . ," and then go on to offer a response to that potential objection. The task is to show why the position you are defending is more acceptable than alternative positions, thus some discussion of the strongest arguments for competing positions is always in order. The body of your paper, then, should not just include a statement and positive defense of your views; it should also include recognition of the most serious objections that can be raised against your arguments and positions and your best attempt to meet those objections.

A well-organized paper should end with a clear summary of what you believe you have accomplished in the paper. If there are residual problems to be addressed (and there generally will be in any philosophy paper), point this out before concluding and attempt to offer some indication of how those problems might be resolved.

APPENDIX 3: SELECTED ADDITIONAL SOURCES

Abramson, Marcia. "Social Work and the Safety Net." *Hastings Center Report* 12:4 (1982): 19–23.

American Nurses' Association Committee on Ethics, 1980–82. *Ethics References for Nurses.* Kansas City, MO: American Nurses' Association, 1982.

Arras, John D., and Robert Hunt, eds. *Ethical Issues in Modern Medicine,* 2nd ed. Palo Alto, CA: Mayfield, 1983.

Babcock, D. L., and C. A. Smith, eds. *Values and the Public Works Professional.* Chicago: American Public Works Association, 1980.

Barton, Walter E., and Gail M. Barton. *Ethics and Law in Mental Health Administration.* New York: International Universities Press, 1984.

Basson, Marc D., ed. *Rights and Responsibilities in Medicine.* New York: Alan R. Liss, 1981.

Beauchamp, Tom L. *Case Studies in Business, Society, and Ethics.* Englewood Cliffs, NJ: Prentice-Hall, 1983.

———, and Norman E. Bowie, eds. *Ethical Theory and Business,* 2nd ed. Englewood Cliffs, NJ: Prentice-Hall, 1983.

———, and Lawrence B. McCullough. *Medical Ethics: The Moral Responsibilities of Physicians.* Englewood Cliffs, NJ: Prentice-Hall, 1984.

Belsey, Andrew. "Scientific Research and Moral Problems." *New Universities Quarterly* 34 (1980): 429–38.

Bennion, F.A.R. *Professional Ethics: The Consultant Professions and Their Code.* London: Charles Knight, 1969.

Bok, Derek. *Beyond the Ivory Tower: Social Responsibilities of the Modern University.* Cambridge MA: Harvard University Press, 1982.

Bond, Kenneth M. *Bibliography of Business Ethics and Business Moral Values.* Omaha, NE: Creighton University Press, 1985.

Boruch, Robert F., and Joe S. Cecil, eds. *Solutions to Ethical and Legal Problems in Social Research.* New York: Academic Press, 1983.

Bowie, Norman E. *Business Ethics.* Englewood Cliffs, NJ: Prentice-Hall, 1982.

———, ed. *Ethical Issues in Government,* Philadelphia: Temple University Press, 1981.

Boyajian, Jane A., ed. *Ethical Issues in the Practice of Ministry.* Minneapolis, MN: United Theological Seminary of the Twin Cities, 1984.

Braybrooke, David. *Ethics in the World of Business.* Totowa, NJ: Rowman and Allanheld, 1983.

Cahn, Steven M. *Saints and Scamps: Ethics in Academia.* Totowa, NJ: Rowman and Littlefield, 1986.

Callahan, Daniel, William Green, Bruce Jennings, and Martin Linsky. *Congress and the Media: The Ethical Connection.* Hastings-on-Hudson, NY: Hastings Center, 1985.

———, and Bruce Jennings. *The Ethics of Legislative Life: A Report by the Hastings Center.* Hastings-on-Hudson, NY: Hastings Center, 1985.

Carroll, Mary Ann, Henry G. Schneider, and George R. Wesley. *Ethics in the Practice of Nursing.* Englewood Cliffs, NJ: Prentice-Hall, 1985.

Curtin, Leah, and M. Josephine Flaherty. *Nursing Ethics: Theories and Pragmatics.* Bowie, MD: Robert Brady, 1982.

Davis, Anne J., issue ed. "Ethics in Nursing." *International Journal of Nursing Ethics* 22:4 (1986).

Davis, Bernard D. *Storm Over Biology: Essays on Science, Sentiment, and Public Policy.* Buffalo, NY: Prometheus, 1986.

De George, Richard T. *Business Ethics.* New York: Macmillan, 1982.

———. "The Status of Business Ethics: Past and Future." *Journal of Business Ethics* 6:3 (1987): 281–87.

Des Jardins, Joseph R., and John J. McCall, eds. *Contemporary Issues in Business Ethics*. Belmont, CA: Wadsworth, 1985.

Donaldson, Thomas. *Corporations and Morality*. Englewood Cliffs, NJ: Prentice-Hall, 1982.

———, ed. *Case Studies in Business Ethics*. Englewood Cliffs, NJ: Prentice-Hall, 1984.

———, and Patricia H. Werhane, eds. *Ethical Issues in Business*, 2nd ed. Englewood Cliffs, NJ: Prentice-Hall, 1983.

Elliston, Frederick A. *Police Ethics: Source Materials*. Washington, DC: Police Foundation, 1985.

———, and Michael Davis, eds. *Ethics in the Legal Profession*. Buffalo, NY: Prometheus, 1984.

———, and Michael Feldberg, eds. *Moral Issues in Police Work*. Totowa, Rowman and Allanheld, 1985.

———, and Jane van Schaik. *Legal Ethics: An Annotated Bibliography and Resource Guide*. Littleton, CO: Rothman, 1984.

Ezorsky, Gertrude, ed. *Moral Rights in the Workplace*. Albany: State University of New York Press, 1986.

Feeney, Stephanie, and Kenneth Kipnis. "Professional Ethics in Early Childhood Education." *Young Children* (March 1985): 54–57.

———, and Lynda Sysko. "Professional Ethics in Early Childhood Education: Survey Results." *Young Children* (November 1986): 15–20.

Flores, Albert, ed. *Designing for Safety: Engineering Ethics in Organization Contexts*. Troy, NY: Rensselaer Polytechnic Institute, 1982.

———. *Ethical Problems of Engineering*, 2nd ed. Troy, NY: Rensselaer Polytechnic Institute, 1980.

Gerson, Allan, ed. *Lawyers' Ethics: Contemporary Dilemmas*. New Brunswick, NJ: Transaction, 1980.

Goodfield, June. *Reflections on Science and the Media*. Washington, DC: American Association for the Advancement of Science, 1981.

Gorovitz, Samuel, Ruth Macklin, Andrew L. Jameton, John M. O'Connor, and Susan Sherwin, eds. *Moral Problems in Medicine*, 2nd ed. Englewood Cliffs, NJ: Prentice-Hall, 1983.

Gross, Gerald, ed. *The Responsibility of the Press*. New York: Simon and Schuster, 1966.

Gustafson, Robert, and Frank Schmaller, eds. *The Social Basis of Criminal Justice: Ethical Issues for the Eighties*. Washington, DC: University Press of America, 1981.

Gutman, Amy, and Dennis Thompson, eds. *Ethics and Politics: Cases and Comments*. Chicago: Nelson-Hall, 1984.

Haan, Norma, Robert N. Bellah, Paul Rabinow, and William M. Sullivan, eds. *Social Science as Moral Inquiry*. New York: Columbia University Press, 1983.

Hazard, Geoffrey. *Ethics in the Practice of Law*. New Haven, CT: Yale University Press, 1978.

Heffernan, William C., and Timothy Stroup, eds. *Police Ethics: Hard Choices in Law Enforcement*. New York: John Jay Press, 1984.

Hoffman, W. Michael, and Jennifer Mills Moore, eds. *Business Ethics: Readings and Cases in Corporate Morality*. New York: McGraw-Hill, 1984.

Iannone, A. Pablo, ed. *Contemporary Moral Controversies in Technology*. New York: Oxford University Press, 1977.

Jameton, Andrew L. *Nursing Practice: the Ethical Issues*. Englewood Cliffs, NJ: Prentice-Hall, 1984.

Jennings, Bruce, and Daniel Callahan, eds. *Representation and Responsibility: Exploring Legislative Ethics*. New York: Plenum, 1985.

Jones, Donald G., and Patricia Bennett, eds. *A Bibliography of Business Ethics, 1981–85*. Lewiston, NY: E. Mellen, 1986.

———, and Helen Troy, eds. *A Bibliography of Business Ethics, 1976–80*. Charlottesville: University Press of Virginia, 1982.

Kipnis, Kenneth. *Legal Ethics*. Englewood Cliffs, NJ: Prentice-Hall, 1986.

Knight, James A. "Exploring the Compromise of Ethical Principles in Science." *Perspectives in Biology and Medicine* 27 (1984): 432–42.

Kurtzman, Paul A. "Ethical Issues in Industrial Social Work Practice." *Social Casework: The Journal of Contemporary Social Work* 64:2 (1983): 105–11.

LaFollette, Marcel, issue ed. "Secrecy in University-Based Research: Who Controls? Who Tells?" *Science, Technology, and Human Values* 10:2 (1985).

Lakoff, Stanley, ed. *Science and Ethical Responsibility*. Reading, MA: Addison-Wesley, 1980.

Lebacqz, Karen. *Professional Ethics: Power and Paradox*. Nashville, TN: Abingdon Press, 1985.

Lieberman, Jethro. *Crisis at the Bar.* New York: Norton, 1978.

Lindsey, Jonathon A., and Ann E. Prentice. *Professional Ethics and Librarians.* Phoeniz, AZ: Oryx, 1985.

Lum, Doman, ed. *Social Work and Health Care Policy.* Totowa, NJ: Rowman and Littlefield, 1982.

Martin, Mike W., and Roland Schinzinger. *Ethics in Engineering.* New York: McGraw-Hill, 1983.

Merrill, John C., and S. Jack Odel, eds. *Ethics and the Press.* New York: Hastings House, 1983.

Nelkin, Dorothy. *Science as Intellectual Property: Who Controls Scientific Research?* New York: Macmillan, 1984.

Pence, Terry. *Ethics in Nursing: An Annotated Bibliography.* New York: National League of Nursing, 1983.

"The Public Duties of the Professions." Special Supplement, *Hastings Center Report* 17:1 (1987): 1–20.

Reich, Warren T., ed. *Encyclopedia of Bioethics.* New York: Macmillan, 1978.

Sieber, Joan E., ed. *The Ethics of Social Research.* New York: Springer-Verlag, 1982.

Snoeyembos, Milton, Robert Alemeder, and James Humber, eds. *Business Ethics: Corporate Values and Society.* Buffalo, NY: Prometheus, 1983.

Solomon, Robert C., and Kristine R. Hanson. *Above the Bottom Line: An Introduction to Business Ethics.* New York: Harcourt Brace Jovanovich, 1983.

Veatch, Robert M. *Case Studies in Medical Ethics.* Cambridge, MA: Harvard University Press, 1977.

Wachs, Martin, ed. *Ethics in Planning.* New Brunswick, NJ: Rutgers University Press, 1985.

Walters, LeRoy, and Tamar Joy Kahn, eds. *Bibliography of Bioethics.* Washington, DC: Kennedy Institute of Ethics, 1985.

Werhane, Patricia H., and Kendall D'Andrade, eds. *Profit and Responsibility: Issues in Business and Professional Ethics.* New York: Edwin Mellon, 1985.